DOMINIC SANDBROOK

Seasons in the Sun
The Battle for Britain, 1974–1979

PENGUIN BOOKS

PENGUIN BOOKS

Published by the Penguin Group
Penguin Books Ltd, 80 Strand, London WC2R ORL, England
Penguin Group (USA) Inc., 375 Hudson Street, New York, New York 10014, USA
Penguin Group (Canada), 90 Eglinton Avenue East, Suite 700, Toronto, Ontario, Canada M4P 2Y3
(a division of Pearson Penguin Canada Inc.)
Penguin Ireland, 25 St Stephen's Green, Dublin 2, Ireland (a division of Penguin Books Ltd)
Penguin Group (Australia), 707 Collins Street, Melbourne, Victoria 3008, Australia
(a division of Pearson Australia Group Pty Ltd)
Penguin Books India Pvt Ltd, 11 Community Centre, Panchsheel Park, New Delhi – 110 017, India
Penguin Group (NZ), 67 Apollo Drive, Rosedale, Auckland 0632, New Zealand
(a division of Pearson New Zealand Ltd)
Penguin Books (South Africa) (Pty) Ltd, Block D, Rosebank Office Park,
181 Jan Smuts Avenue, Parktown North, Gauteng 2193, South Africa

Penguin Books Ltd, Registered Offices: 80 Strand, London WC2R ORL, England

www.penguin.com

First published by Allen Lane 2012
Published in Penguin Books 2013

009

Copyright © Dominic Sandbrook, 2012

The moral right of the author has been asserted

Typeset by Jouve (UK), Milton Keynes
Printed and bound in Great Britain by Clays Ltd, Elcograf S.p.A.

A CIP catalogue record for this book is available from the British Library

ISBN: 978-0-141-03216-0

www.greenpenguin.co.uk

PENGUIN BOOKS

SEASONS IN THE SUN

'Charming, insightful and thoroughly compelling . . . For those of us who grew up in the Seventies, it's like sitting down with a friend to talk about old times' Keith Lowe, *Daily Telegraph*

'Sandbrook has created a specific style of narrative history, blending high politics, social change and popular culture . . . always readable and assured . . . Anyone who genuinely believes we have never been so badly governed should read this splendid book'
Stephen Robinson, *Sunday Times*

'A remarkable achievement . . . entertaining . . . there is something worth reading on nearly every page' Vernon Bogdanor, *New Statesman*

'An entertaining analysis of a decade of great change . . . most importantly, Sandbrook argues that, far from dwindling in the 1970s, "many of the phenomena we lazily associate with the late 1960s" (from long hair, obscenity and drugs to flares and hippy slang) achieved mass purchase only in the following decade' David Edgar, *Guardian*

'The first three volumes of Dominic Sandbrook's epic history of Britain between 1956 and 1979 were exceptionally good. The fourth, *Seasons in the Sun*, is magnificent . . . marked by its pace, style, wit, narrative and characterisation as by its exhaustive research'
Roger Hutchinson, *Scotsman*

'Richly descriptive, anecdotal and often humorous. It should be required reading for all potential and practising politicians'
Richard Ormond, *Tablet*

'Exhausting though it must have been to write, *Seasons in the Sun* is exceptionally easy to read. Ranging widely across politics, economics, society and culture (both high and low), and displaying a wonderful eye for detail, Sandbrook drives the narrative along with enviable pace, power and authority . . . His cast of heroes and (particularly) villains adds enormously to the book's verve and readability . . . Nobody, presumably, will ever read *Seasons in the Sun* in one sitting. But read it you should' John Benson, *Times Higher Education*

'Magisterial . . . For those of us who lived through the period, the book conjures it to mind as if it were yesterday. Sandbrook himself was only a toddler at the time, but his rigorous research and sound judgment have resulted in a work astonishing in its detail and narrative sweep'
Christopher Gray, *Oxford Times*

ABOUT THE AUTHOR

Born in Shropshire ten days before the October 1974 election, Dominic Sandbrook was educated at Oxford, St Andrews and Cambridge. He is the author of three hugely acclaimed books on post-war Britain: *Never Had It So Good*, *White Heat* and *State of Emergency*, and two books on modern American history, *Eugene McCarthy* and *Mad as Hell*. A prolific reviewer and columnist, he writes regularly for the *Sunday Times*, *Daily Mail* and *BBC History*. His BBC2 series *The 70s*, adapted from his books, was broadcast in 2012 to widespread acclaim.

For my mother, Hilary Sandbrook (1945–2011),
with love

We had joy, we had fun, we had seasons in the sun.
But the wine and the song, like the seasons, are all gone.

Terry Jacks, 'Seasons in the Sun' (1974)

A huge icy fist, with large cold fingers, was squeezing and chilling the people of Britain, that great and puissant nation, slowing down their blood, locking them into immobility, fixing them in a solid stasis, like fish in a frozen river: there they all were in their large houses and their small houses, with their first mortgages and second mortgages, in their rented flats and council flats and basement bedsits and their caravans: stuck, congealed, amongst possessions, in attitudes, in achievements they had hoped next month to shed, and with which they were now condemned to live. The flow had ceased to flow: the ball had stopped rolling: the game of musical chairs was over. Rien ne va plus, the croupier had shouted.

Margaret Drabble, *The Ice Age* (1977)

Contents

PART THREE
Terminal Stasis

PART FOUR
We Can't Go On Like This

List of Illustrations and Cartoons

Cartoons

Preface: A Long Time Ago . . .

Everything was fantastic. Whoever wrote it had a fantastic imagination!
Woman after seeing *Star Wars*, BBC news, 26 December 1977

On the morning of 7 April 1976, a film called *Star Wars* began shooting in suburban Hertfordshire. Its American producers had decided to film in Britain because it was much cheaper than staying in Hollywood, and as their principal base they had chosen the vast Elstree studio complex just off Shenley Road, Borehamwood. Once, Elstree had been among the world's most prestigious facilities, the home of *Goodbye, Mr Chips*, *The Dam Busters* and *The Avengers*. But by the time the Americans arrived in this quiet corner of suburban Metro-land, it had long since fallen on hard times. The days when millions of people had gone to the cinema every week were now a distant memory; many cinemas had been converted into bingo halls or simply knocked down. With the domestic film industry in ruins, business had dried up, staff had been laid off and the 28-acre Elstree complex now survived on the income from cheap sex comedies like *Confessions of a Window Cleaner* and its sequels. When the Americans arrived, they found it almost deserted. Like so many British institutions in the mid-1970s, it felt broken, listless, a decaying monument lamenting its vanished glories. 'Drab, ugly, cold, depressing,' was how the producer's assistant later described it. 'But they couldn't have found a better location for privacy. *No one* walked in off the street.'[1]

On the surface, *Star Wars* seems an odd choice to reflect British life in the late 1970s. The brainchild of a Californian television addict, inspired by Westerns, comic strips and Hollywood film serials, it ostensibly has little in common with the world of Jim Callaghan, the Sex Pistols and *The Good Life*. Yet in Britain it was by far the most popular film of the decade, attracting an audience of almost 21 million people. Among post-war films, only *The Sound of Music* has ever done better. More to the point, it was largely a British endeavour. The script, the money and the three lead actors came from Hollywood, but with the exception of some location footage from Tunisia and Guatemala, *Star Wars* was filmed in the heart of the Home Counties. The cinematographer, the set designer and the costume designer were British; so were the art directors, the cameramen, the electricians, the carpenters, the stuntmen, even the orchestra. Almost all of the faces on screen, too, were British. Alec Guinness and Peter Cushing were already household names. Dave Prowse, the West Country actor who played Darth Vader, was familiar to millions of children as the Green Cross Code man. Peter Mayhew, who played the furry Chewbacca, was a porter at King's College Hospital. Of the actors who played R2-D2 and C-3PO, Kenny Baker had appeared in circuses across the country, while Anthony Daniels was an up-and-coming West End actor. And even in 1977, when the film was first shown in London, a few eagle-eyed viewers might have recognized Denis Lawson, who had been in *Dr Finlay's Casebook* and *Survivors*; or Don Henderson, once of *Crossroads* and *Poldark*; or even Malcolm Tierney, who had performed with the Royal Shakespeare Company and later had a regular part in *Brookside*.[2]

As though confirming the bleak reports of British decline in the mid-1970s, the production of *Star Wars* had been a tortured process. The actors' union, Equity, were initially reluctant to allow the film's three American leads into the country, relenting only when the producers pointed out that hundreds of British jobs were at stake. The film's nominal star, the unknown Mark Hamill, had never before visited Europe. When he went into a London hotel to ask for directions on his second day, the receptionist assumed he was an IRA bomber and called the police. The shy young director, George Lucas, felt equally adrift. Although his temporary home in Hampstead was lavish by local standards, he complained that he could not get a decent meal and his wife could find nothing to watch on television. To add insult to injury, the house was burgled while they were filming, the thieves making off with Lucas's colour television and his wife's jewellery. Even at work he never felt at home; to his British crew, he seemed aloof and unfriendly. He sacked the editor halfway through production, while relations with his cinematographer, the old Hitchcock hand Gilbert Taylor, came close to collapse. Lucas wanted the film shot in soft focus to give it a fairy-tale feel; Taylor refused to use soft-focus lenses. Lucas took the script extremely seriously; Taylor regarded it with amused contempt. 'Bring the dog in,' he remarked whenever the action called for Chewbacca. 'Put light on the dog.' Lucas would have sacked him, too, had he not been afraid that the rest of the crew would walk out in sympathy.[3]

Taylor was not alone in his bewilderment at the young Californian's impenetrable adventure story. By far the best-paid actors in the film were the veterans Alec Guinness and Peter Cushing, who were meant to supply some much-needed gravitas. But neither had any idea what was going on. Guinness even threatened to walk out when the director decided to kill off his character halfway through, and, although he relented, he told the *Sunday Times* that he was 'pretty lost as to what's required of me . . . What I'm supposed to be doing, I really can't say.' Cushing, too, admitted that 'a great deal of the script' went completely over his head. 'Many of the stagehands came up to me and asked, "What is all this about? I can't understand a word of it",' he later recalled. 'I told them, "Neither can I. I'm just saying the lines and trying to sound intelligent."'[4]

One sliver of good news for the producers was the collapse of the British pound, which had begun a few weeks before they arrived at Elstree and culminated with the national humiliation of an IMF bail-out. With the exchange rate plummeting – in March 1976, a pound was worth more than $2, yet by the time Lucas returned home, it was barely $1.67 – they found themselves with an unexpected $500,000 windfall. But other events seemed to be conspiring against the project. The summer of 1976 was the hottest in history: every day during the last week in June and first week in July, temperatures in southern England reached at least 90 degrees. Every morning, millions awoke to a blazing sun in a clear blue sky. Outside, children frolicked in parks and fountains, while thousands of workers found excuses to slip off to the seaside. 'Fucking amazing weather continues,' the novelist Kingsley Amis wrote to his American friend Robert Conquest at the beginning of July. 'It'll be 90 today and the front lawn is mostly straw. At least the Arabs who are buying up London will feel at home.' But the Americans at Elstree were not happy at all. In order to film against a blue screen, the crew had put up huge arc lights, which sent the temperatures even higher. In the rafters, electricians fainted from heat exhaustion. On set, Peter Mayhew, the actor playing the 'dog', collapsed from dehydration.[5]

If there was one thing that really shocked George Lucas, though, it was the crew's working habits. Since the beginning of the 1970s, American commentators had held up Britain as an object lesson in the dangers of socialism. For *Time* magazine it was a model of 'labor indiscipline and overly ambitious welfare-statism'; for *Commentary* it was an 'industrial slum'; for the *CBS Evening News* it was 'sleep-walking into a social revolution'; for the *Wall Street Journal* it was simply the 'sick man of Europe'. These were caricatures, of course: if the condition of Britain had really been that bad, Lucas would never have chosen to film there. Even so, he was infuriated by his crew's tightly regulated routine. Every morning they began work at 8.30 before a mandatory tea break at ten. At a quarter past one they had an hour-long break for lunch. At four o'clock they had another tea break, and at 5.30 they finally packed up. At first, Lucas assumed this meant they would begin wrapping up, but by the second day of filming he realized that stopping at 5.30 meant stopping at 5.30. Even if he were in the middle of a scene, the crew would stop dead when the clock reached the half-hour. The remaining shots would have to wait till the following morning, which then meant a further delay while they moved all the equipment for the next scene. Already infuriated by Hollywood restrictions, Lucas could barely believe his eyes. He asked if they would consider working overtime, and discovered that they would have to vote on it every morning. Whenever he mentioned it, they always voted no.[6]

But by Boxing Day 1977, when the film opened in London, all the arguments seemed like ancient history. As Fleet Street triumphantly put it, this 'galactic *Gone with the Wind*', which had smashed all American box-office records, had been 'made in Britain'. Outside the first West End showings in Leicester Square and on Tottenham Court Road, queues began forming as early as seven in the morning. Evening performances were sold out for weeks ahead; outside the cinemas, kiosks sold *Star Wars* brochures for 50p, paperback novelizations for 99p and T-shirts for £3. Tickets swapped hands at exorbitant prices: one 8-year-old boy, Jason Usher, managed to get a seat by writing to the BBC's *Jim'll Fix It*, adding that he was desperate to be an astronaut. And as the box-office takings poured in, at least one member of the *Star Wars* cast found himself with a dilemma he had never expected. Having bargained for 2 per cent of the profits, Sir Alec Guinness was about to become very rich indeed – and, as the *Daily Express* put it, the Inland Revenue were 'already preparing the armoured trucks to haul away 83 pence in every pound'. 'Cut and run,' friends told him. 'Get out while you can.' But Guinness was going nowhere. 'I would keep more if I went to America,' he remarked, 'but I'd go mad.' He did, however, have one request. 'You'd think Denis Healey might send me a letter of thanks for staying,' he mused. 'But I don't suppose he will.'[7]

Not everybody liked *Star Wars*. It was a 'wretched disappointment', Bernard Levin told readers of *The Times*, declaring it 'technically inferior to *2001* and lacking in imagination by comparison, too'. The plot was 'incoherent', the dialogue was 'unintelligible' and it had 'the least attractive hero and heroine I have ever seen'. Yet even Levin recognized that it was more than 'simply a film about a war between stars'. For one thing, he admitted, its clear, unambiguous distinction between good and evil was 'now sufficiently rare, in a film of any pretensions, to be refreshing'. For another, he was impressed that, far from celebrating technology, as so many films had done in the last decade or so, *Star Wars* ostentatiously rejected it. In *2001* (which had been filmed in another corner of the Home Counties, Shepperton), the sets had been painted a gleaming space-age white. In *Star Wars* they were deliberately battered and dirty. Throughout the picture runs a healthy distrust of technological modernity, a message that would have resonated with millions of British filmgoers in an age of resurgent environmentalism, economic decline and cultural nostalgia. And beneath the breathless kinetic spectacle, as so often in the mid-1970s, there was a thick layer of New Age spirituality. Even at the crucial moment, Levin pointed out, the hero turns off his battle computer, preferring to rely on his own instincts, informed by the vaguely spiritual Force.[8]

And this was not the only sign of the times. On the surface, *Star Wars* seems just another slice of nostalgic escapism: there is no moral doubt, no self-hatred, no racial issues, no women's liberation and no sex, while even stylistically there are no flashbacks, no unreliable narrators, no alarming jump cuts or juxtapositions. Like so many British cultural phenomena of the mid-1970s, from the music of David Bowie to the buildings of James Stirling, it is an exercise in cannibalism, a collage of references and allusions. Lucas himself called it a 'combination of *2001* and James Bond', a 'kids' film' that would 'introduce a kind of basic morality'. But had *Star Wars* been entirely reactionary, it would never have been so successful. It presents us with a princess in a dress, certainly, but she knows how to use a gun. At a time when historians and novelists from Jan Morris to George MacDonald Fraser were presenting the British Empire in a much darker light, its anti-imperialist message could hardly be clearer. Peter Cushing's character, after all, is the very model of a British colonial official, coolly unflappable to the last. Its enthusiastic militarism, too, was very much of the moment, reflecting a time when détente with the Soviet Union was unravelling, the temperature of the Cold War was falling and the Leader of the Opposition was calling herself an Iron Lady. Even its moral conservatism matched the wider mood: only two days before Lucas started shooting at Elstree, Britain's new Prime Minister, Jim Callaghan, had promised to return to traditional 'values and standards'. *Star Wars* was a fairy tale, poised between old and new, both excitingly modern and defiantly backward-looking. And in the depths of a cold British winter, with the headlines full of decline and discontent, that was precisely what people wanted.[9]

Seasons in the Sun tells the story of the British experience at a pivotal moment in our recent history. It opens on 4 March 1974, when the unprecedented economic and political crisis created by the OPEC oil shock, the three-day week and the collapse of the Heath government brought Labour's Harold Wilson back to Downing Street as the head of a minority government. And it ends on 4 May 1979, when, after an extraordinary series of strikes had ripped the heart out of Jim Calla-ghan's administration, Margaret Thatcher walked into Number 10 as Britain's first woman Prime Minister.

By any standard these were extraordinarily turbulent and colourful years: the years of the Social Contract and the IMF crisis, the Birming-ham bombings and the Balcombe Street siege, the Grunwick strike and the Lib–Lab Pact, the Bay City Rollers, the Sex Pistols and Ally's Tartan Army. They culminated in the industrial unrest known as the Winter of Discontent, which, rightly or wrongly, became the most enduring sym-bol of the national experience in the 1970s. Many of this period's cultural highlights are fondly remembered, from novels by Martin Amis and Ian McEwan to television classics such as *I, Claudius* and *Pennies from Heaven*. But there is no getting away from the fact that this is generally regarded as the lowest point in recent British history. 'Do you remember what it was like then in the Winter of Discontent?' asked Anthony Quayle's voice-over in the Conservatives' party political broadcasts in 1983, which began with haunting images of rubbish piling up in Leices-ter Square, railway station boards showing a list of cancellations and pickets gathering outside cancer wards. And those images never went away. More than a quarter of a century later, Francis Wheen, who was 20 in 1977, wrote that the 'defining characteristics of the Seventies were economic disaster, terrorist threats, corruption in high places, prophecies of ecological doom and fear of the surveillance state's suffocating embrace'. And even decades after the event, the Conservative press loved to dig out pictures of the Winter of Discontent. 'Vote decisively,' the *Daily Mail* told its readers in 2010, warning that the hung parliament of

February 1974 had produced 'five years of political paralysis, economic meltdown and national humiliation'.[10]

In many ways this view is a caricature. After all, many people have rather better memories of the decade, recalling the simple pleasures of the *Morecambe and Wise Show* and *The Generation Game*, the excitement of Liverpool and Nottingham Forest's European Cup campaigns and the sheer high spirits of a roller disco. There can be few children of the 1970s who do not feel a small thrill at the memory of *Bagpuss* and *Mr Benn*, a nostalgic frisson at the recollection of Tom Baker's absurdly long scarf, or a pleasurable shudder at the thought of Darth Vader's death grip. And even the economic picture was not quite as terrible as we think. We remember the Conservatives' stark poster 'Labour Isn't Working', but we often forget that the jobless figures in the late 1970s were generally better than during the Blair and Brown years, let alone the Conservative governments of the 1980s and 1990s. For all the clichés of donkey-jacketed men standing around braziers, there were actually fewer strikes per year in Britain than in Canada, Australia or even the United States. It is true that inflation soared and real earnings stagnated, which came as a great shock to people used to the buoyant growth of earlier decades. Still, most people were better off in 1979 than they had been in 1970. They spent more money on entertainment, ate out more, went on more exciting holidays, bought their first colour televisions and even installed their first central heating. A few months after the end of the decade, some even bought their first home computers in the form of the Sinclair ZX80. Pockets of extreme poverty remained; yet for the great majority, wrote the columnist Peter Jenkins in 1978, 'the general quality of life in Britain remains probably as high as anywhere in Europe'.[11]

So was this a lost golden age, a last hot summer of the post-war consensus? Some writers, especially on the left, think so. A radical think-tank, the New Economics Foundation, even worked out that for 'national economic, social and environmental well-being', the best year in Britain since 1950 was 1976, the year that George Lucas and his crew had been working on *Star Wars*. But it must have been using a very peculiar index of national progress, for even at the time most people regarded 1976 as a dreadful year. When it began, British families were still mourning the victims of the IRA's bombing campaign in London, while Westminster was digesting news of the government's decision to bail out the ailing Chrysler car giant. The next twelve months saw riots at the Notting Hill Carnival, the unravelling of the Jeremy Thorpe scandal, the petty sleaze of Harold Wilson's 'lavender list' and a series of appalling sectarian atrocities in Northern Ireland. Even the wonderful weather proved a very mixed blessing, with heatwave turning inexorably to drought. Above all, though, this was a year in which the exchange markets completely lost confidence in the British economy, the pound went into free fall and the government was forced to seek a humiliating bailout from the IMF. Far from being alive and well in 1976, in other words, the post-war consensus was already in its death agonies. This had a profound impact on the lives of Britain's 56 million people: after twenty years of almost unbroken growth, real earnings fell in 1976 and again in 1977. And far from feeling that they had reached some promised land of peace and prosperity, politicians of both left and right recognized that change was coming. 'Do you, like me, sometimes feel that we have been slipping?' said Jim Callaghan, the new Prime Minister, in his first words to the nation that spring. A few months later, he even told the Labour party conference that by trying to spend its way out of trouble, Britain had been living on borrowed time. 'Higher inflation followed by higher unemployment,' he said: 'that is the history of the last twenty years.'[12]

The truth is that, although many people led happy and comfortable lives, Britain was in poor shape in the late 1970s. This was not a last glimpse of sunshine before the advent of Thatcherism. It was an age that saw two Prime Ministers broken by the unions, inflation heading towards 30 per cent, sporting occasions regularly disfigured by barbaric hooliganism and hundreds of people murdered by terrorists not only in Northern Ireland but in the streets of London and the pubs of Birmingham. Even before Mrs Thatcher came to power, the gap between North and South was growing, while the manufacturing industries on which Britain's prosperity had long depended were in deep decline. In the industrial working-class cities, unemployment was mounting; in Westminster, almost everybody, from Tony Benn on the left to Sir Keith Joseph on the right, recognized that Britain was facing an extremely painful transition. A rare exception was Harold Wilson, whose final and frankly rather shabby government between 1974 and 1976 has a good claim to be the worst in our modern history. But the administration that followed, under his old sparring partner Jim Callaghan, has been treated too harshly. Both Callaghan and his Chancellor, Denis Healey, made valiant efforts to get to grips with Britain's economic problems, even if their own party rarely appreciated them. Today, left and right alike see 1979 as a historic turning point. But *Seasons in the Sun* argues that, in many ways, thanks to Callaghan and Healey, Britain had changed course already. Indeed, this book shows that there was rather more continuity between Margaret Thatcher and her avuncular predecessor, 'Sunny Jim', than we often think – even though it would pain both left and right to admit it.

What is beyond doubt, though, is that this was a decisive moment in our recent history. It was in this short five-year period, for example, that the British people chose to remain part of the European Community, with incalculable political and economic long-run consequences. It was in this period that Britain turned its back on full-blown state socialism: Tony Benn's extraordinarily ambitious plans for state intervention in industry never came to fruition, and nobody since then has tried anything remotely similar. This was the period that turned Margaret Thatcher into a national figure, gave British politics its first woman leader, and saw the Conservative Party take a decisive step to the right. It saw the abandonment of full employment, the end of the direct grant grammar schools, the birth of punk rock, the collapse of self-government in Northern Ireland, the first benefits of North Sea oil and the peak of nationalist excitement in Scotland and Wales. On a lighter note, it saw the birth of *Grange Hill*, *The Sweeney* and *To the Manor Born*, the heyday of Rick Wakeman, Elton John and Andrew Lloyd Webber, and an outbreak of entertainingly short-lived hysteria surrounding Scotland's odyssey in the 1978 World Cup. And perhaps above all, it saw the last gasp of an old collective working-class culture and the emergence of individualism as the dominant force in our political, economic and social life. Afterwards, nothing would be the same again.

This book picks up directly from its predecessor, *State of Emergency*, which covered the unhappy years of the Heath premiership. There are inevitably a few overlaps, usually to give a sense of the wider social and cultural developments of the decade as a whole. Since I covered some subjects at length in *State of Emergency*, notably football, feminism, sex, housing and environmentalism, I have not said much about them here. On the other hand, I have finally got around to discussing the rise of nationalism in Wales and Scotland, as well as North Sea oil, law and order, schools and universities, the first computers and the strange career of Larry Grayson. As usual, I have written more about England than anywhere else, and probably more about London than is entirely fair. At the heart of this book, though, are the great political and economic questions that defined the era. Far more than, say, the late 1950s or the 1960s, this was an intensely politicized period. In an age of enormous anxiety about the very survival of the United Kingdom, there seemed to be much more at stake. The debates were shriller, the choices starker, the rhetoric more strident. Even escapist entertainments of the day, from episodes of *Doctor Who* to Hughie Green's diatribes on *Opportunity Knocks*, openly referred to the political and economic headlines. Naturally, therefore, the central characters are the nation's politicians: Harold Wilson and Tony Benn, Jim Callaghan and Denis Healey, Keith Joseph and Margaret Thatcher. Partisan books are boring, and I have done my best to be even-handed. Still, some of these characters struck me as much more sympathetic than others, and that will doubtless come across in the narrative.

Finally, the title. Originally recorded as '*Le Moribond*' by the Belgian singer-songwriter Jacques Brel, 'Seasons in the Sun' is best known in Britain as an unexpected hit for the obscure Canadian singer Terry Jacks. It entered the charts in late March 1974, a few weeks after Harold Wilson's return to Downing Street, reached number one on 6 April and held onto the top spot for a month, eventually yielding to Abba's 'Waterloo'. Like so many mass-market hits of the mid-1970s, from the music of the Wombles to the sitcoms of Richard O'Sullivan, it is often derided as tasteless kitsch. One critic, lamenting its 'hectoring nursery-school simplicity', even calls it the 'unsurpassed nadir of pop music'. Yet there is no doubt that it was popular: despite its mawkishness, people kept buying it, week after week. Perhaps, facing the biggest economic crisis that many of them had ever known, with the long post-war boom a fading memory and the political consensus cracking apart, they were drawn to the last words of a dying man, looking back on his days of wine and song and flowers. More plausibly, though, most saw the song as nothing more than a catchy ditty, offering a quick dose of easy escapism. In an era of almost unremittingly bad news, the headlines dominated by surging prices, terrorist bombings and predictions of disaster, it was hardly surprising that so many people wanted to buy a cheap ballad that would yield a few moments' bittersweet diversion. Nor was it any wonder that so many took refuge in events a long time ago in a galaxy far, far away.[13]

PART ONE

The End of the Line

I

Brave New World

Tomorrow's almost over, today went by so fast
It's the only thing to look forward to – the past . . .
Theme song from *Whatever Happened*
to the Likely Lads? (1973–4)

These days it's not very trendy to declare that you're a
patriot . . . And what does loving your country mean
anyway? Loving the political party in power? The system
of government? The countryside? The people? The lot?
Full-page British Army advertisement,
The Times, 10 January 1975

'What a blessing is a garden in such troubled times,' ran a letter from Mrs Massey of Harefield, Middlesex, to the *Daily Express* on Monday, 4 March 1974. 'A mild winter nearly over and today I'm out in the garden watching goldfish in a small pond. Alongside is a colourful bed of heather, bees buzzing around and a lovely orange and brown butterfly. Looking around I see crocuses, roses, pansies and above, a clear blue sky . . . My husband has even been mowing the lawn.'

In west London, the pleasures of the English garden were much on people's minds. At the giant Olympia exhibition site, workers were putting the final touches to the annual *Daily Mail* Ideal Home Exhibition, due to welcome tens of thousands of visitors the next day. At its heart was the usual display of six furnished homes in a landscaped setting, but, as always, the exhibition was gently moving with the times. Nicely straddling old and new, the National Union of Townswomen's Guilds had put up displays on 'the Townswoman as homemaker, gardener, citizen, liberator, craftswoman and entertainer'. A special exhibition told 'The Story of Glass', and there was even a section promising to recreate the experience of a 'walk through space, an out-of-this-world experience ... that defies description'. For the more practically minded, the Garden Advice Centre featured talks by television stars such as Geoff Hamilton and Geoff Amos, while idealistic visitors were bound to enjoy 'The Fat of the Land', a stall run by the self-sufficiency guru John Seymour, offering demonstrations of meat drying and beer brewing. And if all this were not excitement enough, there was even a special stand on the pleasures of potatoes, complete with a 'working model of "Potatoboro"'.

It was now four days since the British people had voted in the most dramatic general election since the war, and still there was no resolution to the political crisis. Yet while Edward Heath, Jeremy Thorpe and Harold Wilson jockeyed for power, life went on as normal. In Norwich, unofficial industrial action by railway guards meant dozens of trains were cancelled or delayed. In Lincoln, police blamed teenage 'snipers' with air rifles for a spate of recent power cuts. In Worcestershire, the rural dean of Pershore complained that state schools were becoming 'pagan wildernesses' where 'a mild kind of sociology' had replaced Christian values. In Oxford, police were called to suppress fighting between militant and Conservative students outside the University's administrative offices. In Leeds, two Irish republicans were jailed for possession of 62 detonators and 713 rounds of ammunition 'with intent to endanger life'.

For one couple in Retford, Lincolnshire, it was a blessing that they had even made it to the morning alive. On Sunday evening, Henry and Mabel Abraham had been tucked up in bed, enjoying their first few hours in their brand-new terraced house after years in rented lodgings. Then, suddenly, there was a gigantic bang, as an enormous gas explosion blew out the windows, ripped out the floor from underneath them and sent their furniture flying into the street. 'When I looked down,' Henry said, 'there was a gaping hole in the floor and I could see flames downstairs. We tried to get down but found our way blocked by a sheet of flame.' Eventually, firemen managed to get them down; amazingly, they were almost totally unhurt. And there was good news, too, in Cambridgeshire, where police told the parents of the missing 16-year-old Rachael Gathercole that they had tracked her down, safe and sound, in the south of France with her music teacher, 57-year-old Arthur King. The couple had been planning to get married, the newspapers claimed;

indeed, King was something of a serial cradle-snatcher, having married 16-year-old girls twice already. Perhaps his employers should have realized there was something suspicious about him, remarked the *Express*: he 'wears a ginger toupee', and 'speaks several languages fluently'.

For those who saw sport as a reflection of the nation's fortunes, there was bleak news on the back pages, where the England cricket party's dismal ten-wicket defeat in Barbados felt like a bucket of water in the face. 'I have known no more chilling moment on tour,' wrote one reporter. 'The home truths are inescapable. Batting-wise, this England party is arguably the weakest ever sent overseas. It is limited in skill, character and guts.' Still, all was sweetness and light in the Black Country, where football fans were still toasting the goals by Kenny Hibbitt and John Richards that had brought League Cup glory to Wolverhampton Wanderers, pride of the Midlands. Few commentators hid their contempt for Manchester City's star striker Rodney Marsh, who had stormed off at the final whistle without congratulating his opponents or collecting his silver tankard from the Duchess of Kent. 'I doubt if he will ever be totally forgiven,' wrote the *Mirror*'s veteran correspondent Frank McGhee, 'for his sour, rancid attitude and appalling lack of sportsmanship ... Marsh spat on a tradition that in this country the loser is expected to summon up a smile, not run away at the end to sulk and scowl alone.' There was a lesson there, perhaps, for the nation's politicians.

In the City, a takeover bid by Boots for the department store chain House of Fraser was looking decidedly uncertain. In the charts, the sounds of the moment included Suzi Quatro's 'Devil Gate Drive', 'Wombling Song' by the Wombles and 'Tiger Feet' by Mud, although the top spot belonged to Alvin Stardust's 'Jealous Mind'. In the West End, Derek Nimmo was starring in *Why Not Stay for Breakfast?*, Richard Briers and Sheila Hancock in *Absurd Person Singular*, Vanessa Redgrave and Jeremy Brett in *Design for Living*, and Albert Finney, Denholm Elliott and Geraldine McEwan in *Chez Nous*. On television that afternoon, children could enjoy *Play School*, *Huckleberry Hound*, *Blue Peter*, *The Magic Roundabout* and *Jackanory*, while the evening's delights included new episodes of *Z Cars* and *Colditz* as well as a *Panorama* special on the secret police in Grenada and a Scotland versus Wales clash in *Come Dancing*. The *Express*'s television critic was particularly looking forward to seeing the Octettes ('eight youngsters playing two pianos') on *Opportunity Knocks*, followed by the latest episode of ITV's sitcom *Love Thy Neighbour*: an 'amusing series', he thought, despite its controversial racial humour. But he was less enticed by the prospect of *Wish You Were Here*, which focused this week on Majorca. 'Doesn't anyone take a traditional bucket-and-spade holiday these days?' he grumbled.

Although foreign travel dominated many conversations in offices, pubs and living rooms that morning, the mood was unusually sombre. Many people were still digesting Sunday's terrible news about the crash of a Turkish Airlines DC-10 bound for London, which had disintegrated in mid-air over the Ermenonville Forest in northern France. Since the headlines had been full of bombings and hijackings in recent months, many people suspected there must have been a bomb, although in fact the crash was caused by a structural problem with the cargo hatch. But it was the worst air disaster in history, killing all 346 passengers and crew. By a horrible mischance, more than two hundred of them, mostly British, had boarded the plane at Orly at the last moment because their earlier flights had been affected by a strike at Heathrow. Many were returning from the Five Nations rugby match between France and England, and no community was harder hit than the Suffolk town of Bury St Edmunds, where eighteen members of the local rugby club had saved up for the trip to Paris. Many were married: their deaths left ten widows and more than twenty boys and girls without fathers. Among the other victims were four of London's top models, the engineering union leader Jim Conway and the former Olympic hurdler John Cooper, who had won two silver medals in Tokyo in 1964. And in the rubble of the crash site, investigators found the charred fragments of a message, evidently written by a seaman to his sweetheart. The letter told its own story:

To Pat, the one I love and always shall.

I have just spent the last four hours stuck in the engine-room thinking of nothing except you and I feel very depressed and it is getting worse.

My feelings towards you have grown a thousandfold, darling. Nothing in this entire world could ever take the place of you.

I am arranging to have some flowers sent to your mother for her birthday from the both of us. How is saving going my love? Hurry up next year is all I can think of when the greatest day in my life will occur.

Here the letter was burned away; all that was left was the ending:

Pat, my darling, please take extra special care of yourself for me, as I dearly love and miss you very much. When you are by yourself and lonely, as

I often am, please remember there is somebody who loves you more than anything else on this entire earth.

All my entire love, David[1]

*

Harold and Mary Wilson ate breakfast that morning at Grange Farm, their Buckinghamshire country retreat, waiting for the news that would bring redemption. Four days earlier, with the opinion polls forecasting a clear victory for his rival Edward Heath, the Labour leader had been contemplating the end of his political career. Beset by economic and industrial troubles, with the miners out on strike and the nation on a three-day working week, Heath had asked the British people: 'Who governs?' For weeks, the polls had suggested that the Prime Minister would get the answer he wanted. Touring his Huyton constituency on Thursday evening, Wilson had seemed yesterday's man, a downcast little figure trudging through the pouring rain. Behind his bullish public statements, he had even drafted an elaborate escape plan, complete with a last-minute change of hotels and an early morning flight south, so that he could escape the press after his second successive election defeat. But when the first results came in, it had suddenly become clear that he would not need it. For although Heath's Tories had won the most votes, Labour had won the most seats, their total of 301 giving them a tiny four-seat lead. With more than twenty seats going to the Liberals and the nationalists, it was not enough to form a majority. But when Harold Wilson awoke on Monday, he knew that unless Heath had somehow engineered an unlikely coalition with the Liberal leader Jeremy Thorpe, the premiership was his once again.[2]

Late that morning, the Wilsons drove down to their town house in Lord North Street, London, a few tantalizing moments' walk from their old home at 10 Downing Street. It was an unseasonably warm day. By the time that Wilson walked into St Ermin's Hotel for lunch with his press secretary, Joe Haines, his chief policy adviser, Bernard Donoughue, and his political secretary, Marcia Williams, the news was more promising than ever. All weekend Heath and Thorpe had been locked in talks, but a deal seemed increasingly impossible. Despite the staid elegance of the St Ermin's dining room, there was an atmosphere of cheerful excitement as Wilson's aides discussed the new administration – although there was an ominous sign of things to come when Marcia

Williams upbraided her boss for not offering Roy Jenkins the Treasury, leaving him 'white with rage'. But when, just before six that evening, Number 10 rang and told Wilson that the coalition talks had collapsed, the bickering was forgotten. As Wilson shaved for his audience with the Queen, the radio reported that Heath had left for the Palace. At half past six, a removal van turned into Downing Street. Finally, just after seven, the long-anticipated call came. Harold and Mary went on ahead in their little car; behind them, his aides followed in a rented Daimler. They swept through the gates of Buckingham Palace, past the cameras and the small crowd of cheering supporters, and while the Wilsons were shown up to see the Queen, the others waited downstairs in a chilly room and moaned about the lack of drinks.[3]

At eighteen minutes past eight, as Wilson's car cruised back down the Mall, a statement from the Palace confirmed his appointment as Prime Minister, the first to lead a minority government since Ramsay MacDonald in 1929. A few moments later, easing through the crowds of photographers and policemen, his car drew up in Downing Street. It was almost exactly fifty years since Wilson had posed for a family photograph on the famous steps, a cheeky little boy in a big baggy cap and knee-length shorts. It was almost ten years, meanwhile, since he had walked into Downing Street as a dynamic new Prime Minister, the champion of science and modernization. But this time, as he trudged to the familiar spot, the flashbulbs popping and Mary smiling self-consciously at his side, there was little of the excitement that had marked his first victory all those years before. His shoulders hunched, his smile thin, his eyes weary, Wilson looked older than his fifty-seven years, a white-haired little man in a crumpled suit. And as he laconically raised a hand in victory, there were no fine words. 'We've got a job to do,' he said slowly, his flat Yorkshire voice barely audible above the mingled cheers and boos of the crowd. 'We can only do that job as one people, and I'm going right in to start that job now.' Then he went inside, and the heavy black door swung shut behind him.[4]

'It wasn't like old times,' the *Mirror* admitted the next day. 'Things have changed too much for that.' The optimism that had animated Wilson's first years in government, and that seemed so emblematic of the so-called Swinging Sixties, had long since disappeared. For almost eight years, British morale had suffered blow after blow, from the devaluation of the pound and the outbreak of sectarian violence in Northern Ireland to a crippling miners' strike and the collapse of the stock market. In the midst of this litany of disaster, the voters had kicked Wilson out of

Downing Street and replaced him with Heath, another meritocratic modernizer with bold plans to revitalize British industry. But by the autumn of 1973 Heath's ambitions, too, were crumbling into dust. Alarmed by rising unemployment, Heath had told his Chancellor, Anthony Barber, to go for broke. It was one of the greatest economic gambles in modern history: while credit soared and the money supply boomed, Heath hoped to keep inflation down through an elaborate system of wage and price controls. But by October 1973, even as he unveiled Stage Three of his grandiose incomes policy, his hopes were unravelling at terrifying speed. Thanks to the 'Barber boom', the economy went into overdrive, with house prices surging by 25 per cent in just six months, the cost of imports rocketing and Britain's trade balance plunging deep into the red. Above all, just a week after Heath had published the details of Stage Three, the Arab oil exporters in the OPEC cartel announced a stunning 70 per cent increase in the posted price of oil, punishing the West for its support for Israel. It was a devastating blow to the world economy, but nowhere was its impact greater than in Britain.[5]

A few days after Wilson returned to Number 10, the financier Siegmund Warburg warned him that Britain faced 'the most serious economic crisis in its history, a crisis which indeed is not only of a material character but is a crisis of the whole fabric of our society'. He was not exaggerating. With import prices rising, Britain's monthly trade deficit had hit a record £383 million by February 1974. In a desperate bid to reassure the markets, the Bank of England implemented the tightest credit squeeze in living memory, raising the minimum lending rate to an eye-watering 13 per cent and puncturing the last remnants of the property-market bubble. Burned by reckless lending, the so-called secondary banks were in meltdown. House prices, land values, even the markets for antiques and vintage cars, had simply collapsed. The stock market was in cardiac shock, losing a quarter of its value in just a month; by January, share prices had fallen by almost half in less than two years. 'The country is now facing the gravest economic crisis since the end of the war,' Heath's Chancellor had told his Cabinet colleagues in a secret report of unparalleled pessimism. A week before Christmas, he slashed public spending by some £1,200 million (4 per cent), sounding the death knell for an era of economic optimism. Nine out of ten people told the Harris poll that 'things are going very badly for Britain'; only two out of ten thought there would be any improvement in the next year. Labour's Shadow Chancellor, Denis Healey, warned his colleagues that Britain stood on the brink of an 'economic holocaust'. Meanwhile, Heath's Environment Secretary, Geoffrey Rippon, told friends that Britain was 'on the same course as the Weimar government, with runaway inflation and ultra-high unemployment at the end'.[6]

All of this would have been terrifying enough. What made it even worse, though, was the breakdown of relations between the government and the trade unions. After losing one round to the miners two years earlier, Heath had tried desperately to conciliate the union leaders, even offering the Trades Union Congress (TUC) a seat at the table to plan the national economy. But they had turned him down. And when OPEC announced its increase in the price of oil, the miners saw their chance to press for more. In November the National Union of Mineworkers approved an overtime ban. The next day, Heath announced his fifth state of emergency in barely four years. Floodlighting and electric advertising were banned; behind the scenes, the government began printing petrol ration cards. As the railwaymen voted to join the miners in pursuit of higher pay, it seemed that Britain was sliding into darkness. Offices were ordered to turn down their thermostats, while the BBC and ITV were banned from broadcasting after 10.30 at night. On New Year's Day, with fuel supplies running dangerously low, the entire nation went on a three-day working week. But even as Britain shivered by candlelight, peace talks came to nothing. The TUC urged Heath to declare the miners an exception to his incomes policy and give them what they wanted. But he was adamant: nobody must be allowed to break Stage Three. The talks broke down, and on Monday, 4 February the miners voted for an all-out strike. Three days later, exhausted, ill and utterly demoralized, Heath called a general election, begging the public to back the government. His appeal was summed up in a simple two-word phrase: 'Who governs?' But the answer, it turned out, was equally simple: 'Not you.'[7]

Amid all the pressures that had brought down Heath's government – the chronic underperformance of British industry, the seemingly inexorable rise of inflation, the frightening challenges of a post-imperial world and the apparent impotence of the Westminster elite – it was the question of the unions that dominated the headlines. By later standards, their sheer prominence in British life was simply extraordinary. Almost every day the papers carried front-page stories by their labour correspondents reporting on strikes, go-slows, overtime bans and work-to-rules. On the evening news, burly men with steel-grey hair and thick glasses were forever trooping in and out of Number 10, shaking their heads sorrowfully at what their members would think of the government's latest offer. To the left they seemed the defenders of the working classes and the guardians of the socialist flame; to the right they seemed a state within a state, anarchic, ungovernable, even subversive. Membership was close to an all-time peak: by the end of the 1970s, some 13.3 million people, about 56 per cent of the workforce, belonged to a trade union. With many people desperate to protect their living standards against inflation, white-collar unions were buoyant: in just fifteen years after 1964, the membership of the National Association of Local Government Officers (NALGO) doubled, while that of the National Union of Public Employees (NUPE) trebled. And since they appeared so good at protecting their members' interests, there seemed no reason why membership would not keep rising. The unions, wrote the *Economist*'s labour correspondent Stephen Milligan in 1976, had 'more power and influence than [the] political parties'; all in all, they were 'perhaps the major political force' in the land.[8]

Trade union power was perhaps the central theme of British political life in the Wilson years. In 1972 five out of ten people thought the unions were too powerful, rising to six out of ten in 1974 and seven out of ten in 1975. In his first administration, hoping to cut down on unofficial wildcat strikes, Harold Wilson and Barbara Castle had proposed a package of reforms, known as *In Place of Strife*. But the union leaders refused to compromise, some of Wilson's ministers kicked up a fuss and eventually he lost his nerve. Then Heath had a go, passing an Industrial Relations Act that provoked massive union unrest and eventually collapsed around his ears. Perhaps it was no wonder that so many people thought the union leaders – the 'new barons', as Milligan called them – were the most powerful men in the land. Indeed, men like Hugh Scanlon, the dour, goldfish-fancying Marxist leader of the Amalgamated Union of Engineering Workers (AUEW), or Len Murray, the mild-mannered Shropshire farm worker's son who had become general secretary of the TUC, were national celebrities, more famous than most ministers.

At the end of 1976, half the public thought the leader of the Transport and General Workers' Union (TGWU), Jack Jones, was the most powerful man in the country, with only one in four nominating the Prime Minister. The son of a Liverpool docker, a veteran of the Spanish Civil War who had accepted regular KGB donations until breaking with them over the Prague Spring, this bespectacled, bullet-headed man struck fear into the hearts of Middle England. Another union leader remarked that he had 'a smile glinting like the sunlight on the brass plate of a coffin', while the journalist Paul Johnson nicknamed him the 'Emperor Jones', after the Caribbean despot in Eugene O'Neill's play. But nobody doubted that Jones fought hard for his members: the *Financial Times* called him a 'national statesman, devoted to doing what he believes to be best for Britain's workers and their families'. It was a sign of his national standing, as well as the respect he commanded in Whitehall, that the imperial nickname stuck.[9]

Yet the great irony of British life in the 1970s was that trade union militancy was born not out of strength but out of weakness. Far from being bound together by working-class solidarity and a shared dream of a brave new world, most British unions were tiny, fragmented and almost comically old-fashioned. For all the press attention given to the Emperor Jones and his fellow union leaders, they were much less powerful than they looked. Behind the headlines, as the *Financial Times*'s labour correspondent Robert Taylor remarked, they were 'uncertain, rather frightened, reactive and muddled men', adrift in a bewildering modern world. And although the language of class confrontation was everywhere in the late 1970s, most union members were interested only in their pay packets. Most had initially supported Wilson's and Heath's union reforms; as early as 1971, some 68 per cent even thought that their leaders' behaviour was 'a threat to the prosperity of the country'. Many were almost Thatcherites in embryo: a poll in January 1975 found that two-thirds of union members opposed further nationalization, while a survey of manual workers found that 82 per cent endorsed the profit motive, 86 per cent agreed it was important to live in a free-enterprise society and 89 per cent thought it was fair to pay dividends to shareholders. For most people, Taylor remarked, the point of having a union card was not to gain entry to some socialist paradise but 'to gain tangible rewards', from a foreign holiday to a new kitchen. Younger workers were accustomed to the fruits of affluence; what they wanted from their union was not so much the New Jerusalem as a new Cortina.[10]

And while Conservative editorials thundered about the dangers of unchecked union power and Labour ministers bent over backwards to give them whatever they wanted, more perceptive observers could see that change was in the air. The 'forward march of labour', warned the Marxist historian Eric Hobsbawm in the autumn of 1978, was coming to a halt. The days of working-class solidarity, he thought, were over: under the pressures of affluence and individualism, the labour movement had broken up into competing 'sections and groups, each pursuing

its own economic interest irrespective of the rest'. On the left, his analysis provoked a hail of criticism. But in the last months of the decade,
events would prove him devastatingly right.[11]

In 1964, when Harold Wilson had first become Prime Minister, much of
Britain had still been desperately poor. Wandering across the industrial
landscape in the year of that first victory, the travel writer Geoffrey
Moorhouse had chronicled with horrified fascination the world of the
'other England', a country where millions of people ate and slept in
conditions that would have seemed familiar to their great-grandparents;
where thousands of elderly people lived alone in conditions of damp,
darkness and utter isolation; where more than 3 million households
lived without baths, inside toilets and hot running water. Yet by the time
Wilson returned to Number 10, the life of the other England had
changed almost beyond recognition. Reshaped by affluence and technology, Britain was now, wrote an American reporter, a much 'cleaner,
sunnier, brighter place in which to live'. In 1964, fewer than one in ten
households boasted central heating; by 1974, almost half of all homes
were centrally heated. In 1964, only one in three households had a
fridge; by 1974, it was more like nine out of ten, and many had bought
freezers, too. Half of all households had a telephone; about half had a
car, and almost everybody had a vacuum cleaner. Almost everybody had
a television, too, and in 1974, for the first time, colour sets outsold
black-and-white. Even the washing machine, still a sensation ten years
earlier, was becoming ubiquitous. By the time Wilson left public life,
seven out of ten people had one.[12]

And for those who had everything, there was always something new
to buy. By the end of 1978, British consumers had imported more than
136,000 video recorders, and by the following spring's general election,
Sony was marketing a product that would revolutionize broadcasting, or so it predicted. The Betamax video recorder, the adverts boasted,
could record 'up to three and a quarter hours of television on one tape',
and even had a 'unique remote control pause switch, which means you
can edit out any unwanted material without getting out of your chair'.
If you were clever enough to buy one, the campaign promised, you
would soon be 'impressing your friends with your new video recorder',
perhaps by inviting them to 'a private film show in your living room'.
'The real advantage of the Sony Betamax can't be appreciated over a
week-end,' it concluded, with comically disastrous confidence. 'It takes
years.'[13]

For a glimpse of the brave new world of mid-1970s Britain, it is hard to beat Mike Leigh's play *Abigail's Party*, first performed on stage at the Hampstead Theatre and then broadcast by the BBC in November 1977. Although the play is best remembered as a merciless dissection of suburban pretensions, from the ghastly Beverly's fondness for Demis Roussos to her harassed husband's unread volumes of Shakespeare and attempts to entertain guests with Beethoven's Ninth, what it captures above all are the ambitions and anxieties of a society transformed by affluence. In the hands of Alison Steadman, Beverly is a monster of social one-upmanship, but she also reflects a generation enjoying comforts their parents and grandparents could barely have imagined. From the silver plate and faux-leather brown sofas to the bowls of olives and bottle of red wine chilling nicely in the fridge, her drinks party is a monument to the consumerism of the mid-1970s. In their different ways, too, each of the supporting characters is marked by the transformations that had remade British society since the beginning of the 1960s. Her husband, Laurence, is an overworked estate agent, trading in the suburban dreams that drove so many sitcoms in the mid-1970s, and reflecting the enormous new interest in the property market since the credit boom of the Heath years. One of her guests, Susan, is a divorcee with a 15-year-old daughter – an increasingly common figure after the Divorce Reform Act of 1969, even though divorce still carried a potent social stigma. And another, Tony, is a former footballer who now works as a computer operator, one of the foot soldiers in Wilson's predicted technological revolution.

To some commentators, the characters appeared disturbingly rootless: in *The Times*, Bernard Levin lamented that these inhabitants of 'Affluent-Yobbonia' had been 'torn loose from history, faith, spirit, even language', a common criticism of the suburban lower-middle classes since the turn of the century. Indeed much of the comedy of *Abigail's Party* derives from the tasteless vulgarity of the music and design, not least Beverly's horrendous work of erotic 'art', Stephen Pearson's *Wings of Love*, which proved enormously popular in the mid-1970s and sold more than 3 million prints, but which her husband has understandably banished upstairs. But then why would Beverly know any better? Like her guests, she has travelled an enormously long way in a short space of time, from a Britain in which paintings, wine and olives were almost unknown outside the upper-middle classes to one in which millions of ordinary families were in thrall to Robert Carrier and Delia Smith. And to be fair, she is not wrong about everything. At the time, many middle-class viewers famously winced when she puts a bottle of red wine in the fridge; but then as Beverly rightly remarks, 'it's Beaujolais! Fantastic!'[14]

In its narrow focus on the suburban middle classes, *Abigail's Party* was hardly unusual. In plays such as Alan Ayckbourn's trilogy *The Norman Conquests* (1973), as well as long-running comedy series such as *Butterflies* (from 1978) and *Terry and June* (from 1979), similar situations were rarely off the television screens, even though their treatment was often radically different. Even fifteen or twenty years earlier, they would have depicted a world far beyond the means of most ordinary families. But it is hardly surprising that by the mid-1970s suburban comedies of manners had become so popular with tens of millions of people. Escapism had something to do with it, of course. To viewers alarmed by strikes, inflation, hooliganism and pornography, it was comforting to lose themselves in the world of Terry and June Medford, where the worst thing that can happen is that Terry might have to partner his irascible boss at bridge, or look after a frisky terrier for a neighbour, or take delivery of an unexpectedly large consignment of gorgonzola. But *Terry and June*'s domestic setting reflected a world in which home ownership had doubled in just thirty years and in which everyday social life was becoming intensely privatized. More than ever, wrote the sociologists Peter Willmott and Michael Young in 1973, the home was 'the centre of people's lives', not just as a badge of status in a mobile, fluid society, or as the place where people watched television and entertained friends, but as a vital financial asset in itself. 'Houses are one of the few investments to keep ahead of inflation,' the developers Sunley Homes urged first-time buyers in 1977, and of course they were right. In the decade after 1970, the average house price increased tenfold. And with more than half the population owning their own homes, Britain was already well on the way to becoming a property-owning democracy, the dream of the Baldwin era apparently fulfilled.[15]

Since people now spent so much time indoors, they lavished extraordinary attention on their homes. In 1977, a survey found that more than half of all men (and one in five women) had spent time on DIY or household repairs in the past month, while a similar number had also spent time gardening. Neatness and order mattered immensely as badges of status: visiting a suburban bungalow in Blackburn, one writer was struck by its 'severely controlled' front garden, its frosted-glass door, its living room decorated with 'damasked wallpaper, polished metal, chintz, a nest of tables'. And since so many people had grown up in an era of shortages, they were keen to show off their material gains, stuffing their houses with all manner of ornaments. Beverly's living room in *Abigail's Party*, with its trinkets, lamps and violent wallpaper, must have been immediately familiar to millions of viewers. And in her state-of-the-nation novel *The Middle Ground* (1980), Margaret Drabble lists what a visitor might expect to see in a typical lower-middle-class home:

> flowered carpets, best tea-sets, an ingenious variety of draped lace curtains, Spanish-style vinyl tiles, wall clocks rayed like the sun in never-dying Deco, china Siamese cats and pigs and dogs, Toby jugs, glass fish, plastic rabbits, rubbery trolls, outsize turquoise teddies, plastic daffodils, plastic palm trees, fake fur rugs bristling with spidery white acrylic electric light, all the wonderful eclectic bad taste of the English.[16]

In Drabble's words, this was a 'brave new world of synthesis': although affluent, vaguely countercultural youngsters often liked a minimalist, stripped-pine look, many others thought that abundance and style were the same thing. Bit by bit, though, tastes were changing: wallpaper sales fell by 40 per cent between 1971 and 1976, while *The Times* noticed a growing trend for 'timber, cork, stone and brick finishes'. But if one word typified the look of the decade, it was *brown*. 'In my house at the moment,' wrote the same paper's home improvements expert, 'there is a brown, cream and white colour scheme, with cream curtains, wood floors, brown upholstery and white walls in the sitting room, cream long-haired carpet, white curtains and brown walls in the main bedroom, and brown and white wallpaper with brown carpets in the bathroom.' To later generations it probably looked hideous; at the time, however, it must have looked satisfyingly modern.[17]

As *Abigail's Party* showed, the look of the home was not the only thing that had changed. The olives and Beaujolais that Beverly serves at her terrible soirée are themselves revealing indicators of affluence and ambition: even twenty years before, very few suburban estate agents' wives would have ever tasted olives. In a relatively short space of time, however, everyday culinary tastes had been transformed. One obvious factor was immigration: by 1981, the census recorded the presence of some 2.2 million Commonwealth immigrants in Britain, although the true figure was almost certainly higher. Even many small towns now had Indian or Chinese restaurants; by the mid-1970s, an estimated one in eight restaurants served 'foreign' food, and in 1977 the *Good Food Guide* reported that there were now more Chinese takeaways than fish-and-chip shops. Contemplating the drive from Hull to Liverpool along the M62, through some of 'the least lovely landscapes known to man', the *Guide* advised anyone hungry for 'real food' to search for 'the Chinese and Indians, who cook it as though they believed in it', which was not something that could be said for most native chefs.[18]

'Happy indeed,' remarked *The Times*, pondering the twists of fate that had brought so many Italians, Bangladeshis, Cypriots and Cantonese to Britain, 'have been the chances that brought Peking duck, tandoori chicken, moussaka and zabaglione within the purview of the man on the Clapham omnibus.' Especially in London, new flavours were arriving all the time: in September 1978 alone the paper reviewed new Lebanese, Korean, Japanese and Indonesian restaurants. And although Harold Wilson boasted of his fondness for HP Sauce and maintained that English cheese was superior to French, millions of his countrymen had other ideas. In December 1979, an intrepid reporter braved the Channel storms to take the ferry to Boulogne, where at weekends, English customers accounted for four-fifths of the food and wine trade. 'A few years ago the English would come in, touch everything and buy nothing. Now they are reasonable customers,' one cheesemonger remarked. But they were not universally popular. 'It is impossible to shop here on Saturdays,' complained a French customer. 'You cannot get a trolley. The British bag them all and then spend hours arguing interminably about what they should buy.'[19]

The boom in foreign travel explains one of the biggest success stories of the 1970s, symbolized by Beverly's chilled Beaujolais. At the beginning of the decade, foreign package trips still accounted for a mere 8 per cent of the total holidays taken by British families. But as the cost of flights fell and as the government relaxed its currency restrictions, the two-week break in Spain with Horizon or Thomson became one of the great status symbols of the age. In 1971, British tourists had taken some 4 million holidays abroad; by 1973 they took 9 million and by 1981 more than 13 million. And what they brought back, apart from blistering sunburn, a splitting headache and a sombrero, was a taste for wine. Twenty years earlier, almost two out of three people never drank wine at all. But with imports pouring in after Britain joined the EEC, and with advertisers presenting wine as modern, glamorous and sophisticated, Beverly was only one of millions who found they rather liked it. By 1973 the British drank 9 pints of wine per head per year, by 1975 11 pints and by 1980 almost 20 pints. By this stage, according to the wine critic Pamela Vandyke Price, they had 'a wider selection from the wines of the world [and] more in terms of quality from the High Street than anyone else'. Even the critics' tastes could be decidedly eclectic: for Christmas dinner in 1977, Vandyke Price advised *Times* readers to try 'Hungarian riesling or Yugoslav riesling, or any of the reds from Hungary, Rumania, Yugoslavia and Bulgaria'. No doubt this reflected the fact that wine-drinking was still a mild affectation: the middle and upper classes accounted for 61 per cent of all wine sales, and many people, keen to look cosmopolitan, were drawn to more exotic labels. 'I don't think the English know wine is for drinking,' a French wine merchant remarked. 'They think about buying it as they would an important piece of furniture. I think they put it on the shelf and keep it for an ornament for ever after.'[20]

From a culinary point of view, though, the real story of the late 1970s was the stunning boom in convenience food. At the turn of the decade, the typical housewife still went shopping three times a week, usually on her local high street. But shopping habits were changing: by 1973 Carrefour had opened Britain's first 60,000-square-foot hypermarkets in Caerphilly and Telford, and other retailers rushed to follow suit. By the time Harold Wilson returned to Downing Street, Britain boasted almost a hundred out-of-town hypermarkets, including 27 branches of Asda, 23 Co-ops, 21 Fine Fares, 20 Tescos and 11 Morrisons. The 'trendy, out-of-town superstore with its cut-price shopping and easy parking will become a British institution', predicted a spokesman for Debenhams. Some shoppers complained they missed the camaraderie of the high street; others, however, relished the sheer choice of the hypermarket. Interviewed in 1974, one housewife remarked that she loved supermarket shopping, because 'I know I can choose all these lovely foods'. In particular, new supermarkets carried vast freezer chests, exploiting the surging popularity of the deep freeze. In 1972, less than one in ten homes had one; by 1978, almost half. Soon, even small grocery stores stocked Vesta curries, Birds Eye fish fingers, McCain oven chips and Wall's ice cream, while by 1975 there were fifteen Iceland freezer centres across the country. There was even a minor genre of frozen-food cookbooks, advising women how to prepare shepherd's pies, casseroles and goulash in bulk, and how to freeze cottage cheese, pâtés and, bizarrely, sardine sandwiches.[21]

Frozen food succeeded for the same reason that thousands of people went out and bought mashed-potato granules after the first Smash commercials, with their famously annoying Martian robots, aired in 1974. The days when most wives and mothers had remained at home, doing

the laundry and preparing the dinner, were long gone. By 1971, almost
47 per cent of married women were working; by 1981, 54 per cent. A
year after the Smash robots made their debut, even the Conservative
Party elected a leader who relied on her freezer. 'I try to cook two or
three things at the same time to have dishes to put in the fridge or
freezer in reserve,' Margaret Thatcher admitted to her local newspaper.
She used to get up at half past six every morning to make Denis's breakfast, and confided that she was 'so busy getting it ready for the others'
that she rarely had time to eat her grapefruit and boiled egg. This was
by no means unusual: the year after she became Tory leader, a survey for
Kellogg's found that only 20 per cent of people began their day with
bacon and eggs, while 40 per cent had cereal and 25 per cent had nothing but tea or coffee. With so many harassed mothers coming home
from work tired and hungry, fast food had an obvious appeal. And
when a chef called John Docker contacted Marks & Spencer with a
plan for a range of high-class 'ready meals', he was pushing at an open
door. Launched in October 1979, the St Michael Chicken Kiev cost
£1.99 for a pack of two. The group director thought it would never sell,
because customers would be put off by the garlic. But after years of foreign holidays, garlic held few terrors for British diners. Chicken Kiev
flew off the shelves; Marks & Spencer never looked back.[22]

The obsession with convenience also reflected a working environment that felt more hectic and high-pressured than ever. In 1978, in one
of those books that at the time appear powerfully insightful but later
seem painfully wrong-headed, the American journalist Bernard Nossiter
argued that Britain was a 'model of sorts' to the rest of the world, since
its people had come to prefer 'leisure over goods'. British workers might
seem slow and lazy, he suggested, but their relaxed pace meant that they
were also 'pleasanter, easier with each other and with strangers'. This
was to prove very wide of the mark, for even before the advent of
Thatcherism offices were becoming both more open (literally, thanks to
the rise of open-plan design) and more cut-throat. Once, middle-class
executives had counted on having a job for life. Now they were in real
danger of being sacked if profits fell, if they failed to meet their targets
or, even more frighteningly, if a computer could do a cheaper job. In the
City, executive dining rooms were dying out, sandwich bars were on the
rise and even the beloved tea trolleys were being replaced with vending
machines offering a quick shot of Nescafé, the ideal pick-me-up for a
harried employee. Increasingly, executives admitted that they took work
home with them, even poring over their files at weekends. 'If you saw

me very happily sitting in the garden with a drink at my side I might be thinking over a problem,' one suburban executive told Peter Willmott and Michael Young. 'If you came along beside me you might be talking to me for ten minutes and I wouldn't hear you, I'd be so concentrated.' It was no wonder that, after studying work and family life in the 1970s, Willmott and Young predicted that, in the years to come, 'there will inevitably be more divorces'.[23]

The irony was that, even as the demands of the workplace became more intense, the leisure and entertainment possibilities were greater than ever. Critics were always wringing their hands about Britain's cultural decline, yet, as the *Observer* pointed out in September 1975, the arts had never been 'so accessible to so many people', from the booming sales of records, posters and paperbacks to the enormous queues outside the Tate's exhibitions on landscape painting in 1974, Turner in 1975 and Constable in 1976. Never before, the *Observer* added, had 'there been so much do-it-yourself art – amateur acting, music-making, Sunday painting'. Never before, either, had there been 'so much money' for 'institutions, objects and events'. Despite the horrendous economic headlines, business patronage for the arts reached a record £6 million by 1979, while Arts Council funding for regional arts associations more than trebled in ten years. Despite dark mutterings of decline, the book world, too, was booming: between 1970 and 1979 the number of new titles every year rose from 24,000 to 36,000, while library lending reached an all-time peak and book clubs like BCA and the Literary Guild boasted more than a million members.[24]

But of course by far the most popular form of entertainment was the small screen. 'Britain is an armchair nation,' declared the *Guardian* in April 1976. 'Nine out of ten of us watch television as our main leisure pursuit.' Researchers found that people watched television for around sixteen hours a week in summer and twenty in winter, often tuning in for an entire evening. There might have been only three channels, but by any standards the quality was very high: between 1974 and 1979, merely to pick a few examples at random, a discerning viewer might have caught *Abigail's Party*, *A Bouquet of Barbed Wire*, *Dad's Army*, *The Fall and Rise of Reginald Perrin*, *Fawlty Towers*, *Gangsters*, *The Generation Game*, *The Good Life*, *Grange Hill*, *I, Claudius*, *Life on Earth*, *The Morecambe and Wise Show*, *The Naked Civil Servant*, *The Pallisers*, *Pennies from Heaven*, *Porridge*, *Rising Damp*, *Survivors*, *The Sweeney* and *Tinker Tailor Soldier Spy*, which was perhaps the best of the lot. It is true that a rather less discerning viewer might have found himself watching *Space 1999*, *Love Thy Neighbour* or *Man About the House*; even so, the fact that so many of these programmes are so fondly remembered is surely revealing. Viewing figures were enormous: even the dreariest *Play for Today* might get up to 10 million viewers, and sitcoms and light entertainment shows commanded gigantic audiences. Among the most watched programmes of the decade were an episode of *Love Thy Neighbour* in April 1974, an episode of *George and Mildred* in October 1976 and the Christmas Day 1977 editions of *The Mike Yarwood Show* and *Morecambe and Wise*. The latter, the dynamic duo's final show for the BBC, had an astonishing guest cast, including Elton John, Penelope Keith, Richard Briers, Kenneth Kendall, Arthur Lowe, John Le Mesurier, Frank Bough, James Hunt and Angela Rippon, and attracted well over 20 million viewers. In Jonathan Coe's novel *The Rotters' Club* (2001), this edition of *Morecambe and Wise* becomes a fitting symbol of a lost consensus, the teenage hero realizing that, at that moment, Britain really is one nation:

> It came to him that he was only one person, and his family was only one family, out of millions of people and millions of families throughout the country, all sitting in front of their television sets . . . all of them laughing at the same joke, and he felt an incredible sense of . . . oneness, that was the only word he could think of, a sense that the entire nation was being briefly, fugitively drawn together in the divine act of laughter.[25]

Contrary to what we often remember, millions of people watched these shows in black and white. In 1970, only 1.7 per cent of the population had colour sets; only four years later did colour licences overtake monochrome, and as late as 1980 three out of ten people were still watching in black and white. Yet odd though it may seem, it was at these moments, perhaps more than ever before or since, that Britain came closest to being one nation united by a common culture. And given that the culture of the 1970s is often remembered as dark, conflicted and intensely partisan, it is worth noting that the single most popular non-factual programme of the decade was the final episode of the first season of *To the Manor Born*, which attracted almost 24 million viewers on 11 November 1979. There was surely something appropriate about the success of a series set in a bucolic, backward-looking English village, where a self-made millionaire of immigrant stock has bought the imposing Grantleigh Manor, much to the shock of the locals. And on the surface, this was not the only way *To the Manor Born* reflected the times: watching Penelope Keith's formidable Audrey fforbes-Hamilton, many viewers must have been struck by the uncanny parallels with another bossy woman who was rarely out of the headlines. But the resemblance was only skin-deep. Given her fondness for self-made men, Margaret Thatcher would have much preferred the millionaire Richard de Vere to the upper-class, paternalistic Mrs fforbes-Hamilton. In any case, since Audrey often dismisses de Vere as a mere 'grocer', she would never have had much time for a grocer's daughter.[26]

Television played a dominant role in the imaginations of millions of children growing up in the second half of the 1970s: from *Bagpuss* and *Bod* to *The Flumps* and *The Wombles*, from *Mr Benn* and *Captain Pugwash* to *Ivor the Engine* and *Noggin the Nog*, from *The Magic Roundabout* to *Multi-coloured Swap Shop*, the choice and quality were unsurpassed. But these shows were only part of an extraordinarily vivid cultural landscape, a cornucopia of sweets and comics, toys and games, books and records. Even the titles hinted at a world of unimaginable excitement: Flying Saucers and Sherbet Fountains, *2000 AD* and *Captain Britain*, Space Hoppers and *Star Wars* figures, *Doctor Who and the Loch Ness Monster* and *Fungus the Bogeyman*, *Haunted House* and *Offshore Oil Strike* – this last being that rare thing, a North Sea oil-themed board game. Even most working-class teenagers had a disposable income of their own: quizzing sixth-form pupils at a London comprehensive, Hunter Davies found that a third had weekend or evening jobs, earning between 50p and £1 an hour, while just under half had regular pocket money from their parents. Their hobbies and interests were eminently predictable: football and sport came first, followed by films, discos and pop music, board games and drinking. 'Also mentioned', Davies noted wryly, 'were Scouts, Woodcraft Folk, cycling, talking to friends on the phone, smoking, sleeping, Frisbee, poetry, YHA [youth hostelling], climbing, drumming, gardening and sex.' Yet far from being delinquent debauchees, many led quiet lives and held strikingly conservative attitudes: a survey of fifth-form girls in 1975 found that the vast majority dreamed above all of getting married and having children. And although retrospectives of the 1970s are usually full of skinheads, football hooligans and punks, most youngsters were none of these things. Despite being caricatured by the press as a generation of selfish materialists, thousands were keen to get involved in voluntary work, and the number of Community Service Volunteers rose by six times in ten years. In terms of numbers, by far the most successful youth organization of the day was the Scouting movement, whose membership surged from 539,340 in 1970 to a record 641,281 ten years later.[27]

Even young people's musical tastes were much more conservative than we usually remember. For all the fuss about the 'filth and the fury', punk rock had only a very limited appeal. Compared with disco, which was by far the most popular new subgenre, punk's chart impact was negligible. Almost incredibly, George McCrae's 'Rock Your Baby' (1974) sold *forty times* as many copies as the Sex Pistols' bestselling record, 'God Save the Queen' (1977). Most punk albums sold very poorly; by contrast, the most popular albums of the day were records like Mike Oldfield's *Tubular Bells* (1974), Abba's *Arrival* (1977), and the soundtracks of *Saturday Night Fever* (1977) and *Grease* (1978), all of which appealed to young and middle-aged alike. Indeed, to glance through the singles charts for the last years of the 1970s is to enter a world in which punk had never happened: among the bestselling singles of 1978 and 1979, after all, were such edgy, subversive recordings as John Travolta and Olivia Newton John's 'You're the One that I Want', Art Garfunkel's 'Bright Eyes' and Cliff Richard's 'We Don't Talk Any More'. The truth is that punk never appealed to more than a minority, whereas disco was a genuinely national phenomenon, transcending barriers of gender, class and even generation. At the end of the decade, a reporter visited a dancing school in Barnet that offered disco classes alongside old-fashioned ballroom styles. Enthusiastic disco learners, the proprietor explained, were drawn from 'all age groups': he had even arranged special classes for old-age pensioners. 'A lot of ladies who have gone to keep fit classes have found that disco dancing gives them valid exercise,' explained another dancing teacher. 'And they do not have to change into leotards to do it.'[28]

In March 1977, Granada Television's series *This England* sent a camera crew to a miserable, run-down old ballroom a few miles from Harold Wilson's Huyton constituency. Claiming some 100,000 members, Wigan Casino was the most celebrated venue in the country for a craze known as Northern Soul. Originally a Mod club, it played obscure American soul records to young devotees who had travelled from across Lancashire, Yorkshire and the Midlands to dance all night. It was not the only club of its kind – Manchester had the Twisted Wheel, Blackpool the Highland Rooms, Stoke-on-Trent the Golden Torch, Wolverhampton the Catacombs – but it was probably the most celebrated. Every weekend, trains and coaches ferried hundreds of youngsters in

tight-fitting sports vests, wide-collared shirts and high-waisted flares to
this decrepit corner of the industrial North-west. Since the club had no
licence, they did not drink, but many took speed so that they could keep
going into the small hours. But the extraordinary thing, as Granada's
haunting film captured, was the sheer incongruity of the scene. The director, Tony Palmer, intercut shots of youngsters dancing ecstatically
with black-and-white photos of Wigan in its industrial heyday – miners
toiling half-naked in the dark, factory workers staring mutely at the
camera – as well as footage of the town in 1977, the mills empty and
disused, the canals dank and silent. And as the exhausted dancers
poured out of the club at dawn, many filing onto coaches for the journey home, the cameras captured the grim background: the sullen brick
terraces, glistening with the early morning rain; the once-mighty civic
buildings, now damp and stained; the new high-rise council flats, glowering mutely on the horizon; a rag and bone man, forlornly pushing his
cart through the deserted streets.[29]

What made Wigan Casino a compelling symbol of change was not
merely the fact that it attracted thousands of white working-class
youngsters to dance to black American music, but that the evening's
revels took place against a landscape of such dilapidation and decay. 'I
think there's something wrong with the world,' one local fan said sadly,
looking back to 'the Industrial Revolution, when Wigan *was* something
and people cared about each other'. Once a successful textile and coalmining town, it had been badly hit by the decline of heavy industry.
Casual visitors could be lulled into thinking that all was well: most of
the slag heaps had gone, while the town centre had what *The Times*
called 'one of the most attractive covered shopping centres in the North'.
But the bitter irony was that many people could not afford to shop
there. In less than a decade, at least one in ten jobs in Wigan had simply
disappeared, throwing 6,600 people – about 9 per cent of the total
workforce – onto the dole. Across the North-west as a whole, the textile
workforce had fallen by almost two-thirds: in Wigan, there were only a
handful of mills left, most of them relying on machines rather than men,
while the Coal Board had closed all the collieries. Wigan was 'a town
built on physical strength, manual labour', wrote the journalist Jeremy
Seabrook, who visited in the second half of the 1970s. Now, 'most of
that force and strength' had become redundant. 'The sense of loss', he
thought, 'is still overwhelming.'[30]

To Seabrook, Wigan presented the spectacle of an old-fashioned,
male-dominated working-class world in deep decay. Wandering through

the 'abbreviated terraces and derelict sites', past empty shopfronts and abandoned factories, he found a landscape of 'cavities in the road filled with water which make some streets almost impassable on foot, broken-down outhouses, gaping doors and windows, smashed glass and rotting wood, heaps of fallen brick'. On one side 'the sunshine streams through the lattice of a roof without tiles'; on the other, 'a chapel is bricked up like a sepulchre'. It was a similar picture elsewhere. Across the moors, in what had once been the West Riding, he found parts of Bradford looking 'as though they had been abandoned, as though the people had deserted the worn-out housing and exhausted landscape and gone elsewhere'. The ruined streets, the empty work-shops evoked the aftermath of some 'natural disaster', leaving 'a debris of empty cans, cider bottles, ordure and ashes'. For Seabrook, all this reflected a deeper story: 'the desolation of ruined communities and broken human associations', as Britain's working-class culture col-lapsed under the pressures of affluence and individualism. 'Everything speaks, not of the boundless joy that should have come with the release from the old poverty, but of great human pain,' he wrote. And contem-plating the redevelopment of industrial cities like Nottingham, with its new concrete Victoria Shopping Centre, one of the biggest malls in the country, he felt a surge of anger. 'The working-class past is extinguished,' he wrote bitterly. 'It is something ugly and shaming, and the overwhelm-ing need is to expunge it.'[31]

The decline and fall of working-class Britain was one of the most common themes of cultural life in the 1970s. Even the opening credits of the sitcom *Whatever Happened to the Likely Lads?* (1973–4) are drenched in nostalgia, showing how the old landscape of back-to-back terraces and busy factories has given way to a new world of high-rise blocks and suburban estates. Of the two characters, James Bolam's beer-drinking, defiantly masculine Terry Collier now seems painfully old-fashioned; across the country, everything Terry represented was in headlong retreat. With manufacturing in deep decline, the mainstays of working-class life – the factory, the colliery, the pub, the football club, the chapel, the co-op, even the Labour Party – were closing their doors. Across Scotland, Wales, the Midlands and the North, buildings that had stood for generations were ripped down, making way for a new land-scape of flyovers, ring roads, tower blocks and office buildings. Driving out of Bradford in the mid-1970s, along a road often frequented by Peter Sutcliffe, the Yorkshire Ripper, the visitor passed not busy facto-ries and crowded pubs, but a seedy collection of sex shops, betting shops, curry houses and prostitutes' haunts. To the consternation of some older residents, mosques and Sikh temples had replaced churches and cinemas. 'The bands ceased to march,' writes the historian Robert Colls. 'Banners were furled. Methodist chapels, emotional heartlands of the Industrial Revolution, became carpet stores. Pine pews were ripped out and sold as antiques.' And as Terry Collier gazes out over Newcastle from the top of a multi-storey car park, he realizes that almost nothing recognizable is left. 'None of our memories is intact,' he says sadly.[32]

The really interesting character in *Whatever Happened to the Likely Lads?*, though, is not Terry but his go-getting friend Bob Ferris (Rodney Bewes), with his semi-detached suburban house, bouffant hair, pushy wife and skiing holidays. What Bob represents, and what writers like Jeremy Seabrook never quite recognized, is the fact that the working-class past was being extinguished not just by vast, impersonal economic forces, but by the choices of working-class people themselves. It was people like Bob Ferris who *chose* to move into new housing estates and New Towns, breaking the old associations of family and street. It was people like Bob who stopped going to chapels and pubs and dance halls, flocked in their thousands to Nottingham's Victoria Centre every Saturday and unashamedly relished the new consumerism that Seabrook found so repugnant. It was even people like Bob, millions of them, who deserted the Labour Party for Mrs Thatcher's Conservatives in 1979. They were not helpless victims but collaborators in the process of change, even if many observers on the political left refused to see it. 'A great sickness has come over a lot of our working-class traditions; something cheap and gaudy is trying to destroy them,' an old man told Seabrook in Bradford. His words recalled those of the critic Richard Hoggart, who had famously decried the 'shiny barbarism' of mass culture in the late 1950s. Like Hoggart, Seabrook regarded working-class youngsters with bewildered horror. 'Few young people visit the Labour clubs,' he wrote disapprovingly. (His own description of one club, full of pensioners playing bingo, might have told him why.) 'They are anchored in a culture of commodities,' he went on, 'helpless dependants on the fantasies it engenders.' But to many people, a culture of commodities meant real comforts, real opportunities that had been denied their parents and grandparents. They were keen to move on, to look forwards. Seabrook never understood this. Margaret Thatcher did.[33]

All the same, Seabrook's journey into the decaying pockets of industrial Britain exposed a side of life that never appeared in *Terry and June* or *To the Manor Born*. Despite talk of a classless society a decade earlier, Britain in the second half of the 1970s remained deeply divided by birth, wealth and breeding. A Gallup poll in October 1974 found that 49 per cent readily identified themselves as working-class, with 12 per cent calling themselves lower-middle-class, 31 per cent calling themselves middle-class, 2 per cent upper-middle and 0.3 per cent upper-class. These were not nominal or trivial distinctions: the gulf between rich and poor lurked behind the government statistics charting unemployment, infant mortality, alcoholism and cigarette smoking. 'Just about everything', wrote the *Financial Times*'s Joe Rogaly, 'from the newspaper we read through the food we eat to the holiday we take is differentiated by class.' And far from dissolving at the touch of affluence, some distinctions were becoming ever more marked. After a long period of improvement, the gap between rich and poor began to widen again in 1976, almost certainly as a result of the decline in manufacturing. 'In our cities we are developing two nations,' lamented the Conservative politician Peter Walker a year later; 'the inner city and the outer city, with the inner city suffering from increasing unemployment, increasing crime and deteriorating housing.' And for those unlucky enough to live in council estates like Tottenham's Broadwater Farm or Hackney's Holly Street, blighted by vandalism, mugging and gang violence as well as leakages, vermin, poverty and unemployment, the sunny suburban pleasures of *Terry and June* must have seemed like the stuff of fantasy.[34]

Of course, life at the bottom was much better than it had been when Harold Wilson was a boy. Outside a block of council flats in Blackburn, one visitor was struck by the trappings of consumerism jammed into the bins: 'bottles and jars, of milk, sauce, salad cream, pickles, jam; tins of beans, fish, Fray Bentos steak pies, fruit, spaghetti rings, Spam, vegetables; hardened slices of bread fanning from their waxed paper, silver foil trays from the takeaway, egg boxes, plastic containers, dispensers of foams, creams, oils and polish; nappies, tights, old clothing', and so on, right down to the 'transistors, broken cassettes, toys and dolls'. But with unemployment rising, there were no grounds for complacency. The poorest families were still shut out of the brave new world their countrymen took for granted: as late as 1973, a staggering 16 per cent of homes in the north of England still had outside toilets. Six years later, the sociologist Peter Townsend published his landmark survey *Poverty in the United Kingdom*, redefining the poverty line as 150 per cent of supplementary benefit and estimating that around 8 per cent of the population lived beneath it. On the right, his conclusions were bitterly resisted. Yet his survey threw up some extraordinarily moving stories, like that of the Nelsons, an Oldham couple who had been forced out of work by severe epilepsy and bronchitis respectively. They lived in a council flat and rented their television; everything else had been donated by charities and relatives. To provide their three children with school uniforms and a little pocket money, they had no social life, had no breakfast, often went without cooked meals and went to bed early to save fuel. Asked if they had recently had a summer holiday, Mrs Nelson nodded vigorously. 'Oh yes,' she said, 'we saved and saved for weeks.' It turned out that they had been on a trip to see *The Sound of Music* at the local cinema.[35]

For those trapped at the very bottom, any chance of escape seemed worth taking. At the beginning of the 1960s there had been barely 600 registered heroin addicts in Britain. Ten years later there were almost 2,000, although police sources suspected the true figure was nearer 8,000. Once the fashionable drug of the idle rich, heroin was becoming the blight of the urban poor. Home Office addiction statistics were rising year after year, and the Standing Conference on Drug Abuse warned of a sharp increase in 'multiple drug abuse', the latest trend being for a cocktail of heroin, alcohol and barbiturates. Most users, the report added, were poor, lonely, vulnerable people, often 'homeless and root-less'. And while most people stayed clear of hard drugs, there were other means of escape. In the damp-sodden, rat-infested Brutalist tower blocks of Hulme, Manchester, one of the poorest places to live in the country, doctors prescribed a quarter of a million tranquillizers and anti-depressants a month. And in Mike Leigh's *Ecstasy* (1979), a much more powerful play than the better-known *Abigail's Party*, the working-class characters lose themselves in sex, singing and shoplifting, but above all in drinking. 'I drink *all the time*,' sobs the central character, Jean, who works behind the counter in a garage, staring at a 'bloody brick wall all day', and leads a desperately lonely life in her Kilburn bedsit. The irony, of course, was that the people watching the play in the Hampstead Theatre, not far from Jean's fictional flat, came from the very opposite end of the social spectrum, a world of earnest discussions and candlelit dinners. Not for nothing did Leigh joke that he originally wanted to call it 'One Mile Behind You'.[36]

Yet misery and loss were not the whole story. When the Queen celebrated her Silver Jubilee in the summer of 1977, commentators took the opportunity to look back over her reign, and most were heartened by what they saw. For a quarter of a century, Britain had largely been at peace. Most ordinary people were healthier, richer and more comfortable than they had been back in 1952. They were better housed, better fed, better looked after; they were taller and stronger, they spent longer in school, they matured more quickly, they worked in safer and cleaner conditions, they were better paid and they had better pensions. When *The Times* dipped into its archive to run a series of stories from the year of the Queen's accession, many seemed like the stuff of ancient history: twenty-five years on, it was shocking to think that the weekly meat ration had once been barely a shilling. 'It takes less work today to earn the necessities of life than when the Queen came to the throne', declared *Reader's Digest*, estimating that it now took the ordinary worker just eight minutes to earn the price of a pint of milk, compared with thirteen minutes back in 1952. Thanks to paid holidays, cheap foreign travel, the dynamism of the arts and the power of television, cultural horizons were broader; thanks to legal reforms and growing public tolerance, there was much more freedom for those who had once been pushed to the margins. Even in working-class homes, washing machines, telephones and fridges were often taken for granted. And while the pillars of industry were tottering, some old backwaters were experiencing an unexpected revival.[37]

Centuries earlier, East Anglia had been one of the richest parts of the country, basking in the profits of the wool and textile trades. After the coming of the Industrial Revolution it had sunk into decline, its people cast as backward-looking bumpkins. But in the 1970s the picture was changing. Thanks to the advent of industrialized farming and the Common Agricultural Policy, the region's farmers were beginning to get rich. 'Processions of pea-picking machines like mechanical dragons roar into the quiet farms of East Anglia,' one observer wrote, 'racing from one field to the next, working all night under arc-lights to devour their quota.' In 1950, a young mechanic's son from Norfolk had started his own business with an investment of £2.50, twenty eggs and a second-hand paraffin-oil incubator in his mother-in-law's shed. A quarter of a century later, after taking factory farming and food processing to new heights, Bernard Matthews was the biggest turkey farmer in Europe. Having brought self-basting turkeys to the masses, he had the satisfaction of seeing his company listed on the Stock Exchange. He even appeared in his own television commercials, turning 'Bootiful!' into a national catchphrase.[38]

But there was more to East Anglia's success than turkey drummers. 'The port of King's Lynn is thriving,' reported a visitor in 1973, 'and entry into the European Economic Community will certainly be good for it.' That was true not merely of King's Lynn, a prosperous market town with a pioneering pedestrianized town centre, but of the region's ports in general. Felixstowe was already on its way to becoming the nation's busiest container port, profiting from the growing trade with the Continent and avoiding the strikes that had crippled London and Liverpool. Rapid growth deterred industrial militancy; as early as 1975, Felixstowe was turning business away 'for lack of space'. Ipswich, too, was booming, the town's fortunes matched by the splendid success of Bobby Robson's footballers, who brought home the FA Cup in 1978 and the UEFA Cup three years later. Thanks to the demand for farm machinery and fertilizers, as well as its port trade, unemployment was just 5 per cent, well below the national average. Indeed, so bright were Ipswich's economic prospects that the council was struggling to find enough housing to match the demand. It was a similar story in Peterborough, where, thanks to new office developments and easy access to the ports, the population had shot up from 81,000 to almost 120,000 in barely thirteen years. In 1980 the city's Development Corporation even spent £250,000 on an advertising campaign for the 'Peterborough Effect', boasting that they had created a 'British economic miracle'. Four years later, a survey found that Suffolk, Norfolk and Cambridgeshire had become the best places to live in Britain, with low unemployment, low pollution and very low crime. 'Seekers after the good life', declared *The Times*, 'should look to East Anglia.'[39]

It was another East Anglian city, though, that offered the most intriguing glimpse of the future. In July 1975, at a time when inflation was heading towards 30 per cent and the nation's economic prospects had never seemed grimmer, a new Science Park opened in Cambridge. Built with a £650,000 investment from Trinity College, the park was 'the first attempt by an English university to bring industry and science together'. Since it began life with only four tenants, the dream of bringing thousands of high-technology jobs to the city seemed highly ambitious, to say the least. Yet even as the British economy stagnated, the Science Park boomed. By the end of the decade it had twenty-five tenants and had become a model for similar initiatives elsewhere. 'Cambridge is where things are happening,' one consultant confidently declared, while already experts were talking of the 'Cambridge phenomenon' (a very different beast, presumably, from the 'Peterborough Effect'). They were right: twenty years later, the city boasted an estimated 1,200 hi-tech companies employing some 35,000 people. All in all, the transformation of the Fenlands market town had been one of Britain's great post-war economic success stories.[40]

The man who came to symbolize Cambridge's resurgence actually spent most of the 1970s based 15 miles away in St Ives, in what had once been Huntingdonshire. A decade earlier, the 21-year-old Clive Sinclair had founded Sinclair Radionics in a little house on Histon Road, Cambridge, selling components for do-it-yourself radio kits. Since Sinclair had no capital and few qualifications, success seemed highly unlikely. But in 1972, just after moving to a converted flour mill in St Ives, he had a breakthrough with a £79 pocket calculator, the Sinclair Executive. There had been pocket calculators before, but never one so slim or so light. Within a year it had become one of the bestselling calculators in the United States: a case, said one admiring early profile, of selling 'electronic coals to Newcastle'. Suddenly calculators were all the rage. Dixons predicted the rise of 'two and three calculator families'; Boots talked of a 'calculator Christmas'; W. H. Smith said their sales of calculators had gone from 'tremendous to marvellous'. But Sinclair had overreached himself. In January 1976 he launched the digital Black Watch, which cost £24.95, had no buttons and lit up only when the surface was pressed. It was a disaster. Early models went haywire whenever the wearer put on a nylon shirt, while the watch looked, as one reviewer remarked, like 'a give-away in a cereal packet'. Undeterred, Sinclair sank a £650,000 grant from the government's National Enterprise Board into a project to make the world's first mass-market pocket television. 'No other company in the world is remotely close to what we have done,' Sinclair bragged in January 1977. But now the sceptics were circling. 'Who will pay almost £200 for a pocket television set?' wondered *The Times*. The answer was: nobody. The two-inch television was another fiasco, and by 1978 Sinclair Radionics was losing almost £2 million a year. A year later, its pale, bearded founder resigned from his own company.[41]

Sinclair was not finished yet. He now concentrated on one of his other companies, originally called Science of Cambridge and then Sinclair Computers. Even as the government's attempts to drive down inflation provoked mass strikes and walkouts, even as the country shivered through the Winter of Discontent, his new firm was working on designs for a home microcomputer. In May 1979, while most people were digesting the advent of Britain's first woman Prime Minister, his team began work on a new project based on the Zilog Z80 processor. And in the New Year, Sinclair unveiled the result: the ZX80, 'a personal microcomputer that sells for just £100'. Accustomed by now to his grand pronouncements, some observers were sceptical: surely computers were only for hobbyists? Not so: as early as February 1980, Curry's were forecasting that sales might reach as high as 65,000 a year. At the 'Microsystems 80' exhibition at Wembley, one reporter browsed wonderingly through the 'shelves of coloured tape cassettes', the titles – *Mastermind*, *Super Startrek*, *Super Alien Attack*, *Wartrek*, *Deathstar* – like bizarre portents of the future. It was to this strange new world that Sinclair's machine belonged. 'The ZX80 cuts away computer jargon and mystique,' said his adverts. 'The genuine computer understanding it gives you will be immediately useful in any business or professional sphere. And the grounding it gives your children will equip them for the rest of their lives.'[42]

All in all, the ZX80 sold an estimated 50,000 units – chicken feed by later standards, but a staggeringly high amount at the time. To later consumers it would seem primitive and unreliable, but this product of the dying months of the 1970s was one of the most influential British products of the age. One day, suggested *The Times*, families might be able to use 'the household computer to manage domestic finance'. They might be able to 'key in the date' and find out their 'bills still outstanding, their last day for payment, the bank balance and the next payment into the bank account from the employer'. They might be able to check their usage of things like heating and lighting. They could even use the computer to write with: using a word-processing program, said *The Times*, 'letters, essays or personal notes can be written on the screen (using a keyboard)' and saved on a blank cassette. To many readers this must have sounded ridiculous, the stuff of science fiction, no more plausible than the old predictions that people would one day travel everywhere by hovercraft, no more reliable than Harold Wilson's talk about the white heat of technology. 'No computer "expert" has been able to tell me any useful task that I could do in the home with a personal computer that I could not do more cheaply and conveniently with a pocket calculator and an indexed notebook,' wrote a scornful Brian Read of Henley. But *The Times* stuck to its guns. 'By the end of the century,' it predicted, the microcomputer would be 'as common as the telephone'.[43]

2

The Social Contract

*We are finished. We may as well pack up. We have left it too
late. We were warned we had three weeks to clear out of
England. That was three weeks ago. Labour has got in. The
consequence is a victory for the Unions who are the dictators
of the Labour Party. I see nothing but total disaster ahead.*

James Lees-Milne's diary, 1 March 1974

*As Hercules in days gone by
Took out his mighty club
And got his rubber kneeler down
To give the floors a scrub . . .
So forward, Harold, once again
To purge the stables' filth
Your tiny mandate in your hand
And redistribute the wealth!*

'Mrs Wilson's Diary',
Private Eye, 8 March 1974

The day after Wilson's return to power, his senior ministers gathered at
Buckingham Palace for the ritual of kissing hands with the Queen. Ten
years earlier, after his first election victory, the mood had been giddy
with half-suppressed jubilation at the chance to turn principles into
power. This time, however, the atmosphere was rather different, not
least because so many of the Palace's vast rooms had been left unheated
during the energy crisis. The Queen 'played her part as pleasantly as
she always does', observed Barbara Castle, a veteran of Wilson's last
government, but it was a 'very muted affair'. Instead of looking forward

to wielding power, Castle felt only 'a kind of dread at the resumption of a feverish round of meetings and paperwork'. There was, she reflected, 'no stardust left ... I hardly felt my pulse quicken. How very different from last time!' And to her surprise and disappointment, this time the Queen did not even offer them refreshments. 'No tea and cucumber sandwiches,' Castle recorded. 'Obviously the Palace is economizing too!'

At five o'clock, Wilson's ministers assembled in Downing Street for their first Cabinet meeting. 'The first shock', Castle wrote, 'was the sight of the inside of No. 10. Heath must have spent a bomb on having it done up. Gone was the familiar, functional shabbiness. Instead someone with appalling taste had had it tarted up. New old-gold carpeting every-where; white and silver patterned wallpaper; gold moiré curtains of distressing vulgarity; "nice" sideboards with bowls of flowers on top.' The Cabinet Room had not survived Heath's thirst for modernization: gone were the familiar dark-green leather blotters, the worn leather of the chairs, the patchy green felt on the Cabinet table. Instead, Heath's decorators had installed 'a symphony of muted browns': fawn baize on the table, light-brown leather for the blotters, new brown leather for the chairs. Even the paintings of old statesmen were gone, with French pastoral scenes mounted in their place. Some people liked it: Wilson's trusted political secretary Marcia Williams thought it 'all looked elegant and coordinated'. But Castle hated it. 'It looked', she thought, 'like a boudoir.'[1]

The scenery might have changed, but as the new Cabinet took their places around the boat-shaped table, the cast felt very familiar. At the outset, Wilson suggested that they should call each other by their first names, raising ironic cheers around the table. More laughter followed when he added that it was 'not compulsory to smoke in Cabinet', puff-ing clouds into the air from his pipe as he did so. To a casual observer, all this would have looked more like a reunion of old colleagues than the first meeting of a dynamic new administration. As Wilson had boasted during the campaign, his was the most experienced team in living memory, and as he looked around the Cabinet table the familiar faces stared back at him: Jim Callaghan, the big, bluff Foreign Secre-tary; Roy Jenkins, reluctantly back at the Home Office, fatter and more florid, but also palpably semi-detached; Denis Healey, the new Chancel-lor, robust and self-confident beneath the thick black eyebrows. Among the standard-bearers of the left, Castle had been Wilson's friend for almost thirty years, while the new Industry Secretary, Tony Benn, had written speeches for him since the early 1960s. Only a handful of relative youngsters stood out, such as Wilson's latest protégée, the endearingly scruffy Shirley Williams, the new Secretary of State for Prices and Consumer Affairs. By and large, however, it was astonishing how few fresh faces there were, and, while Wilson insisted that this was a government of wise old birds, critics thought it looked more like a gathering of tired old lags. Even the most colourful new addition, Michael Foot, the Employment Secretary, was in his sixties, a white-haired veteran who remembered the days of Attlee and Bevan and often seemed more like a relic from Gladstone's day.[2]

It was the new Environment Secretary, though, who best captured the new mood. In the late 1950s Anthony Crosland had been the swash-buckling intellectual hero of the Labour right, 'Mr Gaitskell's Ganymede'. In the late 1960s he had been a fearless Education Secretary, the champion of the comprehensives, the smasher of the grammar schools. But the man at the Cabinet table that March afternoon, with his thickened features, shaggy sideburns and heavy bags beneath his eyes, was almost unrecognizable as the handsome author of *The Future of Socialism*. Crosland was only in his mid-fifties, but Wilson's aide Bernard Donoughue thought that he looked tired and ill, 'a slow and reluctant decision maker'. Another old friend, the Whitehall mandarin Leo Pliatzky, caustically remarked that Crosland had become a 'failed boy wonder, too lazy and with no political courage'. And behind all this lay a deeper decline. Ever since its publication in 1956, Crosland's manifesto *The Future of Socialism* had been a Bible for a generation of social democrats, imagining an affluent Britain dedicated to opportunity and egalitarianism, a world of open-air cafés and well-designed housing estates, a paradise forged in the crucible of abundance. But in the harsh new world of miners' strikes and oil shocks, with endless economic growth exposed as a fantasy, it felt horribly out of date. A few weeks after returning to office, Crosland published a new book, *Socialism Now*, but it fell painfully short of becoming the new gospel for the mid-1970s. To the problems of international competition, rising global prices and rampant inflation, he could find no answer. It was all 'a bit vague', his friend Wilfred Beckermann told him. 'Your admirers will have expected a new lead ... I rather fear they will be disappointed.' But Crosland's reaction spoke volumes about the sheer exhaustion of the old Labour right. 'Keynes didn't write another *General Theory*,' he snapped. Besides, he added, he was 'too bloody busy'.[3]

Crosland's bewilderment at the onset of stagflation was typical of a

generation of social democrats who had pinned their hopes on economic growth but were now adrift without a strategy. By contrast, the
Labour left did have a strategy, even if it struck horror into the hearts of
their own colleagues. As the left's increasingly messianic champion Tony
Benn recorded in his diary, their priorities were '"a fundamental and
irreversible shift in the balance of power and wealth in favour of working people"; an industrial powers act; planning agreements between
companies, unions and the Government on national economic priorities; a State Holding Company; regional policy; monopolies and
mergers'. All of this, Benn noted, must be based on 'a powerful and
really strong policy alliance with the union movement', as well as a new
partnership with factions to Labour's left such as the Communist Party,
thereby building 'a popular front, rather as in France'. To many of his
colleagues, all this was utter madness: but for the time being the left held
the upper hand. Despite the severity of the economic crisis, the party's
manifesto committed it to building 'greater economic equality in income,
wealth and living standards', including measures 'to make power in
industry genuinely accountable to the workers and the community';
heavy spending on health, welfare and education; compulsory planning agreements with industry; plans to nationalize land, shipbuilding,
the ports and aircraft industries; and a National Enterprise Board 'to
enable the Government to control prices, stimulate investment, encourage exports, create employment, protect workers and consumers from
the activities of irresponsible multi-national companies, and to plan the
national economy in the national interest'. Even Jack Jones, the soul of
the union movement, thought this was all a bit much. 'Why don't you
make a speech on pensions,' he once asked a disapproving Benn, 'instead
of all this airy-fairy stuff?'[4]

Quite apart from whether Benn's vision would have worked, the
obvious problem was that Wilson's ministers arrived in Downing Street
without any real idea how they were going to resolve the economic
crisis. Despite their long list of new spending plans, they had no clear
strategy for bringing inflation down, and no real sense how they were
going to keep the economy running at full employment without driving
wages and prices up. To some extent this was deliberate on Harold Wilson's part; for more than a decade, he had maintained his grip on a
fractious party by practising the politics of ambiguity. To many of his
ministers, though, it was deeply frustrating. The Treasury minister
Edmund Dell thought that they had arrived in office with a policy of
'wishful thinking', while his colleague Joel Barnett thought they had no

'economic or financial policies' of any kind, whether 'short-, medium-
or long-term'. Later, Dell wrote that there had been 'no comparable
example of such political and intellectual incoherence in a party coming
into office' in modern British history, an astonishing thing to say about
a government of which he was a part. But all the evidence suggests he
was probably right. Almost incredibly, Wilson's policy chief Bernard
Donoughue later remarked that he could not remember 'a single sustained discussion in Cabinet or Cabinet Committee of central economic
policy – of fiscal or monetary management, or any direct measures to
curb public expenditure growth or wage inflation – until December
1974', by which time things had got well out of hand. Perhaps it was no
wonder that Dell thought his colleagues were like the characters in Jane
Austen's novels, sipping tea and fluttering their eyelashes while the
Napoleonic Wars raged across the Channel.[5]

Wilson's failure to give a lead was not very surprising. For all his
cleverness, the new Prime Minister had never been particularly interested in ideas. At heart, he remained the eager Huddersfield grammar
school swot who, when his Oxford contemporaries were marching
behind the banners of socialism, had locked himself away with his
books. Ideology left him cold: although he had got 'an alpha-plus in
economic theory', he bragged to the *Guardian*'s John Cole, 'I don't like
theory [and] I never understood it.' He was a tactician, not a theorist.
Whether he was even a socialist was a matter for debate: as a student,
he had joined the Liberal Club, not Labour, and even then rarely went
to meetings. Decades later, when his authorized biographer, Philip Ziegler, told him that he was 'far from being a committed socialist', Wilson
replied cheerfully: 'That's lucky. Nor am I!' Indeed, if anything it was his
boyhood hobby of Scouting, not socialism, that provided his political
philosophy. The motto 'A Scout is a friend to all and a brother to every
other Scout' was one of the guiding principles of his life. His colleagues
often found this ludicrous, but Wilson could not care less. He knew
what he liked: listening to Gilbert and Sullivan, playing with his children's Meccano set, whacking a golf ball, reading Arthur Bryant and
Agatha Christie, admiring the paintings of L. S. Lowry. When this quick-
witted, kind-hearted, unpretentious little man told the *Daily Express*
that he preferred tinned salmon and beer to smoked salmon and champagne, most people thought it was a political gimmick. But he was
telling the truth.[6]

In his first administration, Wilson had done his best to govern as a
one-man band. Ten years on, however, he was determined to do things

differently. The weekend after the election, he told Barbara Castle that, since he had so many 'experienced Ministers this time', he planned to 'work much more as a committee, keeping myself freer than I did before'. Even in the first few days there was an obvious sign of change. Instead of moving back into Number 10, where he had spent so many evenings plotting over late-night glasses of brandy, Wilson decided to stay in Lord North Street, a car bringing him to work every morning at nine o'clock. The days of twenty-four-hour presidential leadership, he explained to Labour's National Executive, were over: 'this time, I am going to run this Government very differently.' He had deliberately surrounded himself with 'the most experienced team in living memory . . . They are going to do the bloody work while I have an easy time.' During his first administration, he told Granada's *World in Action*, 'I had to take corner kicks and penalties, administer to the wounded and bring on the lemons at half time and score all the goals myself. Now I will be the deep lying centre half, concentrating on defence, initiating attacks, distributing the ball for my star forwards. They'll score the goals and, by Heaven, they are scoring goals.'[7]

And yet to insiders such as Wilson's acerbic but doggedly loyal press secretary Joe Haines, there was something disturbing about his enthusiasm for a quiet life. Even during the campaign, the *Sunday Times* had thought that Wilson seemed strangely 'withdrawn, nervous, tentative, apprehensive, not to say distinctly bored with the whole affair'. He was only 57, but the bags under his eyes made him look older. He played golf and went swimming much less than before; his movements were noticeably slower; he often seemed tired, listless, even uninterested, an extraordinary contrast with the sharp-witted know-it-all of 1964. Physically he was in manifest decline: later, Haines recalled that he suffered from 'one cold after another', as well as persistent styes beneath his eyes. Before important meetings, he even complained of 'the squitters', as though hoping to be excused. And although Haines thought these ailments were largely psychosomatic, he later wondered whether Wilson had already been suffering from the Alzheimer's disease that robbed him of his memory a decade later. According to one rumour among Wilson's old confidants, a specialist had warned him that 'physical changes were taking place which were likely to affect his mental powers'. In any case, Haines thought 'the Rolls-Royce mind, as Derek Mitchell, his first principal private secretary, once described it, was failing, and the formerly unquenchable optimistic spirit was dampened, even dying'.[8]

During Wilson's first spell in office, Number 10 had been a hotbed of gossip, paranoia and late-night plotting. After 1974 the atmosphere was quieter, largely because his leadership of the Labour Party was more secure. But it was no less dysfunctional. Given the appalling pressure, perhaps it was not surprising that Wilson turned to the brandy bottle, but even men of the world such as Haines and Bernard Donoughue worried that he was drinking far too much. 'When he drinks, he becomes very strange and aggressive,' Donoughue recorded after only ten days of the new regime. 'His brow lowers and a very strange look comes into his eyes. Rather hunched and brooding.' And as time went on, so the Prime Minister became ever more reliant on the bottle – a fact his aides managed to conceal from the press and the public. On 14 October 1975, Donoughue recorded that Wilson had polished off four brandies before Prime Minister's Questions and two more afterwards. On 30 October he drank five brandies before Prime Minister's Questions, and on 27 November, after a diplomatic lunch at which 'Joe said he was all over the place, and drank too much', Wilson put in a terrible Commons performance, slurring his words while the Tories howled with excitement. It was lucky for him that radio coverage was still a few years away.[9]

As Wilson's ministers took their seats around the Cabinet table, one issue above all dominated the conversation. The miners had now been out for a month, and although the unseasonably warm weather meant that Britain had so far escaped serious fuel shortages, Wilson needed to fulfil his promise that he could get them back to work. That morning, he had already held 'friendly and encouraging' talks with the TUC and CBI. Heath's wage controls were history: 'the Stage 3 limit had been lifted.' The only question was whether the government should give the NUM everything it wanted, which came to about £138 million, or whether they should follow the advice of the Pay Board, which had recommended a settlement of £98 million. Foot, in 'rather sombre' form, explained that he was inclined to offer the miners £113 million, conceding their demands on basic pay but not fringe benefits, 'but might be forced further up'. Nobody disagreed; indeed, Denis Healey remarked that 'it was essential for us to settle with the miners in the next twenty-four hours'. And that was that: after all the months of argument and confrontation, it had taken Wilson just a few hours to give the miners what they wanted.[10]

When the Cabinet met again two days later, the deal had been done.

Foot reported that the NUM had agreed to a wage settlement coming to just over £108 million, almost double what Heath had offered under Stage Three. Originally the miners had wanted a 35 per cent increase; Foot had given them 32 per cent. And although the Prime Minister offered his formal congratulations on the compromise, even Foot could not hide his unease. 'The mineworkers' settlement', he told his colleagues, 'would inevitably have an effect on the general prospect for pay settlements, which was already disturbing.' Under Stage Three, Heath had envisaged an annual increase of 11 per cent on earnings, which was already bad enough. Disastrously, however, Heath had included a mechanism whereby every time the retail price index rose by 1 per cent, workers would get automatic pay increases of 40p a week. At the time, these 'threshold payments' were intended as mere window dressing, since Heath was sure that prices would fall. But thanks to the oil shock, inflation was well out of control. 'On present forecasts,' Foot admitted, 'the threshold agreements would be triggered nine times, starting in April, and by the end of the year earnings would then be 19–20 per cent higher than a year earlier, and prices 15 per cent higher.' He added rather weakly that the union barons had promised to consider the miners' case 'unique', but anybody who remembered the previous three years knew that the TUC would find it hard to make that stick.[11]

In the newspapers, relief and jubilation greeted the announcement that the three-day week was over and the miners were going back to work. Yet in the Conservative press there was also a good deal of disquiet that sheer industrial muscle had prevailed once again and that the NUM had been handed such a generous deal. 'By any standards,' said *The Times* the next day, 'it is a highly inflationary increase', while the *Financial Times*'s commentator Harold Bolter thought that 'as a result of the miners' settlement, Britain is faced with a prices problem of truly enormous proportions'. To some extent Wilson had no choice: public opinion demanded an early settlement, and the Pay Board's report, which concluded that the miners were underpaid compared with manufacturing workers, meant that an offer of at least £100 million was probably inevitable. But while the Prime Minister jauntily remarked to Bernard Donoughue that 'normalcy has been restored', the latter felt a lingering sense of anxiety. 'It was really a capitulation on the miners' terms,' Donoughue later reflected, 'and solved little in the longer term. Final confrontation between the miners and the elected government was merely delayed a decade.'[12]

For the man who had done most to secure the deal, it marked a long-delayed introduction to the compromises of office. In many ways Michael Foot made a very improbable Employment Secretary. With his flowing white locks, soaring rhetoric and literary erudition, he cut an incongruous figure alongside the union leaders who trooped dourly in and out of his office. Nobody had ever seen him as a natural minister: born into a family of West Country Nonconformists, steeped in the radical tradition of Swift and Hazlitt, he had grown up with 'bacon for breakfast, Liberalism for lunch and Deuteronomy for dinner'. For most of his life he had been a pamphleteer, not a politician, never happier than when denouncing the Labour leadership in the pages of *Tribune*. After losing in 1970, however, Wilson had made strenuous efforts to bring Foot into the fold, partly as a way of protecting himself against left-wing attack. Crucially, Foot had the confidence of leading union bosses such as Jack Jones and Hugh Scanlon, who trusted him as a socialist campaigner of long standing and guessed that a patrician idealist would have trouble resisting workers' demands for more money. Even while Wilson was waiting for the call from the Palace, Jones had told him that 'the trade unions would not stand for' Labour's right-wing employment spokesman, Reg Prentice, but must have Foot instead. So Foot got the job.[13]

To many observers, the spectacle of Foot taking questions at the dispatch box as Employment Secretary seemed wonderfully bizarre. In fact, despite his rhetorical gifts, Foot felt less than entirely comfortable; Donoughue noted that he seemed 'the most nervous' of Wilson's team. And although he soon got used to the pressures of office, he remained an extremely unusual government minister. Photographers loved to capture him wandering around Hampstead Heath looking for his dog, while in his new office he installed beloved volumes of Rousseau, Montaigne and Montesquieu, as well as a television set for the cricket. As his biographer Kenneth Morgan puts it, with his shapeless pullovers, long hair and pockets full of books, he 'resembled a dilettante of bohemian inclination unexpectedly summoned to arms from the cafés and pubs of Fitzrovia'. Some of Wilson's advisers considered him totally inept: the Prime Minister's economic adviser Andrew Graham thought Foot had 'absolutely no idea how to run a department or how to take decisions'. But since he was enormously popular with Labour activists, left-wing backbenchers and the union leaders, Wilson considered him an asset. In return, Foot rewarded him with steadfast loyalty. For this old radical, wrote his right-wing colleague Edmund Dell, life in Cabinet, with all its inevitable compromises, was a 'supreme test', but one which 'he passed with flying colours'. That was not something that could be said of all Wilson's ministers.[14]

As Employment Secretary, Foot was responsible for the central element of Labour's manifesto, the promise to implement a Social Contract with the unions. Borrowed from Rousseau's concept of the relationship between a government and its people, the phrase 'social contract' had been much in the air in the early 1970s, reflecting a wider sense that the political consensus was falling apart as Britain slid towards lawless anarchy. In his Fabian Society pamphlet *A New Politics* (1970), Tony Benn had warned of 'a breakdown in the social contract, upon which parliamentary democracy by universal suffrage was based', and argued that the 'contract now needs to be renegotiated on a basis that shares power more widely, before it can win general assent again'. Soon enough, other senior Labour figures seized on the phrase. 'What Britain needs', Jim Callaghan told the party conference in 1972, 'is a new Social Contract.' Unlike Benn, however, he conceived of it in narrow terms: although he later talked of the Social Contract as a way to achieve 'nothing less than the social and economic reconstruction' of Britain, he essentially saw it as a way to win the support of the trade unions.[15]

Labour and the unions had always had an unusually close relationship; after all, unlike other left-of-centre European parties, the Labour Party had originally been established as the parliamentary wing of the trade union movement. In the final years of Wilson's first government the alliance had almost collapsed, but once in opposition Labour's leaders eagerly returned to their old flame. In early 1972 Labour and the TUC formed an official Liaison Committee, effectively giving the union leaders a say in policymaking. For left-wingers such as Tony Benn, this was a source of great delight. The Liaison Committee was a 'very useful alliance', he recorded in December 1973, calling it 'the source of our strength' and predicting that the rekindled love affair with the unions 'will win us the Election'. But not all his colleagues saw the unions through such rose-tinted spectacles. Even at this early stage, Barbara Castle noted that while the union barons were perfectly happy to talk about what a future Labour government could do for them, they never offered concessions of their own, especially on pay. Inflation was already a serious problem, yet 'any mention even of a voluntary [pay] policy was taboo', she wrote. 'When at one of the meetings someone dared to refer to the role of incomes in the management of the economy, Jack Jones jumped in at once: "It would be disastrous if any word went from this meeting that we had been discussing prices and incomes policy."' Even at this early stage, in other words, 'liaison' was largely a one-way street.[16]

The blueprint for the Social Contract, which rejoiced in the exciting title *Economic Policy and the Cost of Living*, was published in February 1973. The 'first task' of a new government, it promised, would be to reach a 'wide-ranging agreement' with the unions on 'the policies to be pursued in all these aspects of our economic life'. On everything from public ownership and industrial investment to controls on the flow of capital and subsidies for food and housing, the unions would get their way. Heath's Industrial Relations Act would be scrapped and there would be a 'wide-ranging and permanent system of price controls', but there was no mention of wage controls. The rather optimistic premise was that if Labour met the unions' demands for better conditions and lower prices, then they would naturally keep their pay claims low. As Wilson's authorized biographer observes, it was 'a programme of pious hopes with precious little evidence offered that either side to the bargain would be willing or able to perform its part'. And even at the time, some Labour insiders doubted it would work. Edmund Dell, soon to become Paymaster General, told his friend Denis Healey that the Social Contract would prove 'a load of codswallop'. Healey disagreed; but he would soon change his mind.[17]

With his romantic faith in the unions' goodwill, Michael Foot seemed the ideal candidate to turn the Social Contract into legislative reality. Three months after taking office, he reached a deal with the TUC. While the union leaders pledged to seek wage increases only to keep up with the cost of living, Foot unveiled a range of policies to improve workers' conditions, from anti-discrimination measures to better pensions and sick pay. The Labour Party and the unions, he said proudly, were 'united as never before', and the result would be 'a new industrial climate, a much wider sense of social justice, a new confidence that the Government will keep faith with the people'. And, by and large, Foot lived up to his side of the bargain. By 1976 he had introduced five major pieces of legislation – the Health and Safety at Work Act, the Trade Unions and Labour Relations Act, the Employment Protection Act, the Sex Discrimination Act and the Trade Unions and Labour Relations Amendment Act – and set up the highly successful Advisory, Conciliation and Arbitration Service (ACAS) to mediate between employers and unions. Never had the unions had such a friend in government. By the time Foot moved on, he had not only restored their legal immunities but given their members a vast range of new rights, from maternity leave to guaranteed short-time payments. He remained a staunch defender of the closed shop, whereby employees were obliged to join the union or face the sack. Even in the case of the Ferrybridge Six, a group of power-station workers who were sacked after refusing to join the union and then denied unemployment benefit, he kept unerringly to the TUC-approved line. With the government delivering the promised food and rent subsidies, pension increases and price curbs, it must have seemed to the union leaders that all their Christmases had come at once.[18]

The entire point of the Social Contract was that, in return, the unions would keep their pay demands in line with the cost of living. But this was based on a fundamental misconception. On paper it looked like a perfectly reasonable attempt to copy the successful arrangements in Scandinavia, the Netherlands, West Germany and Austria, where ministers and union leaders, representing vast interest groups, worked together to plan for growth without inflation. But the situation in Britain, with hundreds of fractious, introverted unions, was completely different. Since the trade unions were intensely competitive, the idea that they would put their differences aside and work together for the common good was a self-deluding fantasy. Even many union leaders privately thought the Social Contract was built on sand: as the TUC's Len Murray later admitted, it made impossible demands of what were basically self-interested organizations. Another moderate, the miners' leader Joe Gormley, thought that it 'put us in a false position. Our role in society is to look after our members, not run the country.' On top of that, the general secretaries' power was weakening by the year, as younger members refused to listen to the old men at the top. 'Workplace culture', the *Financial Times*'s labour editor Robert Taylor wrote later, 'was no longer conducive to collectivist values of solidarity and equity.' To put it more crudely, most workers were out for what they could get. Clinging like a limpet to his beloved Social Contract, however, Foot simply could not see it. 'Even he found living with the trade unions physically and spiritually draining,' Edmund Dell remarked, 'but nothing could exhaust his loyalty to them.'[19]

Even before Wilson had taken power, there were hints of the discontents to come. In January, weeks before the election, Denis Healey had begged the Liaison Committee for 'an indication that, if the Labour Government fulfilled its side of the compact, the TUC for its part would try to make the economic policy work'. But that was too much for Len Murray: 'the greatest disservice the TUC could do a Labour Govern-

John Kent takes a very dim view of the Social Contract in the *Sun*,
15 March 1974. Michael Foot, although splendidly wild-haired, seems
to be wearing an unusually garish tie.

ment', he replied, 'was to pretend it could do more than it could.' And
within a few months of the election it was already clear that the Social
Contract was desperately lopsided. Thanks to the oil shock, economic
reality dictated that most people would have to accept a fall in their
standard of living. But although Murray and Jones urged restraint, the
public sector unions were determined to press home their advantage.
So when Heath's old pay policy ran out in July, the scramble for wages
restarted in earnest, each union trying to get a better deal than the next.
When Barbara Castle, facing a nationwide nurses' strike, asked their
loudly self-promoting leader Clive Jenkins: 'Will you help me?', his
reply spoke volumes about the balance of power. 'He spat out "No",'
she recorded, and then 'proceeded to be as insulting as he knew how
and told me his union would enter into widespread and destructive
industrial action immediately'. In the end, Foot declared the nurses a
special case, alongside the teachers and postmen. Other employers drew
the appropriate lesson: by September, just seven months after their last
rise, Ford car workers had won a further 37 per cent increase, and a few
weeks later the BBC offered its staff 28 per cent. As the postmen's leader
Tom Jackson remarked, it was as though the unions had discovered 'a
gigantic Las Vegas slot machine that had suddenly got stuck in favour
of the customer'.[20]

In later years, members of Wilson's Cabinet queued up to disavow the
Social Contract. The unions were too 'conservative [and] self-interested',

Shirley Williams reflected. 'I came away with a slightly stale feeling in my mouth. This was not what I thought democratic socialism was going to be.' The unions had 'defaulted on their part of the contract', agreed Denis Healey, while his Treasury deputy Joel Barnett put it even more bluntly: 'To my mind the only give and take in the contract was that the Government gave and the unions took.' Another government might have tried to hold the line against wage inflation, or at least tried harder to persuade union members of the risks of such reckless pay increases. But with no parliamentary majority and a second election looming, Wilson's ministers had no desire to antagonize their partners. They evidently 'regarded themselves as living on the lower slopes of a mountain which nurtured higher up a number of dangerous wild beasts', wrote an increasingly depressed Roy Jenkins. 'The bigger ones were known as union leaders and the smaller ones as constituency parties, and . . . when they did come down they must on no account be enraged.' There was certainly no danger of that. By the summer of 1974, the crippling strikes of the spring, the blackouts and the three-day week, had become a distant memory. The unions had no need to strike; they were getting everything they wanted. And even as annual wage inflation headed towards 20 per cent, the slot machine continued merrily to pour out their winnings.[21]

On the morning of 14 March, Wilson's Cabinet met to discuss the state of the economy. As the Chancellor, Denis Healey, began to outline the position, a gloomy silence fell over the room. 'The country confronted an economic situation', recorded the minutes, 'which might well be the worst which had ever been faced in peacetime, and which was deteriorating.' Thanks to the oil shock, the puncturing of the Barber boom, the reckless expansion of the money supply, the collapse of the secondary banks and the devastating impact of the three-day week, the government had inherited a perfect storm. Inflation, Healey explained, was certain to reach 15 per cent by the end of the year. The balance of payments deficit had reached a record £1.5 billion and was likely to widen, public borrowing had soared to a record £4 billion and 'growth had virtually come to a halt'. There would, he said, 'be no scope for any increase in living standards this year', and thanks to the threshold agreements inherited from Heath, the government's freedom of movement was severely limited. Cuts were inevitable, 'but not so rapidly as to dislocate the economy and lead to large increases in unemployment'. All in all, it was a catastrophic picture.[22]

On the face of it, there were few better candidates to take command of the economy than Labour's new Chancellor. A former grammar school boy from West Yorkshire whose brains had taken him to Balliol College, Oxford, where he became a close friend of Edward Heath, Denis Healey had been the landing officer for the British assault team at Anzio before entering Parliament as MP for Leeds East. As his friend Edward Pearce later wrote, there seemed to be two Healeys: 'the roisterous, noisy' Healey, who once cornered a Scottish left-winger in the Commons and shouted at him again and again: 'You fucker, you fucker'; and the withdrawn, sensitive Healey, who spent his weekends reading the poetry of William Blake and Emily Dickinson. In an age of increasingly careerist politicians, the poetry-loving, bushy-browed Chancellor seemed a throwback to an earlier era, an eighteenth-century statesman who would have enjoyed downing bottles and swapping epigrams with Charles James Fox. For his colleague Edmund Dell, Healey was a study in paradox: a man of 'deep seriousness worn lightly, sometimes perhaps flippantly', but whose 'outward ebullience concealed inner doubts'; the 'most brilliant of Chancellors intellectually' but 'with a common touch which attracted a wider public'; 'the most cultured of Chancellors', but also 'the greatest bully'.[23]

Not surprisingly, many reporters found Healey irresistible. 'He loves fighting,' wrote the journalist Anthony Sampson, 'and can be rude and bullying to anyone he thinks weaker; he is a relentless talker, and likes to lay down the law not only about all aspects of politics, but about culture too.' The *Guardian*'s John Cole, meanwhile, thought it took 'a refreshing irreverence to be an intellectual robust, overweight, workaholic, long-suffering Chancellor ... with a gusto for music, the visual arts and photography, and yet retain a self-image of the cheeky chappie who can't resist making sharp remarks'. Others tired of Healey's eagerness to remind them how clever he was: as the economist Richard Holt later remarked, his Treasury advisers must have got sick of hearing what John Donne or W. B. Yeats had thought about something. Yet by comparison with his colleagues, Healey stood out as a diamond amid lumps of coal: an enormously engaging, intelligent and complicated man, who thought nothing of sitting up drinking with Helmut Schmidt until four in the morning, or of teaching his fellow finance ministers to sing French revolutionary ballads – or of shoving Roy Hattersley so hard before a Cabinet meeting that he nearly broke his nose.[24]

In the spring of 1974, Healey was best known to the general public for the much-misquoted promise that if elected, he would 'squeeze the property speculators until the pips squeak'. In fact, like many former student Communists, Healey was now firmly on the right of the Labour Party, a staunch Cold Warrior who never tried to curry favour with the activists or the unions. His florid features, enormous eyebrows and irreverent manner made him a gift to the caricaturists, and, thanks to the BBC's impressionist Mike Yarwood, he became a popular figure of fun. Healey even adopted Yarwood's trademark phrase 'Silly billy', which he had never used himself. 'It was less offensive', he explained, 'than the expressions I found coming more naturally to my lips.' And yet despite his flippant ebullience, Healey remained a bit of a loner, a family man who spent his weekends playing practical jokes on his children's friends or answering the phone in the broken English of a Chinese laundry proprietor. Threatened by his intellectual arrogance, many MPs could not stand him. So he relied on his Treasury team: the level-headed Chief Secretary, Joel Barnett; the rigorous Paymaster General, Edmund Dell; and the rich, shrewd and hugely affable Chancellor of the Duchy of Lancaster, Harold Lever, who had a Lebanese wife, a taste for silk dressing gowns and a pronounced disregard for his own party. 'I had a very sceptical view about most of our programme,' Lever said later; 'all this crap about Benn and his industrial planning. I knew it was going to be a dud.'[25]

As he contemplated the wreckage of the nation's finances, Healey faced an appalling dilemma. With the government's parliamentary position so fragile and a second election inevitable, it was imperative to please Labour supporters and reach out to floating voters. At the same time, however, the obvious way to deal with the international crisis was to slash government spending, hold down salaries in the massive nationalized industries and deflate consumer demand, a course of shock therapy that would help to get inflation down, even though it risked tipping the economy deep into recession and driving up unemployment. High unemployment remained the ultimate taboo in British politics: not only did bitter memories of the 1930s run deep, but the bruising experience of the Heath government, when unemployment had briefly gone above one million, apparently proved that the voters would not stand for it. And even though Healey had inherited relatively decent unemployment figures, with just over half a million people out of work, the consensus was that the total simply must not rise any higher. In December 1973, immediately after the oil shock, Anthony Barber had already made record spending cuts. At the Treasury, Edmund Dell recalled, the fear was that further deflation 'would make bad worse'. Interestingly, not only union bosses but business leaders took the same view: inside the CBI, the consensus was that worldwide austerity 'would result in a pointless, beggar-my-neighbour cutting of imports'.[26]

Since their manifesto had promised major spending increases on pensions and social security, most of Wilson's ministers hated the thought of deflation. It was with great relief, therefore, that they seized on the advice of the International Monetary Fund, which had publicly called for members not to cut spending too much, but to 'sustain appropriate levels of economic activity and employment'. In reality, as Dell admitted, this advice was meant for high-performing economies like West Germany and Japan, with their minuscule deficits and healthy finances, rather than big-spending Britain, with its exhausted reserves and enormous debts. For Healey, however, the IMF's advice presented the perfect excuse to put away the hair shirt. Instead of cutting spending to take account of the oil shock, he 'decided to maintain our expenditure plans and borrow to meet the deficit', as Joel Barnett later put it. So while almost every other nation in the Western world deflated, Britain kept on spending: in the fiscal year 1974–5, public spending went up in cash terms by a staggering 35 per cent. To borrow a metaphor from the economics writer David Smith, the party went on 'longer in Britain than anywhere else, even though the champagne had gone distinctly flat'. But as anyone who has ever held a party knows, the longer it goes on, the longer it takes to clear up afterwards – and the heftier the final bill.[27]

Healey unveiled his first Budget on 26 March. In a marathon speech that lasted almost two and a half hours, he delivered on most of Labour's manifesto pledges, from £1.2 billion in higher pensions and £500 million in food subsidies to 'the redistribution of the burdens of taxation on to the broadest backs', as *The Times* put it. Even this was not enough for Labour's hard left: when Healey announced that he was not yet ready to legislate for an annual wealth tax, the Bolsover firebrand Dennis Skinner stormed out of the chamber in disgust. What preoccupied the press, however, was Healey's uncompromisingly redistributive taxation. In total, taxes went up by some £1.4 billion, with the standard rate of income tax up to 33 per cent, the higher rate raised to 83 per cent, corporation tax up to 52 per cent and tax on unearned and investment income up to a record 98 per cent. In the City, the reaction was utter horror: within four days the FT30 Index had fallen by 30 points. Financial insiders joked that they were 'on the tumbril', rolling 'towards the Tower or Tyburn tree', while the CBI, with unusual vitriol, called it 'an attack on a minority class, pandering to the forces of envy'. To middle-class conservatives across the country, it proved that Healey really was a Balliol Bolshevik, squeezing the wealthy until the pips squeaked. 'It penalises the rich,' howled the upper-class diarist James Lees-Milne, pillar of the National Trust and horrified voice of Middle England. 'This ex-Communist announced his intention of penalising them further. His motives are wholly political. They do nothing to save the economy, nothing to boost industry. Everything this new government has done and said is intended to placate the Trades Unions. My worst fears are being realised.'[28]

In later years, Healey looked back on his first Budget with deep regret. Keen not to push the economy into recession, but conscious that he could not afford to alienate the markets, he had told the Commons that his Budget was 'broadly neutral on demand, with a bias, if any, on the side of caution'. Unfortunately, this was based on inaccurate figures. Even as the Chancellor was announcing his measures to the Commons, the state of the public finances was much worse than anyone realized. While the Treasury had forecast that his Budget would slash public borrowing to £2.7 billion, it actually had the opposite effect. By April 1975, borrowing had increased to £7.6 billion, almost £5 billion more than predicted. Not surprisingly, Healey was appalled: far from being 'neutral', his Budget had proved hideously inflationary. As Chancellor, he naturally took the blame. 'I was too inexperienced', he said later, 'to appreciate the full horror of the situation.' It was not really his fault, but it was a disastrous and immensely costly mistake all the same. If only his team had known, his deputy Joel Barnett later remarked, they would never have relied so heavily on borrowing and would never have 'increased public expenditure to the extent we did'. And then, he added, 'the whole course of the next five years might have been different'.[29]

At precisely the point when he ought to have been most cautious, therefore, Healey allowed himself to be tempted into catastrophically crowd-pleasing measures. Haunted by memories of the Hungry Thirties and obsessed by the looming election, many Cabinet ministers insisted that the priority must be to bring down unemployment. In fact, unemployment at around 550,000 was not, by historical standards, all that bad; it was certainly a lot better than it had been under Heath or would become in the Thatcher years. With hindsight, it is obvious that full employment as it had been understood in the 1940s and 1950s was on its way out; beginning with Wilson's first administration, successive governments were forced to run the economy at higher levels of unemployment simply to keep inflation in check, and even during the fat years under Tony Blair full employment never returned. But of course nobody knew that at the time. In the press, unemployment over 500,000 was generally seen as a recipe for electoral disaster, while for men and women of Healey's generation it remained the supreme political nightmare, the great evil that the post-war settlement had been built to banish for ever.[30]

Almost as soon as he had unveiled his Budget, therefore, Healey came under pressure from his colleagues to reflate the economy and go for growth – the classic recipe for a glorious party on election night and a terrible hangover the next morning, as practised for decades by Conservatives and Labour alike. When he raised the prospect of spending cuts, which were now becoming inevitable, his colleagues suggested that he should simply borrow more money. 'We are the party of public expenditure,' Peter Shore told him on 10 April to 'murmurs of approval' from the rest of the Cabinet. As for Wilson, he was characteristically preoccupied by the need for unity. A month later, Donoughue reported to the Prime Minister that the Labour left were already calling for 'faster redistribution and lower unemployment': if Healey slammed the brakes on, Michael Foot might even walk out. But there was no danger of that. After all, Healey was a politician to his fingertips; he wanted to win the election as much as they did. The government had 'one overriding objective in its economic policy', *The Economist* said caustically: 'to be returned to power with a comfortingly higher share of the vote at the next general election'. At lunch with Foot and Castle during an all-day session on Labour's next manifesto, Healey 'grew mellow over stilton and burgundy'. 'You must admit,' he said cheerfully, 'I am the most political Chancellor you have ever had.' 'I do,' Castle replied, 'and I appreciate it.'[31]

For the time being, Healey was as good as his word. In July, he unveiled a new set of economic measures to gladden the heart of Labour loyalists, cutting VAT by 2 per cent, promising another £50 million in food subsidies and offering 60 per cent relief for taxpayers whose local rates had risen sharply in the last year. 'Labour backbenchers whooped their delight,' one reporter wrote, while the Tories 'privately conceded that Mr Healey had probably taken one or two useful tactical tricks in the election campaign'. Not all of the Cabinet were impressed, however: Healey's old rival and predecessor as Labour Chancellor, Roy Jenkins, thought that with inflation now approaching 17 per cent 'this seemed to me a frivolous way of proceeding, even if an election was only two months away', like 'throwing stones at a potential avalanche'. And even inside the tight-knit Treasury team, unease was settling in. Dell and Healey had already had a 'flaming row' about the Chancellor's plans to give away £1.5 billion in pre-election sweeteners, while Barnett thought that the VAT cut was the product of 'a collective guilt complex round the Cabinet table' and 'a move in absolutely the wrong direction'. But this, he remarked, was merely characteristic of 'the first few months of the new Government, [which] were characterized by our spending money which in the event we did not have'.[32]

In the long run, the government's attempt to spend its way out of stagflation was a disaster to rank alongside the Barber boom. As some of Wilson's ministers later admitted, to increase public spending by 35 per cent in cash terms in 1974–5 and a further 25 per cent in 1975–6, at a time when inflation was hurtling through the roof, was an act of breathtaking irresponsibility. The borrowing figures were even worse: given that, at the start of the decade, Roy Jenkins had managed to coax the nation's finances into surplus, it almost beggared belief that public borrowing reached £8 billion in 1974–5 and almost £11 billion a year later. Even Healey later admitted that his extravagance had been a 'mistake', and, coming from him, that was saying something. A short dose of austerity to get inflation under control, as in France, West Germany and the United States, would have been a much better bet. It would have meant pain in the short term, of course, but recovery would have come quickly. Instead, by trying to spend his way out, Healey unwittingly helped to push up inflation to four times the level in West Germany, and set the British economy on the path that led to humiliation at the hands of the IMF. In his defence, he was under intense Cabinet pressure to keep spending high and postpone the inevitable cuts. Almost all Chancellors usually succumb to such pressure, and, with a second election just weeks away, perhaps it was hardly surprising that a self-described 'political Chancellor' acted as he did. What set him apart, though, was that he learned from his mistakes. In the future, Britain would see a very different Denis Healey.[33]

Perhaps the most extraordinary thing about the government's economic strategy in the summer of 1974 was that so many of its members could see the writing on the wall. Even Healey himself warned the Ministerial Economic Committee on 17 June that 'inflation was worse than we had thought', with prices rising so fast that Stage Three's threshold agreements would be triggered twelve times by the end of the year. The obvious solution would have been to cancel them, but of course that would have meant a clash with the unions. 'We aren't going to drop them; we daren't,' recorded Barbara Castle. In the meantime, the Prime Minister's advisers were becoming increasingly frantic in their efforts to coax Wilson back towards economic discipline. As early as mid-May, his Policy Unit's chief economic adviser, Andrew Graham, warned that ministers were 'not fully facing the inflation this year and next', with sterling bound to face enormous pressure and the Treasury likely to demand gigantic cuts. But it was no good. A few weeks later, chatting over a drink with the Cabinet Secretary, Sir John Hunt, Bernard Donoughue confessed that 'economic strategy and incomes policy' were 'just not being properly grappled with':

> It is not properly in the government machine at all ... Nothing has come before ministers. Also the Treasury computer has broken down, so their forecasts are late. We agreed to put it all to the ministerial committee on Economic Strategy over the next two weeks – it has not met for the past two months! Economic policy is simply operating privately in the minds of Healey and Foot. It must be brought out and made coherent, and the PM must take hold of it. My excellent economics adviser Andrew Graham, the economics fellow from Balliol College, Oxford, is very pessimistic, believing that the whole thing will fall apart at the seams in the autumn. He says the Treasury is simply waiting, cynically and fatalistically, for that to happen, so they can move in and impose a massive freeze.

Donoughue and Graham were not alone in fearing disaster. That very evening, Harold Lever put in a 'devastating memo ... warning the PM of a total collapse in financial and industrial confidence unless we reassure people more'. Yet nothing happened: indeed, as Donoughue noted, 'Anthony Wedgwood Benn's machine is roaring on, with proposals for government intervention in industry on an incredible scale ... Totally unrelated to the real world of industry.' Visiting Wilson in early June, his friend and unofficial adviser Siegmund Warburg was stunned by his 'unbelievably detached attitude regarding his colleagues, regarding the Opposition, regarding the trade unions, and really regarding everyone and everything of importance'. And when Donoughue and Graham returned to the fray at the end of July, trying to persuade Wilson that he must 'prepare ministerial and public opinion for the expenditure squeeze and switch to an incomes policy which lay inescapably ahead', he showed no signs of listening. 'The Prime Minister has his head in the sand,' Graham noted grimly as they broke for the August holiday.[34]

So inflation continued its terrible advance. Figures later showed that, during the six months of Wilson's minority government, the Retail Price Index had risen by 10 per cent and wages by 16 per cent, and the final figures for 1974 as a whole showed that wages had gone up by a staggering 28 per cent. In the City, where morale was badly bruised by the secondary banking crisis and the implosion of the property market, few analysts could hide their despair. On 19 June, Sir Peter Tennant, industrial adviser to Barclays Bank International, wondered whether the government and the unions were determined to 'drive us all into self-destruction before they understand what inflation means, or is it possible that they are following Lenin's dictum about destroying the currency in order to destroy capitalism?' That same day, the FT30 Index reached a new low: in the last twenty-five months it had fallen by 53 per cent, further even than in the Great Depression. In July it continued to slide: by the end of the month it was down to 236.4, its lowest level for fifteen years. But as the horrific trade and borrowing figures poured in, worse was to come. By the middle of August, the index was down to just 210.3, and on 19 August it dipped below 200 points for the first time since the 1950s. The news had 'a devastating psychological effect', recalled one investment analyst; afterwards, 'a paralysing pessimism took hold'. In journals such as *The Economist* and the *Banker*, panic was setting in: while the former warned of 'Latin American modes of both price inflation and societal decay', the latter thought that there was only one more chance 'for the parliamentary system to cope with Britain's economic problems'.[35]

Outside the City, however, there was little sense of danger. That summer, as teenage bedrooms echoed to the sound of George McCrae's 'Rock Your Baby', the Rubettes' 'Sugar Baby Love' and the Three Degrees' 'When Will I See You Again', and as millions tuned in to watch Johann Cruyff, Gerd Müller and Billy Bremner in the 1974 World Cup, the headlines had their fair share of bad news. In June and July, the IRA exploded bombs at the Houses of Parliament and the Tower of London, killing one person and injuring dozens. Yet the mood seemed calmer than in the final months of the Heath premiership. Thanks to generous subsidies of bread, butter, cheese and milk, food prices rose by only 5 per cent between April and September, while Shirley Williams cut an amiably reassuring figure as the new Prices Secretary. With Foot approving one pay deal after another, the unions seemed unusually quiescent; as promised, Labour seemed to have lanced the boil of wildcat strikes. Even in Northern Ireland, far fewer people died in 1974 than at the peak of the conflict, two years before. It was a mark of the new mood that Wilson's major public relations initiative that summer was not some grand corporatist incomes policy, but a campaign entitled 'Little Things Mean a Lot', covering such issues as the preservation of local breweries, the rights of people who lived in caravans, the abolition of hare-coursing, a new May Day bank holiday and the expansion of Scottish Gaelic radio. The days of bitter industrial confrontation were over, and millions breathed a sigh of relief: in the opinion polls, the government held a steady lead of between 5 and 10 per cent. Good old Mr Wilson, it seemed, had pulled it off.[36]

And yet as inflation continued silently, inexorably to mount, Wilson's advisers were not the only people convinced that Britain was sleepwalking into disaster. For the self-employed or those on fixed incomes, rising prices spelled disaster. 'Deep freezer sales are holding up,' *The Economist* reported in July, 'but sales of other consumer durables have fallen.' There were also stories, it added, of homeowners deliberately avoiding visits from the Gas Board 'so that they can read their own meters in order to send in exaggerated readings which pre-empt price increases'. More and more, informed observers began to wonder whether Britain was heading for hyperinflation. 'We are in for the biggest slump since the Thirties,' recorded the National Theatre's Peter Hall, formerly a keen Labour supporter, now moving to the right. Even the historian A. J. P. Taylor, who prided himself on his left-wing iconoclasm, predicted massive unemployment and a return to the riots, revolution and totalitarianism of Europe in the 1930s. 'Pray for the recovery of capitalism,' Taylor urged his Hungarian lover. 'You can't realise how near we are to catastrophe: all our banks may close their doors in a few months' time ... You are lucky to be living in a Communist country and safe from such things.'[37]

But even relatively sober commentators were now becoming genuinely alarmed for the future of the nation. On the first day of July, in a 'Doomwatch report on the state of the economy', *The Times*'s Peter Jay predicted that historians would look back on the summer of 1974 as 'the moment when the last chances of fending off political and economic disaster were forfeited'. The first few months of the Labour government, he thought, bore out the golden rule of post-war British politics: in a society attached to full employment and collective bargaining, in which the two parties competed to offer bread and circuses, no government could ever resist the demands for greater monetary expansion. 'When, in 1980 or so, democracy as we know it has been suspended and people have accepted that the depression is established for a decade or so,' Jay wrote grimly, 'the question may be asked: "Where did we go wrong?"'[38]

3

King Rat

*[Harold Wilson] was pleading for food, for sandwiches, but
Marcia insisted that he sign her letters before he got his
sandwiches. So he sat there signing and grumbling, but
chuckling away as Marcia was strict with him and ordered
him to do his job before he got his reward.*

Bernard Donoughue's diary, 21 March 1974

*As a good socialist I'm going for the money. As a good capital-
ist, I'm sticking with the revolution, because if you can't beat it,
spy on it. Don't look like that, George. It's the name of the game
these days: you scratch my conscience, I'll drive your Jag, right?*

Roy Bland, in John le Carré, *Tinker Tailor Soldier Spy* (1974)

Harold Wilson had been in Downing Street for two days when the fighting started. On Tuesday, 4 March, his first full day back as Prime Minister,
he had enjoyed a pleasant lunch upstairs with his closest aides, Marcia
Williams, Joe Haines, Bernard Donoughue and Albert Murray. To his
delight, the meal was classic English fare: roast beef, cheese and biscuits
and plenty of wine. He disliked French food, he explained. But when Wilson trudged upstairs the next day, having spent a long morning with
Labour's National Executive discussing his government's political strategy, the atmosphere was very different, as the baffled Donoughue recorded:

Terrible lunch. We all go upstairs to the small dining-room. We discuss the
CPRS [Central Policy Review Staff] and appointments.

Suddenly Marcia blows up. Already upset because we were eating whitebait. She says she hates them looking at her from the plate. The PM

solemnly announced that they were from the Home for Blind Whitebait,
so she need not worry. I added they were also volunteers.

Broke the tension for a while, but then she blew up over Harold and
me having a polite and friendly conversation together. She said that it was
disgraceful . . . She stalked out. HW followed, his meal unfinished. Gloom.

When Donoughue caught up with her, Marcia Williams had put her
coat on and told him she was 'leaving for ever'. It took him two hours
to talk her round. But the very next day there was another lunchtime
bust-up, this time about Wilson's decision to leave Bill Rodgers out of
the Cabinet. 'At the end of the meal Marcia walks out in a temper and
HW is clearly upset,' Donoughue noted. 'She had attacked him viciously
in front of the waiter.' This time she claimed to have a temperature and
went straight home. But when Donoughue got home that night, he
found a message asking him to call her. It was past midnight, but he
rang anyway. 'She is very depressed and neurotic,' he wrote. 'Says we are
all out for ourselves. Ganging up against her. And that I am out to
replace her. She says she will retire to her country home and wait for
HW to sack us all and come personally to ask her to return.'[1]

Harold Wilson's extraordinary relationship with his political secretary remains one of the strangest stories in prime ministerial history.
The daughter of a Northamptonshire builder, Marcia Williams had met
Wilson while working for the Labour Party in the 1950s. By the following decade she had become his private secretary and indispensable right
hand; by the time he returned to office in 1974, she was widely regarded
as one of the administration's most influential figures. To her admirers,
she was bright, loyal and ruthlessly efficient; to her critics, such as
Wilson's astringent press secretary Joe Haines, she was unreliable, tempestuous and utterly egotistical. Yet Haines recognized that she was
almost a second partner to Wilson, for while his wife Mary hated politics, Marcia lived for nothing else. 'She met for a great many years a deep
craving within him,' Haines wrote in 1977, 'for someone else to whom
politics was meat and drink and the very air that was breathed; someone who, at her best, had a political mind capable of testing and
matching his; someone who, again at her best, possessed a deadly ability
to slash her way through the woolliness and verbiage of political argument to get to the heart of an issue.' But Haines also wondered whether
there was more to their relationship than met the eye. Time and again,
he recalled, Marcia would 'lift her ever-present handbag', tap it meaningfully and announce: 'One call to the *Daily Mail* and he'll be finished.

I will destroy him.' Indeed, Wilson himself once claimed that after a particularly blazing row, Marcia had gone to see his wife Mary and announced: 'I have only one thing to say to you. I went to bed with your husband six times in 1956 and it wasn't satisfactory.' At the time, Haines believed his boss's insistence that Marcia was making it all up. But later he pondered Wilson's parting words that day: 'Well, she has dropped her atomic bomb at last. She can't hurt me any more.'[2]

Marcia Williams always denied the truth of these stories, and in many ways it is irrelevant whether the relationship was physical or not. What ultimately mattered was her extraordinary hold over him. At one level it was rooted in sheer possessiveness: not only did she demand total control over his diary, but she hated the thought of sharing access and influence with other advisers. Even the pettiest detail, from the food served at lunch to the seating plans when Wilson travelled around the country, could throw her into a rage. But to her colleagues, her tantrums were no laughing matter. She had 'a debilitating effect on our everyday life working for Wilson', wrote Donoughue. Every day 'was like walking through a minefield, constantly wary, looking and listening for any signs of where the next hidden explosive might be'. Her influence was 'destructive to the point of being catastrophic', agreed Haines; even the typists 'went in dread of her', and 'the roll-call of girls and women who were reduced to tears by her sarcasm was a long one'.

Yet as far as Wilson was concerned, Marcia could do no wrong. Within a few weeks she had persuaded him to take his lunch on his own in the Number 10 flat, leaving his aides to eat the same food in the dining room below. Sometimes he would sneak downstairs for a cup of coffee, although only when he was sure she would not find out. Even when she upbraided him in front of other officials, he seemed quite unperturbed. On one occasion, when she had ordered Wilson to join her at a House of Lords reception, he and Haines bunked off back to Number 10, where she found them a little later. 'You little cunt!' she exploded. 'What do you think you are doing? You come back with me at once!' Even the hard-bitten Haines was shocked at that. 'As ever, the purpose was to humiliate him and she didn't care if there was a witness. Indeed, a witness was important,' he reflected. 'But to me, the use of such language was beyond comprehension' – as was the fact that Wilson tolerated it.[3]

At a time when Britain teetered on the brink of economic collapse, it seems barely credible that scenes like this were unfolding inside Number 10 on a more or less regular basis. What is even more incredible is that, by the early summer of 1974, Wilson's personal doctor, Joe (later Lord) Stone, was considering a drastic solution to what advisers called the 'Marcia problem'. Some time before June, Stone dropped into Haines's office and asked if they could 'discuss ways of taking the weight of Marcia off the Prime Minister's mind'. He explained that he 'could "dispose" of her in such a way that it would seem to be from natural causes. He added that he would sign the death certificate and that there would not be a problem.' Even Haines thought this was going a bit far, but Stone seems to have been quite serious. During a prime ministerial visit to Bonn a few weeks later, he again floated the idea of murdering Marcia to Haines and Donoughue, the latter describing it in his diary as an 'interesting conversation'. And although they hastily squashed the idea, Stone did not give up. In December, Wilson was in Paris renegotiating Britain's EEC membership when Marcia sent a message to him in the conference hall, announcing that her brother Tony was ill and that Wilson must return at once to London, bringing his doctor with him. At that, Stone muttered to Donoughue that she was not 'properly balanced' and that they should think of 'putting her down'. Perhaps he was only joking, but Haines certainly thought he was serious. 'Whatever Marcia had done,' he wrote earnestly, 'she didn't deserve that kind of end.'[4]

That three of Wilson's most trusted aides seriously discussed murdering his political secretary speaks volumes about the atmosphere inside Number 10 after March 1974. The extraordinary thing, though, is that Wilson tolerated all this with such good cheer. One incident in Bernard Donoughue's diaries says it all. On Thursday, 7 March, three days after he had resumed office, Wilson was due to host a small party at Number 10 to celebrate his victory. Unfortunately this was the same day that Marcia stormed out at lunch over Bill Rodgers's exclusion. While Donoughue was out at the London School of Economics, giving a last lecture before he took up his position as head of Wilson's new Policy Unit, she arranged for the party to be cancelled. As a result, when Donoughue and his wife Carol turned up at 8.30, they were the only guests. In the event, they had a pleasant evening drinking with Wilson in the study; even so, this was a bizarrely demeaning way for Labour's most successful election winner to celebrate his return to power.

Edward Heath would have considered the situation utterly intolerable, yet the Donoughues found Wilson on 'relaxed and very funny form'. It was all a 'pantomime', he laughingly explained to Carol Donoughue. 'It is a riot, quite chaotic . . . Nobody outside would believe it. A total pantomime.' At that moment the telephone rang. It was

Marcia. Donoughue hastily ushered his wife out of the room, and they wandered around Number 10 while Wilson was on the phone. Forty minutes later, the Prime Minister emerged from the study to say good-bye. 'He said nothing', Donoughue recorded, 'about the telephone call.'[5]

On Monday, 18 March 1974, two weeks after Labour's return to office, the new House of Commons assembled for the vote on the Queen's Speech. 'The vote will take place', reported *The Times*, 'in an atmosphere of suspense which Westminster has rarely experienced since the last days of the Chamberlain government.' Outnumbered by the combined forces of the Conservatives, the Liberals and the various nationalist parties, Wilson's new government ran a real risk of being defeated. If the House rejected the Queen's Speech, many insiders expected him to ask for an immediate re-run of the general election. Even as MPs were filing into the chamber, his closest aides were making plans for the campaign. Behind the scenes, however, many senior Conservatives worried that a second election so soon meant annihilation. Heath's former Lord Chancellor, Lord Hailsham, warned his colleagues that it was in 'the interests of the [Conservative] Party' that the government survive. 'I do not think we stand to win if Wilson resigns,' he wrote bluntly. And in the end, it was the Tories who blinked first, withdrawing their threat to introduce a rival amendment. 'Anarchic atmosphere. Shouting and drunkenness,' wrote Donoughue, who watched the debate from the gallery. 'Whitelaw spoke reasonably, if too loud, but when he announced the Tories would withdraw their amendment our side erupted. Derision. Tories looking sheepish and Heath years older and thinner.' Afterwards, he recorded, 'HW was on excellent form. Triumph and revenge written over his face. We all had drinks and laughed and joked.'[6]

Amid all the excitement, few people noticed the story buried on an inside page of that morning's *Daily Mail*. Under the headline 'The Case of Ronald Milhench and his £950,000 Land Deals', it told the story of a flamboyant, bouffant-haired Wolverhampton insurance broker who had been negotiating with Marcia Williams's brother, Tony Field, to buy some land on the edge of Wigan. A former geologist and quarry manager for a cement company, Field had borrowed money in the late 1960s to buy a 30-acre slag site, and had then set up a second company to work a nearby gritstone quarry, with his sister Marcia as one of the directors. While this was going on, he worked for two years in Wilson's Commons office. In 1973, however, Field left Wilson's employment and began to dabble in property speculation, taking advantage (as so many people did) of the unprecedented property bubble caused by the Barber boom. At the time, Wilson and his colleagues were mercilessly attacking 'land profiteering', a particular target being speculators such as Harry Hyams, who had refused to find tenants for Centre Point on Tottenham Court Road, gambling that he could make more money by waiting for a single blue-chip occupier. In February 1974, Labour's manifesto even promised that 'land required for development will be taken into public ownership, so that land is freely and cheaply available for new houses, schools, hospitals and other purposes'. Yet all the time Field was himself trying to make money from buying land at knock-down prices, getting planning permission for development, and then selling it on at a handsome profit. In fact, he was not very good at it. But the crucial point was that, as a director of one of his companies, Marcia stood to gain if he made money. At the very least, this made her (and by extension Wilson) look deeply hypocritical. 'During the election we heard a great deal about Mr Harry Hyams,' one Tory MP said later. 'But Mr Hyams didn't work in Mr Heath's private office.'[7]

At first there was no hint that the Field–Milhench story would turn into a major scandal, although a few days after the *Mail*'s story Bernard Donoughue noted that Marcia Williams was staying away from her office and refusing to answer calls. But then on 3 April the *Mail* unleashed a second bombshell, revealing that Field had sent a letter to Milhench on House of Commons notepaper, apparently bearing the signature of Wilson himself. Not surprisingly, Wilson was furious. For almost a decade he had nursed a virulent hatred of the press, verging on paranoia. Now all his old anxieties returned. 'If they want it dirty, they can have it dirty,' he told Donoughue. If the newspapers attacked him, he raged, he would unmask 'Tory ministers' who had been involved with prostitutes during the Heath years, 'Jeremy Thorpe and alleged homosexuality, including alleged blackmail' and even 'Max Aitken, the proprietor of the *Daily Express*, and his Australian mistress'. Almost incredibly, Wilson proposed to do this on the floor of the Commons, which his aides thought was madness. 'I said he should forget this muckraking and not stoop to the gutter levels of the press,' Donoughue recorded. 'He should elevate the issue on to a political level and say the press campaign was the rich hitting back at Budget redistribution.'[8]

But Wilson was not listening. The following morning, Haines had to interrupt Cabinet with an urgent memo to stop the Prime Minister from reading a furious personal statement to the Commons. Disastrously, however, Wilson could not restrain himself from lashing out when teased about his position on property speculation by the Conservative MP Kenneth Baker. He was the victim of a 'smear by the Tory press', he said furiously. There was 'a difference between property speculation and land reclamation' – and at that, there were great roars of laughter and derision from the Opposition benches. 'This is not a laughing matter,' Wilson shouted, angrier than ever. 'My hon. Friends know that if one buys land on which there is a slag heap 120 feet high and it costs £100,000 to remove that slag, that is not land speculation in the sense that we condemn it. It is land reclamation.' Even coming from the man who had told the British public that the pound in their pockets was not being devalued, this was a singularly ill-judged thing to say. As so often, Wilson's belief in his own cleverness, his confidence that he could argue his way out of the tightest spot, had led him astray. In fact, Barbara Castle had overheard him using the same line that morning before Cabinet, telling Shirley Williams that his critics did not realize 'the difference between speculation and reclamation'. It was a poor line then, but it sounded even worse in the bear pit of the Commons. 'It went down as badly as it deserved to,' Castle noted. 'I'm afraid he has got himself into a corner here quite unnecessarily.'[9]

To Wilson's closest aides, it was almost incomprehensible that he had allowed himself to be sucked into a debilitating row when he was so plainly innocent. Nobody doubted that the signature on the letter was a forgery, and it eventually turned out to be the handiwork of Milhench himself, a fantasist trying to get money and attention after his wife had died in an accident and his businesses had collapsed. But in the meantime the press had a field day. Reporters laid siege to Marcia Williams's home, while the atmosphere inside Number 10 became what Donoughue called 'a jungle of hysteria'. On Sunday, 7 April, he recorded, 'Marcia phon[ed] HW and scream[ed] at him ... saying he was a machine, not a human being, and that he had always promised her this would not happen and that he would protect her. She accused him of abandoning her and hiding. She was savage and threatened "to tell everything" about him.' Joe Haines insisted that she was 'just sick'. But on and on it went, reaching a peak the following Wednesday. That morning, Haines warned that the Tories were spreading rumours that MI5 wanted Marcia out on security grounds, while the Express had reportedly got hold of Wilson's tax returns after a burglary at his home. A little later, Wilson, now 'very rattled', asked Donoughue to reassure Marcia that they would protect her. But after a 'crazy, incoherent, violent' telephone call, Donoughue decided that he had had enough. 'It was absolutely ridiculous that a Labour government elected to help millions of people, and its PM, should be totally absorbed in comforting and being attacked by this woman,' he thought. 'Her insistence on attacking all who try to help her, on insisting that they put her before everything else, is intolerable.' When he asked Marcia 'if she was going to the Scillies with HW for Easter,' her answer spoke volumes. 'Yes, if it will embarrass the King Rat,' she spat back. 'That is what he is. A King Rat.'[10]

In the end, the scandal petered out. Milhench went to prison, Wilson withdrew his threats to sue the newspapers for libel and both Marcia Williams and Tony Field won considerable damages. But while the *Observer* described it as a controversy of 'Lilliputian' proportions, it had taken a heavy toll on Wilson's reputation. Property speculation and petty corruption were emblematic issues of the day: as recently as February, the crooked West Yorkshire architect John Poulson, whose contacts included a vast network of politicians and council officials, among them the former Conservative Home Secretary Reginald Maudling and Newcastle's charismatic Labour leader T. Dan Smith, had been imprisoned for flagrant corruption. In Birmingham, the case of Alan Maudsley, the city architect accused of taking bribes from architects and housing companies for high-rise contracts in the West Midlands, was only two months from coming to trial. Even on the London stage, audiences were flocking to David Hare's play *Knuckle*, which had opened in the first week of March and explores the seedy underbelly of life in suburban England, where developers have forced an elderly woman into a lunatic asylum so that her house can be replaced with 'seventeen floors of prestige offices crowned with an antique supermarket'. As *Knuckle*'s central character puts it, Britain has become 'a jampot for swindlers and cons and racketeers. Not just property. Boarding houses and bordellos and nightclubs and crooked charter flights, private clinics, horse-hair wigs and tin-can motor cars, venereal cafés with ice-cream made from whale blubber and sausages full of sawdust.'[11]

Against this backdrop, many commentators saw the slag affair as a British version of Watergate (which was at its height in the spring and summer of 1974): a scandal tapping wider public anxieties and opening the lid on a broader story of political and economic sleaze. As Wilson's biographer puts it, the land deals seemed 'merely the symptom of a deep and many-tentacled corruption', with the careworn figure of the Prime

Minister at its heart. Even Wilson's denials only made matters worse. When he went on Granada's *World in Action* to insist that Tony Field had actually been doing a noble public service, removing a 'terrible eyesore' at great personal cost and even breaking his leg by falling off a slag heap, the press reacted with hilarity and contempt. 'Sad, vindictive, and utterly predictable,' was the *Mail*'s verdict. In the press, Wilson's reputation could hardly have been lower: day after day, editorials dismissed him as 'unprincipled, sleazy and weak'. For Labour loyalists, the slag story undermined all their pledges to end property speculation and take land back into public ownership. And on the left, nothing better symbolized a supposedly introverted, self-interested governing culture, and a shabby, cynical, treacherous politician, surrounded by a cabal of corrupt advisers. 'We didn't just feel bloody, most of us,' wrote the Labour MP Maureen Colquhoun. 'We felt down, all our hopes and ideals crushed. It destroyed us as socialists.'[12]

On Marcia Williams, too, the affair took a heavy toll. Both in Fleet Street and in Westminster, the knives had been out for her for ten years. Many people could not disguise their loathing of a self-proclaimed left-winger who, by the mid-1970s, owned a mews house in the West End and a country home not far from Chequers, maintained two cars and three servants, sent her illegitimate sons to private schools, and, as Joe Haines later caustically put it, retained Lord Stone as her doctor, Lord Goodman as her personal adviser and Lord Weidenfeld as her escort. Never the most stable or secure of women, she retreated further into isolation and paranoia: Haines thought she was 'never the same person again'. But at least there was some consolation. On 24 May, to universal astonishment, Downing Street confirmed that Marcia was among fifteen new life peers ennobled at Wilson's request. In his diary, Tony Benn recorded that her elevation to Lady Falkender was 'amusing'. To almost everybody else, though, it was an outrage. 'In a way,' said Dennis Skinner, the 'Beast of Bolsover', 'her peerage will assist in driving another nail into the coffin of the Lords, which will greatly please me.' At Westminster, Conservative MPs recalled that the Roman emperor Caligula had tried to make his horse a consul; in Downing Street, aides were 'sunk in gloom'. Until the very last minute, Haines and Donoughue had tried to change the Prime Minister's mind, but to no avail.* Even the

---

* According to Donoughue, Wilson even drafted Marcia's letter accepting the peerage himself. Almost unbelievably, however, she corrected it a day later, crossing out the word 'happily', as if to suggest that she accepted her elevation with great reluctance.

Queen was reported to have raised a quizzical eyebrow when she was shown the final list. 'If the Prime Minister should wish to change his mind about this,' she was said to have remarked, 'he can, of course, do so at any time.' But, of course, he never did.[13]

In the aftermath of the slag furore, not even Harold Wilson's closest intimates could pretend that he still had the slick, modernizing image with which he had first come to power in 1964. His appearance shabby, his eyes weary, even his Commons repartee increasingly slow and downbeat, Wilson seemed a depressingly backward-looking figurehead for a nation in apparently irreversible decline. On the day before Marcia Williams's peerage was announced, Donoughue noted that the Prime Minister drank three neat whiskies before lunch and three large brandies afterwards. 'I shall have to stick to water tonight,' Wilson muttered. The next day, Donoughue recorded that the Prime Minister was 'tired, edgy . . . He looks 10 years older. Is much less cheerful. Looks like he did at times in the February election, surly and lowering.' On 21 June: 'He looks more tired and his political judgement is off . . . And he is *drinking* more – brandy from midday til late evening when he was very slow and slurred.' On 3 July: 'He went out with the press and apparently was the worse for drink. This was embarrassingly obvious when the Cabinet committee on Energy met in the late afternoon. He rambled and ministers looked embarrassed.' All in all, Donoughue found it a depressing picture. There was 'no impression of energetic radicalism', he lamented. 'I smell a massive financial and economic crisis. Nobody in the government seems aware or concerned.' Others felt the same way. When Sir Nicholas Henderson, then Britain's ambassador to Bonn, talked to Wilson in June, he found him in nostalgic form, his conversation a long monologue about Oxford before the war and the right position for Billy Bremner in Scotland's World Cup showdown with Brazil. The Prime Minister, Henderson wrote that night, was 'living in the past'.[14]

What especially alarmed Wilson's colleagues, though, were signs that he was succumbing to paranoia. On 10 April, in the midst of the slag scandal, he gave his Cabinet an extraordinarily melodramatic warning, telling them that 'there are two other members of the Cabinet, whose names wild horses wouldn't draw from me, who are being pursued by the press. One has been tailed for five years and on the other they have got a dossier two feet thick. They both would be regarded as being in the leadership stakes if I went. So I just want to warn you.' The incident 'showed him in his cheapest light', thought Tony Benn. Yet it also reflected Wilson's growing sense, building since the late 1960s but now approaching a climax, that his enemies in the press and in the corridors of power were out to get him. To his increasingly fevered mind, the land-deal controversy was part of it; so were the rumours in the Commons that MI5 wanted Marcia out, as well as the stories that the *Mail* and the *Express* had got hold of his financial records and were about to accuse him of tax evasion. In the spring of 1974, personal tax papers were stolen from Wilson's house at Lord North Street, while his secondary office in Buckingham Palace Road, where he stored other financial documents, was raided a few weeks later. The offices of Wilson's lawyer Lord Goodman were burgled twice in a few months, while his former private secretary Michael Halls, Bernard Donoughue, Marcia Williams (both in London and at her country house), Tony Crosland and Tony Field all reported burglaries at around the same time. Of course this might easily have been a coincidence: after all, burglary figures were rocketing, especially in London. To Wilson, however, it smacked of an orchestrated conspiracy. He was 'rattled', writes his authorized biographer; 'irritated, baffled, and a little apprehensive'. But that greatly understates the case. As time went on, Wilson became not just rattled, but genuinely disturbed. A 'Dirty Tricks Department', he told friends, was out to get him, run from within his own security services.[15]

Wilson had been fascinated by intelligence and espionage since the early 1960s. His path to power had been smoothed by a series of extraordinary security scandals, notably the revelations that an Admiralty official, John Vassall, had been passing secrets to the KGB, and that Macmillan's Secretary of State for War, John Profumo, had shared a call girl with a Soviet attaché. Not surprisingly, therefore, Wilson took intelligence matters exceptionally seriously. As one official said later, the Prime Minister was 'obsessed by intelligence' and 'extremely interested in getting it – not only about the Russians, foreign policy, defence and so on, but also information from the security services about people in this country'. When the seamen had walked out in 1966, causing a dispute that almost derailed Wilson's first premiership, he relied heavily on MI5 wiretaps showing that the strike was partly being run from the Communist Party's headquarters in King Street. But there were other reasons, too, why he was so interested in intelligence. During his first administration he had been alerted to several parliamentary coup attempts, usually masterminded by close colleagues such as Jim Callaghan and Roy Jenkins, and in 1968 the chairman of the IPC newspaper empire, Cecil Harmsworth King, had even tried to persuade Lord Mountbatten to step in as the titular head of an Emergency Government. Of course none of these plots had come to anything, but, given the persistent disloyalty of his own colleagues, it was no wonder that Wilson was obsessed with knowing what was going on. Over time, his obsession curdled into paranoia: a few weeks before King's bizarre coup attempt, Tony Benn had recorded that 'Harold is very paranoid, and . . . in a sense, creating the very thing he is afraid of'. But as Henry Kissinger once remarked of another embattled politician obsessed with the secret world, Richard Nixon, even paranoid people often have enemies.[16]

Not only was Wilson fascinated with the security services, but they were also extremely interested in him. As early as 1945, when he first became an MP, MI5 opened a file on him under the codename 'Norman John Worthington' – the reason, apparently, being that a Communist civil servant had been heard praising Wilson's political outlook. What really attracted MI5's interest, though, was Wilson's appointment as President of the Board of Trade two years later, which meant that he undertook several trips to Moscow. At this stage, nobody really thought that Wilson himself was a Communist. What worried MI5 was that he continued to visit Moscow in the 1950s as a consultant for a firm of timber importers, which meant that he was in regular contact with Soviet officials and Communist sympathizers. Among his acquaintances were at least two KGB officers working undercover at the Soviet embassy, while his close friends included a strange gaggle of shady businessmen with Jewish backgrounds and Eastern European connections, such as the raincoat king Joseph Kagan, the publisher Robert Maxwell and the petrochemicals tycoon Rudi Sternberg. Precisely why Wilson chose to surround himself with such disreputable characters baffled many of his colleagues. The most likely explanation is that they shared his tastes for golf and spirits, contributed to his office expenses and made undemanding and obsequious companions. Intellectuals and pillars of the establishment left him cold, but self-made men evidently fascinated him. For his aides, however, his tolerance defied reason. After Wilson invited a bizarre collection of businessmen to watch him receive the Freedom of the City of London in December 1975, Joe Haines even 'looked around to see if Inspector Knacker of the Yard was keeping the ceremony under observation'.[17]

As MI5 saw it, Wilson's links with such men were at best extremely reckless and at worst deeply suspicious. The Austrian-born Rudi Sternberg, for example, had made vast amounts of money by trading with

East Germany and the Soviet Union. An MI5 report noted that he had made his fortune 'by methods which seem frequently to have been on the fringe of respectability', and counted among his acquaintances more than thirty Eastern European intelligence officers. In his diary, Bernard Donoughue recorded that the Foreign Office had 'told me privately that he is a double agent', while another official told Joe Haines that 'Sternberg was a Soviet spy'. When a shocked Haines raised the matter with Wilson, the Prime Minister 'said cheerfully that he had always thought so too, but that when he checked with the security services he had been told that Sternberg was a double agent'. Perhaps he was. Other acquaintances, however, were even less salubrious. The financier Harry Kissin spent so much time with prostitutes that MI5 asked the Cabinet Secretary to tell Wilson that he was 'obviously not a man to be trusted with confidences'. Like Sternberg, Kissin picked up a peerage in Wilson's resignation honours list.

But the man whom MI5 distrusted most was Joseph Kagan, who manufactured Wilson's famous Gannex raincoats and still had close links with his native Lithuania. Having fled the Soviet Union after the war, Kagan made his way from Bucharest to Bradford, became a successful textile manufacturer and inveigled his way into Wilson's inner circle, where he acted as 'part court jester, part obliging uncle, part boon companion'. He was an inveterate womanizer, claiming to have kept forty different mistresses by the time he was 60; disturbingly, however, he was also very close to a Lithuanian KGB officer at the Soviet embassy, with whom he played chess. When MI5 interviewed Kagan, he admitted that he often supplied 'gossip' to his Lithuanian friend, and that he had tried to get Jewish groups in Britain to call off protests against the oppression of Soviet Jews – all of which, as his interrogator pointed out, meant that he was acting as a KGB 'agent of influence'. Yet even when MI5 warned Wilson about Kagan in October 1972, the Labour leader refused to break with him. Kagan had only two faults, Wilson said affectionately: 'he cannot stop gossiping or chasing women.'[18]

Since even Wilson's closest advisers were bewildered by his fondness for glorified crooks like Sternberg and Kagan, it is hardly surprising that others drew more sinister conclusions. MI5 was not a happy place in the early 1970s. Humiliated by the defections of Burgess, Maclean and Philby, it had become not merely introverted and run-down but deeply paranoid in its own right. Even the former Director General, Sir Roger Hollis, was thought by some officers to have been a Soviet mole. In particular, some MI5 officers had fallen under the influence of the CIA's

eccentric spymaster James Jesus Angleton, who was convinced that the
Western intelligence services had been thoroughly penetrated by the
KGB. By the early 1970s, Angleton had completely lost the ability to
distinguish between fantasy and reality. Not only did he think Harold
Wilson was a KGB agent, he also suspected the Canadian Prime Minister, Lester Pearson, the West German Chancellor, Willy Brandt, his own
Secretary of State, Henry Kissinger, and even President Gerald Ford of
being Soviet moles or dupes. Demented as all this sounds, Angleton's
ideas made a powerful impression on some British officers, notably the
inveterate conspiracy theorist Peter Wright, who had led the witch-hunt
against Sir Roger Hollis. In particular, Angleton persuaded Wright that
the death of the Labour leader Hugh Gaitskell in January 1963 had
been no accident. According to Angleton, Gaitskell had not died of a
rare autoimmune disease, but had been poisoned by the KGB to make
way for their sleeper agent, Harold Wilson. There was no evidence for
this, of course. But as any decent spycatcher knows, lack of evidence is
often the most suspicious thing of all.[19]

On the face of it, the notion that the Prime Minister was a Soviet
mole seems utterly laughable. Still, there is no doubt that MI5 was
unusually sensitive to questions of left-wing subversion in the early
1970s. This was, after all, a time when the miners had brought down
the Heath government, paramilitaries had brought Northern Ireland to
the brink of civil war and the international headlines were full of terrorist bombings, coups and counter-coups. In his controversial memoir
Spycatcher (1987), Peter Wright even alleged that 'up to thirty' officers
shared his concerns about Harold Wilson and joined a secret campaign
to undermine the Labour leader. Later, an internal investigation found
no evidence to support his claims, and Wright eventually admitted that
instead of having 'up to thirty' collaborators, he really had only 'eight or
nine', which he then whittled down to three. Asked how many people
actually joined him in trying to force Wilson out, he replied: 'One, I
should say.' And yet the conversations he claimed to have had with
other MI5 officers – 'Wilson's a bloody menace and it's about time the
public knew the truth . . . We'll have him out, this time we'll have him
out' – do have the faint ring of plausibility. Anecdotal evidence suggests
that many officers held political views well to the right of the mainstream, making them suspicious of a Labour Party that seemed to be
swinging far to the left. Even Edward Heath, hardly Wilson's greatest
admirer, recalled meeting 'people in the security services who talked the
most ridiculous nonsense and whose whole philosophy was ridiculous

nonsense. If some of them were on a tube and saw someone reading the *Daily Mirror*, they would say, "Get after him, that is dangerous. We must find out where he bought it."' But perhaps Heath was a Soviet agent, too.[20]

In his official history of MI5, Christopher Andrew concludes that the 'Wilson plot' was a fiction, a product of Peter Wright's febrile imagination rather than a serious conspiracy against a sitting Prime Minister. One obvious drawback in the conspiracy theory is that, far from being toppled by a nefarious plot, Wilson actually won four out of five general elections and ran the country for almost eight years. Even a security service as demoralized and dilapidated as MI5 would surely have done a better job than that. Yet given the weight of anecdotal evidence – not just Wright's memoirs, but the burglaries, the rumours, the apparently planted stories in the press and the Prime Minister's own suspicions – it is very hard to believe that there was no substance in the stories whatsoever. Revealingly, some of Wright's claims tally closely with allegations made by Colin Wallace, a former Ministry of Defence press officer in Northern Ireland. According to Wallace, MI5 officers working on the 'Clockwork Orange' counter-intelligence programme, which had been set up to discredit the IRA and other paramilitary groups, deliberately tried to smear Wilson as a KGB agent after the February 1974 election. They even claimed that Labour's goal was to force Northern Ireland into a 'Red Shamrock Irish Workers' Republic'. It is just possible that Colin Wallace's story, which he backed up with contemporaneous handwritten notes, was an elaborate forgery.* But it seems more likely that he was telling the truth, and that a tiny cabal of intelligence officers, perhaps orchestrated by Peter Wright, did make haphazard efforts to discredit Harold Wilson, their allegations eventually filtering down to 'small fry' like Colin Wallace. If so, the one consolation for Wilson was that they made such an inept job of it. As Ben Pimlott remarks, people would need to have been very gullible indeed to believe such 'crude and unconvincing political fantasies'.[21]

At one level, of course, all of this was beside the point. Since Wilson

---

* Forensic testing showed that the notes had indeed been written in the mid-1970s, as Wallace claimed. To complicate matters further, he later resigned from his post in very strange circumstances. He alleged that the security services had covered up a child abuse scandal at the Kincora boys' home to protect one of the staff, the leader of the loyalist Tara movement and an MI5 informant. What was more, Wallace was sent to prison in 1981 for manslaughter, only for his conviction to be quashed years later when new evidence suggested he had been framed. These are murky waters indeed.

retired at a time of his own choosing, the conspiracy, if it existed, was remarkably ineffective. And yet there is no doubt that by 1974 the *idea* that he was a subversive influence, perhaps even a KGB agent leading a party of crypto-Communists, had become remarkably widespread on Fleet Street. To people who knew Wilson's deep cultural conservatism, understated patriotism, admiration for the monarchy, distrust of radical ideology and faith in the Atlantic alliance, this obviously sounded absurd. Yet after the turn of the decade it became increasingly common to hear stories that Wilson was actually an enemy agent, controlled or manipulated by the KGB through Joseph Kagan. In October 1971, the front page of the *News of the World* even suggested that 'prominent Labour Party figures' had been 'murdered by Russian killer squads', so that 'in the Labour Movement, right-wingers hostile to Communism could be replaced by left-wingers with very different views'. This was pure James Jesus Angleton, but it also bore a remarkable similarity to stories being fed to *Private Eye*'s anarchic diarist Auberon Waugh. Since Waugh freely admitted that his column was partly devoted to 'telling lies', it was never easy to disentangle polemic from self-parody. Even so, it is surely no coincidence that in the early 1970s his treatment of Wilson became increasingly vitriolic, with frequent references to his Moscow trips, relationship with Kagan and supposed links to the KGB. In June 1975, for example, Waugh reported that some incriminating photographs had 'come into my possession', and a year later he claimed that they showed Wilson and Marcia in a compromising position, and had been used by the KGB to force Wilson's collaboration. 'I have never attempted to hide my belief', he wrote in September 1975, 'that Harold Wislon [*sic*] is [a Soviet agent], recruited in Moscow and London in 1956–8, although I have no evidence to support this apart from intuition.'[22]

There seems little doubt that Waugh was getting some of his informa-tion from Peter Wright, or at least from one of Wright's allies. In his official history of *Private Eye*, Patrick Marnham writes that Wilson's return to power 'was followed by a barrage of anonymous information concerning his activities since the 1940s' which the editors felt 'was extremely detailed and convincing'. In retrospect, Marnham admits, 'it seems likely to have been supplied by someone with connections in the security service', not least since it bore a remarkable similarity to the information given to Colin Wallace in Northern Ireland. In any case, from March 1974 the *Eye* ran a host of stories about Wilson's trips to Moscow, his links with Kagan, Sternberg and Kissin, his private finances and Swiss bank account, his supposed closeness to Jewish financiers and the Israeli secret service, and his relationship with Marcia Williams. Later, Marcia herself remembered hearing rumours about 'close liaisons with KGB colonels', 'mysterious East European "benefactors"' and 'drugs, orgies and nameless vices in mysterious blocks off Baker Street', as well as a stream of bizarre stories about left-wing ministers such as Tony Benn and John Silkin. One story alleged that the party's deputy leader Ted Short had been taking money from Newcastle's corrupt council leader T. Dan Smith, which he had supposedly deposited in a Swiss bank account. In fact the documents sent to the *Eye* had been forged, and Short was entirely innocent. But to readers who already distrusted Wilson as a cheap political fixer, and who had followed the bizarre developments of the slag-heap affair every morning in the *Mail* or the *Express*, it seemed perfectly plausible that he and his ministers might be dangerously subversive. The stories 'came and went', recalled Wilson's old friend George Weidenfeld, but they were 'repeated in clubs, in drawing-rooms, in country houses, and retold, embroidered second and third hand'.[23]

The ironic thing is that, while all of this left little impression on the wider political landscape, it had a powerful effect on Wilson himself. When he returned to office, most of his suspicions were directed at the South African intelligence service, BOSS, and the CIA. But by the autumn of 1974 he had become convinced that MI5 was out to get him, and by the end of 1975 relations between Downing Street and the security service had almost completely broken down. When MI5's director general, Sir Michael Hanley, tried to clear the air with the Prime Minister, their meeting went disastrously wrong. Wilson himself told aides that he had shouted and sworn at Hanley, while the latter recalled that they had a 'terrible row . . . He got the idea I was his worst enemy. I did not know what to do.' But by this stage, Wilson was long past being mollified. He even told his Cabinet Secretary, Sir John Hunt, that 'MI5 was conducting some sort of vendetta against him', and that he was 'being watched or monitored, observed, by both hostile and some friendly intelligence services'. And when the new head of the CIA, George Bush, paid a courtesy call to Number 10 in early 1976, he emerged from his meeting in shaken disbelief. 'Is that man mad?' he asked Hunt. 'He did nothing but complain about being spied on!'[24]

Perhaps a more stable person would simply have shrugged off the smears, especially after winning two elections in less than a year. But even in the 1960s Wilson had been a notably insecure, mistrustful politician, forever looking out for plotters in the dark. And as his health deteriorated and his mental faculties declined, he gradually succumbed to a corrosive paranoia that even his closest allies found extremely worrying. On 18 February 1976, for example, Wilson spent much of the afternoon discussing burglaries with Bernard Donoughue, who had just suffered a break-in, and then saw a private security expert about 'the possible bugging of his study'. Donoughue shared some of his chief's suspicions: he too believed that his office phone was being tapped, but nevertheless 'tried to resist the kind of paranoia which surrounds Harold and Marcia'. The ever-caustic Joe Haines, meanwhile, thought the discussion of burglaries and bugging was 'paranoid' and 'hysterical'. But by this stage, the Prime Minister could not be deflected. Chatting to Haines one day in the Downing Street study, Wilson suddenly astounded him 'by putting his finger to his lips'. He then walked across to a portrait of Gladstone, 'raised it and pointed to the wall behind'. 'We will have to go for a walk in the open,' he hissed melodramatically. On another occasion Wilson told Shirley Williams that there was a bug in the Cabinet Room ceiling, and whenever he chatted to colleagues in the Number 10 lavatory he made a point of turning on all the taps and gesturing towards the light fitting. Again and again, though, he came back to the Gladstone portrait, even calling in a security firm, Argon Ltd, to investigate a mysterious hole in the wall behind it. 'He called Ken Stowe [his principal private secretary] in and put his hands to his lips and said, "Shhh!", pointing to the hole,' Jim Callaghan told a fascinated Tony Benn a few years later. 'Harold is just a Walter Mitty.'[25]

Ultimately, of course, Callaghan was right. Wilson had always been something of a fantasist, and by the mid-1970s his Walter Mitty side had become unhealthily pronounced. Yet there is an intriguing coda to the story of Gladstone's portrait. In the summer of 1977, when Wilson's bugging allegations surfaced in the *Daily Express*, Callaghan ordered a confidential inquiry, which concluded that they were quite untrue. Those who had known Wilson 'for many years', Callaghan breezily told the Commons, 'know that he has a great capacity for illuminating a truth long before it becomes apparent to other people', which was a polite way of saying that he was paranoid. And yet when the official history of MI5 was published some thirty-three years later, it emerged that the security service *had* installed listening devices in Downing Street after all. During the Profumo scandal, Harold Macmillan had asked them to put bugs in the Cabinet Room, a waiting room and the Prime Minister's study. The relevant MI5 files apparently contained 'no product' – which suggests that the bugs were never monitored – but it was not until 1977, after Wilson had left, that they were ripped out. This does not prove, of course, that he was the victim of organized dirty tricks, or even that anybody was listening to his conversations. But it is a reminder that beneath the thick layers of fantasy, behind all the alarmist stories and fears of conspiracy, there was at least a tiny grain of truth.[26]

4

A Third World Country

*Life in London gets more and more impossible – traffic, trains,
soaring prices, the sheer effort to get anything of any sort done
drives one mad.*

Roy Strong's diary, 9 February 1974

*I see a face in the street sometimes. I hardly recognise it, it's
changed so much. Exhausted, eaten into. Without a job, of
course, they always are, or just about to lose one, limping
along, unable to do anything, almost broken, no life for
anything. Shadows. Just shadows, of course.*

Stephen Poliakoff, *Strawberry Fields* (1977)

Harold Wilson was not the only tired little man in a battered mackintosh making an unlikely comeback in the spring of 1974. 'Small, podgy
and at best middle-aged, he was by appearance one of London's meek
who do not inherit the earth,' runs the description of George Smiley in
the opening pages of John le Carré's novel *Tinker Tailor Soldier Spy*,
published a few weeks after Wilson's return to Number 10. Like Wilson,
Smiley is physically unprepossessing: we learn that 'his legs were
short, his gait anything but agile, his dress costly, ill-fitting and extremely
wet', and his estranged wife calls him a 'toad'. Like Wilson, he suffers
from the condescension of more patrician colleagues; like Wilson, he
seems the absolute antithesis of heroic leadership, a frustratingly wily,
ambiguous figure, always slightly out of focus. In the 1960s, Wilson's
critics had joked about the 'ten faces of Harold'; in le Carré's novel
Smiley's People (1980), one character reflects that Smiley has 'not one
face at all' but a 'whole range of faces'. And while Wilson seemed

obsessed with conspiracies from the moment he entered Downing Street, Smiley has been a creature of the secret world since leaving Lincoln College, Oxford, just across the street from Wilson's old college, Jesus. 'I have learned to interpret the whole of life in terms of conspiracy,' he reflects at one point. 'That is the sword I have lived by, and as I look round me now I see it is the sword I shall die by as well.'[1]

In *Tinker Tailor Soldier Spy*, Smiley is summoned out of retirement to investigate rumours of a Soviet mole inside the 'Circus', the nickname for MI6. For all its introversion and secrecy, the Circus is contemporary Britain in microcosm. But it is sadly diminished since the days when Smiley was first recruited, its morale corroded by office politics, budget cuts and a cancerous culture of suspicion. 'Divide and rule, that's the principle these days,' remarks its ineffectual chief Percy Alleline. 'We're losing our livelihood. Our self-respect.' Deceit and betrayal have become part of the fabric, and while Smiley, perhaps the only sane man left, has been forced out, mediocrity has risen to the top. Under Alleline's weak, ingratiating leadership, the Circus has fallen apart. When Smiley visits the training school and interrogation centre at Sarratt, Hertfordshire, he finds it a 'sorry place after the grandeur which [he] remembered'. The trees have been cut down by the Dutch elm disease that struck Britain in the late 1960s; the main house has 'come down a lot since the heyday of the Cold War'; pylons tower over the cricket field. And, if anything, the Circus headquarters in central London is even worse: a shabby, peeling relic, steadily slipping into dereliction amid the bustle of the capital. Even the lobby, with its three old lifts, its poster for Mazawatee tea, its Scenes of England calendar and 'line of mossy telephones', feels embarrassingly outdated. 'Time you oiled this thing,' says Smiley's colleague Peter Guillam as the lift squeaks upwards. 'We keep asking,' says the doorman. 'They never do a thing about it.'[2]

In its decay and disrepair, the Circus headquarters is entirely typical of much of the city that surrounds it. By the time of Harold Wilson's unexpected comeback, the fantasies of Swinging London had long since evaporated. The capital's days as a working port were fast fading; its car and vehicle-parts factories were struggling to stay afloat; its long traditions of engineering and furniture making seemed destined for the scrapheap. With skilled working-class families moving out to the suburbs of Hertfordshire, Essex, Surrey and Kent, entire districts were being utterly transformed. The West End, said *The Times* sadly in October 1974, was in a 'sorry state', with parts of Shaftesbury Avenue and Charing Cross Road 'in the sort of condition that, in Birmingham or

Manchester, would qualify them for wholesale slum clearance'. London had become 'a semi-derelict slum', agreed the journalist Clive Irving the same year: a city blighted by 'tacky porno shops, skin movies, pinball arcades, and toxic hamburger joints', while 'behind neon façades the buildings are flaking and unkempt'. Even the Underground, once the capital's pride and joy, had become a symbol of decline, thanks to the dreadful Moorgate disaster in February 1975, when a Northern Line train smashed into a bricked-up tunnel and killed forty-three passengers. Nobody ever explained why it had happened; nobody had an answer to the city's problems, either. After spending all day at a conference entitled 'London Looks Forward' in July 1977, the Whitehall mandarin Ronald McIntosh recorded that he 'found it all rather depressing'. 'London is evidently losing population quite heavily [and] services are steadily deteriorating,' he wrote, 'and nobody seems to have the least idea of how to deal with it.'[3]

During Wilson's first term, London had been a worldwide symbol of modernity and hedonism, hailed by American journalists as 'the most exciting city in the world'. By 1974, though, all that was merely a faintly embarrassing memory. Smiley's London is the city of the Sex Pistols and *The Sweeney*, not the Beatles and *The Avengers*; a city of tramps and hooligans, hustlers and muggers, the downtrodden and the disappointed, haunted by the deadly figure of the IRA bomber. In Martin Amis's novel *Success* (1977), one of the book's narrators hurries through Queensway, where 'up-ended dustbins and capsized vegetable barrows are being sick all over the pavement; rubbish bags slump like tramps against shop windows; rabid pigeons, too fat to fly, squawk among the filth'. Writers often lamented the demise of an older working-class London: many of its Victorian terraced streets had fallen beneath the bulldozer, while a forest of tower blocks dominated the skyline like prisons for the city's poor. When one character revisits her old working-class neighbourhood in Margaret Drabble's novel *The Middle Ground* (1980), she finds it 'derelict, abandoned', its unfinished tower blocks 'raw, ugly, gigantic in scale', a 'wilderness of flyovers and underpasses and unfinished supports', a 'no man's land' in the aftermath of war. Even the young Jonathan Raban, one of a new breed of middle-class gentrifiers, was struck by the physical decay of his Notting Hill neighbourhood. With its transient population of struggling young mothers, unkempt bohemians and West Indian youngsters, he wrote, it might be picturesque in the sun, but 'on dull days one notices the litter, the scabby paint, the stretches of torn wire netting, and the faint smell of joss-sticks competing with the sickly sweet odour of rising damp and rotting plaster'.[4]

London was not alone in presenting a remarkably shabby image to the world in the mid-1970s. The suburbs of Middle England might be prospering as never before, but the nation's great old cities seemed in sad decline: Manchester crippled by the plight of manufacturing, Liverpool cursed by the decline of the docks, Glasgow scarred by the planners' efforts to turn it into a Stalinist high-rise wasteland. Even where the architects had done their best to drive Britain into a brave new world, there seemed a pervasive sense of degradation and neglect. During Wilson's first term, Birmingham had been hailed as 'the most go-ahead city in Europe'; now, *The Times* admitted, it looked like a 'large and chaotic building site', its Victorian heritage smothered beneath a sea of concrete. High-rise buildings were now symbols of the failure of modernism, most famously in J. G. Ballard's fantasy *High Rise* (1975), in which life in a brand-new tower block degenerates into a cannibalistic struggle for territory. Visiting Southampton's Millbrook, 'a vast, cheap storage unit for nearly 20,000 people', Jonathan Raban found a dismal scene of rain-sodden towers and deserted grassland 'patrolled by gangs of sub-teenage youths'. Inside, most of the people he interviewed complained of theft and vandalism; even their milk-money regularly disappeared, and many admitted that they would not risk hanging their clothes in the communal drying areas. And when Christopher Booker visited Sir Denys Lasdun's groundbreaking sixteen-storey Keeling House (1957) in Bethnal Green in July 1976, he found a 'tatty and forlorn' council block, 'its concrete cracked and discolouring, the metal reinforcement rusting through the surface, every available inch covered with graffiti'. Inside, only one lift was working, 'piles of old cigarette packets and broken bottles' lay in the corners, and there was an overwhelming 'stench of urine'. Here, he thought, was the story of modern Britain: 'the bright, anticipated dream followed by a seedy, nightmarish reality'.[5]

As foreign visitors often remarked, Britain's infrastructure seemed old and dilapidated, its public services often broken down and unreliable, its hospitals struggling to cope with an ageing population, its railways grimy and underfunded. There was a palpable sense, thought the Labour MP Phillip Whitehead, of physical decay: whereas, twenty years earlier, 'travellers had come back from France regretting what they had experienced in the way of shabby streets, late trains, graffiti in the subway and nauseous public lavatories, it was now the French who went home from Britain with the same impression'. Conversely, when British travellers went abroad, they were often embarrassed by the contrasts. Visiting the 'handsome, well-appointed and clean' Juilliard School in New York in December 1978, the National Theatre's director Peter Hall 'found it depressing to compare it with our own already run-down, ill-maintained South Bank building'. The problem, he thought, was only 'partly the difference in money'; in truth, 'the English apparently no longer care about material surroundings. They even seem to take a positive pleasure in defiling them.'[6]

Novelists often took great delight in chronicling the degradation of public spaces, not least as a way of puncturing the idealism of the late 1960s. So when the loathsome sociology lecturer Howard Kirk visits a new shopping precinct in Malcolm Bradbury's *The History Man* (1975), he walks from the car park, 'devoid of people, a place for machines only', to the lift, its walls covered with 'aerosoled scribbles' reading 'Agro', 'Boot boys' and 'Gary is King'. In the corridor leading to the shops, he passes piles of 'human excrement against the walls of the brightlit passage'. Even in the precinct itself, surrounded by 'the economy of abundance', there are signs of disrepair: 'a waterless fountain contains much litter'. Meanwhile, Howard's university campus, originally a temple to the utopian modernism of the 1960s, now seems 'smaller and darker', shrunken by disappointment and neglect. 'In the rain the buildings are black; the concrete has stained, the glass grown dirty, the services diminished,' the narrator tells us. 'The graffiti experts have been at work, inscribing "Stop Police Brutality" and "IRA" and "Spengler Bootboys" on concrete and steel; there has been a small fire in the library; rapes and muggings occur occasionally in the darker corners of this good society.'[7]

Graffiti and litter were common features of mid-1970s fiction. In the opening scene of Colin Dexter's early Inspector Morse novel *Last Seen Wearing* (1977), a man waits at an Oxford bus shelter, 'its wooden walls predictably covered with scrawls and scorings of varying degrees of indecency', from the inclinations of 'several local tarts' to demands that 'all Fascists should go home immediately and freedom should be granted forthwith to Angola, Chile and Northern Ireland'. A window has been smashed: 'slivers of glass sparkled sporadically amid the orange peel, crisp-packets and Cola tins'. In the same year, as one character walks through St Pancras in Margaret Drabble's *The Ice Age*, she surveys 'this vast quantity of garbage and newspaper and plastic bags, this sea of rubbish' and draws a miserable comparison with the great Gothic arches of the station façade:

> Victorian England had produced them. She had so loved England. A fear and sadness in tune with her own breathed out of the station's shifting population: old ladies with bags, a black man with a brush and bin, pallid girls in jeans, an Indian with a tea trolley, a big fat man with a carrier bag, they all looked around themselves shiftily, uneasily, eyeing abandoned packages, kicking dirty blowing plastic bags from their ankles, expecting explosions. It can't be like this, thought Alison: how can it have got to be like this. Who has so undermined, so terrified, so threatened and subdued us?

Would she have been better off at another station? Probably not. Piers Paul Read's novel *A Married Man* (1979) finds the central character at Paddington, sitting on a 'grimy chair drinking insipid tea' and gazing at 'the squalor around him – the scruffy travellers and the listless slut serving tea behind the counter. It is a sign of a nation's decline, he thought to himself, that its people no longer take the trouble to dress themselves decently or keep themselves clean.' And the trains themselves – often grubby, underfunded and unreliable – were hardly a great advertisement for the nation that had invented them. Taking the train from Victoria to Brighton in February 1978, Michael Palin found the dirty carriage 'quite an embarrassment as I hear guttural continental voices in the compartment next door'. He was not alone in seeing the condition of the trains as a symptom of national decline. 'Those filthy carriages on the trip down yesterday which annoyed Jane so much, is the nation completely rotten?' wondered Alan Clark in April 1979. 'Yes,' he concluded bleakly, 'and has been since 1916.'[8]

In an early chapter of *Tinker Tailor Soldier Spy*, Smiley visits a drab, drizzly Oxford to find his old friend Connie Sachs, formerly the Circus's chief researcher but now a needy semi-alcoholic. 'It was a good time, do you hear?' she mumbles, looking back on the early Cold War. 'A real time. Englishmen could be proud then . . . Poor loves. Trained to Empire, trained to rule the waves. All gone. All taken away.' This was no exaggeration: since the beginning of Harold Wilson's political career, the transformation in British power had been simply astonishing. In 1945, Britain had still ruled much of Africa, the Caribbean and South East Asia, as well as the Indian Raj. Three decades on, however, the picture

could hardly have been more different. Now Britain ruled only a handful of tiny territories such as the Seychelles, St Helena, Hong Kong and
the Falkland Islands. At first, people had told themselves that Britain
had left a fine legacy of democracy and civil rights. But as one by one
the old colonies fell under one-party rule, any illusions of post-imperial
peace and prosperity were rudely punctured. By 1978, when Jan Morris
published the final volume of her epic history of the British Empire,
Farewell the Trumpets, a naively cheerful verdict would have seemed
absurd. Some imperial achievements, 'like the roads, railways and
telegraph systems', had endured, but others, such as 'parliamentary
democracy' and 'the importance of the individual', had not. 'The rule of
law proved transitory when the imperial policemen were withdrawn,'
Morris wrote, 'and tyrants more fierce than any colonial governor swept
away the baubles of democracy. Nations gently nurtured into statehood
fractured themselves in civil war, or were curdled in corruption.' Had it,
she wondered, 'all been a colossal mistake?'[9]

In some quarters, criticism of Britain's imperial legacy remained
deeply controversial. When the BBC broadcast a thirteen-part series on
the history of the British Empire, developed with the Royal Commonwealth Society, in the spring of 1972, many academic historians praised
its intellectual honesty. But hundreds of ordinary viewers were clearly
horrified by the focus on slavery, repression and imperial self-interest,
by the 'relish' with which the producers supposedly approached 'their
parade of cruelty and aggression', and by the commentary, which one
irate viewer thought 'consistently rich in pejorative tones and twists of
phrase'. *The Times*'s critic Louis Heren was shocked by the show's
unsympathetic tone, remarking that he could 'not recognize the Empire
I knew', which had 'implanted in every continent ... the English language, British attitudes, fair play and prejudices, institutions, the limited
liability company and much else'. The letters pages, meanwhile, smouldered with fury. 'I cannot conceive what the purpose behind this series
can be, unless it is to make us ashamed, and our children, of what is not
an inglorious past,' wrote an outraged Brigadier Sir Bernard Fergusson,
the former Governor General of New Zealand. The episode on India,
agreed Lord Ferrier, was 'a misleading travesty of a great partnership
story'. Even Charles Gibbs-Smith, Keeper of Public Relations at the
Victoria and Albert Museum, wondered why the '*British* Broadcasting
Corporation' had set out to emphasize 'the so-called past wickedness of
British imperialism', and 'why they decided against showing a series of
our achievements. Or is it now held that we have no achievements?'

Since this 'anti-British' series was aimed partly at children, there must be a sinister answer: 'Have certain quarters in the BBC decided the time has come, not only to chip away at the nation's public image, but to erode our patriotism, particularly amongst the young?'[10]

Despite the furore, the intellectual tide was irresistible. By the mid-1970s, fictional visions of Britain's colonial past were a far cry from the uncomplicated patriotism that had infused the works of H. Rider Haggard or G. A. Henty. As the critic D. J. Taylor points out, writers of the decade often looked back to a past that was 'inglorious or violent', evoking 'defeat rather than victory, stupidity and arrogance rather than heroism'. The most popular example was almost certainly Paul Scott, whose *Raj Quartet* (1966–75) became a hugely successful television series a decade later. Set in the 1940s, Scott's books undermine the preening myths of Britain's mission in India, showing colonial officials as weak, flawed, bigoted, even violent. 'At the end,' Scott told an interviewer, 'there was a kind of moral vacuum ... How did we walk out with such a high sense of duty performed?' But he was far from the only writer who wrote with a 'sense of astonishment and even shame', as he put it, at Britain's colonial history. In his masterpiece *The Siege of Krishnapur* (1973), the Anglo-Irish writer J. G. Farrell recreates the Indian Mutiny in blackly comic fashion, mocking the prejudices of the besieged British, their naive faith in Western progress, their self-deluding obsession with their moral mission. By the end, even the scientific idealism of Hopkins, the Collector, has collapsed under the pressure of the siege; a broken man, he is last seen 'pacing the streets of London, very often in the poorer areas, in all weathers, alone, seldom speaking to anyone but staring, staring as if he had never seen a poor person in his life before'.[11]

What was perhaps most telling was that even avowedly right-wing novelists were covering similar territory. In Simon Raven's hilarious *Sound the Retreat* (1971), set in India in the turbulent final months of the Raj, the British occupiers are almost without exception cowards, philanderers, blackmailers and cynics. None of them, though, holds a candle to the most entertaining imperial anti-hero of them all, Sir Harry Paget Flashman, Tom Brown's tormentor at Rugby School and by his own admission 'a scoundrel, a liar, a cheat, a thief, a coward – and oh yes, a toady'. Reviewers often treated George MacDonald Fraser's series as pure entertainment, and during the grim days of the three-day week and the Winter of Discontent thousands of readers must have taken solace in Flashman's adventures in Afghanistan, the Crimea and the Duchy of Strackenz. But, as Taylor points out, these books were more than merely historical pastiches, and it is perfectly possible to read them as 'exposés of the imperialist sham'. In *Flashman at the Charge* (1973), for example, the Crimean War is revealed as 'an ignoble fiasco, characterised by criminal mismanagement and military incompetence'. Flashman's own attitude remains ambiguous: well aware of the hypocrisies of empire, he nevertheless relishes the chance to deflower native women, skewer nationalist insurgents and carry off as much booty as he can carry. But, as the historian John Burrow perceptively remarked in his review of the first instalment, *Flashman* (1969), his 'lying, brutality, lechery and Falstaffian attitude to honour' made him 'as suitable a hero of our time as his old opponent was of the 1850s'.[12]

Although Flashman had met his fair share of African villains, he surely would have raised an eyebrow had he glimpsed *The Times* on 10 April 1975. 'In view of the success of my economic revolution in Uganda,' announced President Idi Amin, 'I offer myself to be appointed head of the Commonwealth.' Of course, Amin's bid to supplant the Queen was entirely typical of his increasingly buffoonish international image, from his offer to mediate in Northern Ireland to his peculiar obsession with liberating Scotland from English oppression. From the British point of view, though, the real embarrassment lay not in his outbursts but in his personal history. There might be plenty of post-colonial dictators, but none was such an indelibly British creation. Once, Amin had been one of only two black Ugandan officers in the British Army: when he first seized power in 1971, Fleet Street hailed him as a loyal friend and ally. But by 1975, when he threatened to execute Denis Hills, a British lecturer who had called him a 'village tyrant', his image had radically changed. The Ugandan President was 'one of the most brutal butchers since Adolf Hitler', said the *Daily Express*. 'He delights in insulting and provoking Britain . . . in seeing Britain squirm, in insulting British diplomats in Kampala and in demonstrating his power to those in Africa who admire him.'

Humiliatingly, Amin turned down an appeal for mercy from the Queen, relenting only when the Foreign Secretary, Jim Callaghan, agreed to visit Kampala to 'solve the misunderstandings' between their countries. By any standards, it was an excruciatingly demeaning moment. Two decades before, Amin had been following orders; now he was effectively giving them. 'On Bended Knee For Mercy' read one shocked headline in June 1975, above the suggestive subheading 'Amin Considers Reprieve – In His Mud Hut'. And although Callaghan carried off his mercy mission with relative dignity, many people were horrified at the reversal of fortunes. In Margaret Drabble's condition-of-England novel *The Ice Age*, one character reflects miserably on 'the way in which other nations had turned against England':

> England was a safe, shabby, mangey old lion now: anyone could tweak her tail. So the Indians imprisoned schoolteachers and writers, the Ugandans threatened to execute British offenders, schoolgirls were tried for currency offences in Kenya, a mere child was jailed for drug smuggling in Turkey. Malice and justice united, to persecute the once so prosperous, once so arrogant, once so powerful of nations, the nation on whose empire the sun had never set. Powerless, teased, angry, impotent, the old country muttered and protested and let itself be mocked.

To those who remembered the Second World War, like the mole in *Tinker Tailor Soldier Spy*, this was a comedown indeed. The mole was 'an ambitious man', le Carré tells us, 'born to the big canvas, brought up to rule, divide and conquer', driven to disillusionment and betrayal by the reality of modern Britain, 'a poor island with scarcely a voice that would carry across the water'.[13]

Millions of ordinary people, too, shook their heads sadly at the humiliating headlines. 'When you were a child, you had it drilled into you that Great Britain was great,' remarked a Black Country shop steward. 'But what are we today? When a tuppenny-ha'penny sergeant like Amin takes the urine out of Britain, it's a pretty mean level we have sunk to.' 'We've gone soft, whatever way you look at it,' agreed a street cleaner from Coventry. 'I reckon this country's finished. We're pushed around by anybody.' And even relative newcomers were struck by the change in Britain's international reputation. Chatting to the journalist Jeremy Seabrook in a Blackburn café, surrounded by formica-topped tables, Subbuteo games and pinball machines, an Indian bus driver waxed lyrical about the decline of the nation's morale. He had fought for Britain during the Second World War, he said, but now he had lost all respect for his new countrymen:

> What is your country now, anyway? Look at its currency, it is worthless. You couldn't keep your empire, you are in debt. You think that a few barrels of oil are your salvation. You are the laughing-stock of the world. English people don't want to work. What a mess you are in. Your whole world has crumbled. You need us, but you hate us because we still have a lot of things we believe in. We have our holy places still. What do yours mean to you?[14]

With Britain so impotent on the world stage, it was no wonder old-fashioned heroes seemed so few and far between in the popular culture of the mid-1970s. In the literary novel, as Taylor notes, '"virtue" found itself fighting a savage rearguard action'; instead, rising stars such as Martin Amis and Ian McEwan tended to write about 'rapists, violent criminals, child-abusers, moral invertebrates'. In the bestseller lists, there seemed no place for uncomplicated heroism: by the early 1970s, the idea of a British hero saving the world from disaster was too outlandish even for Alistair MacLean, who dropped British characters entirely from many of his final books. Of course there was always James Bond; yet Bond in the Wilson and Callaghan years, portrayed by the distinctly unthreatening Roger Moore, was a very different proposition from his earlier incarnations. Ten years earlier, the Bond films had seemed not merely groundbreaking but positively liberated. Now even admirers described them as reassuringly old-fashioned: 'a nostalgic journey down memory lane'. And unlike Sean Connery's square-jawed sex symbol, Moore's Bond was a pastiche, albeit a rather implausible one. 'In scene after scene, as he seduces Egyptian girls or quips with CIA operatives or faces off against remorseless Indian industrialists, the tension is almost intolerable,' writes one aficionado. 'Will they or won't they all just start laughing at him? At his clothes? At his country?' Perhaps it was no wonder that when Michael Palin took his son to see *The Spy Who Loved Me* three days into 1978, he judged it 'the sort of mindless garbage Britain has no reason to be proud of . . . The American-inspired and scripted *Star Wars* was a far, far better adventure.'[15]

Sadly, it would take more than Scaramanga's solex agitator, a device to 'convert solar radiation into electricity', to solve Britain's economic problems. At the time of the first Bond films, wrote the sociologist Krishan Kumar, all the talk had been of Britain's 'youth and vigour'. Now, however, 'the country's problems seem to be the product of illness and senescence', with commentators often diagnosing a 'British disease', its symptoms 'economic inefficiency, antiquated attitudes and institutions, national complacency, a general and deep-seated inability to pull ourselves out of a growing pit of declining standards in all areas of society'. The paradox, of course, was that despite rising prices and steadily mounting unemployment, most ordinary families led more comfortable lives than they had ten or twenty years earlier. And yet, in competitive terms, the facts of Britain's fall from grace made depressing and unambiguous reading. In 1950 it had commanded a share of about 25 per cent of the world trade in manufactures; by 1970 its share was barely

10 per cent, just half that of West Germany. Indeed, almost every measure, from investment and productivity to the rate of GDP growth per head and the growth of average real earnings, showed Britain falling behind its European rivals, let alone the United States and Japan. When Wilson's Cabinet discussed the European question in April 1974, the paper before them predicted that in GNP per head, Britain would be the EEC's second poorest member by the end of the decade, ahead only of Ireland. As Tony Benn remarked, it seemed that Britain was 'heading for development area status in the EEC . . . with Germany more than twice as rich as we are'.[16]

In some ways the pathological fear of decline was nothing new: ever since the late Victorian period, commentators had been obsessed with the idea that Britain was industrially complacent and technologically backward, its politicians short-sighted and venal, its people lazy and materialistic. Eighty years on, their warnings seemed to have been vindicated: among the political classes, as the *Guardian*'s Peter Jenkins wrote in 1978, 'the notion of Britain in decline has become a commonplace'. Since the Second World War, the thinking ran, Britain had been living beyond its means. Now that its wartime adversaries had eroded its historic lead, its chronic weaknesses were clear for all to see. 'For generations,' said Wilson's former Minister of Labour, Ray Gunter, 'this country has not earned an honest living.' And although Peter Jenkins thought that league tables of GDP growth were 'not something people talk about in pubs', declinism was not confined to politicians and intellectuals. Between 1973 and 1977, the proportion of the public who thought their financial position 'very strong' fell from 18 to just 5 per cent, while the proportion feeling 'very weak' doubled from 13 to 26 per cent. Few had great hope for the future; the number expecting their standard of living to 'fall sharply' in the next decade had doubled too. 'They all tended to rate Britain low, and lower than their own position,' wrote *New Society*'s Tom Forrester. 'Respondents in this survey seem to be saying that the country is going to the dogs.'[17]

For all the gaudiness of Rod Stewart and Elton John, for all the flamboyance of Martin Amis's prose and Zandra Rhodes's clothing designs, British culture in the mid-1970s was saturated with dilapidation and decay. From the crumbling terraces of Wembley Stadium, a temple to a national game that itself seemed in deep decline, to the gory visions of James Herbert's pulp bestsellers *The Rats* (1974) and *The Fog* (1975), from the animal savagery of Ted Hughes's poetry to the grotesque short stories in Ian McEwan's collection *First Love, Last Rites* (1975), a deep sense of pessimism had seeped into national cultural life. Even pop music often reflected the prevailing mood. David Bowie's concept album *Diamond Dogs* (1974), for example, was born out of his fascination with George Orwell's book *Nineteen Eighty-four*, which Bowie had hoped to adapt for the stage. For all the glam-rock trimmings, songs like 'Future Perfect', Bowie's vision of 'Hunger City', with 'fleas the size of rats' and starving men and women roaming like 'packs of dogs', or 'Big Brother', a hymn of love to the totalitarian state, hardly made for comfortable listening. Suggestively, though, Bowie was not the only musician of the day to be heavily influenced by Orwell. In January 1977, Pink Floyd released their typically ambitious concept album *Animals*, loosely based on the class system in *Animal Farm*. The *NME* called it 'one of the most extreme, relentless, harrowing and downright iconoclastic hunks of music to have been made available this side of the sun'. Perhaps it was not surprising, then, that although the album sold well, it never toppled Abba's *Arrival*, the Shadows' *Twenty Golden Greats* or Frank Sinatra's *Portrait of Sinatra* from the top of the chart.[18]

In literary fiction, meanwhile, the same themes – death, decline, desolation, disillusionment – recurred in book after book, from Angela Carter's feminist parable *The Passion of New Eve* (1977) to Iris Murdoch's haunting Booker Prize-winner *The Sea, the Sea* (1978). 'Love *can't* mean anything any more,' says one of the characters in Martin Amis's black comedy *Dead Babies* (1975), at once a radical reimagining of the country-house novel and a horrific vision of permissiveness run riot. 'That's hippie talk. Love's through. Love's all fucked up.' Even more conventional novels reflected the same sense of despair at the passing of the optimistic dream. In Drabble's novel *The Ice Age*, Britain is 'sliding, sinking, shabby, dirty, lazy, inefficient, dangerous, in its death throes, worn out, clapped out, occasionally lashing out', while in John Fowles's *Daniel Martin* (1977), it is 'a thing in a museum, a dying animal in a zoo. No pride left (or what pride there is in the wrong things) and so all intent on dying nice and quietly.' Later, Fowles remarked that he had lived all his life 'with the strong supposition that England is in grave decline, and is done for'. 'Distaste, disdain, revulsion – the nouns of withdrawal, of contact rejected, or scorned – these evoke the characteristic behaviour of only one country,' agreed Kenneth Tynan. 'They are the nouns of England.'[19]

On the stage, recalled the critic Michael Billington, the prevailing themes of many new plays were 'disappointment, disillusion and a pervasive sense of despair'. So Howard Brenton's *The Churchill Play* (1974) is set in a government internment camp ten years in the future, while Trevor Griffiths's *Comedians* (1975) opens in a dilapidated secondary school classroom, the maps on the wall fraying and torn, the graffiti on the blackboard reading 'UCKOFFNOBHOLE'. 'We thought, wrongly, as it turned out, that England was in a state of apocalyptic crisis,' David Hare said later. 'We had lost faith in its institutions, we thought that Britain's assumption of a non-existent world role was ludicrous, and we also thought that its economic vitality was so sapped that it wouldn't last long.' Even the Royal Shakespeare Company reflected the wider trend, putting on the first performance of *Destiny*, David Edgar's brilliant theatrical analysis of the rise of the far right, at The Other Place in 1976 and then transferring it to the Aldwych. The following year the RSC opened the Donmar Warehouse, although as Billington noted, many of its productions merely repeated the theme that 'there was something rotten in the state of England'. He jokingly drafted a scenario for an 'archetypal Warehouse play' which he called *Scavengers*, featuring 'a gang of articulate hobos on a savage journey through England in search of the killer of one of their clan'. Their quest, he thought, might involve 'a brief encounter with a black suspendered Cabinet minister's wife (the minister would be the one in suspenders) outside a motorway café', as well as a charity ball in Market Harborough and a showdown with 'a homosexual policeman' in the forecourt of New Scotland Yard. 'I exaggerated,' he wrote later, 'but only just.'[20]

Not everybody yielded to the temptations of negativity. After a while, as Dennis Potter pointed out in 1977, all of this 'wilful pessimism' could become wearyingly predictable. 'Violence and corruption take the centre of the stage,' he complained, 'and there is nothing else in the wings.' Perhaps that was why so many people preferred more escapist fare: only a year later, Andrew Lloyd Webber and Tim Rice's *Evita* opened at the Prince Edward Theatre in the West End. In the *Sunday Times*, Bernard Levin called it 'one of the most disagreeable evenings I have ever spent in my life', while the National Theatre supremo Peter Hall returned home depressed at the 'cult of kitsch ... inert, calculating, camp, and morally questionable'. But even he admitted that he was 'out of step with popular taste': that very month, *Jesus Christ Superstar* became the longest-running musical in theatrical history, having been seen by almost 2 million people – a sign of the craving for old-fashioned escapism in an age of austerity.[21]

In the long run, the staggering box-office success of *Star Wars* and the invention of the video game *Space Invaders*, which made its Japanese debut in the summer of 1978, were to transform everyday escapism far more than anything Lloyd Webber ever wrote. For the time being, though, many people sought refuge from the gloomy headlines in looking backwards. Museums were one of the great success stories of the age, numbers of visitors doubling between 1971 and 1987, while membership of the National Trust swelled from 158,000 people in 1965 to 539,000 in 1975 and more than a million in 1981. 'Heritage', much mocked by intellectuals, was big business: thanks to the public appetite for Victorian romanticism, Laura Ashley's turnover increased from less than £500,000 in 1970 to some £25 million a decade later, while enthusiasm for Portmeirion's 'Botanic Garden' ceramics range was such that the firm could not produce enough to meet the demand. In fashion, the ultra-modern look of the mid-1960s was long dead, replaced by retro pastiches from Pre-Raphaelite romanticism and art deco elegance to the swirling plums, browns and purples of Biba in its final days. In bookshops, the demand for nostalgic reassurance made unexpected successes out of Edith Holden's rediscovered *The Country Diary of an Edwardian Lady* (1977) and Mark Girouard's *Life in the English Country House* (1978), as well as the Yorkshire vet James Herriot, eight of whose gentle rural titles appeared on the bestseller lists in 1976. On television, the public thirst for a quieter, gentler world of hierarchy and consensus meant that the past was never far away, from *Upstairs, Downstairs* and *The Onedin Line* to *Colditz* and *I, Claudius*, from *Pennies from Heaven* and *The Duchess of Duke Street* to *Dad's Army* and *Last of the Summer Wine*. And at the cinema, only feeble sex comedies and backward-looking adventure stories were left in the debris of the British film industry. As the EMI studio boss admitted, Agatha Christie adaptations such as *Murder on the Orient Express* (1974) and *Death on the Nile* (1978) had been conceived as a deliberate antidote to 'all the gloom and doom in the country'.[22]

To many intellectuals, especially on the left, the popular fascination with the past was a sign that 'something in British culture had gone wrong'. National cultural life, wrote Robert Hewison, 'has been crippled by nostalgia: for the innocence of childhood, for pastoral life, for the world of the country house, for some moment in the not-too-distant past when the community seemed whole'. Of course there was a heavy dose of cultural snobbery in all this: the intellectuals who derided National Trust members for trudging round country houses were not so different from the left-wing barrister in Piers Paul Read's novel *A Married Man* (1979), who is embarrassed by his mother's cherished china statuettes because her 'bad taste betrayed not only her origins but also her pretensions, for she believed that her collection, although not quite equal to the treasures of Castle Howard, was a step in that direction'. In any case, there was more to the vogue for looking backwards than naive nostalgia, as one of 1975's most successful programmes proved very well. This was Peter Hall's *Akenfield*, adapted from Ronald Blythe's bestselling oral history of a Suffolk village. Unlike many re-creations of recent history, Hall's film switched effortlessly between past and present. Made with only a skeleton script and a cast of 150 amateurs, it was an astonishingly austere and evocative depiction of rural life from courtship and marriage to education and work, based around a young man's dilemma about whether to leave behind the familiar rhythms of the countryside for a new life elsewhere. Although it premiered at the London Film Festival in November 1974, it reached its widest audience in January 1975 when almost 15 million people tuned in to watch it on ITV. The next day, even Hall's taxi driver told him how much he had enjoyed it.[23]

By and large, though, most excursions into the past appealed because of their sheer escapism. When researchers asked viewers of *The Onedin Line*, an enormously popular BBC drama based around a Victorian shipping company, if they thought James Onedin's 'commercial struggles' had 'any relevance to the industrial problems of today', most saw no link at all. 'I enjoy the drama and don't look for hidden meanings' was a typical response. For most people, wrote Roy Strong, director of the Victoria and Albert Museum, the national heritage represented 'a happier world which we have lost':

> We are all aware of problems and troubles, of changes within the structure of society, of the dissolution of old values and standards. For the lucky few this may be exhilarating, even exciting, but for the majority it is confusing, threatening and dispiriting. The heritage represents some form of security, a point of reference, a refuge perhaps, something visible and tangible which, within a topsy and turvy world, seems stable and unchanged. Our environmental heritage is therefore a deeply stabilising and unifying element within our society.

Yet, as Strong knew only too well, the environmental heritage was a lot less stable than it seemed. Industrialized agriculture had transformed the rural landscape, tearing out hedgerows, woodlands, meadows and wetlands, as birds, butterflies, animals and flowers were sacrificed to the insatiable demands for cheap food and instant profit. City centres, meanwhile, had been remade in glass and concrete by developers and planners, historic skylines bulldozed over in the name of progress. And even the country houses to which so many families flocked on weekend afternoons, looking forward to a tour of the drawing room and a nice cup of tea, were not impervious to the winds of change.[24]

In October 1974, the V&A mounted one of the most celebrated exhibitions of the decade, 'The Destruction of the Country House', a lament for the damage wreaked on so many magnificent houses by inheritance tax, changing family patterns and the decline of the aristocracy. At its centre, Strong recalled, was a gigantic mock-up of a country house façade, 'but it was tumbling down, falling on to the visitor. Each block of masonry was a photograph of one of the thousand homes which had been demolished in this century. In the background a tape conveyed the sound of burning timbers and crashing masonry, while a voice read the names of those houses like a litany.' The figures were indeed horrifying: in 100 years, some 1,364 country houses had been pulled down, and although much of the destruction had come during the inter-war years, 250 or so had disappeared since 1945, with the remaining 1,000 still under serious threat. 'Who would have thought that death duties and the demolition contractor had undone so many?' asked Philip Howard in *The Times*. Here, he thought, was a 'catastrophic catalogue of sad stories', of some houses burned down, some converted into schools, 'some buried beneath housing estates, some fallen into decay and demolished piecemeal, one turned into a prison and burnt by the inmates, all murdered'. Quoting the famous lines 'The stately homes of England / How beautiful they stand', he remarked mordantly: 'Not any more, they don't.'[25]

For some houses, of course, the heritage industry meant salvation. Although Howard mocked the 'relays of trippers peering warily at the furniture in the Adam suite, a postcard kiosk in the gun room and cream teas in the servants' parlour', Disneyfication nevertheless saved many country houses from the wrecking ball. But there was another route to survival, as the seventh Lord Rosebery discovered in the late 1970s. Facing an eye-watering £5 million estate-duty bill after his father's death, Rosebery decided he had no option but to sell his magnificent Buckinghamshire mansion, Mentmore. Built in fairy-tale neo-Renaissance style by Baron Mayer de Rothschild during the 1850s, Mentmore had passed by marriage to the fifth Earl of Rosebery, who served as Prime Minister in the 1890s, and was a sumptuous museum of eighteenth- and nineteenth-century art and furniture. At first the seventh Earl offered the contents to the government in lieu of inheritance tax, but they turned him down. Next, Rosebery offered to sell them the house as a museum, but they could only find £1 million towards his £3 million asking price. Reluctantly, therefore, he threw open the doors and sold the entire contents for almost £6.5 million, more than enough to cover his tax debts. Much of the press saw the sale as a tragedy, but then the story got worse. In November 1978, the house and gardens were bought for £240,000 by the Maharishi International College, part of the gigantic business empire run by the self-styled Maharishi Mahesh Yogi. Already a household name because of his association with the Beatles, the Maharishi made a very unlikely country landowner indeed. By the early 1980s he was using the house as a fudge factory.[26]

For the *Daily Express*'s William Hickey gossip column, the only surprise about Mentmore's fate was that 'the buyer wasn't an Arab'. Until the mid-1970s, the idea that Arab money might become an important element in British life would have seemed ludicrous. Thanks to the oil shock, however, the balance of power had irrevocably shifted. 'You can hardly open your newspaper these days without reading of some new Arab "takeover",' wrote the *Guardian*'s David Hirst in September 1976. 'Hotels, hospitals, and historic mansions all seem to be falling like ninepins into the hands of the new-rich potentates from the fabulous shores of the Persian Gulf.' Their coffers swollen with oil revenues, the Arab emirates poured much of it back into the City of London, depositing an estimated $2.5 billion in London's banks by the autumn of 1974 and inadvertently helping to transform the City into the crucible of a new, aggressive globalized capitalism. But not everyone was delighted by the transformation in fortunes, and when Arab investors visited London to spend their winnings in the boutiques of Bond Street, they often met with a cool reception. One broker remembered some of his colleagues being 'rude and flippant' when a group of Arabs visited the Stock Exchange. 'I don't think I should do that if I were you,' he said, conscious not only of the demands of hospitality, but of the importance of the visitors' money.[27]

Strolling through west London in the hot summer of 1976, contemplating the 'flowing robes and headgear' on the streets, the copies of 'al-Ahram, al-Anwar, al-Ray, al-Amm' on the news-stands, the fast-food joints selling 'shawarma, hommos and other Arab foods', David Hirst thought he 'might almost be [in] Kasr al-Nil Street in Cairo, or Phoenicia Street in Beirut'. The capital's major hotels each catered to a different group: 'Saudis in the Grosvenor, Kuwaitis at the Churchill and the Portman, Lebanese at the Hilton and Londonderry, Gulf Arabs at the

Gloucester, and Iraqis at the Penta'. From there they descended on Oxford Street, Bond Street and Knightsbridge, sometimes buying a hundred suits at once or carrying off 'armfuls of gorgeous evening dresses' without a thought for the cost. In the evenings, they headed for exclusive Mayfair clubs and casinos such as Crockford's, which advertised in Arabic magazines and boasted an 'Arab room' with Egyptian hostesses, or the Omar Khayyam, with 'an ambience, décor, floorshow, staff and clientele so completely Oriental' that it was a shock to emerge and find oneself in Regent Street. Yet even as Mayfair, Marylebone and Bayswater ('Beirut-on-Thames') were being transformed by Arab money, some residents found it hard to conceal their distaste. 'I think some of them are a little unfamiliar with the Western lavatory,' an almost implausibly upper-class Mayfair man told the BBC in 1974. 'Quite obviously, rather than use it, an awful lot of them would prefer to use the floor, and unfortunately without clearing up some of the mess over a long period.' The 'main unpleasantness', he complained, was the smell, especially on hot summer days. 'I must say that the aroma of Levantine remains will be with me until the day I drop.'[28]

There was more to this, surely, than Middle Eastern unfamiliarity with British plumbing. As David Hirst noted, the newcomers were not merely 'super-rich tourists'; they were 'humiliating reminders of Britain's fallen place in the world ... coming here as the conquerors, with money as their weapon'. To novelists of the late 1970s, they were an irresistible symbol of Britain's international eclipse, their white robes standing out against the shabby streets like 'the white gowns of a new and suddenly universal priesthood of pure money', as V. S. Naipaul put it. In Anthony Burgess's dystopian novella *1985* (1978), for example, we are plunged into a capital transformed by Middle Eastern immigration, where the London skies resonate with the call to prayer, half-moon banners flutter from street corners, and Arab sheikhs own the 'Al-Dorchester, Al-Klaridges, Al-Browns, various Al-Hiltons and Al-Idayinns', with no alcohol in the bars and no bacon at breakfast. And in 'Mrs Wilson's Diary', *Private Eye* imagined a group of Arab investors, led by 'Sheikh Yamani Oryalife', visiting Harold Wilson with 'a reasonable cash offer for the British Isles, to be obtained by a compulsory purchase order'. But Wilson turns them down. 'You are spending too much time with these camel-dung wallahs,' he tells Denis Healey. 'When [North Sea] oil is flowing the market will soon look up. We will sell, but when the time is right.'[29]

*

To thousands of ordinary readers, the picture of the dilapidated Circus headquarters in *Tinker Tailor Soldier Spy*, with its grubby telephones and creaking lifts, must have seemed immediately familiar. 'It sits there for months, and when you actually have a fire, when you actually *need* the bloody thing, it blows your head of!' explodes the proprietor of *Fawlty Towers* after a fire extinguisher goes off in his face in 'The Germans' (1975). 'I mean, what is happening to this country? It's *bloody Wilson*!' Yet Basil's tribulations were as nothing compared with those by Edward Heath's aide Douglas Hurd in August 1971, a long list of frustrations that spoke volumes about the shoddiness of British service:

> All the mechanics of life crumbling around us – heating, cars, telephones, etc . . . Telephone mended, light fuses blow. No progress on cars or heating . . . Demented by no progress at all on selling car or repairing heating . . . The bloody paper fails to insert my ad . . . Still getting nowhere on central heating . . . Finally we have two cars which work, and boilers, taps and radiators ditto. This has taken three months.

The telephone service, then managed by the General Post Office, was a common source of aggravation. As the writer Francis Wheen recalled, even the most mundane call might involve 'a mechanical chorus of clicks, wheezes and crossed lines, as of a thousand boiled sweets being unwrapped simultaneously during a tuberculosis epidemic'. When the diarist James Lees-Milne tried to ring a Bath number in June 1974, it took him three-quarters of an hour. 'Three times I rang the exchange, three times the supervisor,' he recorded. 'Finally, I was driven so mad with rage that I shouted abuse down the mouthpiece and smashed the telephone to smithereens on the hearthstone.' It cost him £50 to replace it, he admitted, but 'it was worth it'. Even the great and the good had to put up with abysmal treatment. In September 1978, Jim Callaghan complained to his Cabinet colleagues that 'he had recently telephoned the Post Office accounts department about his telephone bill' – a strange way, it has to be said, for the Prime Minister to spend his free time. 'I didn't say who I was, didn't give my name, and I was treated disgracefully,' Callaghan said. 'I was told they couldn't answer over the phone, I had better write in, and finally they just rang off.'[30]

Callaghan's experience was entirely typical of British service culture in the 1970s. Sitcoms like *Fawlty Towers*, which revelled in Basil's refusal to serve dinner after nine, his reluctance to book taxis for his guests and his failure to honour even the most basic precepts of hospitality, would never have struck such a chord had they not been rooted in reality. In June 1975, Michael Palin was filming *Three Men in a Boat* on the Thames when he had the misfortune to spend a night at the Swan Hotel, Streatley, where he and his friends arrived 'tired and hungry after a long day'. When he asked if they could have something to eat, the receptionist said curtly: 'It's after quarter to nine.' 'A sandwich . . . or just a piece of cheese?' Palin asked optimistically. 'No,' she said shortly, finally recommending 'a Chinese in Pangbourne', but then adding: 'We close the hotel at 11.30 and there are only two keys.' Deflated, Palin and co. decamped to a pub up the road, where their entreaties again fell on stony ground. 'Oh no,' the barwoman said when they asked if there was anything to eat. 'There's nothing left now.' Eventually, albeit with 'heavy reluctance and much raising of eyes to heaven', she agreed to let them have some nuts and crisps. Palin asked for some pickled onions, but they never came. When he asked again, she said: 'No, I can't give you any.' 'What?' he said, more in disbelief than anger. 'I'm not allowed to,' she said simply. In his diary, Palin could not contain his fury. 'This is Southern England with a vengeance,' he wrote. 'We feel like lepers as we walk down the pretty, the fucking pretty little main street, clutching some of the crisps she was good enough to let us have.'

Of course Palin should have known what to expect. After all, his friend John Cleese had got the idea for *Fawlty Towers* from a real-life establishment, the Gleneagles Hotel in Torquay, where the *Monty Python* team had stayed in 1970. Of course not all hoteliers were quite like the Gleneagles' owner Donald Sinclair, who harangued Terry Gilliam for his American table manners, tossed a timetable in the face of a guest who asked about the next bus to town, and had Eric Idle's bag thrown out of the hotel in case it was a bomb. 'We've had a lot of staff problems lately,' he explained when they asked why anybody would want to blow up the Gleneagles. But in Harold Wilson's Britain, almost anybody who had ever stayed in a hotel, eaten in a restaurant or tried to get a telephone installed had become depressingly familiar with sullen and surly service. Perhaps this explains why *Monty Python*'s 'Dead Parrot' sketch, first broadcast in December 1969, became so popular. Millions of people had met somebody like Palin's stubborn shopkeeper, who insists that the dead Norwegian Blue is merely 'pining for the fjords'. Indirectly, this too was based on a real incident, having been inspired by Palin's frustration when a garage mechanic, despite all the evidence to the contrary, claimed there was nothing wrong with his car.[31]

Whether the fault lay with the trade unions, instinctively hostile to reforms that might involve job losses, or with nationalized industries, too often reluctant to embrace change and competition, or with the sheer complacency, amateurishness and indifference of bosses and managers – or, more plausibly, with all of them – Britain in the mid-1970s often resembled what one of Kingsley Amis's protagonists called 'the land of sorry-sir (sorry sir bar's closed, sorry sir no change, sorry sir too late for lunch, sorry sir residents only sir)'. Amis himself thought that 'Sod the public' was the 'working slogan not only of government, the service industry and the retail trade, but as also, as "sod the customer", "sod the audience" and other variants, that of interior designers, providers of culture, playwrights, composers and many more'. Chief among his targets, not surprisingly, were British hotels. 'No other institutions quite touch these,' he wrote, 'in their single-minded devotion to the interests of those who work in them and indifference to those who use them.' But if the experience of Wilson's Defence Secretary, Roy Mason, was any guide, then Whitehall ran them close. Towards the end of July 1974, Turkey invaded Cyprus, where two key British military bases were located. Yet despite the urgency of the crisis, Mason was astonished to find that '*neither* the permanent secretary nor the relevant private secretary [could be] bothered to come in to the office', since the Turks had been inconsiderate enough to invade at a weekend. On Saturday morning, Mason insisted on going in anyway. But as Bernard Donoughue recorded with amused horror, Mason 'couldn't get into his office, then couldn't work his intelligence telephone because his civil servants were not there. A private secretary had the master key – and apparently "does not like coming to work on Saturdays".'[32]

Given the pervasive impression of apathy and neglect, the state of Britain's cities and the atrocious performance of its heavy industries, perhaps it was little wonder that when commentators looked for parallels, they often looked to the grim societies behind the Iron Curtain. In Paul Bryers's pulp thriller *Hollow Target* (1976), one character remarks that London reminds him of 'Eastern Europe', with 'creeping socialism, high taxes, austerity, cold porridge and power cuts'. Parts of Britain, agreed the political scientist Stephen Haseler in his tract *The Death of British Democracy*, published the same year, 'possess some of the atmosphere of the debilitated physical environment of Eastern Europe of the forties'. Behind this, of course, was an obvious ideological subtext. More than 'any other advanced nation', Haseler thought, Britain was close 'to a sea-change', having been pushed towards fully fledged state socialism by 'unparalleled' borrowing, 'out of control' public spending and 'untrammelled trade union power'. This line naturally appealed to the right, for whom even Denis Healey's social democracy seemed dangerously close to Eastern European socialism. Thanks to 'increasing nationalisation', 'inexorably growing central government expenditure' and 'an obsession with equality', claimed Sir Keith Joseph, Britain was charting a 'unique course, as it slides from the affluent Western world towards the threadbare economies of the Communist bloc'. His closest ally agreed: in 1975, Mrs Thatcher told an audience that 'the distribution of incomes in Britain is surprisingly similar to that in Poland – which is a rather shattering conclusion to reach'. Two years later, she asked her party conference to imagine Labour winning the next election: 'What then? The trap is sprung. And Labour's extremists resume the drive towards a Britain modelled on Eastern Europe . . . the total Socialist state.'[33]

It was at the very top of society – among those people who suffered most from the collapse of the stock market, the fall of property prices and the rising tax burden, who were also those most likely to travel abroad and draw unflattering comparisons with other European countries – that pessimism ran strongest. The country was 'heading for disaster', Roy Jenkins burst out to his old sparring partner Barbara Castle one day in the summer of 1974. 'I can't stand by and see us pretend everything is all right when I know we are heading for catastrophe.' 'Are you suggesting we are going Communist?' she asked. 'No,' he said, 'it wasn't as crude as that.' Of course Jenkins was no more than a semi-detached member of the Labour Party, sidling towards the exit. But even Wilson's policy chief thought that Britain was in deep decline. After a month's holiday in France that summer, Bernard Donoughue wrote that he could now 'see England a little clearer. It looked in a terrible mess. Falling apart socially as well as economically. Seems very frail compared with France, which is becoming a giant again.' And despite his reputation for blind optimism, the Prime Minister himself had to admit that Britain in the mid-1970s cut a sadly reduced figure from the great international empire of his youth. The nation's economic problems, he conceded in the Commons, were partly caused 'by our own failure . . . over a quarter of a century under successive Governments'. Characteristically, Wilson insisted that Britain would soon recapture its former glories, but not all his colleagues agreed with him. 'Our place in the world is shrinking: our economic comparisons grow worse, long-term political influence depends on economic strength – and that is running out,' Jim Callaghan told the Cabinet in November 1974.[34]

For some people, especially the young, the only solution was to get out. Thanks to the death agonies of the Heath government, interest in building a new life overseas had reached a post-war peak in the spring of 1974, with long queues outside the various Commonwealth High Commissions, applications for Canada up by 65 per cent in a year and applications for Australia up by half. Demand to move to New Zealand, meanwhile, was so great that in April the Wellington government announced unprecedented controls on British entrants. New Zealand had no choice, explained its Prime Minister, Norman Kirk: for a country of only 3 million people, an annual inflow of more than 25,000 Britons meant intolerable pressure on housing, jobs and public services. With Australia imposing similar controls a year later, people desperate to escape strikes, power cuts and rising prices turned instead to South Africa, overlooking its wretched international image and the growing tension in the black townships. In 1975 alone, some 29,000 people from the managerial classes moved to South Africa, much to the consternation of the *Daily Express*. Indeed, with a total of 269,000 people packing their bags to leave and just 184,000 coming the other way, Britain's population in 1975 fell for the first time since records began. It fell in 1976, too, and again a year later. By February 1977, one in three people said they would like to move abroad, including half of all under-25-year-olds. In Lancashire, Jeremy Seabrook found that 'nearly all the young people' talked as though Britain was becoming 'uninhabitable'. 'I could go anywhere, be anybody,' said an unemployed young man from Bradford. 'I might go on an oil-rig. This country's finished. Nobody's got any ambition. My mother and sisters, what have they got, what have they done? Nothing.'[35]

'We must stop taking so much in tax from those who create the wealth that the effort is no longer worth while,' insisted Margaret Thatcher in July 1975, at the peak of the emigration panic. 'If we do not, we are in danger of a brain drain such as we have never seen before. Our best and most creative people, whether carpenters or plumbers, craftsmen or scientists, doctors or engineers will not stay here to be harried and abused.' Perhaps she was thinking of Roger Moore, for this ornament of the acting profession was among many who fled Britain to avoid falling into Denis Healey's higher tax brackets. Meanwhile, since changes to the tax system meant that resident Americans were liable for tax on their worldwide earnings, many Hollywood stars now refused to film in Britain. So many stars were fleeing abroad, wrote the critic Alexander Walker, that there was barely room in the papers' classified sections for all the abandoned 'homes in Belgravia, Hampstead or the more secluded stretches of the Home Counties'. The directors John Schlesinger and Karel Reisz both left for Hollywood, while Richard Lester shot *Robin and Marian* (1976) in Spain, where Sean Connery had moved because, he said, he refused 'to pay a fortune to a Labour Government for the "privilege"' of working in his home country. Michael Caine crammed his British commitments into three months a year to escape paying taxes, while Pinewood Studios lost an estimated £120,000 when the producers of *Gold* (1974) moved shooting to Malta so that they could still use Roger Moore's eyebrows. Even James Bond became a tax exile: not only did the franchise's legendary producer Albert R. Broccoli move back to California after a quarter of a century in Britain, but in 1978 he shifted *Moonraker* from Pinewood to France, insisting that 'they' – meaning the government – were 'turning people out'.[36]

'Where have all the rock kings gone?' asked the *Daily Express* in August 1976. 'Into exile every one.' The trend had started with the Rolling Stones, who had fled to the south of France so that they could avoid paying tax on their earnings for 1969–70. Since the Stones, despite their image, were intensely patriotic, the decision came as a wrench. 'I love my roots, and swapping my beautiful country home, Gedding Hall in Suffolk, for an alien territory and culture didn't promise much,' Bill Wyman wrote later. But he had no choice: 'if we stayed in England, we stood no chance of paying off our outstanding tax bills of over £100,000 each.' Other artists found themselves in a similar position. Thin Lizzy, whose single 'The Boys are Back in Town' and album *Jailbreak* had earned an estimated £200,000 between them, were left to share just £34,000 after the taxman had taken his slice. For their next album they went to West Germany, where the top tax band was only 56 per cent. In 1974 David Bowie moved to New York, while Rod Stewart left for California a year later, applying for American citizenship in his bid to escape the tax authorities. And even though the world's most successful recording artist remained in Britain, he did so at enormous financial cost. One in every hundred records bought in the mid-1970s had been made by Elton John; in 1975 alone he sold 28 million albums, and his record company was estimated to be making £90,000 a week. But since he was taxed at 98 per cent on his investments as well as 83 per cent on much of his income, he was not quite as rich as many people thought. 'His own reward', claimed the *Express*, 'is just 2p in every pound.'[37]

For the mouthpiece of Middle England, the flight of Britain's rock stars was merely one symptom of a wider malaise. 'British managers, doctors, engineers – not to mention dockers – are finding that all over the world there are opportunities for them which will net them a great deal more take-home pay than in Britain,' said a sombre *Express* editorial. 'Are we content with a situation in which foreign companies and Governments go searching around Britain for the best talent, rather like vultures looking for choice pieces on a rotting carcass?' Of course this was easily overstated: for a hundred years, Britain had generally been a country of emigrants. But what alarmed even sober observers was the surge in emigration among doctors, who were horrified by Barbara Castle's proposals to renegotiate consultants' contracts and scrap the lucrative pay beds. As early as July 1974, the journal *General Practitioner* was reporting 'an unusually high interest in emigration', and by May 1975 some 284 consultants and 40 senior registrars had moved overseas in just twelve months. Where the doctors led, others followed: according to the manpower consultants Robert Lee International, the number of professional people wanting to move abroad rose by 35 per cent between January and July 1975, almost certainly as a reaction to Wilson's re-election, the increase in the tax burden and the surge of inflation. Interest was keenest, said the firm's chairman, among engineers, accountants, scientists and teachers. 'The quality of these people is disturbingly high,' he added, 'and the country is losing too many of its brains.'[38]

What most alarmed many columnists, though, was the transformation of Britain's image. During the Victorian era, the Ottoman Empire had earned the nickname 'the sick man of Europe'. By the mid-1970s, however, the label belonged to Britain. 'The game is coming to its end; the pageant is crumbling,' wrote the journalist Clive Irving in *Pox Britannica* (1974), a lament for vanished greatness. The British had woken up one morning and 'found themselves the paupers of Europe'; in ten years' time they would be 'lagging behind Spain, Austria and Greece'. What pathetic figures, Irving thought, they must cut in the eyes of their EEC partners:

To the rest of Europe, the British look like somebody staggering home, slightly tipsy, from a fancy-dress ball, still absurdly costumed and in the mind still living the part. As this bizarre figure knocked on the door to beg admittance, it blinked in the unwelcome light of reality and turned surly and regretful that the dream was ended. Strutting, posing and posturing, vain and patronizing, the apparition has the brittle charm of a Shakespearian fool – sometimes to be pitied, sometimes exasperating, occasionally droll. Britain is a victim of the timewarp, promising to reform but really not grasping either the extent of its waywardness or the means of curing it.

The Economist's Robert Moss, meanwhile, thought that Britain had become a laughing stock. 'I am sad to confess that every time I fly back to London from any other major Western capital, my heart sinks,' he told readers of the American journal *Commentary* in February 1977. The United Kingdom was 'fast becoming an offshore industrial slum, where most executives earn less than a good secretary in Washington, D.C.' Even a 'gringo complex' might be on its way: 'the Arabs, who look different, talk different, and spend sterling as if it were confetti, may turn out to be Britain's gringos.' And his conclusion was memorably bleak. 'The more I compare Britain with the countries that it still regards as its peers,' he wrote, 'the more I succumb to the uneasy feeling that [it] is becoming a Third World country.'[39]

For many American observers, Britain's fate was an object lesson in the folly of social democracy and the dangers of unchecked trade union-ism. 'Hardly anybody needs to be told now that Great Britain is the sick man of Europe,' wrote the managing editor of the *Wall Street Journal*, the excellently named Vermont Royster. 'Everywhere you look the evidence abounds.' Other American commentators drew similar conclu-sions: for the Harvard political scientist James Q. Wilson, Britain was in deep 'political and economic decay' and 'very near to collapse', while a long essay in the *New York Times* worried that 'the fabric of British society is about to be ripped up'. Under the title *The Future that Doesn't Work*, one highly conservative commentator, R. Emmett Tyrell, com-piled a collection of essays on such horrors as 'nationalized health care' to dissuade Americans from heading down the British road. And *Time* magazine was positively obsessed with the plight of the British econ-omy, 'the product of a vicious circle of industrial inefficiency, labor indiscipline and overly ambitious welfare-statism'. Labour's 'lofty pol-icy of equality', *Time* claimed in 1975, had 'degenerated into the petty politics of envy'. As proof, the magazine produced its expert witness, the actor Douglas Fairbanks Jr., 'a lifelong Anglophile'. 'In America,' Fairbanks explained, 'the workingman will see someone drive by in his Cadillac and he'll say, "That guy has a Cadillac and I don't. Some day I am going to have two Cadillacs." In Britain, the instant reaction is: "That man has a Rolls-Royce and I don't. He is going to come down to my level."'[40]

Shock and contempt at Britain's condition were not confined to the

American press. On the first page of his book *Britain Against Itself* (1982), the Harvard political scientist Samuel Beer recalled asking one of his students a few years earlier why she had chosen his class. 'It was my father's advice,' she replied. 'He said, "Study England, a country on its knees. That is where America is going."' For the New York-based Hudson Institute, meanwhile, the future for Britain, 'unstable', 'socially divided' and 'economically depressed', seemed bleak indeed. 'The nation is failing,' concluded a report published in September 1974, adding that 'even Italy, supposedly the other sick man of Europe', had 'better reason for optimism'. 'If the economic problems are not solved,' the report ended, 'there is serious reason to fear an eventual social and political upheaval.'[41]

In fairness, the Hudson Institute's report was not entirely convincing, not least because it mentioned neither inflation nor, bizarrely, the trade unions, and thought that the Labour left were 'Selsdon Men', a strange interpretation of recent history. But its conclusions were widely shared. 'One of the principal preoccupations of reasonable men and women across the world – in Washington, in the Commonwealth countries, in the European capitals – is the question "Will Britain founder?"' wrote Alastair Buchan, professor of international relations at Oxford. And in Washington's corridors of power, officials shook their heads in horror at Wilson's attempt to beat stagflation by borrowing and spending. In a note for President Ford in April 1975, his chief economic adviser Alan Greenspan wrote that Britain faced 'a dangerous situation' and that 'the frightening parallels ... should give us considerable pause'. And in his farewell remarks after losing the presidential election a year later, Ford had a warning for his listeners. 'It would be tragic for this country,' he said, 'if we went down the same path and ended up with the same problems Great Britain has.'[42]

The moment that best captured American horror at the condition of Britain, though, came in March 1979, when the most famous hotel in television history had the pleasure of a guest from across the Atlantic. Everything about Fawlty Towers might have been calculated to infuriate Mr Hamilton, the square-jawed, tough-talking American who has never met anybody with Basil's sense of customer service. Mr Hamilton's very first words capture the tone: 'What a drive, eh? Everything on the wrong side of the road – and the weather, what do you get for living in a climate like this, green stamps? It's terrible ... Took five hours from London. Couldn't find the freeway. Had to take a little back street called the M5.'

'Well, I'm sorry it wasn't wide enough for you,' Basil says sarcastically. 'A lot of the English cars have steering wheels.' 'They do, do they?' Mr Hamilton snaps back. 'You wouldn't think there was room for them inside.' And so it goes on. Mr Hamilton wants to book a table for dinner; Basil is horrified by the very notion of eating after nine. Mr Hamilton wants a drink before settling down at his table; Basil suggests a drink after dinner instead. When Mr Hamilton asks for something hot, Basil suggests a toasted sandwich; when he asks for freshly squeezed orange juice, Basil produces 'freshly unscrewed'. 'Can you believe this?' the American says in disbelief. 'What the hell's wrong with this country? You can't get a drink after three, you can't eat after nine, is the war still on?' And when he discovers that Basil has been lying to him, pocketing £20, pretending to keep the chef on and trying to cook the dinner himself, he explodes with rage. 'What I'm suggesting', he yells, 'is that this is the crummiest, shoddiest, worst-run hotel in the whole of Western Europe!'

Of course Fawlty's regulars take a different view. 'No! No! I won't have that!' says the Major. 'There's that place in Eastbourne!' 'Ladies, are you satisfied?' Basil asks Miss Tibbs and Miss Gatsby. 'Oh yes, thank you, Mr Fawlty,' they chorus, 'and thank you for asking.' At that, Basil draws himself up and launches into his finest Churchillian rhetoric:

> You see – satisfied customers! Of course, if this little hotel is not to your taste, then you are free to say so. That is your privilege. And I shall of course refund your money. I know how important it is to you Americans.
>
> But you must remember that here in Britain there are things that we value more, things that perhaps in America you've rather forgotten, but which here in Britain are far, far more important . . .

So carried away is Basil, in fact, that he barely notices the guest standing behind him, or hears the voice saying quietly: 'I'm not satisfied.' It belongs to Mr Johnson, and it is his view that prevails. In Harold Wilson's Britain, there were plenty of Majors, and plenty of Misses Tibbs and Gatsby, too. But there were more than a few Mr Johnsons, their numbers growing by the day.[43]

5

Anarchy in the UK

I suggest that representatives of the Catholic and Protestant communities in Northern Ireland as well as representatives of your government come to Uganda, far away from the site of the battle and antagonism, for a conference on how to bring peace to their province.

Telegram from Idi Amin to Harold Wilson, 30 May 1974

On Sunday, 10 March 1974, six days after Harold Wilson's return to office, two teenagers were killed in South Armagh. Like so many victims of the conflict in Northern Ireland, Michael McCreesh and Michael Gallagher had been tragically unlucky, caught by an IRA bomb left in a parked van and intended for a British Army patrol. McCreesh was just 15, Gallagher 18; both were Catholics. On Monday, another Catholic civilian, George Keating, was killed in Belfast when a gunman opened fire on the Bunch of Grapes pub on Garmoyle Street. The next day, just across the border in Monaghan, the Fine Gael senator Billy Fox was murdered by the IRA: punishment, it was thought, for being one of the only Protestant politicians in the Irish Parliament. On Wednesday, a young British gunner, David Farrington, who had been in the army for only nine months, was shot and killed in Belfast from the steps of a Catholic church. On Thursday, George Robinson, a middle-aged Protestant civilian asleep in bed above his mother's confectionery shop, was shot dead at point-blank range by two Catholic youths who had broken into the shop in the small hours of the morning. And on Friday, a Protestant civilian, Adam Johnston, was killed when a lorry bomb went off in County Derry; a young Catholic man, Noel McCartan, was shot dead by the Ulster Volunteer Force while he was walking along the road in

Belfast; and two IRA volunteers accidentally blew themselves up in a timber yard in County Tyrone. With four more soldiers and Royal Ulster Constabulary men killed over the weekend, it had been Northern Ireland's bloodiest week of the year.[1]

The slaughter in Northern Ireland cast a dark shadow over life in Britain in the mid-1970s. Since the resurgence of the Troubles during Wilson's first premiership, the death toll in the province had reached horrific proportions, with 171 people killed in 1971, 479 the following year and 253 the year after that. And although Wilson had originally sent in the British Army to protect Catholic areas from Protestant rioters, trust between the army and the Catholic population had long since been destroyed by a series of catastrophic blunders, from the bungled introduction of internment to the tragedy of Bloody Sunday. In the spring of 1973 the violence had spilled onto the mainland, thanks to the Provisional IRA's decision to launch a bombing campaign in Britain. They had to bring the struggle 'to the heart of the British establishment', one bomber said, because 'it doesn't seem to matter if it's Irish people dying'. Her name was Marion Price; at the age of just 19, she had helped to set off car bombs outside the Old Bailey and in Whitehall, killing one person and injuring 238. As *The Times* observed, the psychological shock of the bombs was simply incalculable. 'Many of us in London', the paper said grimly, 'had not heard a bomb explode since 1944 and many young Londoners have never heard a bomb explode at all.' Watching events in Belfast on the news was one thing; to have them brought to the streets of the capital, to hear the bang, the screams and the sobbing, to see the plumes of black smoke and streets of shattered glass, the dismembered bodies and white-faced policemen, was something quite different.[2]

Since the turn of the year, the Provos had stepped up their mainland bombing campaign. Almost every month now brought some new horror, from February's M62 atrocity to June's bombing of the Houses of Parliament, from July's callous attack on tourists at the Tower of London to November's bombing of pubs in Guildford, Birmingham and Woolwich. The bitter irony, though, was that the bombing campaign was utterly ineffective. 'What they cannot conceivably do', *The Times* remarked, 'is to make the average Londoner say to himself: "My goodness, the IRA may blow me up if I do not create a united Ireland, so I will go and do so forthwith."' And beyond that lay something the paramilitaries never understood: deep down, most people in Britain simply could not care less about Northern Ireland. Although more than a million Irishmen lived in Britain in the mid-1970s, the Troubles never became a major electoral issue, and although the Troops Out movement picked up support among students and the far left, it never came close to being a mainstream political organization. Even in April 1973, with the conflict at its height, fewer than one in ten people described the conflict as Britain's biggest problem – a proportion that steadily fell in the next few years. For most ordinary people in Aberdeen and Aberystwyth, Wandsworth and Wolverhampton, the plight of the economy was far more pressing: for the rest of the decade, the news from Belfast was like a grim soundtrack playing quietly in the background. Callous as it might sound, remarked one observer, the 'televised spectacle of suffering in Ulster', the images of weeping relatives and bombed-out streets, had grown 'stale with repetition'.[3]

Hard though it might be to believe, Northern Ireland in the spring of 1974 was supposed to be moving into a new age of peace and prosperity. Two years earlier, with the streets of Belfast torn apart by gun battles between the terrorists of the Provisional IRA and the vigilantes of the Ulster Defence Association, Edward Heath had suspended the Stormont Parliament and imposed direct rule from Westminster. But this was only ever meant to be a short-term measure. At the end of 1973, his Secretary of State, Willie Whitelaw, had unveiled a new blueprint for Northern Ireland, with a legislative assembly elected by proportional representation, a power-sharing executive and a Council of Ireland so that North and South could discuss common issues. After long negotiations, the official Ulster Unionists, the nationalist SDLP and the non-sectarian Alliance party had agreed to take seats on the new executive, and two weeks later, at the Civil Service Staff College in Sunningdale, Berkshire, they joined the first full Anglo-Irish talks on Northern Ireland since the early 1920s. A new era, it seemed, was at hand. On New Year's Day, buoyed by messages of goodwill from across the world, the power-sharing Executive took office. 'We want the New Year to see the beginning, not just of a new system of Government, but of a new spirit,' read their statement. 'Let 1974 be the Year of Reconciliation.'[4]

Even before it had taken office, however, the Executive faced an almost insurmountable challenge. Although fewer people had died in 1973 than the year before, the Provisional IRA remained convinced that they could bomb the British out of Northern Ireland, while loyalist vigilantes continued their campaign of terror against Catholics who happened to be in the wrong place at the wrong time. Almost every night, against a dark backdrop of working-class poverty and economic stagnation, the paramilitaries played out their rituals of prejudice and hatred. So much blood had been spilled already that, as the Irish journalist Kevin Myers put it, the mood on the Belfast streets was 'clinically insane'. The city's grey, graffiti-stained estates were 'dreary and cold', he wrote, playing host to 'a seventeenth-century religious conflict bottled in a late twentieth-century industrial decline'. Only those who had spent time there, agreed the *Sunday Telegraph*'s Ian Waller, could

> fully comprehend the shattering effect of the escalation of violence: the wrecked buildings, the talks behind sandbagged windows; the routine frisking when entering hotels; the disruption of ordinary life – three times while writing this I have been warned of a bomb scare and asked to leave my room; the deserted city centre at night. The fear, above all, of another explosion or burst of fire.

By now many people defined themselves by the conflict. Myers thought that 'hatred infected entire areas', and that 'it was this ruthless malignancy that gave them a common, almost reassuring identity'. One young woman, just 19, told the BBC that many of her friends were 'so bitter and biased that they just don't care how long the trouble goes on, providing that it turns out the way their people want'. She doubted it would ever stop. 'People have given up hope', she said sadly, 'of Ulster ever being a normal country.'[5]

Goodwill for the power-sharing experiment was in very short supply. Many Catholics had lost confidence that the majority Ulster Unionists could ever be trusted; by contrast, many working-class Protestants were terrified that their politicians were about to sell them out. The leader of the Unionist Party, Brian Faulkner, was a brusque, dynamic, fiercely ambitious man, with a reputation for getting things done. Closely linked to the province's business interests, Faulkner had long presented himself as the champion of law and order. But even before he had taken office as the province's first Chief Executive, his credibility was slipping away. To many working-class Protestants, their fears of Irish Catholicism stoked to boiling point by the bombs of the IRA and the bombast of the hardliners, Faulkner was signing away everything that Ulster represented. On the very first day of the Sunningdale conference, the Ulster Unionist constituency associations, together with 600 Orange Order delegates and various hard-line loyalist groups, announced their shared determination to smash power-sharing and the Council of Ireland. 'Mr Faulkner says that it will be hands across the border to Dublin. I say that if they do not behave themselves in the South, it will be *shots* across the border!' roared the Protestant preacher Ian Paisley. Worse was to come. Three days into the New Year, the Ulster Unionists voted by 427 to 374 to repudiate Sunningdale. Faulkner immediately resigned as party leader, although he remained as head of the Executive. At the press conference afterwards, noted *The Times*, he seemed 'pale and drawn'. When he insisted that he would not alter his principles, a man by the door shouted: 'Then we'll alter them for you!'[6]

On his return to Downing Street, one of the first things Harold Wilson did was to assure Faulkner of his unbending support. 'It was vitally important to make the Executive and power-sharing work,' he told Northern Ireland's chief executive at a meeting a few weeks after the election. 'There was no chance that anyone would bomb the British Army out,' he added, reiterating his 'absolute determination . . . not to give in, or pull out'. Yet as Faulkner well knew, this was not entirely true, for Wilson had never made any secret of his view that the solution to the Troubles might lie in a united Ireland. In opposition, Wilson had not only put forward a plan for Irish unity, he had even held secret, informal talks with representatives of the IRA, although they came to nothing. Even now, behind the scenes, Wilson quietly encouraged his advisers to consider radical answers to the conflict, including the 'Algerian solution' of immediate withdrawal whatever the consequences. 'It was agreed, again under the highest secrecy, that we would begin considering the implications of a total withdrawal,' recorded Tony Benn after a Cabinet meeting in April 1974. 'Of course, if that got out, it would precipitate bloodshed but we felt we simply had to do it.' A month later, Wilson told Bernard Donoughue that they must 'consider "the unmentionable" – British withdrawal from Northern Ireland'.[7]

Despite the death toll, British withdrawal was never likely. When Wilson mentioned his idea to an SDLP delegation in June 1974, they were horrified. Only the British Army, they argued, stood between Northern Ireland and civil war. Even more significantly, the Irish government was appalled by the thought of British withdrawal. Observers overseas often thought that while Britain was desperate to cling on to Northern Ireland, the Republic of Ireland was desperate to get it back. In fact, the situation was the exact reverse. When rumours emerged of Wilson's intentions, memos flew back and forth between Irish ministers panicking at the thought of inheriting a civil war. Dublin must encourage 'the British [to] continue in Northern Ireland in the hope that a solution may be found in time', wrote one senior Irish official. Later, he even told the Irish premier that the 'advantages' of a continued British presence were 'so great, that we should do everything possible to ensure it comes about'. Meanwhile, Ireland's Foreign Minister Garret FitzGerald secretly briefed journalists in an attempt to harden British opinion against withdrawal. At one point he even asked the American Secretary of State, Henry Kissinger, to help stiffen Britain's resolve – an extraordinary step from the foreign minister of a country that still publicly laid claim to Northern Ireland.[8]

In the meantime, the initiative lay with Wilson's Northern Ireland Secretary, Merlyn Rees. The Labour MP for Leeds South, who cut an endearingly donnish figure, had been an RAF squadron leader during the Second World War, which astonished people meeting him in later life, as well as a schoolmaster, which surprised nobody. His shoulders seemed permanently stooped, his suit was shabby and crumpled, his expression was always worried, and his glasses teetered on the brink of slipping off his nose. He was a middle-class Labour man of the old school: decent, earnest and serious, representing the best of the old dissenting tradition. He was an excellent listener, too, although his officials were infuriated by his inability to make up his mind. 'I don't mind Merlyn wrestling with his conscience for ages over every issue,' one civil servant remarked. 'What I mind is the result always seems to be a draw.'[9]

But Rees was no fool. As soon as he arrived in Belfast as Secretary of State, he realized that power-sharing was in serious trouble. Since the turn of the year, loyalist crime had increased enormously, reflecting Protestant fears of being sacrificed to a united Ireland. In March the UVF bombed a Catholic bar in Greencastle, killing two people; in May they bombed the Rose and Crown on the nationalist Ormeau Road, killing six more Catholic civilians. The 'men of violence', Faulkner gloomily said, wanted to 'kill off the Executive', which, as even he admitted, had 'lost its initiative'. Two weeks later, Rees warned the Cabinet that 'the security situation in Northern Ireland was cause for great concern and the political situation, which was already bad, could deteriorate dangerously. The pattern of violence had changed and consisted largely of attacks with fire bombs prepared and placed by women, and the placing of car bombs by civilians who were not themselves terrorists but who were acting under extreme duress.' In Belfast's loyalist heartlands, any hint of accommodation with the Republic of Ireland was simply unacceptable. And although the Executive staggered on, the atmosphere remained extraordinarily rancorous. In the Stormont Assembly, one official recalled, 'Faulkner was spat upon, jostled, reviled

and shouted down. It was sad to see him spat upon by lesser men, political pygmies and procedural bullies and wild men of the woods and
bogs.' Once Faulkner had been Unionism's golden boy; now he seemed
lost, bewildered, adrift in a sea of sectarian hatred. 'I cannot carry it,' he
told Rees privately. 'I have lost my reason to be. I'm beaten, overwhelmed
by the vote against my sort of unionism.'[10]

On Tuesday, 14 May, with London basking in early summer sunshine, the House of Commons approved Rees's plan to legalize the UVF
and Sinn Fein, which he hoped would draw them back into the political
process. Hundreds of miles away, the Assembly in Belfast was voting on
a loyalist motion condemning the controversial Council of Ireland. For
the last few days there had been rumours that loyalists would call for a
general strike if the motion was defeated, but few people seemed particularly worried. There had been loyalist strikes before – a one-day
general strike in February 1973 to protest against direct rule, for
example – but they had always fizzled out. Neither Faulkner nor Rees
paid much attention to the rumours, and when, just after six that evening, a shipyard shop steward called Harry Murray announced that the
Ulster Workers' Council was calling a strike, almost nobody took him
seriously. Few had even heard of Murray; fewer still had heard of the
Ulster Workers' Council. Even when he claimed that Ulster's power
workers intended to cut the supply to offices, shops and industry, few
people were seriously alarmed. 'There seems little or no enthusiasm
among loyalists for an all-out strike,' wrote *The Times*'s Robert Fisk the
next day, 'and the UWC's claim to a membership of 58,000 should be
taken with a very large pinch of salt indeed. The Government remained
apparently indifferent to the threat of a power strike last night, and it
seems likely that Belfast will suffer no more than a slight loss of power
during the daytime hours.'[11]

The Ulster Workers' Council had been planning the strike for months.
It had been set up in the dying weeks of 1973 by a small group of loyalist trade unionists, convinced that they could bring down the supposedly
crypto-republican Executive and restore either Ulster self-government
or direct rule from Westminster. British union leaders often shuddered
at the comparison, but in a sense the UWC and their British equivalents
were part of the same phenomenon: a defensively minded workers'
revolt against the forces of political and economic change. The difference was that the UWC had unmistakable sectarian associations.
Harry Murray had been a prominent member of the Loyalist Association of Workers, while Glenn Barr, who headed the strike coordinating

committee, was the economics spokesman for the hard-line Vanguard movement. A shrewd operator, with a smooth public manner, Barr was the perfect front man for the UWC. Crucially, he had once been the union convenor at the Coolkeeragh power station, and still had good connections among the electricity workers. It was important, Barr thought, that they keep trouble to a minimum. If the strike became violent, then the security forces would inevitably step in; if it was peaceful, they had a chance of winning. But he was well aware that paramilitary support might be crucial for victory. Not only was Barr himself a member of the vigilante Ulster Defence Association, he was very close to its chairman, Andy Tyrie. From the very beginning, strike leaders kept in touch with the so-called Ulster Army Council, a loyalist umbrella organization, and every Wednesday trade unionists and paramilitaries met secretly to hammer out their plans. And on 14 May, just moments after Murray's announcement that the strike would start the next morning, the Ulster Army Council issued a statement of its own. 'If Westminster is not prepared to restore democracy, i.e. the will of the people made clear in an election,' it declared, 'then the only other way it can be restored is by a *coup d'état*.'[12]

On the first day of the strike, Wednesday, 15 May, a *coup d'état* still seemed very unlikely. At nine that morning, almost every major road into Belfast was still open, and businesses reported that nine out of ten workers had turned up as usual. Even the strike leaders' own families seemed oblivious to their plans, which does not say much for their domestic arrangements. When Harry Murray failed to go to work that morning, his puzzled wife asked him what on earth he was doing, while another strike leader's wife refused to believe his explanation until she went to make his breakfast and found that the electricity was off (which she blamed on a dodgy fuse). But by late morning the power workers' strike was already having an impact, with the electricity supply across the province down to just 40 per cent. By lunchtime, major factories were reporting problems in maintaining production, and at the Harland and Wolff shipyards, UWC speakers warned the 8,000 workers that after two o'clock that afternoon, any cars found in the employees' car park would be set on fire.

Not surprisingly, most of the shipyard workers immediately went home, and by mid-afternoon the strike was clearly gaining momentum. At the Sirocco factory a mile away, 3,000 more workers walked out, while masked men carrying guns and clubs persuaded employees at Mackie's, Belfast's biggest engineering plant, to follow suit. By late afternoon, there were reports that groups of men with UDA insignia were touring Protestant areas, warning shops and businesses that they must comply with 'the will of the majority'. In Larne, County Antrim, armed UDA men in combat jackets marched down the High Street, forcing traders to close their shops, blocking the harbour road with hijacked cars and lorries and shutting down the ferry service to Scotland. And while Faulkner maintained that most Protestants were ignoring the strike, there was no ignoring the fact that electricity in County Derry was down to just 25 per cent, or that many people were now experiencing power cuts four hours long – an ominous echo of the events that had brought Heath down just months before.[13]

At first, Faulkner predicted that any strike seeking 'to hold a gun to the head of the civilian population' would fail 'no less dismally' than the IRA's efforts to bomb Ulster into a united Ireland. But by Thursday morning his words already rang hollow. As the people of Belfast streamed into work, they found that the UDA had been busy, erecting barricades across the capital and effectively choking off the city centre. Since anyone tempted to cross the roadblocks was effectively deterred by the presence of masked men with baseball bats and guns, the strike was now well on the way to becoming general. Outside one factory, Catholic men arriving for work were beaten up by club-carrying pickets, while at a Post Office maintenance depot the UDA told staff that unless they went home their cars would be burned and their Catholic employees executed. Without orders to quell the uprising, the security forces seemed powerless to intervene: at Harland and Wolff, one reporter saw paramilitaries jumping on the hood of a car carrying terrified executives while armed Protestant policemen looked on indulgently. And although the army and the police did clear some barricades later that morning, it was too late to have any effect. From the farms came reports that unprocessed milk was being dumped; from the supermarkets came news of food shortages. That afternoon, hijacked cars and lorries burned across the city, and by evening the UWC confirmed that it had ordered all bars, clubs and hotels in Belfast to shut down. But they had no intention of allowing Northern Ireland to slide into chaos, for that would defeat the point of the strike. Instead, they proposed to set up their own administration to guarantee essential services – an uncanny preview of what was to come in parts of Britain during the Winter of Discontent.[14]

By Friday, the UDA's campaign of intimidation was virtually over – not because the army had stopped it, but because it had achieved its

goal. In Belfast the streets were almost entirely deserted, save for Protestant paramilitaries touring building sites to take the names of anyone
still working. Power cuts now lasted six hours at a time, and there were
rumours that the electricity would soon be turned off completely. In
London, Harold Wilson asked his aides to 'investigate the possibility of
deploying a nuclear submarine to Belfast to provide an emergency
power supply'. Unfortunately, they reported, 'electricity generated by a
nuclear submarine is not compatible with the national grid'. Meanwhile, Larne Harbour was at a standstill, Belfast's two major power
stations were almost out of coal, and in the docks 2,000 mailbags lay
unopened. Hospitals had now run out of milk, while farmers had
reportedly poured 200,000 gallons into ditches before it turned sour.
On the mainland, many people wondered why the army did not step in,
yet the British commander in Northern Ireland, General Sir Frank King,
maintained that the worst possible outcome would be for his men to
become targets for the Protestant majority. So the army did nothing and
ordinary life gradually dribbled to a halt. 'It was a curious experience to
sit each evening in the gathering dusk – no street lamps anywhere, only
the faintest of flickering lights in the windows of neighbouring homes –
isolated in the midst of a community that had suffered almost total
social break-down; wondering what would happen next,' a Belfast lawyer wrote later. 'The feeling of helplessness was very great; no positive
action whatever was possible. Was it a bit like this in the drawing rooms
of St Petersburg in October 1917?'[15]

But the worst news of the day came from south of the border, where,
at half past five that evening, as Dublin's streets were packed with shoppers and commuters, three car bombs exploded almost simultaneously,
killing twenty-three people immediately and three more as a result of
their injuries in the next few days. An hour and a half later, a fourth
bomb exploded in Monaghan, killing a further seven people. Yet again,
witnesses could barely bring themselves to describe the appalling horror
that had visited Ireland's streets: the babies blown out of their prams;
the 21-year-old bride-to-be who had spent the previous night writing
her wedding invitations, now lying dead on a Dublin pavement; the
expectant mother, another 21-year-old, killed along with her unborn
child. The culprits, it turned out, were the Ulster Volunteer Force,
'returning the serve', as one later put it, for the IRA's Belfast bombs.
And while most people in Britain were horrified by the carnage, few
Ulster loyalists shed tears for the slaughter in the south. 'I am very happy
about the bombings in Dublin,' announced Sammy Smyth, press officer

for both the UDA and the UWC. 'There is a war with the Free State – and now we are laughing at them.'[16]

Terrible though the Dublin and Monaghan bombings were, it was the strike that preoccupied the power-sharing Executive. By the weekend it was patently obvious that the army lacked the stomach for a confrontation, leaving the UDA in control of the streets. When a delegation from the UWC went to see Merlyn Rees, promising power for essential services if he would agree to cut commercial and industrial consumers from the grid, he dismissed them out of hand. Of course he had no choice: he could hardly be seen to kowtow to the paramilitaries. But this left the UWC with the initiative, and they proceeded to use it. For Faulkner and his British allies, it was a total humiliation. While they sat on their hands, armed UDA men took control of local areas, orchestrating the shipment of supplies, strutting around like medieval barons surveying their domains. Setting themselves up as an alternative administration, they issued detailed guidelines for the supply of power and services to dairies, farms and hospitals, confounding the government's predictions that the strike would quickly collapse. When the reporter Peter Taylor visited the UWC's strike headquarters, he had to wait behind 'queues of people waiting for passes and permits to provide essential supplies like bread and milk'. It was bizarre, he thought, that the people deciding these issues were not 'the elected politicians sitting powerless in the Executive half a mile away up the road at Stormont, but a mixture of paramilitaries and workers, most of whom had probably never run a raffle'.[17]

'Northern Ireland faces a near total standstill in its daily commercial life,' reported *The Times* on Monday morning. 'The province will once again be without three-quarters of its electricity, without its heavy and light industry and transport, and may, despite the [UWC]'s promise, face food and water shortages.' Although the government had sent more troops to Belfast, there now seemed a serious danger of law and order breaking down completely. More than 150 barricades blocked the roads into Belfast, Larne was under paramilitary control and Carrickfergus had been cut off by barricades of stolen cars. 'To move around Belfast during the day was an eerie and frightening experience,' wrote Robert Fisk.

Gangs of Protestants, some masked and others carrying cudgels and sticks, roamed the main roads into the city, stealing cars, lorries, buses and even a crane before setting them on fire. They yelled abuse from behind smouldering barricades at the end of deserted streets, and the few brave people who had tried to brave the 'constitutional stoppage' thought better of their judgment and returned to their candle-lit homes.

Everywhere Fisk saw milk floats and food lorries pulled over and set on fire. Near Sandyrow he saw 'children and several middle-aged women looting a stolen milk lorry'; elsewhere, he saw gangs of youths invading a milk distribution plant, smashing dozens of crates and selling the rest at 5p a pint to desperate locals. That such anarchy – reminiscent of some post-apocalyptic drama – was taking place on the streets of the modern United Kingdom was bad enough; what was worse was that the army refused to intervene. 'Motorists, vainly trying to leave the city, were repeatedly searched at army checkpoints only about five hundred yards from where masked or uniformed Protestants patrolled unmolested,' Fisk noted. 'At one point on Lisburn Road during the morning, troops were still ritually searching incoming motorists in case they were carrying bombs in their cars, while Ulster Defence Association men were openly driving a stolen tipper truck down the street just round the next corner.'

'It's Anarchy,' shrieked the front page of the *Express* the next morning, painting a picture of milk deliveries drying up and taps running dry, 'fresh fruit and vegetables rotting in windows of closed shops' and bakeries rationing customers to 'one small loaf', as an entire province was 'forced to its knees not by terrorism but by a national strike'. A few hours later, the TUC general secretary Len Murray flew into Belfast to lead a 'back to work' march to the shipyards. The 'vast mass of people in Northern Ireland', he told an interviewer, 'want to go to work today and tomorrow and next week and all the time' – a refreshing thing to hear from a union leader in the mid-1970s. But the march was a disaster. Of the 10,000 shipyard workers Murray had summoned to join him, fewer than 200 turned up, and as they began to march, women chanting 'No surrender!' pelted them with eggs and tomatoes. By the time they reached the Harland and Wolff gates, Murray himself was engulfed by a seething mob. One woman spat directly into his face, while local youths pelted him with bits of iron piping. A second march that day was even worse, attracting just twenty supporters. It was obvious to everyone that the mild-mannered Midlander was painfully out of his depth: nothing had prepared him for the intensity of the hatreds on the streets of Belfast. 'These people have come and have stood up for the right to work,' Murray said defiantly of his little band of resisters. But he never came back to Northern Ireland.[18]

By Thursday, 23 May, the Executive was close to breaking point. At a meeting with trade unionists and business leaders, Faulkner admitted that 'the UWC appeared to be steadily tightening its grip on the country'. Some of his ministers wanted to open talks with the strike leaders; others warned of 'a possible Vietnam situation developing with complete devastation of Northern Ireland'. The next morning, with the strike ten days old, Faulkner flew to England for talks with Harold Wilson. 'We have come to the crunch,' Faulkner said bluntly. With every passing hour, 'it became increasingly evident that the administration of the country was in fact in the hands of the Ulster Workers' Council. The issue was now not whether the Sunningdale agreement would or would not survive. The outcome which the Protestant extremists sought was without question an independent, neo-fascist Northern Ireland.'[19]

This was strong stuff, outweighing even Wilson's instinct for keeping his head down. At a Cabinet meeting that evening, the Prime Minister and his Labour colleagues agreed that they must assert their authority, although, revealingly, the Defence Secretary, Roy Mason, warned that they could not expect too much of the army. The troops simply did not have the know-how to take over the power stations, he pointed out, and 'we might find that the demonstration of our will and capacity to govern was less than convincing. It would not be possible for the armed forces to take over the running of the country if the UWC secured the withdrawal of labour generally.' As so often, therefore, Wilson decided that muddling through was the best approach. The army would take over selected petrol stations and maintain essential supplies, but without provoking clashes with the Protestant militants. Meanwhile, he would give a prime ministerial broadcast the next evening. Perhaps his silver tongue would succeed where others had failed.[20]

Wilson already had a history of unfortunate broadcasts, with his 'pound in your pocket' address in 1967 representing something of a nadir in prime ministerial oratory. For sheer misjudgement, though, his address to the nation on Saturday, 25 May 1974 stands supreme. Few people could disagree with his opening words, as he warned that 'Northern Ireland faces the gravest crisis in her history'. But as the leaders of the UWC listened to Wilson's next few lines, they realized that he was playing right into their hands. 'What we are seeing in Northern Ireland is not just an industrial strike,' he said contemptuously. 'It is a deliberate and calculated attempt to use every undemocratic and unparliamentary means for the purpose of bringing down the whole constitution of Northern Ireland so as to set up there a sectarian and undemocratic state, from which one third of the people of Northern Ireland will be excluded.' Then he came to the passage for which the speech would be remembered:

> The people on this side of the water – British parents – have seen their sons vilified and spat upon and murdered. British taxpayers have seen the taxes they have poured out, almost without regard to cost – over £300 million a year this year with the cost of the Army operation on top of that – going into Northern Ireland. They see property destroyed by evil violence and are asked to pick up the bill for rebuilding it. Yet people who benefit from all this now viciously defy Westminster, purporting to act as though they were an elected government; people who spend their lives sponging on Westminster and British democracy and then systematically assault democratic methods. Who do these people think they are?

Spongers! Even as Wilson said the words, even as millions of British listeners were nodding in agreement, Brian Faulkner was turning pale with horror. Joe Haines had tried to strike out the offending words, but Wilson had put them back in. He thought they sounded tough and decisive, reflecting the views of ordinary voters. But on the streets of Northern Ireland, where it really mattered, they sounded crass and insulting. Even afterwards, Glenn Barr laughed when he remembered Wilson's speech. 'I thought, great stuff,' he chuckled. 'This is fantastic. We'll make him an honorary member of the UDA after this.'[21]

Wilson's broadcast was a disaster. The next day Protestants took to wearing pieces of sponge in their lapels, reflecting their anger at his intemperate words and their pride in their communal identity. And although the army finally took over petrol depots, tankers and roadside stations on Monday morning, nobody now doubted that the strike was virtually unbreakable. When the UWC called for a complete stoppage, announcing that the army would have to handle all essential services themselves, including deliveries of bread and milk, it was clear that the province was on the brink of chaos. At Stormont, SDLP ministers told Rees that they planned to resign unless he sent troops to put down the strike, while unionist ministers were almost beside themselves with rage and despair. 'How can we escape the suspicion that Britain has deliberately let us down and that she wants to undermine us and reimpose direct rule?' one of Faulkner's allies demanded. 'Why has not Wilson done what he said he would? How can the British possibly ask the Dublin government to deal with the IRA and criticize them when they do not, and then refuse to take action against a loyalist strike?' But in London, support for the Executive had ebbed away. 'While the Northern Ireland Executive remain in being, there can be no real movement,' Rees wrote to Wilson that afternoon. 'From our point of view the most desirable situation now is that they should go of their accord.'[22]

By now the situation had deteriorated so far that not even an offer of mediation from Idi Amin, taking a break from his busy schedule of murdering his own people, offered a solution.* As Faulkner flew into work on Tuesday morning, commuting by helicopter because of the UDA roadblocks and petrol shortages, gloomy reports poured in from across the province, 'stories of how the rebels were in control and the community was taking the soft option of giving them at least passive support'. As Faulkner looked down over the Stormont estate, he could see gangs of loyalists gathered around Sir Edward Carson's statue, as well as an incongruous ring of tractors, driven overnight by Protestant farmers determined to bring him down. There was no way back. Meeting his Executive colleagues a few hours later, Faulkner suggested opening talks with the strikers, but even as he said it, he knew that Rees would never agree. A few hours later, with jeering loyalists held back by a line of troops, he read out a brief statement announcing that he and the other Unionist members of the Executive had decided to resign. Afterwards, he walked silently back to his office with Kenneth Bloomfield, the Stormont mandarin who had been with his unfortunate predecessors, Terence O'Neill and James Chichester-Clarke, too, in their final hours. 'Quite without shame, I wept,' Bloomfield later wrote. 'I wept for the success of the hard men with the dark glasses, the balaclava helmets and pickaxe handles; I wept for the inevitability of a sweeping British judgement that we were all hopeless cases, doomed to endless conflict in an inferno of our own creation; I wept for the eclipse of local democracy.'[23]

The strikers had won. Sunningdale was dead, power-sharing was dead and the Stormont Assembly was officially dissolved. In Protestant areas of Belfast, crowds marched behind Orange bands, singing and chanting; that evening, celebratory bonfires burned long into the night. The next day, as workers streamed triumphantly back to their factories,

---

* 'As the general's messages go,' the Foreign Office told Wilson, 'this is one of his more lucid and although it is as preposterous as one might expect, the acting high commissioner believes that it was sent with the best of intentions.'

the UWC called off the strike. The day after that, Britain resumed direct rule over Northern Ireland. In London, Wilson told his advisers to prepare a 'Doomsday scenario' for immediate withdrawal.[24]

Outside Northern Ireland, the collapse of power-sharing was universally seen as a catastrophe. The entire peace process, remarked *The Times*, was 'shattered', and there was 'no use hoping to stick it together again'. Conspiracy theorists, especially on the left, suggested that the British Army had colluded in the collapse of the Executive by refusing to intervene until it was much too late. Some even suggested that rogue elements within British intelligence had played a part in the Dublin and Monaghan bombings, giving aid to the UVF as part of their campaign to crush the Provisional IRA – although there was never conclusive proof either way. What is certainly true, however, is that even at the time many people thought Merlyn Rees was far too slow to crush an illegal and clearly political strike. If, his critics argued, he had acted swiftly and decisively, sending in the army to tear down the barricades and arrest the UWC leaders, then the strike would never have secured the support of the Protestant middle classes, and would have fizzled out after a brief spasm of angry confrontation.[25]

In many ways, this is one of the most compelling counterfactuals of the entire Troubles. Rees himself, however, insisted that early intervention would have made no difference. 'I didn't let them win,' he later said wearily. 'They were going to win anyway. It wasn't like a coal miners' strike in Sheffield . . . The police were on the brink of not carrying out their duties and the middle class were on the strikers' side. This wasn't just an industrial dispute. This was the Protestant people of Northern Ireland rising up against Sunningdale and it could not be shot down.' Crucially, this was also the view of General Sir Frank King, who warned the government that the army would turn themselves into sitting ducks if they took on the Protestant majority. 'If Rees had ordered us to move against the barricades,' he said later, 'we would have said, "With great respect, this is a job for the police. We will assist them if you wish, but it's not terrorism."' But Rees could hardly rely on the Royal Ulster Constabulary to beat the strike, because so many Protestant police officers shared the strikers' feelings. As he knew, hostility to Sunningdale was widespread throughout the Protestant majority. Even Robert Fisk, who was fiercely critical of the police and the army, doubted that the security forces could have broken the strike without bringing the entire Protestant population onto the streets. After years of sectarian bloodshed, too many unionists felt sold out by Sunningdale for power-sharing to have survived. The depressing truth is that, with or without the strike, the Executive was probably doomed anyway.[26]

So the killing went on. Any illusions that there might soon be a peaceful settlement had now disappeared; instead of searching for a political solution, Rees and Wilson contented themselves with measures to bring down violence to what Reginald Maudling had once called 'an acceptable level'. The following February Rees managed to negotiate a ceasefire with the IRA, but nothing came of it. Even while the truce was supposedly in force, the sectarian killings continued. In July 1975, the UVF carried out one of the most senseless atrocities of the entire conflict, killing three members of the popular Miami Showband as they were driving back to Dublin after a concert in County Londonderry. Six months later, the UVF were responsible for another appalling massacre, breaking into two houses in South Armagh and murdering six Catholic civilians. The very next day, the IRA responded with an act of chilling brutality, flagging down a minibus of textile workers outside the village of Kingsmill, separating the workers into Catholics and Protestants, and executing the latter in cold blood. All in all, republican paramilitaries murdered 148 people in 1974, 125 people in 1975 and 154 people in 1976, while the loyalists' gruesome tally was 123, 121 and 116. (By comparison, the security forces killed 41 people in three years.) But even as the bloodletting continued, the new generation of Provisional leaders maintained that victory would come eventually. They must dig in for a 'long war', insisted the young Gerry Adams; they must organize themselves into little terrorist cells, continue the bombing campaign in Britain and wage a war of attrition that would make Northern Ireland ungovernable. 'Make no mistake about it,' declared the *Republican News* at the beginning of 1976. 'Britain's days in Ireland are numbered; the Irish people recognise it, the world at large recognise it, and the Irish Republican Army certainly recognise it.'[27]

But Britain, too, was prepared for a long war. 'We should not revert to the active search for a solution,' a government memo explained in November 1974. 'We should, for a time at least, concentrate on administering the Province. Government should be low key.' And although Rees did not entirely give up on the political process, he was beginning to devise a new approach in tandem with the army, treating the conflict as a security issue rather than a political one. By the summer of 1976 the 'criminalization' of the Troubles was already under way, with the government building new H-blocks in which paramilitaries were stripped of their special status and treated like common criminals. Meanwhile, under its new Chief Constable, the former Met commander Kenneth Newman, the RUC began to take over on the front line. As a secret government document entitled 'The Way Forward' explained, the new strategy was to treat the conflict, not as a war, but as a campaign against criminal gangs. The British Army faded into the background, while Westminster channelled funds to the RUC, setting up new regional crime squads backed up by the locally recruited Ulster Defence Regiment. And while Rees made an unlikely figurehead for a hard-nosed battle against terrorism, his successor, who took over in September 1976, clearly loved the job. A former South Yorkshire miner on the Labour right, a working-class patriot with fierce populist instincts, Roy Mason made up for his lack of inches with a self-consciously blunt, aggressive style. Somewhat incongruously, he was also an enthusiast for amateur cravatology: the art of designing neckties. He had no interest in constitutional initiatives or political deals: his job was to 'take on the terrorists'. The army and the RUC loved him; even years later, mention of his name would bring unionist applause.[28]

Mason certainly had his critics: Catholics and left-wingers saw him as a brutal hard man, while even his admirers were disconcerted by his public enthusiasm for the RUC's ultra-aggressive interrogation techniques. 'I was being as tough as I could be,' he later said, 'and though my policy was undeniably a ruthless business, it at least meant that the level of violence was beginning to come down.' He was right about that. In 1974, some 294 people had been killed; the year after, 260 people; the year after that, 295 people. But in 1977, Mason's first full year in charge, the death toll fell to 111, and a year later it was down to just 82. Thanks to Mason's policy of taking the troops out of the front line, British Army casualties fell to a handful. Meanwhile, as the Provos' Martin McGuinness put it, 'Mason beat the shit out of us,' with the new interrogation techniques and aggressive RUC policing severely damaging the IRA as a street-fighting force. And as the threat from the Provos lessened, so loyalist paramilitary groups lost their appeal. When Ian Paisley tried to organize another general strike in 1977 it proved a miserable failure. With Mason in charge, ordinary Protestants felt no need to rebel against the current regime. UDA recruitment dried up, while other paramilitary groups shrank into squalid criminal gangs, spending much of their time feuding with one another. And even though they dared not admit it publicly, both the SDLP and the Irish government privately applauded Mason's hard line. Some even wished he had been in office earlier.[29]

By now the conflict had become part of the fabric of everyday life. 'Except for the passionately dedicated,' wrote Christopher Thomas in *The Times* in December 1979, 'the war has become a matter of confusion, anger and dazed acceptance.' In the meantime, despite enormous subsidies from Westminster, Northern Ireland had slipped further into poverty, unemployment and deep industrial decline. 'The deprivation in parts of Belfast is frightening,' Thomas wrote. 'Anybody who feels like risking a drive through Turf Lodge, Whiterock, Ballymurphy or the Lower Falls district cannot avoid being moved. There, fear is the master.' The city had long since been carved up into working-class Catholic and Protestant areas, each identified by its murals and graffiti; 'but wherever you are the scene is the same: relentless rows of centuries-old terraces, some of them bombed and bricked up; Army vehicles everywhere; barbed wire and great walls of corrugated iron protecting vital installations; roads strewn with bricks and stones that have been hurled a thousand times at military vehicles. Hope, tragically, is in short supply.' The Peace People, a non-sectarian women's group that had rocketed into the headlines in 1976, had been and gone; the killing, however, continued. Since 1970, Thomas remarked sadly, 'the headlines have carried a grisly message of violence, political failure and dashed hopes'. In the decade to come, he predicted, that message would barely change.[30]

6

Could It Happen Here?

I think it very possible that there may be fighting within four months. If Heath gives way to the Unions this time, the moderates who make up eighty per cent of the population will be in despair. The extremists will press their demands and have to be resisted in force by a super-leader.

James Lees-Milne's diary, 6 January 1974

JOBY: Ten years, the country sliding down. Through the nineteen seventies. Guns. Barbed wire. The woods stripped clean a their leaves. Journalist I were. Good story that. But I never noticed.

Howard Brenton, *The Churchill* Play (1974)

To most people in mainland Britain, the success of the UWC strike came as a terrible shock. When readers of *The Times* opened the paper at breakfast on 28 May, it told them that it was of 'paramount importance that the strike in Northern Ireland be defeated'. By the afternoon, the strikers had won. For 'fifteen unprecedented, historic days', wrote Robert Fisk, 'a million British citizens, the Protestants of Northern Ireland, staged what amounted to a rebellion against the Crown and won with scarcely a shot being fired'. And to the conservative middle classes, what happened in Belfast – the scenes of barricades on the streets, masked men openly carrying weapons, mobs hijacking cars and burning buses while the army looked on powerlessly – seemed a terrifying preview of what might one day come to the streets of Middle England. Since the strikers had 'defied and defeated the democratic process', wrote the academic Richard Clutterbuck, the lesson was that 'intimidation was seen to prevail'. It could hardly have been a more 'dangerous precedent', because it 'provided both encouragement and vicarious experience for those who wish to use industrial action – whether their philosophy tends towards Marxism or Fascism – to defy or destroy parliamentary democracy in Britain'.[1]

In a year of unrelentingly miserable news, against a backdrop of political uncertainty and soaring inflation, the success of the UWC strike seemed an ominous portent of what might be coming to the mainland. And the Provos' attacks on the Houses of Parliament and the Tower of London that summer were not the only signs that violence was steadily seeping into public life. On 15 June, a 21-year-old student, Kevin Gately, died of his injuries after violent clashes between marchers and police at a demonstration against the National Front in Red Lion Square, London. The exact circumstances – he was killed by a blow on the head, possibly from a truncheon, or perhaps by being trampled beneath a police horse – were never determined, but he was the first person killed in a political demonstration since 1919. Two months later, fighting again dominated the front pages, this time at Windsor Great Park, where hundreds of Thames Valley policemen broke up an illegal Free Festival. Some 220 people were arrested and 116 injured; although more than half of the wounded were festival-goers, the public, as usual on such occasions, sided with the police. 'There is no pause in violence,' *The Times* said sadly, lamenting that Britain had apparently moved into 'a world increasingly ruthless and increasingly irrational, a world in which the principle of order is by its nature exposed to furious attack'. The 'vanguard of anarchy', it thought, was 'loose in the world'.[2]

Of course it is easy to exaggerate the breakdown of order in the early 1970s. Most people never joined a strike, were untouched by terrorism or serious crime and continued to lead more comfortable lives than ever. And yet the fact remains that, since the election of Edward Heath in 1970, the United Kingdom had suffered the most traumatic period in its modern political history, with five states of emergency, two successful miners' strikes, countless industrial stoppages, the collapse of the government's authority and the eruption of brutal sectarian anarchy in Northern Ireland. Indeed, in 1974 political violence in mainland Britain claimed more lives than in the rest of the century combined, with forty-four people killed by IRA bombings and one in Red Lion Square. 'Lawlessness is on the increase and "political" lawlessness even more so,' wrote the political scientist Stephen Haseler, a member of the Greater London Council. 'Violent crime is increasing and football vandalism shames the British reputation at home and abroad. Bombing campaigns kill and maim innocent people.' British society, Haseler thought, had become 'increasingly fractured': if the current trends continued, it would simply 'degenerate into an anarchy of warring camps', with Parliament and the unions 'locked in mortal combat'.[3]

When people opened their morning papers, it sometimes seemed that law and order were disintegrating across the world. In May 1974 the West German Chancellor, Willy Brandt, resigned when it was revealed that one of his personal assistants was an East German spy; three months later the President of the United States, Richard Nixon, resigned in disgrace after the Watergate scandal. Terrorism haunted the Western world: in the summer of 1974, dozens of people were killed by political extremists in Italy, a far-left bomb killed eight people at the Mitsubishi factory in Tokyo, and eighty-eight people were killed when TWA Flight 841 was blown up en route from Tel Aviv to New York. If anything, 1975 was even worse, with sectarian violence breaking out in Lebanon, the Baader–Meinhof gang and the Red Brigades on the rampage in Europe and the IRA bombing their way across central London. On 28 October, *The Times* devoted its front page to terrorism, noting that in the previous twenty-four hours bombs had gone off in eight major cities across the world. The bomb, it remarked, had 'developed into the standard international method of urban protest . . . even the world of literary criticism was invaded yesterday with a petrol bomb attack on the Paris home of a member of the committee which selects the Prix Goncourt winner'. Two months later, Carlos the Jackal launched a daring raid on the OPEC headquarters in Vienna, eventually escaping with more than sixty hostages to Algiers and Tripoli. Three days after that, the CIA chief in Athens was shot dead by Greek Marxists. Finally, two days before the end of the year, a bomb killed eleven people in New York's LaGuardia Airport. Nobody ever discovered who was behind it.[4]

To many observers, what was distinctive about Britain was the fact that the state itself had manifestly lost its authority. For a decade, politicians of both parties had been victims of events, buffeted to and fro by the winds of economic change and national decline, powerless to implement their manifesto promises, powerless to steer the ship towards calmer waters. Years of affluence had eroded the old values of social solidarity and individual self-discipline; fattened by prosperity, modern voters wanted jam today, tomorrow and always. Both Wilson and Heath had promised painless modernization, yet neither had delivered.

As growth stalled and living standards stagnated, working-class union members pressed for more; as the government gave way, it inevitably alienated middle-class voters frightened of being overtaken. At Conservative Central Office, messages poured in from constituency associations reflecting a wider 'confusion, helplessness and a growing belief that those in authority were out of their depth'; in the spring of 1973, one Tory advisory committee reported 'a general fear about the state of our society, a feeling that we are not in control'. Now good old Mr Wilson was back in charge, yet not even his fiercest partisans believed he would bring radical change. 'Britain today, unfortunately, seems all too often to settle for the average, the mediocre, the corrupt – the man with a vested interest in the system,' wrote a despairing Stephen Haseler two years after Wilson's return. Parliamentary politics, he thought, had 'patently failed' to address the crisis; meanwhile, Britain 'has tottered to economic breakdown and civil strife'. 'We face the final collapse of the Social Democratic Age,' he wrote sadly. 'As with Liberal England before it, it will pass into the history books. It will be, can only be, supplanted by a totalitarian state.'[5]

Four decades on, the prediction that Britain was heading for totalitarianism sounds ridiculous. To Haseler's readers, however, it was nothing of the kind. Just as many people thought it inevitable that the United Kingdom would disintegrate under pressure from Celtic nationalism, so many political commentators thought that the state had simply failed. 'Why is Britain becoming harder to govern?' asked the political scientist Anthony King in three late-night programmes for BBC1, broadcast in February 1976. The reason, King thought, was that people expected too much, with government cast as 'the sorcerer's apprentice', rushing about with his bucket as the waters carried on rising. The distinction between private and public had become 'hopelessly blurred'; whenever a big firm ran into trouble, from Rolls-Royce and Upper Clyde Shipbuilders to Chrysler and British Leyland, everybody expected the government to bail it out. But even as the state was 'trying to play God', its grasp, in a globalized world dominated by giant multinational corporations, was more enfeebled than ever. The results lay all around: 'the failure to achieve a higher rate of economic growth, the failure to bring inflation under control, the failure to put right the balance of payments, the failure to build enough houses, the failure to reduce the level of violent crime, the failure to reform the trade unions, the failure to make a commercial success of Concorde'. Little wonder, then, that deference and authority were in such manifest decline. And even though King doubted that democracy would collapse, he thought 'the fact that people are talking about the possibility at all is in itself significant'. Britain might not be facing revolution. But it was facing the kind of crisis it had 'not known since 1832, possibly not since the seventeenth century'.[6]

At the time, the striking thing about King's analysis was that, by the standards of the mid-1970s, it was actually quite optimistic. Many perfectly rational observers were far gloomier, perhaps the most influential being Samuel Brittan, economic commentator for the *Financial Times*. As Brittan told the British Association for the Advancement of Science in September 1974, 'liberal representative democracy' had proved incompatible with two relatively new developments: 'excessive expectations' among the public, and 'the pursuit of group self-interest in the market place'. To put it very simply, voters had been spoiled by affluence. They had unrealistic expectations of becoming richer and richer – a report by the Social Science Research Council in 1973 showed that two out of three thought they were entitled to a higher standard of living – and voted for whichever party promised them the goods. If reality failed to live up to their fantasies, then they went on strike to get what they wanted. The unions, Brittan thought, were now so powerful that a democracy could not control them; the result was that 'within the lifetime of people now adult', liberal democracy would give way to the 'petty despotism' of a 'right-wing authoritarian' regime.[7]

Brittan was no right-wing reactionary; indeed, he had briefly been an adviser at George Brown's Department of Economic Affairs in the mid-1960s. And he drew on the ideas of another nominal Labour supporter, Peter Jay, the economics editor of *The Times*, who had already argued that, in the long run, free collective bargaining, full employment and economic stability were simply incompatible. Over drinks in November 1975, Jay nodded as Tony Benn propounded his view that 'ballot box democracy was becoming incompatible with the capitalist market economy and the inequalities inherent in capitalism'. The present drift would go on for eighteen months, Jay predicted, 'culminating in a massive crisis'. The government would then swing back towards 'sound financial and monetary politics involving massive slashes in public expenditure'; then there would be 'a coalition which Harold probably wouldn't join, an election which the Tories would win, the whole Labour movement would come out against the Tory Government and law and order would break down, leading to domination by an authoritarian figure of the Left or the Right'. To some people, this sounded like the stuff of fantasy.

But Jay was not alone in his belief that Britain was probably going the same way as Greece, Turkey, Portugal and Chile, all of which had fallen victim to recent coups. The relevant parallel, explained the conservative economist Milton Friedman in 1976, was 'Chile, with first Allende, and then the takeover by a military junta . . . That's the road Britain is going down and that is the ultimate outcome . . . That's the only outcome that is conceivable.'[8]

There was, of course, a chilling precedent for the collapse of democracy in a major European country. For two decades, Britain had been saturated in nostalgia for the victory over Hitler's Germany. Thanks to an endless flow of war films, boys' comics, television documentaries and paperback bestsellers, the spirit of Dunkirk, the Battle of Britain and the Blitz had long since become a familiar mainstay of national cultural life. What had changed by the early 1970s, though, was that pride in victory had faded into the background, replaced by a morbid fascination with the beaten enemy. Judging by the decade's bestseller lists, wrote the critic John Sutherland, fascism was 'immensely glamorous, inexhaustibly interesting'. Packaged in 'shiny black with prominent Nazi insignia', book after book promised to uncover 'the evil of the Third Reich', while pulp novelists such as Frederick Forsyth and John Gardner sold thousands of copies by suggesting that the Nazis had survived the fall of Berlin and were preparing for an international comeback.* And with the world economy tottering, inflation rising and European capitals haunted by terrorism, even sober observers, noted *Time* magazine in 1974, feared for 'the very future of traditional parliamentary democracy'. One of Willy Brandt's aides remarked that the West German Chancellor saw 'everything breaking apart'. If extremism went unchecked, he said, 'parliamentary democracy in Western Europe could disappear in 20 or 30 years'. The resurgence of Nazism might not be such a fantasy after all.[9]

But was that Nazism in Germany, or Nazism in Britain? When Robert Skidelsky published his groundbreaking life of Sir Oswald Mosley in 1975, dragging the fascist leader out of the gutter and putting him back into the mainstream of recent British history, some reviewers were horrified that he had treated Mosley's ideas with respect. Yet as *The Times*

---

* In Forsyth's *The Odessa File* (1972), a German reporter discovers that a secret Nazi network has been smuggling former SS war criminals to South America; in Gardner's *The Werewolf Trace* (1975), a young boy named as Hitler's heir, smuggled out of the Berlin bunker, is now masquerading as a 'respectable British businessman'.

admitted, Skidelsky's book posed 'a number of questions that remain uncomfortably without answer'. Was fascism inherently un-British, or could it really have happened here? Len Deighton certainly thought it could: his novel *SS-GB* (1978) imagines an alternative 1941 in which Churchill has been executed, Buckingham Palace is in ruins and the King is a prisoner in the Tower of London. The SS have their headquarters in Whitehall, German bands play 'Greensleeves' in the centre of London and the Royal Albert Hall has been converted into a holding pen for civilian internees, and yet the really chilling thing is that for most people, *life goes on*. Deighton's book was a huge hit: the hardback alone sold more than 100,000 copies, while the paperback topped the bestseller lists two years later. But perhaps the most effective rewriting of the Second World War was the BBC series *An Englishman's Castle* (also 1978), a portrait of Britain three decades after its occupation by the Nazis. The Jews have been exterminated, the SS have been and gone; once again, though, life goes on. In a nice twist, the lead role is played by Kenneth More – most famous for his role as Douglas Bader in *Reach for the Sky* (1956), but now playing a willing collaborator. When the *Radio Times* asked how it felt to play a traitor, More shook his head. 'Oh no,' he said. 'You wait and see. It's easy to understand him if you're of my generation and have been through the war. I might have gone the same way so easily myself.'[10]

These were not merely escapist fantasies: with the headlines full of violence, the far right parading openly in the streets and the far left talking eagerly of the coming revolution, they offered an unsettling glimpse of what might be just around the corner. So when Sir Alec Guinness donned the dictator's uniform for *Hitler: The Last Ten Days* (1973), he drew an explicit parallel with current events, telling reporters that 'the situation in England strikes every month a decadent, yes *decadent* note. All these depressing things. People say, why not get someone else to sort it all out for them . . . a strong man.' Only a few years earlier, this would have sounded absurd; as the *Guardian*'s Martin Walker reflected, the British had long nurtured a myth of their 'divine right to stability and political level-headedness', convincing themselves that a 'disintegration of national morale could not happen here'. But the 'slow explosion of Ulster' was only one of the cracks in the national façade: thanks to 'the imminent economic crisis, the permissiveness of cultural life spilling over into the sordid lasciviousness of Soho, the new blunt power of the trade unions, inflation, the impotence of Government, there was a sense of the brink, of instability and of fearsome, frightening collapse'. Even

"Mon Dieu! THIS exercise must be a Colonels' Régime practising for a coup d'état against the Establishment!"

Outlandish as they now seem, rumours of a military coup were taken surprisingly seriously. Here the *Daily Express*'s cartoonist Michael Cummings fantasizes about the army using an exercise at Heathrow as a pretext to arrest Edward Heath, Harold Wilson and the miners' leader Joe Gormley (9 January 1974).

'the prime custodian of the national myth, *The Times* itself', was now 'musing on the likelihood of a military coup'.[11]

For some people, the prospect of a coup and an authoritarian government was long overdue. 'The country's sick of it,' insists the Home Secretary in Arthur Wise's extraordinary thriller *Who Killed Enoch Powell?* (1970). 'Sick of permissiveness, sick of teenage drug merchants, sick of youth-worship, sick of being "swinging". You know what it wants? It wants a strong man – the iron fist.' In Wise's book, Powell's assassination in a village hall is the trigger for rioting across the country and the rise of a military strongman, General Monkton, an old war hero summoned out of retirement to restore order. Monkton sees 'a country losing its shape and coherence, a country in desperate need of discipline'. Inheriting Powell's mantle, he whips up public support by targeting the 'foreign bodies' that have invaded England's green and pleasant land. Absurd as this might sound – although the Sheffield *Morning Telegraph* found it 'frightening' and thought 'all this could happen' – it was a popular theme in bestsellers of the early 1970s. In George Shipway's *The Chilian Club* (1971), a group of retired servicemen decide it is time to fight back against the 'wildcat strikers, agitators, anarchic students and such allied vermin' who have infected the body politic. Britain's enemies 'are fighting in our midst, protected by sympathizers and our own stupid laws', one old soldier says. 'They must be killed.' And so they are: one by one, our heroes knock off the dockers' leader, a Chinese-trained Black Power agitator, a left-wing bishop and a student revolutionary, giving conservative readers plenty to cheer. These unlikely national saviours 'were young when England ruled the world', another character remarks admiringly.

Their manhood saw her empire shredded, her glory tarnished; in old age they see their country become decadent and corrupt, governed by men at best incompetent and at worst stark traitors, riddled with the doctrines of an alien creed. They were soldiers once. Now, in their dotage, they have recognized an enemy whom nobody seems willing to fight. They have answered the call to arms, and oppose him as best they can.[12]

During the the first months of Wilson's new administration, analogies with the rise of Nazism seemed inescapable. In February 1974, James Lees-Milne's stockbroker friend Lord Roger Manners warned him that the City expected 'a complete economic collapse any day, when we shall be in the same condition as Germany in 1923. We must expect chaos, the £ to be worth 1 penny, if we are lucky, and the oil sheiks buying up our industries.' Lees-Milne wrote sardonically that this was a 'jolly prospect'; many people, of course, would have found it highly implausible. But as inflation continued to mount, the comparison began to seem rather less hysterical. Discussing the hyperinflation of the early 1920s, the economist David Laidler thought that 'we are close enough now that I think we ought to be feeling uncomfortable,' while Lord Robens, the former chairman of the National Coal Board, told *Newsweek* that Britain was 'almost at the stage of the Weimar Republic before Hitler. The political consequences of that are a dictatorship of right or left. I wouldn't care to say which.' In July, the veteran Conservative politician Lord Hailsham told the journalist Hugo Young that 'at this rate of inflation, democracy cannot survive'. Eventually, Hailsham thought, 'people will not put up with the law being broken and factions of the workers getting away with it with impunity. People will take control into their own hands, or a strong government will use the public forces to take control. People will get hurt. Quite likely there will be a lot of violence one way or another. But in the end there is a limit to what middle-class people will tolerate.'[13]

The fall of the Weimar Republic was not the only popular analogy in the turbulent years of the mid-1970s. On the left, many activists were frightened that Britain might go the way of Chile, with a weak government ousted by a right-wing military coup. In the autumn of 1973 there was much talk at the Labour party conference of solidarity with Chile, and the left-wing MP Eric Heffer insisted that 'we should introduce trade unions into the army to prevent a development of the Chilean situation here'. A few weeks later, with Heath in confrontation with the miners, the *Spectator*'s Patrick Cosgrave argued that 'we have gone measurably down the road' towards a Chilean-style military coup. Oddly, though, once Wilson returned to power, the Chilean analogy began to lose traction. Instead, observed Martin Walker, the fashionable parallel now was with France in the late 1950s, just before the crisis that brought Charles de Gaulle to power – 'France fighting a war in the "metropolitan homeland" of Algeria, France fighting desperately against the terror bombers and assassins of the OAS, France with inflation, with strikes, with impotent and quarrelsome parliaments and intelligentsia which campaigned against the war, against the torture it involved and the methods that it used – France, where a kind of democracy was saved by a kind of dictator'. What made the analogy so compelling was the running sore of Northern Ireland, which had forced 'the never-militarized British people to grow accustomed to its own aggressive soldiers patrolling familiar British streets, guarding familiar British chain stores, shooting at people like themselves'. The military occupation of Ulster was a 'cancer', Joe Haines told Bernard Donoughue after visiting the province in April 1974, calling it 'Britain's Algeria, brutalising the whole community'.[14]

Parallels between Algeria and Northern Ireland were particularly popular on the far left, where many people saw the British Army's operations, from internment without trial and the shooting of protesters to allegations of torture and rumours of collusion with loyalist paramilitaries, as the warm-up act for an inevitable intervention on the mainland. At this stage, few people had heard of Clockwork Orange, the army's secret disinformation campaign in Northern Ireland, which allegedly tried to smear a bizarrely wide range of politicians from Harold Wilson and Tony Benn to Edward Heath and Ian Paisley; yet on the left, many observers were already convinced that the army was preparing a right-wing coup. 'The British Army is being dangerously brainwashed,' wrote the Communist activist Jack Woddis, 'and acquiring the harsh outlook of a repressive, counter-revolutionary, anti-working class and anti-democratic institution which looks on those who are demanding democratic and national rights as the enemy.' And in David Edgar's state-of-the-nation play *Destiny* (1976), we meet Major Rolfe, a disaffected former officer who served in the last days of the Raj. Now, sick of the 'flaccid spongers' state', tired of England as 'Europe's whipping boy', Rolfe has moved to the far right, bankrolling the fascist group Nation Forward. In the play's final scene he hears that his son, a soldier serving in Belfast, has been shot by a sniper on the Lower Falls, a 'schoolkid' with a 'Russian rifle'. 'We are at war,' a weeping Rolfe tells the audience. 'Same war. In Belfast. Bradford. Bristol, Birmingham, the one we lost in Bombay thirty years ago, the one we're going to lose in Britain now. Unless you see in time.'[15]

At the time, military intervention on the mainland was not quite the outlandish prospect that it seems today. During the course of the 1970s, the army not only provided cover for dustmen, ambulance drivers and firemen but also intervened in industrial disputes on twelve separate occasions. For the conspiracy theorists, exhibit A was a book entitled *Low Intensity Operations: Subversion, Insurgency and Peacekeeping* (1971), written by Brigadier Frank Kitson during a sabbatical at Oxford. A well-read man who had masterminded counter-insurgency operations in Kenya, Malaya and Cyprus, Kitson thought that in future the British Army would need to deal with 'political and economic pressure, strikes, protest marches and propaganda'. Northern Ireland was an obvious example; but there were 'other potential trouble spots within the United Kingdom which might involve the Army in operations of a sort against political extremists who are prepared to resort to a considerable degree of violence to meet their ends'. Accordingly, Kitson wrote, they should prepare 'specialised individuals or units' to 'run ports, railway stations, power stations and sewage works as well as supervise the operations of mines and many types of industrial plants'. To the conspiracy theorists, the subtext was obvious: the army was preparing for a coup. Indeed, interviewing officers at the UK Land Forces headquarters in Wiltshire, one reporter heard plenty of dark mutterings about 'anarchy', 'subversive forces' and 'growing pressures'. Crucially, however, there was absolutely no sign that the officers genuinely fancied a crack at running the country. 'While you may think that we chaps at Wilton were just itching to go in and sort out the miners, that is the last thing we wanted to do,' one brigadier said. 'We know it would have provoked a general strike.'[16]

Rumours about a military coup reached their peak in the spring and summer of 1974, when the second miners' strike, collapse of the Conservative government and minority Wilson regime suggested to more excitable observers that parliamentary democracy was finished. 'If a minority British Socialist Government ever sought, by cunning, dupli-

city, corruption, terror and foreign arms, to turn this country into a
Communist State,' wrote the *Telegraph*'s Peregrine Worsthorne after
touring Pinochet's Chile as a guest of the regime, 'I hope and pray our
armed forces would intervene to prevent such a calamity as efficiently
as the armed forces did in Chile.' He was not alone: a few months later,
the former newspaper tycoon and full-time fantasist Cecil King told the
Foreign Office's Denis Greenhill that Britain was 'heading for a dictatorship, either of the Right or the Left, and much would turn on the
attitude of the Army'. Since the late 1960s, King had fancied himself as
the saviour of the nation. 'A sufficiently ruthless man, with all the
machine-guns and the power of the Government behind him, could
surely be decisive,' he added optimistically. Greenhill thought this was
ridiculous. 'Then you think a Communist takeover inevitable?' snapped
King, who thought his companion 'quite futile'. He did not, however,
give up. A year later, invited to address a dining club at the Army Staff
College, King told them that 'only the armed forces could save the country from chaos'. 'I had no doubt I was listening to a treasonable attempt
to suborn the loyalty of the Queen's officers,' wrote the military historian John Keegan, who was in the audience. But the result was not quite
what King had expected. For half an hour his listeners – 'the brightest
young officers in the Army' – bombarded him with questions 'which
began as hostile and grew increasingly derisive'. Taken aback, King
became 'defensive, then irritable and finally silent'. Eventually he
announced: 'I want to go home,' and went off to find his chauffeur. If
ever proof were needed that the British Army had no intention of
launching a coup, there it was.[17]

As inflation mounted in the summer of 1974, it was a rather older
character who stepped forward as Britain's Pinochet. At the age of 61,
General Sir Walter Walker seemed like a relic of the Raj. His grandfather had been decorated during the Indian Mutiny; his father rode
with the Assam Valley Light Horse and was a superb polo player. Sir
Walter himself had gone to boarding school in England, and even in
those days cut a hilariously forthright figure. To his disappointment, he
found his fellow boys a 'motley bunch of idle, unpatriotic, unkempt,
and "couldn't care less" type of youths', and decided to 'straighten them
out' by handing out 'a straight left to the nose or an uppercut to the
jaw'. His headmaster tried to explain 'the difference between leading
and driving'; whether Walker ever learned it, however, is very doubtful.
But he was undoubtedly a superb soldier, joining the 1/8 Gurkhas and

being mentioned in dispatches for his bravery on the North-West Frontier. In the Second World War he earned a DSO in Burma, and in Malaya and Borneo he won a reputation as Britain's leading jungle commander, ruthlessly crushing Communist guerrillas, stamping out unrest in Singapore and mobilizing English settlers into a civilian volunteer force. To his men, he was the ultimate 'soldier's general'; to the Gurkhas, he was nothing less than a hero.

Unfortunately, not everybody held this proud, single-minded man in such high regard. In Whitehall, Walker was seen as a loose cannon, and although he was recommended for a knighthood after Borneo, he had to wait another five years. By the time he had been promoted to Commander-in-Chief Allied Forces Northern Europe, he was convinced that the 'ungrateful army hierarchy' had stabbed him in the back. Horrified by the social and cultural changes that were transforming British life, he had a particular horror of homosexuals, who 'use the main sewer of the human body as a playground'.* And he was appalled by what he saw as the spinelessness of the Continent's politicians. When he was interviewed for a Tyne Tees documentary called *A Day in the Life of a General*, his superiors were so shocked by his remarks about Europe's lack of military spirit that they had the film banned on security grounds. So by the time he retired in February 1972, he was sick of the lot of them: the 'ceasefire soldiers', the 'sanctimonious creeps', the 'old men of Vichy', the 'fat cats of the Establishment'. A few months later, asked how he would deal with Northern Ireland, Sir Walter did not mince his words. 'I have engaged in campaigns against blacks, yellows and slant-eyes,' he said. 'Why should we have one rule for the whites and one for coloureds? We have to decide if Northern Ireland is part of Britain or not – and, if so, to act accordingly. We should cut off their petrol, gas, electricity and stop food going in, soften them up and then go in. Give warning so that they can get their women and children away before we go in, but go in.'[18]

During the next two years, General Walker became a star turn at meetings of right-wing groups like the Monday Club and the World Anti-Communist League, for whom the collapse of the West was never more than a few months away. One of these groups, well under the radar of much of the press, was Unison, set up in 1973 by George Kennedy Young, former deputy director of MI6, chairman of the liber-

---

* Deviancy of any kind was not to Sir Walter's taste; under 'recreations' in *Who's Who*, he wrote simply: 'normal'.

tarian Council for Individual Freedom and leading member of the Monday Club. But Unison was slightly different from other cranky far-right organizations. Rather than being a pressure group, it was supposed to be a domestic equivalent of the Special Operations Executive, responsible for spying and sabotage behind enemy lines during the Second World War. Unison was a 'formidable vigilante group to help protect the nation against a Communist takeover', Young told the *Express*'s security correspondent Chapman Pincher in February 1974. In a crisis, it would intervene to 'preserve the law and the Constitution if the Government of the day fails to rise to a major threat of civil conflict'. Rather more disturbingly, he claimed to have been 'taking note of disloyal groups and subversive elements'. But precisely how all this would happen was never clear. Young claimed to have the support of 'former Service chiefs' and 'leading business men', and insisted that he had 'contact arrangements' with the Home Office, the police, local authorities and various MPs. But these probably existed more in his own mind than in reality.[19]

Ludicrous as it might sound, not everybody dismissed Unison as a joke. By July 1974, even *The Times* was reporting that 'retired senior army officers and their business associates' were recruiting volunteers in case of 'a breakdown of law and order'. 'We have men in all parts of England,' declared Major Alexander Greenwood, founder of the group Red Alert. 'The great majority are members of the professional classes who are desperately concerned about the way things are going.' But the name that leaped out of *The Times*'s story was that of General Sir Walter Walker. Unison, he explained, was 'entirely non-militant'; it would step in 'only if there was a collapse of law and order'. In a letter to the *Daily Telegraph* that same month, though, he was rather more explicit. 'The Communist Trojan horse is in our midst,' he claimed, 'with its fellow-travellers wriggling their maggoty way inside its belly.' What Britain needed, therefore, was 'dynamic, invigorating, uplifting leadership. A true leader who inspires trust and confidence, who puts love of country before all else ... who puts country before career; the national interest before party politics; who has the moral courage to expose and root out those who try to rot us from within and hold us to ransom by anarchy, blackmail and brute force.' And what better candidate than the hero of Borneo?

As soon as Walker's letter was published, replies flooded in. Many of them enclosed donations; among his correspondents, he recalled, were doctors, lawyers, estate agents and small businessmen, as well as

'Admiral of the Fleet Sir Varyl Begg, Marshal of the Royal Air Force Sir John Slessor, a number of British generals, ex-MPs, the popular Goon comedian Michael Bentine and the shipping magnate Lord Cayzer.'* In reply, Walker sent a form letter denouncing the 'small minority of hard-core militants' in the unions, whom he called 'lackeys of their Russian masters'. More than one in ten union officials, he explained, were 'Communists or far-left revolutionary Marxists'. Unless they were stopped, 'Russia would achieve her aim without having to fire a shot'. The answer lay in his group Civil Assistance, a spin-off from Unison, which would step in to assist the authorities when the crisis came. 'The silent majority has decided at last to stand up and be counted,' Walker declared on 9 August, adding that 'the crunch could well occur this winter'. In a front-page interview with the London *Evening News*, he nodded when asked whether 'the Army might take over Britain, as the Army has taken over so many South American republics'. 'Perhaps', he said, 'the country might choose rule by the gun in preference to anarchy.' Would he accept office himself, as a kind of British de Gaulle? 'I shall be sixty-two in November,' Walker said, 'but I hope to have some years of activity ahead . . . I think it is the duty of all of us who care about Britain [to] try to waken the country from this awful sleeping sickness.'[20]

To some people, this reincarnation of P. G. Wodehouse's Roderick Spode was the hero for whom they had long waited. At a time when Britain was 'in deadly danger from various forms of subversion', here was a 'new Churchill', insisted Paul Daniels, chairman of the British Military Volunteer Force, a tiny group of ex-servicemen who had sent volunteers to the Congo and the Yemen. Daniels was not, perhaps, the ideal salesman for Walker's brand: the manager of a small chemicals firm, he was vague about the nature of Britain's economic problems, but 'thought pornography had something to do with it'. In truth, though, Walker himself had now crossed the thin line between reactionary extremism and outright absurdity. By the middle of August, he was boasting to the press that Civil Assistance had 100,000 volunteers and 40 'local controllers', who were urged to 'compile a register of trustworthy citizens whose unswerving allegiance and loyalty is to the Crown and who have a high respect for law and order'. They should reject applicants with 'character defects' or a history of alcoholism and

---

* Precisely what role Bentine would have played in the new regime (Minister for Fun?) is not clear. In fairness, though, he was keenly interested in military matters; later, he was even credited with having influenced the foundation of the SAS counter-terrorism unit.

drug use which 'might leave them open to blackmail', he added, while members must not carry 'any form of weapon, uniform, headgear or armband'. And as the days went by, Sir Walter's proclamations became ever more grandiose. Interviewed on radio's *The World at One* on 27 August, he predicted that membership would reach 'three million within a month', with a Civil Assistance controller in 'every hamlet, village and town'. Sadly, this forecast proved a little over-optimistic: two months later, he told the press that membership was only 'half a million'. But General Walker remained defiantly optimistic. Since each member had been asked to recruit 'another 30 members', he insisted, 'the total membership could become something in the order of 13,500,000'.[21]

For all his extravagant claims, Walker was not the only candidate to become Britain's military strongman. Since May 1974, the Scottish laird, war hero and founder of the SAS, Colonel David Stirling, had been sounding out friends and comrades about a new organization he called GB75. In August, at the height of the fuss about Sir Walter Walker, his proposals were leaked to the pacifist newspaper *Peace News* and then reprinted in the *Guardian*, where they were presented as a blueprint for a private army. Given Stirling's background in the SAS, as well as his links to mercenary groups in Africa and the Middle East, this was hardly surprising. Yet Stirling insisted that GB75 was merely a group of 'apprehensive patriots' who were training 'to keep public utilities such as power stations running during anything like a general strike'. None of his members, he claimed, had military connections, since 'anything that smells of the military is wrong in this sort of context'. In fact, most of the funding for GB75 came from a millionaire arms dealer, Geoffrey Edwards, while many of Stirling's early recruits were old SAS comrades. Similarly, although Stirling insisted that his movement was 'apolitical' and tried to distance himself from Civil Assistance (which he called '*very* Right-wing' and 'neo-fascist'), the leaked GB75 documents dripped with loathing for 'Wedgwood Benn', whom they accused of planning to wreck 'the private enterprise system'. And, as *The Times* pointed out, when Stirling talked of volunteers intervening in a general strike, 'it is clear that he is not thinking of undergraduates cheerfully driving trains without conflict'. 'If there is a sit-in,' he wrote at one point, 'we might be obliged to round them up.'[22]

The obvious difference between Stirling and Walker, though, was that while Sir Walter loved the limelight, Stirling hated it. As soon as news of GB75 reached the press, he announced that he would make way for a new director with no military background. And with the police, the Ministry of Defence and the Conservative Party hastily ruling out any collaboration with Stirling's organization, GB75 rapidly disintegrated. By the following April, even Stirling had conceded defeat, announcing that he would pour his energies instead into an anti-Communist lobby group within the trade unions, which proved an even damper squib than GB75. On the surface, all of this meant that Sir Walter Walker stood unchallenged as Britain's General Pinochet. Disappointingly for those hoping to see a military dictatorship, however, Walker's cause was flagging. After Harold Wilson's re-election in October, Civil Assistance went very quiet. By January 1975, even the British Military Volunteer Force had jumped ship. 'General Walker was too right-wing,' his erstwhile admirer Paul Daniels said sadly. Undeterred, Walker gave a public lecture to an eclectic gathering of old soldiers and financial executives at St Lawrence Jewry a month later, and issued another call to arms at a City lunch in March. But he was wasting his time. For all their loathing of the Wilson regime and their disquiet at the tax burden, the rise of inflation and the prominence of Tony Benn, the idea of General Walker mounting a military coup would have struck most City figures as simply laughable.[23]

By the middle of 1975 Walker had almost vanished from sight. And by the time his organization opened merger talks with the National Association for Freedom a year later, it claimed not 13.5 million members but barely 15,000 – and that was probably a very generous estimate. The would-be national saviour had become a national joke. Even the sitcom *The Fall and Rise of Reginald Perrin*, first broadcast in 1976, had great fun with Geoffrey Palmer's character Jimmy Adamson, a former serviceman who keeps a cache of rifles in his bedsit in case the 'balloon goes up':

REGGIE: So, come on, Jimmy, who are you going to fight when this balloon of yours goes up?

JIMMY: Forces of anarchy: wreckers of law and order. Communists, Maoists, Trotskyists, neo-Trotskyists, crypto-Trotskyists, union leaders, Communist union leaders, atheists, agnostics, long-haired weirdos, short-haired weirdos, vandals, hooligans, football supporters, namby-pamby probation officers, rapists, papists, papist rapists, foreign surgeons, head-shrinkers (who ought to be locked up), Wedgwood Benn, keg bitter, punk rock, glue-sniffers, *Play For Today*, squatters, Clive Jenkins, Roy Jenkins, Up Jenkins, up everybody's, Chinese restaurants – why do you think Windsor Castle is ringed with Chinese restaurants?

REGGIE: Is that all? I see. You realise the sort of people you're going to attract, don't you, Jimmy? Thugs, bully-boys, psychopaths, sacked policemen, security guards, sacked security guards, racialists, Paki-bashers, queer-bashers, Chink-bashers, basher-bashers, anybody-bashers, Rear Admirals, queer Admirals, Vice-Admirals, fascists, neo-fascists, crypto-fascists, loyalists, neo-loyalists, crypto-loyalists.

JIMMY: Do you really think so? I thought support might be difficult.[24]

Yet despite the utter failure of Civil Assistance, and despite the total indifference of the vast majority of the population, rumours of coups never entirely disappeared. When the army released a new advertisement in January 1975, asking readers if they were 'prepared to fight if necessary to prevent people taking control of this country by force or other unconstitutional means', the Labour left-winger Frank Allaun jumped to the conclusion that they were preparing for a putsch. Tony Benn, too, could never banish the suspicion that he was about to be carted off to an internment camp. When Benn visited the National Defence College to give a lecture in 1978, the commander, Major-General Bate, suggested that he read Frank Kitson's book to get a sense of modern military thinking. To Benn, that merely proved that 'they are really training up people for a military situation in Great Britain, no doubt drawing heavily on the experience of Northern Ireland'. General Bate even told his guest that he had heard rumours of a movement called 'PFP – Prince Philip for President' backed by the Paras and the army in Northern Ireland. This was pure fantasy, of course, but Benn believed it. Even Harold Wilson succumbed to coup hysteria in February 1976, when the headlines were full of British mercenaries being executed in Angola. 'He was completely taken up with the question of Angolan mercenaries,' wrote Bernard Donoughue. 'He is genuinely petrified of a right-wing coup in Britain using ex-servicemen as the shock troops ... Since there are few troops based in the UK they could, he believes, carry out a coup d'état.' Wilson even held a meeting in the Cabinet Room to discuss changing the law; but, Donoughue recorded, 'I did not bother to go. It all seems to me like *Boy's Own* comic stuff and I don't see the point of wasting time on it.'[25]

In May 1974, a week before the beginning of the UWC strike, Howard Brenton's new play opened at the Nottingham Playhouse. Set in the mid-1980s, *The Churchill Play* takes place in 'the twenty-eighth internment camp in the British Isles', where the inmates are putting on a play for a group of visiting MPs. The United Kingdom, it emerges, is now governed by a Conservative–Labour coalition, who have taken authoritarian powers under the Special Powers Act of 1977 and the Emergency Provisions and Industrial Relations Acts of 1981. We discover that for ten years the country has been 'sliding down' towards anarchy and fascism, while the guards' conversation makes it clear that the army lurched to the right after its experience in Northern Ireland. 'Ten years o' yer own streets, yer own kith an' kin,' explains the gruff sergeant:

> Ten years the ordinary soldier has scrubbed your bedpan. That you may not smell the terrorist in the street. Soldier Tom doorway to doorway, bullet in the jugular, bullet in the crotch. Ten years down Ulster then English streets. Then the late seventies and the laws against industrial unrest. Soldier boy at the picket line, working men 'is own kind comin' at 'im yellin' Scab Scab. (*Scoffs.*) I went down a mine, a corporal then, in the strike o' nineteen eighty. The miners o' that pit tried t'kill us, y'know that? Only time I've ever been in Wales. Women spit very 'ard. At Corporals anyway. (*Formal again.*) The British Army's got politicized, y'see, Sir. You should be very glad we've not gone red.

The camp itself, with its low huts and barbed wire, is based on an Ulster precedent: the notorious camp at Long Kesh, later rebuilt as the Maze. But the internees are not terrorists: they are journalists, trade unionists, dissidents, used as guinea pigs for Ministry of Defence torture techniques, from the 'sensory withdrawal' of imprisonment in a white-painted room to the implantation of 'electrode controls'. The sergeant, however, prefers the old-fashioned approach. 'What do you do with a slobbering, rabid dog?' he asks. 'Don't let it go round infecting us all, do you Sir? Y' take it out and shoot it, don't you Sir? Like we did in Ireland.'[26]

Watching Brenton's bleak depiction of 1984, all bullets and barbed wire, some theatregoers must have wished they had gone to see Michael York and Oliver Reed in *The Three Musketeers* instead. For all his radicalism, Brenton's vision was hardly unusual, and although predictions of the future often tend to be pretty depressing, the mid-1970s undoubtedly marked something of a low point. As one critic notes, the same themes – 'industrial confrontation, class warfare, terrorism, regional tensions, conflict between the races and genders' – appeared again and again, with writers queuing up to depict 'a society on the verge of disintegration, or even civil war'. In Doris Lessing's *Memoirs of a Survivor* (1974), we are in 'a decaying and threatened city some time in the near future, public services cut off, air poisoned, looted buildings standing empty', while in Anthony Burgess's novella *1985* (1978), Britain is rebranded as 'Tucland', where the trade unions are all-powerful, pay demands are automatically granted and dissenters are 're-educated' at Soviet-style psychiatric hospitals. 'The time's coming, and it won't be long,' one union official says, 'when every strike will be a general strike. When a toothbrush maker can withdraw his labour in a just demand for a living wage and do so in the confidence that the lights will go off and people will shiver and the trains won't be running and the schools will close.' There is no sense of redemption: as the writer Philip Hensher later remarked, 'these novels peer ahead, compellingly but uncertainly, into the gloom, without seeing any resolution or salvation.'[27]

Televised depictions of the future, meanwhile, were almost unremittingly depressing. In the BBC series *Survivors* (1975–7), all but a handful of the world's population are wiped out by a terrible pandemic. Without food, electricity, order or civilization, the survivors are reduced to trudging across the countryside in their parkas, eventually forming a primitive commune in an abandoned farmhouse. Tellingly, though, one of their greatest adversaries turns out to be a former union general secretary, whose talk of socialism is merely a front for his own power-hungry, authoritarian instincts. The show's creator, Terry Nation, then produced an even grimmer vision of the future in *Blake's 7* (1978–81), later remembered for its extravagant costumes, cardboard sets and gloriously histrionic performances. Beneath the gaudy veneer, however, the premise is pure Orwell. As in *Star Wars*, the galaxy is run by a fascistic military regime, the Federation, which maintains order by brainwashing and pacifying the masses with drugged food, water and air. When Blake (Gareth Thomas) dares to resist, his mind is systematically wiped; later, when he sees dissidents being massacred and his memories return, the authorities frame him for (of all things!) child abuse. Escaping from a prison ship, Blake leads a tiny band of convicts in rebellion against the Federation; in stark contrast to *Star Wars*, however, it all ends in tears when he turns traitor, betraying his friends to the Federation. In the series' unforgettable last scene, the rebels are gunned down one by one, a thoroughly downbeat conclusion for a show that had spanned some of the gloomiest years in modern British history. But the really depressing thing about *Blake's 7*, remarked the *Daily Mail*'s Shaun Usher, was that it showed 'the future as being much the same as the present, Lord help us – only worse'.[28]

The most compelling small-screen vision of the future was Wilfred Greatorex's BBC show *1990*, which ran for two series in 1977 and 1978 and was in many ways a kind of science-fiction equivalent of an editorial in the *Daily Express*. 'It was all infinitely shabbier than they had prophesied,' reflects Edward Woodward's character, the dissident reporter Jim Kyle, in the tie-in novel. 'God was in his heaven, the State controlled and "necessity" was the in-word in 1990. After the twenty-five years during which the pound had sunk too low to be salvaged even by international blackmail, it had finally become necessary to waive freedom.' In this vision of the near future, a bankrupt Britain, having banned emigration and suspended habeas corpus, is governed under a permanent state of emergency by a coalition of politicians and trade unionists. 'I live in a country where, if you don't hold a union card, you starve: where jobs, food and housing are rationed,' says one dissident. By law, trade unionists sit on every company board, and union representatives make up just under half of Britain's MPs. Eton has become a comprehensive school for politicians' children, the *Daily Mail* has been closed down and its headquarters demolished, and the words 'social contract' have become a mild obscenity ('Where the social contract are you?' mutters one character). While ordinary Londoners queue for their meat rations, most West End stores have been boarded up. Only Bond Street still thrives, a Mecca for 'the new elite of bureaucrats and trade union officials'.[29]

As the BBC admitted, *1990* was not really about 1990 at all. It was a 'disturbing vision of what life might be like for all of us here in Britain in thirteen years' time: a bureaucracy run riot, top heavy with administrators, all controlling our every step', explained an article in the *Radio Times*, sounding rather like a passage from the Conservative manifesto. The series was 'going to create a furore', predicted Edward Woodward (wrongly, as it turned out). 'In political terms, it says quite daring things about our system, our form of government, our way of life.' Since Woodward loathed the 'vast, glutinous, jelloid attitude whereby individualism has become a dirty word', he was instinctively sympathetic to Greatorex's vision. Occasionally the script struck him as far-fetched. But then, he said, 'I would pick up a newspaper and read some ordinary item of day-to-day life – and there it all was already. Red tape, the VAT man, forms, identification. It's much more frightening than *1984* because it's closer to us than Orwell's book was to his own generation. It's really just around the corner.'[30]

By far the most elaborate portrait of what lay ahead, though, came in

Robert Moss's book *The Collapse of Democracy* (1975). Once again Britain is effectively run by the TUC ('known as the Upper House') in alliance with the Communist Party, who have taken power after a general strike. The Royal Family have fled to New Zealand, Buckingham Palace is now the Ministry of Equality and Scotland has become independent. In Moss's scenario, government inspectors roam the land confiscating 'paintings, furniture, jewellery and other "anti-egalitarian" possessions'; the streets are patrolled by Volunteer Constables, drawn from the 'factory militias' who prevailed in the general strike; and there are plans for an electrified fence along Hadrian's Wall to prevent emigration from the rump republic. The exchange rate has been frozen at £48 to the dollar, while British citizens found with foreign currency face ten years behind bars. Government ministers boast that 'inflation was used to destroy the middle class', rationing remains in force, and a gin and tonic costs £250. Moss's fantasy (supposedly a 'Letter from London') ends with a few lines on schools, where the day begins with an hour of 'social education' and history lessons are 'all about peasant revolts, trade union martyrs and Marx's travails in the British Museum'. 'Mind you, I suppose it was getting like that when you left ten years ago,' muses the anonymous writer. 'Weren't they studying Marx and Mao Tse-tung, along with abortion and the pill, in religious education classes?'[31]

Just as many left-wing writers genuinely believed that parliamentary democracy would soon fall victim to a military coup, so Moss was convinced that Britain was terrifyingly close to Marxist dictatorship. An Australian-born academic who had become a special correspondent for *The Economist*, occasionally wrote speeches for Margaret Thatcher and was obsessed with international terrorism, Moss thought Britain was 'steaming at full speed' towards 'egalitarian socialism' under 'a crew who, having squandered their fuel, have begun throwing the ship's timbers and the lifeboats into the furnaces'. This, of course, was precisely what most Conservatives thought; the difference was that, for Moss, Harold Wilson and his colleagues were not merely misguided but positively malignant. Even after Wilson had given way to the much more conservative Jim Callaghan, Moss remained convinced that the most powerful man in the country was really union leader Jack Jones. The Labour Party, he thought, could no longer distinguish 'between social democracy and totalitarian Communism'. 'Britain has travelled more than two-thirds of the way toward becoming a fully communist society,' he wrote sadly. 'It is increasingly probable that it will either complete the journey or have to endure the most shattering social and constitutional crisis the country has known since the 17th century'.[32]

Strident as all this might sound, Moss was not the only commentator who thought full-blown state socialism was at hand. In February 1975 the former Labour minister Alan Chalfont, who had once worked for Wilson but had since shot off to the right, treated the House of Lords to a fifty-minute lecture on 'subversive and extremist elements in our society', claiming that both the TGWU and the AUEW had been penetrated by 'Communists or Communist sympathizers'. Chalfont even found room for the Workers' Revolutionary Party pin-up Vanessa Redgrave – who, for her part, thought that 'the Government were preparing concentration camps in Britain and that the Army was being prepared to repress the workers in Great Britain as it had done in Northern Ireland'. And although Chalfont disavowed any 'emotional or alarmist spirit', many of his old colleagues were horrified when he later presented an ITV documentary, *Who Says It Could Never Happen Here?*, claiming that 'the Communist Manifesto was being implemented bit by bit in Britain'. Brandishing a clipboard in front of Karl Marx's grave, Chalfont solemnly explained that Marx had listed ten conditions for the triumph of Communism – and that in Harold Wilson's Britain, seven of them had already been met. 'It was frightening,' thought Tony Benn. Watching the parade of contributors – the anti-Communist electricians' leader Frank Chapple, the former Labour MPs Reg Prentice and Woodrow Wyatt, the Tory frontbencher Lord Hailsham – Benn decided he was 'looking at the faces of the Junta'.[33]

At one level, all this was totally absurd. Far from being two-thirds of the way to Marxist despotism, Harold Wilson's Britain remained one of the most important members of the Western alliance and a pillar of the capitalist world. Yet to anyone horrified by the collapse of the Heath government and the bloodshed in Northern Ireland, Chalfont's case was not as obviously ludicrous as it now appears. Barely a week went by without the *Express* or the *Mail* lamenting the looming triumph of Communism, while in the summer of 1975 the *Telegraph* ran a long feature on the 'creeping, insidious, cancer-like growth' of Marxist ideas, promoted through the 'treachery, deceit and violence of a small minority'. Even Stephen Haseler, who co-founded the Social Democratic Alliance in 1975 to fight for centrist principles inside the Labour Party, predicted 'the emergence of untrammelled trade union power in a state within the Parliamentary state'. First, he thought, would come a 'desperate economic crisis' forcing Britain to turn to the International Monetary Fund – as indeed happened a year later. Then would follow 'an industrial and political struggle' between the government and the unions, ending with 'capitulation to the TUC'. The settlement, he suggested, would probably involve import controls, a siege economy, the nationalization of the banks and insurance companies, 'limitations on the freedom of the media' and 'eventual British withdrawal from NATO', all under the guise of another Social Contract. 'Everything would look relatively normal,' Haseler predicted, but the reality would be 'a new Marxist revolutionary order for Britain'.[34]

What is really striking about all these forecasts, of course, is not just how pessimistic they were, but how far they fell short of reality. Occasionally the crystal ball offered tantalizing glimpses of Britain under Margaret Thatcher. In July 1976, for instance, BBC2's *The Money Programme* presented two possible versions of the 1980s, one of which, the 'do-it-yourself society', imagined an ultra-Thatcherite Britain in which public spending has been slashed to the bone, there is no money for rubbish collection or road maintenance, automation has thrown 2 million people out of work, there has been 'a gradual erosion in the power of the trade union movement', and the struggle to survive is 'making capitalists of us all'. Ironically, though, few contemporary observers seem to have found it very convincing. In the same year, Haseler praised Mrs Thatcher and Sir Keith Joseph as 'the latter-day saints of a classical age, who keep reminding us ... that certain eternal liberal values are still worth fighting for'. 'Even so,' he added, 'a classical liberal future for Britain is improbable. Even the most optimistic of the ultra-liberals realise that they are essentially engaged in a rearguard action against increasing state control of economic life.' As a proportion of GDP, he pointed out, public spending had risen from 45 per cent to 58 per cent in just ten years. 'To roll back this process to anything approaching a proper market economy would be a daunting prospect which could involve the nation in considerable social upheaval' – and for that reason, it was never going to happen.[35]

Throughout all the predictions of coups and counter-coups, revolutions and disasters, there often ran a thick but perversely entertaining streak of paranoia. The poet Philip Larkin, the Humberside Eeyore, believed that there would 'never be another Conservative government' but 'a series of Labour governments that will bankrupt the country so that we are all starving, at which point the Ruskies will step in', while his friend Kingsley Amis, fast becoming a reactionary caricature, half-seriously declared that October 1974 would mark Britain's 'last free election'. Two years later, Amis published an alternative history of a totalitarian modern Britain untouched by the Reformation, *The Alteration*, in which a thinly veiled Harold Wilson has become Pope while the Inquisition is represented in Britain by its dreaded officials Foot, Redgrave and Lord Stansgate. Entertaining as the novel is, however, Amis was not even half-joking. In April 1976 he invited the left-wing Kenneth Tynan and his wife for dinner. 'Over liqueurs, Kingsley calmly says that I am a lover of tyranny and that I propose to turn England into a vast prison,' Tynan recorded in disbelief. When Tynan weakly protested, Amis insisted that his guest and his 'fellow Lefties' were planning 'the establishment of a police state in which he will be executed, probably after a spell on the Gulag Archipelago. What's more, he says, I would unhesitatingly connive at his execution; might, indeed, be garnering evidence against him at this moment.' Accusing one's guest of being a Communist informer was, by any standards, unusual dinner-party banter. It was certainly too much for Tynan, who found it 'chilling to have an otherwise intelligent man uttering opinions like these'. 'At this point I quietly leave the party,' he recorded, 'since there is no way of accepting hospitality from someone who is sincerely convinced that one is involved in a conscious plot to destroy him!'[36]

And yet of course neither Amis nor Tynan was really representative of the great mass of the British people in the mid-1970s. Most people, after all, were not particularly interested in politics. The vast majority merely got on with their lives, some cheerful, some grumbling, none of them delighted with the state of the nation, but many of them largely indifferent to the major events of the day. After all, by far the most popular vision of the future (despite being set 'a long time ago') was *Star Wars*, which had little immediate political resonance. And while *Survivors* and *1990* were successful enough, most people preferred small-screen escapism such as *The Generation Game*, *George and Mildred* and *Robin's Nest*. Even the most celebrated politician of the age, who had little time for either high culture or populist entertainment, was unimpressed by Amis's predictions of looming disaster. Invited to a Downing Street party in 1980, at a time when a change in government seemed to have done little to restore Britain's fortunes, Kingsley Amis took along a copy of his new book. Another gloomy exercise in science fiction imagining a future Britain brutally cut off from its language, culture and traditions, *Russian Hide-and-Seek* had been published that very day, and at the party he presented it to the new Prime Minister. 'What's it about?' she asked. 'Well, in a way it's about a future Britain under Russian occupation,' Amis proudly replied. 'Huh,' said Margaret Thatcher. 'Can't you do better than that? Get yourself another crystal ball.'[37]

7

The Election that Never Was

FLETCHER: *Cheer up, could be worse. State this country's in,
you could be free. Stuck outside, with no work and a
crumbling economy. How horrible that'd be!*
Porridge, 'New Faces, Old Hands', 5 September 1974

*This is an hour of the greatest importance to our country. Our
futures depend on it.*
Alistair Burnet, *BBC Election 1974*, 10 October 1974

Saturday, 5 October 1974, was a big night for Paul Craig and Carol
Burns. By coincidence, their birthdays fell on the same day, and Paul,
who was due to turn 22, thought it would be nice to have a little party.
Only a few weeks earlier, Carol, three years his junior, had been accepted
into the Women's Royal Army Corps, so they had something special to
celebrate. She chose the venue, a pub not far from her barracks, recommended by some of her new WRAC friends who used to meet their
boyfriends there on Saturday nights. Meanwhile, Paul had a surprise up
his sleeve. Unbeknown to Carol, he had invited her parents down from
Boreham Wood for the evening, and, when she left headquarters, all
three of them were waiting outside to greet her. They walked on to the
pub, the Horse and Groom in Guildford, which was already filling up.
The atmosphere was noisy, happy: many of the drinkers were soldiers
and their girlfriends, enjoying a night out. The Burns family found a
table in an alcove by the jukebox. Carol disappeared to the toilet for a
minute or two; when she came back, Paul had moved up and taken her
seat, so she slipped in beside him. It was almost nine o'clock. Then,
quite suddenly, there was a gigantic bang and everything went black.

The next thing Carol knew, she was lying on the ground, her ears full of 'buzzing', her mouth full of smoke and dust. 'Someone was lying on the floor beside me,' she said later. It was Paul.

Paul Craig was one of five people killed in the Guildford pub bombings, victims of a six-pound explosive planted in the alcove by the Provisional IRA. Had he not shifted places when Carol went to the toilet, she would probably have been killed instead. As it was, she and her parents were seriously injured: her father was so badly hurt that it took him five weeks to recover consciousness. In total sixty-eight people were badly injured, while two other WRAC girls – Ann Hamilton, 18, from Crewe, and Carolyn Slater, just 17, from Cannock – lost their lives, as did two young Scots Guards, 18-year-old William Forsyth and 17-year-old James Hunter, lifelong friends from the same Renfrewshire street, who had joined up together only a month before. 'They were just wee lads,' a neighbour said the next day. 'Why should they be killed? It's madness, absolute madness.' 'I hope the people who did this don't rest in their beds,' agreed Carolyn Slater's mother Delphine, who had been looking forward to her daughter's first leave in a few weeks. 'To kill innocent people in cold blood is terrible. They are mad.'[1]

Around the country, the Guildford bombings produced a wave of shock and outrage. 'I loathe and detest the miserable bastards . . . savage murderous thugs,' wrote Lord Arran in the *Evening Standard*. 'May the Irish, all of them, rot in hell.' But in the long run the horrific attack was probably best remembered for the miscarriage of justice that followed. Under pressure to find the culprits, the police charged three innocent young Irishmen and one English woman, who remained in prison for fifteen years until their sentences were overturned. In fact, the real culprits were almost certainly the so-called Balcombe Street gang, Eddie Butler, Harry Duggan, Joe O'Connell and Brendan Dowd, whose bombing campaign in central London dominated the headlines a year later. On trial in February 1977, Joe O'Connell told the Old Bailey that 'four totally innocent people' were in prison for bombings he had carried out, but the authorities refused to listen. Yet while the Balcombe Street gang were quite happy to admit responsibility for their actions, they felt no remorse. In court, O'Connell insisted that he would admit to 'no crimes and to no guilt, for the real crimes and the real guilt are those of British imperialism committed against our people'. Another O'Connell, the Provo leader David, made the message clear in a statement in November 1974 after his comrades had bombed a pub in Woolwich, killing an off-duty soldier and a sales clerk. 'Responsibility rests squarely

and clearly with the British government,' he told the television programme *Weekend World*. 'The British government have simply to say we
are not going to stay in Ireland.' In the meantime, the carnage went on.[2]

Coming just five days before the British people went to the polls, Guildford cast a dark shadow over what had been the dullest, gloomiest
election campaign in living memory. With no absolute majority in Parliament, it was always inevitable that Wilson would call another election.
Yet when he fired the starting gun in the middle of September, even the
most partisan activists struggled to muster much enthusiasm for a second
contest in just seven months. Announcing his decision on television, Wilson claimed it was time for a Labour majority 'to make government and
Parliament work'. There was no question of a coalition, he added, warning that it would lead to 'fuzzy compromises' when the country needed
'clear decisions'. But in East Anglia, where he had been watching Ipswich
Town in the UEFA Cup, Edward Heath struck a very different note. The
country faced such a crisis, he said, that the goal must be 'national
unity': should he win the election, he would 'immediately consult with
the leaders of the other parties' to find common ground. Neither man
sounded very inspiring, and optimism was in short supply. No election
since the war had 'been held in such a mood of public uncertainty and
depression', said *The Times*. 'The probable outlook for the next Parliament is of depression with continued inflation in the short term, and
accelerated inflation in the medium term, and both the depression and
the inflation will be worse than anything in post-war British experience.' Indeed, it added with cool prescience, 'this could well be an
election which will damage or even destroy the party which wins it.'[3]

As the campaign began, there was good news for Wilson in the polls,
which predicted a Labour lead of about 8 per cent and a clear Commons majority. Behind the scenes, though, all was confusion. Even on
the day of the election announcement, Marcia Williams had made the
Prime Minister rewrite his television address because she thought it was
full of clichés. 'He was not good, no style, just flat and all the predictable
phrases,' wrote Bernard Donoughue, who had struggled all day 'to
make something out of his rambling prose'. Almost unbelievably, the
first meeting of Wilson's election team had been 'shuffled from room to
room' on Marcia's orders, in an attempt to stop Donoughue and Haines
getting in. 'Absolutely ridiculous,' the former wrote wearily. 'It is a
pantomime farce, but too petty to be funny.' As the evening wore on,
Wilson began 'drinking brandy heavily', even though he was scheduled

to go on television later, and finally had a blazing row with Marcia in front of his other aides. Two days later, after another terrible argument with Marcia, Donoughue found the Prime Minister knocking back 'stiff brandies', 'sweating and looking very upset'. But Wilson was nothing if not a survivor, and over the first weekend his spirits recovered. When they drafted a long speech on Sunday evening, Donoughue thought he was 'on splendid form, though drinking too much ... We had a very jolly evening. He said to me that he "hated all elections" but was relieved now that this was under way.'[4]

Exactly ten years earlier, Harold Wilson had led Labour into a general election as the apostle of dynamic change, the incarnation of economic modernization and technological revolution. In October 1974, however, his message boiled down to three words: a quiet life. In this, his fifth campaign, he seemed a calm, reassuring, unflappable figure, 'as familiar as an old slipper'. In his speeches and in party propaganda, he empha-sized his 'winning team', making a virtue of the lack of new blood in his Cabinet, while newspaper advertisements boasted that Labour had put an end to the strikes that had blighted Heath's final months. Almost every time he spoke, he invoked the Social Contract as the guarantee of national peace; as the Nuffield study of the election remarks, it became Labour shorthand for 'social justice, conciliation and co-operation', as opposed to Heath's impatient and confrontational style. As Wilson reminded his listeners, his predecessor had been 'at war with millions of our people'. But then:

> On our first day, the Tuesday, I appointed the Cabinet. We met the TUC at once. Our first priority was to end the miners' strike. We did that on the Wednesday. We ended the state of emergency. The lights went on again. We brought the heating back. We did what we said we would ... On our fourth day in office, we imposed a total freeze on the rents of council houses ... In that same week in office – we were three days old – we agreed the terms of the most progressive and radical Queen's Speech since 1943 firmly based on our manifesto ... And as we started to act in those first few days, so we have continued ever since.[5]

But while Wilson was boasting of his achievements, he was keen to keep his more radical colleagues out of the headlines. In particular, he did his utmost to keep Tony Benn ('The Man the Tories Love to Hate', as the Sunday Times called him) out of sight, worried that the Industry Secretary's strident rhetoric would turn off moderate voters. For his part, Benn was convinced that the CIA was about to 'engineer a run on

Few Conservative papers were convinced by Harold Wilson's moderation during the October campaign. In this typically restrained cartoon for the *Express* (14 October 1974), Cummings warns that 'Dracula' Healey, 'Frankenstein' Foot and 'Madman' Benn are lurking in Wilson's chamber of horrors.

the pound or provoke some crisis during the Election'. Friends told him that on Fleet Street 'a big financial scandal or smear was being prepared against me for the last week of the campaign', while Donoughue heard a rumour that the newspapers were preparing allegations about Benn's sex life. The editor of the *Sunday Mirror* even heard that Benn liked to smoke cannabis and take part in orgies at Bickenhall Mansions, an Edwardian block of flats in Marylebone, a story he duly passed on to the Prime Minister. Bizarrely, Wilson did not dismiss it out of hand, despite the fact that Benn was a notoriously puritanical teetotaller with a conspicuous devotion to his wife. At one point Wilson even rang his Industry Secretary to ask whether it was true. Perhaps it was hardly surprising that Benn, like his leader, occasionally seemed to be succumbing to paranoia. 'I just don't think this is going to be an ordinary Election,' he recorded on the first day of campaigning. 'I think something very big is going to blow up on us – I just feel it.'[6]

For the Conservative leader, Edward Heath, however, there were few such excitements. Defeat had taken a heavy toll: not only were Heath and his colleagues exhausted after four intensely gruelling years, but their unexpected repudiation seemed to have left them intellectually adrift, lost in the wilderness with no ideological compass. To be fair, Heath was in an unusually weak position, akin to 'a football manager whose team has narrowly lost the first leg of a cup tie, and who finds that his opponent is allowed to write his own rules for the rematch'.

Stubborn as ever, he showed no sign of learning from the mistakes that had brought his government down, and refused even to inject new blood into his Shadow Cabinet. The same old faces – Willie Whitelaw, Robert Carr, Jim Prior, even Sir Alec Douglas-Home – gazed out from the Tory front bench, but the overall impression was that of a party in shock. And Heath himself seemed in remarkably listless form, like some great bear miserably licking his wounds. Not only was he suffering from an undiagnosed thyroid problem, but fate had turned against him: in September, his beloved boat *Morning Cloud* sank in a gale off the Isle of Wight with the loss of two crewmen, one of them his godson. Poor Heath was grief-stricken, yet inside the Tory Party sympathy was running out. The years of abrasiveness, awkwardness and sheer rudeness had taken their toll, and his personal ratings lagged consistently behind Wilson's. While more than half of all voters personally approved of the Labour leader, only one in three approved of Heath, falling to just 27 per cent by the autumn. Even a groundbreaking visit to China over the summer, during which he managed to secure two pandas for London Zoo, failed to re-ignite his popularity. 'Mao was the first person he had seen in months', a friend remarked, 'who was actually pleased to see him.'[7]

For some Conservatives, notably the handful of right-wingers who thrilled to the uncompromising rhetoric of Heath's old adversary Enoch Powell, defeat back in February proved that they had been wrong to abandon the radical, free-market promise of their first months. Even as Heath was licking his wounds, his former Social Services Secretary, Sir Keith Joseph, was moving sharply rightwards and developing many of the ideas that would become the foundations of Thatcherism. But inside Central Office, leadership loyalists drew very different conclusions from the party's defeat. According to the party's private pollster, February 1974 proved that the voters hated abrasiveness and 'confrontation', both of which they associated with Heath himself. For the party to regain power, it would have to win back millions of middle-class voters who had defected to Jeremy Thorpe's Liberals, and the best way to regain their trust was to drop all talk of social or ideological conflict, and emphasize conciliation and consensus.[8]

This was anathema to the party hawks, of course, but it dovetailed perfectly with Heath's own instincts. Despite his abrasive image, he had always seen himself as a One Nation moderate, bringing different groups together to plan for the common good. What was more, it chimed with a growing consensus in the broadsheets that Britain's economic problems were so deep-seated that no one party could possibly solve them. The *Guardian*'s editor Alastair Hetherington was one of many senior journalists who believed that since Britain had become 'ungovernable', the only solution was a 'government of national unity'. What the public wanted, a *Guardian* leader claimed, was a 'Grand Coalition of all three parties, possibly with Mr Thorpe at its head'. For the paper's political columnist Peter Jenkins, the ideal scenario was a centre–left coalition of Liberals and Labour, what he called a 'government of all the talents'. And in *The Times*, almost every day brought new appeals for a centrist coalition led by a reassuringly solid figure such as Willie Whitelaw or Roy Jenkins. In June 1974, for example, a leader bearing the unmistakable stamp of the paper's economics editor Peter Jay insisted that 'only a coalition government can gain the degree of political consent' to carry out the required measures to bring inflation down. 'We are at present in a situation in which the avalanche [meaning the economic crisis] is coming down the mountain but has not yet arrived,' the leader explained. But 'at some point, a national coalition of all parties is likely to be necessary to rebuild the village after the avalanche has struck'.[9]

If Heath had been the abrasive reactionary of Labour rhetoric, then he would never have been tempted by talk of national unity. Yet inside the upper ranks of the Conservative Party, plenty of people welcomed the idea. Sir Ian Gilmour, for example, wrote in *The Times* at the beginning of May that the Conservatives should put 'nation before party' and reach out to the 'six million Liberal voters' by forming an anti-socialist alliance with Thorpe's party. On 26 June, Heath himself gave a remarkably conciliatory speech promising to adopt a 'programme for national unity' behind which 'the overwhelming majority of people' could unite. Two days later, Harold Macmillan's son Maurice called for 'a real government of national unity' including both Tories and Liberals. And two days after that, Heath's protégé Peter Walker called for a new government based on 'the middle ground of British politics'. So it was not surprising that the new Conservative manifesto, largely written by Gilmour and a young Oxford graduate called Chris Patten, struck a notably consensual note. Emollient and conciliatory where the February version had been strident and confrontational, it insisted that the Conservative Party was 'free from dogma and free from dependence on any single interest'. A new Tory government would 'not govern in a narrow partisan spirit' but would 'confer with the leaders of other parties' and 'invite people from outside the ranks of our party to join with us'.[10]

Almost without exception the press loved it. Heath had shown his 'political courage' in putting nation ahead of party, said *The Times*, while the *Mail* called it a 'survival kit for the nation' and the *Guardian* thought it 'well conceived and well directed'. Only the *Mirror* sounded a dissenting note, pointing out that for all Heath's moderation, his rhetoric 'could mean anything or nothing'. And heart-warming though the manifesto's appeal to national unity might be, it never spelled out precisely what a Conservative government would do. With Heath opposed to electoral reform and unable to give journalists the names of any Labour or Liberal heavyweights who might be persuaded to join his Cabinet, 'national unity' seemed more of a slogan than a solution. On economic policy, too, the elegant rhetoric concealed a lack of specifics. When Heath was asked at a press conference what a Tory government would do if the unions defied his incomes policy, his response – 'It conciliates. It arbitrates. It persuades. It cajoles. It seeks ways round. It gathers public support' – was basically meaningless. And even the manifesto's commendably frank admission that there was 'no quick or simple way of defeating inflation' testified to a broader confusion, even impotence in the face of the economic blizzard. 'We are in a new and dangerous situation,' one Tory aide explained helplessly. 'We need a new Keynes.'[11]

Indeed, when the Conservatives did come up with a concrete economic proposal, promising to cap mortgage interest rates at 9.5 per cent, the press reacted with scornful outrage. The scheme was 'grotesque bribery', said the *Spectator*'s George Gale, while the *Financial Times*'s Samuel Brittan awarded it 'the prize for economic illiteracy' and *The Times*'s Bernard Levin wrote that it 'must have done much to drive further towards despair those who know what o'clock is now striking in the ears of the deaf'. But Heath's Shadow Environment Secretary, Margaret Thatcher, insisted that her mortgage plans were 'absolutely unshakeable' and would be in place by Christmas. For good measure, she promised to replace the rates with 'taxes more broadly based and related to people's ability to pay', a pledge she would have done well to remember fifteen years later. Revealingly, the criticism did not deter her in the least, and she featured more prominently in the Tories' party political broadcasts than any other shadow minister – including, ominously, Heath himself. And even though polls revealed deep (and entirely justified) public suspicion of such an expensive mortgage pledge, the fact that she was so forceful, and clearly had the government rattled, naturally appealed to Tory activists exasperated by Heath's moderation. It was no surprise when, a few weeks later, the *Sun* reckoned that she had been the only Conservative 'star' of the campaign, matched only by Shirley Williams for Labour and Jeremy Thorpe, John Pardoe and David Steel for the Liberals.[12]

On Heath's broad shoulders, by contrast, there was very little stardust in the autumn of 1974. Earlier in the year he had campaigned and lost as the lonely, courageous man of destiny. Now his aides persuaded him to adopt a new style, which he called 'quiet, reasonable conservatism', but which journalists saw as a misguided attempt to make him look 'cuddly', even 'jovial'. He made few formal speeches at large rallies, and did not even chair most of the Tories' press conferences. Instead, he spent most of his time meeting small groups in local meetings, often in his shirtsleeves. The presidential rhetoric had vanished: in his first election broadcast, Heath told the audience that politicians 'lead people to expect too much of them' and suggested that 'there ought to be a little more modesty and humility all round'. This was an astonishing departure from February; some Tories, however, felt that, given the urgency of the economic crisis, Heath and his advisers had gone rather too far down the road of moderation. At his first public meeting in Cardiff, he 'spoke for an hour in his new style without a single burst of applause', which was hardly the ideal way to fire up the electorate. And at his first press conference, speaking so quietly that journalists at the back struggled to hear him, Heath was so non-committal that even the famously terse Clement Attlee would have sounded ebullient by comparison. Asked what his first move against inflation would be, he said simply: 'To see precisely what the situation is.' And what would be his next move? 'To take the appropriate action.'[13]

Heath's neutered public appearances set the tone for the dullest, most downbeat election campaign in modern history: the 'election that never was', as The Economist called it. 'God knows how we'll keep it going for another ten days,' one Tory strategist confided to reporters. There was none of the rowdiness or heckling that had characterized the February campaign; indeed, most meetings were abysmally attended. The broadcasters scaled back their television coverage, correctly reckoning that most viewers were sick of electioneering. Even the weather was cold and dreary: it rained more heavily in October 1974 than in any other post-war campaign. And, with the possible exception of Heath himself, almost everybody accepted that Labour would win. Polls gave the government a steady lead of between 5 and 10 per cent, and, as far as individual issues were concerned, they led the Conservatives by 24 per cent on unemployment, 23 per cent on pensions, 20 per cent on inflation, 20 per cent on the NHS and a staggering 33 per cent on strikes – a testament to the apparent success of the Social Contract. Poor Heath seemed powerless to shift public perceptions. Two days before polling day, the Tory leader admitted that 'politicians, including myself . . . may not have been clear enough, blunt enough, soon enough. Perhaps our language hasn't been the right language.' But when he claimed that Britain was facing economic meltdown, his words fell on deaf ears. Most voters preferred a more reassuring message. 'What the people want,' Harold Wilson told an audience in Bolton, 'what every family needs, is a bit of peace and quiet so that they can plan for the future on a basis of real security for the whole family.'[14]

And yet, deep down, it was hard to miss the lingering unease even among Labour supporters. For all that Wilson and his ministers talked up the Social Contract, more than four out of ten people thought it would 'never be kept by the unions if Labour win the election', while 46 per cent agreed that Labour had 'given in to the unions by agreeing to the Social Contract and have got no real concessions in return'. There was certainly no great enthusiasm for the government: polls showed that 55 per cent of the electorate thought that Labour's performance had been poor, while only 51 per cent had any confidence that either party could solve Britain's problems. 'The fight has been taken out of the people,' remarked a young Birmingham housewife. 'You have Labour in, then suddenly the Conservatives come back, and then Labour again. It's like another cook taking over the stove and buggering the dinner. I don't care who does it just as long as something is done!'[15]

In February, disgruntled voters had turned to the Liberals. But this time the party's momentum seemed to have stalled, not least because Jeremy Thorpe spent the early weeks of the campaign on a preposterous hovercraft tour of English seaside resorts, providing broadcasters with plenty of pictures of himself 'struggling ashore in bedraggled oilskins' while aides toiled miserably to restart his unreliable vehicle. By the time the tour reached Sidmouth the writing was on the wall for the battered hovercraft. 'The first wave struck just as the craft was turning off the beach to head away to the Isle of Wight,' a reporter wrote the next day. 'I was pulling on one rope just behind the Liberal leader and he was nearly swept into the sea by some breakers.' As the hovercraft filled with water, Thorpe and his colleague John Pardoe struggled manfully to salvage their belongings, but the battle was lost. 'When Mr Thorpe left the beach,' the reporter continued, 'the craft lay forlornly on the shingle, its sides broken in and its passenger accommodation filled with water.' At least outwardly, Thorpe remained undaunted. 'This is a great British machine,' he said defiantly. 'If the British hovercraft has any future, then we must continue to use it.' Sadly, however, the hovercraft had no future. Neither, it turned out, did Thorpe.[16]

With just a week to go, Heath's advisers made one last effort to change the narrative. Ever since the summer, Thorpe had rebuffed the Conservative leader's talk of national unity, dismissing him as 'the architect of confrontation'. But on Friday, 4 October, Heath's closest advisers met to discuss taking unprecedented action. The Tory leader, they argued, should use Sunday's press conference to make the 'supreme sacrifice', offering to step aside in the event of a deadlocked election so that another leader – almost certainly Willie Whitelaw – could form a Conservative–Liberal coalition. As they saw it, such a magnanimous gesture could only work to his advantage. In the event of a hung parliament, his leadership would come into question anyway. But if by some miracle the Tories did win a majority, the offer could be quietly forgotten.

Not unpredictably, however, Heath hated the idea. Defeat in February had made him more stubborn than ever; he had not fought so hard to become leader of his party, he had not striven so much as Prime Minister, to throw the leadership away so easily. His one concession was to alter his final message to Conservative candidates, using the word 'coalition' for the first time. 'I have no doubt', he proclaimed, 'that the real hope of the British people in this situation is that a National Coalition government, involving all the parties, should be formed, and the party differences could be put aside until the crisis is mastered.' If he won, he said, he would form 'a government representing men and women of good will of all parties and of none'. But it was not enough to recapture public attention, and Harold Wilson reacted with memorably withering scorn. Talk of coalition, he said, was 'a desperate attempt by desperate men to get back into power by any means . . . Coalition would mean Con policies, Con leadership by a Con party for a Con trick. And how long would it last? About as long as it would take to get the country back to last February, back to the other "cons" – confrontation and conflict.'[17]

Behind the scenes, however, Wilson was rather less bullish than he sounded. Although the polls still showed a clear Labour lead, word had reached his inner circle that the *Daily Mail* was preparing a huge exposé on the Prime Minister's personal finances. On 5 October, discussion of the *Mail*'s plans ('a story about HW's wealth') dominated their strategy meeting. 'Marcia has completely collapsed,' Bernard Donoughue noted.

'Trembling, afraid, taking sedatives and showing little interest in the campaign or the speeches.' Even Wilson seemed to be 'losing his nerve', and by Sunday the 6th, with the headlines full of the Guildford atrocity and the *Mail*'s bombshell expected that night, he was clearly cracking under the pressure. 'He wants to *write an article* in the *Mail* on Tuesday refuting all allegations about his so-called wealth and tax affairs and claiming that they had stolen the documents from his house,' a horrified Donoughue recorded. Intriguingly, nobody had any idea what the *Mail*'s revelations would be. Almost certainly they concerned the royalties from Wilson's book on his first administration – most of which he had paid into a trust, but some of which he had given to Marcia Williams in trust for herself and her children – as well as the Swiss bank account he used for office expenses. In the meantime, all they could do was wait, the tension building as rain poured down outside Number 10. Reports came through of a bomb scare in the *Mail* building, followed by 'some kind of dispute in the "reading room"'. And then, at last, the first edition: no revelations, but a long front-page letter, addressed to Wilson, denying that the paper had ever had any intention to run a smear story. Almost incredibly, under pressure from Wilson's lawyer Arnold Goodman, the *Mail* had lost its bottle. 'General relief that nothing today in the *Daily Mail* – and clearly won't be anything in the press now,' Donoughue recorded the next morning. On Tuesday evening, they sat up with brandy and cigars, looking forward to victory. 'The electoral games are over now,' Donoughue wrote. 'Reality from now on.'[18]

But while Wilson's aides were toasting their inevitable victory, few commentators hid their disillusionment that the campaign was drifting to such a miserable conclusion. For *The Times*, what was at stake in the coming year was 'the survival of the present social and political system of Britain', or, as the *Sun* put it, 'we're flat broke, and our democracy is in real danger'. Yet as the *Guardian*'s Peter Jenkins wrote on the final day of the campaign, 'the crisis has been neither adequately explained nor understood'. No party, he noted, had published realistic economic plans, and only Heath had come close to telling 'the people the truth, which many must have discovered from their own pockets, which is that their standard of living is in fact declining and that there is no way of avoiding this without making things worse'. Somehow it spoke volumes about the muted, dreary nature of the campaign that after the high passions of February, only three papers – the pro-Conservative *Telegraph* and *Express* and the pro-Labour *Mirror* – felt able to give unequivocal endorsements to one of the two major parties. The

Guardian unambiguously backed the Liberals; *The Times* and, surprisingly, the *Mail* called for a Tory–Liberal coalition; and the *Sun* urged voters to elect 'any able politician who could properly describe himself as a social democrat', urging the next government to bring in 'the ablest people in the land, irrespective of politics'. Few people, however, held out much hope. As the playwright John Osborne told the *Observer*, the politicians' 'ritual incantation of phrases – as if they were *things* – like "Inflation", "National Unity", "Priorities" and "Social Contracts"' only concealed 'the nasty reality of the awful brutishness of most of English life today'. 'I shall vote Labour once more,' Osborne wrote, 'but with an even emptier heart than usual.'[19]

Polling day, 10 October: a dreary, drizzly, miserable day. In Bristol, Tony Benn toured his constituency with a flask of tea, sipping from his tin mug on top of his car, wrapped in an anorak and a blanket to keep out the cold. In Bexley, Heath made a last tour of his constituency, oddly cheerful and relaxed, even though the polls forecast a clear Labour majority. His lieutenants were less upbeat: many Tories were terrified that their vote would collapse, giving Wilson a last-minute landslide. At Labour's London headquarters, Donoughue found the Prime Minister in confident form. The final polls gave his party a comfortable lead: 9 per cent, according to an ORC survey in *The Times*, while Gallup put Labour's lead at 5 per cent, Harris at 8 per cent and Marplan at 10 per cent. Some of Wilson's aides, remembering how badly wrong the polls had been before, refused to believe it. When the Labour team flew up to Wilson's Huyton constituency that afternoon, Donoughue noticed that Marcia Williams was 'jumpy' and kept 'swallowing sedatives washed down by brandy'. And when they reached Wilson's suite in the Adelphi Hotel, where they had watched his unexpected win unfold on television seven months before, the mood seemed 'prickly and sour'. When Donoughue and Haines went off for a quick drink, Marcia lashed out, accusing them of 'going off to plot'. 'I didn't like the feel of it,' Donoughue wrote later.

By the time he and Haines returned it was 9.30 and the Prime Minister had joined them. The atmosphere was heavy with tension. 'We were all subdued,' Donoughue recorded, 'eating sandwiches, drinking beer and waiting for the 10 o'clock news.' He called Transport House for updates, but they had no idea what was happening. 'It had been raining,' he noted caustically, 'and the general party organisation is awful.' But now the television coverage had started; on BBC1, Alastair Burnet was announcing the results of the first exit poll, which gave Labour a big win with a majority of perhaps 150 seats. 'For a few moments we were elated,' Donoughue wrote. But then the first results – Guildford, Cheltenham, the two Salford seats – started to come in, showing a swing to Labour of just 2 per cent, and reality came crashing down. The BBC hastily adjusted their prediction, first to 66 seats, then to just 30. In the Adelphi, somebody reported that turnout in Labour areas was heavily down: according to some reports, by almost 10 per cent. At that, Wilson suddenly became agitated. 'We might as well go home,' he said abruptly. 'We've lost.'[20]

Wilson had not lost. In the end, he chiselled out a tiny majority of just 3 seats, only 18 more than in February, but a working majority nonetheless.* Turnout had fallen by about 6 per cent, but it was Conservative voters, above all, who had stayed at home. While Labour picked up 11.5 million votes (down from 11.6 million in February), the Tory vote dropped from 11.9 million to 10.5 million, their worst performance since 1945. Not only had Heath led the Conservatives to their fourth defeat in five elections, but their share of the vote was down to a feeble 36 per cent, the lowest level in their history. Only among the elderly were they still the 'natural' majority party; among voters in their twenties, the Conservatives had little more than half the support of Labour and were dead level with the Liberals.

But while the Tories had nothing to celebrate, the extraordinary thing about the October 1974 result was that nobody else had, either. The Liberal breakthrough had once again failed to materialize: this time, their vote fell from 6 million to barely 5 million, and they lost one of their 14 seats. And by many standards, Labour's performance was deeply disappointing. Their total vote was the party's smallest since 1935, while for the second successive election they had fallen below the 40 per cent threshold. What should have been most worrying of all for Labour, though, was that exit polls showed they had won just 55 per cent of trade union members and 55 per cent of the working-class vote. The party's core constituency was breaking up; mass affluence and disillusionment at industrial unrest were taking a heavy toll. In the excitement surrounding Wilson's narrow majority, few people paid much attention

---

* Labour won 319 seats, the Conservatives 277, the Liberals 13, the Scottish Nationalists 11, the Ulster Unionists 6 and Plaid Cymru 3, with the rest going to smaller Northern Irish parties.

to these figures. In the long run, though, they presaged a political earth-quake.[21]

In Huyton there was little jubilation as the results came in, just more bickering. Before Wilson's team left for his personal count, Marcia Williams took the Prime Minister aside. 'I stood near the door and listened,' Donoughue recorded. 'She was demanding that Albert [Murray, one of his most faithful and self-effacing aides] should *not* be allowed into the count and also attacking Harold for giving Joe and me tickets to the count.' When they emerged, Wilson did as he was told, confiscating Murray's ticket. In solidarity, Haines and Donoughue joined him in a lounge outside the hall, watching the results on television instead of listening to their leader's speech. Afterwards, Wilson sheepishly announced that none of them was welcome at the Huyton Labour Club victory party, either. Not surprisingly, Haines was furious: after all, he had written thirty-three speeches for the leader in just nineteen days. 'HW suggested that we stay there and take down the results for him,' Donoughue noted. 'But we said fuck it, we would go back to the hotel.' There they sat watching television until three in the morning, when Wilson rather shamefacedly rejoined them. Champagne was produced, 'and we drank to victory, although totally without enthusiasm'. After a few moments, Donoughue slipped away and went to bed. 'Joe did the same,' he wrote. 'It was a dismal and sour end. No doubt our victory, but no pleasure in it.'[22]

The next morning they flew back to London. It was another grey, dreary day, and just before they left there was another embarrassing scene, as Wilson debated kicking Donoughue, Haines and Murray off the flight, as Marcia had requested. In the end he relented, and they were beside him that afternoon at Transport House for the official victory party. Given that it marked his second election triumph in seven months, it was an astonishingly downbeat affair. 'Whatever has divided us in this keenly fought election campaign,' Wilson said grimly, 'we have all agreed that Britain faces, and has indeed for a considerable time been facing, the gravest economic crisis since the war. And everyone in industry and in our wider national family now needs to work together, sharing the effort and sharing the burdens of Britain's economic fight.' But he had only just finished speaking when the alarms went off for an IRA bomb scare, and aides began ushering people out. 'It was too much for me,' Donoughue wrote. 'The comic opera stuff had gone on long enough. So I evacuated back to No. 10 and packed my stuff for the weekend.'

Just before he left, however, Donoughue had a visit from Wilson's principal private secretary, Robert Armstrong, bringing bad news. The Prime Minister had just instructed him that from now on, there would be no more Number 10 lunches. For Donoughue, it made a suitably banal end to a thoroughly miserable day. 'I hope [Wilson] gets a minute to think about the country's economy, in between acting as messenger for Marcia's hostilities,' he wrote that evening. 'The nation is going bust. He is at a moment of political triumph. And he spends his time as a messenger on these pathetically trivial matters of who eats lunch in No. 10.'[23]

8

For God's Sake, Britain, Wake Up!

*The depressing pattern of grey skies, rain and dark days is
matched only by the news ... This evening there are two
explosions in Birmingham pubs ...*

Michael Palin's diary, 22 November 1974

*John puffed at his cigar ... 'Most people in this country feel
greater loyalty to the unions than they do to the state.'*
'But they don't want inflation,' said Henry.
*'Quite. And if they thought about it they might concede that
annual increases in their wages of twenty or thirty per cent will
inevitably lead to inflation. But they don't think about it.'*

Piers Paul Read, *A Married Man* (1979)

Another crowded, happy pub, six weeks after Guildford. Thursday was
pay day in Birmingham, and, as darkness fell, the city's bars were heaving
with young workers intent on spending their hard-earned wages. In the
Tavern in the Town, a basement pub not far from New Street station, it
was already packed, the air thick with conversation and cigarette smoke.
Just after quarter past eight, a few drinkers near the door heard a muffled
thump from outside. Though none of them knew it, a bomb had ripped
through another pub, the packed Mulberry Bush at the foot of the
twenty-five-storey Rotunda, a few moments' walk away. Exactly ten
minutes later, there was a gigantic bang and the roof fell in on the Tavern
in the Town. And as the survivors staggered outside, they found a scene
of unimaginable horror: bodies strewn across the pavement, the wounded
limping across the street with blood streaming from their faces, broken
glass and dismembered body parts everywhere, like something from 'a

First World War casualty clearing station'. One woman, who had come into the city from Solihull for an evening meal, stood swaying in a daze of shock while the police desperately tried to clear the area. 'I ran down the street,' she told a reporter. 'Then I saw the front of the place almost opposite [the Tavern in the Town] blow out.' Another bystander, shaking with shock, told the press he had seen people 'weeping and screaming. I saw bodies and blood everywhere.' 'There were women and young girls screaming, blood pouring everywhere,' a third witness said. 'I saw one man who seemed to have half his body blown off. It was horrible.'[1]

In total, 21 people were murdered in Birmingham that terrible night, Thursday, 21 November 1974, and some 182 injured. Once again their killers were the Provisional IRA, who had telephoned the *Birmingham Post* at 8.11 that evening with a warning that there was a bomb in the Rotunda, but had offered no more details. The warning was pathetically inadequate: even as the first bomb went off, the police had only just begun clearing the Rotunda's upper floors, and the second bomb in the Tavern in the Town had been deliberately timed to catch the crowds outside. Minutes later, a third bomb went off in a wine bar on Corporation Street, although mercifully nobody was killed. By no stretch of the imagination were these military targets: the pubs were nowhere near an army base, and the victims were ordinary men and women, many in their teens or early twenties, enjoying an evening out in England's second city. As one police officer emotionally remarked, it was 'the slaughter of the young innocents'. Each of the bombs weighed more than 15 pounds: in the Mulberry Bush, the explosion blew a hole through the 9-inch-thick reinforced concrete ceiling, leaving customers crushed under twisted girders and gigantic concrete blocks. Trapped inside, many never stood a chance: as a St John's Ambulance woman later put it, the scene was 'like a slaughterhouse'. A fireman who was one of the first into the pubs after the bombs recalled seeing a 'torso, with no arms or legs, and a spongy mess where its head had been. The torso was not only wriggling; it was also, through the spongy mess, screaming.' The fireman begged the police to let the television crews film it; if the IRA saw the consequences of their actions, he said, there would be no more bombs. But they refused. If the pictures went out, they said, the reprisals would be too awful to contemplate.[2]

Birmingham after the IRA bombings was a city in shock, traumatized by a horror it had never expected. When the Home Secretary, Roy Jenkins, arrived the next day, he found it 'one of the most difficult, draining and unpleasant' visits he had ever made. 'It was a dry, still, misty, rather cold day,' he remembered, 'and the atmosphere in the unusually deserted centre of the city hung heavy with some not wholly definable but unforgettable and oppressive ingredients . . . Partly it was the lingering scent of the explosions, but there was also a stench of death and carnage and fear . . . a pervading atmosphere of stricken, hostile resentment such as I had never previously encountered anywhere in the world.' Towards the IRA, most people felt a surge of uncontrollable rage. 'Just call them bloody bastards,' said 18-year-old Michael Wills, who had staggered bleeding and dazed from the Tavern in the Town; 'just call them bloody murderers.' The director of the city's biggest A&E department, who told a reporter that he had seen a 'pretty girl about 20 years of age' blinded by metal shrapnel in both eyes, remarked that he had never approved of scrapping the death penalty. 'I hope the people who have voted for abolition', he said bitterly, 'will change their minds now.'[3]

Throughout the city, there was talk of bringing back hanging for convicted terrorists. Nationwide support for the death penalty, which had always struck a chord with a majority of the population, surged to almost 90 per cent. 'The death penalty', said Percy Grieve, the Conservative MP for Solihull, 'should be the ultimate weapon in the armoury of society against this kind of outrage,' while another West Midlands MP, Halesowen and Stourbridge's John Stokes, insisted that 'the great majority of our people' wanted the death penalty for terrorists. For a time, Jenkins, who hated hanging and had given staunch support to the abolitionist lobby when Home Secretary in the 1960s, was seriously worried that public pressure would force a U-turn. But when the Commons debated the issue a few weeks later, he was relieved to find that both Edward Heath and Willie Whitelaw shared his revulsion. Indeed, Whitelaw told the House that the death penalty for terrorism would greatly increase the threat to British forces in Northern Ireland, and the effort to restore it eventually fizzled out.[4]

Jenkins returned from Birmingham 'dismayed and shattered'. In the streets he had heard people calling not only for the death penalty but for the expulsion of the city's Irish population, some 100,000 strong. At a press conference at the end of his tour, he made a point of begging local residents not to 'take it out' on their Irish neighbours. The Prime Minister, too, went out of his way to appeal for calm, telling the press that 'the overwhelming majority of Irish people in Britain condemn and detest these wicked attacks as much as anyone else', while the Lord Mayor of Birmingham begged local residents not to take reprisals against the city's Irish population, 'who have been doing a good job for a long time'. In the immediate aftermath of the bombings, however, these entreaties fell on deaf ears. Across the country, there were stories of Irish people being refused service in shops, thrown off buses, threatened in pubs. By Saturday morning petrol bombs had been thrown at an Irish-run pub in Ealing and an Irish tobacconist's in Streatham, while in Birmingham another petrol bomb was thrown at an Irish pub in Kingstanding.[5]

Although the bitterness never came to anything, for a few days the government was seriously worried that Britain, like Northern Ireland, might find itself infected by the virus of sectarian hatred. 'The damage done to Irish people here, even though they may be Protestants, is terrible, every one a victim of this same awful process of escalating violence,' wrote Tony Benn the day after the attacks. When the Cabinet met the following Monday, their priority was to stop outrage from boiling over. 'The Birmingham incidents had violently aroused public opinion,' the minutes recorded, 'and unless the Government showed a firm determination to act against terrorism there was likely to be an intensified reaction against the Irish community here.' In private, Benn recorded his 'very real fear that we might awaken deep sectarian feelings against the Irish and against the Catholics which had been quiescent for over a hundred years'. But anti-Catholicism had long since disappeared as a serious force in English life, and most people did not distinguish between republicans and loyalists, but blamed all Irish terrorists equally. And while there was plenty of bar-room outrage, and although Irish citizens in Britain during the 1970s often found themselves being snubbed or abused, serious attacks remained mercifully rare – which in itself was a tribute to the intrinsic decency of the people of the West Midlands.[6]

Even so, the government could hardly be seen to do nothing in response to such a terrible atrocity. 'This Can't Go On,' read the banner headline in the country's bestselling newspaper, the *Mirror*, on Saturday morning, insisting that 'the British people will no longer tolerate the murderous outrages of the IRA' and demanding immediate 'emergency measures'. Even Jenkins recognized that he had to do something: only hours after the bombings, he announced his decision to bring in a temporary Prevention of Terrorism Bill. The new Act – which became law just 180 hours later – made it a criminal offence to belong to the IRA, to solicit or provide funds for it or to give it active support. It gave the government additional powers to deport foreign-born immigrants who supported terrorism; it gave the police the power to demand proofs of identity from people crossing to Britain from any part of Ireland; and it allowed them to hold suspects for questioning for seven days, rather than just two. In private, Jenkins frankly admitted that some of these measures were window dressing. The police had told him that banning the IRA in Britain would not do much good, but he knew that it would be 'welcomed by public opinion and would help in discouraging people from taking the law into their own hands'. But the important thing was to strike a balance between appeasing public outrage and preserving the liberties on which British democracy depended. 'We are in greater danger of justifiable criticism if we do too little than if we do too much,' he wrote. 'We must, moreover, take action which is firm enough to pre-empt action by self-appointed vigilantes.'[7]

What is striking now is not how severe the government's response was, but how muted. There was a great clamour for the introduction of identity cards, yet, as Jenkins pointed out, 'apart from creating difficulties for ordinary people, [they] would be extremely expensive and largely ineffective'. Even the Prevention of Terrorism Act, later damned by critics on the left as a step towards a police state, was widely regarded as very mild: as one writer pointed out a few years later, its 'restriction of the liberty of the ordinary citizen was, in practice, nil'. Jenkins could hardly have done more to resist the pressure for reprisals, and the *Sunday Times* later praised his 'sensitivity' in gauging the public mood and coaxing it back towards the middle ground. Unforgivably, however, the police were rather less adept. Under intense public pressure to find the bombers, they beat confessions out of six Irishmen who had lived in Birmingham since the 1960s. Sentenced to life imprisonment in August 1975, the six men were only released in 1991, and the true perpetrators were never charged. It was one of the many tragedies of the case that, as time went by, Birmingham became synonymous with the miscarriage of justice and the brutality of the police, rather than with the suffering of the families whose lives had been devastated by the IRA.[8]

For Roy Jenkins, the Birmingham bombings, striking at the heart of the city in which he had built his political career, represented the low point of his second period at the Home Office.* During the late 1960s he had been one of the government's most assured performers, a reforming Home Secretary, a disciplined Chancellor and a Labour leader in wait-

---

* Jenkins had been MP for Birmingham Stechford, 5 miles to the east of the city centre, since 1950.

ing. But as an ostentatiously civilized grandee inspired by the legacy of Edwardian Liberalism, and as the darling of the pro-European dinner-party circuit, Jenkins found himself increasingly out of touch with the left-wing activists who dominated many local constituency parties. When he resigned as deputy leader in 1972, horrified at Wilson's decision to call for a referendum on British membership of the EEC, he had lost his credibility on the left of the party. Now, for all his superficial charm, this sleek and self-consciously sophisticated lover of fine wines and aristocratic women cut a very disconsolate figure. An outcast in much of his own party, he had never expected Wilson to regain power in February 1974; indeed, privately he thought Labour deserved to lose. When they won, he told friends that he was 'very depressed' and 'felt like a prisoner'. A few months later, Jenkins even confessed that he was 'thoroughly fed up with the party system', which was 'a conspiracy against the people'. And although he handled his duties at the Home Office competently enough, old admirers were disappointed by his transparent indifference. 'He has completely dropped out of the government,' Bernard Donoughue lamented that summer. 'He is just a sleeping partner ... aloof, disdainful, unhappy, trying to avoid contamination from his own party.'[9]

Jenkins was not alone in returning to office after October 1974 with a sense of weary resignation. When Barbara Castle rang Wilson at Chequers on the Sunday after the election, she found him nursing a heavy cold, a preview of the endless ailments that blighted his final years in office. Two days later, when the Cabinet met for the first time since the election, the mood was remarkably downbeat, the tone set by a very miserable Jim Callaghan. The middle classes had got into 'a great state of defeatism', he said. He personally was 'gloomy about the economy' and thought 'public expenditure has to be reined back pretty severely if we are to get through'. He was well known as a champion of the unions, he added, so he could be frank: 'There is a great fear of the power of the unions; they have got too much influence on all Governments and we must rectify and remedy the situation.' Other ministers then chimed in: Foot thought they might need 'emergency measures', Crosland that 'sacrifices' were inevitable. The unions were 'too powerful', the latter added, 'and wherever you had a strong trade union, equality was set back'. Listening in disgust, Tony Benn told himself that the Cabinet 'will have to be cleaned out one day ... You can't go on with a bunch of right-wing people like that.' The only consolation, he thought, was that 'there will be a bust-up some time, whether it is over Europe or whether it is the breakdown of the Social Contract'.[10]

A bust-up, though, was the last thing Harold Wilson wanted. Peace and quiet he had promised; peace and quiet was what the nation would have. It was a long time since he had promised to build a New Britain in the white heat of the technological revolution. Now he seemed palpably old and weary, bowed and careworn, shrunken and shabby. He had avenged his defeat by Heath, won a record fourth election for Labour and secured his place in history, yet he took little pleasure in the challenge of leadership. Rumours of his drinking were now common currency in Westminster and Whitehall: civil servants gossiped that during ministerial meetings he would often send out for whisky and water, while he needed at least a couple of large brandies for any major meeting. Even the loyal Haines recognized that 'he was drinking too much' and that 'the zest had gone'. He seemed plagued by stress, by stomach upsets and eye infections: on 12 December he walked out of a Cabinet meeting and sent for his doctor, Joe Stone, because he was worried about his 'racing heart'. 'He could not remember what he had read in his briefs this morning,' he told Haines. Stone prescribed three days' rest. But Wilson was like a man trapped on a treadmill; the problems kept on coming, an endless flow of meetings and paper. On top of everything else, Marcia Williams was still trying to purge his inner circle. Even lunch, almost incredibly, remained a minefield: as late as May 1975, Wilson's aides were still squabbling over a 'compromise package' under which Marcia conceded that they could indeed eat lunch, 'but not in the dining room'. 'The PM's behaviour', his principal private secretary Robert Armstrong remarked to Bernard Donoughue one day, 'was "utterly contemptible",' an extraordinary thing for such a discreet man to say.[11]

Hanging over everything was the great black cloud of the British economy. Even before the election, Donoughue had warned his boss that, with output and exports stagnant, unemployment approaching one million and inflation heading towards 20 per cent, the economy must be 'the only question: all other policies must go overboard'. In the long run, the most worrying problem was inflation: only days before the election, in a bid to end a crippling rash of strikes, Ford had offered its 53,000 workers a 38 per cent pay rise over two years, adding an estimated £63 million to the car giant's wage bill and raising the spectre of even greater wage inflation to come. For the time being, though, what really worried the Treasury was Britain's record borrowing. By 25 October, the Chancellor's advisers had revised their borrowing projections, and they made for horrendous reading. Instead of borrowing £2.7 billion in 1974–5, as predicted, Britain would actually need to borrow

£6.3 billion, rising a year later to a barely credible £8.5 billion. Not even a Chancellor with Healey's self-belief could ignore figures like that, and when he unveiled yet another Budget three weeks later, his Cabinet colleagues were horrified by the forecasts. 'There was a shocked silence at first,' recorded Barbara Castle, then 'whistles through the teeth when Denis said the borrowing requirement would have to be doubled'. Yet although Healey announced that annual public spending increases would be held at just under 3 per cent for the next four years, there was no talk of cuts and no sign of the government changing course. Inside Number 10, Wilson's chief economic adviser, Andrew Graham, despondently told Donoughue that 'everybody was terribly complacent'. Evidently there would have to be 'a terrible crisis, probably a foreign exchange crisis, before anything will be taken seriously', Graham said – words that were to prove very prescient indeed.[12]

On 17 November, the Cabinet assembled at Chequers for an all-day strategy meeting of unparalleled gloom. It was the first time most of them had visited the great house since 1970, and they were astonished by the extent of Heath's changes. Once again, Barbara Castle had her doubts about his taste; though she liked the displays of china treasures and carefully placed urns of flowers, they 'made everything look so much more *feminine*'. The surroundings, however, were quickly forgotten, as Wilson's roving troubleshooter Harold Lever opened with a paper of extraordinary pessimism. 'We have only a 50 per cent chance of avoiding world catastrophe,' he said bluntly, outlining the international slump, the pressure on resources and the problem of worldwide inflation. His fellow ministers were little more cheerful. Eric Varley thought that the 'miners' attitude was frightening'; Roy Mason felt that there was a real 'danger of war in the Middle East'; Shirley Williams predicted 'inflation of 26–30 per cent next year'. 'We are not giving enough priority to the problem of inflation,' Jenkins agreed. 'This could actually destroy society.' Even Crosland, supposedly the great ideas man, admitted that he had no idea what to do. 'All we can do', he said, 'is to press every button we've got. We do not know which, if any, of them will have the desired results.' But if there had been a medal for the biggest pessimist, it would have gone to Jim Callaghan. 'When I am shaving in the morning,' he remarked gloomily, 'I say to myself that if I were a young man I would emigrate. By the time I sit down to breakfast I ask myself "Where would I go?"' Everybody laughed, but Callaghan was only half joking. There was a serious prospect, he said, that Britain would 'go on sliding downhill for the next few years', perhaps even losing its seat on the United Nations Security Council. 'Nothing in these papers makes me believe anything to the contrary. I haven't got any solution.'[13]

While Callaghan only talked about emigrating, one of his colleagues took matters rather further. Just three days after the Chequers meeting, the Labour MP for Walsall North, John Stonehouse, disappeared from a hotel in Florida, where he had been on a business trip. The last person to see him alive had been a secretary at the beach club, to whom Stonehouse had handed his clothes before going for a swim. Had he drowned, perhaps? Only a few months earlier, he had asked the Home Secretary to 'review arrangements for preventing drowning accidents', so perhaps he had had a premonition of his own demise. But the Miami lifeguards thought that was impossible: not only had nobody seen Stonehouse go into the water, but drowned bodies always washed up after two days. Even more suspiciously, Stonehouse was in serious financial difficulties: his creditors were circling, he faced the real possibility of having to leave the Commons and he had recently taken out an insurance policy giving his wife £125,000 in the event of his death. 'People don't believe he's dead,' wrote Tony Benn a few days later. 'They think that with the financial trouble that he's in, he's just disappeared.' So indeed it proved. On Christmas Eve, the *Mirror* broke the sensational news that in Melbourne, Australia, where the authorities were looking out for the fugitive Lord Lucan (who had been on the run since 8 November after murdering his children's nanny), the police had apprehended a man who looked uncannily like John Stonehouse. When they allowed him one phone call, he chose to ring his wife Barbara. 'Hello darling,' he said cheerfully. 'I am so very sorry.' He sounded, she said, 'like a naughty little boy who had just been found out'.[14]

In many ways Stonehouse's attempt to flee his creditors and start again in Australia was merely a Reggie Perrin-style sideshow, a ludicrous distraction from the economic plight of his native land. Unfortunately for the government, not only did his escapade reduce their wafer-thin majority by one, but Stonehouse's bizarre story proved even more embarrassing than they had initially feared. During the late 1960s, Stonehouse had served as a junior minister in the first Wilson government, and it now emerged that he had been under 'constant security watch' as a possible Communist agent. Although Wilson angrily denied it in the Commons, it transpired that Stonehouse had been passing information to Czechoslovakian intelligence. In his semi-autobiographical spy novel *Ralph* (1982), Stonehouse explained that he had fallen victim to a honeytrap in the 1950s, his lover sending 'sensations of joy to every crevice of his brain' and spurring him on to one last 'magnificent thrust' – after which he realized he was being filmed through a mirror in the ceiling.

For a former minister to be exposed as a crook, adulterer, Communist agent and substandard erotic novelist was bad enough, especially with Wilson himself beset by rumours of spying and treachery. What was worse, though, was that Stonehouse defended himself by turning on his own party. In his final Commons speech before making his break for freedom, he had not only dismissed the Social Contract as a fraud, but had reminded his listeners that, in the last decade, Britain had been the 'second worst' performing country in Europe. 'The kidding had to stop,' he said:

> For too long we have fooled ourselves and have tried to fool others that Britain would somehow muddle through. For too long Britain has allowed itself indulgences which a successful and expanding country would hesitate to allow itself. Our problem is deep-seated, and can be best summed-up as 'the end of Empire syndrome'. It is a failure to adjust to our new situation in the world, which does not owe us a living and is making it extremely difficult for us to earn one.
>
> Our decline first set in during those first 13 wasted Conservative years which have been followed by 10 years of almost constant electioneering, with the wasteful posturing and manipulating that go with it.

Stonehouse might have been a fraud and a fantasist, but several million people would probably have agreed with much of this. Once he was back from Australia, he went even further. With his trial delayed until 1976, he insisted on retaining his seat in the Commons, defying the hecklers with increasingly bizarre interventions. When he rose to justify his conduct in October 1975, for example, it is a safe bet that the Palace of Westminster had rarely heard a more outlandish speech. Referring to himself in the third person and borrowing liberally from the psychobabble of the day, Stonehouse explained that he had suffered 'psychiatric suicide':

> It took the form of the repudiation of the life of Stonehouse because that life had become absolutely intolerable to him. A new parallel personality took over – separate and apart from the original man, who was resented and despised by the parallel personality for the ugly humbug and sham of

the recent years of his public life. The parallel personality was uncluttered by the awesome tensions and stresses suffered by the original man, and he felt, as an ordinary person, a tremendous relief in not carrying the load of anguish which had burdened the public figure.

The collapse and destruction of the original man came about because his idealism in his political life had been utterly frustrated and finally destroyed by the pattern of events, beyond his control, which had finally overwhelmed him.

For the 'new' Stonehouse, nothing better encapsulated the 'humbug and sham' of British life than the trade unions. They were no longer the champions of the workers, he said, but a 'Mafia', a 'protection racket': 'The trade unions have developed too much power and they abuse it ... Someone some day must say something about it.'[15]

Had they been able to overlook his treachery, fraud and therapy-speak, the Conservative middle classes would have found much to applaud in Stonehouse's analysis. He was not, after all, the only person driven towards desperate measures by the state of his finances in the dog days of 1974. Its morale shattered by the secondary banking disaster, the government's record borrowing, the collapse of the stock market and an ongoing liquidity crisis, the City of London found itself in dire straits after Wilson's re-election. 'This bear market is the financial equivalent of the Great War,' the stockbrokers Rowe & Pitman's monthly circular lamented in November. 'Lamps going out, end of an era, casualties numbered in millions, does the country know what's *happening*, will it ever end?' Even NatWest, which had lent massively to the property sector, was rumoured to be struggling: although the Bank of England denied that it was planning a rescue mission, the FT30 Index continued to fall. On 12 December, the same day Healey announced a record monthly trade deficit of £543 million, it closed at just 150.0, a figure David Kynaston wryly calls 'satisfying only for its roundness'. One banker remembered seeing Coleman Street 'cordoned off because someone had jumped out of the window, committing suicide'; another City insider recalled that he 'thought it was the end of the capitalist system, I really did'. And one stockjobber, Brian Bishop, was so disillusioned by the long days with little business that he set up a sideline selling bric-a-brac in New Caledonian Market. Eventually, he and his wife bought a shop in the King's Road and turned it into an antique shop. He got up at five every morning and went down to Portobello Road, then spent most of the day at the City before 'going around to buy stock in the evening'. One morning, coming back to the shop as dawn broke, he bumped into a friend from the Stock Exchange. 'He literally was selling carpet squares,' Bishop remembered, 'and he was making a living that way.'[16]

Behind the anguish of the City lay not just the pathetic debris of the stock market crash, but the stark reality of an economy lurching drunkenly towards the rocks. With unemployment, inflation and public borrowing all heading inexorably upwards, it was hardly surprising that November's Industrial Trends Survey found eight out of ten firms preparing to run down their stocks, squeeze their debtors and borrow heavily merely to survive. Profits had never been so tightly constricted: after tax, the rate of return on trading assets was falling below 4 per cent, the lowest level since the war. In a typical week that autumn, a firm was going bankrupt in the Companies Court every forty-five seconds. On 3 December the British Rail chairman, Richard Marsh, told Ronald McIntosh of the National Economic Development Council that he could actually see the 'loss of confidence' on the faces of the nation's businessmen. The CBI, he said, were 'in a mood of near despair about their relations with government and had a terrible inferiority complex about it. They knew that Healey had complete contempt for them and were convinced that neither Foot nor Benn would pay any attention to what they said.' Even within the government, confidence had reached its lowest ebb. Six days before Christmas, Wilson's informal adviser Thomas Balogh forwarded him a paper predicting that if just one major corporation went bust, the result might be 'a wholesale domestic liquidation' – in other words, economic Armageddon. 'The magnitude of this threat is quite incalculable,' it went on. 'The collapses which have occurred up till now, and even those which have been prevented, can really be likened to the tip of an iceberg.'[17]

'Doesn't it sound strange, 1975?' asks Meg Richardson, Britain's best-loved Birmingham motel owner, in the New Year's Eve episode of *Crossroads*. 'Well, let's hope it's an improvement on 1974,' replies housewives' favourite Hugh Mortimer. 'Two elections, a disastrous summer, one crisis on top of another . . .' But he was not alone in looking back with distaste and forward with trepidation. 'Where do you stand at the end of this bewildering year?' asked James McMillan in that day's *Daily Express*. It had been 'a good Christmas for most people. The shops are full and the sales are on.' And yet, he thought, 'Britain is in for very difficult times', facing 'a year or two with no rise in living

Emmwood's New Year's Resolutions, published in the *Daily Mail* on
31 December 1974, give a flavour of Fleet Street's contempt for the Social
Contract and alarm at Tony Benn's plans for industry.

standards for the nation as a whole – which, as we all know, means a
rise in the living standards of those in the powerful trade unions and a
drop for the rest of us'. Most people, it seemed, agreed with him: when
Gallup asked about their expectations for 1975, 40 per cent expected
the economy to 'deteriorate a lot' and 26 per cent to 'deteriorate slightly',
while only 8 per cent thought it would 'improve slightly' and a minuscule 2 per cent 'improve a lot'. In a letter to a Dutch friend, Roy Strong
captured the general mood:

> The weather has been foul, matching the economic and political situ-
> ation. In the country we till the land, eat our own veg grown from
> seed, stack high the deep-freeze with the fruits of summer ... it's just like
> World War II again ... Everything is in the doldrums. It is said that six
> theatres will close in the West End next year due to lack of money to put
> on new shows ... Seats at Covent Garden have just hit £9 a go, which
> makes one wince. We never go except to see something new. I live in
> dread of vast slashes to museum spending and facing 1975 with no
> money, the exhibition schedule in ruins and the [V&A's] new Oriental
> wing stopped. The post is now on strike in WC1, so don't write to the

British Museum. The Bakerloo and Circle Underground lines are so bad that they might just as well not exist. Sugar and salt are unobtainable. Olive oil, we discovered, has gone up 60% this year, the first of a long list of such rises.

Strong had done his 'winter shop' in August, hoping to beat the price rises. His list said it all: 'vast mounds of tinned and frozen foods, every sort of candle, matches, oil heater, oil lamp, Calor gas, the lot'. Britain, he thought, was 'at a crossroads and it is incredible how many dodge the issue'. But he tried to put a brave face on things. 'Never mind,' he wrote, 'keep smiling . . .'[18]

It was left to Hughie Green, the unctuous host of ITV's talent show *Opportunity Knocks*, to sound an unlikely clarion call for national renewal. To most viewers, 'fast-talking Hughie' was the incarnation of commercial populism, a shameless showman whose performances on *Double Your Money* and *Opportunity Knocks* horrified critics but had paved the way for younger entertainers such as Bruce Forsyth and Leslie Crowther. Yet despite his dissolute private life, Green was an admirer of Mary Whitehouse, a fierce critic of socialism and a keen supporter of Margaret Thatcher. Every year he argued that at least one edition of *Opportunity Knocks* should be filmed on, say, a nuclear submarine or a NATO airbase, although he never got his way. But now he was determined to say his piece. Addressing 18 million viewers on 30 December, his tone suddenly sombre, his faux-American accent becoming mysteriously more clipped, Green abruptly launched into a cod-Churchillian rallying cry:

> Friends, it is the end of the show. Tomorrow is the end of the year. Let us work with all our might to see that 1975, with the gathering storm of despair ahead, will not be the end of our country. Lest we perish, friends, let us all together say in 1975, both to the nation, to each other and to ourselves: 'For God's sake, Britain, *wake up*!'

As Green's words died away, the house band swelled and a choir broke into a chorus of 'Land of Hope and Glory'. It seemed a remarkably inappropriate anthem for a country bereft of either.[19]

On Monday, 6 January, the stock market reached a new and singularly depressing low. That night, the FT 30 Index closed at just 146.0, a fall of 73 per cent in less than three years. It was its lowest level since Roger Bannister had broken the four-minute mile, more than two decades before – an event that seemed to belong to a different world. Even the supposedly Swinging Sixties were now an increasingly distant memory: two days later, after years of wrangling, the Beatles' partnership was officially dissolved in a private hearing in the High Court. 'Another sign of the times,' recorded Michael Palin. 'The feeling in the press is that we have a bad year to come – increasing unemployment, steeply rising prices, etc, etc . . . Everywhere the talk is of cuts, savings and "trimming back".' Palin rather optimistically thought that the worst was over, and that the bad economic news would be enough to 'bring out all the Dunkirk spirit'. But harder-headed observers did not agree. Britain, declared the financial magazine *International Insider*, was now 'a second-rate credit and is fast turning into a borrower to be classed alongside an undeveloped country'.[20]

Lunching a few weeks later at the Carlton Club with a group of City partners, Ronald McIntosh found them all 'very gloomy', and there was 'much talk of collapse and perhaps authoritarian rule'. The very next day, the Cabinet Secretary, Sir John Hunt, told him despairingly that Whitehall had no answer to the crisis. Most civil servants, said Hunt, thought the government would soon 'do all the right things', but he was 'quite sure they will not'. McIntosh worked out an elaborate joke imagining Britain as the *Titanic*, with the TUC cheerfully claiming that the iceberg was really the Northern Lights, the CBI down in the bar singing 'Not so much a contract, more a way of death', and the ship's officers 'holding a referendum on whether to put the helm to port or starboard'. Deep down, however, he too had a terrible sense of looming disaster. 'The two main headlines in the *Times* today are "Militant consultants threaten to close NHS hospitals" and "Troops to move into Glasgow tomorrow",' he wrote on 15 March.* 'This really does look like a collapsing society.'[21]

To those, like McIntosh, who knew the history of the inter-war decades, nothing was more frightening than the advance of inflation. By the time of the second 1974 election, Heath's infamous threshold payments, which the new government refused to scrap for fear of alienating working-class voters, had been triggered eleven times. In just twelve months, the Retail Price Index had risen by 17 per cent; wages, mean-

---

* The headlines actually read: 'Militant Consultants Ready To Close NHS Hospitals' and 'Troops May Move Into Glasgow In A Few Days'. The former referred to the consultants' bid for better pay and conditions; the latter to plans to clear Glasgow's streets of rubbish after a dustmen's strike.

while, had risen by an astonishing 22 per cent. People might not yet need wheelbarrows filled with money to buy a loaf of bread, but if inflation continued to rise at the current rate, Britain's garden centres would soon find themselves besieged by customers. During the election, Wilson had argued that the great merit of the Social Contract was that it would hold inflation back. What was now clear, however, was that he had merely handed the unions a blank cheque, with wage inflation hitting a record 26 per cent by January 1975. Perhaps it was unrealistic to expect the union leaders to show heroic self-restraint: under intense pressure from their members, Jack Jones and Hugh Scanlon insisted that they were merely trying to protect ordinary workers against the ravages of higher prices. The inevitable result, however, was that pay bargaining turned into a frenzied scramble for higher wages, each union frantically trying to outbid its rivals, each settlement bigger than the last. By December, even civil service permanent secretaries had won an extra £120 a week each. And with NHS consultants poised to secure almost 40 per cent increases, wrote Bernard Donoughue glumly, 'the whole wage front is collapsing'.[22]

He was not far wrong By February 1975, the miners had won a whopping 35 per cent settlement, costing the National Coal Board some £140 million, although the Yorkshire NUM president, one Arthur Scargill, claimed that a 'more determined and militant approach' would have secured even bigger rewards. As *The Times* wearily pointed out, the miners' new surface rate of £41 per week would now 'become the target for at least two big groups of public sector workers who are next in the queue: the railwaymen and the electricity supply workers'. British Rail immediately offered the railwaymen 20 per cent, while the Electricity Council offered its employees a sliding scale of increases from 20 to 31 per cent. The unions turned them down. An arbitration tribunal offered the railwaymen 27½ per cent; once again, it was flung back in their faces. As the railwaymen's leader Sid Weighell defiantly explained, they would never accept 'something lower than a whole range of other public sector workers. I don't see why I should say to my members that they have to slip further away from people such as the miners, the postmen and the power workers.'* The rail unions called for a national strike; the government, inevitably, gave in. On 20 June, just three

---

* 'You've just turned down 27.5 per cent. You must be barmy,' said Weighell's father, a former signalman. 'I didn't try to explain,' Weighell said later. 'It just showed how the world had changed in one generation.'

days before the strike was scheduled to begin, British Rail handed its employees a 30 per cent pay increase, putting them level with the miners. As usual, Michael Foot insisted that the award breached neither the spirit nor the letter of the Social Contract. By now, not even government insiders believed him. 'Foot recommended giving way,' recorded Donoughue, 'saying, as always, that this was not the claim on which to make a stand, but also describing a 30% settlement as OK because it was the "going rate". If any rate that is the going rate is OK, then *any* going rate must be OK – so why not 50%!'[23]

By this point, it was clear that things simply could not continue as they were. According to government figures, prices in March had risen at an annual average of 27 per cent, while price inflation for April was even worse, hitting an all-time record 33 per cent. To put this into context, prices in Britain were rising *five times* faster than in any other major European country. What was more, although the Social Contract was supposed to insulate the economy against the global downturn and stop workers losing their jobs, unemployment had almost doubled in twelve months and was just short of the dreaded million mark – a level for which Labour had pilloried Heath three years before. Britain was trapped in a vicious circle: as prices rose, ordinary households howled with pain, the unions pressed for wage increases, profits fell, businesses buckled under the strain and prices inevitably rose again. Inevitably, millions blamed the unions: an NOP poll found that more than 83 per cent of people thought both high prices and trade union power were serious threats to the survival of democracy. Even inside the government, ministers were bewildered by the apparent unwillingness to challenge the TUC. Edmund Dell thought that one problem was the Employment Secretary's middle-class guilt: since Foot was hardly a horny-handed proletarian himself, 'day by day he had to convince himself that he was their man'. In any case, it was now painfully obvious that the Social Contract was a sham. 'PM at a liaison meeting with the TUC and the NEC on the social contract,' Donoughue recorded on 21 April. 'He later said it was "very friendly" – which means they did not deal with it honestly. With wages going up at 30% there is no social contract. It works only one way.' It was 'humbug', agreed Joe Haines, 'and everyone knew it'.[24]

Perhaps the most astonishing thing about the great inflation of 1975 is that although Wilson's advisers desperately tried to persuade him of the urgency of the crisis, he showed little inclination to do anything about it. To some extent, Whitehall was still in shock; recent history offered no precedents for such a challenge. More pertinent, though, was Wilson's sheer passivity, his fundamental unwillingness to do anything that might upset the unions or the electorate. In January, when the Policy Unit begged him to 'take a grip', he simply ignored it. In February, Donoughue and Graham sent him another paper, insisting that he simply must choose '*one* unpleasant option', and suggesting a mixture of spending cuts and wage controls. 'Again,' wrote Donoughue, 'no response'. The irony, though, was that, even as Wilson twiddled his thumbs, the union leaders – the very people who were supposedly preventing him from taking action – were becoming seriously worried. Behind the scenes, the TUC's general secretary Len Murray found one colleague after another approaching him and muttering: 'We can't go on like this.' As Murray recognized, pay increases at 30 per cent a year were a recipe for economic meltdown. Even the AUEW's Hugh Scanlon, by repute the most militant of the union barons, told the TUC-Labour Liaison Committee that it was time for some 'straight talking'. The only sensible line, Scanlon said, was for workers to have 'only one increase a year, and that within the cost of living, and if we mean that why don't we say so?' His listeners could hardly believe their ears. 'Wonders will never cease!' wrote Barbara Castle. But as a good Marxist, Scanlon knew that economic self-destruction was not the road to socialism. He even thought that the government should cut back its welfare commitments and release more money for industry, promoting recovery by putting greater 'emphasis on those who make and sell', rather than channelling resources into the public sector. This was good advice. Nobody listened.[25]

Although Harold Wilson refused to give a lead, his Chancellor was poised to set out on the road to Damascus. For nine months, Denis Healey had stubbornly ignored warnings that the economy was heading for oblivion, but by the New Year his senior Treasury officials had decided that enough was enough. According to his colleague Edmund Dell, they told the Chancellor that 'while they were sorry about any political difficulties their advice might cause him, there was no longer support for his policies within the Treasury'. For all his combativeness, Healey was a man who appreciated frankness, and he was intelligent enough to see the writing on the wall. On 10 January, addressing a meeting in Leeds, he gave the first hint of a historic shift in public policy. The timing could hardly have been more appropriate: a few days later, government figures suggested that if earnings carried on rising, inflation would soon hit a staggering 37 per cent. So when Healey announced that it was time to rethink the Social Contract, his words found a receptive audience. To put Britain back to work, he said, it was essential to get inflation down. 'It is far better', he added, 'that more people should be in work, even if that means accepting lower wages on average, than that those lucky enough to keep their jobs should scoop the pool while millions are living on the dole.' This, as *The Times*'s economics editor Peter Jay noted, was to turn 'conventional economic wisdom on its head', identifying inflation, not unemployment, as the government's real enemy. But as Healey explained to the union leaders, 'you can bankrupt a nation by excessive wage demands'. They 'simply had to get wage settlements down', he said, 'above all in the public sector'. Barbara Castle thought this was extraordinarily brave of him. But it was telling that the union men 'watched him transfixed as he spoke', and that Len Murray was 'barely able to refrain from nodding'. Even they recognized that with inflation now out of control, something had to change.[26]

In the next few weeks, Healey's reincarnation began to take shape. No longer shielding his Cabinet colleagues from the consequences of their commitments, he almost relished delivering the most appalling tidings. 'Our credit, he said, was low and falling,' Castle wrote after a meeting on 25 March. 'The borrowing requirement was much too high for comfort and we might get a sudden collapse of confidence.' He 'didn't want to be too nasty', but they simply had to start cutting spending, starting with £1 billion off their plans for 1976–7. As it turned out, that was nowhere near enough to restore confidence in the British economy. But it was far too much for many of his colleagues. Cutting spending at all was 'totally unacceptable', grumbled Tony Benn, because 'we'd be abandoning measures to which we were committed through the Social Contract'. Yet in stark contrast to his attitude a year earlier, Healey seemed determined to go down as an Iron Chancellor, not a political one. Borrowing was 'terrifying', he told Barbara Castle a couple of weeks later. 'He just had to cut back public expenditure. The Social Contract wasn't working. Inflation was getting out of control.' And, unlike some of her colleagues, Castle recognized that he had a point. The government was 'caught in that sense of inevitability when social democratic dreams come up against the realities of the mixed economy', she admitted on 14 April, when Healey presented yet another Budget to the Cabinet. 'We all know that, whatever the reasons that got us into the mess we are in, we have little alternative.'[27]

When Healey unveiled his new strategy to the Commons the next day, there were gasps of disbelief on the government backbenches. This time, he had no gimmicks to please the crowds or presents for the Labour left. His Budget, he said bleakly, was 'a hard one for all of us in Britain', but it was 'dictated by the harsh reality of the world we live in'. The Social Contract was simply not working: according to the latest figures, prices were rising at an annual rate of 20 per cent, with wage inflation forecast to reach 29 per cent. Hoping to squeeze the inflation out of the system, Healey raised the basic and higher rates of income tax by 2 per cent each. He increased VAT to 25 per cent on electrical appliances, radios and television sets, cameras, jewellery, boats, aircraft and caravans; he cut food subsidies, housing subsidies and foreign aid; he put up duty on cars, alcohol and cigarettes; and above all, he confirmed that he was cutting spending in 1976–7 by almost £1 billion. And in case there was any doubt about his new strategy, Healey spelled it out, loud and clear. He knew that the left wanted him to loosen the purse-strings. But 'when 5p in every pound we spend at home has been provided by our creditors abroad and inflation is running at its current rate', Britain simply could not afford it. 'Moreover, a Rake's Progress of this nature could not last for long. The patience of our creditors would soon be exhausted. We would then face the appalling prospect of going down in a matter of weeks to the levels of public services and personal living standards which we could finance entirely from what we earned. I do not believe that our political or social system could stand that strain.'

On the Labour benches, there was a long, horrified silence. 'It was an exceptional Budget,' one political correspondent wrote the next day, 'because it raised no cheers at all from the backbenchers or frontbenchers garrisoning the Government side of the Commons.' For a Labour Chancellor to put up taxes and cut spending at a time when unemployment was so high was not merely a shock; it was a watershed. In the next day's *Times*, an approving Peter Jay wrote that Healey had 'finally and totally broken with post war orthodoxy' and 'abandoned full employment'. Since the government's unbridled spending had failed to stop unemployment rising towards one million, Healey could well have replied that full employment had abandoned him, rather than the other way round. Even so, the fact that he had switched his attention to bringing inflation down was a hugely symbolic moment. And when Healey looked back, he recognized that his Budget – even more than the IMF crisis a year later – had been a watershed in post-war economic history. 'I abandoned Keynesianism in 1975,' he wrote later.[28]

Even as Healey tried to change course, the outside world was coming to its own bleak conclusions about Britain's prospects. During the Great Depression, when Keynes had first elaborated his famous theories of demand management, Britain had been the world's most respected power. As late as the mid-1960s, when Healey and his colleagues first got their hands on the reins of power, Britannia still had pretensions to world leadership. Yet by the spring of 1975, viewed from overseas, the condition of England had become an object lesson in economic indiscipline, moral dissipation and social fragmentation. 'Britain is a tragedy,' the US Secretary of State, Henry Kissinger, told President Ford at the beginning of the year. 'It has sunk to begging, borrowing, stealing until North Sea oil comes in ... That Britain has become such a scrounger is a disgrace.'[29]

The United Kingdom was 'going down the drain', agreed the chairman of the Federal Reserve, Arthur Burns, a few months later. And unfortunately for Britain's self-image, this view was not confined to the corridors of power. The old country was 'sinking', announced a much-quoted editorial in the conservative *Wall Street Journal* at the end of April, lamenting Britain's 52 per cent corporate tax rate, its 83 per cent top tax rate on earned income, and its 98 per cent marginal rate on unearned income. To the *Journal*, the workshop of the world had become a study in the perils of socialism:

> Britain's current contribution to the world is to reveal the ultimate result of economic and social policies [which hold that] the state must fulfil all needs ... The British government is now so clearly headed toward a policy of total confiscation that anyone who has any wealth left is [taking] any chance to get it out of the country ... The price can only be still slower economic growth and still lower living standards for all the British, rich and poor. Goodbye, Great Britain, it was nice knowing you.

If that sounded melodramatic, it was as nothing compared with the message that the veteran correspondent Eric Sevareid had for the audience of the *CBS Evening News* a week later. The problem with Britain, he said, was not merely 'that her military strength is ebbing and her economic strength weakening', but that it had fallen victim to 'doctrinaire socialists, the true believers, for whom the picture in their heads is more real than the reality around them'. Under their influence, 'Britain is drifting slowly toward a condition of ungovernability [and] sleepwalking into a social revolution, one its majority clearly does not want but does not know how to stop'. It was 'at the stage of Allende's Chilean Government when a minority tried to force a profound transformation of society upon the majority – not that the backlash in Britain need be militaristic, but some kind of backlash is building up'.[30]

Harold Wilson reacted to Sevareid's broadcast with his usual indifference, dismissing it as the tittle-tattle of the 'cocktail circuit'. But Sevareid was no mere gossip: liberal-minded, Anglophile and highly respected, he had made his name reporting on the fall of France in 1940. In Britain's embassy in Washington, officials were reportedly distraught at the blow to their country's image. In London, meanwhile, his report caused enough of a stir for *The Times* to afford it a long editorial. The Chilean analogy, the newspaper said, was overblown: 'there is no armed left-wing movement; there is no sign of a military movement of the authoritarian right.' There, however, the disagreement ended. 'His grave diagnosis is all the stronger,' *The Times* thought, 'because it agrees with the view of many other friendly observers.' Britain's inflation rate was the highest in Europe, the pound was 'the weakest of the major world currencies', unemployment was rising and the economy depended 'entirely on massive borrowing from abroad'. 'These facts are well known to the world,' *The Times* said sadly, 'where British prestige has not stood so low since Charles II was the pensioner of Louis XIV. They are well known in Britain where we are far too sensible not to feel the silent lash of self-contempt … We need nothing less than a revolution in the spirit of the nation if we are to preserve the historic values of the nation.' In short, the situation was 'disastrous'. Britain had reached 'the end of the line'.[31]

PART TWO

A Damn Good Thrashing

9

A Clever Bit of Propaganda

The pupils of William Tyndale Junior School are having a very hard time trying to cope with their teachers. Some of these teachers are polite and hard-working. Others are high-spirited but bright enough and likely to do well. A very few, however – probably those from problem homes – are very disturbed, and every pupil knows that just one such teacher can completely disrupt a classroom.

Guardian, 27 October 1975

'The only way to change society is to change people and the only way to change people is in the schools.'
    'By brainwashing them?'
    'Call it what you like,' said Graham.

Piers Paul Read, *A Married Man* (1979)

All Tracy wanted was to be allowed to wear her platform shoes. They were a present from her aunt, who had bought them for Tracy's first day at her new school. It was well known in the Liddon family that Tracy was nervous about moving to Creighton. She had enjoyed her local primary school and had set her heart on Hornsey Girls, but her mother had said no. Hornsey Girls was a long bus ride away, while Creighton was just a short walk from their home on the Coppett's Wood estate. In any case, her brother Gary was already there and her mother thought it would be nice for them to go to school together. So Creighton it was: a big, bustling school, with boys as well as girls.

Tracy could not disguise her nerves, so a few days before the start of term her mother explained that although she might get a 'few clouts from the older girls', if she worked hard and kept her head down, she would be all right. That made Tracy feel better; but then came the shock about the shoes. Not only did her mother refuse to let her wear them, she vetoed eyeshadow and earrings too. To her horror, Tracy was not even allowed to wear the knee-length skirt she had bought for the disco a few weeks earlier. That put her in a bad mood, and she was trembling with nerves as she left for school in the late summer sunshine. Gary predictably disappeared as soon as their mother was out of sight, and when Tracy reached the gates she felt terrified at the sheer size of the place. Only one of her primary school friends was in her class, and Tracy was so nervous that she wanted to cry. But then she noticed something. 'None of the girls were in high shoes,' she recalled. 'They all had on flat shoes, like me. So my mum was right. She always is.'[1]

The daughter of a Post Office engineer from the north London suburbs, Tracy Liddon was one of thousands of British children making their worried way to a new school that sunny morning in September 1974. There was nothing extraordinary about her: like so many of her contemporaries, she spent most of her time thinking about David Cassidy, the Osmonds and the Bay City Rollers. What made her distinctive, though, was that she had caught the attention of the journalist Hunter Davies, who had been sent to Creighton by the *Sunday Times* to write a series of articles about life in a comprehensive school. Having written the biography of the Beatles and spent a year behind the scenes at Tottenham Hotspur, Davies might have found the project mundane. In fact, he fell in love with it, staying on even after the articles had been published to gather material for a book. Comprehensives such as Creighton, he wrote in the preface, had become associated with 'lowering standards, ill-discipline, mugging, football hooliganism, illiteracy, strikes, pornography, illegitimacy, unemployment, and why England failed to win the World Cup'. The reality, he discovered, was rather more complicated.

Situated on a quiet street in suburban Muswell Hill, Creighton hardly looked like the cradle of national degeneracy. It had been formed in 1967 from the enforced merger of two Haringey schools, a grammar school and a secondary modern, and every day its concrete and glass buildings rang with the voices of some 1,500 pupils of all classes, races, religions and abilities. Many were from first- or second-generation immigrant families: scanning the noticeboards on his first day, Davies estimated that one in three surnames was Indian or Greek Cypriot, and he was startled to see older boys with full beards. Almost seventy pupils, he discovered later, had to attend remedial English classes, most of them

Cypriots, Chinese and the odd Moroccan. But Davies himself was not the only high-profile newcomer to the school in the autumn of 1974. For Creighton had a new headmistress: Molly Hattersley, a 'tall handsome lady of forty-three', married to one of the rising stars on the right wing of the Labour Party, Roy Hattersley. As the former senior mistress of Sheffield's first comprehensive, Mrs Hattersley was in no doubt that comprehensive schools represented social progress. 'Separating the clever and the less clever', she explained, 'is bound to create two communities, perpetuating the divisions in society.'[2]

In some ways, Creighton lived up to a *Guardian* reader's dream of a progressive comprehensive school. Classes were run on a mixed-ability basis, which Davies found exhausting, even though he had studied for a teaching diploma as a young man. The school rules were only one page long and were mainly devoted to hours and attendance. There were no prefects and few punishments, except for suspension for serious offences and detention for the youngest children. There were no uniforms, since they had been voted down in a referendum of staff, pupils, parents and governors. There were no duties or positions for older pupils, and no merit awards, badges or colours. There was, however, a sixth-form common room, where pupils listened to rock music and smoked in the garden, and a democratically elected sixth form committee. Davies was struck by the older pupils' pride in their school's progressive reputation: they were 'obsessed by not competing', and it was seen as 'anti-social to want to beat other people'. This naturally infuriated the sports teachers: one confided to Davies that the abolition of the house system had made it impossible to organize internal competitions. 'Avoiding competition in Sport', he said, 'is avoiding human nature.' But the school's new headmistress was delighted by its anti-competitive ethos. Addressing a parents' meeting, Mrs Hattersley insisted that she did not want a school where the children told each other: 'I'm better than you and I've just proved it.' She was 'in the business of avoiding labelling children', she said, and the business of 'avoiding distinctions'.[3]

Mrs Hattersley was not, of course, the only teacher with progressive opinions. Davies was astonished to see younger teachers in jeans and jumpers, while the art department looked like a 'squatter's paradise', a 'wonderland of shocking pinks and purples'. And some teachers came deliciously close to being *Private Eye* caricatures. 'I don't agree with schools,' said Tracy Liddon's form tutor Dave Matthews, a 26-year-old Swansea graduate and former grammar school boy. 'I don't think kids should be made to come to school. It turns schools into prisons.' He was 'against all laws', he added. 'Kids who can't work or don't want to work should be allowed to do nothing.' On the walls of his classroom, he had put up two displays. One, headed 'The Myth', was a collage of army recruiting posters, showing handsome young men skiing, swimming and operating radios. On the other, 'The Reality', he had stuck pictures of soldiers being shot and killed in Northern Ireland. This, he said proudly, was a 'clever bit of propaganda'. Whether his pupils took much notice, however, is doubtful. Tracy Liddon told her mother that, although Mr Matthews was nice enough, she wished 'he wasn't so soft and the class wasn't so noisy'.

Mr Matthews was not alone in his radical commitments. Another splendid example of a trendy teacher was Andy Dorn, 27, who always wore jeans, a sweater, a denim jacket and a political badge. When Davies met him, the badge read 'Liberate the Arab Gulf States'. Not unpredictably, Mr Dorn was the middle-class son of a middle manager and had been educated at prep school, Brighton College and the London School of Economics. He too looked forward to the abolition of exams and thought that 'the present system only perpetuates the inequalities in the class system.' Meanwhile the 37-year-old head of Religious Education, John Bamford, taught a very different kind of RE from the subject Davies had studied back in the early 1950s. Many classes focused on the issues of 'sex, drugs and violence', and Mr Bamford prided himself on attracting a wide range of speakers, including prison workers, Hare Krishna practitioners, Lord Longford and representatives of the Gay Liberation Front. However, even Molly Hattersley had her limits, and when a visiting speaker proposed to show slides on the difference between pornography and erotica, she put her foot down. Mr Bamford was deeply disappointed. 'It was only going to be soft porn, not hard porn,' he reflected later. 'It would have helped the students to make rational judgments, to have discriminating tastes.'[4]

And yet it was a myth, Davies found, that the staffroom was full of 'raving young Marxists, plotting insurrection, leading the kids to revolution'. In fact, what really surprised him was how many teachers held 'strong conservative, right-wing views'. Even many of the younger teachers had distinctly old-fashioned opinions, especially those who were from working-class backgrounds and owed their achievements to their grammar school education. But it was the older teachers, not surprisingly, who were most disturbed by the advance of progress. Miss Stevens, the 60-year-old head of Commerce, insisted that girls tie their hair up during her classes, made them take off their high heels and jewellery and dispose of their gum, and even made them button up their cardigans. It was getting harder to keep them in line, she confided, although 'I find Indian children very well behaved'. Overall, she thought, standards were slipping, and 'the permissive society is to blame', with parents 'giving in every time their children demand something'. These views were echoed by the second-year head Mr Hart, a local lad who had left school at 13 and was now almost 60. In the old days, he said, 'everyone knew where they were'. But now 'society generally has become more lawless and the crime rate has risen dramatically'. He was still not convinced by the comprehensive principle, but what really disturbed him were the tumbling standards of the younger teachers. 'Look at this photograph from the *Daily Telegraph*,' he said to Davies. 'It's a group of teachers on a union demonstration. Did you ever see such a scruffy bunch? What a rotten image to present to the public!'

What Hunter Davies found so fascinating about Creighton was that it seemed so delicately poised between old and new, straddling a cultural gulf that some teachers found increasingly intolerable. At the end of the year, Miss Stevens shocked her colleagues by handing in her notice. In a letter to Davies, she explained that she was 'sick and tired of pupil abuse, swearing, discourtesy, inattention, indifference to work – i.e. I am completely disenchanted with State education'. At the same time, Dave Matthews also resigned, explaining that the school was not liberal enough. 'I disagree with teaching more than ever,' he said. 'All it's doing is preparing kids for a capitalist, materialistic society. It encourages them to be competitive and blow everyone up.' He hoped to come back when 'exams have ceased to exist', in which case he was in for a long wait. He was last heard of 'heading west for a farming commune in Wales'.[5]

Yet most teachers held much less apocalyptic views, and were content to potter along somewhere in the middle, rather like the teenagers they taught. When a small group of outspoken sixth-formers demanded the right to send representatives to staff meetings, they provoked fierce debates among the staff. In the end the teachers voted by 33 to 18 to admit them. But although Davies made the staff meeting debate the centrepiece of his book, he recognized that most pupils simply did not care. In a survey of the sixth form, half turned out to be totally indifferent, and more were firmly *against* the staff-meeting scheme than were for it. Most of them, like teenagers everywhere, were too busy thinking about Rod Stewart and Led Zeppelin, or Chris Evert and Kevin Keegan, or *Doctor Who* and *The Lord of the Rings*, to worry about school politics. Most said they liked the school, citing sport and drama as particular highlights. And even Tracy Liddon was getting on well. She had had a few fights, and had even played truant one day, but her popularity was reflected in her election as her class's representative to the School Council. In the summer of 1975, playing on her estate, she met some local children who were moving on to Creighton next term. What was it like, they wondered: was it too strict? 'You behave yourself and don't give no cheek,' Tracy said, 'and you'll get on okay.'[6]

Few issues in the 1970s were more divisive than education. It was the stuff of impassioned editorials in the national newspapers, angry exchanges on *Question Time* and innumerable debates around suburban dining tables, the atmosphere dropping to freezing point as guests lectured one another across the sherry trifle. For generations of parents, the right to educate their children how they wanted, often at their own expense, was a crucial element of their social position. The school tie was the supreme badge of class identity: when Captain Mainwaring's resentment against the debonair Sergeant Wilson boils over in *Dad's Army*, he angrily contrasts Wilson's 'tuppeny-ha'penny public school' ('Well, I wouldn't call Meadowbridge *that*,' objects a pained Wilson) with his beloved Eastbourne Grammar. But in a fluid society where exams and qualifications meant the difference between moving up or staying down, education loomed larger than ever. Schools became a battleground not only between working-class ambition and middle-class idealism, but between traditionalists and radicals, old and young, left and right, and, crucially, between two different incarnations of middle-class identity. On the one hand, to put it crudely, were the well-meaning readers of the *Guardian*, who dreamed of a more egalitarian society where children from all backgrounds learned and played together; on the other were the people who read the *Mail* and the *Express*, who glowed with pride at their social gains and were determined to ensure that their children reaped the full benefit of their hard work. Between the two there was little common ground.[7]

The drive to turn Britain's schools comprehensive was not, as is often thought, motivated merely by left-wing egalitarianism. By far the most important factor was the consensus that the existing system, with most children taking the eleven-plus to decide whether they went on to grammar school or a secondary modern, was simply not working. Most grammar schools were excellent, but many secondary moderns were terrible. Since the typical grammar school had three times the resources of the typical secondary modern, success or failure at just 11 could determine a child's entire educational career. If you failed the eleven-plus, you were very unlikely to go on to university: although 56 per cent of children went to secondary moderns in 1968, less than 2 per cent of them were still in school at the age of 17. More disturbingly, though, it was now clear that success in the eleven-plus had more to do with class than with merit. In working-class Gateshead, just 8 per cent of children got into grammar schools, while in neighbouring rural areas more than two-thirds made it. In the inner-city Nottingham district of St Ann's, almost none of the children went to grammar schools, compared with six out of ten in the city's middle-class suburbs. And although much of the noise surrounding comprehensive schools came from left-wing schoolteachers, the decisive factor was middle-class parents' anxiety that little Timmy might fail the eleven-plus and be condemned to life as a failure. Of course there was an element of snobbery in all this, but since secondary moderns were vastly inferior to grammar schools, it was also a matter of simply wanting the best for one's children. Anything, most parents thought, would be better than a secondary modern.[8]

When Margaret Thatcher became Education Secretary in June 1970, the tide had been flowing in favour of comprehensives for almost a decade. Already there were 1,145 comprehensives in Britain, catering for one in three children. But although polls showed a clear majority against the eleven-plus, they also showed large public support for keeping grammar schools. Parents and local authorities alike, not least Labour ones, were justifiably proud of institutions that had done much to encourage social mobility, and were appalled at the thought of losing them. Keeping the grammar schools, however, had not been a priority for Wilson's first government; indeed, Tony Crosland (a former public school boy) told his wife that he hoped 'to destroy every fucking grammar school in England'. These words would have horrified many working-class parents, for whom grammar schools represented a precious opportunity, and they would doubtless have appalled Mrs Thatcher, too. She had no patience, she said, for what she called 'the equalisation rage at the time, that you mustn't select by ability. After all, I had come up by selection by ability. I had to fight it.' But if she really meant to fight it, she had a very funny way of going about it. For while she found more money for direct grant schools and always stuck up for the private sector, the plain fact is that between 1970 and 1974 she closed more grammar schools and approved more comprehensives than any other Secretary of State in history. In less than four years, the proportion of children in comprehensives doubled to 62 per cent, and out of 3,612 comprehensive schemes submitted to her for inspection, she approved 3,286. In a supreme irony, one of the schools affected by the changes was Kesteven and Grantham Girls' School, her own alma mater.[9]

The underlying reality was that, until February 1974, education was governed by an unspoken consensus. Comprehensives were the wave of the future; it was pointless to resist. But once Harold Wilson returned to power, the consensus began to disintegrate, not merely because of parents' protests, but because the government adopted a much more interventionist, top-down approach. In their October manifesto, Labour promised to complete the comprehensive revolution as quickly as possible, mopping up the last pockets of resistance irrespective of what local authorities wanted. On top of that, they promised to remove tax relief and charitable status from independent schools in order to end the culture of 'fee paying in schools'. But what loomed largest in the middle-class imagination was the threat to abolish Britain's direct grant grammar schools. Unlike ordinary grammar schools, these highly successful institutions, many of which had been going for centuries, were a curious state–private hybrid. Every year they offered a quarter of their places free of charge for local primary school children, with another quarter paid for by the local authority and the rest claimed by fee-paying parents whose children had passed the eleven-plus. In 1975 there were 174 such schools, generally single-sex, some of them with boarding places. Most were run by large charitable foundations or religious teaching orders, especially the Catholic Church. They were concentrated in the north of England, with 46 in Lancashire and a further 18 in West Yorkshire, including such prestigious names as Leeds Grammar and Bradford Grammar. Many, such as Manchester Grammar and King Edward's, Birmingham, were easily as good as the best public schools; indeed, their university admissions rates put very famous boarding schools to shame. The difference, of course, was that many of their pupils came from families that would never have been able to afford school fees. In this respect, as *The Times* put it, the direct grant schools were not merely 'pinnacles of academic excellence in secondary education'; they were narrow but well-trodden avenues 'for the educational progress of able working-class children'.[10]

Given that so many direct grant schools had old boys in Harold Wilson's government – Denis Healey, for example, had been to Bradford Grammar, while Harold Lever was an old Manchester Grammar boy – it is surprising that the new administration proceeded against them with such severity. But education reform was a relatively easy way to please the Labour left, and in March 1975 the new Education Secretary, Reg Prentice, announced that the direct grant schools must go comprehensive by the end of 1976. The National Union of Teachers was delighted, hailing it as a 'big step forward towards the removal of elitism from British education'. More sensible observers, however, pointed out that since most of the schools were threatening to become independent if the grant was cut off, Prentice's decision was utterly self-defeating. Manchester Grammar, for example, announced that if the government withdrew the direct grant it would go private, pushing the fees up to £500 a year. As the chairman of the governors admitted, this would 'inevitably tend to exclude children of poor parents, contrary to every instinct and desire of the school, and contrary, one would have thought, to all egalitarian principle'. He was sorry about that, he said, but to preserve the ethos of the school, he simply had no choice. As *The Times* put it, the government's plan would therefore 'reinforce both the principle of selective secondary education and the power of the independent schools', sacrificing genuine mobility to 'the demands of egalitarianism without any corresponding gain'.[11]

Many direct grant schools were genuinely distressed at the choice between becoming comprehensives – which effectively meant forfeiting their identity – and going independent. At Red Maids' School in Bristol, founded for poor women's daughters in 1634, one in five girls came from an unskilled working-class family, and a further one in seven from a semi-skilled household. The oldest girls' school in Britain, Red Maids' now became a private school. So did another Bristol school, Queen Elizabeth's Hospital, whose headmaster thought it 'insane' that 'an historic bluecoat school with nearly 400 years of service to the less well-off boys of Bristol behind it is now being forced by a central socialist government to go independent, raise its fees in consequence and thus move beyond the reach of the very people the socialists have traditionally wanted to help'. Trying to fight back, teachers and parents in the West Country organized a campaign to hand out 14,000 information packs and 18,000 'Save Our Schools' car stickers in black and yellow, the traditional colours of the local Labour Party. In the north of England, the Catholic Church backed a Direct Grant Action Committee to save its schools, most of which were too poor to contemplate going private. Meanwhile, half a million people signed a national petition organized by the free-market Institute of Economic Affairs. 'I think one has to look into the political motives of certain people who do not want our children to have a proper education,' declared the television presenter Hughie Green, the first man to sign. 'I love this country and I do not want to see the citizens of tomorrow becoming servants of another power.' But it was no good: backed by the teaching unions, the government stuck to its guns. In the end, the Catholic schools went comprehensive, a handful of schools closed and the vast majority joined the private sector. It was a strange and rather sad irony that the Wilson government had managed to create more private schools than any administration since the reign of Edward VI.[12]

Having disposed of the direct grant schools, Wilson's ministers turned their attention to the few local authorities that still had grammar schools. The time for persuasion was over: in 1976 a new Education Act ordered them to submit plans for comprehensives. But the atmosphere had subtly changed since the heyday of the comprehensive ideal ten years earlier. Squeezed by taxes and inflation, frightened by headlines about union power, horrified by the apparent spread of crime and disorder, many middle-class parents saw the attack on their beloved grammar schools as the final straw. The new Conservative education spokesman, Norman St John Stevas, helped to organize another petition signed by more than half a million people, while Tameside's Conservative council took the case for their grammar schools to the House of Lords. Yet although the defence of local grammar schools became a potent doorstep issue, the Education Act was practically irresistible. Eight local authorities, including Trafford, Essex, Sutton and Kingston, fought on, hoping that a future Conservative government would eventually save them from the axe. But most gave way. By 1979 there were just 150 grammar schools left in Britain, while almost nine out of ten children went to comprehensives. On the left, some insisted that the destruction of the grammar schools was a price worth paying for a truly comprehensive system. But since many middle-class parents turned instead to private education, reinvigorating a sector that had once been in danger of dying out, the new order was arguably *less* egalitarian than the old. Indeed, since the grammar schools had done such a superb job of educating bright lower-middle-class and working-class children, it is hard to see their disappearance as anything other than a disaster.[13]

The campaign against grammar schools horrified many middle-class voters. Previously the debate had focused on the unfairness of the eleven-plus, but by the mid-1970s both left and right had shifted positions. Little now was heard of the eleven-plus. Instead, *Guardian* readers typically condemned grammar schools as anachronistic and reactionary, while *Daily Mail* or *Daily Telegraph* readers hailed them as temples of excellence and competitiveness. This was not just a debate about education; it was a debate about class, culture and what seemed a generalized assault on middle-class values. The *Mail* described the attack on grammar schools as part of an onslaught against 'anything that is middle-class', including 'respect for truth, the desire for objectivity, the love of scholarship'. Some classrooms, it claimed in 1975, were even run by 'revolutionary socialist teachers who regard it as their task to indoctrinate their children in militant working-class attitudes'. But there was also a 'watered down' threat: the feeling that 'schools should not require intellectually difficult studies since these are – or are believed to be – harder for working-class than for middle-class children.'[14]

What the *Mail*'s words made clear was that the argument about education in the mid-1970s was not just about different *kinds* of schools, but about what was taught inside them. For at least a decade, 'progressive' theories had been gaining ground in teacher training colleges. The system that most parents remembered, with children sitting meekly in orderly ranks while the teacher drilled them in facts and figures, was now considered old-fashioned; instead, educationalists believed that learning should be 'child-centred', emphasizing group projects and encouraging children to learn for themselves. Education must be a 'continuous process of interaction between the learner and his environment', declared the Plowden Report in 1967, encouraging children to 'live first and foremost as children and not as future adults'. In fairness, the Plowden Report was much less idealistic than is often remembered, emphasizing the importance of 'neatness, accuracy, care and perseverance, and the sheer knowledge which is an essential of being educated'. But in its disapproval of corporal punishment and its vision of a school in which children 'would move freely about ... without formality or interference', while teachers 'would be among the children, taking part in their activities, helping and advising', it seemed a long way from the classrooms their parents had inhabited in the 1940s and 1950s.[15]

In some ways, progressive methods marked a great leap forward. By the late 1970s, many schools were undoubtedly much happier and more creative places, with children encouraged to think for themselves in a much friendlier, more supportive atmosphere. But as the *New Statesman*'s Peter Wilby astutely pointed out in 1975, the great misapprehension about progressive schools was that they needed less planning and less structure than old-fashioned ones. In fact, they needed a lot *more* planning. As Wilby remarked, the secret to successful progressive schools such as Prior Weston Primary, Islington, was nothing more exotic than 'hard work, careful preparation, skill, patience and good record-keeping' – precisely those virtues that had underpinned good schools from time immemorial.[16]

Unfortunately, not all schools were like Prior Weston. Too often in the mid-1970s, progressive education degenerated into a disorganized free-for-all. When one writer in *New Society* called for comprehensives to embrace 'chalking on walls', 'pulling a motor bike to pieces' or 'girls dolling up each other's hair', with teachers going into the streets and 'putting on children's chalking competitions, building runnable cars out of junk', and organizing 'dress making' and 'street theatre', the grammar school ethos seemed a long way away. But to many idealistic young teachers, the idea that comprehensives might be grammar schools for all, as Harold Wilson had once promised, was anathema. Some saw themselves as a revolutionary vanguard liberating the oppressed proletariat of 9-year-olds: the NUT's Rank and File group, mostly made up of International Socialists, even called for 'classroom democracy' and 'a shift of power from the minority, authoritarian position of the headmaster' to 'students and the community at large'. Absurd as this might sound, Rank and File actually had more than 2,000 active members and could count on the informal support of thousands more. In 1975 the *Guardian* reported on a conference in London at which some senior teachers openly described 'the big influx of middle-class children' into comprehensive schools as a 'threat'. Some 'even went so far as to admit to definite prejudice against the middle-class child', the paper reported. Almost unbelievably, 'this included their own children'.[17]

For earnest young teachers whose eyes had been opened by university or training college, progressive education was a chance to change the world, one child at a time. But it is not hard to see why parents reared on quadratic equations and the Battle of Agincourt would be horrified by schools like Countesthorpe in Leicestershire. A grey brick circle rising from 'a sea of mud in the midst of a middle-class housing estate', Countesthorpe was hailed by *The Times* as the 'school of the future'. By any standards it was an extraordinary place. There were no classrooms, only 'spaces and recesses'; there were no set periods, 'no sanctions, no formalities'. There were not even traditional subjects: instead of English, history and geography, Countesthorpe divided the humanities into 'the study of the individual and his group' (known as IG), 'creative and expressive work in words, music and movement' (CW) and 'creative and expressive work in two and three dimensions'

(2D-3D). Some aspects were almost beyond parody. Badly behaved children were invited 'to work on motorbikes to satisfy their aggression', while, instead of writing essays, pupils were encouraged to express themselves with portable tape recorders, because 'the spoken word is more important for most than the written word'. Not unpredictably, children addressed the teachers by their first names, while rules and timetables were agreed by a democratic school council. There were no separate toilets for staff, pupils and teachers were expected to queue together for meals, and every day the teachers ran a 'lunch time discotheque'. And there was no headmaster, just 'Tim', the warden. When a reporter asked how he spent his days, Tim explained that he pottered about the school 'talking to staff and children'. He had no office of his own, because he did not 'approve of private rooms'.[18]

Although some Countesthorpe parents were pleased that their children seemed happy at school, many were 'a little worried' at its radical innovations, while a small group were 'appalled' at their children being used as guinea pigs. And to its critics, the school was a symbol of everything that was wrong with progressive education. The backlash had been under way since 1969, epitomized by the infamous *Black Papers*, a series of pamphlets edited by two English lecturers, Brian Cox and Tony Dyson. Far from being fire-breathing Tories, both Cox and Dyson had been active in CND and were regular Labour voters, and while Dyson had founded the Homosexual Law Reform Society, Cox had actively campaigned for Harold Wilson in 1966. Like many other grammar school boys of their generation, such as the novelist Kingsley Amis and the poet Donald Davie, they were deeply worried by the new educational trends. But they were hardly knee-jerk reactionaries. Brian Cox disliked the eleven-plus and had even sent his children to a progressive primary school in Hull, where to his horror they 'wander[ed] around aimlessly all day choosing to do whatever takes their fancy'. What he and Dyson despised, however, was 'the belief that children must find out everything for themselves, must never be told, never be made to do anything, that they are naturally good, must be free of all constraints of authority'. And while they welcomed change, they believed that 'standards of excellence must be maintained' and that their rejection was 'particularly harmful to working-class children' – as indeed it was.[19]

When the first *Black Paper* had appeared in March 1969, its attack on the collapse of standards provoked howls of fury from the left. The *New Statesman* called its editors 'a decrepit bunch of educational

Powellites', while the *Evening Standard* called them 'elderly reactionaries', both of which were absurd things to say about two 40-year-old Labour supporters. Meanwhile the Education Secretary, Ted Short, made a fool of himself by claiming that the publication of the *Black Papers* was 'one of the blackest days for education for the past hundred years', thereby giving Cox and Dyson all the publicity they could have wanted. Inadvertently, he also brought them an influential new ally, the headmaster of Highbury Grove boys' school in north London. A former Labour councillor who ran his school on traditional lines, with a house system, strict regulations and frequent use of the cane, Dr Rhodes Boyson cut an unashamedly old-fashioned figure, his mutton-chop whiskers and Lancastrian accent making him immediately recognizable to millions. In Boyson's view, Trotskyist 'destroyers and wreckers' were using schools to undermine the British way of life. The remedy was to give each child 'security, order, his own book, a regular timetable, his own desk and his own coat peg'. Yet although Boyson was easily caricatured as a reactionary enthusiast for corporal punishment, he was by all accounts a very effective headmaster, and Highbury Grove was regularly oversubscribed. He was also to prove the *Black Papers'* most vigorous cheerleader, becoming co-editor in 1975 – by which point he had also become a ferociously right-wing Conservative MP.[20]

Although Cox and Dyson protested that they were not automatically opposed to innovation, the tone of the *Black Papers* was unrelentingly apocalyptic. 'Anarchy is becoming fashionable,' the editors warned in the very first edition, quoting the admittedly ludicrous opinion of Roger Poole, an English lecturer, that a teacher's job was to 'decode' the 'radical critique of the young'. The idea that comprehensive schools inevitably brought social equality, they went on, was 'so much moonshine'; by contrast, grammar schools upheld 'the finest academic and cultural values' and offered 'genuine equality of opportunity'. Other contributors were even more outspoken. Egalitarianism was a recipe for 'uniform mediocrity' and 'social *in*justice', insisted the right-wing Conservative MP Angus Maude. The fashionable new subject of sociology, wrote the poet and historian Robert Conquest, was a 'shallow' species of intellectual 'barbarism'. In universities, argued the Oxford don Bryan Wilson (a sociologist, as it happened), 'more *has* meant worse'. And Conquest and his friend Kingsley Amis had great fun compiling a 'Short Educational Dictionary' satirizing the excesses of the progressive ethos. The word 'better', for example, is defined as 'a divisive term . . . reproducing bourgeois ideology and/or irrelevant facts with greater servility', while 'history' is 'bourgeois propaganda incompatible with the principles of sociology' and 'spelling' is 'a bourgeois pseudo-accomplishment designed to inhibit creativity, self-expression, etc.' The entry for 'discipline', however, invites readers to 'see *Fascism*'.[21]

By 1975, with the direct grant schools under threat and the headlines full of progressive excesses, the *Black Papers* had taken on an even darker tone. 'The educational scene is very sick indeed,' wrote Cox and Boyson in their opening 'Letter to MPs and Parents'. From hundreds of letters sent in by parents and teachers, it was clear that 'adolescent violence' was increasing, while hypocrisy had become 'commonplace' as 'our educational rulers' sent their own children to schools 'they would prohibit for other people's children'. (Both Harold Wilson and Jim Callaghan, it is worth noting, sent their children to private schools, as had Attlee and Gaitskell before them.) Teachers had been 'brainwashed', claimed G. Kenneth Green, a former comprehensive headmaster, into treating 'academic', 'traditional' and 'intellectual' as words of abuse, while 'progressive' and 'forward-thinking' were 'words of divine revelation'. And Cox and Boyson ended their introduction with a desperate appeal to parents to fight back against the 'dangerous fashions' that had corrupted so many teachers. 'Attend parents' meetings,' they wrote. 'Apply pressure on your local school to maintain standards. Do not be put off by progressive excuses about low standards of reading, writing, spelling and arithmetic. Demand higher standards of behaviour in schools.' And if anyone accused them of exaggerating, Cox and Boyson had the perfect two-word answer: William Tyndale.[22]

On the morning of 22 May 1974, Mrs Dolly Walker, a part-time teacher of remedial English, walked into the staffroom at William Tyndale Junior School, Islington, and pinned four typewritten pages on the noticeboard. 'This school is suffering from a malaise,' her statement began, before accusing the headmaster, Terry Ellis, of presiding over 'a free-for-all atmosphere of total self-indulgence'.

> Chaos and anarchy are in possession. Discipline is frowned on as 'old-fashioned.' Children are being seduced to behave in ways which are detrimental to them, both in their progress in learning anything and in producing anti-social behaviour. They are growing up ignorant, selfish, rude (to the extent that even those manners they learn at home are being eroded), lazy, effete . . . The fault for this state of affairs is constantly placed

on the home background – whereas it is almost entirely due to the School atmosphere. (Too true – Abandon hope all ye who enter here!)

If the headmaster did not immediately agree to meet concerned parents, Mrs Walker's diatribe concluded, she would call a public meeting. But she clearly had little hope of success: Terry Ellis, she noted, was 'the biggest buck-passer I have ever met'.[23]

Dolly Walker's manifesto was the first shot in a struggle that became an irresistibly symbolic confrontation between two very different visions of education. From the summer of 1975 to the spring of 1976, when the furore was at its height, every week brought new headlines: 'Head Who Thought Writing Was Obsolete' (*Mail*); 'Parents Boycott "School Of Shame"' (*Telegraph*); 'I'm No Blackleg, Says Boy Who Fled Strike School' (*Express*); 'Trotskyist Teachers' Warning To Parents' (*Evening News*). And to those papers that loathed comprehensive schools and progressive teaching, the case was a gift. 'Another Term Of Trial For The Class Of '75' began a typical story in the *Daily Express*. 'Allegations flew thick and fast outside the trouble-hit William Tyndale Junior school ... of teachers smelling of drink after lunchtime pub sessions; of a child being hit on the head with a pair of scissors; of nine year olds still unable to read and write; of Left-wing subversion by the teaching staff.' To the school's defenders, this was a classic case of a right-wing media conspiracy against dedicated teachers who had tried to give their pupils a genuinely enriching educational experience. But to its critics, William Tyndale was a symbol for everything they loathed about left-wing progressivism: its disregard for traditional standards, its contempt for order, and its arrogant indifference to the very people it was supposed to defend. 'Here among the drama, comedy and absurdity of it all,' declared the *Express*, 'is sandwiched the future of British schools.'[24]

In July 1973, when Alan Head retired after five years running William Tyndale Junior School, most people would have described it as a fairly happy, successful institution. Advertising for his successor, the Inner London Education Authority explained that it was a small school of 250 children from 'a wide range of backgrounds', just off Upper Street in the London borough of Islington. Most of its pupils in the early 1970s came from poor working-class families; many were first- or second-generation immigrants of West Indian, Pakistani or Cypriot stock. It served a relatively tough area: local planners' reports noted the rise in 'hard-core malicious vandalism', and the last census had found that for overcrowded housing, shared toilets and male unemployment, only Glasgow was a worse place to live. And yet Islington was also a laboratory for a new kind of city living, as young middle-class couples, often vaguely bohemian or countercultural, moved into the Victorian terraces of nearby Canonbury, took over the local Labour Party, and began to fight for change on everything from conservation areas to traffic flow. For the newcomers, the pot-plant and whitewash and white wine and marijuana brigade, what had been good enough for their predecessors was not good enough for them.[25]

While Alan Head had managed to satisfy both working-class and middle-class parents, his successor proved rather less adroit. In his early thirties, Terry Ellis was a great believer in the principle of a community school; in his application, he explained that a school should 'interest itself in the wider aspects of the life of its pupils'. And when he arrived at the school in January 1974, his progressive intentions were immediately obvious. By the summer he had instituted weekly staff meetings, hoping to replace his own power with that of a 'genuine teachers' cooperative'. And as he withdrew, so another teacher emerged to become the dominant personality. A charismatic young man who had trained under one of Britain's most progressive headmasters, Brian Haddow passionately believed in a radical new approach to education. One colleague described him as 'a hard person, a trouble-maker and an ideologue', although he was also clearly a talented and innovative teacher. Now, with Ellis's consent, he threw away the rulebook and invited his pupils to come and go as they liked, watching television or playing table tennis as the mood took them. Within weeks some parents – encouraged by Dolly Walker, the rebellious remedial teacher – were beginning to complain.[26]

In a different world, in which teachers were sensitive to parents' ambitions for their children, the William Tyndale affair would have unfolded very differently. At the time, though, Ellis and Haddow had absolutely no interest in what the parents thought. Like their more conservative predecessors, they were convinced that they knew best; as a *Times Education Supplement* report put it two years later, 'accountability to parental consumers was not yet part of a teacher's vocabulary'. Hilariously, when the teachers did call a meeting in June 1974, it was not to discuss their new methods but to ask parents to support a one-day strike for an increase in their London allowance. They were stunned, therefore, when 'about forty-five parents turned up, and they made it plain that they were not, on the whole, interested in the London Allowance. Several angrily denounced the way the school was being run: it was not a question, they said, of how their children were being taught, but that they were not being taught at all.' A second meeting in July was even worse. When a parent had the temerity to ask a question about his teaching methods, Haddow simply walked out, followed by most of his colleagues.

By this point, trust between teachers and parents had almost entirely broken down. The problem for William Tyndale, though, was that Islington's population, like that of other inner London boroughs, was in steep decline, which meant that every other local school had open places. When the school reassembled after the summer of 1974, one in four children had gone elsewhere. By now, the air was full of recrimination and suspicion; when the school's external managers tried to discover what had gone wrong, the staff closed ranks and refused to cooperate. Wild rumours circulated that teachers were using games of Monopoly to 'show the children how to undermine capitalism', while the headmistress of the neighbouring infants' school made an official complaint about the noise and violence of William Tyndale's pupils, later adding that 'black children were being favoured at the expense of white'. One of the school managers organized a petition calling on the Inner London Education Authority to take 'urgent action'. But the education authority, frightened of offending the powerful teaching unions and provoking mass teacher strikes, hesitated to step in.

So the decline continued: from 220 pupils in January 1974, the roll dropped to just 144 by Easter 1975, with more defecting every week. Finally, the teachers put themselves beyond the pale. In an extraordinary attempt to bully parents into backing down, they persuaded other local teachers to blackball children taken out of William Tyndale. Even more self-destructively, they banned all visits of their managers during school hours, somehow believing that this would save them from official intervention. At this the local authority decided to order a full ILEA inspection – at which point Ellis, Haddow and five allies walked out on strike. 'The ILEA are trying to open your school with blackleg labour,' read their letter to the parents. 'Support your teachers. Don't send your children to school.' By this stage, the affair had reached the national press: by the third day of the strike, with numbers down to a pitiful 63, parents at the school gates were almost outnumbered by reporters, policemen and picketing teachers. 'My kid was struck on the head by a teacher with a pair of scissors, and the teacher had been drinking,' one West Indian mother told the man from the *Express*. 'There is no discipline, they swear at the teachers and they learn nothing,' agreed another mother, adding that her son was 'nine and can barely write'. There were now effectively two William Tyndale schools, one in the usual buildings, run by the inspectors using more traditional methods, the other in a nearby chapel, run by Ellis and his allies on staunchly progressive lines. Had the victims not been working-class children, it would have been hilarious.[27]

Eventually the warring parties agreed to abide by the results of an inquiry chaired by Robin Auld, QC, which ran from October 1975 until February 1976, took evidence from 107 witnesses and cost some £55,000 – although by now public interest was so great that the ILEA recouped its costs in sales of the official report. It proved an extraordinary public circus, conducted in a sour and combative atmosphere. Most attention focused on the central figures in the progressive camp, Terry Ellis and Brian Haddow, and what shocked many commentators was their unashamed belief in education as a vehicle for radical social change. Even the *Express* conceded that despite his 'greying shoulder-length hair' and 'Victorian-style sideburns nudging each other for space as they almost meet at his chin', Ellis was an 'engaging performer'. Yes, he said, he had run the school on democratic principles, letting children 'eat sweets when they liked'. Yes, he had allowed them to skip arithmetic to play table tennis in the yard ('We had some very good players'). No, he did not think reading and writing were 'vitally important'; typewriters were 'taking over from writing anyway'. And in their own account of the affair, Ellis and Haddow explained that their approach was 'democratic, egalitarian and anti-sexist'. Traditional schooling, they wrote, was 'concerned with social control' through 'religious sanctions and petty secular rules'. They made 'no false distinctions between work and play'; they 'rejected arbitrary standards of attainment and behaviour'; and they were keen to 'exercise positive discrimination towards the disadvantaged' – which suggests there may have been a grain of truth in the claim that they favoured black children over white.[28]

As if these ideas were not shocking enough to older teachers, the way they were implemented was positively inflammatory. As the inquiry revealed, Ellis had begun his tenure as headmaster by recommending that his own position be abolished and all decisions taken democratically. He also suggested opening up the staffroom to children and allowing them democratic input into decisions, despite the fact that none was older than 11 and many could not speak English. Whenever his ideas were challenged, he charged his opponents with belonging to an 'anti-progressive' conspiracy: when the infants' headmistress complained about the constant disruption, he accused her of having 'sold out to the middle classes'. In the meantime, Brian Haddow had turned his classes into an open-plan radical workshop, with children free to choose how they spent their days. 'All we ever did', said one 10-year-old boy, 'was play snakes and ladders.' 'No place in the school was put out of bounds to them, not even the staff common-room and lavatories,' reported the *TES*. 'They were allowed to eat sweets whenever they wanted, wherever they wanted. To all intents and purposes, there were no rules at all.'[29]

By the end of 1974, the inquiry found, the school was already 'in complete turmoil'. Not only were children roaming freely around, picking up and dropping activities as the whim took them, but even teachers themselves turned up late for lessons. A local Labour councillor reported seeing children swearing at their teachers and dropping milk-bottles from first-floor windows onto infants in the neighbouring playground, while the infants' headmistress told the inquiry that William Tyndale children had been 'throwing stones and spitting through the windows of the infants' school during class periods; knocking infants' work on window ledges to the floor; [and] throwing articles from upstairs windows into the playground', as well as 'bullying infants; laughing and swearing at teachers; and abusing the dinner ladies and playground supervisors'. In perhaps the outstanding case of ill discipline, one West Indian boy climbed up to the roof of the toilets and refused to come down, hurling milk-bottles at anyone who tried to approach him. Eventually the only teacher who had any influence with him – Brian Haddow – talked him down, and then had to drag him home all the way along Upper Street, while the writhing boy 'screamed racial insults' at bewildered passers-by.[30]

When Auld's report finally appeared in July 1976, its conclusions were unsurprisingly withering. There was plenty of criticism for the school managers and the ILEA, whose ham-fisted interventions had come far too late, but the full weight fell on Terry Ellis and Brian Haddow, who had pursued their ideological objectives with contemptuous indifference to the interests of their pupils. Six teachers, including Ellis and Haddow, were summarily dismissed by the ILEA and eventually drummed out of the profession. Meanwhile, William Tyndale was merged with the neighbouring infants' school under the very headmistress who had complained about its children's behaviour; ironically, she considered herself a progressive teacher, albeit of a rather saner kind than her predecessor. As *The Times* noted, the real lesson of the report was that, while 'progressive methods are not in themselves harmful', they needed a lot more planning, preparation and sheer hard work than Ellis and Haddow had been prepared to put in. And of course the real losers were not the teachers, 'so carried away by the passionate conviction that they were right, that there was no way in which they could bring themselves to think that they might be mistaken'. The real losers were the children, forgotten 'in the fury of ideological controversy', for 'it was they who suffered a year of being taught little but argument and distrust of authority'.[31]

Even supporters of progressive education were shocked by William Tyndale. Margaret Maden, the headmistress of Islington Green comprehensive and a firm believer in progressive principles, was appalled by the Tyndale staff's 'arrogance and refusal to be accountable to anybody'. Their attitude to teaching, she said, was 'ideological claptrap about working-class kids', who really needed 'sweat, detail and rigour' rather than woolly ideas about smashing capitalism. What distressed her most, though, was that the affair handed such ammunition to progressive education's critics, confirming everything the *Black Papers* had been saying about the decline of standards. The case became a symbol of the dangers of radicalism, and when the playwright Shane Connaughton tried to defend the Ellis camp in *Sir is Winning*, which ran at the National Theatre in 1977, he was drawing attention to an affair that progressive champions would rather forget. To their opponents, however, it was a gift. The William Tyndale affair 'demonstrates only too clearly how teaching power can be abused', warned the *Express*. In future, parents must ask themselves: 'Could it be that the William Tyndale syndrome is at work in my youngster's classroom?'[32]

For the Conservative press, the race was now on to find the most egregious examples of progressive folly. The *News of the World* quoted a north London mother whose daughter had been told that, at Sports Day, no pupil would be allowed to win more than one race, while the *Daily Mail*, the market leader in these kind of stories, condemned the ILEA for encouraging teachers 'to ditch textbooks that show boys in too dominant a role'. Rhodes Boyson, meanwhile, was much in demand, enthusiastically retelling his favourite story of the teacher who 'refused to teach decimals because it was used in the form of accounting which accompanied the capitalist system'. Behind the scenes, he had played a key part in the William Tyndale affair as an unofficial adviser to D. Walker. Yet he and his allies always insisted that far from runnir

"Parents! Mind your own business! Give us your
child at the age of six and he's ours for ever!"

What made the schools issue so emotive was that it tapped so many anxieties, from the widespread dislike of progressive education to the growing alarm at football hooliganism. The *Sunday Express*'s Michael Cummings was not alone in deciding that it was all the fault of bearded teachers (17 April 1977).

coordinated campaign, they were merely reflecting the views of millions of ordinary families. 'Parents throughout the country are becoming increasingly frustrated by the lack of discipline and the low standards of state schools,' claimed the *Mail* in January 1975, while fifteen months later the same paper reported that 'millions of parents are desperately worried about the education their children are receiving'. 'Order and discipline have been abandoned,' agreed the *Sunday Express* in July 1976. 'Idiotic theorists and political mischief-makers flourish. And standards are falling almost week by week . . . Has ever a nation's youth been let down so dismally by its educators as in Britain today?'[33]

But this was not just reactionary scaremongering. Many parents were deeply worried about putting their children into a system that had changed so much since their own younger days. As the *Guardian*'s Jill Tweedie pointed out, most working-class parents had 'so many prob-ems of their own to do with exhausting employment or no employment, aking roofs or no roofs, that they really [haven't] the time or the ources to appreciate free expression'. They themselves had not been taught to 'write, read, talk, add or multiply too well'; deep down, they knew that 'if their kids weren't taught too well either, nothing was going to change'. One father, a Yorkshire-born fireman who lived near the school, spoke for the overwhelming majority when he explained that he wanted his daughters to learn 'stability, discipline and the three Rs, the basic tools to do the job'. He was bewildered by the teachers' radical approach. 'When I was at school, it was a miners' school, but no one mentioned politics,' he said. 'They just drummed the Rs into us and then we read newspapers and books and made up our own minds.' What angered him most, though, was the support for progressive methods among a handful of middle-class parents whose children were likely to do well in any case. 'I think the working class see the better-off depriving their kids of education to suit themselves, because they don't have to worry,' he said bitterly. 'We know what it's like to do without so we want our kids to better themselves.' Listening to his words, Tweedie felt a rush of sympathy. Nothing was more patronizing, she thought, than for a progressive middle-class teacher to tell working-class parents: 'You do not know what is best for you. Do as I say because I say so.'[34]

Ironically, given the radical teachers' vociferous anti-racism, they managed to alienate thousands of immigrant parents who were horrified by progressive teaching methods and classroom indiscipline. To parents from India, Pakistan, Africa and the Caribbean, traditional education was the obvious route to respectability, and they were appalled that instead of being encouraged to knuckle down and work hard, their children were invited to learn through group projects and play. 'Where's the homework? Why aren't you doing homework? Where's the books? Why aren't you sat down with the books?' one Caribbean man, a schoolboy in the late 1960s and 1970s, remembered his mother asking. Some immigrants thought that the schools had been better back home: the writer Mike Phillips, for instance, was stunned by the contrast between his old school in Guyana and his new one in north London. When the teacher came into the room on his first day, Phillips jumped to his feet, as he had been taught in Guyana, only to find the other pupils 'laughing and swearing at me'. 'All the mistakes I made in the first week or two were to do with being polite, with treating the school work as if it was a good thing to do,' he said ruefully. 'Back home when the teacher asked a question you stuck your hand up if you knew the answer. Here they all sat there, swearing.' In Guyana, Phillips had been a great reader; in London, he found he 'couldn't talk to them about books'. 'What are you reading now, Phillips?' a teacher asked one day, and when the answer turned out to be the *Meditations* of Marcus Aurelius, the teacher 'pissed himself laughing'. It was hardly surprising that more affluent immigrant families sent their children to private schools.[35]

But it was not just progressive education that came under attack in the mid-1970s; it was the comprehensive ethos itself. Now no longer grammar schools for all, they were increasingly associated with low standards, ill discipline and incompetent teaching, and blamed for social ills from sexual promiscuity to football hooliganism. In the newspapers, the criticism was unrelenting. In July 1974, *The Times*'s columnist Ronald Butt wrote of his horror at the 'obscene language and graffiti' in London comprehensives, especially the 'four-letter words' used freely by girls, which he blamed partly on 'the books which they are given to read in English classes'. He was equally appalled by the abolition of uniforms, noting that some middle-class children came to school wearing 'provocative "badges"' on their clothes, although he admitted that their teachers were no better, affecting 'to dress like tramps'. And his was not an isolated voice. In the *Mail*, comprehensives were frequently portrayed as bloated, dissolute and undisciplined, while even the *Guardian* regularly ran letters from teachers demoralized and exhausted by the problems of keeping order in a gigantic big-city school. 'Violence and bullying are commonplace and no child will complain about the behaviour of another because they are afraid,' one teacher wrote in the *Black Paper 1975*, adding that she had lost count of the times she was 'told to f— off' or 'had chairs thrown at me'.[36]

Even in fiction, comprehensives came in for a rough ride. When Colin Dexter's detective Inspector Morse (at this stage a thinly disguised vehicle for his creator's cultural conservatism) visits schools in the mid-1970s, he is typically confronted by weak and untrustworthy teachers in beards, jeans and sweaters. In *Last Seen Wearing* (1977), set in an Oxford comprehensive school, all kinds of sordid things are going on beneath the veneer of peaceful civility, but none worse than what the children are studying. Morse can barely hide his disdain for 'Environmental Studies . . . little more than a euphemism for occasional visits to the gas-works, the fire-station and the sewage installations', while 'for Sociology and Sociologists he had nothing but sour contempt'. In Piers Paul Read's novel *A Married Man* (1979), meanwhile, we meet the despicable Graham, a comprehensive headmaster who arrives at a drinks party in denim jeans, a denim jacket and a 'blue silk polo-necked sweatshirt', and boasts that he 'no longer owned a suit or a tie'. Educated at a grammar school and University College London, Graham wears a droopy moustache and affects a Liverpool accent, which he sees as 'advanced professional qualifications'. During dinner, he explains that his chief priority is to 'overcome the prejudices my kids bring from their home environments and open their minds to more liberated attitudes of which socialism would be one'.[37]

No doubt Graham would have gone down well in Wilfred Greatorex's dystopian BBC series *1990*, in which British children are force-fed socialist propaganda in multi-storey concrete monoliths and encouraged to betray their parents 'through essays and competitions carefully set at school'. And he would also have fitted nicely into the most famous fictional comprehensive of all, Phil Redmond's *Grange Hill*, which first appeared on BBC1 in 1978 to the horror of sensitive middle-class parents. The series was often accused of encouraging bad language, vandalism and bullying, yet Redmond was no uncritical admirer of the education system. 'I was a social experiment,' he said later, 'which I wasn't pleased to be. I came out at 17, factory fodder assigned to the scrapheap, and fought my way back.'[38]

Of course there was another side to the picture. What rarely made it into the newspapers were the experiences of children at happy, successful comprehensive schools. In Hampshire, for instance, the Conservative local authority enthusiastically adopted the new system, transforming local grammar schools into comprehensives and building acclaimed new institutions such as Henry Beaufort School in Winchester. And while generations of bright working-class children were denied the boost of a grammar school education, others were spared the misery of life at a dilapidated secondary modern. Schools like Creighton were not without their problems, but these were reflections of the pupils' lives and backgrounds. Standards had not fallen since Creighton became comprehensive; in its first seven years, the number of children going to university had risen threefold. The children might look scruffy and dissolute, but Hunter Davies was impressed by their sense of 'tolerance, freedom, equality, fairness and democracy'. And he was struck by the verdict of the head of English, a dapper man with an RAF moustache who had spent eighteen years teaching in a grammar school. There were only two things that mattered, the man explained, discipline and hard work, and both of those were perfectly attainable in a comprehensive school. 'There are definite social advantages in comprehensives,' he concluded, 'and I don't think academically that children do any worse than they did in the old days.'[39]

Yet there is no avoiding the fact that for the government, the schools furore proved enormously damaging. When people thought of Labour and education, what often came to mind was not the opening up of new opportunities, but the indelible image of bearded do-gooders teaching their 'kids' how to undermine capitalism. And given the modernizing ambitions that had surrounded comprehensive schools in the early 1960s, it is extraordinary how low their reputation had sunk in some quarters a decade later. In his introduction to Hunter Davies's book, Professor Maurice Peston, a former government education adviser, complained that, for the press, 'all our problems, economic, social and political, are attributable to the comprehensive schools. Any story of juvenile violence, any example of educational failure, even structural damage to a building, is written up with maximum publicity to imply that had selection at 11+ only been retained, all would have been well.' He blamed the sheer 'malice' of the Conservative press, but there was more to it than that. In some comprehensive schools, discipline slipped to dreadful levels; in others, as a detailed study in 1975 revealed, the crude application of progressive principles left many children without skills and qualifications. And plenty of working-class parents – the very people the comprehensives were meant to benefit – deeply resented the end of the grammar schools. One working-class boy from East London who had won a place at a voluntary-aided grammar school later admitted that he 'hated the Labour Party' for closing his old school. It had given him a 'fantastic opportunity', he said – an opportunity now open only to the rich.[40]

The winner from all this, ironically, was the very person who had closed more grammar schools and opened more comprehensives than any other. 'EDUCASHUN ISNT WURKING' read the caption on Conservative posters towards the end of the decade, chalked on a blackboard by a straining schoolboy. And although Margaret Thatcher never restored grammar schools, the eleven-plus or old-fashioned rote learning, she tapped a deep, formless sense that something had gone wrong in the heart of British schools. 'We have got to stop destroying good schools in the name of equality,' she told the Conservative Party conference in 1977, insisting that the 'main victims' were 'able children from the less well off families'. As so often, she used her own personal history as a powerful political prop. 'People from *my* sort of background', she added with relish, '*needed* grammar schools to compete with children from *privileged* homes like Shirley Williams and Anthony Wedgwood Benn'. The use of Benn's full name was a ruthlessly populist touch.[41]

10

Nutty as a Fruitcake

MRS HOWARD: *I am afraid that the Party is not what once it was. It has become craven. Once it represented all the finest values of the middle class. Now, gangrenous . . . I'm sure it's infiltrated. From the left. The cryptos. Pale-pinks. Sure of it.*

David Edgar, *Destiny* (1976)

Until this speech, the people of Britain have been like sheep without a shepherd. But now they have found one.

Mary Whitehouse in *The Times*, 21 October 1974

The leader of the Conservative Party spent the weekend after the October 1974 election in his beloved Kent, staying at his friend Toby Aldington's country house. Edward Heath had hoped that he might now be in Number 10, making the final touches to his new government. Instead, on Sunday he returned to his home town, Broadstairs, to see his father William, whose eighty-sixth birthday had fallen on election day. In the next day's papers he cut a remarkably cheerful figure, grinning for photographers in his houndstooth jacket. 'Still Smiling', read the *Mirror*'s headline: 'The Man With His Future In The Balance'. But although Heath gave no sign of wanting to step down, the general assumption was that after two defeats in nine months, he could not possibly survive as party leader. 'Virtually nobody could be found yesterday who believed that Mr Heath (played four, lost three) will lead his party into the next contest,' wrote the *Guardian*'s Peter Jenkins on Saturday morning. 'The question is not if he will go but when and how.' 'Ted has to go,' one senior Tory remarked two days later, 'and the sooner the better. If he doesn't quit quietly and quickly he'll have to be sacked.'[1]

Even some of Heath's closest political friends agreed that it was time for a change. Already the faithful Jim Prior had advised him 'to submit himself to re-election', arguing that only a renewed mandate would allow him to carry on. But to Prior's disappointment, Heath refused. As so often, his innate stubbornness and injured pride made it impossible for him to listen to sensible advice; instead, he surrounded himself with flatterers like Aldington, who told him that if only he sat tight, the critics would lose heart. Heath's biographer, John Campbell, suggests that if he had submitted himself for re-election immediately, he might well have won; in the worst-case scenario, he would probably have been succeeded by a close ally such as Willie Whitelaw, allowing him to become Shadow Foreign Secretary, like Sir Alec Douglas-Home before him. But giving ground to his opponents would have taken more subtlety, more flexibility and more humility than Heath possessed. Instead, he was determined to cling on, blind to political reality, like some tin-pot dictator holed up in his palace while rioters set fire to his capital. The irony was that by staying so long, he made it impossible for one of his allies to succeed him.[2]

Although Heath's lieutenants controlled most of the levers of power inside the Conservative Party, his position was much weaker than it looked. For the past four years, many Tory backbenchers, notably his old adversary Enoch Powell but also economic liberals such as John Biffen and Jock Bruce-Gardyne, had been increasingly disturbed by his apparent retreat from free-market principles and his embrace of incomes policies and industrial intervention. 'Ted donned the rather tatty fabrics of socialism,' the maverick Biffen remarked, 'and they didn't look any more decorative on him than they had on Harold Wilson.' As early as September 1973, a group of disaffected right-wingers had set up the Selsdon Group, convinced that Heath was bent on appeasing the unions and returning to inflationary public spending. And their views chimed with those of grass-roots Tory activists for whom the headlines in the Heath years – full of strikes and demonstrations, pornography and football hooliganism, the student sit-ins, feminist protests and Ugandan Asian immigrants – made deeply alarming reading. When they studied their copies of the Telegraph, the Mail or the Express every morning, middle-class Tories saw a breakdown of politeness and public order, a collapse of discipline and self-restraint, a mounting sense of vandalism, greed and self-interest, embodied by individuals from Arthur Scargill to

1. For many people, the IRA attack on the Palace of Westminster in June 1974, *above*, was an abiding symbol of national decline. With bombs going off in Guildford, Birmingham and central London, *below*, almost every week seemed to bring some terrible new atrocity.

2. Facing an unprecedented economic crisis, the nation had recalled Labour's Harold Wilson, *left*. In private, he told his aides that he had only 'the same old solutions for the same old problems'. But his blend of nostalgia and inertia had a strong appeal to people like these Devon pensioners, *below*, pictured playing bingo in 1975.

3. Almost unnoticed, globalization and technology were reshaping British life, and by 1979 computers were becoming distinctly fashionable. *Above*, the new World Money Centre at the NatWest headquarters; *below*, a shopper shows off her new video-games console.

4. The most compelling figure in the political life of the mid-1970s was the clever, ebullient and bushy-browed Chancellor, Denis Healey, *above*. But Wilson's most trusted confidante remained his political secretary, the controversial Marcia Williams, *right*.

5. As champions of the rival Labour factions, Tony Benn and Roy Jenkins aroused love and loathing in equal measure. *Top*, Benn meets representatives of the ill-fated Meriden and NVT motorcycle firms. *Above*, Jenkins is hit by a flour bomb at a public meeting in Newham, 1975.

6. Many people considered the TGWU's Jack Jones to be the most powerful man in the country, though his successor Moss Evans cut a much less impressive figure, *top*. Abroad, British workers had become infamous for their interminable tea breaks. These Ford car workers, *above*, pictured in 1979, certainly seem to be enjoying themselves.

7. The Ulster Workers' Council strike, which brought down Northern Ireland's executive in May 1974, seemed a terrifying sign of the state's impotence in a violent world. *Above*, Protestant crowds celebrate the Executive's fall; *below*, bonfires burn in the streets of Belfast.

8. Although Edward Heath's advisers tried to rebrand him as a cuddly chap in a woolly jumper, he lost his second successive election in October 1974, *left*. Still, his problems were nowhere near as bad as those of his Liberal rival Jeremy Thorpe, pictured, *below*, outside the Old Bailey in 1979.

George Best. 'Honest middle-class people, good citizens, people with principles and standards' had been left 'in a vacuum', one local official complained to Central Office. There was 'a general fear about the state of our society', the party's Advisory Committee on Policy reported in March 1973, and a 'feeling that we are not in control'.[3]

What this meant was that when Heath fell from office after February 1974, there was strikingly little goodwill for him inside the Conservative Party. On the right, some people actively rejoiced at his defeat: the director of the neo-liberal Institute of Economic Affairs, Ralph Harris, later admitted that he had voted Labour to get rid of Heath. 'The squatter in No. 10 Downing Street has at last departed,' exulted an editorial in the *Spectator*. 'A ludicrous and broken figure, he clung with grubby fingers to the crumbling precipice of his power . . . And yet there is one further step to be taken in his humiliation: he must resign the leadership of the Conservative Party.' Even moderate backbenchers thought the writing was on the wall: as early as July, one told the mandarin Ronald McIntosh that 'there was a lot of opposition in the Tory party to Heath continuing as leader'. And when Heath suffered a second successive defeat, even loyal activists began to wonder whether they could ever win with him at the helm. A group of Manchester activists told a television interviewer that if 'Wilson took them on a bus ride to Victoria they would end up at Waterloo, [but] with Heath they would not even get out of the garage'. And in Enoch Powell's heartland of the West Midlands, Heath had become a symbol of the snobbish, haughty and unresponsive elite at the top of the party. In Dudley, where the handsome Conservative club was closing down, one councillor explained that people had 'lost interest in a party which is being run in the way it is from Westminster, without any real regard for the views of the people who do all the work out in the constituencies'. 'Nowhere in the Black Country have I been able to find any support for Mr Heath,' wrote John Groser in *The Times*. 'Local politicians, party workers and voters all say that their message to their respective MPs is the same: "Heath must go."'[4]

The irony, however, is that although the revolt against Heath is often seen as an ideological turning point, what really did him in was his personality. Ever since becoming leader, he had struggled to hide his distaste for the blue-rinsed ladies and retired colonels who stuffed envelopes and organized jumble sales on the party's behalf. Even more damagingly, he treated his own backbenchers 'as cattle to be driven through the gates of the lobby', as the *Spectator*'s columnist Patrick Cosgrave put it, while one backbencher confided to Simon Heffer that Heath had once told him there were 'three sorts of people in this party: shits, bloody shits and fucking shits'. Yet even after October 1974, when it mattered most, Heath could not bring himself to be polite. The backbencher Julian Critchley was having dinner with Jim Prior and two other MPs in the Commons a few weeks later when Heath materialized at their table, chatted to Prior for a few minutes and then stalked off, not even acknowledging the existence of the others. 'What can I do with him?' Prior asked helplessly. He was one of Heath's greatest admirers; but even he was 'surprised by the number of people who were saying that they disliked him, and by the degree of bitterness and the spiteful determination that he had to go'. And this was no isolated incident: other MPs recalled the times Heath had snubbed them in the Commons tea room or ignored them when passing in a corridor. 'Look, Jack, we're not going to get anywhere while Ted is leading us. He's had it,' the newcomer Alan Clark told the Tory whip Bernard 'Jack' Weatherill in the dying days of the October campaign. 'Later,' Weatherill said ominously. 'That comes later. Leave it for the moment.'[5]

Given Heath's refusal to throw in the towel, the only question after the October election was when the challenge would come. It took just three days. On Monday afternoon, just hours after Heath had got back from Kent, the chairman of the backbench 1922 Committee, Edward du Cann, told him that it was time for a contest. But as Heath well knew, du Cann had leadership ambitions of his own. Smooth, rich and ruthlessly self-promoting, he was an old Oxford friend of the writers Kingsley Amis and Philip Larkin and a significant player in the City of London. He had an unrivalled reputation for self-serving slipperiness: other Tory MPs nicknamed him 'Uriah', while one recalled asking du Cann the time and getting the answer: 'What time would you like it to be?' Heath utterly despised him, and even as the press speculated about du Cann's 'Milk Street Mafia' (named after the City street where his merchant bank was based), the Tory leader kept up his limpet impersonation. But when Tory backbenchers handsomely re-elected du Cann as chairman of the 1922 a few weeks later, Heath made a small but crucial concession, asking Sir Alec Douglas-Home to draw up new procedures for a leadership contest. When the new rules were published, his survival suddenly became much harder. To force a contest, a challenger needed only two nominations; but to stop it going to a second ballot, Heath had to win by at least 15 per cent of the eligible voters – not an easy undertaking, especially after losing two elections.[6]

'Heath's critics are delighted,' wrote the journalist Walter Terry when the new rules were published in December: 'the dice is [*sic*] loaded their way.'* Even so, the prospect of defeat clearly never crossed Heath's mind. Despite the speculation in the press, his lieutenant Willie Whitelaw remained steadfastly loyal, while du Cann's business interests, as well as his long list of enemies, held him back from declaring his own candidacy. With polls showing that, despite their anxieties, a majority of constituency chairmen and 54 per cent of Tory voters wanted Heath to remain, the consensus was that no serious rival would stand against him. If he stayed on, predicted the *Express*, 'the Tory Party and the country will come to be grateful for his fighting qualities'. *The Times* noted that there were rumours of a dark horse candidate, 'but the Conservative Party does not seem to want a woman leader'. Instead, it looked as though Heath might just survive to lead his party into a fifth general election in the late 1970s. 'After all the fret and fume,' the editorial concluded, 'this difficult but determined man re-emerges out of the fog, like some grey rock emerging out of the Atlantic mist. Mr Heath is not like the radio character who said "I go, I come back."† He never goes.'[7]

'For the Conservative Party, 1975 is the year of opportunity,' wrote Edward du Cann in an essay for the *Daily Express* to mark the New Year. 'Every day is a day nearer the next General Election. Every working hour must be a step on the path to defeat Socialism.' And yet, du Cann admitted, the party was in poor shape. In the North of England, in Scotland and Wales, and in many larger cities, its image had taken a terrible battering, while party membership was lower than ever. As du Cann saw it, there was an obvious explanation:

> There is little to attract recruits, neither cause nor success.
>
> In the eyes of the general public, our party seems to lack a clear philosophy and therefore credibility. So intellectually bankrupt have we become that the language of most political debate, in the university or public bar, is now habitually the Socialistic language of the Left . . . Socialism advances apace as free enterprise and the habit of independence stagger . . .
>
> Public opinion must be mobilised to stop it.

---

* What is not clear is whether Sir Alec did this deliberately, perhaps even as some elaborate and long-delayed revenge for his own defenestration ten years earlier. But given that he had served loyally as Heath's Foreign Secretary, it seems more likely that it was an accident.

† Even then a curiously dated allusion: younger readers would probably never have heard of the character Ali-Oop in the 1940s radio comedy *ITMA*.

It is our task in the Tory Party to make clear the choice, and make it clearer than we have to date. It is our duty to speak out boldly.

Other Tory MPs echoed du Cann's diagnosis. Heath had run a 'Roundhead administration' with 'far too many management consultants, analysts, lawyers and accountants', agreed the Hendon North MP and founder of the Middle Class Association, John Gorst. He must yield to a 'Cavalier' with 'flair and feeling', who was 'thoroughly Conservative in the sense of being dedicated to Conservative principles'. And at the grass roots, too, activists demanded a new tack. 'The choice of Mr Heath as leader has proved disastrous to both the party and our country,' one P. Palmer-Jones of Sevenoaks wrote to *The Times*. Under his leadership, genuine Conservatives had been 'virtually disenfranchised', while Heath's 'socialist consensus' had brought the country to the brink of ruin. It was time for 'a Tory who is not ashamed of being one', agreed the playwright William Douglas-Home, brother of Sir Alec, demanding a leader who would tell voters to 'buy your Rolls-Royce and cigars, if that is what you want . . . and send your boys to Eton and, if any man attempts to say you nay, salute him with two fingers in the shape of an inverted V sign'. Ted Heath, needless to say, was not that man.[8]

Contempt for Heath's appeasement of socialism, his alleged U-turns in office and his high public spending was nowhere greater than among the small group of thinkers and journalists associated with the Institute of Economic Affairs (IEA). Probably the most influential think-tank in modern British history, the IEA was the brainchild of Antony Fisher, an RAF veteran who had been awarded the Air Force Cross for inventing a gunnery-training machine during the Second World War. Horrified by the Attlee government's programme of public ownership and central planning, Fisher read Friedrich von Hayek's broadside *The Road to Serfdom* and became convinced that Britain was heading for totalitarian socialism. Fisher was not short of a few bob, having made millions by introducing American-style broiler chickens to Britain, and in 1955 he founded the IEA to fight for free-market policies. It was Fisher who chose the Institute's first director, a Cambridge-educated lecturer and former Conservative backroom boy called Ralph Harris, who was soon joined by another Cambridge economics graduate, Arthur Seldon, as editorial director. Between them, Harris and Seldon ran the IEA for three decades. Interestingly, however, they came from very different backgrounds from the Old Etonian Fisher. Brought up in working-class north London, Harris was the son of a tramways inspector, while Seldon had been born to Jewish refugees in the East End. In their own minds, they were outsiders leading a revolution against the welfare state and the patrician old guard at the top of the Conservative Party. 'You have never been poor. I have,' Seldon once wrote to a Tory critic. 'We were not conventional; we were not congenial. We were tearaways!' the dapper Harris told an interviewer. But as Richard Cockett puts it in his history of the IEA, they were trailblazers, representing 'the first stirrings of the Thatcherite revolt against paternalists and middle-class socialists'.[9]

To reread the papers pumped out by the IEA during its first decade is to have a sneak preview of Thatcherism in action. One paper, published in 1963, argued that, by closing 350 coal pits, the government could ensure a 'vigorous free market' in the energy industry; another argued that the 'telephone service would be better off divorced from the public sector'. In 1960 one IEA paper urged the government to finance university education through student loans; in 1967 Arthur Seldon argued for a return to selective, rather than universal, benefits; in 1972 Friedrich von Hayek, whose libertarian ideas had played such a key part in the IEA's foundation, contributed a trenchant paper on the need to curb union power. Few of these papers had an immediate effect: slowly, however, their ideas filtered into the political mainstream, the classic example being a paper arguing for the abolition of Resale Price Maintenance,* which was turned into law by, of all people, Edward Heath. But even though Harris and Seldon saw many of their ideas rejected as heretical lunacy, they succeeded brilliantly in making the IEA interesting. Visitors included not only young right-wing Conservatives such as John Biffen, Patrick Jenkin and Sir Geoffrey Howe, but Labour figures such as Douglas Houghton, David Owen and Brian Walden, and as the years went by, the IEA moved into a smart terraced house in Lord North Street, a few doors down from the Wilson residence. But what never changed was the emphasis on free-market ideology and the lively exchange of ideas. At lunchtime seminars there was always plenty of wine, and Harris made sure everybody had a good time. 'I thought, "People are going to come to the IEA,"' he said later. 'They ought to go away feeling they'd enjoyed themselves.'[10]

Ironically, the politician who seemed closest to the IEA philosophy was probably the last man in Westminster whom colleagues would

---

* The system whereby manufacturers fixed the retail prices of their goods, effectively preventing shops from competing with each other.

associate with boozy conviviality. Presented with merciless logic but held with hot-blooded fervour, Enoch Powell's free-market opinions might have come straight from one of Arthur Seldon's pamphlets, although Powell characteristically insisted that he had come to them entirely on his own. During the mid-1960s, however, his smouldering rhetoric echoed the IEA's views on everything from the horror of incomes policies and the urgency of trade union reform to the folly of corporatism and the importance of privatizing the Post Office. To the general public the Wolverhampton MP was best known for his heretical views on immigration, which earned him the sack from Heath's Shadow Cabinet after his infamous 'rivers of blood' speech. In the long run, though, it was his views on economics and the state that proved more influential. As early as 1968, for example, he was calling for the next government 'at once to dismantle state socialism in industry and re-organize it on capitalist lines', and at the Conservative party conference that autumn Powell argued that they could slash income tax in half and abolish capital gains tax completely if they only had the courage to sell off nationalized industries, tear up the apparatus of the corporate state and cut grants, subsidies and foreign aid. As usual, his prescriptions were largely ignored, the *Observer* even describing his plan as 'utter rubbish'. But of course the attraction, as well as the weakness, of Powell's philosophy was its simplicity. He was a romantic nationalist prophet, not an economist; he sometimes claimed that on his knees in church, he thanked God for the free market.[11]

During Ted Heath's unhappy three and a half years in office, he had no more incisive critic than Enoch Powell. In 1971 Powell played a leading role in the battle against entry into the EEC, warning that Parliament faced 'a life and death struggle for its independence and supreme authority', and a year later he spearheaded the campaign against the arrival of the Ugandan Asian refugees. What most appalled him, though, was Heath's introduction of the most elaborate pay and price controls in modern history. Powell agreed that inflation was the supreme danger, calling it 'a social evil, an injustice between man and man, and a moral evil'. But Heath's clumsy attempts to contain it, he said, were 'totalitarian' and 'Fascist'. This was strong stuff, to which nobody had a very convincing answer: even Tony Benn was impressed by Powell's 'brilliant academic analysis' and wrote that other MPs were 'fascinated by his intellect and clarity'. And although Powell committed political suicide by standing down as an MP in the election of February 1974 and encouraging his admirers to vote Labour, his words lingered in Tory supporters' ears. None of the parties had any idea how to 'cure this disease of inflation', wrote one J. C. Binns of Ilford in July 1974, yet 'Mr Powell diagnosed it 20 years ago and has been consistently right in his forecast . . . He is the only man who can lead a Government to carry out the necessary measures to preserve this nation.' Powell had 'made an ass of himself at the past election', agreed R. L. Travers, writing from the Army and Navy Club, 'but the fact remains that he is a man of integrity and ability and has supporters on all sides. He is the only man who can pull this country together, and unless he is given a chance to do so this country will go the way of the Weimar Republic.'[12]

In reality, Powell's career in the Conservative Party was over. Having stood down in February 1974, he spent the summer mulling over his alternatives before announcing that he would make a comeback as an Ulster Unionist. Elected to represent South Down in October, he remained in the Commons for the next thirteen years, like some spectral reminder of what might have been. Yet at the very moment that his chances of regaining office evaporated, the economic ideas he had championed for so long were finally winning acceptance. In the climate of the early 1970s, with commodity prices out of control, economic growth stagnant, unemployment rising and the government apparently powerless to resist the unions' wage demands, Powell was not alone in thinking that Keynesian tax-and-spend economics had smashed into the buffers. Increasingly, British commentators were looking for inspiration across the Atlantic, where the Chicago professor Milton Friedman had cut a swathe through the staid world of academic economics. Like his friend Friedrich von Hayek, Friedman saw himself as a classical liberal, harking back to the good old days of Adam Smith and John Stuart Mill. What made him a worldwide celebrity, though, was his doctrine of monetarism. To put it very simply, Friedman demolished the notion that by carefully managing demand, governments could achieve a 'trade-off' between inflation and unemployment. There was, he insisted, a 'natural level of unemployment', and when the government tried to push it down further, it merely sent inflation through the roof and thousands more out of work. Instead, the government should restrict itself to regulating the money supply, using strict targets to prevent it from growing too quickly. If politicians yielded to public pressure and allowed inflation to get out of control, there was only one remedy: a severe contraction of the money supply, irrespective of the temporary cost in failing business and disappearing jobs. For Friedman, as for Powell, unemployment was unfortunate. But inflation was a cancer.[13]

On paper, monetarism was not necessarily right-wing. Although Friedman himself was firmly on the right, there was nothing to stop a Labour politician from agreeing that inflation was 'always and everywhere a monetary phenomenon', or from thinking that the government's main economic duty was to set clear targets for the growth of the money supply. The obvious problem for the left, though, was that Friedman thought full employment was an illusion and deplored government intervention in the economy, which directly contradicted Labour thinking since the 1940s. By contrast, monetarism had an immediate appeal to the economic liberals at the IEA, since it apparently confirmed everything they had suspected about the delights of the free market and the folly of big government. In 1969 one of the IEA's brightest stars, the young London School of Economics professor Alan Walters, published a pamphlet explaining Friedman's ideas for lay readers. Suggestively, Walters was yet another outsider: the son of a grocery-store clerk from Leicester, he had failed his eleven-plus, left school at 15 to work in a shoe factory and gradually hauled himself up the academic ladder. His pamphlet had an enormous impact, and when Friedman himself gave a lecture at the IEA in 1970, he found a large and enthusiastic audience – among them Labour's Jim Callaghan, later arguably Britain's first monetarist Prime Minister. The next day, Friedman had a brief audience with Edward Heath. Perhaps, *The Times* suggested mischievously, the Treasury might even take down the picture of Lady Keynes that hung in 11 Downing Street, and to replace it with one of 'Mrs Milton Friedman'.[14]

Although Heath largely ignored monetarist remedies during his turbulent spell in office, Friedman's ideas now had tremendous momentum. At the IEA, Friedman and Walters poured out papers preaching the virtues of the new creed. At the Bank of England, officials were already setting informal monetary targets. In the City, monetarist ideas were making headway thanks to the success of analysts like Gordon Pepper, whose economic forecasts were proving uncannily accurate. At Westminster, many younger Tories were now strongly sympathetic, among them future Thatcherite ministers such as John Biffen, Jock Bruce-Gardyne and Nicholas Ridley. And even in university departments, where, as the economics writer David Smith remarked, to be a monetarist in the 1960s had been 'like having an unfortunate but embarrassing affliction which people were usually too polite to mention', the plates were shifting. In 1971, for example, David Laidler and Michael Parkin won a grant to set up the Manchester Inflation Workshop, while at the

LSE Harry Johnson's new Money Study Group left a deep impression on a generation of students. Many went on to be university lecturers, City economists or Treasury officials, such as Patrick Minford, who studied for his doctorate at the LSE during the Heath years and then carried the torch north to Liverpool. His uncompromising blend of monetarism and 'rational expectations' made him one of Mrs Thatcher's favourite economists.[15]

Perhaps the most striking example of the transformation in monetarism's image, though, came on Fleet Street. For most of the 1960s, monetarists had generally been regarded as crackpots. Enoch Powell, for example, was often treated as an extremist ploughing a very lonely furrow. But as inflation rose, economics writers began treating Friedman's ideas with interest and respect. Not surprisingly, the *Daily Telegraph* had long been an admirer of the IEA: under the editorship of Maurice Green and his deputy Colin Welch, it devoted considerable space to liberal economic ideas. And while the *Telegraph* played a key part in converting much of the Conservative Party, the *Financial Times* was performing a similar role in the City. Its most respected columnist, Samuel Brittan, had formerly been an adviser at Harold Wilson's ill-fated Department of Economic Affairs. Yet after reading Friedman, Brittan became convinced that 'full-employment policies are futile [and] likely to lead not merely to inflation but to accelerating inflation'. Once 'a fashionable growth man', he became what he called 'an IEA sympathizer', and by the mid-1970s he could often be found advocating monetarist solutions to Britain's economic problems.[16]

The most celebrated advocate of the new doctrine was the economics editor of *The Times*, Peter Jay, who was best known to the general public as the presenter of London Weekend Television's current affairs flagship *Weekend World*. The crucial thing about Jay was that not only was he *not* a Conservative, he could hardly have been closer to the heart of the Labour aristocracy. His father, Douglas Jay, had been a left-wing economist in the 1930s, a Keynesian Treasury minister under Clement Attlee and President of the Board of Trade in Wilson's first government; his mother, Peggy Jay, was a prominent Labour councillor in London for more than three decades; even his wife, the television producer Margaret Jay, was Jim Callaghan's daughter. Tall, languid and self-consciously clever, Jay had worked at the Treasury as a young man and considered himself a 'twenty-four-carat Keynesian'. In the late 1960s, however, he visited economics departments in Chicago, Stanford and St Louis, and by the time Edward Heath came to power, Jay's conversion was complete. During the next few years, nobody on Fleet Street did more to popularize Milton Friedman's ideas for a lay readership or to puncture the hubristic assumptions behind Heath's dash for growth. It was 'time to break the familiar economic cycle we stagger round each year', Jay told his readers three days before the October 1974 election, and time to abandon 'the meandering progress of post-war politics towards the brink of hyper-inflation'.[17]

By the middle of 1974 there was a palpable sense of momentum among the IEA's friends and supporters. Later, they became known as the 'New Right', although nobody used that label at the time. Many described themselves as liberals rather than conservatives; in many ways, they were united only by their shared hatred of socialism, state interference and the trade unions. But as inflation soared during 1974 and 1975, the free-marketeers picked up more and more adherents, not least in the Federation of Conservative Students, in strongly Tory universities such as St Andrews and in business groups like the Institute of Directors. By 1976 the Conservative historian Lord Blake thought he could detect 'a wind of change in Britain and much of the democratic world ... one of those rare and profound changes in the intellectual climate which occur once or twice in a hundred years'. Only ten years previously, agreed *The Times*'s Ronald Butt, the IEA had been seen as 'a bit of a joke by economics writers'. Now, thanks to 'the pressures of real life, it has shifted some of the best known economic writers in its direction and a good deal of the most influential economic thinking comes from the IEA'. They might not have won the battle of ideas, but they were more than holding their own. Now all they needed was a champion.[18]

The man who stepped forward as the standard-bearer of the new liberalism was not, on the surface, an obvious candidate for political stardom. Memorably described by Harold Macmillan as 'the only boring Jew I've ever known', Sir Keith Joseph made many people feel faintly uncomfortable. As the heir to the Bovis construction giant, he was a child of privilege, but he could not have been more different from the country squires who traditionally dominated the Conservative Party. Educated at Harrow and Oxford, he had been wounded at Monte Cassino, laid bricks and dug trenches to earn a licence from the Institute of Building, won a prize fellowship at All Souls and was elected MP for Leeds North East in 1956. He was an intense, gaunt, sickly man; having been bullied at school as a Jew, he had a profound sense of being an outsider. Perhaps because he felt overshadowed by his father, a former Lord Mayor of London who had been awarded a baronetcy, Joseph seemed permanently uneasy, crippled by 'an exaggerated feeling of underachievement and a vague sense of guilt'. Few politicians had a keener social conscience: as a schoolboy, he used to take food from his Chelsea breakfast table to a beggar on the street, and no Conservative politician seemed more passionately interested in alleviating poverty. He was a pale, priggish man, physically writhing with guilt about the plight of his social inferiors, yet utterly detached from the concrete realities of ordinary life. He seemed more comfortable with schemes for improving people than with people themselves, a kind of Tory Robespierre.[19]

One of the paradoxes of Joseph's career was that he combined his intense social conscience with the kind of policies associated with the Conservative right. As early as 1958 he could be heard enthusing about the need for 'more competition, production, and to be quite brutal, more bankruptcies', and he soon became a regular visitor to the IEA, picking up all sorts of ideas about welfare reform, capitalist competition and economic liberalism. By the late 1960s he was talking eagerly about the 'failure of many of our public enterprises' and the need to tear off the 'socialist shackles' and unleash the full power of the free market. Yet when he got into government in 1970, running the massive Department of Health and Social Services, he proved to be rather less radical than his rhetoric suggested. Not only did he introduce new benefits for the disabled and the long-term sick, he increased benefits for widows and pensioners and he spent more money on the health service at a faster rate than any of his Labour predecessors. What was more, he even told Tory activists at their 1973 party conference that they were wrong to bang on about 'scroungers' and should 'face the fact that there are a large number of people who are not employable ... Should their children starve? Of course they should not.' It was no wonder that the *Sunday Mirror* called him 'The Tory Minister Who Really Cares', or that he got a standing ovation at a Child Poverty Action Group conference. And perhaps it was little wonder, either, that his old friends at the IEA were distraught at his performance. After the February 1974 election, Joseph recalled, Alan Walters could barely bring himself to speak to him. 'He refused to shake my hand,' Joseph admitted. 'And he was quite right.'[20]

What happened next was probably the most famous conversion in recent British history. 'It was only in 1974 that I was converted to

Conservatism,' Joseph wrote later. 'I had thought that I was a Conservative but I now see that I was not really one at all.' Of course this was
slightly disingenuous. What the talk of 'conversion' concealed was the
fact that Joseph had long been an admirer of free-market ideals and had
dropped them when it seemed convenient during the Heath government. Now, in opposition, he picked them up again. It was probably no
coincidence that one of the companies hardest hit by the property crash
of 1973–4 was Bovis, which stayed afloat only by accepting a derisory
takeover bid from P&O. The virtual collapse of the family firm hit
Joseph hard and was surely a key factor in his intellectual crisis. In any
case, the result was that after the February election he returned to his
old themes, albeit with greater intensity than ever. 'This is no time to be
mealy-mouthed,' he told an audience at Upminster in a speech that has
gone down in Thatcherite legend:

> Since the end of the Second World War we have had altogether too much
> Socialism. There is no point in my trying to evade what everybody knows.
> For half of that thirty years Conservative Governments, for understandable
> reasons, did not consider it practicable to reverse the vast bulk of the
> accumulating detritus of Socialism which on each occasion they found
> when they returned to office. So we tried to build on its uncertain founda-
> tions instead . . . I must take my share of the blame for following too many
> of the fashions.
>
> We are now more Socialist in many ways than any other developed
> country outside the Communist bloc – in the size of the public sector, the
> range of controls and the telescoping of net income.

The Conservatives, Joseph said, had tried to make 'semi-Socialism'
work, and failed. It was time for a radical new approach based on 'competitive free enterprise' – and time for his party to 'decide whether to go
down with Benn or on to a more rational economy'.[21]

After the February election, Joseph persuaded Heath to let him establish a new think-tank, the Centre for Policy Studies (CPS), which he
privately hoped would 'convert' the Conservative Party to free-market
liberalism. Its guiding spirit, Alfred Sherman, was the man who wrote
the Upminster speech, a former Communist from Hackney who had
fought in the Spanish Civil War. Short, bald and pugnacious, Sherman
was possibly the only man in Britain more zealous than his boss. An
obsessive critic of collectivism, he would happily talk for hours about
Heath's appeasement of socialism, the evils of black immigration and

the supernatural virtues of the free market. 'He thought that a firing-squad was too good for anyone who disagreed with him,' the journalist Bruce Anderson recalled decades later. 'Mean-spirited, spiteful, envious and resentful, he never had a good word to say about anyone else's intellect and overvalued his own.' Yet, as Anderson recognized, this unpleasant little man, who never lost the sectarian mindset of his Communist youth, played a key role in the intellectual transformation of the Conservative Party. Sherman not only provided the CPS with dynamic leadership, he relentlessly bullied Joseph into taking ever more outspoken positions. With his friend's caustic words ringing in his ears, Joseph made a vain effort to get the Shadow Cabinet interested in a more monetarist approach. But although Margaret Thatcher and Geoffrey Howe expressed qualified interest, the rest of Heath's team preferred to stick to Keynesian orthodoxy. That left him with no alternative but to go to the people.[22]

It was on 5 September, in Preston's Bull and Royal Hotel, that Joseph made his great break with post-war orthodoxy. Sherman provided the speech, with some help from Alan Walters and Samuel Brittan, and even though Howe and Thatcher had persuaded Joseph to tone it down, it was still shocking enough. He began in apocalyptic vein. 'Inflation', he said, 'is threatening to destroy our society. It is threatening to destroy not just the relative prosperity to which most of us have become accustomed, but the savings and plans of each person and family.' It had been fostered by 'successive governments' going back to 1950, thanks not least to incomes policies that were the equivalent of 'trying to stop water coming out of a leaky hose without turning off the tap'. The underlying problem, Joseph explained, was the government's relentless 'creation of new money'. Conservatives since the war had been 'haunted by the fear of long-term mass unemployment, the grim, hopeless dole queues and towns which died. So we talked ourselves into believing that these gaunt, tight-lipped men in caps and mufflers were round the corner, and tailored our policy to match these imaginary conditions.' It was time, he said, to stop 'over-reacting to temporary recessions' and to stop inventing 'temporary jobs' to get unemployment down. The cure would be painful: unemployment would temporarily rise. But the alternative was bleak:

> If we do not get the trend of the increase of the money supply over
> the next few years on to a steady and low rate, more and even more
> rapid inflation will follow. We will destroy our monetary system; we will

make all our existing problems worse – and will add as yet undreamed nightmares beside. Continued rapid inflation will destroy every plan and every prospect; jobs and savings will evaporate; society will be fractured. It was not for nothing that Lenin recommended inflation as the arch destroyer of what he called bourgeois democracy and we call democracy.[23]

To monetarist commentators like Peter Jay, Preston seemed a moment of glorious hope. *The Times* reprinted the speech in full, while its leader hailed 'The Sharp Shock of Truth'. Even the *Sun*, not usually fascinated by economic theory, gave it extensive coverage. And yet the praise was more than balanced by the voices of criticism. For *The Economist*, Joseph seemed to think that 'Britain should parachute to safety with something closely resembling a pocket handkerchief', while the *New Statesman*'s Roger Opie thought his analysis was 'muddled, naive, assertive and tendentious'. As Opie noted, the speech had been notably light on specifics: 'We must get the money supply right, he says – not too high or too low. Which money supply? How high is too high, how low is too low?'* And crucially, within Heath's Shadow Cabinet there was still little support for Joseph's ideas. When the Conservatives published their October manifesto, price controls and incomes policies were still there. Heath's old collaborator Reginald Maudling spoke for most senior Conservatives when he wrote that Joseph was 'totally divorced from reality'. In private Maudling went further: Sir Keith, he thought, was as 'nutty as a fruitcake'.[24]

If Joseph had kept his head down after Preston, he might have been a serious challenger for the Tory leadership. Within days of the October election, disgruntled backbenchers were asking him to throw his hat in the ring. On the 13th a group of right-wingers met at Nicholas Ridley's Pimlico flat to discuss Joseph's campaign, with his friend Margaret Thatcher already eyeing up the job of campaign manager. What came next, however, was a catastrophic gaffe that seemed conclusive proof of Maudling's diagnosis. Like Enoch Powell before him, Joseph went to a Birmingham hotel to give a speech. But whereas Powell's famous address in the Midland Hotel had been devoted to immigration, Joseph's speech on Saturday, 19 October was about the evils of the permissive society. This seemed smart politics: in an era of soaring divorce and illegitimacy

---

* These were prescient words: when the Thatcher government actually put monetarism into effect, it proved extraordinarily difficult even to define what the money supply was, let alone to set the right targets – most of which the government missed.

statistics, with headlines dominated by pornography, drug use and the impending annihilation of middle-class values, talking about the family seemed an excellent way to appeal to ordinary Tory voters. Only days before the end of the October campaign, Joseph had already warned that Britain was becoming 'a nation of hooligans and vandals, bullies and child-batterers, criminals and inadequates', for which he blamed the 'facile rhetoric of total liberty', the absence of 'rules of community, place and belonging, responsibility and neighbourliness' and the 'commercial exploitation of brutality in print and in film'. This was good rousing conservative stuff, the kind of thing that people like Mary Whitehouse and Lord Longford had been saying for years. Of course it sat rather uneasily with Sir Keith's neo-liberal economics, which held up individual freedom as the great god, and *Private Eye* sarcastically wondered whether he was going to 'renounce his faith in the free enterprise system'. But like so many Thatcherites after him, Joseph never seemed to notice the contradiction.[25]

At first, Joseph's speech to the Edgbaston Conservative Association in Birmingham's Grand Hotel followed the usual lines. British life, he said, was increasingly defined by 'delinquency, truancy, vandalism, hooliganism, illiteracy, decline in educational standards. Some secondary schools in our cities are dominated by gangs operating extortion rackets against small children. Teenage pregnancies are rising; so are drunkenness, sexual offences, and crimes of sadism.' Universities had fallen to the 'bully-boys of the left', while the welfare state had given rise to 'drugs, drunkenness, teenage pregnancies, vandalism [and] vagrancy'. So far, so predictable. But then Joseph committed the blunder for which posterity has never forgiven him. During his time at the DHSS, he had become fascinated by cycles of deprivation, with poverty and delinquency apparently being passed from parents to children. Now he returned to the issue. 'The balance of our population, our human stock is threatened,' he announced, quoting research by the Child Poverty Action Group, allegedly showing that 'a high and rising proportion of children are being born to mothers least fitted to bring children into the world'. These were young women, he said, in 'social classes 4 and 5', many of them unmarried, many 'of low intelligence, most of low educational attainment'. They were producing 'problem children, the future unmarried mothers, delinquents, denizens of our borstals, sub-normal educational establishments, prisons, hostels for drifters'. There was an obvious answer: the NHS must 'extend birth-control facilities to these classes of people, particularly the young unmarried girls', even though it might seem like 'condoning immorality'. But the alternative would be even worse: 'it is degeneration.'[26]

Like Powell's speech six years earlier, Joseph's trip to Birmingham became an overnight sensation. The next morning, Mary Whitehouse, despite her well-chronicled suspicion of birth control, pronounced herself 'tremendously grateful' and declared that the people of Britain had found their 'shepherd'. Like Powell, Joseph claimed to have had thousands of admiring letters. But in the press, voices of support were drowned out by those expressing derision or outrage – not least at that disastrous phrase 'our human stock is threatened', which sounded like something from the Third Reich.* Joseph was a 'saloon-bar Malthus', wrote the *New Statesman*'s Alan Watkins, while the Labour MP Arthur Latham claimed that his message was simple: 'castrate or conform'. Even *The Times*, which agreed with his remarks about the permissive society, thought he had been disastrously reckless to invoke the spectre of eugenics, which had long since become utterly unacceptable. And to make matters worse, the next weekend's *Sunday Times* published a long analysis showing that Joseph had completely misrepresented the Child Poverty Action Group Study on which his closing arguments were based. Far from rising, the working-class birth rate was actually falling, while the study's authors had gone out of their way to point out that birth control was 'no cheap solution to all the problems of child poverty'. All in all, the newspaper concluded, his 'statements on the relationship between social class and the birth rate are just not true – and no amount of constituents' letters will make them so'.[27]

It is just conceivable that, if nothing else had gone wrong, Joseph might have ridden out the storm over his Edgbaston speech and retained his credibility as a leadership challenger. His critics, of course, took enormous pleasure at his discomfiture. 'It's great fun to see somebody else getting into hot water over a speech,' Enoch Powell mordantly remarked. 'I almost wondered if the River Tiber was beginning to roll again.' To Powell, Joseph was a traitor who had meekly gone along with Heath's policies 'until he no longer had cabinet office, salary, car and chauffeur to sacrifice' – an assessment that was harsh, perhaps, but not unfounded. What finally killed Joseph's chances off, though, was an

---

* Most people assumed Sherman had written the offending words, but fifteen years later Joseph told *The Times* that he had personally inserted the phrase over Sherman's objections. In 2010, however, the barrister and historian Jonathan Sumption, who occasionally wrote speeches for Sir Keith, told the same paper that they were his handiwork.

interview he had already given to the *Observer*'s young reporter Polly Toynbee. Although the paper's editor David Astor spiked it, a copy made its way to *Private Eye*, and for Joseph's partisans it made excruciating reading. Evidently overwrought, he had lapsed into long silences before pounding the table and declaring that Britain was 'doomed' and needed 'a new prophet'. Bizarrely, he broke off at one point to declare that the country needed 'more lavatories. I'm in favour of lavatories. Very much in favour of them.' Coming from somebody else, it might have been funny. Coming from a man already widely believed to be 'as nutty as a fruitcake', it was a catastrophe. With each gaffe, the chances of the Tories electing a man who seemed a combination of 'Hamlet, Rasputin and Tommy Cooper' (as Denis Healey put it) became more remote. Joseph was 'dotty and lacks moral fibre for high office', Lord Hailsham recorded in his diary. 'A silly man and always wrong.'[28]

By the middle of November, the man *Private Eye* now called 'Sir Sheath' knew that his leadership challenge was in ruins. 'I know my own capacities,' he said later, with commendable self-knowledge. 'Had I become party leader, it would have been a disaster for the party, country and me.' Even so, his place in Conservative history was assured, not least as the first Tory frontbencher since the 1930s to revive what Simon Jenkins calls 'political masochism' – the idea that 'to govern was to be unpopular, to endure pain', a notion that would have seemed utterly alien to consensual crowd-pleasers like Harold Macmillan or Harold Wilson. And in the years to come, Joseph had to endure his fair share of pain. Touring the country to give dozens of speeches at universities and colleges, he was frequently bombarded with abuse and missiles. At Essex in February 1977, for example, he was pelted with eggs and flour bombs for half an hour while lecturing the students on the case for capitalism. His campus crusade was not entirely fruitless, though: among the young men inspired by his ideas were future Conservative stars such as William Hague, Peter Lilley and David Willetts, while the original treatment for the sitcom *Minder* noted that the would-be entrepreneur Arthur Daley 'admires Sir Keith Joseph'.

Yet just as Arthur Daley's moneymaking ventures invariably had more than a hint of the absurd, so Sir Keith's increasingly apocalyptic denunciations of Marxist subversion and the permissive society were not always sensibly directed. Only Joseph would have chosen to open the Camping and Outdoor Life Exhibition at Olympia in January 1975 by lecturing an audience of camping enthusiasts about the threat of the Soviet Union. To get the full flavour of the occasion, *The Times*'s diarist explained, readers must picture the speech 'being delivered to an audience of apparently non-political campers, many with young children, who were standing in front of a mock woodland area'. The freedom to go camping, Joseph grimly told them, was one of the delights of democratic capitalism; if socialism prevailed, it might be stamped out. 'It does strike a chill,' he concluded. 'Are we sure that we shall not eventually be subject to movement permits if socialism advances here? Don't be too sure.' Afterwards, while parents and children were still shaking their heads in disbelief, Joseph explained that his words had been 'lighthearted'. In that case, remarked *The Times*, people must hope 'he did not have many more New Year jokes of a similarly macabre kind'.[29]

Joseph abandoned his leadership challenge on 14 November, telling his chief backbench supporter, the young Norman Fowler, that under no circumstances would he be a candidate. On the same evening, Heath gave his first speech to the 1922 Committee since the election, giving no sign that he intended to bow out. To Joseph's supporters the news could hardly be worse. But for those who wanted the Conservative Party to swing towards the right, the day did have a silver lining. Almost unnoticed in all the fuss about Heath's intentions, one of Joseph's closest friends in the Commons was making her debut as the Tories' deputy Treasury spokesman. During Margaret Thatcher's time as Education Secretary, nobody had ever associated her with great oratory or a sense of humour. Yet she was 'in sharpest claw', said the *Express* the next day, hailing the 'savage irony' with which she had laid into Healey's latest Budget. Even the *Mirror* thought that she had 'staked a claim to be the next Tory Chancellor', especially if Joseph became the new leader. They had been friends for years, and she was convinced that the tortured baronet was the right man to challenge Heath. But when, on 21 November, he walked into her Commons office and confirmed that he was not running after all, Mrs Thatcher was horrified. Almost without thinking – as she later remembered it – she burst out: 'Look, Keith, if you're not going to stand, I will, because someone who represents our viewpoint *has* to stand.' In that moment, the new liberals found their champion.[30]

11

Housewife of the Year

*I would not wish to be Prime Minister, dear. I have not enough
experience for that job. The only full ministerial position I've
held is Minister of Education and Science. Before you could
even think of being Prime Minister, you'd need to have done
a good deal more jobs than that.*

Margaret Thatcher on BBC1's *Val Meets the VIPs*,
5 March 1973

*Peter Carrington is back. He has had Ted Heath for the
w/end . . .*
Peter: 'I told him he ought to have gone around during the past
few months being a good loser, kissing Margaret on every
possible opportunity and saying what a splendid woman she
was. He looked at me in absolute amazement: "Why on earth?
I do not think she is any good. I am much better and I ought
to be there still."'

Lord Hailsham's diary, 20 January 1976

Shortly before the outbreak of the Second World War, when a Lincolnshire schoolgirl called Margaret Roberts was in her early teens, the
Grantham Journal decided to take on the little market town's critics.
Some people had been complaining that Grantham lacked 'the excitement and amenities of other ultra-modern places and was just content
to jog along in an imperturbable way'. But the *Journal* thought they
were wrong. Grantham had no business copying the hectic lifestyle of
more 'fashionable' places, for its townsfolk much preferred the 'price-
less atmosphere of peace and contentment'. And so indeed it proved.

The years passed; engineering and food processing took over the town's economy, new housing estates sprawled out into the countryside, and Miss Roberts became Britain's first woman Prime Minister. But the pace of life in Grantham seemed barely to change at all. Four decades on, the *Sun* called it 'the most boring town in Britain', while the *Guardian*'s Hugo Young thought it 'the epitome of Middle England, a place that prides itself on the ordinariness of its daily life, the unexciting decency of its people and the slowness of their responses to change'. All in all, Grantham's former town clerk remarked, it remained 'a narrow town, built on a narrow street and inhabited by narrow people'.[1]

Narrowness can be an asset as well as a weakness, and so it proved for the woman who toppled Edward Heath as Conservative leader in 1975. As the first professional scientist to rise to the summit of British politics, Margaret Thatcher was often derided as a soulless philistine, knowing the price of everything and the value of nothing. Even in the late 1940s, when she was a student at Somerville College, Oxford, her college principal had dismissed young Miss Roberts as a 'second-class chemist', and never invited her to weekend dinners because 'she had nothing to contribute'. This was unfair: although Mrs Thatcher was hardly one of the great intellectuals of her generation, she was sufficiently well read to appreciate Rudyard Kipling, dislike T. S. Eliot and enjoy books by Alexander Solzhenitsyn and Harold Bloom. And yet there *was* a narrowness to her: what her biographer John Campbell calls a 'rare moral certainty and unreflective self-righteousness'. Like some Dickensian personification of all Grantham's alleged failings, she had no time for irony and little sense of humour, showed scant interest in contrasting opinions and remained snug in the inflexible certainty of her own rectitude. In the long run, this was to prove her greatest flaw; but amid the confused retreats and seedy compromises of the mid-1970s, it was her greatest strength. 'Methodism, science and suburbia', the journalist Simon Jenkins, both an admirer and a critic, wrote later, 'had armoured her in self-confidence and self-righteousness.'[2]

Margaret Thatcher's background has entered political folklore. Born to a prosperous Grantham grocer in October 1925, she literally grew up above the shop, imbibing the values of small-town entrepreneurship, thrift, hard work and good housekeeping. As an independent councillor and chairman of Grantham's Finance and Rating Committee, her father, Alfred Roberts, was a local bigwig. Eventually he became an elected alderman (and briefly, mayor), as well as chairman of the local Rotary Club, director of the Trustee Savings Bank and governor of both the town's secondary schools. No doubt this helps to explain why his second daughter was interested in politics. But the most important thing he handed down to her – apart from his beliefs in balanced budgets, hard work and the importance of public service – was his Methodist faith. His was a particularly respectable form of Methodism, and the Roberts family worshipped at the Wesleyan Church in the centre of town, not the more downmarket chapels nearer the shop. But it was also a strict faith, frowning on frivolity and indolence, with a strong emphasis on individual self-improvement. Years later, the *Guardian*'s Peter Jenkins, recalling his own Wesleyan boyhood in East Anglia, wrote that it was 'the religion of prosperous shopkeepers and farmers, a pious celebration of the work ethic and discharge of the religious duty which accompanied the ownership of property'. And it left a deep imprint on the young Margaret Roberts, who was taken to church three or four times every Sunday, always perfectly turned out. In a sense, all her political and economic views stemmed from her religious upbringing. 'We were Methodists,' she explained in 1978, 'and Methodism means method.'[3]

Although Mrs Thatcher came from a very different background from most of her Conservative predecessors, it is not entirely true that she hauled herself up by her bootstraps. Her father arranged private tuition for the Oxford entrance exam, and then funded her through Oxford even though she had missed out on a scholarship. Once there, she rapidly became involved in the Conservative Association (OUCA), eventually becoming its president. This was no small feat: it meant that she hobnobbed with the great and the good, and opened up 'a gilded path to the top'. Indeed, even at this early stage she was leaving the grocer's shop far behind. Paradoxically, although she later became famous as 'the grocer's daughter' and eagerly reminded interviewers of her modest provincial background, she showed no such sentimental attachments as a young woman. After leaving Oxford, she rarely returned to Grantham. By 1951, when she married the rich businessman Denis Thatcher, the Methodist grammar school girl seemed to have given way to a Home Counties Tory, complete with extravagant hats and cut-glass accent. She won a seat in a suburban London constituency, sent her children Mark and Carol to expensive private schools, and even embraced the Church of England, traditionally the religious equivalent of the Conservative Party. As Campbell remarks, it is a supreme irony that the grocer's daughter broke with her father's austerity in almost every particular, from her comfortable Chelsea flat to her encouragement of consumerism. A few traces remained: the occasional word of Lincolnshire dialect (famously, 'frit', meaning frightened, during a Commons clash in 1983), as well as an understandable chip on her shoulder about the old boys' network. But it was highly suggestive that when Brian Walden asked about her father's death during an interview, her assistant had to check the date for her.[4]

Although the new Mrs Thatcher initially worked as a research chemist, she made no secret of her political ambitions, winning selection for the unwinnable Dartford seat in both 1950 and 1951. After her second campaign, the area agent sent a note to Central Office enthusing about her 'excellent' performance: 'She is an amazing young woman with experience and knowledge far beyond her years ... she is quite outstanding in ability and has, in addition, a most attractive personality and appearance.' Even at this early stage she was firmly on the right: at Oxford, she had co-written a paper asserting that 'individual enterprise is the mainspring of all progress', and during her Dartford campaigns she talked enthusiastically of 'freedom and liberty'. But even though her robust views ought to have appealed to Conservative activists, she did not make it to Parliament until 1959, when she secured a safe seat in Finchley. The reason was obvious: not only was she a woman, she was a young mother whose place was at home, looking after her children. Indeed, even after being adopted as Finchley's candidate she found that many local Tories were suspicious of her femininity. 'I am learning the hard way', she told a friend, 'that an anti-woman prejudice among certain Association members can persist even after a successful adoption meeting.'[5]

Mrs Thatcher never thought of herself as a feminist, and most feminists utterly loathed her. And yet in her own way she was a compelling standard-bearer of women's liberation. 'Some men I know are far too ready with the phrase "woman's place is in the home,"' she wrote in the Young Conservative journal in 1954, 'forgetting that their own daughters will almost certainly have to earn their living outside the home, at any rate for a time.' If a woman had talent and ambition, she thought, 'it is essential both for her own satisfaction and for the happiness of her family that she should use all her talents to the full'. Of course her femininity counted as an asset, up to a point: once she made it to Parliament, it meant that she stood out from all the men in grey suits, and gave her an extra weapon with which to charm Tory grandees. But it also worked against her: because she was a woman, the press focused unerringly on her outfits, her hats and her efforts to juggle work and family; and because she was a woman, her colleagues took her less seriously and dismissed her ideas. Her femininity also made it harder for her to win the admiration of her leader, because there was nothing Edward Heath liked less than a strident Home Counties woman. Only with great reluctance did he accept his friends' advice that he needed a 'statutory woman' in his Shadow Cabinet and that Thatcher was by far the most talented available. 'Once she's there,' Willie Whitelaw muttered miserably, 'we'll never get rid of her.' He was not the only MP who despaired at the prospect. 'Anti-feminists may feel that she is the sort of thing that happens if you allow women to go into politics,' Woodrow Wyatt told the readers of the *Sunday Mirror* in December 1969. 'Her air of bossiness, her aptitude for interfering, can be very tiresome and irritating to easy-going men who do not always want to be kept up to scratch, particularly by a female.'[6]

Given their historic enmity, it is easy to forget that Margaret Thatcher and Edward Heath were remarkably similar. As their biographer John Campbell notes, both came from modest provincial backgrounds and owed their elevation to grammar school and Oxford. Both were ferociously ambitious; both were doggedly pragmatic; both suffered from a distinct lack of a sense of humour. There was, however, a crucial difference. As the son of a Kentish builder, Heath was steeped in the values of 'deferential working-class Toryism'. From Oxford onwards, he had tried to copy the habits of his social superiors, from classical music to his peculiar strangulated accent, but he never lost sight of his obligations to those at the bottom of the ladder. But the young Margaret Roberts's background was subtly different. Her father was a successful small businessman who had made a name for himself in local politics. She was steeped in the values of middle-class entrepreneurship, of getting ahead and making no apologies for it. Unlike Heath, she had no need to take up upper-class habits, preferring the suburban gentility of a Home Counties lifestyle. And unlike Heath, she had little time for the privileged paternalists who dominated the Tory establishment. To the grocer's daughter, the old world of country estates, tweed suits, hearty chaps and bleeding hearts was utter anathema. 'She doesn't like country gents much,' one of her MPs remarked. 'There's a natural suspicion there.' And it flowed both ways: Willie Whitelaw thought her 'governessy', Francis Pym remarked that she was a 'corporal' rather than a 'cavalry officer' and Sir Christopher Soames even called her a jumped-up 'housemaid'. But she had the last laugh.[7]

Secure in her lower-middle-class values, Thatcher automatically gravitated to the right of the Conservative Party. On social and cultural issues she was not automatically reactionary: although she remained a steadfast supporter of capital punishment, she voted to liberalize the laws on both abortion and homosexuality. But there was no doubt that she was well to the right of Edward Heath. In her most important speech before she entered the Cabinet, the annual Conservative Political Centre lecture at the party conference in 1968, she gave a resounding endorsement of free-market values, demanding 'a far greater degree of personal responsibility and decision, far more independence from the government, and a comparative reduction in the role of government'. Above all, she anticipated two of the key themes of mature Thatcher-ism. 'There is nothing wrong in people wanting larger incomes,' she said: it was a 'worthy objective for men and women to wish to raise the standard of living for their families and to give them greater opportun-ities than they themselves had'. And although money was 'not an end in itself . . . even the Good Samaritan had to have the money to help, other-wise he too would have had to pass on the other side'.

By the 1980s, this would be standard Conservative stuff; in the late 1960s, however, it sounded more like Enoch Powell than Edward Heath. No doubt it also reflected the influence of the Institute of Economic Affairs, where Mrs Thatcher was an occasional visitor. Intriguingly, though, some IEA stalwarts wondered whether she went too far. 'I am not at all sure about Margaret,' the economic liberal Geoffrey Howe wrote to Arthur Seldon a year later:

> Many of her economic prejudices are certainly sound. But she is inclined to be rather too dogmatic for my liking on sensitive matters like education and might actually retard the case by over simplification. We should certainly be able to hope for something better from her – but I suspect that she will need to be exposed to the humanising side of your character as much as to the pure welfare market monger. There is much scope for her to be influenced between triumph and disaster.

In many ways, of course, these were remarkably prescient words.[8]

Howe was not alone in his view that Mrs Thatcher was rather too strident to become a star. When she became Education Secretary in June 1970, her civil servants found her something of a shock. Compared with her self-consciously urbane predecessors, she came across as bossy and intense. 'She had a totally unoriginal mind,' one mandarin com-plained, while the head of her private office thought she was 'really quite narrow' (that word again), with only a 'weak' grasp of 'the human-ities, arts, music, literature, history, languages, which, in an education minister, was something of a handicap'. Most officials admired her appetite for hard work, but resented her habit of talking down to them 'like a very well-spoken nanny'. Even her permanent secretary, Sir William Pile, thought she was 'narrow-minded, emotional, impossible to argue with [and] driven by passions which he found "abhorrent"'. What he found most revealing, though, was her disbelief when she heard that one of her Cabinet colleagues, the Leader of the Lords, Earl Jellicoe, had been visiting call girls. After visibly 'steeling herself up', she asked Pile: 'Did men really pay that kind of money for that sort of thing?' Her sheer naivety left him stunned. 'She lives in a world apart, unaware how most of the population lived,' he told Roy Strong. 'Her knowledge of history was nil.'[9]

Mrs Thatcher was not popular with her senior colleagues. Willie Whitelaw complained that she was 'apt to lecture and bulldoze her way', while Reginald Maudling frequently complained about 'that bloody woman' who 'never listened', and privately referred to her as 'that bitch'. Above all, Edward Heath made little secret of the fact that he found her extremely tiresome. Whenever she embarked on one of her tirades, he would drum irritably on his blotter, and on more than one occasion he had to tell her to shut up. And yet despite her abrasive style, she was a highly competent departmental minister. Her tenure at the Department of Education is now remembered for the fuss about her decision to scrap free school milk for primary school children over 7, which prompted the tabloids to call her the 'Milk Snatcher'. In fact this was a completely 'bogus' issue, to borrow Hugo Young's words. Free school milk was a hangover from the Attlee years, designed to address the malnutrition of the Depression; ironically, the Wilson government had already implemented a much bigger cut a few years earlier by scrapping milk in secondary schools. And the Milk Snatcher business obscured the fact that, when it came down to it, Mrs Thatcher was a thoroughly conventional Education Secretary who saved the Open University from the Treasury axe, fought to raise the school-leaving age to 16, and closed more grammar schools than any minister in history. 'In several respects,' the *Guardian* admitted afterwards, she had been a 'more egalitarian Minister than her Labour predecessor. Her support for primary schools, polytechnics, the raising of the school-leaving age, and the new nursery programme will all provide more help to working-class children than the Labour programme actually did.'[10]

What this reflects is the overlooked fact that in the final analysis, Mrs Thatcher was a thoroughly pragmatic career politician. She betrayed few hints of dissatisfaction with Heath's policy contortions, his decision to go into Europe, his attempt to build a corporatist consensus with the unions or his adoption of an extraordinarily elaborate incomes policy. Like her colleagues, she nodded meekly at every decision, and while some of her acolytes later claimed that she had really been wringing her hands with horror in private, there was little evidence of this at the time. The famous U-turns passed without a squeak of protest, and during the tumultuous crisis of 1973–4, she steadfastly supported Heath's pay and prices policy, even arguing that the government should stiffen it further 'if necessary'. Perhaps it was no wonder, then, that in Heath's very last Cabinet meeting, only Mrs Thatcher roused herself from the general gloom to praise the 'wonderful experience of team loyalty' she had shared since 1970 – a marvellously ironic moment, given what was to come.[11]

By this point, her place near the top of the Conservative Party seemed assured. In the October general election she played a key role in the Tory campaign, appearing in more television broadcasts than any other shadow minister, and eagerly pushing the party's pledge to cap mortgage interest rates at 9.5 per cent. Of course this flew in the face of free-market principles, but, in public at least, she seemed to have few qualms about it. And by the end of the campaign, her vigorous appeals to what she called 'the non-militant, non-organised, non-political people who feel they have been forgotten' had marked her out as one of the party's rising stars. Privately she hoped to become Chancellor, which had long been her dream job. But already there were rumours that she might set her sights higher. As early as March, the Exeter MP John Hannam told Alan Clark that she might be 'a possible successor to Heath'. And once Heath had lost the second election, the murmurs became louder. On 16 October, Piers Dixon, who had just lost his seat to the Liberals, told friends that she was 'now [the] front runner for the leadership of the Tory Party if Heath resigned'. In the *Sunday Times*, meanwhile, Ronald Butt wrote that 'Mrs Thatcher, because of sheer ability, is a real contender, despite the apparent handicap that she is a woman'. But that, of course, was the problem. For as she had once told her local newspaper, 'there will never be a woman Prime Minister in my lifetime – the male population is too prejudiced'.[12]

To her family, Mrs Thatcher's decision to throw her hat in the ring came as a complete shock. 'You must be out of your mind,' remarked her husband Denis. 'You haven't got a hope.' Heath himself was incredulous: when she visited him at the House of Commons on 25 November, he did not even bother to get out of his chair, but merely shrugged and said: 'You'll lose.' In the press, she was seen as a stalking horse for Willie Whitelaw: *The Economist*, for example, thought that she was 'precisely the sort of candidate . . . who ought to be able to stand, and lose, harmlessly'. Not only was she a woman, and therefore unelectable, but she was much too 'narrowly suburban, middle-class and southern in image and appeal', as her biographer puts it. The *Daily Mirror* mocked 'her plummy voice and her extravagant hats and her Dresden-shepherdess appearance'; the *Sunday Mirror*'s Woodrow Wyatt, later a staunch admirer, called her a 'limited, bossy, self-righteous and self-complacent woman'; even the *Daily Express*'s Derek Marks thought she was 'totally out of touch with anybody but carefully corseted, middle-class, middle-aged ladies'. The Conservative Party would never elect her, Enoch Powell confidently predicted. 'They wouldn't put up with those hats and that accent.'[13]

Her candidacy benefited from two great strokes of luck. The first stemmed from Heath's decision to reshuffle his front-bench team, making her deputy Treasury spokesman under his Shadow Chancellor, Robert Carr. From Heath's point of view, this was a grievous mistake, allowing her to take the lead in opposition to Denis Healey's Finance Bill, her fighting spirit shining all the more brightly beside Carr's rather lacklustre moderation. On 22 January she made a famously ferocious intervention, launching a blistering attack on Healey's Capital Transfer Tax and defending inheritance as one of the pillars of a free society. When the Chancellor derisively called her the '*Pasionaria*' of privilege', she hit back in memorable style. 'I wish I could say that the Chancellor of the Exchequer had done himself less than justice,' she said witheringly. 'Unfortunately, I can only say that I believe he has done himself justice. Some Chancellors are macroeconomic. Other Chancellors are fiscal. This one is just plain cheap.'[14]

The Tories roared with delight: for once, as her friend Nicholas Ridley put it, 'here was a senior figure who didn't seem beaten at all; she exuded confidence and certainty'. Even the Heathites were impressed: 'amidst the shambles and doubts of that time,' remarked Francis Pym, 'here was one person who could articulate a point of view with conviction.' And to Conservative supporters in the country, the contrast with the weak-kneed advocates of 'national unity' could hardly have been starker. If the country was to survive, wrote Bernard Levin in the next day's *Times*, 'a Tory leader will one day have to fight under pure Tory colours'. Sooner or later, he thought, 'this country will have a woman for Prime Minister ... I suspect that the time may be right already.'[15]

The second stroke of luck was the withdrawal of Edward du Cann, who pulled out of the race in early January after deciding that he did not want the press raking over his finances. Slightly bizarrely, he invited the Thatchers to his house in Lord North Street, a few doors down from Wilson's house, to announce his decision. They sat on his sofa, he recalled, 'like a housekeeper and a handyman applying for a job'. The real benefit for Mrs Thatcher, though, was that she inherited the services of du Cann's campaign manager, the former intelligence officer and Abingdon MP, Airey Neave. By any standards, Neave was a remarkable character: imprisoned by the Germans in Colditz during the Second World War, he escaped during a theatrical production and became the first British officer to make it all the way home, his route taking him through Germany, Switzerland, France, Spain and Gibraltar. Above all, though, he nursed a fierce hatred for Heath, who had told him that he was 'finished' after a heart attack in 1959. Unseating Heath had become an obsession for Neave, and, having already offered his skills to Joseph, Whitelaw and du Cann, he now turned to Mrs Thatcher. In the next few weeks, he arranged for Tory MPs to meet her in small groups for a cup of tea, emphasizing her accessibility and informality. Crucially, he deliberately played down her chances, telling wavering MPs that the only way to get a serious candidate like Whitelaw was to vote for 'the filly' on the first ballot. So, for example, Norman Tebbit persuaded Michael Heseltine, 'who was a Whitelaw man, that unless he voted for Margaret on the first ballot there would be no second ballot and no opportunity for Willie to stand'. It was political chicanery of the highest order – but it was to prove highly effective.[16]

One of the great strengths of Mrs Thatcher's campaign was that it turned her greatest drawback – the fact that she was a woman – into an asset. She did not present herself as a feminist, even though the vogue for feminist ideas and the advance of working women, especially in the professions, made it easier for her to be taken seriously. Instead, she sold herself as an old-fashioned housewife. 'I am a very ordinary person who leads a very normal life,' she told the *Mirror*. 'I enjoy it – seeing that the family have a good breakfast. And shopping keeps me in touch.' The irony, of course, was that as a working mother who had always put her career first (and had a very rich husband), Mrs Thatcher was the antithesis of a submissive Stepford wife. But now she played up to the image of the lower-middle-class housewife, ditching her extravagant hats, going shopping with her sister and a *Daily Mail* photographer, and putting on a 'pantomime of housework' for the *Mirror*. 'First there was the kitchen to tidy,' the paper wryly remarked. 'Then the bathroom, a dash round with the duster and on to the shopping and the laundry. And after that she had to tidy up the Tory party, polish off Ted Heath and give Britain a good spring cleaning. With Margaret Thatcher it is sometimes a bit hard to tell whether she wants to be Prime Minister or housewife of the year.'[17]

A common criticism in February 1975 was that Mrs Thatcher was merely a television politician, all style and no substance. 'In barely two weeks,' complained the *Guardian*'s Peter Jenkins, 'viewers and voters have learnt more than they need to know about her family life, her domestic habits, her wardrobe and hairstyling.' By contrast, they had 'learnt next to nothing of the substance behind the image and the reason for that is that there is as yet very little substance there'. But this was unfair. To anybody who had paid any attention to politics for the last ten years, Thatcher's right-wing stance was very well known. And despite the emphasis on her dress sense and shopping habits, her convictions were plain for all to see. What she offered was a more populist version of Sir Keith Joseph's free-market credo, 'defining freedom in the daily concerns of individual taxpayers, homeowners and businessmen'. Setting out her rationale in the *Daily Telegraph* on 30 January, she embraced the accusation that she was the champion of middle-class values:

> Well, if 'middle class values' include the encouragement of variety and individual choice, the provision of fair incentives and rewards for skill and hard work, the maintenance of effective barriers against the excessive power of the State and a belief in the wide distribution of individual *private* property, then they are certainly what I am trying to defend . . .
>
> If a Tory does not believe that private property is one of the main bulwarks of individual freedom, then he had better become a socialist and have done with it. Indeed one of the reasons for our electoral failure is that people believe too many Conservatives *have* become socialists already. Britain's progress towards socialism has been an alternation of two steps forward with half a step back.
>
> If every Labour Government is prepared to reverse every Tory measure, while Conservative Governments accept nearly all socialist measures as being 'the will of the people', the end result is only too plain. And why should anyone support a party that seems to have the courage of no convictions?

These were not the words of a bland television politician. Neither was her conclusion. 'My kind of Tory party', she wrote, 'would make no secret of its belief in individual freedom and individual prosperity, in the maintenance of law and order, in the wide distribution of private property, in rewards for energy, skill and thrift, in diversity of choice, in the preservation of local rights in local communities.' Here was Thatcherism in embryo.[18]

To the grandees around Edward Heath, the idea that a suburban middle-class woman could become leader of the Conservative Party was simply absurd. Their champion's own background should have reminded them that the party was changing, yet most shared Sir Ian Gilmour's view that Mrs Thatcher would corral the Tories 'behind a privet hedge into a world of narrow class interests and selfish concerns'. Her basic problem, Douglas Hurd told the *Sunday Times*'s Hugo Young two weeks before the first ballot, was 'her narrow horizons. No vision, no broad sweep. An inability – not unlike Ted's, but more acute – to put herself in others' shoes.' There was some insight in this, but more than a little snobbery, too. And since Heath's team found it impossible to take Mrs Thatcher seriously, his own campaign was extraordinarily complacent. Fatally, his campaign managers, Tim Kitson, Kenneth Baker and Peter Walker, were loyalists who never understood the smouldering dissatisfaction of many backbenchers. And where Thatcher's *Telegraph* article was clear and punchy, even the sympathetic John Campbell admits that Heath's riposte was 'extraordinarily woolly', a bland appeal to national unity without any thrust or specifics. Yet even as the first ballot approached, Heath's team saw no way he could possibly lose – even though their own figures showed him struggling to win much more than half of the parliamentary party.[19]

Tuesday, 4 February, the day of the first ballot, dawned cold and cloudy. In the press, the overwhelming consensus was that Heath would win. The day before, a poll for the *Daily Express* had found that 70 per cent of Conservative voters still preferred him to any other possible leader – although this was less a ringing endorsement of Heath than a damning indictment of his lethargic colleagues. In the Tory press, only the *Mail* expressed even vague enthusiasm for Mrs Thatcher's cause: the *Telegraph*, though critical of Heath, urged him to pay more attention to the right after his inevitable victory, while *The Times*, attached like a limpet to the middle of the road, expressed great enthusiasm for Willie Whitelaw but barely mentioned Mrs Thatcher at all. Even the omens were promising: from Baker Street came good news for Heath on one of

In this *Daily Express* cartoon, published on 3 February 1975, the day
before the first Tory leadership ballot, Cummings perfectly captures
Mrs Thatcher's appeal as the 'saviour of the middle classes' and
'scourge of the lower orders and the Left'.

the pivotal days of his life. He had jumped three places to finish runner-
up in the 'list of political heroes' in the annual poll of visitors to Madame
Tussaud's, beaten only by the reigning champion, Henry Kissinger. In
the list of those 'who inspire hate and fear', Kissinger's former boss
Richard Nixon had fallen to third, beaten by Adolf Hitler and – of all
people – Harold Wilson. 'I get the feeling', remarked *The Times*'s diarist,
'[that] the list is compiled by Conservative Central Office.'[20]

Heath cast his ballot in Committee Room 14 at around three o'clock,
shortly before the poll closed. Even at the last, his campaign managers
were confident of victory: Tim Kitson bet his opposite number a pound
that Heath would get more than 130 votes. Then Heath retired to his
Commons room to wait for the result, surrounded by his faithful
courtiers. Kitson went off to get the figures. While he was gone, they sat
quietly in a mood of gathering suspense. Then the door opened, and
Kitson came in, his face a mask of shock and disappointment. Heath had
not won more than 130 votes; he had won just 119. Against all expectations, Mrs Thatcher, the woman he had snubbed and scorned, the woman
none of them had taken seriously, had won 130 votes, and was now the
frontrunner. Outside, as they sat there in horrified silence, the right-wing
maverick Alan Clark was shouting 'She's won, she's won!' But in Heath's
room there was an atmosphere of utter disbelief. Many of his friends,
including the irredeemably emotional Lord Hailsham, were in tears;
characteristically, Heath himself remained calm, handing around large

glasses of whisky. Although his face 'showed it had been a bitter blow for him', one observer wrote, he managed to hide his agony, even mustering a laugh 'when someone managed to dredge up a joke'. But his old rival Reginald Maudling spoke for them all when he burst in with the words: 'The party's taken leave of its senses. This is a black day.'[21]

In Downing Street, Heath's defeat came as a total surprise. A few days earlier, Joe Haines had suggested that Wilson give Mrs Thatcher a police escort, 'to help her subtly in the leadership contest with Heath'. His rationale was that 'we wanted Heath beaten', because 'he is still the most dangerous', but Wilson was not so sure. 'He said he feared Thatcher as well, especially as a woman,' recorded Bernard Donoughue. When the news came through, Wilson was astonished, although he still thought that 'the Conservative Party would not be willing to have her as leader and that Whitelaw would win in the second ballot'. But other Labour ministers were more acute. Tony Benn thought that Thatcher would 'sweep the board, because the opposition has become a completely negative "Stop Thatcher" campaign, which I think will bring her tremendous support'. Her victory, Benn thought, would be a healthy development, 'because the Tory Party will be driven to the right and there will then be a real choice being offered to the electorate'. (It evidently did not occur to him that such a choice would work in her favour.) Even more enthusiastic, though, was Barbara Castle, who thought Mrs Thatcher had campaigned with 'grace and charm' and had 'never been prettier'. Despite all the pressures, Castle recorded, 'she sails through it all looking her best. I understand why. She is in love: in love with power, success – and with herself. She looks as I looked when Harold made me Minister of Transport. If we have to have Tories, good luck to her!'[22]

In the Thatcher camp, all was jubilation. 'The champagne flowed,' ITN's Norman Rees reported from a victory party in Airey Neave's Westminster flat, 'with pro-Thatcher MPs beaming rather bewilderedly, one thought, in a glare of so much publicity.' But while Mark Thatcher was palpably thrilled by his mother's success, her husband was in more taciturn form:

> REES: Was the result a surprise to you?
>
> DENIS THATCHER: Are you recording this? No, no, it wasn't.
>
> REES: Do you expect Mrs Thatcher's support to hold up under the next ballot?
>
> THATCHER: Yes, yes, I would, wholly.

REES: You say you fully expect your wife to be leading a Conservative party, do you?

THATCHER: I do.

REES: How do you feel about it?

THATCHER: Delighted. Terribly proud. Naturally. Wouldn't you?

Mrs Thatcher herself showed no signs of getting carried away. Leaving the family home in Chelsea the following morning, she found a horde of reporters on the doorstep, eager to hear what she had had for breakfast (her usual 'fruit and an egg', apparently). There were gracious words for her defeated opponent – 'One is very sad because ten years is a long period to be leader of a party and Prime Minister. It was an enormous achievement and one must thank and applaud him for it' – but she was not yet ready to declare victory. And amid the pleasantries, there was a brief flash of steel. As the photographers were pestering her to turn this way and that, she drily remarked: 'One thing no politician can do and that is turn in several different directions at the same time – physically.' 'How do you feel this morning?' a female reporter asked. 'I feel as I look,' was the curt reply. 'How is that?' the reporter persisted. 'Well, my dear,' Mrs Thatcher said, 'you can see me, I can't.'[23]

She had won only the first battle, of course, not the war. Although Heath now withdrew from the contest, four new contenders – not merely Willie Whitelaw but also the bluff Jim Prior, the acerbic John Peyton and the dry Sir Geoffrey Howe – threw their hats into the ring for the second ballot. Even so, the momentum was clearly running in her favour: as the *Telegraph* remarked, it looked as though 'a whole herd of fainthearts left it to a courageous and able woman to topple a formidable leader' and then 'ganged up to deny her her just reward'. The real threat was Whitelaw, who picked up endorsements from the *Sun*, the *Express* and *The Times*. Unfortunately, his delay in entering the contest, as well as the contrast with Thatcher's focus and drive, only accentuated his image as a bumbling booby. Beside her uncompromising enthusiasm for middle-class values, his talk of 'unity' sounded woolly and hollow. When one Conservative MP told him that he should stop agreeing with whatever the last person said, Whitelaw nodded eagerly and said: 'I agree, I agree.' The low point came when his campaign managers allowed him to be photographed at the kitchen sink, apparently in an effort to reclaim the title of housewife of the year. 'Anybody can do the washing up,' Johanna Darke of London NW5 wrote to

The Times a few days later. 'What this country needs is someone to lead us away from our own sense of doom while putting the place to right at the same time. This will require rare qualities of personal magnetism, sagacity, guts and a determination to get on with the job.' Sadly for Whitelaw, these were not qualities that sprang to mind when he rumbled into view. As one Conservative MP later remarked, 'the choice was between a woman and an old woman'. He voted for the woman.[24]

The second ballot was scheduled for Tuesday, 11 February. As luck would have it, Carol Thatcher was due to take one of her Law Society exams that afternoon, but only one thing dominated conversation in the Thatcher household. 'You can't be as nervous as I am,' her mother remarked that morning, ostentatiously crossing the fingers on both hands. Afraid to tempt fate, she had made no preparations for a victory party. But she need not have worried. Just after four that afternoon, ITV broke into its television coverage with the news that she had won 146 votes, far ahead of Whitelaw on 79, Prior and Howe on 19 each and Peyton on just 11. It was, by any standards, a stunning victory. Yet when Mrs Thatcher met the press ninety minutes later at Conservative Central Office, she was the very picture of quiet confidence. Asked if her sex had been an issue, she said simply: 'I would like to think it was merit.' When the questioner asked her to expand, she replied: 'No, it doesn't need expansion. You chaps don't like short answers. Or direct answers. Men like long rambly, waffly answers.' Even the pestering of the photographers failed to shake her composure. 'I am going to take a turn to the right,' she said, revolving for the cameras, 'which is very appropriate.' Only on the BBC news that evening did she betray some of the emotion that must have been surging through her on such a historic day. 'My predecessors, Edward Heath, Sir Alec Douglas-Home, Harold Macmillan, Anthony Eden, then of course the great Winston,' she said breathily, 'it is like a dream. Wouldn't you think so? I almost wept when they told me' – and then, biting her lip, her eyes welling up – 'I did weep.'[25]

'The Lady Is A Champ' roared the front page of the *Daily Mail* the next day, exulting that the Tories had 'chosen a woman of ambition, nerve and brilliance to lead them'. On the left, however, there was a palpable sense of glee that they had made such a disastrous appointment. Marcia Falkender recalled seeing a group of ministers after the news broke, 'laughing, joking and slapping each other on the shoulders . . . "That's it, we're home and dry," was the general tenor. "No need to worry about the next election. It's a foregone conclusion."' But they were not all so complacent. Both Tony Benn and Peter Shore thought Mrs Thatcher would be hard to beat, while the handful of female Labour MPs welcomed her success. Gwyneth Dunwoody professed herself 'very pleased', while Joyce Butler was 'delighted', adding: 'It is time we had women in the top jobs.' In her diary, Barbara Castle, surely concealing a twinge of jealousy that she had been overtaken in the race to become Britain's first woman leader, was even more excited:

> I have had a growing conviction that this would happen: she is so clearly the best man among them and she will, in my view, have an enormous advantage in being a woman too. I can't help feeling a thrill, even though I believe her election will make things much more difficult for us. I have been saying for a long time that the country is ready – even more than ready – for a woman Prime Minister. The 'it's time for a change from the male sex' version of the old election slogan. After all, men have been running the show for as long as anyone can remember and they don't seem to have made much of a job of it . . . I think it will be a good thing for the Labour Party too. There's a male-dominated party for you . . . I believe Margaret Thatcher's election will force our party to think again: and a jolly good thing too.

One Labour figure who was rather less thrilled, however, was the Prime Minister. 'He looked a bit down when he heard,' recorded Bernard Donoughue. 'Because he now had to face a new opponent.' Characteristically, Wilson thought entirely in terms of tactics. 'After ten years of studying the opponent like a hawk, learning every part of his character,' he said sadly, 'now, at my age, I've got to begin all over again'. Equally characteristically, 'he then poured himself a stiff brandy'.[26]

In what had once been Conservative high command, all was consternation. 'My God! The bitch has won!' exclaimed one Tory vice-chairman when the news came through. Whitelaw had been braced for bad news, but not for defeat by such a humiliating margin. The worst of it, he later admitted, was that his elderly mother never forgave him for letting himself be thrashed by a woman. Commiserating with his campaign team on Tuesday night, he wept openly, and when he addressed a Conservative dinner in Winchester a few days later, he again burst into tears. In the audience, recalled Simon Jenkins, many people were 'sobbing'. The atmosphere in the room was 'quite extraordinary': even as Whitelaw swore undying loyalty to the new leader, his listeners were telling themselves: 'We've just made the most terrible mistake . . . We owed it to him, and we've got this mad woman instead.' At Westminster, too, many of the Tories' rising stars were appalled by her victory. Paul Channon thought she was 'a right-wing fanatic who could never win the middle ground', while Norman Fowler considered her a 'throwback' and Kenneth Clarke shuddered at the thought of a right-wing 'counter-revolution'. Yet from East Sussex, home of Heath's old mentor Harold Macmillan, came a surprising message of support. Macmillan was delighted by 'the breakthrough of women's lib into the Conservative party'. Mrs Thatcher, he told a friend, was a woman of 'strong character and good sense' who had 'taken the leadership in her stride amid universal acclaim'. And in Hull, one staunch Conservative was overjoyed by her elevation. 'She has a pretty face, hasn't she,' the poet Philip Larkin wrote to his mother. 'I expect she's pretty tough, too.'[27]

The most common interpretation of Margaret Thatcher's rise to the Tory leadership holds that it was an accident. It was 'an unintended consequence', writes Simon Jenkins, 'a fluke of circumstance, the result of Heath's ineptitude'. There is certainly no doubt that she had been very lucky. If Enoch Powell had not committed political suicide, if Reginald Maudling had not been brought down by financial corruption, if Willie Whitelaw had had the courage to stand earlier or if Sir Keith Joseph had not shot himself in both feet, she would probably never have risen so far. But, as Jenkins suggests, the person she really had to thank was Edward Heath. Had it not been for his refusal to give in to the miners, his botched calling of the February 1974 election, his half-hearted national unity campaign and, above all, his self-destructive refusal to step aside, Margaret Thatcher would have remained a footnote in history. 'She didn't rise to power,' Enoch Powell once remarked with a combination of jealousy and approval. 'She was opposite the spot on the roulette wheel at the right time, and she didn't funk it.' Still, it had taken exceptional single-mindedness, courage and timing to ensure that she was in the right place when the wheel stopped turning. As the 9-year-old Margaret Roberts had told her Grantham headmistress after picking up a school poetry prize: 'I wasn't lucky. I deserved it.'[28]

It is a myth that Conservative MPs had no idea what they were voting for. In fact, the leadership election always had a clear ideological dimension. Analysis of both ballots has shown that members of right-wing factions such as the Monday Club, as well as MPs close to Enoch Powell or those who had rebelled over the EEC, Rhodesia and immigration, were much more likely to vote for Thatcher, while Heath and Whitelaw attracted heavy support from the more moderate One Nation factions. But there were other factors, too. Tory MPs who had been to prestigious public schools were much more likely to remain loyal to Heath, as were Oxbridge graduates and members from Scotland, Wales and the North of England. In the second round, regional and educational factors loomed even larger. While Old Etonians were far more likely to vote for Whitelaw, Thatcher's typical supporter was a former grammar school boy representing a constituency in the South of England. It was no wonder that she later described her victory as a 'shattering blow delivered to the Conservative establishment. I felt no sympathy for them. They had fought me unscrupulously all the way.'[29]

Mrs Thatcher's elevation marked something much more profound, therefore, than a backlash against poor Ted Heath. It marked the resurgence of a free-market tradition that had been underplayed since 1945 because senior Conservatives were desperate to banish memories of the Great Depression. But it also represented a seismic social shift. Since the mid-1960s, surveys had shown that constituency parties were no longer run by rural landowners, retired colonels and local bigwigs, but by middle-class professionals and suburban small businessmen – the 'sharp young men with coloured shirts and cockney accents' that one character deplores in David Edgar's astute political play *Destiny* (1976). As Labour's Dennis Skinner quipped, the estate agents were taking over from the estate owners. These were people like the character Paul Merroney in the television series *The Brothers*, a self-made City whizz-kid who prefigures the yuppies of the 1980s, or the impatient go-getter in John Betjeman's poem 'Executive' (1974), a young man with a Slimline briefcase, company Cortina and scarlet Aston Martin. In the words of the self-made grammar school boy Leslie Titmuss, the mouthpiece for Thatcherite values in John Mortimer's novel *Paradise Postponed* (published in 1985, but looking back to the late 1960s), they were 'tired of being represented by people from the City or folks from up at the Manor'. They saw themselves as 'people who know the value of money because they've never had it . . . people who've worked hard and don't want to see scroungers rewarded or laziness paying off'. And it was these new Conservatives who were to become the rank and file of Mrs Thatcher's army. As the American embassy reported to Washington just a few days after her coronation, 'hers is the genuine voice of a beleaguered bourgeoisie, anxious about its eroding economic power and determined to arrest society's seemingly inexorable trend towards collectivism'.[30]

Of course other people had laid the ground for her. In their different ways Enoch Powell, Sir Keith Joseph and even Heath himself had anticipated her appeal, from Powell's misty-eyed nationalism to Joseph's intense monetarism and Heath's talk of economic modernization. But Mrs Thatcher gave the Conservatives something different: a much greater populist appeal. She never pretended to be an intellectual, like Powell and Joseph, or a pillar of the Establishment, like Heath. She not only exploited popular ambitions and anxieties, she embodied them. She was the ideal candidate to reflect public unhappiness at the rise in crime, the disintegration of old values and the merciless inroads of inflation precisely because she gloried in her ordinariness. 'I'm a plain straightforward provincial,' she told Anthony Sampson in 1977. 'I've got no hang-ups about my background, like you intellectual commentators in the south-east.' Unusually for a Tory leader, she actually liked her activists. 'Harold Macmillan had a contempt for the party,' Nigel Lawson later recalled. 'Alec Home tolerated it. Ted Heath loathed it. Margaret genuinely liked it. She felt a communion with it, one which later expanded to embrace the silent majority of the British people.' And while her seafaring predecessor had been reluctant to exploit his humble background, she had no compunction about mentioning hers. 'I represent an attitude, an approach,' she told *World in Action* on the eve of the first ballot, 'borne out by the development of my life: going to an ordinary state school, having no privileges at all except perhaps the ones which count most – a good home background, with parents who are very interested in their children and in them getting on.'[31]

The great irony, of course, was that Mrs Thatcher had spent much of her life leaving 'the most boring town in Britain' behind. But now boring old Grantham had become terribly important to her. Invoking the grammar school and the Methodist chapel was the ideal way to insulate herself against criticism of her husband's wealth, their privately educated children and their gin-and-tonic lifestyle. The Burmah Oil director's wife had become a 'plain straightforward provincial' again. Even her father's grocery shop became the Conservatives' equivalent of Abraham Lincoln's log cabin, the perfect populist base for a new leader hoping to win over working-class voters. As the *Telegraph* exultantly put it the day after her second-round victory:

Mrs Thatcher is a bonny fighter. She believes in the ethic of hard work and big rewards for success. She has risen from humble origins by effort and ability and courage. She owes nothing to inherited wealth or privilege. She ought not to suffer, therefore, from that fatal and characteristic 20th-century Tory defect of guilt about wealth. All too often this has meant that the Tories have felt themselves to be at a moral disadvantage in the defence of capitalism against socialism. This is one reason why Britain has travelled so far down the collectivist road. What Mrs Thatcher ought to be able to offer is the missing *moral* dimension to the Tory attack on socialism. If she does so, her succession to the leadership could mark a sea-change in the whole character of party political debate in this county.

Some of this was political spin, but not all of it. Thatcher would never have been able to sustain the populist image for so long had it not been built on strong foundations. It was years since she had lived in Grantham, but it was still in her blood. Later, a journalist asked Alfred Sherman how much Friedrich von Hayek had inspired her. 'She came from Grantham with her mind made up,' Sherman said. 'She brought Grantham with her. I doubt whether she ever read Hayek.'[32]

On her first full day as Conservative leader, Mrs Thatcher visited her predecessor in Wilton Street, Belgravia. It was not a success: although she made it clear she would welcome Edward Heath into her Shadow Cabinet, he had already announced his intention to retire to the back-benches. They spoke for only a few minutes, the atmosphere ice-cold. Afterwards, her partisans claimed that Heath had behaved like a sulky child, dismissing her invitation with the words 'Won't' and 'Shan't', and even stacking books on the chairs beforehand so that she would be unable to sit down. Perhaps this was an exaggeration, but it certainly sounds plausible. In years to come, Heath stubbornly refused all entreaties to reconcile himself to the new regime, preferring to lick his wounds abroad. In the next few months, he undertook a kind of private farewell tour, visiting six European countries, the United States and Canada, China, Japan and Hong Kong. But his travels did nothing to heal the scars: when Willie Whitelaw tried to organize a rapprochement at the party conference that autumn, Heath refused point-blank to meet his successor. Thatcher and Joseph, he told friends, were 'traitors'; their policies would 'destroy the Party and the country'.[33]

If Heath had made even a feeble show of swallowing his pride, he would have made a much more effective critic of Mrs Thatcher's policies in the 1980s. Instead, he wallowed in one of the most spectacular sulks in British political history, an epic tantrum that lasted until his death thirty years later. No Conservative leader had ever behaved with

such ostentatious lack of grace towards his successor. And as he maintained his lonely position on the backbenches, glaring frostily at Mrs
Thatcher whenever she rose to speak, struggling to suppress a smirk
whenever she made a mistake, 'a smouldering volcano always liable to
erupt at any moment', he became the most famous bad loser in the land,
his refusal to play the game a feat of superhuman self-pity. As an accomplished sailor, he might have heeded the words of another Tory moderate,
four decades earlier. 'Once I leave, I leave,' Stanley Baldwin had promised. 'I am not going to speak to the man on the bridge, and I am not
going to spit on the deck.' But this naval metaphor held little appeal for
the Tories' old helmsman. Like some latter-day Captain Bligh, Heath
never saw his conqueror as anything other than a mutineer. And as the
decades went by, he never gave up hope that one day his chastened crew
would applaud him back to his place on the bridge.[34]

In the meantime, Fletcher Christian was finding her feet on the deck
of the Commons. After her meeting with Heath, Thatcher returned to
Westminster for her first appearance at Prime Minister's Questions. It
was not an auspicious debut. 'She looked very pale and tense throughout, realising what an uphill task she has,' wrote Bernard Donoughue.
By contrast, he thought Harold Wilson was 'quite brilliant. Destroyed
the opposition on both sides. Witty thrusts. Standing at the despatch
box in complete command.' Ironically, Wilson had been 'very nervous
and gloomy' beforehand, downing three brandies to steady his nerves.
But he had been taking questions for eleven years; he knew the game.
The future Iron Lady did not. 'She still looks scared stiff and does not
take him on,' Donoughue noted a month later. And after watching
another clash on 17 April, he recorded that 'the only interest is to see
Margaret Thatcher sitting there looking petrified, like a rabbit in front
of a stoat. And Ted Heath sitting, waiting, stonily in the corner seat
below the gangway, with no sign of life until HW puts the boot into
Mrs Thatcher, when a wintry smile crosses his face.'[35]

Since Mrs Thatcher had been propelled into the leadership on the
back of her barnstorming Commons performances, her woeful showing
horrified her backbenchers. Week after week, she seemed painfully earnest and over-rehearsed, especially opposite someone as fluent and
relaxed as Wilson, even with all the brandy. After a debate on 22 May,
the *Sunday Times* lamented that her speech had been a 'disappointing
flop' and that her voice had 'its usual garden party quality', while in the
Commons Denis Healey mocked her 'disconnected little homilies ...
charged with all the moral passion and intellectual distinction of a rail-

way timetable'. Her approval rating, which had been a healthy 64 per cent in February, was in free fall, down to 41 per cent in May and a feeble 35 per cent in June. She was, it seemed, a dud, an aberration, an error crying out for correction. The Tory old guard reassured each other that it would soon all be over. 'She'll be out by Christmas,' Lord Carrington told his friends.[36]

12

The Economics of Peter Pan

*We are getting more worried about Tony Benn. He is handing
out money to whoever is broke and to any group of shop
stewards who threaten a work-in. No discipline, no criteria.
Total scandal in some cases but the Treasury seems to have no
fibre, no control. Demoralised.*

Bernard Donoughue's diary, 28 October 1974

*The other programme was a documentary about the workers at
the Meriden motorcycle factory who, when the company decided
to close the plant fifteen months ago, responded by occupying it
and announcing they could run it themselves ... Listening to
these vigorous, inventive, dedicated men, I had a new surge of
certainty that this was the answer to the collapsing West.*

Kenneth Tynan's diary, 13 January 1975

The last months of 1975 were a grim time for the British car industry.
The headlines were dominated by threats of strikes: when workers at
British Leyland returned from holiday at the beginning of August, more
than 16,000 of them were left idle because of a minor pay dispute at a
components plant. On 13 August, a dispute involving just twenty-nine
men brought production at Ford's giant Halewood plant in Liverpool to
a complete standstill. The next day, sales figures indicated that foreign
cars now accounted for a record 41 per cent of the domestic market,
with Datsun and Volkswagen leading the way. In September, Chrysler
put all its British workers on short time because of falling sales, and a
month later *The Times* broke the news that the American car giant, itself
in deep financial trouble, was planning to wind up its British operation.

The position could hardly have seemed worse. In just six months, Chrysler UK had lost almost £16 million, thanks not least to its spectacularly bad record of unofficial strikes. Only a few months earlier, Harold Wilson had promised that he would not spend 'a single penny of taxpayers' money' to bail out Chrysler if strike action forced it under. For the 27,000 people who worked in the American firm's factories in Scotland and the West Midlands, it seemed bound to be a bleak Christmas.[1]

The most memorable sign of the times, though, came one grey October evening in Torquay, where a local proprietor had tried to reinvigorate his hotel business by launching a gourmet night. Disaster struck when the chef collapsed in a drunken stupor, but the hotelier seemed to have retrieved the situation by picking up some meals from a local restaurant. As he was driving back, however, his red Austin 1100, long Britain's best-selling car, chose the worst possible moment to give up the ghost. 'Come on, start, will you?' Basil Fawlty screamed in front of millions of laughing viewers. 'Start, you vicious bastard! Come on! Oh my God, I'm warning you!' Anybody who had ever driven a British car could surely empathize with what happened next. 'Right! That's it!' Basil explodes. 'You've tried it on just once too often! Right! Well, don't say I haven't warned you! I've laid it on the line to you time and time again! Right! Well, this is it! I'm going to give you a damn good thrashing!'[2]

In its way, Basil's frenzied attack on his car says as much about Britain in the 1970s as any number of scholarly dissertations. As a middle-class veteran of the Korean War (or so he claims), he could hardly be expected to do anything other than buy British. But cars are a source of endless worry: almost four years later, in the episode 'The Kipper and the Corpse', they are still on Basil's mind. 'Another car strike,' he says, looking wearily at the paper:

> They ought to get Butlin's to run our car factories . . . Marvellous, isn't it? Taxpayers pay 'em millions each year, they get the money, go on strike. It's called socialism. I mean if they don't like making cars why don't they get themselves another bloody job designing cathedrals or composing violin concertos? The British Leyland Concerto in four movements, all of them slow, with a four-hour tea break in between. I'll tell you why, because they're not interested in anything except lounging about on conveyor belts stuffing themselves with my money.

John Cleese was not alone in his contempt for the British car industry. Struggling to write a novel in October 1977, his friend Michael Palin lamented that he was 'as bad as Leyland Cars in the constant failure to reach my production target'. And even at the very top, plenty of people empathized with Basil's rage. In the summer of 1978, Downing Street ordered two new prime ministerial Rovers from British Leyland, customized with bulletproof windows, a special radio and armour plating. On arrival they were found to have thirty-four mechanical faults, and were promptly sent back. 'When they returned,' Bernard Donoughue recorded, 'the PM went for a trip in one. He decided to open the window for some fresh air and pressed the button which does this electronically. The result was that the window immediately fell in on his lap.' According to his driver, Jim Callaghan said nothing, but his 'face turned dark'. When they had reached their destination, he simply handed the driver the window and said: 'Don't bring this car again.'[3]

The death of British car-making was one of the great industrial tragedies of the century. The motor vehicle industry had once been an authentic British success story: during the 1930s, British firms had produced more cars than any of their European competitors. The next few decades should have been golden ones: by the early 1970s, Britain had become a nation of drivers, with the number of cars on the roads surging from less than 2 million to almost 13 million in thirty years. But Britain's car manufacturers blew it. Assuming that European car firms would serve their own markets, they concentrated on cheap models for the Commonwealth, ignoring the threat from rising powers such as Volkswagen, Renault and Fiat. Insulated by high tariffs from European competition, hobbled by atrocious labour relations and doomed by the catastrophic decision to merge almost all the remaining firms into the industrial leviathan of British Leyland, the domestic car industry began its long slide towards oblivion. By the late 1970s, productivity had fallen well behind the levels overseas: while each British worker produced 5 cars, a Japanese worker produced 12 and an American 15. Exports collapsed: by the end of the 1970s, German manufacturers sold ten times as many cars abroad as their British competitors. By then, sick of the endless faults and delays, even British drivers were opting for foreign models. In 1955, just 2.2 per cent of all cars bought in Britain had been foreign-made. By 1975, however, the proportion was 33 per cent, and by 1980 it was almost 57 per cent. In just ten years, Britain's position as a major car manufacturer had effectively been wiped out.[4]

In the meantime, British Leyland had become a byword for industrial failure. Created in 1968 through a disastrous merger of the two biggest remaining groups, Leyland and British Motor Holdings, it found itself in deep trouble almost from the outset, caught between the competing demands of high-volume mass production and high-end specialist cars. Its first new models were generally fiascos: the Morris Marina never matched the popularity of the Ford Cortina, the Rover saloon fell well short of its sales targets, and the Austin Allegro, with its unflattering 'flying pig' shape and rectangular steering wheel, was widely regarded as the worst British car ever made. Its labour relations, meanwhile, were ludicrously bad. With the fragmentation of the unions exacerbated by the bewildering structure of the car giant, management had to deal with 58 different bargaining units at 34 plants. Shop-floor pay bargaining was a mess: many unofficial disputes were provoked by 'differentials' between different plants, and executives estimated that they were involved in labour negotiations for nine months a year. At some plants, such as Cowley or Longbridge, there were stoppages almost every day. Yet despite the papers' attacks on militant conveners like Derek Robinson ('Red Robbo'), this was not entirely the shop stewards' fault. British Leyland's management was notoriously incompetent, and workers often complained that their advice on improving the companies' cars was ignored. 'If the workforce had any say,' one man remarked on television of the error-plagued new Triumph TR7, 'that could be a good car, [but] a plant of 2,500 men doesn't even have a suggestion box.'[5]

Although the car industry was the best-known example of manufacturing decline, it was not, unfortunately, the only one. British Steel's productivity record, for example, was simply atrocious. In 1975, National Steel (USA), Thyssen (Germany) and Nippon Steel (Japan) produced 280, 370 and 520 tonnes of crude steel per man per year, respectively, yet a British Steel worker produced only 122 tonnes. What was more, the quality of British steel was dubious at best: in the same year, the Ford car giant complained that unless the quality of material from the Llanwern works improved, they would start buying steel from abroad. Underperformance became a vicious circle: when the government brought in Charles Villiers to modernize the industry in 1976, his dream of a comprehensive deal with the unions fell on stony ground and his restructuring plans only provoked more strikes. By the end of the decade, steel output had fallen from 28 million to 11 million tonnes in just ten years, while the workforce had been slashed from 250,000 to just 166,000. Given the role steel had played in the Industrial Revolution, there could hardly have been a more potent symbol of decline. Contemplating the unions' resistance to the closure of several plants, including the Ebbw Vale steelworks that had long been a symbol of

Wales's industrial heritage, *The Times* noted sadly that if British Steel had not been state-owned, it 'would have already become insolvent'. Job losses were regrettable, it said mournfully. 'Yet the facts must be faced. Without higher productivity, there is no future for Britain as a steelmaking nation.'[6]

Of course British manufacturing did have a few successes, notably the pharmaceutical industry, where innovative research and clever marketing made Beecham, ICI and Glaxo enormously profitable. That was little consolation, however, to the hundreds of thousands of men employed in struggling industries. The Lancashire textile industry was in virtual collapse by the end of the 1970s: having gambled on standardization and scale, companies like Courtaulds were unable to compete with European firms which put more emphasis on design, marketing and technical expertise. In engineering it was a similar story, with GEC, GKN and Thorn rapidly losing ground to Japanese and European competitors. And in shipbuilding, major companies like Cammell Laird, Harland & Wolff and Upper Clyde Shipbuilders were in terrible trouble by the end of the 1960s, apparently unable to compete with the resurgent Japanese. Government intervention staved off disaster for the time being, and in 1971 Upper Clyde employees staged a famous work-in to keep the yards open. But shipbuilding remained what one historian calls a 'ward of the state', and in February 1977 the government had to set up a shipbuilding intervention fund, doling out £65 million to subsidize specific orders. A few months later the remaining companies were nationalized as British Shipbuilders, the latest in the endless reorganizations that plagued British industry in the post-war years. But the story remained the same: when the corporation published its first accounts in March 1979, they showed a loss of £100 million.[7]

All of this added up to a seismic shift in the everyday working experience of millions of people. As early as 1971, Anthony Sampson had wondered whether 'the first industrial nation [would] become the first to opt out of mass industry', with the British people 'reverting to their pre-industrial values – to their skills in farming, trading, insurance or entertainment'. More and more, people bought their goods from abroad: in 1970, imports accounted for 15 per cent of the British market, but by 1980 they accounted for almost 30 per cent. As a result, an old industrial working-class world, a world in which millions of men spent their lives doing skilled and unskilled manual labour, walking or cycling to the local factory every morning, never even thinking about another job, was dying. At its post-war peak in the mid-1960s, manufacturing employed some 8.5 million people, accounting for 36 per cent of the overall workforce. But by the end of the 1970s the total had fallen below 7 million, accounting for less than 28 per cent. Of course other Western economies were experiencing similar problems, but nowhere was the trauma so marked as in Britain. At the time, there was talk of a surge in white-collar jobs, especially in the financial, scientific and service sectors. By the late 1970s, some 3.6 million people were employed in professional and business services, 1.9 million in social services, a million in education, another million in insurance and banking and almost 500,000 in the civil service. But the historian Kenneth Morgan's quip that Britain was being transformed from the workshop of the world into its secretarial college was only half right; unfortunately, there were never enough desk jobs to go around.[8]

A common explanation for manufacturing's plight is that it was killed off by strikes, a view encapsulated by Basil Fawlty's belief that car workers spent their time 'lounging about on conveyor belts stuffing themselves with my money'. There is certainly no doubt that Britain's fragmented labour movement, with hundreds of little unions competing for members, made for much more difficult industrial relations than in, say, West Germany. But as the former *Financial Times* editor Geoffrey Owen points out in his history of post-war industry, a glance at the figures tells a surprising story. Most workers were relatively unaffected by strikes, which tended to be concentrated in specific industries, above all cars, coalmining and shipbuilding, which were already suffering from much more serious problems. What was more, these were bad years for labour unrest not just in Britain but around the world, as affluent workers tried to protect their livelihoods from the ravages of inflation and de-industrialization. Between 1970 and 1979, the country worst hit by strikes was actually Canada, with an average of 1,840 working days lost per 1,000 workers in major industries. Next came Italy (1,778 days lost), then Australia (1,298), then the United States (1,211), and only then Britain (1,088). Indeed, industrial unrest in Britain wiped out only two in every hundred working days in the 1970s – well below the figures for accidents and illness. 'Surely there is something wrong with the numbers,' the American commentator Bernard Nossiter wryly remarked in 1978. 'They must not count unauthorized or wildcat strikes. They must leave out the thousands sent home in a car plant when one key shop walks out.' In fact, he noted, both of those things had been taken into account. Astonishing as it might sound, by international standards 'Britain is not especially strike-prone'.[9]

Even Nossiter, who wrote a thoughtful book defending Britain against its critics, recognized that its factories were grotesquely over-manned, its workers were too inefficient and its productivity figures were simply abysmal. But the well-known symptoms of the 'British disease' – late starting and early stopping, poor timekeeping, the inter-minable tea breaks that infuriated George Lucas while filming *Star Wars* at Elstree – were the fault of management as well as labour. Indeed, many observers thought the real causes for British decline could be found in the boardroom, not on the shop floor. In many factories, the divide between management and workers remained absurdly stark, with different entrances, different canteens and different toilets. Writing to *The Times* in 1970, one man complained that at his factory, the bosses had individual towels and fancy soap, the senior staff had rolling towels and decent soap and the workers had 'rough towels' and 'cheese-cake soap'. Anybody who doubted that Britain was a divided society, argued the Labour MP Robert Kilroy-Silk six years later, need only look to 'the factories where manual workers enter by one gate, eat in segregated canteens and work longer hours in worse conditions than their "betters"'. And although British workers were mocked abroad as greedy and lazy, more than a few observers thought the accusation should really be aimed at their bosses. 'The executive rush hour in Lon-don begins well after 9.30 AM,' wrote Bernard Nossiter. After a 'leisurely mid-day break' in the 'panelled executive dining room', the bosses were on their way home again to 'Belgravia, Surrey or other executive haunts' by 4.30. 'An hour later,' Nossiter thought, 'the only executive cars on the road are those bound for some social engagement.'[10]

Of course this was just as much of a caricature as the idea that all British workers were shiftless layabouts. But Nossiter was not the only commentator who thought management was far from perfect. The men who ran British companies, wrote the BBC's economics correspondent Graham Turner in 1969, lacked 'the will to do better. They aim low and are satisfied with modest performances; exhibit a marked lack of the self-critical faculty; and put a quiet (though not ostentatious) life high on their list of priorities.' They were sunk in 'apathetic drowsiness', agreed Stephen Haseler seven years later, accusing them of keeping their heads 'well below the parapet' and accepting a 'vicious cycle of ineffi-ciency and unproductivity'. Even the financial sector was not immune from criticism: in May 1980 the *Financial Times* declared that there was 'something seriously wrong with Britain's retail banking system', blam-ing a management elite that was 'sleepy', 'class-based' and 'wholly in-bred'. And those at the very top often shared these bleak views. In June 1974, the former deputy chairman of ICI and chairman of the Electricity Council, Sir Peter Menzies, told Ronald McIntosh that there were 'only a handful of good people among the senior management of the electricity industry'. 'This confirms my own impression,' McIntosh wrote. 'I think people underrate the damage done by the mediocrity of the general run of managers in nationalised industries.'[11]

Behind all this, some commentators argued, was a social sickness that stretched back for generations. The origins of 'Britain's economic malaise' lay 'deep in the social system', announced a report by the Brooking Institution, one of the United States' most prominent think tanks, blaming an inbuilt 'upper-class disdain for industry'. Perhaps because it repeated so many clichés about the class system, this analysis proved extremely popular. For the journalist Clive Irving, Britain was led by an incompetent elite of 'Greeks wrestling with the Roman world'; for the academic Martin Wiener, Britain had been losing its 'industrial spirit' since the Victorian era, when self-made men had given way to gentlemen amateurs; for the military historian Correlli Barnett, the public schools had created a 'governing class ignorant of, and antipathetic to, science, technology and industry'. But although these ideas proved very popular with Mrs Thatcher's ministers, they failed to stand up to scholarly scrutiny. As the historian David Edgerton points out, twentieth-century Britain was actually a thoroughly technocratic state with high standards of technical education and scientific innovation. The real problem with British management was not that it was inbred or upper-class; it was that it was fatally complacent, lulled into a false sense of security by the weakened competition and soft markets of the 1950s. By the time Britain entered the Common Market, crucial momentum had been lost. In two decades after 1950, Britain's share of the world export market for manufactures had fallen from 25 per cent to just 9 per cent, while West Germany's had surged from 7 per cent to more than 22 per cent. In itself, that statistic explains much of what went wrong in Britain during the 1970s and 1980s.[12]

Against this background, the narrow-minded self-interest of the trade unions made a bad situation worse, effectively making it impossible for companies to implement the radical reforms they needed to survive. But successive governments could not escape their share of the blame. In 1964, Harold Wilson had promised to rebuild British industry in the white heat of the scientific revolution, but his government's attempts to intervene in steel and shipbuilding were no more than ham-fisted meddling. In particular, his lieutenant at the Ministry of Technology, Tony Benn, enthusiastically promoted a bout of 'merger mania', which saw the concentration of Scottish shipbuilding in Upper Clyde Shipbuilders, the consolidation of the computer industry in International Computers Ltd (ICL) and the creation of the behemoth that was British Leyland. By and large, however, the state-sponsored mergers of the late 1960s were a shambles. Size did not automatically guarantee success. Instead, it became a cover for inefficiency, encouraging firms to grow by acquisition rather than by investing in new factories or searching out new markets, and fostering the delusion that there would always be more public money to bail them out.[13]

A consistent fallacy at the top of British politics was that ministers could wave a magic wand, transforming chosen industries into world-beaters by throwing money at them. Even Edward Heath ended up giving tens of millions to the National Coal Board, the machine tools industry and the ICL conglomerate, as well as backtracking on his plans to wind up the shipyards on the Clyde. The interventionists claimed that they were merely copying what President de Gaulle had done in France; they might have noted, though, that the most successful European economy in the 1970s, West Germany, was also the one in which the government intervened least. Instead of propping up industries that were clearly doomed, a better strategy might have been to embrace change, explaining to the public that in an age of global transition some firms were bound to fail, and encouraging a more competitive climate that rewarded high productivity. But since that would have meant losers as well as winners, it would have taken immense political courage. At a time when Conservative politicians still embraced state intervention and when the Labour left were hoping to impose compulsory planning agreements on industry, it was never likely. 'Nationalisation is no good. People don't want it,' the TGWU leader Jack Jones told Tony Benn in the summer of 1974. 'Well,' Benn replied, 'we may have no alternatives if firms go bust.' 'You don't want to do that,' Jones said. 'You don't want to save every lame duck.' But, as events were to prove, he was wasting his breath.[14]

Two men called Benn loomed large in the British imagination in the mid-1970s. One wore a bowler hat, lived at 52 Festive Road and frequently visited a local fancy-dress shop, his time-travelling adventures delighting millions of diminutive television addicts. The other Mr Benn was one of the most controversial characters in modern political history.

To many Labour activists, Tony Benn was the champion of socialism and the greatest hero since Aneurin Bevan. Yet to many of his Cabinet colleagues he seemed a sanctimonious hypocrite, while the Conservative middle classes often saw him as a deranged extremist, hell-bent on turning Britain into a canine-friendly version of North Korea. He inspired extraordinary levels of abuse: Sir Keith Joseph called him 'Dracula', sucking the blood out of British industry, while his former Labour colleague George Brown called him 'an enemy of democracy'. For the Tory moderate Peter Walker, Benn was 'the dominant voice in British politics', a man of 'ability, energy and fanatical determination', yet a propagandist comparable 'with some of the most dangerous figures in political history'. He was inundated with death threats; his rubbish was stolen; his phone may well have been bugged. Yet despite it all, this unflinching, courteous, tea-drinking man never doubted that he spoke for the people, that he alone had the answer to Britain's problems, and that eventually he would lead the Labour Party to the promised land of socialism.[15]

Born into the heart of the political establishment, Anthony Wedgwood Benn came from a long line of Liberal MPs. His father, Viscount Stansgate, left the Liberals to join the Labour Party but lost his seat after refusing to follow Ramsay MacDonald into the National Government, an episode that left a deep impression on his son. His mother, meanwhile, was a Congregationalist theologian and passionate feminist who brought up her children in an atmosphere of high-minded progressivism: by the time he was 12, young Anthony had already met both Gandhi and Lloyd George. And although Westminster and Oxford smoothed his path to the top, he was steeped in the values of the class Michael Frayn famously called the Herbivores: the 'gentle ruminants who look out from the lush pastures which are their station in life with eyes full of sorrow for less fortunate creatures, guiltily conscious of their advantages, yet usually not ceasing to eat the grass'. A teetotaller and a puritan, Benn was the epitome of Nonconformist enthusiasm, always trying to follow John Wesley's apocryphal rule: 'Do all the good you can, in all the ways you can, to all the souls you can, in every place you can, at all the times you can, with all the zeal you can, as long as ever you can.' In a less amiable man, this might have seemed cloyingly self-righteous. But when Benn first came to public attention in 1960, fighting a successful battle to disclaim his peerage and stay in the House of Commons, he was generally well liked. As Postmaster General and Minister of Technology in the first Wilson administration, he was really a middle-of-the-road modernizer, despite his futile attempt to take the Queen's head off the stamps. As late as 1970 he seemed an unlikely candidate to become the tribune of the left. To the historian Kenneth Morgan, he appeared 'a loyal and acquiescent lieutenant of Harold Wilson, the dutiful technocrat to the end'.[16]

But when Wilson lost the 1970 election, his gadget man turned almost overnight into the self-styled heir to the Levellers and crusader for the hard left. There was a large dose of opportunism in this: with Labour in opposition, reinventing himself as the left's answer to Enoch Powell was an ideal way for Benn to appeal to the party's disgruntled activists. In particular, he was keen to reach out to the unions. In September 1970 he published a Fabian pamphlet urging the party to embrace 'industrial democracy' and 'workers' control', and a year later he returned from a trip to Tito's Yugoslavia enthused by 'the lessons of their self-management applied to our industrial policy'. To many of his colleagues, all this was utterly bewildering: as a patrician public school-boy, Benn knew nothing at all about how working-class people lived and thought. But this only made it easier for him to romanticize them, for, as the Labour MP Austin Mitchell remarked, the former Viscount Stansgate worshipped 'the working class, its traditions and institutions and particularly the trade unions, as only someone from an upper-class background can'. Whenever they failed to live up to Benn's high expec-tations, it proved only that they were the prisoners of false consciousness. 'He dismisses the views of the great bulk of workers and shop stewards, and blames the media for brainwashing them,' complained the electri-cians' leader Frank Chapple. In all his years of public life, Chapple added, 'there was no one for whom I felt such profound contempt'.[17]

By now the boyish champion of modernization was dead; in his place stood Chairman Tony, the unions' friend. On the right, Benn's increas-ingly strident attacks on the media and the EEC, as well as his demands for a closer alliance between Labour and the unions, made him a bogey-man. As the journalist Michael Hatfield put it, Benn's name was now synonymous with 'demagoguery, populism, public ownership, syndical-ism, and workers' control'. For the *Express*'s cartoonist Michael Cummings, he was a Nazi, kitted out in full SS regalia; for the *Sunday Telegraph* he was 'Bolshevik Benn'; for the *Observer* he was 'hysterical'; for Thames Television's *Today* programme he was simply 'the most hated man in Britain'. But by this stage, buoyed by the applause of the left, Benn saw abuse as a badge of righteousness. It was as though he had been born again: in August 1972 he decided to 'resign my Privy

Councillorship, my MA and all my honorary doctorates in order to strip myself of what the world had to offer'. He at least had the nous to see that he 'might be ridiculed' for doing so. 'But "Wedgie Benn" and "the Rt Honourable Anthony Wedgwood Benn" and all that stuff is impossible,' he wrote in his diary. A year later he asked the BBC to call him 'Tony'; in the meantime, he struck out all references to Westminster and Oxford from his entry in Who's Who. By 1976 his entry was down to just two lines, and in 1977 it vanished entirely. When he returned in 1983 it was as 'Tony Benn', with no education at all. He had even deleted the reference to his rank in the wartime RAF. Perhaps not surprisingly, his old friend Tony Crosland thought he was becoming a 'fanatic', driven by a toxic blend of personal ambition and ideological zeal. 'We all know he occasionally lies,' Crosland told his wife, 'but no one doubts his sincerity in seeing himself as a Messiah.'[18]

Crosland's caustic view was not shared by thousands of Labour activists, especially the young, well-educated idealists who increasingly dominated constituency parties in cities and university towns.* As the Guardian's Peter Jenkins observed, the 'head boy of the class of '68' had a tremendous appeal to 'the burgeoning and growingly radicalised ranks of the public sector, to the lumpenintelligentsia of new university, polytechnic and comprehensive school'. And as the Heath government lurched towards disaster, Benn's flame burned ever brighter. The party must build 'a powerful and really strong policy alliance' with the shop stewards, he told his colleagues at the beginning of 1973, and the next Labour government should simply 'ask the workers two questions': 'Are you in favour of public ownership?' and 'How would you like the management run?' What was more, it was now time for Labour to embrace Marxism, 'because the Party without Karl Marx really lacks a basic analytical core'. This kind of talk horrified many of Benn's colleagues. But attending a May Day rally in Birmingham, gazing with pleasure at 'all the sects . . . the International Marxists with Red Weekly; the Socialist Labour League with Workers' Press; the International Socialists with the Socialist Worker; the Communist Party with the Morning Star; the Labour Party with Labour Weekly', Benn felt a great rush of enthusiasm. 'It was all tremendously informal and friendly,' he wrote afterwards. 'A marvellous meeting.'[19]

---

* A good fictional example is Reggie Perrin's son Mark, an unemployed young actor. In David Nobbs's original novel The Death of Reginald Perrin (1975), he wears a T-shirt with the slogan 'Wedgwood Benn for King'.

Benn was particularly attracted to the ideas of Stuart Holland, a former Wilson aide who argued that the emergence of massive multinational corporations posed a new challenge to the state. To reassert economic sovereignty, Holland thought, the next Labour government should set up a 'state holding company' to buy a stake in Britain's leading companies, using planning agreements to ensure greater efficiency. This new National Enterprise Board should acquire a 'portfolio' including 'twenty leading manufacturing companies, one of the big three leading banks and two or three leading insurance companies'. This was music to Benn's ears. Through massive state intervention, he wrote, Labour could bring about 'a fundamental and irreversible shift in the balance of power and wealth in favour of working people and their families'. That phrase horrified the City, the press and the right wing of his party, but it nevertheless made it into the Labour manifesto. So, after a long battle, did the left's strategy for intervention in industry, which committed the new government not only to nationalizing the ports, shipbuilding, marine engineering and aero-engineering, but to taking over 'individual firms in those industries where a public holding is essential to enable the Government to control prices, stimulate investment, encourage exports, create employment, protect workers and consumers from the activities of irresponsible multi-national companies, and to plan the national economy in the national interest'. In his diary, Benn could barely contain his excitement, looking forward to wielding 'emergency powers'. 'We will have to carry reform through on the wave of the capitalist crisis,' he wrote eagerly. 'These are very stirring times.'[20]

Almost from the moment he took office in March 1974, however, the new Secretary of State for Industry ran into trouble. His new permanent secretary, the veteran Sir Antony Part, made no secret of his anxiety at Benn's plans. 'Minister, do you really intend to go ahead with your National Enterprise Board, public ownership and planning agreements?' Part asked. 'Of course,' Benn said. 'If you do it,' Part said worriedly, 'you will be heading for as big a confrontation with industrial management as the last Government had with the trade unions over the Industrial Relations Act.' Not surprisingly, Benn concluded that Part was out to block him at every turn. 'The Department [is] sabotaging my industrial proposals,' he complained a few weeks later. 'They just turf back things I want with their objections, and I then have to force them to carry out my wishes.' Within Whitehall, their deteriorating relationship became common knowledge, and by the late summer relations had reached rock bottom. After a blazing row about his plan to send out a million copies of a 'popular version of the Industry White Paper', Benn seriously considered asking for Part to be replaced, which was almost unheard of in Whitehall. 'Part treats me like a consultant psychiatrist would a particularly dangerous patient,' Benn complained. 'At any moment I expect him to ring a bell and a fat, male nurse in a white jacket will come and give me an injection.'[21]

Yet Benn's rapport with his chief civil servant was positively cordial compared with his relationship with his Cabinet colleagues. Once considered a courteous, charming man with mildly amusing eccentricities, he now struck some Labour MPs as a self-appointed saviour playing to the public gallery. As two future SDP sympathizers recalled, 'most right wingers in the party positively loathed his self-serving sanctimoniousness'. Even some of the old left were horrified by his indifference to the urgency of the economic crisis. When Benn subjected a dinner of left-wing ministers to a long lecture about the dangers of moderation, for example, Michael Foot was 'almost snarling' with anger. 'Mike obviously thinks he is obsessed by ambition,' Barbara Castle noted. 'The rest of us, who are on [Benn's] side on policy, are getting a bit sick of his clear determination to strike attitudes publicly, whenever he can.' Indeed, Castle and Benn had already had a blazing row about what she called his 'unctuousness' and 'ambition' – specifically, his decision to hand out copies of his industrial policy blueprint to MPs, which was a blatant attempt to blackmail the Cabinet. He was deliberately 'embarrassing [his] colleagues who knew the money was not available', she told him bitterly, reminding him about 'the doctrine of collective responsibility'. But Benn could not care less. 'My God, Barbara's hatred really came out,' he wrote. 'I think she is feeling guilty.'[22]

By now Benn was deaf to criticism. Like so many messiahs, he seemed almost to revel in the abuse, seeing it as confirmation of his own righteousness. Instead of trying to persuade his colleagues of the merits of his plans, he toured the land like a revivalist preacher, addressing trade union groups on the need for massive government intervention in industry. But the more that Benn inhaled on his own rhetoric, the closer he came to self-parody. A few weeks after returning to office, he instructed the Post Office to produce 'a set of stamps featuring the trade unions', only to be rebuffed because they were too 'political'. A few weeks later, he decided that the answer to Britain's difficulties was to have a 'secondary power structure' run by the TUC. 'This concept of a working-class power structure, democratic and organised in parallel with the Government structure – in effect joint government of the country by the Labour

No minister in living memory had inspired so much outright loathing as Tony Benn during his time at the Department of Industry. Here, John Jensen conflates Benn's nationalization plans with a controversial rape case before the House of Lords (*Sunday Telegraph*, 4 May 1975).

Party and the trade unions – makes an awful lot of sense,' he wrote. If he seriously thought that the Cabinet would support it, then he really was deluded. But by now he was fundamentally not interested in what his colleagues thought; indeed, far from being diluted by the pressures of office, his plans for industry were grander than ever, envisaging a National Enterprise Board imposing planning agreements on the private sector and spending £1 billion a year to buy up British companies. 'As I look at it,' Benn told his diary, 'I can see my way through now in breaking industry's resistance to my policies.'[23]

Although Benn's industrial plans would be unimaginable today, globalization having rendered them redundant, they did not seem inherently ludicrous at the time. For many academic economists, massive state intervention to build up 'national champions' seemed a perfectly rational response to the rise of multinational capitalism. Even in the mid-1970s, the defects of state planning in Eastern Europe were far from obvious, while many academics admired the results of 'indicative central planning' (*dirigisme*) in France. The problem, though, was that whereas French central planning was associated with highly trained bureaucratic mandarins, the messianic Benn made a very controversial champion of state intervention in Britain. On Fleet Street his name was now a dirty word: for the *Daily Express*'s political correspondent Walter Terry, for example, he was the British Allende, a 'dedicated Marxist' who had nothing in common with 'old-fashioned, semi-virtuous British Socialism'. On 13 June, Edward Heath called him a Soviet 'commissar' who was copying 'Stalin's disastrous economic plans for Russia'. The very next day, the head of the CBI, Ralph Bateman, claimed that Benn's policies would mean 'an economic system not unlike that favoured by Communist states'. Benn was 'not just tinkering with our economic way of life', Bateman said: his schemes were 'revolutionary' and would 'inevitably reduce the freedom of the individual'.

Ten days later, after officials had leaked a list of firms contemplated for nationalization, among them ICI, Ford and Esso, more businessmen joined the attack. Benn's plans were 'disastrous', said Tate & Lyle's chairman. 'What does he want? Does he just want power?' wondered the head of Rank Hovis McDougall, the country's biggest bakery company. Under the banner headline 'Benn Widens His Grab Net', the *Express* claimed that the *Daily Mirror*, the *People*, *Woman's Own*, Bowyers sausages, Cow & Gate baby foods, William Hill, Harp, Babycham, Double Diamond and even Berni Inns had been 'lined up for state control'. Yet Benn himself remained calm. 'Fleet Street is having a sort of nervous breakdown,' he recorded, 'because nobody has ever dared to argue the case openly and without embarrassment. If they really thought it was so unpopular, they wouldn't be devoting so much space to trying to stop it . . . So I feel perfectly happy.'[24]

Inside the Cabinet, Benn's colleagues were horrified by the publicity. To more conservative ministers, such as Denis Healey and Jim Callaghan, it seemed insane to be considering massive state intervention when budgets were so tight, inflation was in overdrive and business confidence was at an all-time low. At a meeting with Wilson and his top aides in June 1974, Healey and Callaghan insisted that he address 'the question of Benn'. 'Don't take him seriously,' Wilson said wearily: 'he is not well, not sleeping well.' But Callaghan was having none of it: 'Benn knew exactly what he was doing, a calculated campaign to get the leadership,' recorded Bernard Donoughue. '[Callaghan] rebuked HW very firmly and said something would have to be done about it. Healey agreed.' That afternoon, Donoughue went over to see Benn himself. 'He looked very grey and tired,' he wrote. 'His driver told me that he was working till 3 a.m. every morning and then getting up early. But the gleam in his eye is clear and unwavering. He is certainly odd, but I don't think he will crack. Destiny is guiding him and so he doesn't need sleep. But he was boorishly rude to his officials.'[25]

In the past, the Prime Minister had always stuck up for his old protégé. But now Harold Wilson had run out of patience. 'All reports from departments and committees are that [Benn] is completely in orbit, issuing statements, announcing that he is consulting the shop stewards on every conceivable subject,' Donoughue recorded. 'An increasing number of people say he is bonkers. Ministers at yesterday's Public Enterprise committee have been phoning in to say so.' On the evening of 11 June, Wilson asked Joe Haines to tell the press that 'he was taking over the handling of all Benn's industrial policies. Otherwise there will be a total collapse of confidence and no investment.' 'HW said that Benn is "completely mad,"' Donoughue noted afterwards. When Benn saw the headlines the next day, he was understandably outraged, noting that 'there is a war between us and Number 10'. Two days later, Wilson formally instructed him to stop making speeches on industrial policy. True to form, Benn decided to 'take no notice of that whatsoever'. Wilson promptly summoned him to Number 10, where Benn found his leader 'red and angry'. 'Why are you having this "debate"?' Wilson asked angrily. 'You are only helping the Tories . . . Why don't you work harder instead of making all these speeches?'[26]

Of course the real question was why Wilson did not simply sack a minister who had declared open rebellion against his own colleagues. But Wilson had never been a good butcher, and was almost obsessively afraid of provoking a revolt on the left. So Benn stayed in government, although his colleagues gave him a rough time. At the end of June, when he presented his blueprint to the Cabinet's Industrial Development committee, the blows rained down. 'Healey spoke first and was very rough. He took Benn apart and described the paper as full of irresponsible rhetoric,' Donoughue wrote. 'Callaghan followed and was even more savage. He said he would not have it and they had better understand it was either the paper or him.' When they reconvened a couple of weeks later, the Cabinet Office had eviscerated Benn's radical proposals, making planning agreements voluntary and allowing the National Enterprise Board to control only those industries that had already been nationalized. Benn thought it was a 'disgrace'. Yet when he tried to speak up, Wilson snapped: 'You can't have a marauding NEB going round the country grabbing firms.' That, of course, was precisely what the Labour manifesto had promised; but nobody cared about the manifesto now.

'You can't write a Manifesto for the Party in opposition and expect it to have any relationship to what the Party does in Government,' remarked Jim Callaghan. 'We're now entirely free to do what we like.'[27]

Benn had not given up hope quite yet. But when the Cabinet met on 2 August to decide the issue, the moderates were in brutal form. 'One after another,' wrote Barbara Castle, 'they turned on him.' Denis Healey said that Benn's plan would mean 'the collapse of business confidence'; Harold Lever said it would be 'a ruinous blow to industry'; Shirley Williams insisted that with the country in such a dreadful state, 'we couldn't be tied by what we said before'. ('Shirley is, without doubt, the most reactionary person I know,' wrote Benn, which said something about the kind of people he mixed with.) The real question was whether planning agreements and NEB acquisitions would be compulsory. If they were voluntary, then firms would ignore them, the plan would fall apart and the chance to build a new system of centrally planned socialism would have gone. And on this point, Benn did not stand a chance. The compulsory element was overturned: as the Cabinet minutes put it, 'the rights of private interests' would be 'strenuously safeguarded'. As a satisfied Bernard Donoughue put it afterwards, Benn had been 'completely defeated'.[28]

The National Enterprise Board met for the first time in November 1975. Diluted by endless compromises, it could hardly have been more different from the ambitious vehicle for state socialism of which Tony Benn had dreamed. As chairman, Harold Wilson appointed his 'favourite businessman', Sir Don Ryder, an intense and ambitious man but no revolutionary. And although the NEB spent almost £800 million in four years, almost all of it was swallowed up by long-promised bailouts of struggling companies such as Rolls-Royce (aircraft engines), Ferranti (electronics), Alfred Herbert Ltd (machine tools) and British Leyland, which was now a byword for shoddy management, endless strikes and unreliable products. Not all of its investments were fiascos: ICL produced a decent profit when it was privatized ten years later, while a £50 million investment in INMOS, a small Bristol semiconductor firm, allowed it to capture 60 per cent of the world market in static RAM devices. In general, though, Benn's brainchild had become a life-support system for lame ducks. Far from capturing the commanding heights of the economy, the NEB found itself consoling the waifs and strays: by 1979, no less than 85 per cent of its budget had been soaked up by Rolls-Royce and British Leyland. Originally its intellectual godfather, Stuart Holland, had hoped that the NEB would work to 'reinforce and promote success rather than simply to underwrite or subsidise failure'. In the event, it did exactly the opposite.[29]

The NEB is best remembered as the sponsor of three short-lived experiments in workers' cooperatives, enthusiastically backed by Tony Benn over the opposition of almost all his colleagues. The first, and probably the unlikeliest, was the former Fisher-Bendix washing-machine plant at Kirkby, Merseyside, which had been identified for closure in 1971 and was then occupied by its workforce, who refused to leave the shop floor. The sit-in lasted for nine weeks, the workers relenting only when another company, International Property Developers (IPD), agreed to take over the plant. Whether IPD were ever serious about making it work, however, is very dubious. By the spring of 1974, the factory not only manufactured radiators, storage heaters and car parts, but it also produced orange juice, a very unlikely recipe for commercial success. Eventually IPD announced that it was calling in the liquidators, and once again the workers occupied the factory. This time, however, most observers assumed they were doomed.[30]

From the very beginning, Benn knew that the Kirkby enterprise had serious problems. History offers few examples of successful factories making both car parts and orange juice. But after meeting the works conveners in June 1974, he decided to champion 'the human case against the chartered accountants' case'. 'I felt you could not sack 1200 workers even though it was a bum firm,' he recorded, so he told his officials to buy the factory and 'save the jobs as best we could'. His consultants warned that the factory could sustain only 450 jobs, but when the conveners insisted that 'all of the workers should be employed', Benn immediately agreed. Proudly, he recorded that he had 'worked out on the back of an envelope' that it would be cheaper to keep them in work than to pay them unemployment benefit. This was not, perhaps, the best basis on which to spend public money, and his Cabinet colleagues were aghast when he laid out his plan to spend £3 million on the factory and a further £300,000 to subsidize the 'unutilized labour': in other words, literally paying people to do 'uneconomic jobs'. 'Harold Lever said that this was the economics of Peter Pan,' Benn wrote angrily. 'If these discussions were broadcast, people would leave the Labour Party in droves. There is such cynicism and hostility from Labour leaders about the needs of working people. The gap between me and the right wing, or even the unimaginative, run-of-the-mill Labour politicians, is vast.'[31]

Undaunted by his colleagues' ridicule, Benn drew up his plans for a workers' cooperative. When he presented them to the Cabinet's Industrial Development committee, however, he was shocked at their reaction. 'Harold Lever sat there bursting with laughter,' he wrote piously, 'and Denis Healey thought it was crackers.' As a Merseyside MP, however, Harold Wilson could see the short-term benefits. 'It was in my last Election address,' he said. 'We'll have to do something until the Election is over.' Even Benn thought this 'utterly cynical', but at least he could carry on with the good work. A few days after the October election, the Kirkby shop stewards asked for £4 million in government aid. 'Predictably my officials were totally obstructive,' Benn wrote, listing their objections: 'it isn't viable; it won't work; the manning is too high.' The Treasury was dead against it: if the government backed the shop stewards, Denis Healey wrote, then 'there can be no limit to the demands we should face for public aid to insolvent companies, and logically there would be no economic criteria that we could ever again apply in assessing them. Industry will draw the lesson that the uncompetitive need no longer fear the consequences of failure.' But when the issue came to Cabinet, Benn wore his colleagues down, winning approval for a 'once-and-for-all' grant of just under £4 million. It was 'a terrible defeat on a crucial principle of whether we are rigorous or promiscuous in doling out money to every Tom, Dick or Harry who comes begging,' wrote an appalled Bernard Donoughue. 'The Treasury certainly no longer dominates government business. I always opposed that domination. But now, unless some of it is restored, in the cause of responsible finance, the country will be bankrupted.'[32]

Donoughue was not alone in his view that, by handing so much money to the new Kirkby Manufacturing and Engineering Company (KME), the government was making a catastrophic mistake. Benn's own advisory board accused him of throwing public money down the drain, while in January 1975 *The Times* reported that the department's accounting officer had filed a written objection. As Benn gloomily noted, this was the first time in living memory that a senior civil servant had publicly come out against his own minister, which spoke volumes about morale inside his department. Yet at first the cooperative seemed to confound its critics. By the summer of 1975, radiator production was up to 10,000 units a week, while (almost incredibly) even the orange juice department was making a marginal profit. Unfortunately, although demand for radiators grew steadily and turnover boomed, the consultants had been right all along. By April 1977 the cooperative was losing so much money that the government had to put in a further £860,000. But in September 1978 KME came knocking at the door again. By now they were losing £20,000 a week; they needed £3 million, they said, or the cooperative would go under. In Whitehall, patience had run out: as the Cabinet minutes noted, the government's experts, 'who included trade unionists, had advised unanimously against support'. Two months later, the government announced that KME would be taken over by a Midlands engineering firm, with major redundancies to follow. Merseyside's cooperative experiment was dead.[33]

The sad story of KME was characteristic of Benn's cooperatives. A second venture, the *Scottish Daily News*, was founded in May 1975 when the *Scottish Daily Express* moved out of Glasgow, throwing almost 2,000 employees out of work. From the outset, Benn's colleagues thought it was a bad idea. When Benn arranged a meeting to discuss giving public money to the workers' Action Committee, Harold Wilson immediately cancelled it. The TUC general secretary Len Murray was 'very negative', telling Benn that 'the print unions were in trouble and he can't recommend to his members to help the paper', while Jack Jones bluntly told him: 'You don't want to support the Scottish newspaper workers.' On 5 May, however, some five hundred workers, having put in £200,000 of their redundancy money and obtained a £1.2 million loan from Benn's department, produced the first issue of their new broadsheet. 'All 300,000 copies were sold out and demand greatly exceeded supply,' *The Times* reported admiringly. But once the novelty had worn off, sales plummeted. By August 1975, with circulation barely 80,000, the paper was losing £30,000 a week. Relaunched as a tabloid, it staggered on until November, when the government turned down entreaties for more money. Benn was naturally furious: on 11 November the first line of his diary read simply: 'The *Scottish Daily News* died yesterday.' Actually, this was not quite true. Some of the workforce refused to accept their fate, occupying their iconic art deco building and struggling to produce a rudimentary paper which they sold on the streets of Glasgow. Amazingly, it was not until a year later that the sit-in finally ended, killed by sheer exhaustion.[34]

The most celebrated of Benn's cooperatives was based in the West Midlands. In the summer of 1973, the Triumph motorcycle factory in Meriden, outside Solihull, had merged with the only other remaining British motorbike manufacturer to form Norton Villiers Triumph (NVT). Almost immediately, NVT proposed closing the Meriden factory with the loss of some 1,750 jobs. Copying the Upper Clyde Shipbuilders, the Meriden men promptly occupied the plant and refused to budge, insisting that they could carry on producing profitable motorbikes as a workers' cooperative. Of course Benn loved the sound of it, but when he commissioned a report from his officials, they advised that it would never make money and 'we couldn't go ahead with Meriden'. Undaunted, Benn insisted that they produce a second report, this time 'arguing *in favour* of Meriden'. As usual, his Cabinet colleagues told him it was a bad idea, but Benn 'fought like a tiger' to get an initial bailout of £5 million. In this case, though, he also faced opposition from the workers at NVT's plants in Wolverhampton and Small Heath, who were outraged to hear that the government might fund one of their local competitors. So Benn flew up to Small Heath for 'a very hostile meeting' with some three thousand men. To his horror, not one convener was willing to join him on the platform, leaving him alone before 'a very rough' crowd. 'You're just a tin-pot king thinking you can impose your will,' one convener shouted. 'You don't care about the jobs here. Why should Meriden have help?' It was 'an alarming situation', Benn later admitted. 'There was the militancy of people sticking to their jobs, which I fully support, but at the same time, the fear of slump means that workers will turn against workers and working-class solidarity will be strained to its utmost.'[35]

Given the problems union leaders were having controlling their own men, the episode should have taught Benn that 'working-class solidarity' existed more on paper than in reality. But despite the fury of the Small Heath workers, he was determined to press on. Visiting Meriden one Sunday morning, he found men warming their hands miserably around a brazier while inside their colleagues were planning a new carburettor design. 'It must seem awful to you being here night after night,' Benn told the pickets, 'but if this stopped, Meriden would be dead in twenty-four hours, so you must keep at it and I will do my best for you.' He was as good as his word: by the end of January 1975, he had not only persuaded the Small Heath men to drop their objections, but he offered NVT an £8 million export credit, allowing them to sell Meriden's motorbikes abroad. The cooperative was safe; hundreds of jobs had been saved. But when Benn briefed his Cabinet colleagues on his triumph, not one shared his enthusiasm for the cooperative. Indeed, when Denis Healey found out that Benn had promised the unions more money for NVT, he was furious. 'The Japs are now well entrenched in motorbikes,' said Joel Barnett. 'We can't compete.' Even Jim Callaghan, the unions' friend, thought Meriden had been a victory for 'belligerency, militancy and tenacity' and that 'it will simply spread to other places. We can't have it.'[36]

By the summer of 1975 Meriden had formally reopened as a workers' cooperative. But within months it was clear that there was trouble ahead. One afternoon, after Benn had moved on from the Department of Industry (of which more later), he was lecturing the Cabinet about industrial democracy when the new Industry Secretary, Eric Varley, drew Barbara Castle's attention to a file labelled 'Meriden'. 'It's gone bust,' Varley said contemptuously. He was referring not to the cooperative but to its former owner, NVT, which had been given £10 million in public money but was still in desperate financial trouble. Thanks to the world-wide recession, the overseas motorcycle market had collapsed, leaving NVT with thousands of unsold vehicles. Disastrously for Benn's reputa-tion, the Small Heath conveners now published a letter he had sent them the previous November, promising that the government was 'fully com-mitted to securing the future of the motorcycle industry in this country', and specifically naming NVT as well as the Meriden cooperative. In effect, observed Bernard Donoughue, Benn had given 'assurances of government support without ever getting any government authority for doing so ... Now that Norton Villiers Triumph is bankrupt and has come to us for £50 million, and its shop stewards have Benn's letter in their pocket, the chickens really are coming home to roost.'[37]

When the issue came before the Cabinet's Industrial Development committee, Benn escaped the coming firestorm by walking out before anybody had said a word. He must have 'more pressing business else-where', Varley observed sarcastically. But at a time when all the talk was of cuts, the decision was only ever likely to go one way. Varley's consult-ants estimated that NVT might need far more than £50 million and would probably not break even until the late 1980s. Even with massive public backing, the motorcycle industry would probably 'fail in the face of overwhelming competition, largely from the Japanese'. The figures made for bleak reading: 'the Small Heath factory of NVT produced about 10 motorcycles per man per year, whereas the corresponding fig-ure for Japanese firms was about 100.' The brutal truth was that 'there was no future for the British motorcycle industry'. For once the press was unanimous that the government had done the right thing. 'By say-ing No to NVT,' *The Times* said sadly, 'the Government has at last shown a capacity to undertake the unpleasant. It is the right decision.'[38]

Norton Villiers Triumph did not go down without a fight. In Wolver-hampton, hundreds of workers occupied the factory, hoping to emulate their old rivals at Meriden. In the press their plight elicited a great deal of sympathy: to men with such specialized skills, it seemed utterly unjust that Meriden was 'nourished by the taxpayer' while Wolverhampton was left to rot. 'I just can't understand how they can treat their own people like this,' said one shop steward, who had spent his entire adult life working for the Labour Party. 'Now I see them tear up their commitments and put us on the streets. It's diabolical.' But although 900 workers were still occupying the plant in January 1976, their protest petered out eventually. So too, sadly, did the Meriden cooperative. For all the guts and ingenuity of its workers, the cooperative never stood a chance in a market dominated by gigantic Japanese corporations. By 1977 it was already begging for more public assistance, and three years later the Thatcher government – rather belying its ruthless image – wrote off £9 million worth of debts so that the cooperative could keep going. But eventually the financial pressure was too much. By the beginning of 1983 the Meriden cooperative could not afford to produce a single motorcycle, and that August it was finally wound up.[39]

On the left, Benn's cooperatives are sometimes remembered as a heroic statement of defiance in the face of global capitalism. In the very short term, his interventions saved the jobs of thousands of people who would otherwise have been unemployed. But although it is hard to remain unmoved by the courage of the workers at KME, Meriden and the *Scottish Daily News*, there was nothing heroic about Benn's habit of making promises he could not keep or his enthusiasm for using public money to produce goods nobody wanted to buy. In each case his own advisers, consultants and Cabinet colleagues, as well as the trade union leaders, warned him that the enterprise would be unviable. In each case, he threw money at them anyway. At one stage his special advisers, Frances Morrell and Francis Cripps, even distributed a paper arguing that (as Donoughue put it) 'no firms should be allowed to go broke and no workers should be made redundant', which really was the economics of *Fantasy Island*. Yet there was nothing socialist about misleading anxious workers into thinking they could rely on a bottomless pot of public money. Contemplating the wreckage of the *Scottish Daily News*, Bernard Levin thought that the former Industry Secretary should take a long look in the mirror:

> The question is: has he sent any word of apology, for his conduct, to the poor devils who trusted him and sank their life-savings as well as their redundancy payments into this tartan Titanic? They, after all, were working men who dreamed, as many do, of being their own bosses, of working together with their colleagues in an enterprise that would be their own; it was a laudable aim and the only thing wrong with it was that it had no

hope of success. That being so, it was Mr Benn's duty to tell them as much, and to prevent them from plunging into disaster. Instead of fulfilling that duty, he allowed them to delude themselves. Now they face the bitterness of the inevitable failure: what comfort has Mr Benn for them now?[40]

The truth is that for all the utopian rhetoric of the early 1970s, neither Benn nor his colleagues came close to reversing the sorry decline of British manufacturing. Even Labour ministers themselves recognized that their strategy had been a mess; in 1978, an internal report described it as 'an uninspired and largely ineffective exercise in ad hockery'. One problem was that intervention simply came too late; even so, many economic historians agree that the 'situation at the end of the 1970s was not sustainable: a major restructuring was essential'. Public ownership was no panacea, and while carefully targeted intervention might have made a difference, the hapless efforts of the Heath and Wilson years kept wages and prices high, held back productivity growth and merely delayed the inevitable collapse. And at a deeper level, as some insiders later recognized, they put far too much faith in the state's ability to reverse Britain's deep-seated industrial decline. In an age of fierce global competition, no government could wave a magic wand and turn a struggling business back from pumpkin to stagecoach. 'Looking back,' Bernard Donoughue wrote later, 'it is striking how most of us in that Labour government ... still believed state intervention in the markets and the direction of capital would actually improve the performance of the economy over the longer term. Our subsequent experience in government provided a rude awakening.'[41]

For the time being, however, the government recoiled from the harsh logic of the balance sheet. Once again cars were the supreme symbol of national failure. By April 1975 British Leyland was in deep trouble. At the end of the year it had made a thumping loss of £76 million; had it been a private company, it might have been wound up. The TGWU's Jack Jones thought that the government should get rid of it to a multinational corporation who might at least run it properly. 'Why don't you sell it to General Motors?' he asked Tony Benn, much to the latter's horror.* Instead, Benn commissioned a report from Sir Don Ryder, who

---

* Amusingly, Benn took this as a sign that Jones was just another a closet Conservative. 'When Jack Jones recommends that the British Government sell British Leyland to General Motors of America,' he wrote, 'there is an indication that the criticisms of him from the Left are correct.'

thought it could be re-established as one of the world's top car manufacturers and recommended that the government step in to bail it out.
An alternative report by a House of Commons committee pointed out
that it was madness to keep producing both mass-market and specialist
cars, but its advice was ignored. Instead, the Cabinet followed Ryder's
recommendation that, to check the flood of foreign imports, British
Leyland must carry on making cars for everybody. Following his formula, they agreed to buy out British Leyland's existing shareholders,
turning it into a fully state-owned company under the National Enterprise Board, and put in another £1,400 million over the next eight years.
Only one minister had the nous to speak against this latest experiment
in throwing good money after bad. British Leyland was a 'grandiose
folly', Harold Lever said, calling the report a ' "bad Pharoah's dream" in
which we weren't even promised seven fat years after the seven lean
ones'. But, Barbara Castle noted dismissively, 'he didn't cut much ice.'[42]

Lever was quite right, of course. The Ryder Report was based on the
wildly over-optimistic prediction that, in the next few years, British Leyland's share of the home market would remain constant, while sales in
Western Europe would boom by 25 per cent in seven years. These forecasts were about as accurate as predictions that Scotland would win the
1978 World Cup, the Bay City Rollers would eclipse the Beatles and
Shirley Williams would become the first woman Prime Minister. In fact,
British Leyland's share of the domestic market fell from 31 per cent in
1975 to a pitiful 18 per cent in 1980. Productivity remained very poor,
production targets were routinely missed and, above all, labour relations were still abysmal. In the second half of 1975 alone, unofficial
strikes cost the company 40,000 cars with a showroom value of
£90 million, while another 25,000 cars were held up by faults or missing
parts. It was no wonder so many people were buying Japanese: even the
Board of Trade had to send back three new Princesses because they were
faulty. And by the second anniversary of the Ryder Report, British Leyland was in a terrible state. In the first six months of 1977, strikes had
cost the company 9.3 million man-hours and 120,000 cars, while profits
were down by two-thirds in a year. In July, the group had even been
forced to borrow another £100 million from the National Enterprise
Board merely to keep production of the new Mini going. In desperation,
the government brought in a ruthless South African-born businessman
called Michael Edwardes. But as events were to prove, his idea of turning British Leyland around was very different from Don Ryder's.[43]

Six months after approving the Ryder Report, Wilson's ministers were faced with an even less promising case for treatment. When the news broke that Chrysler was in trouble, the obvious course was to let it fold. Its financial woes had dominated the headlines for months; its management was widely seen as both ruthless and inept; and its labour relations, even by car-industry standards, were atrocious, with 138,000 working days lost already that year. Now its American owners had had enough. Unless the government wrote off Chrysler's £75 million losses and pumped in another £80 million to keep it going, they said, they would close the whole thing down. Since the state had already bailed out British Leyland, though, this would leave the taxpayer subsidizing two competing companies. On top of that, Chrysler's British operations were losing so much money that any investment would be a massive gamble. Only one member of Eric Varley's Industrial Development Authority Board thought the enterprise was at all viable, while a Policy Unit report suggested that the car market was far too crowded. 'All the schemes we have considered would be unviable even on paper,' Varley told the Cabinet. 'The NEB don't want it. Leyland don't want it. Vauxhall are afraid we might help Chrysler. Ford don't want it.' The case against bailing it out was 'quite overwhelming': they 'had better accept the inevitable, let the company wind itself up, and concentrate on a massive redundancy scheme'.[44]

For some of Varley's colleagues, there was little to mourn in Chrysler's troubles. Edmund Dell thought that letting it die would be a 'valuable lesson' for other manufacturers, while even Wilson remarked that it was not so much a lame duck as a 'dead duck'. But, as might have been predicted, Tony Benn was horrified by the prospect of almost 30,000 redundancies. Letting Chrysler fold, he said angrily, would be 'a massive further step towards industrial suicide'. Even to consider the question of profitability, he added, was 'a dangerous doctrine'. Benn's alternative was 'to defend what we have, even if its equipment is lousy, defend it if necessary behind protective walls and then reconstruct it with the help of workers in the industry and make it viable'. This kind of talk, as Barbara Castle noted, always went down very well with party audiences. 'But the constant flaw', she wrote, 'is that Wedgie has never faced up to (or asked his followers to face up to) the problem of where the money would come from, and the sacrifices we would have to make, while we were taking over and reconstructing all these unviable companies.'[45]

Had Benn been his only opponent, then Wilson would probably have let Chrysler die. But almost immediately the Scottish Secretary, Willie

Ross, pointed out that closing the giant Linwood plant would be 'politically disastrous' in Scotland, where Labour seemed in real danger of being overtaken by the Scottish Nationalists. And when Ross and his junior minister threatened to resign, Wilson's instinctive self-interest reasserted itself. By early December, he had decided on a compromise that would 'rescue some of Chrysler for a year or so'. The Department of Industry and the Treasury played along because they were convinced that Chrysler would turn it down. But when the Americans arrived for talks on the rescue package, they proved rather tougher negotiators than their British counterparts. With their 'menacing dark eyes, swept-back greased hair, sharp suits and flashy ties', wrote Bernard Donoughue, the Chrysler chairman John Riccardo and his henchmen looked like 'night club owners from Hollywood thrillers of the 1940s'. Donoughue expected them 'to put on sunglasses at any moment and assumed that they had violin cases under the table'. By comparison, the British officials looked like 'a bunch of country vicars thinking they were coming to a village fete but finding themselves in a downtown casino'.[46]

'This is like a Middle Eastern rug market,' Riccardo said bluntly. 'You've guessed our problem. We will guess yours. You will have real problems if we have to bankrupt in the UK. We came to play as gentlemen, but if you prefer, we won't.' At that, Donoughue half-expected the Americans to reach under the table for their violin cases and 'pump us all on our side of the table full of lead'. Deep down, he knew that the deal made no economic sense. 'But politically,' he thought, 'the government might want to go for it.' Indeed they did. Under pressure from Harold Wilson, Varley finally agreed to bail out Chrysler after all. He made no secret of his deep disappointment. 'It would be presented as a surrender to a multi-national company,' he told the Cabinet. 'It would destroy the Government's industrial strategy and weaken their policy of controlling public expenditure, and create a precedent which it would be difficult to escape when faced by other companies.' The alternative, however, meant accepting 30,000 job losses and handing a gift to the Scottish Nationalists. 'Let's be politicians,' Harold Wilson said. The Conservatives would attack the scheme as a waste of money. But the government could 'take on the Tories – and Eric will have a great parliamentary triumph with our people'.[47]

Unveiled a week before Christmas 1975, the Chrysler deal cost Britain almost £163 million in subsidies and loans over the next four years. By any sensible standard, the government's decision to spend so much money subsidizing a struggling competitor to British Leyland seemed completely deranged; for Denis Healey's biographer Edward Pearce, it appeared 'the embodiment of politically-fuelled weakness, a general instinct to appease, postpone, walk away from confrontation'. That same day the chairman of Rolls-Royce, the state-owned maker of air-craft engines, admitted that the firm was still in deep trouble and would need an injection of £100 million for 1976. 'It annoys me like hell to see this money going into Chrysler,' he said bluntly. In Whitehall, mean-while, the Central Policy Review Staff published their long-awaited report on the future of the British car industry, a sorry story of 'serious competitive weaknesses . . . poor quality, bad labour relations, unsatis-factory delivery record, low productivity and too much manpower'. And in Speke, Liverpool, a dispute was boiling over at Leyland's Tri-umph plant. The problem had originated in the trim shop, where the twenty-one-man workforce had walked out complaining about 'a smell caused by stray cats'. 'Work stopped while cleaners spent 45 minutes scrubbing the floor,' *The Times* reported. 'Then the men protested that the floor was still wet and dangerous to work on.' Two days later the men had still not returned and 600 other workers had been sent home. Such was life in the British car industry.[48]

13
Power to the People!

> You would study a number of themes, including the philosoph-
> ical and historical background to Marxism and sociology, the
> roots of racism and sexism, revolutionary movements and the
> dynamics of domination in industrial societies and the Third
> World ...
>
> Middlesex Polytechnic sociology prospectus,
quoted in The Times, 15 November 1977

> BRIAN: *Excuse me, but are you the Judaean People's Front?*
> REG: *Fuck off!*
> BRIAN: *What?*
> REG (scornfully): *Judaean People's Front? We're the People's
> Front of Judaea!*
>
> Monty Python's Life of Brian (1979)

Early one Monday afternoon in November 1974, a group of middle-
aged men in smart suits gathered at the Polytechnic of North London's
main building on Holloway Road. The welcoming committee was
already in place, and along the main corridors stood dozens of students,
many carrying placards and banners. The director, Terence Miller, hastily ushered his governors into the staff common room, but there was no
escape from the jeers and the chants. At half past two, Miller told the
governors to go through into a secure inner room. It was far smaller
than their usual boardroom, with no natural light, and some of them
had to sit on the floor. But the meeting had barely begun when there
were ominous noises outside: 'a heavy thud, and then the crack of splin-
tering wood as a student hurled himself against the door'. The chairman

of the governors, wrote one observer, was 'clearly shocked: his face was grey and his cheekbones stood out'. He tried to keep talking, but the noise grew steadily louder: 'stamping, chanting, banging on the wall, the metal chairs, the big cauldrons and silver salvers in the kitchen'. From a little side-window with wooden louvres there came a ripping sound, and two of the slats abruptly disappeared, replaced by a loudhailer. 'Get out!' said a metallic voice. 'You cunts . . . Motherfuckers . . . Get out . . . Get out of this polytechnic. Get out!'[1]

To those who had been following recent events at the Polytechnic of North London (PNL), the turbulent scenes on 18 November were nothing out of the ordinary. By the following summer, meetings of the court of governors had been disrupted six times, five of them ending in 'pandemonium'. All in all, PNL had suffered eighteen major disturbances in barely four years, becoming a national symbol of student rebellion. 'If you get a kick out of street fighting and agitation,' boasted the student union handbook, 'you have come to the right place.' The *Daily Express* called it a 'school for scandal'; the former headmaster and Tory MP Rhodes Boyson demanded that it be 'cleansed' of subversive elements, and even the veteran liberal academic Lord Annan thought that PNL offered a chilling example of 'the tyranny of rule by mass assembly'. It had become 'an intellectual concentration camp', agreed *The Times*'s columnist Bernard Levin, who thought that the students' goal was 'the destruction of PNL as part of the wider aim of turning Britain into a totalitarian Marxist state'. And for the new leader of the Conservative Party, the troubles at PNL were a gift, an object lesson in the dangers of unchecked militancy. 'Everyone who believes in freedom', Margaret Thatcher told her first party conference as leader, 'must be appalled at the tactics employed by the far Left in the systematic destruction of the North London Polytechnic . . . No wonder so many of our people – some of the best and brightest – are depressed and talk of emigrating.'[2]

Based mainly in a grim, thirteen-storey concrete block on Holloway Road, PNL had been formed in 1971 from the merger of two smaller polytechnics. In the early years of the decade it attracted some 4,000 full-time students and 3,000 part-timers, taught by about 550 academics. Almost from the beginning, however, it was hit by protests and sit-ins, most of them directed at the director, Dr Terence Miller. A former wartime pilot and Territorial Army officer who had since become an eminent geologist, Miller had served as principal of University College Rhodesia during the late 1960s. Despite accusations of complicity with Ian Smith's breakaway racist government, he had often spoken out against the Smith regime, and lasted just two years before resigning in protest at Rhodesia's new racist constitution. The far right were sending him hate mail before the far left had even heard of him; then the latter started sending him hate mail too. As the student leaders at PNL saw it, Miller had sinned by going to Rhodesia in the first place: for years, posters condemning 'Miller the Racist' confronted visitors to Holloway Road. In February 1971 students held a mass sit-in to protest against his appointment, and from that event flowed all the years of 'endless meetings, negotiations, propaganda, violence'.[3]

The authors of those words were three senior lecturers, Keith Jacka, Caroline Cox and John Marks, who in the summer of 1975 published an exposé of their own institution under the melodramatic title *Rape of Reason*. It was this book that stirred up much of the press furore about PNL: the *Express* made it the subject of a major feature, while Bernard Levin told his readers that it was 'one of the most serious books I [have] had in my hands for a good number of years'. As Levin admitted, it would have been easy to dismiss it as right-wing scaremongering: it was published by Rhodes Boyson's Constitutional Book Club, it carried advertisements for titles such as *Goodbye to Nationalisation* and *Down with the Poor*, and one of the authors, the sociologist Caroline Cox, later became a Conservative peer. Even so, at the time all three considered themselves to be on the liberal left. Jacka had previously been a Communist, while Marks was still a member of the Labour Party. And even allowing for exaggeration, their book was still a frighteningly compelling account of higher education at its worst. When *The Times*'s education correspondent visited PNL, staff reluctantly admitted that the facts were correct. 'Since the [new] polytechnic was formed we have had nothing but strife,' lamented George Dickson, a laboratory superintendent who had worked at the old Northern Polytechnic for twenty-five years. 'The middle ground has been swept away and there is just polarization.' A couple of lecturers, overhearing his interview, interrupted to say that things were not quite as bad as that. Nonsense, Dickson snapped: 'It is the non-academic staff who have to suffer all the disruption ... You science lecturers seem to have your heads buried in the sand. You would carry on lecturing when the water in the classroom is right up round your necks.'[4]

Although Terence Miller's uncompromising managerial style no doubt played its part, the roots of PNL's troubles went back to its foundation. On paper the merger of the Northern Polytechnic and the North Western Polytechnic had made sense, but it brought together two very different institutions. The former was small, conservative and highly specialized, being particularly strong in the natural sciences; the latter had been the biggest polytechnic in London, with a very active student body and a pronounced bias towards the social sciences. Under pressure from North Western's student union, the governors of the newly merged PNL had agreed to an unusually high level of student representation, with students taking more than one in three seats on the academic board. But this was a recipe for catastrophe. Student politics at North Western had fallen under the sway of the International Socialists, a tiny Trotskyite cult that had enjoyed considerable success on British campuses during the late 1960s. Of course most students had no sympathy for Trotskyism, but through sheer persistence the International Socialists secured a grip on the student union, winning almost every post between 1970 and 1976. The presidency, meanwhile, alternated between two outspoken International Socialists: Mike Hill, originally at North Western, and Terry Povey, originally at Northern. Militancy for its own sake was their guiding principle: as early as December 1970, Hill issued a statement promising 'the most serious disturbances this country has yet seen at a polytechnic'. Three years later, Hill and Povey released another statement explaining that 'under capitalism' there could be no 'democracy in education'. Their goal, they said, was 'the destruction of the system itself'.[5]

For people who talked a great deal about tolerance, the militant leaders were hardly models of open-mindedness. Inside the student union, dissenting views were not welcome. Students who tried to work during occupations were relentlessly bullied, while non-Marxist visiting speakers found their lectures picketed and broken up. When one speaker pleaded for tolerance, a student replied: '*You* are the one who counts tolerance as a good thing. *I* don't.' Meanwhile the student leaders demanded half the votes on all major university committees, including the court of governors, board of studies and academic board, and campaigned against governors who disagreed. Almost unbelievably, the student union's official handbook described Terence Miller as 'an incompetent, reactionary and authoritarian buffoon', while Keith Jacka, an Australian mathematician, was dismissed as a 'crude, intellectually barren thug'. Yet the great irony was that most students simply could not care less. Despite the sensational headlines, reported *The Times*, 'most staff shared the view of a woman print assistant that 96 per cent of the students came to the polytechnic to work'. Most simply got on with their studies: despite all the pushing and shouting, political interest was so low that in March 1975, during a by-election to the academic board, the students' elected representatives received just *nine* votes each out of a potential four thousand. The paradox, though, was that apathy was the father of militancy: since the student union had fallen under the control of the International Socialists, most students stayed away, allowing the radicals to tighten their grip.[6]

But life went on. As at other universities, the academic calendar eventually brought an end to the disturbances. The older student leaders moved away, while the new generation, alarmed by rising unemployment and narrowing prospects, kept a lower profile. Gradually, almost unnoticed, the Polytechnic of North London faded from the headlines. Indeed, despite a brief drop in admissions for some courses, it not only survived but prospered, eventually becoming London Metropolitan University. And despite attempts to suspend and even sack him, Terence Miller remained as director until 1979, when he retired with some characteristically trenchant remarks about the future of the polytechnic system. (Polytechnics, he thought, should teach only 'strictly vocational subjects', students should be given higher grants to push them into engineering and the sciences, and there should be a 'ruthless' purge of the 'dead wood' in the staff common rooms.) And for those who had suffered during the campaign of disruption, there was at least one consolation. After taking seven years to finish his maths degree, Terry Povey, the long-haired face of student militancy, found himself lost in the world of the job market. He tried to qualify as a schoolteacher, his wife told the press, 'but they said he had handed in his essays three days too late'. He went up to Scotland to work on a building site, but after six weeks he was back in London. When last heard of, he was trying to become a bus conductor.[7]

In some ways, the mid-1970s were surprisingly good years for Britain's universities. Once open only to a privileged few, university education had undergone an enormous boom: by the time the Polytechnic of North London opened for business, there were no fewer than fifty-three universities and a further thirty polytechnics. Conservative and Labour ministers alike agreed that increased university education was crucial to Britain's economic success: when Margaret Thatcher had unveiled her big-spending Education White Paper in 1972, for example, she envisaged an extraordinarily ambitious expansion of 60 per cent in just nine years. And when she gave way to Labour's Reg Prentice in 1974, there were almost 500,000 students in higher education, a gargantuan figure compared with the few thousand during her own student days. It is true that, thanks to the economic downturn, Britain fell short of her original target of 750,000 full-time students by 1981, while capital spending cuts and stagnant pay left many academics with an acute sense of decline. Even so, there was no doubt that by the end of the 1970s most campuses were busier, livelier, more diverse places than they had been ten years earlier, with expanding courses and broadening horizons. For students who benefited from generous government grants, life was not bad at all.[8]

When universities appeared in the media, however, it was rarely in the context of opportunity and scholarship, and more often in terms of strikes, sit-ins and general absurdity. Although British students had long had a reputation for conservatism, the late 1960s had seen a sudden surge of demonstrations, largely in imitation of events overseas. At institutions across the country, students protested against the Vietnam War, claimed the right to sit on university councils and demanded the abolition of entry requirements, exams and a defined curriculum. But although student protests are usually seen as part of the fabric of the 1960s, they were much more widespread in the years that followed. Indeed, by the early 1970s they had become far more extravagant in motivation and form, with left-wing students keen to champion the workers' cause against the heartless Heath and the gutless Wilson, those running dogs of bourgeois imperialism. The more prestigious the institution, it seemed, the more likely it would attract trouble: at Oxford, for example, the winter of 1973–4 was notable for innumerable occupations by students convinced that, by winning the right to a student union building, they would help to liberate Britain's exploited masses. Despite their noisy clashes with the local police, however, the Oxford students' appeals to proletarian solidarity fell on very stony ground. No doubt the car workers of Cowley were less than impressed to hear that the Balliol College room where the militants held their meetings had been turned into an 'undergraduate cabaret', with tickets, 'including a bottle of bubbly', on sale for £2.50 each.[9]

The epicentre of student protests in the mid-1970s was Essex, a new campus university built a decade earlier along the lines of an East German power station. Here the culture of protest became especially deep-seated: every time the authorities tried to deal with the legacy of some disturbance, their measures set off yet more demonstrations. Some of these were frankly preposterous, such as the 'revolutionary festival', at which, according to New Society, 'a car was set on fire and a student and a mathematics professor struggled over possession of a hosepipe', while behind them a wall slogan proclaimed: 'DON'T JUST STAND THERE – WANK'. Yet student militancy was no laughing matter, and for years life at Essex was dominated by a culture of complaint, hanging in the air alongside the faint smell of marijuana smoke, stale beer and unwashed clothes. In March 1974 hundreds of students occupied university buildings, demanding higher grants and complaining, as always, that the authorities were being too hard on those involved in previous sit-ins. At one stage dozens of students were arrested after pitched battles with the police, and *The Times* reported that the scenes of mass brawls, missile-throwing and attacks on police vans had been 'some of the worst disturbances ever seen at a British university'. Meanwhile the vice chancellor, Dr Albert Sloman, a shy scholar of Spanish literature, seemed overwhelmed by the protesters' fury. When some seventy students burst into his office, Dr Sloman sat 'neatly in a grey suit and tie', smiling nervously while 'the students, with studied loutishness, put cigarettes out on the floor, swigged Coca-Cola from bottles and called him Albert'. Several called him a fascist. One girl called him a 'silly old sod' before storming out of the room. 'Albert, you're a bloody boring little academic,' said a student with 'a wispy Ho Chi Minh beard'. It was hardly surprising that as the *Sunday Times* laconically put it, 'the discussion was not considered fruitful by either side'.

So the protests continued: as the students broke up for their Easter vacation, 'imposing barricades of the Falls Road variety' were still up at the main entrance. 'Essex began as an idealistic dream that was going to fundamentally alter the character of university life,' one lecturer said sadly. 'But that has turned very sour in the last few months.' As though to confirm his judgement, his voice was promptly drowned out by rock music from a loudspeaker put up by protesters outside the main office building. Of course the sensationalist headlines did not tell the whole story: most students, admitted *The Times*, had taken no part in the demonstrations, let alone the violent clashes with the police. 'The silent majority is here, but as long as it remains silent, no one takes any notice of it,' one physics student complained. 'Hundreds of us just want a quiet life, but what hope have we got?'[10]

What really infuriated militant students was the fact that nobody took them as seriously as they did themselves. The vast majority of the general public had not benefited from a university education and deeply resented being lectured by middle-class youngsters who had. Gallup found that barely one in ten people sympathized with student protests, while the *Sunday Telegraph* was struck by the 'almost vindictive hostility to the student population'. Despite the apocalyptic headlines in the *Mail* and the *Express*, however, most people saw student militants as essentially comic, even ridiculous figures, which only infuriated them all the more. The 'British revolutionary', remarked the *Sun*, 'usually has eyes that are close together, and he wears a satisfied smirk'. He had 'badges in his lapels', was 'a martyr to acne', and used the word 'irrelevant' 'as many as ten times in a sentence'. Britain's student protesters, the *Sun* said, were 'firmly against violence, except when they are being violent', yet 'could not organize a church bazaar'. In popular culture, meanwhile, students were generally shown as ludicrous rather than threatening. In the sitcom *Rising Damp*, Richard Beckinsale's medical student Alan conforms to every conceivable stereotype. A self-proclaimed Maoist, he decorates his room with a poster of Che Guevara, wears his hair so long that Rigsby accuses him of looking like Rasputin, and on one occasion disrupts a National Front meeting and 'accidentally' hits a policeman. Yet to Rigsby (and to the audience), he is an ineffectual, amiable layabout, so effeminate that he looks like Veronica Lake, so lazy he even shaves 'lying down'. Given the restrictive tightness of Alan's trousers, as well as the fact he is terrified of horror films, society has little to fear. 'Look what happened when we watched *Psycho*,' Rigsby jeers. 'You went to the toilet fourteen times!'[11]

In fact, even Alan was probably more militant than most of his classmates. Surveys consistently found that most students were far more interested in putting away a few pints of Watney's, listening to grandiose concept albums, passing their exams and getting decent jobs than in smashing the system or having more representatives on the university council. Six months after a major sit-in at Leeds, for example, a poll found that six out of ten students had been against it and almost nine out of ten thought student politics were 'boring'. But perhaps this was not surprising. The vast majority of students still came from affluent middle-class backgrounds, and they were far better treated than their counterparts overseas. Tuition was free, almost all living costs were covered by the state grant, and they were taught in small classes and seminars, not in gigantic Continental-style lecture theatres. Even the idealistic usually channelled their enthusiasm into worthy causes: when the Conservative MP Ian Gilmour made a throwaway jibe about the 'inmates' of Britain's universities in November 1974, a professor at York angrily replied that most students were 'decent young people destined to fill responsible positions in our society'. One of the most active societies at York, he pointed out, was the Social Service Organization, which 'makes no national headlines; but many local people have reason to know it is there'.[12]

By this point the momentum behind student protest had peaked. Even at Essex the older student organizers were moving on. Many proved to be more interested in climbing the greasy pole than in fomenting world revolution: the president of the National Union of Students between 1975 and 1977, describing himself as a 'Marxist to the left of Mr Benn', was one Charles Clarke, former head boy of Highgate School and future spear-carrier for Tony Blair. Yet by the time he stepped down from the union presidency, Clarke was out of step with the general trend. Most students, as opposed to student politicians, were increasingly worried about getting a decent job in a country haunted by rising unemployment. As early as 1975, *The Times* rejoiced that many had 'rejected the frivolity and superficiality that was once a feature of student life' and had adopted 'a much more mature and perhaps even puritan approach to their own lives and their hopes for the future of our society'. A year later, during the long hot summer of the IMF crisis, a survey of 250 students at London, Sussex and Warwick found that their economic and political attitudes were surprisingly conservative. Two out of three agreed that 'competition tends to ensure the lowest prices and the best quality for goods and services', while fewer than one in three approved of government support for industrial lame ducks. For those who fondly remembered the heady days of the late 1960s, these were sobering figures indeed. By 1978, the socialist playwright David Hare was complaining that the new generation had 'given up on the possibility of change'. Thanks to the darkening economic picture, 'anxiety and diffidence' were now the norm, agreed the LSE's director Ralf Dahrendorf. 'Gone are the high spirits, the clever ideals, the great hopes of the 1960s.'[13]

It was in the common room, not the student union bar, that the flame of revolution burned brightest. Expanding rapidly to cope with rising student numbers, many university departments, especially in newer disciplines such as political science and sociology, were taking on new staff. These younger lecturers rarely conformed to the tweedy stereotype: if they wore a uniform, it was of the polo neck, denim jacket and wooden earrings variety. Often from lower-middle-class or even working-class backgrounds, and having come of age in the late 1960s, they burned with the fire of moral indignation. As Donald MacRae, Professor of Sociology at the LSE, pointed out, there had been only five

sociology professors in the entire United Kingdom in 1960. Seventeen
years later, with the subject taught in every university except St Andrews,
the picture had changed completely. 'What you got,' Professor MacRae
told *The Times*, 'was a flooding into universities of people who considered themselves sociologists but were in fact simply Marxists. The
one was simply a substitute for the latter.' Perhaps this was an exaggeration; then again, perhaps not. 'The whole air has a definite texture to
it,' complained the Polytechnic of North London's director Terence
Miller, no great fan of sociology. 'The whole atmosphere of Marxism
and its assorted paraphernalia of women's liberation, anti-abortion [*sic*:
presumably he meant pro-abortion], Chile and Northern Ireland
impregnates everyone, just like coal dust gets into a miner's skin.'[14]

Of course there had always been plenty of Marxists in British academic life: a generation earlier, historians such as E. P. Thompson and
Christopher Hill had earned well-deserved praise for their intellectual
labours. By the mid-1970s, however, a very different kind of Marxism,
inspired by Gramsci, Marcuse and Foucault, had permeated deep into
British university life. In the words of another Marxist historian, Perry
Anderson, it had created a 'new radical public sphere', spreading from
universities and polytechnics out into a booming 'metropolitan counterculture'. It was there in the common rooms, where bearded young
lecturers eagerly discussed 'hegemony' and 'false consciousness'; it was
there in the pages of *Screen* magazine, where Marxism, feminism and
post-structuralism flowed together in a mighty river of left-leaning film
criticism; it was there in the new Women's Studies and Black Studies
courses at Kent and Sussex; it was there in the Centre for Contemporary
Cultural Studies at Birmingham, run by the Jamaican Marxist Stuart
Hall, which poured out papers on everything from the mass media to
the panic over mugging. It was there in the journal *History Workshop*,
established in 1976 as 'a journal of socialist and feminist historians', the
first issue beginning with a marvellously Spartist statement from the
'editorial collective' promising 'democratic scholarship' that questioned
'the structures of power and inequality in our society'. And by the end
of the decade, it was even there in the pages of the *New Statesman*,
whose writers were, as the Labour MP Austin Mitchell put it, increasingly 'writing for each other about Marxist economics, Marxist
sociology, feminism and race'.[15]

Since nothing dates quicker than intellectual fashion, the temptation
to poke fun at the academic world of the 1970s – its obsession with
subcultures, minorities and plural abstractions, its abasement before

French critical theory, its devotion to jargon, its scorn for readability and above all its towering, world-class earnestness – is almost overpowering. From the Open University biology professor who insisted that scientists needed to fight against the 'undemocratic' nature of their discipline, with its 'racist' and 'sexist' emphasis on 'experts' and 'Western modes of thought', to the Polytechnic of North London sociologists who dismissed the 'parent-child relation' as 'part of bourgeois ideology' and the health services as 'institutions of violence, whose function is to repair human labour power for capital', there was plenty of material for the satirist. Even at the time, some found it irresistible. David Lodge, for instance, drew on his experiences teaching English at Birmingham for his comic novels *Changing Places* (1975), *Small World* (1984) and *Nice Work* (1988). And Malcolm Bradbury, who taught at the University of East Anglia, produced one of the most celebrated campus novels of all in *The History Man* (1975), which tells the story of Howard Kirk, lecturer in sociology at 'Watermouth' (based on Sussex), the most repellent fictional monster of the decade.[16]

What makes Howard Kirk so obnoxious is not just his preening conceitedness, his duplicitous departmental backstabbing or his predatory stalking of students and colleagues alike. It is not even his Zapata moustache, 'hairy loose waistcoats' and 'pyjama-style blue jeans', which came as standard-issue in the common rooms of the mid-1970s. No, what makes Howard so unpleasant is his sheer, intolerant self-righteousness. As a fashionable media don with a renovated Georgian house full of scrubbed-pine furniture, African masks and earnest political tracts, he never, even for a moment, doubts his own rectitude. When Carmody, a conservative student dressed in a blazer and tie, reads out a formal, well-argued paper in one of his sociology classes, Howard is outraged, denouncing it as 'an anal, repressed paper in every way'. 'Do I have to agree with you, Dr Kirk, do I have to vote the way you do, and march down the street with you, and sign your petitions, and hit policemen on your demos, before I can pass your course?' Carmody asks in frustration. Even Howard allows that this is 'not required', although 'it might help you see some of the problems inside this society you keep sentimentalizing about'. Later, when Carmody says that he believes 'in individualism, not collectivism', and in culture as 'a value, not an inert descriptive term', Howard snaps that he must 'accept some sociological principles', or he will fail. But the truth is that Carmody is already doomed, a victim of Howard's narrow dogmatism. 'There are two sides to every question,' the head of the sociology department suggests weakly. But to Howard, this is anathema. 'You'll just sink into your liberal mess if you accept that,' he says contemptuously.[17]

Howard Kirk was, of course, a caricature – albeit one containing a considerable grain of truth. In some seminar rooms, passion did tip over into intolerance, with faintly comical results. One student who arrived at Middlesex Polytechnic in 1974 remembered that 'the teaching staff all called themselves Marxists' and told their students not only that most historians were 'apologists for capitalism', but that 'the law was a blunt instrument of capitalism'. Even in the law faculty, students would be 'howled down for disagreeing with Marxism in a seminar'. 'You couldn't get away from it,' he mused. 'There would be political speeches being made in the refectory as you were having your lunch.' It was the same story at the Polytechnic of North London, where student militants drew support from a small faction of Marxist academics who wanted to turn the university into a vehicle for revolution. The sociology department was such a Marxist hotbed that some students talked of coming to PNL 'to learn "the Gospel"', and refused to take courses taught by more conservative lecturers. Even some staff believed that academic standards were 'social [and] political constructs' and instruments of capitalist repression. During strikes and sit-ins, these lecturers were eager to mount 'alternative education' classes in the ominously named 'Occupied Sector': sample course titles included 'Perspectives for the British Class Struggle' and 'Social Workers Pick Up What Lawyers Smash'. And yet, tempting as it is to laugh at the academic world of the mid-1970s, it is worth bearing in mind that its influence has never died out. From postmodernism and post-colonialism to media studies and 'subaltern studies', the intellectual ideas pioneered by Howard Kirk's real-life equivalents shaped generations of scholars and students alike. Given that their proponents loudly claimed to be fighting for democratic values, there is a nice irony in the fact that such ideas drove a wedge between the campus and the general public, most of whom found them baffling and repellent. But then Howard's interest in the common man was never more than skin deep.[18]

Confined to their seminar rooms, the Howard Kirks of British academia would have been no more than an eccentric distraction from the grim challenges of the 1970s. But like Howard himself, who writes articles for the newspapers, appears on television and is a 'thorn in the flesh' of the local council, plenty of idealistic young intellectuals were determined to get involved in the political process. The obvious destination was the Labour Party, not just because it was the party of the left, but also because its institutional decline meant lots of opportunities for newcomers. Between 1964 and 1979, the party's active membership fell by more than half. Only twenty-five constituency parties had more than 1,500 members; many had only a handful, and one had just 14. For the outspoken and ambitious, it could hardly have been more promising territory; as a result, the party's social profile began to change dramatically. In cities like Birmingham and Liverpool, the typical Labour member had once been a 'lorry driver, bricklayer or miner'. But by the mid-1970s, many members were teachers, social workers or local government officers, with a good education and a vested interest in the public sector; and many, of course, were women. 'Everything's changed,' remarked an octogenarian farm worker in Somerset, who had been one of the founders of his local branch after the First World War. 'Even the Labour Party is like the rest of the world, it's got so educated that they aren't the same as they used to be. Everybody's so clever, 'tis hard to explain.'[19]

Nowhere was this process more apparent than in London areas such as Lambeth, Brent and Tower Hamlets. As skilled working-class families moved out and students, immigrants and young professionals moved in, moribund constituency parties became heartlands of support for feminism, gay rights and Irish republicanism. As the historian Jerry White remarks, left-wing politics in the city was now characterized by 'factionalism, shifting alliances and internecine strife' on a scale not seen for fifty years. Race and gender drove deep dividing lines through the Labour coalition: in areas like Hackney, for example, West Indian, Asian, Jewish and other immigrant communities competed for influence. Ironically, the one thing that was lost was a strong sense of collective class identity; increasingly, activists threw their energies into an eclectic collection of single-issue pressure groups, including 'conservationists, environmentalists, squatters, anti-nuclear campaigners, roads protesters, lobbyists for single mothers or playgroups, [and] protesters against abortion or kerb-crawling'. And many could not contain their contempt for the party leadership: 'an awful right-wing lot' and 'a disgrace to any Government', as a young Camden councillor called Ken Livingstone put it. The likes of Callaghan and Healey, agreed Valerie Wise, the 25-year-old vice chairman of the Greater London Council's Industry and Employment committee, had 'betrayed the working people of this country [and] given Labour a bad name. The sooner they go, the better.'[20]

To older Labour supporters, the influx of so many newcomers, often bitterly opposed to their own leadership and indifferent to the concerns of their working-class neighbours, was deeply worrying. 'Terrible,' wrote a depressed Bernard Donoughue after a meeting of the St Pancras North management committee in June 1976. 'Constantly passing mad motions denouncing the government. If ever the Party – and government – is really controlled by these middle-class, left-wing neurotics, who represent and are typical of nobody but themselves, then that is the end of either the Labour government or of Britain.' But he was fighting a losing battle: by the end of the decade many urban constituency parties were dominated by teachers, lecturers, social workers and lawyers. As the journalist Anthony Sampson remarked, 'the armies of young post-graduates and teachers had the time and the zeal to spend long evenings in local Labour party organisation, outlasting their more moderate rivals'. To the *Observer*'s Alan Watkins they were the 'polyocracy'; to the *Guardian*'s Peter Jenkins they were the 'lumpenpolytariat'; to the Grimsby MP Austin Mitchell they were the 'polyTrotracy'. But Donoughue, who watched in horror as they gradually took over in St Pancras North, preferred a rather more caustic term. 'What a bunch of wankers!' he wrote in September 1977. 'Not a serious working person there. All part-time polytechnic lecturers!'[21]

As a result, the Labour benches in Parliament were beginning to look different. It was harder than ever to keep order in the ranks, the Chief Whip told Wilson at the end of 1974, since the left-wing Tribune Group was 'more arrogant than ever'. Moderates and pro-Europeans found it increasingly hard to win selection as parliamentary candidates; instead, activists wanted people who reflected their ideals. A typical example was the MP for Bedwellty, elected in 1970 when he was just 28. Like many of his contemporaries, Neil Kinnock was reasonably well edu-cated: the son of a coalminer, he had been president of the Cardiff student union, pouring his energies into politics and graduating at the second attempt with a bare pass degree in history and industrial rela-tions. He was scornful of Parliament, a 'leather-bound supporters' club for Party leadership', but thought the unions could do no wrong. 'We are at the dawn of the age', he said proudly, 'when the power of democ-racy is moving out of its single base of the ballot box periodically on to the shop floor.' And like so many Labour activists, Kinnock and his wife Glenys, a schoolteacher who had joined CND in her teens, regarded Harold Wilson and his colleagues as Tory traitors. 'Don't be stupid, Neil,' Glenys remarked, puncturing his enthusiasm after the February

1974 election. 'These are the people who sold us out last time and they'll do just the same next.'[22]

For some activists, even the Labour left represented too much of a compromise with bourgeois capitalism. According to the tiny Workers' Revolutionary Party, which had no more than 3,000 members and was more of a cult than a political movement, Labour was a party of 'class traitors'. Parliamentary democracy, explained the WRP's best-known supporter, Vanessa Redgrave, was merely a 'façade to hide the conspiracies taking place outside'. As an Oscar-winning actress, Redgrave bestowed an incongruous sense of glamour on her political comrades, especially when she stood for Parliament in Newham North East in February 1974. Sadly, it was not accompanied by any sense of perspective or, indeed, humour. (Her brother Corin, who recruited her to the party, once remarked that humour was 'the last bastion of the bourgeoisie'.) Donning a guerrilla's khaki bonnet in a futile attempt 'to look unfeminine and proletarian', Redgrave declared that she wanted to 'rally the workers to smash all the power and class structures of capitalism'. The workers refused to be rallied: on election day, she won a grand total of 760 votes. But there was a genuinely sinister side to the WRP. Its veteran leader, Gerry Healy, took money from the Libyans and the Palestinian Liberation Organization, stole from party funds, beat up subordinates who disagreed with him and sexually assaulted dozens of female supporters. His so-called 'youth camps', held on a Peak District estate bought with Redgrave money, gave the tabloids something to get excited about, but most people saw him as a bully leading a handful of fanatics. Still, Vanessa Redgrave never lost the faith. 'I can truthfully say that I remain absolutely convinced of the necessity of Marxism and that not for a single day has my conviction been shaken,' she wrote many years later. She attributed this to 'the training and education I received from the party I joined, and from the man who led it for almost all those years, Gerry Healy'.[23]

For some strange reason, the WRP had a particular appeal to the acting profession. Another keen member, for example, was Frances de la Tour, who played Miss Jones in Rising Damp. 'I think it appeals psychologically to some of them,' remarked the general secretary of Equity. 'There is an air of drama to a life based on a belief in imminent revolution.' The party's popularity was particularly marked among the writers, directors and producers who worked on the BBC's Play for Today strand, such as Ken Loach, Roy Battersby, Colin Welland, Trevor Griffiths, Kenith Trodd, Roland Joffé and Tony Garnett, all of whom held more or less militant views.* This would have been no surprise to viewers who watched, say, Colin Welland's play *Leeds – United!* (November 1974), which meticulously recreated a strike by female clothing workers four years earlier, showing how the strikers had been sold out by their own leaders. *The Times*'s critic thought it was 'sad, savage and sincere', although he noted that, as so often on *Play for Today*, the employers and union leaders were 'prissy, devious or bovine', while the strikers were suspiciously saintly. Welland's play caused great offence to an eclectic collection of people, including Mary Whitehouse, the clothing employers and even the National Union of Tailors and Garment Workers, who were outraged at being shown as capitalist lackeys. But he was unapologetic. It had evidently 'touched on a very raw nerve', he remarked, 'which is exactly why I wrote the play in the first place'.[24]

Betrayal was a common theme of these painfully earnestly political dramas. In Trevor Griffiths' series *Bill Brand* (1976), for example, we follow a young left-wing Labour MP into Parliament, where he is horrified by the compromises and hypocrisies of political reality. 'We've had these buggers leading us before,' one character bitterly remarks of the party leadership. 'They're like dry rot . . . They think capitalism's a coat of paint, like a veneer, and underneath is the structure. And it isn't: capitalism IS the structure.' A similar message underpinned Jim Allen and Ken Loach's series *Days of Hope* (1975), which explores working-class life during and after the First World War. The point, explained its producer, Tony Garnett, 'was to show ten years of betrayal in the Labour Party and [the] trade union leadership. It ended up in defeat and the idea was that, if we showed how that came about, we could warn everybody to ensure it did not happen again.' Each episode had a fierce didactic thrust, from the plight of the working-class Tommy on the Western Front to the violent repression of Irish nationalism and the unions' alleged betrayal of the General Strike, which hardly endeared it to the more traditionally minded newspapers. After the final episode, the BBC ran a special edition of *Tonight* featuring a debate between the Trotskyite director Jim Allen and the *Telegraph*'s Bill Deedes, who called it 'sheer propaganda'. 'I was so angry,' the conservative novelist John Braine told the *Mail*, 'I couldn't take any more and almost kicked the set in.'[25]

---

* MI5 was sufficiently alarmed to warn the BBC that it was harbouring a cell of dangerous subversives. Some found themselves quietly dropped: Roy Battersby, for example, was effectively blacklisted by the BBC for years.

Much of the WRP's rhetorical ammunition was aimed at rival Trotskyite groups with distractingly similar names. Among the 'thick-bearded men and patch-jeans girls', as Anthony Sampson called them, there was precious little solidarity. The biggest group was the International Socialists, whose membership increased fourfold between 1970 and 1974, and who renamed themselves the Socialist Workers' Party two years later. Their greatest appeal was always on campuses (as remains the case today), but by the mid-1970s it had become clear even to the SWP that since students lacked any political or industrial muscle and had a national reputation for slothful inactivity, they were not a very good revolutionary vanguard. In the second half of the decade, therefore, the SWP launched a new offensive to win over trade union members, the Right to Work campaign, which provoked a punch-up with the police at Hendon but otherwise had few lasting results. More successful, at least in terms of publicity, was their drive to recruit black and Asian members, presented as an 'anti-fascist' campaign against the National Front. Under the guise of the Anti-Nazi League, the SWP helped to organize the giant Rock Against Racism concerts and clashed with the National Front in Southall in April 1979, an event that became notorious for the death of the teacher and SWP member Blair Peach. All the same, what was most striking was not the party's success but its failure. For all its efforts, it still had no more than 5,000 active members by the end of the decade.[26]

Still, numbers were not everything, as the most controversial far-left group was to prove. Its founding father was Ted Grant, a South African activist who in 1964 founded a Trotskyite newspaper, *Militant*. Its supporters, known as the Militant Tendency, called for the immediate introduction of full state socialism, including massive nationalization and workers' control. Unlike most far-left sects, they saw no problem with joining the Labour Party; indeed Grant and his allies positively encouraged it. Their aim, said the paper's editor Peter Taafe, was 'to carry the message of Marxism to the ranks of the labour movement and to its young people', largely by joining local constituency parties and converting them to the gospel. And as the Wilson government ran into trouble in the late 1960s, so Militant began to build momentum, especially among young activists disillusioned by the compromises of office. The key to Militant's success, as the journalist Michael Crick later explained, was that its supporters moved carefully and quietly. They started by joining the local Labour branch, selling newspapers and suggesting speakers, and before anyone knew it they had become a majority.

By 1970 they had taken over the Labour Party youth section, although at this stage there were only about a hundred active Militant supporters. Four years later, however, membership was around 500 and by 1979 it was more like 1,500.

On the surface, these figures were pretty poor: even the Doctor Who Appreciation Society had more members than that. One reason Militant's appeal was so limited was that its members were expected to lead a 'semi-puritanical lifestyle', keeping their hair short and wearing collars and ties. Smoking pot was a 'petty-bourgeois deviation'; rock music was not encouraged; feminists were not truly working-class. On top of that, life in Militant was expensive, since members were expected to hand over at least 10 per cent of their income in subscriptions. And it was boring: night after night selling newspapers, listening to speeches and attending committee meetings was not many people's idea of a good time. Yet those who stuck it out were extremely effective. Disciplined, punctual, apparently tireless, they made ground simply by outlasting their opponents, who often decided that they had better things to do. And by the mid-1970s, with the economy in ruins, social democratic politicians floundering helplessly and the world crisis creating a genuine sense of excitement on the far left, morale was buoyant. 'We must dig the roots in the wards and the constituencies as we have in the [Young Socialists],' declared a secret Militant policy statement in 1974. 'Many are still shells dominated by politically dead old men and women. They are now ossified little cliques. They will begin to change with an influx of new members ... Enormous opportunities will open up and we must be ready organizationally and politically to take advantage of them.'[27]

Even at the time, it was tempting to laugh at the sheer earnestness of all these would-be revolutionaries. Indeed, probably the most influential fictional personification of the far left was Robert Lindsay's 'Wolfie' Smith in the sitcom *Citizen Smith* (1977–80), the self-proclaimed leader of the Tooting Popular Front, whose Che Guevara beret and 'Power to the People!' slogan cannot disguise the fact that he is essentially an unemployed waster with an overdeveloped imagination. To many senior Labour figures, however, Militant infiltration was no laughing matter. Briefing the new Home Secretary, Merlyn Rees, in November 1976, the director general of MI5 found him 'fully seized of the importance of subversive penetration of the Labour Party ... He had spent his life in the Labour Party, but unfortunately the Labour Party was no longer what it had been.' Even Rees's Leeds South constituency had been infiltrated: according to MI5, the chairman of the local Young Socialists was 'in touch' with Militant, while the party chairmen in the neighbouring constituencies were both Militant members. Harold Wilson, too, was well aware of the problem. At the 1975 Labour conference he publicly rebuked 'subversives and trouble-makers' and lamented the 'infestation' of the 'so-called extreme left' in a few constituency parties. 'I have spent thirteen years so far trying to keep the Party together,' he mournfully told the National Executive Committee, 'and I do not like what is going on.'[28]

Characteristically, however, Wilson was reluctant to do anything about it. That autumn, Labour's National Agent, Reg Underhill, prepared a report on Trotskyite entryism, based on reports from regional offices and conversations with local party officials. Most of it was devoted to Militant, and Underhill quoted liberally from pamphlets in which the far left openly discussed their strategy to infiltrate the Labour Party. But when Underhill presented his report to the National Executive, many of the old left, such as Michael Foot and Barbara Castle, thought it smacked of the anti-Communist purges of the 1950s, while a Militant-backed Young Socialist member of the Executive insisted that their paper was no different to *Tribune*. As for Wilson, he merely read out an evasive statement from a piece of paper poorly concealed under the table. In the end, they agreed to let the report 'lie on the table with no further action'. This was typical Wilson: as Roy Hattersley remarked, he was unwilling ever to 'meet [the party] head on', but preferred to keep his head down and avoid any trouble. 'I saw Shirley Williams,' Bernard Donoughue recorded afterwards, 'and she was furious. She asked me to tell Healey when he arrived, and he reacted equally strongly.' But Wilson could not have cared less. He was, he admitted, 'totally bored of the whole business'.[29]

In the long run, the rejection of the Underhill report cost Labour dear. Leaked to *The Times* a few weeks later, it painted a clear picture of Trotskyite infiltration at the grass roots, providing both Conservative columnists and Militant's Labour critics with all the ammunition they could want. Some party members tried to fight back: in 1976, hoping to recapture the National Organization of Labour Students from Militant control, a group of moderate students launched the short-lived 'Operation Icepick', named after the weapon that had been used to kill Trotsky. But Militant's sheer discipline made it a tough opponent, and by 1977 MI5 reported that it had 'gained a foothold' in eighty-eight individual constituency parties. Despite growing criticism, the group sheltered under the protection of left-wingers like Tony Benn, who insisted that Marxism had always been 'a legitimate strain of thought' within the Labour Party. When the National Executive returned to the subject in January 1977, the left-wing MP Eric Heffer dismissed anti-Militant reports as 'Tory-inspired' and said he 'had known the Militant Tendency for a long time and the issue had been blown up out of proportion'. To his credit, Michael Foot warned that, by ignoring the Underhill report, they were 'helping our opponents', but nobody listened. A few months later, the National Executive agreed not to publish the Militant documents that Underhill had collected. 'There were always Marxists in the Party,' they concluded; 'there always had been and always would be.'[30]

For the time being, therefore, Militant's strength grew unchecked. And in the meantime, it was the Labour right that found itself under intense pressure. Ever since Wilson's defeat in 1970, the hard left had been demanding revenge for the betrayal of socialism. Incensed by his indifference to grass-roots opinion, they wanted the annual conference and the National Executive Committee to have greater control over party policy, with senior MPs effectively reduced to mouthpieces for the movement. In the summer of 1973, after Wilson had watered down Tony Benn's plans for massive public ownership, a dozen activists founded the Campaign for Labour Party Democracy (CLPD), calling for conference decisions to be 'binding'. And although Labour won power a few months later, the CLPD went from strength to strength, reaching out to civil liberties groups, nuclear disarmament campaigners, students and trade unionists. In 1974 they had the registered support of just 4 constituency parties, but by 1979 they had 77, as well as a further 85 trade union branches, most of them in white-collar public sector unions. By this stage they were demanding that MPs undergo 'mandatory reselection', so that apostates and appeasers could be rooted out. In 1976 reselection motions came in from 45 constituency parties, and in 1977 there were 79 more. A year later, the CLPD were convinced they had mandatory reselection in the bag. Only a blatant bit of political gamesmanship by the Amalgamated Engineering Workers' leader Hugh Scanlon, who claimed he had 'lost' his union's block vote, saved the day for the right. Despite the activists' outrage, however, they only had another year to wait.[31]

By this point the left had already taken two notable scalps. In the summer of 1972, left-wing activists in Lincoln voted by 75 votes to 50 to kick out their MP, the urbane Dick Taverne. The dispute had a long history: a decade before, when Taverne had first been selected, a hard-left activist called Leo Beckett had complained that he was too moderate. When Taverne defied the party whip to support Britain's membership of the EEC, Beckett saw his chance to strike. At first Taverne trusted that the party leadership would reverse the Lincoln activists' decision. But as hope began to fade, he took the spectacular gamble of resigning his seat to force a by-election in March 1973. Clearly he could not stand as a Labour candidate, so he ran under the banner of Democratic Labour, which earned him expulsion from the party. To universal surprise, however, he won the seat, beating the official Labour candidate. That only enraged the activists further: there were extraordinary scenes after the count, with the beaten Labour candidate snarling that Taverne was a 'freak' and one senior activist even trying to punch him. For a brief, shining moment it seemed that Taverne was the herald of a new politics: there was talk of his supporters becoming the nucleus of a new social democratic party, and Taverne begged his friend Roy Jenkins to leave Labour and campaign at his side. But Jenkins turned him down, preferring to 'go to ground like a skulking fox'. Labour had not yet swung definitively to the left; the social democrats' day had not yet dawned. And although Taverne held onto the seat in February 1974, he was beaten the following October by a young party apparatchik called Margaret Jackson. The man who masterminded her campaign was Leo Beckett. A few years later, she married him.[32]

Taverne's story was not unique. On the eve of the February 1974 election, Blyth deselected their MP Eddie Milne as punishment for blowing the whistle on the corruption inside the Labour-run local authorities in the North-east. Like Taverne, Milne ran as an independent and retained his seat, only to lose it the following October. But the case that captured most attention came two years later, when the activists in Newham North East turned on their MP, Reg Prentice. Having entered the Cabinet in 1974, first at Education and then at Overseas Development, Prentice had earned a reputation as the government's most right-wing minister, anxious about inflation, sceptical of the Social Contract and alarmed by what he saw as the abuse of union power. Unlike some of his natural allies, he was no claret-sipping dilettante, but a pugnacious former union official. Perhaps this inflamed his critics all the more; in any case, by the summer of 1975 his local party had turned against him. Newham was classic hard-left territory, a crumbling inner-city seat whose moribund Labour Party had few members and was ripe for a takeover by left-wing idealists. Some of these newcomers, though not all of them, were Militant members. But the Campaign for Labour Party Democracy also played its part; more than any other event, this was the moment that catapulted the CLPD into the national headlines. The irony, of course, was that for a movement supposedly dedicated to democracy, it showed remarkably little interest in what Prentice's constituents wanted. Despite the left's claims that Prentice had neglected the people of Newham, a straw poll found that at least seven out of ten people on the streets of east London supported him. As far as his opponents were concerned, though, that was totally irrelevant.[33]

So the Prentice affair dragged on. His fellow ministers lined up to back him; more than half of all Labour MPs spoke up in his support; even Harold Wilson, breaking his pledge not to interfere in constituency affairs, denounced the 'small and certainly not representative groups' who were infiltrating the Labour Party. Many people thought this was a crucial test case: praising Prentice's courage and honesty, *The Times* remarked that 'if a man like him cannot keep his place in Parliament, other Labour politicians can be expected to draw their own conclusions'. But work on what the paper called the 'Newham Scaffold' went on: at the end of July 1975, Prentice's activists deselected him. His friends rallied to his side: at a spectacularly bitter public meeting in East Ham, Roy Jenkins was heckled with shouts of 'Traitor!' from angry anti-immigration women, while assembled activists, some from Militant and the Socialist Workers' Party, others apparently from the National Front, bombarded him with flour bombs. While this eclectic gaggle of demonstrators exchanged punches in the aisles, Jenkins delivered a memorably blistering speech from the platform. Surrender to the hard left, he said, would be 'a possibly fatal perversion of the process of democracy so that it enthrones the minority, debases or destroys the man of courage and conviction, and further alienates from politics the majority of reasonable, sensible, moderate people . . . If Reg Prentice goes down, it will be the end of free speech and democracy in this country.'[34]

But go down he did. Although Prentice initially commanded considerable sympathy within the Labour Party, his outspokenness dismayed many of his own supporters. The Newham left-wingers, he claimed, were a 'little gang [of] Communists' who had gone 'completely round the bend'; by contrast, his own activists, who included the future Conservative MP Julian Lewis, struck some of his colleagues as worryingly right-wing.* At the Labour conference in September 1975, Prentice gave a remarkably inflammatory speech dismissing the left as 'bitter, class-consciousness and dogmatic', and by the following year, when he rejected Labour's latest policy document as 'irrelevant and irresponsible', his cause was rapidly withering. Not even his bitterest enemies, however, could have anticipated what he did next. Four days before Christmas 1976, Prentice melodramatically resigned from the government, declaring that Britain needed 'new leadership' to tackle its deep-seated economic problems. Ten months later, to the dismay of his friends and the delight of his critics, he announced that he was taking the Conservative whip. He had been converted, he said, not merely by his horror at the events in Newham, but by his admiration for Mrs Thatcher and Sir Keith Joseph. 'The Conservative Party today', he claimed, 'represents all the people, not just the privileged.' For his old party, however, Prentice had no such warm words. 'The only way we can prevent this country going on a further lurch down the Marxist road', he told *Weekend World*, 'is for the Labour Party to be soundly beaten at the next election.'[35]

For the hard left, the Prentice affair seemed the perfect gift. All along they had argued that the Labour right were a gang of crypto-Conservatives; now, it seemed, Prentice had furnished the proof. 'The CLPD and the movement for accountability,' said the hard-left activist Chris Mullin, later a Labour MP, owed Prentice 'a great debt of gratitude'. But that was not, of course, how everybody saw it. Prentice was 'well out of it', thought Bernard Levin, for whom the social democrats had 'already accepted so many of the Marxists' premises that, even if they were prepared to stand and fight (and most of them are not), they would have nothing to fight with'. That was Prentice's own view, too, and once the dust had settled he went on the offensive. 'The nature of the Left has changed,' he wrote in 1978. On the right, the moderates had 'lost their will to fight'; on the left, the 'starry-eyed idealists' of the past had given way to 'hardline, dogmatic Marxists'. All the time, he said, he was getting letters from people saying: 'I got so fed up with all the left-wing talk that I don't go any more. It is no longer the party I joined.'[36]

---

* Later, in an almost incredible twist, it emerged that Lewis had been secretly funded by the National Association for Freedom, which had decided to infiltrate the Newham constituency from the right.

Had Prentice been merely a lone eccentric, it would have been easy to ignore him. But he was not the only Labour MP to have walked out on his party. During Wilson's first administration, two right-wing back-benchers, Desmond Donnelly and Woodrow Wyatt, had rebelled over steel nationalization; curiously, both ended up writing for the *News of the World*.* Another Labour moderate, Christopher Mayhew, a junior minister under both Attlee and Wilson, defected to the Liberals in July 1974. His old party, he said mournfully, had become 'too vulnerable to the extreme left and too dependent on the unions'. The former Foreign Office minister Lord Chalfont gave similar reasons when he, too, quit the Labour Party the following September. Even Lord George-Brown, who had once been Wilson's deputy and Foreign Secretary, noisily walked out of the party in 1976, claiming that it no longer stood for 'individual freedom'. Brown's well-deserved reputation for drunken misbehaviour, however, meant that his departure was less damaging than it might have been. He had been inspired to leave, he told a television interviewer, after watching a BBC programme about Alexander Solzhenitsyn, which had filled him with 'tremendous guilt' about his position in the party. On his way home from the studio, Brown rounded off a memorable evening by collapsing drunkenly in the gutter. All the same, said an editorial in *The Times* the next day, he was 'a man of strong mind and strong heart who cares for the defence of the freedoms of his country . . . Lord George-Brown drunk is a better man than the Prime Minister sober.'[37]

Politicians had, of course, been swapping parties for generations. But there was something distinctive about the mid-1970s. Even at the time, commentators detected a shift away from the Labour Party, and by the end of the decade many of Mrs Thatcher's loudest cheerleaders were converts from the left. The historian Hugh Thomas, author of a defini-tive account of the Spanish Civil War, had once been a keen socialist. In October 1974, however, he voted Conservative for the first time. By 1977 he was writing speeches for Margaret Thatcher and in 1979 he became chairman of the Centre for Policy Studies. But Thomas was only one of a generation of public intellectuals who had once seen themselves as radical outsiders but were now swinging rapidly to the right, from the sociologist Caroline Cox and the columnist Bernard Levin to the novelist Kingsley Amis and the playwright John Osborne. Often from

---

* Donnelly killed himself in April 1974. Wyatt, however, became one of Mrs Thatcher's great confidants as well as a notoriously indiscreet diarist.

lower-middle-class grammar school backgrounds, they were horrified by the changes in education and intellectual fashion. The so-called Movement poets – Amis, Robert Conquest, Donald Davie and their friends – had come to prominence in the early 1950s, when they had been the outsiders. Now they were middle-aged, comfortably off, *established*: the kind of people threatened not just by Denis Healey's tax policies, but by the emergence of a new generation who despised their ironic detachment and talked instead about authenticity, self-expression and class struggle. For Amis, often regarded as one of the voices of his generation, this new style was utter anathema. Once a keen Labour supporter, he now thought it was the party of the 'abortion-divorce-homosexuality-censorship-racialism-marijuana package'. He had come round, he said, to 'grudging toleration of the Conservative Party because it is the party of non-politics, of resistance to politics'.[38]

Since Amis's conversion came in 1967, he was slightly ahead of the pack. Bernard Levin, for example, did not definitively change camps until ten years later, in a *Times* column full of contempt for Labour's 'incompetence', 'deceit' and 'shabby excuses'. Still, Levin was positively mild compared with the journalist Paul Johnson. Formerly an intemperate left-wing admirer of Aneurin Bevan, Johnson evolved almost seamlessly into an intemperate right-wing admirer of Margaret Thatcher. As another conservative polemicist, Christopher Booker, remarked at the time, Johnson had always had an uncanny resemblance to Sir Herbert Gusset, the splenetic reactionary invented by *Private Eye*, so his conversion was a bit less surprising than it might seem. All the same, it was pretty spectacular. Once, Johnson told the readers of the *New Statesman*, he had believed that Labour 'stood by the helpless and persecuted, and by the angular non-conformist who – wrong-headedly perhaps – reserved the right to think for himself'. But now, he realized, the people's party had become a 'repository of destructive envy and militant failure, a party of green-eyed monsters'. And as it 'drifted into collectivism', he saw that it posed a deadly threat to 'the individual conscience, the most precious gift humanity possesses'. The party was heading, Johnson wrote darkly, towards 'left-wing fascism', marked by 'an utter contempt for human life'.[39]

Given Johnson's history of extravagant rhetoric, the sheer violence of his tirade came as little surprise. What was notable about his latest effusion, however, was where it appeared: a slim volume entitled *Right Turn: Eight Men who Changed their Minds*, edited by the Conservative MP Patrick Cormack and published in the autumn of 1978. Each contributor had made a similar political journey. 'The authors of these essays have turned right,' Cormack wrote in the introduction, 'because they believe there is a *real risk* that our society will be replaced by the sort of materially, intellectually and spiritually impoverished tyranny that so many millions suffer from, and seek to escape from, in Eastern Europe, if the Labour Party prevails at the polls.' For the political journalist Edward Pearce, the 'politics of the mob' was likely to become an everyday part of British life; for Hugh Thomas, the apparent triumph of socialism was nothing more than 'fascism with a human face'. The Labour Party, agreed Lord Chalfont, would not rest until it had achieved the total 'nationalization of business and industry'. Even free speech, wrote the Cambridge don Graham Hough, was in grave danger. The real aim of the Social Contract, he explained, was 'a permanent tyranny; and naturally the leader in this field is Michael Foot'. If Foot got his way, 'articles such as this one will soon have to appear in *samizdat* form. The champions of liberty and fraternity will see to that.'[40]

Paranoid as it now sounds, *Right Turn* undoubtedly struck a chord. 'It cannot be entirely insignificant', wrote Ronald Butt in *The Times*, 'that so many intelligent men who have seen the effects of socialism at close quarters think that Labour is no longer a party for the freedom of the individual'. Reading the book on the train to Blackpool before the Labour Party conference, his colleague David Wood drew a similar conclusion. It was 'no more than two hours reading', he remarked, 'yet it has an importance surpassing a ton of doctoral theses ... for here we are brought to face questions that drive to the heart of things'. And it was not only journalists who thought so. Inside Conservative high command, the idea of building on the defections of former left-wingers had already occurred to Margaret Thatcher's advisers. A year earlier, the director of the Centre for Policy Studies, Alfred Sherman, had argued that the Tories should present themselves as the true heirs to the tradition of Keir Hardie and Ernest Bevin, who would have had 'much more in common with us than with Benn, Mikardo and the Tribuneites'. By using 'Hugh Thomas and his group of ex-Labour friends', Sherman wrote, 'we open a path to our door for many who are disgusted at Labour'. Margaret Thatcher loved the idea. 'She would like you to go ahead as soon as possible with the theme of "We are heirs to the Social-Democratic heritage,"' her political secretary told Sherman a few days later. But only after she had made it into Downing Street, boosted by millions of working-class votes, did it become clear how much the left had played into her hands.[41]

14

The Great Referendum Sideshow

BASIL: *We are all friends now, eh? All in the Market together,*
old differences forgotten, and no need at all to mention the
war. Sorry!

Fawlty Towers, 'The Germans', 24 October 1975

Benn has taken over this referendum. He will lose it, but it has
been his referendum, from inception to the end.

Bernard Donoughue's diary, 28 May 1975

In November 1974 the Labour Party conference met at Central Hall, Westminster, to celebrate a second successive election victory. Thanks to the IRA bombings, security was stiflingly tight, but one foreign intruder did manage to penetrate the cordon. At Harold Wilson's invitation, Helmut Schmidt had been invited to deliver fraternal greetings from the Social Democrats. The omens were not promising. Only the day before, the conference had voted to support British withdrawal from the European Economic Community, and there were rumours that left-wing delegates would stage a mass walkout during the West German Chancellor's speech. But as soon as Schmidt got to his feet, the mood lightened. He came, he said, as a friend and comrade; although he hoped Britain would stay in Europe, he felt rather like 'a man urging on a Salvation Army meeting the advantages of drink'. The delegates laughed; he had them. 'How handsome and relaxed he looked!' admitted the sceptical Barbara Castle. 'His speech was masterly: it was a joy to hear how skilfully he dodged all the pitfalls and how cleverly he played on those emotions in his audience which were most likely to be favourable to him . . . Above all he had them rolling in the aisles and once again I was surprised to realize what a good sense of humour Germans have.'[1]

The next day's papers were full of Schmidt's triumph. 'He made some good jokes, quoted Shakespeare, spoke flatteringly of the Labour Party's historic contributions to trade unionism and the welfare state, and in general cut the ground from under the feet of [the sceptics],' thought the Foreign Secretary, Jim Callaghan. Even Tony Benn, a ferocious critic of the Common Market, allowed that the German Chancellor had been 'very witty and amusing'. On the right of the Labour Party, meanwhile, many listeners wished they could keep Schmidt and send Harold Wilson off to Bonn. 'In its confidence, crispness, political agility, its relationship to the world of political ideas, and even its use of the English language,' wrote the GLC councillor Stephen Haseler, Schmidt's speech had made for a 'stark contrast to the third-rate performances of the British politicians. To those who observed this spectacle it represented a poignant picture of the decline of British political leadership.' But among those who hated the idea of European speakers at Labour conferences, old attitudes died hard. 'I smell a plot to fiddle the Common Market referendum next year,' declared John Ryman, the backbench MP for Blyth. 'The speech by the West German Chancellor was an impertinence. Why should this patronising Hun lecture the great British Labour Party?'[2]

Memories of the struggle against the Hun were everywhere in the mid-1970s. 'Every game, every conversation, every television programme seemed in some way to spring from the War,' wrote one child of the Wilson years, recalling 'a ceaseless round of Airfix model planes, *Commando* comics, *Dad's Army*, military games, Action Man and dreams of visiting the Imperial War Museum, a form of childhood that had been consecrated in Britain since the War itself'. Comics recreated a world in which plucky Tommies were forever hacking their way past square-headed sadists, while 'every playtime seemed to be devoted to loving reconstructions of El Alamein or D-Day'. On television, meanwhile, the Second World War seemed to have taken over the schedules, from the anti-German jokes in *Till Death Us Do Part*, *Whatever Happened to the Likely Lads?*, *Fawlty Towers* and *Rising Damp* to the sententious brilliance of *The World at War*, which ran for 26 episodes over the winter of 1973–4. The biggest hit of the season, though, was the BBC's *Colditz*, which concluded in April 1974 with audiences of almost 19 million people. Escapist entertainment it may have been, but it was firmly rooted in memories of the war: in January, the Imperial

War Museum invited veterans of the camp to a reunion party, where they mingled with actors and production staff.

Even *Are You Being Served?*, which began life in 1973, found it hard to escape the shadow of the war. In its third episode, the staff at Grace Brothers find themselves stranded by a transport strike and are forced to spend the night in the store, sleeping in tents and telling old war stories. 'Some people seem to forget,' says Mr Rumbold, 'that men like Captain Peacock and myself were instrumental in making this a country fit for heroes to live in.' In April 1975, meanwhile, the store holds a 'German week', decorating the shop floor with German flags, playing German music and serving German wines. It is, of course, a disaster. 'I won't forget being thrown flat on my back on Clapham Common by a landmine. And the German air force was responsible,' Mrs Slocombe says darkly. 'All the other times she was flat on her back,' Mr Lucas puts in helpfully, 'the American air force was responsible.'[3]

'World War II has turned from history into myth,' *Colditz*'s producer Gerard Glaister told the *Daily Mail* in 1977. Aged just 24, Glaister had joined the RAF in 1939, captained a Blenheim bomber and flew reconnaissance missions over the Western Desert, earning the Distinguished Flying Cross. As he saw it, the war was 'our last frontier, the English equivalent of the Western'. But although politicians never wearied of appealing to the spirit of Dunkirk and the Blitz, the contrast between the imagined unity of wartime and the 'conflict, envy and cynicism' of the present was painful to contemplate. Watching a documentary on the late Richard Dimbleby in September 1975, Bernard Donoughue, who was only 11 when the war ended, wished he could have been 'a war correspondent, in a genuine war I believed in, when Britain mattered'. Three months later, one of the war's great chroniclers, A. J. P. Taylor, told an interviewer that he wished Britain could turn back the clock to 1940, 'the best time we ever had, in my lifetime, when the country was best run, the most egalitarian society and the most efficient'. Perhaps, he mused, 'we might consider having a war with somebody – but it would have to be someone just big enough to give us a fright, and yet not big enough to defeat us'. A few weeks later Taylor told his wife that he had abandoned plans to revise his classic book on Britain between the wars. It would 'destroy the spirit', he explained. 'When I wrote [it] I still had great hopes for the future. Now I have none.'[4]

What made memories of the war particularly painful was the fact that Britain seemed to have fallen so far behind its former enemy. Since the early 1960s, the comparison between the British and German economies had been simply embarrassing, and it got even worse in the decade that followed. Britain's inflation rate for the 1970s was 13 per cent; West Germany's was just 5 per cent. Britain's unemployment rate was 4 per cent; Germany's was 2 per cent. Britain's productivity growth rate was barely 1 per cent; the Germans' was more than 3 per cent. 'At the moment,' admitted the *Express* the day after Schmidt's appearance at the Labour conference, 'the Germans are top dogs. After the awful destruction of the war, Germany started from scratch and everything from factory management to parliamentary government is geared to the present. The admirable cooperation usually shown in German industrial relations contrasts with British discord and Germany's enormous balance of payments surplus puts everyone else to shame.' The Cummings cartoon on the same page rather said it all: wearing a Wehrmacht uniform adorned with the Red Cross, Schmidt is dragging the battered figure of Harold Wilson along on a trolley marked 'Britain – Sick Man of Europe'. 'You WANT Britain in Europe, Herr Schmidt?' reads the caption. 'Then you must either be the greatest humanitarian since Florence Nightingale or be off your head!'[5]

Even on the football field the Germans had become the model. When West Germany humiliated England 3–1 at Wembley in April 1972, the newspapers could not contain their admiration for the victors. 'From the cool heads in defence to the glittering flair of the forward line', wrote the *Daily Mail*'s Ian Wooldridge, this was a 'team to make nonsense of the pulp magazine conception of the German character and to make a few million adults realise that their prejudices are as obsolete as Bismarck's spiked helmet.' 'No Englishman', agreed the *Observer*'s Hugh McIlvanney, 'can ever again warm himself with the old assumption that, on the football field if nowhere else, the Germans are an inferior race.' But by now the idea of the Germans as inferior, given their economic accomplishments, was simply laughable. 'Hello Germany!' proclaimed a four-day *Daily Mirror* feature in May 1975, looking enviously at the 'golden journey' of 'one of the richest nations in the world', where, unlike in Britain, the unions held 'a solid and united front against inflation'. For many British politicians, West Germany was the ideal: strolling around Bonn one summer, Bernard Donoughue was amazed 'how clean and optimistic everything was, how smart and efficient the shop assistants are'. This was, he wrote enviously, 'the spin-off of a successful nation'. Even Margaret Thatcher, not known for her fondness for all things German, told the Commons in November 1975 that 'Germany is doing four times better in dealing with inflation than we are and therefore can speak with more authority. The Prime Minister has to rely on Germany and America to reflate because he has lost control of the economy here. He has to go to other private enterprise economies to try to get the Socialist-run economy of this country out of its financial mess.'[6]

But German observers, too, were conscious how the balance of power had shifted. Ten months after his Labour conference speech, Helmut Schmidt told the *Guardian* that although 'a very anglophile person', he was sorry that Britain had become so 'damned class-ridden'. 'I would not feel that Britain is advanced,' he said sadly. 'By no means – not regarding her social set-up, not regarding her industrial set-up, and not even regarding her political set-up. I think that the English nation for too long a number of years has taken too many things for granted.' He had harsh words for Britain's 'outmoded' trade unions: while he thought German unions 'behaved extremely sensibly', he was appalled that in Britain 'ten, twelve or fifteen times' more working days were lost to strikes every year. 'British trade unionists', he remarked, 'are the right-wingers because they don't really want to have a say in the British economy and society.' He was right about that. Only a few months later, Harold Wilson set up a committee under the historian Alan Bullock to discuss copying European models of industrial democracy, with workers' representatives sitting on companies' boards. When the committee reported in January 1977, it had warm words for the West German system, seeing a 'strong and direct connection' between their excellent labour relations and their economic miracle. But its recommendations never made headway. Condemned by the right as a surrender to union power and by the left as an attempt to co-opt the forces of progress into bourgeois capitalism, the Bullock report withered on the vine – just as Helmut Schmidt might have predicted.[7]

When Harold Wilson returned to power in 1974, Britain felt more like part of Europe than at any time in living memory. The previous January, after a gruelling parliamentary battle, Ted Heath had taken the United Kingdom into the European Economic Community. Nine million people a year now holidayed outside Britain's shores, turning Benidorm and Torremolinos into household names and bringing back a dubious taste for sun, sangria and sombreros. From duvets and au pair girls to tourism and town-twinning, from the *Eurovision Song Contest* and *It's a Knockout* to Abba's 'Waterloo' and Sylvia Vrethammar's 'Y Viva España', European influences seemed to be everywhere. And yet exceptionalism – the belief that Britain was different, and should steer its own course free from Continental entanglements – died hard. Millions of Britons might sear themselves on the beaches of Spain, yet they insisted on surrounding themselves with reminders of home, from fish and chips and warm beer to the *Daily Mirror* and kiss-me-quick hats. There had been no referendum on European entry, and many people still deeply disliked the idea. Even on the day that Britain entered the EEC, a poll for *The Times* had found that only 38 per cent of people were pleased at the prospect, with 39 per cent unhappy and 23 per cent undecided. And a year later, two out of three people agreed that Britain should have 'developed links with the Commonwealth' instead. 'Now that we are in the Common Market,' one Black Country shop steward told an interviewer, 'we are just like all those other countries who have foreigners making decisions for us.'[8]

As the product of a lower-middle-class Huddersfield home, Harold Wilson looked across the Channel with deep suspicion. In the late 1960s he had made a doomed bid to join the EEC, but at heart, he admitted, he had always been 'a Commonwealth man'. He was 'basically a north of England, non-conformist puritan', wrote Bernard Donoughue. 'The continental Europeans, especially from France and southern Europe, were to him alien.' On top of that, Wilson's party was deeply divided over Europe. Most right-wing ministers, such as Roy Jenkins, Shirley Williams and Bill Rodgers, were passionately for it, while outspoken left-wingers such as Tony Benn, Peter Shore and Barbara Castle regarded it as a terrible capitalist cartel. When Heath announced that he was taking Britain into Europe, therefore, Wilson refused to back him. Instead, Wilson supported Tony Benn's plan for a national referendum, giving the British people the right to decide whether they remained in the Common Market. In the February 1974 manifesto, he promised that Labour would renegotiate Heath's terms to get a better deal on the Community budget and Common Agricultural Policy. If better terms were forthcoming, Wilson explained, the government would advise people to vote Yes in the referendum. If not, it would support withdrawal.[9]

Since Britain had been in Europe only since January 1973, Wilson's new partners were less than impressed by his demand to renegotiate the terms. In the French news magazine *Le Point*, a cartoon showed Harold Wilson as a *pétanque* player, invited by Helmut Schmidt and Valéry Giscard d'Estaing to join them instead of playing on his own. First Wilson demands that they carry his balls for him; then that they let him throw with his feet apart; then that he be allowed to throw outside the circle. 'Pick up my balls for me, please,' he says. 'I can't bend down. Public opinion won't stand for it.' They humour him, and at the end, Giscard asks: 'Well, do you like *pétanque*?' 'No!' Wilson says, walking away. 'You Continentals don't have any sense of sportsmanship!' Another cartoon, published in the satirical magazine *Le Canard enchaîné* (the French answer to *Private Eye*), made the point rather more graphically. Wilson, a diminutive and frankly ridiculous figure, is in bed with a gorgeous naked woman, who wears a crown labelled 'EUROPE'. Positioned between her thighs, he gazes plaintively into her eyes. 'Get in or get out, my dear Wilson,' she says wearily. 'But do stop all this ridiculous coming and going.'[10]

What really shocked European observers, though, was that Wilson's representatives seemed oblivious to the courtesies of international diplomacy. When the new Foreign Secretary, Jim Callaghan, met his counterparts in Luxembourg in April 1974, he opened with a speech that was regarded as 'blunt to the point of rudeness'. Unless Britain's partners gave ground, Callaghan said brusquely, he would advise the electorate that the terms were 'unacceptable' and ask them to support 'withdrawal of the United Kingdom from the Community'. By the staid standards of European diplomacy, this was sensational stuff: over the next few days, Callaghan's rudeness was the talk of the chancelleries of Europe. Yet beneath the John Bull exterior, the Foreign Secretary was nothing if not a pragmatist, and by the late summer he was beginning to mellow. As he admitted, the terms were hardly the stuff of life and death, and when he found himself haggling over 'import levels of apricot halves' and the precise distinction between 'mutton and lamb', he felt 'not so much a Foreign Secretary as a multiple grocer'. One low point, he recalled, came when 'nine Foreign Ministers from the major countries of Europe solemnly assembled in Brussels to spend several hours discussing how to resolve our differences on standardising a fixed position of rear-view mirrors on agricultural tractors. I wondered what Palmerston, Salisbury or Bevin would have made of it.'

By the end of the year an agreement seemed close. At a summit in December, Wilson promised that he would support Britain's European membership if Schmidt and Giscard agreed to amend the Community budget, and when they reconvened at Dublin in March 1975, the deal was done. Precisely what had been gained was not obvious, since the terms were remarkably similar to Heath's. Even a Foreign Office diplomat admitted that renegotiation 'never produced any financial results'. In essence, it was nothing more than a gigantic public relations exercise, designed to mollify the Labour left and prepare the ground for the referendum campaign. But it was not entirely pointless; as David Butler and Uwe Kitzinger point out in their definitive analysis of the referendum,

In this glorious cartoon for the *New Statesman* (13 December 1974), Nicholas
Garland has great fun with Wilson's efforts to renegotiate the European terms.
Among the details are a tiny George Brown, a prostrate Ted Heath,
a champagne-quaffing Roy Jenkins and a suitably haughty
Valéry Giscard d'Estaing.

'time was of the essence'. By the spring of 1975, the British people had
had two and a half years to get used to European membership, strengthening their sense that it would be better to stick with the status quo than
to face an uncertain future alone. If the referendum had been held earlier, it might have produced a very different result.[11]

On 17 March, Wilson reported to the Cabinet that the talks had been
a glorious triumph. 'We have substantially achieved our objectives,' he
said proudly, since the Community was 'now operating much more
under the political direction of the Governments of member states' – a
very dubious assertion indeed. 'The cohesion of Western Europe might
well be disrupted if we were to leave the EEC, and the British people
might be misled into taking the view – which had bedevilled British policies for decades after the Second World War – that we remained a great
major world power in our own right,' recorded the Cabinet minutes. On
top of that, 'the Community was not now developing in a federalist direction; as long as we remained members we could prevent it developing
in that way.' (This, as later events would show, was even more dubious.)
Not all Wilson's colleagues, though, were convinced. 'The Community

will destroy the whole basis on which the labour movement was founded, and its commitment to democratic change,' insisted Tony Benn, who predicted that Britain would find itself on a 'federal escalator'. 'We're giving up so much,' agreed Michael Foot. 'We shall dismember Parliament and the UK.' In the end, the Cabinet voted 16 to 7 to recommend staying in. In other circumstances, the split would have been a disaster, but Wilson had already promised that during the referendum campaign ministers would be free to campaign on either side. 'It is a triumph for HW,' wrote Bernard Donoughue. 'He has held the party together and put us in a position to stay in the Market. Nobody else could have done that.'[12]

The referendum was set for Thursday, 5 June, and the question – 'Do you think the UK should stay in the European Community (Common Market)?' – could hardly have been simpler. On the face of it, this was a seismic moment: not merely the first national referendum in Britain's history, but an opportunity for its people to choose between proud isolation on the one hand, and closer union with the Europeans on the other. But it did not seem that way at the time. Coming so soon after two general elections, the referendum never really caught the imagination. For one thing, the campaign had no shape, only spluttering into life around the middle of May, when both camps began holding press conferences. Unlike in a general election, the Prime Minister never really threw himself into the campaign, giving just eight very unenthusiastic speeches, while his Foreign Secretary was even more elusive. 'I am not pro, nor am I anti,' Callaghan told Robin Day during a phone-in show. 'What are you doing on this programme?' asked a mystified Day. 'You're here to advise people to vote "Yes", aren't you?' But the truth was that neither Callaghan nor Wilson could muster any passion for their cause. Wilson was 'clearly unhappy at having to come out so firmly in favour of the Market', noted an amused Donoughue. 'He is required to be in favour but he is really a Little Englander, and at heart he agrees with every word that Peter Shore says. So he fights to the end against actually telling people to vote yes.'[13]

Wilson's ambiguity was symptomatic of the entire campaign. Confusingly, the battle lines were blurred. Seven Cabinet ministers opposed European membership, while 145 Labour MPs had voted against the government's recommendations and the party's special conference had voted by a huge majority to pull out of the European Community. The unions, too, were divided: although the TGWU, ASTMS and the printing unions recommended a No vote, the GMWU, APEX and the railwaymen all supported the Yes campaign. But while Wilson hesitated to pin his colours to the mast, the new leader of the opposition had no such qualms. Since Conservative voters were overwhelmingly pro-European, Margaret Thatcher had nothing to lose by backing the Yes campaign. There was 'not a genuine alternative' to British membership, and Europe's future depended on 'working closely together on trade, work and other social matters which affect all our peoples'. The Conservative Party, she told her first campaign press conference, 'has been pursuing the European vision almost as long as we have existed as a Party . . . We are inextricably part of Europe. Neither Mr Foot nor Mr Benn nor anyone else will ever be able to take us "out of Europe", for Europe is where we are and where we have always been.'[14]

Rather awkwardly, Mrs Thatcher was joined at her first press conference by the unsmiling figure of Edward Heath, who had agreed to be the chairman of the Conservative Group for Europe. Perhaps wisely, Thatcher chose to play the modest protégée rather than the Iron Lady. 'It is especially appropriate that we should open the Conservative campaign to keep Britain in Europe under your chairmanship,' she said bashfully, 'because you have done more than anyone else for the Conservative cause in Europe, and to see that Britain's place is in Europe. Naturally, it's with some temerity that the pupil speaks before the master, because you know more about it than any of the rest of us.' These words cut no ice with Heath; as she was speaking, the camera caught him glaring at her with undisguised loathing. And although he quoted her statement in his memoirs, he then declared that he had been 'disappointed' by her efforts.* But it is a myth that she did nothing to help. She visited the European Assembly, gave television interviews and a few speeches, and most memorably, posed in front of Churchill's statue in Parliament Square with nine women in woolly jumpers, each decorated with the flag of a European member state. She might not have shared Heath's passion; but nobody listening to her in the summer of 1975 could have doubted that Mrs Thatcher was a keen European.[15]

By and large, it was the Tories who provided the backbone of the official Yes campaign, Britain in Europe (BIE), handing out leaflets, booking speakers, organizing rallies and getting out the vote on Refer-

---

* An ITN clip of the Thatcher–Heath press conference can be seen on YouTube, though it is easy to be distracted by the comments below it. 'What a wicked man he was,' writes 'realzoomy'. 'Yes, wicked as in awesome,' replies 'Sir Edward Heath'. 'He was a great, imposing, impressive, astonishing, awe-inspiring man, unlike you, you spent old has-been hag.'

endum Day. Even the campaign headquarters off Piccadilly was borrowed from Mrs Thatcher's future confidant Alistair McAlpine, then treasurer of the European League for Economic Co-operation. The campaign was not entirely a Conservative affair, of course: the Liberals were staunchly pro-European, while the Labour Campaign for Britain in Europe, run by Shirley Williams and Dick Mabon, boasted 88 MPs, 21 peers and 25 senior union officials. BIE also commanded the keen support of the Confederation of British Industry, which set up a European Operations Room and sent out a million documents encouraging a Yes vote. Businessmen had long supported membership of the Common Market: in a poll for *The Times* in April, 415 out of 419 chairmen of major companies said they wanted Britain to stay in. As a result, BIE had no problem getting money. Shell, Marks & Spencer, ICI, GKN and Vickers each donated £25,000 to the campaign; Ford, IBM, Rank and Reed all gave £20,000; and Legal & General, Royal Insurance, Sun Alliance and Unilever each gave £15,000. With the government giving a further £125,000 to both camps, the BIE campaign had a war chest of almost £1.5 million. Not even the Conservatives had ever spent as much on a national campaign.[16]

Branded with a Union Jack-coloured dove in flight, the Yes campaign's advertisements were everywhere in the weeks before Referendum Day. Many played on the perennial concerns of jobs and prices, insisting that families would be much more prosperous if Britain stayed in, but some other old favourites crept in, too. On 8 May, for example, newspapers ran the following ad:

> Thirty years ago today, the war in Europe ended.
>
> We called that day – VE Day.
>
> Millions had suffered and died in the most terrible war Europe had ever seen.
>
> On VE Day we celebrated the beginnings of peace.
>
> Vote Yes to make sure we keep it.
>
> Keep Britain in Europe.

But not all their ads were quite so solemn. Another trumpeted the Yes campaign's long list of celebrity supporters, from Alec Guinness and Peter Ustinov to Susan Hampshire and Joyce Grenfell, from Graham Greene and Stephen Spender to Don Revie and Derek Dougan. The nation's favourite policeman, *Dixon of Dock Green*'s Jack Warner, shared his pro-European enthusiasm with the readers of the *Daily Mail*, while Henry Cooper and Brian Close appeared in television commercials. Even Kenneth Williams recorded a pro-European message for the BBC, though not all his *Carry On* comrades shared his views. 'Lunch with Bernard [Bresslaw] (Anti-EEC) and Elke (Sommer) and me who are pro-EEC,' he recorded on 10 April. 'Quite long discussion. Bernard maintains it is a false union and that it will inevitably lead to trouble.' But even Bresslaw admitted that the referendum 'will be won by the Marketeers'.[17]

BIE's greatest asset was that its spokesmen were among the most popular public figures in the country. According to a Harris poll, the politicians most respected by the public were Harold Wilson and Ted Heath (each admired by 42 per cent), followed by Jeremy Thorpe (40 per cent), Roy Jenkins (34 per cent), Willie Whitelaw and Shirley Williams (both 33 per cent) and Jim Callaghan (31 per cent). Of these six names, four were active in the BIE campaign, while Wilson and Callaghan made vaguely supportive noises. The real star was Heath, who hammered away with an articulacy and passion that astonished his critics. Only inside Europe, he insisted, could the British 'fulfil ourselves as a nation'; as for the sceptics, 'their talk of sovereignty would only make sense if the Royal Navy ruled the waves and gunboats could be dispatched anywhere in the world'. At rallies around the country, he cut an implausibly dashing figure, bounding on to great torrents of applause. 'There was no doubting [his] new-found, or rediscovered, popularity when he appeared, looking aggressively bronzed, to address a Britain in Europe rally in Leeds Town Hall yesterday,' reported *The Times* on 2 June. As he entered the stage, flanked by Cyril Smith and Reg Prentice, 'the 2,000-strong crowd rose cheering and clapping'. 'That's for Mr Heath,' an elderly man whispered to the watching reporter.[18]

In an age of deep ideological polarization, the experience of the BIE campaign came as a welcome tonic to its chief spokesmen. Behind the scenes the key figures were Roy Jenkins and Willie Whitelaw, who set the tone of good-humoured collaboration. The steering group, one member said later, 'was one of the best committees I have ever attended . . . Perhaps we were all on our best behaviour. Perhaps there was an unusually high proportion of professionals who knew how to fight elections and just got on with it.' For Jenkins, an increasingly lonely figure inside Wilson's Cabinet, the experience of working with similarly centrist figures was 'a considerable liberation of the spirit'. Men like Whitelaw, he thought, 'epitomised the feeling that the "yes" side was the side of sense, substance and public spirit'. Like many of his supporters in the media – especially in *The Times* – Jenkins hoped that the campaign might lead to a political realignment, producing a coalition that would address Britain's 'gross inflation and subservience to the unions'. But of course the realignment never happened: too many people were still attached to their tribal loyalties. Looking back later, Jenkins lamented that he had not done more to keep the BIE spirit alive. 'I look back on 1975', he wrote, 'as a great missed opportunity for Heath and Whitelaw and a whole regiment of discarded Conservative "wets" as much as for Shirley Williams and Steel and me.'[19]

At the grass-roots level, too, the Yes campaign often looked uncannily like a dry run for the launch of the SDP. For the journalist Hugo Young, its activists were 'a fraternity of the middle-minded'; for the Marxist historian E. P. Thompson, it was conducted through 'a haze of remembered vacations, beaches, bougainvillea, business jaunts and vintage wines'. Despite his sneering tone, Thompson was not far wrong. In Huntingdon, the local Yes group was set up by an export manager who had joined the Tories in 1961, 'flirted with South Kensington Liberals in a vegetarian restaurant' and became a Liberal activist in 1974. In Aberystwyth the key figure was a Liberal postgraduate student; in Sussex, one group was 'formed over gin-and-tonic one Sunday morning in February'. By May there were more than 300 such groups, and by Referendum Day the total had reached 452. Like high-minded groups through the decades, they depended on the voluntary efforts of middle-class women who put up posters, organized lunchtime lectures and evening discussions, and sent speakers to Rotary Club lunches, Townswomen's Guilds and school debates. Cannily, their pamphlets often played on local concerns: 'Nuneaton and Bedworth will be better off within the EEC'; 'Rugby, the hub of the British road and rail networks communicating with Europe, is ideally placed to benefit'; 'The Border area has proved to be highly suitable for the growing of vegetables, especially peas. Access to the European Common Market will offer greater opportunities for the full development of this potential.'

The really extraordinary thing, though, was how well different activists worked together, perhaps because they came from similar backgrounds and identified with the moderate wings of their respective movements. In Nottingham, one Labour activist fondly remembered, 'the Conservatives were a wow at welcoming people', even putting on 'lilac or plum-coloured ties instead of the usual blue, as a conciliatory gesture to the Socialists'. Outside Bristol, the Tories sent their loudspeaker car to advertise the visit of a pro-European Labour MP; in East

Grinstead, the local Conservative MP toured the constituency trailing all three party colours. Interviewed afterwards, many activists described the campaign as a 'joy', 'refreshing' or 'invigorating'. 'It was marvellous to be free of the traditional restraints; the caution of agents, the touchiness of the old guard, the parsimony of treasurers, the endless cups of tea,' said one Labour MP. 'It had all the improvisation of Dunkirk and much of the steadfastness of the Battle of Britain.'[20]

The No camp – officially the National Referendum Campaign (NRC) – was not a happy ship. While the pro-Europeans cultivated a moderate image, many Get Britain Out branches were rather less keen to stick to the middle of the road. In Braintree, the local Get Britain Out group was almost entirely Communist-dominated; on Merseyside the Communists were 'so much in evidence' that some Labour activists refused to join the campaign; in Ipswich, the No campaign was staffed by a peculiar alliance of Labour activists, Communists, disaffected Tories and a married couple described as 'not quite National Front, but close'. This was not a recipe for success: in Burnley, the chairman was an avowed anarchist, the secretary a Communist and the Treasurer a Labour supporter, while other activists included a 'solitary member of the Conservative Party' who was said to feel 'rather out of place'. Some people found this collaboration invigorating – a woman from Norfolk was pleasantly surprised to find that 'not all Trade Unionists are selfish left-wing extremists but are in many cases more patriotic than many a Tory and certainly as hard working as many employers!' – but others were less enthused. Only her 'passionate love of this country', a Twickenham woman said, had given her 'the stomach ... to consort with Communists, International Socialists, Labour Party members and Maoists'. And many groups were frankly a mess. 'Our campaign was a shambles from beginning to end,' one activist wrote, blaming Communist infiltration for alienating 'all [the] moderate and right-wing voters'.

At the national level the No campaign was little better. An uneasy coalition of hard-left and hard-right groups, the NRC was terribly short of money. While their opponents had £1.5 million to spend, the anti-Europeans had a derisory £133,630. Embarrassingly, all but £9,000 had come from the government. One commentator thought the competition was like a race between a Formula One car and a bicycle, while a visitor from the Yes camp 'stumbled out of the NRC offices saying that it was like taking candy from a baby'. Looking back, Butler and Kitzinger thought the No campaigners did tremendously well to hold their own, despite the great gulf in 'money, facilities and in many respects, professionalism'. But they could not match the glitter and glamour of their opponents: the only celebrities who actively supported the campaign were the unlikely triumvirate of Kenneth Tynan, Harry H. Corbett and Paul Johnson. To make matters worse, Paul McCartney announced that he would be voting No for patriotic reasons. Since the referendum came only a few days after Wings released their fourth album, the result can perhaps be explained by the fact that his musical crimes were so fresh in voters' minds.[21]

The NRC's other obvious problem was the lack of a popular spokesman to match Heath, Jenkins and Whitelaw. An incisive cartoon in the *Evening Standard* showed a 'Get Britain Out' march led by Tony Benn, Enoch Powell and Michael Foot, surrounded by banners reading 'Trotskyists', 'National Front', 'Orange Order', 'Communist Party' and 'IRA'. None of these men had a moderate reputation: by far the most popular was Powell (liked by 33 per cent of voters), while only 17 per cent liked Benn or Foot. As the polls suggest, every time they spoke they probably lost votes rather than gained them. On top of that, the senior figures never worked well together. Their catering was adventurous enough: when they met to plan their strategy on 16 March, Barbara Castle served 'taramoosalata' and goulash, an oddly Continental choice for such an occasion, which left Jack Jones 'a bit apprehensive'. But after speaking to 2,000 people in Manchester's Free Trade Hall, Castle admitted that their case was 'over-simplified extremism', and that despite the revivalist atmosphere inside the hall, they were struggling to win over moderate opinion. Characteristically, however, Benn drew an entirely different conclusion from the same event. 'It was one of the best meetings I have ever attended,' he recorded afterwards, flushed with millenarian enthusiasm. 'That great tide of public opinion cannot be held back now, of that I am sure.'[22]

Probably no minister in modern times has suffered the abuse directed at Benn during the month-long campaign. By now it was almost impossible to exaggerate the loathing he inspired in City executives and conservative columnists, and even to many Labour sympathizers he had become a 'cult hate figure', the Red Menace in human form. His sheer prominence was simply extraordinary: in just over a month, the *Guardian* devoted 829 column inches to him, *The Times* 586 and the *Telegraph* 505, in each case overwhelmingly negative. 'Benn Factor Now Dominant Issue in Campaign' read one *Telegraph* headline, while the *Guardian* thought he had 'dominated the campaign single-handed, making the headlines day after day'. Not one of those headlines was positive. By the spring of 1975, most newspapers habitually described Benn as either a madman or a Communist: the *Daily Express*'s William Hickey gossip column ran a photograph sent in by a reader who thought Benn looked like Hitler, while the *Sunday Telegraph*'s cartoonist drew him as a rapist dragging off the screaming figure of Industry with the words 'Good Heavens! Everyone knows that when a woman says "NO" she really means "YES"!' Benn had become a 'dangerous politician who stirs up and exploits political forces that will first bring Britain to economic ruin and then possibly use the rubble as the foundations for a collectivist regime, which would immediately discard him as the Kerensky whose work was done', agreed *The Times*'s David Wood. And even when Benn tried to improve his image, giving an interview to the *Mirror* denying that he was a 'Dracula-like bogeyman', the front-page headline read simply 'BENNMANIA'.[23]

On 16 May, Benn gave his critics all the ammunition they could want with a disastrous gaffe that sealed his fate. Staying in Europe, he said, would bring 'industrial disaster' and 'mass unemployment'. What was more, there had been 'nearly 500,000 jobs lost since we entered the Common Market'. At the very least he was guilty of creative arithmetic, and the following morning the pro-Europeans returned fire. Benn's 'Sunday scare story' had stood 'the truth on its head', declared Willie Whitelaw. It was an 'absolute lie', concurred the Liberal man-mountain Cyril Smith, while in the Commons even Harold Wilson admitted that he 'did not agree with those figures'. Up went the cheers from the Tory benches. 'Is he a liar? Sack him!' they yelled, their fingers jabbing at the white-faced Industry Secretary. But it got even worse for the beleaguered Benn. On 26 May, making a rare intervention in the campaign, Denis Healey issued a statement slamming his 'falsehood' and condemning those who tried to 'escape from real life by retreating into a cocoon of myth and fantasy'. The next day, Roy Jenkins told a press conference that he found it 'increasingly difficult to take Mr Benn seriously as an economics minister'. Behind the scenes, this brought a furious rebuke from Wilson, who was appalled by the spectacle of his ministers throwing mud at each other in public. But the damage was done. Even the *Mirror* now twisted the knife, devoting its front page to an attack on 'The Minister of Fear'. 'Mr Benn bears the heavy responsibility of misleading the country. Of trading on fear,' it declared, noting that not even Michael Foot had backed him up. 'There is no mystery about what others of Tony Benn's colleagues think. They think Mr Benn is not telling the truth.'[24]

It was to Benn's credit that he somehow kept going under the pressure. On 17 May Special Branch warned him that 'there may be a risk of you getting biffed or attacked in some way', while two days later he was besieged by rumours that one of his children had secretly been admitted to hospital. A few weeks after that, he was sent a death threat signed, bizarrely, under his wife's maiden name, while his daughter heard a previous conversation being played back to her on the phone, suggesting that the line was bugged. Equally disturbingly, his rubbish disappeared every morning, almost certainly stolen by journalists. Yet among his comrades on the anti-European left, there was surprisingly little sympathy. 'He's losing us the referendum,' Barbara Castle's special adviser Jack Straw told her despairingly. This was no exaggeration: a Harris poll found that Benn's efforts actually made voters *less* likely to vote No, while a poll for the *Sun* found that only four in a hundred people had been persuaded by his arguments. 'Mr Benn often complains that the press and television are biased against the anti-marketeers,' agreed the *Telegraph*'s John O'Sullivan. 'And he is absolutely right. They keep on reporting him.' 'Wedgie Has Decided Me,' read the headline on John Akass's *Sun* column on the last day of the campaign: 'I'm Going To Vote Yes.'[25]

Looking back, the striking thing about the referendum campaign was that it was such a non-event. Despite the fuss about Tony Benn, the tabloids were more exercised by the crimes of the Cambridge rapist, the misbehaviour of the nation's football fans and the triumphs of the Bay City Rollers. The BBC and ITV struggled to show much enthusiasm for the campaign, and even the broadsheets devoted more attention to the tribulations of Chrysler and the horrific inflation figures. Only very occasionally did the campaign threaten to burst into life. On 27 May, Edward Heath was addressing a packed house in Lancaster when the head of the Blackpool Get Britain Out committee, Harry Bucklitch, shouted that he was a traitor and ought to suffer the fate of Lord Haw-Haw. At that, a nearby woman, later identified as a senior member of the Lancaster Conservative Association, 'smacked Mr Bucklitch in the face and was slapped back before they were separated'. 'I have never hit a lady before,' Bucklitch said afterwards, 'but I did not think she could be one, so I struck back.'[26]

By and large, though, the campaign never took off. The weekend before polling day, both sides told the *Sunday Times* they had been disappointed by the voters' 'horrible lack of enthusiasm'. Most people were much more interested in prices, jobs and the state of the economy: in a poll only a few months before, just one in ten had ranked Europe as an important issue. And it is not true, as is often claimed, that people were never told about the consequences for British sovereignty. At rally after rally, Foot, Shore and Powell warned that the EEC posed a deadly threat to Britain's political independence. The implication of a Yes vote, Shore claimed, was that 'the long and famous story of the British nation and people has ended; that we are now so weak and powerless that we must accept terms and conditions, penalties and limitations, almost as though we had suffered defeat in war'. These were stirring words, but most people took absolutely no notice. As Hugo Young observed, the truth was that public opinion about Europe remained 'changeable, ignorant and half-hearted'. Even in the week of the vote, for example, Michael Palin recorded that he was 'still undecided':

> In both cases it boils down to having confidence in Britain. Either to stay in Europe and keep up with the fast rate of material progress which undoubtedly have made France and Germany quite attractive places to live in, or to have the confidence to break from the incentive and the protection of Europe and become a one country independent free trader, as in the good old days. Neither decision I think involves the downfall of our nation. Once a decision is taken it will all be absorbed into the system and the country will carry on working (or not working) as it always did.

Palin's instinct was to vote No in protest against the 'smugness and complacency' of the Yes camp. But eventually he changed his mind, following the advice of one of his favourite columnists, the *Mirror*'s Keith Waterhouse, who thought that 'a thousand years of insularity' had produced only the 'bingo parlour, carbonised beer and *Crossroads*'. Palin's experience was not unusual: although most people remained suspicious of European collaboration, they followed the advice of the politicians and commentators they most respected. And at a time of terrible economic anxiety, with headlines showing that wage inflation had reached a record 30 per cent, few people wanted to gamble with Britain's future. 'It's damn cold outside the European Economic Community,' remarked the former Conservative MP and European Commissioner Sir Christopher Soames, 'and in our present parlous position, this is no time for Britain to be considering leaving a Christmas club, let alone the Common Market.'[27]

The opinion polls tell the story. As late as January 1975 they had suggested a clear No vote: while fewer than one in three people thought Britain had been right to join the EEC, half the electorate thought it had been a mistake. But when Wilson and Callaghan announced they had been converted to the European cause, the picture changed. By the beginning of April, 60 per cent said they would vote Yes, and by Referendum Day the Yes campaign's majority had surged from 8 per cent to 34 per cent in just three months. No doubt economic uncertainty had a lot to do with it, but in the final analysis, most people probably voted as their favourite politicians recommended. At open-air meetings in Blackburn shopping centre in the final days, women crowded around Barbara Castle. 'How can I choose?' they asked her. 'I don't know enough about it.' She particularly remembered one woman who listened to her arguments 'with respectful appreciation' before asking worriedly: 'Then why does Harold Wilson take a different view?' 'I realized then', Castle wrote, 'that Harold's identification with the pro-Market cause would be decisive for most Labour voters. People still vote party rather than ideas.'[28]

The other obvious factor was, of course, the media. In most papers, as Tony Benn complained, the No campaign was almost drowned out by the cacophony of abuse.* To take them in circulation order, the *Mirror* ran 2,436 column inches on the pro-EEC case and only 533 on the antis; the *Sun* ran 1,408 for and 529 against; the *Express* ran 1,722 for and 665 against; and the *Mail* ran 1,672 for and just 476 against. Given the supposedly non-partisan nature of the debate, this was partiality carried to extremes: some 69 per cent of the *Mirror*'s content was aggressively pro-European, with only 15 per cent critical. And as polling day approached, the coverage became more strident. The *Sun* ran a gigantic leader promising that jobs would be more plentiful and prices lower if Britain stayed in the EEC: 'Yes for a future together, No for a future alone'. The *Mail* ('Vote YES for Britain') ran a long feature imagining the future if Britain left the Common Market: 'A Day in the Life of Siege Britain ... No Coffee, Wine, Beans or Bananas, Until Further Notice'. And the *Mirror* outdid itself with a huge picture of nine small boys from an international school in Brussels, eight huddling cheerfully together, the ninth standing miserably alone. That ninth boy was, of course, British. 'He's the odd lad out,' the paper explained, no doubt wiping away the tears. 'FOR THE LAD OUTSIDE, VOTE YES.'[29]

In the final days, both the BBC and ITV mounted referendum spectaculars. On Tuesday evening, Granada's *State of the Nation* team organized a two-hour debate, with Heath and Jenkins leading the

---

* There is an obvious parallel here, of course, with the referendum on the Alternative Vote in 2011.

pro-European team and Powell and Shore spearheading the anti-European response. The real story was the non-appearance of Tony Benn, who, unlike his colleagues, refused to share a platform with a Conservative. The producers offered him seven different seating options, including a gangway that would physically protect him from Conservative contamination, but Benn was not having it. Intrigued by the prospect of a debate crossing party lines, 9 million people tuned in, and despite a blistering closing speech from Peter Shore, who told viewers that they were being 'asked to renounce our freedom [and] the rights of our Parliament and people', the Yes camp were thought to have carried the day. The Metropolitan Police commissioner Robert Mark, who had previously been undecided, was probably not alone in finding it all very one-sided. 'My God! If that's the lot who want us to come out,' he remarked, 'let's get up early and go to vote to stay in.'[30]

The following evening, the BBC followed suit with a two-hour debate live from the Oxford Union, pitting Heath and Thorpe against Shore and Castle. By any standards, this was an extraordinary occasion: to viewers more accustomed to, say, *It Ain't Half Hot Mum*, it must have seemed like some baffling upper-class ritual from the dawn of time. Heath and Thorpe, both former presidents of the Union, arrived in their dinner jackets, while Castle, a graduate of St Hugh's, was wearing a sixty-year-old 'suffragette blouse' that had turned up among her mother's old things. Despite her long experience, she felt 'paralysed' with nerves, and when the speakers walked into the Union, her worst fears were confirmed. The place was 'packed to the ceiling', and while she and Shore were 'greeted with catcalls and boos, there was warm applause for Jeremy and a crescendo of adulation for Heath, who took it with a new dignity'. And although Thorpe's wisecracks had the audience 'rolling in the aisles', the real star was Heath. 'The audience was his,' Castle recorded admiringly, 'and he responded to it with a genuineness which was the most impressive thing I have ever seen from him. He stood there, speaking simply, strongly and without a note. They gave him a standing ovation at the end, and he deserved it for the best example I have ever seen of The Man Who Came Back.'

Afterwards, as they had drinks in the president's room, everyone was around Heath, congratulating him and shaking his hand. Even Castle, trying to ignore 'the slow stain of the misery of failure', told him how good he had been. He was 'at his warmest and most natural', she recalled almost in disbelief, 'and thanked me genuinely for the nice things I said to him'. It was the greatest rhetorical triumph of Heath's career, all the sweeter for coming on his old stamping ground. 'It obviously attracted some celebrated viewers,' he wrote years later, full of Pooterish pride, 'as I received congratulatory letters from Kenneth Williams, star of the *Carry On* films, and the comedian Dave Allen.'[31]

On the last evening of the campaign, it was clear that the life had gone out of the No campaign. At a final press conference, flanked by the odd couple of Jack Jones and Enoch Powell, Wilson's dissenting ministers begged voters to make Thursday 'Britain's independence day', but even the press seemed barely interested. The Yes campaign's only fear was that turnout would be too low, thereby keeping the issue alive, and when Roy Jenkins awoke on Thursday, 5 June to pouring rain, he feared the worst. Visiting a polling station in Birmingham, he posed for photographs in a 'sodden playground'; then, not untypically, he went down to London for lunch. By the time he emerged, however, a 'miraculous weather transformation had occurred'. The sky was clear, the sun was out and all seemed right with the world. A couple of miles away, in Westminster, Harold Wilson told Bernard Donoughue that he thought the turnout would be surprisingly high. Wilson himself had voted early and was hoping for a big victory: interestingly, though, both his wife Mary and Marcia Falkender had voted No. That evening, Donoughue walked to Soho for a quiet pint, standing outside and watching the world go by. The evening headlines, he noticed, were already predicting a landslide. As he walked home across Hampstead Heath, watching the 'families playing on the grass', he felt 'no sense, however, among the people around of a great day of decision. They did not look as if they had voted!'[32]

Unlike in a general election, the referendum votes were counted not by constituency but by counties and regions, with Northern Ireland's votes calculated separately. The count did not unofficially start until nine on Friday morning, and within two hours the first results were in: a 75 per cent Yes vote in the Scilly Isles, a 72 per cent Yes in Cumbria, a 71 per cent Yes in Gwynedd. In Number 10, Donoughue listened to the results with a celebratory bottle of champagne. Outside, he noted, it was 'a gloriously sunny day – European weather'. And as the figures flooded in, it was obvious that the Yes campaign had won a smashing victory. Turnout was just under 65 per cent (compared with 78 per cent in February 1974 and 73 per cent in October), and in total, 67 per cent had voted to stay in Europe, with every county and region recording a Yes vote. Pro-European sentiment was weakest in Northern Ireland and Scotland, while it was strongest in affluent Conservative counties such as Buckinghamshire, Surrey and West Sussex. The explanation was simple: the vast majority of Conservatives had voted Yes, while Labour supporters divided fifty–fifty. Perhaps not surprisingly, richer and better-educated voters, who were more likely to have travelled abroad, had rallied to the European banner. Yet Butler and Kitzinger thought that, rather than being suffused with European enthusiasm, most voters were motivated by fear that Britain would sink if left on its own. It was lucky for the pro-Europeans that the economy was in such a mess: had the referendum been held a few years earlier, or indeed a few years later, the instinctive insularity of the British people might have swung the result the other way.[33]

In the press, all was jubilation. 'Full hearted, whole hearted and cheerful hearted', the result was a 'tonic for Britain and a tonic for Europe', gushed the *Guardian*. It was 'the most crushing victory in British political history', agreed a delighted *Daily Mail*, which thought 'the effect of this thunderous YES will echo down the years'. The *Sunday Times* even thought it 'the most exhilarating event in British politics since the war'. Many commentators thought it had also been a vindication for Harold Wilson, whose machinations had managed to secure Britain's European future without a split in the Labour Party or the loss of a single Cabinet minister. The referendum had been 'quite frankly a triumph for Mr Wilson', announced the *Telegraph*, not normally among his admirers. But if it was a victory, he seemed remarkably disinclined to enjoy it. That evening, his aides arranged a little party at Number 10. When they were all ready, however, Wilson said: 'I had better go to see Marcia,' and disappeared to her room to drink champagne. Eventually Haines and Donoughue got bored and went off to watch television instead.[34]

By and large, the anti-Europeans took their defeat with good grace. 'I have just been in receipt of a very big message from the British people,' Tony Benn told the press, showing remarkable good humour after enduring such abuse. 'I read it loud and clear.' As for the victors, their joy was unconfined. At a celebratory press conference at the Waldorf, Roy Jenkins noted that it was the anniversary of D-Day, 'when we had to fight a more painful campaign to end our exclusion from Europe'. Yet even Jenkins had to admit that the star of the campaign, 'as impervious to the waves and as reliable in his beam', had been his old Oxford friend Ted Heath. For *The Times*, the former Prime Minister was 'the Achilles of the European cause', while the *Sunday Express* thought that 'Britain in Europe is Edward Heath's achievement. Twice rejected by the electors and finally disowned by his party, Mr Heath has known the cruelty of public life. But he has the richest of consolations, that he has left an abiding mark on his country's destiny.' Even Mrs Thatcher paid tribute to her predecessor on the Monday after the vote, declaring that 'all of us on this side of the House, and many on the other, would wish to hand the campaign honours to my right hon. Friend the Member for Sidcup'. At that, all eyes turned to Heath. Surely such a generous tribute could not fail to elicit a smile? But Heath had not changed one iota. 'Head in hand, stony-faced,' remarked *The Times*, 'he made no acknowledgement.'[35]

The European referendum was one of the decisive moments in modern British history. If the result had gone differently, then Wilson and the Labour moderates would have been grievously, perhaps fatally damaged. For the left, victory would have been a tremendous boost; for Benn, it would have been a crucial stepping stone to the leadership. Abroad, a No vote would probably have done terrible damage to Britain's reputation. If the United Kingdom really had pulled out of Europe in the summer of 1975, then the collapse of the pound would almost certainly have happened earlier and been even more devastating. As it was, however, the result broke the left's momentum. From this point onwards, although Benn and his allies still made an enormous amount of noise, they posed no serious threat to the more moderate triumvirate of Wilson, Callaghan and Healey.

Four days after the referendum, Wilson reshuffled his government. In theory, the reshuffle was meant to be a definitive reassertion of his authority; in practice, it was merely an embarrassing reminder of his failings. Hoping to balance left and right, he had conceived an elaborate plan to demote the right-wing Education Secretary, Reg Prentice, to Minister of Overseas Development, while promoting the left-wing Overseas Development minister, Judith Hart, to Transport. But when both refused to budge, the scheme exploded in Wilson's face. Prentice eventually moved but kept his place in Cabinet, while Hart refused to accept her new position and therefore got the boot. Embarrassingly, Wilson sat meekly through furious lectures by Roy Jenkins and Michael Foot, leaders of the rival factions, on his folly and perfidy. It was totally 'humiliating', wrote Bernard Donoughue. 'He should never have allowed it to happen. Attlee would never have tolerated it. It was part of the erosion of HW's power. Just like a 15th-century monarch, when the feudal barons had excessive and independent powers.'[36]

The big development, though, was the emasculation of Tony Benn. As soon as the referendum results were in, Wilson made his long-rumoured move, shifting him from the battlefield of Industry to the backwater of Energy. Although Benn suspected what was coming, having been spotted 'glowering blackly' on his way into Number 10, he made no attempt to conceal his anger:

> 'You've got lots of energy, if you know what I mean,' [Wilson] said smiling.
>   I did not smile.
>   'You'd enjoy it,' he said. 'It's a very important job.'
>   I said nothing.
>   'Well, haven't you got any questions?'
>   'No,' I replied, 'except how long are you going to give me to think about it?'
>   'I must know soon. Two hours.'
>   'Overnight.'

In the end Wilson gave Benn until the following afternoon. But by four o'clock the next day, there was no reply. 'Nobody has seen Benn,' Donoughue wrote. 'He is not in his ministry. Neither did he turn up at the House, so the committee stage of his Industry Bill was abandoned. A chaotic atmosphere. The House and the lobby are now full of rumours.'

At last, shortly before seven, Benn appeared in the doorway of Wilson's office. 'What is your answer?' Wilson asked, staring at him intently with what Benn called 'his piggy little eyes'. Benn promptly launched into a long tirade. 'What you are doing', he spat, 'is simply capitulating to the CBI, to the Tory press and to the Tories themselves, all of whom have demanded my sacking ... You are capitulating and if you think this is going to save you, you've made a great mistake because they'll be pleased for twenty-four hours and then they'll turn on you.' That was too much for Wilson. 'You don't speak for the movement,' he snapped. 'I know as much about the movement as you do.' A few moments later Benn walked out, slamming the door behind him. It seemed obvious that he had resigned. But when Wilson emerged, 'his round face looking battered and blank', it turned out that Benn had taken the Energy job after all. It was now 'transparently clear', Donoughue thought, 'that there was no humiliation which he would not swallow in order to stay in the Cabinet'. Amazingly, though, Benn was more convinced than ever that history was flowing his way. 'Wilson has made a fatal error,' he wrote, 'and he will not be Leader of the Labour Party by the end of the year.'[37]

The next day's papers interpreted the reshuffle as a turning point, not only in Benn's career, but in political history. Yet behind all the headlines about comings and goings, the basic economic reality had not changed a jot. On the very day of the reshuffle, with Arab petrodollars rushing out of London, the pound hit a record low, while new figures showed that manufacturing investment was falling at an unprecedented rate of 15 per cent a year. 'When the edge was off the thrill of victory and the agony of defeat,' wrote one American reporter, 'Britons were reawakened to the fact that all of their old problems were still with them.' In the *Sun*, a cartoon showed Wilson and his ministers as animal tamers at a circus, gathered around a table labelled 'REFERENDUM SIDESHOW', waving their whips at a tiny little mouse. Behind them rears the gigantic figure of a tiger labelled 'ECONOMIC CRISIS', its teeth bared to strike, saliva dripping from its fangs. 'Right, lads,' a bystander says nervously, 'now you've finished playing with the mouse . . .'[38]

15
The Bells of Hell

> *What really broke Germany was the constant taking of the soft*
> *political option in respect of money . . . Inflation aggravated*
> *every evil, ruined every chance of national revival or individual*
> *success, and eventually produced precisely the conditions in*
> *which extremists of right and left could raise the mob against*
> *the state . . .*
>
> Adam Fergusson, *When Money Dies: The Nightmare*
> *of the Weimar Collapse* (1975)

> FLETCHER: *Do you know this country is on the verge of*
> *economic ruin? This once great nation of ours is teetering on*
> *the brink of an abyss?*
> GODBER: *By the time you lot get out, there'll be nobody worth*
> *robbing.*
>
> *Porridge*, 'Disturbing the Peace', 7 November 1975

At seven o'clock on a warm evening in August 1975, a skinny 19-year old boy walked into the Roebuck pub on the King's Road, Chelsea. The son of working-class Irish immigrants, John Lydon had grown up in a dilapidated council flat in Finsbury Park, north London. His was a boyhood of poverty and violence, dirt and peeling wallpaper: his father was often away on building sites, his mother suffered a series of miscarriages, and in the evenings he hung around with a gang of local children, throwing stones and breaking into the nearby factories. As a teenager he rebelled against authority, growing his hair long in the fashion of the early 1970s. His father told him to get it cut, so he had it cropped to the scalp and dyed it bright green. When his father threw him out, he joined a group of hippies squatting in a run-down Victorian building. He got a job in a sewage farm, then in a shoe factory, then cleaning the kitchens in a vegetarian restaurant. At weekends he and his friends hung around on the King's Road, where they drifted in and out of the local boutiques, pocketing whatever they could get their hands on. And it was there that he came to the attention of one of the proprietors, a would-be impresario called Malcolm McLaren, who was looking for a front man for his new band.

When Lydon walked into the Roebuck that August evening, he cut an outlandish figure. Thin, hunched, aggressive, his spiky hair still lurid green, he wore a tattered Pink Floyd T-shirt, held together with safety pins, which he had improved by scratching holes in the group's eyes and scrawling 'I HATE' in felt-tip pen over their logo. To the three teenagers waiting by the bar, who had already seen several other candidates for the job, he 'looked really interesting', but his attitude – threatening, sneering, supercilious – put their backs up. Trying to calm them down, McLaren suggested that they should go back to his shop for an impromptu audition. There he handed Lydon a shower attachment to use as a microphone, put Alice Cooper's 'Eighteen' on the jukebox, and ordered the others to move back. By his own account, Lydon was terrified. But, encouraged by the others, he began to leap and jerk around, inventing his own lyrics, spitting out the words. At the sight of this scrawny boy with green hair screaming tunelessly and jumping about, the others burst out laughing. 'We thought he was really funny,' one of his future band-mates recalled. 'I thought he was hysterical.' The only one not laughing was McLaren. 'It was a gut feeling,' he said later. 'I thought he had something.'[1]

In its way, the state of British pop music spoke volumes about the nation's morale in the summer of 1975. Exactly a decade earlier, the Beatles – the group that Malcolm McLaren most despised, but also the group he dreamed of emulating – had been at the height of their fame, playing before vast crowds on the last leg of their American tour. Thanks to their extraordinary commercial success, British youth culture had then been at the height of its international popularity; as the editor of the *NME* had put it, 'we may be regarded as a second-class power in politics, but at any rate we now lead the world in pop music!' But ten years after 'Yesterday', '(I Can't Get No) Satisfaction' and 'All Day and All of the Night', the mood felt very different. The British Invasion was a distant memory, the boutiques of Carnaby Street had long since closed down, and even James Bond had been reduced to battling it out with a heavily perspiring midget. The list of the year's top singles made for spine-chilling reading: ten years after the Beatles had been at their peak, Britain's most popular acts were the Bay City Rollers, followed by such glittering musical talents as Telly Savalas, Billy Connolly and Windsor Davies, all of whom recorded number one singles in 1975. After the heady optimism that had suffused British popular culture a decade earlier, it felt like a humiliating comedown. In 1965 the Beatles and the Rolling Stones had missed few opportunities to boast about Britain's renaissance; a decade later, however, their successors struck a very different note. 'Everyone is paranoid,' remarked the Stranglers' guitarist Jean-Jacques Burnel at the end of 1976. 'There's decay everywhere. We've always lived with the assumption that things were getting better and better materially, progress all the time, and suddenly it's like, you hear everyday there's a crisis, financial crisis. Things being laid off, people not working. Everything's coming to a grinding halt.'[2]

For the green-haired young man singing along to the jukebox that evening in August 1975, the naive optimism of Swinging London had never been anything more than a sick joke. In place of the peace and love espoused by the Beatles, the Sex Pistols offered violence, anarchy, contempt and confrontation. But they were not the only rock musicians of the mid-1970s to reflect the darker impulses of a society turning in on itself. For the Beatles' most talented successor, a suburban South London boy who had flirted with psychedelic pop and glam rock, there were no cheeky photo-calls with a grinning Harold Wilson. What Britain needed, David Bowie told the *NME* in October 1975, was not love, but 'an extreme right front [to] come up and sweep everything off its feet and tidy everything up'. The advent of the far right, he thought, would 'do something positive, at least, to cause a commotion in people and they'll either accept dictatorship, or get rid of it'.

The following April, Bowie told a press conference that Britain 'could benefit from a fascist leader', and in May he greeted fans at Victoria Station with what looked suspiciously like a Nazi salute. And in case any doubt remained, Bowie made his position crystal clear in an interview with *Playboy* a few months later:

> I'd adore to be Prime Minister. And, yes, I believe very strongly in fascism. The only way we can speed up the sort of liberalism that's hanging foul in the air at the moment is to speed up the progress of a right-wing, totally dictatorial tyranny and get it over as fast as possible. People have always responded with greater efficiency under a regimental leadership. A liberal

wastes time saying, 'Well, now, what ideas have you got?' Show them what to do, for God's sake. If you don't, nothing will get done.

He was in good company, he explained. 'Adolf Hitler was one of the first rock stars . . . I think he was quite as good as Jagger. It's astounding. And boy, when he hit that stage, he worked an audience. Good God!' Bowie's friends claimed that this was merely irony, a pose to confuse the media. But at least some of his admirers took him seriously. 'I believe in anything to purify the race,' one Bowie fan told the magazine *Let It Rock* in October 1975. 'We should rule the world like we used to.'[3]

Britain ruling the world could hardly have seemed a more implausible prospect in the summer of 1975. Superficially, life seemed good: the weather was hot, the skies blue and cloudless, the parks and beaches packed with sun-seekers. Yet when the Conservative MP Alan Clark contemplated 'the terrible decline of the country' at the end of May, he found the 'whole thing tatty, bad-tempered, lazy, in collapse'. Characteristically, he wondered whether 'perhaps I should go the whole way, stand as National Front candidate'. No doubt Clark and Bowie would have made an entertainingly implausible double-act; yet their diagnosis of decline was widely shared. Touring the country a few weeks earlier, the *Daily Mail*'s Terry Coleman found 'not a sense of approaching cataclysm, but of increasing erosion'. Bumping into his friend Peter Hall at Covent Garden, the composer Sir Georg Solti 'bewailed the collapse of all the democratic and liberal values of England; how we were letting 400 years of achievement slither down the drain through ineptitude and apathy'. The British people had 'woken up one morning', the journalist Clive Irving told American readers, 'and found themselves the paupers of Europe'. To outside observers, Britain must 'look like somebody staggering home, slightly tipsy, from a fancy-dress ball, still absurdly costumed and in the mind still living in the past'. 'The game', Irving wrote sadly, 'is coming to an end; the pageant is crumbling.'[4]

Even inside Downing Street, one of the Prime Minister's closest advisers had yielded to the general sense of hopelessness. In his diary, Bernard Donoughue admitted that he had been 'forced to realise that this nation is in sad decline'. Returning from holiday in France, he found London muggy and rainy, 'shabby' and 'depressing'. Harold Wilson, he thought, was 'completely isolated from the remorseless relative decline of this country' because he took his holidays in the Scillies, 'which is relatively unchanged since 1950, so he thinks the world is unchanged. The same is true of Marcia, Mary and Joe, who all holiday in Britain.' But even the beer and sandwiches served during the interminable pay talks with the unions, 'dry and unappetising', plunged Donoughue into gloom. The Cabinet Office restaurant, too, was 'appalling. Filthy food. Terrible service.' Every night, he went to bed feeling deeply depressed:

> Britain is a miserable sight. A society of failures, full of apathy, and aroused only by envy at the success of others. That is why we will continue to decline. Not because of our economic and industrial problems. They are soluble. But because the psychology of our people is in such an appalling – I fear irretrievable – state. Meanness has replaced generosity. Envy has replaced endeavour. Malice is the most common motivation . . . This is the social personality of a loser. It is time to go and cultivate our gardens, share love with our families, and leave the rest to fester. And if it gets intolerable – because fascism could breed in this unhealthy climate – to emigrate if need be.

For the first time in his life, he admitted, he had seriously thought about a new life in France or the United States, leaving the beer and sandwiches far behind.[5]

What worried Donoughue, as well as millions of ordinary Britons, was the apparently irresistible surge of prices and wages. Gathering momentum with every new pay settlement, the tide of inflation seemed to have reached monstrous proportions: by the spring of 1975, basic wage rates were rising at an annual level of 29 per cent. Not all of this was Wilson's fault: the Barber boom, the OPEC oil shock and Heath's threshold payments had all helped to send inflation into overdrive. Yet it was glaringly obvious that the Social Contract had not merely failed to improve a bad situation; it had, as the journalist Edward Pearce put it, 'made bad unimaginably worse'. Almost every other industrialized country had chosen to take the hit of the oil shock immediately, deflating to keep prices down and swallowing the short-term pain so that they could rebound in the long run. Only Britain had refused to do so, and the contrast was now frankly embarrassing. Everywhere else, inflation was falling; only in Britain was it still rising. In a table of the world's richest nations, the *Mirror* told its readers, Britain was now 'down among the peasants in 19th position, just behind Italy but ahead of Turkey, where inflation is 25 per cent'. On top of that, not only had Britain's GDP fallen for two successive years, but profit levels had hit an all-time low and unemployment was almost one million – the level for which Heath had been pilloried back in January 1972. 'The social contract', said the *Mirror*, 'is a cartoonists' joke . . . Running up bigger debts and printing money that nobody has earned hardly looks the way to stop inflation.'[6]

On Friday, 13 June, the Department of Employment reported that while the average annual pay settlement had now reached 31 per cent, living costs had risen by 25 per cent. In just twelve months, the price of sugar had gone up by 184 per cent, carrots by 137 per cent, electricity by 66 per cent, tinned soup by 54 per cent, orange squash by 51 per cent and coal by 47 per cent. In June 1974, a family paid 94p for a pound of rump steak; now they paid £1.52. Even a pint of milk, which would have cost 4½p in 1974, now cost 7p. And thanks to Denis Healey's tax increases, reported the *Express*, in the past twelve months 'most families would have needed an increase in income of nearly 32 per cent' merely to stand still. A family living in a council house on £39 a week in May 1974 now needed an extra £15 'simply to maintain their living standards', while a family in their own semi-detached house on £72 a week now needed to make £110. In the same period, rail fares had doubled, while even London taxi fares were rising at an astonishing rate. After approving a 26 per cent increase the previous April, Roy Jenkins yielded to cabbies' demands for a further 25 per cent rise in June 1975. Even books were becoming prohibitively expensive: with printing costs up by 30 per cent a year and distribution costs up 400 per cent in just four years, publishers were producing shorter books and ditching the failures more quickly, leading to a proliferation of remainder shops. The price of a typical hardback rose from just £2.78 in 1970 to £6.64 in 1976, but with prices rising so rapidly, many publishers were reluctant to tie themselves down. By the summer of 1975, many books were issued without printed prices, just sticky labels that could easily be replaced as inflation continued to bite.[7]

There were plenty of losers from the great inflation of 1975. Elderly savers watched aghast as the fruits of their working lives were eaten away. A hundred pounds invested in the bank in June 1974 was worth £107.50 a year later, yet in the meantime living costs had gone up by almost 30 per cent. And while workers in powerful unions were generally protected, pensioners, the self-employed and people who did not belong to unions found themselves tumbling down the economic ladder, their incomes stagnant as prices rocketed. Buying in bulk and storing food in the deep freeze was no answer: while a freezer cost less than £10 a year to run in 1974, higher electricity charges meant that it cost more than £15 to run a year later. And even a decent pay rise might not be enough to stand still, as Brian Barker, a 37-year-old employee of an industrial instruments firm, discovered to his horror. Living with his wife and 8-year-old son in a three-bedroom house in Waltham Cross, he had recently been awarded a 6.5 per cent pay rise, taking his salary to £3,000 a year. 'It doesn't sound too bad at all, does it?' he told an interviewer. 'You'd think we would be really comfortable on that. Then the gas bill comes in, followed by the electricity, the rates, the phone bill, and a lot of others.' His wife estimated that the weekly housekeeping bill had risen from £10 to more than £13 in just a year, while she was spending £2 a week extra on her son's clothes. 'I am just one of thousands, I suppose, but there is no comfort in company,' Brian sighed. 'And I've given up any notion of doing any better for my family.' His wife was even gloomier. 'We don't save a penny,' she said. 'We used to think we were really well off. Not any more.'[8]

Young and old, rich and poor, nobody was safe from the ravages of inflation. 'Simpler food. Fewer clothes. Less dining out,' were the *Mirror*'s recommendations after interviewing women across the capital. One of them, the prosperous Julien Pettit, married to a consultant physician from St John's Wood, said she had no longer bought fruit, baked her own bread and 'stopped going to the hairdressers'. 'I don't buy flowers any longer, or sweets and chocolate,' she added. 'I buy fewer clothes and larger sizes for my son so that they last longer ... Holidays? We used to go skiing every year. We haven't thought about it this year.' Another housewife, Vivien Shebson from Finchley, bought all her groceries in bulk, and whenever 'things are cheapest in supermarkets, I buy the most I can, like half a dozen packets of washing powder'. 'We hardly ever eat out now,' she said. 'The money doesn't go nearly as far.' But her life looked almost luxurious beside that of Caroline Booker, a 19-year-old working for an employment agency and sharing a flat in Notting Hill Gate with three other girls. 'Nowadays I wear holey tights under long skirts and trousers instead of throwing them away,' she said. 'I've changed to a cheap kind of make-up and I haven't been to the hairdressers for six months.' Two of her flatmates, she said, were so poor that they had 'cheese instead of a meal some nights'.

Like teenagers everywhere, Caroline had found the ideal solution. 'If I can't afford a proper meal,' she said, 'I go and eat at my parents.' For millions of other people, however, that option was impossible. 'Nearly 700,000 parents go to bed hungry at least once a fortnight just to keep their children fed,' reported the *Mirror*:

For those at the bottom of the scale – the lowest paid and the pensioners – inflation is a nightmare.

THEY ARE the people whose pay packets and pensions fall further and further behind the cost of living.

THEY are the victims who are least able to fight for themselves in a world of catch-as-catch-can.

So long as inflation gets worse and more and more pound notes are printed their plight will get worse.

And – don't let's kid ourselves – more and more people who think themselves all right now will begin to share their plight.

BECAUSE YOU CAN'T PRINT FOOD.[9]

For many people, the really frightening thing was that inflation seemed to be getting even worse. In February, Len Murray had bluntly told Denis Healey that 'the going rate for wage increases was already thirty per cent, although inflation was still only twenty per cent'. Terrified of falling behind, union members were now pressing for even greater increases, yet the government continued to roll over. On 3 April the power workers won a 31 per cent deal; on 14 April the civil servants accepted 32 per cent; on 18 April the doctors won 35 per cent; on 29 April London's dockers settled for 30 per cent. By now, three out of four people thought the government should step in to control prices and incomes, and although the union leaders insisted that they were merely *reacting* to the inflation caused by the Barber boom and the OPEC oil shock, they became the scapegoats. 'The Social Contract', said the *Mirror*, 'is a shameful flop, a national sick joke.' One front-page editorial might have come directly from a Conservative party political broadcast:

Do the unions plead with passion for the poor, the unfortunate, the deprived and the desperate?

Or do they fire their heaviest guns on behalf of those who are already doing very well and mean to do better?

Big Brother Joe Gormley, president of the National Union of Mineworkers, has given his answer in one brutal sentence:

'The miners are going to be at the top of the tree and remain at the top of the tree, and if that hurts somebody then I am sorry.'

Mr Gormley is SORRY. What a comfort for those who haven't the muscle power of the miners or of other big unions . . .

Sorry that Britain is having to skimp on *hospitals* and *schools*. Sorry for the *pensioners*. Sorry for the *disabled* and *sick*.

There will only be crumbs for them because Big Brother Gormley and other Big Brothers intend to walk off with the cake.

This was distinctly mild, however, compared with the verdict of another former Labour sympathizer, the columnist Paul Johnson:

> Rapid inflation inflicts the greatest possible suffering on the very poor, the old, the very young, the sick, the helpless, the physically and mentally handicapped, all the outcasts and misfits and casualties of society. Collectively, they number millions. Collectively, from a trade union point of view, they are powerless ... They cannot batter the public with their fists. Old people open their newspapers with dread, knowing they will read of 30%, 40% and even 60% wage increases, leading inevitably to monstrous rises in the cost of essentials, like electricity and gas, transport and food, and compulsory charges like rates ...
>
> This may be good trade unionism, but it is not socialism as I understand it.

Ironically, many union members themselves agreed with him. Len Murray remembered that 'in tea rooms, in bars, sitting and having a cup of tea, having a glass of beer, the delegates – the same delegates who were voting the 30 per cent wage increases – [were] saying to me directly, "Look, we've got to do something about this. You've got to do something about this. We can't go on like this."' Yet since nobody wanted to fall behind, nobody made the first move. And so the scramble for wages continued, and the prices rose and rose.[10]

It is hard to exaggerate the despair in the press in May and June 1975. For the *Mirror*, the British economy was sinking beneath 'a tidal wave of pessimism'; for the *Sun*, 'the Bells of Hell' were tolling; for *The Economist*, 'Britain's dream of apocalypse is horribly close to coming true'. Few of them could understand why Harold Wilson seemed so indifferent to the urgency. 'Why Are We Waiting?' demanded a banner headline in the *Sunday Mirror*. 'Isn't it obvious that the Government MUST act against inflation? That we CAN'T go on like this?' Yet even to his colleagues Wilson seemed listless and lethargic, paralysed by the fear of alienating the trade unions and dividing his party. 'You know, I love Harold,' the Prime Minister's confidant Harold Lever remarked to his Treasury colleagues, 'but I have to acknowledge that he's a complete coward.' 'Privately we know he is blown, no more interest, no more ideas, no appetite for power,' agreed Bernard Donoughue. As his policy chief saw it, Wilson was 'simply going through the motions, like a veteran boxer. The appetite and the spark have gone. He does not get much kick out of it so he should give up.' Walking home one 'lovely warm

June night', Donoughue reflected that 'there was not much to be proud of. There was a sense of impending collapse. Not of cataclysm. Just of erosion and final decline.'[11]

On 18 June, less than a week after he had been exiled to the Department of Energy, Tony Benn boarded a hydrofoil at Tower Pier, bound for the Medway estuary in northern Kent. 'It was a bright, hot day,' he recorded, 'and even the Isle of Grain, the most ravaged, desolate, industrial landscape in the Medway, looked quite beautiful.' The trip had been scheduled to mark a historic event – the first landing of North Sea oil at a British refinery – and as Benn raised a flask of oil aloft for the cameras, he welcomed a 'day of national celebration'. Privately, though, he was in a foul mood, barely able to contain his scorn for his travelling companions, 'a complete cross-section of the international capitalist and British Tory establishment and their wives', among them dignitaries from various oil companies, the conglomerate Rio Tinto-Zinc and 'the filthy *Daily Mail*'. That evening he and his wife consoled themselves with dinner at the Gay Hussar. 'It cost £10 for the two of us,' he wrote in disbelief.[12]

Two days later, Benn travelled to Chequers for another of Wilson's interminable summits on the economic crisis. It was, thought Barbara Castle, 'a beautiful day and it seemed criminal to incarcerate ourselves in the long room, with its dark panelled walls and sombre oil paintings'. Gazing out on the cows grazing complacently in the meadows, she wondered why 'crises always occur in that incomparable weather in which the English countryside seems to exude a placid security'. Then Denis Healey opened the discussion, and her attention returned to the economy:

> The problem, he said, was more urgent than any of us realized . . . Inflation was 'terrifying'. Borrowing could stop 'overnight'. Anything could trigger off a disastrous run on the pound and force us into £1 billion's worth of public expenditure cuts *this year*. There was not a minute to waste. 'We must have a credible policy by the end of July.' And if we were to get inflation down to single figures, we couldn't go beyond 10 per cent for wages or £5 a week.

To this apocalyptic prognosis, Healey's colleagues reacted with almost scripted predictability. The future Social Democrats were even gloomier than the Chancellor. Roy Jenkins, for example, thought that 'society was breaking down' and demanded spending cuts and a statutory pay policy. 'Are you suggesting putting people in prison?' asked Michael Foot. 'We'll have to face that,' Jenkins said.

Then it was Benn's turn. 'The familiar theme,' Castle recorded. 'We were in 1931 again.' They had to face the fact, Benn said, that 'power has shifted in our society and the ballot box is now incompatible with the market economy as it operates. Power has shifted to people on the shop floor.' The only solution was 'a coalition with the trade union movement' – a fantastic suggestion given that the union leaders could barely control their own members. Not surprisingly, this won little support, and the Cabinet agreed to back Healey's plan for a voluntary pay policy of 10 per cent, with statutory powers in reserve if it failed. Given the situation, this was still pretty feeble. But as Benn walked down the ornate staircase with his fellow left-winger John Silkin, he pointed his finger meaningfully at the portrait of the ill-fated Labour 'traitor' Ramsay MacDonald.[13]

Harold Wilson was eating strawberries and cream at the Royal Agricultural Show in Warwickshire when the crisis came to a head. That morning, Monday, 30 June, the pound had opened at almost $2.23, yet by lunchtime it was already down to $2.17, the biggest slide in its history, sending shock waves through the Bank of England. In Whitehall, recorded Ronald McIntosh, 'there is a mood of near hysteria and incipient collapse'; in Warwickshire, Wilson was inspecting giant marrows, enjoying the summer sunshine and smiling reassuringly for the cameras, the very image of calm complacency. But by the time the helicopter had brought him back to London, both Healey and the Governor of the Bank, Gordon Richardson, were waiting anxiously at Number 10. 'We must act now. We must act *now*,' Richardson announced. 'This government's whole credibility has gone.' It was time, he said, for a statement 'to reassure foreign holders', and time to 'end this nonsense of getting the co-operation and consent of others, the trade unions, the Labour Party. We must act. People are ready to support tough measures.'

Healey, too, was in an apocalyptic mood. Sterling was 'crumbling', he told a hastily assembled meeting that afternoon, and the Bank had already spent $500 million trying to prop it up. 'We have to act to halt the haemorrhage now.' As it so happened, the Treasury had prepared precisely the drastic measures that the crisis demanded: a White Paper banning employers, by law, from granting pay increases of more than 10 per cent, followed by another White Paper announcing massive spending cuts and price controls. This would, of course, mean the end of the Social Contract, and, in the Cabinet Room, there was a moment of 'stunned silence'. 'It was clear to me,' Donoughue recalled, 'sitting there watching the Prime Minister's face, that Wilson was in full retreat towards statutory compulsion. He had, as often before, been converted by the familiar mournful tolling of the sterling bell.'[14]

The obvious attraction of the Treasury plan was that nothing would better persuade the markets that the government meant to get inflation and borrowing under control. On top of that, compulsory wage control was very popular with the general public: according to an ORC poll, 70 per cent of voters and even 63 per cent of trade unionists thought the government simply had to clamp down to prevent Britain sliding into hyperinflation. The obvious drawback, however, was that Wilson had explicitly ruled out a statutory incomes policy. If he went back on his word, he would not only be executing a flagrant U-turn, but he would divide the Labour Party and alienate his union allies. To Joe Haines and Bernard Donoughue, the Treasury plan would 'make the Government put its policies totally in reverse, abandon its manifesto commitments and commit suicide'.

Even as Wilson was welcoming guests to a dinner for the Belgian Prime Minister, Haines and Donoughue installed themselves at his elbow, muttering that compulsory wage control would drive the unions into open revolt. (In its way, of course, this incident speaks volumes about Wilson's authority and governing style.) The battle reached a climax at midnight, when the Treasury sent over a draft of Healey's statement on compulsory wage controls. 'We all agreed it was disastrous,' Donoughue wrote. But Wilson was still tied up at his dinner party, where 'several notable public figures [were] now staggering around full of good drink'. So his aides disappeared up to Haines's room and drafted a response, warning that surrender to the Treasury would mean 'incalculable consequences for the Government and the party'. By the time they had finished, it was one in the morning and the battle seemed lost. But the exhausted Donoughue had just climbed into bed when the phone rang. 'It was Joe,' he recorded. 'The PM had spoken to him on the phone. He wanted us to know that he "agreed with every word in our brief", he was going to forbid Healey to circulate his proposed draft statement and was himself dictating a long minute incorporating our criticisms. Joe was jubilant, and I was relieved sufficiently to compensate for being woken up.'[15]

Would the Treasury plan have averted the IMF crisis a year later? Or would it have provoked rebellion in the unions and divided the Labour Party? We shall never know. When the Cabinet met the next morning,

Healey repeated his apocalyptic warnings, but this time Wilson ruled out a return to wage controls. Instead of adopting the Treasury plan, the Prime Minister turned to a scheme the Policy Unit had drafted ten days earlier, envisaging a voluntary wage increase (or 'norm') of no more than £5 or £6 a week, backed up by 'a massive propaganda exercise'. What made this so attractive was that it had the backing of the ultimate union bogeyman, the TGWU boss Jack Jones – a rather more pragmatic operator than his critics realized. For all his militant rhetoric, noted *The Economist*'s Stephen Milligan, Jones was a 'thoughtful and constructive man: a man who could listen as well as lecture'. And by now Jones had reluctantly conceded that higher wages were indeed driving up unemployment. Unless the unions exercised more restraint, he thought, 'we were going to have hyper-inflation ... and that was no good to the working people of this country'. But Jones had more partisan motives, too. The alternative to voluntary restraint, he told the TUC, would be a 'massive withdrawal of funds by foreign bankers' and the advent of a 'right-wing coalition which would impose a statutory incomes policy, cut living standards and raise unemployment'. Anything would be better than that.[16]

Although a flat-rate policy was far from Healey's first choice, the chance of an alliance with the most powerful of the union barons proved irresistible. After spending a month haggling over the details, they compromised on a pay increase of no more than £6 a week, which worked out at about 14 per cent a year. This was neither a statutory nor a voluntary policy, but something vaguely in between: although the government had no powers to back it up, Healey issued an undefined 'threat to take reserve powers if necessary'. Even this was much too much for the hard left, for whom any talk of restraint, despite the palpable evidence of soaring prices, was unacceptable. In the Commons, Norman Atkinson complained that Healey had ripped up the Labour manifesto, while Brian Sedgemore colourfully called it a 'political and economic cock-up'. The scheme was 'unjust', 'unsocialist and 'a total sell-out', agreed the Yorkshire miners' leader Arthur Scargill, pledging to do all in his power to undermine it. And of course Tony Benn considered the entire thing utterly appalling. Arriving for the decisive meeting, he had walked into Number 10 with the Labour manifesto tucked ostentatiously under his arm: this was 'intended', he wrote, 'as a tremendous message to the movement, done without any breach of Cabinet loyalty'. Of course, he might have resigned, as some activists were urging. As usual, however, Benn had worked out a rationale for keeping his ministerial car. 'If you come out,' he wrote, 'you're accused of rocking the boat . . . The best strategy is to develop the campaign for Labour policy from inside the Government.'[17]

Benn, however, was in a minority, for, as the *Mirror* told its readers the next day, the new '£6-a-week-and-no-more rule has two great merits. It is socially fair. It is simple and straightforward.' Importantly, the scheme had something for everybody: the left were mollified by the fact that low-paid workers gained most from the flat-rate formula, while the Treasury were pleased that the level had been set at just £6, rather than the £10 Jones initially wanted. It was egalitarian, but, unlike many wheezes dreamed up in the name of equality, it actually worked. In twelve months, hourly wage inflation fell from 33 per cent to 18 per cent. This was not as radical or as fast as the markets wanted: price inflation in late 1976 was still about 15 per cent, well above the Treasury's goal. Still, that was still an awful lot better than 30 per cent: at last the government had stepped back from the brink. In the *Mirror*'s words, they had lifted 'the pressure on every union to grab every last penny because that is what every other union will try to grab'. And even years later, some of Wilson's aides remained proud of their achievement. The formula proved 'remarkably successful', insisted Bernard Donoughue, for whom it was 'a more humane way of controlling inflation than relying on the harsh deflationary impact of Mrs Thatcher's later four million unemployed'.[18]

Yet even at the time, it was painfully obvious that the settlement was built on wobbly foundations. From the outset, more militant union leaders bitterly opposed the scheme: it was 'atrocious, the totally unacceptable face of coalition policies', said Mick McGahey, the Communist vice president of the miners' union, while Alan Fisher, general secretary of the National Union of Public Employees, called it 'disgraceful'. When the TUC voted on the plan, some of the biggest and most influential unions, such as the AUEW, ASTMS and NUPE, came out against it. In the end, it was only when Len Murray and Jack Jones put their credibility on the line that the trade unions eventually came round. Britain could not 'go about spending money as we like with somebody else's cheque book in our pocket', insisted Murray, while Jones warned that unless they showed restraint, 'unemployment will become Britain's incomes policy for a very long time to come' – a pretty accurate prediction, as it turned out. But the very fact that Jones needed to stake all his political capital to get it through should have been deeply worrying for the government. No other union leader could match his prestige, popularity or flint-like charisma; without his influence, the unions could easily have turned it down. An economic policy so dependent on the support of a man in his early sixties was no recipe for long-term success.[19]

There were deeper problems with the flat-rate limit. For one thing, it came much too late: as events were to show, international confidence in the British economy had now almost evaporated. What was more, the cure was just as dangerous politically as the disease. Although £6 a week sounded like a raise, it was actually nothing of the kind. For a very low-paid worker on just £24 a week, £6 sounded like a 25 per cent pay rise. But since *prices* were still rising by 27 per cent, that actually meant a slight drop in his living standards. For a typical manual worker on £50 a week, meanwhile, £6 represented only a 10 per cent net increase, which meant an even bigger drop in his standard of living. And although Harold Wilson might talk about pulling together in the national interest, many ordinary people could not care less about working-class brotherhood. People like Hugh Scanlon's engineering workers wanted to preserve their standard of living, not to give it all up in the name of some seemingly illusory greater good. For the time being they held their tongues. But as their pay slipped behind and they found themselves forced to postpone their plans for a new car, a new cooker or a new holiday, resentment began to build.[20]

Depressingly, inflation was only the most obvious of Britain's economic woes. While almost every other Western country had reacted to the oil crisis by cutting spending, electoral pressures had deterred Denis Healey from putting the brakes on. In 1974–5, public spending had risen in cash terms by a staggering 35 per cent, while in 1975–6 it rose by a further 25 per cent. In accordance with Labour's manifesto promises, much of this money went on health, education, pensions and benefits: indeed, since 1960 the welfare state's share of GDP had increased from about 11 per cent to almost 20 per cent. Much of it, too, was devoured by local authorities, which had taken to throwing money around as though it would never run out. In four years, local government spending had risen by a barely credible 40 per cent, while local authorities had taken on an extra 800,000 staff in just over a decade, despite the fact that, in the same period, private sector employment had fallen by one million. All this was funded not just by higher taxes, but by unprecedented borrowing. In Heath's last year, borrowing had reached a record £4.5 billion, provoking great wailing and gnashing of teeth. But under

Wilson, borrowing reached £8 billion in 1974–5 and almost £11 billion in 1975–6, even more than the Treasury had predicted. As one American observer put it, Britain was like a 'debtor whose creditors can ill afford to force him under because they would lose too much in the process'. All the same, he noted, 'the dependence on foreign money is not only humiliating for the nation that was once the world's greatest financial power, it is risky in the extreme'.[21]

Not all Wilson's ministers were oblivious to the danger. The position was 'infinitely more serious than any of the crises we have faced over the past 20 years', Tony Crosland told local authorities in May 1975. 'For the time being, at least, the party is over.' His old friend Roy Jenkins went even further, pointing out that as a proportion of GDP, government spending had risen from 44 per cent to 60 per cent in just ten years. If it went any higher, Jenkins warned, 'freedom of choice' would be threatened: 'We are here close to one of the frontiers of social democracy.' What was more suggestive, though, was that even left-wing union leaders agreed with him. As the champion of the engineering workers, Hugh Scanlon consistently urged the government to spend less on public services and more on manufacturing. Lasting recovery, he remarked in 1976, would come not through employing an ever-growing army of social workers, but 'on the basis of a viable, efficient manufacturing industry with emphasis on those who make and sell and, if necessary, somewhat less emphasis on those who serve'.[22]

For months the Treasury had been working on a way to get spending under control, and on 1 July Denis Healey unveiled it to the Commons. The plan, he explained, was to 'fix cash limits for wage bills in the public sector', which sounded sensationally dull, but was to have enormous repercussions over the next decade. In the past, public spending had been worked out in terms of volume: the government agreed to finance a given project, and if the costs ballooned, then the Treasury found the money somewhere. But under the new system, departments were given a fixed limit for each project in current cash terms. If they went over budget, there was a small contingency fund, but then the money dried up. It was a brilliantly simple device to keep budgets down – and the Labour left hated it. Healey's strategy, grumbled Tony Benn, was 'pre-Keynesian and a recipe for a major slump' (a prediction that turned out to be quite wrong), while the National Executive meeting on 9 July was dominated by a blazing row between the Chancellor and the hard-left Ian Mikardo. 'I sometimes wonder where my colleagues live,' Healey said angrily. He had been 'talking to miners' in his Yorkshire constituency, and they all agreed with what he was trying to do. 'It's about bloody time,' they had told him. But all this was lost on his more idealistic colleagues. 'I see no reason for the existence of a Labour Government,' lamented Barbara Castle. 'We have adopted the Tory *mores*. The only difference is that we carry out Tory policies more efficiently than they do.'[23]

Taken together, the £6 pay deal and the introduction of cash limits managed to steer Britain away from hyperinflation. In August 1975, inflation stood at 27 per cent; twelve months later, it had fallen to less than 14 per cent. On the left, however, satisfaction with falling inflation was outweighed by horror at rising unemployment. By the summer of 1975, more than a million people were unemployed, with the jobless total peaking at 1.4 million the following January. 'Mrs Thatcher is now referring to us as the natural party of unemployment,' grumbled Tony Benn. Again and again he lectured his colleagues that they were re-enacting the treachery of Ramsay MacDonald: after one meeting, Castle noted that he had a 'routine speech about how this was 1931 all over again'. But when the left-leaning ministers dined at the Gay Hussar to discuss their approach, Benn's unctuous protestations of his own right-eousness drove Michael Foot into a towering rage. After listening to the familiar litany ('Our first job as a Labour Government is to defend the trade union movement ... Now as in 1931 we are selling them out'), Foot could stand it no more. 'You are dodging it,' he exploded. 'The best way to defend the trade union movement is for them to have a policy that deals with the country's problems.' Benn could no longer 'run away from the fact', he added, 'that inflation threatened to un-dermine everything we were trying to do'. But Benn knew what was going on: Foot and the others were really right-wingers in disguise. 'If I want to do anything other than frolic around on the margins of British politics,' he decided, 'I must be Leader of the Labour Party and Prime Minister.'[24]

Much as it would have horrified Benn's colleagues, this did not seem such an unlikely prospect in the late summer of 1975. Although the press had reacted favourably to the new pay settlement and Healey's introduction of cash limits, many Labour activists were outraged at the betrayal of socialism. A perfect example was the Welsh MP Neil Kin-nock, his rhetoric as red as his thinning hair, who was already making a name as the left's most flamboyant young talent. To Kinnock, the government's belated offensive against inflation was merely yet more treachery. 'When shall we in the Labour movement realize who are our supporters to whom we owe our existence, and when shall we start rewarding them for that?' he demanded in frustration. And, like Benn, he knew who to blame: the traitors in the Cabinet, who had ducked the challenge of 'taking on the Daleks in the Treasury, taking on the sterling holders, taking on the greed of the creditors,' and had fallen for 'the arguments of capitalism'. There must be no more 'concessions to our enemies', Kinnock said. 'In the nostalgic vocabulary so fashionable now, that is not the spirit of Dunkirk, it is the tragedy of Munich.'[25]

With the air hot with accusations of betrayal, the autumn's Labour Party conference was a thoroughly miserable occasion. The mood was 'appalling', Bernard Donoughue thought; 'an atmosphere of envy, hate and pettiness, which cannot produce good government or a decent society'. The party rewarded Denis Healey for his efforts, for instance, by kicking him off the National Executive, an extraordinary humiliation for an incumbent Chancellor. But delegates showed more tolerance to Michael Foot, whose speech begging them to get behind the government was one of his greatest rhetorical performances:

> We face an economic typhoon of unparalleled ferocity, the worst the world has seen since the 1930s. Joseph Conrad wrote a book called *Typhoon*, and at the end he told people how to do it. He said: 'Always facing it, Captain MacWhirr. That's the way to get through.'
>
> Always facing it – that's the way we have got to solve this problem. We don't want a Labour movement that tries to dodge it; we don't want people in a Labour Cabinet who try to dodge it. We want people who are prepared to show how they are going to face it . . .
>
> I am asking this movement to exert itself as it has never done before, to show the qualities which we have, the socialist imagination which exists in our movement, the readiness to re-forge the alliance, stronger than ever, between the government and the trade unions, and above all to show the supreme quality in politics, the red flame of socialist courage.

The irony was that although Foot's 'red flame of socialist courage' is often remembered as a paean to socialist idealism, it was actually a rhetorical device to persuade left-wing delegates to support spending cuts. Behind the 'gale of oratory and eloquence', wrote a bitter Tony Benn, Foot had 'misled the Conference'. There was a huge ovation, Benn noted, but 'I didn't stand'.[26]

It was the following evening's Tribune rally, though, that best captured the febrile atmosphere inside the Labour Party. First up was Eric Heffer, who told the crowd that 'we could end up like Chile', before a bravura performance by Neil Kinnock. Then came the veteran MP Ian Mikardo ('Mik' to his friends), who had already handed out a statement 'savagely attacking Jack Jones and the TUC and claiming that the poor had got poorer under this Government'. As Barbara Castle looked on in fascinated horror, the meeting rapidly descended into pandemonium:

> The hall was packed, the TV lights picking out the baroque moulding at the back of the platform, which gave the whole scene an air of dramatic intensity . . . Mik proceeded to read the speech he had handed out, piling selective statistic on selective statistic to give a hostile distortion of the work of the Government. Suddenly out of the crowded aisle where he had been standing leapt Jack Jones, up onto the platform, jabbing an accusing finger at Mik like an Old Testament prophet. As Mik had the microphone and Jack had not, all we could hear were a few snatches of what Jack said. 'I detest these attacks on the trade union movement' was all I caught. But he stood there for a full minute, jab following jab with inarticulate shout after inarticulate shout. It was electrifying.

Beside her, Tony Benn even thought that the confrontation might boil over into 'physical violence'. Disappointingly, however, Jones ran out of steam and sat down, allowing Mikardo to rattle through his denunciation of the TUC for selling out the workers' interests. When he had finished, there was a huge gale of applause, and some people gave him a standing ovation. After that there was only one man who could save the day. Once again Michael Foot was in outstanding form, making 'the pay policy sound like a socialist crusade'; once again the audience rose like the congregation at a revivalist prayer meeting. Ominously, however, not all the delegates were impressed. A row or two in front of Castle, a woman hissed angrily: 'He's sold out,' and gave the Communist salute.[27]

With the confrontation played out in front of the world's press, it is hardly surprising that the markets were losing faith in the government's ability to turn Britain around. The really surprising thing, in fact, is that confidence had not already evaporated completely. Although few ministers seem to have realized it, Britain had actually been extraordinarily lucky. For two years the pound had been propped up by the Arab oil producers, who had deposited a large proportion of their massive winnings in sterling, more out of a sense of tradition than out of any great faith in Britain's prospects. But this happy situation was never going to last for ever; as Edmund Dell remarked, 'it could only be a matter of time before the oil-rich countries realized the unwisdom of what they were doing.' Most foreign observers still took an extremely dim view of Britain's prospects: in August, the *Wall Street Journal* had warned that the government's policy of 'spend and spend, tax and tax, inflate and inflate' was 'a model study in how to bring to ruin a once-vigorous nation'. And by the autumn of 1975 the pound was already in deep trouble, the exchange rate beginning to slide as countries drew down their sterling balances. In nine months the Bank of England spent some £800 million trying to defend the pound. But in the long run the only solution was to win back international confidence – and that would mean spending cuts.[28]

It was a sullen autumn. In scruffy venues at colleges across London – St Martin's College of Art, Westfield College, Chelsea School of Art, City of London Polytechnic – Malcolm McLaren's new band played to indifferent audiences. They were 'very slow, very amateurish', one early listener remembered. Afterwards, he recalled, 'one of them was crying because they were so terrible'. Like so many avant-garde rock groups before them, the Sex Pistols picked up a handful of fans, often bored teenagers from outer London's dormitory towns and suburbs. Many already wore the ripped clothes and scalped haircuts that would become synonymous with the Sex Pistols. As yet, though, they were a tiny minority: in the charts and on the airwaves, the sounds of the autumn were Rod Stewart's 'Sailing', Hot Chocolate's 'You Sexy Thing' and Queen's 'Bohemian Rhapsody'.[29]

The headlines, however, belonged to Britain's football hooligans, who had marked the new campaign with an orgy of violence surpassing anything that had gone before. On the very first day of the new season, hundreds of Manchester United fans ran amok in Wolverhampton, stabbing fourteen people and causing thousands of pounds' worth of damage. 'It must have been bottling up inside them,' a police spokesman said gloomily, 'all through the long, hot summer.' But worse was to follow. When Chelsea visited Luton on the last Saturday in August, enraged away fans invaded the pitch, attacking players and officials, punching the Luton goalkeeper to the ground, and leaving one steward nursing a broken nose and another with stab wounds. After the final whistle, they ran wild in the streets, vandalizing cars and shops; on the way home, they burned out a railway carriage, threw seats and toilet fittings out onto the track, and forced the guard to lock himself in to protect the mail. On the same day, fifty Manchester United fans were arrested after fighting broke out in Stoke, sixty Rangers fans were arrested outside Ibrox, and dozens of Liverpool supporters set fire to the train carrying them home from Leicester, causing £70,000 worth of damage. 'To travel to and from matches', lamented *The Times* two days later, 'is to run the gauntlet with these packs of marauding fiends as they terrorize the community at large.'[30]

London that autumn felt like a city under siege. With a small Provisional IRA cell at loose in the capital, barely a week seemed to go by without reports of another atrocity. Their campaign began in earnest on the evening of 28 August, when they hid a bomb above the Peter Brown men's outfitters on Oxford Street, detonating it at precisely the point when the pavements were packed with theatre-goers, drinkers and late-night shoppers. Miraculously, only seven people were injured. But this was only the beginning of the horror. The very next night, a bomb-disposal officer was called to investigate a box in the doorway of a shoe shop in Kensington Church Street. When he opened it, a bomb went off in his face, killing him instantly. After that, nobody going out in London after dark could not be sure that they, too, would not fall victim to what the papers called the 'New Blitz'. On 5 September, a bomb killed two people and injured sixty-three in the lobby of the Hilton on Park Lane; a month later, a bomb exploded in a bus shelter on Piccadilly, killing one man and injuring twenty, many of them children heading home after an evening out. And early on 23 October, just as Tony Benn was getting ready for work, he heard 'the most enormous explosion'. Immediately assuming it was an attack on Roy Jenkins's house down the street, he dashed to the front door. 'Through the trees in Campden Hill Square,' he recorded, 'I saw flames licking up twenty-five to thirty feet and realised that the explosion was over by Hugh Fraser's house.' The car bomb had indeed been intended for Fraser, a right-wing Tory MP. Tragically, it killed Professor Gordon Hamilton Fairley, one of the world's leading cancer specialists, who had spotted it while walking his dog and gone over to investigate. He left a wife and four children.

Even by the standards of the IRA, the murder of a man who specialized in curing children with leukaemia was a grotesque obscenity. 'Will the men of blood never realise', asked the *Mirror* the next day, 'that every bomb HARDENS the nation's feelings against them? And STRENGTHENS the nation's determination never to give in until they join their partners in death behind bars?' But the IRA took no notice; instead, they switched their attention to the capital's nightlife. On 30 October they detonated a bomb in the doorway of a West End Italian restaurant, the blast so great that Michael Palin, eating a Chinese takeaway several streets away, heard the terrifying 'dull thud'. Two weeks later, they threw a bomb through the window of Scott's in Mayfair, killing one diner and seriously injuring eighteen. Six days after that, a man threw another bomb through the windows of Walton's in Chelsea, killing two people and injuring twenty. In each case, the attacks were designed to cause as many casualties as possible. Not only did the bombers strike at peak times, but they packed their devices with nuts, bolts and ball bearings, ensuring the maximum suffering for those caught in the wrong place at the wrong time. There seemed no escape from the horror: after another car bomb near Marble Arch, Scotland Yard warned that the IRA might strike 'anyone at any time', and urged drivers to check underneath their cars every morning. 'Are you sure you're not living next door to terrorists?' asked the grim commentary on the Metropolitan Police's public information film *Time of Terror*. 'Wherever you are, beware.'[31]

The London bombings made for a sombre conclusion to a thoroughly miserable year. Six out of ten people told Gallup that they were worse off than in 1974; four out of ten thought things would be even worse in 1976. Opening the International Boat Show at Earls Court at the turn of the year, Prince Philip defiantly insisted that 'the country has a long history. We've been through these storms before and we'll certainly get through this one.' But not everybody shared his optimism. When the *Daily Mirror*'s panel of experts unveiled their predictions for 1976, they made for singularly depressing reading: 'Street violence will increase and so will crime among juveniles ... Wage rises will be smaller. Living standards will fall. Unemployment will continue to rise, with more and more people chasing fewer and fewer jobs ... Common Market rules will force up the price of our butter, cheese and beef ... Several big firms will go bust.' Perhaps it was no wonder that even as some 50,000 revellers were toasting the New Year in the West End, Bernard Donoughue sat wrapped in gloom. 'What a grubby world,' he wrote that night in his diary. 'I cannot say that 1976 holds any fine prospects ... Further political, social and economic deterioration in Britain.' Fortunately, he consoled himself, he had his family, 'compared to which nothing else matters'.[32]

16

Our World is in Danger

The Sergeant looks at England, and it's changed before his eyes;
Old virtues, thrift and prudence, are increasingly despised;
Old values are devalued as the currency inflates;
Old certainties are scoffed at by the new sophisticates . . .

David Edgar, *Destiny* (1976)

LEELA: *These 'taxes': they are a sacrifice to the gods?*
THE DOCTOR: *Well, roughly speaking, but paying taxes is*
more painful.

Doctor Who, 'The Sun Makers', 26 November 1977

For one man, the lesson of the London bombing campaign was that, in the war against terrorism, there was no room for half measures. On 4 November 1975, the day after a car bomb in Connaught Square had almost crippled an innocent London solicitor, Ross McWhirter decided it was time to take a stand. For years he had fought trade unionists, pacifists, socialists and Communists. Now he took on the IRA. Unveiling his 'Beat the Bombers' campaign at a sparsely attended press conference, the co-editor of the *Guinness Book of Records* warned that Britain was 'gradually wallowing into a situation of terror and violence'. The answer was simple. All 'Southern Irish nationals' should carry identity cards, and leave copies of their passport photographs and signatures with the police. On top of that, the government should reintroduce the death penalty for terrorists, while McWhirter himself promised to pay £50,000 for information that secured a conviction. When one of the reporters asked if he was worried about becoming a target himself, McWhirter agreed that it was a possibility. 'But when you feel as strongly as I do about the need for the murderous and senseless bombings to cease,' he said passionately, 'then it is not something you can worry about.'

To most people in the autumn of 1975, Ross McWhirter was one of the eccentric *Record Breakers* twins, more famous for his television banter with Roy Castle than for his views on the death penalty or his role in the right-wing group Self-Help. Few people paid much attention to his words that day; but the IRA did. On the evening of Thursday, 27 November, McWhirter's wife was getting out of her car outside their house in suburban Enfield when two men with guns rose suddenly from the shrubbery. At the sound of her tyres on the gravel her husband had already come to the door, and as it swung open the gunmen fired two shots. Hit in the head and the chest, McWhirter did not stand a chance. Although he was rushed to hospital, he died on arrival, the first victim of a political assassination on mainland Britain in living memory. 'England should be weeping this evening,' said his friend Rhodes Boyson in the first of many tributes, 'for the death of law and order.' And at the House of Commons the next day, Margaret Thatcher made no effort to disguise her shock and grief. She 'knew Ross McWhirter well and admired him a great deal', she said. 'He was one of the finest people of his generation. He was never timid or passive about his belief in liberty. He was active each and every day in protecting and preserving individual liberty. The terrorists may have killed him and others, but . . . they must never conquer that indomitable spirit of unhesitating courage without which freedom would perish.'[1]

McWhirter's killers, who had escaped in the family Ford Granada, were captured two weeks later after one of the most extraordinary sieges in London's history. Having noticed that the IRA men tended to return to the same targets, the Met had flooded the West End with plain-clothes officers. And when, on the night of 6 December, the gang attacked Scott's restaurant for a second time, the police were ready for them. After a dramatic car chase through Mayfair and Marylebone, the four gunmen fled on foot down Balcombe Street, next to Marylebone station. Ducking through the first open door they found, they eventually ended up in No. 22B, a council flat belonging to the dumbfounded John and Sheila Matthews. Within hours the flat was surrounded by police marksmen, but the IRA men refused to budge, using Mr and Mrs Matthews as human shields and demanding safe passage to Dublin. For six days the siege continued, a stalemate played out in front of hundreds of onlookers. Driving home from a party four days into the siege,

Michael Palin stopped at the traffic lights and saw the flat illuminated by gigantic floodlights, surrounded by 'groups of police, smiling, telling jokes', as well as a Thames Television van with a camera crew. But on 12 December, after the police had cut off their electricity and hot water, the gunmen gave in. Eventually all four were given life sentences at the Old Bailey, only to be released twenty years later under the Good Friday agreement. Gerry Adams called them 'our Nelson Mandelas', although it is hard to imagine Mandela drafting a list of targets that included Madame Tussauds, the National Gallery and University College London, all of which were on the gang's 'death list'. No doubt the families of those killed or maimed in Piccadilly, Kensington and Mayfair would have chosen a rather different comparison.[2]

In the meantime, Ross McWhirter's work went on. For years this pale, passionate, tenacious man had campaigned against what he saw as the advance of socialism. In 1964 he had stood as the Conservative parliamentary candidate in Edmonton, but his most notable efforts came in the courts. His career as a litigant had begun ten years earlier, when, not yet 30, he had sued the National Union of Journalists for defaming his twin brother Norris. In the same year he co-founded the bestselling *Guinness Book of Records*, and over the next two decades led a bizarre double life, both record-breaking front man and libertarian crusader. In 1967 he launched four separate legal cases to stop Enfield's grammar and secondary modern schools being turned into comprehensives; in 1968 he successfully forced the Home Office to recount the votes in Enfield's local elections; in 1969 he challenged Jim Callaghan's handling of the new parliamentary boundaries; in 1970 he took the Independent Broadcasting Authority to court for transmitting subliminal messages during a Labour party political broadcast. Two years later he claimed that Edward Heath had acted unlawfully in signing the Treaty of Accession to the Common Market, and in his last case, in October 1975, he used a High Court injunction to free passengers' vehicles from a P&O ferry that had been held up by a labour dispute in Southampton. To some he was a hero, to others a bore. But he never gave up.

By the early 1970s McWhirter, like many other right-wing campaigners, had become convinced that Edward Heath's Conservatives were colluding in the betrayal of Britain. Court actions, he realized, would not be enough, and while he had plenty of time for Margaret Thatcher, he had nothing but contempt for the 'Old Gang' of Heath, Whitelaw and Prior, 'a bunch of political failures'. At the beginning of 1975 he set up the Current Affairs Press, with a budget of £100,000 and a fortnightly newsletter, *Majority: The Journal of Free Enterprise and Self-Help*. Its main purpose, McWhirter said, was 'standing up to the unions', and the newsletter gave useful advice on how to set up generators, pool car resources, break strikes and so on. In the event of a national strike, McWhirter added, he would be able to print 3 million newspapers a day, while 'Operation Road-Lift', relying on volunteer drivers, would break any nationwide rail strike. To many observers this seemed dangerously close to General Sir Walter Walker territory, and indeed some of McWhirter's pronouncements did carry a strong whiff of paranoia. As always, however, he was indomitable. In June 1975, a week after the European referendum, he had lunch with the war hero and former Conservative minister Viscount de L'Isle, VC, who shared his view that somebody had to stand up against the Communists in Westminster and Whitehall. A month later, after a larger meeting at the Grosvenor House Hotel on Park Lane, they agreed to set up a new group to rouse public support for conservative values. McWhirter had just finished work on its founding document, a fifteen-point Charter of Rights and Liberties, when the gunmen struck.[3]

In his loathing of the welfare state, his rejection of the post-war consensus and his contempt for the nation's politicians, Ross McWhirter spoke for an increasingly assertive section of Britain's conservative middle classes. The mid-1970s were 'a time of crisis for the middle classes, who are subjected to unprecedented pressures and, at the same time, to unprecedented denigration', wrote Patrick Hutber, the City editor of the *Sunday Telegraph*. The Oxford-educated son of a civil servant and a doctor's daughter, Hutber himself lived in rural Buckinghamshire with 'four children, three cats, one dog, two horses and a pony'. Like many of his readers, he derived 'warmth and comfort' from his middle-class background, and saw no need to apologize for it. Yet when he invited his readers to write to him about 'their hopes, their fears and their finances', he was struck by their overwhelming pessimism. 'Just who the hell do they think they are to tell me what I can buy or what I cannot,' ran a typical letter from a *Telegraph* reader, horrified by the 'growth of crime, hooliganism, pornography, violent vandalism and terrorism' as well as inflation and 'strangling controls'. Another man wrote of his 'deep sense of helplessness, the feeling of utter frustration, at being unable to do anything to improve the situation'. 'It is my belief that the way things are going, the middle classes are doomed to a gradual extinction over the course of the next generation or two,' agreed a woman from London; 'and with their disappearance, we shall have lost the last bulwark of democracy.'[4]

Hutber's call to arms, published in 1976 as *The Decline and Fall of the Middle Class – and How it Can Fight Back*, formed part of a swelling chorus of discontent. In the *Evening Standard*, the columnist Alan Watkins warned of a 'middle class revolt'; on ITV, an hour-long documentary investigated 'the mangling of the middle classes'. In *The Times*, the historian Ian Bradley announced that, after years of dominance, middle-class influence was in deep decline. 'Thrift, self-help and the gospel of work have been casualties in an age of instant credit and raging inflation,' he explained. 'Permissiveness has swept away the puritan moral code and threatened to destroy the sanctity of family life. More and more, the real power in the country is coming to lie with the trade union bosses and the captains of industry.' In the next few days, letters poured in from readers delighted that somebody had articulated their anxieties. 'It is time we, the so-called and much maligned middle class, cried "Enough!",' wrote F. E. Rogers from Essex, whose father had been a labourer and who now owned his own business. He was not alone. 'The people who've been hardest hit in this country', remarked a woman from a manicured middle-class suburb of Blackburn, 'are what are called the self-employed, such as we are, middle people. If you have any personal ambition, if you have any money left to build up the firm, it's taken away.' Sometimes, she said, it felt 'almost as if it had been diabolically arranged. Squash the middle people.'[5]

As the product of a middle-class upbringing and an old-fashioned education, Patrick Hutber was typical of thousands, even millions of people who feared that everything they believed in was falling apart. The very phrase 'middle-class values', Hutber lamented, was now used in a pejorative sense: even the General Synod of Church of England now made vague noises about shedding 'its middle-class image'. 'The values we've believed in – the king, the empire, a hierarchical society – they're all seen now not just as old-fashioned but as downright wrong,' says a retired brigadier in Piers Paul Reid's novel *A Married Man* (1979). Plenty of people would have agreed with him, for as middle-class readers pored over their copies of the *Daily Express* and the *Daily Mail*, it genuinely seemed that their world had changed. If the papers were to be believed, the schools were full of juvenile drug-takers, the universities were crammed with Marxist radicals and the streets were teeming with muggers, immigrants, feminists and sociologists. This was a caricature, of course, but even many liberal-minded people thought it contained a grain of truth. Shortly before his death in 1975, the great comic song-writer Michael Flanders told Kenneth Tynan that it 'puzzled and saddened him to think that all the things he was, and had been brought up to be proud of – professional middle-class, well-educated at non-snob public school, liberal with a small "l" in politics and morals – had suddenly become bad things, to be ashamed of. He said he couldn't really adjust to this new image of himself.' And two years later Roy Strong complained in his diary that 'the virtues of talent, hard work and rewards' were in deep decay, thanks largely, he thought, to the government's high taxation. 'The middle and the professional classes', he wrote, 'have had their incomes and their values seemingly flung to the wall.'[6]

Behind all this talk of decaying values was the stark reality of the financial squeeze. After years of growth, real net earnings* fell by an estimated 18 per cent during 1975 and 1976, which came as a terrible shock to a generation fattened by affluence. What was more, in stark contrast with the Great Depression, the burden fell most heavily on the rich and comfortable – people like Patrick Hutber, Michael Flanders and Roy Strong. Their earnings were eaten away by inflation; their investments were subject to heavy taxation; their share values had been slashed by the stock market crash; their dividends had been wiped out by the collapse of business profits. Even their homes were worth a lot less than they had paid for them during the heady days of the Heath administration. During the Barber boom of 1972–3, with banks throwing money at property developers, house prices had rocketed by a stunning 70 per cent, the biggest margin in living memory. Young middle-class couples, who might once have spent years renting, had jumped aboard the property bandwagon, priding themselves on their stripped-pine furniture, their painstakingly restored fireplaces, their gigantic pot plants and expensive faux-rustic crockery. But now the bubble had completely burst. In 1974 house prices fell by 13 per cent. A year later they fell by another 16 per cent; a year after that they fell by a further 8 per cent. 'Everything had started to slump and slide and crack,' reflects Anthony Keating, an amateur property developer, in Margaret Drabble's novel The Ice Age (1977). 'Caught in a trap of his own making', Anthony contemplates the collapse of his ambitions, his 'imagined fortune' now merely 'a tangled mess of unsaleable liabilities'. And he was

---

* This takes into account not just the economic slowdown, but price rises, energy and transport costs, and, of course, the effect of increased taxation.

far from alone. The middle-class family was 'up against the wall,' remarked one of Hutber's correspondents. 'I haven't seen a play in London in two years. I only eat in restaurants on business. Can't afford the gardener once a week any more. You start adding it up and it amounts to a social revolution.'[7]

For Hutber, the greatest threat to the comfortable classes was inflation, which struck at 'the most vital elements of [middle-class] existence – thrift, responsibility, forward thinking and stability'. Far more than foreign holidays, brand-new cars or piano lessons for the children, he thought, savings and investments were the essential accessories of a middle-class lifestyle. But with prices rising so quickly and Denis Healey taxing investment income above £1,000 a year at 45 per cent, many *Telegraph* readers complained that it was pointless trying to save money. 'Although I am placing £50 a month with a building society, I am acutely aware that this is being continuously eroded by inflation and although I could save more there seems no point in doing so,' explained one reader. As Hutber pointed out, the shock of rising prices fell heaviest on particular middle-class groups, notably self-employed professionals, small businessmen, shopkeepers, workers on fixed incomes, workers who did not belong to trade unions and, above all, the elderly. Indeed, to pensioners who had spent years putting money aside, inflation seemed a moral as well as an economic challenge. 'I think people of my generation have had a very rough deal, living through two world wars and being brought up to recognize hard work and thrift as virtues,' lamented another *Telegraph* reader, calling himself 'embittered, frustrated and apprehensive'. Like many pensioners, he felt 'cheated' by the government. His only consolation was that he would not long 'remain to be cheated for ever'.[8]

Public outrage at rapid inflation, however, was as nothing compared with middle-class fury at the rising tax burden. As recently as the mid-1950s, relatively few families had suffered the taxman's close attentions. In 1955 a married father of two, earning about the national average, had paid less than 4 per cent in income taxes and National Insurance. But as government spending rose, so did the tax burden: by 1975 a married man on average earnings paid about 25 per cent of his income. Taxation, wrote Anthony Sampson, had 'become as much part of Englishness as the food and the weather', its impact reflected in 'the spate of weddings in autumn, the rush of dons to lecture in America, the proliferation of private dining-rooms, the fondness of authors for living abroad, and the nomadic existence of stars and pop singers'. Conservative newspapers howled that high taxation was holding Britain back; only by cutting taxes, they argued, could the nation compete with its European rivals. In fact, the overall direct tax burden in Britain in the late 1970s, at 26 per cent of GDP, was actually lower than in France (27 per cent) and West Germany (28 per cent). What *was* true, however, was that marginal rates, paid by the very richest people in society, were much higher in Britain, which explains the outrage of the Conservative press. Indeed, by later standards income taxes for the rich were very high indeed. Under Wilson and Healey, the top rate of earned income tax (for those making more than £24,000 a year), reached 83 per cent, while the top rate on investment income (which, in fairness, very few people paid) was a staggering 98 per cent. And since tax bands were deliberately *not* increased in line with inflation, thousands of people found themselves pushed up towards the higher tax brackets – which only heightened the impression that, as the papers claimed, Healey was determined to squeeze the middle classes 'until the pips squeak'.[9]

Complaints about high taxes were the stuff of countless dinner-party conversations in the mid-1970s. Even before Labour had returned to office, Tony Crosland had been struck by the 'exceptional resentment of high taxation', and Healey's decision to increase income tax only inflamed middle-class passions. For the 80,000 people at the top of the earnings pyramid, the 83 per cent rate seemed a terrible affront: the theatre director Peter Hall worked out that to afford the £1,500 to send his son to Cambridge, he needed 'another £7,000 or £8,000 to have that clear after tax'. One King's Road nightclub proprietor warned his customers that whenever they ordered champagne at £17 a bottle (which, it has to be said, was exorbitantly expensive by the standards of the day), they needed to earn £100 to pay for it. But the culture of complaint was not limited to the rich and famous. 'There's so many different taxes,' grumbled a young man from one of Blackburn's suburban estates. 'You can't name a thing you're not taxed on. Soon we'll be handing our wage straight to the government and they're gonna say, "Here's a couple of quid for you," and we'll say, "Oh, thanks very much."' Not surprisingly, therefore, few days seemed to go by without some new feature in the *Daily Mail* about the swelling ranks of tax exiles, from Roger Moore and Rod Stewart to Billy Butlin and Engelbert Humperdinck. Even the England football manager Don Revie pointed an accusing finger at the tax laws when he defected to the United Arab Emirates in July 1977. For a man who had grown up on the poverty-stricken streets of Middlesbrough, the chance to earn

"OF COURSE THERE'S NOT MUCH TO TAKE — YOU KEEP ROBBING THE SAME COACH!"

Although very few *Sun* readers would have paid Denis Healey's top tax rate of 83 per cent, Stanley Franklin's cartoon, published on 14 April 1975, reflected the growing anxiety that the bushy-browed Chancellor was determined to squeeze the middle classes for every penny.

£340,000 in four years, tax free, was simply too good to resist. The Arab sheikhs' offer was 'an unbelievable opportunity to secure my family's future', Revie told the *Mail*, adding that the British 'tax structure, let alone the salaries available, makes it impossible to earn this kind of money at home'. It did not save him from the fury of the press, though.[10]

By far the most entertaining shriek of rage against Healey's tax policy, however, came from a very unlikely source. At the beginning of 1977 Robert Holmes, the script editor of *Doctor Who*, found himself enmeshed in a byzantine battle with the Inland Revenue over the taxes due on his freelance earnings. Exasperated by his failure to make headway, Holmes poured his frustrations into the script for one of Tom Baker's stranger adventures. 'The Sun Makers' finds the Time Lord travelling to Pluto in the distant future, a society dominated by the corrupt, bureaucratic and avaricious Company. The people of Pluto live in vast Megropolis tower blocks, where they are ground down by eye-watering taxes. Each Megropolis is governed by a Gatherer, and each Gatherer reports to the Collector, a grotesque little man who commands the dreaded Inner Retinue and says things like: 'Grinding oppression of the masses is the only policy that pays dividends.' As usual in *Doctor Who* in the 1970s – not least because inflation had eaten away at the show's budget – much of the story involves people running interminably up and down corridors, but even these are named after tax forms. The Doctor joins forces with a small band of tax dodgers, and despite the Collector's bravado ('An ongoing insurrectionary situation would not be acceptable to my management. This fiscal period we're aiming for a seven percent increase in the gross planetary product'), the villains are, as always, overthrown. Gatherer Hade, whose red face, bushy eyebrows and orotund rhetoric are suspiciously reminiscent of Denis Healey, is thrown off the top of a tower block, while the Collector dissolves into a kind of intergalactic seaweed. 'I fed two percent growth tax into the computers,' says the Doctor. 'Index linked. Blew the economy and he couldn't take it.' No doubt plenty of viewers wished their own tax problems could be solved so easily.[11]

Back on Earth, what really infuriated many people was the belief that their tax money was being frittered away on waste and welfare. The middle classes had been complaining about waste for decades, and Viscount Rothermere had set up an Anti-Waste League as early as 1921. Half a century on, their complaints were more anguished than ever, largely because the government was spending so much more money. In 1963, the last full year before Harold Wilson's rise to power, public spending had been just 35 per cent of GDP. By 1973 it was more than 40 per cent; by 1976, after three years of extraordinary growth, it was almost 60 per cent. And to the fury of the Conservative press, a lot of this money went on the welfare state. In 1946, social security, health and education had accounted for just 6 per cent of Britain's national income. Three decades on, however, these three leviathans of the welfare state accounted for about 20 per cent, a level that remained more or less constant for the next thirty years. But although conservative analysts claimed that this over-generosity lay behind Britain's competitive decline, the facts tell a different story. As the journalist Bernard Nossiter pointed out in 1978, Britain spent 7.7 per cent of GDP on unemployment benefit, old age pensions, family allowances and sickness benefits. That might sound like a lot. But it was far less than the totals in Belgium and Holland (14 per cent), France and Germany (12.5 per cent), Italy (10 per cent), or even the United States (8 per cent). Even before Mrs Thatcher came to power, in other words, welfare spending in Britain was actually lower than almost anywhere else in the industrialized world.[12]

Yet at a time when so many people were feeling the pinch, all of this seemed beside the point. The press seized gleefully on cases of 'dole queue scroungers', such as Patrick Deevy of Liverpool, who claimed in 1977 that he had fraudulently collected £36,000 in benefits. His facts did not quite add up, but the newspapers did not care: what mattered was the moral impact. These stories often had a racial dimension: in pubs and clubs across the country, people exchanged urban legends about 'sponging' immigrants, almost always passed on via some mysteriously untraceable 'mate' or 'friend of a friend'. 'My mate works in a garage,' one woman told a journalist. 'This black comes in with his car, you know. American job with leopard-skin upholstery, bunch of plastic tulips in the back. My mate says, "Okay, come back Monday." He comes back. It's a big job, eighty quid. He drives off, winds down the window and says, "Send the bill to Social Security."' It was sheer myth, of course, but none the less potent for that. 'You can get a television from Social Security,' another elderly woman explained. 'They buy one with doors, like a cabinet. Then, you see, it's classed as a piece of furniture ... I've got a friend who works in Social Security, she told me that's how they do it, so I know it's true.'[13]

Although polls found that most people remained deeply attached to the principle of the welfare state, attitudes to recipients were rather different. Hostility to 'scroungers' and 'spongers' seems to have been particularly marked among the elderly, among whom it blurred into shock at the erosion of the self-discipline they had once taken for granted. 'The Welfare State has weakened the moral backbone of the country. People get to demand and expect things to be done for them instead of learning to do them for themselves,' complained a retired local historian from Blackburn, now in his seventies. 'The Welfare State and do-gooders, they're undermining the guts and morale of the people of this country,' agreed a former Lancashire cotton-worker. 'There's not enough self-reliance today, there's too much help.' But younger people, too, often shared their scepticism about the plight of the unemployed. 'Most people on the dole could find work if they wanted to,' said a young man from a middle-class estate. 'A lot of people just don't want to work,' said Mrs Goatley, a policemen's wife in her mid-thirties. 'They're quite content to live on unemployment, and really, well, they're just suckers on society, aren't they? They're just draining the country of its life-blood.'[14]

Although some politicians shuddered to hear such talk, even Labour insiders thought there was some truth in it. Bernard Donoughue, for example, thought that 'welfarism' was becoming a 'national way of life', with the interests of public sector workers 'given priority over the millions of ordinary citizens who paid for it and were its users'. And at one Cabinet meeting in November 1975, Denis Healey took a similar line. 'At the Labour clubs,' he said, 'you'll find there's an awful lot of support for this policy of cutting public expenditure. They will tell you all about Paddy Murphy up the street who's got eighteen children, has not worked for years, lives on unemployment benefit, has a colour television and goes to Majorca for his holidays.' 'If that's the case,' grumbled Tony Benn, 'I'd be interested to know how many people who frequent the Labour clubs actually vote Labour.' But if the former Viscount Stansgate thought he knew what people in the old-fashioned Labour clubs really thought, then he had a shock coming.[15]

So-called scroungers were just one group among many enemies lurking at the fringes of the middle-class imagination in the mid-1970s, from hooligans and terrorists to sociologists and pornographers, from progressive schoolteachers and radical social workers to interfering bureaucrats and militant trade unionists. Even *Coronation Street*, the nation's most popular slice of working-class nostalgia, reflected the sense of middle-class resentment. As a proprietor of a struggling photographic firm, Ernie Bishop can barely hide his bitterness at the 'great conspiracy' to do him down. 'Why, if you're ordinary and honest and you slave away, why does life just become more and more impossible every day?' he bursts out. 'And don't tell me it's not the government. They don't care. If the TUC barks, they throw them a bone. And where does the bone come from? From the skeletons of all the rest of us.'

In what the press saw as a sign of the times, poor Ernie eventually comes to a sticky end, killed by burglars during an armed robbery. But as Alwyn Turner remarks, 'the dissatisfied and disgruntled cynic, the personification of raging impotence' was very common in the mid-1970s. Some of the most popular television characters of the day were mouthpieces for reactionary anxieties, from Alf Garnett, forever inveighing against feminists, 'coons', 'Micks' and 'Commies', to Basil Fawlty, who blames 'bloody Wilson' for his inadequate fire extinguisher, thinks modern men look like 'orang-utans' and is disgusted by the 'riff-raff' who patronize his hotel. Then there is *Rising Damp*'s Rupert Rigsby, a mean-spirited miser who worships the Royal Family, loathes the Labour Party and makes no effort to hide his contempt for his student lodgers. In 'Stand Up and Be Counted' (1975), Rigsby throws himself into a local by-election, enthusiastically canvassing for the Conservatives, blaming 'Russian gold' for the three-day week and waxing lyrical on the need to bring back hanging. 'Our world is in danger!' he tells Miss Jones. But like so many lower-middle-class businessmen, he never quite clicks with the Tory old guard, especially when the patrician candidate not only gets his name wrong but condemns his boarding house as 'the unacceptable face of capitalism'. 'The people can do without people like you, Ragsby,' says Colonel DeVere-Brown. 'And I can do without you, you great public school twit!' Rigsby spits back. 'Just because I wasn't born without a silver spoon in my mouth! Yes, well, I can get along without you mate, I'm a self-made man.' The new Conservative leader herself could hardly have put it better.[16]

Although few people were quite as outspoken as Leonard Rossiter's splendid creation, the penny-pinching landlord's contempt for those below and above him was far from unusual. 'We struggle to buy our own homes and send our children to good schools, while the poorer people live in council estates and have everything done for them,' one suburban London couple told researchers. In a Blackburn bungalow, a young woman told Jeremy Seabrook that 'the average working man has it very easy. They're always on strike for more holidays and more pay.' And another upper-middle-class woman went even further:

> I can't understand people who feel guilty about the working classes. People will always be different, even if everyone has the same houses and the same money. We would always be richer in our minds than the working classes, just by reading books ... All they are concerned with is revenge, in the petty ways of their minds. Jealousy and bitching is their main occupation ... There is always going to be envy, there's always going to be people who are better off than others. It annoys me when people vote Labour out of emotionalism. My best friend voted Labour once, just out of emotion, because she felt it was the right thing to do. Edgar said: 'Are you mad? They are going to nationalise everything and you'll lose all your shares!' She was horrified. 'Oh God, what have I done?' she said. She's mad, completely mad![17]

As this might suggest, Britain in the mid-1970s was still a deeply snobbish society. A spectacular example was the country-house historian James Lees-Milne, whose diaries blazed with hatred for his social inferiors. 'One is suspicious of them all,' he recorded after discovering that his gardener might be looking for a new job. 'They have no loyalties, no morality, no gratitude, no decency – all those virtues for which *one* is so conspicuous. They think only of themselves and of money, and more money, and employers are "they", to be rooked, tricked and deceived.' By Lees-Milne's standards this was actually quite generous. In January 1974, as the country slid into economic crisis, he decided that 'the morale of the British Mr Average has never been lower, his values more debased, his covetousness, greed and lack of self-respect more conspicuous'. And after paying his domestic staff that summer, he wrote simply:

> I loathe and detest them. All they want is less work and more money. They have no decent feelings, no regard to truth. They are spoilt and rotten. I hope unemployment leaps to astronomical proportions, and that they are humiliated and come begging cap in hand for work. I shall be prepared to undergo every personal deprivation for the satisfaction of seeing them reduced to starvation.[18]

Although few people were quite so open about their prejudices, Lees-Milne was not the only distinguished writer smouldering with reactionary rage. 'Fuck the non-working classes,' Philip Larkin wrote to his friend and fellow poet Robert Conquest in 1971, 'fuck the students (fuck you students everywhere), fuck the Common Market e'en. Hurray for Ian Smith, Ian Paisley (fuck all branches of the IRA).' Complaints about unemployment, he told his friend Kingsley Amis, were 'canting nonsense'. People should tell the working classes ('an idle shower') that the 'filthy money-grubbing unions have priced your products out of the world markets, just as we said they would, and nobody wants them'. Meanwhile Amis himself, though originally a Labour supporter, was scarcely less reactionary. As a regular panellist on Radio Four, a columnist for the *Express* and a guest star in advertisements for Sanderson fabrics and W. H. Smith, he was probably the best-known literary novelist in the country, but he was also one of the most conservative.[19]

In *Jake's Thing* (1978), for example, we encounter Jake Richardson, a middle-aged Oxford don who has lost his libido and finds himself thoroughly alienated from the modern world. Exhausted, disillusioned and impotent, Jake finds himself beleaguered by immigrants, teenagers, left-wingers, feminists and psychotherapists, a Chamber of Horrors from the conservative imagination. When we first meet him, his Harley Street doctor is rushing through their consultation to make way for his appointment with an Arab oil sheikh. On his way out Jake tries to hail a taxi, but finds that 'no sooner had one black, brown or yellow person, or group of such, been set down on the pavement than Americans, Germans, Spaniards were taken up and vice versa'. His London street has been invaded by young couples and 'pairs of homosexuals'; his Oxford college is even planning to admit women. As Amis's biographer remarks, Jake is 'menaced by a falling real income, a decline in status and the emergence into power and affluence of uncouth persons who sneer at what he feels and stands for'.* In this, as in so much else, Jake is not merely an updated version of *Lucky Jim*'s Jim Dixon, but an accurate reflection of the sentiments of millions of middle-class readers.[20]

Amis was only the best-known member of a generation of writers who poked fun at the liberal values of the so-called permissive society, from Malcolm Bradbury (*The History Man*) and Piers Paul Read (*The Professor's Daughter*, *A Married Man*) to Margaret Drabble (*The Ice Age*, *The Middle Ground*) and Penelope Lively (*Next to Nature, Art*). In what the critic D. J. Taylor calls the 'anti-Sixties novel', the same themes crop up again and again: the hypocrisy and self-importance of the bohemian world, the folly of fashionable educational theories, the corruption of modern politics, the destructiveness of the new morality, and so on. Yet, as Taylor observes, the one thing that these novels rarely explored in any depth was the very thing for which the period is best remembered: the issue of the trade unions. A few left-wing writers tried to defend their working-class brethren: Barry Hines's books *The Price of Coal* (1979) and *Looks and Smiles* (1981), for example, are steeped in affection for the dying world of the industrial North. By and large, though, working-class people rarely appeared in the literary fiction of the late 1970s. The grammar school generation had long since moved to leafy, comfortable north London, while their successors, such as Martin Amis and Ian McEwan, had little interest in the kind of kitchen-sink realism that had been so popular twenty years previously. As a rule, therefore, the right had things their own way. 'In 1982 our last Conservative government was deposed by the trade unions, over whom it had attempted to assert its democratic authority,' runs a typical sentence in Julian Fane's *Revolution Island* (1980) – a line that might have come from some doom-laden exercise in futurology in the *Daily Express*.[21]

The 'filthy money-grubbing unions', as Larkin called them, haunted the conservative imagination in the 1970s. Middle-class hostility to the

---

* Some twenty years earlier, Amis had used these very words to describe the ideal readers of the long-forgotten conservative novelist Warwick Deeping.

unions stretched back for decades: ever since the Attlee years, Tory activists had persistently urged their leaders to take a tougher line against strikes and stoppages. Thanks to the Social Contract, however, Britain now had the most unambiguously pro-union government in its history. To Michael Foot and his colleagues, the Trade Unions and Labour Relations Act (1974) and the Employment Protection Act (1975) were laudable measures confirming the unions' legal immunities, guaranteeing employees' rights and protecting vulnerable workers from company fines and arbitrary dismissal. Yet even some of Foot's Cabinet colleagues, reflecting on the miners' victories over the Heath government and the alarming surge in wage settlements, felt they were going too far to appease the unions. At one point, Foot even wanted to give official pickets the right to block the highways, flagging down drivers and persuading them to support their strike – an idea he had got, not surprisingly, from the TUC. Almost unbelievably, there was even talk of making it a criminal offence *not* to stop and listen to pickets, which, as the police pointed out, was a recipe for disaster. In the end the Home Secretary, Roy Jenkins, managed to persuade his colleagues that there was a strong possibility of 'potentially violent scenes' unless the plan was dropped. Even so, left-wing activists remained confident that in time, they could strengthen the unions' role in British society. It was time, a Fabian Society pamphlet remarked, for the law to recognize that 'the idea of individual freedom is a middle-class concept which is often in conflict with the fact of working-class advancement through solidarity'.[22]

Strident predictions of trade union tyranny, which were very common in Conservative newspapers in the mid-1970s, concentrated above all on Foot's support for the closed shop – the system whereby a firm hired only members of a particular union. Abroad, the closed shop was rare: in the United States and many European countries it was legally banned. It was not particularly popular: a Gallup poll in 1973 found that even 53 per cent of trade union members themselves were opposed to it. All the same, it was gaining ground. In 1970 some 16 per cent of the British workforce belonged to a closed shop, rising to 23 per cent by the end of the decade. To union leaders, it ensured that workers stuck together and maximized their bargaining power; to their critics, it represented an intolerable restriction on personal freedom. In some quarters, Foot's enthusiasm for the closed shop provoked virtual apoplexy. Many freelance writers, including occasional columnists and critics, were horrified by the prospect that they would be forced to join the National Union of Journalists, whether they wanted to or not. At various points, scores of distinguished writers and academics, among them Rebecca West, Isaiah Berlin, Veronica Wedgwood, Arthur Koestler and J. B. Priestley, who were hardly card-carrying reactionaries, wrote to the *Times Literary Supplement* attacking Foot's labour laws as an assault on freedom of speech. In the end their protest fizzled out, but the issue never quite went away. A particular sore was the case of the Ferrybridge Six, a group of Yorkshire power station workers who had joined a breakaway union, were sacked under a closed shop agreement and were then denied unemployment benefit. This was 'pure undiluted fascism', claimed the Conservative MP Norman Tebbit, calling Foot 'a bitter opponent of freedom and liberty'. The next day *The Times* weighed in too, defending Tebbit for using the 'fascist' label 'in a legitimate descriptive sense'. The real question, the paper thought, was not 'is Mr Foot a fascist' but 'does Mr Foot know he is a fascist?'[23]

Given Foot's passionate commitment to the traditions of parliamentary democracy, to call him a fascist was simply ridiculous. But intemperate political rhetoric was very common in the mid-1970s, especially where the unions were concerned. They were a 'brotherhood of national misery', the formerly left-wing Paul Johnson wrote in the *New Statesman*. The union leaders were 'gangsters . . . conspir[ing] together to squeeze the community', while their 'Mark of Cain' was the closed shop: 'the right of union bureaucrats and bully-boys to coerce individuals into collective conformity, as a prelude to further erosions of human freedom'. As always, this was a bit extreme, but even many liberal-minded commentators agreed with Johnson's verdict. During the February 1974 election, the *Observer* had melodramatically warned that 'the arrival of the militants', backed up by a handful of 'fashionable Marxists', posed a serious threat to 'a free society'. And even inside the Labour Party, some thought that union power was becoming a threat to democracy. The unions were 'much too powerful', Jim Callaghan, once their great champion, told Tony Benn in January 1974. 'This is our problem.' Given how they later treated him, this showed remarkable prescience.[24]

But it was on the Conservative right that anti-union sentiment blazed most fiercely. The union leaders, wrote the High Tory columnist Peregrine Worsthorne, were 'brazenly and ruthlessly concerned about promoting a sectional interest, however this may "hurt" anybody else'. Alone among public figures, they were 'totally unencumbered by a sense of guilt', which allowed them to display 'a truly aristocratic disregard for public approval'. Time after time, they had reduced Britain 'to chaos far more effectively than the Luftwaffe was ever able to do', not least because their affluent opponents were far too polite to fight back. But the Queensberry Rules were 'wholly unsuited to the new reality of class war created by trade union militancy': the middle classes must 'tell them to get stuffed'. 'Herr Hitler was not a gentleman,' wrote Worsthorne. 'Nor are the Communists in the unions who are fighting to win.' It was time, he concluded, to take to the barricades, and 'fight for bourgeois values against overwhelming odds'.[25]

But who would lead the charge? Surely not the Conservative Party, which, after ten years with Edward Heath at the tiller, seemed painfully out of touch with middle-class hopes and fears. Despite his humble background – or, perhaps more accurately, precisely because of his acute social insecurity – Heath had never tried to articulate popular anxieties about crime, immigration, pornography and morality, while his corporatist economic policies were widely seen as an betrayal of middle-class interests. The party leadership, claimed the Worthing Conservative Association in 1973, showed 'an undue lack of appreciation of the aspirations and desires of those who would normally be expected to vote for the Conservative candidate'. And when Heath famously asked 'Who governs?', he discovered that many middle-class voters had run out of patience. In February 1974, the Tory share of the middle-class vote fell by a staggering 16 per cent, with most of the defectors turning to the Liberals instead. And worse was to come: when Heath led the Tories to defeat in October, he attracted less than 36 per cent of the national vote, the party's worst performance in its modern history.[26]

With the Conservative Party in the doldrums, many activists felt they had no alternative but to take up arms themselves. Grass-roots citizens' groups had never been as common in Britain as in, say, the United States, largely because the Tories had been so successful at reflecting middle-class interests. But 'respectable rebels' were not unknown. During the late Victorian and Edwardian period, middle-class activists had joined the Liberty and Property Defence League, the Anti-Socialist Union, the Middle-Class Defence League and the Personal Rights Association, which seethed with fury at the 'confiscatory' taxation and 'socialist' measures of Gladstone and his Liberal heirs. During the 1940s, too, fears of socialism had seen the rise of free-market groups such as the Economic League, Aims of Industry and the Society for Individual Freedom. Many were basically pro-business lobby groups, but they also attracted middle-class activists who felt the Tories were letting them down. By the post-war years, they were appealing to people in the lower echelons of the middle classes – small shopkeepers, garage owners, caterers, builders and grocers – who felt squeezed between an increasingly centralized, bureaucratic state on the one hand, and an articulate, aggressive trade union movement on the other. Such people were usually instinctive Conservatives: both Edward Heath's father, a successful Kentish builder, and Margaret Thatcher's father, a prosperous Grantham grocer, had belonged to this class. But now, as they contemplated their soaring costs and rising taxes, they felt friendless, abandoned by their old political allies. In future, some thought, they would have to fight for themselves.[27]

With inflation rocketing, the Tories divided and the newspapers full of Tony Benn's plans for British industry, the twelve-month period after February 1974 was a fertile time for middle-class protest groups. Across the North of England, for example, ratepayers' groups blossomed, reflecting public anger at the local authority rate rises announced in March and April. Thanks to inflation, the heavy-handed reorganization of local government and some very overenthusiastic council spending, the average increase in England and Wales was an excruciating 30 per cent. In Yorkshire, Humberside and the North East, most districts increased their rates by more than 50 per cent, and some even increased them by 100 per cent. 'My rates have gone up from £118 to £193 in a year,' a Newcastle man complained. 'When I opened my rates demand my mouth just fell.'

That summer, the new National Association of Ratepayers' Action Groups (NARAG) picked up an estimated 350,000 members, and in some Yorkshire towns it aspired to become the major challenger to the Labour Party. As Newcastle's *Evening Chronicle* put it, 'the great North East rates revolt is on'. As so often, though, it proved very difficult to turn a single-issue pressure group into a lasting political force. With Tony Crosland hastily promising £150 million in tax relief for hard-pressed ratepayers, and with the NARAG leadership squabbling among themselves about broadening their approach, the ratepayers' revolt fizzled out. But it cast a long shadow. 'The present system of rates is both old fashioned and increasingly unfair,' Margaret Thatcher admitted in a party political broadcast in the late summer of 1974, promising to 'replace it with a different system of taxes, a system that relates to what people can afford to pay'. But Britain would have to wait more than a decade to discover what she had in mind.[28]

Soaring rates were only one among several middle-class concerns during Wilson's first year back in Downing Street. Another was the increased tax burden on the self-employed, which had been compounded by Heath's introduction of VAT in 1973. At first it applied to some 1.3 million companies, with the registration threshold set at a non-indexed £5,000 a year, but as inflation mounted, more and more small businesses found themselves pushed into the VAT bracket. To add insult to injury, Denis Healey promptly served them with a new National Insurance bill, insisting that the self-employed pay Clause 4 National Insurance at 8 per cent on their gross profits. More 'than any other single measure', thought Patrick Hutber, this convinced the self-employed that they were being 'unfairly treated'. Among them was a retired army captain called Norman Small, who had worked as a recruiting officer for the small shopkeepers' unions and now invited like-minded people to defend 'the only free-thinking individualists in our society today' and 'save Britain from the slow Hari-Kari she is now intent on committing'. By the end of 1974 his National Federation of the Self-Employed (NFSE) had 10,000 members, and by the middle of 1975 it had more than 30,000. Such was the torrent of enquiries, indeed, that not even the tireless Small could keep up. After spending months touring the country on a 'diet of pep-pills', he eventually suffered 'a complete collapse' and was forced to resign on the grounds of ill health.[29]

Most of the NFSE's members seem to have been drawn from the lower-middle and upper-working classes. One survey found that 8 per cent were farmers, 6 per cent were garage proprietors and 5 per cent were builders, while the remainder included hoteliers, caterers, grocers, confectioners and road hauliers. But although the NFSE made a lot of noise about VAT, it had 'no discernible impact' on Healey's policies. Indeed, some small businessmen preferred to join a rival group, the Association of Self-employed People (ASP), which recruited members through advertisements in the *Daily Express* and *Daily Mail*. Its appeal was more limited but its ideological thrust was rather more strident, thanks largely to its libertarian founder, Teresa Gorman. As with the rates protest, however, the various self-employed groups eventually faded into the background, their themes absorbed into mainstream Conservative rhetoric. 'What hard working person, what skilled person, manager, professional person, farmer, small businessman, doesn't react against a government that takes away the fruits of their labour in tax?' Margaret Thatcher demanded in 1979. Her dream, she said, was to set people free 'to start up their own businesses, free to carry on with their farms and hand them from father to son, free to pass [*sic*] small business and keep it into the family, free to build up a little bit of capital out of earnings. That's what we ought to be able to do, each and every person in this country.' Ironically, though, one of the first things she did on reaching office was to increase VAT.[30]

As single-issue protest groups, neither the rates groups nor the self-employed organizations were ever likely to become major national forces. On the surface, a more plausible contender was the Middle Class Association (MCA), launched in November 1974 by the colourful Conservative MP John Gorst and his ex-Ulster Unionist colleague Captain Lawrence Orr. A former public relations man who had become a withering critic of Ted Heath, Gorst hoped to unite people from 'professional, managerial, self-employed and small business occupations', who were 'suffering disproportionately from inflation and massive erosions of savings and investment'. In essence, his organization was Thatcherite before the term had been invented, blaming 'successive Governments since the Second World War' for depriving the middle classes of 'a fair return for their industry, enterprise or thrift' and for allowing Britain to drift towards 'a collectivist society and the loss of individual liberty'. But despite its broad approach, the MCA never got off the ground. By the summer of 1975 it had only 4,000 recruits, and Gorst was ousted in a palace coup after missing a committee meeting so that he could move house. The leadership passed to an anti-Communist Irish millionaire with the tremendous name of John Martyn-Martin, under whom the MCA drifted into oblivion. But by this time public attention had switched to a new and much more successful middle-class protest group – the crusading organization on which Ross McWhirter had been working when the IRA gunmen struck him down.[31]

The National Association for Freedom was launched at a press conference near the Tower of London on 2 December 1975, just six days after Ross McWhirter's death. On the platform his twin brother Norris, still under plain-clothes police guard, insisted that the British people must not 'bow to the threats of intimidators who seek to destroy us'. By his side, Viscount de L'Isle grimly agreed that his late friend's work must go on. The first two points in McWhirter's Charter of Rights and Liberties, he observed, were 'the right to be defended against the country's enemies' and 'the right to live under the Queen's Peace'. Few people would quibble with those, but some of the others were much more obviously libertarian: the freedom 'not to belong to a trade union', for instance, or freedom 'from oppressive, unnecessary or confiscatory taxation', or even 'freedom of choice in the use of state and private services'. And in the new group's paper, the *Free Nation*, the tone was little short of paranoid. British freedom, it explained, was under threat from Marxist subversives, 'trade union militants' and soft left-wingers who had turned a blind eye to 'the menace of Soviet military expansion' and the danger of 'terrorists inside our own frontiers'. In future issues, Britain was permanently on the brink of disaster and the Communists forever hammering on the gates: sample headlines included such gems as 'We Launch Another Vital Campaign – Stop the Scroungers', 'Labour Goes Leninist', 'Council Houses: Give Em Away!', 'Why the Zambezi is OUR Front Line' and the chilling 'Revealed: Labour Plan to Nationalise Football'. 'It's now or never,' shrieked a recruiting leaflet, warning that Britain was on 'the road to totalitarianism'. Ordinary people must 'speak now in strength or – forever be silenced!'[32]

Had it not been for Ross McWhirter's murder, then the National Association for Freedom (or NAFF, as it was rather embarrassingly known) would probably have received little attention. But with McWhirter dead and his killers on the run, it attracted more publicity than almost all the other middle-class groups put together. The press pored over its list of supporters, who included the Conservative MPs John Gorst, Winston Churchill and Rhodes Boyson as well as the IEA director Ralph Harris, the journalist Peregrine Worsthorne, the novelist John Braine, the philosopher Antony Flew and even the chairman of the England cricket selectors, Alec Bedser, though in most cases their contribution was pretty nominal. Although NAFF presented itself as an entirely new organization, it drew on the resources of two older libertarian factions, Aims of Industry and the British United Industrialists. But while these were basically lobby groups, NAFF appealed directly to the general public. In two years it held almost 150 public meetings, generally attended by between fifty and a hundred people. 'Freedom Proclamations' regularly appeared in national newspapers and magazines, and some younger members even took to the streets, copying their hard-left counterparts by handing out pamphlets in shopping centres and inviting passers-by to sign petitions. By February 1978, it claimed a membership of about 20,000 people – 'then a huge figure', remarks one historian, 'for a fringe political organization'. Most came from the Home Counties, with very few in traditional working-class areas. There were fourteen branches in London, for example, but only five in Scotland and two in Wales. One edition of the *Free Nation* listed forthcoming events in East Surrey, Weybridge, West Kent, West London, East Sussex, North

West London, Wiltshire, Buckinghamshire and Worcestershire – but only one (in Cheshire) north of the Trent.[33]

NAFF is often seen as one of the key institutions of the New Right, a reactionary vanguard preaching a heady blend of free-market libertarianism and authoritarian conservatism. In fact, apart from its populist appeal, there was nothing very new about it. Even its first director, John Gouriet, was precisely the kind of old soldier who had been active in similar organizations in the past. After Charterhouse and Sandhurst, Gouriet had served as an intelligence officer in Malaya, Borneo and Aden, and then joined the merchant bank Rea Brothers just in time for the great City meltdown. Having served on the front line against Communism and seen the stock market crash at first hand, he was astonished by his colleagues' apathy. 'It's no use complaining, then doing nothing,' he impatiently told friends on a grouse-shooting expedition early in 1974. The exchange stuck in his mind: a little later, fired with crusading spirit, Gouriet applied to join the Monday Club. Through its economic committee, he became friends with the IEA's Ralph Harris, who then introduced him to Ross and Norris McWhirter. Gouriet loved their idea of a new grass-roots organization to fight socialism; what was more, it was originally his idea to offer a £50,000 bounty for the IRA bombers. And although he was shaken by Ross McWhirter's death, the former major never wavered in his commitment. 'We felt that 1975 and the years that followed were really a watershed in British politics,' he said later. 'We had to decide which way we were going to go: down the slippery slope towards communo-socialism and a satellite state of the Soviet Union at its worst, or were we going to claw our way back?' The remark was typical Gouriet: a gentlemanly birdwatcher who enjoyed the finer things in life, he was nevertheless a man of extraordinary, even apocalyptic zeal. Many mainstream commentators thought he was a fanatic; his left-wing opponents sometimes likened him to General Pinochet. Gouriet rather liked the comparison.[34]

Over the next two years, Gouriet proved a tireless advocate for the libertarian cause, travelling the country to give an estimated 138 speeches. 'It is time to stand up and be counted,' he melodramatically told his audiences, 'or run the risk of losing our freedom for ever.' Above all, inspired by his late friend Ross McWhirter, he believed the best way to fight the left was 'to use the law wherever the law could be used'. In one notable case, he put up almost £40,000 in legal fees for three British Rail staff who had been sacked under a closed-shop agreement, taking their case all the way to the European Court. In another, NAFF promised to pay the legal fees of the Tameside Parents' Education Group, who took their local council to court in the summer of 1976 to block its plans for a comprehensive-school system. 'I believe in competition, initiative and ability, and comprehensive education to me destroys competition, initiative and ability,' one of their spokesmen said. 'If we can put back socialism twenty years in the next two years, that's what we'll do.'

These were fighting words indeed. But neither of these cases quite captured the public imagination. What Gouriet needed was a real cause célèbre, a story that would command front-page headlines and make the libertarian crusade the centre of national attention. Then, in the autumn of 1976, he read a little story in the *Evening Standard* about a photo processing company in the suburbs of north-west London, which was facing a postal boycott after refusing to recognize a union. Intrigued, Gouriet picked up the phone. The company's name was Grunwick.[35]

17

It's Bloody War Now

We portray what is necessary. I believe we portray truth. When people get hurt, they bleed. If some people had their way ... we would end up with Mary Poppins twenty-four hours a day. Violence exists in real life and people are hiding from it if they think otherwise.

Lewis Collins, discussing *The Professionals*, 1979

RIGSBY: *We'll have none of that talk around here. This is a respectable house.*

ALAN: *Times have changed, Rigsby. We believe in love without fear.*

RIGSBY: *Love without fear? I seem to remember the last time you indulged in love without fear, you spent three days under that bed hiding from her father.*

Rising Damp, 'The Permissive Society', 7 November 1975

It was the milkman, making his rounds shortly before eight o'clock one foggy October morning, who spotted the body. Alan Routledge had just unloaded a crate outside the community centre off Scott Hall Avenue when he caught a glimpse of what looked like a bundle of rags, half-wreathed in the early morning mist, just past the edge of the playing field. As he walked towards it, the outline became clearer: a human shape, probably a children's guy, abandoned six days before Bonfire Night. Then, as he came a little closer, he realized that it was not a guy at all. It was the body of a woman, her white flared trousers pulled down to her knees, her blue jacket ripped apart, her body stabbed repeatedly in the chest and abdomen. Her auburn hair spilled across the grass; her red handbag lay on the ground beside her, the strap still circling her hand. This was the body of 28-year-old Wilma McCann, a mother of four from Chapeltown, Leeds. The previous evening, after going out for a few drinks and a takeaway, she had accepted a lift from a man in a green Ford Capri. The driver's name was Peter Sutcliffe, and Wilma McCann was the first victim of the Yorkshire Ripper.[1]

When the police were called to her body on the morning of 30 October 1975, they had no inkling that they were dealing with one of the most vicious killers in British history. Despite attempts to rebrand it as the modern Motorway City, Leeds had a reputation as a hard town, a town of chimneys and factories and back-to-backs, its people tough and tribal, its skies and streams black with soot. 'The City of Dreadful Something', the poet Martin Bell called it: a city with 'rain one day, snow the next, and sleet and fog the next day', an inferno with 'special subways for mugging'. Chapeltown, where Wilma McCann's body was found, was one of northern England's most notorious red-light districts, the 'Mecca of vice'. Like many decaying industrial neighbourhoods, it had been transformed by the influx of low-paid Jamaicans, Indians and Pakistanis, its Methodist chapels converted into mosques, its nightlife dominated by shabby drinking clubs, where, as one writer put it, 'drugs, jewellery and sexual favours were indiscriminately bartered, wrangled over, sometimes even bought and sold'. Casual violence was common and women were often the victims: wives thumped by their husbands, girls slapped around by their boyfriends, prostitutes beaten up by their pimps. Only a few days before Wilma McCann's murder, one battered wife, Juanita Greening, strangled her husband with the telephone cord after he had tried to stop her dialling 999. Barely two months later the Bingley teenager Mark Rowntree murdered an 85-year-old widow in her terraced cottage. A few days afterwards Rowntree stabbed another teenager at a bus stop, and in the New Year he killed a prostitute in her Leeds flat, as well as her 3-year-old son. When the police caught him, he explained that he had always been 'hurt and let down by girls'.[2]

Against this background, the chief investigating officer, Detective Superintendent Denis Hoban, saw Wilma McCann's death as nothing out of the ordinary. Known locally as 'the Crime Buster in the sheepskin coat', Hoban knew the city's underworld intimately and had already solved almost forty murders. At first he was keen to play down McCann's history of prostitution, knowing it would lose her public sympathy. Instead, the police emphasized the four children she had left behind, and the next day's papers described her simply as a 'young mother'. By the

New Year, however, the investigation had got nowhere: although Hoban's team had called at 5,000 houses, taken 538 statements and produced 3,300 index cards, he was no closer to catching the killer. But when Sutcliffe struck again, stabbing to death 42-year-old Emily Jackson, both the police and the media drew a link between the crimes. On 23 January 1976, the *Sun* ran the headline 'Ripper Hunted in Call-Girl Murders', coining the nickname for which Sutcliffe became famous.[3]

The police now went to greater lengths to publicize their manhunt, sending out loudspeaker vans begging for witnesses and a Range Rover with a giant photo of Emily Jackson, and interrupting cinema screenings and bingo sessions to appeal for help. But Leeds's red-light districts were effectively closed communities: neither pimps nor prostitutes talked to the police, while their male clients were hardly likely to volunteer information. In Chapeltown, fear and mistrust descended like a thick fog, but most working girls simply could not afford to stay indoors. 'There is always a danger when you do this game, but you have got to find a quiet spot, a dark spot,' one said. 'If I thought about the Ripper every time I was on the street, I'd run home and lock the door,' another told the *Halifax Courier*. 'I stop myself thinking about him by thinking about *money*. It always works.'[4]

Once again the trail went cold. In February 1977 Sutcliffe bludgeoned to death another prostitute, Irene Richardson, leaving her body in Roundhay Park, and two months later he claimed a fourth victim, Patricia Atkinson, whose battered body was found in her Bradford flat. Tellingly, however, it was not until his fifth murder that the Ripper really captured national attention. On the evening of Saturday, 25 June 1977, a pretty 16-year-old girl, Jayne MacDonald, was walking home along Chapeltown Road when Sutcliffe hit her from behind. For the first time he had killed somebody who was clearly not a prostitute, but simply a fresh-faced teenager who worked in a local supermarket and spent her free time roller-skating, shopping for clothes and dancing with her friends. For the police and the press, Jayne was the first 'innocent victim', and the public reaction was noticeably stronger. 'Hang the Ripper' graffiti appeared on Chapeltown walls, while an open letter to the killer in the *Yorkshire Evening Post* asked: 'How did you feel when you learned your bloodstained crusade had gone so horribly wrong? That your vengeful knife had found so innocent a target?'[5]

For all the efforts of the West Yorkshire Police, however, Sutcliffe's rampage went on. In October he murdered a Manchester prostitute, Jean Jackson, dumping her body in some nearby allotments. In her handbag the police found a five-pound note: by tracing it to banks in Shipley and Bingley, they were able to narrow down the list of suspects, and in the next few years they interviewed Sutcliffe nine times. In a pre-computer age, however, the investigation was drowning in pieces of paper, and since Sutcliffe's wife gave him an alibi, he slipped through the net. So the killings went on: in the first three months of 1978, Sutcliffe murdered Yvonne Pearson, Helen Rytka and Vera Millward. The pressure from the media was now more intense than ever: 'Why Can't They Catch the Ripper?' demanded the *Daily Express*. And with operational costs soaring, West Yorkshire's finest were getting desperate. 'The public have the power to decide what sort of society they want. If they want murder and violence they will keep quiet. If they want a law-abiding society, in which their womenfolk can move freely without fear of attack from the individual we are seeking, then they must give us their help,' insisted Assistant Chief Constable George Oldfield. In desperation, he went on Radio Two's *Jimmy Young Show*, reminding listeners that the Ripper was 'someone's neighbour and he is someone's husband or son'. Some of his fellow officers muttered that he was adrift in a sea of index cards, but Oldfield blamed the public. 'Fifteen or twenty years ago,' he told the press, 'we'd have been holding the public back, so many would have been anxious to give us information. We'd have wrapped this one up by now.' Instead, he said, 'life's become very cheap in this civilised country of ours. There's a general state of apathy, of unconcern at violence.'[6]

In fact, most people were horrified by the crimes of the most brutal serial killer in living memory. In the next three years, public fascination with the case swelled to unprecedented proportions, especially after the police released the 'Wearside Jack' tape, which claimed responsibility for the murders but proved to be a hoax. When Sutcliffe killed the Bradford University student Barbara Leach, in September 1979, the papers were beside themselves. By now the police were warning women 'to use lighted streets and to walk home with someone they know', while the *Bingley Guardian* warned that the cost of defying the warnings 'could be a hideous assault ending in death'. By the end of 1979, 2 million copies of a special newspaper had been sent to homes across the North of England, the Wearside Jack tape was being regularly played at pubs, clubs and football grounds, and more than 5,500 gigantic posters had been put up on billboards across the country. 'THE MAN NEXT TO YOU MAY HAVE KILLED TWELVE WOMEN,' the message began. 'He may be sitting next to you in your pub, club or canteen. Or in a queue. Or in a bus. He may be working at the next machine, desk or table. But he is in fact a vicious, deranged maniac . . .' There had never been a media blitz like it, yet the police seemed no closer to catching the culprit. By November 1979 their list of possible suspects stretched to 17,000 names. 'The fact is,' said a damning editorial in the *Sun*, 'they seem no nearer capturing this monster than they were four years ago.'[7]

For local women, the Ripper's rampage was a terrifying reminder of the unspoken violence that lay beneath the civility of everyday life. By the end of 1979, many local firms, shops and colleges were organizing lifts for women after dark, while attendances at evening classes and bingo sessions dried up and even restaurants and pubs reported dwindling numbers. A year later, after Sutcliffe murdered another student, Jacqueline Hill, who was on her way home from a seminar in Leeds, the panic reached a peak. Many female students told reporters they were too frightened to go out, while the vice chancellor of the University of Leeds, Lord Boyle, told students that they should 'under no circumstance be out alone after dark'. Quite understandably, many women were outraged that they had to pay the price for the Ripper's crimes. Hundreds joined Reclaim the Night and Women against Violence against Women marches; in the centre of Leeds, feminists invaded a screening of the film *Dressed to Kill*, throwing rotten eggs and paint bombs, while in Chapeltown a sex shop had its windows smashed and graffiti ('No men after dark') painted on the walls. And in Bradford the student union promised to support any woman who carried a knife or pepper spray, while eleven feminist protesters were arrested for picketing an Odeon showing the film *Violation of the Bitch*.

In *The Times*, the University of Bradford sociologist Hilary Rose argued that the Ripper case had merely made 'public and unavoidable' something feminists had been campaigning against for years: 'the high level of violence against women whether in the home or on the streets'. The hunt for the killer, she wrote, 'is not merely an urgent matter in its own right, but it has become part of a long battle against the sexual violence which deforms our society'. The next day a man from Surrey, one W. M. Newte, sent in a letter of agreement. For years, he said, people had been mocked when they warned that sex and violence on the screen would undermine the moral health of the nation. 'Can we not now', he asked, 'agree that this may well be true, and not have to listen to the sniggers and sneers of our worldly-wise critics and commentators when ordinary people express their anxieties?'[8]

Thanks to David Peace's intoxicating 'Red Riding' novels, the crimes of the Yorkshire Ripper have become a familiar symbol of the 1970s,

unfolding against a background of smoke-filled rooms, relentless violence and terrible wallpaper. Contrary to what Peace's books suggest,
however, there was nothing intrinsically Northern about Peter Sutcliffe's
murders. Indeed, although nobody knew it at the time, the Ripper's
crimes coincided with another killing spree in Gloucester, where Fred
and Rosemary West tortured and murdered eleven young women
between 1971 and 1979. In London, meanwhile, the Scottish-born civil
servant Dennis Nilsen killed at least fifteen young men in the five years
after 1978, often chopping them up and burying bits under his floor-
boards. Of course it is possible, as W. M. Newte had implied, that such
terrible crimes were more likely to happen against the disorientating
backdrop of the 1970s, a world of pornography on the news-stands
and nudity on the television, a world of splintered families, atomized
communities and moral confusion. That was certainly the view of the
anti-permissive campaigner Mary Whitehouse, who wrote to *The Times*
citing another case in the north of England, where a 60-year-old man
had been convicted of buggery and indecent assault on his 6-year-old
niece, apparently copying the pornographic magazines he read so avidly.
But there have been serial killers throughout history; that so many were
active in the late 1970s is surely a hideous coincidence rather than a sign
that the post-war decades were incubators of evil. And although it is
possible that, as feminists later argued, Sutcliffe's upbringing in the
aggressively masculine world of working-class Bingley contributed to
his hatred of women, the fact remains that Yorkshire in the 1970s was
full of men who had grown up in similar circumstances and went on to
become decent and loving husbands.[9]

Yet the Ripper's atrocities fuelled a growing sense in the late 1970s
that violent crime was running out of control. Long-term trends in
crime are notoriously difficult to measure, but it seems clear that, as the
bonds of family and community frayed, unskilled and manufacturing
jobs dried up and the old moral sanctions came into disrepute, crime
rapidly increased. By 1972, when the word 'mugger' first appeared in
British newspapers, Home Office statistics showed that violent crime
had risen by 62 per cent in just five years. By 1974, every single category
of crime was showing a significant annual jump: the figures for theft, for
example, were up by 42 per cent overall and a staggering 71 per cent in
London. And by the end of the decade, not only had the annual number
of violent crimes almost doubled, but the number of serious firearms
offences had increased threefold. Barely a day passed without new scare
stories about terrorists, muggers and serial killers: in the early months

of 1975, for example, the headlines were dominated by the hunt for the 'Black Panther', the armed robber Donald Neilson, who kidnapped the 17-year-old heiress Lesley Whittle and left her to die in a Staffordshire drainage shaft. Even Britain's most waspish political interviewer became a victim of crime: when Robin Day was mugged near Holland Park that July, suffering a broken jaw and a black eye, his plight made the front pages. 'I had become a part', he later reflected, 'of the deeply disturbing criminal statistics.' 'Why Didn't You Use the Bow Tie, Robin?' one newspaper wondered.[10]

For the Conservatives, the rising crime figures furnished merely more proof of Labour's incompetence – which conveniently ignored the fact that the biggest increase had come during the Macmillan years. In 1974, Sir Keith Joseph claimed that 'for the first time' since the days of Robert Peel, 'areas of our cities are becoming unsafe for peaceful citizens'. A few months later, the former Home Secretary Reginald Maudling – himself no stranger to lawbreaking – loudly lamented 'the crumbling of discipline, the growth of crime, and the apparent erosion of the sense of personal responsibility'. (Interestingly, Maudling blamed the disappearance of 'the old disciplines of mass unemployment and grinding poverty', which certainly made a change from people arguing that unemployment and poverty were to blame.) And in 1978, the future Thatcherite minister David Howell warned that Britain was regressing to a state of 'medieval ferocity . . . reminiscent of a much more savage past, where people were killed for the hell of it, almost for sport'. This kind of talk horrified the Labour left, but it went down well with more old-fashioned ministers such as Jim Callaghan. In 1974, Callaghan even remarked that he 'greatly admired' the section on law and order in the Conservative manifesto and 'wished we had anything as good as this in ours'. 'Hear, hear!' said Denis Healey loudly, much to the disgust of Barbara Castle.[11]

But it was Callaghan, not Castle, who reflected the public mood. Although academics often dismissed anxieties about crime as middle-class paranoia, talk of 'Britain's Streets of Fear' seemed all too real to the working-class people, trapped in dilapidated Victorian terraces or damp council flats, who suffered most. In an increasingly individualistic society, where the younger generation had moved away, the familiar brick terraces had been torn down and the old physical and cultural landmarks had disappeared, older people often felt isolated and unsettled, frightened even to ask their neighbours for help. The character in Margaret Drabble's novel The Middle Ground (1980) who reflects on 'the terror we each now feel when walking down a concrete underpass, when we fumble for a key on our own doorstep with the sound of footsteps behind us, when an unknown car pulls up at a kerb' was effectively speaking for millions. Even the elderly were not always to be trusted: in April 1977, the 85-year-old William Benions tottered into the dock at the Old Bailey, accused of mugging an 81-year-old woman for her daily groceries. 'It's disgraceful someone like you going around bashing and mugging a defenceless woman,' said the judge, giving him a twelve-month conditional discharge. 'You ought to know better at your age.' Little wonder, then, that so many people reached for comparisons with the supposedly barbaric past. In the midst of unprecedented affluence, lamented Max Caulfield, 'bus conductors are now being murdered in London. Thugs rob or beat up old ladies, old men, women and girls on the London Underground. The thin veneer of civilisation that has kept the brute within all of us at bay has been deliberately cracked and we are back in the eighteenth century.'[12]

Public anxiety about law and order was also driven by the changing image of the police. In May 1976, the nation's most beloved policeman, Sergeant George Dixon, hung up his helmet after a staggering 432 episodes. Created by the Labour-supporting playwright Ted Willis, *Dixon of Dock Green* had been the supreme expression of paternalistic, consensual values for twenty-one years. Its star, the 80-year-old Jack Warner, was one of the most familiar faces in the country, and his favourite expression, 'Evening all', had become a national catchphrase. Yet by the mid-1970s, this reassuringly nostalgic Sunday serial, whose lead actor had served in the Royal Flying Corps, felt like a relic of ancient history. To younger viewers, the series that really captured the image of the modern Metropolitan Police could hardly have been more different. Originally devised as a one-off play for Thames Television, *The Sweeney* offered a self-consciously realistic version of life in the Met's Flying Squad. Its creator, Ian Kennedy Martin, was the brother of the man who had devised *Z-Cars* in the early 1960s. But Kennedy Martin thought that *Z-Cars* had gone soft. He wanted to write a series in which the police officers were men who shouted and swore, men with pasts and prejudices, men with broken marriages and drinking habits. His new series, he hoped, would reflect the realities of life in the 1970s, a world of terrorism, corruption and armed robberies, with no place for George Dixon. 'It's war, it's bloody war now,' says the central character, Detective Inspector Jack Regan. 'When you stop a kid in a stolen car, you can't be sure he isn't tooled up and ready to blow your face off.'

Written specifically for Kennedy Martin's friend John Thaw, the character of Regan could hardly have been more different from Jack Warner's saintly bobby. A working-class Northerner who has moved to London and become one of the Flying Squad's most effective officers, Regan has an ex-wife and a daughter. He ostentatiously smokes, drinks and enjoys female company, and thinks nothing of breaking into properties, planting evidence and lying to his superiors if it will secure a conviction. 'You can't operate unless you break the rules. Everybody knows that,' explains his sidekick, George Carter (Dennis Waterman). And while it is hard to imagine Jack Warner saying 'Shut it!' or 'Get your trousers on, you're nicked!', it is downright impossible to imagine him saying: 'We're the Sweeney, son, and we haven't had any dinner yet, so unless you want a kicking . . .', or the classic line: 'Look, slag, I don't give a toss who you have in your bed.' Yet as Alwyn Turner points out, we are never in doubt that *The Sweeney*'s central characters are fundamentally decent people: when a senior officer is accused of corruption, it soon transpires that he is being 'stitched up by villains'. The series effectively invites us to sympathize with the plight of the modern policeman, beleaguered not merely by robbers, pimps and murderers, but by do-gooders, *Guardian* readers and well-paid lawyers. 'You try and protect the public and all they do is call you fascist,' Regan says. 'You nail a villain and some ponced-up pinstriped amateur barrister screws you up like an old fag packet on a point of procedure, then pops off for a game of squash and a glass of Madeira.'[13]

Even conservative reviewers liked *The Sweeney*. Jack Regan might be 'a million light years from the wooden Scotland Yard men of yesteryear', wrote one critic, but 'at last, we're getting a genuine insight into the behaviour of the real cops and robbers who live in the primitive frontiers of London's underworld'. Evidently millions of ordinary people agreed: by the time the second series started in September 1975, it was attracting more than 17 million viewers a week, making it the second most popular programme in the country. It was, said the *Daily Express*, 'the most violent and brutal police series ever to reach British screens', full of 'sadistic beatings', 'bloodletting' and 'bad language' (although by later standards, of course, it was positively tame). Yet the producers prided themselves on their authenticity, employing a retired Flying Squad inspector to advise on procedure, and filming as much as possible on the streets of London. Policemen themselves reportedly loved it, the only caveat being that 'Regan and Carter give their wives nasty suspicions because they appear to fall casually into bed with too many attractive ladies'. Waiting patiently for the team to finish filming in a London street, one young officer confided that *The Sweeney* was his favourite show. 'I always try to arrange my shifts so that I'm off on Monday to watch,' he said. 'It makes our job seem so exciting.'[14]

Other television companies now rushed to make hard-hitting police dramas of their own, notably London Weekend Television's *The Professionals*, which ran for five series from December 1977. Supposedly about a special investigative unit answering only to the Home Secretary, it kept closely to the *Sweeney* template, with Martin Shaw and Lewis Collins playing hard-drinking agents who hated bureaucracy, liked a ruckus and had a barber with a cruel sense of humour. To millions of viewers, this was merely an hour's worth of diverting entertainment; to some academics, however, its overt celebration of a violent anti-terrorist unit marked the triumph of 'New Right authoritarianism'. At the very least, the fact that it had been devised and written by Brian Clemens, the brains behind *The Avengers*, symbolized how much the popular mood had changed since the carefree days of bowler hats, catsuits and suburban robots. Indeed, it was telling that when ITV tried to revive the two most successful adventure series of the 1960s in the form of *The New Avengers* (1976–7) and *Return of the Saint* (1978–9), neither really caught on. Gritty authenticity was the order of the day. Even the emblematic British comic-book character of the period, making his first appearance in *2000 AD* in March 1977, was the square-jawed, leather-clad Judge Dredd, who enforces the law in the apocalyptic world of Mega-City One with pitiless brutality.[15]

The most self-consciously realistic vision of modern-day policing, however, was G. F. Newman's BBC series *Law and Order* (1978), which provoked fierce protests from the Police Federation, outrage among some Conservative MPs and a debate in the House of Lords. The series explores the case of a career robber, framed for a crime he did not commit. At its heart, Newman told the *Radio Times*, was the idea that 'detectives and villains . . . talk the same way, think the same way and often behave the same way'. In *Law and Order*, the police are just as corrupt as their adversaries, and we see detectives consorting with prostitutes, beating up suspects, paying off informers, planting evidence and lying in court. Crucially, the series was filmed with painstaking authenticity: the actors were relatively unknown, the shooting style was austere, the characters feel real and the corruption seems banal and everyday. But to *Law and Order*'s critics, that was precisely what was so alarming about it. The Police Federation insisted that the BBC was peddling 'absolute fiction'; the new head of Scotland Yard, Sir David McNee, said it 'insulted every honest and hard-working CID officer'; and the Conservative MP Julian Critchley claimed that it had 'offended millions'. Judging by the BBC's audience research, this last statement was totally untrue. Surveys found that viewers loved it: 'so good that I thought at first it was a documentary', one wrote. Even serving CID officers privately remarked that it was 'like a documentary'. The fuss, however, was unrelenting: the former Labour minister Patrick Gordon Walker initiated an anti-BBC debate in the House of Lords, while the Police Federation's parliamentary spokesman, the Tory MP Eldon Griffiths, claimed that 'no single emission' had done more to damage the police. The BBC refused to apologize; still, despite its undoubted merits, the series was not repeated for thirty years.[16]

What *The Sweeney*, *Law and Order* and even *Judge Dredd* reflected was a public image of the police that had changed enormously in the past two decades. 'At one time people thought of the police force in terms of the strong arm of the law, the warm protecting father's arms,' wrote the dramatist Jeremy Sandford. But now, as the policeman rode by 'on his jabbering motor cycle', the phrase that came to mind was 'the surly lip of the law'. Throughout the 1970s allegations of police abuse regularly made the headlines, from the wrongful convictions of the Birmingham Six, the Guildford Four and the mentally disturbed Judith Ward to the horrendous miscarriage of justice in the Lesley Molseed murder case, which saw an entirely innocent man, Stefan Kiszko, forced into a confession and sentenced to life in prison. Black and Asian immigrants had particular reason to fear the law: in parts of London, wrote Mike and Trevor Phillips, the police were seen as 'a natural hazard, like poisonous snakes or attack dogs off the leash', who might strike at any moment through the stop-and-search 'sus' laws. In Nottingham, one in three West Indians and Pakistanis told a survey that the police gave them 'less favourable treatment'; even more disturbingly, one in five Nottingham residents claimed that the police regularly beat up blacks and Asians. And in Leeds, two policemen were sent to prison at the end of 1971 for assaulting the Nigerian immigrant David Oluwale, a homeless vagrant whose body was found floating in the River Aire. The case left a terrible stain on the constabulary's image. 'Leeds Murder Squad,' ran a popular joke of the day: 'Who do you want murdering today?'[17]

What did most damage to the reputation of the police, though, were the corruption allegations that erupted in London at the turn of the decade. Since 1829 the Metropolitan Police had answered only to the

Home Secretary, while allegations of serious misbehaviour were automatically investigated by the plain-clothes Criminal Investigation Department. CID therefore enjoyed what one group of reporters called 'absolute power', and by the end of the 1960s its detectives had become 'a law unto themselves', accepting favours from major criminals, dropping charges in return for bribes and fostering an extraordinary climate of corruption and collusion. 'I'm in a little firm inside a firm,' one detective sergeant told his criminal contact in a secretly recorded conversation, explaining that 'anywhere in London I can get on the phone to someone I know I can trust'. South of the Thames, CID men sold 'licences' to commit crime: in the autumn of 1969, for example, a convicted burglar, who had gone on the run while on home leave, bought a string of £5 licences so that he could commit more break-ins to provide for his wife. To supplement their income, some officers planted contraband material and then demanded that the victims pay up to avoid prosecution. They were also notably unfussy about catching the actual perpetrators of crimes, happily 'fitting up' people who had crossed them. 'If there's anybody that's ever done you a mischief,' one corrupt inspector told a dodgy car dealer in another taped conversation, 'that wants seeing to . . . you know what I mean?'[18]

When *The Times* uncovered this cosy world in November 1969, the reaction was widespread shock. Yet far from being congratulated for their efforts, the reporters were treated like criminals, while a Home Office inquiry under the former Cumberland chief constable Frank Williamson proved a total shambles. From the outset, Williamson found himself 'isolated and undermined, working with sullen, uncooperative officers'. Documents mysteriously went missing, officers were quietly tipped off and CID sources spread rumours that Williamson was out of his depth in the big city. Almost incredibly, even the Met officer assigned to work alongside him, Bill Moody, was later jailed for corruption, having been a key figure in the notorious Obscene Publications Squad. The fact that Moody drove a 2.5-litre Triumph and a 1.5 Lancia and took holidays in Switzerland on a superintendent's salary was something of a giveaway: when he saw Williamson's battered Austin 1800, he said contemptuously: 'Is that the best you can do?' Eventually, an exhausted Williamson resigned in frustration. There were, he thought, only three kinds of Met detective: 'those who were themselves corrupt, those who knew that others were corrupt but did nothing about it, and those who were too stupid to notice what was going on around them'. As a result, he was denied his expected promotion to Chief Inspector of

Constabulary, which meant he also missed out on a bigger pension and a knighthood. Such were the rewards for integrity.[19]

The Williamson debacle was a sign that the sickness at the Met went well beyond a few bent coppers. In 1970 *World in Action* began investigating rumours of corruption inside the Drug Squad, which was not only paying West Indian informers in cannabis, but was selling 'licences' to favoured dealers. Yet this was small beer compared with the activities of the Obscene Publications Squad, which, as a judge later put it, had become a 'vast protection racket'. In their Soho heartland, the 'Dirty Squad' accepted hefty bribes in exchange for turning a blind eye to the burgeoning sex trade: one prostitute paid £40 a week as well as rendering 'other services', while wholesale publishers paid £50. One porn baron, Bernie Silver, paid Commander Wallace Virgo £2,000 a month as well as a £2,000 Christmas bonus, the equivalent of an annual £500,000 today. In 1972 the *Sunday People* revealed that another porn millionaire, James Humphreys, had even taken the head of the Flying Squad, Commander Kenneth Drury, and his wife on a free holiday to Cyprus. Amazingly, Drury had not only signed the hotel register with his police rank but actually gave his address as New Scotland Yard. It transpired that their families had become great friends; in Cyprus, they had discussed buying a hotel together, even going out to inspect potential properties. It would have been hilarious had it not been so shocking. When the case came to trial in 1977, thirteen officers were sent to prison. Virgo was sent down for twelve years; Drury went down for eight. 'Ken's trouble', his wife insisted, 'was that he gave too much to the job.'[20]

By this point, the Met was in the throes of a long revolution. At the end of 1971, the Home Secretary, Reginald Maudling, had appointed a new chief at Scotland Yard. Like Jack Regan, the new man was a Northerner who never forgot his roots. Born in Manchester, Robert Mark had worked his way up the ranks, joining the local police as a cadet, becoming Britain's youngest Chief Constable and building a reputation as an honest officer who spoke for the uniformed rank and file. Even so, cleaning up the Met was a challenge worthy of Hercules, and Maudling's rather loaded invitation – 'Will you do this fucking job for us?' – suggested the scale of the challenge. 'Though I had known wrongdoing,' Mark wrote later, 'I had never experienced institutionalized wrongdoing, blindness, arrogance and prejudice on anything like the scale accepted as routine in the Met.' Meeting CID representatives, he bluntly told them that it 'had long been the most routinely corrupt organization in London [and] that nothing and no one would prevent me from putting an end to it'. To break their closed circle, he ordered thousands of CID men to report to uniformed commanders instead of their old detective commanders. Meanwhile, he set up a new department, A10, to investigate corruption allegations, and in the course of his five-year reign he forced out 478 officers suspected of misconduct. 'A good police force', he once remarked, 'is one that catches more crooks than it employs.'[21]

Sadly, the sickness at the heart of the Met was too deep-rooted to be cured in five years. 'The corruption at the top is almost institutionalized,' the filmmaker Simon Albury told his friend Michael Palin after working on *World in Action* in 1974. Even raw recruits, it seemed, were being inducted into wrongdoing by falsely arresting down-and-outs in order to boost their arrest figures. Four years later, alarmed by claims that Flying Squad officers were in cahoots with professional criminals, the Home Office approved a major new investigation, run by outsiders from the Dorset constabulary. The biggest and most controversial exercise of its kind ever conducted, Operation Countryman lasted six years, cost more than £4 million and proved a terrible fiasco. Consistently obstructed by senior officers at the Met and constantly squabbling with the Commissioner, Sir David McNee, the team from Dorset was eventually replaced by a new team from Surrey. Yet when the investigation was wound up in 1984, not a single Met officer had been successfully prosecuted. In terms of public relations, it was a disaster. And to many observers, it merely confirmed that the Met remained irredeemably corrupt.[22]

Of course there were plenty of honest coppers, but there were plenty of wrongdoers, too. In Liverpool, one policewoman told the BBC that after joining the force in the early 1970s, she had regularly seen 'brutality and drug planting and harassing of minority groups'. Officers often talked of 'agriculture', and when she asked what it meant, they explained: 'Planting – but you can leave that to us.' And even people who instinctively defended the police could not excuse abominations such as the beating of confessions from three innocent teenagers for the murder of Maxwell Confait in Catford in 1972, or the horrifying case of the Gateshead electrician Liddle Towers, who died of his injuries in 1976 after the police had given him 'a bloody good kicking'. Yet despite the torrent of accusations, the public remained deeply attached to *Dixon of Dock Green*'s sentimental vision. Between 1972 and 1975, with the corruption storm at its height, LSE academics carried out a major survey into attitudes to the Metropolitan Police. Even the Met was astonished by the results: to their amazement, 96 per cent of people said they were 'satisfied' with the police, 93 per cent 'liked' them, 90 per cent 'trusted' them and 98 per cent 'respected' them. In an age of deep disillusionment, millions of people still told themselves that the police fought for the common man against the forces of disorder. The old stereotypes died hard: people might enjoy watching Jack Regan, but they still wanted to believe in George Dixon.[23]

On 23 October 1975, a week before Wilma McCann's body was found in Leeds, the state-educated son of a Wigan miner was unveiled as the new Chief Constable of Greater Manchester. Outspoken, media-friendly and devoutly religious, James Anderton soon became the most controversial policeman in the country. Modern Britain, he lamented, had 'spawned an undisciplined and ailing offspring', yet whenever the police tried to apply the obvious remedies, the 'moral degeneration' of public opinion held them back. When Anderton threw police resources into a string of vice raids, seizing hundreds of thousands of pornographic magazines, his own councillors accused him of wasting time and manpower, while critics called him a 'crank, an outdated Puritan, a do-gooder crackpot and a religious fanatic'. Yet he continued to court the limelight. In April 1978, just days after complaining that he had been attacked for trying 'to uphold the law', he went on television to defend the Manx practice of birching young offenders, warning that crime had 'soaked into society like water into a sponge' and calling for the return of 'selective corporal punishment'. Liberals loathed him, yet the letters pages glowed with approval. Anderton was a 'tough, lucid and rather populist policeman', said an editorial in the *Daily Express*, predicting that he would become 'a hero or a monster to the next generation'. It was time, the paper said, to turn back the clock: 'We have had 20 years of enlightenment and 20 years of rising crime . . . Mr Anderton is right.'[24]

By the late 1970s, James Anderton's diagnosis was eminently familiar. In the newspapers, allegations about the decline of the family, the collapse of school standards, the indulgence of the judiciary, the corruption of the police, the folly of social workers and the debauchery of the young had become well-worn clichés, and although these had been common themes for decades, they now carried greater force than ever. The dirtiest word of all, though, was 'permissiveness', the supreme scapegoat for the nation's ills and a 'political metaphor' with connotations of decadence and decline. Permissiveness had its 'civilised' side, conceded the *Daily Express* in December 1977, but 'freedom must have its limits'. Tolerance had gone too far, bequeathing 'more violence, more venereal disease, more unmarried mothers and one parent families than ever before'. Even *The Times*, usually self-consciously measured, agreed that 'permissive agnosticism' had spun out of control, unleashing a wave of 'hooliganism, theft, violence to other pupils, violence to teachers – as well as illiteracy and academic failures' in Britain's schools, especially 'large inner-city comprehensive schools'. The public, it said sternly, demanded a 'general restoration of discipline in our society'.[25]

In many ways that was quite true. Opinion polls had always shown strong opposition to the abolition of capital punishment, as well as considerable unease about the liberalization of the divorce, homosexuality and abortion laws. Asked to rank possible explanations for crime in September 1973, six out of ten people thought the main causes were 'a general breakdown in authority' and laws that were 'too lenient'. About half, meanwhile, nominated the 'bad example' set by parents and the rising use of drugs, with issues such as poverty and unemployment relegated to also-rans. 'The quest for freedom has moved us too close to licence,' remarked Fred Smithies, general secretary of the National Union of Schoolmasters/Union of Women Teachers, arguing that far too many children, 'brought up in the permissive environment', had become virtually uncontrollable. 'In the past two decades standards and values have so deteriorated,' one woman wrote to the *Daily Mail*, 'that materialism and selfishness have become the norm.' All people cared about in the 1970s, she lamented, were 'wealth, permissiveness [and] "doing one's own thing" regardless of the consequences to others'.[26]

At the heart of all this was the single most emotive symbol of all the changes that had transformed British life since the war: sex. Although we often think of the supposedly Swinging Sixties as the heyday of the sexual revolution, it was actually only in the early 1970s that its consequences really became apparent. It was only in this period, for example, that many single women got hold of the Pill. Even during the Heath years, the government had resisted introducing free birth control, afraid of the tabloid reaction to 'sex on the rates'. But when Harold Wilson returned to office, prescription charges for birth control were abolished. Family Planning Association clinics were gradually absorbed into the NHS, while a £300,000 government advertising campaign asked: 'What are your chances of getting pregnant tonight?' By the end of the decade, about eight out of ten young women had taken the Pill, and it had become by far the most popular form of contraception among young married couples. The fertility rate dropped by 30 per cent between 1971 and 1977, allowing more women to pursue careers. On top of that, the Pill helped to transform attitudes to sex before marriage, once a potentially life-changing pleasure, but now one apparently free of consequences. Waiting until your wedding night was becoming obsolete: three out of four women who got married between 1971 and 1975 had already had sex with their husbands, and by the beginning of the following decade, more than nine out of ten women in their early twenties had lost their virginity before their wedding night. Indeed, girls were now losing their virginity earlier: between the early 1950s and the late 1970s, the average age dropped from 21 to about 18.[27]

Of course all this did not come without a cost. For millions of couples, marriage was no longer a permanent contract: in the course of the 1970s, the divorce rate doubled among people over 25 and trebled among those younger. In 1960 there had been just 2 divorces per 1,000 married people, yet thanks to the reform of the divorce laws by 1980 there were 12, a breakdown rate that would have been almost unthinkable a few decades earlier. Single-parent families were becoming increasingly common: in 1974 there had been just one in eleven, but six years later the proportion had already risen to one in eight. To the horror of more conservative observers, many of these families were headed by girls who were still at school themselves. Teenage pregnancies were the 'problem that will not go away', wrote *The Times*'s medical correspondent in 1978, noting that in the previous year some 30,000 children had been born to unmarried teenage mothers, while a staggering 28,000 teenage girls had had abortions. Like most observers, he thought the answer lay in sex education and birth control: even the *Mail* conceded that 'in an unhappy choice between two evils, contraception is preferable to pregnancy for a 12-year-old'. Yet by 1979 there were 74,500 teenage extramarital pregnancies in England and Wales alone, of which some 10,000 were to girls aged 15 or younger. More and more teenage girls were having abortions, too, with the level up to almost 35,000 a year.[28]

In Wigan, Jeremy Seabrook overheard two elderly women chatting on a bus. 'They're sex mad if you ask me,' one said. 'All these kids at mixed schools, they're down the park every dinner time. How can they expect to learn anything? Sex is eating their brains away.' But although teenagers were often denounced as slaves to their passions, the truth was that most youngsters still led humdrum, vaguely frustrated lives, convinced that everybody else was having a much better time than they were. Their attitudes were clearly more liberal – by 1980, only 8 per cent of those aged between 15 and 24 thought it was wrong to live together outside marriage – but their behaviour was not necessarily more licentious. After interviewing 376 men and women in their early twenties for his book *Promiscuity* (1976), Michael Schofield found that only 17 per cent had had sex with more than one partner in the previous year. Interestingly, the more promiscuous were not noticeably immoral; they were merely more talkative and self-confident, as well as better educated and better paid. Going away to university was undoubtedly a key factor in their more varied sex lives; by contrast, early school-leavers often married young. But this sometimes had baleful consequences of its own since, as Schofield pointed out, couples who married very young were more likely to split up.[29]

Often seen as the great engine of moral transformation, television furnished some memorable examples of disquiet at the pace of change. 'Just remember the permissive society stops at that front door,' Rigsby tells his lodgers in *Rising Damp*. 'We don't want any of it in here.' Occasionally he admits to a few adventures: he once visited a brothel in wartime France, but 'nothing happened. The Germans scored a direct hit on the bedroom. I thought, "If this is sex, you can stuff it."' But of course attitudes were different when he was young: 'Our idea of a dirty weekend was cleaning out the coal shed.' And as an instinctively conservative middle-class man with a military moustache and an apparently sexless marriage, the manager of Fawlty Towers deplores the new morality and clearly loathes the young. At the beginning of 'The Wedding Party' (October 1975), Basil reprimands the maid Polly for kissing her boyfriend ('What sort of place do you think this is, a massage parlour?') and tells her off for wearing a tight T-shirt ('I'm afraid we've abandoned the idea of the topless afternoon teas'). A few minutes later, greeting an affectionate young couple in their twenties, he is horrified to discover that they are not married. 'I can't give you a double room,' he snaps. 'It's against the law.' 'What law?' 'The law of England. Nothing to do with me.' Later, hoping to find some batteries for his electric razor, the young man asks if the local chemist is open. As usual, Basil jumps to the wrong conclusion. 'Now look! Just don't push your luck. I have a breaking point, you know,' he says. 'I only want some batteries!' the man insists. 'I don't believe it!' Basil says in horror. 'You disgust me. I know what people like you get up to and I think it's *disgusting*.'[30]

To most viewers, Rigsby and Basil were figures of fun. But to older people brought up in a more restrictive moral climate, the sexual landscape of the 1970s *did* seem deeply shocking. Contemporary life, remarked an elderly Lancashire woman, was 'a mockery of all the things we fought for . . . You're not put here just to enjoy yourself.' And when Jeremy Seabrook talked to men in the Conservative Club in Blackburn, among them a lorry driver, a schoolteacher, a hairdresser and an undertaker, he found considerable unease at the 'permissive society'. Girls were becoming 'pregnant at fifteen', one man said, 'because they take all this as a matter of fact, they've had that much of it at school . . . They indulge, because they think they know the answers, and consequently they get in this predicament.' At the root of it, said another man, was 'lust. Just dirty lust . . . It's getting to the stage now, when they don't think of anything else but sex . . . The whole obsession of their mind, from morning till night, is just sex.' A third man suggested that things had not really changed that much. No, the second man insisted: 'Married life and sex should be exalted as a chastity. You're forgetting the old words, you're forgetting purity and chastity and the very things that make life on earth bearable. And that means the home, gentlemen. The home is the foundation of everything.'[31]

Thanks to television, however, not even the most conservative home was entirely safe. So-called industrial language was becoming much more common: as the journalist Ian Jack put it, 'the old Anglo-Saxon has crept out of its prison in the mines, the mill and the public bar and is now threatening an assault on the living room'. The dramatist Alan Bleasdale, the son of a Liverpool factory worker, left Britain to teach abroad in 1971, returning three years later. 'When I left,' he recalled, 'I'd never heard a girl pupil swear. When I came back, I found beautiful little eleven-year-olds shouting, "you f. . .ing twat" down the school corridor. I was appalled.' Even more shocking for some viewers was nudity, which had been almost entirely taboo in the 1950s and 1960s. 'Did you see that couple on television last night, doing it like, you know, in a boat?' one woman asked another on a Wigan bus. 'I didn't know where to put myself, and I was on my own. If he'd been there [presumably meaning her husband], I would have had to turn it off.' And television certainly was much more graphic in the mid-1970s, reflecting the changing values of writers and producers. The BBC's adaptation of *I, Claudius* in the autumn of 1976, for example, positively revelled in nudity, lust and incest. 'The high point of debauchery', remarked *The Times*'s critic Stanley Reynolds, was the career of the Empress Messalina, who 'staged a sort of Roman version of *It's a Knockout*, challenging the chief whore of the empire to see how many chaps they could exhaust in a single day'.[32]

The bacchanalian orgies of *I, Claudius* attracted surprisingly little comment, almost certainly because the classical setting had given it a patina of respectability. By contrast, LWT's adaptation of Andrea Newman's novel *Bouquet of Barbed Wire*, shown earlier that year, was far more controversial. For the *Daily Express*, this story of a contemporary London family ripped apart by incestuous passion and domestic violence was a 'sick joke', the characters' behaviour 'so grotesque it's almost comical'. Plenty of readers wrote in agreement, among them Mrs Stevenson of Richmond, who worried that 'children watching must think that all adults are immoral and sex mad'. 'As soon as a television or even radio play is announced, my husband and I begin to worry,' agreed Margaret Picco of Thornton Heath, Surrey. 'We can be almost certain it will be offensive.' Even some television professionals shared her concerns: a few days later, the *Express* ran a long piece by George Markstein, the former script editor of *The Prisoner*, who thought too many people sneered at 'so-called middle-class entertainment'. 'We're knocking our values, all the things that made this country great,' he complained. Yet it is worth noting that, like *I, Claudius*, *Bouquet of Barbed Wire* was an enormous popular success, pulling in more than 20 million viewers every week. Perhaps all those viewers were sado-masochists, tuning in so that they could be shocked, but it seems unlikely. As the *Express*'s television critic had remarked only a few months earlier: 'Nudity on television hardly raises an eyebrow nowadays – a fair reflection of how viewers' toleration has expanded in recent years.'[33]

Compared with what some people were reading, even *I, Claudius* seemed tame. Thanks to the relaxation of the obscenity laws, the development of cheap printing technology and the ease of importing European materials, hard-core pornography had been one of the few growth industries of the Heath years. By 1971, when Paul Raymond relaunched the lifestyle magazine *Men Only* as a rather different publication, there were about fifty hard-core retailers in Soho alone, each taking in an estimated £10,000 a week. Readers were not merely lonely old men in dirty mackintoshes; according to a survey in the early 1970s, eight out of ten soft-core readers were under 45, with a third of them earning over £2,000 a year (almost £40,000 today). Attempts to crack down were futile: time after time, juries acquitted proprietors accused of corrupting public morals. The pendulum had swung decisively against state regulation of private morality, and by the mid-1970s three out of four people agreed that 'adults should be allowed to buy whatever indecent erotic books and magazines they like, so long as they are not on public display'. 'Where no one is hurt and the experience brings pleasure,' a consulting psychiatrist at St Thomas's Hospital, London, wrote to *The Times* in February 1976, 'the law should mind its own business.'[34]

By this point, pornography had become part of the fabric of national life, its presence on the top shelves a standing affront to moral conservatives. 'On every bookstall there are glossy magazines with pictures of naked women fondling themselves,' lamented the columnist George Gale. 'It is almost certainly impossible now to write a book which would attract prosecution for obscenity.' He was not exaggerating: by 1975, *Men Only* commanded an estimated 1.85 million readers, with *Mayfair*'s readership put at 1.67 million, just ahead of its great rival *Penthouse*. Four years later, the Williams Committee, which had been asked to suggest reforms to Britain's chaotic obscenity laws, estimated that about 8 million people frequently read 'up-market' magazines, most of them under 35, with readership strongest among the skilled working classes. Even in mainstream fiction, references to pornography had become routine. In the first Inspector Morse novels, *Last Bus to Woodstock* (1975) and *Last Seen Wearing* (1977), Colin Dexter's detective is a connoisseur of porn magazines and a frequent visitor to strip-clubs. An even more unlikely symbol of change, meanwhile, was George Roper, the inept landlord played by Brian Murphy in the sitcoms *Man About the House* (1973–6) and *George and Mildred* (1976–9). In the first series, George is a conservative, even sexless figure, a stuffy middle-aged counterpart to Richard O'Sullivan's hedonistic young tenant in the flat below. Yet by 1977 we discover that even George has a taste for pornography when his wife gives his old 'gardening magazines' to the vicar for a jumble sale. Only the 'top layer', it emerges, would appeal to Percy Thrower or Geoff Hamilton; the other hundred have titles such as *Nudge*, *Wink* and *Titter*.[35]

Against this background, what had once seemed excitingly naughty now felt downright dated. With audiences dwindling, even the producers of the ailing *Carry On* films felt under pressure to include more explicit material. 'Breasts are on parade this time,' the *Observer*'s critic remarked of the execrable *Carry on England* (1976), lamenting the passing of the 'mere coy bulbousness of seaside-postcard days'. Worse was to follow two years later in *Carry on Emmannuelle*, a shameful parody of the soft-core French films. 'Make no mistake about it, this will be a sex film,' the director, Gerald Thomas, told the *Daily Mail*. 'We are out to titillate. This is no Disneyland job.' But for some of the regulars, this was a step too far. 'You begin with her wanking a Steward on the Concorde,' Kenneth Williams wearily recorded after receiving the script. 'I found it monotonous and unfunny. When you get to her having the PM, the Judge, the Commissioner of Police, etc. etc. with no variations whatsoever, the credibility is gone & there's nothing *funny* to redeem it. It's so far away from the sort of story which a Carry On used to have. All this seems to do is to attempt to shock.' Soon after filming had started, Williams opened his morning paper and read that Barbara Windsor had walked out, lamenting the death of 'good family entertainment'. A few minutes later the phone rang. 'This is the *Evening News* ... could you comment on Barbara leaving your film? She says it is just pornography.' 'Yes! so do I,' Williams thought, although he did not say so. But thanks to its AA certificate, which meant that children under 14 were barred, the film was a well-deserved disaster. 'Crass', 'tired' and 'rootless' were some of the more complimentary critical verdicts.[36]

Mary Whitehouse was no admirer of the *Carry On* films. For more than a decade this retired Shropshire schoolmistress had campaigned against the evils of nudity, obscenity and pornography, her tirades against Alf Garnett and Alice Cooper making her a household name. To many commentators she seemed a crank, a ludicrous, reactionary figure whose outbursts against sex education in schools or 'obscene vegetable matter' in *Doctor Who* alienated people who might otherwise have shared her anxieties. And yet, like another middle-aged, middle-class provincial woman who thought that Britain teetered on the brink of irreversible moral decline, Whitehouse was often greatly under-estimated. The *Sun* might well demand: 'How many of us does Mary Whitehouse really speak for?', but she certainly spoke for the 31,000 members of the National Viewers and Listeners Association (NVALA). This was no marginal group: its membership (largely female, elderly, middle-class Christians) was roughly the same as that of the Communist Party and much bigger than the National Front or the Socialist Workers' Party. Her undeclared national support, meanwhile, was almost certainly much wider. Her Nationwide Petition for Public Decency, calling for stronger obscenity laws, attracted a staggering 1.3 million signatures, making it by far the most successful petition for forty years. And she was not entirely without influence: in January 1975, for example, she played a key role in defeating the Greater London Council's bid to end film censorship in the capital. It was, she said, 'a wonderful example of the way ordinary people can make an impact on the great issues of our time'.[37]

By the mid-1970s this dogged woman's admirers included the most influential prophets of what would soon be called Thatcherism. Writing in the *News of the World*, Enoch Powell praised her for fighting back against a movement that had 'swept around the world like an epidemic', using 'obscenity of every kind as a battering ram . . . to break down the walls of civilized society'. And in his notorious 'human stock' speech in October 1974, Sir Keith Joseph singled her out for praise:

> Let us take inspiration from that admirable woman, Mary Whitehouse. I do not accept all her ideas, she will not accept all mine. Yet we can see in her a shining example of what one person can do single-handedly when inspired by faith and compassion. An unknown middle-aged woman, a schoolteacher in the Midlands, set out to protect adolescents against the permissiveness of our time.
>
> Look at the scale of the opposing forces. On the one side, the whole of the new establishment, with their sharp words and sneers poised. Against them stood this one middle-aged woman. Today, her name is a household word, made famous by the very assaults on her by her enemies. She has mobilised and given fresh hearts to many who see where this current fashion is leading . . .
>
> We too can take courage from her, and dedicate ourselves to fighting back on issues which will decide the nation's future far more than economics, however important it remains.[38]

Despite the controversy that became attached to this speech, Joseph continued to bang the anti-permissive drum. In April 1975, after Margaret Thatcher had become party leader, he circulated some 'Notes Towards the Definition of Policy', some of which sounded as though he had been taking dictation from deepest Shropshire. 'In matters of behaviour,' Joseph wrote, 'we have gone along with what claimed to be progressive views. The result has been suffering for many.' The surge in violent crime, for example, was the result of 'our well-intentioned destruction of communities and the extended families they contained', as well as 'the educational fashions we permitted'. And, like Mrs Whitehouse, Joseph saw the small screen as one of the biggest threats of all. British children, he noted, watched more television than any other children outside the United States, and there must be 'a link between delinquency and violence and the television programmes' they watched. What was worse, the BBC now propagated 'a range of alien values based on variants of tyranny and anarchy'. It was time to fight back. Television must be monitored for 'lack of objectivity', while teachers must 'pledge themselves not to propagate any other system than democracy'. So much for the free market. Still, there were limits to Joseph's authoritarianism. A truly free society, he thought, should 'do nothing to suppress pornography for those who seek it out' – a line that showed how far the moral centre had shifted in just a few decades.[39]

What was revealing, though, was how few of Joseph's colleagues agreed with him. Peter Carrington thought the paper was a 'recipe for defeat', Francis Pym called it a 'recipe for disaster' and Reggie Maudling said he did 'NOT agree with ONE little bit'. Indeed, far from waging a culture war against feminists and homosexuals, the Conservatives said remarkably little about the permissive society in the late 1970s, preferring to talk about economics and the unions. Occasionally they made supportive gestures to the anti-permissive lobby: in 1978, for example, Willie Whitelaw delivered the keynote address at the NVALA conference, promising to 'conserve the moral standards on which our society has been based, and so preserve them for future generations'. But this was pretty woolly stuff, and in any case, a big, bumbling, amiable man like Whitelaw hardly made a plausible Savonarola.[40]

As for Mrs Thatcher, she remained, as so often, quietly ambiguous. In January 1970 she had told her local paper that she wanted to see 'a reversal of the permissive society', but now, apart from making vague noises about spiritual rebirth, she hardly mentioned the subject at all. In almost four and a half years as leader of the Opposition, she only twice publicly used the word 'permissive': once when talking about vandalism, and once when talking about trade union balloting procedures. But perhaps this was not surprising. As a working mother who believed women should compete with men for the top jobs, Mrs Thatcher was herself a powerful symbol of cultural change. What was more, only ten years earlier she had voted *for* such permissive reforms as the Abortion Act, the legalization of homosexuality and the reform of the divorce laws. Perhaps it was just as well, then, that the political battleground in the late 1970s never turned into an American-style 'culture war', for it is not necessarily obvious which side she would have been on.[41]

With the Conservatives apparently reluctant to discuss moral issues, it fell to Mary Whitehouse to carry the standard against the permissive society. Much of her energy in the late 1970s was poured into a campaign against the apparent rise of paedophile pornography, for by this time police raids were turning up growing quantities of magazines with titles like *Lolita*, *Children-Love* and *Lust for Children*. 'I have been in the police force a long time, and I thought that it was impossible to shock me,' one officer remarked after raids in Manchester had yielded thousands of books, magazines and films. Now, he said, he felt 'sickened . . . If I can feel like that, I wonder how ordinary members of the public would react'. Yet some people defended child pornography, and the so-called Paedophile Information Exchange (PIE) even held workshops, distributed newsletters and organized public meetings. Public opinion, however, remained implacably hostile: when PIE members assembled at Conway Hall, London, in September 1977, reported *The Times*, they were 'jeered, spat upon and pelted with stink bombs and rotten eggs by a screaming crowd'. That same month, Mary Whitehouse arranged a meeting with Mrs Thatcher to discuss the surge in hard-core pornography, securing a promise that the Conservatives would legislate immediately on taking office. (She was 'particularly concerned', she said, 'about the use of coloured children'.) A few weeks later the NVALA launched a petition against what Whitehouse called the 'kiddie porn industry'. 'Stamp It Out, This Abominable Evil,' read a headline in *The Times*. The government took note: a year later, the Protection of Children Act appeared on the statute book, making it an offence to make, show or distribute indecent pictures of children.[42]

But while few people could seriously object to Whitehouse's campaign against child pornography, her most famous cause proved rather more controversial. In November 1976 she received a cutting in the post. It came from the fortnightly paper *Gay News*, founded four years earlier by the Gay Liberation Front and the Campaign for Homosexual Equality. With a circulation of about 18,000, *Gay News* was a powerful symbol of the new freedoms enjoyed by homosexual men and women, even though many major retailers, such as W. H. Smith, refused to stock it. But now, Mrs Whitehouse thought, it had gone too far. The cutting came from an issue in early June: it was a poem entitled 'The Love that Dares to Speak its Name', written by the lecturer James Kirkup. As she read on in mesmerized horror, it became clear that the poem described a homosexual encounter between a Roman centurion and the crucified body of Christ. Not only do we discover that Christ had 'had it off with other men', from John the Baptist to Judas Iscariot ('a great kisser'), but the loving description of his naked body, ecstatically penetrated by the centurion, leaves nothing to the imagination. 'I think it shook me more than anything I had seen or come into contact with all the time I had been campaigning,' Whitehouse said later. 'The only thing it seemed to me I could do at all, was to see if it was blasphemous, if we could take action under the law.'

But this was not quite the whole story. As Michael Tracey and David Morrison showed three years later in their excellent study of the Whitehouse phenomenon, she had been hunting for a blasphemy case for months. As early as May, the NVALA had asked for legal advice on testing the public blasphemy laws, and now she had what seemed like the perfect opportunity. As Tracey and Morrison pointed out, she needed a case that was not merely clear-cut, but would have 'enormous symbolic importance'. And since Kirkup's poem was both shockingly explicit and unambiguously blasphemous, she could hardly have asked for a more ideal target. Even the team at *Gay News* had hesitated before publishing it. The editor, Denis Lemon, was 'doubtful', but his research editor, the literary scholar Rictor Norton, thought it was 'sincere and serious' and advised that 'although the poem was in many ways shocking, it clearly was not pornographic because it was not obscene simply for the sake of obscenity'. Lemon was pleased with the advice, because he always enjoyed annoying gay Christians. Revealingly, though, he did not consult the solicitor Richard Creed, one of the directors of *Gay News*, or other, more conservative members of staff. Indeed, Norton recalled that some of them 'resented Denis's unilateral decision to publish the poem', especially when 'letters of complaint began to stream into the GN offices'. It was clear, Norton thought, that 'we had given great offence to a significant number of our readers. We had stepped too far across the boundary of good taste.' What he never imagined, though, was that they would soon find themselves in the dock.[43]

Ten days after receiving a copy of the poem, Whitehouse launched a private prosecution for the long-forgotten common-law offence of blasphemous libel. At first she hoped to retain Lord Hailsham as prosecuting counsel, thereby dragging the Conservative Party into the case; sensibly, however, he turned her down. The Director of Public Prosecutions made vague noises about stepping in but eventually held back, which meant Whitehouse had to cover the costs herself. Donations flooded in from NVALA members, but she was disappointed not to get more help from the Christian Churches themselves. Writing to the archbishops of York and Canterbury a few months later, she declared herself 'dumbfounded' by their refusal to intervene. 'In no way could I ever have imagined that this poem could have done anything but rouse the Church to action,' Whitehouse wrote. 'Now I find myself alone – that is irrelevant in terms of what happens to me, but that the idea that the Lord was homosexual, and that the perverted practice on His dead body will not be seen to be blasphemous if the case is lost – about that I am lost for words!' What made this even worse, she thought, was that the entire 'homosexual/ intellectual/humanist lobby' had rallied behind *Gay News*, from writers and artists to gay rights campaigners, the Young Liberals and even some Labour MPs. 'I came under attack from just everybody – dons, religious leaders, the media people,' she reflected bitterly. 'I was completely overwhelmed by the extent of the opposition, and the silence of the church.' By declining to comment on the affair, the Anglican hierarchy had turned its back, she thought, on the timeless truths of Christian belief. 'The church has compromised where homosexuality is concerned,' she said scathingly, 'and it was afraid to come out and say anything about the poem.'[44]

Whitehouse's self-image as a plucky underdog battling the establishment would have raised eyebrows inside the offices of *Gay News*. Yet she always saw herself as the victim in the case, reacting fiercely whenever she was accused of waging a campaign against homosexuality. The trial was 'not about homosexuality' at all, she told *The Times*, but 'the right of Christians and sympathizers with the Christian faith not to be offended in the matter of their religious feelings'. But although Whitehouse angrily denied that she was 'involved in a campaign against homosexuals', this was not very convincing. Homosexuality was at the heart of her case: her whole point was that Kirkup's poem was blasphemous *because* it was homosexual. And although Whitehouse claimed that she was 'not against homosexuals as people', her repeated insistence that 'homosexual practices are evil', her belief that homosexuals were afflicted by a 'deficiency' or 'illness' and her claim that at least half of them could be 'completely cured and moved into a heterosexual position' hardly made her look a paragon of tolerance. To her admirers, she was a Christian crusader, standing alone against a tide of permissiveness. To her critics, she was an antediluvian bigot, trying to turn back the clock to the days when homosexual love had been punishable by law. Between these two positions there was little middle ground.[45]

In the short term, Whitehouse won. On 11 July 1977 a jury found both *Gay News* and its editor, Denis Lemon, guilty of blasphemous libel. The next day the judge, Alan King-Hamilton, handed out fines of £1,000 to the magazine and £500 to Lemon, who was also given a nine-month suspended sentence. 'It is perhaps being a little too optimistic in this era of obscenity,' King-Hamilton said, 'but it is possible to hope that by this verdict the pendulum of public opinion is beginning to swing back to a more healthy climate.' But he was in for a big disappointment. Far from being silenced, *Gay News* continued to thrive, its circulation reaching a peak thanks to the free publicity. Even the judge's order that the defendants pay most of Whitehouse's costs had little effect, for *Gay News* had amassed a £26,435 fighting fund, testifying to its support among affluent liberals as well as militant activists. When all the dust had settled, the magazine was actually left with a small surplus, which it donated to various gay rights organizations. Meanwhile, Whitehouse found herself under fierce attack. The *Tablet* thought her case had been a 'misapplication of the criminal process', while the *Church Times* felt she had been 'foolish' in drawing attention to a profane poem that would otherwise have gone virtually unnoticed. The Church was no longer in the business of condemning homosexuals, the Bishop of Gloucester told the BBC. Whatever homosexuality's cause, 'in so far as it is leading and helping and guiding some people to loving relations – responsible, tender, loving, caring relationships one with another – that must be good, that must be of God'.[46]

The truth is that, with barely one in fifty people going to church every week, Mary Whitehouse's vision of a God-fearing Britain was simply a fantasy. Decades earlier the stigma attaching to homosexuality would probably have deterred *Gay Times*'s supporters from speaking out. Yet now letters poured in to the newspapers, while thousands of gay rights campaigners marched to Trafalgar Square, handing out leaflets showing Whitehouse as another Hitler. Polls showed that in ten years since the legalization of homosexuality, public attitudes had gradually shifted from the widespread intolerance of earlier decades. In August 1977, Gallup found that three out of five people thought homosexual relationships should remain legal, while a majority thought gay men should be allowed to serve in uniform (although most opposed their being doctors, prison officials or junior school teachers). In taking on *Gay News*, therefore, Whitehouse was not only taking on a vast network of gay groups and self-help organizations, she was defying a growing liberal trend among younger and more affluent Britons. Only two days before the verdict, *The Times* had run a feature on the growing popularity of political badges, many carrying slogans such as 'Glad to be Gay' and 'How Dare You Presume I'm Heterosexual?' And in November, Granada's music show *So It Goes* featured the first live television performance of the Tom Robinson Band's 'Glad to be Gay', which reached number 18 in February 1978. The fact that the BBC refused to feature it on *Top of the Pops*, preferring another track from the same EP, made its success all the more impressive.[47]

Just two months after 'Glad to be Gay' had peaked in the charts, there came another little sign of change. Following Bruce Forsyth's defection to ITV, the BBC needed a new host of the hugely successful Saturday night show *The Generation Game*, and their choice fell on the unashamedly camp Larry Grayson. Of course there had been camp comedians before, but never one as overt as the toothy veteran from Nuneaton, never one with such limp wrists, never one who took such delight in announcing that it would be a 'gay day today'. Yet when Grayson went head to head with his predecessor in October 1978, the results left no room for doubt. While *Bruce Forsyth's Big Night* was a ratings disaster, Grayson's *Generation Game* was soon pulling in 24 million viewers a week.

Some gay rights activists complained that this was merely homophobia with a smiling face. 'Laugh at Larry Grayson and You're Laughing at Us' read a banner at one Gay Pride march. 'As far as we are concerned,' an activist said, 'they do not come much lower than Larry Grayson.' But Grayson, who disliked being labelled ('I am what I am. It's just me,' he explained when asked about his sexuality), returned their contempt with interest. 'Gay!' he said scornfully. 'I've never seen a more serious, miserable lot in my life.' Even conservative newspapers liked him: the *Express* thought that 'at a flop of the wrist, Larry Grayson has done more for Gay Liberation than a full-scale Hyde Park rally to their cause. He's legalised camp, playfully knocked over sex barriers, taught women to laugh and men not to sneer.' In its way, thought the interviewer Jean Rook, Grayson's rise to fame after decades of obscurity was a powerful symbol of popular tolerance. 'The almost total heterosexual acceptance of Grayson's high camp', she wrote, 'should be a gay day for homosexuals. Laugh and the world laughs with you – and if it doesn't see it your way, it may at least view you with a more tolerant eye.'[48]

PART THREE

Terminal Stasis

18

Evening All

Presumably he's getting out while the going's good. Still, he's been PM for nine years and was becoming as secure a British institution as the Queen or Bovril.

Michael Palin's diary, 16 March 1976

At about 12.30 Laurena telephoned and told me that Harold Wilson has resigned! What a time to leave the sinking pound!

Kenneth Williams's diary, 16 March 1976

One afternoon in December 1975, Bernard Donoughue sat in on a Cabinet committee meeting on defence cuts. It was a typically bruising occasion, and soon after the start there was a telling exchange between the Prime Minister and his Chancellor. 'When it emerged that the Cabinet might need to meet on Friday,' Donoughue wrote, 'HW said he might not be able to be there.' At that, in full view of everybody else, 'Healey rounded on him and said, "It might be better for all of us if you were not there."'

By any standards this was an extraordinary thing to say to the Prime Minister. What was even more extraordinary, though, was that Wilson simply pretended not to hear. A few minutes later, he got up and went out to the toilet, where Donoughue later found him standing with his head in his hands. 'I am so exhausted,' Wilson said miserably. During his last government, he said, he had enjoyed taking his dog for a walk to the pub near Chequers, but even that was too much for him now. He used to play a lot of golf; now he never found the time. 'I don't get any relaxation,' he said gloomily. 'I'm so tired.'[1]

Bored, listless, physically and mentally worn out, Harold Wilson had cut a ghostly figure ever since the European referendum. He 'felt exhausted', he told his press aide Janet Hewlett-Davies, 'and the job gave him little satisfaction'. Talking to Donoughue a few weeks afterwards, he muttered: 'I have been round this course so often that I am too bored to face jumping any more hurdles. The trouble with me now is that I only have the same old solutions for the same old problems.' He used almost exactly the same words to Joe Haines a little later. Working on a speech for the Durham Miners' Gala, Wilson had produced a draft that his aides thought 'stale, boastful, full of his old clichés, with whole paragraphs repeated from previous speeches'. When Haines pointed out that there was nothing new in it, Wilson said sadly: 'Well, I don't have anything new to say, do I?' 'Well, you might put some of your old ideas in new words,' Haines snapped back. But he was fighting a losing battle. The causes of Wilson's lassitude were partly physical – he seemed permanently afflicted by colds, styes, stomach complaints and bouts of flu – but there were moral and intellectual factors, too. His verbal sharpness had deserted him, while his famously brilliant memory had deteriorated to the point that, as one civil servant later recalled, whenever Wilson 'quoted a date or a reference at least one figure was bound to be wrong'.[2]

Conscious of his waning powers, Wilson cut back on his committee assignments, cancelled trips abroad and ignored all but the most pressing papers that landed on his desk. More and more he took refuge in his pet theories about burglaries and bugging, convinced that MI5, the CIA and the South African Bureau of State Security were plotting to undermine him, and that the unfolding Jeremy Thorpe scandal was merely one of their schemes. As one writer puts it, his mind was a 'simmering goulash of half-remembered incidents and unexplained mysteries'. Meanwhile, his reliance on the brandy bottle was worse than ever: by January 1976, Donoughue thought he had become 'a part-time Prime Minister firing on only two cylinders'. With most of his responsibilities handed over to Callaghan and Healey, he had 'almost ceased to function except in the House of Commons, at Cabinet once a week, and on isolated big issues'. Even his red boxes often went unopened, a cardinal sin in the eyes of his officials and something almost unimaginable ten years earlier, when Wilson had tried to do everybody else's jobs himself. He was 'grey and tired', his policy chief thought, 'just a shadow of the man of two years ago'. And when they went for lunch at the *Guardian* on 3 March, there was a tiny but highly revealing moment. At first, Wilson seemed in good form, chatting animatedly about Thorpe and the South

Africans. Then the political columnist Peter Jenkins asked him 'some pertinent questions about the future of Britain and how to arrest the decline in British power'. There was an embarrassing pause. 'HW just looked blank,' Donoughue wrote sadly.[3]

Wilson had been dropping hints for years about his desire to resign, and it says a great deal about his reputation that his colleagues never took them seriously. In the spring of 1970, he had told Roy Jenkins that he planned to go in three years' time, when he would overtake Asquith's record as the longest-serving Prime Minister of the century. The result of the next general election put paid to that. But although Wilson was determined to have a last taste of power, he kept telling people that he would only serve two years. In 1972 he told Denis Healey that he would not serve another full term, and before the February 1974 election he told Tony Benn that he would 'do two more years and then resign'. Since few people expected him to regain power, it sounded like an empty promise. But when victory was assured, he advised Bernard Donoughue to get leave from his LSE teaching job 'until Easter 1976, because I will retire then'. And as Barbara Castle later recorded, he told the Queen, too. 'When I became PM this time I told the Queen the date on which I would retire from this job,' he explained to Castle in 1976. 'She's got the record of it, so no one will be able to say afterwards that I was pushed out.'[4]

By the summer of 1975 Wilson was determined to walk away. On 14 July he told Haines that he wanted to go 'sooner rather than later'. 'He felt it was time to give the others a chance,' the latter reported to Donoughue. 'He said that Healey and Crosland were already in their mid-fifties and he "must not stand in their way". He also said he was totally fed up with the party and found its behaviour intolerable. He was very tired after 29 years in high politics.' Left to his own devices, Wilson might have resigned that autumn. But as Donoughue recorded, 'he gave way under strong pressure' from Marcia Williams, 'who argued that there would be an international and a financial crisis if he went – it was not clear whose financial crisis was being referred to, perhaps hers. He yielded, but insisted that under no circumstances would he go on beyond Christmas.' Once again, though, Marcia worked her magic, persuading him to keep going until the New Year. Haines and Donoughue were not pleased. 'The effrontery of this choked us both,' the latter recorded. 'HW had given way again, agreeing to go on until March, although he is worried that Mary will be furious again [a clear sign that his wife was pressing him to walk away]. I was furious. Because it is a sign of his weakness. He should take a decision and stick to it.'[5]

But not even Marcia could delay the inevitable for ever. In October Wilson's private secretary, Ken Stowe, confirmed to Buckingham Palace that he would go in the spring, and on 6 November Haines drafted the timetable for Wilson's resignation and the handover to a new leader, suggesting a three-week transition in February or March. Meanwhile, Wilson had already broken the news (or, perhaps, reiterated it) to the Queen when he and his wife were staying at Balmoral. If his own account is to be believed, the circumstances were bizarre, to say the least. Leaving her officials and bodyguards behind, the Queen drove Harold and Mary to a small lodge on the estate, where she busied herself making tea while Mary laid the table. Afterwards, the Queen put on an apron and began washing the dishes while her Prime Minister leaned on the worktop and explained his plan to resign. At this stage there was still no definite timetable, but at their regular audience on 9 December, Wilson finally mentioned a date, '11 March or thereabouts', which would give his successor time to bed in before the next Budget.[6]

Although Wilson had his qualities, keeping a secret was not among them. By the end of 1975, rumours that he was planning to walk away were swirling around Whitehall. On Boxing Day, his lawyer Arnold Goodman told Roy Jenkins that Wilson was 'resolved to resign in March, probably on his sixtieth birthday'. A few days later, Jim Callaghan had a visit from another of Wilson's confidants, Harold Lever, reporting that 'the Prime Minister had made a firm decision to resign in March, and I must prepare myself to take over'. For almost a decade, Jenkins and Callaghan had been the two leading candidates for the succession. The fact that Callaghan was working when he heard the news, whereas Jenkins was at a lunch party with Isaiah Berlin and Anne Fleming, spoke volumes about the gulf between them. Characteristically, Jenkins spent the next few weeks languishing with what he called a 'psychosomatic' flu, whereas Callaghan immediately called his friend Merlyn Rees to plan his campaign. In the meantime, the news was gradually seeping out, albeit in a very garbled form. On 4 March Wilson told Barbara Castle, 'I don't intend to be in this job much longer,' explaining that he had 'spent thirteen years trying to keep this party together and it's been a pretty thankless job'. Castle could not quite believe it: when the *Observer*'s columnist Alan Watkins predicted that Wilson might go after the Queen's Silver Jubilee, she wrote: 'I can't see him missing that.'

Meanwhile Tony Benn had heard 'a very strong rumour that Harold Wilson is about to retire'. As usual, Benn jumped to a melodramatic conclusion, suggesting that 'some papers which were stolen from Harold's desk may envelop him in some way in a scandal' – a baseless rumour that never entirely disappeared.[7]

Wilson originally planned to announce his resignation on Thursday, 11 March, his sixtieth birthday. That idea bit the dust, however, when the pound was sucked into the worst currency crisis since his return to power. With the British economy in such a mess, it was a miracle that disaster had not struck sooner, and it was lucky that the plight of the dollar had taken some of the pressure off the pound. Indeed, some Treasury officials thought that the pound was rising a bit *too* high, making exports expensive and hamstringing British manufacturers. On 4 March, therefore, the Bank of England announced that it was selling sterling, and on the next day it cut interest rates by 0.25 per cent. It was a terrible mistake. Even as the Bank was selling sterling, other traders, especially the Nigerians, were getting rid of their holdings, too, and within hours the pound's value had begun to collapse. By the following evening, it had fallen from $2.05 to $1.98, the lowest level in its history, and in the next few days it continued to plunge. In desperation, the Bank tried to change course: in two weeks, according to *The Times*, it spent a staggering one billion dollars trying to prop up sterling's value. It did little good: by 10 March, the pound had fallen to $1.92. 'Everything the authorities are doing seems designed to weaken the pound in the most dramatic way,' a youthful Conservative spokesman drily remarked. His name was Norman Lamont.[8]

The cruel irony was that the markets had lost confidence in the British economy only *after* Healey had begun to get the public finances under control. Thanks to his spending cuts, inflation fell from almost 30 per cent to 13 per cent in just nine months, while the deficit fell from more than £3 billion in 1974 to less than £1 billion two years later.* Inside the Treasury, recalled the mandarin Leo Pliatzky, there was a sense 'that we had turned the corner'. Yet as Healey's colleague Edmund Dell admitted, Britain had been extraordinarily lucky to get away with its apparently blithe indifference to inflation for so long. When the Bank of England made its ham-fisted attempt to sell sterling, it was as though the

---

* By comparison, Japan's inflation rate for 1976 was just 8 per cent, the American inflation rate was 7 per cent and the West German inflation rate was less than 4 per cent: figures that, as so often, put Britain to shame.

market woke up 'to what it should have been perceiving for months': the facts that sterling was overvalued, inflation was still too high, and the Labour Party had still not grasped the urgent need for financial discipline. Often decried as the sworn enemies of socialism, the markets had actually showed surprising tolerance in putting up with Britain's flagrant indiscipline for so long. But by March 1976 they had run out of patience. What they wanted now was blood.[9]

On 10 March, with the pound now down to just $1.91, the Commons voted on Healey's latest cuts. With the left-wing Tribune group in uproar, there was a palpable sense of mutiny: by the time Barbara Castle reached the House, 'the air was electric with the message: "We are going to be defeated tonight."' When she saw Bob Mellish, the Chief Whip, he seemed 'pale with fatigue and almost heartbroken'. 'Some of these rozzers aren't the old Tribune group at all,' he said gloomily. 'They're just thugs.' And when the tellers came back in and the Opposition Whips took their place on the right-hand side, a great bellow of delight burst from the Tory benches. With thirty-seven Labour MPs having abstained, the government had lost by 28 votes. 'Suddenly,' Castle noted, 'the rumble went round the House: where was Harold?' That the Prime Minister had left the Commons at such a crucial moment seemed not merely incredible but disgraceful, and for fully three-quarters of an hour the Speaker struggled desperately to restore order. 'Somehow, eventually, the hubbub died down,' Castle recorded. As the MPs streamed out, she asked Mellish why Wilson had been missing. 'You know him as well as I do, duckie,' Mellish said. 'He just said he would keep out of this.' Nearby, a Conservative MP muttered: 'I wonder if there will be any sterling left tomorrow.' But not everybody was displeased by the result. It had 'transformed the situation', wrote a jubilant Tony Benn, who had somehow brought himself to vote for his own government. 'It has ended the phony peace and people see now that the Government is supported by the right-wing forces in society.'[10]

The Tories would have been even angrier if they had known where Wilson was. It was Lady Falkender's birthday, and since Wilson's own birthday fell the next day, their friend George Weidenfeld had organized a little party at his Cheyne Walk flat. Wilson had briefly slipped out to vote at the House, and 'as if on impulse', he invited Jim Callaghan to come with him in the car. As the car sped along the Embankment, Wilson for the first time told his old rival that he was planning to quit. He would tell the Cabinet, he said, on Tuesday, 16 March, and in the meantime, Callaghan 'should begin to make preparations for the inevitable contest'. Despite Harold Lever's tip-off, Callaghan was in shock: he walked through the division lobby, he later remembered, 'in a bemused state, hardly grasping that the Government was actually in the throes of a crisis'. Even as their car headed back towards Marcia's party, Callaghan's mind was racing. It would be wrong, he told Wilson, 'to resign at such a moment'. But Wilson was past caring; he had made up his mind. It was 'not the happiest conclusion', Callaghan thought, 'to the Prime Minister's birthday party'.[11]

When the Cabinet assembled the next morning, neither man breathed a word of their conversation. Instead, Wilson insisted that the government must demand a vote of confidence that evening. Since it was his birthday, they broke for a celebratory coffee, and Shirley Williams dutifully struck up a chorus of 'Happy birthday, dear Harold', which most of them seemed to enjoy – except, of course, Tony Benn, who thought it 'odious'. The rest of the day, though, was pretty miserable, with the Labour whips forced to arrange ambulances so that sick and elderly MPs could be counted in the confidence vote. In the end the rebels fell into line and gave Wilson a 17-vote majority. But although nobody knew it at the time, the night was a crucial moment in the battle for the succession. At the dispatch box, Denis Healey blazed away contemptuously at the left-wingers who had tried to 'blackmail' the government. They had betrayed 'the hopes of those in the trade union movement who have made sacrifices to help the Government and the country', he said bitterly: if they rebelled again, they would 'betray the whole of our Labour movement to its enemies'. This was sensational stuff, leaving some of Healey's colleagues frozen with embarrassment. 'Stalinist! Stalinist!' Eric Heffer yelled at the Chancellor as they walked through the lobby, while his fellow left-winger Russell Kerr shouted 'Bastard! Bastard!' This was Healey's kind of talk. 'Go and fuck yourselves,' the Chancellor yelled back, 'you fuckers!' It was an appropriate response, perhaps, but hardly the ideal warm-up for a leadership campaign. Healey's 'verbal behaviour was unprintable and obscene in the extreme', one backbencher, Tom Litterick, complained a couple of days later. 'He came across like a drunken oaf.'[12]

Wilson spent the weekend after the confidence vote at Chequers with his wife and sister. On Monday morning, he was in the car back to London when the radio reported that the currency markets were quiet. 'It is all systems go,' Wilson said softly. When he reached Number 10 he disappeared upstairs with Ken Stowe, making their final preparations.

Later, Stowe told Donoughue that the Queen was 'very concerned' about Wilson's plans and had toyed with asking him to stay on. Everybody agreed that this would be a bad idea. 'He has lost the appetite for power and the will to govern,' wrote Donoughue. 'That is why he has no alternative.'

When Donoughue went into Number 10 early on Tuesday morning, there were so many aides milling around that it was obvious Wilson was going ahead with his plan. Even the policemen on the door realized something was up: the rumour, one of them confided, was that 'Crosland is resigning'. Yet when Wilson's ministers began gathering for their regular Cabinet meeting, none of them seemed to have any idea what was coming. Only Harold Lever sidled up to Donoughue and whispered 'D-Day?' Upstairs, Jim Callaghan was closeted with the Prime Minister. On his way down, Callaghan looked 'totally winded', and when Joe Haines wished him a good morning, he gloomily replied: 'Is it?'* Wilson then called Denis Healey into the little toilet just off the Cabinet Room to tell him, too. But when the rest of the Cabinet filed in a few moments later, most had still not heard the news. Without any preamble, Wilson started reading a typed statement. He had just returned from the Palace, he said, where he had told the Queen of his 'irrevocable' intention to resign. He had been Labour leader for thirteen years, and it was time to give others a chance and to have fresh ideas at the top. While he was still speaking, aides discreetly distributed signed copies of the statement.

When Wilson had finished, there was a long, stunned silence. 'Harold is not a man who arouses affection in most people,' Tony Benn reflected, although he too was in a state of shock. Eventually Ted Short, whose eyes were red with tears, 'blurted out something incoherent about what an appalling shock and blow this was'. 'Another silence,' noted Barbara Castle. Then Callaghan – halting and hesitating, according to Castle, although Benn thought he 'found it hard to conceal his excitement' – paid an emotional tribute, ending with the words: 'Thank you, Harold, for all that you have done for us.' Then, embarrassingly, there was another long silence. Castle found herself biting back the tears. Finally Wilson said that he had to inform Jack Jones and Len Murray, so he

---

* This was now the third time Callaghan had been told. The fact that he was *still* shocked suggests that he never really believed Wilson would go through with it. After working so closely with Wilson for more than a decade, he evidently did not have much faith in the Prime Minister's word.

would let Short chair the rest of the meeting. When he got up, waiters appeared in the background with cups of coffee. Wilson's ministers all looked 'poleaxed', Donoughue noted with amusement. When he told his staff at the Policy Unit, many of them could barely believe it. At lunch, the atmosphere was subdued. Upstairs, Wilson ate on his own, in the flat.[13]

By now the news had reached the streets of London. In Harvey Nichols, Wilson's old rival was signing copies of his new book *Sailing* when he was called to the phone. Entirely characteristically, Ted Heath returned 'looking quite impassive'. 'Are you going to have to dash away, sir?' a shop assistant asked worriedly. 'I think I might have to,' Heath said, sitting down, picking up his pen and flashing an unsettlingly large smile at the next customer. He did not tell anybody the news; instead, he merely went on signing books, studiously ignoring the journalists gathering behind him. The BBC rang, but Heath carried on signing. 'By the time he got up,' an onlooker wrote, 'the BBC had either hung up or had been cut off. Heath went back to the job.' By now the rest of the store had heard the news. 'So that makes it a lovely day,' one said to Heath. 'Does it?' he said. 'Isn't it marvellous?' asked another. 'It is certainly extraordinary,' Heath said impassively. But the crush of reporters was now so great that he had to stop signing, so he withdrew to the fridge-freezer department to ponder his reaction. Three minutes later he was ready, delivering his statement while 'leaning nonchalantly on an Italian deep-freeze'. It was not an ideal time for Wilson to go, he said, but he admired his rival's skill in staying at the top for so long. Then he went back to signing copies of *Sailing*. 'The reason you look so well is the restful life you have been having,' one woman gushed, clutching her prize. 'Harold Wilson will be looking fit and well and signing books all over the world quite shortly.'

On the streets, the *Times* diarist found that people were shocked and bewildered by the news. 'I think it's a great pity,' said a Scottish army officer, who always voted Conservative. 'I think he's ratted out on us. He's picked a bad time and one wonders why. Is there some great scandal?' At that point, not inappropriately, the clouds burst and the rain began to stream down, so the reporter ducked into a pub behind Mount Pleasant post office. 'You can't control a Government with people going against you,' said an elderly man in a suit and cardigan, who worked for the Law Society. 'I'm a Labour man – I have to be because I come from Durham – and I say that the trouble with the party is that there's too many of those Left-wingers in it.' Nearby, a 78-year-old former council worker in a flat cap, who had voted Labour all his life, agreed that it was the left's fault. They were 'always having a go at him,' he said. 'There's only so much a man can stand ... I hate those Left-wingers. I despise them. Wilson knew his job. He was the finest politician in the world, bar none.' What about his successor? 'Callaghan, probably,' said a young man who identified himself as a floating voter. 'He's very astute, but a bit of an opportunist. But then so was Wilson. He's always been able to find out the prevailing mood and move with it, rather than divide the party. But he's always kept the chap-next-door image you can trust.' His friend, a Labour voter, agreed that Callaghan was the man for the job: 'I'd let him take my dog out for a walk, yes.'[14]

In the next day's papers, the predominant reaction was sheer disbelief. Wilson's resignation was 'yet another characteristic confidence trick', thought the *Sunday Telegraph*'s Peregrine Worsthorne, 'a final brilliant act of legerdemain'. Barbara Castle, too, thought that there must be some secret explanation, even though Wilson had explicitly told her that he was tired of the job. 'What exactly *was* Harold up to?' she wondered. 'More than had met the eye, I have no doubt.' The reality, of course, was that he had long since lost his enthusiasm for politics, but many people refused to accept such a transparent explanation. With memories of the Watergate scandal still fresh, conspiracy theorists insisted that there must be some murky link to the Jeremy Thorpe scandal, an explanation Wilson himself encouraged after leaving office. Another theory held that he was planning a dramatic comeback at the head of a coalition government; others suggested that his enemies in the security service had forced him out, or that he had resigned because of some terrible financial or sexual scandal. Implausible as all these theories were, they reflected a widespread sense that Wilson's dominant characteristics had been deviousness and cunning. He had been 'an incomparable political stunt man', wrote Bernard Levin in *The Times*, marvelling at his ability to keep his party united. 'His tragedy', agreed the *Express*, was that 'he has been obsessed by the necessity to keep the Labour Party intact. As a result he has not only seemed, at times, to put the party before country but he has actually done so.'[15]

On 22 March, three days before the first ballot to determine his successor, Wilson held a farewell dinner in the dark-panelled surroundings of the State Dining Room. His ministers all sat in their usual places, so that, as Barbara Castle remarked, it felt 'just like a Cabinet meeting with food'. The only memorable moment came when a waiter managed to pour hollandaise sauce all over Denis Healey. Luckily, 'he was in a very jolly mood and laughed loudly', recorded Tony Benn. The speeches afterwards, however, were terrible, and after Wilson had said a few words ('boring', according to Benn; 'curiously toneless and emotion-less', according to Castle), there was a long silence. To everybody's relief, Benn jumped in and told a funny story about being asked to write Wilson's obituary for the BBC. But Castle thought 'the life soon fizzled out of the occasion', and she went home feeling thoroughly miserable. 'The pathetic thing about tonight', agreed Benn, 'was that nobody is sad that he was going. He hasn't inspired any affection, he's just done his job like a Civil Service Prime Minister for years, fudged every issue, dodged every difficulty, but kept us in power, kept us together, ground out the administrative decisions. It is difficult to feel warmth for him though, as a matter of fact, I get quite soft when I think of his kindness.'[16]

The following night Wilson hosted a dinner for the Queen and Prince Philip, who did him the honour of coming to Number 10 as they had done for Churchill. Once again all his aides turned out in their finery. Marcia 'gave a deep and well-practised curtsey', noted an amused Donoughue, 'as only one member of royalty can do to another'. What all these farewells could not disguise, however, was the fact that the life had been sucked out of Number 10. Wilson was like a man wandering in a deep sleep, Haines and Marcia were already planning for life after Downing Street, and the rest of his aides were waiting nervously for the results of the leadership election. The house was 'like a small liner whose engines had stopped', wrote Donoughue, 'and she lay becalmed in the waters of Whitehall'. Looming on the horizon was the small but very dark cloud of Wilson's resignation honours list. But in the meantime, Donoughue was getting ready for the Policy Unit's farewell bash. It was somehow entirely fitting that Wilson showed up two hours late after having been closeted with Marcia. Even more fitting, perhaps, was the fact that 'most of the guests were happily drunk – but nowhere near as under the weather as HW'. The Prime Minister was 'walking slowly and heavily', Donoughue recorded, 'his face vacuous and his eyes glazed'. Wilson stayed for three-quarters of an hour, then 'walked through the door and looked totally lost', and had to ask somebody to show him the way back.[17]

Wilson said farewell to Number 10 on Monday, 5 April. After all the bickering about lunch over the previous two years, he had planned a lavish farewell meal for his personal staff. At the appointed hour they assembled for drinks, standing around awkwardly and making small talk while they waited for Marcia to join them. Finally she hove into view, a mere forty-five minutes late. 'The Prime Minister and his wife, on their last day in 10 Downing Street, at their last meal there as Prime Minister, were kept waiting three-quarters of an hour,' recorded a disbelieving Donoughue. But even he admitted that it was oddly appropriate. 'Harold Wilson went out as he came in, a remarkable man but too often humiliated and made shabby by this sad association.'

Afterwards, Wilson went across to the Commons to get the result of the Labour leadership election before a last interview with the Queen. There was a rumour that the Prime Minister might go straight from the Commons to the Palace, but Donoughue insisted that he simply must 'come back and say goodbye to his devoted staff', and at least show his face at Joe Haines's farewell party. At last, at 5.30, Wilson appeared in the doorway, and the staff struck up 'For he's a jolly good fellow'. When the song died down, he turned and walked back to the hall, waiting while the car drew up outside. And then, almost twelve years after Harold Wilson had become Prime Minister for the first time, and more than half a century after he had first posed for a photograph on the steps of Number 10, the black door opened for the last time. 'He just walked out,' Donoughue wrote, 'slightly stooped, brushing back his grey hair, a plump little man in a crumpled suit, casting aside without a second thought or backward look the office, the house, which is the supreme object of many politicians' dreams and ambitions.' One moment he had been the dominant figure in British public life. The next, he was gone.[18]

At the time, Wilson's departure seemed to close a chapter in British politics. Not only was he was the last Prime Minister to serve non-consecutive terms, but his record of winning four out of five elections has never been equalled. Like Stanley Baldwin, another phlegmatic, kindly and inscrutable man, he seemed destined to leave a deep stamp on history. Many commentators thought that the 1960s and 1970s would be remembered as the 'Wilson era'. And yet the astonishing thing, given his political longevity, was how completely he disappeared after leaving office. The day after his departure, his successor joked in the Commons that he expected a short honeymoon, followed by 'the well-known cries of "Bring back Harold"'. But that never happened: indeed, people seemed to forget that Wilson had ever existed. Even in the newspapers, he was only ever mentioned in the context of his controversial resignation honours, which did enormous damage to his reputation, or his overheated allegations about spying and dirty tricks, which made him look like a paranoid fantasist. Only a week after Wilson had gone,

Tony Benn spotted him pottering aimlessly around the House of Commons and was struck by his utter lack of presence. 'He has absolutely shrunk,' Benn wrote. 'It shows that office is something that builds up a man only if he is somebody in his own right. And Wilson isn't.'[19]

Twelve years before, when Wilson had come to power as a dynamic modernizer promising to rebuild Britain in the white heat of the technological revolution, such a verdict would have seemed unthinkable. With his cheeky charm and Gannex raincoats, he had seemed the personification of modernity itself: after a string of tweedy Tory patricians, here was a technocratic populist who would drag his country into the scientific age. The longer Wilson stayed at the top, however, the more damage he did to his own image. By the time he bowed out of public life, even his famous raincoats had lost their sheen. Cheap, crumpled and shabby, they aptly symbolized Britain's endemic seediness. It is true that Wilson inherited a terrible economic mess from the hapless Heath, and he deserves some credit for calming the passions aroused by the miners' strike and three-day week. But thanks to his refusal to deliver bad news, his reluctance to take decisions and his preoccupation with the ludicrous feuding inside Number 10, his two-year administration after March 1974 was probably the worst in modern British history.

Wilson was one of the cleverest and kindest men ever to inhabit Number 10; sadly, he was also one of the weakest. At a time when his energies should have been devoted to turning the economy around, he wasted his time arguing with Marcia Williams, sorting out the bizarre squabbles about lunch arrangements or consoling himself with the brandy bottle. 'Thanks almost entirely to Wilson's most characteristic weakness, his invariable wish to avoid immediate trouble at the cost of storing up much worse for the future, Britain was allowed virtually to dig its own economic grave,' wrote the conservative journalist Christopher Booker in June 1976. Such views were not confined to the right. A year later, even Donoughue admitted that 'those first eighteen months under HW were sadly wasted'. In his memoirs the head of Wilson's policy unit concluded that he had totally failed to address the 'chronic weakness in British industry' or to overhaul 'Labour's antique ideological commitments'. Other Labour verdicts were even more damning. For the former MP David Marquand, a close friend of Roy Jenkins, Wilson 'presided over record levels of inflation and unemployment', 'did enormous damage to Labour's self-confidence and unity' and 'was, by any reckoning, a bad Prime Minister'. But the last word belongs to Denis Healey, who had served under him since 1964, first as Defence Secretary

"... AND THE SUN SMILING BRIGHTLY ON HIM, AND ALL NATURE JOINING IN A CHORUS OF APPROVAL TO THE SONG OF SELF-PRAISE THAT HIS OWN HEART WAS SINGING TO HIM, TOAD ALMOST DANCED ALONG THE ROAD IN HIS SATISFACTION AND CONCEIT."

(The Wind in the Willows)

Garland's cartoon in the *Telegraph* (18 March 1976) reflects the widespread public disillusionment at Harold Wilson's record in his final years. 'It's no good, Toady,' says the Rat in Kenneth Grahame's *The Wind in the Willows*; 'you know well that your songs are all conceit and boasting and vanity ...'

and then as Chancellor. Wilson, he mused later, 'was a terrible prime minister'.[20]

What happened to Wilson after 1976 was one of the saddest declines in political history. He had never had many close friends, and after leaving office he seemed to vanish into a 'black hole', abandoned by his cronies and hangers-on, lost and listless in a world that had passed him by. Already he was showing signs of the Alzheimer's disease that would blight his final years, his famously sharp mind fading fast. In December 1978, Donoughue had lunch with Wilson's old driver, Bill Housden, who was in very gloomy form. 'He said [Wilson] still drinks much too much, and that his memory is completely going – he cannot remember where he is going in the evening, even though Bill keeps reminding him,' Donoughue wrote. 'Harold apparently sits most of the day in his room in the Norman Shaw building finishing his book on the 1974–76 government. Bill says that nobody visits him and he has no friends. "It is very sad."'[21]

Ten days later, Wilson had one last turn in the limelight, appearing on the *Morecambe and Wise* Christmas special and cracking weak jokes about 'the pound in your pocket' in front of 20 million horrified viewers. Like the former Prime Minister, his hosts had recently made a breathtaking career decision, leaving the BBC for more money at ITV. Their debut on commercial television, however, was not a success. 'Ghastly,' wrote Peter Hall in his diary, while viewers told the *Express* that the show was 'very weak' and 'nothing like their old style', and the *Mirror* thought it 'a hefty helping of cold Christmas pud – with soggy lumps of custard'. For Wilson, as for Morecambe and Wise, it was a sad let-down. Even more depressing, perhaps, was the fact that nobody was very surprised. 'They all refer to his having "shrunk" physically as well as in reputation,' Donoughue wrote. 'A sad, but inevitable end. Everybody uses the word "shabby".'[22]

For more than a decade, Westminster had simmered with rumours of conspiracies to seize the Labour leadership, with Roy Jenkins often identified as Wilson's most likely successor. Even now, with fulsome endorsements from the Conservative papers and *The Times*'s star columnist Bernard Levin, the Home Secretary remained the favoured son of Fleet Street and St James's. Unfortunately, Bernard Levin's backing was not much of an asset in a Labour leadership race. 'With his big smooth head he looks like an aristocratic egghead,' one journalist wrote of the Home Secretary, noting that Jenkins made 'the most improbable leader of a workers' party'. To make matters worse, the left had never forgiven his pro-European enthusiasm, and at Westminster he was widely perceived as fastidious and aloof. Even Wilson's resignation statement had a dig at Jenkins's supposed preference for the lazy world of letters over the hard graft of politics. (Being Prime Minister was a 'full-time calling', Wilson wrote, adding that 'these are not the easy, spacious, socially-orientated days of some of my predecessors'.) Later, Neil Kinnock liked to tell a story about being in the Commons tea room with a group of Labour MPs when one of the Home Secretary's disciples came bounding up. 'Will you be voting for Roy Jenkins?' he asked brightly. 'No, lad,' a Yorkshire veteran said firmly, shaking his head. 'We're all Labour here.'[23]

Jenkins's fall from grace left a vacancy at the head of Labour's social democratic wing. One possible contender was his old friend Tony Crosland, the Environment Secretary: indeed, in the summer of 1975 Bernard Donoughue had recorded that he was 'very much HW's chosen successor these days'. Crosland certainly had the intellectual pedigree, but as Donoughue noted, there was 'something of the detached amused Oxford don about him', and it was never clear that he would do the 'tough and detailed things which are distasteful but have to be done'. With his Keynesian assumptions apparently discredited by the onset of stagflation, even old admirers were losing their faith: as the right-wing Labour MP David Marquand told Hugo Young, Crosland seemed a 'busted flush', trading on lazy clichés about the 'voters of Grimsby'. Like Jenkins, though, he threw his hat into the ring, albeit more in hope than expectation. Even his most ardent disciple, Roy Hattersley, suggested that he ought to step aside, but Crosland simply ignored him. 'The important thing now', he said, 'is to get a decent vote. I take it you'll vote for me.' Sheepishly, Hattersley said that he did not want to waste his vote. 'You'll not vote for me?' Crosland asked in disbelief. 'Even on the first ballot? Then fuck off.'[24]

The truth is that neither Jenkins nor Crosland stood a chance of winning the Labour leadership in 1976. In many ways the more obvious candidate was Denis Healey, who boasted more courage and self-belief than most of his colleagues put together. Had Jenkins and Crosland put their personal ambitions aside and rallied behind the Chancellor, his momentum might have been unstoppable. But neither was known for his humility, and both had the intellectual's distaste for a man who liked to get his hands dirty, as Healey manifestly did. And despite his obvious qualities, Healey suffered from some glaring weaknesses. Unlike Jenkins, he had never bothered to cultivate a network of allies, while his unashamed combativeness and intellectual arrogance meant that more sensitive souls could not stand him. If the election had been held a few weeks earlier, the Chancellor might have stood a better chance. But since it came so soon after his 'drunken oaf' performance, he was never more than a dark horse. Indeed, it was only after much persuasion that his Treasury colleagues managed to get him to enter the race at all. 'He admits to his friends that he may not always, or customarily, be a sweet and lovable, or even tactful person,' remarked David Wood of *The Times*. 'But ... he has to put down his marker for the not too distant future as a potential party leader.'[25]

All of this meant the way was clear for the obvious candidate of the centre. In a race dominated by Oxford old boys, Jim Callaghan was the only contender who had never been to university. A failure at the Treasury in the 1960s, the Portsmouth petty officer's son had rebuilt his reputation as Home Secretary and Foreign Secretary and was regarded as one of the government's most confident performers. 'Jim has become very much the conservative elder statesman,' wrote Donoughue a few days before Wilson's resignation, noting that Callaghan now spent more time talking about his Sussex farm than he did plotting for the leadership. Even Wilson, after years of mutual distrust, had come to rely on his experience. Nobody had better connections with the trade unions or the Labour Party machine, and nobody better reflected the traditional values of the self-styled people's party. On top of all that, Callaghan had had weeks to plan his campaign, which now moved smoothly into life under the management of his old friend Merlyn Rees. Cleverly, he took a deliberately presidential approach: alone among the candidates, he drafted no platform, gave no interviews and did not even appear on television. Everyone knew Big Jim; there was no point descending to the others' level. Only the day after Wilson's resignation, *The Times* was already reporting the view 'on the left and right that the only conceivable successor to Mr Wilson must be Mr Callaghan', while the *Mirror*'s front-page story began with the stark words: 'Jim Callaghan for Prime Minister. That was the betting at Westminster last night.' Even Wilson thought it was 'all sewn up for Callaghan'. 'Jim was so confident of victory', he told Donoughue, 'that he was "almost preparing to come and measure up for new curtains at No. 10".'[26]

Any doubts about Callaghan's victory were dispelled by the first ballot, on 25 March. On the left, Michael Foot won a surprisingly high 90 votes to Tony Benn's 37, leaving Foot as the undisputed standard-bearer of parliamentary socialism. The real question, though, was whether anybody could check Callaghan's momentum on the right and centre. But when the result was announced that evening, Callaghan had picked up 84 votes, while Crosland had a derisory 17, Healey a disappointing 31, and Jenkins a surprisingly poor 56, far fewer than many people had predicted. Jenkins knew what was coming: not untypically, he had spent the afternoon having lunch with a Foreign Office mandarin to discuss becoming the President of the European Commission. He promptly dropped out, as did Crosland. Only Healey, bloody-minded to the last, fought on, but in the second ballot five days later he won just 38 votes to Callaghan's 141 and Foot's 133. Since Healey's supporters were bound to turn to the Foreign Secretary, the contest was all over bar the shouting. With strong support from English, Welsh and Scottish MPs, from union groups and from both the soft left and the pro-European right, Callaghan was the undisputed unity candidate. Perhaps no leadership battle in Labour's history had been more eagerly anticipated; yet as Barbara Castle reflected, it had all been 'a bit of an anti-climax'.[27]

Callaghan was alone in his room at the Commons when, at lunch-time on Monday, 5 April, the chairman of the parliamentary party, Cledwyn Hughes, brought him the news he had wanted for so long. He had beaten Foot by 176 votes to 137: a clear victory, albeit one that testified to the surprising strength of the Labour left. Callaghan had never been a sentimental man, yet even he could not hold back the tears. 'Prime Minister of Great Britain,' he said slowly, almost as if he could not believe it. 'And I never went to a university.' 'You are in good company,' Hughes said reassuringly. 'The two greatest Prime Ministers of the century did not go to university – Lloyd George and Churchill.' The exchange said a great deal about Callaghan's self-image. A few hours later he told an aide: 'There are many cleverer people than me in the Labour Party, but they're there and I'm here.'

No doubt it was sweet satisfaction to hear those clever people clapping and cheering when, at four that afternoon, the result was announced in a packed Committee Room 14. 'There was a lot of wooden applause from the Callaghanites,' noted a disappointed Tony Benn. 'The Footites, including myself, were sitting pretty quietly and applauding a bit – that was the least one could do.' Still, even he was impressed by Callaghan's speech of acceptance, which promised to 'wipe the slate clean' of the feuds of the past, and that there would be 'no insiders or outsiders'. It was 'very emotional', Benn thought. 'To become Leader and Prime Minister together must be an overwhelming experience, and Jim is a human guy.' Indeed he was. An hour later, as the car carried him towards Buckingham Palace, the former Ordinary Seaman reflected on the great names of the past – Pitt, Gladstone, Disraeli and Lloyd George – that he had studied at school. Now he was following in their footsteps. 'For me,' he wrote later, 'it was a boyhood dream come true.'[28]

That night, Callaghan addressed the nation on television for the first time as Prime Minister. He had written much of the speech himself, revising his aides' draft 'with more emphasis on restoring the traditional values'. And to listeners used to Wilson's reassuring platitudes, his opening words must have come as a shock. His priority, he said, would be 'the vital job of bringing down the rate of inflation', and he made no attempt to disguise the scale of the challenge:

> We cannot have a prosperous industry in this country if we are unable to sell our goods overseas. No one owes Britain a living, and may I say to you quite bluntly that despite the measures of the last twelve months, we are still not earning the standard of living we are enjoying. We are only keeping up our standards by borrowing, and this cannot go on indefinitely.
>
> There is no soft option. I do not promise you any real easement for some time to come. There can be no lasting improvement in your living standards until we can achieve it without going deeper and deeper into debt as a nation.

But government, Callaghan said, was not just about managing the economy. He promised never to appease 'the greedy or grasping or selfish'; he pledged to defeat 'vandalism and violence'; he insisted that families were 'at the heart of the battle for our national survival'; and he asked parents 'to stand firm in your attitude both to our values and to our future'. 'Do you, like me, sometimes feel that we have been slipping?' he asked. 'Then join me, join all of us, in a national effort to uphold our values and our standards.'

It hardly sounded like the red meat of socialism; even the *Express* thought it was an appeal 'to which many conservative-minded voters could respond'. But then what did they expect from PC Jim, the former parliamentary adviser to the Police Federation? As an amused Kenneth Baker put it, Britain now had 'the Prime Minister of Dock Green'. All that was missing was the catchphrase: 'Evening all.'[29]

19

A Great Detective Exercise

*By his last act of patronage Sir Harold has succeeded in
reducing himself, and not only himself. He has demeaned the
office of Prime Minister and embarrassed his successor.*

The Times, 29 May 1976

*The most disappointing result has been Jeremy Thorpe's
success in North Devon. Thorpe was already conceited enough
and now threatens to become one of the great embarrassments
of politics. Soon, I may have to reveal some of the things in my
file on this revolting man.*

Auberon Waugh in *Private Eye*, 8 March 1974

Harold Wilson's aides had known for months that his resignation
honours list was going to cause trouble. In December 1975, Bernard
Donoughue recorded that there had been a 'terrible row' between the
Prime Minister and Lady Falkender over peerages. When Marcia
reminded him 'of his obligations to her from long ago', Wilson replied:
'That does not mean I have to spend 20 years' penal servitude.' As
always, however, Wilson's resolve soon evaporated. The day after the
Prime Minister had announced his resignation, his principal private sec-
retary, Ken Stowe, told Donoughue that he was seriously worried about
Wilson's plans for resignation honours:

This is supposed to be a small list of those who have worked personally
for the P.M. But Marcia has a book – which Albert [Murray, Wilson's chief
bag-carrier] has seen – which contains an enormous long list of names –
with a lot of show-biz characters such as Lew Grade and David Frost as

well as [George] Weidenfeld. It includes people already committed to pay HW and MF for books and TV series.

This was Marcia's 'last chance to influence honours', Donoughue mordantly remarked, 'and she is going for the lot'. Stowe was adamant that it must never get through, not least because it was bound to infuriate Wilson's successor. But Donoughue could see 'a big battle ahead. HW is trying to slip it through before he leaves but there is bound to be trouble.'[1]

Two weeks later, Donoughue was working quietly in his Downing Street office when Joe Haines appeared in the doorway, 'very depressed'. According to the former's diary, Haines had just laid eyes on the most infamous honours list in history: 'Some fifty names for peers and knighthoods all in Marcia's handwriting on a sheet of lavender-coloured notepaper and simply ticked by HW. It is a most odd list, led by David Frost and John Vaizey. Joe and I know the reason for the proposed peerages in most cases.'* According to Haines, Wilson had only crossed out one of the names: Will Camp, a corporate publicist who was apparently 'too close to *Private Eye*'. Many of the other names, however, were financiers, media moguls and businessmen who were reportedly close to Marcia: very few were Labour Party insiders. 'Some of them', Haines said grimly, 'are people that Scotland Yard might in due course wish to interview.' Not surprisingly, both men thought the list was a disaster. That evening, after Wilson's drunken appearance at the Policy Unit farewell party, they tried to talk some sense into him. 'He was not prepared to listen,' Donoughue wrote sadly. 'He is suicidal. He doesn't seem to care about the reaction to this final and scandalous use of patronage. He just wants to be rid of the whole thing and to buy off some peace with Marcia.' Even hours before Wilson was due to walk out of Number 10, Donoughue was trying to change his mind. By this stage, the Bank of England, the Home Office and the Inland Revenue had all lodged objections to some of the names on the list. But Wilson was deaf to criticism. 'I don't understand why I am being attacked over the honours list,' he said plaintively. 'I have barely ever met half of them.'[2]

Originally the honours list was supposed to be published on 15 April.

---

* Although the story of the lavender notepaper is supported by both Donoughue's diary and Haines's autobiography, Lady Falkender has always denied it. In 2007 she won a handsome settlement from the BBC after it broadcast Francis Wheen's drama *The Lavender List*. 'As [Harold] Wilson always made clear throughout the period after he left office,' she explained, 'and as I myself have always made clear, the 1976 list was his own work and included only those individuals he himself believed ought to be honoured.'

But when the day came and went, the newspapers' antennae began to twitch. On Fleet Street, rumours abounded that the list had run into trouble with the Scrutiny Committee, which usually rubber-stamped the outgoing Prime Minister's suggestions. On 2 May, the *Sunday Times* claimed that three names – 'a City financier', 'a financier and impresario' and 'a minor businessman' – were causing real problems, and that Wilson had already been forced to delete some of his recommendations. The weeks went by: 'the suspense', said the *Sunday Express*, was 'unbearable'. And then, on 27 May, the list appeared at last – and it was even worse than predicted. In total, forty-two people carried off honours. Most were unexceptionable: there were medals and MBEs for various Downing Street and Chequers cleaners, policemen, housekeepers and stewards, while there were knighthoods for actors Stanley Baker and John Mills and an OBE for the impressionist Mike Yarwood, then at the height of his popularity. The final ten names, however, were genuinely shocking. Peerages for the Russian-born impresarios Sir Bernard Delfont and Sir Lew Grade baffled many Labour partisans, while a life peerage for Wilson's publisher George Weidenfeld smacked of blatant favouritism. But even his fiercest critics could hardly believe that Wilson had given knighthoods to the property tycoon Eric Miller and the corporate raiders James Goldsmith and James Hanson, both of whom were keen Conservative donors, or that he had really given a peerage to the Gannex tycoon Sir Joseph Kagan, presumably for services to raincoats. 'That he should pick inadequate, buccaneering, sharp shysters for his honours was disgusting,' wrote Tony Benn the next day. 'It was unsavoury, disreputable and just told the whole Wilson story in a single episode.'[3]

For once, Benn was perfectly in tune with the Westminster consensus. 'The names on the list have nothing to do with the promotion of socialism which is what the Labour Party and the Labour Government mission is supposed to be about,' complained the Labour MP Sydney Bidwell, while his colleague Jeff Rooker remarked that there were '50 people in my local party who have done more individually than this lot put together'. It was a list of 'cronies and associates', agreed the Conservative MP Teddy Taylor, while his fellow Tory Neil Macfarlane thought it symptomatic of the way Wilson had 'demeaned and debased' Britain's political life. The outrage at Westminster, however, was as nothing beside the contempt of the newspapers. The list, said the *Telegraph*, was a 'fitting legacy from an in many ways absurd Prime Minister', while even the *Guardian* declared that Wilson had gone beyond 'the point at which personal patronage has to stop'. And while *The Times* thought it 'rather pleasant to see the wilder shores of capitalism once again hung with coronets', it found it 'very odd that such a scene should be set by the ex-Prime Minister of a socialist party'. Men like Miller and Goldsmith, after all, were 'the contradiction of everything for which the Labour Party stands. Is it really true that these are the people he most admires? Is it really true that they are the people he wants to thank for having helped him with his administration? Are they his friends for whom he feels the warmth of personal gratitude?'[4]

Behind these words, of course, was the strong suspicion that the real author of the list was not Harold Wilson at all. Two days later, *The Times*'s George Hutchinson made the charge explicit. The list, he wrote, was no trivial matter: it had left Wilson's reputation 'irretrievably damaged', 'injured the Labour Party, and thereby the Government' and 'brought so much discredit to the honours system that it may not survive in its present form'. But while Wilson deserved most of the blame, Hutchinson thought that 'Sir Harold's amanuensis and adviser (one might almost say accomplice) can hardly be exonerated'. Lady Falkender had 'claimed too much influence and responsibility in the past to escape comment and attention now', and Hutchinson recommended that she 'lie low for a while, perhaps a long while, avoiding the House of Lords'. That was too much for Marcia. Two days later, *The Times* printed her 2,000-word shriek of rage, in which she furiously insisted that the list was 'Harold Wilson's list and his alone' and dismissed the criticism as 'unadulterated snobbery' and 'covert anti-semitism'.[*5]

Marcia has clung to this line all her life. When Joe Haines published his memoirs in February 1977, repeating his claims about her lavender notepaper, she rushed back into print, dismissing his 'wild and intemperate' allegations. Even Wilson waded into the fray, denouncing Haines's book as a 'farrago of twisted facts' – although, as the press noted, it seemed telling that he issued his statement only after spending almost an hour closeted with Lady Falkender. The headlines – 'Marcia: The Truth About *That* Honours List', 'The Cross We Had To Bear: By Top Wilson Aide' (this, gloriously, above an advert headed 'Painful

---

* Many of the controversial names, such as Goldsmith, Miller, Kagan, Weidenfeld, Grade and Delfont, were Jewish, as were other businessmen on the list such as Sir Max Rayne and Sir Sigmund Sternberg. Wilson had always had a soft spot for Jewish businessmen, perhaps because he was drawn to outsiders. To accuse his critics of anti-Semitism, though, was going too far; what people disliked about, say, Goldsmith was his business ethics, not his religion or ethnic background.

Piles'), 'Carry On Slanging', 'Miaow!' and 'Still They Claw And Scratch' –
could hardly have been more damaging. Less than a year before, Wilson,
Haines and Marcia had been running the country; now they were brawling in the gutter. Between them, one paper remarked, they had 'presented
a million votes to the Conservative Party'. For George Hutchinson, however, the damage went much deeper. 'Small wonder if Mr Callaghan is
looking on with distaste, not to say disgust,' he wrote. For the effect of
the furore 'must be to undermine confidence in our institutions and in
the probity of public life, to encourage scepticism and promote disillusion. No one can gain from that, except our enemies.'[6]

Since the infamous lavender list has never been found, we will never
know for sure who drew it up.* Certainly Haines and Donoughue were
convinced that it was Marcia's responsibility. Haines claimed that James
Goldsmith, an outspoken right-wing Tory whom Wilson had barely
met, had offered to make Marcia a director of Cavenham Foods, while
Donoughue heard that Goldsmith had paid the school fees for one of
her sons. As for the Peachey Properties boss Eric Miller, Donoughue
claimed that he and Marcia had been so close that many Downing
Street officials expected them to get married. Lord Goodman even
claimed that Miller had paid for Marcia's second home in Wyndham
Mews, which the two were planning to use as a 'love nest' until Miller's
wife intervened. Quite possibly these stories were exaggerated, distorted
or plain invented. In any case, the ultimate responsibility lay with
Harold Wilson. Whether through weakness, indolence or corruption, he
had contrived to bring the honours system into utter disrepute. And as
the months went by, the list looked even worse. In May 1977, facing
accusations of fraud, theft and forgery, Sir Eric Miller shot himself. A
year later, Lord Kagan was charged with tax evasion. Like Miller, the
raincoat tycoon stood exposed as a cheat and a fraud: he had even
stolen four drums of indigo dye from his own firm. Stripped of his
knighthood, he remained a peer of the realm. After serving ten months
in prison, where he was a 'prodigious sewer of mailbags', he unashamedly returned to the House of Lords and became a keen advocate of
penal reform.[7]

Wilson was not the first Prime Minister whose reputation was tarnished
by his handling of the honours system. Coming when it did, however,

* If the list really existed, it was probably not lavender. When Haines showed his wife an
example of Lady Falkender's notepaper, she said: 'That's not lavender, that's lilac.'

the lavender list left a considerable dent in the image of British politics. Thanks to the Watergate scandal, anybody who had opened a newspaper in the last few years was eminently familiar with dodgy political contributions and dirty tricks, while the fate of the disgraced Reginald Maudling, who had become embroiled with both the corrupt property developer John Poulson and Wilson's friend Eric Miller, was a reminder that British politicians were no strangers to rampant greed. And not even the figurehead of England's national game, it seemed, was immune. In September 1977, Bernard Donoughue had 'dinner with Ted Croker of the FA, who told me some alarming corruption stories about Don Revie, [the former] England team manager'. A few years earlier, Leeds United had been the finest football team in the country; now, according to a *Daily Mirror* exposé, it appeared that their manager had 'planned and schemed and offered bribes, leaving as little as possible to chance'. Despite the torrent of allegations from rival managers, as well as a confession by Revie's goalkeeper Gary Sprake, the accusations were never proved. But like the stories about Marcia Falkender and the lavender list, they lingered in the air like a bad smell, the stuff of speculation for years to come.[8]

There was one corruption story, however, beside which the lavender list, the Revie match-fixing scandal and the revelations about Reggie Maudling paled into insignificance. It was the story of a man who had inherited the mantle of Gladstone, Asquith and Lloyd George, who was seen as a kingmaker in the febrile political world of the mid-1970s and who was even mentioned as a future Prime Minister. It not only dominated the headlines, it came to haunt the fevered imagination of Harold Wilson, becoming inextricably entangled with fears of burglaries and bugging, rumours of South African conspiracies and gossip about coups to bring down the government. At its peak, it became the supreme embodiment of what contemporaries saw as Britain's political seediness and moral degeneracy, and yet at its heart were some of the most basic human urges of all: lust, fear, pride, ambition. Above all, it featured a cast of characters too strange for even the most imaginative novelist: a dashing national party leader with a taste for rough trade, a hysterical male model who kept trying to kill himself, a failed Liberal MP who moved to California, a professional killer with a phobia of dogs, a fruit-machine dealer who fancied himself as a murder mastermind, and a cut-price carpet dealer called John Le Mesurier. And, of course, a dead dog called Rinka.

At the centre of the story was one of the most colourful characters in

British politics. The son and grandson of Conservative MPs, Jeremy Thorpe had been educated at Eton and Oxford, where he was president of the Liberal Club, the Law Society and the Union. Even in those early days he cut a dash, thanks to his showy dress sense, expensive tastes and witty repartee. He was a brilliant mimic, a dazzling raconteur and a ruthless self-promoter: the historian Keith Kyle, whom he beat to the presidency of the Union, remarked that 'he was a bounder but, by Jove, a bounder with style'. Superficially the moribund Liberal Party seemed an odd choice for such an ambitious young man, but it made an excellent vehicle for such a flamboyant force of nature. In the humdrum world of Liberal politics, Thorpe stood out like a jewel in a slag heap. And when he was elected to represent North Devon in 1959, he stood out in the Commons, too. A fine speaker, a devastating heckler, a keen advocate of human rights and civil liberties, he was immediately recognized as a star of the future. When he succeeded Jo Grimond as Liberal leader in January 1967, he seemed set for a long and glittering career.

Even at this early stage, though, there were whispers about Thorpe's private life. In 1960, when his Old Etonian friend Antony Armstrong-Jones got engaged to Princess Margaret, Thorpe was mentioned as a possible best man. But when MI5 asked the Chief Constable of Devon to confirm his suitability, the latter reported that Thorpe had 'homosexual tendencies'. Rumours of his fondness for handsome young men swirled around Westminster, and at least one Liberal MP bumped into one of Thorpe's disgruntled ex-lovers at the House of Commons. At this stage homosexuality was still illegal, which made Thorpe's indiscretion all the more reckless. He was well aware of the dangers. 'If I'm ever driven out of public life in Britain for a gay scandal then I shall settle in SF!' he wrote to a gay friend in San Francisco in 1961.* Yet he refused to moderate his behaviour, often taking his old Oxford friend David Holmes, now a Liberal fund-raiser, on hedonistic Mediterranean holidays. 'When he was in London he loved the danger,' another friend said. 'That was half the attraction of it all. He had an enormous thirst for getting into really tricky situations. But there was a sense, I think, of liberation in going abroad.' At the time, this was a common recreation for gay men; still, Thorpe was taking an enormous risk. After a break in Greece, he returned with gonorrhoea after having had sex with a male

* The most striking thing about this letter is Thorpe's use of the word 'gay' a quarter of a century before most dictionaries recognized it – which suggests how deeply he was embedded in London's gay subculture.

prostitute on a beach. Afraid to visit his own doctor, he ended up going to a Hampstead doctor recommended by a friend.[9]

Sometime in late 1960 or early 1961, Thorpe met a mixed-up young stable boy called Norman Josiffe, who was working at the Kingham Stables outside Chipping Norton. Just 20, Josiffe was greatly impressed by his suave new friend. In November 1961, having fled the stables after a row with the owner, he decided to visit Thorpe at the House of Commons. Perhaps surprisingly, Thorpe agreed to see him, and Josiffe poured out a long story about how he had been badly treated and had fled Kingham without his National Insurance card, which he needed if he wanted to work again. It should have been obvious that Josiffe was not a very secure young man; indeed, he had been sectioned under the Mental Health Act a few months previously. But instead of passing his case to the local MP, Thorpe took Josiffe to his mother's country house in Essex. There, according to Josiffe, Thorpe seduced him, calling him his 'poor bunny'. Afterwards, Thorpe arranged for Josiffe to be installed in a cheap Chelsea bedsit – a kind of reward for services rendered.

Had it ended there, the story of Thorpe and Josiffe would have remained entirely inconsequential. Unfortunately, it did not end there. Josiffe was a deeply troubled man, at once greedy, resentful and paranoid. Despite the fact that Thorpe had given him money and arranged a job for him, he became convinced that the Liberal MP had treated him disgracefully, and even went to the Metropolitan Police, alleging that they had had 'homosexual relations'. The police took little notice, but the story was duly sent to Special Branch and MI5. Disastrously for Thorpe, Josiffe also handed the police a stash of Thorpe's letters, including an indiscreet postcard about Princess Margaret's marriage to his friend Armstrong-Jones, in which Thorpe had recorded his ambition to 'marry the one and seduce the other'. For the time being, though, the security services did nothing. When Thorpe became Liberal leader in 1967, the MI5 chief Sir Martin Furnival Jones told the Home Secretary that Josiffe (who was now calling himself 'Norman Scott') had been making complaints of 'buggery' against him. 'Thorpe's homosexuality was common knowledge in the House,' Roy Jenkins replied, so there was no need to do anything about it. That was a relief to Furnival Jones. 'We had never investigated Thorpe,' he told the Home Secretary, 'and would not at all welcome a request to do so now.'[10]

By now Thorpe had enlisted the help of his fellow Liberal Peter Bessell, who was MP for neighbouring Bodmin, to keep Josiffe quiet by paying him a weekly retainer. By any standards, Bessell made a very unlikely confidant. An unscrupulous wheeler-dealer whose schemes – a chain of motels, a luxury hotel at Heathrow, a business making plastic egg-cartons – had never come off, he was basically a real-life version of Rick Pym, the con man who stands as a Liberal candidate in John le Carré's novel *A Perfect Spy* (1986). He was hardly the ideal person to sort out other people's problems, since his own finances were such a mess that he had started embezzling party funds from Liberal donors. By contrast, Thorpe was riding high: not only had he been elected leader, he had acquired a beautiful young wife, Caroline Allpass, who worked at Sotheby's. But that only made it all the more urgent that he shut Josiffe up for good. Convinced that his former lover had letters that could destroy him, Thorpe spent hours discussing ways to deal with him. In December 1968, he allegedly asked Bessell if he realized 'what a predicament and black crisis he faced every night of his life'. 'We've got to get rid of him, it's the only way,' Bessell remembered him saying. 'It's the only solution. If I don't, this man is going to haunt me all my life. It is no worse than shooting a sick dog.'

Can Thorpe genuinely have said this? The last line, at least, is surely too good to be true. Thorpe always denied the entire conversation, and Bessell was hardly the world's most reliable witness. Yet Bessell's allegations went further. In another conversation, he claimed, Thorpe suggested that his friend David Holmes pose as a German journalist, lure Scott to a deserted site in Cornwall, and murder him by breaking his neck. Alternatively, he mused, Holmes could lure Scott to a Cornish pub, poison his drink and dispose of his body down an old mineshaft. Even Holmes thought that was a bit much, pointing out that it might look 'rather odd' if Scott suddenly fell off his bar stool, 'stone dead'. Perhaps Thorpe was joking; both his friends, however, thought he was serious. Braver men might have told him to drop the idea, but they continued to humour his increasingly bizarre schemes. Indeed, Bessell claimed that at the end of 1970 they cooked up an even more outlandish plan. 'It's got to be the ultimate solution,' Thorpe supposedly told Bessell. 'We daren't let Scott go near a court.' The ideal scenario, he now thought, was for Holmes to lure Scott to Florida, a suitably exotic location for a plot becoming more flamboyant by the day, kill him and dump his body in the Everglades, to be eaten by the local alligators.

In the meantime, Scott was becoming ever more unstable. In the spring of 1971 he secured an audience with the Liberal Chief Whip, the 33-year-old David Steel, and told him the whole story. Horrified by Scott's letters, which proved that he had been taking money from Bessell and Thorpe, Steel set up a secret inquiry. But Scott performed so abysmally, sobbing and whingeing, that the Liberals dismissed him as a paranoid fantasist. In desperation, he tried to sell his story to the *Mirror*, only for them to turn him down. But now the story took a strange twist. At a *Mirror* reporter's suggestion, Scott took his tale to a freelance journalist called Gordon Winter. He found Winter a willing listener; so willing, indeed, that the two men sealed the deal by going to bed together. But Winter had a secret of his own. He was no ordinary journalist; he was an informant for BOSS, the South African Bureau of State Security, then one of the world's most effective intelligence outfits. Since Thorpe was a fierce critic of the South African regime, Winter passed Scott's story on to his paymasters. They told Winter to sit tight. In the event of a close election and a possible Labour–Liberal coalition, they thought, he could use the story to destroy Thorpe and make sure the Tories stayed in power.[11]

Although the BOSS element has always fascinated conspiracy theorists, it was no more than an outlandish sideshow, distracting attention from the real story: Thorpe's terror that his homosexual past would come out and that he would lose the leadership of the Liberal Party. The irony was that, as the Heath administration staggered towards oblivion, his star was rising higher than ever. Witty, sardonic, his relaxed moderation a stark contrast with the partisan pieties of his rival party leaders, he was the undisputed star of the February 1974 election, which gave the Liberals more than 6 million votes, almost 20 per cent of the total. Once the leader of an obscure, even derided political party, he now found himself a kingmaker, dashing to London for talks with Edward Heath on a possible coalition. Power was so close he could almost touch it, and there was even talk of Thorpe as Home Secretary – which would have put him in charge of MI5, who now had a thick file on Scott's allegations. Of course the talks never came to anything, and Wilson took over instead. But with another election bound to follow, Thorpe stood every chance of playing the kingmaker again. The stakes had never been higher; silencing Scott had never been more urgent.[12]

According to the prosecution in Thorpe's trial – when he was, in fairness, acquitted – the Liberal leader decided to make a move against his old lover after the first election. On 10 April 1974, he wrote to the property developer and philanthropist Jack Hayward, a regular Liberal donor, asking for £10,000 to cover his expenses in the last election. Hayward, a decent and patriotic man, promptly sent a cheque. According to the police, the money had been earmarked not for Thorpe's expenses in

North Devon, but for Norman Scott's killer. Unfortunately, the chief plotter was Thorpe's ineffectual crony David Holmes, who had no experience of murdering people. He could hardly advertise for a hit man, so he enlisted the help of his friend John Le Mesurier, a salesman from Bridgend and no relation to the splendidly suave *Dad's Army* actor. No doubt Le Mesurier was the ideal man to handle the purchase of a cheap carpet – although, having said that, his business was on its last legs – but he was an unorthodox choice to arrange a political assassination. Still, he refused to let any trifling moral objections get in the way of helping a friend. 'David told me that Thorpe was so obsessed by the threat posed to his political career by Scott that he had conceived an almost manic desire to have Scott killed,' Le Mesurier recalled. 'I could see that David was at his wits' end and he was immensely relieved when I said I'd help.'

Le Mesurier now approached a man called George Deakin, who sold fruit machines to clubs across South Wales. A quintessential self-made man of the early 1970s, Deakin wore sharp suits, drove cars with personalized number plates and lived in a big mock-Tudor monstrosity. Mildly comic as it might sound, the slot-machine world was no place for shrinking violets, and Deakin had few qualms about the job in hand. In February 1975 he approached a young airline pilot called Andrew Newton, telling him that he wanted somebody for a 'professional frightening job'. The exact arrangement remains unclear, since Newton, Deakin, Le Mesurier and Holmes all told different stories. Holmes and Le Mesurier admitted hiring Newton, but insisted that they just wanted him to intimidate Scott. But this seems very implausible. After all, people had been trying to bully Scott into keeping quiet for ten years, and it had not done the slightest good. Rather more telling, perhaps, is the fact that they agreed to pay Newton between £10,000 and £20,000, an enormous sum of money for a pilot earning £6,000 a year. As Newton remarked, they would hardly have paid him so much just to frighten somebody.[13]

Of course the plot was completely deranged. Even the most amateurish conspirators, if they had an ounce of sense, would have kept the hit man at arm's length so that they could deny all involvement if it went wrong. Yet Holmes and Le Mesurier not only went to see Newton, they told him the whole story about Thorpe and Scott. Afterwards, Newton set the operation rolling in a very strange fashion. On 12 October 1975 he introduced himself to Scott in Barnstaple with the peculiar cover story that he had been asked by 'a friend' to protect him from assassination. 'You're going to be killed,' Newton told Scott. 'A man has been paid a five-figure sum to kill you.' Twelve days later, he arranged to meet Scott again, but this time he brought an antique Mauser pistol. The plan was that he would pick up Scott in the village of Combe Martin, supposedly to discuss the plot against his life. Then he would drive to a deserted spot on Exmoor, shoot Scott and claim his reward. But when Newton arrived to meet his victim, he discovered that something was wrong – for instead of coming alone, Scott had brought his beloved dog Rinka, a Great Dane bitch.

As luck would have it, Newton was terrified of dogs, At first he refused to let her into the car, only relenting when Scott made a fuss. Eventually, after Newton had had a break to steady his nerves, they made it onto the moors. By now it was night, the pouring rain scouring the black sky, and both men were becoming increasingly uneasy. Assuming his friend was tired, Scott offered to take over the driving. Now events took a farcical and sinister turn. Newton pulled over, and both men got out. In the general confusion, Rinka assumed she was about to be let off for a run, and she jumped out too. At the sight of the dog leaping around in excitement, Newton panicked. 'Oh no,' he exclaimed, 'this is it.' With that, he pulled out the Mauser and shot Rinka in the head.

At first Scott did not realize what was going on; indeed, he knelt down and tried to revive her. But then the penny dropped. 'You've shot my dog,' he burst out. 'Oh no, not my dog . . . You can't involve Rinka. You can't involve the dog.' Newton now seized the moment, putting the Mauser to Scott's head and pulling the trigger. But in another of the twists in this absurd story, the gun jammed. The next thing Scott knew, his would-be assassin was crouched over by the headlights, fiddling with his gun and muttering: 'Oh fuck, oh fuck'. Assuming that he was going to die, Scott ran over to Rinka's body, so that he could be with his beloved dog in the final moments. But Newton was shaking so violently that he could not fix the gun. After a few moments of blind panic, he jumped back in the car and screeched away, leaving Scott sobbing by the roadside. A few minutes later, an AA scout came over the horizon and saw a hysterical man framed in his headlights, weeping and wailing over the body of a dead dog. 'Oh please,' the man screamed, 'someone's shot my dog and someone's tried to shoot me.'[14]

Rinka's story first surfaced in the pages of the *West Somerset Free Press*, appearing alongside pieces on the state of the public toilets in the local park and stamp thefts at the local sub-post office. 'Mystery of the dog in the fog,' read the headline. The piece explained that the Devon and Corn-wall police were investigating 'a mystery as impenetrable as moorland fog', in which a local 'dog owner' claimed that he had been attacked on Exmoor by a man who had shot his dog. When the paper dug deeper, it discovered that the dog owner somehow knew Jeremy Thorpe. But when the *Free Press* asked Thorpe for a comment, the Liberal leader treated the story very lightly. 'Are they hunting dogs on the moors these days?' he joked. It was a disastrously unwise remark. For as luck would have it, one of the local paper's subscribers was Auberon Waugh, the conserva-tive satirist who wrote *Private Eye*'s regular Diary column and lived nearby. Waugh was not a Thorpe fan by any means, and in December he decided to share the story with his readers. 'West Somerset is buzzing', he wrote, 'with rumours of a most unsavoury description . . . about an inci-dent which occurred recently on Exmoor.' As Waugh noted, Norman Scott claimed 'to be a great friend of Jeremy Thorpe, the Liberal states-man . . . My only hope is that sorrow of his friend's dog will not cause Mr Thorpe's premature retirement from public life.'[15]

Just over a month later, in the incongruous surroundings of a magis-trates' court in Barnstaple, Norman Scott blew the case wide open. Facing charges of social security benefit fraud, he took the stand and almost immediately began to sob and shake. 'It has been fifteen years,' he burst out. 'I really would like to get this matter cleared up. It has become so sick. I am being hounded all the time by people just because of my sexual relationship with Jeremy Thorpe.' The clerk of the court tried to shut him up, but it was too late; the words had come out. As it happened, that afternoon Thorpe was awaiting the report of a govern-ment investigation into the collapse of London and County Securities, a secondary bank consumed in the crisis of 1973. Thorpe had been a dir-ector of the bank: very unwisely, many said. That evening, his solicitor issued two statements. One welcomed the government report, which acquitted him of malpractice. The other responded to Scott's claims. 'It is well over twelve years since I last saw or spoke to Mr Scott,' Thorpe said. 'There is no truth in Mr Scott's allegations.'[16]

Despite Thorpe's denials, many Liberal insiders immediately sus-pected that there was more to the story than he was letting on. Their flamboyant leader did, however, have one very powerful supporter, who unquestioningly accepted his explanation that he was being framed by the South African secret police. Although Harold Wilson and Jeremy Thorpe were ideological rivals, they had long had an excellent relation-ship. Wilson had a soft spot for cheeky adventurers and enjoyed the younger man's wit, charm and sense of style. Crucially, Thorpe was also a great favourite with Marcia Williams, who explained that 'Harold and I used to giggle at his impersonations. He was a colourful addition to any dinner party.' What was more, a Prime Minister obsessed with spies and security was bound to be intrigued by the suggestion that the whole thing was a BOSS plot. The fact that Wilson had briefly contemplated using Thorpe's homosexual past to scupper a possible Conservative–Liberal coalition was quietly forgotten. Instead, at Thorpe's invitation, Wilson gladly plunged into the murky waters of a South African conspiracy theory.[17]

Wilson's obsession with the Thorpe affair was an embarrassing reminder of his detachment from the business of government. Only four days after Scott's outburst, Wilson told Joe Haines that 'foreign espionage agents are trying to destroy British politicians. That the South Africans have planted the homosexual scandal on Jeremy Thorpe. And that the CIA have tried to get him.' Precisely why the South Africans would waste so much time discrediting a party leader with only thirteen MPs never seems to have occurred to him; like much of the British press, Wilson credited BOSS with almost supernatural powers. On 2 February 1976 he asked the Cabinet Secretary for a report on 'the activities of the intelligence agents of [the] CIA, Russia and South Africa', and three weeks later he summoned his Intelligence Coordinator, Sir Leonard Hooper, to complain that MI5 were not taking the South African threat seriously. A few days later, Wilson told Bernard Donoughue that he and Thorpe had met late one night and talked for three hours. 'He is absolutely convinced that the South Africans are behind it all,' Donoughue recorded. 'The PM is loving it all, since it appeals to all his obsessions with plots, spies, leaks, conspiracies, etc.' The irony, of course, was that according to the prosecution, the only conspiracy worthy of the name had been the sensationally inept enterprise orchestrated by Thorpe himself.[18]

Not all Wilson's confidants were swept along by his theories. At lunch on 4 February, Wilson told Barbara Castle that the affair was 'all a plot to discredit Jeremy, set up by agents of the South African Government because the Liberal Party had opposed South African policies. He hinted darkly that he knew all about that sort of thing and had his spies working on it, because he had been the victim of it: the theft of his own confidential papers.' This was pure fantasy, of course, and Castle despaired of her friend's 'erratic and dramatic Goldfinger' style. But the next day Wilson buttonholed her again, suggesting that she find out why her department had prosecuted Scott for fraud and given him the platform for his denunciation. 'How did it originate? How was he discovered? Did he even volunteer the information on which he was prosecuted?' Castle passed the message on to her special adviser, a young man called Jack Straw, who 'went off to do some ferreting'. But when Straw handed in his report, it showed that 'Jeremy's relationship with Scott had been longer and more domesticated than he had so far admitted'. This was not good news for Wilson's conspiracy theory, and Castle warned him 'against going overboard for Jeremy too recklessly'. But Wilson took no notice. Like any self-respecting fantasist, he saw no reason to let the facts get in the way of a good story.

A week before his resignation, Wilson decided it was time to go public. At lunch on 9 March, he told Castle that BOSS was definitely behind the Thorpe affair. 'It's been a great detective exercise, I can tell you,' he said gleefully. 'Detective Inspector Falkender has been up to her eyes in it. I've got conclusive evidence that South African money has been involved. After all, she's been through the same thing. So have I. No Minister or political party is safe unless we expose this.' Not surprisingly, Castle was 'completely mystified':

> I couldn't quite see why they should pick on the Liberals, a spent force, rather than us. 'They have already picked on me,' Harold explained. 'But they believe it was the Liberal intervention that let us into office and the first thing we did was to stop arms for South Africa.' 'Are you saying that there was nothing in the Jeremy–Scott affair and they have been inventing it, or that there *was* something and they were exploiting it?' I asked. 'I dare say there may have been something at some time,' Harold said indifferently, 'but they are out to destroy the Liberal leader and they would destroy any successor to him. There is big money involved in this.'

That afternoon, Wilson made his move. 'I have no doubt at all that there is strong South African participation in recent activities relating to the right hon. Gentleman the Leader of the Liberal Party, based on massive reserves of business money and private agents of various kinds and various qualities,' he solemnly told the Commons. 'Anyone in the House who is concerned with democracy will feel revolted by the fact that we have to face this sort of thing in this country, so far as leaders of any party or all parties are concerned.'[19]

What Thorpe made of all this can only be imagined. By now his position was desperately fragile: alarmed by rumours of homosexual skulduggery and financial impropriety, many Liberals were keen to get him out. Only a few days before, David Holmes had admitted paying Scott £2,500 for a bundle of letters, thereby apparently confirming that there *was* a link between the former stable boy and the Liberal leader. 'I Paid £2,500 To Norman Scott, Says The Godfather' was the excited headline in the *Mirror*, playing on the fact that Holmes was godfather to Thorpe's son Rupert. Now everybody began to panic. Thorpe gave his side of the story to the *Sunday Times*, while Bessell, who had fled to California, started talking to the *Daily Mail*.[20]

Then came the bombshell that destroyed Thorpe's political career. Fourteen years earlier, Scott had given the police a pile of letters from the Liberal leader. Having been leaked to Harold Wilson's lawyer, Lord Goodman, copies then found their way to the *Sunday Times*. On 9 May the paper published them in full, and although most of their contents were perfectly anodyne, one line leaped out. In February 1962, Thorpe had ended an affectionate letter with the phrase 'Bunnies can (and will) go to France', apparently a reference to Scott's ambition to study dressage across the Channel. As most commentators observed, men very rarely call each other by the pet name 'Bunny'. Thorpe was finished: the next morning, he resigned as Liberal leader. Yet even now he could not resist distorting the truth, claiming that he was quitting to save the party from a 'campaign of denigration' and a string of 'plots and intrigues'. 'From the beginning,' he added, 'I have strenuously denied the so-called Scott allegations and I categorically repeat those denials today.'[21]

Even now, Harold Wilson still believed Thorpe had been framed. On 12 May, barely a month after leaving office, the former Prime Minister telephoned a young BBC journalist called Barrie Penrose and announced that he had a story for him. As Penrose later reflected, he had never spoken to Wilson, 'was one of dozens of television news reporters and was hardly the obvious choice for an ex-prime minister to summon for an exclusive chat'. But he duly presented himself at Lord North Street alongside his old friend Roger Courtiour, a researcher in the BBC's current affairs department. It had been a warm day, and as they sat sweating in their heavy dark suits, the shirt-sleeved Wilson lowered himself into an armchair and lit a cigar. 'I think that democracy as we know it is in grave danger,' he said solemnly. The security services, he explained, had been trying to discredit him. Some of them were 'very Right-wing', and had come to believe that 'Socialist leaders were another form of Communism. They are blinkered: the sort of people who would have spread the stories of No. 10 and the Communist cell.'

Barely able to believe their ears, Penrose and Courtiour asked Wilson to explain what he meant. 'They were saying that I was tied up with the Communists,' he said calmly. 'The link was Marcia. She was supposed to be a dedicated Communist.' Norman Scott, Wilson went on, was a South African agent, part of an international conspiracy including Peter Bessell and Gordon Winter. If Penrose and Courtiour cracked the case, it would become the 'British Watergate'. They would face implacable opposition from within the Establishment, but they could come to him for guidance whenever they wanted. Then Wilson said the words for which this extraordinary interview would always be remembered: 'I see myself as the big fat spider in the corner of the room. Sometimes I speak when I'm asleep. You should both listen. Occasionally when we meet I might tell you to go to the Charing Cross Road and kick a blind man standing on the corner. That blind man might tell you something, lead you somewhere.'

Only a few weeks before, the man responsible for these words had been Prime Minister of the United Kingdom. Now he seemed to be auditioning for a part in *Tinker Tailor Soldier Spy*, or, perhaps more fittingly, in some madly overwrought Roger Moore Bond film. And he was not finished yet. As he ushered Penrose and Courtiour downstairs, he told them not to trust the telephones or the post. On the way out, he showed them a seven-foot safe he had installed in his living room. 'There should be no security problems now,' he said happily. 'Make certain your own security is as good.' Noting their disbelief, he gave a little smile. 'When you've had as many robberies as we have,' he said, 'you'll begin to understand.'[22]

In the long run, Wilson's ludicrous outburst about the blind man on the Charing Cross Road did irreparable damage to his reputation. Later, both Wilson and Lady Falkender claimed that he had been joking, but Penrose and Courtiour were convinced that he was in deadly earnest. After all, he had been complaining about bugs and burglaries for months, and his resignation was evidently the cue for a descent into full-blown paranoia. At first, however, the two journalists kept quiet about his allegations. For the next few months they worked tirelessly to follow up his leads, investigating Scott's background, the South African connection and a weird mishmash of conspiracy theories dating back to the late 1960s. The irony, of course, was that the real story was the Scott–Thorpe affair, yet Wilson had succeeded in thoroughly muddying the waters. Their editors even told them to drop the Thorpe element, which might have led them to the truth, and concentrate on the South African intelligence angle, which was largely fantasy. Eventually the BBC shut down the investigation, prompting Penrose and Courtiour to sell the details to the press. The papers were naturally delighted to get their hands on such sensational material, and the *Mirror*'s inimitable headline 'Wilson Feared Marcia Was Being Lured Into A Sex Orgy' gives a sense of the general tone. But the real losers were Wilson and Marcia, who came across as fantasists of the most deluded kind. When readers learned that Wilson blamed his 'fourteen robberies and break-ins' on South African intelligence, or that Marcia wanted to know 'why MI5 would want to neutralise Jeremy Thorpe and want to get at Harold and myself', they must have wondered whether they had been governed by escapees from a lunatic asylum. And when Tony Benn asked the new Prime Minister about Wilson's accusations, he got the only appropriate response. 'Oh,' Jim Callaghan sighed, 'Harold is just a Walter Mitty.'[23]

While Wilson was flirting with the wilder shores of the secret world, the net was closing around Jeremy Thorpe. After the shooting on the moors, the police had quickly tracked down Andrew Newton, who was charged with possession of a firearm with intent to endanger life and sent down for two years. For the time being, Newton kept his mouth shut; in return, David Holmes paid him £400 in cash and promised a further £5,000 after the trial. It was only a matter of time, however, before Newton's greed got the better of him, and on 19 October 1977 the *Evening News* led with the banner headline: 'I Was Hired To Kill Scott. Exclusive: Gunman Tells of Incredible Plot – a Murder Contract for £5,000'. At this stage, though, Newton refused to name names. On his release he fled to Rhodesia, hoping to start a new life as a pilot, but he was promptly sent back to Britain. In the meantime, the *Evening News* had signed up Peter Bessell, who was hoping to cash in on his knowledge of the alleged conspiracy. From this point onwards, Thorpe must have realized that disaster was inevitable.[24]

On 27 October, the former Liberal leader gave 'an extraordinary and tense news conference' at the National Liberal Club, insisting that he had never discussed 'any proposed murder or attempt to harm' Norman Scott, and that 'no sexual activity of any kind' had taken place. *The Times* thought that Thorpe had 'carried off magnificently his act of appearing relaxed and scornful'. But it was no good: behind the scenes, the Director of Public Prosecutions had already ordered an inquiry into Andrew Newton's claims. At last, on 3 August 1978, Thorpe, Holmes, Deakin and Le Mesurier were summoned to Minehead Magistrates' Court, Somerset, and formally charged with conspiracy to murder.

Dapper and composed as ever, Thorpe said nothing except for his name and address. That evening he attended a drinks party organized by the local Liberals, where several hundred people greeted him with applause and cheers. Inside, said *The Times*, he 'went round shaking hands and told party supporters that he was still their MP and he intended to carry on his public engagements. Today he will attend a flower shower at Bishops Nimpton, near his home.'[25]

What Thorpe did next spoke volumes about his superhuman vanity. Initially he had promised his successor as Liberal leader, David Steel, that if he faced criminal charges, he would step down as an MP and stay away from Liberal gatherings. But now that the charges had come, Thorpe refused to quit, even though his very existence had become a hideous embarrassment to a battered, bruised and bankrupt party. Infuriated, Steel sacked him as the Liberal spokesman for foreign affairs and asked him to stay away from the party conference in Southport. But staying away was not Jeremy Thorpe's style. On the last day of the conference, moments after the party had approved the slogan 'Break with the Past', Banquo's ghost made his grand entrance. 'He didn't just appear,' Steel recalled, 'but, with his usual showmanship, the doors at the back of the hall were flung open and he marched down the crowded aisle with [his second wife] Marion to a half-standing ovation.' When Thorpe reached the platform, Steel reluctantly shook him by the hand, although, as one reporter remarked, he looked 'as though he would rather have gripped him by the throat'. The audience roared, and Thorpe half rose to acknowledge them. Then, with impeccable timing, the chairman said: 'I have a police request . . .', and Thorpe adopted a puzzled expression, pretending that he could barely hear. It was a consummate performance by a man who had brought his party to the brink of oblivion.[26]

In November 1978, with the Winter of Discontent just weeks away, Thorpe returned to Minehead for his committal hearing. Shabby, decaying, its former visitors having long since decamped to Malta and Majorca, the little seaside town made an oddly appropriate venue for the beginning of the end. Yet its residents showed remarkably little interest in the extraordinary events taking place in their red-brick courthouse. 'Go to a local pub,' wrote the *Mirror*'s Paul Callan, 'and you will find the locals slightly embarrassed by it all.' 'He's a very popular man round here,' said Marty Jenkins, a 28-year-old farm worker. 'He's a good man – at least that's what we all think.' Perhaps that explains why, when the committal hearing opened, ordinary spectators were heavily outnumbered by reporters, photographers and television crews from across the world. 'There were rumours of a Japanese television crew in the town,' one reporter noted, 'but it was not seen. Perhaps, like a German press photographer, it got lost in the winding lanes of north Somerset.'[27]

The Japanese cameramen were missing a treat. Day after day the courtroom played host to a bizarre gallery of characters, more like the cast of some Tom Sharpe novel than regular guests of the local constabulary, from Peter Bessell, boasting 'hair that appeared to have been dunked in luminous orange paint', to Andrew Newton, dressed like a 'golf professional' and wearing a balaclava to hide his features. Even the legal eagles cut weirdly exaggerated figures. Thorpe's solicitor, the former Law Society president Sir David Napley, rode around in a Rolls-Royce with a supply of champagne in the boot, while the clerk of the court, for reasons never explained, had been issued with a microphone that had to be strapped to his face like an oxygen mask. Perhaps it was no wonder that some visitors queued for hours to claim the twenty public seats. Yet amid the chaos, it was easy to forget that at the centre of the hearing was a plot to end a man's life. And as Bessell, Newton and Scott told their stories to the enraptured courtroom, Jeremy Thorpe's last hopes of saving his political career dribbled away.[28]

By mid-December, the magistrates had ruled that there was enough evidence for Thorpe and his fellow conspirators to face trial at the Old Bailey. Thanks to the looming election, however, the trial was postponed until May, allowing Thorpe to take his case to the people of North Devon. It was not a happy occasion: with the Liberal vote in meltdown, few observers thought he could cling on. Just in case there was any danger of forgetting that Thorpe was shortly due to face trial for conspiracy to murder, his old enemy Auberon Waugh threw his hat into the ring, too, representing the Dog Lovers' Party. He was hoping for 40 votes, he said. In interviews, he refrained from attacking Thorpe personally, but insisted that 'dogs have had a very poor deal'.

As in campaigns past, Thorpe trudged the streets in his uniform of battered brown trilby, fawn overcoat and yellow tie. But he had lost the fizz, the zest, the style of old. 'Behind the smile and the easy words,' one reporter wrote, 'the eyes of Mr Thorpe have the look of a man still in a state of shock at what has happened to him. The face is tired, the figure stooped, the manner subdued and grave . . . There is none of the wisecracking sparkle and show-business gimmicky of the old barnstorming days.' And yet Thorpe remained the 'uncrowned king of North

Devon'; wherever he went, 'people stop and shake his hand and warmly wish him luck'. Few voters seemed disturbed by his alleged homosexuality: a sign, perhaps, of how attitudes had changed since his brief affair with Norman Scott. 'He is innocent until proven guilty,' said the trade union representative at a local chipboard factory. 'I shall vote for him because of what he has done for North Devon.' 'I shall certainly be voting for him,' agreed Georgina Campbell, a seamstress for a Bideford sailmaker. 'If he is found guilty . . . well, everybody's human.'[29]

In the event, Thorpe lost only 5,000 votes. It was not enough, though, to hold off the Tory candidate Tony Speller, a popular local businessman, who took the seat with a majority of more than 8,000. (Auberon Waugh, meanwhile, had the satisfaction of finishing third from bottom, with 79 votes.) For Thorpe it was a shattering blow: on television he looked gaunt, drained, his cheeks hollow, his eyes empty. Yet even his critics admitted that he took it with courage. 'It didn't matter what you thought of Jeremy Thorpe before,' conceded the *Express*. 'He took the hardest defeat in Britain like a man . . . Everyone might be able to see, shining in his eyes, the regret that 20 brilliant years had been thrown aside. But he kept his cheeks dry.' In the old days he would have celebrated with a torchlight parade. Now he merely drove around the area's towns to thank his volunteers. 'It wasn't a big shock,' he insisted the next day. 'It is unlikely I will be leaving politics.'[30]

On 8 May Thorpe's trial opened at the Old Bailey. The courtroom, wrote Jean Rook in the *Express*, was 'like a scene from Madame Tussaud's . . . Jeremy Thorpe sits stiff as his dapper little waistcoat, as unmoved as wax. Under the neon lighting, his tan is yellow as candlegrease and his round, brown, glass marble eyes are fixed on Norman Scott – the man he's alleged to have conspired to murder.' But while Bessell, Newton and Scott all had their moment in the limelight, there was disappointment for those hoping to see Thorpe in the witness box. Since the Crown's case was based on the evidence of 'Scott, a vengeful hysteric, Bessell, a self-confessed fraud, and Newton, a braggart who would say anything for money', all the defence lawyers had to do was discredit their story. There was no point putting Thorpe himself on the spot. And while Newton, Scott and Bessell floundered under cross-examination, Thorpe played the underdog fighting overwhelming odds, the drowning man struggling to keep his head above water.[31]

This certainly seemed the view of the judge, Mr Justice Cantley, a famously unworldly man who was said to have remained a virgin until marrying in his mid-fifties. When Cantley described Thorpe as 'a Privy

Counsellor, a former leader of the Liberal Party and a national figure with a very distinguished public record', he was playing into the defence team's hands. Equally, when he described Bessell as 'sexually promiscuous, and therefore a humbug', or Newton as 'a chump, a conceited bungler', the Crown's lawyers must have felt utterly downcast. Above all, Cantley described Scott in such damning terms that he made it almost impossible for the jury to believe him. 'He is a crook,' the judge said sternly. 'He is a liar. He is a fraud, a sponger . . . He is a whiner. He is a parasite. But of course he could still be telling the truth.' It was no wonder that only ten days later, during the *Secret Policeman's Ball* show to raise funds for Amnesty International, Peter Cook mercilessly lampooned the judge's summing-up, dismissing 'Norma St John Scott' as 'a scrounger, parasite, pervert, a worm, a self-confessed player of the pink oboe'. If the two speeches had been put side by side, it would have been hard to tell them apart.[32]

On 22 June, Thorpe was enjoying a lavish lunch of smoked salmon, roast beef and claret, courtesy of his friend Clement Freud, when he heard that the jury had finished their deliberations. Flanked in the dock by Holmes, Deakin and Le Mesurier, he stood pale and impassive, gazing straight ahead. One by one the verdicts came in: 'Not guilty', 'Not guilty', 'Not guilty', 'Not guilty'. Deakin slumped forward, tears running down his face; Holmes swayed back and forth; Le Mesurier grabbed Thorpe's arm in delight. For a moment, Thorpe barely moved; then he grinned at his wife and said: 'Darling, we won!' The showman was back. A few moments later, he strode out towards the crowds waiting in the sunshine, a conquering hero pumping his arms in the air. 'There were cheers and some jeers,' said the *Express*, 'as Mr Thorpe, wearing his famous hat at a rakish angle, dashed for the TV cameras.'

Five years earlier, in the final days of the February 1974 campaign, Thorpe's star had seemed one of the brightest in the firmament. Had things turned out only a little differently, he might have found himself sitting at the Cabinet table, perhaps as Home Secretary. In itself the resurgence of Liberalism was a highly suggestive story, reflecting popular alienation from the two larger parties, the decay of old collective identities and the emergence of a much more individualistic political landscape. Perhaps, if Thorpe had been a different character, he might have exploited public dissatisfaction with Heath and Wilson and laid the groundwork for an even greater Liberal surge. Instead he became a byword for the sleaze and self-interest that seemed to be washing over public life in the 1970s, the lurid allegations about his private life part of a larger mosaic of seediness and corruption. Even the festivities after his acquittal spoke volumes about his thirst for attention. That night, after celebrating with champagne at home near Hyde Park, he appeared on the balcony, waving at supporters as though marking some extraordinary political triumph. But hundreds of miles away, on Dartmoor, there were no such scenes of delight. 'I have been thinking of a holiday,' Norman Scott told reporters from his isolated little cottage. 'In Tibet.'[33]

9. Schools were the focus of intense controversy in the 1970s. *Above*, sixth-formers hold a discussion group at Parmiter's School, Hertfordshire. *Below*, a progressive teacher from Central Casting organizes a frankly extraordinary-looking lesson in London, 1974.

10. In the mid-1970s, popular television programmes could easily command tens of millions of viewers. *Top*, *Doctor Who's* Tom Baker and his Zygon friend drop in on the American embassy; *above*, *The Sweeney's* Regan and Carter contemplate the iniquity of people who read the *Guardian*.

11. For flares, sequins and silly hats, the popular culture of the mid-1970s was unsurpassed. *Top*, Elton John, the most successful singer of the decade, in 1975. *Above*, the splendidly camp Larry Grayson in rehearsals for *The Generation Game*, 1978.

12. In June 1975 the British people voted in the first referendum in their history. Most followed Richard Briers's advice to stay in Europe, *above left*, while Tony Benn managed to put people off the No campaign, *above right*. The real star of the referendum, though, was Margaret Thatcher's jumper, *below*.

13. Jim Callaghan's conservative style went down very well with the general public, although not with the students who barracked him at Ruskin College, Oxford, *above*. His Chancellor, Denis Healey, takes on the left during Labour's tumultuous Blackpool conference, 1976, *left*.

14. The summer of 1976 was the hottest in British history. *Above*, the Taf Fechan reservoir, South Wales, on 12 August. *Below*, black residents take on the police at the Notting Hill carnival, two weeks later.

15. The Grunwick strike, *above*, began as a protest by Asian workers at an obscure photo processing plant. But by the summer of 1977 it had become the most violent industrial confrontation of the decade, the strikers' cause overshadowed by the chaos in the streets, *below*.

16. Public life in the mid-1970s seemed to have taken on a much more aggressive, even violent edge. *Top*, police hold back thousands of National Front marchers, 1974; *above*, anti-fascist demonstrators attack an NF member in Birmingham, 1977.

20

Jim's Facts of Life

*The summer's disorder, those hot lazy mobs, made him wish
for a cleansing holocaust – some visible crisis, black frost
combined with an economic crash. It was certainly coming: a
slump, a smothering heaviness, a power cut and a blinding
storm stopping lifts between floors and silting up the Thames,
and but for the tolling of funeral bells there would be silence.*

Paul Theroux, *The Family Arsenal* (1976)

*Economic policy can destroy a Government. Our problems are
deep-seated and daunting . . .*

Bernard Donoughue to Jim Callaghan,
'Themes and Initiatives', 15 April 1976

On Tuesday, 6 April, Jim Callaghan walked into Number 10 to find the
place stripped almost bare. The atmosphere felt odd, almost provisional.
Outside his new study, the display cabinets stood empty. In the upstairs
drawing room, the photographs and mementoes that had marked
Harold Wilson's time in office had disappeared. In the Cabinet Room
Callaghan worked alone, eating a solitary lunch in his study. The next
morning, summoning Bernard Donoughue to discuss the work of the
Policy Unit, Callaghan confessed that he felt 'lost', 'isolated', 'a prisoner'. To Donoughue, there could hardly have been a greater contrast
than with the gossipy, whisky-swilling Wilson. 'Jim is slower,' he
recorded after three days with his new boss. 'Likes less paper. Gets tired
easily – he looked old and grey last night. He has left everybody jumpy.
He plays his cards close to his chest . . . Yet he is refreshing in many
ways after Wilson and more direct, and with no hidden influences (or

none we have seen so far).' And at 64, the teetotal Callaghan had learned how to pace himself. Whereas Wilson used to relax after lunch with couple of large brandies, his successor preferred a short nap. 'Better well rested,' he told his aides, 'than well briefed.'[1]

More than any other modern Prime Minister, Callaghan was shaped by Britain's maritime tradition. His father had been a Chief Petty Officer in the Royal Navy, and young Len (as he was then called) grew up in the shadow of Portsmouth's docks.* He loved the ethos of the Navy – its pride, its solidarity, its dogged patriotism – and in later life he decorated his Sussex farm with naval prints, even using a old ship's rope ladder to get up to the attic. His mental world, writes his official biographer, 'was one in which Britannia really ruled the waves . . . and where Jolly Jack Tar with his pigtail, in contrast to the soldiers of a potentially oppressive standing army, was the people's instrument of national freedom'. It was an intensely moral world, for like many Labour politicians of his generation, Callaghan was steeped in the culture of religious Nonconformity. Not only was his mother a strict Baptist, but he had attended Sunday School every week and learned passages of the Bible by heart. The blend of naval and Baptist traditions gave him a strong sense of service, but also a profound cultural conservatism. He was a big man, a bruiser, even a bully, but beneath the superficial breeziness, he was sometimes crippled by self-doubt. In a stark contrast with his Cabinet colleagues, he had left school at the age of 17, becoming a tax clerk. With characteristic tactlessness, Denis Healey used to tease him about his education: whenever Callaghan used a foreign expression, Healey playfully asked him to translate it 'for the benefit of us simple-minded fellows'. It was a sign of how much the former Portsmouth Northern Secondary School boy liked the ex-president of the Balliol Junior Common Room that he let him get away with it.[2]

Above all, Callaghan was devoted to the Labour Party. He was still in his teens when he first joined; later, his stubborn fidelity to the trade unions, most famously when he helped to block Barbara Castle's reforms in 1969, prompted the journalist Peter Jenkins to nickname him 'the Keeper of the Cloth Cap'. But unlike many of the Labour politicians who fawned over the unions, he was never a militant. From the day he entered Parliament as MP for Cardiff South in 1945, Callaghan

---

* Since Callaghan was christened Leonard James, his family always knew him as Len. He adopted James (or Jim) in 1945, when he first ran for Parliament, perhaps because it had been his late father's name.

was a man of the Labour right. Solid, sensible and pragmatic, the heir to the working-class patriotism of Ernest Bevin and the businesslike moderation of Clement Attlee, he made an appropriate parliamentary adviser to the Police Federation. His critics saw him as a machine politician, but unlike his donnish rivals, Callaghan had the common touch. To watch him on the streets of Cardiff, wrote the historian Kenneth Morgan, was 'to see a master craftsman at work, his technique tempered by a genuine humanity and directness'. Indeed, perhaps only somebody so rooted in the values of working-class voters could have rebuilt his career after Callaghan's disastrous stint as Chancellor in the mid-1960s, although it took a fair bit of resilience, too. 'You know,' Roy Jenkins once remarked, 'there is nobody in politics I can remember and no case I can think of in history where a man combined such a powerful political personality with so little intelligence.' But Callaghan had the last laugh. Only one man in history has ever held all four Great Offices of State: Home Secretary, Foreign Secretary, Chancellor and Prime Minister. That man was not Roy Jenkins.[3]

By the early 1970s, Callaghan cut a much calmer figure than the ambitious political climber of his younger days. Having bought Upper Clayhill Farm in the east Sussex countryside, he had transformed himself into a successful small farmer. Even as Prime Minister, he liked to spend weekend mornings tramping around the fields to check on his cows and making his daily rain check (something he kept up for more than a quarter of a century). Farming might seem an incongruous recreation for a Labour politician, but in many ways it was a very canny choice. Pictures of Farmer Jim trudging across his fields to inspect his cattle, a tweed hat jammed on his head, reinforced his avuncular, reassuring image, the soul of small-c conservatism in a changing world. Now in his sixties, he was no longer a young man in a hurry; indeed, in 1973 he seriously considered an offer to become the new head of the International Monetary Fund (a wonderfully ironic moment, given what was coming). On television, he spoke slowly and directly, his rounded Hampshire accent redolent of a quieter, gentler age. And when Labour returned to office in 1974, he spent his time working with Harold Wilson rather than plotting against him, as in the old days. They were 'more than colleagues, more than allies if still less than friends', thought Joe Haines. The memories of their past battles had 'acquired a certain nostalgia'; they 'still probed each others' guard', but without the bitterness of old.[4]

Callaghan was well aware that Wilson's last years had not been a

golden age of British government. One of his aims, he told his biographer, was to 'redeem the tawdriness' of his predecessor's final years.
The days of blazing rows behind closed doors were gone: whereas Wilson had loved to mull over events with Joe Haines and Marcia Williams,
Callaghan relied on civil servants such as his press secretary, Tom
McCaffrey, the head of his political office, Tom McNally, and his
principal private secretary, Ken Stowe. But as Bernard Donoughue
remembered, the biggest difference was that Callaghan had a 'strong
sense of values – really like those of a Nonconformist Victorian, with
deep feelings of responsibility towards the under-privileged and a strong
sense of right and wrong'.[5]

Indeed, on moral issues Callaghan sometimes sounded downright
reactionary. He told Donoughue that he was an 'old-fashioned male
chauvinist', and would never want a 'woman private secretary'. During
a friendly lunch with his Policy Unit in September 1978, he confessed
that he was 'embarrassed by nudity, on TV or on the stage', and said 'he
felt embarrassed in the company of his children – even though they were
now in middle age and had children themselves'. What shocked him
most, however, was homosexuality. In 1979 he returned from the *Evening Standard* theatre awards to meet his advisers at the Commons, and
as Donoughue recorded, the discussion took an unexpected turn:

> Somehow the conversation moved from the theatre and the drama awards
> to homosexuality. [Callaghan] said he was completely unaware of homo-
> sexuality until well into adult life – it was the notorious behaviour of the
> Labour queer Tom Driberg that brought it to his knowledge. He said, 'They
> say we are all repressed homosexuals. But it all puzzles me. There have
> always been so many attractive girls.' He seemed surprised when we pointed
> out that there were a number of well-known homosexuals in the present
> House. He obviously knows nothing of those in his government.

The Lancashire MP Roger Stott then did an impersonation of a 'homosexual cook who had once served on ship with him when he was in the
navy,' which most of them found hilarious. Callaghan, however, 'looked
very shocked, and said he "never came across anything like that" when
he was in the navy'. Afterwards, when the Prime Minister had gone,
Tom McNally remembered a similar conversation on an international
trip. 'You won't tell these stories in front of Audrey, will you?' Callaghan had asked anxiously at the end. 'She would be very shocked.'[6]

Callaghan's own life was the model of respectability: he had met his
wife Audrey when they were just 17 and 16 respectively, and they were

one of Westminster's most devoted couples. Even before the phrase 'the permissive society' had been coined, he had a horror of moral and sexual dissolution, and for a nominally left-wing politician he could be intensely conservative. Any criticism of the police, the armed forces or the trade unions was guaranteed to provoke him, while, like Wilson, he nursed a profound admiration for the Queen and the Boy Scouts. To the schoolteachers and social workers who increasingly dominated Labour's local constituency parties, this was disgracefully reactionary stuff. But at a time of deep public anxiety about crime and morality, Callaghan's old-fashioned views were a powerful asset, especially among older voters. It did Labour no harm to have a figurehead who loved the songs of music-hall stars such as Marie Lloyd and Vesta Victoria, who liked nothing better than spending a weekend on the farm, and who, like any decent Englishman, knew that the French were fundamentally untrustworthy.

Callaghan needed no spin-doctor to sell him as Labour's Baldwin; his moderation was unforced, his populism genuine. His big frame and heavy features, his slow speech and old-fashioned expressions ('Oh boy!', 'Well I never!', 'My goodness!'), even his gigantic thick-rimmed glasses, all identified him as a solid, reassuring figure who looked back to Britain's great seafaring tradition and had an unconditional respect for the monarchy and the family. Certainly he aroused none of the contempt that had surrounded Harold Wilson during his final years, and despite all the vicissitudes of his premiership, his personal ratings remained remarkably high. His nicknames – 'Big Jim', 'Uncle Jim' and especially 'Sunny Jim' – were always affectionate, and, unlike other Prime Ministers, he never had to suffer a fortnightly parody by *Private Eye*. (Perhaps an agricultural theme, along the lines of *Spitting Image*'s 'One Callaghan and his Dog' might have been appropriate, with, say, Roy Hattersley as the dog.) He never quite shed the image of a backroom fixer who knew where the bodies were buried. But all in all, as Peter Hennessy memorably puts it, he was 'a rather gnarled tree with huge, sturdy roots, a magnificent piece of political foliage which, in its prime ministerial flowering (except for those last dreadful months) was rather glorious to behold'.[7]

Callaghan's first task was to reshuffle his Cabinet. The principal casualty was his old enemy Barbara Castle, who immediately got the boot. Roy Jenkins was also on his way, off to Brussels to become President of the European Commission. In the meantime, there was a promotion for Callaghan's old ally Tony Crosland, who became Foreign Secretary, while Denis Healey remained in charge of the Treasury. Although they were never great friends, Callaghan and Healey became extremely close partners. Indeed, recent history offers few examples of a Prime Minister and Chancellor working so well together, especially given the intense pressures of a vanishing majority and embattled pound. But on Healey in particular the pressures took their toll. Not only did he face the appalling challenge of defending sterling against the international speculators, but he was in charge of pay deals with the unions and sat on more Cabinet committees than any other minister. It was no wonder that, as one gruelling day followed the next, he looked increasingly unhealthy, his features thickening, his face flushed, his eyes puffy with tiredness. But he was still the same old Healey, a practical joker with a taste for poetry. As one old friend remembered, people who rang his private number continued to be greeted in 'fractured English by someone who claimed to be from the local Chinese laundry'.[8]

The Lepidus of Labour's ruling triumvirate was the new Leader of the House, Michael Foot. On the surface this seemed a bizarre appointment, but it was actually a very clever one. Despite their differences, Foot and Callaghan had a shared love of England's naval history and soon struck up an excellent working relationship. More importantly, Foot was the ideal man to hold Labour's factious backbenchers together, thanks not only to his left-wing credentials, but to his personal decency, courtesy and knowledge of parliamentary tradition. While Callaghan toured the country and Healey pored over the books, it was Foot who kept things ticking over in the Commons. He was like 'the ravens in the Tower of London', wrote the journalists Simon Hoggart and David Leigh: 'as long as he remained, the government would, in some magical way, survive'. Even Callaghan admitted that without Foot's 'protection and personal loyalty', the government might not have lasted as long as it did. 'There were occasions when he had to swallow his views in order to bolster our position,' Callaghan wrote, 'but he never failed to do so. He was a true comrade.' But Foot's record made for a stark contrast with another of their Cabinet colleagues, who often described himself as a comrade but rarely acted like one. Like Wilson, Callaghan could never bring himself to get rid of Tony Benn. But in private he made no secret of his views: Benn, he told his aides, was 'a canting hypocrite'.[9]

The Callaghan government marked a clear shift to the right. It was not entirely without talent, and there were promotions for youngish moderates such as Shirley Williams, Edmund Dell, Bill Rodgers and Roy Hattersley. But there were an awful lot of grey men: even at the time, few voters could have picked out Fred Mulley, David Ennals, Albert Booth or Bruce Millan. There was a dearth of 'weight and personality at the top', Donoughue recorded after only ten days. 'The new men lack charisma and magic.' A year later, even Callaghan confided that his government had 'too little political sex appeal'. But there was hardly a great pool of talent to choose from, and in any case he liked having a compliant Cabinet. Despite the nickname 'Sunny Jim', he could be a brutal bully, but after years of drift, most ministers were happy to have a strong hand on the tiller. Many remembered him as a direct, avuncular boss, sometimes impatient and bad-tempered, but generally sympathetic to their personal problems. In Cabinet he reigned supreme, firm and fair, but a Prime Minister rather than a pseudo-president. Donoughue was not exaggerating when he described these years as 'the peak and the final performance of classic British Cabinet government'. And yet, touchingly, Callaghan never lost a slight sense of disbelief that he had made it to Number 10. Having lunch with his officials, he once asked: 'Do you ever stop and think that Baldwin and Neville Chamberlain had lunch here, in this small dining room?'[10]

From his first days in office, Callaghan was determined to banish the defeatism that he felt was holding Britain back from regaining her rightful place at the top table. 'What we need is not so much a change in economic policy as changes in attitudes,' he told an interviewer after his first few weeks.

> This country has felt too long that it has been on the losing side. Well, I think that a country which can be self-supporting in energy (as we shall be in 1980), a country which has skilled scientific manpower and a technological base, a country that has a self-disciplined population – don't tell me that this country can't succeed. Of course it can. We've got to give our people confidence that there is something on the other side of the hill and stop the loser mentality.

In an article for the *Mirror*, meanwhile, he told its largely Labour-supporting readers that the problem was simple: Britain was 'spending more than we produced and earned, and the enemy at the gate was inflation'. Cutting spending and slowing wage rises, he explained, would be his chief aims.[11]

Even with a clear mandate and a firm majority, this would have been difficult enough. But if Callaghan had any illusions about the scale of the challenge, they were dispelled within hours on his first full day. Early that morning, the news came that Brian O'Malley, a bright junior minister who had been working under Barbara Castle, had died in hospital after delicate brain surgery. In itself, O'Malley's death meant that the government had lost its Commons majority, and the next day there was more bad news as the John Stonehouse saga took a new twist. Accusing the Labour Party of 'prejudging' his case, Stonehouse announced that he was resigning the party whip and called for an immediate general election. 'The Prime Minister', he declared, 'does not have a mandate to cope with the serious economic problems of the nation.'[12]

Nobody cared what Stonehouse thought. The problem, though, was that the parliamentary arithmetic now left Labour with 314 seats and the other parties 316. Two Irish nationalist MPs, Gerry Fitt and Frank Maguire, generally sided with Labour in crucial divisions, so Callaghan was not quite finished yet. But now every vote was on a knife-edge; to get its legislation through, the government needed to pull every trick in the black book of parliamentary skulduggery. And as early as 27 May, just weeks into Callaghan's premiership, it seemed that the game was up. The issue was the nationalization of aircraft and shipbuilding, and the tension in the final moments of the debate was excruciating. Even the usually courteous Michael Foot lost his cool under fire from Michael Heseltine and Norman Tebbit, claiming that 'the jobs of workers in the shipbuilding and aerospace industries' were being 'put in jeopardy by a semi-drunken Tory brawl'. The House then voted on a Conservative amendment to declare it a 'hybrid' bill, which would delay its passage, but the result was a nail-biting 303–303 tie. That left the Speaker, George Thomas, with the casting vote: following precedent, he voted with the government. So the bill went directly to the decisive vote – and this time the result was 304–303 in Labour's favour. 'Word spread like wildfire', recorded Tony Benn, 'that the Chief Whip, Mike Cocks, had allowed one of our MPs, who had paired with a Tory, to vote, thus breaking a pair, to which he had been strictly tied, without warning.'

The Labour benches were jubilant, and as the tellers came back in they started singing 'The Red Flag', which infuriated the Tories even more. There were scenes, reported *The Times*, of 'wild disorder' as 'the anger of the Conservative Opposition, frontbench and backbench, passed all bounds'. The Tory elder statesman Geoffrey Rippon 'abused the Government backbenchers around him in the roughest words'; the Tory Michael Spicer and Labour's Tom Swain exchanged punches before being dragged apart by their colleagues; the Serjeant at Arms was knocked almost to the ground while trying to restrain another group of brawling MPs; and most famously, Michael Heseltine charged through the bedlam, grabbed the Mace and brandished it wildly over his head, as though he were a caveman about to beat his adversaries' brains out.* The Speaker had to suspend the session, and Heseltine apologized the next day. But behind all the headlines about the shocking parliamentary punch-up, everybody knew that the government had survived only by the most unscrupulous of tactics. 'The fact is', Benn wrote, 'we cheated . . . Now we are in a hell of a mess.'[13]

The mess that most concerned Callaghan was, of course, the state of the economy. He had been Prime Minister for only a few hours when the Policy Unit's Gavyn Davies warned him that the pound was still coming under intense pressure, its weakness such that devaluation by at least 10 per cent was widely expected. In the last month the Bank of England had spent a record £600 million supporting sterling; yet in the past few weeks alone, the value of the pound had fallen by 7 per cent. Since the end of fixed exchange rates in 1971, it had lost a stunning 35 per cent of its value against other major currencies. Meanwhile the Bank of England went on spending: eleven days later, when Callaghan held his first official meeting with his Chancellor, he was horrified to hear that since January it had spent $2 billion, a third of its total currency reserves. His next visitor, the Governor of the Bank of England, Gordon Richardson, brought even worse news. The situation, he reported, was one of 'unparalleled uncertainty and loss of confidence': the government was still borrowing far too much, and a begging mission to the IMF seemed inevitable. Callaghan later wrote that if he had not been inoculated against the disease he christened 'Governor's Gloom', then 'the only thing to do would have been to throw myself out of an upper-floor window on to the Downing Street pavement'.[14]

The irony, of course, was that the markets had lost confidence in Britain at the very moment when inflation was falling and the economy seemed to be improving. But as a report by Barings in mid-April explained, 'currencies are not judged solely on the basis of purely economic criteria', but on more intangible factors, too, such as 'confidence and political capacity, judgement and popular willingness to take and accept those actions generally seen to be the minimum necessary to translate a bad situation into an acceptable one'. At a moment of unexpected political flux, with a new Prime Minister in Downing Street and

---

* Hence the nickname 'Tarzan', which Heseltine enthusiastically embraced, even calling his autobiography *Life in the Jungle*.

the Commons so precariously poised, perhaps it was hardly surprising
that the markets should have got the jitters. Even inside Whitehall, confidence was hardly robust: on 12 April, the NEDC's Ronald McIntosh
wrote that 'foreigners simply don't believe we are capable of managing
our affairs effectively . . . It seems quite likely that before the end of July
we shall experience a financial crisis so severe that it brings about some
kind of political realignment.' And unlike some of his Cabinet colleagues, Denis Healey himself recognized that arguing about economic
statistics was pointless; confidence was all that mattered. There was not
much point, he wrote, 'in complaining when the financial markets
behave like hysterical schoolgirls. You can not buck the markets.'[15]

If Healey wanted to reassure the markets, he needed to prove that the
government would keep up the fight against inflation. In his Budget on
6 April he had offered the unions a naked bribe, promising £1,000 million in tax relief if they agreed to a 3 per cent pay increase for the
following year. The Tories claimed that he was handing over power to
the union leaders, with Thatcher charging that Healey was 'disregarding
the interests of the majority' by allowing the TUC to decide whether
or not people got the promised tax relief. But although Callaghan laid
on a Berni Inn-style menu of smoked mackerel, steak and kidney pie
and ice cream with black cherries at Number 10, a far cry from the pro-
verbial beer and sandwiches, the union leaders proved as stubborn as
ever. After almost a month, as Donoughue recorded, the talks were still
deadlocked:

> Healey reported, very pessimistically, that he was still trying for 4½%, but
> the TUC would not budge and wanted 5%. Jim was terrifically firm. He
> said 5% would damage the government's credibility and might destroy
> the currency. So the ministers went off to see the TUC again and we went
> back to No. 10 . . .
>
> [Later] We reassembled in the Cabinet Room . . . They reported progress.
> The TUC would not shift. Healey wanted to settle for 5%. Jim said no –
> go away again and tell them that 5% would damage the currency. We sat
> there chatting and Healey came back alone. No progress. He wanted to
> settle at 5%. Jim said no – it would destroy the credibility of his govern-
> ment. So Healey went off again.

At this point, Callaghan announced that unless the unions gave way, 'he
was prepared to resign'. But this was an empty promise, for when the
TUC barons trooped back into the Cabinet Room at 1.30 in the morning, there was no talk of resignation. Callaghan ordered his officials out

of the room, but, by lurking near the door, Donoughue overheard what was going on. 'They went around the table,' he recorded afterwards. 'Jim made his appeal. [Len] Murray, [Jack] Jones and the rest of the trade unionists said that 5% was the least that they could sell. They were not willing to bargain. So Jim said OK that is that.' The deal was done; the unions had got their way.[16]

Visibly exhausted, Healey unveiled the deal in the Commons the next day. In place of Jack Jones's flat rate, he announced, pay increases would be limited to between £2.50 and £4 a week, amounting to 5 per cent a year. Of course this was a good deal more than the Chancellor had promised in the Budget, but it was a sign of the unions' stranglehold over government pay policy that even this result was generally seen as a great achievement – especially when compared with the gigantic increases of 1974 and 1975. Lapsing into the language of some sheep-skin-jacketed football manager, Callaghan spoke warmly of his pride in 'Denis and all the rest of the lads,' while Michael Foot sent a warm note of congratulations for 'a Herculean feat'. For their part, the TUC seemed happy with the new arrangement: at a special conference in June, their members endorsed it by a margin of almost 9 million votes, and there was even talk of a 'Social Contract Mark II'.[17]

And yet amid the backslapping, there were signs of trouble ahead. The interminable rounds of talks, the pictures of union leaders trooping in and out of Number 10 and the endless discussions about pay rates and differentials gave an impression of vast union power. But the real threat to Callaghan's government was that as month followed month, the eld-erly union leaders were gradually losing power over their own members. Sick of pay restraint and spending cuts, unimpressed by fine words about patriotism and responsibility, shop stewards and left-wing activists alike had little faith in the Social Contract. 'We now call Jack Jones a Fascist,' the chairman of the Blackburn Labour Party told a horrified Barbara Castle in March 1976. What was more, the new pay deal meant that, over the next nine months, prices rose by 15 per cent but wages by less than 8 per cent, meaning an inevitable drop in many workers' standard of living. Only a month into the new agreement, Jack Jones warned Cal-laghan and Healey that they should consider 'an orderly return to free collective bargaining' by the summer of 1977. Quietly, almost imper-ceptibly, the seeds of the Winter of Discontent were being sown.[18]

In the short term, the problem was the markets. Once again, it looked to the outside world as though economic policy was being made in the TUC, not the Treasury. By the middle of May it was painfully clear that, as *The Economist* memorably put it, holders of sterling 'put no more value on a British pound than on an ice-cream sundae'. On 3 June sterling fell to just $1.70, a drop of more than 10 per cent since the beginning of March. What was worse, the Bank of England's reserves were now almost totally dry. Even the $2 billion it had borrowed from the International Monetary Fund at the beginning of January had disappeared in the despairing struggle to prop up sterling's value. This left Healey facing an agonizing choice: massive spending cuts on one hand, or another international loan on the other. The latter, his Treasury mandarins told him, was 'the most sensible and also the most painless course', and at first it seemed that he would get $3 billion from various central banks and $2 billion from the Federal Reserve in Washington. But on Saturday, 5 June, the American Undersecretary of the Treasury, Ed Yeo, arrived in London to discuss the loan – and at that moment, it became clear that the picture was rather more complicated.[19]

Ever since the International Monetary Fund had been set up in 1945, easily its biggest single contributors had been the Americans. Not surprisingly, they demanded a big say in the conditions governing the IMF's loans. Unfortunately for Healey, the orthodoxy in Republican-dominated Washington was well to the right of the consensus in London. The American view, recalled the Federal Reserve chairman Arthur Burns, a self-confessed 'Neanderthal conservative', was that Britain's 'profligate government' needed to learn a harsh lesson in financial discipline. If anything, the United States Treasury Secretary, William Simon, was even more hawkish: as he wrote in his autobiography, he saw nothing wrong in helping an American ally, but had no desire to play 'host to a parasite'. Healey thought that Simon was 'far to the right of Genghis Khan'. But as Edmund Dell mordantly remarked, 'debtors cannot always choose their creditors'; if the British government really wanted to avoid dealing with him, they should not have got into such a mess in the first place. And although Simon makes a suitably terrifying scapegoat for what followed, he was far from the pantomime villain of journalistic accounts. Even Healey admitted that he was a 'good colleague ... always firm and sometimes flexible'. In any case, Simon was far from alone in his hostile view of Britain's woes. 'The Fund were pretty appalled, really by the management of the economy,' explained one IMF director, William Ryrie. As a former British Treasury official, Ryrie recalled sadly, 'I was ashamed.'[20]

The upshot was that although Healey got his $5 billion, there was no provision for the loan to be renewed indefinitely, as was usual. Instead,

Britain had six months to pay back the money. If, on 9 December, Healey could not pay it back, then he would have to make a formal application to the IMF – meaning not only utter humiliation, but swallowing their demands for spending cuts. Some Labour insiders were convinced that this was all a gigantic Treasury conspiracy with the IMF to 'bounce' the government into massive cuts. Two days after the announcement, Bernard Donoughue told Callaghan that he was 'sure that the Bank will spend the new swap facility quickly and we will be forced to go to the IMF for a full loan and then will have the cuts forced on us'. Certainly the Treasury had its fair share of spending hawks. But as Dell points out, opinion inside the Treasury was far too divided to support a conspiracy, and the Americans hardly needed encouragement to take a hard line. In any case, as Callaghan told his policy chief, the brutal truth was that 'we had to make cuts', whatever the situation with the Fund. One of the great myths of the IMF crisis is that the cuts were forced on Britain by the wicked Americans. The reality is that, whether Callaghan's ministers liked it or not, cuts were always coming.[21]

In the newspapers, attention had switched to the record-breaking summer temperatures. The next morning's headlines made depressing reading for those sick of the sweltering temperatures. 'Sweat It Out For Fifty Years' read the headline in the *Express* on 26 June, explaining that thanks to the newly discovered 'greenhouse' effect, Britain would soon become a 'hothouse'. That afternoon, a government car collected Donoughue for the big government summit on economic strategy. 'We drove to Chequers in enormous heat,' he wrote: 'the last stretch of winding country road was melting and the sticky tar slowed the car and made an odd tearing sound.' When he arrived, Denis Healey had already been swimming, though it was 'so warm', the Chancellor said, that he could not really enjoy it. And when they sat down, Healey presented a bleak picture. They simply had to make deep cuts, he said, partly to release 'resource space' for manufacturing, and partly to restore 'currency confidence'. It was, he explained, 'the size of expenditure programmes and of the borrowing to finance them which, in the eyes of the financial world, were at the heart of our problem', and he wanted to cut spending by around £1.25 billion, the equivalent of a cut of 2½ per cent in every programme. Even Callaghan blinked at that. Mollifying the markets, he pointed out, could easily bring down the government. He could probably get the cuts through Cabinet. But he was 'not sure we would have a Party at the end of it'.[22]

In the first three weeks of July, often working in punishing heat, the

Cabinet met seven times to discuss Healey's proposals. Not surprisingly, the Chancellor faced fierce opposition: to many Labour ministers, the very idea of such deep cuts was utter anathema. Chief among them was the Keynesian champion Tony Crosland, now Foreign Secretary. Crosland hated the idea of cuts, which undermined all his social democratic dreams, but the hard left's alternative of a siege economy and import controls left him cold. He seemed exhausted, impotent in the face of the economic blizzard: he 'looked terrible', Donoughue thought, his face 'puffy and ashen grey'. When journalists asked him at lunch what he would do about the pound and the IMF, Crosland said wearily: 'There isn't a solution.' In his commonplace book, he scribbled his despair at the 'illiterate and reactionary attitude to public expenditure' gaining ground on all fronts. 'Now no sense of direction and *no* priorities,' he wrote gloomily; 'only pragmatism, empiricism, safety first, £ supreme ... grave loss of welfare, security, choice: very high price to be paid for deflation and negative growth.'[23]

Healey's other major opponent, by contrast, was as spirited as ever. Despite his exile to the Department of Energy, Tony Benn was convinced that he had got his hands on the secret formula for economic recovery. The premise of the so-called Alternative Economic Strategy was that, in a globalized world, Britain could only reboot its stalled economy by temporarily cutting itself off from external pressures. Under this strategy, the government would introduce stringent controls on foreign imports and the flow of capital, effectively throwing up a protectionist barrier to stop too many foreign goods getting in. Behind this trade wall, they could adopt a properly socialist policy, with full employment, steadily rising wages, booming demand and hence a resurgent manufacturing sector, all under the direction of a souped-up National Enterprise Board. This sounded good on paper; but since it would be incompatible with membership of the Common Market, let alone the free-market trends across the Western world, most ministers thought it was madness. When Benn first floated it early in 1975, Healey snapped that it was 'not a strategy at all' but a 'caricature' that would produce 'a run on sterling [and] a cut of 6 per cent in our living standards'. Edmund Dell, too, thought it was lunacy: if protectionist controls were ever introduced, he wrote, Britain would become a 'pariah among nations'. Even Benn's former industrial guru Stuart Holland was horrified by his enthusiasm for a North Korea-style 'siege economy'. 'The hard left cherished the thought of a Fortress Britain, in a world whose boundaries ended at Dover,' Joe Haines wrote later. 'They wanted a perennial political Dunkirk, because in their minds Dunkirk was a victory, if only because it got us out of Europe.'[24]

As usual, Benn stuck to his guns. The Alternative Economic Strategy, he wrote, was a 'real Labour policy of saving jobs, a vigorous micro-investment programme, import control, control of the banks and insurance companies, control of export, of capital, higher taxation of the rich, and Britain leaving the Common Market'. The question of international confidence, he told his colleagues, was irrelevant. 'The IMF is in a position to press anything on us once we accept the confidence argument and there will be no end to it,' he said dismissively. Instead, 'we should fight for our own people . . . We should adopt import controls because what is happening is that our manufacturing base has shrunk and there is nothing in this which will allow it to grow as it should behind a wall of protection. And we should have compulsory planning agreements to see that investment occurs.' This left most of them aghast: as Dell remarked, the idea that the IMF would pour out 'financial assistance unconditionally to thirsty borrowers' was simply absurd. But Benn was in fighting form, ending on a note guaranteed to infuriate the former Major Healey. 'I think', he said defiantly, 'that the British Establishment is now infected with the same spirit which afflicted France in 1940, the Vichy spirit of complete capitulation and defeatism. It is that which is going finally to destroy us. I hope nobody will take this as being offensive but my Privy Councillor's oath requires me to disclose my opinions in the Council and this is what I have done.' Afterwards, he recorded proudly, 'Denis sat there scarlet. He always blushes when he is in difficulty and the argument is gaining force.'[25]

But it was Healey who carried the day. On Wednesday, 21 July, the Cabinet finally agreed a cuts package worth £954 million, as well as a 2 per cent surcharge on National Insurance contributions to raise another £1 billion. Afterwards Benn trudged outside 'absolutely dazed and stunned by the magnitude of the deflation that had been undertaken'. The next day, when Healey announced the cuts to a stunned House of Commons, Benn sat a few feet away on the front bench, but only because Callaghan had specifically told him to. 'I suppose it looked as if I was sunk in gloom,' Benn wrote grumpily, 'but, in fact, I was sound asleep.' Callaghan was not impressed: on Friday, he rang Benn to warn him that if he made trouble, he would be sacked. 'We should be so lucky!' Donoughue wrote in his diary. But when Benn met his local Labour activists that night, it was clear that most of them shared his horror at the government's austerity. People in Bristol, said a young shop steward, were asking 'Where's your Tony Benn now? What sort of a battle is there now?' 'It was a tremendous attack,' recorded a satisfied Benn. 'Nobody had a good word to say for the Government.'[26]

Jim Callaghan spent much of the August holiday on his Sussex farm, helping to bring in the harvest. Usually, this meant 'a combination of physically tiring work, long hours, frustration when it rains or the machinery breaks down', and then 'a growing sense of satisfaction as successive fields are cleared, and of immense fulfilment as the final trailer-load is tipped in the barn'. But this year was different. The heat wave had taken its toll; up and down the country, fields were parched and dry. That summer, Callaghan recalled, 'the harvest was easy but light, some wheat and barley died in the ear, there was little fodder, the grass dried up, turned brown and even crackled underfoot in the baking heat'.[27]

Meanwhile, Denis Healey was taking his wife on a tour of Scotland. Up they drove, through the Lake District towards Ardnamurchan, then on to Skye and up the west coast of Scotland towards Ullapool, where they stopped at a little hotel on the quayside. Even there, however, the Chancellor was unable to put the plight of the economy behind him. 'After a pleasant supper of Loch Broom smokies,' he recalled, 'we went to bed.' But what followed was a 'night of French farce'. Scarcely had he laid his head on the pillow than the telephone rang downstairs. So he trooped back downstairs, wearing a raincoat over his pyjamas, to the phone in the hall. It was the police, calling with the unhappy news that there had been a bomb threat against him and Special Branch were on their way from Inverness. Healey had barely got back to his bedroom before the phone rang again, so he trudged wearily back downstairs. This time it was the Treasury, reporting that sterling had come under renewed pressure. A third call inevitably followed from the Bank of England, asking for approval to spend $150 million defending the currency. Healey agreed. 'Finally,' he recorded laconically, 'I got back to bed for a few hours' sleep.' What his fellow guests made of it all can only be imagined.

By the time the Healeys returned to London, the news was even worse. On 3 September, 21,000 workers at British Leyland walked out after a demarcation dispute at the Castle Bromwich plant. In the previous two months, strikes had cost the company £20 million in car sales, but not even the most rabidly anti-union columnist could have made up this latest dispute, which hinged on the responsibility for pressing the buttons on a new control panel. 'The state-controlled car company's plight is assuming crisis proportions,' said *The Times* grimly, noting that at Longbridge there had been eleven major strikes in six months. 'I am totally opposed to it,' said an angry Callaghan, adding that 'we cannot afford this kind of sudden stoppage'. Even most union leaders deplored the strike: the AUEW's Terry Duffy, soon to succeed Hugh Scanlon, insisted that the shop stewards were 'just putting their fingers up to union officials. It is apparent to me there is anarchy reigning at Longbridge . . . Their attitude is wrong, and I condemn it.'[28]

But no amount of condemnation could ease the pressure on the pound. On Monday, 6 September, fourteen unions joined forces in demanding that the government adopt a 'socialist economic and industrial policy'. The next day, Labour's National Executive called for the government to nationalize Britain's four biggest banks as part of the Alternative Economic Strategy. On Wednesday, the National Union of Seamen announced a national strike to begin at the weekend in pursuance of its £6 a week pay claim – a decision that stunned not only the government but the TUC. Meanwhile the drought was getting worse: by mid-September it had officially become the worst for 250 years. And given this barrage of bad news, the markets were rapidly losing faith in the government's ability to keep order. On Wednesday morning, recorded Bernard Donoughue, Healey and the Governor of the Bank of England warned Callaghan that they had 'already spent £175 million defending the currency by the time they met at 10 a.m.!'

Horrified, Callaghan told them to stop throwing away their reserves: 'either we had a floating rate or we did not', and the Bank should stop trying to defend it at $1.77. But with Thursday's papers leading on the seamen's strike, confidence was seeping out of the economy like air from a popped balloon. 'Sterling fell like a stone to $1.73,' Donoughue noted. 'The Bank threw away $100 million in the first ten minutes and then withdrew support, following [Wednesday's] instructions from the PM.' On Friday morning, Healey raised the Bank's minimum lending rate to 13 per cent – a level reached only once before in its history, for a few weeks at the end of 1973. 'The increase brought immediate help to the hard-pressed pound,' reported the next day's *Times*. But it came at a heavy price, for such a high rate was not only a disaster for anybody borrowing money, it was bound 'to slow down the economic recovery, with all the implications that this must have for the level of employment'.[29]

By now, faced with the impossibility of defending the currency as well as paying back the IMF, the Bank of England was effectively staring into the abyss of bankruptcy. And as September wore on, the pressure on the pound intensified: standing at $1.75 on the 10th, it was down to barely $1.70 by the 24th and finally hit $1.63 on the 27th. By this time, the Treasury had given up any illusions that they might escape a humiliating mercy mission to the IMF. On Thursday, 23 September, Healey bluntly told the Cabinet's Economic Strategy Committee that Britain faced a 'very gloomy future . . . we should have to go to the IMF for another loan next month. Even that would only tide us over until the end of 1977 . . . Our reserves are down to £4 billion – and the deficit this year and next will absorb that. Sterling is at an all-time low. Inflation is no longer falling. The incomes policy is lacking. We have record interest rates to protect sterling and finance [public borrowing]'. Worst of all, wrote Bernard Donoughue, 'the siege economy is a little nearer. Benn and Shore sit and wait for it. We may just avoid it by the skin of our teeth. But I see no chance of winning an election before 1979.'[30]

As luck would have it, the following weekend marked the opening of the Labour party conference in Blackpool. In many ways the old resort made an appropriate venue for a party hidebound by its own history: indeed, only a few months earlier, Blackpool had celebrated the centenary of its incorporation. Like Britain itself, it was grudgingly moving with the times. 'Boarding houses are now guest houses, [while] the special attractions listed in the windows have changed from hot and cold running water and free sauce through foam rubber mattresses to colour television,' wrote one visitor that May. 'Now they feature electric-razor points, licensed bars, and, perhaps significantly, full fire-precaution certificates.' Yet part of Blackpool's charm – like the Labour Party's appeal – was that it remained defiantly old-fashioned. Which other town, after all, would have chosen to celebrate the centenary with a flying display, a carnival and, inevitably, a 'bathing beauty competition'? And despite the rise of foreign package holidays, Blackpool remained staggeringly popular with working-class holidaymakers from the north of England. Sixteen million bookings were expected during 1976: well down from the inter-war years, but still an awe-inspiring total. Evidently not everybody agreed with the acerbic MP Alan Clark, who had not enjoyed his visit to the Lancashire resort three years earlier. 'Isn't Blackpool appalling, loathsome?' he wrote in his diary. 'Impossible to get even a piece of bread and cheese, or a decent cup of tea; dirt, squalor, shanty-town broken pavements with pools of water lying in them – on the Promenade – vulgar common "primitives" drifting about in groups or standing, loitering, prominently.'[31]

Even by the standards of Labour conferences in the 1970s, the mood was ugly. Even the weather had changed, rain pouring down from slate-grey skies. In the very first session on Monday morning, fumed Bernard Donoughue, 'five of the first eight speakers were Trotskyites'. (Beforehand, Callaghan's aides had prepared a list of likely speakers who were thought to be Marxists: a revealing sign of the mood at the top of the party.) And as day followed day, speakers lined up to demand an end to Healey's cuts, the imposition of import controls and the nationalization of the banks. 'Most of the votes went against the platform,' Donoughue wrote on Thursday. 'The easiest way to win votes and cheers was to attack the Labour government. It was really terrible and everybody was depressed. Jim said to me that it was worse than ever before.' But at least one minister enjoyed himself. To great cheers from the hall, Tony Benn told his comrades that Labour must drive 'back the blunt and inhuman force of the market economy'. The main enemies, he said, were 'monetarists, nationalists and racialists' who sought to 'divide working people from each other'. But there were enemies within, too. 'We are also paying a heavy price,' Benn said grimly, 'for the 20 years in which we have, as a party, played down our criticism of capitalism and soft-pedalled our advocacy of socialism.' The delegates loved it: in the National Executive elections Benn again topped the poll, increasing his majority by 4,000 votes. 'You know, young man,' Jack Jones remarked, 'you'll be Prime Minister next.'[32]

Jim Callaghan, however, had rather different ideas about the future of socialism. When he stood on Tuesday afternoon for his first conference speech as party leader, the pound was in freefall, tumbling towards a record low of $1.63. The storm had broken; the crisis had come. But as Callaghan rose in his smart dark business suit, he looked the very picture of calm professionalism. Beforehand, he had been 'jumpy' about his speech, and perhaps it was no wonder. For although much of it was devoted to the ritual attack on the Conservatives, one passage had the delegates staring open-mouthed. It began with words that not even the most dogged militant could possibly dispute. 'For too long, perhaps ever since the war, we postponed facing up to fundamental choices and fundamental changes in our society and in our economy,' Callaghan said bluntly. 'That is what I mean when I say we have been living on borrowed time. For too long this country – all of us, yes, this Conference too – has been ready to settle for borrowing money abroad to maintain our standards of life, instead of grappling with the fundamental problem of British industry.'

It was what he said next, though, that really shocked his listeners. To gasps from the hall, he began by burying full employment, one of the assumptions of British life since the Second World War. 'The cosy world we were told would go on forever, where full employment would be guaranteed by a stroke of the Chancellor's pen, cutting taxes, deficit spending – that cosy world is gone,' he said. And instead of making lofty promises about banishing unemployment, he went on to discuss its root cause:

> Quite simply and unequivocally: it is caused by paying ourselves more than the value of what we produce. There are no scapegoats. This is as true in a mixed economy under a Labour Government as it is under capitalism or under communism. It is an absolute fact of life which no Government, be it left or right, can alter . . .
>
> We used to think that you could spend your way out of a recession and increase employment by cutting taxes and boosting Government spending. I tell you in all candour that that option no longer exists, and that insofar as it ever did exist, it only worked on each occasion since the war by injecting a bigger dose of inflation into the economy, followed by a higher level of unemployment as the next step. Higher inflation followed by higher unemployment . . . that is the history of the last twenty years.

To many of his listeners, this was horrifying stuff. For a Labour Prime Minister to be ditching full employment was bad enough, but for him to bury Keynesian economics was barely believable. But Callaghan was not finished yet. The only route to prosperity, he said sternly, was for Britain's labour costs to become 'at least comparable with those of our competitors'. Next, there must be a big improvement in 'the productivity of both labour and capital'. And finally, he said, 'we will fail – and I say this to those who have been pressing about public expenditure . . . if we think we can buy our way out by printing what Denis Healey calls "confetti money" to pay ourselves more than we can produce'. No full employment; no spending your way out of a recession; no confetti money. It felt like the end of an era.[33]

Although Callaghan's address became one of the most celebrated political speeches of modern times, he did not write it himself. The controversial section on the death of the post-war consensus was actually the handiwork of his son-in-law, Peter Jay, still nominally a Labour supporter despite his reputation as Fleet Street's most enthusiastic monetarist. To most party members, however, Jay's words felt like a bucket of cold water in the face. Bernard Donoughue, who considered the famous passage 'remarkably courageous', recorded that there were 'few cheers' and 'no standing ovation'. Tellingly, many members of the National Executive did not even clap when Callaghan had finished, which his aides thought a stunning exhibition of disloyalty. Tony Benn, the chief dissenter, thought that Callaghan had given 'the most patronising lecture', and wrote (yet again) that 'the smell of 1931 is very strong in my nostrils'. By contrast, the Tory newspapers, almost despite themselves, were impressed: even the *Express* welcomed 'Jim's facts of life warning'. When Callaghan rang President Gerald Ford to discuss the state of the pound the next day, even he was taken aback to be greeted by the words: 'Jim, you made a helluva speech yesterday.' And monetarism's founding father was enormously impressed by Callaghan's courage. 'The most hopeful sign I have seen in Britain', Milton Friedman told *The Money Programme* three months later, 'was the talk which your Labour prime minister gave to the Labour conference at the end of September. That was, I think, one of the most remarkable talks, speeches, which any government leader has ever given.'*[34]

It was also a landmark in British political history. For the first time a Labour Prime Minister had publicly abandoned the consensus built on deficit spending and full employment; as the economics writer David Smith puts it, Callaghan had 'effectively sounded the death-knell for post-war Keynesian policies'. It also marked the long-overdue recognition of the impact of globalization: at last, rejoiced Edmund Dell, a Labour leader had had the guts to admit that 'Britain was not an island' and that the rest of the world did not 'intend to arrange its affairs to ensure Britain a living'. Yet Callaghan himself saw the speech in much narrower terms. Years later he explained that, rather than wanting to ditch Keynesianism, he had really been aiming at the 'unrealistic' proposals of the hard left. He was 'exasperated by left-wing extremism and economic illiteracy amongst his Labour comrades', he told his biographer, Kenneth Morgan, and intended to show them 'that they must face up to reality'. To some extent, then, his speech was merely an exercise in telling his left-wing critics a few home truths – as well as telling

---

* Three months later, Friedman paid Callaghan the ultimate compliment by quoting the speech in his Nobel Prize lecture, in which he argued that Keynesianism had failed because it needed 'larger and larger doses of inflation to keep down the level of unemployment'.

the nation's international creditors what they wanted to hear. The irony, though, was that by using Peter Jay as a scriptwriter, Callaghan gave the impression that he was fully converted to the monetarist argument, which made it more difficult for him to pour cold water on it later. The lesson, remarked Denis Healey, was clear: 'Never have your speeches written by your son-in-law.'[35]

Healey was not in Blackpool to hear his colleague's speech. That morning, he was due to fly to Hong Kong for a Commonwealth finance ministers' meeting before moving on to Manila for the annual meeting of the IMF. 'Packed in morning. £ still falling heavily,' the Chancellor recorded in his diary. By the time he left for Heathrow, grinning cheerfully for the cameras, the flight from sterling had become a mad stampede. Every few minutes the car telephone rang with bad news from the Treasury, and during the hour-long journey to the airport, the pound dropped by another two cents. By the time Healey walked into the VIP lounge at the terminal, he was facing an awful dilemma. If he boarded the plane, he would be cut off from London for seventeen hours; but if he changed his plans and stayed at home, he might send the markets over the edge. For half an hour, pondering over a large gin and tonic, he hesitated. He rang Callaghan at the Imperial Hotel in Blackpool, where the Prime Minister was just about to leave for his landmark speech. 'Denis told me that Bank of England experts were forecasting gloomily that sterling would continue to fall … as low as $1.50,' Callaghan remembered, 'and no one could tell whether it would then stop.' He agreed that Healey should turn around. Fifteen minutes before the flight was due to depart, aides began loading the Chancellor's bags back into his official car. An hour later, he was back at the Treasury. And that night, even as the newspapers were preparing elaborate analogies with Napoleon's retreat from Moscow, Healey yielded to the inevitable. There was no alternative: Britain must go to the IMF.[36]

Healey spent the next day barricaded inside the Treasury. The news was worse than ever: at the Ford plant in Dagenham, the workers had walked out after a dispute about the doors on the new Cortina, smashing factory windows and making a bonfire of old boxes. Even the pugnacious Chancellor had reached rock bottom: as the tabloids gleefully noted, he seemed so helpless in the face of events that he had not even had time to change the jacket and slacks he had first put on for the flight to the Far East. Later that morning, the Treasury confirmed the grim news that Britain had applied to borrow the maximum $3.9 billion

(£2.3 billion) from the IMF, a humiliation almost beyond precedent. 'Dance Of The Puppets' shrieked the *Express*, explaining that Callaghan and Healey were 'dancing to the IMF's tune, like puppets on a string attached to the life-saving loan'. On the front page, a table showed the decline of the pound in just twelve months, down from $2 to just $1.67. 'Prices of all imported food – from fruit, meat and dairy produce to tea, coffee and spices – will rise as soon as present stocks run out,' the newspaper predicted. And when Healey emerged for an interview on *News at Ten*, he stuck an even more pessimistic note. The only alternative to the IMF, he said bleakly, 'would be economic policies so savage, I think they would lead to riots in the streets, an immediate fall in living standards, and unemployment of three million'.*[37]

In Blackpool, the atmosphere had now reached a peak of hysteria. Ladbrokes were even offering odds of 3 to 1 against Callaghan's resignation, responding, a spokesman said, 'to public demand'. As luck would have it, on Thursday afternoon the conference was due to debate the economy, and at breakfast Healey rang the Prime Minister, asking permission to fly north and make his case. 'Jim doesn't want me in Blackpool,' he recorded, since it would 'weaken [the] repair of calm'. On top of that, Callaghan reminded him that, as he was no longer a member of the National Executive, he could not speak from the platform. With the IMF application already lodged and the pound 'fragile but stable', the Chancellor therefore found himself at a loose end. To pass the time, he went off to the National Gallery 'to choose an Ostade and a Wouwerman for my office at the Treasury, and a Van den Neer for No. 11.' But Healey's break in the Dutch Golden Age did not last long; at 11.30 a Treasury aide burst in with the news that Callaghan had changed his mind. A plane was waiting at RAF Northolt, but by the time Healey got there rain was pouring down and the runway was flooded. He sat there for almost an hour, and then at last the plane took off. At 2.30 he touched down in Blackpool, where a motorcycle escort was waiting to convey him to the Winter Gardens. At three o'clock, damp, red-faced and excited, the Chancellor walked into the conference hall. 'When I came in,' he remembered, 'they started booing.'[38]

Not even the government's severest critics could have scripted what happened next. While Healey took a seat near the back, scribbling notes and shaking his head, the conference debated the National Executive's

---

* Intriguingly, this reads now as a reasonably accurate prediction of what did indeed happen a few years later.

plan to take Barclays, Lloyds, the Midland Bank and the NatWest into public ownership. The text of the resolution speaks volumes about the atmosphere in the party:

> This conference believes that there can be no advance to and maintenance of full employment except by means of a planned economy and public control of all sources of money supply for commercial and industrial investment ... Only by the creation of a state monopoly of credit and finance, with a state bank and a state credit corporation under the control and management of the democratic organisations of the working class, [can] integrated socialist planning be implemented ...

As one speaker after another rose to demand compulsory planning agreements and import controls, Healey buried his head in his hands. 'If we are to restore confidence in this country behind a socialist banner and a socialist programme,' thundered Norman Atkinson, the new party treasurer, 'then unfortunately we have to sacrifice the confidence of those who are now telling us what the terms are for us borrowing their money.' What Healey thought of that is probably unprintable.

At last it was Healey's turn. And somehow it says it all that the Chancellor at the eye of one of the greatest financial storms in British history had to speak from the floor for no more than five minutes, just like any other delegate. As he stood up, waving a sheaf of papers, his face flushed, his tie askew, some people cheered; but more booed. For one anonymous Labour MP who later joined the SDP, this was the moment the left finally went too far. 'He was booed all the way to the rostrum,' the MP said later. 'I was horrified. I hated it; that bloody mob, those clenched fists, those pointing fingers.'[39]

'I do not come with a Treasury view,' Healey began, almost shouting to be heard above the jeers. 'I come from the battlefront.' He begged the delegates to 'recognize that statements and resolutions are not just words that die when the echoes fade in the Winter Gardens. They are heard in the real world in which the Government must act. An unwise resolution, an ill judged statement, could knock £200 million off the reserves in a minute.' At that there were more boos, but Healey was merely warming up. 'There are some people who would like to stop the world and get off,' he yelled scornfully. 'They say, "Let us go to a siege economy." But they want a siege economy of a rather odd type. They want to stop the imports coming in but to get total freedom for exports to get out.' Now people were shouting from the floor, but the Chancellor ploughed on. 'Oh yes,' he said mockingly, 'you want the exports to go out, you want the jobs in the engineering factories to increase as the exports increase, but you want to stop other people having the advantage of selling their goods to us . . . I have never heard of a siege in which you keep the enemy out of your castle but the enemy allows you to come and go as you please through its ranks.'

The only result, he said, would be 'a return to the conditions of the 1930s'. Within months the Tories would be back in power, bringing massive spending cuts and high unemployment:

> If you do not want this then we have got to stick to the policy we have got [*Shouts of 'A Tory policy!'*].
>
> I am going to negotiate with the IMF on the basis of our existing policies, not changes in policy, and I need your support to do that. But when I say 'existing policies', I mean things we do not like as well as things we do like. It means sticking to the very painful cuts in public expenditure [*Shouts of 'No!'*] on which the Government has already decided. It means sticking to a pay policy which enables us, as the TUC resolved a few weeks ago, to continue the attack on inflation [*Shouts of 'Resign!'*] . . .
>
> That is what it means! That is what I am going to negotiate for! And I ask conference to support me in that task!

With that, Healey walked back towards his seat, more florid than ever, engulfed in a cacophony of cheers and boos. For a moment he sat down. Then he got up again, pumping his fists in the air like Muhammad Ali, his eyes blazing, his clothes disordered, his face glistening with sweat. On the platform, Callaghan gave a small smile of satisfaction. 'I couldn't even clap him,' Tony Benn angrily recorded, 'his speech was so vulgar and abusive.'[40]

Even Healey's critics had to admit that he had shown extraordinary courage. But in the City, admiration for the Chancellor's defiance was eclipsed by horror at the conference's vote to nationalize the banks and at the fact that he had been so violently booed. As Barings Bank's report put it, 'the spectacle of the policies of the Chancellor being rejected so vociferously' was a disaster for confidence. But by this stage the problem was not so much the speculators as the IMF. Everything now depended on the government being able to reach a deal with the Fund's negotiators. Talking to the BBC's Robin Day a few hours after Healey's belligerent intervention, Callaghan refused to admit that the loan might mean 'higher prices, higher mortgage payments, higher rates [and] higher unemployment', as the papers were predicting. 'Pure newspaper speculation,' he said, smiling and shaking his head. 'Speculation. Speculation.' But when Day asked if failure to overcome the crisis might mean the collapse of British democracy, the smile disappeared. 'You're right,' Callaghan said grimly. 'If we were to fail – and I don't particularly want to make a party point – I don't think another government could succeed. I fear it would lead to a totalitarian government of the left or right.'[41]

21

Money, Money, Money

*Perhaps the politicians, who have got us into our present mess,
would like to know what the British people are fed up with
most of all . . . Not the fall in the pound. Not ever-rising food
prices. Not the erosion of their pay packets. Not even the
weather. What the British people are fed up with most is feeling*
ASHAMED.

Sunday Mirror, 31 October 1976

LEELA: *What is he saying, Doctor? I do not understand.*
THE DOCTOR: *He can't make ends meet. Probably too many
economists in the government.*

Doctor Who, 'The Sun Makers' (1977)

It was a dreary autumn, the cracked fields sulking under lowering
clouds. The summer's carefree pleasures were now fading memories.
'Everything here in Britain is so gloomy,' wrote Roy Strong at the beginning of October.

> I keep looking for GOOD NEWS – WHERE IS IT? The main theme is can
> or can we not survive until the 1980s without a collapse of society as we
> know it. It all seems so incredible compared with five years ago that it is
> terrible to grasp. One is confused, bewildered, despairing. Well, one can
> only plough one's lonely furrow in as true a way as one can, and that's that.[1]

In student unions across the country, a new kind of music was
gathering momentum, 'coming straight from the straight-out-of-school-
and-onto-the-dole deathtrap,' said the *NME*, 'which we seem to have
engineered for our young: the '76 British terminal stasis, the modern

urban blind alley'. On 21 September, one of the new groups, the Damned, were performing at the 100 Club on Oxford Street when another young musician, who called himself Sid Vicious, threw a beer glass at the stage. Shards flew everywhere, one hitting a girl in the eye and blinding her for life. Two days later, the *Evening Standard* drew public attention to the new craze, noting that one group, known for its 'harsh dogmatic attitude', had 'recently been attracting a great deal of attention from leading record companies'. On 8 October the Sex Pistols signed their first record deal with EMI. Exactly a week later, the *Sun* devoted a two-page spread to the new movement, illustrated with shocking pictures of safety pins, handcuffs and swastikas. The new groups, the paper explained, looked like 'Hell's Angels in a *Clockwork Orange* nightmare'. The piece quoted the Pistols' lead singer, the staring, spiky-haired John Lydon. 'We want chaos to come,' he said. 'Life's not going to get any better for kids on the dole until it gets worse first.'[2]

Inside the corridors of power, the mood was grimmer than ever. The party conference, thought Bernard Donoughue, had shown 'the appalling mess in the Labour Party – full of lunatics'. Even at Number 10, tempers were close to fraying, and when Healey asked permission to raise interest rates to a record 15 per cent, Callaghan turned him down. For a few hours, unknown to the public, the government teetered on the brink of collapse: after a blazing row with Callaghan's ally Harold Lever, Healey stormed back to Number 11, intent on resigning. He had barely had time to calm down, however, when Callaghan's private secretary Ken Stowe stuck his head around the door. 'Excuse me, Chancellor, but the Prime Minister has asked me to tell you that he was only testing the strength of your conviction,' Stowe said. 'Of course he will support you.'

It was a pivotal moment. By the end of the week, high-street lending rates had reached 16½ per cent and mortgage rates 12¼ per cent, a brutal squeeze indeed. In Cabinet, ministers seemed 'mesmerised' by the horrendous figures. 'This is a very difficult time for all of us,' Callaghan told them grimly. 'If you will forgive a little homily, we have got to stick together now.' As Donoughue watched the rain pour down outside the windows, he felt utterly 'depressed by the drift of economic events'. In the long run, the credit squeeze probably did as much as anything to reinvigorate the gilt market, fund the debt and restore confidence in the British economy. But it came at a heavy price, not least in unemployment. When the jobless total had hit one million under Ted Heath, there had been uproar. Now, under Callaghan, it was heading towards a peak of 2 million. In some areas, such as Scotland and the North-east, the unemployment rate was far above the national average; for young people in particular, the prospects were terrifying, with almost half of all under-25-year-olds out of work by 1979.[3]

While the tabloids were becoming increasingly disturbed by the rise of what critics called 'dole queue rock', the markets seemed as febrile as ever. When the *Sunday Times* rashly claimed that the IMF wanted the pound to fall to $1.50, there was yet another plunge in confidence: by lunchtime on Monday, 25 October, sterling had fallen 7 cents in just a few hours. That evening, Healey went along to see the Queen open the National Theatre on the South Bank. Given the rigours of the day, he was in remarkably cheerful form, but it was a suitably miserable occasion. Outside, bedraggled brass bands, funfair vendors and hot-dog sellers shivered in the driving rain, while republican demonstrators chanted: 'Whose National Theatre? Whose National Theatre?' The new trumpet setting of the national anthem 'nearly blasted most of the audience out of their seats', while the play, Tom Stoppard's *Jumpers*, seemed to provoke only 'utter boredom'. The event was 'a washout', recorded Roy Strong, 'in every sense of the word'.[4]

A week later, the IMF team flew into London. Their very arrival was seen as a moment of overwhelming disgrace, as though Britain were some Central American republic incapable of running its own finances. The papers were naturally fascinated by the six men who would decide the nation's future: an Englishman, an Australian, an American, a German, a New Zealander and a Greek, who sounded like the introduction to some elaborate and deeply offensive joke, or perhaps the supporting cast for some terrible European-funded spy caper. In keeping with the traditions of international espionage, they had travelled separately to avoid detection, and had even booked rooms under false names in the elegant surroundings of Brown's Hotel, off Piccadilly. Usually they would have spent a day settling in before going over the nation's accounts, but when they visited 11 Downing Street, the Chancellor had some bad news. The books, Healey explained, were not ready: the IMF would have to wait. The truth was that not only was the Treasury divided about how much should be cut from public spending, but its officials could not even agree how much Britain was currently borrowing. To the IMF, however, this smacked of obstruction: 'doors were being closed deliberately,' they thought, 'and the British were consciously delaying.' Behind the scenes, the IMF's patience was wearing thin. Yet in public, its six smart negotiators presented an image of cool equanimity. 'Ask any bank manager,' remarked the *Express*; 'the bigger the overdraft, the better they treat you.'[5]

While the IMF team were kicking their heels, Callaghan was engaged in one last effort to avoid humiliation. Deep down, he feared becoming another Ramsay MacDonald, broken and ostracized because of his fealty to the markets. One day in early November, Edmund Dell was chatting to Healey in a Commons corridor when 'Callaghan came up to us and said, "Tony Crosland tells me it is all a bankers' ramp like 1931. I think I agree with him."' At that, Dell recalled, 'Callaghan walked off into the Chamber. Healey turned to me in near despair: "What can I do now?"'[6]

In fact, the Prime Minister had his own ideas about how to deal with the IMF. Interviewed on *Panorama*, he dropped heavy hints that Britain might have to withdraw its troops from West Germany to save money. Meanwhile, he begged Gerald Ford and Helmut Schmidt to call off the dogs, even sending Harold Lever on a secret mission to Washington. But he was wasting his time. Not only was Ford a lame duck, but Washington and Bonn refused to give ground: it was time for Britain to learn a hard lesson in financial discipline. Lever's presentations, one IMF negotiator remarked later, 'just didn't seem to be taking the problems seriously and this just confirmed the US view that we had to go through with this. This was the last throw to get some American influence to moderate the IMF line, and I think it convinced Callaghan that it wasn't going to succeed and he had to bite the bullet.'[7]

The difficulty with biting the bullet, however, became clear when the Cabinet's Economic Strategy Committee met on 3 November, two days after the IMF negotiators had arrived in London. While Healey insisted that 'cuts in public expenditure would be very welcome', even suggesting that benefits might be cut so that 'we could reduce the rates of tax on higher incomes' and 'have more incentives for our managers', Tony Benn felt 'almost sick with anxiety and disgrace to hear people who were elected with the support of Labour people talking in that way'. Benn's alternative followed the well-worn lines of planning agreements, quotas and a siege economy, but nobody was really listening. Indeed, by now Benn's pronouncements were more extravagant than ever. 'The market is the big spanner in the works and we have to find a way of getting it out,' he told the Cabinet a few weeks later, which must have had Healey and Dell burying their heads in their hands. And when Mao Tse-tung died that autumn, Benn was outraged that his fellow ministers refused to pay him a handsome tribute. At the very least, he wrote afterwards, 'Mao merited a moment of reflection in the British Cabinet . . .

In my opinion ... he will undoubtedly be regarded as one of the greatest – if not the greatest – figures of the twentieth century ... he certainly towers above any other twentieth-century figure I can think of in his philosophical contribution and military genius.'[8]

Had Benn won the day, and had Britain retreated into a siege economy behind protectionist quotas, then the history of the next few years would have been utterly different. But he was never close to commanding a majority, and while Benn continued to make a lot of noise, the real threat to Healey's position came from his old friend Tony Crosland. For the author of *The Future of Socialism*, giving in to the IMF would mean abandoning all his commitments to redistributive taxation, generous public spending and full employment. As Crosland saw it, the government had cut more than enough already; there was no basis, he thought, for the IMF's prescriptions. On top of that, there was the question of sheer self-interest. Crosland had already seen off one right-wing rival in Roy Jenkins. He knew that, at 64, Callaghan would not be Prime Minister for long, and that Healey would be a strong candidate to replace him. Coming out against the cuts not merely allowed Crosland to appeal to the Labour left; it was an opportunity to humiliate a rival whose job he rather fancied for himself.[9]

Crosland made his move at a secret meeting of senior ministers on 18 November. By this time the IMF had already made their opening bid, demanding that Britain slash borrowing to around £6.5 billion a year. Since Treasury estimates put annual borrowing at about £11 billion, this meant spending cuts of £3 billion in 1977–8 and £4 billion in 1978–9, beyond even the pessimists' wildest nightmares. Crosland was having none of it. There was no economic argument for cutting spending, he said, because more than a million people were already out of work, inflation was falling and the cuts would destroy the Social Contract. In many ways this was a perfectly legitimate argument: only weeks before, the *Investors' Chronicle*, hardly a beacon of socialist thinking, had announced that all the economic indicators were 'moving in the right direction'. But at a deeper level, Crosland was missing the point. As Edmund Dell wrote with mordant contempt, his was 'the kind of argument that might impress in the Senior Common Room of an Oxbridge college but which was hardly relevant to the political and economic realities of the moment'. The brutal truth was that only one thing now mattered: the confidence of the markets. Britain desperately needed a loan, and only the IMF could supply it. Like it or not, the government had no choice but to dance to the bankers' tune.[10]

For Callaghan, the rift between Healey and Crosland posed a dreadful dilemma. He had been in power for barely six months, his majority had disappeared and on 5 November Labour had been humiliated in the Walsall and Workington by-elections. In these circumstances, a Cabinet split might be fatal. His solution, however, was a stroke of genius. Instead of wading into the argument, Callaghan decided to sit back and let the heavyweights talk themselves into exhaustion, acting as a benevolent, unflappable umpire while they slugged it out. Every minister had his turn in the limelight; even Benn's Alternative Economic Strategy had a long hearing. Of course all this was enormously time-consuming: in two months the Cabinet met no fewer than twenty-six times. Yet with Britain's economic fortunes teetering on the brink, time and chance had thrown up the right man for the moment. Getting into the prime ministerial Rover one afternoon in the midst of the crisis, besieged by paperwork, beset by competing advice, Callaghan noticed that his parliamentary private secretary, the young Jack Cunningham, seemed overwhelmed by the pressure. 'Relax,' the Prime Minister said with an avuncular smile. 'I know you're feeling the strain. But when you've been through one or two of these, you know how to deal with them. It gets easier.'[11]

With Callaghan taking a back seat, the burden of argument fell on his exhausted Chancellor. The scale of the challenge was monumental: not only was Healey in charge of negotiating with the IMF, he needed to keep an eye on the markets, retain the confidence of his Treasury team, and somehow seduce his colleagues into accepting heavy cuts. A lesser man would have collapsed under the strain: day after day Healey rose at six, went straight to the Treasury and worked until well after midnight, making do with just a few hours' sleep. It was hardly surprising that he came down with a nasty case of shingles. The really astonishing thing, though, was that, as one meeting followed another, as the evenings drew in and the rain poured down, the Chancellor simply gritted his teeth and kept going. During Labour's first months in office, he had made his fair share of mistakes. But in the drab, dying weeks of 1976, he more than made up for them. It could have been 'the nadir of Healey's career', wrote his friend Edmund Dell, who was sometimes his only supporter. Instead, 'it was the supreme achievement of a Chancellor who, having been for months under intolerable strain, was now drawing on what were, perhaps, his last resources of courage and intellectual power'.[12]

*

On Tuesday, 23 November, the drama approached its climax. When the Cabinet met that morning, Callaghan announced that they had twenty-four hours to make their minds up. With that he turned to Healey, who reported that the IMF had made a revised offer, asking Britain to cut spending by £1.5 billion in 1977–8 and another £3 billion a year later. It would be 'painful', Healey admitted, 'but it would be made with the full endorsement of the IMF and our major allies. It could transform our international position and have a very important effect on domestic confidence.' Then Crosland spoke up. 'In terms of the Social Contract,' he said bitterly,

> there was absolutely nothing to be said for the proposal. The case for a reduction in public expenditure had not been made out; and there was an impressive body of opinion among economists of all political shades against such a move. Further public expenditure cuts would have a disastrous effect upon the public service unions, and the Social Contract would certainly break down as far as the public sector was concerned.

He accepted that the government had to make some savings to appease the markets, but these needed only be cosmetic. They should tell 'the IMF, the Americans and the Germans: if you demand any more of us we shall put up the shutters, wind down our defence commitments, introduce a siege economy'. This, Crosland said dismissively, 'would be sufficient to persuade the Fund to lend the money without unacceptable conditions'. Curiously, therefore, Britain's very weakness was its greatest strength: 'if the Government kept its nerve, it could insist on its own terms'. It was time, Crosland said loftily, 'to stop paying "danegeld"'.[13]

Listening to his old rival, Healey realized that he had once again missed the point. What Crosland refused to face, the Chancellor said later, was that 'when you have a deficit, you can only finance it by borrowing and you've got to persuade people that it's worth lending money to you and that they'll get their money back … There is no way of escaping it.' If the British economy was to be dragged back from the brink, all that mattered was regaining the confidence of the markets through a deal with the IMF. But as Dell later put it, Crosland's solution amounted to blackmail by 'petty menaces', with Britain threatening to scrap its international commitments, pull its troops out of West Germany and turn itself into the Western equivalent of North Korea unless the IMF paid up. This was not only wildly irresponsible, it was utterly implausible. In his characteristically arrogant way, Crosland had failed to see that there was no way the IMF would step meekly into line, because the Fund itself was answerable to its American and German paymasters. If the IMF allowed Britain to flout the basic rules of financial housekeeping, then the markets would lose confidence not just in Britain, but in the IMF itself. And even if, by some bizarre stroke of luck, the IMF *did* go along with Crosland's scheme, it would have destroyed Britain's reputation as an honest broker and its standing inside NATO. 'The folly of these threats', Dell wrote, 'confirmed my view that Crosland could no longer be trusted ... His remarks showed a Crosland who had lost all power of judgement. Indeed, it was difficult to know how seriously to take such proposals. I was certain they would never be implemented.'[14]

Yet since Crosland had told them precisely what they wanted to hear, most ministers took a rather different line from the icily rigorous Dell. Once again, therefore, the meeting broke up with nothing resolved. While Healey went grumpily off to the Treasury to lick his wounds, the various camps mustered their forces. On Wednesday evening, Tony Benn joined a cabal of left-wing ministers in Michael Foot's room to plan their strategy. 'We agreed that we would have to stand firm,' Benn recorded, 'and they were all very optimistic about Tony Crosland's position, saying we should rally round him.' Benn himself had not yet abandoned his siege-economy scheme; even at that moment, he was working on a detailed paper for the next Cabinet meeting. But Foot, the lodestar of loyalty, was anxious about party unity. He was 'worried and thought that Jim was going to come down against Denis, and Denis might resign'. Even Benn recognized that this would be a disaster: 'if he does resign, the pound will go through the floor, even if we get the IMF loan.'[15]

In fact, Healey was determined to fight to the finish. But as the week drew on, the pressure was building. On Thursday, issuing an obvious warning to the party leadership, *Tribune* reprinted the minutes of the Cabinet meeting about spending cuts that in 1931 had brought down Ramsay MacDonald's government and split the Labour Party. But when the Cabinet met that morning, there was no showdown. There was no need to rush, Callaghan explained, for the IMF team were happy to wait another week. Next Wednesday, the Cabinet would talk everything through one last time, and then they would make a final decision. Characteristically, Healey could not restrain himself from a pre-emptive effort to sway his colleagues. 'We had to remember that the money-lenders did determine the value of our currency,' the Cabinet minutes recorded. 'We were spending more than we were earning ... So long as we lived in an open and mixed economy, we shall depend on the market judgment to determine our future.' Equally characteristically, Crosland then interjected that 'he didn't believe further cuts were sensible or necessary'. But it was the Prime Minister who had the last word, intervening to mop their fevered brows. 'The situation was very grave,' recorded Tony Benn, 'but somebody said you shouldn't ever lose sleep over public affairs, and Jim agreed with that.'[16]

Behind the scenes, Callaghan was still undecided, but events were coming to a head. Over the weekend, the US Treasury Secretary, William Simon, visited London to stiffen the Treasury's resolve, holding an impromptu meeting with British officials at, of all places, his Mayfair tailors. The next day, Callaghan and Crosland flew in pouring rain to The Hague for a meeting of the European Council. Callaghan had not entirely given up hope of persuading Helmut Schmidt to approve a softer line, but when they had breakfast together on Tuesday morning, Schmidt said there was nothing he could do. 'I was not surprised,' Callaghan wrote later. Crafty as ever, he had asked Crosland to have breakfast with them precisely because he thought Schmidt might say no. It was the perfect way to show his Foreign Secretary that it was pointless to fight the IMF. A few hours later, as they flew back to London, Callaghan broke the news that he had decided to back Denis Healey. 'I knew where I stood,' Callaghan wrote later; 'what would he [Crosland] do? I reminded him that he had great influence with a section of the Cabinet and must decide where to throw his weight.' The implication was obvious: it was time for the Foreign Secretary to concede defeat. When Crosland arrived back at his London residence, his wife noticed, he seemed 'sad'.[17]

Wednesday, 1 December, the decisive day, began with a secret meeting between Callaghan and Johannes Witteveen, the managing director of the IMF, who had flown in that morning from Washington. According to the only onlooker, Callaghan's aide Ken Stowe, it was a 'really tough meeting. Witteveen insisted on £2 billion of public expenditure cuts. The PM said that was not economically sensible or politically possible. He would do £1 billion – or it meant a break with the IMF.' In a nicely melodramatic gesture, Callaghan promptly picked up the phone and rang President Ford to 'put the boot in', as Stowe later put it. Despite the bluster, though, this was something of a breakthrough. For the first time, Callaghan had explicitly committed himself to cuts and the IMF had come down to a figure he could accept. The trick now was to persuade the Cabinet to go along with it. Even as Callaghan was on the phone to Washington, the first ministers were coming through the heavy black door. By the time Tony Benn arrived, Cabinet had been put back by half an hour, which made him suspicious. 'You don't normally delay a Cabinet of that importance unless there's some hiccup,' Benn wrote, 'and we wondered whether Jim and Denis were having a set-to; in fact when we went into the Cabinet, Denis was coming out, so I think they must have had a talk.' In fact, Callaghan had merely been briefing his Chancellor on the latest position. But now it was 10.30: Callaghan's ministers took their places around the long oval table, and one of the most critical Cabinet meetings in modern British history began.[18]

Callaghan's strategy was simple but deadly. One by one, he asked Healey's critics to introduce their suggested strategy, kicking off with Tony Benn. This was Benn's big moment, the chance to convert his colleagues to the joys of a siege economy; but it backfired horribly. Unknown to Benn, Callaghan had quietly passed a copy of his paper to his Policy Unit, and asked them to prepare a comprehensive demolition job. Not only had Donoughue's team drafted a list of questions for the Prime Minister, but they also circulated advice to moderate ministers such as Shirley Williams and Bill Rodgers, giving them the ammunition to take Benn out of the debate.* Even as Benn was cheerfully extolling the virtues of import and exchange controls, his colleagues were readying themselves to strike, and when he had finished, the questions came flying in. Did he really want the loan? Did he not realize that there would be massive retaliation against British manufacturers? Did he really think that he could get such a radical scheme through the Commons? Where would Britain get foreign currency from if it had exchange controls?[19]

Benn was like a boxer reeling on the ropes as blows rained down from all sides. When he weakly told Callaghan that 'the IMF would help us because it would be in their interests to do so', or when he told Shirley Williams that he was sure Britain's trading rivals would not retaliate, or when he admitted to Bill Rodgers that he could not be sure what would happen to unemployment because 'I hadn't got a Treasury

---

* As the Policy Unit paper noted, the repercussions of the Alternative Economic Strategy would be enormous: 'It would be damaging to the EEC, damaging to international co-operation in trade and payments policy, and damaging to NATO. Once this damage had been done, it would be extremely difficult to re-establish ourselves in the Atlantic Community. Our former partners would be reluctant to trust so unreliable an ally again, and we would be liable to find ourselves left economically protectionist, and politically isolated.'

computer to mislead me', he was hammering the nails into his own coffin. 'It became a game that no-one took seriously,' Rodgers reflected later, 'as Benn's proposals were stripped bare of credibility.' At one point, Callaghan even had to remind his colleagues that Benn 'should be listened to with respect'. And at another particularly memorable moment, Denis Healey was cutting articles out of the morning's newspapers, as he often did in Cabinet, when he heard Benn say that his solution would avoid the need for deflation. 'Denis did not look up from the surgery he was performing on *The Times*,' recalled Roy Hattersley, 'as he asked Tony to name one reputable economist who supported the idea of a painless solution to Britain's economic problems.' Benn did not hesitate: 'Wynne Godley,' he said confidently. What followed was classic Healey knockabout:

> Denis carved on as if he had been confounded. Then, dramatically, he held up a couple of column inches which he had pruned from the letters page. There followed a few minutes of theatrical business of which Donald Wolfit would have been proud – smoothing the paper, focusing on the type and trying to pronounce the words. Eventually he managed to read the brief but authoritative assertion that the Alternative Strategy had to be accompanied by severe deflation. Then, after a titanic struggle with palate, teeth and tonsils, Denis pronounced the signature: 'Wynne Godley, King's College, Cambridge.'[20]

Benn had been thoroughly routed. Next came Peter Shore, whose paper also called for import controls, but on a much more limited basis. He got a more respectful hearing, but when Healey forced him to admit that import controls might drive up unemployment just as much as spending cuts, the case for a siege economy began to fall apart. Finally, it was Crosland's turn. Although he now knew that Callaghan was likely to back Healey, he began in extraordinarily cavalier style, even by his own standards. 'I think the proposals I wish to put forward will command more support than Tony's or Peter's,' he said languidly. To cut spending by a billion pounds was 'unacceptable, and the IMF won't really press us for it. If they do, we should resist and threaten a siege economy, or talk about our role in Cyprus or our troops in Germany, or our position in Rhodesia, membership of the EEC, etc. Schmidt and Ford would soon give way.' Unfortunately for Crosland, some of his colleagues were getting cold feet about the idea of holding the Atlantic alliance to ransom. 'What if the IMF say no?' Benn asked. 'We won't accept it,' Crosland said. 'But what if they stand firm?' Healey asked.

'We would have to defend ourselves,' Crosland said dismissively. But all this was utterly fantastical, and the more Crosland talked airily about blackmailing the IMF, the more his support evaporated. Perhaps he was merely going through the motions, conscious that his cause was doomed. Either way, it marked the sad nadir of a career that had once glittered so brightly.[21]

That evening, Benn tried to calculate the balance of forces, giving Healey eight supporters, Crosland seven and himself six. But the truth was that since most ministers were always likely to follow the Prime Minister, the Treasury was bound to win the day. And that night, as the whips were discussing their strategy for getting the cuts through the Commons, Crosland discovered that his support was collapsing. One by one, ministers came to his room in the Commons to break the news that they were voting with Healey. In the end, even Crosland had to face facts, although only he could have been quite so arrogant about it. 'Since I now propose to give my reluctant support to Jim,' he told Roy Hattersley, 'you must do the same. No time for heroics – or for you to think that your judgement is better than mine.' A few minutes later, he knocked on Callaghan's door. 'In Cabinet tomorrow,' he announced, 'I shall say I think you're wrong, but I also think that Cabinet must support you.' Afterwards, Crosland invited Hattersley to drown his sorrows in a drink. 'We never could have won anyway,' he told his young disciple. But Hattersley thought he was wrong about that. 'Beating the Chancellor of the Exchequer – and by implication the Prime Minister – would have been a catastrophic mistake,' he wrote later. 'Denis Healey would have been forced to resign, the Party in Parliament would have split down the middle, sterling would have collapsed and the government might well have been brought down. But it could have been done.'[22]

Thursday's headlines were dominated not by the intrigues at Westminster, but by rather more shocking developments in the studios of Thames Television. '4-Letter Words Rock TV,' read the *Telegraph*'s headline, while the *Mirror*, unforgettably, led with 'The Filth and the Fury'. But as Callaghan's exhausted ministers dragged themselves to yet another Cabinet meeting, the Sex Pistols' outrageous television appearance was the last thing on their minds. With Crosland in retreat, the momentum clearly lay with the Treasury. Public borrowing, Healey announced, was now forecast to be more than £10 billion, which meant there had to be cuts. He therefore proposed to raise £500 million by selling Burmah Oil shares, to cut spending in 1977–8 by £1 billion, and to cut spending in 1978–9 by a further £1.5 billion. At that, Callaghan announced that 'the time had now come to make decisions', and he had decided to back the Chancellor. A few moments later, Crosland threw in the towel. He still thought Healey's plan was 'wrong economically and socially destructive of what he had believed in all his life . . . but the new factor is your view, Prime Minister. What would be the consequence of rejecting the Prime Minister? The unity of the party depends on sustaining the Prime Minister and the effect on sterling of rejecting the Prime Minister would be to destroy our capacity. Therefore I support the Prime Minister and the Chancellor.' And that, in effect, was that. 'It will be the death warrant of the Labour Government if we accept this,' Benn said bitterly. But nobody was listening.[23]

There was one little bit of drama left, since the IMF team still had to be convinced that Healey's plan was stringent enough to please the markets. The next day the Chancellor had a blazing row with their chief negotiator, shouting that the IMF could 'go and take a running jump' if they seriously wanted deeper cuts. With a typically melodramatic touch, Healey even threatened that, unless the negotiators gave ground, 'we would call a general election on the issue of the IMF versus the people'. His bravado won the day: on Sunday morning, the IMF agreed a deal for cuts of £1 billion in 1977–8 and £1.5 billion a year later. On Monday, the Cabinet met yet again (they must have been sick of the sight of each other by now) to decide exactly where the cuts would fall. Nursing a bad cold, Callaghan was in no mood to mess about. When the Cabinet reached Tuesday lunchtime without getting to £1 billion, he 'exploded and said they had to settle it one way or the other *today*, and they would meet again this evening at the Commons'. Some of his ministers suspected he was only pretending to lose his temper. Either way, it worked, and by the end of the evening the details had been finalized, with defence, foreign aid, food subsidies, building programmes and regional employment measures paying a heavy price. The only minister who refused to face up to his responsibilities, reported Ken Stowe, had been Benn, who 'wriggled, ducked and weaved' and 'looked very cowardly and diminished before his colleagues'. Afterwards, Donoughue found Callaghan in his room reading some papers:

> He looked tired – grey, with little voice left, and constantly coughing. He said he was pleased they had tied up the package and he had got the figure he had gone for. He thought the Party would hold together on it, but he was less confident about the reaction in the markets. I said we could now

JAK's Cartoon Annual, published by Beaverbrook Newspaper rz, is available from newsagents and booksellers, price 50p.
"What does your group think of the latest IMF conditions?"

With the Sex Pistols dominating the headlines, Jak could not resist the
chance to give the IMF crisis a twist in this cartoon for the *Evening Standard*
(7 December 1976). It has to be said that Callaghan's senior ministers
make surprisingly convincing punks, not least Michael Foot,
with his fondness for *Sniffin' Glue.*

set about the recovery programme, and plan on an election in 1979. He
said, 'I will be dead by then, given how I feel tonight.'²⁴

Callaghan's handling of the crisis had been a remarkable achievement. Given that he had been in office for only a few months, and had
inherited from Wilson a horrendously beleaguered pound and a wafer-
thin Commons majority, he had worked miracles to mollify the markets,
strike a deal with the IMF and keep the government united. Later, he
wrote that the atmosphere had always been 'good-tempered', with a
'minimum of personal backbiting, very little malicious leaking and a
strong feeling of solidarity'. But he deserved a lot of the credit. A lesser
man would have broken; even Harold Wilson, with all his wiles, might
have struggled to hold the government together. That Callaghan had
done it without losing a single minister was a great tribute to his leadership. Denis Healey thought that 'the consummate skill with which he

handled the Cabinet was an object lesson for all prime ministers', but the dissenters, too, were impressed by Callaghan's patience in guiding them towards a conclusion. Even Tony Benn could not help but admire his leader's virtues. 'Jim is a much better Prime Minister than Wilson,' he wrote at the end of December. 'He is much more candid and open with people and he does not try to double-talk them as Wilson did. Wilson has just simply disappeared from sight. Once his patronage has gone, there's nothing left. Nobody thinks about him any more.'[25]

Denis Healey unveiled the IMF deal in a notably sombre mini-budget speech on 15 December. At the news of the cuts in defence and foreign aid, housing and employment, nationalized industries and food subsidies, not to mention the higher charges for gas and telephone services, backbenchers grimly shook their heads. The Chancellor's 'credibility was at a very low ebb', remembered his deputy Joel Barnett, 'and the House was unsympathetic; he was received with jeers by the Tories and stony silence from our side'. Healey himself was expecting an even worse reception. 'Not so bad,' he scribbled in his diary. The press, however, was unforgiving. 'Britain's Shame', screamed the headline in the *Sun*. Many observers were impressed by the Chancellor's courage under fire – as David Wood noted in *The Times*, 'nobody in Westminster politics today shows sturdier spirit under assault' – but the Conservative papers were unanimous that he should have gone even further. He 'could have cut public spending by about £4 billion,' said the *Daily Express*. 'Of course there would have been an enormous outcry from the looting classes. The Labour Left would have been on the march . . . But at least the country and the world would have known that Britain had an iron Chancellor who meant business.'[26]

There is no escaping the fact that the IMF crisis was a national humiliation. As Callaghan's biographer Kenneth Morgan rightly notes, it had laid bare all Britain's persistent weaknesses, from its overvalued pound and financial indiscipline to its sclerotic unions and tribal politics. On the international stage, Britain stood exposed as 'an incompetent beggar', one hand holding out a bowl for alms, the other holding up two fingers to the rest of the world. And yet the crisis never had the seismic impact that contemporaries expected. Despite all the predictions about a split in the Labour Party, Callaghan's backbenchers trooped into line, and despite all the warnings about the terrible damage the cuts would do to Britain's economic recovery, none of them came true. Almost as soon as the IMF team had packed their bags, the pound's value began to soar and interest rates gradually came down. Inflation continued to fall, and by the middle of 1977 Healey felt able to cut taxes and stimulate growth. Even unemployment went up much less than Benn had predicted. 'In all honesty,' admitted Peter Shore, who had been one of the Chancellor's most stubborn adversaries, 'it didn't have that dramatic deflationary impact which I so feared at the time.'[27]

The biggest irony of the IMF crisis, though, was that it was based on dodgy figures. In an almost unbelievable twist, it transpired that the Treasury had been far too pessimistic about Britain's position. Instead of borrowing almost £11 billion a year, Britain was actually borrowing only £8.5 billion, which meant that Healey only needed half of the IMF's money and was able to repay it more quickly than anybody had expected. Some observers have even concluded that the whole crisis was a nefarious plot by 'right-wing' Treasury officials and grasping American bankers to drag Britain away from socialism. But this is nonsense. There was no Treasury plot, not least because Healey's senior officials were so divided about the right course. The exaggerated borrowing figures were the result of cock-up, not conspiracy. As Healey himself noted, the Treasury consistently got its forecasts wrong: only two years earlier, it had underestimated public borrowing by a massive £4 billion. There was nothing suspicious about this: despite its image of Machiavellian omnipotence, the Treasury in the mid-1970s was muddled and confused, struggling to make out the contours of a new landscape through a fog of uncertainty. Against a background of soaring inflation and stagnant growth, forecasting had become a mug's game.[28]

In essence, though, the issue of the forecasts was completely irrelevant. Given the horrendous pressure on the pound, all that mattered was to satisfy the IMF and the markets. And what the markets cared about, as the Treasury official Sir Derek Mitchell later remarked, was 'not the reality but the sentiment'. Britain was paying the price for the course it had taken since the spring of 1974, when Wilson and Healey had refused to squeeze inflation out of the system, as every other major Western country had done. The markets had seen plenty of rosy Treasury forecasts in the past, and had long since learned not to trust them. The government might well protest that the economy was improving, but they had heard it all before. They wanted a symbolic display of contrition, a ritual demonstration of hair-shirted repentance, a 'penalty for past misbehaviour', as Edmund Dell put it. In this context, the only thing that mattered was to win back their confidence, and that meant big sacrifices. 'Denis was right,' Professor Maurice Peston, then Roy

Hattersley's chief economic adviser, later admitted. 'If the IMF had said that the entire Cabinet had to jump off Westminster Bridge, you would have had to jump off Westminster Bridge.'[29]

On the left, the government's decision to put international confidence first was seen as a disgraceful betrayal of its socialist commitments. As the years went by, hard-left activists came to see this as the moment when socialism was definitively betrayed, casting Callaghan and Healey as the road-sweepers who cleared the way for Margaret Thatcher. 'The IMF counter-revolution', claimed the activist Ken Coates four years later, had forced Labour 'into reneging on its fundamental post-war commitment to welfare, and [into] major concessions to monetarist prescriptions'.[30]

Tony Benn, too, claimed that the IMF crisis marked 'the beginning of what subsequently came to be known as Thatcherism'. Of course he might have resigned in protest. As usual, though, he preferred to polish his principles in a nice ministerial office rather than in the cramped conditions of the back benches. In Whitehall he cut an increasingly lonely, semi-detached figure. His permanent secretary at the Department of Energy told Bernard Donoughue that Benn '*never* takes decisions, never commits himself, never forms a firm policy – because he doesn't want to offend any political interests, especially the unions . . . Much of the time of Benn and his special advisers is spent dealing with these outside interests, in the unions and in the Party.'[31]

Benn's alternative strategy would probably have been a catastrophe. For one thing, he consistently refused to accept that a siege economy would probably annihilate what was left of British manufacturing. What was more, he seemed completely indifferent to the importance of financial discipline and international confidence, as though he could simply wish away the new world of global competition and fluctuating exchange rates. 'What the left don't realize', the Labour moderate David Owen told Hugo Young in September 1976, 'is that literally no policy can succeed which does not have international support.' For Callaghan and Healey, as for much of Britain's political and financial elite, the IMF crisis marked the moment when globalization really sank in; the moment when Fortress Britain, whether socialist or not, crumbled into dust. Yet in Benn's imagination the rest of the world appeared as a sinister conspiracy of American bankers, European moneylenders and multinational corporations, plotting to undermine British socialism. And while Callaghan recognized that the nation-state was not necessarily the answer to everything, Benn remained a Little Englander to the last. One exchange tells a wider story. In March 1979 Benn complained that British businesses were allowed to order coal from Australia and ships from Japan because they were cheaper than the domestic alternatives. 'We mustn't be insular,' Callaghan said wearily. 'This is a world problem ... The state can't do much to stop it. Nobody knows the answer. I cannot offer a plan.' Benn was horrified. 'This is Jim abandoning his role as a British Prime Minister,' he wrote afterwards, 'let alone as the Leader of the Labour Party.' But at least Callaghan could see that the world was changing. For Benn, it was as though the summer of 1945 had never ended.[32]

The IMF crisis is often described as a watershed in modern British history. Yet what is remarkable is how *little* changed, not how much. It is a myth, for example, that the IMF forced Healey to concentrate on fighting inflation. In fact, he had been trying to get inflation down since the beginning of 1975. It is a myth that it ushered in an age of cuts, for he had been cutting spending for months already.* It is a myth, too, that the IMF forced the government to adopt cash limits on public spending. In reality, cash limits had been introduced the previous summer, covering about 80 per cent of public spending by the autumn of 1976. Far from the IMF forcing the government to abandon the post-war consensus, therefore, it actually gave its seal of approval to policies that Healey had been pursuing *already*, much to the displeasure of the left. Indeed, the untold story of the IMF crisis is the extent to which Healey used the issue of international confidence, personified by the bankers in grey suits, as a way to get his cuts through the Cabinet. Years later, Callaghan claimed that he, too, had always been in favour of cuts. 'I had no doubt about that, irrespective of the International Monetary Fund or anything else,' he said, 'although it's easy for people to say, "Oh, the IMF did it." The IMF, of course, were an instrument in it, but they certainly didn't do it. I myself was convinced after a few months as Prime Minister.'[33]

The other common view of the IMF crisis is that it was a milestone in Britain's conversion to monetarism. But here too the story is rather more complicated than a simple tale of wicked IMF bankers imposing monetarism on a helpless government. For years the Bank of England had been flirting with elements of monetarism, and by late 1973 the

---

* Of course, the December 1976 cuts were slightly different: for the first time Healey was cutting the total level of spending rather than merely the *growth* of spending. The fact remains, though, that cuts had been on the agenda for more than a year; all that had changed was their severity.

Bank had adopted secret money supply targets. And Peter Jay was not the only Labour supporter who thought that, at a time of runaway inflation, monetary targets might have something to offer. Even Bernard Donoughue thought that 'crude Keynesianism', with its apparent obsession with high public spending, was driving up inflation and unemployment. As early as May 1974, he had sent Harold Wilson a paper by Andrew Graham suggesting a special Cabinet committee on monetary policy, which Wilson promptly ignored. Nineteen months later, the Policy Unit again wrote to Wilson suggesting 'a stricter monetarist approach to government finances'. Once again he did nothing. In the end, it was not until July 1976 that money supply targets were published for the first time. And though Healey made little fuss about it, casually mentioning the new target in the middle of his cuts announcement, *The Times* thought it merited a front-page story, calling it 'a major innovation in economic policy'.[34]

The irony was that, although his critics claimed he was a Tory monetarist in sheep's clothing, the Chancellor was never a true believer. In his memoirs, he called himself an 'eclectic pragmatist', borrowing from the latest theories whenever it suited him. He started publishing monetary targets, he admitted, purely 'in order to satisfy the markets'. If they cared about such things, they could have them, even though he never really believed in them himself. In fact, he wrote later, he had 'never met a private or central banker who believed the monetarist mumbo-jumbo', not least because 'no one has yet found an adequate definition of money, no one knows how to control it, and no one except Friedman himself is certain exactly how the control of money supply will influence inflation, which is supposed to be its only purpose'. All the same, Healey took 'a grim satisfaction' in the fact that he actually proved a much more effective monetarist than his successor. 'Geoffrey Howe, who unlike me was a believing monetarist, let the money supply expand twice as fast as I had,' he noted gleefully, 'and overshot his monetary targets by 100 per cent in his first two and a half years.'[35]

What the IMF crisis really marked was not so much the advent of monetarism as the death knell for Keynesianism. If Callaghan had pronounced the last rites at the Labour Party conference, then the deal with the IMF was a long wake, albeit one with some of the mourners protesting that the deceased was still breathing. Keynesianism had now fallen a long way from fashion: it seemed fitting that its most stubborn defenders, Tony Crosland and Reggie Maudling, were both decrepit boy wonders, characterized in the one case by physical deterioration, arrogance and indolence, and in the other by physical deterioration, arrogance, indolence and corruption. But this was not just a British phenomenon: across the Western world, Keynesianism seemed in headlong retreat. In May 1977, Healey and Callaghan discussed the impossibility of returning to full employment, 'because all the other countries were against any action on growth and employment'. 'Keynesianism has failed,' Healey said bluntly. And when Helmut Schmidt returned to London a year later, he sounded a very similar note. He had no intention of reflating the German economy, he told them, because 'it did not work. We no longer knew what "demand" was and how it worked. The attempt to stimulate economies artificially simply produced inflation and not growth.' The Prime Minister himself could hardly have put it better.[36]

Callaghan ended the year 'tired but relieved'. Despite being a teetotaller, he cut a cheerful and avuncular figure at Whitehall's Christmas parties, and spent the holiday with his grandchildren at Chequers. Few modern Prime Ministers had endured such a baptism of fire; few had come through so skilfully. But there was no escape from the pressures of the job: even on Christmas Day, messages poured into the Chequers communication room, where, he recalled, 'the duty clerks handled them amid mince pies and turkey'.[37]

His Chancellor, meanwhile, was in Sussex, hosting his 90-year-old father and 87-year-old mother at the family cottage. 'Our day's very ordinary, and traditional, and ritualistic,' Healey told the columnist Jean Rook, pointing out the tree decorations he had owned for more than twenty years. The Healeys never went to church, but they had a ceremony of their own: every year they did 'the choo-choo train', parading 'in a long line round the house, singing carols'. They always had turkey and, when they remembered, they usually listened to the Queen's Christmas message. As for presents, Healey always gave records or second-hand books, and expected exactly the same in return. 'Clothes are wasted on him,' sighed his wife Edna. But, like middle-aged men up and down the country, what he really enjoyed, 'the most marvellous ritual', was getting out 'the colour slides of the family since the year dot'. The twist was that Healey liked to provide an appropriate musical accompaniment. 'When we get to the holidays in the Alps,' Edna explained, 'he yodels. Then we all fall about, killing ourselves and shrieking, "Oh, God, don't tell me I looked like that!"'

The headlines were dominated by what the press called 'the great Christmas rip-off', with grocery shops supposedly selling vegetables 'at jewellers' prices', while the tabloids had got excited about the birth of a baby boy to television's newest star, the 'pretty, blue-eyed' *Nationwide* presenter Sue Lawley. The race for the Christmas number one was something of a non-event, since everybody knew that Johnny Mathis's saccharine 'When a Child is Born' was bound to win. A more appropriate winner might have been Abba's number three hit 'Money, Money, Money'; no doubt Denis Healey, who had indeed worked all night and worked all day to pay the bills he had to pay, would have sympathized with the sentiment. But as always, it was the small screen that dominated the festive season, with Christmas Day offering such treats as the *Rod Hull and Emu* Christmas special, the *John Curry Ice Spectacular* with Millicent Martin and Wayne Sleep, and the now traditional *Morecambe and Wise*, with Elton John, Des O'Connor and Dennis Waterman, as well as the high-kicking Angela Rippon. And as the Prime Minister was enjoying a bracing walk around the estate, drinking in the winter air, even his critics found a little Christmas spirit. Perhaps, mused the *Express*, 'we are quite lucky in old Jim Callaghan. He has his faults – which we have dwelt on before, and will do so again – but there is a certain decency about the man.'[38]

Some things, though, never changed. On Boxing Day British soldiers shot and killed a Catholic man in County Tyrone; four days later, a 67-year-old security guard died in hospital after having been shot by republicans planting a bomb in a Portadown pub. And on 1 January, just hours into the New Year, one-year-old Graeme Dougan was killed when an IRA car bomb exploded just yards away from his parents' house in Glengormley, County Antrim. The killings were a brutal reminder that, for all the festive cheer, Britain still had more than its fair share of problems. Opinion polls found that fully 64 per cent disapproved of the government's record, easily the worst figure since Wilson's nadir in the late 1960s. What might be called the 'feel-bad factor' could hardly be more alarming: 24 per cent thought the economy would 'deteriorate a lot' and 27 per cent that it would 'deteriorate a little' in the next twelve months, with only 1 per cent thinking that it would 'improve a lot'. And once again, Hughie Green had a patriotic message for the viewers of *Opportunity Knocks*:

In your farewell to 1976, did you see Britain old and worn, on the brink of ruin, bankrupt in all but heritage and hope, and even those were in pawn? Where do we go from here, if time, bought with borrowed money, is lost for lack of conscience?

We British – Scots, Welsh, English, Irish – who in the past earned respect throughout the world – have one more loan to come. One more transfusion for the nation that twice, twice nearly bled to death for freedom. The nation that Churchill offered only blood and toil, tears and sweat. Have we really lost what he once inspired in us – the dignity of work, the urge to salvage honour, the will to win? Do we need loans for these?

Let us take – yes, take – not borrow, this year of 1977. Let it be our year to lift up our heads and resolve that this time next year, we can say, 'We did it, and it cost nothing but determination, hard work, freedom from strikes, better management, and from all of us, *guts*,' lest without these virtues, we lose our freedom for ever.

Sadly for Green, although not for anybody else, his New Year turned out rather differently. Although he released his lecture as a single, accompanied by a massed choir singing 'Stand up, and be counted / Take up a fighting stance / This year of 1977 may be our final chance!', it failed to make the charts. A few months later, exasperated by his fondness for political asides, Thames Television gave him the boot. For the channel's director of programmes, Jeremy Isaacs, Green's 'mixture of patriotism and propaganda' had been both 'excruciating and inappropriate'. In his place Thames hired Capital Radio's young disc jockey Kenny Everett, whose derisive style could hardly have been more different from Green's ingratiating patter. For the man who had given Britain such delights as Paul Daniels, Les Dawson and Little and Large, it was a sorry comedown. 'My crime', Green said later, 'is that I always aimed my shows at an audience that lived beyond the borders of Eaton Square.' And like so many commentators in the mid-1970s, he drew an ominous conclusion. 'The Reds aren't under the beds, they're right in there running programming,' he fumed. 'Why else did they stop me praising our heritage, and giving viewers good old rousing patriotic stuff to get this country back on our feet?'[39]

22

The Break-up of Britain

*Down to Llandovery for lunch. Lavish buffet at the King's
Arms for £1, drinkable wine 30p the beaker. Low-beamed hall
thronged with feasting sons of Dyfed. Loudspeaker plays God
Bless the Prince of Wales, and Glyn points out gloomy red-
bearded customer, retired C-in-C, Free Wales Army. 'Got his
lawyer with him' – 'He would have, it's court day.'*

Guardian, 18 January 1975

*They're both stylish, tough, great performers and they're both
proven winners. Great British winners.*

Scottish World Cup-themed advertisement for
the Chrysler Avenger, May 1978

Amid all the headlines about terrorists, strikers and hooligans, one menace above all haunted parents in the mid-1970s. Like so many plagues,
the tartan terror had begun innocuously enough. The first signs of infec-
tion were apparent just before Harold Wilson's return to office, when
'Remember (Sha-La-La)' reached number six in the singles chart, but at
that stage the epidemic seemed unlikely to survive the summer. But then
more hits followed. In late May, 'Shang-A-Lang' peaked at number two,
and a few weeks later 'Summerlove Sensation' reached number three. By
late October, when 'All of Me Loves All of You' peaked at number four,
it was clear that the plague would not easily be beaten. And as Britain's
new pop sensations launched their first nationwide tour, the *NME*
reluctantly conceded defeat. 'In the same week that Muhammad Ali
regained his heavyweight boxing title,' the magazine announced at the
end of the month, 'the featherweight crown of pop, too, has changed

hands. It now rests firmly on the well-coiffured heads of the Bay City Rollers.'[1]

To those old enough to remember the early days of the Beatles, Rollermania seemed distinctly familiar. Like their predecessors, the Bay City Rollers had evolved from an amateur band, formed in the late 1960s by teenage brothers from Edinburgh, Alan and Derek Longmuir. Like the Beatles, they owed much of their success to a domineering manager – in their case Tam Paton, a Prestonpans potato merchant's son who was later convicted of abusing teenage boys. And, like the Beatles, the Rollers broke through as an unthreatening, family-friendly band, appealing not just to teenage girls, but to older listeners, too. 'We've got mums and dads in the fan club – everyone from ten years old to 60,' boasted their lead singer, Les McKeown. 'We've even got some grannies.' Not surprisingly, older rock writers despised them. 'They're young, polite and pasteurised . . . attentive, mild and housetrained,' complained the *NME*'s Pete Erskine. But in an age of deep moral anxiety, those values were the key to the Bay City Rollers' appeal. 'Don't you think, in this day and age,' asked Tam Paton, 'when we have so much trouble and terrorism and blowings up and things laik [*sic*] that, the kids want to be happy and go along to a concert where they can scream, wet their knickers and have a really great time? Really? I mean, isn't that what music's all about?'[2]

For all the sneering, the Rollers' formula worked. By the end of 1974, their debut album was selling more than 75,000 copies a week, and when the guitarist Eric Faulkner celebrated his twenty-first birthday, fans sent him an estimated 25,000 cards and 5,000 parcels. And by the spring of 1975, Rollermania seemed irresistible. Released in March, 'Bye Bye Baby' held the top spot for six weeks and sold more copies than any other single of the year. 'The Rollers inspire extremes of emotion – slavish adulation from their hardcore fans and out-and-out resentment from those who see them as the lowest common denominator in music,' remarked the *NME*. 'But, like them or loathe them, sales are hard to argue with.' Even more striking than their sales, though, were the scenes that greeted the five young Scots when they played at theatres across the country:

> The Rollers play exactly the same set every night and receive exactly the same uncritical response from a houseful of teenage girls decked out in tartan scarves and wearing the identikit shortened trousers.
>
> Their audience is aged between 10 and 15, and their enthusiasm can realistically be compared with Hitler's Nuremberg rallies.

The hysteria is akin to rolling snowballs down hills – it needs just one fan to rush the stage before scores of screaming girls will push, fight, scratch and kick their way forward to obtain a better view or even to touch a Roller's stacked sole.

The group's music is barely audible, partly because of their woefully inadequate PA and partly because 2,000 schoolgirls can create a horrendous din if the mood takes them.

Even the *NME* thought that the hysteria was getting out of hand, especially when the Rollers played in their native Edinburgh. 'Girls were being trodden underfoot in the melee,' wrote one observer, 'and the front row of seats became dislodged from the floor and smashed as more and more surged into the crowd. There were at least a dozen cases of fainting, and twice girls pretended to be overcome in order to be lifted up stagewards.'[3]

The Rollers dominated the newspapers that summer. In Cardiff, more than 70 girls were injured when fans tried to storm the stage; in Hammersmith, another 250 girls had to be treated for 'hysteria and shock'; in Oxford, 60 girls had to be given first aid after fighting broke out when two St John's Ambulance men 'grabbed a hysterical girl who had jumped from the front row into the orchestra pit'. In every town in the country, girls 'in their standard uniform of half-mast trousers with tartan stripes, ringed football socks and tartan scarves' thumbed excitedly through the latest Roller magazines. All this was irresistibly reminiscent of the Beatles' breakthrough twelve years before: the same talk of girlish 'hysteria', the same anecdotes about teenagers leaving venues sodden with sweat and urine, the same tabloid headlines about sieges and mobs. There was, however, one glaring difference. Whereas the Beatles' success had been built on the songwriting talents of Lennon and McCartney, the Rollers were little more than backward-looking teenyboppers, repackaging old hits for prepubescent girls. By the end of 1975 they were running out of steam, and when their founder Alan Longmuir walked out a few months later, it was clear that the Bay City Rollers' golden moment had passed. In wardrobes across the country, tartan-trimmed cut-off jeans gathered dust, embarrassing relics of a craze that had burned itself out.[4]

In a way, though, those tartan trousers were wonderfully suggestive. Only a few years before, the notion that tartan might become a teenage fashion symbol would have seemed absurd, for while Scotland had produced plenty of outstanding musicians, it was often seen as a bit of a

cultural backwater. But by the mid-1970s all that had changed. For the
Scottish football fans who followed their national team to the 1974 and
1978 World Cups, tartan was a symbol of their new self-assurance, a
reminder that their heroes had succeeded where England's finest had
failed. Basking in the anticipated benefits of North Sea oil, many Scots
looked forward to a new golden age of cultural and political
independence – and they were not alone. In Wales, where there were
now sixty-two primary schools and seven secondary schools teaching
entirely in Welsh, talk of potential independence was no longer seen as
a ludicrous fantasy, but as a possible long-term objective. Grand imperial allegiances seemed to be dying out; in an age when small was
beautiful, local identities were at last reasserting themselves. Once seen
as erratic and eccentric, Celtic nationalism was in danger of becoming
fashionable: for thousands of Scottish Bay City Rollers fans or Welsh
rugby supporters at Cardiff Arms Park, their Celtic roots were something to celebrate. And now that the British Empire had disappeared,
some asked, how long before the United Kingdom followed suit?[5]

One cold morning in February 1975, Michael Foot paid an unhappy
visit to his Ebbw Vale constituency. Addressing 2,000 steelworkers at
Ebbw Vale Civic Centre, the white-haired champion of the left stood
alone on the platform while his constituents jeered for ten minutes.
'Traitor!' they yelled. 'Go back to Devonport! Give Foot the boot!'
'Never', wrote one observer, 'has an MP in this Labour fortress been so
unpopular.' But it was not hard to see why. A few days before, the
nationalized British Steel Corporation had announced it was closing the
Ebbw Vale steelworks, throwing almost 5,000 people out of work
almost overnight. In what *The Times* called a 'one-industry valley', the
news was a disaster; across Wales as a whole, however, it was becoming
a familiar story.[6]

For decades, steelmaking and coalmining had been the twin pillars of
working-class Welsh identity. But now, with British industry under terrible pressure from new global competitors, those pillars were tottering.
In 1960 some 106,000 Welshmen had worked down the mines; by
1979, however, there were just 30,000. Across the principality, unemployment remained stubbornly high: a few months after the Ebbw
Vale closure, the Welsh TUC described job prospects for school-leavers
as 'the worst for 30 years'. 'These are difficult days for optimists,' admitted *The Times*. 'To many Welshmen the prospect from Snowdon this
morning seems decidedly dismal ... against a background of rising

unemployment, clouds thicken over the steel towns of Wales.' Even the capital, Cardiff, seemed in deep trouble. Visiting Tiger Bay, the novelist Gwyn Thomas lamented that 'the noise and the passion are gone. The mountains of coal that once went out from the bunkers of these docks have dwindled to molehills hardly large enough to sustain comfort in an average vestry.' Even the 'portentous exchanges', where once 'India and Africa were regarded as suburbs of Loudun Square and Cathedral Road, Cardiff', were now 'as quiet as the grave'.[7]

In Scotland, which was even more dependent on the old heavy industries, the situation was even worse. Even before the downturn of 1973–4, male unemployment in Glasgow was running at almost 10 per cent. More than thirty men were chasing every job, most of them in their twenties or thirties and more than half without any skills at all. On the banks of the Clyde, the success of the Upper Clyde Shipbuilders' work-in could not mask a growing sense of decay and dilapidation. In the mid-1950s, Scotsmen had built more than one in ten of the world's ships; by the early 1970s, overtaken by foreign competitors, they made less than one in a hundred. As a result, unemployment was far higher in Scotland than in the South of England or the Midlands, and only marginally better than in the North, reaching more than 8 per cent by 1978. In some areas the levels of deprivation seemed almost Victorian: according to a report in 1976, Clydeside accounted for 90 per cent of the most concentrated urban poverty in Britain. Although both Heath and Wilson tried to attract new investment through regional planning, much of Scotland seemed in danger of turning into a ward of the state. By the mid-1970s, the Scottish share of public spending per head was already 20 per cent higher than that in England. And by the end of the decade, no fewer than 54 per cent of Scottish households lived in rented council accommodation, a higher proportion than in many states of the Communist bloc.[8]

To some of those left high and dry by the tides of globalization, the answer was obvious: Wales and Scotland must cast off the shackles of British oppression, and step forward as independent nations. Both nursed a strong sense of cultural distinctiveness. In Wales, for example, the all-conquering rugby side of Gareth Edwards, Barry John and Phil Bennett became the focus for intense national pride. Singing 'Hen Wlad fy Nhadau' before each match became the supreme ritual of Welsh patriotism, while some spectators even wore T-shirts proclaiming their support for the tiny Free Wales Army. The crowds 'swaying sparkle-eyed' at Cardiff Arms Park, wrote one observer, 'are involved in a great communal experience, in the electric unity of tribalism ... Many of them do not know the meaning of the Welsh words of the anthem that they learned parrot-fashion at school or chapel or grandfather's knee. Yet there is an element in their singing of affirming their identity.' Managers and players alike saw rugby as a channel for the national spirit: Clive Rowlands, the Welsh coach until 1974, urged his players to perform 'not just for yourself but for your father, your mother, your long-lost aunt, the miners, the steelworkers, the teachers, the schoolchildren'. And in 1977 Phil Bennett delivered a famously nationalistic call to arms before Wales's match against England, capturing the feelings of thousands of his fellow countrymen. 'These English you're just going out to meet have taken our coal, our water, our steel; they buy our houses and live in them a fortnight a year,' he told his comrades. 'Down the centuries these English have exploited and pillaged us – and we're playing them this afternoon, boys.'[9]

For some observers, Wales's stunning record between 1969 and 1979, when they won three Grand Slams, two Triple Crowns and eight Five Nations titles in all, was entirely fitting. 'I do not think that it is mere fancy to say that in some ways Welsh rugby reflects the mood of modern Wales, the new confidence and pride in Welshness,' wrote Trevor Fishlock, an English journalist who lived in Wales, in 1976. And by many standards, Welsh cultural identity genuinely seemed more vibrant and self-confident than at any point in living memory. The long battle for language rights had been won: the Welsh Language Act of 1967 had given Welsh equal status in law and government, bilingual signs were becoming the norm, and in 1977 the BBC launched the Welsh-language Radio Cymru. Meanwhile, the Party of Wales had come a long way from the days when its members had been mocked as eccentric folk enthusiasts. In 1966, Plaid Cymru's mild-mannered, cricket-loving leader Gwynfor Evans had won its first Westminster seat at the Carmarthen by-election. And although both the Tories and Labour treated Plaid with contempt (it offered 'flower politics for flower people' was Edward Heath's rather peculiar verdict), it won two seats in February 1974 and a third in October. Rural, moderate, pacifist and liberal-minded, Plaid seemed ideally placed to profit from a cultural climate in which green was good and small was beautiful.[10]

From another perspective, though, the mid-1970s were frustrating years for Welsh nationalists. Polls showed only a tiny majority in favour of devolution, and nationalist support was weak outside the Welsh-speaking west and north, where Plaid had effectively succeeded the Liberals. In the Labour strongholds of South Wales and the mining valleys, which had attracted large numbers of English and Irish immigrants, many people viewed the nationalist cause with deep suspicion. The Party of Wales was nothing more than a vehicle for 'irrational, insatiable ... vulgar and aggressive nationalism', the Labour MP for Pontypool, Leo Abse, said contemptuously, mocking 'the mumbo-jumbo of primitive nationalism'. For the young Neil Kinnock, meanwhile, Celtic nationalism was a bourgeois 'distraction' from the real issues. Kinnock loathed Plaid Cymru, seeing them as 'mournful Druid fanatics'. He even detested Welsh-language television, claiming that most people would rather watch an imported Western than 'the fascinating story of Roman gold mining in Dyfed as told in Welsh'. And for all the ostentatious passion of the Welsh rugby supporters, there were limits to their patriotic zeal. Even their crushing victories over England, thought the Welsh historian Kenneth Morgan, were 'a peaceful therapy to suppress embarrassing political aspirations ... Most of the Welsh were content to have it that way. They rejoiced in their rugby skills, made no protest, and asked few questions.'[11]

It was a similar story in Scotland. There too a nationalist party, founded in the 1930s, had struggled to shed its image as a 'tartan ghetto' for students, poets and bohemian aristocrats. As late as 1960 the Scottish National Party had fewer than twenty active branches and no more than 2,000 members. Like Plaid Cymru, however, the SNP made tremendous strides in the following decade. In November 1967 it won its first parliamentary seat when Winnie Ewing, a Glasgow solicitor, won the Hamilton by-election, attracting more press coverage than the party had enjoyed in the previous twenty years put together. With the aristocratic and amateurish Scottish Conservative Party in long-term decay, space had opened up for the SNP in the New Towns of central Scotland, which had been badly hit by unemployment and surging inflation. SNP activists were no longer just professors and eccentrics: they were clerks, decorators, salesmen and surveyors, drawn from the lower-middle classes. As in Wales, though, there seemed a limit to what they could achieve. Polls showed that three out of four Scots liked the idea of Home Rule – a far higher proportion than in Wales, reflecting the fact that Scotland still had its own legal system, school system and national church. But although the SNP put up a record 65 candidates in the 1970 election, 43 of them lost their deposits, their overall vote fell and they won only one seat (the Western Isles). At that stage there seemed little prospect of a major breakthrough. What changed things was oil.[12]

'The wind-whipped waters of the North Sea usually roil in a fit of rage, the skies are oppressively gray, and the fog hangs on for weeks,' declared *Time* in the spring of 1973. For more than a decade, rival companies had been scouring the sea between Scotland and Norway, gambling that the freezing waters concealed major oil and gas reserves. By November 1969 some 32 wells had been drilled on the continental shelf, not one yielding reserves in commercially viable quantities. After so much money and effort, the oil companies were close to throwing in the towel. But a few days after the Apollo astronauts had landed on the moon, the rig *Ocean Viking* made a stunning find in the Ekofisk field. Studying a sample brought from 10,000 feet beneath the seabed, the rig's superintendent could barely contain his excitement. 'What the astronauts have done is great,' he told his geologist, 'but how about this?' He held up the sample: it had a glossy, golden sheen, the sign of very high quality. A year later BP struck oil in the Forties field, on the British-side of the demarcation line. In the next day's *Times* it was the lead story. Oil was no 'magic solution to Britain's economic problems', cautioned an editorial; still, this surely meant 'a fundamental change in the country's economic prospects'. Other papers, however, threw off the shackles of caution. 'The prospects are glistening,' exulted the *Express*. 'Jackpot!'[13]

The technical challenges were enormous. Stormy, cold and unpredictable, the North Sea was widely regarded as 'one of the world's most inhospitable places to look for oil'. So deep and fierce were the waves that the drilling platforms were built 700 feet tall, the size of Europe's tallest office buildings. They stood on a treacherous base of mud, quicksand and clay, buffeted by winds that often approached hurricane speeds. Nobody had ever tried to drill for oil through deeper waters – and once the drill reached the seabed, it still had to travel thousands of feet through rock. And because the choppy waters made it difficult and dangerous to load the oil onto tankers, the oil companies had to install two gigantic floating platforms with huge storage tanks. Each cost an estimated $300 million; merely towing them into place (162 miles to one field and 225 to the other) cost a further $3 million, making it the most expensive tugboat operation in history. But the story of North Sea oil was a feat of human courage as well as an extraordinary marvel of engineering. With the weather changing three or four times a day and ferocious storms likely at any moment, the risks to life and limb were immense: by September 1975, some twenty-one men had been killed in drowning and mechanical accidents. Visiting the first working platform, Tony Benn marvelled at the bravery of the workers, who were flown in by helicopter and toiled in desperately difficult conditions. 'In the middle of winter when the conditions are exceptionally rough, it must be absolute hell to work there,' he thought. 'It is a complete science fiction world and it is a sobering thought that our future as a nation depends upon the Forties Field and others like it.'[14]

Benn was not alone in his view that North Sea oil had the potential to transform Britain's future. Ever since its discovery, the black gold had been hailed as a gift from heaven, a miracle that would drive a new technological revolution. That the discovery had arrived just before the 1973 oil shock only made it appear all the more exciting. Nature's bounty had arrived in time 'to save us from relegation to the third division', wrote the Conservative MP Laurance Reed. 'The 1980s will be Britain's decade. We shall become one of the most influential of nations.' This might sound wildly over-optimistic, but even abroad his view was widely shared. 'In Britain, North Sea oil stands for nothing less than national survival,' explained *Time* magazine in September 1975. 'It offers an opportunity for Britain to become not only self-sufficient in energy but also a modest exporter, probably in the 1980s, pumping oil revenues into its sick economy, wiping out its balance of payments deficit and reversing 30 years of economic decline.' Inside Wilson's Cabinet, too, there was great excitement. Puffing on his pipe in the Downing Street study in the summer of 1975, Wilson told the *New York Times* that North Sea oil would fundamentally transform Britain's economic prospects. Perhaps, he mused, he might become chairman of OPEC in five years' time.[15]

In Scotland the oil bonanza had a dramatic effect, from the spectral silhouettes in the foggy seas to the newfound excitement in Edinburgh's moribund merchant banks. Later there was fierce criticism of the Heath government's largesse with exploration licences, which were given away free to the oil companies in 100-mile-square 'blocks'. Even its tax arrangements seemed remarkably overgenerous, with the British exchequer collecting only 60 per cent of the oil profits, compared with the typical 75–80 per cent share in the Middle East. The government had behaved like a 'gullible Sheikhdom,' declared a scathing report by the Public Accounts Committee. Only when Harold Wilson returned to office was the situation properly addressed, with the publicly owned British National Oil Corporation (BNOC) set up to buy 51 per cent of landed oil and sell it on at a profit. Yet it was not until the following decade that the Treasury really reaped the rewards. By the end of 1975, the oilfields were still producing only 34,000 barrels a day, and even in

Labour's last full year in office, North Sea oil production was barely 1.2 million barrels a day, less than half of its peak a few years later. Jim Callaghan had once described North Sea oil as a gift from God. Unfortunately for him, though, the Almighty had addressed it to a woman.[16]

Meanwhile, even remote corners of Scottish life were being radically transformed. In the Shetlands, the local council set up a trust to spend its winnings on a brand-new infrastructure of schools, hospitals, leisure centres and care homes, effectively creating a little state-funded paradise. But the biggest beneficiary of the oil bonanza was Scotland's third largest city, Aberdeen. By 1973 some 250 new companies, many of them American-owned, had moved in to supply everything from helicopters to packaged hot meals, while unemployment had fallen to less than half the Scottish average. When a reporter visited two years later, he thought that the Granite City had turned into a 'tartan Texas with an ego to match'. From the hilltops, the glass and concrete headquarters of the oil companies – Shell, BP, Occidental, Total – gazed down on the city; in the pubs, Stetson hats and cowboy boots had become familiar sights. Elsewhere, the Scottish economy was moribund, yet the labour exchange was giving away jobs 'at salaries which three years ago would have been unbelievable'. The airport was Britain's busiest outside London, while house prices were higher than almost anywhere outside the South-east of England. And plenty of people worried that amid all this money, Aberdeen's character was being lost. Once, wrote Roger Nicholson of the local *Press and Journal*, 'you could live and work anywhere in the city and be golfing, fishing and sailing within 10 minutes. Your children could go through primary school to a PhD without having to miss a midday meal at home.' But now, with the roads choked with commuter traffic and new housing developments sprawling along the Dee, 'all this is threatened'.[17]

North Sea oil transformed Scotland's political culture. For years, the SNP had struggled to counter the argument that if Scotland broke away from the United Kingdom, it would face a miserable, impoverished future. But as the Nationalist MP Margo MacDonald later reflected, the sense 'of just being too poor, of being the fag end, being the recipient of English largesse, was turned on its head when oil was discovered, because that knocked the economic argument out of the window'. For the first time, *The Times* admitted, 'independence becomes an option . . . Suddenly oil has done for the [Scottish National] party what its manipulation of the statistics of public finance could not.' Indeed, if the nationalists were to be believed, the Scots would be much richer if they rid themselves of the 'dead weight of England's colossal problems'. And as the Whitehall mandarin Sir Kenneth Berrill warned ministers in 1975, there was a lot of truth in the SNP's case. Given the likely oil profits, Berrill wrote, 'Scotland could go it alone quite comfortably.' Indeed, far from exaggerating the benefits of North Sea oil, the nationalists had actually *under*estimated them. 'All that is wrong now with the SNP estimate is that it is far too low,' reported the government economist Gavin McCrone at the beginning of 1974. If Scotland went it alone, he thought, oil revenues would put it 'in chronic surplus to a quite embarrassing degree', as well as giving it the strongest national currency in Europe. England, meanwhile, would be left 'in dire straits'. Not surprisingly, his report was never made public.[18]

In the meantime, the SNP were trying to turn black gold into votes. 'It's Scotland's Oil' ran the party's new slogan, while posters asked bluntly: 'Rich Scots or Poor Britons?' In January 1973 the campaign almost paid immediate dividends when the SNP came within just 1,200 votes of winning the Dundee East by-election, and by May's annual conference it was hard to miss the sense of expectation, even euphoria in the air. The United Kingdom was 'disintegrating', declared Donald Stewart, the Nationalist MP for the Western Isles, and Scotland must 'get out', lest it be dragged down by an England that was being 'eaten by the maggots of permissiveness and decay'. The conference even boasted a production of the controversial play *The Cheviot, the Stag and the Black, Black Oil*, written by the passionately left-wing dramatist John McGrath and performed by his touring company 7:84 – its name derived from the statistic that just 7 per cent of the British population owned 84 per cent of the nation's wealth. Tracing the capitalist exploitation of the Highlands from the days of the Clearances to the arrival of the oil companies, this was agitprop at its most uncompromising, seething with rage at the English ruling classes and their American allies. Revealingly, however, many of the company were uneasy about performing for an audience they regarded as 'bourgeois nationalists' and 'tartan Tories'. 'Nationalism is not enough!' insisted the socialist actress Elizabeth MacLennan when the play was over, much to the displeasure of many of her listeners.[19]

The next twelve months were an *annus mirabilis* for the Scottish Nationalist cause. In November 1973 the party contested another by-election, in Glasgow Govan, a solid Labour seat since the First World War. With thousands unemployed and the skyline dominated by concrete tower blocks, Govan was a byword for inner-city poverty. Trudging around the constituency, canvassers were horrified by the neglect, the deprivation, the rats scurrying along the gutters, the brick tenements with sheets of polythene over the windows. Almost nobody imagined that Labour could lose, but they had not bargained on Margo MacDonald, the SNP's outspoken young candidate. 'She has a sharp sense of humour and a skilful way of putting over the SNP political line . . . that all Scotland's and Govan's troubles could be overcome if Scotland had all the profits from North Sea oil,' wrote one correspondent. And when the votes were counted on 8 November, MacDonald had taken the seat with a staggering 27 per cent swing, sending shock waves through Westminster. Although she lost it in February 1974, the wider results were a triumph for her party, which took 22 per cent of the Scottish vote and sent seven MPs south to London. Within six months, the SNP had established more than 140 new branches; indeed, such was the popular enthusiasm that it ran out of membership forms. And when the dust had settled after the October election, the SNP had made even greater gains, winning more than 30 per cent of the vote and eleven seats. In terms of popular support – if not yet in seats – the nationalists were now Scotland's second biggest party.[20]

In London, the nationalist renaissance did not go unnoticed. In the late 1960s both major parties had established commissions to look into regional devolution, and in 1970 Edward Heath came out in favour of a new single-chamber Scottish assembly. Three years later the Kilbrandon Commission reported in favour of directly elected 100-member assemblies for both Scotland and Wales, much to the delight of nationalists everywhere. With Wilson finally committing Labour to assemblies on the Kilbrandon model, devolution seemed unstoppable. It even served as the premise of a pulp thriller, *Scotch on the Rocks* (1971), co-written by Heath's young aide Douglas Hurd and the *Private Eye* founder Andrew Osmond, which imagines a Scottish Liberation Army launching a violent uprising against their English neighbours, seizing the town of Fort William. After a brief struggle the terrorists are vanquished, but London concedes Home Rule and the SNP leader becomes Scotland's first Prime Minister. Two years later the BBC turned it into a five-part television series, provoking howls of anguish from Scottish nationalists unhappy at the implicit comparison with the Provisional IRA. Even the BBC's Programme Complaints Commission conceded that it had been a mistake to associate the SNP with revolutionary violence, and the series was never shown again. Still, it had at least one admirer north of Hadrian's Wall. Forty years later, Scotland's First Minister good-humouredly admitted that *Scotch on the Rocks* was one of his favourite books. It was, said Alex Salmond, 'a cracking read'.[21]

In its melodramatic way, *Scotch on the Rocks* reflected a growing sense that the United Kingdom was unlikely to survive for long in its current form. It was clear, for example, that with class loyalties being eroded by education, affluence, mobility and generational change, the days of stable two-party politics had gone for good. And perhaps, some thought, Britishness itself was in decline, too. 'The nation is beginning to look too big,' wrote Anthony Sampson in his astute *New Anatomy of Britain* (1971); 'it finds itself increasingly unable to provide the sense of identification, of belonging, or providing a convincing community to which its citizens can feel loyalty.' In a series of highly influential articles for the *New Left Review*, the academic Tom Nairn went even further. Britain, he claimed, had always been 'tied up with its empire ... No other nation was so dependent on imperialism or had got more out of it.' But with the empire long gone and Britishness itself associated with 'rapidly accelerating backwardness, economic stagnation, social decay and cultural despair', the United Kingdom was 'at the point of disintegration'. Celtic nationalism, Nairn thought, had become 'the grave-digger of the old state in Britain': a political revolution was at hand. A few years later, even the arch-Tory historian Arthur Bryant gave up the ghost. 'There is no unifying faith,' he wrote, 'to bind us together.'[22]

As events were to prove, Nairn's predictions of the imminent break-up of Britain were wildly overheated. Although almost all Scottish and Welsh voters were keenly patriotic, the great majority had no problem reconciling their Celtic and British identities. Polls throughout the mid-1970s found that only one in five Scots favoured independence, while in Wales the proportion was more like one in ten. In some ways the nationalist surge was a reflection of deep dissatisfaction with the Wilson and Heath governments, a Celtic equivalent of the Liberal renaissance in Middle England. Still, there was more to it than a middle-class protest vote. In Scotland, nationalism tapped a broad seam of patriotic sentiment, appealing to affluent working-class areas and rural towns as well as leafy middle-class suburbs. 'The Nationalists were always considered a bit of a giggle, but the giggle now is that I keep running into people who I had no idea were voting SNP,' remarked a Perthshire dairy farmer at the end of 1974. 'If we can say to the militant in the Clyde Valley and the right-wing estate owners, "Look here, we established this government together," why can't we also sit down and get on without all this class crap they have in England?' asked Pat Stewart-Blacker, a professional heraldist who had defected from the Tories. 'Well, that's Utopian, but there is a lot more confidence that we can come closer to it on our own up here. People no longer feel self-sufficiency is just a dream. This isn't a warning. The chips are down.'[23]

Behind the scenes, however, unity proved rather more elusive. For the SNP's young, upwardly mobile voters, there was more to life than patriotism, and as the party became more successful, it came under pressure to clarify its positions on economic issues. As the journalist Andrew Marr wrote a decade later, SNP spokesmen often tried to blur the question by talking about the 'New Politics', but in practice this usually meant 'blaming the English for everything and promising gurgling barrels of oil-rich dosh'. By the second half of the 1970s, party conferences were often dominated by bitter rows between left and right, with some delegates arguing for a more pragmatic, devolutionist strategy, others insisting on full independence, and a third group demanding a full-blooded socialist approach to Scotland's economic woes. At one point, relations between the SNP's Scotland-based leadership and its Westminster MPs almost broke down completely, with one meeting descending into acrimony when somebody threw a punch at the party's heroine Winnie Ewing. Fractious and divided, the SNP's senior figures were palpably struggling to cope with their own success – as indeed were the higher echelons of Plaid Cymru, torn apart by bitter bickering between former Labour left-wingers and middle-class mystical nationalists, as well as between pro-devolution moderates and pro-independence ultras.[24]

And yet as Wilson and Callaghan floundered in the face of the economic storm, success flowed the nationalists' way. In December 1975 polls put the SNP ahead of both Labour and the Conservatives for the first time, with support at 37 per cent. In May 1977 it made record gains in Scotland's local elections, making big inroads in Glasgow and the central industrial belt, and breaking the government's control of Edinburgh, Aberdeen and Dundee. Looking back later, the journalist James Naughtie remembered 'a heady sense of self-importance, an almost incestuous interest in all our institutions'. In nationalist circles there was a palpable sense of 'excitement', with some people expecting to see 'Embassy Row springing up somewhere in the terraces of Edinburgh'. In *The Times*, Peter Jay declared that if the Scots seized the chance 'to break away from the more malign aspects in the English financial tradition', encouraging inward investment and keeping inflation low, their future would be 'exceptionally bright'. Meanwhile, senior Scottish Nationalists were

WELCOME TO THE STATE OF SCOTLAND!
- LAND OF OIL AND OPPORTUNITY!
"The fairest sight to the Englishman's eye is the broad highway that leads to Scotland"

PASSPORT CONTROL

NEWS FROM ENGLAND GHASTLY AS USUAL

Cummings

"Unless we bring in an immigration act soon, there'll be more Englishmen
than Scots in Scotland, and Loch Ness will start running with blood . . ."

With Scottish self-confidence running high, even the ultra-conservative
Cummings began to wonder whether an oil-rich Scotland might be
better off on its own. Lurking in the queue of immigrants are
Denis Healey and Jim Callaghan, the latter disguised as an elderly
woman (*Daily Express*, 1 December 1976).

busy planning everything from the 'titles of district officers' to 'the size
of farms that would be permitted'. The chairman of their Defence Committee even spent 'hours and hours' discussing 'epaulettes and badges for
the regiments that would be taken out of the British Army' – an unusual
hobby, perhaps, but no doubt very satisfying.[25]

To most English observers, of course, all this seemed utterly bewildering. One typically insular middle-aged Englishman, his horizons
bounded by Agatha Christie, *Morecambe and Wise* and HP Sauce, told
friends that he found devolution 'a bit of a bore'. Yet, as always, Harold
Wilson was nothing if not pragmatic. Conscious that the surge in
nationalist sentiment threatened Labour's electoral hegemony in Wales
and Scotland, he saw devolution as the ideal way 'to weaken the forces
of separatism'. When the Cabinet discussed the issue in January 1975,
some of his ministers warned that 'we were on [a] slippery slope towards
the break-up of the UK'. 'The workers were against devolution,' added
Tony Benn, 'because it would break up the UK trade union movement'
(though what evidence he had for this is not at all clear). For once, however, Wilson's position was decisive. Devolution, he said, was 'the only
way to avoid separatism', and would stop the haemorrhage of Labour
voters to the SNP. 'We must get devolution rolling forward.'[26]

In November 1975 the government unveiled plans for a 142-member
Scottish assembly and a government run by a Cabinet chief executive,

with powers over local government, health, social services, schools and planning. Wales, meanwhile, would have a 72-member 'executive assembly', run on a committee system. Predictably, the plans drew criticism from all sides: the Tories claimed that the government was 'wrecking the United Kingdom', while the Liberals, the SNP and Plaid Cymru proclaimed themselves 'appalled' by the government's lack of 'courage and conviction'. 'We were promised more. We want more!' thundered the *Daily Record*. Yet it was revealing that, for all the talk of an irresistible tide of nationalism, public opinion remained divided and half-hearted. Polls carried out for the BBC showed that only 20 per cent of Scots favoured complete independence, while 30 per cent favoured an elected assembly with power to tax and spend, 30 per cent wanted a more limited assembly and 20 per cent wanted no change at all. In Wales, meanwhile, the polls made even less dramatic reading. Only 10 per cent of Welsh voters wanted independence, compared with 39 per cent who liked the idea of an elected assembly and 51 per cent who were dead against Home Rule. As for the English, most seemed to like the United Kingdom just as it was: two out of three said they saw no need for regional devolution at all.[27]

Devolution's progress through Parliament was almost comically tortuous. Under ferocious attack from both the Conservative right and the Labour left, the Scotland and Wales Bill staggered painfully through the Commons, receiving its second reading in December 1976. By this time Wilson had given way to Callaghan, who was even less interested in the issue than his predecessor. Indeed, most senior ministers thought the Cabinet committees on the devolution bill were 'immensely tedious', and many tried to get out of serving on them. Even Michael Foot, who was in charge of getting the bill through, found the endless meetings 'extremely boring'. His officials complained that whenever they tried to talk to him about the subject, Foot would turn on his television for the latest from the Test series between England and the West Indies. Given the sheer complexity of the Scotland and Wales Bill, though, few could blame him. 'It is more like some obscure Private Bill obsessed with its own tedium than a great constitutional document,' remarked the Tory MP Leon Brittan. Even the human rights lawyer Anthony Lester, who had been Roy Jenkins's special adviser until 1976, called it one of 'the worst conceived and executed constitutional measures to have been introduced by any modern British Government'.[28]

To the press and public alike, the interminable struggle over devolution seemed utterly baffling. Writing in November 1977, *The Times*'s

David Wood estimated that devolution would take up two-thirds of the government's time in the new Commons session, leaving very little room for any other legislation. Yet most voters, he pointed out, regarded it as a total distraction from the terrible realities of economic decline. What was particularly bewildering was the sheer confusion of the various positions. The Labour leadership supported devolution, but many left-wing Labour MPs were against it. In Wales, Neil Kinnock was only one of several Labour MPs fiercely opposed to the bill; in Scotland, Labour MPs such as Tam Dalyell and George Cunningham did all they could to derail it. As Dalyell pointed out, the creation of Welsh and Scottish assemblies would create a bizarre constitutional anomaly (the 'West Lothian question'). Under the government's plans, the MP for West Lothian would still be free to vote on English issues, yet English MPs would have 'no say on the same matters in Scotland, Wales and Northern Ireland'. This, Dalyell insisted, was 'a basic design fault in the steering of the devolutionary coach which will cause it to crash into the side of the road before it has gone a hundred miles'.* Other Labour MPs were even more scathing. Celtic nationalism, said Neil Kinnock, must be 'killed by the education of minds and the exposure of its idiocies'. 'Not a single interest of people anywhere in Wales – whether be it democratic, cultural or political,' he declared, 'will be advanced one inch by devolution.'[29]

Meanwhile the Conservatives were edging away from their former commitments. Visiting Edinburgh for the first time as leader, Margaret Thatcher claimed to be 'absolutely in tune with the theme of devolution', which turned out to be completely untrue. 'The establishment of a Scottish Assembly must be a top priority,' she even told an audience in Glasgow, 'to ensure that more decisions affecting Scotland are taken in Scotland by Scotsmen.' But she soon changed her tune. In her bones she was a classic middle-class Little Englander, devoted to the Union and bewildered by the strength of nationalist feeling. By the end of 1975, as her biographer notes, her commitment to devolution was already hedged with 'reservations and conditions', and she was quick to denounce Wilson's devolution plan as a recipe for bloated bureaucracy. As the Scotland and Wales Bill came up for its second reading, she

---

* He was wrong about that. When the Scottish and Welsh assemblies opened two decades later, the anomaly remained: the MP for West Lothian could vote on issues affecting West Bromwich, but the MP for West Bromwich had little real say over the affairs of West Lothian. But the predicted English revolt never materialized, and the coach stayed on the road.

persuaded her Shadow Cabinet colleagues to vote against it, provoking her Scottish spokesmen, Alick Buchanan-Smith and Malcolm Rifkind, to resign. In their place she promoted Teddy Taylor, a staunch unionist who liked nothing better than getting stuck into the SNP. By 1979, devolution had completely disappeared from the Conservative manifesto, which talked only of 'discussions about the future government of Scotland' and 'proposals for improved parliamentary control of administration in Wales'. From being the party of change, the Conservatives had returned to their natural position as the party of the Union – and of England.[30]

In the meantime, to widespread public indifference, the parliamentary battle dragged on. In February 1977 the Labour rebel Leo Abse forced through an amendment insisting that referendums be held in Scotland and Wales before the new assemblies could come into operation. Disastrously for the bill's fortunes, this alienated the SNP and Plaid Cymru, who wanted devolution without a referendum campaign. With its majority almost non-existent, the government had run out of room for manoeuvre, and when Foot tried to bring down the parliamentary guillotine, it was defeated by 312 votes to 283. So he had to start all over again, this time dividing the legislation into separate bills for Scotland and for Wales. Both passed their second readings in November, which meant that devolution seemed to be back on track. But on 25 January 1978 – Burns Night – the independent-minded Labour backbencher George Cunningham, who represented Islington South and Finsbury, made a crucial intervention. Amid extraordinary scenes – at one point the Serjeant at Arms was asked to clear the lobbies after reports that government supporters were staging a sit-in – Cunningham moved an amendment which required that for each referendum to pass, at least 40 per cent of the *entire electorate* – not just those voting – must vote Yes. A simple majority, in other words, was no longer enough.[31]

Although Cunningham was a Scotsman, he was no friend of devolution. The Labour leadership, he said later, 'were committed to go on marching into the sea, deeper and deeper, until their hats floated. It was necessary for someone else to call halt, and that's what we did.' He had got the idea from the young Edinburgh MP Robin Cook, a fierce critic of the Callaghan government, who initially suggested a 30 per cent threshold. It was Cunningham's idea to raise it to 40 per cent, which completely transformed the position. Given the polls, a Scottish Nationalist referendum victory had never been a sure thing; now it became a real challenge. Quite understandably, therefore, the nationalists were outraged. 'When the English start losing they change the rules of the game,' said the SNP's Douglas Henderson. 'If they're losing at football, they tell you it's cricket they're playing.' If the 40 per cent rule had applied to parliamentary elections, he pointed out, twentieth-century Britain would never have had a government. In Wales, meanwhile, Cunningham's amendment made victory virtually impossible. Only a few weeks earlier, a poll had found pro-devolution support falling to just 27 per cent, with opposition at 41 per cent. Even the secretary of the Welsh Labour Party, no devolutionist, thought the rule 'absurd, illogical and unfair', while Plaid Cymru's leader Gwynfor Evans was distraught. 'When a referendum comes,' he told one of his Labour friends, 'we shall lose disastrously.'[32]

A few weeks after Cunningham's intervention, the SNP had a chance for revenge. Thanks to the tragically early death of the Labour MP Alexander Wilson, there would be a by-election in his Hamilton constituency. Located on the south-eastern edge of the Glasgow conurbation, with an unemployment rate of 10 per cent and a high proportion of jobless school leavers, it seemed perfect nationalist territory. The SNP selected their 'prime crowd-puller', the passionately left-wing Margo MacDonald, briefly MP for Govan and widely seen as their 'warrior queen'. By contrast, Labour's candidate, a full-time trade union official called George Robertson seemed positively bland, a lamb to the slaughter. Most commentators expected the nationalists to win: after all, they only needed a swing of 4.6 per cent. And if they could do it, then they had a good chance of winning ten seats where they needed smaller swings, scything into Labour's Scottish heartlands. With a general election looming, declared *The Times*, Hamilton could prove 'a political and emotional watershed'.[33]

Although by-elections are traditionally held on Thursdays, Hamilton was brought forward to Wednesday to avoid clashing with the opening ceremony of the World Cup in Argentina. Of the home nations, only Scotland had qualified, and many observers thought that a triumphant Scottish campaign could have seismic political consequences. 'With their lips Jim and Maggie may be shouting for Scotland,' remarked the *Daily Mail*. 'But in their political hearts they'll be rooting for those bonny outsiders from Peru and Iran' – a reference to Scotland's likely victims in the group stage. Indeed, if the worst happened and the Scots actually won the tournament, thought the *Mail*, then Celtic pride 'would be like distilled firewater. Hooched up on that, the nationalists could rampage to victory up there in any general election that followed.'[34]

For both sides, therefore, Hamilton was more than an ordinary by-election. The final days of the campaign coincided with the SNP's annual conference in Edinburgh, but the party laid on shuttle buses so that delegates could spend their evenings canvassing in Hamilton. The conference itself was an extraordinarily rousing affair, the atmosphere so heady that the delegates spent hours discussing the structures of government in a sovereign, independent Scotland. Western culture was 'sick', claimed the party chairman, William Wolfe, nodding approvingly as speakers debated a resolution on Scotland's 'post-independence economic strategy'. In Hamilton, meanwhile, Margo MacDonald was leading the charge in typically swashbuckling style. It was time, she said, for the Scots to show that their pride lasted for 'more than 90 minutes in Argentina'. In answer, Labour sent Tony Benn, a committed anti-nationalist, to rally the troops. Hamilton, he said grandly, had 'an appointment with destiny': its result would show 'the future shape of British politics'.[35]

On polling day both campaigns pulled out all the stops, commandeering hundreds of cars to ferry their voters to the polls. From Margo MacDonald there came one last jab at her opponent, whom she called 'a Dark Age politician who believes Labour is due Hamilton's loyalty as of right, not because they have earned it'. But when the votes were counted, it was George Robertson – apparently so stolid, so unspectacular, so uncharismatic – who had the last laugh. With Jim Callaghan having steadied the ship in the aftermath of the IMF crisis, nationalism's appeal as a protest vote had taken a severe hit. Many potential voters, it turned out, were put off by the heady fantasies of Scottish independence; what was more, the interminable devolution battle had clearly sapped their appetite for nationalist rhetoric. After all MacDonald's sound and fury, Labour almost doubled their majority, while the SNP vote actually fell by more than 5 per cent. The result did not mean that 'Scottish Nationalism is dead', said *The Times*. But its momentum had clearly been checked. And with Hamilton lost, those who dreamed of a nation proud and free were left to console themselves with a campaign that kicked off just three days later: Scotland's quest for World Cup glory.[36]

At half-past six on a warm May evening, a few days before the people of Hamilton went to the polls, almost 30,000 people stood on the terraces of Hampden Park, Glasgow in a state of almost hysterical excitement. Festooned with flags, scarves and banners, they had come to wish good luck to their nation's World Cup squad before their flight to Argentina. They cheered and applauded as ten massed pipe bands took to the field. They laughed and sang along with Andy Cameron, the comedian whose anthem 'Ally's Tartan Army' had proved an unexpected hit. Finally, they roared their adulation as the twenty-two members of the Scottish football squad stepped sheepishly out onto the red carpet, followed by their manager Ally MacLeod, the hero of the hour. Rarely had a British team departed with such high hopes; certainly none had ever had such a spectacular send-off, broadcast live on television. And as the squad's coach carried them south towards Prestwick Airport, thousands of people lined the road. One man, who had just jumped out of the bath, was dripping wet. Others held up children and babies to see the bus; housewives waved tea towels; bridges were draped with flags and banners. At Prestwick, hundreds of people gathered on the beach to wave as the plane lifted into the air, euphoric in the knowledge that they were watching the future world champions.[37]

For decades, football had been a central element in Scottish national identity, transcending boundaries of class and region. In the world's first international match, played in Glasgow in 1872, the Scots had played England off the park thanks to their emphasis on collective endeavour rather than individual skill. And over the next hundred years the 'Hampden roar' had become one of the most celebrated emblems of Scottish pride, a tidal wave of sound propelling them to victory over the Auld Enemy. Beating the English was the supreme expression of Scottish uniqueness: as Margo MacDonald later recalled, the SNP 'used to print leaflets and stuff that made reference to the football because it was such a big part of Scottish life, Scottish social life, Scottish cultural expression'. Yet although the Scots produced plenty of excellent players, from Denis Law and Billy Bremner to Kenny Dalglish and Graeme Souness, they always underperformed on the biggest stage. At the 1974 World Cup in West Germany, Willie Ormond's squad had included some of the biggest names in European football, yet after beating Zaire they could only draw with Brazil and Yugoslavia, bowing out unbeaten on goal difference. Given the talent in the squad, many commentators felt they had failed to do themselves justice; even so, an estimated 10,000 people welcomed them home at Glasgow Airport. It was merely the first in a long line of heroic failures.[38]

In May 1977, with qualification for the next World Cup still in the balance, Scotland appointed a new manager whose rhetoric matched the fans' ambitions. Lanky and fair-haired, Ally MacLeod might look a lugubrious character, but in patriotic passion he was second to none. Although he had never played for his country, his record with Ayr United and Aberdeen marked him as an inspirational coach. And from his very first press conference, when he told reporters that he was 'born to be a success', to his first words to his players – 'My name is Ally MacLeod and I am a winner' – he seemed a kind of Caledonian Brian Clough: cheeky, loquacious and endlessly enthusiastic. Even his fondness for the safari suit seemed a welcome sign of modernity and innovation. And when MacLeod's team immediately crushed the Auld Enemy at Wembley, it seemed he really did have the Midas touch. Afterwards, as drink-sodden, sweat-stained Scottish fans tore handfuls of turf from the Wembley pitch, it felt as if MacLeod's players had banished centuries of inferiority. Fleet Street was predictably outraged – the 'Scottish hordes', said the *Mirror*, had 'mutilated' Wembley's 'hallowed turf' – but there was no denying the symbolism of the moment. The atmosphere, one reporter wrote, 'was overwhelmingly influenced by Scotland, and Scotch. It was at once powerful and obscene, and gave no comfort to England who might have been on Scottish soil.' On and off the pitch, Ally's Army reigned supreme.[39]

That autumn, MacLeod's men secured their place at the World Cup finals, something that had proved well beyond their English rivals. Expectation was high: with the Netherlands, Peru and Iran waiting in the first round, Ladbrokes made the Scots 8–1 to win the tournament. Unfortunately, tickets for the matches in Argentina were in very short supply, with only 500 on sale in Scotland, and official package tours cost a staggering £2,000 each. One fan told the press that he planned to hire a submarine to take him across the Atlantic, while an enterprising travel agent toyed with organizing Boeing 707 flights from a runway on the Shetlands. Some fans hoped to work their passage on a boat from France or Spain; 'several dozen more', according to *The Times*, had flown to New York and were working their way down to Mexico, 'after which their travel plans are, to say the least, vague'. Meanwhile, commercial sponsorship had reached levels unimaginable only ten years before. To the amazement of the press, British firms paid out £5 million to support the squad, with Chrysler at the head of the queue. The Trustee Savings Bank produced a special booklet, 'The Flowers of Scotland', while the Valentine greeting-card company paid the squad £25,000 for the rights to sell their official team photograph in newsagents across the country. At Esso garages, drivers could pick up beer glasses engraved with the players' signatures for just 40p each, while other World Cup-themed products included T-shirts, shampoo, aftershave, talcum powder and, slightly bizarrely, a Scottish-themed 'soap on a rope'.

These novelties were positively tasteful, however, compared with the real crime of the summer, the squad's World Cup single 'Olé Ola / I'd Walk a Million Miles for One of Your Goals', recorded with Rod Stewart, who had become a kind of bottle-blonde team mascot. At one stage, Stewart even dropped in by helicopter to don the national shirt and have a kick-around with the squad. But the anthem that best captured the national mood was the work of Andy Cameron, a stand-up comedian from Glasgow:

> We're on the march wi' Ally's Army,
> We're going tae the Argentine,
> And we'll really shake them up
> When we win the World Cup
> 'Cos Scotland is the greatest football team.

Almost unbelievably, 'Ally's Tartan Army' lurched up the charts to peak at number six. On *Top of the Pops*, Cameron cut a splendidly incongruous figure even by the standards of the 1970s, cavorting in his Scotland shirt, tartan cape and tam o'shanter while the audience cheerfully sang: 'And England cannae do it 'cos they didnae qualify.'[40]

Instead of dampening the flames of excitement, as a more experienced manager might have done, MacLeod gleefully poured on the petrol. On the eve of Scotland's warm-up games, he announced that he planned to use England ('a second-class nation') for 'target practice'. Then he went even further:

> You can mark down the twenty-fifth of June 1978 as the day Scottish football conquers the world. For on that Sunday I'm convinced the finest team this country has ever produced can play in the final of the World Cup in Buenos Aires and win.
>
> We have the talent. We have the temperament and the ambition and the courage. All that stands between us and the crown is the right kind of luck. I'm so sure we can do it that I give my permission here and now for the big celebration on the twenty-fifth of June to be made a national holiday: a national Ally-day.

Not even defeat to England could dampen MacLeod's confidence. His players had treated the game purely as a training exercise, he explained, and now he was off home for a few days' rest before the flight to Argentina. He would be using the break, he said, to do some last-minute DIY: 'I'm putting in a new corner unit to hold the World Cup.'[41]

Almost from the moment that the Scotland squad arrived in Argentina, things began to go wrong. Far from being an 'Argentinian Gleneagles', as team officials had claimed, the squad's hotel in Alta Gracia, a small town not far from Córdoba, was blatantly substandard, with no water in the swimming pool, no net on the tennis court and plaster peeling from their bedroom ceilings. It was a familiar situation for thousands of British package tourists, perhaps, but hardly ideal surroundings for future world champions. Bored and disappointed, the players spent much of their time arguing about their bonuses, and with the hotel's training pitch intolerably bare and bumpy, they were forced to take the coach into Córdoba every morning to practise at the stadium. Every day they whizzed past rows of hunchbacked shacks, a glimpse of everyday life under Argentina's authoritarian regime breaking through the clouds of sporting hype. Every day, too, they passed the bodies of two dead horses, lying forgotten by the side of the road – another bad omen, the more superstitious players thought.[42]

Even so, when Scotland took to the field on Saturday, 3 June for their opening game against Peru, most observers expected a comfortable victory. After fourteen minutes they even took the lead, but in the second half everything fell apart. The Peruvian goalkeeper saved a Don Masson penalty, the South American playmaker Teófilo Cubillas blasted home two superb goals, and before they knew it, the Scots had contrived to lose 3–1. After just ninety minutes, MacLeod's plans to bring home the trophy were in tatters. 'Barring the kind of miracle that no one here is prepared to believe,' wrote the *Observer*'s football correspondent, Hugh McIlvanney, 'the party is surely over and the Scots are left with little but dirty glasses and the stale smell of spent euphoria.'[43]

At first, the press reaction to Scotland's opening defeat was remarkably restrained. Even the English papers were relatively benign: the *Express*, for example, thought that the Scots had 'lost honourably while trying very hard', and had 'nothing to apologise for.' The next day's headline, however, told a rather different story. 'Cup Star Banned For Life' screamed the front page above the news that West Bromwich Albion's 'fiery winger' Willie Johnston had failed a drug test after the game. The drug in question was Reactivan, a mild stimulant which was nevertheless on FIFA's banned list. Nobody seriously thought Johnston was a cheat; he had merely forgotten (or ignored) the Scottish officials' warnings about taking any kind of medicines. All the same, they were left with no choice but to send him home, prompting a full-blown media furore. With their second game scheduled for the very next day, Scotland's march of destiny was beginning to look more like a night at the circus. 'The match against Iran', said *The Times*, 'clearly becomes the most testing in the history of Scottish international football. They are a team in disgrace and badly need to win to avoid further bad publicity.'[44]

What followed was the most humiliating ninety minutes in the history of Scottish sport. As against Peru, Scotland's fans expected a comfortable victory; as one supporter later put it, the Iran game seemed 'the perfect tonic' after the weekend's bad news. But while MacLeod shuffled his pack, there was still no place for Liverpool's dynamic young midfielder Graeme Souness. And for all the manager's rousing rhetoric, invoking the spirit of Bannockburn and insisting that 'nothing less than victory' would do, Scotland never got going. Jeered by a pitiful crowd of less than 8,000, MacLeod's players toiled drearily until just before half time, when the Iranians decided to help them out by scoring an own-goal of farcical proportions. Surely now the floodgates would open? Not a bit of it: sixteen minutes into the second half, after Scotland had sunk back into their torpor, the Iranians profited from some slack defending to score a deserved equalizer. On the bench, MacLeod sat alone, his head buried in his hands, a picture of utter misery and helplessness. Even his own players thought he was 'distraught', 'destroyed'. At the final whistle, he trudged off to a chorus of boos.

To Scottish fans who had spent hundreds of pounds travelling to Argentina, the shame of Córdoba was almost too much to bear. As the players trooped disconsolately towards the tunnel, they had to run the gauntlet of men in tartan tam o'shanters aggressively flicking V-signs at them. Later, while their bus was waiting to leave the stadium, they were surrounded by jeering supporters, some chanting 'You only want the money'. That evening, fifteen Scottish fans were arrested after a punch-up at a local restaurant, compounding the general sense of ineptitude and chaos. 'MacLeod ought to be ashamed of himself,' one man, magnificently turned out in kilt, cape and tam o'shanter, his voice trembling with fury, told the television cameras. 'It was an absolute shambles and a disgrace to Scottish football.' Not surprisingly, the next day's papers agreed with him. Scotland might have drawn 1–1, wrote the veteran football correspondent Norman Fox, 'but this was an even worse performance than against the Peruvians simply because Iran are such outsiders in the world of football'. Recalling with grim irony 'the fanfares with which Scotland left home', Fox thought they had played entirely 'without soul'. 'Never', he wrote sadly, 'have they been so humiliated.'[45]

The next day, Chrysler pulled its adverts involving the Scottish World Cup squad. For many observers, the campaign had now reached depths of 'shame and humiliation' almost unmatched in British sporting history. And for the tabloids, poor MacLeod had become the perfect scapegoat. After all the hype, the headlines – 'Scotched!', 'All This Way For SFA', 'Dead End Ally' – were predictably unforgiving. To his credit, the beleaguered manager did his best to shoulder the criticism. 'I am ultimately to blame,' he told the press after the Iran debacle. 'It's no good the players taking the blame. I am responsible.' But that cut little ice with his critics; as one correspondent wrote, 'his attitude throughout has been that the opposition would fall beneath the weight of his own chauvinistic statements. The World Cup is no place for such shallow ideas.' In Dundee, one record shop slashed the price of 'Ally's Tartan Army' singles from 65p to just 1p, urging customers to buy as many records as they wanted and smash them to pieces on the counter with a hammer. Even the Tories got in on the act, with Sir Geoffrey Howe making a laboured comparison between the beleaguered Scottish manager and the Prime Minister: 'the manager, Dead End Cally, who carries the can'.[46]

For many commentators, the implosion of MacLeod's ambitions was a damning indictment of a national culture of self-deluding arrogance. Drunk on his own predictions, the Scottish manager had arrived in Argentina 'more as a cheer leader than as team manager', remarked Norman Fox in *The Times*, yet 'his attitude of "let the opposition worry about us" was typical of a certain school of thinking that has too many followers in Britain'. In the *Observer*, Hugh McIlvanney, himself a proud Scot, saw MacLeod's fall from grace as a lesson in the perils of Celtic chauvinism. 'The seeds of the small disaster', he wrote, 'are to be found in the natures of the people most devastated by it.' For as he pointed out, Scotland's manager had hardly been alone in his predictions of glory:

> As they approached the World Cup finals, most Scottish supporters gave every indication of being happy to be on the march with Ally's Army, of sharing the outrageous, patently unjustified optimism of Ally MacLeod ... They believed him because they wanted to believe him, because he talked like one of them, indeed could contrive, when utterly

sober, to sound as the wildest of them might sound after a night on the liquid hyperbole. In the run-up to the tournament he behaved with no more caution, subtlety or concern for planning than a man getting ready to lead a bayonet charge. The fans echoed his war cries, never bothering to wonder if the other contenders for the world title would be willing to stand still and be stabbed.

At the root of all this, McIlvanney thought, was a culture of chauvinist exaggeration, rooted in a historic sense of grievance. Eager to make 'aggressive declarations about themselves to the rest of humanity', the Scots had sent out their 'nearest thing to a gunboat'. Unfortunately, as the debacle of Córdoba had proved, Ally MacLeod's team was 'hopelessly ill-equipped to carry the burden of emotional expression the Scots seek to load upon it'. And now, in the ruins of humiliation, they were left with 'the realisation that something they believed to be a metaphor for their pride has all along been a metaphor for their desperation'.[47]

There was, however, a twist in the tale. On the day McIlvanney's piece was published, Scotland had one last chance to redeem themselves against the Netherlands, who had been runners-up in the last World Cup and were many people's favourites for the trophy. Needing an implausible three-goal victory to stay in the tournament, MacLeod at last yielded to reason, picking Graeme Souness to run his midfield. But although the Scots got off to a flying start, with the tireless Souness apparently everywhere, it was the Dutch who scored first from a soft penalty. So far, so predictable: Kenny Dalglish preserved a glimmer of hope for Scotland by volleying home an equalizer, but at the break there seemed little chance that Scotland could confound the bookies' predictions. A minute into the second half, however, another penalty gave Scotland a 2–1 lead. And then came the moment that is still etched into the memories of every Scottish fan. In the 68th minute, the ball broke to Nottingham Forest's dour little midfielder Archie Gemmill, just outside the Dutch penalty area. 'Good play by Gemmill!' exclaimed the BBC's commentator David Coleman, his voice rising as the little man dodged a Dutch tackle. 'And again!' as Gemmill slipped inside another challenge and suddenly found himself with only the goalkeeper to beat. And then, half a second later: 'Three-one! A brilliant individual goal by this hard-working little professional has put Scotland in dreamland! The miracle is beginning to happen! They need one more to qualify!'

Dreamland lasted for three minutes; then the Dutch striker Johnny Rep bludgeoned home a spectacular goal to make the score 3–2. It was 'a dagger through our heart', said the Scottish captain Bruce Rioch. The momentum was lost, and with Scotland needing to score two more, time dribbled away. When the referee blew for full time, the Scots were out – albeit after a heroic victory. Later, the match became famous as a magnificent failure, a kind of sporting Culloden, while Gemmill's extraordinary goal even crops up in the film *Trainspotting* (1996).* Yet as the next day's *Scotsman* remarked, it was a victory 'more vainglorious than glorious', the team's courageous performance making what had gone before seem 'all the more excruciating'. Revealingly, the players flew home to a distinctly glacial reception. Collecting their bags at Glasgow Airport, some were even jeered by the local baggage handlers. 'We had people spitting on the bus, a welcoming committee with all the gear on, calling us everything under the sun,' remembered Joe Harper, who had played as a substitute against Iran. 'It was pathetic . . . "You're a wee bastard; you've let us down; you've done this and that."' 'Even the airport people were baying for blood,' recalled the goalkeeper, Alan Rough. 'It was like a hanging mob the way they were screaming at us. It was pretty much fever pitch; pretty bad.'[48]

After all the expectation, Scottish football's pretensions had been exposed before millions of viewers across the world. Even the British chargé d'affaires in Buenos Aires sent a damning report to his Foreign Office superiors, remarking that the Scots had seemed 'provincials out of their depth in international waters'. As Scottish commentators pointed out when the document was released thirty years later, there was in this more than a little Anglo-Saxon satisfaction. 'English sportswriters have sportlessly wallowed in the mud we've slung at the tattered Tartan Army. We've called them posers, big-heads, Ally's Follies, a "sick joke of a team". We've put in the boot, trodden on their bowed necks, danced on the graves of their hopes, and drunk their spilt blood like whisky,' wrote the *Express*'s famously severe Jean Rook. She blamed not Ally MacLeod, who stepped down a few months later, but 'Margo MacDonald and her English bashers', who had 'alienated everybody south of the border she would have liked to put up between England and Scotland'. Even so, Rook thought that the Scots' neighbours should be more gracious:

---

* 'I haven't felt that good since Archie Gemmill scored against Holland in 1978,' says Ewan MacGregor's character after having sex. After seeing the film, Gemmill was not quite sure how to take the compliment. 'To be fair, I was a bit embarrassed by it,' he said sheepishly.

Admittedly, the kilt-swinging, plaid-waving Scots can be an intensely irritating people, especially when they're roaring like rampant lions about devolution, or gushing about their oil.

If they had their way, they wouldn't spare an Englishman a drop to grease his bike.

But blood – even if it's in the veins of a bloody-minded Scot – should be thicker than water . . .

The Scots are our brothers, or at least our cousins.

And however much you dislike your relatives, you do not allow perfect strangers to kick them to chips.[49]

But as the letters pages were to prove, plenty of English observers had rather different ideas. Still smarting from 'the insulting things Ally MacLeod said about England', Miss R. W. Beard of Cornwall wrote that she was 'sick of the whole boasting, bragging, loud-mouthed pack of them'. The Scots 'had rammed themselves down our throats', agreed G. Bevan of London. 'I don't suppose they have learned their lesson, but it gives the rest of us a chance to have a go at them for a change. Come to think of it, I might just go round and dig up a few Scotsmen's garden lawns.' And just to show that old prejudices died very hard indeed, the *Express* reacted sceptically to the suggestion that, given their 'enormous' sponsorship deals, the Scottish players 'should make some personal monetary contribution to those dedicated people who travelled so far and at such expense to support them'. That, the paper thought, was very unlikely. *'Ever tried getting money from a Scotsman?'*[50]

23

No Fun at All

*Ever since that Bill Grundy interview with the Sex Pistols,
adults have been brainwashed into believing that all teenagers
have been taken in by the punk rock craze.*

*Well, it's not all of us who waste our time and money on
these talentless 'musicians'. We know of far better groups to
listen to when it comes to musical quality.*

Letter from Clive Weatherley (15) of Harlow,
Essex, to the *Daily Express*, 3 February 1977

I work for the Inland Revenue. Am I still allowed to be a punk?
Letter from Steven Morrissey
of Manchester to the *NME*,
9 April 1977

In the summer of 1975 the Empire Pool at Wembley played host to one
of the most extraordinary entertainments the crumbling old arena had
ever seen. An instrumental adaptation of *The Myths and Legends of
King Arthur and the Knights of the Round Table* would have been outlandish enough; the fact that it was *on ice*, however, lifted it to an
entirely new level. On his way in, the critic Philip Norman had desperately hoped that it was all a joke. But no: 'the sight of the blue ice-rink,
and an island in the centre of it packed with the New World Symphony
Orchestra, the English Rock Ensemble, the Nottingham Festival Vocal
Group and much other orchestral hardware, all bespoke a motive anything but lighthearted'. In barely an hour, Rick Wakeman distilled
everything its critics said was wrong with modern rock music – the
unsmiling seriousness, the extravagant costumes, the earnest medieval-

ism, the interminable keyboard solos – and, as he might have put it, turned it up to eleven.* While Norman watched in horror, 'pasteboard knights, ladies in see-through gowns and horses moving backwards' swooped across the ice. Somewhere in the middle was Wakeman, hunched over his keyboards, dressed in a silver cloak and chain mail. As an encore, he played the whole of his last composition, *Journey to the Centre of the Earth*. It was an evening, wrote *Rolling Stone*'s Paul Gambaccini, that 'literally had to be seen to be believed'.[1]

If nothing else, Wakeman's career was an illustration of the enormous possibilities that had been opened up by the rise of pop culture. A former grammar school boy from the west London suburbs, he had trained at the Royal College of Music before joining the group Yes in 1971. Pale, lank-haired and apparently very, very serious – an impression he corrected after his subsequent reincarnation as a reliably amusing panel-show guest – he manned the keyboards on the band's increasingly grandiose albums for the next three years, before packing it in to go solo. But his idea of a solo career turned out to be very different from, say, Cilla Black's. His first album, *The Six Wives of Henry VIII* (1973) was a collection of six instrumental pieces about the Tudor king's ill-fated consorts. Not surprisingly, Wakeman's record company steeled themselves for disaster; amazingly, however, *The Six Wives* sold more than 2 million copies worldwide in its first year. Next, in January 1974, Wakeman recorded a forty-minute interpretation of Jules Verne's *Journey to the Centre of the Earth* at the Royal Festival Hall. *The Times*'s critic noted, almost in awe, that the climax involved 'more than 150 instruments and voices', though he was less impressed by 'the inescapable pretentiousness of the rockaphonic style'. But when the album was released a few months later, it went straight to number one. Wakeman had been vindicated. 'At 26,' an admiring profile declared, 'he has all the trappings of super success – a £120,000 mansion, 17 luxury cars, including eight Rolls-Royces, and the title of "world's top keyboard musician".'[2]

To his critics, Wakeman's success was a reflection of pop music's sheer exhaustion. For all the lurid glamour of *Top of the Pops* and the scantily clad charms of its dance troupe Pan's People, for all the exuberant showmanship of Abba, Elton John and the Bay City Rollers, the music industry was not in great shape in the mid-1970s. Annual singles

---

* To be fair, though, the record's title track, 'Arthur', made a splendidly rousing election theme for the BBC. First used in 1979, it was disgracefully dumped in 2010.

sales had reached a peak of 63 million in 1974; then, worryingly for the record companies, they began to fall, tumbling to 57 million two years later. The market had become irredeemably fragmented: between the bloated solemnity of progressive rock and the superficial frivolity of teenybopper pop, there seemed little middle ground. Industry insiders talked endlessly of finding the 'new Beatles' or the 'next big thing', but executives seemed shy of anything even vaguely radical. Independent record shops were beginning to die out; by the mid-1970s, most listeners were buying their records from major stores such as Boots, Woolworths and W. H. Smith, which stocked a smaller range of heavily discounted bestsellers. As a result, marketing and recycling seemed to matter more than musical innovation: by 1976 compilation records accounted for an estimated 30 per cent of all album sales, with nine compilations in the Top Twenty alone. That the bestselling albums of 1975 and 1976 included *Elvis's 40 Greatest Hits*, Jim Reeves's *40 Golden Greats* and Glen Campbell's *20 Golden Greats* spoke volumes about the pop world's sheer inertia. 'At the heart of the Rock Dream,' lamented *Melody Maker*, 'is a cash register.'[3]

By far the most easily lampooned genre of the mid-1970s, as well as the most colourful, ambitious and self-consciously serious, was progressive rock. Groups such as Yes, Genesis and Emerson, Lake and Palmer, as well as slightly less successful outfits like King Crimson, Barclay James Harvest and Van der Graaf Generator, saw themselves as being in the business of art, not entertainment. And although the 'images of long solos, overlong albums, fantasy lyrics, grandiose stage sets and costumes, and a dedication to technical skill bordering on the obsessive', as one account has it, are a bit of a cliché, it was still a cliché grounded in reality. While teenage-friendly pop stars sang about the excitement of falling in love, prog rockers often drew inspiration from Arthurian romances (as in Led Zeppelin's preposterous 'The Battle of Evermore') or *The Lord of the Rings* (as in Barclay James Harvest's 'Galadriel', Rush's 'Rivendell' or Camel's 'Nimrodel/The Procession/The White Rider'). Some prog albums were almost beyond parody, such as Genesis's *The Lamb Lies Down on Broadway* (1974), which tells the story of a Puerto Rican called Rael who finds himself in a netherworld beneath New York and has to fight the degenerate Slippermen, a race of sex-crazed monsters; or Hawkwind's *Warrior on the Edge of Time* (1975), which boasted lyrics by the science-fiction writer Michael Moorcock based on his idea of a multi-dimensional Eternal Champion and set on the planet Megadon in the Solar Federation.* By these standards, concept albums like David Bedford's *The Rime of the Ancient Mariner* (1975) seemed positively austere.[4]

Not all prog rockers were as overblown as Rick Wakeman; many toiled in relative obscurity, playing for love rather than money and performing to small student audiences. Success, however, seemed to go hand in hand with grandiose pretensions of the most risible kind. For their world tour to promote *The Lamb Lies Down on Broadway*, Genesis required seven slide carousels holding 1,500 pictures, allowing them to project the images of, say, 'a greatly magnified and grotesque insect against a stolid fifties Ford', or 'a snowy white feathered heart nestled in crimson satin drapery'. On stage, Peter Gabriel wore a string of outfits that might easily have got him locked up, including a clinging bodysuit designed to glow under the stage lights and, infamously, the Slipperman costume, a kind of lump-encrusted sub-*Doctor Who* monster suit, complete with inflatable genitals. In a class of their own, meanwhile, were the super-group Emerson, Lake and Palmer, whose album *Brain Salad Surgery* (1973) included one track, 'Karn Evil 9', so long they had to split it across the two sides of the record. Their shows included such delights as a flying Persian carpet, a spinning grand piano and a rotating drum platform, while for their 1977 American tour they required three enormous trucks (decorated in turn with the gigantic words EMERSON, LAKE and PALMER), a fifty-eight-piece symphony orchestra, a choir, a portable stage with a hydraulic lift and a road crew of 120 men. The Beatles in Hamburg seemed a long way away.[5]

Progressive rock had no monopoly on pretentiousness or avarice. Even the Beatles, after all, were not exactly renowned for their indifference to money ('Taxman' springs to mind), while records like the Rolling Stones' *Their Satanic Majesties Request* had hardly been models of stripped-down austerity. All the same, there is no doubt that the inflated earnings and swirling cloaks of the mid-1970s drove a wedge between musicians and their audiences. The appeal of Paul McCartney and Mick Jagger, at least at first, had depended on their seeming to be just like the teenagers who bought their records. But nobody thought that Rick Wakeman or Keith Emerson was just like them. Indeed, Emerson

---

* Hawkwind delivered Moorcock's lyrics, reported *Melody Maker* on 10 May 1975, 'with all the emotion of Davros being exterminated by renegade Daleks'. Later, the band's bassist, 'Lemmy' Kilmister, described the album as 'a lot of fucking rubbish'.

emigrated to Switzerland because, he said, Denis Healey's tax policies were 'way out of order'. 'Go to any major pop concert these days and you will wonder what ever happened to rock and roll,' remarked the *Daily Express*. 'You will be one of thousands paying £3 or more to squeeze into a seat and watch a group appearing, dot-like, on stage. At the end T-shirted security guards will ensure that no-one gets so much as a peep of the "stars", who are escorted to a waiting limousine and driven to the best hotel in town.'[6]

At Britain's biggest selling music paper, the *NME*, letters poured in from readers complaining that the 'superstars with champagne and coke parties' had lost sight of their audience. Rock had become 'big-time', 'tax-exile, jet-set', part of the 'turgid mainstream of traditional show business', lamented the writer Mick Farren. Many younger listeners, he noted, were infuriated at the rise of stadium rock, finding themselves pinned in their 'numbered, regimented seats', unable to dance or express themselves:

> You all seem to have had it with The Who and Liz Taylor, Rod and the Queen, Jagger and Princess Margaret, paying three quid to be bent, mutilated, crushed or seated behind a pillar of PA stack, all in the name of modern, 70s style super rock . . .
>
> People are tired of having their booze confiscated and being ordered to stop dancing. Maybe they're also sick of seeing the vibrant, iconoclastic music whose changes did, at least, shake the walls of the city a little, being turned around, sold out, castrated and co-opted.
>
> Did we ever expect to see The Rolling Stones on *News at Ten* just like they were the Badminton Horse Trials or the Chelsea Flower Show?[7]

Even *The Times*, of all papers, thought that rock music was 'in the doldrums'. It had become 'a world of hairy, pot-bellied guitar heroes and expensive, extravagantly packaged multi-record albums of flatulent electronic doodling,' wrote the paper's critic Tony Partington in the summer of 1977. 'You cannot get farther from the spirit of rock 'n' roll than that.'[8]

Progressive rock was not, of course, the only game in town. As far as many teenagers were concerned, the biggest stars of 1974 and 1975 were the likes of the Bay City Rollers, Showaddywaddy and 10CC, with Abba breaking through a year later. In an increasingly fragmented musical landscape, some were drawn to the aggressive hyper-masculinity of heavy-metal groups like Black Sabbath (who released their first album in 1970) and Judas Priest (1974) who appealed overwhelmingly to working-class boys and young men. Most heavy-metal stars came from similarly proletarian backgrounds: both Black Sabbath's guitarist Tony Iommi and Judas Priest's Glenn Tipton, for example, had previously worked in the steel industry. No doubt this explains the rhythmic violence of the heavy-metal sound: as Tipton later recalled, he only became a professional musician after working in 'a massive steelwork labyrinth, riddled with polluted canals, massive grimy workshops, foundries and steam hammers'. It also explains why heavy metal was so popular in the West Midlands: Judas Priest and Black Sabbath both came from Birmingham, while Led Zeppelin's frontman Robert Plant was born in West Bromwich and later became vice-president of Wolverhampton Wanderers. In an age when genuine metal-bashing was dying out, heavy metal seemed a defiant statement of sweaty authenticity, in stark contrast to the lurid affectations of prog rock. And like the skinhead craze that had briefly flourished at the turn of the decade, it appealed to teenage boys who felt alienated by feminism, homosexuality and middle-class bohemianism, offering what one account called 'a reassertion of solid, male, working-class toughness'.[9]

A second alternative, which flourished in London in the first half of the 1970s, was so-called pub rock. The antithesis of progressive rock, performed in obscure bars across the capital, it was punchy, intimate and self-consciously simple. Bands like Brinsley Schwarz, Dr Feelgood and Eddie and the Hot Rods saw themselves as preserving the true spirit of rock and roll, a spit-and-sawdust ethos that could not have been more different from the grandiose pretensions of Emerson, Lake and Palmer. Like their punk successors, they looked back for inspiration, playing aggressive, intense rhythm and blues before small, admiring audiences. And although pub rock made virtually no impression on the charts and was barely noticed by those outside the circuit, only a very thin dividing line separated it from punk. The singer Ian Drury started out as a pub rocker with Kilburn and the High Roads, was later hailed as a punk musician and achieved his greatest success as an exponent of the so-called New Wave. The Clash's front man Joe Strummer originally played pub rock with the 101'ers; similarly, the Stranglers, who began life as a Guildford pub rock group in 1974, were later seen as a typical punk band. The truth, of course, is that all these labels were slippery and artificial. To those people who disliked rock music – a group that probably included most people over 40, as well as many of their juniors – they all sounded the same anyway.[10]

Pub rock was not the only backward-looking trend of the day. In the early 1970s, barely noticed by the newspapers or the rock press, there was a brief Teddy boy revival, with youngsters dusting down the old frock coats and drainpipe trousers in an early sign of pop's fixation with its own past. Among them was an irreverent young man from Stoke Newington called Malcolm McLaren, who co-owned a boutique at 430 King's Road, Chelsea with his girlfriend, the designer Vivienne Westwood. Born a few months after the end of the Second World War, McLaren had left home as a teenager and drifted through a string of art colleges, never really settling down or finding his vocation. In the late 1960s, like so many disaffected art college youngsters, he became interested in radical 'Situationist' ideas, especially the notion that bourgeois society could be undermined if artists put on increasingly outrageous and offensive public spectacles. What really dominated McLaren's imagination, though, were the stories of rock and roll impresarios such as Larry Parnes, the flamboyant promoter who had groomed late-1950s stars such as Billy Fury, Johnny Gentle, Vince Eager and Duffy Power. It is no exaggeration to say that McLaren was obsessed with Larry Parnes: indeed, for all his bohemian patter and Situationist rhetoric, for all the provocative designs on sale in the King's Road boutique, what McLaren really wanted was to become a pop Svengali in his own right. But this seemed very unlikely. The Teddy boy revival burnt itself out, while Vivienne Westwood began to look even further back for ideas, producing extravagant lime-green zoot suits and biker-inspired leather dresses. Bored and frustrated, McLaren persuaded her that they should try their luck across the Atlantic.[11]

McLaren's brief stay in New York, where he spent most of the two years after 1973, was a key moment in the evolution of British punk. Thanks to punk's reputation as either the 'sound of the suburbs' or 'dole queue rock', its American provenance is often overlooked. But when McLaren arrived in Manhattan, he found a thriving prototypical punk scene. The very word 'punk' – derived from a long-forgotten English word meaning prostitute or sodomite, now carrying overtones of snarling youthful rebelliousness – was already current among American rock critics. They first applied it to the amateurish garage bands of the mid-1960s, but by the beginning of the 1970s it had taken on a slightly more bohemian edge. Some proto-punk groups like the MC5, the Stooges and the Ramones were content to play austere, direct, hard-hitting music – one early reviewer defined their style as 'heavy, monotonous, industrial, mechanical' – but others, like the Velvet Underground and

Television, had more highbrow, vaguely arty aspirations. What they had in common was their distaste for prog rock's self-indulgence and their insistence on a spare, stripped-down style. McLaren's particular favourites were the New York Dolls, who combined an aggressive sound with a flamboyant glam-rock look. Self-consciously provocative, the Dolls often wore lipstick and high heels and behaved outrageously on stage. Some critics saw them as the triumph of style over substance: 'Whispering' Bob Harris, presenter of *The Old Grey Whistle Test*, dismissed them as 'mock rock'. But McLaren loved the Dolls' penchant for shocking their audiences, and even briefly acted as their manager. And although the band was already in irreversible decline, the experience convinced him that his Larry Parnes fantasy was not entirely far-fetched. Returning to London, he decided to find a British equivalent of the New York Dolls – a group that would be at once aggressive and theatrical, bohemian and unsentimental, nostalgic and uncompromising. 'As far as I'm concerned,' he told the *NME* in 1976, 'they were *the* group – the *single* most important rock band. They were certainly the prime motivators behind what's happening now.'[12]

Some time in 1973, McLaren had taken under his wing an amateur group called the Strand, founded by two teenage dropouts who used to hang around his King's Road shop. Steve Jones and Paul Cook had both grown up in working-class west London, and Jones, an occasional football hooligan, had a string of petty criminal convictions. Neither had any grand musical ambitions; as they saw it, the band was merely a convenient excuse for bunking off school. Like so many teenage amateurs, they played the music they had grown up with: in this case, Small Faces-style Mod, seasoned with a few fashionable glam-rock flourishes. Before leaving for New York, McLaren had found them a new bass player – a shy, grammar-school-educated student called Glen Matlock, who occasionally worked at the shop – and asked a friend to look after them. Now, back in London and at something of a loose end, the would-be Larry Parnes picked them up again. He sacked the lead guitarist, moved Jones from vocals to guitar, and began to audition potential front men. For a while the trail ran cold: both Midge Ure, later of Ultravox, and Kevin Rowland, who subsequently founded Dexy's Midnight Runners, turned him down. At last, in August 1975, an increasingly desperate McLaren approached a skinny, green-haired boy whom he had noticed skulking in the shop. The other band members were not terribly impressed by John Lydon, but McLaren thought he had something. A few weeks later they changed their name to the Sex Pistols, largely because they thought it might get them noticed.[13]

At first the Sex Pistols seemed a very unlikely prospect for national stardom. For nine months they played to indifferent audiences in half-empty clubs, student unions and art colleges. To most of their listeners, recalled the writer Jon Savage, an early fan, their music was merely 'scraping and gnawing sounds', but their confrontational style always struck a chord with one or two. The standard seems to have been fairly abysmal: one of their first fans, who heard them at St Albans Art School in the autumn of 1975, recalled that 'they were terrible. We thought they were a piss-take of a sixties group: afterwards one of them was crying because they were so terrible.' All the same, he was irresistibly drawn to their style – the scalped hairstyles, the ripped T-shirts, the general air of casual aggression – and as the Pistols toured the dormitory towns of the South-east, they began to pick up admirers. Contrary to myth, these early fans were not unemployed working-class school leavers, but arty sixth-formers and college students, precisely the kind of people who had previously been drawn to David Bowie and Roxy Music. Revealingly, they were attracted to the band not by their sound, which was dreadful, but by their look. And instead of copying McLaren's boys, many of these early admirers were already wearing punk-styled clothes, suggesting that an embryonic proto-punk subculture, characterized by pierced ears, cannibalized clothes and luridly dyed, close-cropped hair, existed even before the Sex Pistols became famous. 'We liked to be noticed,' one said. 'We were influenced by Bowie, Roxy Music and *Clockwork Orange*, but we were doing it in our own way.'

In the late spring of 1976 the Sex Pistols were still toiling in utter obscurity, having picked up no more than about fifty serious fans. As the temperatures soared, however, their momentum, almost imperceptibly, began to build. In an odd way, the extraordinary weather worked in their favour: their audiences' inhibitions seemed to evaporate in the stifling heat, and as John Lydon ('Johnny Rotten') strutted and shuddered on stage, sweat pouring down his face, his listeners responded with growing excitement.* The other key factor was the resurgent popularity of amphetamines – speed – which had played a vital part in

---

* It is worth pointing out that Lydon was absolutely central to the Sex Pistols' success: without his extraordinary, hyper-theatrical stage persona, their impact would probably have been negligible.

Mod's success in the mid-1960s and meant that listeners were more receptive to harsh, aggressive music. Watching them play in a 'tiny basement just off Leicester Square', just weeks before they made their national breakthrough, Savage found the violent atmosphere intoxicating. On stage, Lydon gyrated in a 'filthy white T-shirt, round-collared with pinholes, festooned with "I survived the Texas Chainsaw Massacre" stickers', which never quite covered the burn marks on his arms. In the audience, Savage noticed two girls tied together with a dog-chain, both wearing bin liners, while nearby stood a man in a Cambridge Rapist mask. 'People get up and dance on the stage and pour beer over each other, while the singer insults the audience and goads them to jump on each other,' Savage recorded. He loved it.[14]

By now the Pistols had come to the attention of the music press. The *NME* first mentioned them while reviewing an all-night ball at Queen Elizabeth College, London in December 1975 ('they are all about 12 years old . . . and they're going to be the Next Big Thing'), while an article two months later called them 'spiky teenage misfits' playing '60s styled white punk rock'. It was a piece by the *NME*'s star writer Charles Shaar Murray in September 1976, though, which really marked their breakthrough. By now their performances had noticeably improved. 'They play loud, clean and tight and they don't mess around,' Shaar Murray wrote. 'The first thirty seconds of their set blew out all the boring, amateurish artsy-fartsy mock-decadence that preceded it purely by virtue of its tautness, directness and utter realism.' Like so many writers who followed him, he saw them as the voice of a generation, screaming with frustration at the cold reality of economic decline. 'Their music is coming from the straight-out-of-school-and-onto-the-dole deathtrap which we seem to have engineered for our young,' he wrote: 'the '76 British terminal stasis, the modern urban blind alley . . . You wanted Sex Pistols, and now you've got 'em. Trouble is, they look like they aren't going to go away.'[15]

Like the Beatles thirteen years earlier, the Sex Pistols seemed an ideal match with the dominant political themes of the moment. Just as the Beatles' northern backgrounds, irreverent populism and good-humoured optimism had matched the public mood in the second half of 1963, so the Sex Pistols seemed the perfect musical accompaniment to the plight of the pound, the surge in youth unemployment and the gnawing humiliation of the IMF bailout. Ten years earlier, their style would have been wrong, but in the summer of 1976, the growing violence that accompanied their appearances – leading to bans from the

Marquee and Nashville clubs – seemed entirely appropriate. The more
they provoked audiences, the more publicity they got, which explains
why Malcolm McLaren and Vivienne Westwood were so keen to egg
them on. The Sex Pistols were 'programmed for confrontation', Savage
writes; 'as [McLaren's] instrument, they would act out his fantasies of
conflict and revenge on a decaying culture.'

From the media's point of view, this made perfect copy: what better
symbol could there be of Jim Callaghan's Britain? The Pistols, wrote the
NME's Tony Parsons in October 1976, were the quintessential 'product
of the United Kingdom in the nineteen-seventies . . . The music they play
reflects their times, no more, no less.' By this stage McLaren's boys had
come to the attention of the record companies, and on 8 October they
signed a two-year deal with EMI. A month later, they were featured on
the BBC show *Nationwide*, where they were described as the leaders of
a new youth cult 'as big as the Mods and Rockers of the sixties', and on
28 November they appeared on Thames Television's *London Weekend
Show*. Three days later, when EMI's biggest band, Queen, pulled out of
Thames's early evening show *Today*, their publicist suggested the Sex
Pistols instead. Their appearance lasted barely four minutes, but it
changed their lives for ever.[16]

The striking thing about the Pistols' infamous exchange with *Today*'s
ill-fated presenter, Bill Grundy, which went out live on 1 December
1976, is how comical they all looked. The Pistols, accompanied by four
hangers-on, slouched uncomfortably on the sofa, trying their best to
look unconcerned. In his hastily written introduction, Grundy made it
obvious he had never heard of them. 'They are punk rockers. The new
craze, they tell me,' he began. 'Their heroes? Not the nice, clean Rolling
Stones; you see they are as drunk as I am. They are clean by comparison.
They're a group called the Sex Pistols, and I am surrounded by all of
them.' Later, Grundy insisted he was merely playing up to the image he
cultivated in his articles for *Punch*, where he had called himself 'the
greatest drunk in the world', although the Pistols certainly thought he
had been drinking. What is beyond doubt, though, is that Grundy completely mishandled the interview. His first question concerned their
reported £40,000 advance: did that not conflict with their 'anti-materialistic way of life'? (He seems to have confused them with hippies; at
this stage, there was no reason to think the Sex Pistols were especially
anti-materialistic.) 'We've fucking spent it, haven't we?' said Steve Jones.

But Grundy seemed not to notice the swearing. Clearly amused by his guests' adolescent awkwardness, he embarked on a bizarre new line of questioning:

> GRUNDY: Beethoven, Mozart, Bach and Brahms have all died—
>
> JOHN LYDON: (*rocking back and forth*) They're all heroes of ours, ain't they?
>
> GRUNDY: Really? What? What were you saying, sir?
>
> LYDON: They're *wonderful* people.
>
> GRUNDY: Are they?
>
> LYDON: Oh yes! They really turn us on.
>
> GRUNDY: Well suppose they turn other people on?
>
> LYDON: (*whispering*) That's just their tough shit.

At this point, with only sixty seconds left, Grundy could easily have steered the conversation into calmer waters. Instead, inexplicably, he asked Lydon to repeat himself. 'Nothing, a rude word. Next question!' Lydon said, giving Grundy a last chance to move on. Instead, self-destructively, Grundy kept going: 'No, no. What was the rude word?' Like a naughty schoolboy, Lydon said: 'Shit.' Then Grundy switched to the girls behind the sofa. 'Are you worried, or just enjoying yourself?' he asked the 19-year-old Siouxsie Sioux. 'Enjoying myself,' she said. 'I've always wanted to meet you.' And this was where Grundy really lost control:

> GRUNDY: We'll meet afterwards, shall we?
>
> STEVE JONES: You dirty sod! You dirty old man!
>
> GRUNDY: Well keep going, chief, keep going. Go on, you've got another five seconds. Say something outrageous.
>
> JONES: You dirty bastard!
>
> GRUNDY: Go on, again.
>
> JONES: You dirty fucker! (*The others laugh*)
>
> GRUNDY: What a clever boy!
>
> JONES: What a fucking rotter!*
>
> GRUNDY: Well, that's it for tonight . . .

Who knows what Grundy thought he was doing? Afterwards, he told the press that he had set out 'to prove that these louts were a foul-mouthed

---

* As is often pointed out, this was a very strange thing to say: outside Billy Bunter adaptations, nobody had used the word 'rotter' for decades.

set of yobs'. But most of the swearing only came *after* he started goading the group. Would, say, Michael Parkinson or Frank Bough, going out live at teatime, have asked their young guests to 'say something outrageous'? Surely not. Yet Grundy was an experienced broadcaster who had been on screen for twenty years and had interviewed hundreds of celebrities. Some accounts suggest that he lost his temper, but he never looked very angry. Perhaps it was the drink talking.[17]

Since *Today* only went out in London, far fewer people saw the interview than is often thought. But the ensuing moral panic was not entirely whipped up by the media, for almost immediately complaints jammed the Thames switchboard. What was really damaging was that the show had gone out live at 6.25 in the evening, when many children were watching. To hundreds of thousands of horrified viewers, it was as though the sneering menace of punk rock had crashed through the television set into the heart of the living room. 'I can swear as well as anyone,' a lorry driver told the *Mirror*, 'but I don't want this sort of muck coming into my home at teatime.' Incensed that his 8-year-old son had heard such bad language, he claimed he had kicked in the screen of his brand-new colour television. (This seems pretty unlikely; to a lorry driver, a £380 set was not something to be sacrificed lightly.) But to the tabloids, the affair was a godsend. In barely two minutes, the Sex Pistols – 'obnoxious, arrogant, outrageous, the new pop kings' – had unmasked themselves as the greatest folk devils of all. 'The Foul Mouthed Yobs', roared the front page of the *Evening Standard*; 'Fury At Filthy TV Chat', howled the *Express*; and above all, 'The Filth and The Fury', shrieked the *Mirror*, writhing in anger at 'the filthiest language ever heard on British television'.[18]

For Bill Grundy the affair was a catastrophe. After suspending him for two weeks, Thames cancelled his show in the New Year. He ended up presenting a books programme on Sunday mornings, remembered for ever as the man who had goaded the Sex Pistols. Most of the newspapers' fury, however, was directed at the Pistols' record company, EMI. 'Never mind morals or scandals,' said a leader in the *Daily Mail*: 'the only notes that matter come in wads.' The blame, it thought, lay with 'the ultimate pedlars of the pop industry – slick, agile of brain, fast of mouth', who cashed in on 'young people's instinct to outrage the older generation'. The *Express* agreed, warning that the publicity would only reward 'the group's four-letter outburst' and that the 'real four-letter word behind it was CASH'. People would be wrong, wrote the columnist George Gale, to blame 'these ignorant and ill-educated youngsters', who freely admitted 'that they roam the streets, have been out of work, despise the rich establishment of rock stars and hate the present state of the country'. Bizarrely, Gale thought that the lion's share of responsibility lay with the BBC, which 'panders to the ignorance and tastelessness of those who enjoy the noises of punk rock'. Given that the programme had not even been on the BBC, this seemed a bit harsh. But Gale was outraged that the Corporation had refused to ban 'Anarchy in the UK' from being played on the radio. Like so many conservatives before and since, he missed few opportunities to throw mud at the state broadcaster.[19]

The Grundy interview transformed the lives of the Sex Pistols. When they woke on Thursday, 2 December, they found themselves national celebrities, their faces plastered across every newspaper in the land. Glen Matlock's mother even complained that when she went in to work at the Gas Board, everybody called her 'Mrs Sex Pistol'. Although it was Steve Jones who had done almost all of the swearing, it was Lydon, the staring-eyed singer with the lurid red hair and 'Johnny Rotten' stage name, who became the chief folk devil, the demonic incarnation of disorder, Middle England's worst nightmares made flesh. And although notoriety usually means commercial success, in this case it created a host of difficulties. McLaren had been planning a national tour, but within two days of the *Today* broadcast seven dates had been cancelled. The next day, Derby's Labour councillors demanded that all punk groups audition before their Leisure Committee, a comic hurdle which meant that gig was off, too. Eventually, only six of the planned nineteen dates went ahead, which was no way for the Pistols' record company to make money. To their fans, they had become the victims of a witch-hunt. They had broken no laws and hurt nobody, yet few venues would accept bookings – and whenever they *did* manage to play, the pressure from the media, the excitement of the crowd and the expectations of violence meant that their music was almost an afterthought.[20]

Life now became a whirlwind of cancelled concerts and lurid allegations. With 'Anarchy in the UK' banned from most commercial radio stations, sales were poor and the single peaked at number 38. Despite pressure from the media, EMI initially refused to cancel their contract, and one executive drew a parallel 'with the early Rolling Stones when they aroused similar outrage'. But as the furore rumbled on, EMI's board decided that the group would have to go. On 5 January 1977, after allegations that the Sex Pistols had 'vomited and spat their way to an Amsterdam flight' – a story that proved almost totally untrue – EMI brusquely terminated the Pistols' contract. By now the band had become a freak-show turn, and any pretensions to musical quality disappeared completely when, a few weeks later, they kicked out Glen Matlock. (He had been sacked, McLaren claimed, for being too keen on the Beatles.) In his place they appointed Lydon's friend Sid Vicious, a self-harming heroin addict who looked good with a bass guitar but had no idea what to do with it. Another record company, A&M, threw them a lifeline, organizing a signing ceremony outside Buckingham Palace; but when Vicious celebrated by smashing up the company's offices, horrified executives ripped up the deal. Eventually Richard Branson offered the Pistols a home at his upstart label Virgin Records, hoping to cash in on their forthcoming single 'God Save the Queen'. But with Lydon and Vicious electing to play up to the violent roles the newspapers had invented for them, their musical career was already tailing off. For early fans like Jon Savage, they had ceased to be a musical outfit; instead, they had become a 'total spectacle ... flies in the amber of notoriety'.[21]

Almost overnight, the Grundy affair had turned punk from a little-known musical subculture into a universally recognized emblem of youthful disorder. From the purists' point of view, it also turned it into a self-parody, a 'shrink-wrapped' product, with every band sounding exactly the same. Just as during the beat boom of 1963–4, record companies rushed to sign up groups who looked just like the Sex Pistols. CBS snapped up the Clash and the Vibrators; EMI signed Wire, the Tom Robinson Band and X-Ray Spex; Polydor signed the Jam, Sham 69 and Siouxsie and the Banshees; United Artists signed the Stranglers, Buzzcocks and 999. By the spring of 1977, three-minute songs and sneering aggression had become a predictable formula, every band having the same 'stiff rhythm sections, overamplified guitar and harsh, almost characterless vocals'. And like so many teenage subcultures before them, punks adopted a kind of uniform: black leather jacket; ripped graffiti-covered T-shirt; tight, narrow trousers; dyed hair rubbed with Vaseline; identikit sullen leer. 'From something artistic and almost intellectual in weird clothes,' sighed Siouxsie and the Banshees' guitarist Marco Pirroni, 'suddenly there were these fools with dog collars on and "punk" written on their shirts in biro.' The torch had passed, agreed the journalist Peter York, to 'provincial kids out at the back of beyond'. Once, the 'proper' punk had been a rebellious art-school dropout. Now he was 'a nice little fifth former from, say, Muswell Hill,* who gets his

---

* The fact that York defined Muswell Hill as provincial is wonderfully revealing; whatever would he have made of someone from, say, Dudley?

hot tips from *NME* and *Sounds*, and three years before would have been a hippie'.[22]

There was a heavy dose of cultural snobbery in all this. Punk might never have become so successful had it not been championed by a new generation of rock writers, notably Tony Parsons and Julie Burchill, who joined the *NME* in August 1976 after answering an appeal for 'hip young gunslingers'. But although the critics loved punk – not least because, as York pointed out, it made them feel important – they hated the fact that so many other people liked it too. To its early fans, punk's very obscurity had been a guarantee of avant-garde authenticity. Nothing was more alarming than the prospect of success: as early as November 1976, one Peter Knife of London had written to the *NME* to wonder 'how long before the racks are filled with K-Tel's "40 All-Time Punk Greats"', warning that soon '"Punk" as a word' would become 'meaningless'. And it did not take long for Parsons and Burchill to decide that punk had got too big for its boots. It had fallen victim, they lamented in March 1977, to 'poseurs, businessmen and bandwagon-jumping musicians ... who memorise the right platitudes and wear the right clothes'. Yet their own coverage of punk was not quite as unsparing as they liked to suggest. Their *NME* cover piece on the Clash in April 1977, for example, portrayed the group as stereotypical 'ex-skinhead Maoists from a new brutalist landscape'. There was no mention of the fact that like so many bands before them, the Clash had all been to art school, or that their lead singer was an old boarding school boy. That would have spoiled a good story.[23]

That punk genuinely horrified many older people is beyond any doubt. At one of the last performances in the Pistols' national tour, at Caerphilly in South Wales, the tension between young and old resulted in what one reporter called 'a classic generation gap standoff'. Inside the Castle Cinema the Sex Pistols played to a small but rowdy audience. Outside, in the car park, stood a little crowd of local councillors and Pentecostal chapel-goers who had tried to get an injunction to ban the concert and, on failing, had decided to put on a carol service instead. They were, said Councillor Ray Davies, merely reflecting the views of the community, which was probably true. 'The people of Caerphilly, because it's an area well known for its culture, felt it deplorable that this Punk Rock group should have been brought in after it had been rejected in other parts of the country,' he said. 'Are children's minds to be vandalised and prostituted? This group not only come out with obscenities in their programme, but they also bring all the dope peddlers and filth peddlers in their wake.'[24]

As Councillor Davies's remarks suggest, one of the keys to punk's shock value was its provocative lyrical content. Even the bands' names – the Clash, the Damned and the Stranglers, for example, or Vermin, Electric Chairs and Slaughter & the Dogs – were deliberately outrageous, celebrating things that made most people recoil in horror. Often overflowing with obscenities, their lyrics sometimes seemed to have been written purely to provoke, with Nazism, torture, bondage and sadomasochism being particular favourites. Yet while previous teenage crazes had offended moral conservatives by their emphasis on sex, punk often seemed extraordinary sexless. In his analysis of the fifty bestselling singles in Britain in 1976, Dave Laing found that thirty-one concerned 'romantic and sexual relationships', ten addressed 'music and dancing' and the remainder were either novelty records or first-person narratives. Love, sex, dancing: these had been the central concerns of pop songs for decades. But punk was different. As Jon Savage points out, there was a puritan streak in McLaren and Westwood's fetish imagery; although their shop was called SEX, their clothes turned sex into an 'abstraction', stripping it of its erotic associations. And despite their name, there was nothing even faintly pornographic about the Sex Pistols' lyrics. 'The strongest element to come over from their songs', writes Savage, 'is sexual disgust.' To those weaned on the cheery optimism of the 1960s, this was shocking stuff. 'I think it's disgusting the way these punks sing about violence all the time,' said Radio One's Tony Blackburn, pop's answer to John Ruskin. 'Why can't they sing about beautiful things like trees and flowers?'[25]

Still, the fact is that since commercial radio stations refused to play their singles, most of the Sex Pistols' critics never heard their lyrics. What they were really objecting to was their image. Indeed it is hard to exaggerate just how important punk's image was. 'From the start I realised that the Pistols as a band were not relevant strictly for the music,' McLaren candidly admitted before the Grundy affair. 'That was in fact all very secondary to the image they were projecting.' One of the great strengths of the punk look was that it was so immediately recognizable; another was that it was very easy to reproduce. Unlike, say, Mod fashions, remarked the *NME*, 'the gear is made from objects that cost nil or nearly nothing', including 'safety pins, antique gym shoes, tattered Levis and all manner of refuse and castoffs'. But its appeal to teenagers was also rooted in the fact that it was such a reliable way of upsetting their elders. Swastikas and razor blades, safety pins and dog collars, fishnet tights and leather trousers: these not only marked a radical break with their older siblings' hippy look, but were guaranteed to upset middle-aged parents. And while cultural historians have spent entire careers discussing the ideological subtexts behind all this, the driving force was surely the perennial adolescent desire to shock. Wearing swastikas 'was always very much an anti-mums and anti-dads thing,' Siouxsie Sioux later remarked. 'We hated older people – not across the board but particularly in suburbia – always harping on about Hitler, "We showed him", and that smug pride. It was a way of saying, "Well, I think Hitler was very good, actually": a way of watching someone like that go completely red-faced.'[26]

With its atmosphere of simmering aggression and its studied contempt for social taboos, punk could not have been better designed to alienate Middle England. Previous pop crazes had often hinged on the spectacle of teenage girls sobbing with excitement. But with their gleeful displays of casual violence, compounded by the 'gobbing' rituals that left performers dripping with saliva, punk concerts had a far more hostile atmosphere. 'I bet YOU don't hate US as much as WE hate YOU,' John Lydon would sneer at his fans – a sentence unimaginable from, say, Paul McCartney. Even Rob Tyner, formerly of the proto-punk group MC5, was shocked when he visited London in the autumn of 1977. 'The levels of violence around here are weird and random,' he told the *NME*. 'At least, back in the USA if you're getting the shit kicked out of you, you know exactly who is doing it and why. Here, it seems to just erupt and could easily spill over your innocent lap.' When he had talked to 'cabbies and milkmen and postmen and cops about Punk', he said, their responses had been unanimously damning. 'Every time I see one of these bleeders, walking around with safety pins and swastikas all over their arses,' a London cabbie remarked, 'I look up to God and curse the seven years of my life I spent fighting the Nazis in the big war.' 'If they like to fight and spit so much,' agreed a policeman, 'perhaps a couple years militia would sort them out. Then they could work off that spunk fighting for England and not bashing innocent people in the face.'*[27]

On the surface, punk seemed to mark a radical break with the musical past. For almost a decade, 'serious' rock musicians had prided themselves on their growing levels of expertise and complexity. To some

---

* These remarks are perhaps worth taking with a pinch of salt: did cabbies and policemen really go around talking about 'bleeders' and 'spunk' in 1977?

critics, albums like Emerson, Lake and Palmer's *Brain Salad Surgery*, with their symphonic orchestration and twenty-minute songs, were a sign of rock's maturity. But to punk's new breed, the sight of Keith Emerson playing the synthesizer upside down was utter anathema. Progressive rock was pompous, elaborate, contemplative; punk was curt, urgent, brutally aggressive. Prog rockers toiled for weeks to achieve a smooth, clear sound; punk bands not only welcomed distortion and feedback, but went out of their way to create the improvised feel of a live recording. Unlike their predecessors, they gloried in their very *in*expertise, an amateur ethos that felt like a slap in the face to older musicians who had learned their craft. In some cases this was a bit disingenuous: many punk stars, including members of the Clash, the Damned and the Stranglers, had experience as professional musicians. But musical skill seemed to go against everything punk stood for. 'You can't play,' a listener told the Sex Pistols after one of their first performances. 'So what?' said Glen Matlock.[28]

For some people, all this was genuinely intoxicating. Across the country, hundreds of amateur punk bands now sprang into life, not unlike the skiffle and beat groups of two decades earlier. Punk felt like liberation, recalled the producer Mark Reeder, who grew up just outside Manchester and turned 16 in 1976: 'It was the feeling of people wanting to have something different. Young people not being able to relate to stadium rock bands like Yes.' To middle-aged moralists, the spectacle of young men in ripped T-shirts loitering around street corners or outside pubs and clubs seemed an alarming sign of national degeneration. But to the writer and DJ Dave Haslam, a teenager in Birmingham in the late 1970s, it felt as if 'a new generation was out there reclaiming our cities'. The seaside town of Brighton, for example, boasted an eclectic range of punk bands with a nice line in song titles, from the Dodgems' 'Lord Lucan Is Missing' to the Piranhas' 'I Don't Want My Body' – although as Haslam observes, Joby & the Hooligans' song 'Looking Through Gary Glitter's Eyes' was surely a step too far. And punk's do-it-yourself spirit gave rise not only to a rash of self-published fanzines – most famously *Sniffin' Glue*, but also titles such as *Blam!*, *Chainsaw*, *Jamming* and *ENZK* – but to a string of independent punk labels. One estimate suggests there were about 120 'Xerox' labels by 1978, from Duff Records of Bangor to Vole Records of Wolverhampton. Few of them lasted very long. But Factory Records, founded by Tony Wilson and Alan Erasmus in 1978, played a key role in the pop culture of the next decade, while Rough Trade, founded by Geoff Travis, remained an influential player in the twenty-first century, its survival a tribute to punk's ethos of independent self-reliance.[29]

But although punk is often seen as a radical departure, it was nothing of the kind. The atmosphere certainly felt very different, but the stage antics of John Lydon were not so far removed from the theatricality of glam rock stars like Marc Bolan. An even more obvious antecedent, meanwhile, was David Bowie, whose spectacular blend of pantomime, self-parody and artifice, inspired by his art school training, had made him a household name in the early 1970s. As early as 1972, one reviewer of Bowie's album *The Rise and Fall of Ziggy Stardust and the Spiders from Mars* had praised his combination of 'thoroughly punky aggressiveness, urgency and non-seriousness with a view of the world that's simultaneously personal, apocalyptic and radical', a description that might easily have been applied to many punk bands. Even Bowie's colourful, androgynous appearance anticipated what was to come: long before John Lydon dyed his hair bright orange, critics were mocking Bowie's 'hair like an orange lavatory brush'. This implies that punk's roots went back even further than the glam-rock craze of the early 1970s, for Bowie had made his breakthrough playing vaguely psychedelic folk rock, and in many ways was the very model of a prog rocker. Indeed, it was no coincidence that punk, as Peter York remarked, took up residence in 'precisely the same areas and social mix' that had produced the hippy movement a decade earlier. 'You saw punks where you used to see hippies,' he wrote, principally 'Notting Hill/Ladbroke Grove/Soho and Camden/Islington/Round House'.[30]

Although Malcolm McLaren loved to pour scorn on the dreamy utopianism of the late 1960s, deep down he was just another art school armchair radical, talking airily about smashing the system. Like so many who had drunk deeply of the intoxicating bohemianism of the counterculture, McLaren was rarely happier than when harking back to a lost golden age: in his case, the era of Teddy boys, skiffle music and garage bands, when he had been a teenager. Even the Bay City Rollers spent their time looking backwards, copying the family-friendly pop music of the late 1950s. And although punk fans would shudder at the comparison, it is hard to deny that, in essence, the Sex Pistols were not so different: a glorified tribute band playing punchy three-minute pop songs. Not for nothing did early articles on punk style emphasize their debts to the Teddy boys and the Mods, while the *NME*'s first proper review of the Sex Pistols described them as playing '60s styled white punk rock' and noted that their repertoire included plenty of 'Small

Faces numbers' and 'early Kinks B sides'. Indeed, when *Sounds*' critic Alan Lewis reviewed 'Anarchy in the UK' nine months later, he pointed out that it had 'so many of the traditional ingredients of high-energy rock that it makes nonsense of all those hysterical letter-writers who see the Pistols as a threat to Music as We Know It. Conversely, it also makes nonsense of any claims that the Pistols are revolutionaries.'[31]

Of course the idea of punk as a decisive break is so deeply embedded in our collective wisdom that it will never disappear. It is revealing, though, that the producer of 'Anarchy in the UK', Chris Thomas, was an old hand who had worked with the Beatles, Pink Floyd and Roxy Music. Thomas did not see the Sex Pistols as anything radical: recalling the moment he first heard their demo tapes, he remarked: 'It wasn't a transition for me. It was all just music to me . . . I thought, "This has the potential to be the best English rock band since The Who. It's a three-piece again – guitar, bass and drums."' Other punk groups were similarly backward-looking: the Jam's Paul Weller, for example, told the *NME* that he had been 'besotted' with the Beatles and was inspired above all by Pete Townshend and the Who. Even the *Daily Express*'s critic, trying to define punk for readers who found Ralph Vaughan Williams a bit daring, explained that it had 'the raw energy of mid-fifties rock or the early sixties beat boom'. Ironically, though, few veterans of the 1960s were keen to acknowledge their progeny. They were getting old now; they resented the new kids on the block. 'If any of them punk rockers gets anywhere near my drumkit I shall kick 'em square in the knackers,' snapped the Who's drummer Keith Moon in October 1977. 'I got fifteen years in this bloody business and what the hell do those bastards know?'[32]

From an early stage, punk was seen as a scream of rage against Britain's economic decline. 'Dole queue rock 'n' roll', Tony Parsons called it in the autumn of 1976; a 'gut-level reaction' taking in 'aggression, anger, frustration and . . . hope'. A year later, reflecting on 'the year of punk', the feminist writer Angela Carter concluded that it was a music born of unemployment, the sound of 'those who cannot work because there is none to be had and so make their play, their dancing, their clothes into a kind of work'. Even the *Daily Mirror*, lambasting the government for tolerating high unemployment, agreed that punk was an expression of despair. 'It's not much fun to be young today,' began an editorial entitled 'Punk Future' in June 1977, pointing out that in the previous month '104,000 school leavers have gone straight from their classrooms to an idle and purposeless life on the dole'. 'Is it any wonder', the paper asked, 'youngsters feel disillusioned and betrayed? Is it any wonder they turn to anarchistic heroes like Johnny Rotten? . . . Punk rock is tailor made for youngsters who think they only have a punk future.'[33]

Although the Sex Pistols had been founded in the summer of 1975, when inflation, not unemployment, was the big economic story, it was not hard to see why so many people associated their music with the plight of jobless youngsters. About half of all teenagers left school at 16, yet as manufacturing stagnated and Denis Healey's cuts began to bite, growing numbers found that there were simply no jobs for them. In the first half of 1977, some 252,328 youngsters under the age of 20 were out of work, more than three times the number a decade earlier. By the end of the decade, four out of ten under-25s were out of work, a glaring indictment of British industrial underperformance as well as a reflection of the turbulence still convulsing the Western economy. 'In towns like North Shields, Sunderland, Hartlepool and Consett, and also in the big urban centres of Tyneside and Teesside, most school-leavers expect to go on the dole', wrote the journalist Ben Pimlott. 'Older children in Newcastle schools are taught how to sign on for social security, and everywhere there is a coffee-bar society of unemployed teenagers.' Later, some youngsters described how 'frightening' the situation had been. 'At school, you'd be told that most of you would leave and not find a job,' one reflected. 'None of us expected to get jobs when we left school,' said another. 'So many people felt as though they were on the human scrap-heap, especially those who came from a deprived background.'[34]

Whether McLaren ever intended the Sex Pistols to have any political significance seems very doubtful. Despite his enduring interest in the revolutionary Situationist International, it seems much more likely that, at the beginning, he saw the Pistols as no more than 'a nine-month wonder, a cheap vehicle for some fast money, a few laughs, a touch of the old épater la bourgeoisie', as the critic Greil Marcus puts it. Only once the band became notorious did he begin to play up the political angle, not just because it allowed him to dust down some of his old adolescent anarchist rhetoric, but because it went down so well with highbrow critics. 'Punk rock lyrics certainly go along with terrifying the bourgeois,' said one Observer piece, quoting one of McLaren's more inflammatory statements: 'They are England's next generation and we will be proud of them. It's a class war; they want to destroy society.'[35]

On the face of it, talk of punk as class war was not so far-fetched. For one thing, John Lydon sang with a pronounced working-class accent, a kind of 'stage cockney' that came as a shock to audiences used to the deliberately Americanized intonation of most rock musicians. A survey by the academic Dave Laing shows that many punk songs explicitly mentioned social or political themes, among them 'royalty, the USA, dead end jobs, the police, watching television, record companies, sexual hypocrisy, war, anarchy and riots'. Lyrics were often fiercely anti-consumerist, too. 'Don't be told what you want / don't be told what you need,' sings Lydon on 'God Save the Queen', while fanzines like *Sniffin' Glue* could barely contain their contempt for the 'big companies' that were supposedly trying to 'tidy up the acts' just so they could 'make more money'. And whereas protest songs of the late 1960s often had a rather wishy-washy feel, punk lyrics were often nakedly confrontational. 'I hate the Civil Service rules / I won't open letter bombs for you,' runs the Clash's 'Career Opportunities'. 'You sit up there deciding my future / What the fuck do you think you are,' sing the Slits in 'Number One Enemy'. Indeed, many songs might have been written deliberately to annoy the respectable middle classes: in 'Mr Clean', for example, the Jam pour scorn on a *Times*-reading commuter, with his smart blue suit and Cambridge degree: 'I hate you and your wife / And if I get the chance I'll fuck up your life.'[36]

Yet despite punk's image as a kind of working-class protest music, there were more than a few middle-class punks. Profiling the Stranglers, the *Daily Express* noted that Jean-Jacques Burnel was 'a restaurant owner's son from middle-class Guildford'. A trained classical guitarist, Burnel had studied at the Royal Grammar School, Guildford before reading history at the University of Bradford, while his band-mates included 'former research student Hugh Cornwell', who had studied biochemistry at Bristol, and 'ex-university student Dave Greenfield', a medieval re-enactment enthusiast. As always, most rock stars liked to play down their suburban origins: as Peter York remarked, there was 'a lot of class tourism going on'. Yet a study of punk musicians' backgrounds shows that 43 per cent came from middle-class homes, compared with 48 per cent of beat musicians in the early 1960s, while 29 per cent had been university students – up from 22 per cent during the beat boom.[37]

Indeed, perhaps the biggest influence on British punk were the same art colleges that had influenced the psychedelic counterculture of the late 1960s, and even the rhythm and blues boom of a few years earlier. Malcolm McLaren, of course, had been to art college, as had Glen Matlock, while the Clash were essentially an art school band. 'The instigators of punk', the director Derek Jarman recorded in August 1976, 'are the same petit bourgeois art students who a few months ago were David Bowie and Bryan Ferry look-alikes – who've read a little art history, and adopted Dadaist typography and bad manners, and are now in the business of reproducing a fake street credibility.' And while there is no doubt that many working-class teenagers loved punk, its heartland remained the London art schools. 'A Punk Rock concert is simply the latter-day equivalent of the old art school hops, pitched at a slightly different social level,' wrote Richard Williams after seeing the Damned at the Marquee in July 1977. 'It is unabashedly an opportunity to wear fancy dress, to jump up and down oblivious to the welfare of one's neighbours and to score points for the best combination of pose and costume.'[38]

While barely half of all punk musicians were working-class, very few were genuinely political. Even *The Times* was struck by punk's lack of ideological content. Its 'half-formed anarchism' was 'an appeal to the emotions, not the intellect; an attitude, not a message', wrote Tony Partington in July 1977. 'Politically, the new wave has been more of a damp squib than the Sex Pistols' "potential H-bomb".'* Of course this contradicts the common view that punk was politically subversive; but, as Laing points out, far from having strong political commitments, most punk bands admitted that modern politics left them bored and apathetic. 'No-one sees any heroes,' remarked Jean-Jacques Burnel, the Stranglers' guitarist and one of punk's most articulate spokesmen. 'The politicians have lost their credibility; political philosophies are no longer relevant.' Like many of his contemporaries, Burnel had little faith in the left, claiming that 'leftist heroes' were 'all intellectuals' with no appeal on the streets. 'Democracy has totally collapsed, it's lost all its credibility,' he said. 'So we're due for tyranny. People laugh at that, because England is the last place for that, but I really think it could happen.'[39]

Burnel thought this explained the vogue for Nazi fetishism: young people, he said, 'want to believe in something. And that is a very strong image. They definitely don't wanna be associated with leftist things.' There was a lot of truth in that. Many punk bands seemed much keener on images of the far right than the far left, perhaps because, given the legacy of the Second World War, they seemed so shocking. The post-punk band Joy Division, founded in Salford by a group of friends inspired by the Sex Pistols, took its name from the sex-slave wing of a

---

* A line from the Sex Pistols' 'God Save the Queen', then much in the news, which claims that the 'fascist regime . . . made you a moron / A potential H-bomb'.

Nazi extermination camp in the Holocaust novel *House of Dolls*. The cover of their first EP, *An Ideal for Living* (1978) was a picture of a member of the Hitler Youth, drawn by the band's guitarist Bernard Sumner; the first song, 'Warsaw', meanwhile, was a lyrical biography of Rudolf Hess. And when they were not trying to shock, punk musicians often came over as much more conservative than we remember. Chatting to the *NME* in May 1977, the Jam's Paul Weller remarked that he was a big fan of the monarchy, explaining that the Queen 'works harder than what you or I do or the rest of the country'. He was planning to vote Conservative at the next election, he added. 'It's the unions who run the country.'[40]

The one genuinely political major punk group was the Clash. 'They talk of the boredom of living in the council high-rise blocks, of living at home with parents, of the dole queues and the mind-destroying jobs offered to unemployed school-leavers,' wrote Barry Miles after interviewing them in December 1976. 'They talk about there being no British clubs that stay open late, of how Britain has no rock 'n' roll radio stations, of how there is nothing to do.' As usual, this was slightly misleading: the singer Joe Strummer was a diplomat's son; the bassist, Paul Simonon, had studied at the Byam Shaw School of Art; and although the lead guitarist, Mick Jones, had been brought up on the nineteenth floor of a west London council block, he had still got in to the prestigious Strand grammar school, formerly a hothouse for the civil service. But although the Clash were not quite as proletarian as they appeared, they had a political edge that set them apart from their peers. Their first single, 'White Riot' (March 1977), was written as a reaction to the riots at the previous year's Notting Hill Carnival, where Strummer and Simonon had watched black Londoners fighting the police. With its explicit denunciation of inequality and its praise for black people 'throwing a brick', it was much more engaged than most punk singles, setting the tone for their album *The Clash*, which came out a month later. This was punk as social commentary, songs like 'Career Opportunities' blazing with fury at the plight of school leavers. 'We are dealing', remarked Joe Strummer, 'with subjects we really believe matter.'[41]

What also set the Clash apart was their keen interest in black music. 'The poor blacks and the poor whites are in the same boat,' Strummer told the *NME*. 'They don't want us in their culture, but we happen to dig Tapper Zukie and Big Youth, Dillinger and Aswad and Delroy Washington. We dig them and we ain't scared of going into heavy black record shops and getting their gear. We even go to heavy black gigs where we're the only white people there.' In particular, they had a passion for reggae, which had broken into the charts in the autumn of 1975. Reggae, said Jones, gave black youngsters 'their own culture but the young white kids don't have nothing'. The Clash set out to produce 'white reggae', and as time went by they began to incorporate Caribbean sounds into their own music. In the summer of 1977 they hired the legendary reggae producer Lee 'Scratch' Perry to produce their single 'Complete Control', and a year later they released the groundbreaking '(White Man In) Hammersmith Palais', which begins as the story of a white onlooker at a reggae concert before broadening into an appeal for racial solidarity and 'wealth redistribution'. No punk group had ever attempted such a blend of black and white genres, and none could have pulled it off so successfully. For the Clash, however, this was about more than music: bringing together reggae and punk was a political statement. 'We're hoping to educate any kid who comes to listen to us,' Strummer once remarked. 'I mean, we just really don't want the National Front stepping in and saying, "Things are bad, it's the blacks ..." We want to prevent that somehow, you know?'[42]

While the Clash were expanding their horizons, the Sex Pistols' descent into full-time folk devils was almost complete. At the end of May 1977 they released their long-awaited second single, 'God Save the Queen'. A more provocative title is hard to imagine, especially with the Silver Jubilee just weeks away. In fact, John Lydon had written the song months earlier and wanted to call it 'No Future'. It was Malcolm McLaren, always eager to court publicity and offend Middle England, who insisted on the new title. But this was not the only thing that outraged the press. Lydon's caustic, sneering delivery was as provocative as ever, while the lyrics, with their talk of the 'fascist regime', their mockery of the monarch ('She ain't no human being') and their sheer nihilism ('There's no future'), dripped with bitterness and frustration. Even Jamie Reid's iconic sleeve design, with the title and the band's name stamped in ransom-note script across the Queen's face, was too much for the platemakers, who initially walked out and had to be persuaded to go back to work.

On this occasion, the controversy proved extremely lucrative. Even though both the BBC and the Independent Broadcasting Authority banned the song, and even though Woolworths, Boots and W. H. Smith all refused to stock it, 'God Save the Queen' sold an estimated 150,000 copies in five days, entering the chart at number 11. Then it began to climb, and as Jubilee week approached it seemed that it might even reach number one. In fact it peaked at number 2; the official chart showed that the bestselling single during the Jubilee was Rod Stewart's 'I Don't Want to Talk about It/First Cut is the Deepest', leading to accusations that it had been rigged to prevent an embarrassing victory for the Sex Pistols. We shall probably never know the truth: although it is perfectly possible that the British Market Research Bureau fiddled the figures, that may well be wishful thinking on the part of punk fans. Rod Stewart's single had been selling very strongly for weeks, after all, and its chart performance over the summer as a whole was far stronger than that of 'God Save the Queen'.[43]

What is certain, though, is that 'God Save the Queen' lifted anti-punk hysteria to a new pitch. At a time of mounting unemployment, with Denis Healey's cuts beginning to bite and Jim Callaghan struggling to cling on to power, the tabloids seemed obsessed with a craze that seemed to represent everything supposedly going wrong in Britain. With its aggressive, anarchic overtones, punk appeared a fitting soundtrack for a nation flirting with economic disaster. Even fans like Jon Savage saw it as a shriek of pain against the 'prison' of the post-war liberal consensus, the supreme symbol of a society falling apart. One paper called the Sex Pistols the ringleaders of a 'sick', 'sinister' conspiracy against everything Britain held dear, while for Bernard Brook-Partridge, the Conservative law and order spokesman on the Greater London Council, they were 'absolutely bloody revolting', their attitude a 'deliberate incitement to anti-social behaviour and conduct'. 'Pop music morons', the Conservative MP John Hunt told the Commons, were debasing the morality of the young. 'If Pop music is going to be used to destroy our established institutions,' the veteran Labour MP Marcus Lipton told the *Mirror*, 'then it ought to be destroyed first.'*[44]

By now the rhetorical violence of the Commons chamber and the stylistic violence of punk itself were matched by genuine, terrifying violence on the streets. From the King's Road there came reports of Saturday afternoon punch-ups between punks, skinheads and would-be Teddy boys, who were presumably unaware that their predecessors had

---

* Amazingly, it was Norman St John Stevas, of all people, who spoke up for the nation's youngsters. Not all pop music programmes, he told the Commons, were 'moronic . . . Most of them are entertaining and some of them are even instructive – including the *Jimmy Young Show*, on which I appeared this morning.'

once been such inspirations to Malcolm McLaren. Leaving a pub on Sunday, 19 June, John Lydon was attacked by what he called 'a gang of knife-wielding yobs' shouting 'We love our Queen, you bastard!' Lydon himself thought they were merely 'lads out for violence'; even so, they severed two tendons in his left hand. 'SLASHED!' read the gleeful front-page headline in the *Mirror* two days later. That same afternoon, Paul Cook was attacked by a group of Teddy boys while walking down the Goldhawk Road. 'We were marked,' he reflected later. 'Everybody knew our faces. It was a nasty period.'

To the press, the Pistols were merely reaping what they had sown. But to the group themselves, still in their early twenties, it was a frightening sign that their lives had spun out of control. Once again sheer notoriety propelled their album *Never Mind the Bollocks, Here's the Sex Pistols*, released in October 1977, to the top of the charts, where it replaced Cliff Richard and the Shadows' *40 Golden Greats*. But as always, they were surrounded by controversy. Outraged by the title, radio and television trade associations banned adverts for the record, while a Nottingham record-shop proprietor who put it in the window was charged under the Indecent Advertisements Act. When he was acquitted, the tabloids could not contain their fury. 'Astonishing,' declared the *Sun*. 'That gives Johnny Rotten and his foul-mouthed Sex Pistols the chance to put up two fingers to the world.'[45]

But by this stage McLaren's band was falling apart. In January 1978 he organized a disastrous tour of the United States, booking small venues in the Deep South in order to provoke audiences and generate headlines. For Sid Vicious, now heavily addicted to heroin, it was all too much. In San Antonio he smacked a member of the audience over the head with his guitar; in Baton Rouge he simulated oral sex on stage; in Dallas he spat blood at a woman who had stormed the stage and hit him in the face. The music was now almost entirely irrelevant; all that mattered were the ritualistic displays of violence. At the end of the last gig, at Winterland in San Francisco, Lydon sat on the stage, chanting emptily: 'This is no fun, it's no fun at all.' 'Ever get the feeling you've been cheated?' he asked the audience. Four days later, he announced that he had left the band. The Sex Pistols were dead, but, in traditional rock-star fashion, there was plenty more misery to come. In October 1978 Sid Vicious was charged with murdering his girlfriend in New York. The following February, after a party celebrating his release on bail, he died of a heroin overdose. Five days later the High Court began hearing John Lydon's suit against Malcolm McLaren for non-payment of royalties. The battle only ended in 1986, when Lydon and his former band-mates were awarded control of the Sex Pistols. But by then, very few people cared.[46]

Punk's heyday was brief. By the end of 1977, most observers thought it had simply run out of energy, and the following February the *Evening Standard* bluntly declared that 'punk is dead'. To its original fans, it had long since become predictable, its avant-garde potential frittered away in attention-seeking stunts. Even the punk look, once so shocking, had begun to filter into the mainstream. By the beginning of the 1980s young punks in leather jackets and extravagantly spiky dyed hair had become a familiar sight, memorably parodied by Adrian Edmondson in *The Young Ones*. The 'shocking pink cockscomb', wrote the *Times*'s fashion editor in 1980, was distinctly chic, with fashionable hairdressers having 'absorbed the punks' obsession with dazzling plumage'. (Entertainingly, one cultural critic even suggests that punk's greatest legacy was in the world of hairdressing, with the 'close-cropped and spiky look' becoming a staple part of the post-feminist uniform.) In art, design, fashion and typography, too, punk left a deep imprint: from the clothes of Vivienne Westwood to the layout of magazines such as *The Face*, *City Limits* and even *Smash Hits*, it had an enormous influence on the culture of the next ten years.[47]

Punk's musical legacy, however, is less straightforward. Some groups made the transition into mainstream rock, notably the Stranglers, the Clash and the Police; others, such as Bauhaus, the Cure and Siouxsie and the Banshees, moved into more experimental (if very gloomy) post-punk before descending into the murky world of mid-1980s Goth. But punk's impact on popular music was not entirely healthy. Instead of taking rock back to basics, lamented the novelist and prog-rock fan Jonathan Coe, 'all it did was to make real musicianship unfashionable', ensuring that 'a generation of some of the most gifted rock musicians this country had ever produced suddenly had their already precarious livelihoods taken away from them'. This is probably a bit strong; still, there is some truth in the claim that, in musical terms, punk was a backward step. With its emphasis on speed and simplicity, its disdain for expertise and its contempt for earnestness and experimentation, punk arguably narrowed horizons instead of expanding them. As the writer Ian MacDonald astutely pointed out, it was quintessentially democratic music, 'flattening all distinctions between audience and performer', and allowing even the most unskilled band to imagine they could make it.

But by emphasizing pace and aggression over accuracy and fluency, 'it destroyed the skills base of pop music' in Britain. Of course there were still plenty of talented bands, but with pop music now falling in love with the beat of the drum machine, 'basic musical articulacy became thin on the ground'.[48]

More than any other craze since the early 1960s, punk has become synonymous with its historical moment. On the surface, nothing better symbolizes the tortured politics of the Callaghan years, or captures the disillusionment and anger of Britain's school leavers in the age of stagflation. And yet the fact is that punk was *not very popular*. Beat music makes a fitting soundtrack for the early 1960s because millions of people liked it; by contrast, the vast majority of pop music fans in the late 1970s never listened to punk rock. In 1963–4, no fewer than 88 beat singles had appeared in the Top Thirty; in 1977–8, only 38 punk singles made it. Contrary to popular belief, the list of the bestselling singles in the last four years of the 1970s, reflecting what people actually bought and listened to, was a largely punk-free zone. Only the Boomtown Rats (who were arguably not really a punk band) made much of an impression on the charts, and even their success was dwarfed by much more popular acts like Abba, Boney M and the Bee Gees. In terms of albums, meanwhile, punk made no impression at all, especially when compared with the enormous success of Abba's *Arrival*, Fleetwood Mac's *Rumours* and the soundtracks of *Grease* and *Saturday Night Fever*, which dominated the charts for years. To see punk as the sound of the late 1970s, in other words, is just wrong. It may have delighted the staff of *Melody Maker* and the *NME*, and it certainly had a tremendous influence on fashion and design. But as far as most ordinary record-buyers were concerned, it was irrelevant.[49]

It is not hard to see why punk's impact was so feeble. Its disdain for virtuosity meant that people who enjoyed listening to concept albums about knights and maidens simply loathed it. Of course many young music fans, desperate not to be left behind by fashion, immediately swapped allegiances. Feeling like a 'fickle lover', the future Spandau Ballet songwriter Gary Kemp, who turned 17 in 1976, took his pile of Yes, Genesis and Emerson, Lake and Palmer records to sell at Cheapo Cheapo's record store in Soho as soon as he had heard the Sex Pistols play. But, contrary to myth, punk did not kill off progressive rock entirely. High-concept albums such as Yes's *Going for the One* (1977), Emerson, Lake and Palmer's *Works Volume II* (1977) and especially Pink Floyd's *Animals* (1977) and *The Wall* (1979) continued to sell millions of copies, while the Electric Light Orchestra's splendid *Out of the Blue* and *Discovery* were among the biggest sellers in 1978 and 1979. Meanwhile, the letters pages of the *NME* smouldered with the fury of prog rock fans appalled by critics' enthusiasm for the new trend. 'Each week your paper contains less and less about music, spending more of its space on theatrics, punk rock being the greatest example,' one Birmingham man wrote in December 1976. Punk acts, he thought, 'should be classed with magicians, jugglers, comedians, etc., not musicians whose prime objective is music'. A year later, a reader from Preston sounded a similar note. 'It's a crying shame,' he complained, 'when talented contemporary originals such as Yes, ELP, etc., spend months recording vinyl masterpieces which are biasedly slagged off, yet one-chord wonders like The Adverts get praised for badly played inept garbage which is probably recorded in a public convenience.'[50]

Punk also manifestly failed to win over the teenage mainstream. Most successful records of the day had cheerful or romantic themes; by contrast, punk was associated with violence, negativity, dole queues and depression. As Laing points out, musical trends since the 1960s have usually involved a strong dance element – particularly important for teenage girls – but punk offered few opportunities for dancing. For many teenagers, pogoing was 'not dancing', just as punk was 'not music'. Crucially, too, most punk singles were rarely played on the radio, appearing only late at night or on specialist weekend shows. And on top of all that, punk was eclipsed by a much more successful musical genre that is often overlooked in standard accounts of a bleak, confrontational late 1970s – a genre that was designed specifically for dancing, had a strong appeal to teenage girls and was perfectly suited to daytime radio. That genre was disco, which crossed the Atlantic in the mid-1970s and proved a massive popular success. To most rock critics, disco was anathema, the epitome of mindless commercialized dance music. But to millions of ordinary British teenagers, singles like Donna Summer's 'I Feel Love' and Hot Chocolate's 'So You Win Again', or albums like K-Tel's *Disco Fever* and Abba's *Voulez-Vous*, were catchy, accessible and endlessly entertaining. Punk never appealed to anything more than a minority. But disco, which transcended boundaries of class, race and generation, was nothing if not mainstream. That was why rock journalists hated it; and that was why most people loved it.[51]

Punk's place in the iconography of the late 1970s is, of course, assured. For one thing, it fits perfectly into a narrative of decline and division, with 'dole queue rock' as the musical expression of an economy in meltdown, a political consensus in tatters and a society tearing itself apart. But although things were bad enough in the late 1970s, they were never quite that bad. And a glance at what people actually bought suggests a rather different picture. In terms of total sales, by far the most successful British artists of the decade were Queen, Elton John, Led Zeppelin, Pink Floyd, Genesis and the Bee Gees. None of these groups was remotely as controversial as the Sex Pistols, but they were much more popular. As for Elton John, not for nothing does one writer call him 'the single most representative "sound of the seventies"'. Between May 1970 and October 1979, the former Reg Dwight had no fewer than sixteen Top Fifty albums, four of them reaching number one. Across the Atlantic he was even more popular: twelve of John's singles sold more than a million copies each. As early as 1974 he was earning more money per month than the Beatles at their peak, an extraordinary testament to the breadth of his appeal. Of course, as the leading exponent of adult-friendly 'soft rock', the flight lieutenant's son was very far from being the darling of the rock music press. Yet as *The Times* remarked in 1975, this 'slightly tubby, balding man from Pinner' had not only sold 75 million records worldwide, he was already 'the most popular single performer in the ephemeral history of rock 'n' roll, Britain's true successor to The Beatles'.[52]

Queen's success, meanwhile, was even more striking. Catchy and unthreatening, their cheerful blend of prog rock, pop and glam yielded six hugely successful albums during the lifetime of the Wilson–Callaghan government, all of which reached the top five. Their flamboyant style left many critics unmoved: when Freddie Mercury, Brian May, Roger Taylor and John Deacon played at Earls Court in 1977, *The Times*'s reviewer complained that 'everything was over-inflated' and concluded that 'the future lies in other directions'. But Queen's sales, an estimated 19 million records in Britain alone, told a different story. Far from being stuck in the past, almost everything about them – the theatrical performances, the grandiose sets, the extravagant costumes, the vast sell-out crowds, the restless mixture of styles and genres – anticipated the trends of the decade to come. With the music press rushing to embrace punk's stripped-down austerity, few critics had much time for what *The Times* called Queen's 'triumph of technology over music'. But all the time technology was filtering into the musical mainstream. As early as December

1977, Peter York told the readers of *Harpers & Queen* that the 'brief surge of primitivism' had come and gone. Punk might have attracted more attention, but from Donna Summer's disco rhythms to Kraftwerk's pioneering electropop, synthesizers and computers were steadily redefining what millions of ordinary people listened to every week. '2001', wrote York, 'seems closer than 1984.' In this respect, at least, Rick Wakeman won after all.[53]

24

Carnival Time

Who am I? What am I? Where am I going?
Sign in a hostel for homeless black teenagers in London,
quoted in *The Times*, 30 January 1975

*Black people should not be allowed in England because
England is meant for whites. England is nearly full of black
people. They should be thrown out of England ... It is meant
for white people only.*
Ten-year-old schoolboy, quoted in *The Times*,
14 February 1978

After weeks of sunshine, London was in the mood for a party. It was
'carnival time', announced the *Daily Mirror* on 28 August 1976, looking
forward to the 'irresistible explosion of West Indian colour and music' that
was about to hit 'the grey pavements of London this holiday weekend'.
Established as an annual festival for the capital's Caribbean immigrants,
the Notting Hill Carnival had been held in west London for the last eleven
years. Although there were occasional scuffles with the Metropolitan
Police, the carnival was generally seen as a friendly, vibrant affair, in keeping with the organizers' promise that it would celebrate 'joy, love and fun'.
At the previous year's carnival, the drink had steadily flowed, but there
had been relatively few reports of trouble. Some revellers came as 'demons
and scaly dragons, wearing papier mâché masks', wrote one onlooker, 'or
as angels and butterflies with gilded wings five feet high'. From their windows, local residents leaned out and took photos; on the pavements, stalls
sold watermelon slices, rum punch, curried goat and plantain tart. 'It made
a change', *The Times*'s diarist thought, 'from the Clapham horse show.'[1]

But this time the atmosphere felt different. Partly because of pressure from Kensington and Chelsea Council, which made no secret of its dislike for the carnival, the Met had decided to flood the area with some 1,600 police, who were much more visible and assertive than in previous years. Still, on Sunday the parades passed off as usual, and everybody seemed to be enjoying themselves. 'Dancing In The Rain' read the *Mirror*'s headline the next day, showing a policeman laughing with a black woman, testament to the 'sunshine spirit' that had survived an unexpected downpour. But then, on Monday afternoon, everything changed. At about 4.30 the police tried to arrest some black youths whom they accused of working as pickpockets along Acklam Road. Other West Indian men intervened; tempers flared; and quite suddenly, almost out of nowhere, anger tipped over into outright violence. As bottles flew through the air, some officers seized milk crates and dustbin lids to protect themselves; others drew their truncheons and waded into the crowd. The sound of the steel bands gave way to screams; the streets were suddenly full of running people. One West Indian bystander saw the crowd 'throwing anything they could lay their hands on, bottles, bricks and sticks', while the police sheltered behind their makeshift shields, blood streaming down from beneath their helmets. As police reserves poured into the narrow streets around the Portobello Road, local residents gathered at their windows to shout and jeer. 'Stuff was even coming down on us from the flats above,' one policeman said the next day, barely able to hide his disbelief.

By now the carnival had become a pitched battle. 'I had never seen policemen running away from a situation before,' recalled the future radio presenter Dotun Adebayo, a 16-year-old who had spent the afternoon dancing happily to calypso music. 'I don't know where all the rocks came from but they were raining down on the fleeing cops.' With police cordons sealing off the streets around Ladbroke Grove, many revellers found themselves trapped inside a full-scale riot. And even as a police helicopter circled impotently overhead, it was clear that the Met had lost control. Police car windows were smashed on sight; one supermarket, its windows kicked in, was robbed of all its alcohol supplies. Two reporters captured the apocalyptic scene:

> One gang of young black people made their way up the road smashing
> every window in sight. A girl aged about 14 held a milk bottle and smashed
> it against the plate glass window of a café until the window cracked. Then,
> with the heel of a platform shoe, she kicked the glass until it shattered.

Another gang of youths lobbed a brick through a window of an ice cream van. When a passing middle-aged white man made a comment, the youths turned on him. A young girl was among those kicking the man . . .

Closer to Ladbroke Grove, the side streets off Portobello Road were covered with broken glass and bloodstained rags lay in the gutter.

Motorists driving along Ladbroke Grove found themselves in the middle of the riot as stones bounced off the windows of their cars. One gang of youths moved along the road and turned over two cars, then smashed all the windows in a large private house and began to loot the building.[2]

By the time the fighting died down, some 450 people had been injured, most of them policemen, while 68 people had been arrested. All in all, it was the worst violence seen on the streets of London since the Second World War, eclipsing even the racist hooliganism in Notting Hill sixteen years earlier. And in the next day's papers, all talk of the calypso spirit had disappeared completely. 'Battle At The Carnival', shrieked the *Mail*, horrified by the spectacle of 'Ulster in Portobello Road'. The *Express* shuddered at the rioters' 'animal spirits', the *Mirror* described them as 'an angry army of black youths', and the *Telegraph* conjured up a terrifying image of 'coloured men in screaming groups . . . with bottles and bricks'. And for those people who disliked immigration, the news confirmed everything they had ever suspected. For the *Telegraph*, the root cause was 'the instability of the West Indian family'; for the readers of the *Evening News*, the culprits were 'teachers, social workers and others who have told the young blacks to do their own thing'; for the *Express*, the riots raised the spectre of 'race war in Britain'. And for the *Mail*'s star columnist Lynda Lee-Potter, they were yet another reminder that, in Jim Callaghan's Britain, nothing was sacred and nobody was safe. In the face of such 'vindictive hooliganism', she wrote, law and order were on the verge of collapse. 'In our safe, comfortable homes in the provinces, we're all beginning to know fear . . .'[3]

Not everybody was quite so quick to blame the West Indian community. The *Mirror*'s John Pilger blamed 'police overkill' for the violence, while even the *Evening Standard* suggested that by flooding the streets with officers, the Met had been 'far too heavy-handed'. But Scotland Yard refused to admit fault. 'It's the same old story,' remarked a spokesman: 'a lot of West Indians who intervened and attacked our men did so without bothering to inquire why we were trying to arrest other coloureds.' And for the Met Commissioner, Sir Robert Mark, the riots had been a disgraceful exhibition of 'hooliganism, drunkenness, vandalism and most of all, pocket picking and robbery', resembling 'nothing so much as a return to the sordid celebrations attending the hangings at Tyburn Tree'. The criticism of his men, he wrote later, was easily explained: 'No one is prepared to tell the simple truth when wrongdoing involves coloured people.' The West Indians simply must learn to behave themselves, agreed the deputy leader of Kensington and Chelsea Council, who had earlier tried to ban the carnival entirely. 'This is not Trinidad.'[4]

For the image of the Notting Hill Carnival, the riots of August 1976 were a disaster. As far as Fleet Street was concerned, a celebration of London's ethnic diversity had become a sinister, threatening occasion and a symbol of black criminality. As the journalist Gary Younge later put it, the carnival had 'moved from being a story about culture to one about crime and race'. And when isolated skirmishes broke out the following year, the headline-writers were waiting. 'War Cry!' roared the *Express*. 'The Boot Goes In . . . The unprecedented scenes in the darkness of London streets looked and sounded like something out of the film classic *Zulu*.' The Shadow Home Secretary, Willie Whitelaw, suggested that the risks of holding the carnival now outweighed 'the enjoyment it gives', while the *Mail* warned that 'if the West Indians wish to preserve what should be a happy celebration which gives free rein to their natural exuberance, vitality and joy, then it is up to their leaders to take steps necessary to ensure its survival'. Outside London's Caribbean communities, only a few liberal-minded souls spoke up for the carnival. 'It's so nice to see so many happy, dancing people with smiles on their faces,' said Prince Charles.[5]

Whatever people's views of the Notting Hill riots, one thing was clear. In *The Times*'s words, they had been 'a shock for the nation':

> The incidents were ugly in themselves and were evidence both of the tension that exists between many blacks and the police and of the growing resentment and disaffection among many black teenagers.
>
> That resentment runs deep. Many young blacks are out of a job, have left school with few qualifications and have no prospect of a satisfying career. They often live in poor, cramped conditions in inner city areas where their grievances feed upon each other . . .
>
> What matters most in the long run is to deal with these underlying frustrations. So long as they persist there is the danger that more and more young blacks will turn to crime and that there will be mounting fear and antagonism between the races.[6]

For many of the parents of the black teenagers at the Notting Hill Carnival, Britain had once seemed the promised land, its plentiful jobs and high wages making up for the cold weather, the hard stares and the harsh words. But by the late 1970s the picture had changed. Roughly 2 million people with origins in the so-called New Commonwealth lived in Britain during the Callaghan years.* Some 31 per cent came from India, 13 per cent from Pakistan and 3 per cent from Bangladesh; another 25 per cent came from the Caribbean; just over 8 per cent were East African Asians; and the rest came from Hong Kong, Malaysia, Nigeria and elsewhere. More than half had settled in Greater London, 17 per cent lived in the West Midlands and smaller groups lived in Lancashire, West Yorkshire and the East Midlands. Many were not, strictly speaking, immigrants: they were black and brown Britons, born and brought up on British soil, with local accents, local friends and local tastes. Yet although not all their neighbours agreed that, as the skinhead song put it, 'there ain't no black in the Union Jack', old prejudices died hard. When the Schools Council published a survey of primary school children's racial attitudes in 1978, the results were often shocking. Even the more tolerant white children, the report found, betrayed an 'unquestioning feeling of superiority'. 'Black people are nearly the same as white people ... They are sometimes very nice,' wrote one child from an all-white Midlands school. 'They can't help being black,' wrote another. 'They look like normal people,' agreed a third.[7]

The news was not all bad. Under the 1976 Race Relations Act, which outlawed discrimination on the basis of 'colour, race, nationality or ethnic or national origins' and set up the Commission for Racial Equality, Britain had the most sweeping anti-racist laws in Europe. It was revealing that the new regime won the support of the Conservative front bench; although they had their doubts, explained Willie Whitelaw, opposition 'would not be possible for us as a party to justify'. And although prejudice endured, polls showed that most people believed discrimination was wrong. A survey by the Race Relations Board in 1975–6, for example, found that eight out of ten people opposed job discrimination and seven out of ten were against housing discrimination. In many circles, overt racism was now unacceptable: already many libraries had removed their copies of *Little Black Sambo*, and although the defiantly old-fashioned comedian Bernard Manning remained a fixture in the ITV schedules, the fate of *The Black and*

* The census of 1981 gave a figure of 2.2 million, which may be a slight underestimate.

White Minstrel Show was another sign of change. For years black activists had complained that the programme indulged racial stereotypes, but the BBC had consistently ignored them. Throughout the early 1970s the Minstrels' old-fashioned routines regularly attracted audiences of more than 12 million, but in July 1978 they disappeared from the screen, never to return. And even the relatively conservative Jim Callaghan, no great supporter of immigration, had patently mellowed. Chatting to Bernard Donoughue a year earlier, the Prime Minister dismissed the idea of 'a multicultural society'. Far better, he said, for 'immigrants to marry UK natives, "decent white Britons", and let us have a coffee-coloured community'. He was, he added, 'a supporter of Brazil'.[8]

In many ways, Caribbean and Asian immigrants were becoming absorbed into mainstream British society. Cuisine was the most obvious symbol of assimilation: by the time Harold Wilson returned to Downing Street, Britain boasted more than 2,000 Indian restaurants (most of which were actually Bangladeshi), while even the smallest market town had a Chinese takeaway. But perhaps an even more striking example, because of its sheer visibility, was sport. The nation's best boxer during the mid-1970s, for example, was the light-heavyweight champion John Conteh, born in Liverpool to a Sierra Leonean father and Irish mother, while Clive Sullivan became the first black man to captain a British national side when he led Great Britain's rugby league team to victory in the 1972 World Cup. In football, meanwhile, the tipping point came a few years later when Ron Atkinson's West Bromwich Albion fielded three young black players, Laurie Cunningham, Cyrille Regis and Brendan Batson, nicknamed The Three Degrees after the black singing group. In April 1977, Cunningham became the first black player to pull on the white England shirt, scoring on his debut for the Under-21s against Scotland. A year later, Nottingham Forest's right-back Viv Anderson became the first black player to be picked for the senior side when he played against Czechoslovakia. Unlike earlier pioneers, neither was an immigrant: Cunningham had been born in Archway, while Anderson was from Nottingham. As England's manager, Ron Greenwood, told the press, they were as English as any of their teammates.[9]

Sadly, however, not everybody was quite so open-minded. To succeed on the pitch, black footballers needed a thick skin. Many coaches had decidedly old-fashioned views about black players: when Hunter Davies asked Tottenham's chief scout how a north London club could have no black professionals or apprentices, the latter explained that they 'don't have the determination'. On another occasion, Davies saw the team's assistant manager, Eddie Baily, having a disagreement with a black workman while the players were on a pre-season run. 'Why don't you get back to the jungle and eat bananas?' Baily snapped. Even highly successful players, such as West Bromwich's striker Cyrille Regis, struggled to break down the walls of prejudice. 'There were lots of stereotypes then about black players – that we couldn't handle the cold weather, that we were all flair and didn't have the right temperament – and when you've been brought up in London in that time, as we were, you certainly know you're different,' Regis reflected. Away fixtures were a particular ordeal. On arrival, Brendan Batson recalled, 'you could see the National Front outside, handing out their racist literature', while during the game the opposing fans often chanted racist songs and threw bananas. For the time being, however, the authorities closed their eyes. Critics were being 'a little sensitive', Chief Superintendent David Polkinghorne of Scotland Yard told a conference in 1981. The stadium, he insisted, was 'a ground for racial harmony, where working-class blacks and whites stand side by side. I don't see it as a problem.'[10]

The ugly chants on the football terraces were a reminder that, despite the apparent progress in the previous two decades, there remained a long way to go. And for families who had moved to Britain in the relatively buoyant 1950s, the economic woes of the Heath and Wilson years were a dreadful shock. During the heyday of mass immigration, thousands of newcomers had been drawn to industrial towns like Bradford and Wolverhampton where jobs were plentiful and housing was cheap. But during the downturn of the 1970s these were precisely the places that suffered most from the agonizing death of heavy industry. Wolverhampton, for example, was devastated by the disappearance of Norton Villiers Triumph and the closure of the nearby Bilston steelworks. And as the factories that would once have given newcomers a foothold on the ladder closed down, so black and Asian settlers found themselves condemned to low-paid jobs in increasingly dilapidated dead-end towns. By 1975, government figures showed that unemployment among immigrants was twice the national average, while young black school leavers were four times less likely to find jobs than their white counterparts. Even a good education was not necessarily a passport to success. In 1976 more figures showed that one in four West Indian or Asian university graduates went on to become manual workers, compared with a minuscule number of white graduates. And by the end of the decade, it was clear that the decline of British manufacturing had taken a heavy toll on the ambitions of the immigrant population. In 1984 eight out of ten black men and seven out of ten Asians were still working as manual labourers – compared with only five out of ten whites.[11]

With the economic ladder ripped away, it was little wonder many black youngsters felt they stood no chance of success. In major cities, black families were increasingly concentrated in 'estates where no one else wanted to live'. In London, for instance, they were clustered in damp, dilapidated council estates that had been abandoned by their original inhabitants, especially in areas such as Haringey and Hackney. A good example was the Holly Street estate, Dalston, where between 1977 and 1980 almost eight out of ten flats went to black families. Like so many council estates, Holly Street had originally been a symbol of optimism and opportunity, its four concrete towers and nineteen medium-rise blocks supposedly offering a clean, modern, democratic way of life. Yet by the end of the decade Holly Street had already become a byword for unemployment, vandalism, prostitution, drug abuse and racial violence. In just one week in 1980, the estate suffered twenty-one separate break-ins. 'The corridor is a thieves' highway,' wrote one visitor:

> No one questions the passage of strangers, who may be residents of a distant block taking a sheltered short cut. At the corners where blocks join are dark passages, blind alleys, gloomy staircases. It is easy to get lost in these labyrinths, and easy for robbers to lurk or to lose their pursuers. The fear of muggings is so widespread that people, if they have to venture out at night, stick to the lit areas and walk hurriedly.

The tragedy was that Holly Street was far from unusual. The Broadwater Farm estate in Tottenham was built to hold 3,000 people and finished in 1973. By this point, however, the design flaws were already obvious. Poorly maintained and located a long way from decent amenities, the Farm's flats suffered terrible problems with vermin, leaks and break-ins. Within just three years of the estate's completion, 53 per cent of council tenants were refusing to go there, while more tenants had applied for transfers out than anywhere else in the borough. There was talk of pulling it down, but nothing happened. By 1980, seven out of ten flats were going to homeless families.[12]

Of course not all immigrants lived on sink estates like Broadwater Farm, and most reports played down the fact that half of its residents were white. But in the editorials of Conservative newspapers and the imaginations of the middle classes, council estates became a kind of shorthand for immigrants and criminals. Since the summer of 1972, the tabloids had been full of anguish about 'muggers', almost invariably identified as being black, who were supposedly stalking the city streets, robbing and pillaging at will. In fact, most of the decade's high-profile crimes, from the IRA pub bombings to the murders by the Yorkshire Ripper and the Black Panther, were by white men, although it is true that, in London, six out of ten victims of street crime said their attackers had been black. But it was mugging that really captured public attention. Supposedly inspired by events in the United States, it was alien, threatening, even subversive, hinting at the dangers that lay beneath the surface of modern city life. And through the mugging panic, as a group of social scientists from the University of Birmingham argued in a famous study in 1978, immigrants became identified with age-old racial stereotypes, playing on 'images of sex, rape, primitivism, violence and excrement'.[13]

'It's the coloureds who cause most crime,' explained a Birmingham woman interviewed by the writer Beatrix Campbell:

> The *Birmingham Mail* says the majority of muggings are by coloureds. Muggers should get life as well. What gets up my nose is the jails: they've gone in there to be punished and they might think it's hard, but I don't think it is: they're waited on hand, foot and finger. Hanging should be brought back. And rape – they should be put away for life.

Such views were not confined to West Midlands shop assistants. Neighbourhoods such as Brixton and Clapham, Judge Gwyn Morris told an Old Bailey jury during the trial of five black thieves in May 1975, had once been 'peaceful, safe and agreeable to live in'. But they had been 'radically transformed' by 'immigrant resettlement'. Muggers, he said, were preying on 'honest, innocent and hard-working unaccompanied women . . . I notice that not a single West Indian woman was attacked.' Not surprisingly, his remarks provoked uproar, and Morris hastily issued a statement explaining that he thought most immigrants were 'law-abiding citizens'. But a year later he was at it again, suggesting that white Londoners should set up 'some form or other of vigilante corps' to stop West Indian men preying on white women. Once again, Morris found himself at the centre of a furore. 'We expect these remarks from the National Front,' sighed the director of a charity working with black youths in Brixton. 'But not from a judge.'[14]

What bothered many black activists was not so much the tirades of the judiciary as the attitude of the police. Decades after immigrants had first arrived from south Asia and the Caribbean, Britain's constabulary remained almost entirely lily-white. In 1972 there were just 58 black and Asian police officers in England and Wales out of a total of more than 110,000. Three years later, under pressure from the Home Office, the Met Commissioner Sir Robert Mark launched a recruitment drive with the words: 'The only colour we recognize is blue.' But the results were pretty pathetic: by the middle of 1981 there were still only 286 black and Asian policemen across the country. Police spokesmen insisted that this was because immigrants' own communities discouraged them from joining the police, but even if this contained a tiny grain of truth, it was far from the whole story. Tony Lucombe, who had served as a policeman in Barbados before moving to Britain in the 1960s, was told that 'black officers were not wanted' and became the nation's first black prison officer instead. The handful of black and Asian policemen who joined in the 1970s encountered persistent mockery from their fellow recruits, while a Commons Select Committee on Race Relations and Immigration found that most white officers automatically associated darker skins with criminality. 'There is almost an inbred tendency for the coloured people to believe they ought to be able to do their own thing,' an experienced Brixton policeman told *The Times*. Most officers, found the sociologist Maureen Cain, thought 'niggers' were 'pimps and layabouts, living off what we pay in taxes'. 'Have you been to a wog house?' one officer asked her. 'They stink, they really do smell terrible.'[15]

Against this background, it was hardly surprising that relations between the police and Britain's immigrant communities were so strained. To make matters worse, the Met had become very keen on the so-called 'sus' laws, which dated back to 1824 and allowed them to arrest anyone they suspected of loitering 'with intent to commit' an offence. Not only were these laws invoked more in London than anywhere else, but their targets were disproportionately black. In 1976, for example, the Met brought more than half of all the 'sus' charges in the nation, while four out of ten people arrested under the 'sus' laws were black. Given that black people accounted for just 2 per cent of the national population, it is no wonder that so many people saw this as proof of racism. Other figures hinted at a similar story: the Home Office research unit showed that in 1975, black Londoners were fifteen times more likely than whites to be arrested for petty thefts, even though few people seriously thought they were fifteen times more likely to commit them. As a result, everyday confrontations between white policemen and black youngsters were charged with tension. Overshadowing every encounter, wrote Mike and Trevor Phillips, was the certain knowledge that you were facing a white man who could beat you, or send you to prison, or even kill you, just because of the colour of your skin, and there would be very little that anyone could do about it. But what hurt the most was their casual contempt, the way they flaunted their power over you and their determination to make you understand that you were less than they were.[16]

For some black activists, notably the future Labour MPs Diane Abbott and Paul Boateng, the campaign against the 'sus' laws was the decisive event in sparking their political interests and launching their careers. Most black residents, however, felt sheer frustration. Many young men and women turned inwards, rejecting assimilation into a society they called 'Babylon', and throwing themselves into separatist clubs and self-help projects. Often they sought solace in the intoxicating sound of reggae, which had crossed from Jamaica into Britain during the Heath years, spearheaded by the Jimmy Cliff film *The Harder They Come* (1972) and Bob Marley's album *Catch a Fire* (1973). By the time Harold Wilson returned to power, black British bands were producing their own home-grown reggae, while there were specialist reggae record shops in Birmingham, Leeds and Croydon, as well as the more heavily Caribbean areas of London. For many black teenagers, listening to reggae became a kind of refuge from unemployment, racism and alienation. The aspiring young poet Linton Kwesi Johnson, for example, borrowed its beat for his first album *Dread Beat an' Blood* (1978), which was suffused with the anger that led so many black youths to pick up 'bottles and bricks and sticks'. 'What was happening, for want of a better term, was racial oppression,' Johnson said later. 'I was inspired to articulate in verse how I felt, and how the generation of black youth to which I belonged felt about growing up in a racialised society.'[17]

What no amount of poetry could disguise was the cold, hard reality of the economic downturn. By 1977, the jobless rate for black Britons under the age of 25 was almost 14 per cent, twice that for their white neighbours. Even more disturbingly, black unemployment was growing more than three times more quickly than white. In Brixton, there were barely twenty jobs for every hundred applicants, and for many youngsters the future seemed to offer little hope. Like the earnest young hero in Horace Ové's gritty and compelling *Pressure* (1975), the first black British film, they felt squeezed between the expectations of their parents and the burdens of everyday racism, lengthening dole queues and police harassment. In *Pressure*, the protagonist's hopes of assimilation are repeatedly dashed; unable to get a job, he drifts into a netherworld of petty crime, dope smoking and Black Power politics. And outside the cinema the temperature was rising. After clashes between black and white youths in Wolverhampton in February 1978, local charity workers pointed out that black school leavers were three times as likely to be unemployed as their white counterparts. As usual, the police denied harassing black residents, while the town's Labour council leader insisted that while there might be one or two bad apples, 'things are not too serious'. But local activists told a different story. 'The police have been at odds with blacks in Wolverhampton for years,' one said sadly. 'There have been many previous incidents at schools and other places . . . There will be more, much more.' Sadly, he was right.[18]

Immigration had never been popular. At the end of the 1960s, one in four people thought it had been the single most lamentable development of the decade, while the extraordinary public regard for Enoch Powell – voted the BBC's Man of the Year three times in the early 1970s – was almost entirely based on his opposition to immigration. Although most people liked to think of themselves as open-minded, old prejudices died hard, from the yellowing 'No Coloured' signs in landladies' windows in the 1950s to the stand-up routines in ITV's *The Comedians* two decades later. But somewhere between the OPEC oil shock and the IMF crisis there was a subtle change in the atmosphere. The economic woes and endless disappointments had taken their toll; many people were looking for scapegoats. Racist jokes seemed to have a harder, more aggressive edge; urban myths seemed less patronizing and more resentful. Returning to Blackburn in the late 1970s after an eight-year absence, Jeremy Seabrook found that people were still telling the same anecdotes about Pakistani benefit cheats, but whereas they had once been 'half-humorous', the stories were now charged with bitterness. When he talked to local Asian residents, they told him that 'racialism' was getting worse, that there was more overt hostility than before, that their white neighbours blamed them for everything that was going wrong. They would not have been reassured by a Gallup poll in February 1978, which found that 49 per cent of people thought Caribbean and Asian immigrants should be offered 'financial aid' to return home. That many of them had been born in *Britain* was evidently beside the point.[19]

Nowhere was this culture of resentment better captured than in Dennis Potter's television play *Brimstone and Treacle*, which was made in

1976 but suppressed by the BBC because of its shocking depiction of the rape of a disabled girl. At the centre of the play is the girl's father, Tom Bates (Denholm Elliott). An outwardly amiable middle-class publisher of religious books, Tom has recently joined the National Front, driven partly by his abhorrence of 'drugs, violence, indiscipline, strikes, subversion, pornography', but also by prejudices dating back to the days of empire. Sharing a glass of whisky with Martin, an unexpected visitor who claims to have known his daughter, Tom throws caution to the wind. 'There'll always be an England? Not with half the cities filled with coloured men there won't,' he scoffs. 'Send them back to their own countries.' But then Martin – who agrees with him, but may be the Devil in disguise – gets carried away. 'Send them back to starve . . . Put them in cattle trucks and drive them out!' he says. 'Put them into camps . . . Oh, you'll hear de calypso then all right. You'll hear the darkies sing! You'll see England like it used to be again, clean and white.' This is too much for Tom. 'Stop it!' he says. 'That's going too far!'

> All I want is the England I used to know. The England I remember as a younger man. I don't want anybody to be hurt. But too many things seem to have gone wrong. I just want things to be like they used to be. When there were no bombs and not so much sniggering and you knew where you were, and old ladies could feel safe in the street and – well, yes, I do want the blacks to go.

What makes this so powerful, of course, is that Tom previously seemed such a nice, reasonable chap. 'I simply want the world to stop just where it is,' he says plaintively. 'And – go back a bit.'[20]

In reality, someone as outwardly mild and middle-class as Tom would have been out of place in the National Front. Created by a merger of far-right groups in the mid-1960s, it had slowly gathered momentum during the Heath years, but most of its supporters were working-class voters who saw their bread-and-butter anxieties through the prism of race. In February 1974 the NF had performed very poorly, its candidates attracting an average of just 3.3 per cent of the vote. All the same, it was now the most visible and assertive far-right movement since Oswald Mosley's British Union of Fascists, and there was no reason to think it would disappear overnight. In just seven years, the party had established 30 branches and 54 groups around the country, as well as having an estimated 20,000 paid-up members. Its activists were highly conspicuous on the streets of major cities, distributing leaflets that tackled issues such as crime, inflation, Northern Ireland, Europe and strikes.

Disturbingly, it was now targeting both university students ('Don't be bullied by the crackpots and gangsters of the extreme left') and school-children ('Are you tired of lessons where the teacher continually tries to run down Britain, while at the same time Black kids have "Black Stud-ies" to give them more self-respect?'). But although NF activists tried to exploit public outrage after the Birmingham bombings, handing out anti-Irish literature in local pubs, at the heart of their ideology was pure racism. There was a 'global struggle for survival between various species of humanity', wrote the party's corpulent joint leader Martin Webster in 1974. 'The British people are in the front line of this struggle and must be made to realize it . . . White man, are you ready to fight?'[21]

In what many commentators saw as a chilling echo of the 1930s, the National Front's presence on the streets was a central element of its appeal. In June 1974, almost a thousand NF marchers clashed with anti-fascist students, most of them belonging to the International Marx-ist Group, in Red Lion Square, Holborn. As mounted policemen fought to keep them apart, one student, Kevin Gately, was knocked to the ground and killed. As the first person to die in a political demonstration in mainland Britain for fifty-five years, he became a depressing symbol of the new violence of public life in the mid-1970s. As was their wont, the far left blamed the police; in fact, since none of the other demonstra-tors even saw a policeman near him, it seems more likely that he was accidentally hit on the head, perhaps with a banner pole, by another protester. Afterwards, an inquiry under Lord Justice Scarman blamed the International Marxist Group for causing the violence, concluding that they had deliberately charged the police lines to get at the National Front. For the far left the episode had been a disaster; by contrast, the NF congratulated themselves on a job well done. As one observer put it, by obeying police instructions and keeping their discipline, the far-right marchers seemed to have given 'a display of order and dignity to con-trast with the disorder and violence' of their opponents. This was an illusion, of course: many NF marchers had fitted lethal metal spikes on top of their Union Jack flagpoles. But they could not have wished for better publicity. In the months that followed, new recruits flooded in, and in October their parliamentary candidate in Hackney and Shoreditch won 9.4 per cent of the vote, their best result yet.[22]

As might have been expected, the National Front drew most of its support from cities that had experienced high levels of immigration. Although it boasted 174 regional branches by the end of the decade, its strength was concentrated in London, the industrial West Midlands, the

Lancashire mill towns, South Yorkshire and Leicester. By and large, recruits came from unskilled manual workers and the self-employed lower-middle classes, such as small shopkeepers who resented their Asian rivals, felt squeezed by the major chains and 'needed someone to kick'.* Among the NF's older members were Second World War veterans who felt cheated and abandoned; among the younger recruits, meanwhile, were former Borstal boys and football hooligans who were attracted by its aggressive patriotism and by the prospect of a good punch-up. 'I think there's a lot you can do with a soccer hooligan,' the party's co-leader Martin Webster told *Panorama*:

> I think that people resort to mindless violence and vandalism because they have not been given by society a point and a meaning to their lives. People do like to identify: they do like to associate themselves with something which is big and glorious and noble which they, the little individual, can associate themselves with and feel proud that they somehow belong. And we feel that the very, very fanatical adulation by supporters for their particular clubs is a sort of sublimated patriotism.

'So it's a case of Millwall today and National Front tomorrow?' asked the interviewer. 'We hope so,' Webster said.[23]

What made the National Front's appeal so potent was that it tapped a host of anxieties that had little or nothing to do with immigration. A survey in 1978 found that one in four people thought the NF stood for 'ordinary working people', while a study of its supporters in Harlesden two years later found that its appeal was grounded in mundane bread-and-butter issues such as housing, schools and jobs. Its heartlands had seen tremendous change in the previous twenty years – the kind of change captured in the titles sequence of *Whatever Happened to the Likely Lads?*, as Terry Collier's beloved working-class streets fall beneath the bulldozer, making way for high-rise council blocks. In inner cities across the nation, skilled white families had moved out. Jobs had dried up; slums had been cleared; concrete tower blocks now stood where there had once been long red-brick terraces. And to those who stayed put, the social landscape of the mid-1970s often seemed deeply unsettling, with their values and traditions under siege from muggers,

---

* David Edgar's play *Destiny*, first performed by the RSC in September 1976, is very good on this. One of the central characters, Turner, is a former army sergeant whose West Midlands antiques shop has been scheduled for redevelopment. Blaming 'the multinationals and multi-racial elements in our midst', he turns to the far right.

immigrants, pornographers and developers. In Hackney, Jeremy Seabrook met a woman in her late fifties at a bus stop, her dyed hair swept
back in a style that was already two decades old. 'There's nothing round
here now, it's not Hackney any more,' she said sadly. 'All the people we
used to know, they've all gone. All these that are here now, I don't know
where they come from, who they are.' At the Pensioners' Association in
Dalston, rain coursed down the grimy windows while elderly people sat
over chipped cups of tea, complaining about mugging, television and
the morals of the young. 'It's horrible round here. It isn't Hackney now,'
one said. 'I knew everybody round about where we lived. Now I don't
know anybody.' 'It'll get worse,' another pensioner chipped in. 'The last
ten years, it's rubbish that's here now. Problem families.' 'It's the
schwartzes,' the first speaker muttered, using an old Yiddish term. 'I
don't care what you say.'[24]

To all these resentments the National Front had a simple answer:
they were all the immigrants' fault. As the *Guardian*'s Martin Walker
observed, everything always came back to skin colour. 'Unemployment
was explained as black workers taking British jobs; bad housing as
blacks jumping the council house queue; clogged health and social services were the fault of diseased immigrants taking the place of deserving
Britons; bad schools were the cause of illiterate black kids, and crime
was their fault too.' It was, Walker pointed out, a 'potent and poisonous
combination', not least because 'the bad schools, the bad housing and
the unemployment' were most visible in precisely those 'run-down,
inner-city areas with poor housing in which immigrants have tended to
congregate'. The other great strength of the NF's propaganda was that
it tapped the prejudices with which so many people had grown up. In
an era when millions of people laughed at the racist jokes in *Till Death
Us Do Part* and *Love Thy Neighbour*, even youngsters instinctively saw
blacks and Asians as backward, bestial, dirty and undisciplined. 'You
see them natives on TV, dancing around in the jungle,' remarked Barry,
a disaffected teenager from a north London estate. 'I says, we've got 'em
living next door to us. We don't like that. Their music, the food, the
smell, they're different. Their whole attitude to life is different to ours.
You got to put a gas mask on to get past their door.' And even though
polls showed that public opinion was slowly becoming more tolerant,
Barry was far from alone. 'I don't want to be with black people. I don't
want a multi-racial country,' remarked a Walsall tool-setter. 'Why should
I? I've got nothing in common with them. I want to be able to go into a

pub, I want to be able to go to work without seeing a black face. The National Front is saying the sort of things I want to hear . . . I want to be just with our own.'[25]

The National Front's popularity reached a peak in the long, hot summer of 1976. In May, it capitalized on the press uproar when Malawi expelled its small Goan middle class, some 200 of whom had UK passports and therefore fled to Britain. When West Sussex council put up two Goan families at a four-star hotel, the tabloids went berserk, howling with rage at the 'invasion' of '£600 a week immigrants'.* 'The passport to plenty – more Asians on the way to join 4-star immigrants,' ran a typical headline in the *Express*. NF activists immediately dashed to Gatwick, where with staggering insensitivity they greeted a planeload of new arrivals – many of whom, almost laughably, were American tourists – with the chants 'Don't unpack, you must go back', and, mysteriously, 'This is England, not Pakistan'. And amid the furore, the Conservatives were quick to claim that the government had been far too lax. 'The terrain of race relations in this country', claimed the young MP Jonathan Aitken, 'has been transformed in the last year or two from being a relatively tranquil pasture of tolerance and understanding into a dry and brittle scrubland of tension which could be set ablaze at any moment by a spark of fear, anger or misunderstanding.'[26]

In fact, as everybody admitted, Britain had suffered a net population *loss* for six years in a row – a statistic that told its own story about the nation's miserably low self-esteem in the mid-1970s. There was hardly a risk of overcrowding: even though 28,000 Commonwealth immigrants had arrived in 1975, they were easily outnumbered by the 70,000 people heading the other way. To the National Front, however, this was merely a sign that the nation's essential character was in dire peril, and their message found a receptive audience. In the local elections at the end of May they recorded their best results yet, with eighty of their candidates winning more than 10 per cent of the vote. In West Bromwich, their candidates picked up 17 per cent of the vote; in Leicester 18 per cent; in Blackburn 33 per cent. Indeed, in Blackburn two candidates for the breakaway National Party managed to win council seats – which, as

---

* This was, of course, Fleet Street's perfect story, allowing them to hit at three familiar targets – immigrants, 'scroungers' and local councillors – in one go. Even the broadsheets got in on the act. 'Migrants Here Just For Welfare Handouts', read one *Telegraph* headline, while a *Times* leader carried the solemn headline 'Four Stars Too Many'.

a spokesman for the Board of Deputies of British Jews remarked, 'should serve as a warning to those who still believe that fascism cannot gain widespread support here'.[27]

As the temperatures rose and the nation sweltered through the hottest weather in history, the next few weeks brought worse news for those who feared that Britain was sliding towards racial conflict. The atmosphere felt ugly, wrote Martin Walker, 'with young immigrants clearly moving away from the traditional controls of their parents and elders, and confidence in the capacity of the police to maintain order being lost'. In Blackburn, local officials recorded thirty attacks on Asians and their property in less than two weeks. In east London, what *The Times* called a 'wave of racial violence' prompted frightened Bengali men to organize street patrols after dark. And in Southall, most shockingly of all, a Sikh teenager, Gurdip Singh Chaggar, was stabbed to death by a white gang outside a cinema. A few days later, hundreds of outraged Sikhs staged a protest outside Southall police station, demanding that the authorities find his killers and stamp out the racist attacks. 'But the demonstration suddenly got out of hand,' reported *The Times*. 'A police van window was broken and stones were thrown at cars and shops. A youth was detained and a scuffle started in which a policeman was cut in the face.' As might have been predicted, the tabloids cast the Sikhs as the wrongdoers – 'Rampage Of Vengeance', shrieked the *Mirror*'s front page the next day – although what their protest really revealed, of course, was the sheer frustration on the streets of west London. There was 'an increasing feeling of helplessness among Asian communities throughout the country', explained Shigbat Kadri, general secretary of the Standing Conference of Pakistani Organizations. 'Once colour warfare starts, there is no end to it.'[28]

On 5 August 1976, a few weeks before the Notting Hill Carnival, Eric Clapton appeared at the Birmingham Odeon. Two years earlier, the former Yardbird had played a key role in bringing Bob Marley's music to a white audience, his cover version of 'I Shot the Sheriff' becoming one of his biggest hits. But that night his fans were in for a shock. Clapton was visibly drunk, and in a pause between songs, he muttered angrily that Britain was turning into 'a black colony'.* There were gasps from the audience, but he was only warming up:

---

* Note that the concert was not recorded, and there are slightly different accounts of what Clapton said.

I used to be into dope, now I'm into racism. It's much heavier, man. Fucking wogs, man. Fucking Saudis taking over London. Bastard wogs. Britain is becoming overcrowded and Enoch will stop it and send them all back. The black wogs and coons and Arabs and fucking Jamaicans ... don't belong here, we don't want them here. This is England, this is a white country, we don't want any black wogs and coons living here. We need to make clear to them they are not welcome. England is for white people, man. We are a white country. I don't want fucking wogs living next to me with their standards. This is Great Britain, a white country; what is happening to us, for fuck's sake? We need to vote for Enoch Powell, he's a great man, speaking truth. Vote for Enoch, he's our man, he's on our side, he'll look after us ... Enoch for Prime Minister! Throw the wogs out! Keep Britain white!

From anybody this would have been shocking; from a rock musician who had cut his teeth on American blues, it seemed absolutely extraordinary. Many of Clapton's fans were appalled, and a few days later the rock photographer Red Saunders and the Trotskyite activist David Widgery organized an open letter to Clapton via the *NME*, *Melody Maker*, *Sounds* and the *Socialist Worker*. 'Come on Eric,' they wrote. 'Own up. Half your music is black. You're rock music's biggest colonist.' At the end they added an appeal: 'We want to organise a rank and file movement against the racist poison in music. We urge support for Rock Against Racism.'[29]

There was more to Rock Against Racism (RAR) than met the eye. The signers of that letter all belonged to or sympathized with the little Socialist Workers' Party, the most vigorous of the various Trotskyite sects. Originally strongest on university campuses, the SWP was now trying to broaden its horizons, reaching out to union members, immigrants and low-paid workers. Without its support, Rock Against Racism would probably never have got off the ground; one organizer admitted that they relied on the party's post office box, their print shop and even 'their ability to book coaches for demonstrations'. What is beyond dispute, though, is that RAR brought in thousands of youngsters who would normally have had no interest in far-left politics. Within two weeks the organizers had 600 replies, and in November they organized their first concert in Forest Gate, east London. More gigs followed at the Royal College of Art and the Polytechnic of North London, while sympathizers founded RAR clubs across the country. In Leeds, for example, an NHS clerk set up a club at the local polytechnic, where bands played every Friday night for eighteen months. The most celebrated event, though, came in April 1978, when RAR organized a demonstration against racism in Trafalgar Square, a march to Victoria Park and then a concert headlined by the Clash, the Buzzcocks and the Tom Robinson Band. The organizers had expected 20,000 people; in the event, 80,000 turned up. No doubt many came purely for the music, but as a gesture of contempt for the National Front it could hardly have been more impressive. 'It was an incredibly emotional moment,' one Asian teenager remembered, 'because for the first time I felt that I was surrounded by people who were on my side. That was the first time I thought that something had changed in Britain forever.' Perhaps that was overstating things a bit; even so, the movement undoubtedly had a tremendous effect, not least in making it deeply unfashionable to hold racist opinions.[30]

For some members of the Socialist Workers' Party, concerts were not enough. In May 1977 the National Front won 120,000 votes in the Greater London Council elections, more than their entire nationwide total in October 1974, and some SWP activists decided that it was time to drive them physically off the streets. Drawn to the party by its emphasis on militant confrontation, they dreamed of emulating the left-wing groups who had brawled in the road with Oswald Mosley's Blackshirts in the famous Battle of Cable Street. And in August 1977 they got their chance. The battleground was Deptford and Lewisham, where a year earlier far-right candidates had won 40 per cent of the vote in the local elections. The pretext was a march by the National Front, ostensibly to protest about mugging (which they blamed entirely on West Indians), but in reality to bolster their support among white working-class voters. And the result was some of the worst violence south London had seen for decades, with hundreds of SWP supporters bombarding the National Front marchers with 'bottles, dustbins, timber and chunks of masonry', while simultaneously fighting off hundreds of Millwall football hooligans who were chanting 'Up the National Front! Kill the blacks!' It was just as well that, for the first time, the police were carrying Perspex riot shields; among the weapons they confiscated were knives, ammonia and iron pipes studded with bolts. Six policemen suffered serious injuries, while one was stabbed in his van after demonstrators threw a brick through the windscreen, blinding him with broken glass. Some 134 people needed hospital treatment, 214 were arrested (the vast majority of them coming from outside the neighbourhood), and yet, amazingly, nobody was killed. Many black activists were horrified, arguing that the 'Battle of Lewisham' had only played into the hands of the far right. But the SWP were delighted with their afternoon's work. 'We intend to crush the National Front,' a spokesman said. 'Of course there will be violence. And to achieve our object we will have to condone the use of every weapon that was wielded on Sunday.'[31]

To many observers, the Battle of Lewisham conjured up frightening images of the street fighting of the 1930s. As one commentator put it, the violence – carried out almost entirely by outsiders – had done 'immense damage to community relations in these highly inflammable areas'. 'The inhabitants of this battleground, represented by the sad and angry Lewisham councillors, were, of course, the total losers,' agreed the *Guardian*. But despite a torrent of criticism, the Socialist Workers were totally unrepentant. Living out their Cable Street fantasy, the party's activists now launched a new initiative, the Anti-Nazi League. On the face of it, the ANL was a united front against the far right; in reality, it was yet another organization dominated by the far left. During the final years of the decade, the ANL organized a series of marches, meetings and concerts, appealing in particular to young people and students. In May 1978, for example, the ANL was much in evidence at the demonstrations in Brick Lane after the murder of a Bangladeshi garment worker, Altab Ali. And in September, ANL activists organized a rally in Hyde Park to coincide with a National Front march in the East End. Among the speakers was Tony Benn, who loved it:

> There was a lorry with a steel band playing, and there were tens of thousands of young people. The average age was about twenty to twenty-five, and there were banners and badges and punk rockers, just a tremendous gathering of people ...
>
> A speaker from the Socialist Workers' Party spoke from the platform first, followed by Arthur Scargill and me. Tom Robinson, a gay pop star and a committed socialist, sang. Bill Keys, General Secretary of SOGAT, and Dennis Skinner were there. As far as I know, Dennis and I were the only two Labour MPs. Multi-racial rock music has given the movement leadership and it is a tragedy that the Labour Party can't give a firmer lead, but it has never done so.

Afterwards, Scargill and Benn marched together down to the corner of Piccadilly, though the latter found the crowds a bit oppressive. 'The youngsters were rushing along and pushing ahead,' he recorded. 'It made me feel like an old animal in a herd!'[32]

While Rock Against Racism undoubtedly had an impact on thousands of impressionable teenagers, the ANL's influence is more debatable. Even on the left, many people regarded it as a front for the Socialist Workers, which is why no other Labour MPs joined Benn and Skinner at the Hyde Park rally. Even the trade unions were wary of getting involved: at conference after conference, delegates complained that the 'extremism' of the SWP was deterring 'ordinary trade union-ists' from joining the anti-fascist effort. And as the SWP-supporting journalist Paul Foot later admitted, surprisingly few young black men and women joined the Anti-Nazi League, almost certainly because it struck them as a talking shop for well-educated white leftists. By the beginning of 1979, in fact, the Anti-Nazi League was losing momen-tum. The press, notably the *Telegraph*, had exposed its close financial links to the Socialist Workers' Party, while the violence at Southall in April, when thousands of ANL members fought running battles with the National Front and the police, played into the hands of critics who argued that the two parties were as bad as each other. And although some ANL veterans insist that their efforts precipitated the National Front's decline at the end of the 1970s, the real cause was almost certainly very different. People had joined the National Front because they felt they had no alternative; nobody else, they thought, was articu-lating their resentment, their fears and anxieties. But in 1978, a much bigger, more moderate and more respectable organization than either the ANL or the NF stepped into the immigration debate and whipped the rug out from beneath the far right. Its name was the Conservative Party.[33]

Although a genuine electoral breakthrough by the National Front was never very likely, they would have stood a better chance with a more credible and charismatic leader. In the autumn of 1977, the Tory gran-dee Peter Carrington told Lord Hailsham that, according to rumours, the Front had found their man. 'It was quite certain', Carrington said, that the NF were able to unveil the former Conservative leadership can-didate and anti-immigration firebrand Enoch Powell. Hailsham, who hated Powell, could barely contain his glee. 'Oh,' he burst out, 'I *do* hope it's true.' Winning the sage of Wolverhampton's support would indeed have been an extraordinary coup; not only was he enormously popular with white working-class voters, but even his most dedicated opponents admitted that he boasted a hypnotic style and fearsome intellect. Unfor-tunately for the National Front, the rumour was completely false.

Instead, Powell remained as Ulster Unionist MP for South Down, and never had any dealings with the National Front.[34]

Although Powell's position was always more nuanced than his critics allowed, his rhetoric about immigration was still extraordinarily aggressive. In the West Midlands, he said, politicians were ignoring 'cries of anguish' from people who saw 'their towns being changed, their native places being turned into foreign lands'. 'When he looks into the eyes of Asia,' he went on, 'the Englishman comes face to face with those who would dispute with him the possession of his native land.' The *Guardian*'s Martin Walker was not alone in thinking that this was 'the language of the National Front', and indeed one NF organizer claimed that 'Powell's speeches gave our membership and morale a tremendous boost'. And although Powell slowly faded from the headlines after the fall of his arch-enemy, Edward Heath, he liked to send up a rocket every now and then, as if to remind people he was still there. Speaking to the Monday Club in Croydon in October 1976, for example, he suggested spending £1 billion on a voluntary repatriation scheme to remove the 'alien wedge' from Britain's cities, and to avoid the inevitable 'catastrophe of widespread violence'. As usual, his comments provoked howls of anger: the leader of the Asian Action Committee even demanded that Powell be prosecuted for inciting racial hatred. But there is no doubt that, despite the gradual shift in racial attitudes, many ordinary white people agreed with him. 'I think Enoch is a marvellous man,' one Blackburn woman said earnestly, 'and I hope that some day he's Prime Minister.'[35]

Paradoxically, Powell's outspokenness made it very difficult for other senior politicians to speak out along the same lines. Since being associated with him was politically toxic, many preferred not to mention immigration at all. Even Mrs Thatcher, who is often accused of pandering to populist prejudice, hesitated to break with the liberal consensus, not least because it would have alienated her senior colleagues and scuppered the Tories' attempts to broaden their appeal. In the 1974 elections they had done especially badly among black and Asian voters in marginal seats, and two years later Conservative Central Office set up a special Community Affairs Department, including an Ethnic Minorities Unit, to reach out to immigrant voters. Meanwhile, Mrs Thatcher often seemed more interested in wooing immigrant voters than in tapping white working-class anxieties. In an interview with the *Community Relations Journal* in 1976, she freely admitted that the

Conservatives were keen to attract the Asian vote and were 'trying to have more and more contact with immigrant communities'. In a letter to the *Finchley Times* a few months later, she expressed her 'total condemnation' of 'those who for their own ends exploit the issue of race in such a way that the likelihood of racial violence is increased'. And when, at the Young Conservatives' conference in February 1977, she condemned Conservative clubs that still had a colour bar, some of the audience loudly groaned. 'Look, what are you trying to do?' she shot back. 'To me there is only one way to judge a person, whatever his background, whatever his colour, whatever his religion, and that is what that person is, and not by his race or creed. That is what I believe in, that is what I will tell everyone, and that is what I try to achieve.'[36]

By this point, however, the mood in the party was already shifting. As Mrs Thatcher struggled to make headway against the unflappable Callaghan, a more populist, overtly right-wing approach seemed increasingly tempting. For years the Conservative leadership had been markedly more liberal than its activists, many of whom shared Powell's views on an immigration cap and voluntary repatriation. Given her sympathy with the rank and file, it would have been odd if Mrs Thatcher had *not* moved away from Heath's dogged liberalism. Meanwhile, her closest advisers were pressing her to take a harder line, not least because the National Front threatened to eat into the Tories' potential working-class support. Two months before the Notting Hill violence, for example, Airey Neave warned that the party's 'elitist' attitude was alienating people who thought 'their neighbourhoods [had been] literally taken over'. Thatcher's aide Edward Leigh, meanwhile, reported that one in four letters from the public either touched on or was completely devoted to immigration. Many of the writers, he thought, were working-class: although they were 'not racist', they were full of 'frustration and anger' at the major parties' reluctance to discuss the issue. And in January 1978 her close adviser Nigel Lawson told her that if the Conservatives were serious about striking a 'populist' note, then '*we must not shirk the immigration issue*, which is almost the acid test of whether a political party is in tune with the ordinary people'. In the margin of his memo, she drew a thick black line to emphasize the point.[37]

Mrs Thatcher chose her moment carefully. At the beginning of 1978 the Conservatives were faced with an eminently winnable by-election in Ilford North, where the sitting Labour MP had died tragically young. Although Labour had picked a bright young candidate, a social worker called Tessa Jowell, their majority in October 1974 had been less than

800 votes. This was precisely the kind of outer London marginal that the Conservatives simply had to win, with an upper-working-class electorate who were bound to respond well to a tough line on immigration. And on 27 January, in an interview for Granada's *World in Action*, Mrs Thatcher made her move. 'I think there is a feeling that the big political parties have not been talking about [immigration],' she mused. 'If we do not want people to go to extremes, and I do not, we ourselves must talk about this problem and we must show that we are prepared to deal with it.' Merely talking about the problem was one thing; to send a clear message, though, she picked her words carefully:

> I am the first to admit it is not easy to get clear figures from the Home Office about immigration, but there was a committee which looked at it and said that if we went on as we are then by the end of the century there would be four million people of the new Commonwealth or Pakistan here. Now that is an awful lot, and I think it means that people are really rather afraid that this country might be rather *swamped* by people with a different culture; and, you know, the British character has done so much for democracy, for law and done so much throughout the world that if there is any fear that it might be swamped, people are going to react and be rather hostile to those coming in.

Mrs Thatcher's terminology – 'swamped' – is often described as a gaffe. In the ensuing furore, as ministers, race relations experts and even bishops lined up to deplore her choice of words, her press officers briefed journalists that she had merely slipped up, blaming her 'inexperience' and tendency to 'shoot from the hip'. But this was not true at all: Thatcher rarely spoke without thinking, and she did use the word twice. In another interview a year later, she insisted that she 'stood by it one hundred percent. Some people *have* felt swamped by immigrants. They've seen the whole character of their neighbourhood change.' The reality, of course, is that she had chosen her words to achieve the right political effect. And it was no coincidence that, only a couple of weeks later, her old mentor waded into the debate too. 'There is a limit to the number of people from different cultures that this country can digest,' declared Sir Keith Joseph on a visit to Ilford. 'We ignore this at our peril, everyone's peril.' As so often, he sounded rather like a diluted Enoch Powell.[38]

In an echo of Powell's infamous speech ten years earlier, Mrs Thatcher's words provoked howls of anguish. She was 'cynically encouraging prejudice and blatantly courting the National Front vote', thought

Bernard Donoghue, who noted that when the subject came up in the Commons a few days later, 'Whitelaw, Heath and Walker all looked very uncomfortable'. Her 'vulgar remarks', thundered the Labour MP Bill Molloy, merely echoed 'the cry of all those who favour some form of racialism while looking for someone as a scapegoat on whom to hang their political arguments'. Jim Callaghan declared that she had 'knowingly aroused the fears of thousands of coloured people living in this country', while the *Sunday Times* suggested that she had given 'aid and comfort to the National Front'. Most dangerous for Mrs Thatcher, though, was the fury of her deputy, Willie Whitelaw, who had not known what she was planning to say. Having made a point of criticizing 'extremists' who were 'exploiting fears about the number of coloured people coming into the country', Whitelaw was outraged by his leader's remarks. Three days after *World in Action*, he told Roy Jenkins that he was thinking of resigning and ridding himself of 'that awful woman'. Even after Jenkins had persuaded him merely to 'distance himself', Whitelaw went out of his way to strike a more moderate note. After a notably conciliatory speech in Loughborough, he waited outside in the driving rain to shake hands with Asian protesters. His 3-year-old granddaughter, he said, had plenty of black friends: 'She does not know the difference between them. That gives me hope for the future.'[39]

The great irony of Mrs Thatcher's supposed gaffe was that it was one of the most effective things she ever said. In the two weeks after *World in Action* an estimated 10,000 letters poured into her office, most of them praising her for speaking out. There were even rare words of praise from the dreaded Powell, who welcomed 'the great surge of hope and relief' that she had aroused with just 'a single word'. As usual he was exaggerating, but not by much. An NOP poll taken in February 1978 showed that the furore had pushed immigration to the forefront of people's minds, with the proportion rating it as an 'urgent issue' up from 9 per cent to 21 per cent. More pertinently, though, the Conservatives' poll rating had shot up by 9 per cent, testifying to the immediate impact of Thatcher's remarks. The Tories' private polls were even more encouraging, showing that one in five people were more likely to vote for them if they promised 'to stop all immigration'. 'The Tories, and Thatcher herself, are in much better morale after her immigration speeches,' admitted Bernard Donoughue in the middle of February.[40]

Two weeks later, the voters of Ilford North gave Mrs Thatcher the vindication she wanted. The swing was not especially impressive: at 7 per cent, it gave Callaghan's aides hope that they could cling on in a general election. But in a seat where the National Front had hoped to do well, they had been beaten back, winning barely 2,000 votes and finishing a very poor fourth. The key to the Conservatives' victory had been defectors from the Labour Party. In previous by-elections, many Labour defectors had turned to the National Front; this time, three out of four switched to the Conservatives, and half of them said immigration had been the decisive factor. Many Labour observers could barely contain their fury, and Callaghan claimed that Mrs Thatcher had won by appealing to 'fear and prejudice'. Ilford, thought *The Times*, had shown that immigration would an explosive issue in the coming general election. Much of the public feeling, it said, 'is based on ignorance . . . and sheer racial prejudice, but that will not stop the issue being of political significance'.[41]

For many writers, Mrs Thatcher's 'swamped' interview was an unforgivable excursion into the scaremongering politics of the far right. But this is easily overstated. 'I said that some people felt swamped. Some people *do* feel swamped, that is perfectly accurate,' she told a radio interviewer after the Ilford result. This was, of course, true, although (like Enoch Powell in 1968) she was under no obligation to cast herself as their mouthpiece. What she was doing, of course, was making a calculated bid for white working-class votes. With just one word, she had sent a message to millions of resentful voters, reassuring them that she understood how they felt, and strengthening her image as the populist crusader who would stand up to the liberal establishment. Of course her words also sent a message to thousands of immigrants, suggesting that despite her earlier protestations, the Conservative leader was not really on their side after all. In that moment, as Mrs Thatcher's biographer observes, her 'fundamental instincts' came into sharp focus. Whether they were intolerably cynical or merely ruthlessly pragmatic is in the eye of the beholder; in fairness, by the standards of, say, her Republican friends across the Atlantic, or indeed of Enoch Powell, her supposed rabble-rousing was pretty tame. 'My goodness me,' she remarked, 'if I'm never accused of using any word worse than "swamped" I shall be very pleased.' But then she never had to. As Enoch Powell, of all people, acutely observed, 'if you're trying to convey what you feel to the electorate, you only have to do it once.'[42]

25

A Hot, Hot Day

KEVIN: *People have had enough now – they have! This*
summer is different. Under the heat, it's all changing.
Stephen Poliakoff, *Strawberry Fields* (1977)

Our own industrial troubles are put into perspective by the
horrible picket at Grunwick. The country gets more and more
like Germany in the twenties. And there's clearly a jolly band
of extremist brothers on picket outings at Grunwick to see that
it does.

Peter Hall's diary, 23 June 1977

The summer of 1976 was the hottest Britain had ever known. On 23
June the temperature in the south of England hit 90 degrees, where it
stayed for the next two weeks. Across the country, sunbathing workers
stripped off to enjoy their sandwiches, while teenagers skipped school
to play in lakes and rivers, their radios pumping out Elton John, Demis
Roussos, the Wurzels and the Real Thing. In the tabloids, where headlines greeted the 'Riviera Touch', there was much anxiety at the thought
of ice-cream salesmen 'giving short measure and charging high prices'.
Most people assumed the weather would break eventually. But to universal astonishment, the sun kept on shining. 'ZIZZLER!' gasped the
Mirror, noting that at the Wimbledon tennis championships, where
temperatures had reached a record 104 degrees and male spectators had
stripped 'bare to the waist', the umpires were struggling to stay awake.
In London, the AA were called to 1,500 breakdowns because of over-
heating engines; on the Underground, a signal failure left hundreds of
passengers stranded for hours in appalling heat. In Bristol, 'there was a

slight outbreak of the old Roman custom of bottom pinching against woman shoppers'. But from East Anglia there came an ominous warning. If the hot weather continued, the water authority warned, the reservoirs would soon run dry: people should 'think twice before having a drink of water'.[1]

As the summer wore on, delight at the glorious weather began to turn to disquiet. By mid-July, after less than a tenth of an inch of rain in a month, the Meteorological Office was warning that Britain faced the worst drought since records began. At Lord's, a brief drizzle during one of Middlesex's matches prompted applause from the spectators. But it did not last long; soon the heatwave was back on. The grass turned brown; the crops died; cracks appeared along the façades of stucco buildings. In Surrey, the Fire Brigade struggled to cope with tens of thousands of emergency calls; in Dorset, heath and forest fires broke out almost every day. Often firemen would put a blaze out only to be called back the following morning, the fire having smouldered on underground beneath layers of dry peat. On Horton Common, a dust-devil whipped up a fire a mile wide; in Hurn Forest, an inferno consumed an estimated 50,000 trees; in Ferndown, a wall of flame swept through 250 acres of woodland, forcing a nearby hospital to evacuate hundreds of patients. Only the efforts of 250 firemen and more than 100 soldiers, who pumped water from two tankers commandeered from the Milk Marketing Board, managed to control the blaze. And in South Wales, harder hit than any other part of the country, every evening brought fresh reports of firemen battling terrifying forest fires. 'Wales is a tinder-box,' Monmouthshire's deputy fire chief told the press. 'My boys are stretched to the limit. Our calls have increased tenfold, and some work 72 hours without a break.'[2]

At the beginning of August the government rushed a Drought Act through the Commons, with the colourful Sports Minister, Denis Howell, appointed 'Mr Rainmaker'. Summoning reporters to his house, Howell revealed his plans to save water, including putting a brick in the toilet cistern and sharing baths with his long-suffering wife. People should fill their baths only five inches deep, he said earnestly, urging them to report 'abuses or misuses' by their neighbours. 'The flowers are going to have to wilt,' he added, 'and cars will have to remain dirty.' On his orders, British Rail stopped washing their trains; meanwhile, entrepreneurs sold T-shirts with the slogan 'SAVE WATER, BATH WITH A FRIEND'. In Yorkshire and East Anglia, the regular water supply gave way to standpipes in the street. At London Zoo, every drop of the elephants' bathwater was saved and used to water the plants; in Birmingham, 'hosepipe patrol vans' were believed to be lurking around every corner, looking out for anyone unpatriotic enough to wash the car; in Surrey, angry residents besieged a local golf club, demanding that it turn off its sprinklers. And in South Wales, where householders were banned from washing their cars on pain of a £400 fine, the water supply went off every afternoon at two o'clock, only coming back on the following morning. 'There are no baths, and clothes don't get washed so often,' one Cardiff housewife said miserably. 'I used to use the washing machine every day. Now it is once a week, and we pipe the dirty water from the machine into rubbish bins and keep it for flushing lavatories.'[3]

In London, the searing sunshine exposed the shabby dilapidation of a city that had seen better days. The flowers died; the birds fled; the Tube felt like a sauna. 'It is intolerable in town,' lamented Bernard Donoughue. At night he lay awake, fretting about the plight of the pound, 'too hot to sleep'. Every morning he drove to Whitehall in his vest, which was 'soaking wet' when he got there, and only then put on his shirt. He was not alone in his exasperation at the sweltering temperatures. 'The boiling sun is relentless,' complained Kenneth Williams; 'the sort of weather which one loves on holiday & loathes in London ... One is sweating before the day begins & I have one sheet over me on the bed & it's still uncomfortable.' Walking to the West End, he was shocked to see 'everyone standing *outside* pubs holding beer in their hands', an unusual sight in 1976. 'Don't go in tonight, Kenny!' people shouted outside the theatre. 'There'll be no bugger there!' Meanwhile, in a stifling bedroom south of the river, a young writer called Ian McEwan was working on his first novel, which was published two years later. 'The days were too long, the house was too hot, the house seemed to have fallen asleep,' recalls the teenage narrator of *The Cement Garden*. 'We did not even sit outside because the wind was blowing a fine, black dust from the direction of the tower blocks and the main roads behind them. And even while it was hot, the sun never quite broke through a high, yellowish cloud; everything I looked at merged and seemed insignificant in the glare.'[4]

On the South Bank, where the National Theatre had opened a few weeks earlier, the director Peter Hall was initially delighted by the summer sun. On 17 July he was pleased to see 'crowds of people milling around the theatre this lunchtime: a kite-flying festival by the river, a Dixieland band playing on the terraces, hordes of children watching a puppet show near the main entrance, a full house for the *Hamlet* mat-

inee. It's the way this building has to be – a place for a party.' Yet only a
few weeks later, as the concrete buildings baked in the heat, Hall's mood
changed. Rehearsals for *Tamburlaine the Great*, the play chosen to open
the Olivier Theatre, were going badly, with the actors barely audible
beneath the roaring air conditioning units. On Friday, 13 August – 'a
day which lived up to its reputation' – the stagehands walked out on
strike in protest at being on call for two theatres at once. In the sweltering weather – 'a hot, hot day,' he recorded two days later – tempers
frayed. On Monday morning, Hall issued suspension notices to all those
refusing to work in the Olivier. Unusually, the stagehands' union supported him, warning that strikers would be suspended if they walked
out. But it was no good. 'By just after 2 pm,' Hall wrote, 'the stage staff,
electrics and stage props had left the building on unofficial strike.'

When he arrived for work the next day, there was a 'very unpleasant
atmosphere around the building'. Nobody was working, and there was
'a lot of talk about threats and intimidation, and a rumour that all our
good electrics staff who should have reported for the *Tamburlaine* technical rehearsal last Friday night, and would have reported, were
informed that there'd be some broken limbs if they became scabs.' Wednesday was even worse. 'I can only compare it with a corrida, a bullfight
at full pitch,' Hall wrote with a melodramatic flourish. 'There was a
feeling of destruction, of blood. I am not exaggerating. During the day
the pickets increased and the feeling of imminent violence increased
with them.' At last, after a long, dragging day of talks with the stagehands' representatives ('sweating, twitching and nervous . . . an evil
atmosphere'), Hall gave in. That night he slept for just two hours, 'turning the thing over in my mind', and the next day he broke down in tears.
'I felt so sick of everything and everybody,' he noted afterwards. 'If only
I could care less about this building and what it means to so many
people. It's only a job after all. One thing's certain. I am learning about
industrial relations.'[5]

The next day, Friday, 20 August, was another scorching day. In Hyde
Park, on Hampstead Heath and in parched brown parks across the
country, children played in the baking sunshine. But a few miles out of
the centre of London, in the dusty, nondescript surroundings of Chapter
Road, Willesden, tempers were stretched to breaking point. In the win-
dowless mailroom of Grunwick Processing Laboratories, piles of
photographs had been steadily mounting since the heatwave began.
Most of the workers in the mail order department were Asian women

from East African countries such as Kenya and Uganda, who had fled persecution to start new lives in north-west London. They had been promised air conditioning, but Grunwick's new unit was not yet up and running. So the women sat in their rows at the long tables, hunched over heaps of negatives, their faces taut with concentration, the sticky heat clinging to their saris, the air heavy with the sound of Capital Radio. And all the time, as the temperature mounted, the piles of orders in the long mailroom seemed to get bigger and bigger.

It was around lunchtime, with the temperature almost 75 degrees and sweat clinging to the workers' clothes, that the trouble started. Nineteen-year-old Devshi Bhudia was just heading out for lunch when his supervisor, a pale little man called Malcolm Alden, emerged from his glass box and asked him to sort through an extra thirteen crates for the evening post. But Devshi Bhudia was not only hot, he was sick of being pushed around. He had already had a run-in with his managers after demanding more money, and had even argued that Grunwick's workers should form a union to fight for their rights. A few days earlier he had started looking for a new job, and now he snapped. If he was going to be given extra work, he told Alden, he wanted more money. Under pressure to get the orders sent out before the weekend, Alden said no. Bhudia did not like that answer: encouraged by three students working alongside him, he began a 'go-slow' in protest. When Alden found out what they were doing, he lost his temper, and a few moments later Bhudia and the students walked out. But although they had been sacked, they did not leave the site. Instead they hung around by the gates, waiting for their ex-colleagues to emerge, their tempers still boiling in the summer sun.

In the meantime, the rest of Grunwick's employees were toiling away. Among them was a short, middle-aged woman called Jayaben Desai, whose son, Sunil, also worked at Grunwick and knew Devshi Bhudia. The clock ticked on; the shadows lengthened. At about six o'clock, Mrs Desai stretched and stood up, ready to leave at last, looking forward to the weekend. What happened next is unclear, but it seems that one of the foremen insisted that she sort through some more orders before she went home. By the time Malcolm Alden had come out to see what all the noise was about, Mrs Desai was embroiled in a blazing row with his under-manager. Alden called her aside, but calming her down was impossible. 'I want my freedom,' she kept saying, slipping into Gujerati as her temper flared. And then she snapped. 'I want my freedom,' she repeated. 'I am going. I have had enough' – and she stormed out, her son

Sunil trailing behind her. At the gates they found Devshi Bhudia and his three friends, still arguing with the firm's personnel manager. Bhudia thought they should get revenge by letting the tyres down on Alden's Jaguar. But Mrs Desai had other ideas. Many times, over dinner, her husband had asked why there was no union at Grunwick. This was her chance. 'What should we do?' Bhudia asked her. 'We don't know anything about involving a union,' Jayaben Desai said. 'But let's find out.'[6]

In some ways it was astonishing that Grunwick had not suffered industrial unrest before. The firm had been founded in a garage in St John's Wood in 1965 by an entrepreneur called George Ward, who had moved from New Delhi to London to train as an accountant. Like many children of Anglo-Indian families, Ward never quite fitted in, his dark skin and Indian accent immediately marking him as an outsider. Yet he was clearly a man of great discipline, drive and commercial nous. Thanks to the surge in camera ownership and foreign holidays, photo processing was extremely lucrative. Every summer brought a greater deluge of holiday snaps, and by March 1976 Ward's laboratories were turning over £4.2 million a year, with annual pre-tax profits up by almost 20 per cent. Families who used his mail-order business found it cheap, quick and reliable: indeed, in June 1977 *Which?* named it Britain's fastest processing service, outstripping giants such as Kodak. But the reason Grunwick was so cheap was that Ward kept labour costs very low. He had relocated from St John's Wood to the scruffier surroundings of Willesden to tap the cheap, hard-working labour of the East African Asian immigrants who had arrived in the early 1970s, most of whom earned between £25 and £30 a week (say, about £230 today). This was by no means abominable: indeed, some employers paid less for similar work. But as Lord Scarman's report into the Grunwick affair later concluded, it was undoubtedly 'at the lower end' of the industry spectrum. At Kodak, for example, basic pay started at almost £50 a week.[7]

What really infuriated some of Ward's employees was not the pay but the ferocious discipline. To the casual observer, conditions at Grunwick did not look too bad. The largely female workforce sat at long rows of desks under bright lights, stuffing envelopes, processing cheques and filing invoices. It was a lot better than, say, emptying bins or going down a mine. But Ward and his managers ruled with a rod of iron, keeping their staff cooped up for long hours in hot weather and denying them any opportunity to air their grievances. Since workers had to ask permission even to go to the toilet, it was perhaps not surprising that staff turnover was high and sackings were common. All employees were compelled to do compulsory overtime during the summer, while holidays in July, August and September were strictly forbidden. And above all, Ward was implacably opposed to any efforts to establish a union. When a handful of workers tried to establish a branch of the TGWU in 1973, Ward sacked them without compunction, claiming that 'work was short'. The ensuing dispute lasted for seven weeks, but Ward won the day. He was determined, he explained, to keep the 'arrogant' trade union movement out of Grunwick. Its leaders might claim 'that it stands for workers' solidarity and the "sacred right" of collective bargaining', he said. But 'what it wants is more power'.[8]

Over the weekend, the Grunwick rebels made their plans, and when their former colleagues arrived for work on Monday morning, Mrs Desai and her comrades were stationed outside the Chapter Road gates, waving hand-written placards ('GRUNWICKS IS A ZOO') and a petition for union representation. Even George Ward conceded that they persuaded 'many' people to sign, and at three that afternoon more than fifty people left their desks and walked out to join them. This left the Grunwick management utterly flabbergasted, and when they went out to negotiate with the rebels, there was all sorts of 'shouting and excitement'. The strikers then marched off to the firm's other premises at Cobbold Road, ten minutes' walk away, where they persuaded about twenty-five more people to join the strike. Eventually the police were called, and the strikers moved off. On the face of it, this was bad news for Grunwick: by Friday, 27 August, ninety-one full-time and forty-eight part-time employees had walked out. Remarkably, however, George Ward did not think the furore important enough to interrupt his holiday in Ireland; evidently he was confident that, if necessary, he could always attract other people to do the job. On 2 September, each of the strikers received a letter in the post. 'Your participation in strike action has brought [your] contract to an end,' it read, 'and accordingly your employment with this company has ceased.'[9]

By this point, the strikers had already made contact with a trade union. On the afternoon of the first walkout, Sunil Desai had cycled down to the Citizens' Advice Bureau to get the phone numbers for the TUC, the Brent Trades Council and the Association of Professional, Executive, Clerical and Computer Staffs (APEX). By the following Tuesday, the Grunwick strikers had filled in APEX application forms; by Friday, all ninety-one striking full-timers were members. Like other white-collar, middle-class unions, APEX was experiencing extraordinary growth, membership surging from almost 80,000 in 1968 to more than 140,000 in 1976. It had a reputation as one of the TUC's most moderate unions: its Wimbledon headquarters, wrote the *Financial Times*'s Joe Rogaly, was 'flat and modern', while its staff were 'courteous and friendly'. Its general secretary, Roy Grantham, was widely seen as one of the most right-wing union bosses, a staunch supporter of EEC entry who had shared a platform with Edward Heath during the referendum campaign. Grantham had the demeanour of a 'stubborn chief clerk', but the government regarded him as a man they could do business with. He was Jim Callaghan's kind of trade union leader: calm, decent and thoroughly pragmatic, interested only in getting the best for his members.[10]

It was not Roy Grantham, though, who became the face of the Grunwick dispute, but somebody rather more radical. On Tuesday, 24 August, Mrs Desai and her colleagues had a meeting with the secretary of the Brent Trades Council, a young man called Jack Dromey. Born in Brent, the son of Irish immigrants, Dromey made no secret of his hard-left convictions. 'He would call himself a Marxist,' Joe Rogaly recorded. 'He had no political affiliation except to the Labour Party, but he shared the Marxist view of history and the Marxist economic analysis.' When Mrs Desai came to him for help, he was already fighting cuts to the local NHS and organizing twenty-four-hour pickets at a factory in Brentford, where women had walked out demanding equal pay. But from the first he saw Grunwick as a perfect way to attract low-income immigrant workers to the trade union movement. And for the next eighteen months, nobody worked harder to support the Grunwick strikers. It was Dromey who devised their picket system and drew up their rota, who liaised with the Trades Council and the TUC, who took the strikers to local factories to enlist support, who helped to produce strike bulletins and who got them legal advice – some of it from a young lawyer called Harriet Harman, whom he later married. To the Conservative press, he seemed the archetypal bearded agitator. But unlike other hirsute idealists in the mid-1970s, Dromey had an acute sense of political reality. 'I knew that we were in for a tough fight from the start,' he said later; 'the fact that less than half the workforce had walked out; the fact that we started with no organization at Grunwick ... One of our union convenors said to me: "This is going to be a tough one, Jack."'[11]

The handful of workers at the heart of the Grunwick battle made distinctly unlikely standard-bearers for the cause of the left. Not only was Ward an immigrant employer, but the majority of his staff were immigrants, too. Of 206 employees in early 1977, some 78 were East African Asians, 41 were West Indians, 22 were immigrants from other areas and only 65 were white Londoners. When Joe Rogaly visited the mail order department to interview its predominantly Asian staff, he found that they were almost all 'middle-class, with a strongly motivated desire to work and save'. Most owned their own homes; many were women married to successful small businessmen. Far from being the downtrodden victims of capitalist greed, as some of their allies claimed, they were 'already giving every appearance of becoming an elite' within their own communities. In this respect, the Grunwick strikers were typical of the Kenyan and Ugandan Asians who had fled to Britain at the beginning of the decade. Better educated, more fluent in English, more skilled and often more ambitious than other immigrant groups, they owned shops and small businesses, encouraged their children to go to university and conscientiously saved to buy their own homes. Indeed, by 1977 three out of four East African Asian families owned their own homes, compared with just half the population as a whole. All in all, they were hard-working, serious and thrifty: precisely the kind of people, ironically, of whom George Ward's supporters in the Conservative press usually approved.[12]

During the 1960s the trade unions had shown little interest in championing low-paid Asian or West Indian workers, not least because so many of their white members were so hostile to immigration. By the 1970s, however, things were changing. Successful strikes at Mansfield Hosiery Mills in 1972 and Imperial Typewriters in Leicester two years later demonstrated that East African Asians were ready to fight poor pay and conditions, even though their local unions refused to help. Crucially, these strikes showed that Asians could be extremely stubborn and effective negotiators, partly because their education and experience meant that they understood how their employers thought, but also because exile and resettlement had given them a strong sense of solidarity. Even physically they made an arresting change from the strikers who usually dominated British television bulletins. These were not burly men standing around braziers; they were little Asian women in saris, their quiet courtesy belying their steely resolve. Jayaben Desai, for example, was less than five feet tall. 'Her image is that of the small but determined figure in the posters,' wrote Rogaly, 'the motherly picket surrounded by policemen, the champion of trade union rights.' He thought she was well on the way to acquiring 'as important a place in the British social consciousness as Eliza, tripping across the ice-floes to save her life in *Uncle Tom's Cabin*, did for nineteenth-century Americans'.[13]

There was, however, a crucial difference between the Grunwick strike and *Uncle Tom's Cabin*. Contrary to far-left mythology, the dispute had absolutely nothing to do with racism. Skin colour, said Jayaben Desai, 'has nothing to do with this fight'. It is true that George Ward liked to employ immigrant workers, but from his point of view this was simply good business sense, because (as his own legal advocate admitted) they were more likely to accept lower wages. As Lord Scarman later reported, Grunwick was hardly a sweatshop. 'In so far as it has provided job opportunities in a depressed area for people whose situation in the labour market was weak,' Scarman wrote, 'the company has proved beneficial. It has provided jobs, where jobs were and are urgently needed.' On top of that, it is simply not true that the Grunwick workers were the victims of discrimination. 'The strikers themselves have been adamant in maintaining that their being Asian is irrelevant,' declared the Commission for Racial Equality in a report studiously ignored by many writers on the strike. 'They see the dispute as a conflict between workers and employers.' Indeed, far from being racists, the people the left most abhorred – the workers who kept going in to Grunwick every morning, as well as the man who employed them – were themselves Asian. As the Metropolitan Police Commissioner David McNee remarked, few people seemed to notice that every morning his supposedly racist force put their bodies on the line 'to convey a small group of frightened Asian workers in a double-decker bus into a small factory managed by a rich Anglo-Indian against the massed opposition of white trade unionists'.[14]

On the surface, the confrontation at Grunwick was a minor industrial dispute involving a handful of people in a shabby corner of north-west London. From the very beginning, however, partisans on both sides saw it as a titanic clash of political principle. For the left, the issue was simple: the right of low-paid workers in small companies to join a union and fight for better conditions. The Grunwick workers, their argument ran, were poor, vulnerable people whose grievances should be heard. On top of that, victory would have obvious benefits for the union movement as a whole, for if APEX won then the unions could expect to attract thousands of new immigrant members. Yet the obvious justice of the strikers' complaints did not mean there were not powerful arguments on the other side, too. George Ward might be ruthless and stubborn, his defenders argued, but by keeping costs down he was providing work for dozens of poor Asian immigrants. Small businesses like Grunwick 'could not have come into existence', insisted *The Times*, 'if they did not have a competitive edge, and the only edge they could have is low labour costs and a willing labour force not restricted by trade union attitudes'. For the right, just as for the left, the issue was clear: the right of an employer to run his business as he wanted, without interference from the trade unions. Indeed, for the National Association for Freedom, which contacted Ward in the autumn of 1976 and campaigned unceasingly on his behalf, this was a crucial test of principle. Grunwick, said NAFF's director John Gouriet, was 'one little company that was being bullied' – and he was determined to save it.[15]

At first the Grunwick strikers struggled to attract much attention. Picketing was hard work, and although APEX quickly rustled up some strike pay, at an initial £8 it was barely a quarter of what they had been earning beforehand. Many of them were married women whose husbands expected them to cook and clean, so picket duties had to be arranged around housework. The months went by; summer turned to autumn; the heatwave became a fading memory. In pouring rain and driving snow, the little huddle of Asian women stood in Chapter Road, waving their placards; 1976 became 1977, and still they held their ground. In May three APEX-sponsored Cabinet ministers, Shirley Williams, Denis Howell and Fred Mulley, visited the picket line to offer warm handshakes and encouraging words.* But still the affair failed to capture the public imagination. In the drab street outside the Grunwick factory, the number of pickets steadily dwindled. Delivery vans came and went, while Ward's managers no longer bothered to slow down as they drove past the picket lines. Sometimes, when Jack Dromey turned into Chapter Road, he found there were no pickets at all. It was time, he decided, to go for broke. The call went out across the country: on 13 June, there would be a mass picket at Grunwick. What Dromey hoped to achieve was never clear: perhaps he thought it would stop workers getting into the factory, or even suffocate its business by blocking deliveries. Still, it was bound to attract attention. As he later remarked, the

---

* Shirley Williams was understandably outraged when she was later accused of having given her approval to the violence at Grunwick. As she pointed out, there had been no trouble at all when she visited the picket lines, since the violence only started weeks afterwards.

only things that 'frightened the right more than the dreaded "mass
picket"' were the Red Army and sex education.[16]

Dromey's appeal fell on fertile ground. From a demonstrator's point
of view, Grunwick was the perfect location for a quick outing: not far
from central London, with Dollis Hill station just a few minutes' walk
from the factory. As Rogaly remarked, 'anyone willing to get up early
enough in the morning could be on the picket line by seven o'clock,
shout slogans at the company bus as it arrived within the following
hour or so, and be on the way to a job somewhere in London before
nine'. Even better, the television cameramen could be back at their studios by mid-morning with plenty of potential clips for the evening news.
For activists and broadcasters, it made an ideal story; for committed
militants, meanwhile, it offered an ideal opportunity to attract new
recruits. The Communist Party was quick to join the bandwagon, but
the biggest support came from the Trotskyist Socialist Workers' Party,
which was keen to exploit trade unionists' resentment at Labour's pay
restraint. On 28 May the SWP's official newspaper launched an appeal
to its 5,000 members to join the Grunwick picket, and in the next week
it distributed more than 22,000 leaflets and put up 2,000 posters across
the capital, insisting that 'aggressive picketing can close the factory'.
Not all Dromey's collaborators viewed the intervention of the SWP
with unruffled equanimity. Roy Grantham loathed the party so much
that its members were barred from holding office in APEX, and he was
deeply anxious about this new twist in the Grunwick story. But there
was not much he could do about it.[17]

At six o'clock on Monday, 13 June, 200 people were already milling
about outside Dollis Hill tube station. In the surrounding houses, many
people had not even got out of bed, while Grunwick's workers were not
due to arrive for another two hours. But already there was a heady,
festive atmosphere, thanks partly to the presence of an outspoken
contingent from the Communist Party Women's Group. By the time the
first employees hurried anxiously towards the factory gates, the crowds
had swollen to about 700 people, chanting 'Scab! Scab! Scab!' as the
police battled to get the workers inside. Accounts differ about how the
trouble started: the police claimed they had been attacked with eggs and
flour bombs, while APEX maintained that the police had overreacted to
lawful picketing. But whoever started it, the fighting quickly got out of
control. By the end of the morning eighty-four people, many of them
women, had been arrested and bundled into police vans. What shocked
many observers, however, was the enthusiasm with which the police set

about their opponents. They were trying to clamp down on 'lawful picketing', Labour MPs complained afterwards, while Roy Grantham demanded a public inquiry into 'unnecessary police violence'. Even the *Evening Standard*, which told its readers that 'one demonstrator was dragged to a police van by his hair, and several others were clearly punched during the arrests', was clearly shocked by the Met's enthusiasm for the battle.[18]

The scenes at Grunwick that morning were the first serious clashes between police and pickets since the miners' strike five years earlier. There was, however, a crucial difference. In 1972 the police had been overwhelmed by the sheer numbers of picketing miners. But this time the Met had mobilized about 300 men, held in readiness in buses along the main road. Among them were plain-clothes members of its famously over-zealous Special Patrol Group (SPG), who laid into the demonstrators with unseemly gusto. Determined that the unions would never humiliate them again, police commanders now planned for strikes as though they were medieval battles, sealing off streets, changing the entrances used at factories and going out of their way to intimidate their opponents. In many ways, therefore, the violence at Grunwick anticipated what was coming seven years later, during the miners' final showdown with the Thatcher government. But the violence was hardly one-way. Some policemen 'may have been deliberately provocative, or too free with arrests, or especially rough', wrote Rogaly, but most were not, and 'they took hard knocks'. Another watching reporter, who was horrified to see three SPG men banging a girl's head against the bonnet of their van, thought that there was 'a great deal of provocation dished out to the police'. In some cases, individual constables who became separated from their colleagues were 'beaten and kicked by groups of pickets while [they] were on the ground'. An APEX man shouted 'at the crowd through a loudhailer that they were a disgrace to the trade union movement', but they took no notice: he 'was laughed at and jeered'.[19]

Monday's mass picketing set the tone for the next ten days. Every morning hundreds of activists, students and trade unionists, including radical actors and the president of the Socialist Lawyers' Society, made their way to Chapter Road, where they waited with their flags and banners beside a small, almost unnoticed group of Asian women. After a couple of hours, the bus would appear at the end of the street, and the ritual shouting – 'Scabs! Scabs! Scabs!' – would erupt as the crowd surged towards the road. Sometimes the pickets managed to break through the line of policemen, hammering on the side of the bus, pressing their faces against the windows, their features contorted with rage. 'We know where you live!' they would shout, waving pictures of the strike-breakers. The bus always made it through, disgorging dozens of frightened women to scuttle through the gates. Every day brought more arrests; every day the numbers swelled. By Thursday, there were an estimated 700 pickets and 521 policemen; a week later, there were 2,000 pickets and 793 policemen, enough to restage a decent re-enactment of the battle of Poitiers. And every day brought more violent clashes and more gripping footage of policemen and pickets pushing and shoving, grappling on the ground, exchanging kicks and punches. In total, June and July saw an estimated 18,000 pickets confront 3,500 policemen, with 297 people arrested and 97 policemen injured. Almost overnight a little mail-order firm had become the centrepiece of the bitterest industrial confrontation of the decade.[20]

Grunwick was now front-page news. In the two weeks after 13 June, *News at Ten* devoted almost a third of its total running time to the dispute, while the newspapers frequently ran images of the fighting. But in Downing Street, Jim Callaghan seemed paralysed. He banned his ministers from visiting the Grunwick picket lines, but since George Ward ignored their messages, the government's attempts to mediate fell on deaf ears. On 21 June, after the Attorney General reported that 'the dispute was plainly being manipulated for political purposes', Callaghan warned his colleagues that they 'were liable to lose support if scenes of disorder continued'. Just a few hours later, however, the APEX leadership announced that 'there was no way they could exert much stricter control over the picketing', while another effort to contact Ward got nowhere. 'Senior ministers are profoundly disturbed about the impression created at home and abroad by television reports showing, day after day, fighting between demonstrators and the police,' reported *The Times*. But they seemed completely bereft of ideas: one meeting came to the limp conclusion that there was 'no obvious way through the current difficulties'. Even Callaghan admitted that he was at a loss. After reading a memo reporting that, thanks to sympathetic strike action by Post Office workers, Grunwick's local sorting office was likely to close, he scribbled simply: 'Dear oh dear! I've no suggestions.'[21]

By now Grunwick had become a magnet for the ultra-left. No self-respecting militant wanted to miss a morning's picketing, and every day seemed to bring bigger, more boisterous crowds. 'The whole panoply of the left, from International Marxists to Gay Liberationists parades daily,' remarked the *Sunday Times* on 26 June. 'It is essential to be seen

here,' explained one militant, 'best of all to get arrested.' By these standards, one of the biggest winners was the Labour MP Audrey Wise, who
joined the picket line and promptly tried to stop a policeman arresting
a young female demonstrator. Not realizing who she was, the constable
arrested Wise with the words: 'Never mind, love, you'll do instead.' But
she was merely one of a horde of celebrities who helped to turn Grunwick into 'the Ascot of the left'. A typical morning, remarked Joe Rogaly,
might see 'Mr Norman Atkinson, Labour MP for Tottenham, just
behind Miss Pat Arrowsmith, peace campaigner, or Mrs Regina Fischer,
mother of world chess champion Bobby Fischer', as well as union leaders such as the AUEW's Hugh Scanlon, NUPE's Alan Fisher and
NALGO's Geoffrey Drain. Around them students handed out leaflets
for a bewildering variety of far-left sects: the Communist Party of Great
Britain, the Socialist Workers' Party, the Workers' Revolutionary Party,
the Revolutionary Workers' Party (Trotskyist), the Communist Party of
Britain (Marxist-Leninist), the International Marxist Group, the
International Communist Current, the Indian Workers Movement/
Caribbean Workers Organisation, and so on. No doubt the People's
Front of Judaea were there too, if only in spirit.[22]

The climax of the picketing came on Thursday, 23 June. The day
before, the leader of the South Yorkshire miners, Arthur Scargill, had
promised to bring two coaches of pickets down to west London overnight. To the Grunwick women, Scargill's offer was a mixed blessing:
although he commanded enormous prestige on the left for his role in the
1972 miners' strike, nobody was more likely to inflame moderate and
right-wing opinion. Behind the scenes, Roy Grantham and Len Murray
had tried to deflect 'unwanted help' from the miners, although they
would never admit it publicly. Jack Dromey, however, took a different
view. Only escalation, he thought, would force George Ward to back
down. One warm Sunday afternoon he had secretly driven Mrs Desai
and other strike leaders to Barnsley, where they literally knocked on
Scargill's door and asked for help. As it happened, Scargill had just got
back from the Yorkshire Miners' Gala beauty contest, judged by the
unlikely duo of David Dimbleby and Tom Baker. But as an opportunis-
tic militant with a thirst for publicity, he immediately saw Grunwick's
potential. So it was that just before eight o'clock on Thursday morning,
Arthur Scargill led some 150 miners down Chapter Road towards the
factory. To the demonstrators cheering on the sidelines, it was a wonderful symbol of working-class solidarity. 'They marched in procession,
some eight abreast, below broad scarlet and red banners, and seemed to

fill the narrow road,' the left-wing activist Stuart Weir wrote with misty eyes and a thumping heart in *New Society*. 'Naturally we joked, "The US Cavalry's come at last."'[23]

What followed was not in Scargill's script. In 1972 his flying pickets had generally had things their own way, but now the SPG had different ideas. As the first bus appeared on the horizon and the pickets surged towards the centre of the road, the police began to shove them back, and in the melee tempers snapped. Caught in the crush, his tie flapping from beneath his donkey jacket, Scargill found himself pressed against the sturdy figure of a policeman, and in the next moment the SPG were on him. As the cameras rolled, one man came in from the side, pinning his arm behind his back, while two more bundled the miners' leader towards a police bus, from where his pale face soon stared out from behind a barred window. Perhaps he was lucky to be in captivity, for outside all hell had broken loose. As police and pickets grappled in the middle of the street, more demonstrators broke through the cordon to pile into the fray. The cameras caught it all, a whirlwind of movement and violence: burly men punching each other in broad daylight, pickets kicking policemen on the ground, SPG men administering instant just-ice with their fists. 'I was at Saltley Gate,' one miner later told Capital Radio, 'and it was a children's Sunday picnic by the side of this.' And one image above all came to define the morning's events: a photograph of a uniformed constable, lying motionless on the pavement, blood pouring from a wound in his head. Hit by a bottle, he lay bleeding for what seemed an eternity – even Dromey thought it was a quarter of an hour – before his comrades came to his aid.[24]

On the right, the picture of PC Trevor Wilson, stricken and bleeding outside the Grunwick factory, became the ultimate symbol of industrial unrest. The irony, of course, was that as a member of the SPG, Trevor Wilson was no stranger to rough and tumble. One of his colleagues remarked that the violence was 'chicken feed' compared with what they usually faced on 'the terraces at Arsenal'. But in hospital, where he received ten stitches, Wilson became a national hero. 'I was afraid this would happen,' his wife Janette, who was expecting their first child, told reporters. 'I knew the situation at Grunwick was getting worse, and the fear for my husband's safety was always at the back of my mind.' What was more, *The Times* reported that he would now 'miss a charity sport-ing event next Saturday which he had helped to organize. He had got together a Metropolitan Police team to take part in a raft race aimed at raising £6,000 for an electro-cardiogram machine for a hospital in

" You can be damned sure we're not going to take this lying down."—(Miners' Lodge Leader at Grunwick).

The shocking picture of the wounded Trevor Wilson instantly became the defining image of the Grunwick confrontation, as well as a stick with which to beat the trade unions: Garland in the *Daily Telegraph*, 24 June 1977.

Northampton.' Even the pickets rushed to condemn his attacker, and Jayaben Desai visited the hospital with flowers and chocolates. 'No genuine trade unionist', one of the strike organizers told ITN, 'would have thrown a bottle.' But public opinion was already turning against the pickets. The bottle would 'live for years in British political history', wrote David Wheeler in *The Listener*. 'However good a case the Grunwick strikers may have against the management, television has ensured that what will stick in people's minds is the blood running from the constable's head as he lay unconscious on the pavement.'[25]

This should have been the perfect moment for Jim Callaghan to speak out and reclaim Grunwick for the Labour right. A moderate trade unionist all his life, he abhorred the far left and was horrified by the violence outside the factory gates. The fact that Roy Grantham 'had been spat at when visiting the site', he told his ministers, 'showed that the Government was not dealing with respectable unionism but rent a mob'. Yet Callaghan's dependence on union support for his pay policy meant that he felt unable to say in public what he felt in private. While

PC Wilson was being treated in hospital, PC Jim floundered in the Commons when Mrs Thatcher asked why 'we have had no total condemnation of intimidation and violence on the picketing lines from the Prime Minister – no condemnation at all'. 'She is trying to turn this matter into a political battle,' Callaghan protested, adding that it was 'the job of the police' to protect workers and pickets alike. 'Without bottles,' interjected a Tory MP. 'Of course without bottles,' Callaghan snapped. 'Why does the hon. Gentleman make such obvious remarks? Does he think that it is necessary for me to stand here and defend the police from being hit over the head with bottles?' But this was hardly a ringing condemnation, especially when compared with the outrage of the Tory press. For the next day's *Express*, Wilson's injury was 'THE BLOODY LIMIT'. The British people, an editorial declared, now had 'a better understanding of the real class struggle which is now on. *It is a struggle between civilised men and the voice which shouted from the crowd: "Smash the fuzz's brains in."*'[26]

The widespread horror at Wilson's injury broke the momentum of the Grunwick pickets. In the next few days, Roy Grantham agreed to cut picket numbers to 500 a day, much to the fury of Arthur Scargill and the Socialist Workers. One last mass picket was called for 11 July, and although the other union leaders begged Scargill to stay away, he duly turned up with several hundred Yorkshire miners. This time the march passed off relatively quietly: although about 18,000 people turned up, the police arrested only 69 pickets and suffered 19 casualties. Given the size of the crowds, this was a lot better than many had feared, and no worse than at a typical First Division football match. But as so often, the actions of a few extremists played right into the hands of the Conservative press. The mass picket had been 'hate-filled, violent and bloody', claimed the next day's *Express*, likening it to something from the dying days of Weimar Germany. 'In narrow Chapter Road a constable was knocked to the ground. While he lay there a man deliberately stamped on his leg, breaking it. Another young constable, dripping blood from a head wound, was vomiting over a garden wall,' the paper said breathlessly. 'For a moment the factory boss, George Ward, appeared at the window. Cried the mob: "You're easy – we'll get you . . . You can't beat the workers . . . We'll kill the lot of the bloody scabs." They gave every impression they meant it.'[27]

Although readers of the *Express* could hardly have guessed it, the mass picket on 11 July was the left's last throw. The face at the window that morning was that of a man who knew victory was at hand. Throughout the case, Ward had insisted that his workers did not want a union, and to the horror of his critics, he turned out to be right. When Gallup organized a poll of the 260 remaining Grunwick employees, 83 per cent said they did not want to be represented by a union, 85 per cent were opposed to APEX representation and 80 per cent said Ward should not take back the sacked workers. If anything, the trouble outside the gates had hardened their hearts. One reporter who joined Ward's employees on the buses that brought them to work was astonished to find them staunchly behind their employer. Many were 'clearly frightened', he noted, 'as the buses approached the gate'. But they blamed Roy Grantham's 'bullying' pickets, not George Ward. They were happy with their pay and conditions, they said; as one woman proudly remarked, 'to guarantee a fast service for our customers we have to work hard.' Many said they had suffered intimidation from the pickets; one had come home to find the word 'scab' painted on his front door. They would walk out, they agreed, if Ward gave in and re-employed the strikers. 'All this', said a West Indian man, 'is making me, and everybody else I know, more determined than ever to keep going in. Everybody has been forced into the defensive and we are convinced that we should stick up for the firm. From what we have seen of Mr Grantham and his union, we do not want anything to do with it.'[28]

Despite the extraordinary scenes in Chapter Road, the biggest threat to Ward's position was a boycott of Grunwick's mail by members of the Union of Post Office Workers. The Cricklewood postal workers had launched a preliminary boycott in November 1976, but it lasted only four days before NAFF squashed it in the courts. In June 1977, however, the Cricklewood workers again voted to boycott Grunwick's mail, leaving photographs piling up in George Ward's factory. From his point of view this was a disaster: if he could not deliver people's pictures, they would stop using him. After three weeks, he recalled, 'there were nearly a thousand mail bags containing about a hundred thousand packets of processed mail piled up in every available corner in the Chapter Road works'. But once again John Gouriet came to Ward's aid. Establishing his headquarters in the Waldorf Hotel – a highly appropriate base, it has to be said, for such a right-wing operation – Gouriet rented two large trucks and recruited twenty-five NAFF activists, mostly from the City but also including the Conservative MP John Gorst and his wife. Just after midnight on Friday, 8 July, they collected hundreds of mailbags and drove up to the Oxfordshire town of Burford, where a sympathetic farmer had lent them a barn. There more activists were waiting, and for the next few hours they busied themselves licking thousands of stamps before distributing their haul in postboxes across the land. The mood, Gouriet recalled, was 'euphoric': at last, he thought, they were fighting back against the forces of socialism. By Monday morning, Grunwick's deliveries were in sorting offices across the country, and in the Commons the next day, John Gorst could not contain his glee. The 'action of the Post Office workers at Cricklewood is completely irrelevant', he boasted, for all the mail had been 'posted last weekend'.[29]

On 29 July the postal boycott collapsed, with even the Cricklewood militants returning to work. On the same day the High Court ruled that the mediation service ACAS had been wrong to recommend union recognition without balloting Ward's existing workers. The strike, it seemed, was drawing to a close. And while Ward stuck to his guns, scornfully dismissing a critical report from Lord Justice Scarman, his opponents were falling out among themselves. Behind the scenes, the Grunwick strike committee had a blazing row with the APEX executive, with Dromey arguing for more mass pickets and Grantham threatening to slash strikers' pay from £30 to £12 a week and take control of the strike himself. By this point, the numbers of pickets had fallen sharply. Scargill's miners went off on their summer holidays; the students went home or simply lost interest. By November, Roy Grantham had decided enough was enough. A few weeks later Jayaben Desai and three colleagues went on hunger strike outside the TUC headquarters, begging the unions not to give up on their cause. But it was no good: APEX promptly suspended them for four weeks and cancelled their strike pay. After the summer's heady idealism, it was the saddest of comedowns.[30]

In the courts the case dragged on until December, when the House of Lords upheld the High Court's verdict in the case between Grunwick and ACAS. But to all intents and purposes the battle was over. The scenes of mass excitement in Chapter Road had faded into history, and every morning George Ward's employees walked to work along dark and empty streets, with only a handful of pickets waiting for them at the gates. Many of the workers, Dromey remembered, now chatted to the pickets 'as if nothing had ever happened'. By March 1978 even he had yielded to the inevitable, and when he admitted to LBC radio that the strike was a lost cause, the pickets turned on him, too. A Communist-backed motion censuring APEX's 'treacherous' and 'cowardly betrayal' (even though the union had spent more than £130,000 on strike pay alone) inevitably failed, and on 14 July Dromey announced that the remaining pickets had agreed to give up the battle. They had been fighting for 591 days, but they had lost. Somehow it said it all that, unlike the reports of fighting in the streets, the announcement failed to make the next day's front pages.[31]

To the right, Grunwick had been a gift. 'The issues raised by the Grunwick siege,' Sir Keith Joseph told a Doncaster rally, 'represent a make-or-break point for British democracy, the freedoms of ordinary men and women. The siege has suddenly shown us how far we have drifted, how far power in the Labour Party and unions has slipped into the hands of the authoritarians, the totalitarians, the men of violence for whom law and order are dispensable.' This was strong stuff, even by Joseph's standards, but he was only warming up. Grunwick, he went on, was a reminder that Labour was full of 'apologists for Soviet despotism, mass murder, denial of freedom'. Moderates like Shirley Williams might seem unthreatening enough, but they were merely 'the façade behind which the assaults on our liberties continue, behind which Red Fascism spreads'.[32]

Yet despite Joseph's extraordinary rhetoric, the Tories' emollient employment spokesman, Jim Prior, was much more cautious. Openly contemptuous of NAFF, not least because he wanted to build good relations with the union leaders, Prior stuck to a moderate line, outraging many right-wing activists. The NAFF director Robert Moss, who occasionally wrote speeches for Mrs Thatcher, claimed that Prior had 'an appeaser's contempt for the heroism of the management and staff of a company that has been fighting a battle for us all', while Norman Tebbit declared that men like Prior had 'the morality of Laval and Pétain – they are willing not only to tolerate evil but to excuse it and to profit by doing so'. Instead of sacking Prior, however, Mrs Thatcher stood by him, and although she was close to NAFF, she was careful not to appear too strident. 'What we've seen on the television screens has, I think, horrified many, many people, including many, many trade unionists,' she told *Panorama*, deploring the scenes of 'intimidation and violence and mob rule'. She had, she said, 'the greatest admiration for those people who in the bus have gone through the picket lines day after day ... What we have to get rid of are the *wreckers* in society.' But where the unions were concerned, she still shrank from radical medicine. The best way to discourage mass picketing, she insisted, remained a 'voluntary code of practice'. She did not sound much like an Iron Lady.[33]

For left and right alike, Grunwick seemed a clash of supreme political importance. For the left, the dispute had been a symbol of interracial working-class solidarity. Although the strike might have failed, the spectacle of burly miners marching in support of Asian immigrant women represented something new in British politics. On the right, meanwhile, it became a celebrated milestone on the road to Thatcherism: the moment, as George Ward's supporters saw it, when one man stood up to the massed forces of organized labour. Ward himself embraced the role of a crusader for free-market values: writing in *The Times* in September 1977, he claimed that Grunwick had become 'an exceptional nuisance to those who see Britain's future as that of a collectivist, corporate state, in which any business can be obliged to surrender to coercion and brute force'.* As for the National Association for Freedom, its members were delighted with their efforts. Grunwick brought them tremendous publicity and a flood of donations, and it was no coincidence that their membership doubled while the strike was in the news. For the first time in a generation, they believed, a small group of activists had shown that the unions could be beaten. Indeed, some historians see this as one of the great unheralded turning points in post-war British history, the moment when the New Right, relying on aggressive policing and the compliance of the media, began to roll back the power of the working classes. For the far-left activist Paul Foot it was 'the most appalling defeat'; for the moderate Labour MP Phillip Whitehead it 'marked a point of counter-revolution'. But of course the biggest losers were not really the unions. The biggest losers were a small group of obscure, anxious Asian women, their hopes and fears almost forgotten amid the great clash of political principles.[34]

The real significance of Grunwick was that it cemented the popular association between strikes and violence. When the miners had brought down Edward Heath, they had done so peacefully, conscious of the risks of antagonizing moderate opinion. But the street fighting in north-west London was a terrible blow to the unions' image. It was no use pointing out that APEX was actually one of the more moderate unions, for when most people watched the strike on the evening news they saw streets filled with militants and faces contorted with hatred. The unions' defenders protested that the real culprits were the police; what most people remembered, however, was the picture of PC Wilson lying in a pool of blood. Indeed, it was Trevor Wilson, not Jayaben Desai, who became the lasting symbol of the strike. As the Labour-supporting historian Kenneth Morgan put it, 'Grunwick became not a fight for

---

* Given the striking familiarity of Ward's rhetoric, the piece was almost certainly drafted for him by one of his NAFF allies.

workers' rights but a symbol of mob rule and the uncontrolled threat from trade union power.' And what made it such a potent symbol was that it compounded a growing public anxiety about the trade unions. In May 1975, an Opinion Research Centre/ITN poll had found that three out of four people already thought the unions were 'too powerful'. Despite the unions' defeat, Grunwick added to that impression: by September 1978, MORI found that a staggering 82 per cent of people thought they wielded too much power. Perhaps most revealing of all, though, was the fact that three out of four trade union members themselves thought so too.[35]

Grunwick was only one in a series of strikes that dominated the headlines in the 1970s. It is worth repeating that most businesses remained unaffected, while the strike picture in Britain remained nowhere near as bad as in, say, Canada or Australia. Despite the newspapers' talk of 'mob rule', most strikes were driven not by ideological extremism, but by ordinary workers' material ambitions and fears of falling behind. Many union leaders, as well as thousands of shop stewards, were moderate, decent, sensible men, doing their best for their fellow workers. And yet there is no doubt that the unions were often their own worst enemies; indeed, during the Callaghan years it sometimes seemed that unions and management had entered a contest to see who could orchestrate the most absurd confrontation.

Television, for example, was persistently disrupted by strikes. In April 1977 a cameramen's dispute even forced the BBC to postpone the Eurovision Song Contest (won the previous year by Brotherhood of Man) by five weeks. Two years later came one of the most infamous strikes of the decade, provoked by an argument on 8 March 1979 between Terry Ryan, a light-rigger, and his manager, John Carter. Having assaulted Carter so viciously that he needed nine stitches, Ryan was sacked on the spot; as a result, almost 400 riggers, drivers and crew walked out in sympathy. Once again Eurovision paid the price, with the BBC forced to scrap the evening's live *Song for Europe* show. For a week Television Centre ground to a halt – the second series of *Fawlty Towers* being among the shows disrupted – and only when the BBC agreed to pay Ryan's salary pending an internal inquiry did the technical union go back to work. But the disruption did not end there: in December, yet another strike forced the BBC to abandon the season finale of *Doctor Who* halfway through, much to the disgruntlement of its writer, Douglas Adams.* The corporation's only consolation was that the situation at ITV was even worse. On 6 August 1979, Thames Television's technicians switched off the power in pursuit of a 20 per cent pay increase, plunging the channel into darkness. When the management turned it back on again, the technicians' union called an all-out strike. Almost unbelievably, ITV went off the air for eleven weeks before the independent companies gave in and offered the union almost 18 per cent.[36]

Had there been a prize for the most self-destructive unrest of the late 1970s, though, it would undoubtedly have gone to Fleet Street. With many advertisers having switched to television, the newspaper industry was in a desperate condition. Of the eight national dailies, two were making heavy losses, one was breaking even and the others were making minuscule profits. Its ranks boosted by an influx of outspoken younger members, the National Union of Journalists was so powerful that, as one activist, Roy Greenslade, later recalled, 'no one could be fired, even for incompetence'. At the *Mirror*, the union secured a guarantee that 'layabouts who were useless' would be automatically replaced; at the *Sun*, they even saved the job of a sports writer who, steaming with drink, had jumped onto a table and exposed himself. But the real power brokers were the print unions, who jealously guarded their hard-won privileges, fiercely resisted new technology and could bring production to a halt at the click of their fingers. As Greenslade recalled, their power to stop production meant the printers were infamous for 'their ability to extract the maximum amount of money for the minimum amount of work'. Unlike the owners, for whom the loss of even one issue was a commercial disaster, most printers 'didn't really care whether the paper was published or not'. In 1975 alone *The Times* lost hundreds of thousands of copies, while the *Mirror* group disappeared from the news-stands for ten days. Desperate to keep them happy, the owners consistently broke government pay norms, yet in the first six months of 1978 alone Fleet Street lost 105 million copies to industrial action. It was little wonder some proprietors were already thinking about radical change.[37]

At the end of November 1978 came a moment that, for more conservative observers, seemed conclusive proof that the nation had lost its way. Despite its reputation as the newspaper for 'top people', *The Times* had been haemorrhaging money for years. Unlike other papers, it

---

* Adams did not waste the material, however, recycling it a few years later in his novel *Dirk Gently's Holistic Detective Agency*.

refused to make under-the-counter payments to its print workers, who were therefore paid less than their Fleet Street brethren. That bred discontent in the print room: in the first three months of 1978, strikes cost *The Times* some £2 million. Gambling on the equivalent of a First World War frontal attack, the chief executive, Marmaduke Hussey, handed the print unions an ultimatum. Unless they agreed a new productivity deal, including the installation of computer technology, by the end of November, the *Times* papers would be shut down. The months went by; the deadline approached. On Thursday, 30 November, the paper's main leader warned that 'this will be the last edition of *The Times* to appear for some time'. Its tone was bullish. 'In seeking to deal with the growing anarchy in Fleet Street,' it explained, 'we believe that we are in fact helping the trade unions.' But the printers did not see it that way. For the next eleven months, *The Times* vanished from the nation's newsagents, only reappearing on 13 November 1979. The dispute cost some £40 million; what was more, Hussey had to admit defeat in his crusade for new technology. Two years later, exhausted and dispirited, *The Times*'s Canadian owners sold the paper to Rupert Murdoch. He had rather different ideas about how to drag Fleet Street into the modern world.[38]

To many observers the disappearance of *The Times*, a newspaper that had reported the fall of the Bastille, the death of Nelson and the battle of Waterloo, seemed almost unimaginable. But it was not the only national institution crippled by strikes in the last years of the decade. At the Victoria and Albert Museum, Roy Strong complained that the unions made his life 'absolute HELL' by kicking up a fuss whenever he tried to bring in new curatorial talent. 'Their great objective is to achieve a union closed shop,' he recorded. 'There is to be, in their view, no recruitment from outside except at the very lowest levels, otherwise Buggins' turn all the way. Above all there must be no changes, no new broom, no new ideas . . . It has become total confrontation all the way.' Yet industrial relations at the V&A were positively cordial compared with the situation on the South Bank, where the National Theatre had become a great concrete symbol of the slow death of 1960s optimism. Already crippled by soaring costs and press criticism, and already scarred by the August 1976 strike, Peter Hall's great project was in danger of collapsing into industrial anarchy. In May 1977, for example, a strike broke out over the dismissal of a plumber for gross inefficiency. Unfortunately the plumber was also a shop steward for the National Association of Theatrical, Television and Kine Employees (NATTKE), and the 'workshops, the stage staff and some others' promptly walked out in sympathy. Performances had to be suspended, the losses mounted and eventually Hall backed down. The plumber got his job back. But his work did not improve, and he was finally sacked a year later.[39]

By this time, industrial disputes had become a regular feature of the theatrical calendar. Wage demands were a constant problem: in the summer of 1977, for example, Hall recorded that NATKKE were asking for almost 30 per cent. 'We haven't got anything like it,' he lamented, adding that 'the government pay policy is completely broken'. In the end they settled for 10 per cent, pushing the National's finances closer to the brink of collapse. By November 1977 the press were reporting that the theatre was 'half a million pounds in the red in its current account this year, would shortly not be able to sign cheques, and would be closing down unless more money were found'. This, Hall admitted, was 'fairly near the truth'. Yet on the first day of November 1978 the stage staff walked out yet again, having rejected the maximum pay deal possible under the latest government guidelines. That evening Hall had a visit from his friend Bill Gaskill, who had just directed an acclaimed production of the left-wing classic *The Ragged Trousered Philanthropists*. 'All the men, [Gaskill] declared, should be sacked for unprofessional behaviour,' Hall recorded. 'He also said roundly that he didn't believe in unions. I enjoyed this from the socialist who has just directed the classic of English working-class union life. No, that's not quite fair. He hates unions *now*. And he's bloody right.'[40]

By the middle of November, with NATTKE having voted three to one for a strike against the National Theatre's 5 per cent pay offer, a strike seemed certain. In his diary, Hall lamented the increasingly 'rancid atmosphere of distrust and gloom'. His friend Harold Pinter, whose brilliantly moving new play had been in rehearsal, was 'walking about like a sad zombie, wondering whether *Betrayal* is to open or not'. Hall was sure the theatre would have to close. 'We haven't got the money to get near what the men are demanding,' he wrote, 'and I cannot let us slide into a Fleet Street situation. Otherwise, isn't it possible that in a couple of years' time, our NATTKE branch could decide to take unofficial action if they don't like the particular political content or meaning of a play? Just as printers in Fleet Street ban some cartoons or articles.' The atmosphere deteriorated; at dinner with Bernard Levin, Hall agreed that the National 'would soon be going down the same road as *The Times*'. He asked Levin what on earth Jim Callaghan was doing in Downing Street. 'Hiding under the table,' Levin said.[41]

In October 1974 Hall had voted for Harold Wilson. A Labour

supporter almost all his life, he doubted that he could ever vote for any-body else, remarking that it would be like 'a Catholic leaving the religion he was born to'. Like many prominent figures in the arts world, he saw himself as an instinctively left-leaning sort of person. But as the unrest intensified, he hardened his heart. When the stagehands called an over-time ban in March 1979, he decided to take a tough line. 'The time is right for blood-letting,' he wrote. 'Our political situation is good; the country is strike-ridden and fed up with it; and we have the Board's backing.' A few days later the stage staff walked out. 'Three full houses went down the drain,' Hall wrote. 'This is the big one.' Performances ground to a halt; actors who crossed the picket line were routinely abused; pickets broke into the car of a staff member who had been unwise enough to leave it in the theatre car park. One morning, the pickets stopped Hall's taxi driver and asked him to support 'their fair fight against the corrupt management'. 'Get out of my way,' the driver shouted. 'I know most of your faces, you're all a lot of fucking mini-cab drivers.' At that, the stunned Hall noted, the pickets 'melted away like fog in the sun'. But the strike dragged on for weeks, and in the end it cost the National Theatre £250,000 and the Labour Party at least one vote. That spring, for the first time in his life, Peter Hall voted Conservative.[42]

26

What a Treat to Look at You!

Roddy Llewellyn, the young restaurateur holidaying with
Princess Margaret on the Caribbean island of Mustique, has a
new ambition: to be a pop singer. His experience? Singing the
occasional duet with the Princess . . . Roddy has told friends: 'I
intend to be more outrageous than David Bowie.'

Daily Express, 25 February 1976

The Queen is something – perhaps the last thing – where we are
the best in the world. She is doing very well even if we are not!

Bernard Donoughue's diary, 10 June 1977

One morning in early 1977, Jim Callaghan kicked off the weekly Cabinet meeting on an unusual note. Since the Queen's Silver Jubilee celebrations were approaching, he said, they ought 'to consider giving a gift to the Queen'. Something 'she would really use' would be ideal, he added, at which Shirley Williams brightly suggested a saddle. 'Someone else said don't forget that Parliament gave Charles I a saddle,' noted Tony Benn, 'at which there was a lot of laughter.' But Benn himself was in typically earnest form. 'We are a Labour Cabinet,' he said, 'so if we are going to give her something shouldn't it be uniquely Labour? I am not suggesting a leather-bound copy of our Constitution' – and at that, he recorded, 'there was a sort of groan around the whole Cabinet'. 'Let him finish,' Callaghan said wearily.

'Well, I think we should perhaps give her something that comes out of the labour movement,' Benn went on. 'I have got in my office a vase, given me by the Polish Minister of Mines, carved out of coal by a Polish miner. What about that?' 'Well, in Wales we have beautiful clocks set in carved coal,' said the Lord Chancellor, Elwyn Jones, allowing Benn proudly to record that 'the suggestion wasn't entirely ridiculed'. Fortunately for the Queen, however, Callaghan had other ideas. A month later he announced that she had asked for a silver coffee pot. Audrey Callaghan had duly gone off to buy a Victorian coffee pot, 'and since it will cost each member of the Cabinet £15, it is worth at least £370'. 'I assume that as it is a Cabinet coffee pot it won't leak?' Benn asked. 'You can say that to the Queen yourself,' Callaghan said.[1]

Callaghan made no secret of his admiration for the Queen. He had been brought up to respect the monarchy, and jokes about the Royal Family met with stern disapproval. Although he treated her with greater formality than had Wilson, who was reputedly her favourite Prime Minister, he always enjoyed his weekly audiences. Despite being an avowed republican, Michael Foot, too, was a great fan of the Queen, often chatting to her about history and dogs. Foot even had an excellent rapport with the Queen Mother, who later complimented him on his infamous 'donkey jacket'. And although Callaghan and Foot shared the values of an older generation, their attitudes almost certainly reflected those of the vast majority. Thousands of people turned out to greet the Queen when she toured the country, millions tuned in religiously for her televised Christmas message, and a staggering 28 million people watched Princess Anne's wedding in November 1973. Even though 'a great many Britons had a very low opinion of Parliament and political parties', thought The Times, 'what is reasonably certain is [that] the majority still defer to the Monarchy, if to few other institutions, and that it has been strengthened by the Queen'. Her 'very Englishness . . . her restraint, composure and fortitude' were appreciating assets in a time of extraordinary political uncertainty, economic misery and cultural flux. Even her role as head of the armed forces might prove increasingly important: 'Perhaps only a few Britons know that in the unlikely event of great national dissension and violence the allegiance of the armed forces to the Monarchy would be decisive,' said The Times, 'but the majority senses the stability this ensures.'[2]

Yet not everyone shared Callaghan's admiration. Among left-wing activists, especially the university-educated idealists who identified with Tony Benn, automatic respect for the monarchy was in very short supply. Attitudes had begun to shift in the early 1970s, when the New Statesman led a strident campaign against a planned increase in the Civil List. For the first time in living memory, the Royal Family's finances were the stuff of public debate: in Lambeth, left-wing councillors took down a portrait of the Queen and hid it under the sofa, while the *Sun* (then nominally a Labour paper) devoted two pages to her finances, and claimed that four out of five readers opposed her pay rise. And as big-city constituency Labour parties fell under the sway of younger activists, criticism of the Royal Family became an increasingly easy way to get applause. The first Privy Council after Wilson's return in March 1974 offered a little sign of change: while Barbara Castle deliberately wore 'the old coat in which I had been campaigning', Foot and Benn 'looked as if they had been camping' and 'most people walked back normally to their places instead of feeling their way backwards as one is supposed to do'. A year later, when Denis Healey increased the Civil List to £1.4 million to keep up with inflation, 89 Labour MPs voted against it, while another 50 deliberately abstained. Conservative votes ensured that the Queen got her pay rise, but *Private Eye*'s memorable cover – 'WINDSOR WOMAN IN MASSIVE £420,000 POOLS WIN', above a picture of the Queen saying: 'It will not change my way of life' – demonstrated how attitudes had changed. One day, insisted the republican Labour MP Willie Hamilton, 'the Monarchy and all its prostituted entourage' would be 'dumped in the garbage can of history'.[3]

Since respect for institutions was declining across the board, it would probably have been impossible for the monarchy's lustre to remain untarnished into the 1980s. To some extent, though, the Palace was responsible for its own problems. In the pioneering fly-on-the-wall documentary *Royal Family* (1969), the Windsors had partially lifted the veil of secrecy. By later standards its tone was almost excruciatingly deferential, yet as the royal biographer Kenneth Rose remarked, once people had seen 'Prince Philip cooking sausages', they would 'want to see the dining room, the sitting room, then everything except the loo'. And with the tabloids fighting an increasingly bitter circulation war in the early 1970s, Prince Charles's love life and Princess Anne's equestrian feats became regular front-page highlights, reflecting a new appetite for populist sensationalism. Indeed, even though the public voted for Anne as BBC Sports Personality of the Year in 1971, and cheered her on in the Montreal Olympics five years later, they also enjoyed stories about her impatience and prickliness. Few British publications went as far as American papers such as the *Washington Daily News*, which called her 'snobbish, bored, pouting, sullen and disdainful'. But some columnists, notably the *Express*'s redoubtable Jean Rook, came pretty close. 'It still unnerves me to think that Anne might get within a stone's throw of the crown,' she wrote in April 1975. The princess, she thought, was not only 'snappish and easily bored'; she was often 'bloody rude'.[4]

Even these sentiments, unthinkable ten years earlier, paled by comparison with Mary Griffiths's blistering piece in the *Mirror* two years later, which described Princess Anne as 'the Royal Family's own little gift to republicanism':

> She is being paid a lot of money – £35,000 a year – and for that at least you'd expect her to be pleasant. Well, what else is she FOR? . . .
>
> I think I know what's wrong with Princess Anne, or One, as she apparently likes to be known.
>
> She's plain arrogant . . . She really has an uncommon gift for putting her hoof in it. Remember when she called her husband (though some say it was his horse) a bastard when man-and-mount fluffed a fence?
>
> I know you'll remember because it was one of her better days. She gave a tongue-lashing to a cameraman – also, according to her, a bastard – and told a small boy he was a silly bugger.
>
> And these words are not ones which any member of OUR Royal Family ought to bandy about too readily, are they?*

Not surprisingly, the *Mirror* was promptly inundated with letters. Many rallied to the princess's side. 'Three cheers for Princess Anne – a fresh, modern and uncluttered young woman!' wrote Hazel Rowen of Berkshire, while B. Cash of Hornchurch thought the Princess was 'entitled to be as bitchy as she likes. Most members of the human race are beneath contempt and need putting in their places. She has the guts to do it and should be admired for that.' And yet other readers wrote in to congratulate Mary Griffiths. 'What can one expect', added D. Waxman of Hartfield, 'from "One" who at the time of her marriage didn't know what it was like to eat sausages, whose dogs and horses live in conditions far better than over half the population of the world?' 'Thank goodness we have found a person to say in print what so many of us think about Princess Anne,' agreed Mrs D. M. Cox of Basildon. 'I, too, think she is the most disliked Royal we have ever had.'[5]

But Princess Anne's antics were as nothing compared with the scandal that engulfed her aunt's reputation in the spring of 1976. A figure of

---

* The story referred to an incident in September 1976, when Anne snapped at her husband, Captain Mark Phillips, for hitting a show-jumping fence. Discovering that she was being filmed, she mouthed: 'Bastard. What an idiot' at the BBC cameraman, and then lashed out verbally at a small boy who had got under her feet.

almost transcendent fascination to the newspapers since her flirtation with the divorced Group Captain Peter Townsend in the early 1950s, Princess Margaret had always relished her reputation as the monarch's 'wicked' little sister. Her marriage to the playboy photographer Antony Armstrong-Jones (later Lord Snowdon), only added to her lustre, and for the first ten years of their marriage she relished being the centre of a well-heeled society set, hobnobbing with stars like David Niven and Peter Sellers. By the early 1970s, however, her marriage to Snowdon, always highly tempestuous, was falling apart, leaving Margaret to seek solace with the handsome Roddy Llewellyn, a would-be gardener eighteen years her junior. By the beginning of 1976 their affair was common knowledge on Fleet Street, presenting a glaring contrast with the Queen's carefully maintained moral conservatism. But worse was to follow. The day after Harold Wilson had announced his resignation, the Palace confirmed rumours that Margaret and Snowdon were to separate. As Joe Haines later admitted, Wilson had advised the Palace to pick that particular date because the bad news would be overshadowed by his resignation. But he was wrong about that.[6]

In the long run, the collapse of Margaret's marriage was a critical moment for the modern image of the Royal Family. Within hours of the statement from Buckingham Palace, the press had laid siege to Roddy Llewellyn's farm, turning him into a household name. That he was unemployed at a time of rising public antipathy to welfare claimants only made matters worse: 'Margaret's Darling Angel On The Dole' read the gleeful headline in the *News of the World*. By the end of March, the *Express* had paid £6,000 for exclusive pictures of 'The Court Of King Roddy', where he and his upper-class friends posed in some very ill-advised kaftans and drank champagne for the cameras. But Llewellyn evidently had no qualms about milking his unexpected celebrity: in October 1978, he even tried his hand at a pop career, inviting the press to the launch of his execrable record 'Roddy' at the nightclub Tramp. To the press he seemed a wonderfully ridiculous but pleasingly photogenic figure: few weeks in the late 1970s went by without a Roddy story in the gossip columns, and London souvenir shops even sold 'Roddy for PM' T-shirts. 'Hot news: Roddy may join Bruce Forsyth's "Big Night" TV show,' gushed the William Hickey column in the *Express*. 'Where will this madness end?'[7]

No doubt the Queen must have asked herself the same question. For although there was no serious danger of Llewellyn joining the Royal Family, his affair with her sister had smashed their image of manicured respectability into a thousand pieces. Everything Margaret did was now fair game, and the rude, childish and self-indulgent behaviour that had earlier been overlooked now made it onto the front pages. The critics could hardly fail to notice that her public engagements dropped by half in 1977 and 1978, that she spent half her time in the Caribbean, and that she treated the press with wilfully self-destructive contempt. By April 1978, seven out of ten people agreed that Margaret had damaged the image of the Royal Family, and whenever Labour's Willie Hamilton laid into her 'expensive, extravagant irrelevance', people listened. But beyond all this lay a deeper problem for the monarchy. Much of its popularity since the late 1930s had been based on its image as a happy, united churchgoing family, with the Queen and Prince Philip held up as exemplary parents. But thanks to Margaret, that image was becoming unsustainable. 'The Queen and her family reflect as well as represent the community,' *The Times* admitted two years later. 'They are exposed to the pressures of modern life like the rest of us.' In the *Telegraph*, Peregrine Worsthorne suggested that instead of being set apart, the Royal Family should be seen as a 'normal' family in a permissive age, complete with 'royal broken marriages, merry widows, disorderly divorcees, delinquent teenagers'. He was only joking. But in the long run, he was more perceptive than perhaps he realized.[8]

On the face of it, the Queen's Silver Jubilee, marking the twenty-fifth anniversary of her accession in 1952, was the ideal opportunity to rekindle the romance with her people. Similar celebrations in the past had been great orgies of patriotic excitement, complete with firework displays, street parties and loyal addresses from coast to coast. At first, however, the government seemed nervous. With the economy in the doldrums, Celtic nationalism on the rise, the IRA bombing campaign in full swing and national morale at rock bottom, Harold Wilson had dragged his feet, afraid that the celebrations were bound to be a flop. By the time Callaghan took over, however, the Palace had made plans for the Queen to visit Australia, New Zealand and the Pacific Islands before spending three months touring the United Kingdom, culminating in a week of celebrations in London. Whether this would rouse the public, however, seemed very dubious. Many observers thought that the news about Princess Margaret had badly damaged the image of the monarchy, and certainly the Duke of Edinburgh had a funny idea about how to make friends and influence people. Asked to give his views on the state of the nation in the magazine *Director* in January 1977, he suggested that contemporary Britain should 'not concentrate so heavily on the unfortunate, the underprivileged'.

> A hundred years ago everyone knew what he should do. He should go out, work hard, earn a living, provide for his children, provide for health, provide for old age, leave something solid for his children, accumulate some wealth and some treasures of various kinds. He wanted to be remembered for being a successful person, to contribute to charity, to build up something for the community.
>
> If you want any of these things today, they are all cut off. You need not try to provide for your children, because the state says, 'No, we are better able to educate them' . . . You need not try to provide for your old age, because you have got to be taxed to provide other social benefits, and in any case there is a national pension scheme. You must not accumulate wealth (well, it is not a question of must not, but it is so arranged that you should not). We have turned the whole thing, in a sense, upside down.

Not surprisingly, these trenchant views, which might have come from some Freedom Association pamphlet, did not go down well on the Labour benches. The Duke was 'impudent and ill-advised', said the Labour MP James Lamond, while Dennis Skinner thought he had 'no respect for workers'. But the Duke showed little sign of taking any notice. Broadcasting on Radio Clyde a few weeks later, he warned that by the year 2000 Britain would have suffered 'a gradual reduction in the freedom of choice and individual responsibility', from education and healthcare to 'the ability to acquire or inherit personal property' and 'the freedom of the individual to exploit his skills or talents as suits him best'. And a conference on the future of London at the Royal Festival Hall, largely attended by local councillors and planners, found him in similarly forthright form. 'He inveighed against what he called "the nanny society",' recorded one participant, 'and said that in the old days all the people who wanted to tell other people how to run their lives used to go overseas and govern remote parts of the Empire – now unfortunately they stayed at home.'[9]

Had there been a less deferential occupant of Number 10, Prince Philip's remarks might have caused greater offence. It was lucky for the Queen, then, that Callaghan was determined to make the Jubilee a success. Meeting the head of the planning committee, Lord Drogheda, in January 1977, Callaghan remarked that the celebrations 'were falling in a good year this year. Last year the national mood would have been quite wrong.' With national holidays scheduled for both Monday 6 and Tuesday 7 June, Callaghan thought there might be an appetite for old-fashioned patriotic entertainment. 'There would be spontaneous street teas in working class areas if they were given any encouragement at all,' he said, adding that 'the most enjoyable for many people would be children's street teas'. What this really reflected, of course, was the Prime Minister's innate conservatism, although, as it turned out, millions of people agreed with him. The other great benefit of 'street teas' was that they were cheap: as one official wrote, 'to spend too lavishly on the celebrations in current economic conditions would undoubtedly lead to criticism both of the Queen and the Government'. Yet Callaghan was adamant that petty financial considerations should not blight the Queen's long-awaited party. As the big day approached, Lord Drogheda became increasingly frustrated that the Department of Energy was blocking his plans to illuminate the buildings along the Thames during the Jubilee holiday. The fact that this was Tony Benn's department did not escape him, and there were murmurs about the 'anti-monarchist in DoE'. But Callaghan was not going to let Benn ruin a good party. 'Bloody nonsense,' he scrawled on a letter complaining that Energy officials were dragging their feet. 'This is pernickety bureaucracy. Let them light up for a bit during the main summer weeks.'[10]

For all Callaghan's enthusiasm, the general expectation at the beginning of 1977 was that the Jubilee would be a very damp squib indeed. During the spring there were reports of street parties being cancelled for lack of interest, while local authorities were said to be making little effort. With official expenditure on flags and bunting in the City of London expected to come in at about £150, the complaints about a 'Jubilee on the cheap' seemed distressingly well founded. And although the Queen's Pacific tour could hardly have gone better, her appearance at Westminster to receive the loyal addresses of both Houses of Parliament on 4 May provoked fierce complaints. 'I cannot forget', she said, 'that I was crowned Queen of the United Kingdom of Great Britain and Northern Ireland. Perhaps this Jubilee is a time to remind ourselves of the benefits which union has conferred, at home and in our international dealings, on the inhabitants of all parts of this United Kingdom.' To Scottish and Welsh nationalists – not to mention Catholic nationalists in Northern Ireland – this statement, drafted in Buckingham Palace, seemed an intolerable affront. Even *The Times* thought that it had broken 'the convention that the Sovereign does not descend to the arena of party political controversy', while the SNP leader Donald Stewart warned that if Scottish nationalists were forced to choose between the monarchy and independence, 'we would choose independence'. 'She knows we're slipping out of her clutches,' one Edinburgh man said, 'and she's panicking.'[11]

And yet while the Scots seemed a little more resistant than their neighbours to the magic of monarchy, the Queen returned from her Caledonian tour in high spirits. The Scottish crowds had been far larger than even the most optimistic had expected, the pavements teeming with flag-waving children. Polls showed that barely 13 per cent of the population could imagine Britain without its Royal Family, and suddenly Jubilee merchandise was everywhere: not merely the inevitable mugs, tea towels and commemorative coins, but Union Jack underwear, Portmeirion pottery, Robert Lacey's bestselling book *Monarchy*, and even special Jubilee editions of *Penthouse*, *Mayfair* and *Forum*. Breweries sold barrel upon barrel of Queen's Ale and Silver Jubilee Ale. On the streets of London, hawkers offered Jubilee-themed jewellery, T-shirts, beer mugs, jeans, even egg timers, thermometers and ashtrays. And one enterprising Soho sex shop even sold Jubilee lingerie emblazoned with an image of the State Coach.

The most celebrated Jubilee tie-in, of course, was the Sex Pistols' infamous single 'God Save the Queen', a commercially astute scream of rage against 'the fascist regime'. But even those who loathed punk rock had to admit that this was not quite the musical nadir. That distinction surely belonged to the dreadful hymn written by the Poet Laureate, John Betjeman, for children to sing at the Royal Albert Hall: 'From that look of dedication / In those eyes profoundly blue / We know her Coronation / As a sacrament and true.' 'Worse than this we cannot go' was the *Guardian*'s verdict. Perhaps it was just as well that the nation's outstanding poet, Philip Larkin, kept his Jubilee tribute to himself and a few friends:

> After Healey's trading figures
> After Wilson's squalid crew
> And the rising tide of niggers
> What a treat to look at you!

Given the Queen's well-chronicled love of the Commonwealth, as well as her evident enthusiasm when greeted by flag-waving black and Asian children, it is a safe bet that she would not have been amused.[12]

*

The centrepiece of the festivities began on the evening of Monday, 6 June, with the Queen and her family climbing Snow Hill in Windsor Great Park. It was a bitterly cold, rainy night, yet an estimated 300,000 spectators gathered to clap and cheer as she lit a great bonfire, answered in the night sky by 101 other beacons across the country. Pictures of her grinning with delight appeared prominently in Tuesday's papers, making the perfect introduction to a day of patriotic jubilation.

Once again the weather had done the Queen no favours; as Britain awoke to its national party, the skies were grey, a cold breeze was blowing and rain was pouring down. Yet even as the monarch was having her breakfast, tens of thousands of people were lining the streets from Buckingham Palace to St Paul's, standing twenty deep along the Mall. By the time Tony Benn left for the morning service of thanksgiving, the streets were 'packed with people behind crush barriers . . . and there was sand on the roads and soldiers and Gurkhas, airmen and sailors, some with fixed bayonets. Crowds and crowds, all waving Union Jacks and cheering.' Even Benn's republican heart melted at the spectacle of so many people in such excitement. It was 'rather fun, to be honest', he admitted. The car dropped him in Fleet Street, and he walked the last few yards to the cathedral past the crowds. He was wearing a 'slightly old but warm suit with my medals' – his daughter Melissa had remarked that he 'looked like a member of the National Front' – and as he passed, 'a few people cheered me and gave a special wave'. Not everybody, though: 'one or two', he conceded, 'shouted "Rubbish!"'[13]

The Queen left for St Paul's at a quarter to eleven, her every move tracked by the television cameras. Defying the rain in the gilded State Coach, waving cheerfully to the crowds, she was greeted by a fanfare of the Household Cavalry trumpeters on the cathedral steps and ushered inside by the Lord Mayor of London. Many of the spectators pressing around the cathedral had slept on the pavements to guarantee a good spot, and were still damp from the overnight showers. 'It was worth it,' insisted Karen Budford, a nursery nurse from Southend. 'We got a superb view, and she will pass by us as she comes out.' Despite all the fuss in the newspapers about punks and hooligans, many people were surprised to see so many teenagers carrying banners and badges reading 'Liz Rules OK' and 'Cool Rule Liz', or chanting 'Two, four, six, eight! Who do we appreciate? LIZZIE!' Even Benn found the spectacle of so much pageantry and patriotism 'extraordinary', though he was less impressed by the Archbishop of Canterbury's sermon with its emphasis on 'penitence, reconciliation and thanksgiving'. It was 'awful', Benn

thought, 'full of the old reactionary ideas – prayers about the Commonwealth and prosperity, trust in God and so on – awful opium of the
people stuff'. What he had expected the Archbishop to say is not clear;
perhaps he was upset that Dr Coggan had had what sounded like a dig
at the trade unions, warning of 'the hollowness of a way of life which
seeks to build on a basis of materialism, of each for himself, or each for
his own sectional interest, and forgets the good of the whole'.

For many people, however, the real highlight came afterwards, as the
Queen left the cathedral and walked down to the Guildhall, shaking
hands and accepting flowers as she passed along Cheapside. By now the
rain clouds had cleared, and as the cries went up of 'We love you, Liz!',
the mood was one of joy unconfined. 'It was the happiest and most
good-natured of crowds,' wrote one observer, 'with none of the supposed British reserve about talking to strangers. Children were passed
overhead to the front to sit on the kerb. The variety of costume was
extravagant, from Union Jack kilts to red, white and blue bowlers, and
blouses decorated with portraits of the Queen.' As the royal party
passed, the hands stretched forward with cards and bouquets. 'Did you
pick them yourself?' the Queen asked 13-year old Jennifer Williams
from Tottenham, who was shyly holding out a bunch of roses. Prince
Philip, meanwhile, was in typically mordant form: spotting a woman
from Sydenham with a Jubilee-themed shopping bag, he asked if she
had just been out for her groceries. Older onlookers remembered
the Coronation, but there was one obvious difference: this time, not all
the faces were white. An American reporter thought that the Queen
'appeared to pay particular attention to black and brown faces in the
crowd'. 'Are all these yours?' she asked Viveth Parkinson, born in
Jamaica but now living in Edmonton, north London, who was accompanied by 'six smiling children'. Only three were Mrs Parkinson's, it
turned out; the others were nephews and nieces, who had not wanted to
miss the big day and could not believe their luck.[14]

The climax to the day was the Queen's traditional appearance on the
balcony of Buckingham Palace, where she and her family gazed down
on what *The Times* called 'an astonishing sea of waving flags and a tide
of roaring throats assembled in the tribal arena of British patriotism'.
Despite all the foreboding in the press, at least a million people were
estimated to have swarmed onto the streets of central London, possibly
even eclipsing the crowds at the Coronation in 1953. They were basically 'middle-class British', thought the watching Roy Strong, with plenty
of 'educated voices' and 'men in suits' carrying Union Jacks tied to their

umbrellas. But it was a young, noisy crowd, and despite the rain there was plenty of cheering, 'followed by the singing of the national anthem or "Rule Britannia" and then more cheers'. When the Royal Family walked out onto the balcony, Strong wrote, 'the roar below was deafening', while 'the surge of emotion and the lump in the throat was almost tangible'. 'Close to me,' he recorded, 'a group started to sing the national anthem, which was taken up across the tide of humanity. One could not help finding it deeply moving, as indeed was the cry of a cockney nearby who yelled up to the Queen: " 'Ave a good sleep."'

Yet what distinguished the Silver Jubilee was not the orgy of pageantry in the capital, but the unexpected outpourings in unsung neighbourhoods across the country. In Havering Street, Stepney, a banner strung across the road proclaimed 'Liz Rules OK'. The area had changed enormously since the journalist Louis Heren had grown up around the corner, but when he returned on Jubilee Day, he found that even the presence of new high-rise flats at the end of the street had not broken its community spirit. Havering Street felt a long way from Buckingham Palace: seen from the commuter trains that ran across the end of the road, Heren thought, 'it must look like two rows of mean cottages'. Many had outside toilets and no bathrooms, yet as an electrician told him, 'there are worse places to live, like those flats'. Their residents were not wealthy, but they were staunchly patriotic: Mrs Anscombe at number 46 had been collecting money at the bingo hall since September and had raised the princely sum of £621, enough for twenty street parties. Many people were defiantly backward-looking: old Mrs Hart at number 40, who had worked at Dr Barnardo's until she was 86, could clearly remember Queen Victoria's last Jubilee. Heren wondered whether the Jubilee was merely 'an excuse for a good knees up', but the locals soon put him right. 'She's a good queen,' one woman said. 'She's Britain, yer know.' 'I'm a monarchist myself,' agreed another. 'Always 'ave been. Who'd want to live in a republic?' Almost despite himself, Heren loved it. There was a 'tea party and a fancy-dress competition for the kids', he wrote, 'bottles of booze and dancing for the grown-ups and lashings of Cockney kindness and good humour for everybody'.[15]

Many readers would have expected nothing less from a traditional Cockney neighbourhood. But the party spirit knew no class distinctions. In lower-middle-class Daffodil Street, Hammersmith, householders displayed portraits of the Queen in their windows and hung bunting across the road. In upper-class Kensington, a policeman wearing two Union Jacks in his helmet led a conga of 300 residents, including four Conservative MPs and two diplomats. 'It was quite amazing,' one woman said. 'You found yourself talking to the most unlikely people and we ended up after midnight drinking brandy in the house of someone we'd never met before.' In the Children's Hospital on Great Ormond Street, parents were invited to a Jubilee tea and children were presented with Jubilee crowns. On Merseyside, some 2,500 street parties were reported 'in streets decorated with flags, bunting and balloons'. In Mansfield, 400 bakers refused to work over the holiday because, they said, it was 'a once-in-a-lifetime occasion'. Even *Coronation Street* marked the occasion with a 'Glamorous Granny' competition, with an irate Elsie Tanner making it all the way to the final. The centrepiece of the *Street*'s celebrations, though, was a 'Britain through the Ages' float for the Weatherfield city parade, decorated by Ken Barlow and driven by Stan Ogden. After a great deal of bickering, the line-up was agreed: Annie Walker would play Elizabeth I, Ena Sharples would be Queen Victoria and Barlow himself would play Sir Edmund Hillary. Disastrously, however, Stan Ogden left the lorry's lights on all night before the big day, draining the battery and spoiling everybody's fun. Tried by a kangaroo court in the Rovers' Return, poor Stan was sentenced to buy everyone drinks. In the end, though, everybody enjoyed themselves, although more sensitive viewers had to avert their eyes from the spectacle of Bet Lynch dressed up as Britannia.[16]

Everywhere there were street parties and hog roasts, fêtes and raffles, puppet shows and picnics. 'My liver is damaged beyond repair, my waistline has disappeared,' wrote the columnist Jilly Cooper. 'I've been sabotaged by street parties, but I've never enjoyed a summer more.' Driving south from the Scottish Borders, the journalist Neal Ascherson, who had been impressed by the patriotic bunting in his native land, realized that he had 'seen nothing as soon as I reached the first English streets at Longtown. The place had vanished under red-white-and-blue billows of flag and ribbon, and every small town southwards was the same.' In Ellesmere, Cheshire, a giant crown floated on the lake while little girls in Union Jack knickers ran about in the rain. In Shilton, Oxfordshire, the village's sixty residents gathered in the evening with flaming torches and marched in procession to the top of the nearby hill before coming back to the Old School for drinks and a hoarse rendition of 'Land of Hope and Glory'. In Shurdington, Gloucestershire, the holiday brought a bonfire organized by the Scouts, a special service in the parish church, a fancy dress competition on the village green, the coronation of Miss Jubilee, a 'novelty cricket match', a tug of war, the 'weigh-in of sponsored slimmer Mr Paul Baker', and a 'floodlit disco'. And in nearby Chedworth, not even the hail 'drenching the T-shirted spartans in the three-legged race' could spoil the party atmosphere. 'The church bells were ringing a quarter peal of bob doubles,' wrote one observer, 'and the entire population, in rosettes, ribbons and toppers, were out in the lanes.' Almost as soon as the afternoon's races had started, the rain came pouring down and the villagers feared for their barbecue. 'But they sat down in the village hall and ate the village tea,' *The Times* reported, 'paid for by two money-raising dances. And the rain stopped, and the sun dried the puddles and made the sporting spartans' T-shirts steam. It was just perfect.'[17]

In the face of all this popular excitement, the anti-monarchist critics who had predicted a Jubilee flop looked distinctly sour. One moment they had been congratulating the public on their apathy; the next, they were deploring the vulgarity of popular taste. The 'excessive public adulation of the Queen,' grumbled the Labour MP Raymond Fletcher, reflected only 'a popular desire to live in Dreamland, where Britain is always Great, its Queen always good and its rituals far more splendid than anything those crude Americans and Germans can manage'. What made the pill even harder to swallow was the fact that republican efforts to capture public attention had been an unmitigated failure. The *New Statesman* published a spectacularly feeble anti-Jubilee edition, its case rather undermined by the fact that its chief historical expert, Kenneth Morgan, thought that 'for the sake of a democratic Britain, perhaps even a democratic socialist Britain', it might be better to keep the monarchy after all. The magazine did offer more trenchant opinions: one contributor wrote that the Queen had 'a big mouth like Jaws* and shes an old bag shes only wants money and to be rich' [*sic*], but the fact that the *Statesman* had been reduced to running pieces by north London schoolchildren rather said it all. The Socialist Workers' Party handed out stickers with the slogans 'Stuff the Jubilee' and 'Roll on the Red Republic', while the Movement Against a Monarchy sold car bumper stickers proclaiming 'Rot All Rulers'. But most republican events were a total washout. One rally attracted just eight people; another, arranged on Blackheath by the Libertarian Communists, attracted a grand total of five and was rained off.[18]

---

* Possibly the shark, but more plausibly Roger Moore's sinister steel-toothed adversary in the James Bond film *The Spy Who Loved Me*, which was released that summer to enormous audiences.

As a monarchist and a patriot, Jim Callaghan loved the Jubilee. His favourite moment came when the Queen invited him and Audrey to join her aboard the royal yacht *Britannia* for the naval review at Spithead. 'I was determined not to miss this,' he wrote afterwards, explaining that his father had served as a seaman aboard the royal yacht's predecessor, the *Victoria and Albert*, when it carried King George V to his Coronation Review in 1912. 'My father had taken me aboard the *Victoria and Albert* when I was a toddler,' Callaghan recalled, 'but I do not suppose it ever crossed his mind that one day his son would be invited to return as the Prime Minister of the United Kingdom.' That night, as the royal party enjoyed a lavish reception and the Royal Marines beat the retreat, he felt his spine 'tingle as dusk fell and the ceremony drew to an end'. At the close, as the deck lights were switched on so the crowd on shore could see more clearly, he stepped backwards with the rest of the party to leave the Queen alone before her cheering people. Lord Mountbatten encouraged him to join her at the front in taking the applause, but Callaghan was having none of it. 'It was the Queen everyone wanted to see,' he recalled, 'not me.'[19]

As always, of course, there were those who refused to enter into the party spirit. 'Everything seems utterly bleak to me and all these Jubilee celebrations malapropos,' wrote the ever-cheerful Kenneth Williams. 'In a time of economic recession, the Queen should have set an example of austerity: thousands of pounds wasted on processions and bonfires, which could have been used for better purposes.' But he was hardly one to talk about austerity, since he spent the day drinking champagne with his mother and admiring the Queen's 'good-humoured composure' on television. And given the context of financial crisis, political uncertainty and general gloom, as well as the wet weather, even the most ardent royalists were stunned by the success of the Silver Jubilee. The 'explosion of genuine popularity and emotion', said *The Times*, had 'taken most onlookers by surprise':

> It has not just been the fact that literally millions of people have been out on the streets of Britain to see her and cheer her – unprecedented though that has been, even including the VE-day celebrations; nor is it that those crowds contain as many young people as old; that spontaneous gestures such as flowers and bouquets have appeared without any prompting or pre-programming; or that the spontaneity and good spirit of the jubilee spread to street parties and fetes, throughout the land, however distant from the royal itinerary. The response has shown itself in the quality of

the post-bag being received at the Palace, where 50,000 letters have already been delivered containing people's own personal gestures of commitment and gratitude to the sovereign for the example she has given.

Even the Queen herself was reportedly stunned by the nation's enthusiasm. 'I am simply amazed,' she told one of her ladies of the bedchamber. 'I had no idea.' And at one level this was simply the reward for a quarter-century of sheer hard work: as an American observer told his readers, 'the vast majority of her subjects clearly appreciate the manner in which she has fulfilled her unique constitutional role: embodying the nation's unity, providing historical continuity, standing above party strife and class divisions.'[20]

But there was surely more to it than that. At a time when the political parties, the civil service, the trade unions and even the nation itself were coming under attack, observed an internal Conservative Party report nine months later, there was evidently an intense thirst not merely for '*national pride* and *national unity*', but for '*continuity* . . . in a bewilderingly changing world'. Similarly, at a time of fierce controversy about family life and sexual morality, the Queen seemed an unshakeable pillar of respectability. 'Through a period of fluctuating fashion and considerable moral disintegration,' wrote John Grigg in the *Observer*, 'she has lived up to her own high standards . . . [and] has shown how much family life means to her, and has stood rock-firm for all it represents.'* And at a time of fierce controversy about moral and aesthetic values, her conservatism, her ordinariness, her very lack of glamour, seemed glittering virtues. 'If she would rather go to Ascot than peer at a lot of dirty nappies in the Institute of Contemporary Arts,' asked the *Telegraph*, 'what is wrong with that?' Thank goodness, agreed Jean Rook in the *Express*, she was 'the same tidy, dedicated, undramatic, magnificently "dull" woman' as always. 'While her head is on even the sinking £ note, I feel we could survive.'[21]

Yet as Rook's last words suggest, there was a more sombre note amid the unexpected enthusiasm. Only a few months earlier, after all, the country that had once been the workshop of the world had been forced to go cap in hand to the IMF in a moment of supreme humiliation. When the Queen attended a Commonwealth summit the day after the Jubilee climax, joining her various prime ministers to watch a spectacu-

---

* There was a lovely irony in this: twenty years before, Grigg had been the first man to criticize the Queen in print, infamously claiming that her court was too stuffy and her accent a 'pain in the neck'.

lar firework display on the South Bank, it was a vivid reminder of how rapidly Britain's imperial power had collapsed since her accession in 1952. The Queen might be 'a worldwide symbol of GREAT Britain', conceded the *Mirror*, but as her prestige had risen, so 'Britain's power in the world has declined'. And not even the most enjoyable party could banish the nagging anxieties for long. As *The Times* admitted:

> The popular imagination can no longer feed on the glories and wonders of empire . . . Nor, it has to be admitted, does the Britain of 1977, relieved of almost all its imperial baggage, present the sort of spectacle to light in the mind the bonfires of national rejoicing . . .
>
> Behind the better living standards, Britain's decline in relative power, influence and wealth is universally perceived. The everyday symbol of that decline is the common token of exchange, the pound note, bearing the Queen's image, and now having a value one quarter of the value it had when the Queen came to the throne.
>
> What is more, the very integrity of the kingdom is under attack in Northern Ireland and is called in question in Scotland; and some of the old assurance with which these threats might have been repulsed is lacking . . .
>
> So it is that the time is less apt than at previous royal jubilees for the nation's celebration of its own fortune or contemplation of its density. This jubilee is more than ever the Sovereign's jubilee, a celebratory punctuation of her reign, a popular thanksgiving for her person.[22]

No doubt there were millions of people, cheerfully stuffing themselves at street parties, dancing in the rain and waving their bedraggled Union Jacks, who would not have agreed with a word of this. Yet it was suggestive that even the Jubilee edition of *Coronation Street*, the most watched programme of the week, faced up to the issue of national decline. When Ken Barlow comes to commiserate with Annie Walker about their float's non-appearance, reassuring her that nobody missed them anyway, his words fall on very stony ground. 'I'm sorry, I can't see it in that easygoing, don't care attitude,' says Annie, still in costume as Elizabeth I, her voice trembling with regal passion. 'I'm surprised to hear it from you. That's one of the things that's wrong with the country today. Nobody tries hard enough any more, and when things go wrong, nobody seems to care any more.'

She might have been speaking for millions of people who thought that things *had* gone wrong since the Queen had come to the throne, who were sick of the betrayals and humiliations, the strikes and the crises, and who felt that for all their wealth and comfort, they had lost something in the process. And even the most sympathetic foreign observers shared Annie Walker's view that Britain was no longer what it had been. 'Despite her success as a sovereign,' said *Time* magazine,

> Elizabeth II has not presided over a new Elizabethan age – for which her subjects, perhaps unrealistically, hoped when she ascended the throne . . . Indeed, the past quarter-century has witnessed enfeeblement and decline – the end of an empire, the shrinking value of the pound sterling, near stagnation of a formerly innovative economy. It is this grim reality that the Jubilee briefly banished. But it will still be there to challenge Britons when their party is over.[23]

PART FOUR

We Can't Go On Like This

27

The Shades are Closing In

Disgruntlement hangs in the air; it hangs in the air like
migraine.

Martin Amis, *Success* (1977)

RIGSBY: *This country gets more like the boiler room on the*
Titanic *every day – confused orders from the bridge, water*
swirling round our ankles. The only difference is they had a band.
Rising Damp, 'The Good Samaritan', 3 May 1977

Tony Crosland was working on some papers at home in Oxfordshire
when the stroke hit him. It was mid-morning on Sunday, 13 February
1977, the day after his thirteenth wedding anniversary. 'I can't feel my
right side,' he said suddenly to his wife Susan, his pen poised in mid-
sentence. At first, the doctors thought it was a brief spasm; within hours,
however, they knew it was something more serious. Even if he survived,
they told his wife, he would probably be paralysed for life. By Monday
morning, with Crosland still unconscious in intensive care, the news
was all around Westminster. That afternoon, Susan Crosland rang
Number 10 from the hospital and told Callaghan that there was no
hope: 'The damage is still going on. It can't be reversed. We're not going
to put him on one of these life-saving machines.' Friends had been worried about Crosland for a while: as his junior minister David Owen put
it, 'his lifestyle, the long hours, good food, little exercise, alcohol and
cigars could not have helped'. Only days before, Bernard Donoughue
had been shocked by his colour at a Cabinet committee meeting. Nothing, however, could possibly compensate for the shock. At dinner that
evening, another aide thought he 'could sense the anxiety of the political

wives there – Edna Healey, Audrey Callaghan, Molly Hattersley – that it could have been them in Susan Crosland's place'.[1]

Crosland died the following weekend. 'He was a major political figure of the present generation, gifted beyond the reach of many of us,' the Prime Minister told a subdued House of Commons. 'He combined physical courage, mental toughness and great personal charm, and, although he always carried the aura of the university don even into his local Labour club, it was never resented.' Many commentators saw Crosland's death as a shattering blow to the government's prospects: in the *Financial Times*, David Watt called it a 'major public calamity', and predicted that Labour would soon become a party 'without a doctrine'. 'The brains and quality and style has gone out of the moderate wing of the Party now,' Bernard Donoughue privately agreed. 'Now there are too many second-rankers, decent but without charisma.' And coming so soon after the IMF crisis, Crosland's loss seemed to mark the end of the heroic age of social democracy. He had been 'the high priest of revisionism or social democracy in the Labour Party', wrote his old friend Tony Benn. But now social democracy, like its author, was dead, its expectations about 'mass abundance' undermined by the cold realities of stagflation and globalization. There could be no greater contrast, wrote the conservative columnist Colin Welch, than that between the 'open-air cafés, brighter and gayer streets' that Crosland had imagined in *The Future of Socialism*, and the 'shabby, decaying slum' of contemporary Britain. 'All around us,' Welch lamented, 'we see frustration, failure, hopelessness, the very soil in which alone can thrive (apart from punk rock, and whatever *that* rough beast may portend) those sour and mad fanatics whom he detested so much.'[2]

To replace Crosland as Foreign Secretary, Callaghan made one of the most unexpected promotions of modern times. 'Jim Calls In Dr Who' read the headline in the *Express*, which must have had some readers thinking that Callaghan had offered Tom Baker the Foreign Office. In fact, Crosland's replacement was his 38-year-old junior minister David Owen, a former doctor, who now became the youngest Foreign Secretary since Anthony Eden. But he did not seem likely to last long. The previous November, Labour had lost previously safe seats at Workington and Walsall North, and Callaghan's parliamentary position was desperately difficult. In barely three years the government's majority had been whittled to nothing: by now the whips were in almost daily negotiations with the Scottish and Welsh nationalists to get their legislation through. The late nights were eating away at Labour's morale:

barely a week seemed to pass without one nail-biting defeat or other. The Tories scented blood, and with abrasive figures such as Norman Tebbit and George Gardiner harrying the government at every turn, the mood inside the Palace of Westminster felt more confrontational than at any time since the war. Many of Callaghan's backbenchers were old men, fond of liquid lunches and midnight boozing, and the long hours took their toll. Thirteen Labour MPs died between 1974 and 1979, the majority of heart attacks. The Chief Whip, Michael Cocks, was not alone in blaming the tight parliamentary situation.[3]

On 17 March, the government reached rock bottom. With by-elections looming in Grimsby and Stechford, Labour's strength was down to just 312 seats. That night, faced with a potential left-wing rebellion over his public spending plans, Callaghan ordered his MPs to abstain, giving the Conservatives victory by 263 votes to none. It was a sorry moment indeed: 'a disgraceful and dishonourable episode', Mrs Thatcher called it. 'This country has no government,' she said angrily. 'I have never seen a government flee in the face of the enemy before. Deserters! It is complete dishonour.' Behind the scenes, however, she found it hard to contain her excitement. The arithmetic, it seemed, had taken a decisive turn in her favour: if she could press home her advantage, a general election might be just weeks away. When the Commons reassembled the following morning, Thatcher moved in for the kill, lodging a motion of no confidence for Wednesday, 23 March. It was, as Callaghan put it, 'the moment of truth'. The messages coming into Number 10 were uniformly pessimistic: 'the Irish and the Scots and Welsh Nationalists won't support us,' noted Bernard Donoughue, while with the Thorpe scandal in full swing, the Liberals were 'in a suicidal frame of mind'. 'The shades are closing in on the Government,' Mrs Thatcher's spokesman told the press. 'We must be very near the end.'[4]

For a man whose political life was so close to extinction, Jim Callaghan seemed remarkably relaxed. He spent Friday in Cardiff, ostentatiously enjoying his constituency surgery, and returned to Chequers the next day. There he walked to the top of Beacon Hill with Audrey, 'enjoying the lovely views of the neighbouring counties'. But when he returned to Downing Street on Sunday evening, the position was looking distinctly bleak. 'It's Not Adding Up For Jim', declared the headline in Monday's *Mirror*, predicting that there would be a general election on 28 April. As a solid Labour paper, the *Mirror* was naturally horrified: an early election, it claimed, 'will cause untold damage to Britain's immediate prospects of economic recovery'. The Conservative papers, however, could barely contain their glee. In Monday's *Express*, the latest poll gave the Tories a 7 per cent lead, which 'could give Mrs Margaret Thatcher a 50–60 seat majority'. Inside, the paper's star commentator George Gale advised her to reach a deal with the Liberals based on proportional representation, which would 'most damage the Left' and 'prevent any further extension of creeping Socialism'. All in all, thought the *Express*, the public demanded change. 'The sooner we get it over with, the better.'[5]

Behind the scenes, however, Callaghan had been busy. On Friday, just hours after Thatcher had lodged her no-confidence motion, he had sent Michael Foot to open talks with the Ulster Unionists, hoping that promises of greater devolution and more Northern Ireland MPs at Westminster would be enough to win them round. At the same time, he told the whips to contact the little band of Liberal MPs, led by the young David Steel. On Monday morning, Bill Rodgers reported that Steel was ready to cut a deal in return for extensive policy consultation and proportional representation in elections for the European Parliament and the planned new Scottish and Welsh assemblies. This would clearly be tricky, but the alternatives were running out. When Callaghan met the Ulster Unionist leader James Molyneaux and his chief ally Enoch Powell later that day, they warned that they could not guarantee the support of all their colleagues. Many Unionist MPs wanted the government to crack down even more ruthlessly on republican supporters; even though Callaghan's Northern Ireland Secretary, Roy Mason, was a pretty tough character, they had been shocked by his insistence that Ulster must not be a 'one-party state'. Still, both Molyneaux and Powell agreed to back Callaghan until the end of the parliament, which meant at least two crucial votes were in the bag. 'The PM was pleased,' Donoughue wrote. 'He likes the Ulster Unionists – much more than the Liberals – because they are his kind of straight, tough old-fashioned conservative people.'[6]

In normal circumstances, the prospect of Callaghan doing a deal with the Liberals, a party loathed by many Labour MPs, would have been almost unthinkable. But from the Liberals' point of view, these were not normal circumstances. The shocking revelations about Jeremy Thorpe had badly contaminated the Liberal image, and the heady days of 1974 seemed a very distant memory. Although the party had elected a bright new leader, its performance in recent by-elections had been abysmal, with the Liberal candidate in Walsall North even finishing behind the National Front. But with their activists demoralized, their finances exhausted and their image tarnished, the last thing the Liberals wanted was a general election. The thirteen Liberal MPs were 'hysterical', thought Donoughue; indeed, polls predicted that all but five would lose their seats. For Steel, therefore, a pact with the government seemed unusually appealing, since it would not only stave off an election but allow him to make his name with the public and re-establish the Liberals as a serious party. As early as 17 March, even before Thatcher's no-confidence motion, Steel had quietly indicated to Number 10 that he fancied a deal. He wanted, he said later, 'to get the Liberal Party back into thinking about sharing in power'.[7]

Steel secretly visited the Prime Minister for the first time at six on Monday evening, but it did not go well. It was 'all too vague', Callaghan grumbled afterwards, adding that while the Ulster Unionists were 'serious men', Steel was 'adolescent'. For his part, Steel told Donoughue that he was 'bewildered' by Callaghan's intransigence. The next morning, still playing hard to get, Callaghan told his staff that, instead of doing a deal with the Liberals, he would prefer 'to go off to the farm'. At lunchtime, a letter arrived from Steel confirming the Liberals' terms: a consultative committee on legislation, regular meetings on economic policy, proportional representation in European Parliament elections and a free vote on PR in the new Scottish and Welsh assemblies. 'Well, I cannot take that,' Callaghan snapped immediately, throwing the note onto the coffee table. Somehow his aides managed to calm him down, suggesting that if he let them draft an agreement, they might be able to find common ground. By the early afternoon the ice was thawing, and when Callaghan and Steel met that evening the mood had become distinctly friendly. This time Steel brought with him John Pardoe, his clever and outspoken Treasury spokesman, a clear sign that the Liberals meant business. Pardoe was an old-fashioned Cornish liberal, not a Scottish social democrat like Steel. But, as Steel had earlier told Michael Foot, anything was better than letting the Conservatives in. 'He hadn't come to Westminster to put Mrs Thatcher in power,' he said. 'He would do what his colleagues thought and they would all vote the same way, but he had no doubt that the Government and the Liberals would reach an accommodation.'[8]

On Wednesday morning, with the no-confidence debate just hours away, Callaghan and Foot briefed the Cabinet on the talks. 'As you might expect,' noted Tony Benn, 'the press was full of rumours of deals,' while Downing Street was packed with onlookers. Even on Callaghan the pressure was taking its toll: he was 'absolutely red-faced', Benn wrote, while Foot was 'white and drawn'. Speaking for the majority, Denis Healey remarked that the suggested pact was a lot better than relying on 'Nats and nutters'. It was 'painful and difficult for the Party', agreed Shirley Williams, but 'a Thatcher victory would lead to such a confrontation with the trade union movement that it would be a threat to democracy'. In the end, only four ministers voted against the pact, among them Benn, who complained that it would stop Labour adopting 'a manifesto which is radical and relevant'. All the same, it was a clear victory for Callaghan and Foot, albeit a rather inglorious one. Afterwards, Callaghan 'looked a bit tired, and said it had been a tough meeting', Donoughue wrote. 'He had taken more criticism than he had expected. Obviously the pressure of this crisis is beginning to get to him.'[9]

In the meantime, Benn had dashed to the Commons to round up the usual suspects – Eric Heffer, Norman Atkinson, Michael Meacher, Judith Hart – who were all 'pretty shocked' by the news. As was now traditional, he had no intention of allowing collective loyalty to stop him undermining his Cabinet colleagues. After lunch, Donoughue walked past Benn's room when he heard voices, and before he knew it, he had his ear to the door:

> I could hear Benn asking Ian Mikardo to organise a letter of protest and signatures from Labour backbenchers. Benn said, 'This is just like the Common Market. We need the right to dissent. We can't be bound by this decision.' Benn was of course referring to the collective decision of Cabinet which, barely an hour earlier, he had agreed to be bound by. He was conspiring to organise a left-wing backbench rebellion against the decision he had shared in. Jim had given him the chance to resign, but he had declined. Once again he wanted the pleasure of opposing, without resigning . . . Benn said he 'wanted sixty to eighty signatures', Mikardo said he would go off and do what he could.

From anyone else this combination of self-righteousness and disloyalty would have been barely believable, but not from Benn. Still, his comeuppance was not long delayed. The following evening, he had a phone call from the Prime Minister, who had heard all about the letter and told him not to sign it. 'Well, I've already signed it,' Benn said proudly. 'In that case I want your resignation,' Callaghan retorted. That evidently gave Benn a shock, and a few hours later he was back on the phone to Number 10. 'I've withdrawn my signature,' he said pleadingly. Showing extraordinary patience, Callaghan allowed him to stay, but

Benn's weakness had been exposed for all to see. 'Don't attack me, please,' he begged his political adviser Frances Morrell afterwards. 'Don't criticise me.' At least he had a new toy to cheer himself up: earlier that morning, he had visited the Metyclean shop, 'one of my favourite ports of call when things are going wrong'. There he had bought the latest gadget, 'a Casio quartz clock computer which has the most fantastic facilities – gives you the time, works as a stopwatch and as a calculator, and has four alarms. It weights 4 ounces and fits into your pocket.'[10]

Thanks to the Lib–Lab Pact, Wednesday's no-confidence debate turned out to be an utter non-event. Barely able to contain her frustration, Mrs Thatcher bitterly denounced Labour's 'shabby, devious manipulations', but later even she admitted that she was not on good form. 'It was clear that she was depressed by our deal with the Liberals,' wrote Donoughue, 'and her confidence was gone. Also she made her old mistake of sticking rigidly to the text of the speech, reading paragraph after paragraph, cliché after cliché. She made no adaptation to the fluid and turbulent mood of the House ... and the longer she went on the worse it sounded.' 'She had the House openly laughing at her before she had done,' agreed the sympathetic Barbara Castle. 'So for Jim, practised, relaxed and an outstanding Parliamentary performer – a man speaking to a male audience – it was a walk-over.'

Afterwards, snatching a quick moment with his aides, Callaghan remarked that he thought Thatcher's speech 'very poor'. He returned to the Chamber a few hours later to hear the result: a Labour–Liberal victory by 322 votes to 298. While the Tories waved their order papers and chanted 'Pink Socialists!' at the Liberals, Neil Kinnock led a few lusty verses of 'The Red Flag', much to the amusement of the press corps. Upstairs, Donoughue found Jim and Audrey Callaghan already celebrating. 'He had *even* opened the drinks cupboard and provided a bottle of brandy,' Donoughue noted, 'which is a rare historical event since Jim does not drink and is not overgenerous in encouraging others.' After a few minutes' relaxed conversation, the Callaghans left to get a good night's sleep. 'We stayed behind to finish the brandy,' Donoughue recorded, 'being unwilling to see it disappear back in the cupboard for another twelve months.'[11]

Like any coalition, the Pact was not without its moments of drama. Years later, Denis Healey remarked that the problems could be summed up in 'three words, Pardoe, Pardoe and Pardoe'. The Liberals' Treasury spokesman 'was robust and intelligent enough', Healey thought, 'but sometimes I felt he was simply Denis Healey with no redeeming features'. By contrast, most of their colleagues enjoyed the spectacle of these two combustible men locking horns. During one notable row, Pardoe even walked out while Healey was still talking, an appropriately melodramatic gesture from a former president of the Cambridge Footlights. In future, all their meetings had to be supervised by Joel Barnett and David Steel, 'if only to hold their coats'. Yet the truth is that the Pact worked rather well. Many Labour moderates were greatly taken with David Steel: by 1978, some even muttered that Steel would make a fine Home Secretary in a formal coalition. 'Labour moderates hope very much to see the pact renewed as a way towards their big dream,' noted the journalist Hugo Young; 'a realignment of the parties and a dropping of the *Tribune* and ultra-left fringe. They see Steel as an indistinguishable social democrat.' But his biggest fan turned out to be the Prime Minister himself, who treated him almost as a favourite son. Indeed, Callaghan rather enjoyed working with the Liberals. 'He wants to play the next election as the leader of a left-wing party heading towards the centre,' Steel recorded in February 1978. 'He says he needs a good sized Liberal vote, and that the next parliament may well be hung.'[12]

If the Lib–Lab Pact had failed and Callaghan had been forced to call an early election, he would almost certainly have lost it. Memories of the IMF humiliation were still raw, the government seemed to be drifting and most families had yet to see an improvement in their living standards. Above all, unemployment was shockingly high: figures for February 1977 showed that almost 1.4 million people were out of work, with particularly high levels in Northern Ireland (10 per cent), the North of England (7.5 per cent) and Scotland (7.4 per cent). Even a few years before, these figures would have been unthinkable, but the days of full employment seemed to be dead. 'I don't know the answer,' Callaghan helplessly told Labour backbenchers, while at a conference to discuss youth unemployment, Shirley Williams explained that 'we are seeing the increase of unemployment throughout the industrial world, and it is a problem for which we still have no real answer'.[13]

But although it would have come as little consolation to school leavers unable to get jobs, the medium-term outlook was really not that bad. Now that the markets had been appeased, the pound's value was surging by leaps and bounds, recovering to $1.70 by January 1977 and reaching $1.93 by the end of the year. Foreign capital poured into sterling and gilts, while the official reserves boomed from $4 billion in December 1976 to more than $20 billion by the end of 1977. That in turn allowed the Bank of England to cut its minimum lending rate, which fell to just 5 per cent by October 1977, much to the relief of the suburban middle classes. On top of all that, Britain was finally seeing the benefits of North Sea oil, now pouring forth at a rate of 550,000 barrels a day. 'During 1978 and 1979, the government's take will multiply a thousand times, and by the mid-1980s Whitehall's share will be running at $6.7 billion a year,' wrote an American analyst in *Time* magazine. The North Sea bonanza, he thought, gave 'Britain the chance to start the long climb to price stability and high employment – but it would be all too easy for the nation to blow that chance'.[14]

At the end of April, Healey unveiled a Budget mercifully short of bad news. Giving one of the shortest Budget speeches of modern times (eighty minutes), he promised to cut the basic rate of income tax by 2 per cent if the unions agreed a new pay formula, but otherwise made remarkably few changes. Most commentators focused on his decisions to raise taxes on cigarettes, petrol and vehicle excise duty, which went down very badly with a public not yet enjoying the fruits of recovery. According to Gallup, 54 per cent of the electorate regarded Healey's new deal as 'not fair', making it the least popular Budget since polling began. That night, Labour's pollster Bob Worcester warned that the effect on the coming Stechford by-election was bound to be 'terrible', and the first polls showed voters defecting in massive numbers to the Conservatives. The result on Thursday night was even worse than feared: the Tories took the seat with a swing of more than 17 per cent, while the Liberals once again contrived to finish behind the National Front. But although Labour insiders blamed Healey's budget, the Chancellor himself seemed quite unmoved. At the National Theatre, Peter Hall spotted him looking remarkably 'jovial' in the audience, 'apparently unworried by his budget, and adoring *Bedroom Farce*' – an appropriate choice, some might have thought, given the events of the past few months.[15]

In the midst of the Lib–Lab Pact negotiations, Jim Callaghan found the time to record a historic first. On 24 March he became the first Prime Minister to appear alongside Frank Bough and Sue Lawley on the BBC's early evening show *Nationwide*. His aides wanted him to counteract Mrs Thatcher's popularity among 'working-class women', who rarely watched political programmes. And as Callaghan sat there, his eyes fixed on the monitors showing questioners in studios across the country, he could hardly have been more relaxed. For many families, he frankly admitted, times were 'going to be horrid'. When a Sunderland pensioner asked about rising gas bills, he said confidentially: 'We had a little chat about that in the Cabinet this morning.' When a woman rang in from his Cardiff constituency, he gave her a smile and a wave. 'I hope Cardiff is looking good today,' he said. 'Sorry I am not there.' A schoolgirl asked whether she should become a teacher. 'May I call you Jean?' he asked. 'I beg you to do it, if you have a vocation.' A pools winner asked for advice on how to spend his money. 'Congratulations!' the Prime Minister said. 'Invest it or put it into bricks and mortar: always a good investment.'[16]

Afterwards, as admiring letters from working-class housewives poured into Number 10, Callaghan's aides congratulated him on a job well done. It was a trivial episode and quickly forgotten. But it also reflected a welcome sense of authority at the summit of government. Under the new regime, life seemed much 'cleaner, simpler, more directly concerned with policy', wrote Bernard Donoughue on the first anniversary of Callaghan's accession. Almost without exception, his ministers much preferred him to his predecessor. 'On big issues, he genuinely wants to hear what everyone thinks,' Bill Rodgers told Hugo Young in 1978. 'He is a very good listener.' And in contrast to Wilson, 'who was always plotting, and thus inducing everyone else to plot', Callaghan ran a steady, relatively united ship. 'He has produced stability, a stable style and stable government,' Rodgers said admiringly. 'What he believes in is the regeneration of industry. He likes the company of businessmen, feels at home with them, shares most of the same attitudes. He likes them almost as much as he likes the Labour Party. What he cannot abide is the long-haired intellectual and all his works.'[17]

Of course Callaghan was not immune to gaffes. His decision to send his son-in-law Peter Jay as ambassador to Washington in May 1977 was roundly condemned as shameless nepotism, and the *Express* spoke for Fleet Street in deploring the new vogue for 'young men with modishly tarnished jeans and first-class Oxbridge degrees'. But this was a mercifully isolated incident, and Callaghan was generally thought to have banished the stench of corruption from Downing Street. And at a time when the headlines were dominated by punk rockers and football hooligans, he came over as a reassuringly gruff and genial presence, a champion of law and order and old-fashioned family values. Above all, the public liked him. After dipping during the IMF crisis, Callaghan's personal approval rating reached 59 per cent in October 1977, the highest figure for any Prime Minister for almost twelve years, and remained in the mid-fifties for the whole of 1978. He had proved a 'much more effective Prime Minister than most people had believed possible', conceded the *Financial Times*, and his 'nerve and sense of purpose have been admirable'. 'We have a Prime Minister who is good on television; who looks like Stanley Baldwin; who lives like Stanley Baldwin,' remarked the former Conservative minister Peter Walker in December 1977; 'and Stanley Baldwin with the vote of the Labour Party and North Sea oil is a very formidable opponent.'[18]

Meanwhile, Callaghan's opposite number seemed at a loss how to burst his bubble. Mrs Thatcher had only just been getting used to Harold Wilson, but now she found herself up against an unflappable opponent who deflected her questions with good-humoured chauvinism. Nothing annoyed her more than being patronized by an older man, but Callaghan always seemed to be patting her on the head. 'I am sure that one day the right hon. Lady will understand these things a little better,' he once remarked reassuringly in the Commons. When she accused him of peddling 'avuncular flannel', he said mildly: 'I have often thought of the right hon. Lady in many ways, but never as my niece.' After the failure of her no-confidence motion, he took chauvinist condescension to new heights: 'Now, now, little lady,' he murmured across the dispatch box, 'you don't want to believe all those things you read in the papers about crisis and upheavals and the end of civilization as we know it. Dearie me, not at all.' And when she dredged up an old Wilson quotation about the dangers of a payroll tax and asked him to guess who had said it, Callaghan seemed utterly unperturbed. 'I rather suspect that that is a catch question,' he said cheerfully. 'I might have said it myself some time ago.' Watching in the gallery, Donoughue thought it was 'the most dominant performance I have seen in two and a half years. Totally relaxed and amusing, putting Thatcher down gently but with patronising contempt. Even the Tories were roaring with laughter.'[19]

In the weeks after the Queen's Silver Jubilee, the mood began subtly to change. It was a poor summer, with countless holidays ruined by rain, yet at least there was no repeat of the previous year's drought. For once the economic news seemed to be excellent. 'The pound is up two cents. The payments in surplus. The tax reliefs paid this month. The PSBR well below the IMF ceilings. Massive gilt sales,' wrote Donoughue at the end of August. 'Our side is much more optimistic. The press is talking about us winning the next election – so are the Tories who are clearly getting jittery and warning the electorate not to be conned by a phoney economic boom.' Two weeks later, with the stock market at a new high and a *Telegraph* poll showing the Conservative lead down to just 4 per cent, he recorded that 'the change in the political climate is quite dramatic ... Everyone is in a euphoric mood.' In his autumn Budget, Denis Healey even felt confident enough to present a 'Budget of reward', unveiling £1 billion in tax relief, injecting £400 million into new building projects and giving pensioners a £10 Christmas bonus. And by the beginning of December, the unthinkable had happened. After being behind for so long, Labour had not merely drawn level, they held a slender lead of half a per cent. It was no wonder that at the Number 10 Christmas party, the atmosphere was better than anyone could remember. Callaghan had demanded music, so his staff had borrowed Healey's record player. 'There was dancing, plenty of drink and good food,' Donoughue noted. 'The PM strolled around beaming and chattering. He came over to talk to me and said what a good year it had been and how we must hold the improvement for next year.'[20]

And yet the economic figures did not tell the whole story. Although the balance of payments surplus reached a record £316 million in August and the FT30 Index hit a new high of 592.2 a few weeks later, this was cold comfort to the families who were paying the price for Britain's recovery. The truth was that living standards had been stagnant for four years; indeed, by December 1977 the take-home pay of an ordinary family with two children was worth £4 *less*, in real terms, than at the end of 1973. And rather than blaming the vicissitudes of the international economy or the tides of historical change, most people blamed the government – not entirely without reason. For although the voluntary pay limit agreed in May 1976 had worked wonders in bringing inflation down, it had come at a heavy price, especially for the low-paid. During the first nine months of the new arrangement, earnings rose by just over 7 per cent, which was still rather more than the Treasury had hoped. Prices, however, went up by almost 15 per cent, thanks partly to Healey's decision to scrap food subsidies. In other words, ordinary families' pay packets were not keeping up with the prices on the high street: as the Whitehall mandarin Sir Denis Barnes put it, Healey's latest pay policy represented 'the most severe cut in real wages in twenty years'.[21]

With inflation pushing many people up into tax bands originally meant for high earners, with Healey slashing food and rent subsidies, and with the government approving hefty increases for gas and electricity, public transport and phone charges, many families had experienced the biggest economic shock since the Great Depression. According to one estimate, the typical family's real net earnings fell by a stunning 8.2 per cent between 1975 and 1976, and by another 9.9 per cent by the end of 1977. And precisely because so many people had been so spoiled in the 1950s and 1960s, the shock of the Callaghan years was all the greater. On the surface, Britain might be a far richer, healthier and more comfortable society than ever before in its history. But after two decades of rising expectations, the downturn of the mid-1970s felt like a bucket of cold water in the face. To the young couples forced to postpone their Spanish holiday because they were struggling to pay their bills, the ubiquitous advertisements for consumer luxuries seemed a mocking reminder of what they were missing. And to families compelled to cut down on their children's Christmas presents, the government's rhetoric of national sacrifice fell on very stony ground.[22]

The other obvious flaw in Callaghan's economic strategy was that it seemed to penalize some workers more than others. That almost every family in Britain was far better off than it had been a decade earlier was beside the point, because people compared themselves with their present-day neighbours, not with their younger selves. Like the suburban couples in sitcoms such as *The Good Life* and *Terry and June*, they looked anxiously out of their front windows, taking note when their neighbours took delivery of a new three-piece suite, or brought home a new Ford Cortina, or disappeared for two weeks to the Costa del Sol. What was more, despite the rhetoric of left-wing politicians, solidarity between different groups of workers was very thin on the ground. To technicians and skilled workers, their beloved 'differentials' and 'relativities' were an important symbol of status and respectability, marking them out from the herd. Yet with pay increases limited by Healey's flat-rate policy, these relativities seemed to be disappearing. In June 1971 a skilled engineering worker had earned 38 per cent more than an unskilled worker. Five years later, however, the gap was just 27 per cent. 'Skilled men who had been through several years of training or poorly paid apprenticeship', wrote one observer, 'often earned little more than unskilled process workers with only a few weeks experience.' Indeed, there were some reports that junior managers were taking home less than the men they supervised, who were able to supplement their wages with overtime and bonuses. And as unskilled manual workers caught up, the skilled men who trudged every day into the giant car plants at Longbridge and Dagenham, the 'aristocrats of manual labour', began to chafe under the fetters of pay restraint.[23]

The irony of all this, though, was that as workers rebelled against the

Social Contract, they found themselves taking on the union leaders who were supposed to be defending their interests. At British Leyland, which was dogged by disputes in the spring of 1977, the leader of an unofficial toolmakers' strike complained that he 'couldn't even get into the same room as management or even our own union'. The reason was obvious: elderly general secretaries such as Jack Jones and Hugh Scanlon, with their fine wines and *goujons de sole*, were losing touch with their ordinary members on the shop floor. As the labour correspondent Robert Taylor remarked, there was a vast gulf between 'the settled world of the union leader sitting in head office (usually down in London suburbia a long way from Britain's industrial heartland) and the fluid, informal routine of union life' on the factory floor. To younger workers who lived in a new home on a suburban estate and spent their evenings listening to Rod Stewart and Status Quo, appeals to working-class solidarity fell embarrassingly flat. What did they care for Scanlon's memories of the Great Depression or Jones's experiences in the Spanish Civil War? Indeed, as early as June 1976 Jones quietly warned Denis Healey that if they wanted to keep union members' support, they would soon have to return to 'free collective bargaining'. Times had changed, he admitted to the *Observer*: whenever he visited factories, the 'workers knew what was happening to prices and dividends, and simply shouted at him; though he added that their shop stewards read the *Financial Times*, and it was possible to argue issues out with them'. He was exaggerating, but not by much. Slowly but surely, any hopes that the Social Contract might be the cornerstone of a new relationship between the government and the unions were ebbing away. The unions did not want a new relationship. They wanted to fight tooth and nail for every advantage, as they had in the past.[24]

Ever since the miners' return to work in March 1974, the strike picture had been surprisingly good. But by the aftermath of the Jubilee, the warning signs were clear. At Ford's Dagenham plant and the British Steel works in Port Talbot, workers had walked out; at Heathrow Airport, a stoppage by maintenance engineers had cost the taxpayer an estimated £31 million; at Longbridge, the toolmakers' strike had dragged on for eight weeks, pitting British Leyland's shop stewards against their own representatives in the AUEW and the TUC. 'The toolroom workers', explained *The Times*, 'are a group of skilled workers whose differentials have been severely eroded under the incomes policies of this and the previous Government.' As the toolmakers' leader pointed out, many of them were drifting away to better-paid semi-skilled jobs outside engin-eering, forcing British Leyland to spend taxpayers' money on tools from abroad. And although their strike petered out, the toolmakers were not alone. 'Our factories are raring to go on strike because workers every-where are frustrated in their wage demands by the Social Contract,' Derek Robinson told the press that spring. 'Unless there is some relax-ation, then it is bound to end in conflict.' Once, he said bitterly, Leyland workers had been 'among the best paid in the country'; now, thanks to 'wage restraint, they were falling behind'. At Vauxhall, too, conveners insisted that they could no longer 'stand by and see our members' living standards drop to an all-time low', while the miners' leader Joe Gormley admitted that he would never get support for a new round of pay curbs. And as *The Times* pointed out, Labour's humiliation at the Stechford by-election told a worrying story. In this 'suburb of craftsmen', Labour's defeat hinted at the 'deep resentment ... against a policy which has advanced the interests of the unskilled at the expense of the skilled'. Somehow it said it all that 'Jack Jones, the true architect of this policy, came to campaign in Stechford, and had very little notice taken of him'.[25]

By the summer of 1977 the Social Contract was already on its last legs. 'The unions were simply not prepared to go along with any struc-tured wage policy at all, nor with any figure,' reported Denis Healey after talks on 12 July. The next day, Callaghan called the union leaders to Number 10. 'The package has still not been disclosed,' wrote Tony Benn, 'and the crisis atmosphere is building up.' At five, the union bosses filed into the Cabinet Room, where Callaghan opened the meeting with remarks that, given what was to come, would prove extraordinarily prophetic:

> I want to know if there is to be a confrontation with the TUC. I don't want to end my time as leader of [the] Labour Party like that. I've seen it all before, 1968–70. I don't want to finish my time fighting the low-paid hospital workers in September, fighting Joe Gormley in November–Decem-ber. I would sooner finish now, go to the country, and say I cannot do it.
>
> If I hang on, with high wage claims, the credibility of this government will have disappeared. I am not going to spend twelve months fighting the Labour movement. But I believe in the common sense of you people. Democracy is not always tidy. But I believe we can work it out. It is my own firm view that the government should take a clear position: if we get 10% earnings this year, then it is worth going on. If not Mrs Thatcher will

take over, with so much going well, then she will have to fight you. Now
please tell me.

Coming from the unions' oldest political ally, this was powerful stuff.
But despite Healey's list of 'sweeteners' if the unions agreed on a 10 per
cent pay limit, such as gas and electricity rebates, a rise in child benefit
and a 6 per cent income tax cut, the union leaders were not having it.
With so much pressure mounting on the shop floor, they knew 'they
could not deliver'. Even as Callaghan was still talking, 'Jack Jones sat
uninterested throughout, not taking notes'.[26]

The failure of the Downing Street summit marked the end of the
Social Contract. 'Callaghan's Wake', the *Express* called it, printing sinister mug shots of the 'chief mourners'. Under TUC rules, most unions
were barred from demanding new deals until the summer of 1978,
which at least gave the government some breathing space. In the meantime, the Treasury decided to hold public sector increases to a maximum
of 10 per cent, setting an example for the rest of industry. But as Bernard Donoughue noted, the collapse of the Social Contract had left the
government with a horrendous dilemma. Either they gave in to 'very
high wage settlements', thereby driving up inflation, or they simply had
to confront the rising anger on the shop floor. Callaghan's own position
was clear: he had staked his prestige on bringing inflation down, and
was determined to resist inflationary settlements at all costs. The danger,
though, was that workers' patience was ebbing away: it was telling that
when the Prime Minister attended that summer's Durham Miners' Gala,
the master of ceremonies introduced him merely as 'Kaligan' (*sic*), without any of the usual formalities. In that single word simmered the
resentments that would sweep Labour to the edge of oblivion.[27]

By the time that delegates assembled for the TUC's annual conference in Blackpool, it was obvious that the ageing general secretaries had
lost their grip. On the day before the conference even met, Hugh Scanlon provoked uproar among his own delegation, storming out of a
meeting after telling them that he would vote to support the TUC's
twelve-month moratorium on new pay claims. There was a nice irony in
the fact that, although the union bosses were often accused of being tin-
pot Marxist dictators, Scanlon was actually using his power to protect
the supposedly 'fascist' Callaghan and Healey from the far left. Against
him, demanding a return to free bargaining, was ranged a coalition of
miners, boilermakers, printers, train drivers and civil servants, as well as
the largest union of all, the TGWU, which had stunned observers by

defying its leader. Supposedly the most powerful man in the country, the Emperor Jones could not even control his own union. That summer, attending his last TGWU conference as leader, Jones had suffered the ultimate humiliation, taking to the rostrum to defend the twelve-month rule and then watching in impotent horror as his men voted the other way. 'If you support this motion, you will not assist the government,' Jones begged them, his voice straining above the jeers. 'You will para-lyse it and indeed stand in danger of destroying it . . . You will put back the mighty in their seats and kick the people of low degree in the teeth.' But the members he had protected for so long had heard it all before. Jones himself blamed Communist agitators, which was marvellously ironic given his own history. For thousands of ordinary trade unionists, however, the days of swallowing Whitehall pay limits in the name of the greater good were over.[28]

In the end, Scanlon's high-handedness saved the day. On the third day of the TUC conference, the delegates voted to maintain the twelve-month gap between pay deals, with Len Murray imploring them to 'take into account the profitability of the companies your members work in'. To many people this sounded like plain common sense; to the militants, however, it was a disgraceful surrender. Labour correspondents could barely remember a conference surrounded by such rancour: Paul Routledge could barely credit 'the extraordinary spectacle of [the AUEW] president Hugh Scanlon holding up a voting card for the 12-month rule while most of the members of his delegation stood up and shouted their defiance of it'. It was 'a formula for industrial unrest', said their self-appointed spokesman, Ronald Halverson, still smarting from having had his microphone turned off when he went to the rostrum to speak. Outside the conference, too, passions boiled over: when the min-ers' leader Joe Gormley left to get some lunch, he was jostled for more than ten minutes by Socialist Workers' Party members who chanted 'Scab!', 'Traitor!' and 'Bosses' Man!', and pushed him, punched him and spat at him. With policemen trying to protect him from the crowd, Gormley could not even wipe the spittle from his face because his arms were pinned to his sides. 'Something has got to be done about the laws of the land,' he said afterwards, sounding uncannily like a Conservative law-and-order enthusiast. 'I think we are getting ourselves into a sick and sad society when people who want to express a point of view have to spit in other people's faces . . . If I could have got hold of the bastard who spat at me, I would have done him, and you can print that.'[29]

When Callaghan came to the conference, promising that 'the period of reduction in our living standards is now at an end', nobody spat at him. But like Gormley, the Prime Minister was plagued by hard-left demonstrators, who picketed the hall and screamed 'Coward!' when police spirited him out by a side door. Still, Callaghan was determined to show that nothing would deflect him from the task of driving down inflation. When the Police Federation demanded a pay rise of 104 per cent, PC Jim declared that he was 'prepared to resign' rather than countenance a 'breach in pay policy'. And when the Home Secretary sent him the draft of a speech recognizing the police as a 'special case', Callaghan scribbled in the margin: 'NO. So is beating inflation. Don't use this terminology.'[30]

The bobby on the beat was not the only public servant chafing at the government's pay restraint. 'We are not greedy – we just cannot live on our wages,' wrote Mike Sims, a 40-year-old fireman, on 17 November. A married father of three with seventeen years' service and a weekly take-home wage of just £49, he had an unexpected brush with fame when the *Mirror* ran his open letter to the government on its front page. He had no freezer and 'no HP accounts', he said; his black-and-white television was fifteen years old; his fridge was a second-hand gift from a friend; he was three months behind on his mortgage payments; and his family had last eaten a joint of meat on Christmas Day, when he had spent the whole day on duty. 'We all suffer from conscience regarding our duty to the public to a degree you cannot comprehend,' he wrote. 'We WANT to help but just cannot afford to. Social conscience will not buy meat. Don't treat us as a threat to an incomes policy, but as vital members of our community who only want to live.'[31]

Although nobody could have known it, the Fire Brigades Union's strike in November and December 1977 offered an uncanny preview of the events that destroyed Callaghan's premiership. Like the miners who had brought down Edward Heath, firemen risked life and limb for a pitiful weekly wage. In an interview with *The Times*, Acting Sub Officer Reuben Clarke, whose watch covered 750,000 people in the London borough of Newham, explained that he had been in the service for twenty-three years and took home £270 a month. One of his men, Ron Fairweather, had served for four years and earned just £218 a month. With an extra year under his belt, Fairweather could expect to get a further 3p an hour, and then another 3p if he stayed in the job for fifteen years. For men who worked forty-eight-hour weeks in highly dangerous conditions – their territory included quantities of gun cotton and radioactive materials, and many of Reuben Clarke's men had attended the

Ronan Point and Moorgate disasters – this was hardly a king's ransom. 'Over the years,' Clarke said, 'they have appealed to our consciences but that does not bring a crust of bread. If you go into a shop to buy on hire purchase you feel ashamed to tell them your salary. We are asking for the average bloke's wage. We want what a dustman gets.'[32]

Not surprisingly, even people who thought the government should refuse their 30 per cent pay claim felt sorry for the firemen. 'These men of such courage, who lose a man a fortnight in fires and are paid below the national average income, are now being put in the dock,' lamented Tony Benn on the first day of the strike. Their spokesmen, he thought, 'came over very well'. Asked about their consciences, they replied: 'We have got consciences but a conscience cannot pay the mortgage.' Indeed, public sympathy was so strong that ITN's Gordon Honeycombe, who had been voted Britain's 'sexiest' newsreader and had written a book about firemen called *Red Watch*, took a leave of absence because he felt unable to report the strike impartially. 'I've lost six weeks' money,' he said, 'but it is nothing to what the firemen are losing.'[33]

In Cabinet, Callaghan admitted that the firemen 'had a case, even though there were wider factors which meant it could not be met in full'. The government must not try to 'set public opinion against the firemen', he added, as most people 'did not regard the firemen as irresponsible and might increasingly support their claim'. Yet he remained adamant that breaking the 10 per cent ceiling would set off an explosion of wage claims among local authority and NHS employees: 'if they were breached in any way there would be a flood of exceptions.' To the firemen's leaders, meanwhile, he presented an image of total inflexibility, warning their leaders that they would upset the entire pay balance, sending prices soaring and the pound into freefall. 'I stand or fall', one of the firemen's leaders, Peter Rockley, remembered the Prime Minister saying, 'that no one will beat the 10 per cent this year'. Impressed despite himself, Rockley thought Callaghan was 'the most determined person I had ever met'. Another delegate noticed the tiny JC monogram in the stripes of the Prime Minister's suit, made especially by Moxon's of Yorkshire, and asked if it stood for 'James Callaghan'. 'No,' another delegate butted in. 'Jesus Christ.' It was not the best way to win the puritanical Prime Minister's sympathy; as the meeting broke up, Callaghan said bluntly: 'Your strike will not win. You cannot be allowed to succeed.'[34]

On the first count, at least, the Prime Minister was right. For all the public sentiment, the government stubbornly refused to give ground, using 20,000 soldiers as firemen and mobilizing the famous 'Green Goddesses', as the auxiliary fire engines were nicknamed. Even though fire insurance losses trebled in two weeks, Callaghan stood firm. On 12 January 1978, amid scenes of extraordinary anger, the FBU's general secretary Terry Parry announced that the strike was over. Outside the conference hall in Bridlington, militants jostled and punched their elected representatives. One Scottish executive member was chased down the street, pinned against a wall and kicked to the ground, while policemen had to rescue Parry himself from an enraged mob. 'Some of them', the shaken FBU leader said afterwards, 'behaved like animals with a violence which we cannot stand for and cannot condone ... I appeal to trade unionists in all unions to take a stand against this kind of thing. It is anarchy of the worst kind.' The episode spoke volumes about ordinary union members' fury at the government, as well as the collapse of their faith in their own leaders. 'A lot of us will never vote Labour again,' one fireman at London's Mount Pleasant station told reporters. And there was one more portent of things to come. At the beginning of the strike, the *Daily Express* had predicted that Britain was due for a 'winter of discontent'. As it turned out, the festive season had been more peaceful than most people expected. But a winter of discontent was coming, all the same.[35]

28

Maggie Isn't Working

> What struck me most forcibly was the lack of any kind of
> strategic approach in Mrs Thatcher's comments . . . It was
> painfully clear that she hadn't really got her thoughts on
> anything further ahead than tomorrow or next week – in this
> respect she was very much a Tory Harold Wilson.
>
> Ronald McIntosh's diary, 3 July 1975

> Peter Carrington came into my room at the [House of Lords].
> He is disturbed at the way the party is being run. We are giving
> the impression of an extreme right wing party . . .
>
> We both agreed Margaret an extremely nice person, but I
> said I had never had much confidence in her judgement & my
> fears had been realised.
>
> Lord Hailsham's diary, 29 March 1977

It remains one of the most celebrated images in British political history. Beneath the stark red-and-white sign 'Unemployment Office', a thin line snakes back into the distance: male and female, young and old, businessmen in their smart dark suits, teenagers in their gently flared trousers, working women in their knee-length skirts. At the bottom, in small letters, are the words of hope: 'Britain's Better Off With the Conservatives'. And above, in thick black letters in a white background, the slogan hammers home the message: 'LABOUR ISN'T WORKING'. Nothing better captures the spirit of the election campaign of 1979; nothing better embodies Labour's failure in the last years of the decade, the rising surge of public frustration, the sense of optimism and release as Margaret Thatcher swept triumphantly to victory.

So runs the myth. In fact, Saatchi & Saatchi's famous poster, supposedly such a key part of Mrs Thatcher's armoury in the 1979 campaign, was actually unveiled almost twelve months earlier, at a time when she was flagging badly in the polls and a Labour victory looked increasingly likely. Far from converting millions of voters overnight, it dragged the Tories into an unseemly row and had little impact on their national popularity or the morale of their activists. And far from being a symbol of Mrs Thatcher's radicalism, the poster hints at a rather different story: the story of an anxious, cautious, uncertain woman, struggling to win over her own party, let alone the country.[1]

In the spring of 1978, Saatchi & Saatchi was the brightest star in the firmament of British advertising. Founded eight years earlier by the enterprising brothers Maurice and Charles, who had been born into a Jewish family in Baghdad, the firm had made an astonishing impact on the advertising world. By the beginning of 1978, it not only boasted turnover approaching £50 million, but had captured some of the most prestigious contracts in the country, including assignments from Sainsbury's, British Rail, Black & Decker and the British government. In many ways, therefore, the Saatchi brothers were Mrs Thatcher's kind of people: self-made men, impatient with tradition and keen to find new worlds to conquer. Yet when her publicity chief Gordon Reece handed them the Conservatives' advertising contract, many senior Tories felt a twinge of unease. Inside Downing Street, too, Saatchi & Saatchi's appointment drew raised eyebrows. 'The Conservative Party have moved away from the more traditional, staid advertising agencies they have used in the past,' reported the head of Labour's publicity team, 'and chosen an agency which has a reputation for being aggressive, energetic and creative. Their work may even be considered controversial.' But as Reece freely admitted, he had picked Saatchi precisely because he wanted a clean break with the past, dropping the 'clichés' of Heath's campaigns and 'selling [the] brand in the most acceptable way'. By the time the campaign was over, predicted the advertising trade journal *Campaign*, 'the Tories may well have an election property which party members find difficult to recognise and the electorate finds a complete surprise'.[2]

The Conservatives' brief was astonishingly vague: when the Saatchis' colleague Tim Bell asked to see what the party stood for, Central Office sheepishly told him that nothing had been written down. So Bell commissioned interviews with four groups of target voters, discovering that while voters thought the Tories were better at handling issues affecting individuals, Labour were better at dealing with issues affecting the state. The Conservatives' key themes, therefore, must be freedom, choice, opportunity and minimum state interference. Above all, their adverts must 'make [people] dissatisfied with the government', hammering away at its record on inflation and unemployment. Bell then unveiled his poster ideas, one of which was the 'Labour Isn't Working' design. There was an awkward silence. 'Why is the biggest thing on this poster the name of the opposition?' Mrs Thatcher asked. 'We're promoting the opposition.' 'No,' Bell said calmly. 'We're demolishing Labour.' She paused for a moment. It was a 'simple negative message', she admitted; it stuck in the mind. The more she thought about it, the more she liked it.[3]

The first 'Labour Isn't Working' posters went up on the last day of July 1978, part of an advertising blitz concentrating on the government's record on jobs and prices. ('They doubled prices. They held down your wages. And then they doubled your tax.') Even before the posters appeared, however, the campaign had made headlines. Just a few days earlier, Callaghan had told his colleagues that the Tories were planning 'a propaganda effort unprecedented in British politics, and the party would have to be ready to counter it'. But although Saatchi & Saatchi had booked 1,100 sites, they put up only about twenty 'Labour Isn't Working' posters. Twenty was all they needed: the next day's papers did the rest for them.

The Conservatives were guilty of 'sickening hypocrisy', insisted Labour's Joel Barnett, who accused them of 'playing with the emotions of the unemployed' and accurately predicted that if Mrs Thatcher were elected, unemployment would reach 'two million and more'. But Barnett's rebuttal was lost amid the furore about the poster itself. According to Labour's outraged national agent, Reg Underhill, the dole queue in the picture was made up 'entirely of employees of Saatchi and Saatchi, one of whom appears on the poster five times'. The following day, the Tories shot back that the people in the queue were 'unpaid volunteers'. Actually, most were members of the Hendon Young Conservatives, some of whom had brought their parents along. Since far fewer people had turned up for the photo-shoot than the organizers had hoped, the photographer used a rope to mark out the dole queue and told the little knot of volunteers to move along it, later combining the images into a composite picture. It was pure trickery, of course, but it worked. And when Labour complained that not a single person in the line had been genuinely unemployed, the Tories had what they considered an ideal answer. 'The tragedy of 1,500,000 people out of work', their spokesman said gravely, 'should not be aggravated by their being photographed and possibly recognized on poster hoardings.'[4]

But the really revealing thing about the poster furore was not the commotion about advertising techniques but the Tories' chosen battle-ground. The poster said nothing about Conservative values or policies; there was nothing about how they would address unemployment, and there was no mention of their leader. What was more, unemployment was traditionally a Labour issue. According to the conventional wisdom, the Tories were better off talking about subjects such as waste, crime and national defence. And yet for months, Mrs Thatcher had been attacking Labour as 'the natural party of unemployment', even calling Jim Callaghan 'the Prime Minister of unemployment'. The message was clear: under Labour, unemployment had become intolerable. This was standard opposition stuff, but it also implied that, under a Conservative government, bringing unemployment down would be an immediate priority – an extraordinarily ironic suggestion, given Mrs Thatcher's subsequent record. But these remarks also hint at a rather different Thatcher from the caricature of the Iron Lady: a calculating political opportunist who played down any talk of radical experiments and told the public what they wanted to hear. 'We'd have been drummed out of office,' she remarked in one party political broadcast, 'if we'd had this level of unemployment.' As events were to prove, however, she was quite wrong about that.[5]

From her very first day as leader of the Conservative Party, Margaret Thatcher was acutely conscious of her own weakness. Although she quickly reshuffled her team, appointing the free-market Sir Geoffrey Howe as Shadow Chancellor and inviting Sir Keith Joseph to take charge of policy and research, her Shadow Cabinet was full of Ted Heath's men. None of them thought much of their new leader. 'It is now becoming clear', Willie Whitelaw wrote after only a few days to his old friend Robert Carr, 'that her cohorts (a) have little talent, (b) have no idea at all about running a party.' Three years later, Whitelaw was still telling friends 'how absolutely ghastly life was with that awful woman', and even mused about resigning. That Thatcher stopped just short of pushing him into rebellion was one reason she survived. But as her approval rating sank from 64 per cent in February 1975 to a pitiful 35 per cent in June, many senior Tories reassured themselves that she would soon be gone. 'How are we going to handle this?' many Conservative MPs asked themselves, looking forward to the restoration of the old guard. And in the press, many commentators made no effort to disguise their derision. In the *Daily Mirror*, Terence Lancaster mocked her as 'Mike Yarwood in drag'; in the *Sunday Times*, Dennis Potter remarked that with her 'small pawing gestures' and 'glossy head tilted at a rather too carefully alert angle', she reminded him of 'everyone's favourite cel-luloid bitch, Lassie'. Even the Conservative Research Department used her middle name, which they thought painfully provincial, as a patron-izing nickname. 'It was "Hilda",' Matthew Parris recalled, 'and it was not meant kindly.'[6]

Thatcher's survival was above all a triumph of image. From Febru-ary 1975, public relations occupied a central place in her advisers' thinking. While Heath had been notoriously contemptuous of his own advertising men, she was quick to adopt their suggestions, even down to small details such as putting out more flags and playing Elgar at the party conferences. Her most important image-maker was her cigar-chomping head of publicity, Gordon Reece, a former television producer who commissioned private polls after her early appearances as leader and then showed her the results. Although voters liked her sincerity and single-mindedness, they thought 'her voice was too shrill and upper-class, her style too hectoring, her appearance too austere and school-marmish'. So out went the hats and the pearls, and in came sim-pler outfits, softer hairstyles and gentler make-up. Reece also persuaded her to visit a National Theatre voice coach, who taught her how to lower her voice, speak more slowly and rid herself of the cut-glass accent she had acquired in childhood elocution lessons. As John Camp-bell notes, there was 'nothing magical' in all this; it was merely 'good professional advice'. It was to her credit, though, that she was self-aware enough to heed it; the chances of Ted Heath visiting a voice coach were slim, to say the least. Like her friend Ronald Reagan, she always listened to the team behind the scenes – the mark of a true showbiz professional.[7]

What this meant was that, oddly, Mrs Thatcher seemed younger and more down-to-earth at the end of the 1970s than she had at the begin-ning. That said, she still sometimes came across like the less amiable twin sister of *The Good Life*'s Margo Leadbetter. Indeed, the comparison with Penelope Keith's famously humourless and staunchly Conservative social climber was not entirely baseless, not least because Thatcher's aides tried to present her as the one thing she had never been – a stay-at-home suburban housewife, just like Margo. Crucially, Reece encouraged her to concentrate on tabloid newspapers, women's maga-

zines and middlebrow television programmes; instead of writing worthy
essays in the *Spectator*, she was just as likely to write pieces for *Vogue*
or *Woman's Own*, or to pop up on *Nationwide* or *Jim'll Fix It*. Readers
seeing the headline 'My Face, My Figure, My Diet' in the *Sun* must have
rubbed their hands at the prospect of an illustrated piece on Farrah
Fawcett, only for their faces to drop when they discovered an interview
with the Conservative leader. Indeed, more than any Tory leader before
her, she set out to woo the kind of people who listened to Radio Two's
enormously popular *Jimmy Young Show*, the kind of people who read
the *Daily Mail* and the *Sun* – which returned the compliment by giving
her the affectionate nickname 'Maggie'.[8]

All of this was designed to present Mrs Thatcher as an ordinary
housewife who understood people's daily concerns – an image that outraged feminists but reassured voters. Backward-looking it may have
been, but it was a brilliant political device, allowing her to address the
issues of the day – the soaring prices in the supermarket, the right school
for your children, the worrying levels of public debt – on a reassuringly
domestic level. As she told Shipley Conservatives in 1975,

> Perhaps it takes a housewife to see that Britain's national housekeeping is
> appalling. Britain is producing every week the same as she was in February
> last year. Yet she is spending half as much again. No family could survive
> like that. For a bit they can borrow, buy on HP, and delay paying the bills.
> But in the end the only way to get straight is to stop spending so much.
> What is right for the family is right for Britain.

A few weeks later she announced that 'competition, diversity, a range of
choice are as important in our society as a whole as the housewife finds
them on the supermarket shelves'. And even when the economy began
to pick up in the middle of 1977, she fell back on the same theme. 'I
don't see much improvement when you've still got an annual inflation
rate of 17 per cent,' she told Granada Television that autumn. 'You ask
the housewife.'[9]

But Thatcher's housewife persona was only one of her various roles.
Thus, as John Campbell writes, she was sometimes 'the Teacher, patiently
but with absolute certainty explaining the answers to the nation's problems', or 'the Headmistress exhorting the electorate to pull its socks up',
or 'Nurse Thatcher prescribing nasty medicine or a strict diet which the
voters knew in their hearts would be good for them', or even 'the
nation's Nanny, with overtones of discipline, fresh air and regular bowel
movements to get the country going'. All of these, of course, were drawn

from the stock of bossy female stereotypes; she might have been auditioning for a part in some terrible *Carry On* film. There were other roles, though, such as the coquettish flirt, who delightedly accepted a stack of Valentine cards a couple of days after becoming Tory leader (one of them measuring ten by twelve feet and costing a staggering £300) with the words 'I like to be made a fuss of by a lot of chaps!' Her most celebrated role, however, first surfaced one night in January 1976, when she was addressing the Finchley Conservatives. 'I stand before you tonight,' she began, 'in my Red Star chiffon evening gown, my face softly made up and my fair hair gently waved, the Iron Lady of the Western world. A Cold War warrior, an Amazon philistine, even a Peking plotter. Well, am I any of these things?' 'No!' the audience shouted back amid the laughter. 'Yes,' she said, smiling. 'I *am* an Iron Lady.'[10]

The famous nickname, which had been coined by the Soviet army newspaper *Red Star*, was well deserved. Like her future friend Ronald Reagan, then merely a former Governor of California, Mrs Thatcher saw herself as an ideological combatant on the front line of the Cold War. In an age when Soviet power appeared to be reaching a peak, parallels with the age of appeasement came naturally to her tongue, and for speeches on foreign policy she invariably turned to the anti-Communist historian Robert Conquest, whose classic book *The Great Terror* (1963) was the first comprehensive study of Stalin's atrocities.* To the Tory old guard, however, Thatcher's distaste for détente spoke volumes about her own extremism. Within the higher echelons of the Conservative Party, the general feeling was that unless she headed 'for the centre where elections are won', as *The Economist* advised her, her leadership would be brief. Even the *Sunday Telegraph* warned of the dangers of 'too much preaching of the gospel' and not enough of the 'tolerance' that was part of Tory tradition.[11]

And for at least one of her senior frontbenchers, her attacks on détente proved all too much. As Shadow Foreign Secretary, Reginald Maudling now cut an astonishingly louche figure even by his own standards, regularly downing a jug (a jug!) of Dubonnet and gin during morning briefings, and falling asleep three times during an official trip

---

* At the time, Conquest's views earned fierce criticism from hard-left writers keen to downplay Stalin's crimes. Years later, according to Conquest's friend Kingsley Amis, a publisher suggested issuing a revised edition under a new title. Conquest replied: 'How about *I Told You So, You Fucking Fools?*'

to Paris. He had just enough tattered vigour to make it clear that he not only disagreed with Thatcher's foreign policy but utterly despised her personally, even reassuring Soviet officials that she would not be leader for long. The last straw came at a Shadow Cabinet meeting in November 1976, after she had expressed her doubts about President-elect Jimmy Carter. 'Feed a grub on royal jelly,' Maudling said gravely, 'and it will grow into a queen bee.' Some of his colleagues had to stifle snorts of laughter, but as Jim Prior remembered, 'Margaret was po-faced. I did not fancy Reggie's chances in the next reshuffle.' Sure enough, she sacked him a few weeks later. 'When I told him that he had to go,' she wrote disapprovingly, 'he summoned up enough energy to be quite rude.'[12]

Maudling's fate was only one of many hints that Mrs Thatcher was cut from a rather different cloth from her Conservative predecessors. Few people then used the term 'Thatcherism', which her colleague Nigel Lawson defined as 'a mixture of free markets, financial discipline, firm control over public expenditure, tax cuts, nationalism, "Victorian values" (of the Samuel Smiles self-help variety), privatization and a dash of populism'. Thatcher herself defined her values as 'sound finance', 'living within our means', 'being strong in defence' and 'rolling back the frontiers of the State'. This last aspect is often exaggerated; in many ways, the state became a lot stronger in the 1980s. But although political scientists still argue over definitions of Thatcherism, her basic aims were very clear even in 1975. Her priorities were to wring inflation out of the economy through rigorously controlling the money supply; to slash government spending and reduce the size of the public sector; to limit the power of the unions and liberalize the labour market; and to reassure middle-class voters that law and order were the central principles of British life. Economic liberalism played its part, but so did old-fashioned social conservatism – and so too did even more old-fashioned electoral calculation. Above all, as the historian Richard Vinen points out, Thatcherism was less about ideas than about winning and wielding power. It began 'less as a doctrine', agreed Alfred Sherman, 'than as a mood'.[13]

From the very beginning, Thatcher had to put up with disgruntled muttering from One Nation patricians who considered her ideas utterly illegitimate. One version of her rise to power sees her as an ideological outsider, inspired by the libertarian ideas of Friedrich von Hayek and Milton Friedman, storming the barricades of the establishment and tearing down the pillars of the post-war consensus. Of course Thatcher and her allies were very pleased to have such powerful thinkers on their side. And yet the ideas of 'Fred-what's-his-name', as Norman Tebbit called him, were not so different from what Tory activists had been saying since the late 1940s, when there had been plenty of grumbling about the expansion of the welfare state, the rising tax burden and the influence of the trade unions. Even if Hayek and Friedman had never written a word, the Tory right would still have spent the post-war decades complaining about nationalized industries, Whitehall bureaucrats, heavy taxes and over-mighty unions, a litany of resentment that lay at the heart of Thatcher's rise to power. And of course this explains why the rank and file took to their new leader so quickly. From the moment she threw her hat in the ring, she had merely repeated what many of them had been saying all along.[14]

Of course this clashes with the common view that Mrs Thatcher was not really a Conservative at all. Heath's old ally Sir Ian Gilmour, for example, thought her agenda was merely 'nineteenth-century individualism dressed up in twentieth-century clothes', the bastard offspring of 'Manchester Liberalism' rather than true Conservatism. There was an element of truth in this: with her Methodist middle-class roots, free-market rhetoric and open distrust of the party establishment, Thatcher did sometimes sound like Gladstone's heir – and her father, the sainted Alderman Roberts, had started his political life as a Liberal. All the same, the notion that she was not a true Conservative is complete tosh. Far from being some sort of Liberal sleeper agent, she was, in the words of her adviser John Ranelagh, 'a conventional British Conservative politician, always loyal to the Party', and 'a loyal Minister under Macmillan, Douglas-Home and Heath'. In any case, economic liberalism was not an exclusively Liberal idea. Its place in Conservative tradition went back not just to the tax-cutting, small-state Conservatism of Baldwin and Chamberlain, but to the laissez-faire values of Sir Robert Peel – like Thatcher, a provincial pragmatist seen as the champion of the entrepreneurial middle classes. Of course free-market liberalism often clashed with other Tories' paternalist, hierarchical, organic vision of society. But since the turn of the century, free-market liberalism had been gaining ground within the Conservative Party. Mrs Thatcher's elevation to the leadership merely confirmed its victory.[15]

What disturbed moderates like Gilmour was the fact that Mrs Thatcher's economic liberalism had such an uncompromising moralistic dimension. Perhaps no Tory leader since Lord Salisbury had such contempt for the British left, which she clearly regarded as a halfway house on the road to Communism. And while her predecessors had deplored what they saw as socialism's economic inefficiency, she saw it as a moral outrage. 'We must fight Socialism wherever we find it,' she explained in the summer of 1976, adding that her aim was 'not just to remove our uniquely incompetent Government from office; it is to destroy the Socialist fallacies, indeed the whole fallacy of Socialism that the Labour Party exists to spread'. A few months later, she told the Conservative party conference that Labour's programme was 'frankly and unashamedly Marxist', and that 'the dividing line between the Labour party programme and Communism is becoming harder and harder to detect'. In her final words, she appealed to 'all those men and women of goodwill who do not want a Marxist future for themselves or their children or their children's children', urging them to join her 'crusade not merely to put a temporary brake on Socialism, but to stop its onward march once and for all'. This was a long way from Edward Heath's worthy appeals to national unity. But she meant every word. 'By God,' an admiring Kingsley Amis reported to his friend Philip Larkin after having dinner with her in October 1977, 'she doesn't half hate lefties.'[16]

In contrast to what she saw as the Marxist values of the Labour Party, Mrs Thatcher put her faith in the supreme virtues of the British middle classes. In her leadership campaign she had promised 'to stand for "middle class values"', which she defined as including 'the encouragement of variety and individual choice, the provision of fair incentives and rewards for skill and hard work, the maintenance of effective barriers against the excessive power of the State and a belief in the wide distribution of individual private property'. As the *Evening Standard* remarked at the time, there was 'a considerable air about Mrs Thatcher of "the middle class, *c'est moi*"', while the *Express*'s cartoonist Michael Cummings drew her as 'St Joan Margaret de Finchley, Saviour of the Middle Classes, Scourge of the Lower Orders & the Left'. The general assumption was that she would have to tone this down after winning the leadership; again, however, she stuck to her guns. Addressing a Conservative audience in Harrogate in her first major speech as leader, she ended with words that might have been scripted by her admirers in the Middle Class Association. 'Self-reliance has been sneered at as if it were an absurd suburban pretension,' she warned. 'Thrift has been denigrated as if it were greed. The desire of parents to choose and to struggle for what they themselves regarded as the best possible education for their children has been scorned . . . in the name of equality.'[17]

The concept of 'equality' – which at the time was associated with the debates about direct grant schools and comprehensives, as well as with Labour's sharply redistributive taxation – became one of Mrs Thatcher's chief targets during her years in opposition. 'We are witnessing a deliberate attack on our values, a deliberate attack on those who wish to promote merit and excellence,' she declared at the Conservative party conference in October 1975, before delivering a ringing endorsement of *in*equality:

> We are all unequal. No one, thank heavens, is like anyone else, however much the Socialists may pretend otherwise. We believe that everyone has the right to be unequal but to us every human being is equally important. Engineers, miners, manual workers, shop assistants, farm workers, postmen, housewives – these are the essential foundations of our society. Without them there would be no nation.
>
> But there are others with special gifts who should also have their chance, because if the adventurers who strike out in new directions in science, technology, medicine, commerce and industry [and] the arts are hobbled, there can be no advance.
>
> The spirit of envy can destroy. It can never build. Everyone must be allowed to develop the abilities he knows he has within him, and she knows she has within her, in the way they choose.[18]

If it was hard to imagine Edward Heath saying anything like this, it was even more difficult to picture, say, Anthony Eden or Harold Macmillan doing so, precisely because their privileged backgrounds had given them a sense of *noblesse oblige*. But as Mrs Thatcher never failed to point out, her background might have been a Victorian parable about hard work and opportunity. 'My father left school at the age of thirteen and had to make his own way in the world,' she told *World in Action* in 1975. 'I was brought up in a small town in the Midlands, for which I'm always profoundly thankful, because it's nice to be brought up in a community atmosphere in community spirit where everyone helps everyone else.' What she represented, she claimed, was 'an attitude, an approach, and I believe that that approach is borne out by the development in my own life going to an ordinary state school, having no privileges at all, except perhaps the ones which count most, a good home background with parents who are very interested in their children and interested in getting on'. Getting on: in those two words was her entire philosophy.[19]

Thatcherism's moral dimension was nowhere more apparent than in her attitude to economic policy. For the new Tory leader, economics and morality were inseparable: as her friend Sir Keith Joseph had explained, inflation was a moral scourge threatening thrift, self-discipline, hard work and aspiration. And as Mrs Thatcher argued in her final press conference before the 1979 general election, economic freedom was the only way that led 'genuinely to the greatest good of the greatest number . . . a moral case as well as a material one'. Of course plenty of politicians had argued for the moral dimension of economic policy before. But as many commentators saw it, Thatcher and Joseph were breaking new ground by making an explicit moral argument for very unpleasant economic medicine. Not since the 1930s had the Tory leadership seriously contemplated the prospect of higher unemployment: a necessary evil, Joseph argued, if inflation were to be conquered. 'We all agree that inflation is our most urgent preoccupation,' he had told his colleagues in May 1974. 'If this country is to return to sound money by gradual steps then consistent policies – involving some unemployment, some bankruptcies and very tight control on public spending – will be needed for at least five years . . . Some increase in unemployment will be unavoidable if inflation is to be mastered.'[20]

At the time, Heath had been in charge and unemployment had been the great evil. But Mrs Thatcher's elevation marked a historic shift. While her predecessors had been obsessed with avoiding a return to the mass unemployment of the Great Depression, she rejected Labour's 'policy of resisting any redundancy when bad management, declining markets or advancing technology lead businesses to fail', because it meant that 'workers will not be available to fill tomorrow's jobs'. The crucial question, though, is whether Thatcher consciously planned for the mass unemployment that scarred her first term, as her critics often suggest. In fact, some of the most enthusiastic monetarists denied that the British people would have to pay a high price for their shock therapy. In July 1978 Nigel Lawson even complained that he was 'a little disturbed' by how many Tory frontbenchers thought their economic policy 'would cause higher unemployment'. The true effect of their reforms, he believed, would be 'quite the reverse'. Still, as his note suggests, most of her team *did* think that jobless figures would rise, even if they never realized how high they would get. Her Economic Reconstruction Group under Sir Geoffrey Howe frequently discussed the possibility of higher unemployment, considering how it might be made simultaneously 'harsher', giving a wake-up call to 'those elements of the labour force which were insufficiently mobile', but also 'less harsh', so that it would be 'less unpalatable and likely to cause less social strain'. And Thatcher herself made no secret of the fact that she saw the positive side to higher unemployment. It was time, she said in 1975, to end 'the mindless policy of never having men and women available to move into tomorrow's jobs'.[21]

To many observers, this kind of rhetoric offered conclusive proof that Thatcher and her allies had signed up to Milton Friedman's doctrine of monetarism. The proper role of government, monetarists argued, was to exert strict control over the money supply, intervening in the economy as little as possible and leaving unemployment to reach its 'natural' level. To Sir Ian Gilmour this was yet another Liberal heresy; in reality, though, it was not so different from the sound-money, free-market approach urged by right-wing Conservatives for decades. In 1968, Thatcher herself had told the Tory conference that 'the essential role of government' was 'the control of money supply and management of demand', and called for government 'to exercise itself some of the disciplines in expenditure it is so anxious to impose on others'. By then she was already a regular guest at the IEA, and Friedman later recalled that she 'recognized very clearly the relationship between monetary policy on the one hand and inflation on the other'. During the Heath years she had little chance to follow up her interest. But as inflation ran out of control after 1974 and monetarism became unexpectedly fashionable, so the consensus hardened that Keynesianism had failed. The dream of managing demand so that unemployment could be eliminated, *The Times*'s Peter Jay told his readers in April 1975, had always been an illusion. 'The age of full employment', he wrote, 'is over.'[22]

Whoever the leader was, monetarist ideas would probably have percolated into the higher echelons of the Conservative Party. But since Mrs Thatcher was such a close ally of the zealously monetarist Sir Keith Joseph, the path was much smoother than if, say, Willie Whitelaw had been in charge. By the late 1970s, monetarist economists such as Alan Walters, Patrick Minford and Tim Congdon were familiar figures in Tory policy discussions, while few economic planning sessions passed without a mention of 'monetary discipline' or 'monetary targets'. The priority, Sir Geoffrey Howe told his colleagues in 1975, must be to curb inflation through 'proper management of the money supply' as well as 'greater restraint and economy in public spending', while Joseph suggested that the next government should reduce the government's share of GNP to just 40 per cent and work towards a balanced budget. Many Labour critics thought this was hilariously unrealistic: during a Commons debate in May 1975, Harold Wilson had some fun painting Joseph as Thatcher's wild-eyed 'Rasputin'. But there was no turning back. 'We shall aim to continue the gradual reduction in the rate of growth of money supply, in line with firm monetary targets,' declared *The Right Approach to the Economy*, which outlined the Conservatives' economic strategy in October 1977. 'This is not to say that one has only to follow the right money supply path and everything in the economy will become right. That would be to oversimplify a vastly complicated area of the financial and political system. But it is certainly the case that if the management of money is handled wrongly, everything goes wrong.'[23]

And yet what is really striking about Thatcher's monetarism is how vague, even muted it was. As Howe warned, it was pointless trying to 'popularise' monetarism, because to most people it was simply 'unintelligible'. But in any case, Mrs Thatcher was remarkably reluctant to be seen as an economic radical. When Milton Friedman gave an IEA seminar urging the abolition of exchange controls – later one of the landmark reforms of her first term – she listened intently, but then said that she might not be able to 'carry her party'. Abolishing exchange controls was not mentioned in her 1979 manifesto; similarly, privatization was barely discussed at all. On this point, in fact, Thatcher was so cautious that when Howe suggested selling the government's BP holdings in 1978, she hastily denied the idea in the House of Commons. All in all, nobody reading her economic proposals from the late 1970s could have seen her as an uncompromising radical: in many ways, they offered merely the standard waffle about eliminating bureaucracy, cutting taxes and encouraging enterprise, precisely what Tories had been saying from time immemorial. Even the monetarist elements, often lost amid the ritual denunciations of waste and red tape, were markedly underdeveloped. And for all the talk about strict monetary targets, nobody ever quite spelled out what those targets would be.[24]

Economic policy was not the only area in which Mrs Thatcher was rather less radical than we remember. While Joseph talked of radical surgery to the welfare state, her own rhetoric was much more cautious. 'All men of good will', she told an audience in 1978, 'must be concerned with the relief of poverty and suffering.' This was sensible politics: a Conservative Party promising to slash social services would not have been popular with the electorate in the mid-1970s. Indeed, one of the key differences between Thatcher and Joseph was that, as a much cannier and more instinctive politician, she knew that hair-shirted radicalism would not play with ordinary voters. And since Mrs Thatcher was noth-ing if not supremely pragmatic, it was no wonder that, as the election approached, radical ideas were quietly dropped. The idea of experi-menting with school vouchers, for example, disappeared from the Conservative manifesto. Even in Shadow Cabinet meetings, the welfare state was barely discussed at all. And when Thatcher mentioned it pub-licly, she talked only about making it more effective – not about rolling it back.[25]

The truth is that, although Mrs Thatcher is now remembered as the sworn enemy of caution and consensus, some of her closest allies thought those words summed her up. Her speechwriter Ronald Millar nicknamed her 'Cautious Margaret', while her advisers in the right-wing Centre for Policy Studies thought her 'a supremely cautious politician'. She was interested only in what was 'practicable and achiev-able,' she told the CPS's Norman Strauss, who considered her 'an incremental pragmatist with convictions'. To borrow an image from Ronald Reagan, she hoisted a banner, not of bold colours, but of remarkably pale pastels, presenting herself as the champion of the mid-dle ground against the forces of extremism. It was the left, not the right, that seemed to be reshaping British society between 1974 and 1979, and in this context she posed not as the destroyer of the post-war consensus, but as its defender. Indeed, far from ditching the One Nation message, she did her best to claim it for herself. 'We are one nation,' she told the Tory party conference in 1976, pledging that her party would defend the 'hopes and aspirations of the working people', and that there would be 'nothing narrow or vindictive or self-righteous' about 'our crusade'. A year later, mocking Labour's anthem 'The Red Flag', she declared that the Conservatives always flew 'the flag of one nation – and that flag is the Union Jack . . . So much for my so-called extremism.'[26]

And when, a few months later, her advisers drew up a report on 'Themes' for the next election, it made very striking reading. For one thing, it encapsulated one of Thatcher's great strengths: her ability to bring issues down to a domestic level. '"Capitalism" is *not* a good word, and we do not think even "Free Enterprise" rings many bells,' wrote the authors. They preferred the phrase 'More Choice', while instead of 'Freedom' they recommended 'Stop Messing Us About'. Above all, even though the authors (who included Angus Maude, Norman Tebbit, Nigel Lawson and Rhodes Boyson) were later celebrated as some of Thatcherism's keenest evangelists, they were remarkably anxious to downplay any hints of radicalism:

> We believe people are fed up with *change*, and with new systems that *don't* work. There is a deep nostalgia, in part for what is thought of a comfortable past, but chiefly for a settled, civilised life. Continuity is vital, and that is in tune with a Conservative approach . . .
>
> The conventional wisdom is that we must always appear forward-looking, never backward-looking. We think that at this moment the conventional wisdom may be wrong. The 'change' that people want today is much more a change *back* to known standards than a leap forward into the unknown.
>
> People will be more attracted by a promise – backed by sensible practical proposals – to restore some of the valued things they have *lost* than by promises of a vague, bright tomorrow.
>
> These include a sound currency, living standards, jobs, law and order and physical safety, sound educational standards, freedom from bureaucratic interference, etc. – to say nothing of national pride and a sense of common purpose.
>
> People would welcome a return to settled values and more predictable prospects.

This was not exactly the red meat of Thatcherism; in fact, it sounded more like the kind of thing Stanley Baldwin might have said. Perhaps it was no wonder that Chris Patten, the young director of the Conservative Research Department, worried that his leader was 'so cautious and sympathetic to the tolerant left-wing approach' that she might have a problem 'keeping the right wing happy'.[27]

What most exercised the Tory right in the late 1970s was the question of trade union reform. Mrs Thatcher herself had long advocated union reform: it was 'the individual who needs protection against the power of the unions and the public who need protecting against unofficial strikes', she had told Finchley Conservatives in 1966. And once she became leader, the problem of dealing with the unions became a dominant theme of planning for the next election. The key figures were an unlikely double act at Keith Joseph's new Centre for Policy Studies: John Hoskyns, an urbane ex-military man turned computer consultant, who was convinced that his elaborate flow charts held the answer to Britain's economic problems; and Norman Strauss, an unorthodox Unilever systems analyst who thought the Tories needed to adopt an entirely new vocabulary of change and confrontation. Interestingly, neither was especially partisan: when Alfred Sherman first invited Hoskyns to work with the CPS, the latter replied that he was 'not a committed supporter of the Tory Party', and in February 1976 he told Sherman that he now had 'even less confidence in the ability of the Conservatives to solve the country's problems' than when he started. He remained on board, however, and in late 1977 he and Strauss began work on a blueprint to turn Britain around. They called it 'Stepping Stones', and it was to become one of the most celebrated documents in modern political history.[28]

Hoskyns and Strauss opened in suitably sweeping style:

> The task of the next Tory Government – national recovery – will be of a different order from that facing any other post-war government. Recovery requires a sea-change in Britain's political economy.
>
> A Tory landslide is not enough, if it only reflects the electorate's material dissatisfaction since 1974. A landslide is needed, but it must represent an explicit rejection of socialism and the Labour–trades unions axis; and the demand for something morally and economically better ...
>
> There is one major obstacle – the negative role of the trades unions. Unless a satisfying and creative role can be developed, national recovery will be virtually impossible.
>
> To compete with Labour in seeking peaceful co-existence with an unchanged union movement will ensure continued economic decline masked initially by North Sea oil. It will also make failure to win Office more, rather than less likely, for the Tories. There is nothing to gain (except, just possibly, Office without authority) and everything to lose by such a 'low risk' approach.

What followed was a detailed explanation, complete with flow charts, of the 'high risk' approach. Hoskyns and Strauss outlined four central 'turn-around policies': first, the stabilization of the pound through 'sustained monetary discipline'; second, a shift from income tax to VAT; third, the radical deregulation of the private sector; and finally, the use of North Sea oil revenue to cut public borrowing. None of this would be possible, though, without 'a complete change in the role of the trades union movement'. The Tories must campaign hard against 'the dictatorship of unsackable union leaders' and win a mandate for sweeping reform. Good slogans might be 'Make Maggie's Britain Work', 'Jim's

Britain is a Sick Britain' and 'In Place of Hate', which would 'suggest what we are offering as an alternative to continued class warfare and economic suicide'. Above all, Hoskyns and Strauss thought that union members *themselves* held the key to a Thatcher breakthrough. The ordinary member, they wrote,

> is precisely the man we must get to vote Tory . . . Very few of the silent majority can be proud of the closed shop, picketing, bullying, selfishness, blatant disregard for others, violence and intimidation, particularly as they well realise it could so easily happen to them. So the trend of natural forces is probably now beginning to move in our direction and we suspect that it will continue that way, especially with some delicate help.[29]

To a modern reader, 'Stepping Stones' seems a stunningly prescient blueprint for the Thatcher government. Not only did Hoskyns and Strauss anticipate the central role of union reforms, they were absolutely right to predict that the votes of union members themselves would play a key role in her rise to power. Mrs Thatcher was delighted with the document, telling Hoskyns that it was 'the best thing we've had in years'. And yet what is really revealing is that, instead of being adopted as party policy, 'Stepping Stones' was pushed onto the sidelines. When the Shadow Cabinet discussed it at the end of January 1978, senior figures lined up to dismiss it as too confrontational, too ambitious and too expensive. Even Thatcher herself seemed to share their doubts. 'When [John] Davies argued that if we told the truth about the unions we should certainly lose the election,' the minutes recorded, 'Mrs Thatcher acknowledged that this could not be the centrepiece of our election strategy' – an astonishingly cautious thing for her to have said, given her reputation.[30]

For the time being, therefore, 'Stepping Stones' gathered dust in the equivalent of a locked desk drawer. Indeed, far from welcoming a rematch with the unions, many senior Conservatives shrank from the prospect of confrontation. Memories of their defeats by the miners died hard; as another, far more pessimistic report by Peter Carrington put it, 'there will always be groups with the power successfully to challenge government. In these cases the only possible course is for government to avoid confrontation.' When this report was leaked to *The Times* ('Mrs Thatcher Warned in Secret Report of Defeat in Confrontation with Unions'), many activists were outraged at their leader's defeatism. But it was the Tories' bluff employment spokesman Jim Prior, the image of a jolly country farmer, who set the tone. Talk of trade union reform,

Prior thought, would only alienate working-class voters. And to the consternation of her activists, Mrs Thatcher seemed quite happy to follow his lead. 'There is no problem about my getting on with trade unions or trade unions getting on with me,' she told *Panorama* in February 1976, 'provided we are both interested in getting a flourishing Britain.' Even eighteen months later, after the fighting at Grunwick had seared its way into the national consciousness, she stuck to the same line. She kept hearing, she complained, that 'the Tories won't be able to work with the unions'. But nothing could be further from the truth. 'A strong and responsible trade union movement is essential to this country and its rights must be respected,' she explained. 'We in the Conservative Party look forward to a long and fruitful association with the unions.'[31]

Whether Mrs Thatcher would ever put her promises into effect, however, remained very doubtful. For all the efforts of her image-makers, at least four out of ten voters consistently told pollsters that she was not proving a good Leader of the Opposition. And to the horror of Conservative supporters, the polls showed that the public much preferred the reassuring presence of Jim Callaghan to the novelty of a woman Prime Minister. By the time the Tories assembled for their party conference in October 1977, some 46 per cent of the electorate thought Callaghan would make the best national leader, compared with only 29 per cent for Mrs Thatcher. And as the economy recovered after the IMF debacle, she actually lost support. By the autumn of 1978, even after the 'Labour Isn't Working' posters, Callaghan led her by 50 per cent to 39 per cent. To add insult to injury, she was much less popular would increase their standing by 14 per cent if Edward Heath returned as leader.[32]

It was no wonder that so many people still dismissed Margaret Thatcher as a fluke, an aberration, a footnote in history. Watching her at an arts conference that summer, the National Theatre's Peter Hall reflected that the test of a political leader was that 'he or she must be able to go anywhere and not be out of place. Uncle Jim would be alright down a coal mine, in a factory, in a school, in a hospital, on the lawns of Buckingham Palace, or in a street barbecue in Brixton. Margaret Thatcher wouldn't. I doubt if she'll win.' Even in her own mind, behind the manicured mask of certainty, the doubts occasionally crept in. As a woman, she admitted, she would get only 'one chance' at victory; if she lost, the party's verdict would be swift and brutal. And like her activists, she dreaded the result if her crusade to stop the onward march of social-ism failed at the polls. 'People have always said that the next election will be crucial,' she told Kingsley Amis over dinner. 'But this one really will be, and if it doesn't go the way Denis and I want then we'll stay, because we'll always stay. But we'll work very hard with the children to set them up with careers in Canada.' She never contemplated giving up, of course. But as month followed month and her personal popularity remained stubbornly in the doldrums, it seemed ever more likely that Mark and Carol would be off to Toronto.[33]

29

We'll Beat the Bastards Yet

This is the death of the Labour Party. It believes in nothing any more, except staying in power.

Tony Benn's diary, 15 January 1978

His favourite meal is the archetypal British dinner – roast beef and Yorkshire pudding, even down to potatoes and sprouts. Though steak-and-kidney pie and Mrs Callaghan's rabbit pie are strong runners-up . . .
 Television? Inevitably he is restricted to weekend programmes. He likes Bruce Forsyth and never misses a Morecambe and Wise show if he can help it.

Daily Mirror, 5 April 1978

When Jim Callaghan looked back on his time at Portsmouth Northern Secondary School, even he had to admit it had been less than distinguished. Unlike his two predecessors in Number 10, Callaghan had been a 'bad boy', caned for such misdemeanours as running a sweep on the weekend's football scores, blowing up the geography teacher's red ink bottle and tying a fish underneath his master's table – although, in this instance, he claimed he had been framed. A big, keen boy who devoured classic novels at the local library, he nevertheless found maths and science entirely beyond him. 'With all due respect to some of my teachers, I don't think some of it was very well taught,' he mused later. Compared with the 'clever boys', he felt himself a bit of an idiot, and reflected 'how unfair it was, that old Doggo Croucher the maths master would say it once and these lads would have it [while] I was still thinking about it'. His reports were 'indifferent, if not downright bad', with the holidays often overshadowed by dire warnings that he must buck up his ideas. But like many children, he improved as he got older; at the last moment, he was entered for the Oxford Schools Certificate, which he passed with distinctions in English and history, the first step on the long road to Number 10.[1]

When Callaghan became Prime Minister, one of his priorities was to make a big speech that would identify him as the voice of decent common sense, in obvious contrast to the radical ambitions of the far left. In his first major briefing for his new boss, Bernard Donoughue suggested emphasizing 'the restoration of responsible values in society', particularly in education. This was a subject near to Donoughue's heart: he had four children in Islington state schools, his wife worked as a teacher, and he loathed 'the middle-class Labour people from Islington, the trendy lecturers from higher education' with their '*Guardian*-style ideologies and prejudices'. In a further memo, he suggested that Callaghan 'restate the best of the traditional and permanent values – to do with excellence, quality and actually acquiring mental and manual skills'. This was music to the Prime Minister's ears. Long interested in education, he hated what he saw as the radical middle-class 'irresponsibility' of the William Tyndale teachers, who were giving state education a bad name. He was determined, he said, 'that the Tories were not going to line us up with Tyndale, and every idiotic teacher who was sympathetic to the Labour Party'.[2]

From Callaghan's point of view, moving into the education debate was smart politics. By now the rhetoric of the *Black Papers* had seeped deep into the media coverage of education, and there was a growing sense that teachers were out of control. In the *Times Educational Supplement*, the head of the GEC electronics giant, Arnold Weinstock, accused teachers of being 'feather-bedded and inefficient', and claimed that they were doing 'no service to our children if they prepare them for a world that does not exist', while the Confederation of British Industry's John Methven complained that British youngsters were 'ill-equipped for almost any kind of employment and woefully ignorant about the basic economic facts'. Meanwhile Mrs Thatcher seemed determined to turn education into a major battleground. Socialists were 'increasingly preoccupied' with producing 'children who are "equal", almost regardless of educational attainment', charged the new Conservative manifesto, *The Right Approach*, in October 1976. Parents were rightly 'worried about the moral values taught in our schools; about the decline of religious education; about their lack of influence and choice; about the imposition of one form of secondary education; about the levelling down of standards; about the lack of discipline at many schools'. All this was bound to strike a chord with Callaghan, for whom working-class opportunity was everything. Even the *TES* conceded that there were 'perfectly respectable arguments about the levels of achievement expected of pupils . . . and the methods and styles of teaching appropriate to these expectations'.[3]

Only weeks into his premiership Callaghan called in his first Education Secretary, Fred Mulley, and demanded a full report on the curriculum, exams and the education of sixth-formers. The report finally appeared in October, its cover earning it the nickname the 'Yellow Book', and was promptly leaked to the *TES*. Many teachers were horrified by its contents. In primary schools, the report claimed, the 'uncritical application' of 'newer and freer methods' had clearly back-fired, and it was time for 'a corrective shift of emphasis' back to greater formality. As for secondary education, the Yellow Book acknowledged 'the feeling that schools have become too easygoing', with many teachers too young and idealistic to get the best out of their pupils. The curriculum, meanwhile, did not do enough to prepare children for their 'economic role' in society; indeed, many employers complained that 'school leavers cannot express themselves clearly'. Finally, the Prime Minister should make an 'authoritative pronouncement' to banish for good the canard that 'no one except teachers has a right to any say in what goes on in schools'.[4]

The Yellow Book set the scene for one of the most influential speeches of the late 1970s: Callaghan's address at Ruskin College, Oxford, to mark the foundation of a new residential building. As an institution dedicated to the education of working men, Ruskin held a cherished place in left-wing hearts. Yet even before Callaghan rose to speak, the press was trailing his speech as a dramatic break with post-war orthodoxy. The *TES* predicted that it would mark 'a turning point in English educational history', wresting back control of schools from the teachers' unions to 'the public's representatives'. Revealingly, however, the *TES* thought this a terrible idea, accusing Callaghan of 'selfish political motives' and 'political demagoguery' – which in turn confirmed his contempt for the 'appalling educational snobbery' of the teachers and their supporters. But most of the national papers were more supportive: even the *Guardian*, usually sympathetic to progressive teachers' interests, agreed that, just as the 'clinical independence of doctors' was going to have to be reduced, so was 'the far more recent professional independence of teachers'. It was clear, the editorial said, that 'the State must step into schools'.[5]

When Donoughue went up to Oxford on the big day, he was worried that the speech had been 'trailed and discussed so much in the papers that it was impossible to meet expectations'. What was more, Callaghan had toned it down over the weekend, softening the attack on progressive education so that 'he did not end up in the Rhodes Boyson/Tory camp'. Yet the Prime Minister began with a dig at those telling him 'to keep off the grass [and] to watch my language', noting that 'some people would wish that the subject matter and purpose of education should not have public attention focused on it: nor that profane hands should be allowed to touch it'. His remarks were meant not as 'a clarion call to Black Paper prejudices', but as an appeal for 'a rational debate based on the facts', involving parents and businesses as well as teachers and the government. He was horrified by complaints from industry that school leavers 'do not have the basic tools to do the job', and he shared parents' 'unease' at the 'new informal methods of teaching', which produced 'excellent results when they are in well-qualified hands but are much more dubious when they are not'. The balance, Callaghan said, had been wrong in the past, when children had been bombarded with facts, but there was now a danger of getting it 'wrong again in the other direction'. And he had a warning for the teaching unions. 'You must satisfy the parents and industry that what you are doing meets their requirements and the needs of our children,' he said bluntly. 'For if the public is not convinced then the profession will be laying up trouble for itself in the future.'

Today the Ruskin speech looks pretty innocuous. At the time, however, Callaghan's tone, as well as his talk of a national 'core curriculum' and of 'monitoring' schools to 'maintain a proper national standard of performance', left many teachers appalled. Even at Ruskin there were jeers and catcalls from the audience. Donoughue blamed 'student Trot militants protesting about education cuts', and relished the irony that 'these were the *privileged* students' interrupting a speech meant to benefit 'the underprivileged in education'. Even the girls, he remarked cattily, had beards. There was also an excruciating moment when, as Callaghan was laying the foundation stone for Ruskin's new building, he had to endure a rant from the college's student union president accusing him of 'dancing to the tune of the International Monetary Fund'. The Prime Minister had the last laugh, though, when fifty protesters broke into a spirited rendition of the 'Internationale', only to tail off after a few lines because they could not remember the lyrics. Trying not very hard to suppress a smirk, the Prime Minister asked if they would like him to finish the song – for unlike them, he actually knew the words.[6]

On the Labour left, where talk of standards was seen as a reactionary backlash, all was consternation. Tony Benn's wife Caroline, a champion of progressive education, warned that Callaghan was really attacking 'the "lefties" who are teaching the social sciences', while Benn recorded that the speech had been 'most damaging to the cause of comprehensive education'. Meanwhile the teachers' unions were furious. The general secretary of the National Association of Head Teachers, as though competing in some unofficial overstatement competition, declared that he had been teaching 'in Nazi Germany during the thirties and saw what happened when the curriculum was nationally controlled. My history books were taken out and replaced.' Most vitriolic, though, was the reaction of the *TES*. Callaghan had 'gathered his Black Paper cloak around him,' thundered an extraordinary front-page editorial, accusing him of having 'trotted out clichés from the CBI about the shortcomings of young workers'. He had 'whistled up weasel words to exploit popular prejudices' and to 'divert popular indignation from ... his own management of the economy'.[7]

On the right, however, Callaghan's Ruskin initiative went down very well. Rhodes Boyson called it 'a very good speech', while *The Times* hoped that it heralded 'a reverse swing of the pendulum' reflecting the 'leanness and meanness of the times'. And although Callaghan's new Education Secretary, the amiably earnest Shirley Williams, mildly resented his invasion of her turf, she shared his view that progressive education had gone too far. The new teaching fashions 'hadn't always been thought through', she thought, and in January 1977 she indulged in an enjoyable bout of teacher-baiting, blaming the problems of British education on 'poor teachers, weak headmasters and headmistresses and modern teaching methods'. Yet in the next two years, little actually changed. Teachers and civil servants alike were resistant to the idea of radical reform, and although Mrs Williams tried to purge the Schools Council and scheduled a series of regional conferences to discuss education's 'Great Debate', her Conservative critics pointed out that she had made little concrete progress towards a national curriculum or raising standards.[8]

What had undeniably changed, however, was the mood music. By the late 1970s, Callaghan had helped to set a much more conservative educational agenda, in which teachers were more tightly controlled, the curriculum was more utilitarian, and the general emphasis was on higher standards all round. For the first time, a senior Labour figure had challenged the teachers' professional independence, while his talk of a national curriculum clearly paved the way for the classroom revolution of the 1980s. The Ruskin speech was 'the first time the Prime Minister had actually wandered into the sacred vineyard of the curriculum', said Kenneth Baker, the Education Secretary who introduced Mrs Thatcher's key reforms a decade later. Indeed, the preamble to Baker's Education Reform Act explicitly acknowledged Callaghan's influence. And although many teachers loathed the new emphasis on standards and skills, Callaghan remained enormously proud of his part in the change. The Ruskin speech, he later reflected, 'was like a stone dislodged by the mountaineer's foot which, rolling down the mountainside, precipitates an avalanche'. Bernard Donoughue went even further. 'I wouldn't claim we made great practical progress; we didn't have time,' he wrote a quarter of a century later. 'But "Stop the rot" is a good phrase and it really was a rot. One doesn't often have a chance to do a little that's good in life but I'm proud of that one, I can tell you.'[9]

To Callaghan's left-wing critics, the Ruskin speech was merely one symptom of a disturbing shift away from socialism. 'In my heart of hearts,' wrote a despairing Tony Benn on New Year's Eve 1977, 'I believe the country is moving to the right.' The union leaders, he complained bitterly, 'are so enjoying their corporatist relationship with the Government that they don't want to hear anything about socialism'. At lunch with Hugo Young, Benn explained that social democracy was dead: the only real choice lay between the 'monetarist course', represented by Callaghan, Healey and Thatcher, and his own 'alternative strategy'. Perhaps surprisingly, he now referred to Mrs Thatcher with great interest and respect. 'What she presages is a real polarization,' he told Young in 1978, the latter noting that 'Benn evidently relishes the thought'. Indeed, in his diaries Benn had already recorded that 'things will have to get worse before they get better'. He was keenly looking forward to carrying out major 'mid-Eighties reforms', but thought that 'the public isn't ready'. His time would come, he thought, 'when we have seen the full meaning and effect of Thatcherism'.[10]

Benn's growing fascination with the Conservative leader was not matched by any great affection for his own colleagues. Appalled by the Lib–Lab Pact, he had lost any semblance of respect for his nominal allies around the Cabinet table. One evening in early 1978 he 'reluctantly went to the Foots' house' and 'found it very depressing. For the first time I felt I had nothing in common with any of them.' Even the party, he thought, was irrelevant, since 'all the growth on the left is going to come up from the outside and underneath'. But to his Cabinet colleagues, the sound of Benn's voice droning on about the alternative strategy and the radical potential on the shop floor had become almost intolerable. Listening to Benn attacking pay restraint at another dinner, Michael Foot 'blew his top and shouted, "You just want us to go back to inflation. Face the real problems – you have got to help the low paid."' 'He was red with anger,' Benn recorded afterwards. A few weeks later, after Benn had organized a secret meeting to derail the government's arrangements for elections to the European Parliament, they had another blazing row. 'I think it's bloody crooked,' Foot shouted at him. 'You just want the Tories in . . . you with your halo of martyrdom.'[11]

In many respects, Benn's portrait of Callaghan and Foot as crypto-Conservatives was a ridiculous caricature. Discussing crime and immigration in February 1978, for example, Callaghan said that 'he did not think we could ever win on these issues. They are Tory issues.' Labour must not 'chase the Tories "down every hole" on issues such as immigration and law and order', he repeated a few weeks later. 'We must hold to our principles, and if we lose on it "so be it".' And yet under Callaghan, those principles *did* seem more conservative than under Wilson. In Northern Ireland, the pugnacious Roy Mason treated terrorists as common criminals and turned a blind eye to the excesses of the Royal Ulster Constabulary. In Whitehall, plans to reform the Official Secrets Act were held up in a mess of red tape; in the NHS, the offensives against pay beds and private practice quietly withered away; in education, talk of ending the charitable status of private schools came to nothing. And while Callaghan saw himself as a throwback to Clement Attlee, many activists thought his talk of standards, responsibility and order made him sound like a Tory. 'He's telling people what they want to hear,' admitted the Conservatives' golden boy Michael Heseltine. 'He's playing the Big Uncle, patting you on the shoulder and telling you to relax while he takes the strain.' Even the *Express* called him the 'Iron Uncle', keeping the 'naughty boys and girls' in check. But that, of course, was what most people wanted. Britain was 'not ready for a more radical Prime Minister, certainly not one of the left', remarked *The Times* in May 1978. 'The Labour Party would be massacred under a left-wing leader in any election this year, but Mr Callaghan is reassuring to the electorate. Again and again . . . he leaves the ordinary but interested elector thinking: "that is what I would have done myself".'[12]

Callaghan's more conservative line owed a great deal to the Number 10 Policy Unit. At first, Bernard Donoughue had been ready to pack his bags and go back to the LSE, but on only his second full day as Prime Minister, Callaghan asked him to stay on. 'I am not very clever, as you will know from the newspapers,' he remarked. 'I don't have Harold's brain for bright ideas. But in fact I need the Unit more than Harold did. And although I don't get many bright ideas of my own, I am good at spotting the bright ideas of others and know whether they will work or not.' He was as good as his word: after their first proper strategy meeting three weeks later, an ecstatic Donoughue wrote that Callaghan had been 'first class', calmly laying out his aims and sending them all away 'refreshed and committed to work with enthusiasm'. And over the next three years, the Policy Unit poured forth a torrent of ideas on everything from the school curriculum and economic recovery to exchange rates and devolution. Indeed, although historians often describe the Callaghan government as intellectually threadbare, it is striking how much Donoughue's team anticipated the reforms of the 1980s. Even during the Wilson years, for example, he had recorded his outrage at the 'terrifying growth' of public sector bureaucracy, and in his first major paper for Callaghan he suggested the theme of 'social responsibility', recommending 'tough honesty' on crime ('because there is no doubt that some aspects of the current "permissive" social ethos have produced widespread misgivings') and a new approach to welfare (which, he thought, 'threatens to produce a corrosive dependency'). If Callaghan's grassroots members had caught sight of this, of course, they would have been horrified – although it is tempting to wonder what one young Hackney activist, a left-wing barrister called Tony Blair, would have made of it.[13]

What certainly outraged many Labour supporters was the government's line on the economy. Thanks to Healey's cuts, public spending as a proportion of GDP had fallen from almost 46 per cent in 1975–6 to less than 40 per cent two years later, although it slightly rose again afterwards. Public borrowing, too, had fallen from 10 per cent of GDP in 1975 to just 5 per cent in 1978. Even the tax burden was lighter by the end of the Callaghan administration. For the richest, it fell from a punitive 70 per cent to 65 per cent; for those earning one-and-a-half times the national average, it fell from 35 per cent to 32 per cent; and for those making just half the national average, it fell from 22 per cent to 18 per cent. Contrary to the stereotype, therefore, Britain was not becoming a more socialist or spendthrift state in the Callaghan years. Indeed, in both 1978 and 1979, the government spent proportionately *less* public money than its competitors in France, Italy and West Germany. To the teachers, lecturers, nurses and social workers who dominated many local Labour branches, however, this represented a shocking betrayal. For two decades they had assumed that there would always be more money for the welfare state. Now everything had changed: although Callaghan and Healey were hardly rolling back the state, they were not exactly rolling it forward, either. 'Up to that time in social welfare,' remarked Sir Peter Barclay, chairman of the Social Security Advisory Committee, 'it seemed that all we needed was to identify problems, create an organisation to cope with them, and that would solve it. Social care, social work, social services – we all had unlimited resources, it then seemed.' But 'from 1976 on it became a demoralising fight'.[14]

Behind this lay a deeper intellectual shift. Although neither Callaghan nor Healey was an ideological monetarist, their adoption of money-supply targets has often been seen as a crucial step towards the economics of Thatcherism. To borrow a term from the Governor of the Bank of England, Gordon Richardson, they were 'practical monetarists', taking what they wanted and discarding the rest. Richardson himself thought that monetary targets were an excellent 'self-imposed constraint, or discipline, on the authorities', which is probably how Healey saw them, too. To old-fashioned Keynesians all this was utter heresy: later, the Labour MP Austin Mitchell complained that monetarism had been 'introduced and house-trained by Labour, ready for the Conservatives to turn it into the only instrument of policy'. But one of monetarism's earliest champions had nothing but praise for Healey's courage. The Chancellor had presided over 'a revolution of great significance and import', Enoch Powell told the Commons in July 1977. He had, he mischievously confided, long recognized in Healey a kindred spirit. 'The Chancellor of the Exchequer has been – I know this because I have watched him over the years – a monetarist much longer than anyone has ever suspected of him,' Powell said with relish. 'I used to listen with enjoyment to his speeches in the years 1972 to 1974, and I would shake my head and say to myself, "He will be a good Chancellor of the Exchequer, for he understands the real causes of inflation." Oh, he understands them all right.'[15]

The other obvious continuity between the Callaghan and Thatcher years was the retreat from full employment. Far from being foisted on Britain by Mrs Thatcher in 1979, unemployment had started rising during Wilson's first spell in office. Under Heath it had reached one million for the first time since the war, and after falling during the Barber boom, it had then started rising again. By the spring of 1978 the jobless figure was almost 1.5 million; by 1979 it had risen by 60 per cent in a decade. The government was hardly indifferent to the human cost: in towns across the country, the arrival of Job Centres was a reminder of both the tragedy of unemployment and the government's efforts to address it. But to young school leavers unable to find work, this came as little consolation. Visiting Sunderland in April 1978, one reporter found a town 'dying a slow death'. That July, 4,000 school leavers would begin 'searching for jobs that do not exist'. For with the port moribund, shipbuilding dying and the coal industry in rapid decline, the jobless figures were already twice the national average and steadily rising. Even before the advent of Mrs Thatcher, unemployment was becoming a way of life: 'everywhere,' wrote another visitor to the region, 'there is a coffeebar society of unemployed teenagers.' Even Sunderland's Labour council leader, Len Harper, could see little hope. 'This is no ebb tide of some world economic sea which will turn to flood at some time in the future,' he said bleakly. 'The jobs that are gone are not likely to return . . . The concept of an industrial town in the industrial north is an anachronism.'[16]

Sunderland's plight was merely one example of the way in which Britain in the Callaghan years seemed an increasingly divided society, a world of us and them. For almost twenty years after 1957, income inequality had been falling; from 1976 onwards, however, it had begun to grow again. 'Britain is a good place to live for most of its inhabitants,' wrote the perceptive Peter Jenkins in the *Guardian* in September 1978, 'provided you are not one of the 10.4 million who are living at the supplementary benefit level or no more than 20 per cent above it.' Only eight years after Heath's pledge on the Downing Street steps to 'create one nation', Jenkins thought that Britain seemed closer than at any time since the 1930s to being 'Two Nations'. For the great majority, 'the general quality of life in Britain remains probably as high as anywhere in Europe'. But for the 1.5 million unemployed or the 600,000 people on hospital waiting lists, especially the 40,000 urgent cases, 'life leaves much to be desired'. Roughly speaking, he thought, around one in five people qualified as poor and needy, belonging to the lesser of the Two Nations. Theirs was not the Britain of new cars, foreign holidays, video recorders, *Delia Smith's Cookery Course* and *The Country Diary of an Edwardian Lady*; instead, it was the Britain captured in small-screen masterpieces like *The Spongers*, which ran in the BBC's *Play for Today* slot in January 1978.[17]

The Spongers was written by Jim Allen, a former labourer from

Manchester who became an ardent socialist and wrote a string of fiercely ideological plays for the director Ken Loach. Set against the background of the Silver Jubilee, it follows a Salford single mother called Pauline, who has four children, including a daughter with Down's syndrome. Around her, council workers are excitedly preparing for the Queen's great party. But Pauline has more pressing concerns: the bailiffs are at the door, while her local Labour councillors have just voted to slash benefits for the disabled. Her community organizer urges her to keep fighting, but fate seems against her. Because of the cuts, her disabled daughter is moved from a residential care home to an under-equipped, shabby hostel; worryingly, her doctor admits this may exacerbate her condition. All the time the Jubilee preparations continue, and the play culminates with the joyful street parties of the big day, a savagely ironic counterpoint to Pauline's deepening plight. Unable to meet her arrears, the walls closing in, she cracks. That night, as the Jubilee celebrations are dying down, she gives her children an overdose of antidepressants, and then takes one herself. The last word belongs to a female neighbour, who watches ghoulishly as the bodies are taken away the next morning. 'She had no right to do it,' she says. 'She should have stuck it out like the rest of us, instead of letting them get one over on her.'[18]

In some ways, *The Spongers* conformed absolutely to the stereotype of the ultra-depressing late-1970s *Play for Today*, battering the audience with the plight of the working class and the evils of capitalism. The television critic Michael Church admitted afterwards that he had tuned in 'with deep misgivings', expecting 'a cosy left-wing rebuttal of right-wing social prejudices'. But there was nothing cosy or simplistically left-wing about it. 'Without a trace of mawkishness', Church thought, Allen and his director Roland Joffé had 'manipulated their seedy, down-at-heel material to let the raw tragedy float free'. Tellingly, though, the play made nothing like the impact of earlier works such as *Cathy Come Home*, and the *Daily Express*'s critic doubted that viewers would 'find much sympathy' for a celebration of social security benefits. One reason, no doubt, was that audiences now took this kind of material for granted: in the previous twelve months, *Play for Today* had told the stories of a disillusioned comprehensive school boy holding his teachers hostage (*Gotcha*), a nuclear power disaster (*Stronger than the Sun*), an abortive workers' revolt in Manchester (*Come the Revolution*) and an Alcoholics Anonymous group (*One Day at a Time*) – although not, controversially, Roy Minton's play *Scum*, a brutally hard-hitting portrait of young offenders inside a borstal, which was suppressed by the BBC and eventually remade for the cinema. All these plays tackled worthy subjects, and indeed many of them were exceptionally well written and produced. But to casual viewers they probably seemed like a very gloomy Spartist blur.[19]

Yet there was surely another reason why Allen's play aroused little reaction. From economics and welfare to law and order, public opinion in the late 1970s was unquestionably swinging to the right. Allen's title was of course ironically chosen, yet the press was full of reports of 'spongers': only a few weeks later, the *Express* ran a long story headlined '5 Years On The Sponge' about a 27-year-old Kingston-upon-Thames father of four, who had worked for only three days since 1972 and cheerfully told his social security officer: 'As long as the State looks after us, that's all right by me.' 'The public are sick of spongers,' a magistrate declared, sentencing him to nine months behind bars for 'persistently claiming' benefits.[20]

And if the polls were to be believed, the magistrate was right. In July 1978, when Gallup asked what policies the next government should follow, a majority supported strict pay limits, tougher immigration controls, longer prison sentences, the sale of council houses, the return of grammar schools and the withdrawal of benefits from strikers' families, while most people opposed more nationalization, the nomination of union leaders to sit on companies' boards and the abolition of the House of Lords. This was not, of course, a uniformly conservative picture: as usual, most also wanted extra spending on the NHS, higher pensions and a more dynamic approach to unemployment. But another survey in October told a similar story: seven out of ten felt that the decline of deference had gone too far, six out of ten wanted a crackdown on pornography and more than half thought that Britain should spend more on defence. Perhaps most striking were the attitudes of Labour voters: since 1964, support for nationalization had dropped by 25 per cent, sympathy for the unions by 23 per cent and enthusiasm for greater social spending by 28 per cent. 'At a time when competitiveness is the key to arresting the national decline,' remarked the *Guardian*, 'the mood seems to be turning towards conservatism and resistance to change. There seems to be a feeling after a decade and a half of social engineering ... that change has been tried and found wanting.'[21]

In his moral and cultural conservatism, his old-fashioned patriotism and his unashamed enthusiasm for law and order, Callaghan seemed ideally placed to exploit the shift in public opinion. Once the IMF crisis was behind him, he was much more conservative than is often remembered, just as Mrs Thatcher was rather less radical. Nobody observing his old-fashioned attitudes on crime and education, or his Northern Ireland Secretary's enthusiasm for a hard line in Ulster, could possibly imagine Uncle Jim as the champion of permissiveness or the standard-bearer of the revolution. Above all, the gap between Callaghan and Thatcher on the economy was much narrower than we usually remember: while Denis Healey and Geoffrey Howe were hardly singing from the same songbook, they were at least borrowing from the same library. Later, Healey even remarked that some of Mrs Thatcher's union reforms had been 'absolutely right'. He and his colleagues were a long way short of being Thatcherites, whatever their hard-left critics might say. But it was nevertheless telling that even Mrs Thatcher, interviewed on the *Jimmy Young Show* in January 1978, thought that the choice lay between 'a Conservative government and ... a half-hearted Labour government practising Conservative policies'.[22]

In one crucial area, though, Callaghan's caution infuriated his advisers. At the beginning of the decade the Heath government had made a tentative attempt to sell council houses to their tenants, but local authorities dragged their feet and by 1974 only 7 per cent of the housing stock had changed hands. There was clearly a huge appetite among tenants to liberate themselves from their landlords: as Tony Crosland had conceded in the *Guardian* in 1971, council tenancy carried 'the whiff of welfare, of subsidization, of huge uniform estates, and generally of second-class citizenship'. It was the council, Crosland admitted, that decided 'what repairs are to be done, what pets may be kept, what colour the doors will be painted, what play areas there should be, where a fence should be put up', giving the tenant 'far less freedom than the owner-occupier to do what he likes in and around his home'. In an era of growing affluence, ambition and individualism, this was increasingly intolerable. During the 1974 elections, canvassers reported that tenants often brought the issue up on the doorstep. Polls showed that there was enormous public support for the sale of council houses: in 1974, eight out of ten council tenants liked the sound of the idea, more than six out of ten said the issue was very important to them, and three out of ten were actively interested in buying their own home. Even the director of the Child Poverty Action Group, Frank Field, thought that Labour should 'free the council serfs' and invest the proceeds elsewhere.[23]

Almost as soon as Labour had taken office in March 1974, the Policy Unit had started work on a plan to sell council houses. For Bernard

Donoughue the issue had deep personal resonance: growing up in Northamptonshire, he had experienced the joy of moving into a new council house and 'knew the difference it could make to family life'. Now, as a private owner-occupier in Camden, he was horrified by 'the dogmatic lunacies of our local council', not least its 'Direct Works Department', which was 'distinctly averse to doing any work, direct or otherwise'. His brother Clem, meanwhile, worked as a carpenter for the Manchester Works Department, and used to tell 'how they spent most of their time drinking tea and playing cards'. For Donoughue, therefore, the issue became something of an obsession. In his mind, it was about giving ordinary tenants

> the freedom to decorate their homes as they wished and, very important, to move in pursuit of employment – many inner-city unemployed dared not move to seek jobs because it meant giving up their council homes and going to the back of the council queue elsewhere. I could not see why the middle classes should have this freedom and not the working classes on the council estates. It infuriated me when I raised this issue with my local Kentish Town Labour Party and was dismissed out of hand by a bunch of mainly left-wing activists, many of whom were prosperously middle-class and enjoyed the benefits of owning their own homes in nearby Hampstead and Camden Town.

He found plenty of allies. Gavyn Davies, the Policy Unit's brilliant young economist, estimated that he spent half his time in 1974 working on council house sales, and later waxed lyrical about the 'public accounts advantages' and the 'political liberation for urban working people – our people'. 'We had schemes absolutely fully developed, ready to launch,' he recalled, with subsidies to help tenants buy their homes and plans to reinvest the proceeds in new council houses. Even the tribal Joe Haines was a great supporter of the idea. Unless Labour met working-class voters' demands to own their homes, he thought, they 'would be outflanked on council housing policy' by the Tories. So Haines and Donoughue drew up a plan to give tenants the chance to buy their house at its original cost, minus the amount already paid off on the loan. When the tenant and his dependants died, the house would revert to the local authority. That way, Haines thought, the government would 'overcome the fundamental criticism of many Labour groups' that they would be reducing the total number of council houses available to the poor. There would be plenty of complaints from the left, he conceded: but the advantages were 'enormous for everyone concerned'.[24]

Since the sale of council houses became such a crucial element of Mrs Thatcher's record, it is tempting to wonder how different political history might be if Wilson or Callaghan had heeded the Policy Unit's advice. At first Wilson seemed to like the idea, even telling Donoughue that his plans 'could change history'. Very soon, however, the idea got bogged down in the Whitehall machine. At the Department of the Environment, Crosland was against it because it offended his faith in the public sector, while his special advisers worried that it would alienate local Labour activists. Donoughue countered that 'it would also attract many times that number of local voters'. But by the time Wilson resigned, the project was stuck in limbo. At the Labour conference in September 1976, a motion demanding a law to *forbid* the sale of council houses was 'heavily carried amid applause', and although Donoughue did his best to persuade Callaghan of its virtues, this was one battle too many. By 1978 the council house scheme was dead, handing the issue to Mrs Thatcher on a plate. A year later, the Conservative manifesto promised to give council tenants 'the legal right to buy their homes' at heavy discounts. Donoughue was furious; it was no consolation when, years afterwards, Callaghan's Environment Secretary Peter Shore admitted that they had 'totally misjudged the policy of selling council houses'. 'It was an own goal,' admitted Gavyn Davies. 'A monumental own goal.'[25]

'Hot again,' wrote Michael Palin at the end of May 1978. 'Into the sizzling silly season for the newspapers.' At last, after months of hard slog, the sacrifices seemed to be paying off. With inflation down to single figures, nine North Sea oilfields pumping out their black gold and the Treasury looking forward to an oil bonanza, Britain seemed to be turning a corner. Chase Manhattan's chief European economist even thought that 'the outlook for Britain is better than at any time in the post-war years'. And after four years of public pessimism, Callaghan and Healey had the rare pleasure of basking in the fabled 'feel-good factor': at last, more than 50 per cent of voters told Gallup that they expected things to get better. Healey even felt confident enough to produce from his conjuror's hat that old favourite, a pre-election giveaway Budget. And with house prices buoyant and growth predicted to reach 3 per cent, the Chancellor cut a very jaunty figure that summer. One post-Budget poll gave him a handsome 67 per cent approval rating, ahead of both Callaghan (64 per cent) and Mrs Thatcher (54 per cent). Even in the City, reported the *Express*, there was a growing 'mood of euphoria', coupled with a feeling that Labour would probably be back after an autumn election. 'Much as it hurts them to admit it,' the paper remarked of Britain's financiers, 'they have a sneaking suspicion that Jim Callaghan and Denis Healey have got things right and that a massive change in policies might not be a good thing.'[26]

With consumer spending back up to levels of the early 1970s, sales of appliances up by 24 per cent and new car registrations set to break all records, with road building, arts funding and schools spending buoyant, with more people dining out, taking holidays abroad and spending their money at spanking new shopping centres, it seemed that the upbeat headlines were well deserved. In the summer of 1978, remarked the *Guardian*'s Peter Jenkins, foreign visitors to London would find 'people staggering cheerfully under the burden of prosperity', and they would 'see much the same if they ventured north – a consumer boom reverberating down every high street'. When he canvassed opinion about British decline, the replies – 'What decline?' 'How can there be a decline when everything is going up?' – spoke volumes about the new mood. 'Callaghan is personally very popular at the moment,' wrote Michael Palin at the end of May, 'and Thatcher is not ... I'm better disposed to letting the present Labour government run my country for me than any other group – apart, perhaps, from Pan's People – and I feel better governed (in a moral, rather than material sense) than at any time for many years.'

And yet, as even the Labour-supporting Palin acknowledged, the underlying problems had not gone away. 'I think anyone with any information of substance must realise that Jim's good news basket is a very small one,' he wrote, 'and all the signs are that the present drop in inflation (now down to 7.8%) and unemployment figures cannot be maintained.' Other, more expert commentators were similarly cautious. As Peter Jenkins reminded his readers, Britain's industrial performance was still atrocious. Between 1973 and 1976, the last three years for which figures were available, manufacturing output had grown by 7 per cent in Italy, 5 per cent in France and almost 3 per cent in West Germany, yet in Britain it had actually fallen by 6 per cent. It was no wonder, then, that the former workshop of the world was in such competitive decline. In the last fifteen years, its share of the world car market had fallen from 11 per cent to 5 per cent. In shipbuilding it had fallen from 8 per cent to 4 per cent, in steel from 6 per cent to 3 per cent, in electrical machinery from 14 per cent to 8 per cent, in transport equipment from 16 per cent to 6 per cent. Of course this was only relative decline; most people were more prosperous than ever. And yet 'decline feeds upon itself', Jenkins wrote. 'Its effects become the cause of further decline ... No country has yet made the journey from developed to underdeveloped. Britain could become the first to embark on that route.'[27]

Above all, the apparent calm of 1978 was built on the fragile acquiescence of the unions. The firemen's strike had been a powerful reminder that years of restraint had taken their toll on the morale of low-paid workers, and although the government had won, the underlying problems remained. Furious at the erosion of their differentials, some skilled manufacturing workers were tempted by Mrs Thatcher's promise to restore free collective bargaining; others, such as the British Leyland toolmakers, seemed to be swinging to the left. On the TUC General Council, the militants seemed more vocal than at any time in years: as well as the openly Communist Ken Gill of the Technical, Administrative and Supervisory Section, hard-left general secretaries such as the television technicians' leader Alan Sapper, the seamen's Jim Slater and the print workers' Bill Keys were all pushing for big new deals. After two years of 'flat-rate controls,' warned *The Economist* in January 1978, skilled workers were on the brink of revolt.[28]

What was more, Jack Jones, the man who had almost single-handedly kept them in check, had now withdrawn from the stage, bowing out as leader of the TGWU with an extraordinary gala at the Royal Festival Hall in February. It was a sign of Jones's pre-eminence in public life that not only did Jim Callaghan come to pay his respects, but the performers included Les Dawson, the Nolan Sisters and Mike Yarwood, who had the audience howling with laughter at his impersonation of the Prime Minister. At the end, Jones was presented with a farewell present of £10,000 from his members. As the applause rolled around the hall, he took the envelope, murmured a few words of thanks – and handed it straight back, explaining that he would like it to go towards the union's campaign for pensioners and its convalescent home. 'A great silence fell across the Festival Hall, then a gathering murmur of amazement,' wrote the *Mirror*'s Geoffrey Goodman. A few feet away, Callaghan quietly bowed his head, some said to hide the tears in his eyes. It was, by any standards, a wonderful way to bow out. But as Goodman noted, Jones's departure meant there was bound to be trouble ahead. 'He leaves a scene', the *Mirror* man wrote, 'that can ill afford to be without his talents.'[29]

For the time being, though, the mood inside Downing Street was more cheerful than at any time in the previous ten years. Even Bernard Donoughue's diary entries were positively upbeat. 'The PM was in excellent humour,' he wrote after Prime Minister's Questions on 24

January. 'Indeed it is striking how he has been in very good form for a long time now – because everything has gone well for so long.' Two months later, with the latest poll putting Labour only just behind the Conservatives, 'the PM was absolutely back on his best form. Relaxed . . . The increase in morale on our side was very evident.' The squabbling and paranoia under Harold Wilson were distant memories; more typical was a happy evening when Callaghan invited the triumphant Welsh rugby team to Number 10 for a 'lively and enjoyable, almost riotous' party. It was, Donoughue amusedly noted, the first Downing Street reception at which the waiters had been forced to lock the guests out of the room where the drinks were being prepared. 'Some of the men locked out', he remarked, 'were huge and very thirsty-looking.' But the party went on into the small hours, with Callaghan leading 'the singing in a lovely Welsh hymn'. In fact, late-night singing was something of a trademark of Downing Street life under Sunny Jim. When the American Vice President Walter Mondale visited London in 1977, recalled Denis Healey, Callaghan hosted a 'riotous dinner', after which they sang 'old labour union songs until well after midnight'. Afterwards, one of Mondale's officials took the wine list back to his hotel, worked out the cost and told the press that 'the Labour Government lived in a state of luxury which President Carter would never permit in Washington'.[30]

Much of Callaghan's good humour derived from the fact that in the Commons, he reigned supreme. His aides' strategy was to present Mrs Thatcher as 'abrasive and divisive . . . a dangerous woman who will divide our society and create trouble', casting the Prime Minister as the champion of 'understanding and experience'. After April 1978, parliamentary proceedings were carried on the radio, which worked in Callaghan's favour. Although audiences were shocked by the baying and jeering at Prime Minister's Questions, the consensus was that Uncle Jim, calm, cheerful and authoritative, came over much better than his opposite number. She sounded, said the *Express*, like 'an angry woodpecker'. Week after week, Labour clawed back the Conservative lead in the polls, and by the summer the two parties were neck and neck. And as almost everybody recognized, much of this was down to the Prime Minister. Even right-of-centre papers such as *The Times* acknowledged him as 'the champion of moderation, common sense and national unity', a big man in apparently effortless command of his party and his country.[31]

In the last debate before the summer recess, Callaghan struck at the jugular. For the first time, he told his aides, he had 'decided to go for Thatcher . . . to make a big attack to demonstrate his superiority as well as to give Labour backbenchers a morale booster'. He was as good as his word. Opening the afternoon's debate on economic policy, he ripped into her as never before:

> The right hon. Lady is insulting the intelligence of the British people with her one-sentence solutions to deep-seated problems. That is no way to conduct an Opposition, especially when they aspire to be a Government . . .
>
> The simple truth is this: the right hon. Lady has led the Conservative Party for three years and under her leadership people still do not know what the Conservatives stand for. They still have no clear idea what their policies are on pay, on production, on immigration or on anything else. They do not know because she does not know. She has a distaste for policy-making.
>
> The right hon. Lady's every speech is a rallying cry to prejudice. The Tory Party once aspired to lead one nation and to speak for one nation. Now the Tory Party, many of its members reluctant and sullen, has to listen to the language of division the whole time. That call to division will fall on deaf ears.

Taken aback by his ferocity, Mrs Thatcher struggled to match the mood of the House, reeling off statistics in what the *Financial Times* called a 'nervous and faltering' voice. As she stumbled over her final words, the Labour benches roared in triumph. 'We have been present at a historical occasion today,' Denis Healey said mockingly. 'The axes and knives are already being sharpened.' In the press, where an autumn election was widely expected, her political obituaries were being prepared. Only Thatcher herself, defiant to the last, still kept the faith. 'How are you?' she asked her friend Norman Tebbit afterwards. 'Not depressed? Good. We'll beat the bastards yet.'[32]

With the government's parliamentary position so precarious, Callaghan's inner circle had been discussing election dates for months. Since Christmas the options had narrowed to two: going to the country in the autumn, or hanging on until the spring of 1979. But Callaghan was always sceptical about an early election. The economy might be improving, he told his aides, but 'that did not mean we should hold an autumn election. There was a time lag of six months before the public appreciated events. So if you wanted to capitalise on the autumn well-being you should go in the following spring.' Even so, as Labour's position continued to improve, the merits of an early election seemed increasingly obvious. With growth and wages up and inflation down, advised the

Policy Unit, there would never be a better time to go to the country. Even *The Times* predicted that the economic picture was 'likely to be the most favourable experienced by any government since the 1966 election, which produced a Labour majority of over 100'. And when Tony Benn discussed an early election with Callaghan, he found the Prime Minister reasonably bullish. 'He is convinced that October is right, though he's worried about the long run-up, and what the City might do in the meantime,' Benn noted. There must be nothing 'radical' in the manifesto: no 'wealth tax', for example, because 'Mrs Thatcher would say we were just squeezing the rich'. Hanging and immigration, Callaghan thought would be major issues: 'It will be a very dirty Election and we'll have to fight hard.'[33]

On 3 August Callaghan went off to his farm for a summer holiday, taking with him a pile of books on past elections, as well as reams of analysis from Bob Worcester's MORI pollsters on the state of play in marginal seats. Before leaving, he had learned that the Ulster Unionists and Plaid Cymru would support him into the spring, while both Michael Foot and Michael Cocks, the Chief Whip, thought the government could comfortably go through to 1979. Not even his most intimate confidants were sure what he would do, but most were convinced an autumn election was inevitable. In the Commons, leaving parties had already been arranged for retiring Labour MPs. Tom McNally, perhaps Callaghan's closest aide, advised him to get a smart new suit with a spare jacket and to have his hair cut before announcing the date. On 30 August, while Callaghan was still relaxing at the farm, a group of senior party officials had lunch at the *Mirror* headquarters to discuss themes for the campaign, with 'Heart' and 'Fairness' being the favoured options. By now, noted Donoughue, Callaghan was telling friends that 'he "has made up his mind", but without telling anybody in which direction'. The assumption, though, was that he had decided on early October. 'Election Date Is Likely To Be Announced Within Week', ran the headline in *The Times* on 3 September. 'Ministers would be taken aback,' explained the lead story, 'if Mr Callaghan decided to risk trying to persevere through the winter.'[34]

Two days earlier, Callaghan had invited the six most important union barons – Len Murray, Hugh Scanlon, Dave Basnett, Moss Evans, Geoffrey Drain and Alfred Allen – to dinner at Upper Clayhill Farm. It was a lovely summer's evening, and as they gazed out at the rolling Sussex fields, all seemed right with the world. 'My wife's reputation as a cook was well known,' Callaghan recalled proudly, 'and she presided over a splendid table at which our guests were served by my eldest grand-daughter, Tamsin Jay.' All but one of them encouraged him to go for an October election. If he delayed, they warned, he might risk a wages explosion over the winter as their members threw off the fetters of restraint. Callaghan played devil's advocate, putting the case for waiting until the spring, but they held their ground: only Scanlon thought he should wait. And when they left, amid warm handshakes and back-slapping all round, it seemed that Callaghan had been persuaded. An autumn election it was.

On Tuesday, 5 September, Callaghan arrived in Brighton to address the TUC conference. To most observers he seemed refreshed, confident, ready for the fight. From the platform, he joked that there had been plenty of speculation about the election date, yet 'no one could have been more silent than I'. Teasing his audience, he said that he would not be divulging his plans that afternoon. The newspapers, he said to laugh-ter from the delegates, had 'fixed the month for me. They have even chosen the date and the day.' But he had some advice for them:

> Remember what happened to Marie Lloyd. She fixed the day and the date, and she told us what happened.
>
> As far as I remember it went like this:
>
>> *There was I, waiting at the church . . .*
>
> Perhaps you recall how it went on:
>
>> *All at once he sent me round a note.*
>> *Here's the very note.*
>> *This is what he wrote:*
>> *Can't get away to marry you today –*
>> *My wife won't let me!*

At that the Prime Minister glanced over at his grinning wife Audrey, there were roars of laughter, and some delegates shouted 'More!' 'Now let me just make it clear,' Callaghan said mock-seriously, 'that I have promised nobody that I shall be at the altar in October. Nobody at all.'[35]

The next day's front pages had great fun with the Prime Minister's excursion into tuneless verse. 'Play It Again, Jim!' read the headline in the *Express*, noting that the song actually belonged to one of Marie Lloyd's rivals, Vesta Victoria. In fact, Callaghan had known that all along, but thought Marie Lloyd would be more familiar. It was a moment that spoke volumes about the man, his style and his values.

Many younger trade unionists had never heard of Marie Lloyd, far less Vesta Victoria, but their older comrades loved it. So did the newspapers, which were impressed by his tough noises on economic discipline and pay restraint. 'Tremendous press for the PM,' Donoughue wrote on Wednesday morning. 'Everybody agrees that it was courageous and statesmanlike. Great send-off for an election campaign – assuming there is one.' Everyone, he recorded, was looking forward to the announcement after Thursday's Cabinet meeting. 'No. 10 has a curious atmosphere. No papers coming through ... People wandering around reading the tickertapes or gossiping. The Political Office has its door closed and gives an impression of the Allies' military headquarters on the eve of D-Day, June 1944.'

And when Britain awoke the next morning, election fever had already set in. 'Polling Day Statement Is Expected Today', read *The Times*'s headline, noting that 'outside broadcast units have been summoned to Downing Street'. At last, after all the waiting, the moment of decision was at hand.[36]

30
Siege Conditions

The coming year will clearly be the year of decision and advance. A year in which the British people will be asked to choose the path they intend to follow in the 1980s. It is our achievement that this important decision will be taken in a calmer atmosphere and against a background of greater stability than seemed possible only a few years ago.

James Callaghan's New Year message, 31 December 1978

Up at 7.30 to get the papers: all the talk at the bookstall was about the utter hatred of unions and strikes, etc.: one day, I think this loathing will be channelled into action.

Kenneth Williams's diary, 4 January 1979

It was not until after one o'clock that Callaghan's pre-election Cabinet broke up. Waiting outside for confirmation that the campaign was on, Bernard Donoughue noticed that the ministers all looked uncomfortable on their way out. 'That is the most depressing Cabinet I have ever attended,' Bill Rodgers muttered as he walked past. Donoughue did not, however, have a chance to ask what he meant, because he had to make a lunch appointment. By the time he got back, the television engineers were already setting up for Callaghan's broadcast to the nation that evening. The *Mirror*'s political correspondent, Terry Lancaster, who was hanging about inside Number 10, asked if the election date was definitely 5 October. 'I could not tell him because I did not know!' Donoughue wrote later. 'Then Tom McNally rushed up and handed Terry a piece of paper with "1979" scribbled on it. I could not believe it. No election now!'

Lancaster's immediate reaction was that there must be some mistake, and Donoughue agreed with him. But then reality began to sink in. 'I felt terribly disappointed,' Donoughue recorded. 'At first I thought the PM was mad and badly wrong.' He was not alone: his Policy Unit colleagues were 'flabbergasted', while Callaghan's political aides, who had been nervously putting away large whiskies, could not believe their ears. Even at Cabinet, a few hours earlier, a 'startled silence' had greeted the news. Tony Benn, who had been torn between going to the country early and waiting until the spring, was 'most surprised and, indeed, angry' that Callaghan had made such a dramatic decision entirely on his own. The Prime Minister had decided to hang on, Benn recorded, for 'outright victory. We could win now, but he said the position would be clearer once the improvement in the economy was felt more fully.' To rub salt in the wounds, Callaghan added 'that he would prefer that there be no discussion of this matter because he could not unwrite the letter to the Queen.' At that there was a 'ripple of laughter', but Callaghan did not join in. 'You're laughing now,' he said. 'But if we have trouble with the unions and get forced out in the winter you'll feel differently.' History offered few better examples, thought Roy Hattersley later, 'of prescience and irony combined'.[1]

That night Callaghan addressed the nation. 'Now I'd like to tell you, personally, how I see it,' he said confidingly, his heavy features dominating the screen. Things, he said, were now 'much better', but the improvement would only last if the government followed consistent policies.

> Let us think for a moment of the great domestic issues the country faces now, and ask ourselves whether a General Election now would make it any better this winter.
>
> Would a General Election now make it easier to prevent inflation going up once more? Would unemployment be any less this winter? Would a General Election now solve the problem of how to deal with pay increases during the next few months? Would it bring a sudden dramatic increase in productivity?

Slowly, smiling gently, he shook his head. 'No,' he said flatly. 'We shall face our difficulties as we come to them. I can already see some looming on the horizon.' But the government would go on; there would be no election, after all. 'Instead, I ask every one of you to carry on with the task of consolidating the improvements now taking place in our country's position. Let's see it through together.'[2]

Watching in Downing Street, many of Callaghan's closest aides still struggled to disguise their shock and disappointment. 'Either he is a great political genius,' Tom McNally said quietly, 'or he has just missed the boat.' Other observers were equally astonished: David Steel proclaimed himself 'astounded', while Callaghan's parliamentary aide Roger Stott was 'dumbfounded'. Party officials were 'baffled' and the union leaders were reportedly furious at having been, as they thought, misled. Even the newspapers, which had so confidently predicted an autumn election, were outraged that Callaghan had made them look foolish. He had 'seriously miscalculated', declared the *Financial Times*, while *The Times* lamented that he had 'condemned the country to probably another half year of pre-election tension'. 'Jim Unfixes It,' read the headline in the next day's *Mirror*. And amid the criticism, one voice stood out. Having travelled to the West Midlands to launch her campaign, Margaret Thatcher was said to be 'deeply disappointed' by the news. 'He has lost his majority and when that happens I think you lose the authority to govern,' she said bitterly. 'He should now properly seek the verdict of the people . . . This country belongs to the courageous, not to the timid.'[3]

Jim Callaghan's decision not to call an election in the autumn of 1978 is often seen as one of the greatest blunders in British political history. Yet at the time, it was not such a strange decision. Both the Leader of the House, Michael Foot, and the Chief Whip, Michael Cocks, thought they could get through the next parliamentary session, even without the Liberals' help. Many of the whips were worried that an autumn election would smack of panic or opportunism; others thought that, although Wales and Scotland were safe, Labour was still struggling in the crucial English marginals. Inside the Cabinet, opinion was almost evenly divided. Ten of Callaghan's ministers were in favour of going to the country in October; eight preferred to wait until the spring and give the economy more time to improve. Crucially, the eight included most of the really big names, with Michael Foot joined by the Chancellor, Denis Healey, the Foreign Secretary, David Owen, and the Home Secretary, Merlyn Rees. The most vociferous was Foot, who was convinced that if they held on a little longer, they would soon see the benefits of economic recovery and North Sea oil. The only question was whether, now that the Lib–Lab Pact had expired, they would be able to get their business through the House of Commons, but the whips thought they could manage it. 'We have lived on next to nothing for years,' explained the deputy Chief Whip, Walter Harrison, 'and should have a go at carrying on.'[4]

All his life Callaghan had been a notably cautious politician, and as he brooded over the polls at his farm in the late August sunshine, all his instincts told him to wait. Local election results in the West Midlands, the battleground where Heath had won power in 1970 and lost it four years later, suggested that Labour would struggle in the marginal seats. As Callaghan knew, the trade union vote was unreliable, the party machine was creaking and many of his own activists were deeply disaffected. And although some national polls gave Labour a slender lead, he treated them with suspicion. 'I don't trust them. I don't believe in them,' he told his friend Helmut Schmidt at the end of August. (Indeed, on 4 September the party's private pollster, Bob Worcester, gave the Tories a 2 per cent lead, while two slightly later polls, based on interviews before the non-election announcement, gave the Tories leads of 6 per cent and 7 per cent.) Meanwhile, poring over past election results, Callaghan did some calculations of his own. The most likely result of an October election, he thought, would give the Tories 304 seats and Labour 303 – another hung parliament. After two-and-a-half years scrabbling around for a parliamentary majority, that was the last thing he wanted. On 18 August he telephoned Denis Healey, who had a cottage in nearby Alfriston, and invited himself over for tea. As they sat in the garden, enjoying the late summer sunshine, Callaghan explained that he was 'sick to death of the continual compromises required for our survival'. If the best result in October would be a hung parliament, he would rather wait till the spring and either get a proper majority or lose outright. Healey agreed. 'It was not worth having an election', he thought, 'that would result in a hung parliament.'[5]

It is a myth that Callaghan's caution cost his party victory. Assuming that the polls were right – and it is worth noting that a year later they slightly *under*estimated the Conservative lead – the only likely outcomes in October were another hung parliament or a narrow Tory victory. On the face of it, therefore, waiting till 1979 was an understandable gamble, and Callaghan was convinced he had made the right decision. He was 'in top form', wrote Bernard Donoughue a few days later, 'still delighted with himself for not calling an election, and so making a fool of all the commentators'. But as his biographer remarks, there was a considerable element of hubris in all this. By playing his cards so close to his chest, Callaghan had not only upset many of his own ministers, he had made enemies in the unions, who felt that his 'Marie

Lloyd' speech had made fools of them. Not only in the conference rooms of right-wing newspapers, but in shop stewards' meetings and left-wing Labour constituency parties, the Prime Minister's critics were sharpening their claws. Soon the warm summer weather faded into history. The headlines were full of rumours of strikes; the storm clouds were gathering. On Friday, 22 September, Donoughue heard that Ford car workers had walked out on Merseyside. 'We shall have the most difficult time yet on pay this winter,' he noted, 'and I suspect we will often look back and regret not having taken an election during this beautiful sunny September.'[6]

If Callaghan wanted an outright majority the following spring, he needed to maintain Labour support in places like Chelmsley Wood. A large overspill estate close to Birmingham Airport, Chelmsley Wood was a temple to the optimistic ambitions of the 1960s. It had a relatively new shopping centre, a new library, almost forty blocks of multi-storey flats and a young, working-class population. Almost a decade after the shopping centre had been completed, however, business was stagnating. Closures and cuts had taken their toll; the mood felt pinched and tired. Money was short, explained 24-year-old David Bond, a parks gardener who gave an interview to the *Guardian*. Every week David earned £40 from Solihull District Council; if he did overtime, he got an additional £10. Out of that he paid income tax, then £11 rent for their council house, and then another £13 on electricity and gas. The rest he gave to his wife Lynne to spend on the household and their two small children, keeping nothing for himself. He did not smoke or drink; he had worked for the council for four years and liked his job. The only problem was the pay. 'We have just got a washing machine,' David said, 'but my wife had to get a part-time job to pay for it, and I may be old-fashioned, but I don't really like her going out to work.' Like many young couples, he and Lynne dreamed of a better life, but they saw little prospect of it becoming a reality. 'I want to buy my own home one day,' David said, 'but every time it looks as if I've got enough coming in to reach the repayment levels, the tax system changes or they put up the interest rate, and we're back to square one.'[7]

David Bond's story would have been immediately familiar to millions of working-class Britons in the last months of 1978. Although real net earnings were now rising, the days of buoyant affluence and ever-expanding horizons seemed a distant memory. Between 1975 and 1977, many families had seen their household income fall by more than 10 per cent, forcing them to tighten their belts and postpone their dreams of new homes and foreign holidays. To those at the bottom of the ladder, years of enforced pay restraint had made a mockery of their ambitions. For, say, Manchester sewage workers earning just £54 a week, 'ankle deep in muck and slime', airy talk of the national interest rang hollow.* Yet what really fuelled workers' resentments, noted the *Observer*'s Robert Taylor, was not 'envy of the super-rich', but their eagerness 'to climb a rung or two above those whose pay they traditionally compare with their own'. He drew up a 'wages table', showing that, in three years since April 1975, some groups had forged ahead while others had fallen back. At the top of the table, for example, power engineers had overtaken teachers, office managers and senior civil servants, their pay rising by a hefty 65 per cent, while car workers had jumped from the Fourth Division to the Third with an increase of 53 per cent. By contrast, firemen and water workers had dropped a division, while nurses and Post Office workers had fallen several places. In general there was a clear pattern: public sector workers, especially at the bottom end, had done worse than those in the private sector. Little wonder, then, that the public sector unions were restive.[8]

Faced with rising discontent, a less scrupulous operator, such as Macmillan or Wilson, would almost certainly have relaxed the pay policy and put inflation out of his mind until after he had won the election. But that was not Jim Callaghan's style. Dismissed for much of his career as a supremely tribal politician, he was keen to prove himself a genuine national statesman. As early as November 1977, he had told Donoughue that they 'would have to be tough, and next year's norm would have to be about 5%'. If it worked, they would go into the election 'with inflation down to around 6%, and the Tories having nothing similar to offer'. Of course this was terribly risky, since it might provoke a breach with his old allies in the unions. But beating inflation had become Callaghan's overriding priority, just as he had promised in his very first address as Prime Minister. Denis Healey even thought he was 'obsessed' with it. But Healey, too, told the Cabinet that 'high inflation is not only a major social evil but is also incompatible with high

---

* To put this into context, official figures showed that a typical male manual worker earned £65 a week and £3,385 a year. Non-manual workers earned £81 a week and £4,243 a year. Senior professional people earned between £8,000 and £15,000 a year, while top executives, newspaper editors and bankers earned up to £30,000. Meanwhile, the England football captain Kevin Keegan, who had moved to Hamburg in 1977, took home a reported £125,000 a year. Some things have changed less than we think.

employment'. For years, he argued, Britain had been paying itself more than it earned:

> The central problem of our economy for more than a generation has been that, although productivity has grown more slowly than that of our competitors, we have seen annual wage increases of the same order as theirs. So our inflation has risen faster than in other countries and we have been able to maintain price competitiveness and full employment only by a series of devaluations which have further added to inflation and increased the pressure for excessive wage increases. In the era of North Sea Oil it will be more difficult to devalue our currency to maintain price competitiveness. So unless we can keep wage increases close to the level of productivity increase, we shall face rising unemployment and a further erosion of our industrial base.

Now, Healey thought, there was 'a better chance than ever' of winning support for a really tough pay policy that wrung inflation out of the British system. Trade unionists, he wrote optimistically, were 'tired of being paid in confetti money'.[9]

Callaghan first broached his fateful pay policy with his Cabinet just before Christmas 1977. If they kept on as they were, he said, inflation 'would steadily be reduced to 9 percent', which was 'simply not good enough when compared with the performance of other countries'. They must squeeze the economy even tighter, which meant an official pay guideline of around 5 per cent. Many ministers thought that was far too tight, and Tony Benn good-humouredly called him 'an unregenerate old reactionary', which made Callaghan laugh. For the time being, nothing was decided. But when Callaghan gave a BBC interview on New Year's Day 1978, 'the 5 per cent idea hardened and popped out'. Callaghan's recollection makes it sound like an accident, but he undoubtedly knew what he was doing. Rising prices had determined two out of the last three elections; he wanted to send a signal to the public that he would do anything to get inflation down. Given the phenomenon of 'wage drift', a 5 per cent policy might mean a general 8 per cent increase, pushing inflation down into single figures. Already some union leaders, especially in the public sector, were warning him that their members would never wear it. But Sunny Jim was not for turning. As Donoughue recorded in April 1978, he believed that 'beating inflation is *politically* more important than beating unemployment. So he will go for 5% on wages next year – and is prepared to take the unions on.' And by the middle of July, the policy was set in stone. 'Five per cent it is,' Callaghan told his colleagues, 'and I have told the unions that they have all the weapons. We are naked in their presence and we need their cooperation.'[10]

There was an obvious flaw in Callaghan's strategy. Like Edward Heath before him, he thought that winning support was essentially a matter of getting the union leaders around a table and giving them a good meal. What he never understood was that *within* the unions, there had been a decisive shift in the balance of power. Even supposedly autocratic general secretaries like Jack Jones had bought support by devolving power to the shop floor, while skilled workers were now demanding the right to negotiate their own local deals. Better educated, more ambitious and more independent than ever, many white-collar workers had grown up challenging their parents, their teachers and their employers. The days when they automatically deferred to their elders, if they had ever truly existed, were long gone; as Jack Jones, Hugh Scanlon and Joe Gormley had discovered, they were quick to jeer if their leaders failed to deliver the goods. And behind all this lay a deeper shift. As the Marxist historian Eric Hobsbawm had pointed out that spring, consumerism and individualism had smashed the British labour movement into competing 'groups, each pursuing its own economic interest irrespective of the rest'. Appeals to working-class solidarity had lost their force; having known nothing but affluence, most young workers no longer saw themselves as foot soldiers in the army of labour. They dreamed of new cars, colour televisions and foreign holidays, not the inevitable triumph of socialism. They were tired of being told to wait for jam tomorrow; they wanted jam today, tomorrow and the day after that. They might be children of the 1960s, but they were also Thatcherites in waiting.[11]

Against this background, probably no incomes policy could have succeeded. Although Callaghan and Healey had brought inflation down to single figures, they had done so only by stoking bitterness among millions of ordinary workers, furious at seeing their earnings held back by deals in Downing Street. Those resentments were bound to boil over eventually, and the only remarkable thing is that they did not do so earlier. Polls showed that many people had little confidence in government-sponsored pay restraint: in 1977, for example, only 27 per cent thought it might succeed. Lack of faith became self-fulfilling: because people thought the policy was bound to collapse, they were even keener to grab what they could in case they fell behind. Indeed, even before Callaghan had officially unveiled the 5 per cent policy, miners, road hauliers, car workers, local authority manual workers, doctors, dentists, police officers and civil servants were all protesting that they had been uniquely hard done by and clamouring for new deals. Even people at the very top were demanding big increases: in June 1978 the government's pay review body handed deals worth a whopping 30 per cent to senior judges, top civil servants and the chairmen of nationalized industries, with some getting as much as 70 per cent. In this context, the union leaders were always likely to heed the frustrations of their members. 'There is no ambiguity at all and no qualification,' said Moss Evans, leader of Britain's largest union. 'The TGWU does not support pay restraint.'[12]

If Jack Jones and Hugh Scanlon had still been on the scene, it is just possible confrontation might have been avoided. But it was Callaghan's bad luck that both had just retired, giving way to much less charismatic and experienced men. Scanlon's successor as leader of the AUEW, Terry Duffy, was a relative moderate, but with so many of his members demanding wage increases, he was not strong enough to lend Downing Street much support. The key figure, though, was Jones's successor at the TGWU, the amiable, rotund little Welshman Moss Evans. During his election campaign, Evans had promised to devolve power to the shop stewards, allowing local representatives, not the national leadership, to set the pace in pay negotiations. From the start, he urged Callaghan to '"back off" and let the unions get on with the job of securing the best settlements they could', promising that they could be trusted 'to behave responsibly'. As events were to show, Evans had a funny idea of what constituted responsible behaviour. It is true that he was coming under intense grass-roots pressure to put his members' ambitions first; even so, he was supposed to be a leader, not a ventriloquist's dummy. Denis Healey thought that Evans 'had no leadership qualities and little loyalty to the Labour Party', while the political journalist Edward Pearce thought he lacked 'courage, mind and energy to work even for mitigation of the mood'. Callaghan's biographer, Kenneth Morgan, even blames Evans for 'eleven years of Thatcherism'. Perhaps that is a bit strong; even so, Evans's performance over the next few months made Ally MacLeod look like a model of leadership.[13]

Given these conditions, Callaghan's decision to go for 5 per cent had all the tactical cunning of a general leading his cavalry straight at the enemy batteries. His pay policy, argues one typical academic account, was 'unrealistic' and 'inflammatory', leaving the shop stewards no choice but to lead their men out. Even Denis Healey later claimed that Callaghan had been 'blind' to political reality, lamenting that his 'hubris in fixing a pay norm of five per cent without any support from the TUC met its nemesis, as inevitably as in a Greek tragedy'. (This is more than a little self-serving: after all, Healey had been as involved as anyone in devising the policy.) If the government had merely insisted that all pay settlements come in at under 10 per cent, Healey thought, they would have 'retained the support of the unions, avoided the Winter of Discontent and won the election'. But this is very doubtful.* All the evidence of the previous twelve months suggests that the shop stewards were spoiling for a fight, while even ordinary members were keen to get as much as they could. As Callaghan's special adviser David Lipsey later remarked, it was absurd to imagine that 'if we had had a 7 per cent policy ... the Ford workers would have said, "Ooh, 7 per cent, that sounds quite enough for me", when they could have 17 per cent'. What the Winter of Discontent proved was not that a 5 per cent policy was dead, but that *any* incomes policy was dead, whether 5 per cent, 7 per cent or even 10 per cent. In Lipsey's words, 'it wasn't about the numbers. It became rapidly a trial of strength' – a battle, it turned out, for which very few of Callaghan's ministers had the stomach.[14]

Like Heath before him, Callaghan insisted on appealing to vague ideas of national solidarity. Like Heath, he failed to grasp the gathering resentment on the shop floor, or to see that most union members no longer danced to their leaders' tune. And like Heath, he was essentially punished for doing the right thing. Lipsey later recalled Callaghan's reaction when his political secretary, Tom McNally, questioned whether the 5 per cent policy was realistic. 'Are you saying, Tom, that 5 per cent would not be best for the country?' Callaghan said angrily, thumping the table for emphasis. And of course he was right. A return to high inflation would mean not just higher prices and reduced living standards, but failing businesses, rising unemployment and redoubled misery for the poorest and most vulnerable people in the country. As Callaghan knew, inflationary pressures were growing: with the Shah's regime tottering in Iran, the world was poised on the brink of a second oil shock.

---

* Given that the polls were so close in the autumn of 1978, it is hard to see how Labour could possibly have won in 1979. If Callaghan had given the unions everything they wanted, he would have driven up inflation and pushed non-union and middle-class voters further towards the Tories. On the other hand, if he had browbeaten the unions into accepting his pay policy, many union members would surely have voted Conservative in protest. The truth is that a clear Labour victory in 1978 or 1979 was probably impossible (or at least very unlikely), because middle-class defectors who had voted Liberal in 1974 were *always* likely to return to the Tory fold.

Even a supposedly stringent 5 per cent guideline, reported the Number 10 Policy Unit, would 'simply stop [inflation] from going up'. Pay restraint might be politically difficult, wrote Bernard Donoughue, but it was also 'the only way of avoiding high inflation – and avoiding the monetary squeeze and high unemployment which would inevitably follow such inflation'. It was unquestionably popular: polls showed that even most trade unionists thought Callaghan was doing the right thing. But as Edward Heath could have told him, prime ministers who put economic rigour ahead of narrow self-interest do not always get the rewards they deserve.[15]

It was on Monday, 25 September, in the grey, dusty surroundings of the Ford plant at Dagenham, Essex, that Callaghan's government began to fall apart. A few days earlier, shop stewards at Ford's Escort plant on Merseyside had ordered their men out in protest at the company's 5 per cent pay offer. At Daventry, Swansea, Southampton and Basildon, other men followed suit, but everybody was waiting to see what happened at Dagenham. They did not have to wait long. At eight that morning, some 2,000 body-plant workers crowded into the cavernous factory canteen for a mass meeting. On a bare stage at the far end, a TGWU shop steward with a malfunctioning loudhailer read out the news that Ford had turned down their demand for a thirty-five-hour working week and a pay rise of £20 a week. The firm's annual profits, he said, were £300 million. 'We want some of that money ... If we accept 5 per cent this year, when inflation is at 8 per cent, what will happen next year when inflation is 12 per cent? We will soon be facing legislation for a cut in wages.' The only answer, he said, was 'a cessation of production. We will stop everybody working on this site. We will get the outside contractors off the premises. We will get the security guards off the gates and take them over ourselves.'

Then, amid cheers from the crowd, another shop steward took over the loudhailer: 'We will put it to the vote right away. Now let us have a straight vote, a good clean vote. You all understand what this means, don't you? It means you are on strike from today. Everybody understand that? Right, all those in favour.' At that, a watching reporter wrote, the canteen was 'thick with a forest of hands, white, brown and ebony'. 'Right, hands down,' the shop steward said. 'Any against?' About a dozen hands went up; 'all eyes turned on them and they were roundly booed by the majority.' They had been at work for just sixteen minutes, but the day was over. 'That's it then,' men said to each other as they swarmed towards the exits. Outside, a few made a dash for the bus stop, but most 'hung loosely around the gates, as if thinking it unwise to return to busy wives at 8.30 in the morning'. 'What do we do now?' one young recruit asked. 'Down the social security, innit?' an older man replied. 'Right. Are they open yet?' asked the first man. 'Not yet, stupid,' the second said. 'You get paid this week.'[16]

For the government, the Ford strike was a disaster. The very next day the AUEW made the Ford strike official, while the TGWU confirmed that it would soon follow suit. Ordinary workers, explained the shop stewards in a letter to the Prime Minister, felt 'a deep sense of betrayal'. The policy of wage restraint had done 'irreparable damage to the Labour Party', and at Dagenham there was 'a growing hostility to the continuation of a Labour Government'. Already other unions were pledging support: a spokesman for the National Union of Public Employees (NUPE) told the press that 'the 5 per cent pay policy is just not on. It is not on at Ford and it is not on in the public sector for low-paid workers'. And if Callaghan thought that Moss Evans would assert his authority and restrain his men, he had another think coming. As Evans argued, wages at Ford had been steadily falling behind those at the publicly owned British Leyland, so the shop stewards' demands were perfectly reasonable. The ideal solution, he suggested, would be to give workers in *both* companies a raise of about 30 per cent. That was hardly in the spirit of the Social Contract, but then, as Evans explained to Tony Benn, the Social Contract was dead. He had heard all Callaghan's pieties about the public interest before. 'The rank and file of our people are the public too,' he explained, 'and we are just as much members of the public as those who don't want wage increases.' The TGWU, he added, was ready for a long fight. 'We can take that; we've got £32 million in the bank.'[17]

A week later the Labour party conference met in Blackpool. If the atmosphere was less apocalyptic than it had been three years earlier, during the IMF crisis, it was nonetheless remarkably fractious. On its first full day the conference debated a resolution from Liverpool Wavertree rejecting 'any wage restraint, by whatever method, including cash limits, and specifically the Government's 5 per cent'. From the start it was clear that emotion was running against the leadership. 'You know what percentages do for the lower paid,' Alan Fisher, leader of NUPE, exhorted the delegates. 'It gives least to those who need it most and most to those who need it least.' 'Let us make no bones about it,' agreed another delegate. 'If the Government persist in attempting to impose the 5 per cent limit, they will be committing political suicide. The 5 per cent limit will undermine their support among the working classes. You can only stretch an elastic band so far. Inevitably, it has to snap.'

In reply, Michael Foot gave one of his characteristically impassioned rhetorical performances. 'If we were to see inflation going upwards, ten per cent, fifteen per cent, twenty per cent, it certainly would not assist the low-paid workers,' he thundered. 'If you have a Tory Government, what sort of wages policy do you think you are going to have? You can have a wages policy imposed by mass unemployment, far worse unemployment than anything we have experienced – that is the Keith Joseph–Thatcher policy.' (As Callaghan later remarked: 'No one can complain that Michael did not warn them.') There was also a memorable intervention from the railwaymen's moderate leader Sid Weighell, aimed directly at NUPE's Alan Fisher:

> Look what is lining up ahead. Twenty per cent, 35-hour week, a month's holiday for Ford's. Alan wants forty per cent. This is what they call 'responsible collective bargaining'. Responsible? Really? . . .
>
> My union helped to create this party. The union that sponsored the conference that created the Labour Party. I am not going to stand here and destroy it. But if you want the call to go out at this conference that the new philosophy of the Labour Party is that you believe in the philosophy of the pig trough – those with the biggest snout get the biggest share – I reject it.

But it was Fisher, backed by the TGWU and AUEW block votes, who carried the day. In a stunning humiliation for the government, the conference voted by two to one for the Liverpool resolution. On the platform, Denis Healey, who had given a typically barnstorming performance, looked 'obviously depressed'. And, as had become traditional, Tony Benn struggled to contain his delight at his own government's defeat. 'The result was dazzling,' he recorded, 'and Jim's whole position now is endangered.'[18]

Even now Callaghan believed the union leaders would remain loyal. In his speech the next day, he broke off from his text to chat candidly about his desire for peace, almost apologizing for his failure to win greater support and imploring the unions to act 'responsibly' in the months to come. It was a 'masterly performance', declared the press, and the voters seemed to like it too: the next Gallup poll gave Labour a

5 per cent lead. 'It also shows a massive support for incomes policy, particularly among trade unionists!' noted Donoughue. He was not exaggerating: two out of three voters, as well as a staggering 69 per cent of union members, said they approved of Callaghan's 5 per cent limit. Relations with the TUC top brass were still cordial: at an 'open and friendly' dinner a week later, Callaghan found the union leaders 'anxious to avoid a rift'. 'I keep reading that our 5% is finished,' he told Donoughue. 'But nobody has told me a better way to fight inflation. Of course we shall lose some. But I mean to stick to it. I am not going to give up now.' Healey, too, remained relatively optimistic, telling the Cabinet that he had spent the last few weeks talking quietly to the TUC. He was confident, he said, that they would soon agree a vaguely conciliatory document which would 'restore the TUC to a position of helpful neutrality'. With the TUC withdrawing from the battlefield, the militants would back down, the pay demands would subside and everything would fall into place.[19]

But fate had an unpleasant surprise for Denis Healey. On 14 November the TUC General Council met to approve the statement. The hours went by; no word emerged. 'Then at 5 p.m. we heard the devastating news that the TUC had rejected the pay agreement,' wrote Donoughue. 'Nobody had expected this, [and] now that we had lost it, we all realized how much we wanted the agreement.' What had happened was almost beyond belief. Although the TUC's Economic Committee had unanimously backed the deal in the morning, the General Council then got itself in a terrible mess. When the vote was taken, Sid Weighell was outside giving a broadcast interview, while another moderate, the steelworkers' leader Bill Sirs, voted against the deal because he did not want to alienate his members and was convinced it was going to pass anyway. Most incredibly of all, the TGWU leader Moss Evans – who had co-written the crucial document – had chosen this moment to take a holiday in Malta, and so missed the vote entirely. As a result the General Council was tied at 14–14, and although the chairman, the postmen's leader Tom Jackson, personally favoured the deal, TUC convention banned him from using his casting vote. The upshot was that the deal was dead. As Callaghan's fiercely pro-Labour biographer Kenneth Morgan remarks, 'there could hardly have been a clearer demonstration of incompetence and irresponsibility by the union leaders'. In Downing Street, Healey was furious; even Callaghan had never seen him so 'downcast and disappointed'. But at least one of their colleagues was pleased. 'It's a real kick in the teeth for the corporate state,' wrote Tony Benn.[20]

Meanwhile the Ford strike rumbled into its sixth week. By the beginning of November the company had lost 79,000 vehicles at a cost of some £300 million. In desperation, it made a 'final' offer of 16½ per cent – and to universal disbelief, the TGWU turned it down. Almost a third of the projected increase, union officials complained, was dependent on 'workers turning up on time and avoiding wild-cat strikes'. Who could possibly stand for that? 'We are not prepared to accept a situation,' said the TGWU's chief negotiator Ron Todd, 'where a worker may lose pay on a foreman's say-so simply because he is late in after, for example, taking his wife to hospital.' Other car firms drew the only possible lesson: a few days later, Vauxhall bought off its workers at Luton and Dunstable with an offer of almost 9 per cent. The postmen's leader, Tom Jackson, warned his colleagues against a 'mad wages scramble', insisting that no union had 'a God-given right to 30, 40 or 50 per cent'. But by this stage, Ford had lost their appetite for the fight. 'We were going downhill fast, losing sales to companies that were being subsidised by the Government up in Birmingham,' recalled Ford's industrial director, 'and we thought "enough is enough".' On 15 November they dropped the penalty clause for lateness, and a week later the TGWU concluded a deal giving their men a 17 per cent raise. Callaghan's incomes strategy was dead. 'Management and workers between them', said the *Express*, 'have driven a battle tank right through the Government's five per cent pay limit.'[21]

Watching in horror from Number 10, Callaghan was determined to make an example of Ford by withdrawing government business, as Whitehall had done in the past. The car giant, he thought, was a bellwether – 'where Ford would go the others would follow' – which made it even more important to reassert his authority. Some of his ministers were wavering: at Cabinet on 7 December, even the right-wing Bill Rodgers bluntly asked 'whether it was worth sticking to 5% if it was going to be breached quite often'. Callaghan promptly 'slapped him down'. The policy 'commanded broad support among the public, among Labour Party supporters and among trade unionists', he insisted. His own backbenchers, however, had other ideas. On 13 December a revolt by the left-wing Tribune Group smashed Callaghan's plans for 'sanctions' against employers who broke the 5 per cent guideline. 'Those who most loudly preach socialism also most often practise disloyalty to

Labour and give comfort to the Tories,' observed a caustic Donoughue, who nearly got into a fight with a group of left-wing MPs after telling them that 'Mrs Thatcher was going to put them in her first honours list'. Some ministers thought they should now scrap the 5 per cent policy, or even call an immediate election. Instead Callaghan preferred to soldier on. But as David Owen remarked, 'sanctions were like a finger in a dyke; once removed the whole edifice of restraint collapsed'. It was at that moment, he thought, that the Labour left handed Margaret Thatcher the keys to Number 10.[22]

With sanctions defeated, the wage scramble was on. Low-paid manual workers squeezed after years of restraint; white-collar workers eager to flex their muscles; skilled engineering workers keen to maintain their lead – everybody wanted his share. The bad old days of 1975 seemed to have returned: by the end of November, local authority manual workers had put in for a 40 per cent increase, NHS auxiliary workers for 40 per cent, the miners for 40 per cent, British Leyland's manual workers for 30 per cent, the nation's bakery workers for 22 per cent and British Oxygen gas workers for 20 per cent, in what Callaghan called a 'never-ending stream' of demands. Day after day, he begged the union leaders to remember the virtues of solidarity. What he never grasped, though, was that they too were prisoners of events, swept along like drowning men in a foaming sea. The tanker and lorry drivers, for example, had almost walked out the previous winter, eventually settling after an overtime ban. Now they were impatient to get what they thought they deserved. In 1978, a typical tanker driver earned about £100 a week (the equivalent of around £700 a week today), which meant they were far better paid than many other TGWU members. But they wanted more. On 15 November, the Employment Secretary, Albert Booth, reported that their representatives were demanding increases worth a staggering 60 per cent, well beyond their employers' ability to pay. In reply, Callaghan advised him to recommend 5 per cent, but to go to 8½ per cent if necessary. Confrontation seemed inevitable.[23]

Once again Callaghan hoped that Moss Evans would step in to moderate the shop stewards' demands. Once again the TGWU chief had no intention of putting his neck on the line. His only priority, he announced, was 'to look after my members' pay claims'. As Callaghan later observed, Evans had effectively 'washed his hands of any responsibility for the long-term effect of his actions'. So the dispute headed inexorably towards disaster. By 5 December shop stewards at Esso and Shell had called for a strike in the New Year, while Texaco's shop stewards imposed an immediate overtime ban. 'The oil companies are now seriously concerned at the virtual certainty, in their view, of a national strike in January,' the Prices Secretary, Roy Hattersley, reported to his colleagues. His officials had made it clear that any deal 'must be capable of justification under the 5% guidelines', but he was not optimistic. In fact there was rather more flexibility in the government's approach than is often thought: by 14 December, the oil companies were offering almost 13 per cent, with the increase over 5 per cent to be justified by vague 'productivity proposals'. But it was no good. Just as at Ford, the shop stewards scented blood: they wanted 40 per cent, or they were out. 'Unless the companies seek their own salvation, we are heading for a national stoppage on 3 January,' Hattersley wrote. Inside Whitehall, a mood of grim despair was taking hold. A national strike would 'lead to the virtual stoppage of the road haulage industry, which would affect all sectors of the economy', predicted a confidential Treasury paper. In the middle of winter, fuel shortages seemed inevitable. History was repeating itself: it was the three-day week all over again.[24]

It is a myth that the government was totally unprepared for what came next. As early as 21 November the Cabinet Office's Civil Contingencies Unit prepared a secret plan called Operation Drumstick, which called for troops to be put on seventy-two-hour standby, so that if the government declared a state of emergency, the army could step in and drive the oil tankers. As the blueprint admitted, though, there were obvious risks, notably the 'strong likelihood' that tanker drivers would sabotage their vehicles before the troops got to them. The other problem was timing: the army would need ten days' notice to be ready by the time the government proclaimed a state of emergency, and it would take another seven days before oil distribution was even '30 per cent of normal'. In early December, the Prime Minister's principal private secretary, Ken Stowe, sent him a detailed timetable, requiring Callaghan to declare a state of emergency on 4 January so that the army could be deployed by the 12th. Again, Stowe noted the dangers: even if the police guarded depots 'to stop any attempt at break-in or sabotage', there was still a risk that military preparations would provoke reprisals from the tanker drivers. Moving quickly was 'too risky', concluded a Cabinet committee on 13 December. 'There could be no guarantee that the early steps would remain covert and if they leaked out then any prospects of avoiding a strike would be seriously damaged'. Yet by this stage, rumours that Callaghan would send for the army were already sweeping Whitehall. 'We are still planning to announce a state of emergency,' recorded a worried Bernard Donoughue. 'Hundreds of troops are being specially trained to move in early in the New Year. This will be quite dramatic. Having troops on the streets strike breaking will take us beyond Ted Heath in 1974!'[25]

On 19 December, in the last Cabinet meeting before Christmas, Callaghan briefed his colleagues on the worsening situation. As Energy Secretary, Tony Benn, of all people, was in charge of the timetable. 'The instructors would be training drivers on Boxing Day,' he explained; 'on 29 December we would go to Sandringham for the Privy Council to declare a state of emergency; on the 30th and 31st we would requisition 4000 tankers; on 2 January the strike would begin and we would recall Parliament; on 5 January Parliament would be asked to approve the state of emergency,' and so on. Nobody liked the sound of that. 'The way all this has been described,' Callaghan muttered, 'I can see an enormous Thatcher victory. I wonder whether life in these islands will break down' – an extraordinary thing for the man at the top to say. But for the time being most ministers shrank from the thought of using the army. Two days later, the *Guardian* reported that British units were being 'secretly trained in Germany to run essential services', and on 22 December the same paper claimed that '15,000 soldiers will be mobilised between Christmas and the New Year'. 'If we're going to do it, we're bloody well going to do it well,' one senior officer remarked. Yet behind the melodramatic headlines, there was no political will to declare a state of emergency. At meeting after meeting, ministers pored over the options, yet every time they decided to wait. On 28 December, Callaghan's emergency committee went over the schedule yet again. 'I favoured Option C, which involved not doing anything,' Tony Benn recorded. And as it turned out, so did everybody else.[26]

For Callaghan's dispirited staff, Christmas came as a welcome relief. They were now 'doing little except hanging on to fight inflation', Donoughue lamented on the last day before he left for his Suffolk retreat. 'There is no question of having long-term policies.' More than ever, he regretted that they had not called an election in the autumn, 'a "window" when everything was temporarily going right'. Now, it all seemed to be going wrong. On top of everything else, five days before Christmas thousands of staff walked out at the BBC, complaining at the suspension of eleven process workers who had refused to handle freelance film. For two days both BBC channels disappeared from the airwaves, viewers' screens displaying only a brief message blaming 'industrial action by the Association of Broadcasting Staff'. In the press all was consternation; for many people, the prospect of missing out on the BBC's Christmas extravaganza, which included such delights as *The Sound of Music*, *The Two Ronnies*, an ice-dancing spectacular with John Curry and a celebrity edition of *Blankety Blank*, boasting the glittering talents of Kenny Everett, Beryl Reid, Patrick Moore, Roy Kinnear and Lorraine Chase, was almost too much to bear. At last, three days before Christmas, the government gave the BBC permission to buy off the strikers with a remarkably generous 12½ per cent deal – this on top of the 5 per cent guaranteed by the official pay policy. All talk of restraint was forgotten; what mattered was to keep the viewers happy. 'We sold our pay policy,' one minister remarked, 'to have *The Sound of Music* on Christmas Day.'[27]

The weather that Christmas was terrible: grey, drizzly and bitterly cold. 'As the days get shorter and colder and darker,' wrote Michael Palin, 'a sort of pessimistic gloom descends.' In the streets of London he saw cars queuing outside petrol stations, desperate to fill up before the expected tanker drivers' strike. 'All in all,' he thought, 'it's siege conditions again.' In fact, Shell, Esso and Mobil had already decided to abandon the government's toothless guidelines and give their drivers 20 per cent increases, although Texaco were still holding out. In his New Year message Callaghan begged 'those who possess industrial muscle . . . not to abuse their great strength'. But by now few people were listening. Even the elements had turned against the government: on the evening of Saturday, 30 December, heavy snow began to fall. In Hampstead, Palin looked out 'in glee as the powdery snow, driven by a sharp, south-easterly wind, covered Oak Village'. The next day, driving through a 'wondrously empty' London, he relished the spectacle of the streets 'white with caked snow . . . the Houses of Parliament floodlit and the bridge still uncleared'. And that night the snow kept falling. In Piccadilly Circus and Trafalgar Square, the crowds of New Year revellers were smaller than usual, while in Scotland the roads into Edinburgh were closed by thick snow and freezing fog. On New Year's Day only three out of forty-eight Football League fixtures went ahead, with Ron Atkinson's West Bromwich Albion taking the chance to pull level with Liverpool at the top of the table. The only other First Division match to kick off, between Bolton and Everton, had to be abandoned at half-time after 'driving snow obliterated the lines on the pitch'.

Still the snow came down. On the first evening of 1979, Manchester suffered the worst blizzard since the First World War. On Tuesday morning all postal services and milk deliveries were cancelled, while British Rail forecast 'severe delays' and the AA asked drivers to stay off the roads unless absolutely necessary, and to take a shovel and a flask of tea if they really had to travel. In north Wales the roads were covered with four inches of ice; in Scotland the beer froze in pub cellars. In Lancashire dozens of drivers abandoned their cars and trudged through the snow to find help; in Kent, hundreds of holidaymakers were trapped in the roads outside the Channel ports; in Cornwall, a midwife, armed with three candles and a kettle of water boiled on an open fire, helped a mother give birth in a house cut off from electricity and water. And in south Devon, the newly married Scott and Valerie Healey tramped through the snow-filled lanes in a desperate bid to get to their wedding reception, which was being held in Essex, 300 miles away. 'Hanging onto their suitcases, [they] clambered down a cliff to reach a fishing boat on an isolated beach at South Hams,' a reporter wrote. 'After a 20-mile boat trip they reached Plymouth and caught a train for Essex.' They made it in the end – only twenty-four hours late.[28]

In Downing Street the atmosphere was deathly quiet. Callaghan's right-hand man Ken Stowe had flu, while his private secretary for home affairs, Tim Lankester, was still snowed in. Many of Callaghan's ministers were stranded in their constituencies. Tony Benn, for example, was snowed in at Stansgate, Essex, with his family, although on Tuesday a snowplough cleared a path so they could buy some food from the village. Meanwhile Bernard Donoughue drove back from Suffolk 'in glorious sunshine, but so cold that the car windows kept on icing up on the *inside*'. Every now and again he had to stop, shivering and grumbling, to clear the windscreen. 'Even on the motorway there was only one lane free of snow,' he wrote in his diary. 'The local authorities had made no attempt to clear the roads – still more evidence, if more were needed, that our local government provides *no* services at all now and that local government employees are the worst "scroungers on the welfare state".' He was not alone in his fury: with local authority gritters observing an overtime ban, many roads were in a terrible condition. In Essex, Bedfordshire and parts of Surrey, there did not appear to have been any gritting at all. But in a preview of what was to come, the NUPE boss Alan Fisher refused to accept any blame. 'The roads are in the disgraceful state they are now,' he said defiantly, 'not because of the men but because of the penny-pinching employers.'[29]

On Wednesday the 3rd, Donoughue spent the morning with his son on Hampstead Heath, sledging in the snow. 'It was lovely, very cold and sunny, and the hillside was covered with children,' he wrote. But when he got to Number 10 that afternoon, he found the Prime Minister in remarkably gloomy form. At midnight the Scottish lorry drivers had walked out, and by the early afternoon there were reports of English drivers doing the same. The picture was confused; in Kent the drivers were still on the roads, but in major ports like Liverpool, Tilbury and Hull there was already heavy picketing. 'Things were drifting,' Callaghan muttered bleakly:

> What is going on? This doesn't look good. There is an ominous calm. Everything is quiet here in government. Denis has gone away to the country. But I don't like the smell of it. We shall wake up in a few weeks' time and find that it is too late, everybody is settling for 20%. I have never believed very much in incomes policy: it doesn't make a great deal of difference – except when people start settling for 20%. If they were 'responsible' and settled for 8% it wouldn't matter. But this does not look good. It will destroy our competitiveness, inflation will roar and we shall have more unemployment.

Callaghan had no intention of giving the drivers what they wanted: among his Christmas cards, he told Donoughue, the two most popular messages had been 'Thanks for the £10 pensioners' bonus' and 'Stick at it against inflation'. But he was worried, all the same. 'This could be the domino issue,' he said, 'where, if it falls, everything else will go with it.'[30]

On 4 January the Prime Minister flew to the Caribbean island of Guadeloupe for a summit meeting of the West's 'Big Four': the United States, Britain, France and West Germany. Seeing the bags piled up in the Number 10 hallway, Donoughue felt a 'bit envious, as it was bitterly cold here and it would be nice to lie in the Caribbean sunshine'. The weather was now worse than ever: at Heathrow, Callaghan watched and waited, wrapped up in a heavy coat and Russian-style fur hat, as airport workers dug his VC10 out of the snow. But he was unusually fortunate: later that day, British Airways claimed the conditions were too dangerous for its employees, and all flights were cancelled. And even as Callaghan's plane streaked west, more bad news was pouring into Downing Street. All over England, Wales and Northern Ireland, lorry drivers had walked out, joining their Scottish comrades. At the ports of Southampton, Hull, Liverpool and Tilbury, all work had ground to a halt. And with the transport network crippled by snow and ice, there were already reports of food shortages. 'Country roads are blocked by snow, root vegetables are frozen into the ground and greens have been damaged by frost,' announced that morning's *Express*, adding that not only were leeks 'almost unobtainable at 30p a lb', but 'the 50p cauliflower is on the way'.

Meanwhile Texaco's 1,150 oil-tanker drivers had voted to walk out, while from Scotland and the north-west came scattered reports of garages running short of petrol. And the next day's news was even worse. In Stockport, the schools closed because of shortages of heating oil; in Manchester, the dustmen refused to collect people's rubbish because they said the pavements were dangerously icy; in Hull, all major road junctions were now guarded by small groups of pickets. At Liverpool docks, where no lorries were going in or out, half a million pounds' worth of tomatoes and cucumbers from the Canary Islands lay rotting on the quayside. Butchers were complaining that no meat was getting through; farmers were worried about supplies of animal feed. At Heathrow, dozens of flights were still cancelled because of the weather; in Essex, an 84-year-old widow was found dead in her kitchen, encased in ice after she had collapsed while filling the sink. And in Downing Street the mood was grimmer by the hour. There was 'a smell in the air reminiscent of January 1974', Donoughue thought. That night he took his daughter to see Alan Ayckbourn's play *Ten Times Table* in the West End. 'It was bitterly cold,' he recorded, 'and the theatre was only half full.'[31]

What really worried Donoughue was not just the dreadful news but the '"image" problem' for Jim Callaghan, who had now arrived in Guadeloupe. 'Pictures of him basking in the Caribbean do not look good,' Donoughue thought, 'when Britain is frozen in and coming to a halt.' In fact, despite the pictures of straw huts, palm trees and gorgeous beaches, the occasion was not just a glorified holiday. For one thing, Callaghan took the opportunity to strike a vital deal with Jimmy Carter for the Trident nuclear submarine, cornering the American President in his beach hut while their wives and officials had gone off for a walk.* But when presented with pictures of Carter playing tennis with Valéry Giscard d'Estaing, glamorous young women sunbathing topless on the beaches around the world leaders' bungalows, and Audrey Callaghan sunning herself in a 'Margaret Rutherford-style hat', it was hardly sur-

---

* This incident would surely make a splendid one-act play. Callaghan wrote later that the President was 'a gentle and a good man', which is probably shorthand for 'weedy'. At mealtimes, Carter used to invite everybody to clasp hands while he said grace, which is unlikely to have gone down well with, say, Valéry Giscard d'Estaing. In retirement, Callaghan, Schmidt and Giscard often spent their summer holidays together, usually hosted by their friend Gerald Ford. Carter was not invited.

prising that the tabloids treated it as a 'costly feet up snorkelling junket for the Big Four and their wives'. One afternoon Callaghan took an inflatable dinghy out to sea; later, lubricated by gallons of rum punch, Helmut Schmidt began chopping up coconuts with a machete. To make matters worse, Callaghan had decided to move on afterwards to Barbados, spending three days at Sandy Lane, one of the most luxurious beach resorts in the world. To his aides this seemed merely a sensible way of recharging his batteries before the trials ahead. But in the tabloids, images of a sun-tanned Callaghan emerging from the sea onto the pristine Barbadian sands, as though he were Portsmouth's answer to Ursula Andress, made for a damning contrast with events at home. 'Wish We Were There, Jim!' read an envious headline in the *Daily Express*.[32]

While Callaghan enjoyed the Caribbean sunshine, the lorry drivers' strike had gone from bad to worse. On the evening of Friday, 5 January, the employers rejected a union-brokered deal that would have given the hauliers a 20 per cent increase, while the TGWU confirmed that it would shortly make the strike official. The next morning, the papers carried the first reports of panic buying. In Newcastle, one supermarket manager witnessed 'astonishing' scenes, as women literally fought for possession of the last goods on the shelves. 'Britain At Bay As Strikes Spread Panic', shrieked a typical headline on Sunday morning:

> Housewives ignored 'don't panic' pleas and went on the rampage clearing out many foodstore shelves. Some shops were completely out of frozen vegetables and tinned foods.
>
> 'They've gone absolutely mad,' said Mr Allen Barlow, manager of Bejam's frozen food centre in London's Shepherd's Bush.
>
> From all over Britain came reports of panic buying. One supermarket manager in Hyde, Cheshire, said: 'It's like watching a swarm of locusts.' At some shops there were skirmishes at check-out points, with shoppers accusing each other of switching food from other people's trolleys to their own . . .
>
> One of the biggest supermarkets on the south coast at Langney, near Eastbourne, was being emptied by shoppers faster than assistants could restock the shelves. 'People are coming in from country areas and stocking up with canned and frozen food because they think lorries won't get through,' said a spokesman.

Of course there was plenty of exaggeration in all this, and talk of 'rampages' and 'skirmishes' was over the top. But contrary to what some historians claim, this was not an 'invented' crisis. Across the country, reported the *Guardian*, petrol shortages, empty supermarkets, cancelled buses and deserted schools were adding to the sense of chaos. 'Half the oil company plants are closed either by strikes, like Texaco, or by picketing,' wrote Tony Benn after an emergency meeting with oil executives on Monday morning. 'Oil supplies are down to 50 per cent; a quarter of all filling stations are closed; in Northern Ireland there are no deliveries, as in the north-west, where supplies are down to 5 per cent. The situation is really very serious.' Already Manchester, Nottingham and many areas around London had scrapped bus services to save petrol, while Oldham and Bolton had joined Stockport in closing most of their schools. To make matters worse, the snow was falling again: in Scotland, blizzards made road travel almost impossible, while in Devon, burst pipes left many villages without mains water. And with those petrol stations that were still open now rationing supplies, drivers' tempers were running short. Outside one Willesden garage, twenty cars queued behind a van for an hour before they realized there was nobody in it. Eventually the garage owner had to call the police because, he said, 'drivers have been fighting and arguing'. 'Most garages are closed and the roads probably full of cars, like me, wasting petrol looking for a garage that's open,' wrote Michael Palin after venturing out at lunchtime.[33]

In Downing Street the bad news was piling up like snow on Scotland's roads. The lorry drivers' pickets were tighter than ever, while the train drivers were now threatening to walk out too, just as they had during the last days of Edward Heath. On Monday afternoon, Bernard Donoughue had a long talk with Denis Healey, who had 'drunk a couple of whiskies' and was 'a bit belligerent'. To forestall public sector pay demands, Donoughue thought, they should introduce legislation to keep prices down. Healey shook his head: they had already 'buggered around with industry more than any country in the world'. That evening Callaghan had arranged to ring them from the Caribbean, although his call was an hour and a half late because he was too busy 'enjoying himself in the sun'. 'Something tough would have to be done about the unions,' they all agreed. ('But when? Ever by Labour?' Donoughue wondered.) The next day, however, was even worse. 'The road haulage strike is deteriorating, and the railwaymen are going to strike,' Donoughue wrote. 'Suddenly there is madness in the air.' He thought of telling Callaghan to come home, but said nothing for fear of being thought jealous. 'Well, I am jealous,' he admitted, 'but I think they are mistaken to sit out there in the sun, with photographs of them lazing on beaches surrounded by topless women, while this country is increasingly paralysed.

There will be a backlash, and it won't help the PM's authority when he comes to tell the unions that they must take a more puritanical line.'[34]

Callaghan flew back into Heathrow in the early hours of Wednesday, 10 January. 'Welcome home, Prime Minister,' said a sarcastic editorial in that morning's *Express*. 'The Caribbean must be very nice at this time of year. But back here we have been having some trouble. Now we are hoping that you will succeed where your lieutenants have failed and actually DO something about it.' In fact, Callaghan was in good spirits, pleased at his diplomatic success and refreshed by his break. After a brief sleep on the plane, he held a quick discussion with his closest aides, Tom McNally and Tom McCaffrey, wondering whether he should talk to the press at the airport. McCaffrey thought he should wait until he had got back to Downing Street and had been given a thorough briefing. McNally, however, thought it would be a better idea to face them immediately, reasserting his authority and letting the country feel the smack of firm government. Callaghan agreed: McCaffrey, he said, 'is not a politician like we are'. A few moments after landing, his entourage hovering behind him, the Prime Minister met reporters in a Heathrow corridor. And almost as soon as he had begun speaking, McNally had a terrible sinking feeling. 'I knew in my bones', he reflected later, 'that he had got it wrong.'

Deliberately relaxed, wearing a light grey suit and sporting a slight tan, Callaghan seemed determined to play the reassuring uncle, just as he had in the past. 'Not at the moment, no,' he said dismissively when a reporter asked if he planned to call a state of emergency. 'We've been on the brink of it, I think, once or twice in the last week, but we've stepped back from it. There's no point in declaring a state of emergency.' Then another journalist asked what he thought of the criticism of his trip. And as Callaghan began to reply, McNally knew for certain that they had made a terrible mistake:

> I'm sure everybody would have liked to have been with me, but I don't think anybody except a few journalists are very jealous of it. I think that they feel that we've been working hard, as indeed we have – and do you know, [*sarcastically*] I actually swam! And I know that's the most exciting thing of the visit – but no, I think you should put all of that kind of criticism in perspective. One mustn't allow jealousy to dissuade you from doing what you know is the right thing.

On television the spectacle of a sun-tanned Prime Minister reminiscing about his holidays looked absolutely dreadful. What came next, though,

'Funeral? What funeral?' The *Express* ran this Cummings cartoon on 12 January 1979, two days after the *Sun*'s famous 'Crisis? What Crisis?' headline. Although Callaghan's premiership still had months to run, public opinion had decisively turned against the government.

was even worse. 'What is your general approach, in view of the mounting chaos in the country at the moment?' asked a man from the *Evening Standard*. At that, Callaghan looked irritated:

> Well, that's a judgement that you are making. I promise you that if you look at it from outside – and perhaps you're taking a rather parochial view at the moment – I don't think other people in the world would share the view that there is mounting chaos. You know, we've had strikes before, we've come close to the brink before, there's a need for a great deal of industrial self-discipline in this country, I hope we shall gradually learn it, and I hope we shall avoid hurting each other. But please don't run down your country by talking about 'mounting chaos'.

Again, what was so calamitous was not the words themselves but the way Callaghan said them: casual, condescending, almost self-satisfied. Even the way he rounded off the exchange reflected his complete failure to grasp the public mood. 'Now don't you think that's enough after a nine-hour flight overnight?' he asked jovially. 'And no breakfast!' Grin-

17. To more conservative observers, the Sex Pistols' lead singer John Lydon, *top*, was a symbol of everything going wrong with Britain. Despite its nihilistic image, punk sometimes had a sharp political edge: *above*, fans enjoy a Rock against Racism concert at Alexandra Palace, 1979.

18. To the surprise of the sceptics, the Silver Jubilee in the summer of 1977 was a triumph of popular patriotism. *Above*, crowds welcome the Queen to Ipswich; *below*, residents enjoy a street party in Brunswick Court, Bermondsey.

19. Sport as Celtic patriotism. *Above*, Wales's Phil Bennett takes on England in the Five Nations Championship. *Below*, Ally MacLeod and a cardboard Rod Stewart record the execrable 'Olé Ola' before Scotland's 1978 World Cup campaign.

20. When low-paid workers rebelled against Callaghan's pay policy, Britain was plunged into the Winter of Discontent. Images of burly men standing around braziers, *top*, became a cliché of national life, but women like the COHSE nurses *above* played a large part, too.

21. As the road hauliers' strike began to bite, supermarkets ran out of food, *above*. But perhaps the most memorable images of that terrible winter came from Liverpool, where a council gravediggers' strike meant the dead briefly went unburied, *below*.

22. The pictures of rubbish piling up in the streets of London were a catastrophe for the government. *Top*, shoppers try to ignore the festering bin-bags; *above*, Sir Joshua Reynolds surveys the chaos in Leicester Square.

23. 'Don't wish you were dead! There is nobody to bury you.' By early 1979, public opinion had swung decisively against the unions, as this poster in a grocer's shop suggests.

24. 'Where there is discord ...'
Left, a sun-tanned Jim
Callaghan gives the most
disastrous press conference in
recent political history;
below, Britain's first woman
Prime Minister celebrates
victory in the general election
of May 1979.

ning, he pointed to the man from the *Standard*. 'However, with the mounting chaos he talks about in the country, I doubt if I shall even find a cup of coffee, do you?'[35]

In the past, Callaghan's famous unflappability had gone down very well with the public. Even now, some viewers were impressed. 'One admires his phlegm,' wrote Kenneth Williams, no friend of the Labour Party. But most of the Prime Minister's staff recognized that he had completely misjudged the national mood. 'The danger is that the "unflappable" image will look very complacent,' wrote Bernard Donoughue that evening, while McNally himself thought it had been a 'total disaster'. The next day's newspapers made blistering reading. 'Come Off It, Jim!' scoffed the front page of the *Express*, declaring that Callaghan had carried 'coolness to the point of absurdity'. 'He had better not try that line,' the paper said, with 'workers facing lay-offs, long-suffering railway passengers, farmers whose livestock face death for want of feed-stuffs, nor with those of us forced to produce reduced-size newspapers. There IS a crisis, Mr Callaghan, and the country expects YOU to do something about it.' On the left of the page ran a sidebar:

> *What a Way To Run a Country!*
>   ICI on its knees
>   The sick are hit
>   No rail peace
>   Lay-offs nearer
>   Pickets hit food
>   Calls for action

Even the pro-Labour *Mirror* took a similar line. 'This Is Your Strife' read the bleak headline the next day, above a picture of a miserable-looking Callaghan. 'Now things will get worse,' explained the lead story, reporting that the lorry drivers' strike was intensifying. 'Food will rapidly disappear from supermarket shelves and millions of workers will be in danger of losing their jobs.' The subheading said it all: '*Chaos – Official.*'[36]

But it was the nation's new darling, Rupert Murdoch's revamped *Sun*, which coined the phrase from which Callaghan never recovered. At the beginning of 1978, the *Sun* had overtaken the *Mirror* to become Britain's bestselling paper, a remarkable achievement in just nine years. Although it still called itself a radical paper, its ethos had utterly changed under Murdoch's handpicked editor, Larry Lamb. Brash, aggressive and unashamedly populist, it revelled in sex, sport and scandal, reaching out to millions of working-class readers. Over time the *Sun*'s politics had become markedly more conservative, and Murdoch and Lamb made no secret of their admiration for Margaret Thatcher. Now the paper produced perhaps the most devastatingly effective front page in its history. 'Sun-tanned premier Jim Callaghan breezed back into Britain yesterday and asked: Crisis? What crisis?' began its lead story. 'Not even the threat of up to two million people being laid off work next week worried jaunty Jim. He blandly blamed journalists for talking of "mounting chaos" in strike-battered Britain.' Above, a gigantic headline rubbed salt in the wounds: 'Crisis? What Crisis?' Of course Callaghan had never used those words; indeed, the *Sun* had borrowed them from a headline three days earlier in the *Daily Mail*. But from that day on they hung around his neck: a painful reminder that, when it mattered most, Sunny Jim had lost his touch.[37]

31

Rats on the Town

*This time we are determined that the capital will take notice of
what we are saying, and if it means lives lost, that is how it
must be. We are fed up of being Cinderellas. This time we are
going to the ball.*

> Ambulance drivers' spokesman Bill Dunn, quoted in
> *Daily Express*, 20 January 1979

BILLY FRASER: *We can bring London's hospitals to a complete
standstill. There'll be no blood transfusions during operations, no cancer treatment, nothing – until we have brought
back the compassionate society.*
Yes Minister, 'The Compassionate Society', 23 February 1981

At the beginning of 1979, London shivered beneath a dirty blanket of
snow. In the streets, grubby cars moved gingerly under leaden skies,
their drivers anxious to avoid skidding on black ice. Outside schools
and hospitals, small knots of pickets huddled together to keep warm,
while passers-by, wrapped up in heavy coats and thick scarves, scurried
miserably through the cold, trying to ignore the heaps of sodden cardboard boxes and bursting black bin liners. Perhaps not since the war
had the capital seemed so tired, so gloomy, so downright shabby. As so
often during times of crisis, there was much talk of the 'spirit of the
Blitz'. One nightclub on Great Queen Street was even decorated in
homage to the Second World War, with murals of St Paul's wreathed in
smoke and fighter planes soaring overhead. On bare, stripped floor-
boards, drinkers sat at tables with gingham cloths beneath grimy,
enamel-shaded lamps. On the walls were framed photographs of

Winston Churchill, though his indomitable spirit seemed a very distant memory. Appropriately enough, the club was called The Blitz.

On the night of 6 February, The Blitz tried something a little different. Hurrying through the cold, past the walls of rotting rubbish, regulars found the door guarded by a young Welshman with heavy make-up and extravagantly sculpted hair. At the age of just 19, Steve Strange had persuaded the owners to let him run a regular Tuesday 'Electro-Diskow' night, building on his success at a grubby gay bar called Billy's in Soho. Membership cost £2 and entry £1, but Strange was very particular about the people he allowed in. His approach, he said, was inspired by David Bowie's song 'Heroes': he wanted a club for 'people who created unique identities'. To get in, visitors had to have the right look, the right style; while extravagant make-up, elaborate hair and colourful clothes helped, it was also a question of attitude. 'Maybe a lot of it was escapism, but for me, it wasn't just dressing up for the night,' Strange recalled. The Blitz was not a club for identikit punks; it was a club for their successors, people who stood apart from the crowd. Many early visitors were fashion students from St Martin's College; another was the *Evening Standard*'s pop columnist David Johnson, who recalled that inside, 'Hammer Horror met Rank starlet. Here was Lady Ample Eyeful, there Sir Gesting Sharpfellow, lads in breeches and frilly shirts, white stockings and ballet pumps, girls as Left Bank whores or stiletto-heeled vamps dressed for cocktails in a Berlin cabaret, wicked witches, kohl-eyed ghouls, futuristic man machines.' As the young Gary Kemp recalled, they wore high heels and feather boas, took speed in the toilets, checked their hair in the mirrors in the ladies and 'shouted at each other about Italian futurism, Russian constructivism or English hooliganism'. And in the background throbbed the relentless sound of Kraftwerk, Gina X and Giorgio Moroder: 'hard-edged European disco, synth-led but bass-heavy', a world away from the retro-austerity of punk.[1]

Like so many youth subcultures, the scene pioneered in the shabby surroundings of The Blitz was both nostalgic and forward-looking. Novel as they might seem after three years of spiky-haired, leather-jacketed punks, the wedge haircuts and frilly shirts were nothing new. Steve Strange had cut his teeth as the host of a David Bowie night in Soho, and Kemp, too, was a keen Bowie fan. In part, dressing up was their homage to the great man, a tribute to the art and artifice of the early 1970s. Two or three years earlier they had been punks; but now punk was dying. 'The original glamorous support had melted away, either forming their own bands or going back to the disco,' Kemp recalled. The Sex Pistols and the Clash now left him cold, while his amateur band the Gentry, formed with his brother Martin and a group of school friends, was 'meant to be ironic, an anti-punk statement'. Like so many aspiring pop musicians, Kemp dreamed of escaping the grimy routine of daily life – 'the city was broken, it was a horrible place' – and saw glamour (and glam) as the answer. His schoolmate and later manager Steve Dagger looked back even further, to the nightclubs and discotheques of London in the 1960s, when the economy had been buoyant and British pop stars proudly flew the Union Jack. 'I badly wanted a new swinging London,' Dagger said later. And threadbare and decrepit as it might seen, The Blitz was where their dreams of a new swinging scene began to take shape, fuelled by speckled blue pills and the futuristic sound of the Yamaha synthesizer. 'We are making the most contemporary statement', Kemp told the press a few months later, 'in fashion and music.'[2]

At the time, the so-called Blitz Kids saw themselves as the voice of a generation. 'Young people are no longer prepared to be sold clothes they don't like or go to clubs playing records they don't want to hear, being run by grunters three times their age, and having to pay for the privilege,' explained one regular, a St Martin's fashion student called Chris Sullivan, for whom punk was already the music of the past. Later, music critics often claimed that Strange, Kemp and their friends were pioneering the soundtrack of the New Right, 'style over substance', 'Thatcherism on vinyl'. Yet there was more to their politics than met the eye. Four of the five members of Kemp's band Spandau Ballet had fathers with trade union connections, while all but the lead singer, Tony Hadley, were Labour voters. Their background was working-class, but their ambitions were a long way from Tony Benn's idea of working-class values. Born in 1959, Gary Kemp had grown up in a typical working-class north London household, in a terraced council house with no bathroom and a brick toilet in the back yard. Like millions of other young Britons in the dying days of the 1970s, he dreamed of a better life, a life of style and comfort and material security. Later, when Kemp bought his first house, gazing at his 'church candles and interior magazines on the black enamelled coffee table ... with a glass of claret in my hand and something light and choral on the stereo', he felt a 'strong sense of denying everything my family was'. But that, too, was entirely typical: millions of other people also felt that way. Some were

Thatcher voters, but not all of them; some were even trade union members. And in the opening months of 1979, even as Kemp and his friends were shivering outside The Blitz, they too wanted their seasons in the sun.[3]

When Jim Callaghan got back to Number 10 from Heathrow, his first thought was to ring the trade union leaders and ask for help. Ten years earlier, the Keeper of the Cloth Cap had put his neck on the line for the unions, using all his experience to block Barbara Castle's reforms, and insisting that, if left alone, they would always behave responsibly. But now he was in for a shock. On Thursday, 11 January, the day after Callaghan's return, the TGWU leader Moss Evans declared the hauliers' strike official. In the newspapers, the prognosis was bleaker than ever. In Scotland, more terrible weather meant most roads were completely blocked by snow and ice. In Northern Ireland, 'already half-paralysed by a shortage of oil and a lack of essential raw materials', the heaviest snows for sixteen years brought the entire transport network to a halt. In north Wales the mountain passes were closed by snow; in the north-west, cars struggled along a single lane of the M6. And at an early morning meeting of senior ministers, there were the first signs that Callaghan's colleagues were abandoning ship, with the Health Secretary, David Ennals, begging that NHS workers be made a special case. 'This man has no balls,' wrote a contemptuous Bernard Donoughue. 'His bottle has completely gone. Last November he was all for others taking sanctions to force the Ford management to take on their strike. Now he is facing the crunch in the NHS, where he is the minister responsible, his nerve has gone, he wants to run and even to argue that the whole government should run as well, as cover for his own cowardice.'[4]

A few hours later, Callaghan met his full Cabinet for the first time since December. He was 'all bronzed', yet his mood could not have been more sombre. 'The 5% is not working and it now looks as if we are getting 15–20 per cent settlements,' Callaghan said. 'The TUC simply can't help us at the moment and we can no longer rely on them. I must tell colleagues to prepare for an Election in the near future. We must go to the public, and I don't know whether the unions will come with us because they have not helped us over the last two years.' Benn jumped in and complained that 'there is a mass media attack now on the trade unions of a kind I have never seen before'. 'The trade unions are responsible!' snapped Harold Lever, while Callaghan observed that Moss Evans should 'stand up and take control, as Jack [Jones] would have done'. Yet for the first time there was a sense that Callaghan himself was losing heart. At a committee meeting that evening, he looked 'tired and grey': when one minister asked if they had to stick to 5 per cent for public sector workers, it was Roy Hattersley, not Callaghan, who said: 'Yes.' There was 'a strong whiff of Pétainism in the air', wrote Donoughue, who noted that 'Ennals, Foot and Booth were retreating out of sight'. The election, he thought, was lost. 'We have slipped badly, seeming out of touch, and helpless before the irresponsible power of the trade unions. I think of poor Ted Heath!'[5]

Over the next few days the pickets tightened their grip. In an unprecedented bid to keep supplies to farms, hospitals and nursing homes flowing, Callaghan set up emergency committees in London, Birmingham, Manchester, Leeds, Bristol, Cambridge, Reading, Newcastle, Nottingham, Cardiff and Edinburgh, whose job was to liaise with the local TGWU. The Civil Contingencies Unit, meanwhile, was now sending reports to Downing Street every three hours. Yet for all the impression of activity, the government had effectively been reduced to a spectator. Every day more sleet and snow came down; every day more bad news came in. On Friday, British Airways staff walked out because, in the confusion caused by the bad weather, the airline had put a long-haul plane on the London–Paris route, breaking the agreed demarcation lines. In Manchester the water and sewage workers walked out, defying their union's entreaties to accept a 9 per cent pay offer. In the West Midlands, stoppages in the car industry meant that 750,000 men were scheduled to be laid off, with 50,000 having already been laid off in the North-west and another 10,000 in Yorkshire. With the nation's only rock-salt supplier blockaded by pickets, road conditions were worsening.

And there was more. On Saturday, the papers reported that starving pigs were turning to cannibalism, while fighting broke out between police and bakery workers outside a factory in Berkshire. To add insult to injury, government figures now showed that prices had officially doubled since Harold Wilson's return in March 1974. As the *Guardian* pointed out, this was a reminder of the 'appalling danger' of giving in to the lorry drivers' demands. Yet 'a deal will have to be done', it said miserably, 'even though it means mortgaging our inflationary future still more than it has been mortgaged in recent months'. Even the nation's only liberal paper was losing faith with Labour. 'We need something better,' the editorial concluded, 'because the logic of the present situation is starkly clear: jobs lost, prices soaring. And if it continues much longer then a battered electorate will surely begin to ask: Could it be any worse under Mrs Thatcher?'[6]

Almost every hour, it seemed, brought more terrible news. On Monday the 15th, the Ministry of Agriculture reported severe shortages of 'sugar, butter, salt, breakfast cereals, biscuits and margarine' in the nation's supermarkets. In Scotland, processed and frozen foods had now largely disappeared; in industry, the situation was worse than ever, with the disruption of ICI deliveries affecting 'textiles, footwear, paper, pharmaceuticals, aircraft manufacture and other chemical and plastic manufacture'. In south Wales, a disgruntled farmer fired a shotgun at pickets outside a flour mill in Abergavenny, injuring three of them; in Greater Manchester, a million people were now suffering water shortages, their taps producing only a trickle of black sludge. Slowly but surely, panic was setting in. 'When Radio Blackburn began broadcasting advice on how to prepare for an emergency,' reported the *Guardian*, 'consumers reached for every container in sight and drew off far more water than normal.' And as if life were not already disturbingly close to a scene from the post-apocalyptic series *Survivors*, the train drivers walked out on Monday evening, bringing the entire network to a standstill. The next morning, the Confederation of British Industry predicted that within a week a million people would be thrown out of work. 'The general situation is getting worse,' read Callaghan's civil service briefing, noting that ICI production was down to 60 per cent and British Steel production was at 76 per cent. Even Sainsbury's and Marks & Spencer, those twin pillars of the British high street, were now running out of food.[7]

On Tuesday, 16 January, Callaghan sounded the retreat. Having decided to 'go further in an attempt to ease the situation', he told the Commons, the government was prepared to relax its 5 per cent pay policy for the low paid, adopting a 'comparability' principle for public sector workers that would allow them to claim larger increases. He sounded as cheerful as ever, but there was no disguising the fact that his pay policy was dead. And although Callaghan made a point of condemning the hauliers' 'indefensible' secondary picketing, most observers awarded the laurels to Mrs Thatcher, who had opened with a blazing attack on the unions. 'On this occasion,' declared the *Guardian*, 'it was Mrs Thatcher, waxing furiously indignant, who spoke for the country while Mr Callaghan was the prisoner of the Labour Movement. He was reduced to explaining why this could not be done or that would not be wise and the inevitable effect of such weary urbanity was the impression of a Government strapped for an answer to the country's difficulties.'

Watching from the gallery, Bernard Donoughue thought the Conservative leader had been 'extremely effective, passionate and with a slashing attack on the excesses of union power. Typical of her at her best, articulating popular resentment and prejudices.' Even the *Guardian* thought she had spoken for the nation: 'We can't go on like this.'[8]

While the nation shivered, an extraordinary saga was unfolding on the football field. Scheduled for 6 January, the third round of the FA Cup had been blighted by the terrible weather. One of the few games that went ahead was at Hillsborough, where volunteers cleared snow from the terraces so that Jack Charlton's Sheffield Wednesday, then in the Third Division, could host Arsenal, the previous season's runners-up. The pitch was covered with four inches of snow, the home fans good-naturedly threw snowballs at Arsenal's goalkeeper Pat Jennings, and the match ended in a 1–1 draw. Three days later the two teams met again at Highbury, but once more it was impossible to separate them: after 120 minutes, the score was again 1–1. On 15 January, therefore, they met on neutral territory at Filbert Street, Leicester. Twice Arsenal went ahead; twice Wednesday equalized. With penalty shootouts not yet a feature of English football, this meant a fourth encounter just two days later. Even following it on the radio, Michael Palin, Sheffield born and bred, could feel the tension. 'I could hardly bear to listen,' he wrote in his diary.

> One-nil to Wednesday – heart surges. Arsenal miss a penalty – heart practically bursts. Then a minute later Arsenal equalise – numbness. Then Arsenal draw ahead – feeling of resignation, pulse rate almost down to normal. Then Wednesday equalise two minutes from the end! Extra time again. Over seven hours of football and still tied. Then an extra goal apiece in extra time. Another heroic evening. And they play again – in Leicester next Monday.[9]

Even though Arsenal won at the fifth attempt, Palin thought that 'amidst all this gloom' the epic battle had been a 'golden ring of light'. Like many bright young men who had been at university in the 1960s, he held vaguely left-liberal convictions and usually saw strikes as a 'healthy sign . . . that there are people out there, amongst the computers and the rationalisations'. But now his patience was running thin. 'The two rail unions, ASLEF and the NUR, hate each other,' he noted, 'with the result that, whilst many of the country's road hauliers are on strike, the railways, far from benefiting and offering an uninterrupted service in these cold, grey days – which would win them enormous goodwill – are going on strike too.' Even the weather, Palin wrote wearily, was 'dull, harsh [and] uncomfortable', reflecting the 'spirit of the times'. And he was far from alone. Another habitual Labour supporter, Peter Hall, locked in battle with his own unions at the National Theatre, was similarly appalled by the news that the railway drivers had walked out. 'We are a society of greed and anarchy: no honour, no responsibility, no pride,' he wrote bitterly on 13 January. 'I sound like an old reactionary, which I'm not, but what we have now isn't socialism, it's fascism with those who have power injuring those who do not.' Six days later, flying to Toronto, Hall felt 'sad to leave an embattled England ... to come to a place which is clean, well-organised and efficient'. The British people, he thought, 'seem to be presiding over the collapse of decency and integrity without the energy even to realise what's happening ... God, the tatti-ness of England now.'[10]

In the media, talk of crisis was everywhere. Many newspapers ran 'Britain in Crisis' banners; even the BBC's early evening show *Nation-wide* now began with a 'Britain in Crisis' round-up. The abiding symbol of the dispute became the port of Hull, out on the eastern edge of the country, whose isolation made it easy for the pickets to cut it off. In the more melodramatic newspapers, it had become 'Siege City' or the 'second Stalingrad', a sub-zero battleground where the shop stewards' word was law. The TGWU set up a 'dispensation committee' in their local headquarters, where every morning local farmers and business-men came to beg the shop stewards for supplies. On one occasion, a reporter from the *Sunday Telegraph* watched as a coffin-maker came to ask for wood. 'Nervous and watchful,' the reporter wrote, 'he sat before the table as before a tribunal and answered questions.' In the end the shop stewards granted his request, though only after he agreed to 'donate' money to the widow of an Aberdeen picket who had been run over by a lorry. Yet despite the occasional flashes of Ealing-comedy Eng-lishness, the mugs of tea and polite conversation, there were recurrent hints of violence. One shop steward recalled that some of his lads 'almost pulled a door off a cab' and 'knocked fish off the back of fish trucks'. One picket, he remembered, threw a block of concrete 'over the flyover into the windscreen' of a lorry. And at other ports, too, some hauliers revelled in the discovery of their own power. 'The country can't take it,' exulted a hulking 17-stone picket at London's Royal Docks, when a reporter asked him about public opinion. 'It's not whether or not the country can afford to pay us. It's whether they can afford not to.'[11]

For one enraged burgher of Hull, all this merely confirmed what he had always believed. 'The lower-class bastards', Philip Larkin told his friend Kingsley Amis, 'can no more stop going on strike now than a laboratory rat with an electrode in its brain can stop jumping on a switch to give itself an orgasm.' Amis's own views were scarcely less ferocious. 'If you can think of anything short of, or not necessitating too much, violence that will get these bastards back to work, I wish you'd tell me,' he wrote. 'It would cheer me up, you see.' Of course Amis and Larkin were precisely the kind of middle-class Conservatives who were never likely to sympathize with the hauliers – not least because all the talk of special dispensation committees, civil contingencies units and home defence emergency depots echoed the dystopian fantasies that had fascinated them for years. But it was not only card-carrying reactionaries who were horrified by the pickets' intransigence. The Transport Secretary, Bill Rodgers, whose mother was dying of cancer, was appalled by news that the men in Hull were refusing to release supplies of chemotherapy drugs, materials for penicillin and chlorine for water purification. Even the Archbishop of Canterbury, Dr Donald Coggan, told his congregation that 'Christians must protest' against the 'pitiless weapon' of 'irresponsible strikes which cause suffering and sometimes even death to innocent people and helpless animals'.[12]

For some ordinary people, the Winter of Discontent was merely something they read about in their newspapers – although the papers themselves had been badly affected, with newsprint shortages meaning most were much thinner than usual, while *The Times* had vanished completely. But there is no doubt that on many people, especially in the North, the strikes had a profound impact. Infuriated by the Liberal MP John Pardoe's suggestion that people in the North should 'sweat it out', Nicola Watson of Stockport sent a blistering letter to the *Guardian*:

> Let me tell you what things are like here. Last weekend I could buy neither smokeless fuel nor paraffin and the old lady next door will be unable to get a replacement gas cylinder when her present one runs out. All the local shops were out of stock of decent electric heaters. This last week we have had rush hour buses only and even if I owned a car petrol was virtually unobtainable. Schools, swimming baths and leisure centres were closed, evening classes were cancelled. The buses are back this week but the train drivers' strike on Tuesday and Thursday means a doubling of my journey time to an office where we have no more heating for at least six more days . . .

My friends in North Manchester haven't even access to a safe supply
of water to drink.

She was not alone in her distress at the mounting shortages. 'Wherever
we turn, something has been cut off, due to an industrial dispute,' lamented the columnist Jill Tweedie, the last person anyone would have
accused of being a capitalist mouthpiece. 'Trains, planes, schools, petrol,
newspapers, bread, social services, hospital facilities and water, to name
but a few.' Even when Tweedie went to the supermarket, having obeyed
instructions to refrain from panic buying, she was in for a shock: 'Toilet
paper? Bread? Butter? Marge? Frozen peas? Sorry madam. All that
went at ten o'clock this morning.'[13]

By Wednesday, 17 January, the news was worse than ever. Many
shops, reported the Department of Transport, were completely out of
'salt, sugar, tea, butter and margarine', while 'in the North West Tesco
tinned foods are no longer available'. In the East Midlands, companies
from Golden Wonder Crisps to Pedigree Pet Foods were begging the
government for help; in Yorkshire and Humberside, farmers were preparing to slaughter their famished livestock; across the north of England,
many factories were completely out of oil. Yet despite all the TGWU's
promises to ensure the free movement of essential supplies, it was painfully clear that the strikers could not care less. 'The attitude of pickets
continues to harden,' the Department of Transport told Callaghan. 'In
the North West, Wales, Humberside, Scotland and Northern regions
there have been many reports of pickets not accepting directions from
their district secretaries about the movement of goods on the priority
list. In the South West, South Wales and South Eastern areas the local
strike committees appear to have taken matters into their own hands
and are refusing to operate the priority lists until settlements are
achieved at £65.' At Grimsby, fish piled up uselessly in the docks; on
Merseyside, 'cargoes of fruit are blacked and ready to rot'. Avonmouth
was closed to traffic, Bristol shop stewards were allowing nothing out
at all, and King's Lynn's TGWU branch announced that not even medical supplies would move until they got their money. As if all that were
not depressing enough, wrote Bernard Donoughue, 'some parts of the
North West have had no fresh water for ten days'. That morning he
heard Callaghan's press secretary Tom McCaffrey advising the Number
10 staff to start looking for new jobs. 'We are near the end,' McCaffrey
said bleakly.[14]

Later that afternoon, Callaghan told his senior ministers that it was 'abundantly clear' that the TGWU had lost control over its pickets. It was time, he announced, to call a state of emergency and send in troops to break the strike. Some of his more hawkish colleagues, notably Denis Healey and Bill Rodgers, agreed: unless they acted, 'it would look as though the Government were simply letting the country drift into total breakdown'. Fleet Street had been calling for a state of emergency for weeks, and polls showed that just over half the public were in favour. Using troops was nothing new: even Clement Attlee had done it to break dock strikes in the 1940s. But times had changed. Most Labour ministers shrank from doing anything that might antagonize the unions, and as the doves were quick to point out, there were nowhere near enough trained army drivers to make more than a dent in the strike. Bill Rodgers argued that at least a state of emergency would give the impression of decisive activity, but he was wasting his breath: yet again Callaghan's ministers voted to put off intervention. Unfortunately for the Prime Minister, he had already arranged to see Len Murray and Moss Evans that evening, intending to tell them about his decision. Hamstrung by his own Cabinet, he confined himself to vague threats about using troops unless the pickets mended their ways. But even at this stage, Moss Evans refused to accept even a meagre share of the blame. The only reason the dispute had escalated so quickly, he remarked, was that 'the Government had not given the Unions sufficient notice of what it would have to do in the event of the situation continuing'. How Callaghan restrained himself from sending in the army then and there is one of the great miracles of British political history.[15]

On the next day, the 18th, it snowed again. With the train drivers having announced another one-day stoppage, Britain was once more at a standstill, the roads white with snow, the stations deserted. In Scotland the shortages were now so bad that many firms had moved to a four-day week rather than lay off workers. That morning, Callaghan told his Cabinet that he had definitively ruled out calling a state of emergency. Instead, they agreed to 'tip a wink to the road haulage employers', allowing them to increase prices so that they could afford to offer their drivers more. As for the water workers, Callaghan said gloomily: 'We may be forced to pay 16 per cent. People appear to prefer inflation to the cost of the strike.' 'That means the end of the pay policy,' objected Shirley Williams. 'But a million people are without water in the north-west,' Callaghan said heavily. Afterwards, Bill Rodgers could not conceal his outrage. '"Tipping the wink" to the road hauliers', he wrote privately to Callaghan, would be 'widely seen as giving in to the TGWU and more particularly to Strike Committees and pickets'. For a moderate like Rodgers, surrender was unthinkable. 'I assume that the Government must stand and fight somewhere and at sometime,' he concluded bitterly. 'But in this case the Government is not even in the front line. To suggest to others that they should now give in would be defeatism of a most reprehensible kind.'[16]

Once, Callaghan might have listened. Ever since his return from the Caribbean, however, he had cut an exhausted, even pathetic figure. Even his mastery in the Commons seemed to have deserted him: announcing his decision against a state of emergency that afternoon, he had little response to Mrs Thatcher's withering scorn. 'Well, it will all be over in eleven weeks,' * he told his press secretary. 'How do you announce that the government's pay policy has completely collapsed? I don't want an answer now. Just think about it.' Talking later to his aide Ken Stowe, Callaghan said that they simply must 'bring the strike to an end – by effectively giving in . . . There is no point fighting for a pay policy which has disappeared.' Coming from somebody who had been such a bruiser, this was astonishing stuff. But the truth was that the great survivor had run out of spirit. Everything Callaghan had believed in was crumbling around him. He had 'lost his direction', thought Bernard Donoughue. 'Clearly this onslaught from the trade union movement against a Labour government has stunned him. He has always said that he would not fight the trade unions. Now his dilemma is that unless he fights the unions, he will look weak and will lose public opinion.' As an old union man, Callaghan simply could not bring himself to do it, not least because his party would never forgive him. Instead he retreated to the Number 10 study, brooding in splendid isolation on the collapse of his ambitions. His friends thought he seemed both morally stricken and physically diminished; at least one of his ministers thought he was having a nervous breakdown.[17]

By now the atmosphere inside Downing Street was silent, cold, almost sepulchral. When Callaghan's aides suggested that he go on television to explain the crisis to the British people, he said bleakly that there was no point: he had 'nothing to say'. Ken Stowe told colleagues that it reminded him of the last days of Edward Heath, work grinding to a halt as officials waited to see how the crisis would play out. For the second time in five years, there was a vacuum at the top of the British

---

* Presumably Callaghan was calculating that, having lost the votes on Welsh and Scottish devolution, the government would immediately fall from office and Labour would lose the ensuing election. He was, of course, quite right, although it took a little longer than eleven weeks.

state. Paralysis had taken hold: although the Policy Unit still poured forth ideas, nobody bothered to read them. 'It is all very quiet,' wrote Donoughue. 'There are no papers coming through. Ministers meet regularly to receive reports, but don't seem to have any ideas. The atmosphere is one of quiet despair.' Privately he fumed at the 'cowardice' in the Cabinet; later, he reflected that it reminded him of 'the fall of France in 1940'. But like his colleagues, he could only look on grimly as one terrible headline followed another. They were like passengers trapped helplessly below deck on a stricken ship, some raging, some resigned, as the water rose over their heads and condemned them to oblivion.[18]

As the snow fell in the first weeks of 1979, Penny Hibbins was one of millions of Britons struggling to keep up the routine of ordinary life. A 34-year-old divorcee with four girls aged between 8 and 15, she had been working as a cleaner at Starcross Hospital, Devon, for two years. If she worked weekends and evenings, as well as taking on extra responsibilities of looking after patients, she went home every week with £40. State benefits took her up to almost £50, but after she had paid her mortgage, her rates and her utility bills, she was left with barely £25. 'Food takes another £20 quite easily,' Penny added. That left her with less than £5 a week for herself and her girls. 'At the weekends we make do with a small chicken and I make a pie,' she told an interviewer. 'I can't afford a Sunday joint. I can't afford to take the children on holiday or anywhere else. My eldest daughter wants to go into nursing when she leaves school this summer. I just hope I can get her a grant because I won't be able to help.'

As Penny freely admitted, she was better off than some. Geoffrey Scone, a school caretaker in Bridgewater, Somerset, took home £38 a week, while his wife earned an extra £7 doing part-time work, so that she could feed and clothe their three children. 'I know I could be better off on the dole,' Geoffrey said, 'and it makes me furious when I see some of the people getting more money on the dole than I do for putting in a 40-hour week. But I believe a man ought to work if he is able.' Then there was Peter Ellis, a former Sheffield steelworker who had become a lavatory attendant after being made redundant. It was 'better than being out of work', he said – 'just'. His take-home pay was a mere £34 a week; only if he worked weekends and rest days did he come close to £50. And as Peter Ellis watched the Ford workers winning their 17 per cent pay deal, the road hauliers fighting for their 20 per cent and the water workers getting 14 per cent, he knew that he, too, would have to fight to stay afloat. 'It's no good people in private industry getting 15 and 20 per cent and us any less,' he said. 'We go in the same shops and buy the same things, so we need the same money.'[19]

Penny Hibbins, Geoffrey Scone and Peter Ellis were among more than a million people who worked in the public sector but earned less than £40 a week, the equivalent of perhaps £280 a week today. The issue of low public sector pay had been quietly smouldering for years, exacerbated by fears of rising prices and spending cuts, but also driven by a nagging anxiety that shop stewards in the private sector were aggressively seeking big increases for their members. People like Penny Hibbins were among those who had suffered most from the ravages of inflation; for low-paid workers, surging prices often meant smaller meals. But many commentators saw the issue as one not just of living expenses, but of simple justice. As the *New Statesman* pointed out, while senior civil servants and local authority executives had secured increases of well over 20 per cent, many low-paid public sector workers, from road sweepers and lavatory cleaners to car park attendants and parks gardeners, were taking home less than they could have got on supplementary benefit. 'How Do They Get By On £40 A Week?' wondered a headline in the *Guardian*. Among them were hundreds of thousands of women, who as nurses, teachers, cleaners and clerical staff, had become the bedrock of the public sector. 'Certainly as far as local authority workers go,' the paper explained, 'the majority are part-time and the great proportion of these are women. They are not working for pin-money but to help out husbands who are already in the low-paid sector, public or private.'[20]

While much of British manufacturing struggled during the 1970s, the welfare state had been one of the nation's most spectacular growth areas. Even as the nation's car industry staggered towards disaster, there was always more money for schools, hospitals, universities and polytechnics, welfare schemes and retirement pensions. Much of this went to local authorities; in the first half of the decade, local authority spending went up by 40 per cent, allowing them to take on almost a million new employees. Public sector unions such as the National Union of Public Employees (NUPE), the General and Municipal Workers' Union (GMWU), the Confederation of Health Service Employees (COHSE) and the National Association of Local Government Officers (NALGO) saw their ranks swollen to an extent few could have expected. Between 1964 and 1979, NALGO's membership increased from 338,322 to 753,226, while NUPE's membership went from 240,000 to 691,770.

Born and bred amid rising affluence, these new members were less deferential, more idealistic and more ambitious than their predecessors.
They were also much more likely to be female: more than 450,000
NUPE members were women, reflecting its strength among health
service employees, dinner ladies and cleaners. Inevitably, this meant a
dramatic change in the union's ethos. Under its loquacious leader Alan
Fisher, who had worked for the union since leaving school in Birmingham in 1939, NUPE became one of the most assertive, even populist,
unions of all. Behind the headlines, most ordinary members were largely
indifferent to union politics: a survey in 1974 found that in two-thirds
of NUPE branches, less than 5 per cent of the membership bothered
going to meetings. But Fisher himself rarely missed an opportunity to
condemn the government's pay restraint and Healey's cuts. And by
devolving power to his shop stewards – who tended to be much more
militant than the men and women they represented – he ensured that
NUPE remained firmly on the left.[21]

The government had known for months that trouble was brewing in
the public sector. At the 1978 Labour party conference, Fisher told
Denis Healey that he wanted nothing less than a 50 per cent pay increase
for his members, ten times the government limit. At a Cabinet meeting
on 7 December, meanwhile, Callaghan admitted that 'it's in the public
sector that we shall have the most trouble'. It is a myth that the government refused to compromise: on 18 January, hoping to forestall a wave
of public sector strikes, Callaghan and Healey gave local authorities the
go-ahead to increase their pay offer to 9 per cent, almost double their
original bid. That same day, however, there was an ominous sign of
things to come from the Royal College of Nursing, which threatened to
call out its members unless the government granted 'an immediate 25
per cent award'. As Callaghan's officials had been warning for months,
the unions scented blood. By failing to beat the Ford workers and the
road hauliers, the government had betrayed its own weakness. And for
Alan Fisher, whose success as a union leader had always been based on
his image as an outspoken radical who reliably delivered what his shop
stewards wanted, the opportunity was too good to resist.[22]

On Monday, 22 January, NUPE, COHSE and the GMWU called a
Day of Action in pursuit of a minimum wage of £60 a week. With an
estimated 1.5 million people walking out, it was the biggest and most
effective industrial action since the General Strike of 1926. Almost all
schools were shut; so were all public buildings, museums, parks, leisure
centres, public libraries and airports. In Manchester and West Yorkshire

there were no buses; in universities there were no cooks, cleaners or porters, while hospitals turned away all but emergency cases. The unions, said the *Guardian*, had 'put "closed" signs on Britain'. In London, Birmingham, Glasgow and Cardiff, the army and the St John Ambulance Association provided emergency ambulance services; in Manchester the city centre was almost deserted; across Merseyside there were no burials or cremations. Outside the House of Commons, Tony Benn found tens of thousands of demonstrators carrying placards with the '£60' legend. 'It was biting cold,' he wrote. 'There were gravediggers, dinner ladies, caretakers, ambulance drivers – in short, our constituency, appealing for more money to keep the public services going.' This was not quite true: although the public sector unions were bitterly opposed to Healey's cuts, what most strikers wanted was money for themselves. 'What do we want?' they chanted outside the Commons. 'More pay! When do we want it? Now!' But as so often in the Benn diaries, the real hero of the hour was Benn himself. 'They were very friendly to me,' he noted: '"Tony, how are you? . . . Keep at it . . ."'[23]

Not everyone was so sympathetic to the strikers' cause. 'For many of them,' wrote a contemptuous Bernard Donoughue, 'this will be the first action they have ever seen, as they certainly never do a day's work for whichever local authority overpays them.' And from Leavesden Hospital in South Hertfordshire, one reporter filed a story that would soon become increasingly familiar. Some 500 caretakers, porters and cleaners had gone on strike, complaining that their pay was too low to afford houses in nearby Watford. But unlike in other hospitals, where some patients had volunteered to help, Leavesden was particularly badly hit by the strike because it catered exclusively for the mentally disabled. Nurses prepared the boiled eggs for the patients' breakfasts, but for lunch they had to make do with 'corned beef, grated cheese and a smattering of potato salad nurses had managed to save from the previous day's tea', poor fare even by the standards of the 1970s. They ate off disposable plates because there was nobody to wash up. Nobody swept the wards; nobody washed their clothes or their bed linen. 'If a patient had been taken ill and needed surgery at another hospital,' wrote the reporter, 'there would have been no porter to take them to an ambulance – even if there had been one.' Fortunately, the prospect never materialized. But as the consultant psychiatrist remarked, many patients could not understand 'what is going on, why they are not getting hot meals, or can't get to their special schools or workshops. They just find it disturbing and frustrating.'[24]

The next day, proclaiming themselves 'astounded' by the success of the Day of Action, the public sector unions launched a programme of 'continuous action' to break the government's resistance. The circumstances could hardly have been bleaker; overnight the temperatures had dropped even further, while bickering between the rail unions meant that the trains had been shut down again. 'Freeze Piles On Agony For Labour', read the *Guardian*'s headline the next day, above a series of stories of unparalleled misery. The caretakers' strikes meant hundreds of schools were closed, while all twenty-seven ambulance stations in Liverpool had completely shut down. Talks to resolve the rail dispute had broken up acrimoniously, making a further stoppage inevitable, while in the capital, 'refuse workers, school caretakers, maintenance men, porters, boilermen and sewage workers' had all walked out. In Manchester, the absence of just two men responsible for fire control meant the entire airport had to be closed, since other workers refused to accept their temporary replacements. And then there was the snow, falling steadily and turning the road network into what the RAC called 'a white hell'. In the West Country, 'scores of Somerset and West Devon villages' were completely cut off; in Wiltshire, a lorry driver was killed when his vehicle skidded and fell thirty feet down an embankment; in South Wales, a pregnant woman was stranded in a snowbound ambulance until a police car rescued her and took her to hospital, where she gave birth to twin girls. It was a rare glint of good news amid the gloom.[25]

The next two weeks were among the grimmest in Britain's peacetime history. Where the road hauliers had led, dustmen, nurses, hospital porters, ambulance drivers, caretakers, canteen staff, maintenance men, gravediggers and bus drivers now followed. Already at the bottom of the pay ladder, they were terrified of being unable to afford life's necessities; when NUPE called them out, they readily answered. In towns and cities across the country, amid freezing temperatures and driving blizzards, public services ground to a halt. Children were locked out of schools, 999 calls went unanswered, icy roads went ungritted and suppurating bin bags piled up on the nation's streets. What really horrified the press, though, was the disruption at the nation's hospitals. By the final days of January, all out-patient departments in Northern Ireland were closed, all 172 hospitals in Cumbria and the north-east were accepting emergencies only, and in Birmingham, unforgivably, some cancer patients were sent home. At St George's Hospital on Hyde Park Corner, a walkout by theatre assistants and orderlies meant that surgeons were reduced to doing just eleven operations a day; at another St George's in Semington, Wiltshire, nurses looking after disabled and elderly patients broke down in tears when confronted with 'a mountain of soiled and infected linen'; at the Charing Cross Hospital, Fulham, only one in three wards remained open, while some cancer patients were forced to travel in every day by Tube instead of staying overnight. Television pictures showed distraught old men waiting for postponed pacemaker operations, disabled patients haranguing the pickets, even young nurses ripping up their union cards in disgust, while a walkout at Great Ormond Street Hospital drew predictably ferocious headlines. 'Target For Today – Sick Children', roared the *Mail*, while the *Express* claimed that 'sick children' had become 'the victims of Britain's sickest strike'. As always, the pickets insisted that the media were ignoring the real scandal of their low pay. But if they genuinely thought that walking out at a children's hospital was the best way to advance their cause, then they really were deluded.[26]

In Number 10, Callaghan's aides were numb with shock. In desperation, the Prime Minister implored Alan Fisher to show some restraint, but Fisher was now deaf to criticism. He was 'just a left-wing windbag', Callaghan snarled to Bernard Donoughue. Unfortunately, though, Fisher and his union held the whip hand. 'We'll tell it to you straight,' a group of hospital pickets lectured Callaghan's horrified policy chief. 'Our purpose is to get more than you offer and whatever you offer it won't be enough.' For Donoughue, their attitude was unforgivable: how, he wondered, could self-proclaimed socialists take 'action that is bound to kill people in hospitals'? Even other union leaders were shocked by Fisher's determination to grind the government into the dust, regardless of the consequences for the general public. Most NUPE members, remarked the electricians' leader Frank Chapple, had 'never done a day's work in their lives'. The government simply must stand up to them, he told Donoughue, because whatever Fisher got, the electricians would insist on 'fucking Fisher times two'. Here was the root of so much of the trouble, for as Chapple explained, he was a prisoner of his members' ambitions. 'My executive are enemies of mine, and they are a fucking 'orrible lot,' he sighed. 'In fact my members are a fucking 'orrible lot too.'[27]

With Callaghan sinking into self-pity, the strikes went on. On the streets of the capital, mountains of rubbish were piling up. When Westminster City Council hired private contractors to clear some of the mess, NUPE ordered its street sweepers, lavatory attendants and sewer workers out, too, in retaliation. By early February, the council had been

As the public sector workers walked out and rubbish mounted in the streets, Jim Callaghan seemed to have completely lost his touch: Stanley Franklin in the *Sun*, 10 February 1979.

forced to open more than thirty emergency open-air tips, much to the distress of many residents. Walking through Covent Garden on 2 February, Michael Palin had to 'pick my way through piles of uncollected garbage piled up in the passageway from Monmouth Street'. A week later, he observed that 'the piles of uncollected rubbish are now being blown apart by the wind', leaving the West End resembling 'a tip from which buildings emerge'. Meanwhile, at Berwick Street Market, where boxes and bin-bags had been piling up for two weeks, an ITN camera crew found a gigantic wall of rubbish, twelve feet high. Health officials sprayed the piles with insecticide and laid down rat poison; on the pavements nearby, though, reporters found open bags 'dripping with food scraps and loose rubbish'. 'Rats On The Town', howled the front page of the *Evening Standard*, which had sent its photographer to Leicester Square with orders to find rats scavenging amid the overflowing bags.

But such scenes were not confined to the West End. In Cardiff, Bristol and Plymouth, dustmen's strikes saw 'mountains of rubbish' accumulate on the streets. And in Barking, black bags piled up outside the Frizlands Lane rubbish dump, where reporters found an almost stereotypical group of donkey-jacketed pickets huddled around a smouldering brazier. The caretakers' strike meant that all schools in the borough were closed, but as ITN noted, 'the 27,000 children affected will have to stay at home. There are no parks, libraries or play centres open. The council's lorry fleet is locked up, and the Meals on Wheels service is running down as the strike spreads.' On television, the camera showed a suitably wizened pensioner, hunched over what appeared to be a bowl of Victorian-style gruel. 'Many are already relying solely on their neighbours to bring home food,' the commentary said solemnly. And what if the worst happened? 'The strike has shut cemeteries as well,' the report continued, over an image of a padlocked graveyard. 'The council stopped taking bookings for burials last week as the gravediggers came out. Now undertakers are being forced to embalm or freeze corpses in local mortuaries.'[28]

The image of a padlocked cemetery, snow glistening on the abandoned graves, became the abiding symbol of the Winter of Discontent. Even decades later, the Liverpool gravediggers' strike was seen as the supreme symbol of NUPE's folly and an indelible blot on the unions' reputation. Ironically, NUPE had nothing to do with it at all, since the gravediggers actually belonged to the General and Municipal Workers' Union. They were certainly very poorly paid, most taking home less than £45 a week, and their regional officer insisted that they had gone on strike only very reluctantly. Still, even sympathetic observers agreed with Liverpool's chief medical officer, Dr Duncan Dolton, who found 'this sort of industrial action most distasteful'. In Whitehall there was talk of using troops to dig graves, but the Ministry of Defence objected that very young recruits would be sickened by the work. Some officials suggested using private contractors, but others pointed out that this could provoke 'unseemly scenes at cemetery gates', with pickets and blacklegs fighting in front of the grieving relatives. At one point, almost unbelievably, Liverpool City Council considered asking families to 'make their own arrangements for gravedigging', but this too was rejected on the grounds that few mourners would have 'the skill or the strength' to dig old Uncle Ernie's grave. And all the time, in a disused factory in Speke, the bodies piled up: by the end of January, there were some 225 unburied corpses.[29]

To the Conservative papers, the gravediggers' strike was the perfect gift. Under pressure from reporters, Dr Dolton admitted that if the crisis went on for months, some might have to be disposed of at sea. 'They Won't Even Let Us Bury Our Dead', shrieked the front page of the *Daily Mail*, while the *Express* reported that on Tameside, undertakers were 'asking relatives to take back wedding rings and jewellery from bodies stored in warehouses – in case of robberies'. But most Labour ministers, too, were appalled by the spectacle of mourning families being forced to wait weeks to say goodbye to their dead. In the Commons, the Environ-ment Secretary, Peter Shore, begged the men, 'whatever their grievance, to reconsider their action, to understand the distress being caused to the bereaved, and the deep offence being caused to the overwhelming mass of our people, and to return to work'. When Dennis Skinner dismissed this as 'utter hypocrisy', claiming that the government could best 'get rid of these dead bodies' by giving the gravediggers what they wanted, Shore had a fierce reply. 'Hypocrisy – no; death is not hypocrisy,' he said angrily. 'Nor is human grief. Nor is the sense of common humanity that people have when they share these experiences. Therefore, some sense of common fellowship and decency between members of the same community ought to come across.'

For Callaghan, the gravediggers' strike was a definitive sign that the unions had lost their minds. Even years later, he found it 'painful to write about some of the excesses that took place'. The gravediggers' 'cold-blooded indifference to the feelings of families at moments of intense grief', he wrote, 'rightly aroused deep revulsion and did further untold harm to the cause of trade unionism that I, like so many others, had been proud to defend all my life. What would the men of Tolpuddle have said?' The remarkable thing, though, was that even the men's nom-inal leader agreed with him. Later, Roy Hattersley recalled seeing the General and Municipal Workers' boss David Basnett 'in tears' at the men's behaviour. Having started his working life in the North-west, Basnett felt personally responsible for the agony his men were inflicting on bereaved families. 'Who could have believed that Liverpool Parks and Cemeteries Branch would behave like this?' he asked emotionally. For Hattersley, 'the prosaic – indeed, almost risible – language in which he expressed his distress made his despair all the more moving'. Here was conclusive proof, he thought, that the unions were 'wholly incap-able of dealing with the problems of the modern world'.[30]

On 1 February, with sleet coming down outside, the Cabinet met in an atmosphere of greater 'agony and angst' than at any time since the dying days of the Heath government. 'There is a general sense of unease all over the country,' wrote Tony Benn. 'We are in an atmosphere of siege and crisis which the media are continuing to play up.' The lorry drivers had at last accepted a deal worth between 17 and 20 per cent – a settlement, Callaghan said gloomily, that 'reminded him of Munich' – so the only question was what they should offer the public sector unions. A few younger ministers, notably Bill Rodgers and Roy Hattersley, still had the stomach for a fight; most, including the Prime Minister himself, had simply given up. (Callaghan 'was looking so red-faced,' noted Benn, 'that I thought he was ill'.) 'We had got to the point where indiscipline was threatening the life of the community and the Government must have a clear line,' said Callaghan, according to Benn's account. 'The situation was extremely grave and the Tories could win, giving Mrs Thatcher a mandate for the most violent anti-trade union policy.' Still, Callaghan added bleakly, 'at least the trains would run on time'. His only flash of spirit came when he was discussing picketing with Tony Benn. 'What do you say about the thuggish act of a walk-out, without notice, from a Children's Hospital?' the Prime Minister asked. 'When decent people become irrational,' Benn said piously, 'something else must be wrong if they are driven to such desperate acts.' Callaghan shook his head. He had never in fifty years been so depressed as a trade unionist, he replied. Later he told Donoughue that, were it not for the looming election, he would have sacked Benn forthwith. But Donoughue had heard it all before. 'I wonder,' he wrote sadly.[31]

In the end, the Cabinet agreed to settle at 10 per cent, although even this was much lower than the ministers Donoughue called 'the marshmallows' had wanted. 'Every week we have a "positively last concession",' he remarked. 'At first it was not a penny above 5%. Then it was 8.8%; now it is 10%. If I was a trade unionist, I would just sit and wait for further concessions.' This was a result, he thought, of having 'weak' ministers who were 'never prepared to stand and fight. They would be perfectly capable, in three weeks, of arguing that 30% is not enough and not fair to the low paid, so we ought to offer 100%.' There was probably some truth in this; certainly the likes of David Ennals and Stanley Orme seemed astonishingly keen to run up the white flag. But the truth was that, by now, talk of standing and fighting was meaningless. The government had lost any chance of victory before Christmas, when it failed to stop Ford abandoning the 5 per cent pay line. And when Callaghan failed to call a state of emergency at the beginning of January, defeat became inevitable – not because the army would have broken the strike, but because his inaction showed the public sector unions that he lacked the appetite for battle. To Donoughue, who had spent the last five years wrestling to bring inflation down, everything he had worked for was falling apart. 'I don't feel depressed – just angry that the government has so little fight,' he wrote in his diary. 'I don't mind being beaten, but I cannot bear going down with so little fight.'[32]

Callaghan accepted defeat on 14 February. Appropriately enough, the day began with yet another blizzard. 'The country was paralysed again this morning,' wrote Donoughue. 'It took me two hours to get to work, walking much of the way through beleaguered London ... I sat at Kentish Town Tube station for over an hour without any trains. It was a nightmare.' Across the country, hundreds of schools were still closed; on the roads, cars inched along like men tiptoeing across a tightrope. When Donoughue finally made it into Number 10, he found it full of men from the TUC, who had come to finalize the details of Callaghan's surrender. Unveiled that afternoon, the 'Valentine's Day Concordat' committed both sides to work towards a 5 per cent inflation rate by the spring of 1982. But not even the men smiling for the cameras that afternoon took it seriously. If the Winter of Discontent had proved anything, it was that earnest pieties about the national interest had absolutely no influence on the shop stewards. To the Conservatives, and indeed the public, the Concordat was a joke. As the Tory grandee Sir Ian Gilmour observed, a better term would have been 'Capitulation', recalling, he thought, the treaties under which the humiliated Ottoman Empire had been forced to grant special immunities to foreign citizens. *The Economist* remarked that it was impossible to trust a document that 'says the unions can do the same all over again if they want to', but it was the Shadow Chancellor, Sir Geoffrey Howe, who delivered the pithiest verdict. The so-called Concordat, he remarked, was merely 'the same old cobblers'.[33]

That same day, the former Conservative deputy leader, Reginald Maudling, died of cirrhosis of the liver. Despite their political differences, Maudling and Callaghan had been close friends; later, Callaghan loved to recall Maudling's cheerful insouciance when handing over the Treasury in 1964 ('Good luck, old cock. Sorry to leave it in such a mess!'). For decades, Maudling had been the most articulate champion of One Nation Toryism, a clever, gregarious and permissive man who liked nothing better than a large glass of whisky and a great wad of cash. Yet his personal fortunes had mirrored the decline of the political consensus he tried to uphold. His liberal principles had disintegrated in the furnace of Northern Ireland, while his Keynesian optimism had been blown away by the OPEC oil shock. Even Maudling's fall from grace in the early 1970s, when it was revealed that he had been pocketing bribes from the architect John Poulson, seemed to reflect the moral collapse of a decaying order. And although Margaret Thatcher briefly recalled him to the colours, Maudling already seemed a decrepit, drunken relic. All that he had stood for, all that he believed in, was collapsing in ruins. In his last public speeches he tried to speak up for John Maynard Keynes, to reaffirm the importance of high public spending, to wave the banner of One Nation paternalism. But even though he was not yet 60, he was a man out of time, his morale broken and his principles discredited. By the beginning of 1979, it was hard to remember that Maudling had ever been seen as a serious candidate to lead Britain into a new golden age. As the ambulance rushed him through the snowstorm to the Royal Free Hospital, past the men at their braziers and the women with their placards, it was as though an era was dying with him.[34]

The Valentine's Day Concordat was not quite the end of the Winter of Discontent. With the government's retreat having turned into a rout, other groups now clamoured for increases of their own. The teachers' unions demanded 36 per cent; the civil servants, meanwhile, put in for 26 per cent. On 23 February, civil service pickets even blocked the entrance to Downing Street. Arriving for a Cabinet meeting, Tony Benn earnestly assured them he was 'not going in to do their job or replace their work'. In the end, they won a 24 per cent deal, with some getting as much as 45 per cent. Bernard Donoughue was not alone in being struck by the bitter irony that the very officials who had drafted Callaghan's 5 per cent policy showed such little compunction in securing massive pay increases of their own. But since the civil service refused to let the Policy Unit see the relevant papers, there was no way of stopping them. 'How do you take these people on, Bernard?' Callaghan asked him resignedly. 'It is very difficult to beat them.'[35]

There was one last humiliation before it was all over. Appeased by the Concordat, many local authority workers had gone back to work. Alan Fisher, however, held out until the middle of March, and in the meantime relations between NUPE and the government reached a depressing new low. On 6 March, the mild-mannered Health Secretary, David Ennals, was admitted to Westminster Hospital. A former tank officer who had been captured by the Germans after D-Day, Ennals had never fully recovered from his wartime injuries. At the time, bone from his leg had been used to repair his shattered arm; thirty years on, he was still plagued by thrombosis. Unfortunately, Westminster Hospital was one of the pickets' chief targets. For weeks they had blockaded the hospital entrance, with not even emergency patients allowed in. 'Dirty linen stood in piles in the corridors,' the *Daily Mail* reported. 'Patients ate meals off paper plates.' Sterile materials, heating oil, fresh fruit and vegetables were all turned away, and when managers asked the army to bring in supplies, the pickets slashed the delivery vans' tyres and left them blocking the entrance. Now the chief shop steward, a young Scotsman called Jamie Morris, announced that Ennals – who had been smuggled in through the back – was a 'legitimate target'. His stay in hospital, Morris promised, 'would be made as uncomfortable as possible . . . He won't get the little extras our members provide patients. He won't get his lockers cleaned or the area round his bed tidied up. He won't get tea or soup. He won't get a single smile.'

True to form, Ennals refused to complain, greeting journalists in his hospital bed with a very unconvincing show of cheerfulness. Yet for the Conservative papers, which covered the affair in forensic detail, there could hardly have been a better illustration of the pickets' disregard for human suffering. Ennals had shown 'staggering ineptitude, even by this inept Cabinet's standards', wrote the *Express*'s George Gale. 'But a man who goes into hospital for treatment arising from complications following wounds received in the last war deserves, at the very least, not to be singled out for unfavourable and punitive treatment at the hands of unskilled porters whose greed he has declined to satisfy.' Amid the furore, Jamie Morris's protestations that the real victims were low-paid ancillary workers were ignored; in the press, the long-haired shop steward became the personification of the unions' excesses. Morris was 'a symbol of the age', the right-wing Tory MP George Gardiner told the *Sunday Express*; 'the man who will not work, but cannot be sacked. He represents the barrier to good relations and to a more productive economy . . . the very element in our society that we must overcome if we are to get our country back on her feet again.' Later the incident inspired a memorable episode of *Yes Minister*, as well as Lindsay Anderson's blistering satire *Britannia Hospital* (1982), both of which featured entertainingly bolshie, shaggy-haired shop stewards. But nobody was laughing at the time.[36]

By mid-March, when NUPE accepted the government's offer of 9 per cent and a pay review (giving many members an overall increase of more than 15 per cent), the Winter of Discontent was winding down. Some historians insist that it was nowhere near as bad as the bleak picture painted by Tory propagandists, and indeed it is true that some newspapers blew the crisis out of all proportion. The *Sun*, for example, not only claimed that '3 million face the dole queue', but even ran the extraordinary headline '1,000 Old Could Die Every Day'. The *Spectator*'s reliably unreliable Auberon Waugh announced that while 'rubbish lies uncollected on the street, old-age pensioners are mercilessly raped whenever they venture out after dark, dying like flies in any case and their corpses left unburied'. Even Labour tabloids sometimes played fast and loose with the facts: the *Mirror*, for instance, ran a tear-jerking story about a 7-year-old boy waiting for a life-saving transplant as porters walked out at Westminster Hospital, only at the very end admitting that the boy was actually at a completely different hospital. And behind the headlines, those grim months were never quite as bad as many commentators had feared. Most medical supplies got through eventually, and although many shops ran out of butter, bread and cornflakes, nobody starved. The potential disputes that really frightened the Civil Contingencies Unit – a national water strike and a national power strike – never materialized, and as early as 24 January the *Guardian* observed that the 'more lurid forecasts' had come to nothing. 'We have not seen an additional million thrown out of work,' an editorial said with relief. 'The shops have not been emptied. There is no famine, no pestilence, and – so far at least, on the available evidence – no death.'[37]

All the same, no sane observer could possibly deny that the Winter of Discontent marked a dreadful nadir in modern British history. It might not have been as bad as Tory propaganda later claimed, and not even Moss Evans and Alan Fisher could be blamed for the freakishly bad weather. But even so, this was a crisis that saw ports, schools and railway stations shut down, businesses starved of essential supplies, farmers forced to slaughter their livestock for lack of fodder and thousands of workers defying not just the government but their own representatives. 'Every night,' wrote Denis Healey, 'the television screens carried film of bearded men in duffle coats huddled around braziers.' The sick genuinely went untreated; the dead did go unburied. And what made it so damaging was that it had happened before. In 1970 strikes by the council and electricity workers had seen rubbish piled high in the streets and homes plunged into darkness. In 1972 the miners had brought industry to a standstill, and in 1974 they had brought Edward Heath's government to its knees. Later that summer a general strike had smashed power-sharing in Northern Ireland, and by the following year union pay claims had pushed inflation to almost 30 per cent. For a brief period, Wilson and Callaghan seemed to have restored calm, but that illusion had not just been dispelled by the Winter of Discontent, it had been smashed into a thousand pieces. In 1974 many voters had told themselves that the crisis was all Heath's fault and that a new government would sort everything out. But the Social Contract was dead, the unions had walked out once again, and it was back to the same old headlines about strikes and stoppages, the same depressing footage of pickets and placards. Never had the prospects for industrial peace seemed bleaker; never had the British state seemed so helpless and irrelevant.[38]

At the time, the Winter of Discontent was seen as the triumph of union power. The irony, though, was that, in the long term, it was a catastrophe for the unions. As the *Guardian*'s Peter Jenkins pointed out, it was a myth that the strikes were a victory for the over-mighty union barons. 'If the country threatens to become ungovernable,' he wrote, 'it is rather because of their powerlessness to govern their own members. Their national leaders have lost control. I have never known them to be more alarmed.' They were right to be worried, for the Winter of Discontent completely shattered their popularity among the public at large. A Gallup poll at the end of January found 84 per cent agreeing that the unions were too powerful, the highest figure in the survey's history, while another poll for the *Mail* in early February found that fully 44 per cent believed the unions' very existence was a 'bad thing'. Among all groups – young and old, rich and poor, diehard Tories and traditional Labour voters – there was a marked swing away from the unions. Even among union members themselves, many of whom were appalled by the hospital and gravediggers' disputes, there had been a profound shift. Between 1974 and 1979, the proportion of union members who felt the unions were too powerful rose by 22 per cent. Indeed, in March 1979 Labour's private pollster Bob Worcester reported that a staggering 94 *per cent* of trade unionists supported Mrs Thatcher's plan to have compulsory ballots before strike action – a hugely popular reform that most union leaders and Labour MPs still opposed.[39]

Defenders of the trade unions sometimes claim that the Winter of Discontent was all Jim Callaghan's fault. But this is patently ridiculous. Even if Callaghan's pay policy was too rigid – which is debatable anyway – it still beggars belief that, after everything Labour had done for them, and with an election only months away, the union leaders made such feeble efforts to restrain their shop stewards. Their 'cowardice and irresponsibility', wrote Denis Healey, not only guaranteed Mrs Thatcher's victory, but 'left them with no grounds for complaining about her subsequent actions against them'. Even people who saw themselves as being on the left were appalled by the spectacle of pickets targeting the very young, the very old, the sick, the disabled and the bereaved. The strikes of early 1979, wrote the Trotskyist journalist Paul Foot, were nothing more than 'bloody-minded expressions of revenge and self-interest', while the Communist historian Eric Hobsbawm thought that behind all their talk of socialism, the unions were only interested in 'their members' narrow economic benefits'.[40]

And this, of course, was the greatest irony of all. What drove the Winter of Discontent was not socialism but something often regarded as the core of Thatcherism: the pursuit of material security. The strikers outside ports, schools and hospitals were not campaigning for a New Jerusalem; as they saw it, they were fighting to protect their living standards from the ravages of inflation. In true Thatcherite spirit, they put themselves and their families above nebulous ideas of the greater good. But to a generation of Labour politicians steeped in the values of collective social democracy – politicians who enjoyed comfortable living standards themselves, and therefore found it hard to grasp the sheer anger and anxiety of NUPE's low-paid members – they were traitors to the movement. The strikers were engaged in 'occupational tribal warfare', thought Labour's Peter Shore, 'as though every separate group in the country had no feeling and no sense of community, but was simply out to get for itself what it could'. 'This has nothing to do with trade unionism,' agreed Bernard Donoughue. 'It is hard-faced, grab-what-you-can capitalism with a union card.'

The other big losers were Callaghan and his colleagues, for whom the Winter of Discontent was an unalloyed catastrophe. Not only did the crisis make them look craven, supine and out of touch, but it destroyed their party's greatest asset, the perception that only Labour could handle the unions. In February 1974, voters had turned to Labour, not because they liked its interventionist manifesto – indeed, polls showed that even party supporters heartily disliked it – but because they thought Harold and Jim would guarantee them a quiet life. Even the Social Contract, which allowed wages to spiral out of control until Denis Healey managed to reassert some economic discipline, had seemed a price worth paying for peace on the industrial front. But now it transpired that all those beers and sandwiches at Number 10 had been for nothing; the unions had gone on strike anyway. The only difference between Heath and Callaghan, it appeared, was that while Heath fought and lost, Callaghan did not fight at all. As his own policy chief observed, the Prime Minister was constitutionally incapable of taking on a movement he had joined as a teenager. But if not even Labour ministers could persuade the unions to moderate their behaviour, what was the point of voting them in? 'They no sooner retreat and decide to make a stand than they start retreating again,' Donoughue lamented at the beginning of February. 'This really is the end of the old Labour movement as a potential government.'[41]

By this point, any chance of winning the next election had completely evaporated. By the beginning of January, the Tories were already 8 per cent clear, and then Labour's retreat turned into a rout. By mid-February, only two out of ten people approved of the government's record. Unemployment and the cost of living, the two most pressing issues for the previous twelve months, had been overtaken by strikes as the public's biggest concern. Humiliatingly, just one in ten people thought that the government was doing a good job at handling them, compared with eight out of ten who actively disapproved. By 6 February, MORI was giving the Tories a stunning 19 per cent lead, and even Labour supporters had now given up the ghost. Almost seven out of ten people thought Mrs Thatcher would be the next Prime Minister; only two out of ten picked Callaghan. 'I was not surprised,' wrote Donoughue after reading the MORI poll. 'We have given an impression of weakness and vacillation. So we lose our friends who want firm government, but we don't gain anybody.' Even Callaghan had 'suffered a catastrophic decline in personal popularity', and although it pained Donoughue to say so, his boss deserved it. 'I've been appalled at some of the things that have gone on,' Callaghan told Robin Day on 26 February, 'and I have bitten my tongue more than once.' But that was part of the problem: to the untutored observer, it was awfully difficult to tell the difference between a Prime Minister biting his tongue and a Prime Minister cowering in his bunker.[42]

The big winner was, of course, Margaret Thatcher. Ever since becoming Conservative leader, she had struck a remarkably cautious note on industrial relations, taking care not to say anything that would antagonize union members. But by the end of 1978, the unions' hostility to Callaghan's pay policy had convinced some of her advisers that the time had come for a harder line. 'The public mood *vis à vis* the Unions has changed,' wrote the combative but astute Alfred Sherman in December. 'The Unions' moral ascendancy has been eroded, they are no longer seen as valiant fighters for the underdog but as selfish and often ruthless operators . . . What counts is that "do something about the unions" is again thinkable.' And as the industrial crisis deepened, the Conservative press could barely contain its enthusiasm for battle. 'Now let's take on the union wreckers,' wrote George Gale in the *Express* on 9 January. 'The power of trade union monopoly is exercised as irresponsibly as the harlot's prerogative – but it is not a harlot's power. It is the power, which is far greater and far worse, of the blackmailer.' Strikes must be broken, employers should be supported and the closed shop should be banned, while 'trade unionists must be brought within the law, their legal immunity removed and legal responsibilities imposed'. This was typical *Express* fare, but now even relatively liberal Tories were saying similar things. The unions, wrote Lord Hailsham, were 'selfish, short-sighted and narrow-minded'; they had 'betrayed their membership, their country and their class'. Paradoxically, such criticism often went down well with union members themselves. Polls showed that most of them wanted an end to strikes, were sick of inflation and were desperate for change. In this context, Sherman thought, Mrs Thatcher should argue that 'trade union reform is not union-bashing, but in the interests of trade Unionists'.[43]

As strike followed strike, the Conservative leader began to find her voice. Interviewed by Brian Walden on *Weekend World* on 7 January, Mrs Thatcher announced that she would consider scrapping benefits for unofficial strikers and banning strikes in essential services. Twelve days later, speaking at a Tory rally in Glasgow, she memorably denounced 'the wreckers in our midst', who had done 'as much damage to the decent name of trade unionism as they do to our economy'. But her most notable statement came on 17 January, in one of the most effective broadcasts of her entire career. Speaking quietly but firmly, she presented herself not as a partisan political leader, but as the voice of the nation. 'Yes, technically, this is a Party Political Broadcast on behalf of the Conservative Party,' she began. 'But tonight I don't propose to use the time to make party political points. I do not think you would want me to do so. The crisis that our country faces is too serious for that.'

As expected, she made a great deal of her outrage at the industrial unrest. 'Some of the things I've seen on television, read in the newspapers, and heard directly from you in factories and shopping centres make me wonder what has happened to our sense of common nationhood and even of common humanity,' she said earnestly. Cleverly, however, she did not then lay into Jim Callaghan; instead, she pretended to feel sorry for him:

> I recognise how hard this is for the Labour Party, because of their close connection with the unions. Without the unions there would be no Labour Party. Without union money there would be no Labour funds.
>
> But surely Labour can accept what I think the majority of union members themselves accept, that there are some changes which have simply got to be made if we're to avoid not just disruption but anarchy.

In the name of the national interest, she promised Conservative support for three measures – publicly funded strike ballots, a ban on secondary picketing and no-strike contracts in essential services – that she knew Callaghan could never possibly accept. And with an election only months away, she deliberately ended on a prime ministerial note:

> If the present crisis has taught us anything, it has surely taught us that we have to think of others as well as ourselves; that no one, however strong his case, is entitled to pursue it by hurting others.
>
> There are wreckers among us who don't believe this. But the vast majority of us, and that includes the vast majority of trade unionists, do believe it, whether we call ourselves Labour, Conservative, Liberal – or simply British. It is to that majority that I am talking this evening. We have to learn again to be one nation, or one day we shall be no nation. If we have learnt that lesson from these first dark days of 1979, then we have learnt something of value.[44]

Even her critics admitted it was brilliant. Mrs Thatcher had 'rattled a number of senior ministers' who thought her message would win 'considerable support in the country', reported the next day's *Guardian*. Her television manner was still 'a little too Sandringham-like, the new voice a little too huskily-moderated', thought Peter Jenkins; but he nevertheless admired 'an address to the nation delivered with statesmanlike restraint and free from party rancour'. Yet for all her talk of one nation, there was the occasional flash of steel beneath the manicured image. For four years the Tory leader had gone out of her way to deny that she wanted a confrontation with the trade unions. But when she appeared on the *Jimmy Young Show* on the last day of January, there was a revealing hint of things to come:

> Some of the unions are confronting the British people; they are confronting the sick, they are confronting the old, they are confronting the children.

I am prepared to take on anyone who is confronting those and who is confronting the law of the land . . .

If someone is confronting our essential liberties, if someone is inflicting injury, harm and damage on the sick, my God, I will confront them.

Young wondered whether she might prefer a quiet life, but Mrs Thatcher shook her head. 'It's no earthly use saying "anything for a quiet life",' she said. 'I don't regard this as a quiet life. You can't even get a decent burial.'[45]

32

No Confidence

I think it's time for truth, and the truth is you lost, Uncle Jimmy.

The Jam, 'Time for Truth' (1977)

A night like this comes once a lifetime.

Margaret Thatcher, 28 March 1979

On the first day of March 1979 Britain awoke to yet more atrocious weather. It was St David's Day, the day the people of Wales and Scotland would have their say over their own destiny. If they voted 'Yes' in sufficient numbers, then the Scotland and Wales Acts would give Edinburgh and Cardiff the first democratic assemblies in their history. Yet as the first voters trudged to the polls, snow, sleet and hail were streaming down from leaden skies. In the north-west of Scotland some of the polling stations were almost deserted; although the government had planes, helicopters and even fishing boats ready to bring the ballot boxes from some of Britain's remotest outposts, it seemed as if they would barely be needed. In the morning papers, last-minute surveys showed support swinging away from Scotland's pro-devolution camp. One poll put the Yes and No camps dead level on 38 per cent each, with 24 per cent undecided. Meanwhile, under the headline 'The Stark Choice', the *Mirror* took a different approach to enlightening its readers. 'While the folks back home go to the polls it'll be business as usual for these two lovelies,' the article explained, opposite a gigantic topless picture of 'Scots-born Helen Ferguson and former Miss Wales Sian Adey-Jones'. 'It is widely expected', the piece went on, 'that the girls will get an overwhelming "Yes" vote for their assemblies.'[1]

For the Scottish Nationalist leader William Wolfe, who had launched the 'Yes' campaign a few weeks earlier, the referendum was nothing less than a 'struggle for the soul of our country'. But that was not how it seemed to millions of his countrymen. Even in the Scottish newspapers, the devolution debate was largely overshadowed by the Winter of Discontent, with worthy arguments about Home Rule driven off the front pages by deserted railway stations, rubbish in the streets and empty hospital wards. Nationalists still disagreed whether devolution was an end in itself or merely a necessary step to independence; meanwhile, most Labour pro-devolution campaigners refused to share platforms with the SNP, despite their common goal. Technically, Labour was supposed to be in favour of devolution, but with Callaghan's popularity slipping by the day, their campaign never got off the ground. Instead, it was devolution's opponents who made the running. Chief among them was the Labour maverick Tam Dalyell, who not only bombarded local newspapers with anti-devolution letters and travelled the country delivering blistering speeches, but even went to court to scupper the government's plans for pro-devolution party political broadcasts. It was, wrote the election experts David Butler and Dennis Kavanagh, 'a magnificently single-minded and effective performance'.[2]

For the Conservatives, most of whom had long since abandoned their brief commitment to devolution, the referendum campaign was an ideal opportunity to take potshots at Labour and nationalists alike. Conscious of the need to attract former SNP voters, the Tory leader claimed that she still liked the idea of devolution in principle, but that the proposed assembly would merely create 'another tier of governmental interference in Edinburgh'. 'We have been through a bad patch as a country, and we are still not out of it,' Mrs Thatcher wrote in the Scottish *Sunday Post*. 'Please let us stick together. We need each other now as much as we ever did.' Her MPs, however, were rather less restrained. 'On Tuesday the "Yes" campaign for a Scottish Assembly are holding a public meeting in Dundee,' wrote Iain Sproat, the Tory MP for Aberdeenshire South, in the *Sunday Express*. 'The names of the three main speakers are very interesting. They are: Anthony Wedgwood Benn, Mick McGahey, the Communist miners' leader, and Jimmy Reid, the ex-Communist and current Labour Parliamentary Candidate for Dundee.' Faced with such 'political cockroaches,' he thought, 'most sensible people in Scotland should shout out "No!" at the top of their voices'. In the accompanying Cummings cartoon, a kilted Callaghan dumps the Act of Union in a dustbin. 'So what?' he says. 'It's only another scrap of paper!' Another Cummings cartoon showed Britain smothered beneath overflowing dustbins and bursting bin bags. On top of the pile stands a fat, florid-faced man in full Highland dress, blowing hot air from a set of bagpipes in the shape of Jim Callaghan's face. 'I'm just amazed', Callaghan is saying, 'that there's ANYONE who wants to stay attached to any place I'M in charge of!'[3]

In Wales the contest was even more one-sided. Strictly speaking, the Wales for the Assembly Campaign was meant to be non-partisan. But even its launch in Llandrindod Wells on 6 January was overshadowed by squabbling, with the secretary of the Welsh TGWU refusing to appear alongside Plaid Cymru's veteran leader Gwynfor Evans. Since so many Labour figures also refused to appear alongside their Plaid counterparts, the nationalists ended up shouldering most of the burden: as Evans complained, they had 'prepared every leaflet and arranged which speakers go where and organized all the meetings'. By contrast, the No campaign commanded the enthusiastic support of the Conservatives, many Welsh Labour MPs, many trade unions and most South Wales councils, as well as considerable funding from the anti-devolution Federation of Small Businesses. Not surprisingly, the polls left no room for doubt. On 9 February, a month into the campaign, a BBC survey found that support for devolution had fallen from 38 per cent to 33 per cent. And as defeat became a certainty, the Yes campaign's momentum dribbled away: when the Foreign Office minister Ted Rowlands returned to his Merthyr constituency to address a pro-devolution meeting, not a single voter turned up. Even before the first vote had been counted, Gwynfor Evans had conceded defeat. The campaign had been a useful exercise in 'educating people on the needs of Wales', he said defiantly. But 'when one opinion poll after another goes against you, you have to accept that they probably reflect the situation'.[4]

For the nationalists, the results on 1 March came as a dreadful disappointment. In Scotland, 1.23 million people voted in favour of devolution, with 1.15 million against. With a turnout of less than 64 per cent, it meant that only one in three Scots had voted for an assembly, well short of the required 40 per cent. For the SNP, the result was particularly humiliating. Of the twelve Scottish regions, only the Labour strongholds of Strathclyde, Central and Fife returned decent Yes majorities, while the Highlands, Lothian and the Western Isles voted Yes by tiny margins. Everywhere else the No campaign carried the day. Still, the SNP could console themselves that they had done better than Plaid Cymru, for whom the referendum proved an unmitigated disaster.

Turnout in Wales was a derisory 59 per cent, and of those who bothered to vote, just 20.3 per cent voted Yes, with 79.7 per cent voting No. In some areas, such as Clwyd and Gwent, the result was a total embarrassment, with almost nine out of ten people voting against. When turnout was taken into consideration, this meant that in some areas only *seven* out of every hundred people had voted Yes, a far cry from the 40 per cent needed for devolution to pass. Gwynfor Evans admitted that he felt 'sick', while Labour's Welsh Secretary John Morris said bleakly: 'If you see an elephant on your doorstep, you know what it is.' Another devolution supporter, the veteran Welsh-language journalist John Roberts Williams, chose a rather more colourful metaphor. 'The nation ventured onto the world stage for one brief moment,' he wrote the next day. 'What did we do? We filled our pants.'[5]

Even without the Winter of Discontent, the Welsh referendum would almost certainly have gone against the nationalists. As the historian Kenneth Morgan points out, his countrymen had been lukewarm about Home Rule for almost a hundred years. Internal linguistic and regional divisions died hard, while many families in South and West Wales had recent English roots. In other circumstances the vote in Scotland, which had a much clearer sense of national distinctiveness, might have gone differently, although the 40 per cent threshold obviously presented a formidable obstacle. Admittedly, SNP support had been in decline for more than a year, while Andrew Marr rightly points out that many rural Scots did not share the nationalist assumptions of the 'urban, leftish-leaning establishment'. But what really killed devolution was the Winter of Discontent. As rubbish mounted in the streets and the government's popularity went into free fall, traditional Labour supporters lost interest in the cause. In effect, the Scottish and Welsh referendums had become 'plebiscites on the government's record' – plebiscites which, given the appalling headlines, it was bound to lose.[6]

While the nationalists licked their wounds, devolution's opponents could hardly have been more delighted. 'That should effectively put an end to the whole stupid charade,' recorded a jubilant Kenneth Williams, who 'opened a bottle of champagne and drank the lot, celebrating the devolution defeat & the Conservative by-election victories'. Margaret Thatcher, meanwhile, hailed a 'great day for the United Kingdom', adding that if Callaghan's ministers continued with their devolution plans, as some nationalists were urging, it would be 'the final insult' by a 'dying government'. But Callaghan now faced a dreadful dilemma. 'Pressing ahead with devolution means asking our Party and others to vote to override the 40% clause,' recorded Bernard Donoughue, who had watched the results on television in mute horror. 'But if we don't, the Scot Nats will say they cannot support us on a confidence vote. And the Liberals say they won't anyway. We get more and more boxed in.' The next ten days, Donoughue thought, would be vital. 'There will be a confidence vote some time and, if we are beaten, that means an early election.' Surely, he added, the Prime Minister must be thinking about the road not taken; 'I wonder if he would now like to replay last autumn's "non-election"?'[7]

For Welsh nationalists, there was a very meagre consolation in the aftermath of defeat. On Saturday, 17 March, more than 60,000 passionate Welshmen packed into Cardiff Arms Park for the ritual slaughter of fifteen white-shirted Englishmen. Until the final stages, the score was still close, but in the final minutes Wales cut loose, running in five tries to England's none. Watching in the stands, the MP for Cardiff South East good-humouredly cheered every score. Jim Callaghan had taken up rugby during his days as a young trade union official, playing in the second row for Streatham. On moving to Cardiff, he had adopted the Welsh national team, relishing his rare opportunities to see them in action. But as his biographer Kenneth Morgan notes, Wales's victory that afternoon was a supremely misleading moment. Although they retained the Five Nations championship, they were no longer the dominant force of old. Their outstanding half-backs, Gareth Edwards and Phil Bennett, had retired the previous year: almost imperceptibly, Welsh rugby was entering a period of deep decline. It would be nine years before Callaghan's adopted homeland returned to the top of the Five Nations table. By then, his premiership would seem like ancient history.[8]

Callaghan spent the weekend after the Scottish and Welsh referendums on his farm, as if hoping that the cold air and a little exercise would lift his spirits. On the Sunday, Michael Foot rang with an elaborate strategy for buying nationalist support. Under the terms of the referendum, the government was committed to repealing the Scotland Act. Instead, Foot thought they should lay a Repeal Order before the House, but then urge a vote *against* it. If they made this a vote of confidence, there was a good chance that Labour and the nationalists would vote together. The Scotland Act would not, however, come into force immediately, because the government would delay the necessary Commencement Order until after the election. That way, Foot thought, the

Scottish Nationalists would have no choice but to stick with Labour, allowing the government to stay in office till the autumn. Callaghan was not convinced. At a Downing Street meeting the next day, he pointed out that this extraordinarily complicated scheme was unlikely to impress the public, for whom it was bound to look a very grubby back-room deal. In the meantime, however, the vultures were circling. On Tuesday afternoon, David Steel told Callaghan that the Liberals would not back the repeal of the Scotland Act. But when Callaghan briefed his Cabinet colleagues, he repeated that Foot's wheeze would look dreadful to ordinary voters bewildered by the finer points of parliamentary procedure. There was no need to rush, he said wearily. They should take their time, keep talking to the Liberals and the nationalists, and perhaps something would turn up.[9]

Since becoming Prime Minister, Callaghan had found himself in plenty of tight spots. The difference now was that he was exhausted. The Winter of Discontent had taken its toll: Big Jim, the great backroom fixer, had run out of patience. Meeting the Cabinet's Economic Strategy Committee on Wednesday, 14 March, he announced that he was 'fed up with living from week to week, with his authority slipping away'. 'If the worst came to the worst,' he added, 'we had better leave Thatcher to inherit the situation. If prices rip the Tories will have to cope with it and then we'll get back in again because of their inability to cope.' Not all his aides agreed: a few days later, Donoughue recorded that 'the general view was that we should go on as long as possible, through a crude deal with the Ulster Unionists if need be'. But it was hard to miss the stench of defeatism and decay, the atmosphere of *fin de régime*. Even the weather took another turn for the worse: on the Sunday after the Wales–England game, it snowed so heavily that Callaghan was nearly stranded at Chequers. 'Whole areas of the North are cut off, with drifts up to twenty feet,' Donoughue recorded. Inside Number 10, work had ground to a standstill; even the civil servants seemed to be waiting. 'In the Private Office the secretaries sit there, with their feet on the desks, reading magazines,' Donoughue wrote the next day. 'It is as if this administration is just petering out, not with a bang but with a whimper. There is a sense, in fact, that the government has already ended. We are just going through the final motions.'[10]

By the following Thursday, after days of fruitless talks, the tension had reached breaking point. Before Cabinet that morning, Michael Foot made one last effort, warning that the nationalists would back a vote of no confidence unless Callaghan gave them a full debate on repealing the

Scotland Act, which would allow devolution to go ahead regardless of the referendum result. But Callaghan's patience had run out: when the Cabinet met a few moments later, he repeated that he had no intention of making commitments to the SNP. It was now clear, thought Tony Benn, 'that we can't survive ... Everyone is talking about an Election.' At lunch, 'people round the table looked downcast', recorded Donoughue. Later, at the Commons, the Prime Minister's parliamentary private secretary, Roger Stott, made a last attempt to urge a deal with the Scottish Nationalists. But Callaghan was having none of it. 'He was near the end of his tether,' he told them. 'He had compromised in many areas to achieve majorities for the government. He had done many things he did not believe in. Now he had had enough. And if there was an election, so be it.'[11]

After a desultory session of Prime Minister's Questions, Callaghan retired grumpily to his Commons room. A few moments later, Labour's deputy Chief Whip, Walter Harrison, materialized with the news everyone had expected: the Scottish Nationalists had laid down a motion of censure. It could have been avoided, Harrison said glumly, if they had only given the nationalists a date for the repeal debate. Slumped in his chair, almost uninterested, Callaghan said that it 'would have happened anyway'. The Prime Minister did not seem surprised or depressed, his policy chief thought, just 'a bit edgy'. As for Donoughue himself, he felt increasingly detached from events. 'I really do believe that our side has run out of steam,' he wrote the next day. 'The PM has lost his drive. He is doing nothing to win back the initiative ... Nothing is happening. No policy ideas. No meetings to try to examine how to restart our political momentum. I get the feeling that most ministers have already conceded defeat.'[12]

With the no-confidence debate scheduled for Wednesday, 28 March, the government had six days to cobble together some sort of majority. In Number 10 the atmosphere was almost despondent; in the Palace of Westminster, by contrast, the mood seemed feverishly over-excited, the bars and tea rooms flowing with drunken gossip, the harassed party whips endlessly calculating and recalculating their totals. From the outset it was clear that the vote would be extremely tight. With 279 Conservatives, 13 Liberals and 11 Scottish Nationalists committed to voting against the government, Callaghan's fate would come down to just one or two votes. Yet, almost in disbelief, Donoughue recorded that the Prime Minister had 'forbidden his ministers and whips from doing any wheeler-dealing to gain those key couple of votes'. Even when Michael Foot begged him to make concessions to the nationalists, Callaghan said no. The irony, as Donoughue noted, was that 'Michael's reputation remains that of the unworldly man of pure socialist principle and the PM's is that of the typical Tammany Hall wheeler-dealer . . . the PM was complaining about this at the weekend. He is clearly very upset about this reputation as a "fixer".' Foot, too, was bewildered at the Prime Minister's newfound principles. 'I had the feeling', he said later, 'that Jim had made up his mind to have an election anyhow.'[13]

Callaghan's friends were rather less inclined to throw in the towel. With the figures so close, some of his ministers – notably Foot and Roy Hattersley – made desperate efforts to win over the undecided. Plaid Cymru's three MPs, for example, had initially threatened to vote with the Opposition, but when Foot promised compensation for Welsh quarrymen suffering from silicosis, a cause that had long been dear to Welsh nationalists, they announced that they would back the government after all. Then there were the various Ulster Unionists, most of whom usually sided with the Tories. When Hattersley approached Enoch Powell to see if a deal was possible, he discovered that the Unionists might back the government if Callaghan agreed to increase Northern Ireland's representation at Westminster and to approve a gas pipeline to the mainland. Nervous that he might be given a rollicking for his temerity, Hattersley reported to Number 10 that a deal might be possible. Once again, however, Callaghan refused to budge, repeating that 'his government was not up for auction.' The Prime Minister was determined, Hattersley thought, 'to go down like a noble Roman'. When other ministers heard the news, however, they saw it rather differently. 'He's lost his bottle,' said John Smith.[14]

But Hattersley had not yet given up hope, and at almost the last minute he managed to win over two Ulster Unionists, John Carson and Harold McCusker, with a promise that the government would set up a special price index to keep an eye on inflation in Northern Ireland. On the day of the debate, Hattersley was deputed to keep the two men under close guard in his Commons office, both to secure their votes and to stop them being intimidated by other Unionists. There was a strong element of farce in all this: McCusker drank so much whisky that Hattersley had to borrow another bottle from John Smith, and when Hattersley showed them a draft of their agreement, they made him type it out again because he had signed it in green ink. Even so, it was a notable coup, and when he had the two signatures, Hattersley shot off to tell Callaghan about his accomplishment. 'I went downstairs to his room and gave him the good news,' Hattersley recalled. 'He received it with perfunctory thanks. He knew that it made no difference.'[15]

The problem, as Callaghan knew, was that even with Carson, McCusker and Plaid Cymru, the government would probably fall short. Crucially, his ministers had failed to win over Northern Ireland's two Catholic MPs, Frank Maguire, a self-styled Independent Republican, and Gerry Fitt, leader of the Social Democratic Labour Party. A Sinn Fein sympathizer who had been interned for two years as a young man, Maguire rarely showed his face in the Commons and disliked publicity. Despite his republican connections, he was a man of genial simplicity, spending most of his time refereeing Gaelic football and telling jokes in his Fermanagh pub. Northern Ireland officials reported that matters outside his own constituency barely interested him at all, so in other circumstances Labour might have been able to count on his vote. The problem, though, was that there was no way Maguire's republican backers would let him support a government including the hard-line Roy Mason. On the day of the vote, they persuaded him to fly to London specifically to abstain in person. The minister Stanley Orme told Donoughue that he had seen Maguire in the Palace of Westminster accompanied not only by his wife but by 'two sinister Republican "heavies"', who had come to make sure he did not vote. The moral pressure was clearly immense: Maguire, he added, 'was nearly in tears'.[16]

As an old socialist, Gerry Fitt could hardly have seemed a more natural Labour ally. A former merchant seaman who had fought in the Second World War, supported the Catholic civil rights movement and spoken out bravely against the Provisional IRA, the West Belfast MP usually voted alongside his friends in the Labour Party. Unfortunately for the government, he too had been thoroughly alienated by Roy Mason's enthusiasm for the security forces. Many Labour MPs found it incomprehensible that Fitt would vote to bring down their government and make way for Margaret Thatcher's Conservatives. 'I [have] been a committed Socialist all my life,' he admitted in the Commons on the night of the vote. 'When I came to this House I felt proud and honoured to associate myself with the Labour cause.' But he had been appalled by Labour's 'disastrous' policies in Northern Ireland, from the Prevention of Terrorism Act to Mason's emphasis on a 'military solution'. His greatest loyalty, he added, was not to his fellow socialists, but to the people of Northern Ireland: 'I am speaking with their voice tonight. It is their voice saying that because of what the Government have done in the past five years – disregarded the minority and appeased the black-mailers of the Northern Ireland Unionist majority – I cannot go into the Lobby with them tonight.' 'So we pay the price', wrote Bernard Donoughue, 'for Mason's policy.'[17]

With Fitt and Maguire bound to abstain, the government's hopes came down to one man. Sir Alfred Broughton had been the Labour MP for Batley and Morley since 1949. A former family doctor from West Yorkshire, he was now 77 and in very bad health, spending most of his time in hospital. Some of the Labour whips had long wanted him to retire; others had urged him to stay on, afraid they would lose the ensuing by-election. But now, as Hattersley noted, the only issue was 'whether or not a dying man should be brought 200 miles to the House and left in the ambulance in Speaker's Court while he was "nodded through" the division lobby by a whip'. He thought they should bring Broughton down. So did the assistant whip Ann Taylor, who volunteered to go up to Yorkshire and accompany Broughton in the ambulance. The problem, though, was that Broughton's health was now desperately fragile; some thought he might not survive the journey. In London, the whips hesitated; in Yorkshire, journalists surrounded the Broughtons' house. To complicate matters further, Lady Broughton stopped answering the telephone, and even asked neighbours to tell callers they were away. As the crucial day approached, Labour's deputy Chief Whip, Walter Harrison, was forced to send his wife to push a message through the letterbox. But even as the vote approached, nobody could be sure whether Broughton would make it or not.[18]

The day before the debate was Jim Callaghan's sixty-seventh birthday. After Prime Minister's Questions, recorded Donoughue, he held a meeting with his closest aides:

> He said, 'Well, we are still set to lose.' He then began to talk about the coming election, clearly looking forward to it. He said, 'I am going to enjoy myself. Once the adrenaline starts flowing it will be fine. I think we will win. We should all believe we are going to win. Then we will wake up on the morning after and then we will find out.' Tom McNally asked him straight to his face, 'Are you sure you really want to win?' The PM said yes, but I thought it was a good and brave question.

Callaghan's advisers still thought they should try to win the confidence vote, but when McNally teased him about his reluctance to do deals, the Prime Minister 'bridled and said he was just not going to do it'. Donoughue tried to change his mind, arguing that if they lost, the Labour Party would be demoralized and the Conservatives buoyant ahead of the election campaign, but Callaghan again shook his head. That evening, as they held a little party for the Prime Minister's birthday, the whips reported that the debate was too close to call. 'It still looks very close and may end in a tie, with the Speaker's vote keeping the government in,' wrote Donoughue. 'My instinctive feeling is that we will win by one.'[19]

Wednesday, 28 March: the day of the debate. In Downing Street, Callaghan spent the morning working on his speech, skipping a long-scheduled meeting of Labour's National Executive. After lunch, he retired upstairs for a brief nap; when he came downstairs to leave for the Commons, the Number 10 staff had gathered 'to give him a cheering send-off'. By the time Callaghan's aides reached the Commons gallery, the chamber was packed, with hundreds of MPs squeezed into the green leather benches and some even huddled on the floor. 'In the galleries,' wrote an American observer, 'peers from the House of Lords stood jammed together like asparagus stalks, while Tory wives watched like *Upstairs, Downstairs* aristocracy, waiting for the vote that might cast them and their husbands once again into the front ranks.' Perhaps appropriately, the Palace of Westminster had a funereal atmosphere: in a twist almost too good for fiction, the catering staff was on strike, so all the bars and tea rooms were closed. The Speaker began by warning that if MPs left the House for refreshment, they should make sure they were back for the division at ten o'clock. Then he nodded to the Leader of the Opposition, and at 3.34 p.m., Margaret Thatcher rose to her feet. 'Mr Speaker, I beg to move', she said, 'that this House has no confidence in Her Majesty's Government.'[20]

As so often during her years in opposition, Mrs Thatcher's speech never quite lived up to the occasion. Hoping to keep the atmosphere as flat as possible, the Labour whips had ordered backbenchers not to interrupt or heckle her, and as she worked her way through the well-worn criticisms, the atmosphere felt still, stagnant, almost dead. She began with some familiar economic facts: the intolerably high inflation rate, the shocking level of unemployment, the poor productivity of British industry. Four major flaws, she said, had crippled the Labour government. First, 'far too little attention has been given to wealth creation and far too much to wealth distribution'. Second, 'the Government have concentrated far too much power in the hands of the centralised State and left too little with the individual citizen'. Third, the government had shirked the urgent need for trade union reform. (These first three points, of course, had been standard elements of Conservative rhetoric for decades.) Finally, the government had shown 'insufficient support for the rule of law in this country':

> The phrase 'law and order' does not refer only to vandalism and violence – although that is uppermost in many people's minds. It means that our citizens expect and are not getting an ordered or orderly society. They expect the rubbish to be cleared, the schools to be open and the hospitals to be functioning. They are not. They expect each man and woman to rise to his obligations in an orderly and decent way. They expect bargains to be kept between trade unions and employers. Finally, they expect Ministers to support them in those views.

Labour's failure, she concluded, had not merely been to double prices and double dole queues; above all, it had 'undermined public respect and confidence in the law'. Only a new government could restore them. 'There has been a failure,' she ended, 'not only of policies but of the whole philosophy on which they are based – the philosophy which elevates the State, dwarfs the individual and enlarges the bureaucracy. Across the Western world the tide is turning against that, and soon the same thing will happen here.'

When the Conservative leader sat down, it was the Prime Minister's turn. 'Be kind, Jim,' shouted Eric Heffer, to laughter from the Labour benches. But Callaghan was in his element. Memorably, he began by pouring scorn on the strange coalition of adversaries with which he found himself confronted:

> We can truly say that once the Leader of the Opposition discovered what the Liberals and the SNP would do, she found the courage of their convictions. So, tonight, the Conservative Party, which wants the [Scotland] Act repealed and opposes even devolution, will march through the Lobby with the SNP, which wants independence for Scotland, and with the Liberals, who want to keep the Act. What a massive display of unsullied principle!
>
> The minority parties have walked into a trap. If they win, there will be a general election. I am told that the current joke going around the House is that it is the first time in recorded history that turkeys have been known to vote for an early Christmas.

Even some Liberals laughed at that. The rest of the speech, however, was less memorable, a string of warnings about the dangers of turning to the Tories. 'I know that the Opposition want to forget the years

1970–74,' Callaghan added, to laughter from his backbenches. 'The right hon. Member for Sidcup, the former leader of the party, is removed from Conservative Party collective thinking like Trotsky was blotted out of the photographs of the Stalin era.' At that, some of the Tories started shouting. 'I admit that I am provoking them a little, Mr Speaker,' Callaghan said cheerfully.

Callaghan's aides thought his speech 'quite superb'. But their delight was short-lived, for just after five o'clock one of the whips passed the Prime Minister a note. 'His face dropped,' the watching Donoughue recorded. 'I knew it was bad news.' In the corridor outside, Callaghan said abruptly: 'They cannot get Doc Broughton here. He is too ill. We will lose. Please go and get Audrey. She should know this as soon as possible.' His policy chief was taken aback: would Harold Wilson, he wondered, have spared a thought for Mary? 'I told him that he had made an excellent speech,' Donoughue wrote afterwards. 'He said, "I'm sorry, but speeches don't make any difference. We won't get the votes and that's what matters." '[21]

Broughton had always wanted to come down to Westminster, despite the obvious risks. Just after one o'clock, however, his wife finally rang Walter Harrison. The message was simple: he was 'determined to come to the aid of the party, but it would be madness for him to do so'. Effectively that put the decision in Harrison's hands. An old-fashioned Yorkshireman, he had no desire to drive Broughton to his death. No, he said: Broughton should stay at home. That should have been that – except that Harrison saw one last chink of possibility. Broughton's absence would count for nothing if the Tories agreed to honour the long-standing gentleman's agreement on 'pairing', with one of their MPs abstaining because a government MP was too ill to vote. Unfortunately, this convention never applied in confidence votes: when Harrison approached his opposite number, Bernard ('Jack') Weatherill, the latter gently pointed out that there was no way a Conservative MP would abstain on such a crucial occasion. But then Weatherill hesitated. A former tailor who always carried a thimble in his pocket to 'keep me humble', he prided himself on his sense of honour. 'We've always dealt fairly with each other,' he said slowly. 'I shall not vote tonight. I shall stand out.' It was an extraordinary offer. If Weatherill abstained at such a moment, it would surely destroy his career. 'I'm not going to put you in that position,' Harrison said immediately. 'I didn't want Jack Weatherill put on the rack,' he explained later. 'I was dealing with it straight. I couldn't fetch Doc Broughton in, and I don't see why Jack Weatherill should have sacrificed himself.' It was a noble response to a brave gesture: a sign that, for all the partisanship, there was still a place for honour in politics.[22]

In the Commons chamber, the debate went on. The SNP's Donald Stewart slammed Labour for frustrating 'the Scottish desire for self-government'. Plaid Cymru's Gwynfor Evans waxed lyrical about the government's offer of help for Welsh quarrymen. Gerry Fitt, heard in almost reverential silence, explained unhappily why he could not support the government. Finally, at 9.30, it fell to Michael Foot to wind up for Labour. Speaking largely off the cuff, vaulting from point to point with dazzling spontaneity, he was on tremendous form. His merciless ribbing of David Steel, for instance, has gone down in parliamentary folklore. 'I am sure that I shall elicit the support and sympathy of the right hon. Lady [Mrs Thatcher] when I say that she and I have always shared a common interest in the development of this young man,' Foot said, tongue firmly in cheek. But he would love to know how the Tory–Liberal alliance, 'this most grisly of assignations', had come about. 'I do not want to misconstrue anything,' he said mischievously, 'but did she send for him or did he send for her – or did they just do it by *billet-doux*?' This had even the Tories roaring with laughter, but Foot was not finished yet. 'What the right hon. Lady has done today', he went on, 'is to lead her troops into battle snugly concealed behind a Scottish nationalist shield, with the boy David holding her hand.' He was 'more concerned about the fate of the right hon. Gentleman than I am about her. She can look after herself. But the Leader of the Liberal Party – and I say this with the utmost affection – has passed from rising hope to elder statesman without any intervening period whatsoever.'

As though swept along by the gales of laughter that greeted these words, Foot launched into one of the most memorable perorations in parliamentary history. 'What will once again be the choice at the next election?' he asked. 'It will not be so dissimilar from the choice that the country had to make in 1945, or even in 1940 when the Labour Party had to come to the rescue of the country.' That provoked great bellows of rage from the Conservative benches, but by now Foot was unstoppable, drunk on his own heady rhetoric. 'It is sometimes in the most difficult and painful moments of our history that the country has turned to the Labour Party for salvation, and it has never turned in vain,' he shouted above the din. 'We saved the country in 1940, and we did it again in 1945! We set out to rescue the country – or what was left of it – in 1974! Here again in 1979 we shall do the same!' 'Shame! Shame!'

shouted the Tories, the noise now so loud that the Speaker vainly bellowed for calm. 'I think that it is high time that the Tory Party recovered some sense of humour, even if it has lost everything else,' said Foot, provoking yet more howls of exaggerated anger. 'Conservative Members really ought to have had plenty of practice at laughing at themselves over these recent years, and they should make a better effort on this occasion.'

It was now ten o'clock, and as Foot resumed his seat amid great cheers of encouragement, the House divided. 'The Tories looked down and seemed to expect to lose,' Donoughue recorded. 'One of them who is a friend signalled to me with a thumbs-down.' The lobbies seemed unnaturally crowded; the air was thick with rumour and counter-rumour. On the Labour benches, there was talk of the Liberal MP Clement Freud abstaining, meaning the result would be a draw. Five, ten, fifteen minutes went by. The *Mirror*'s political editor Terry Lancaster watched the Prime Minister return to his seat, 'fiddling with a piece of paper, looking relaxed, even confident'. Callaghan himself thought 'the wait seemed never-ending'. At last he saw the first of the government whips, Jimmy Hamilton, emerging from the crush of MPs at the Bar of the House. As Hamilton reached the clerk's table he gave 'an almost imperceptible thumb's up', and there were murmurs of delight from the government benches. A moment later, the Tory Chief Whip, Humphrey Atkins, pushed his way through to Mrs Thatcher's side and handed her a piece of paper. Atkins's face looked grim, and as Thatcher scanned the figures, Donoughue thought she looked 'disappointed, even angry'. Perched in the members' gallery, Roy Hattersley watched her lips move. 'I don't believe it,' she muttered, and a great gasp of triumph came from the Labour benches. Almost unbelievably, they had done it.*

Then the clerk of the House handed the voting slip to the Conservative teller Spencer Le Marchant, and in that moment the mood changed. Suddenly the government benches were deathly silent; suddenly all the noise was coming from the Opposition. 'Order, order!' said the Speaker, and the House fell absolutely still. 'The Ayes to the right, three hundred and eleven,' Le Marchant said slowly, as though savouring every word. 'The Noes to the left, three hundred and ten.' Even before he had finished, there came from the Tory benches an almost animal roar of

---

* In the tension and excitement, the tellers had got mixed up. The likeliest explanation is that the Labour tellers had forgotten to include the Tory tellers in their adversaries' total.

unbridled joy. On the left, Callaghan and his ministers sat as if turned to stone. On the right, the Conservatives rose as one man to their feet – 'but not,' Lancaster noted, 'as one woman'. Amid all the shouting, Margaret Thatcher remained absolutely motionless, sitting silently in place while her colleagues celebrated. 'Out, out!' they shouted at the government benches, and for a few moments the House seemed engulfed by pandemonium. Then Jim Callaghan got to his feet and the shouting died away. 'Mr Speaker,' the Prime Minister said, his voice slow and heavy, 'now that the House of Commons has declared itself, we shall take our case to the country.'[23]

Callaghan left the chamber with 'The Red Flag' ringing in his ears, an anthem of defiance from the Labour left. When he reached his Commons room, the first thing he did was to call for his wife, Audrey. In the meantime, parties and wakes were under way across the Palace of Westminster, some Tories even doing a conga through the corridors. In the government whips' office, whisky-fuelled recriminations were already beginning. Some of the younger whips thought they should have forced Broughton to come in, regardless of the threat to his health. But Walter Harrison launched into 'a long explanation of why they had decided not to bring in Broughton in an ambulance and get him nodded through. It was a bit emotional.' Bernard Donoughue stayed to the end, knocking back the drink, becoming ever angrier at their 'unnecessary' defeat, 'a self-inflicted wound'. Callaghan, he thought, had been 'too priggish about doing deals. The whips squeamish about bringing in Broughton to vote.' In another corner of the room, Hattersley was drowning his sorrows with the elderly whip Jack Dormand. Trying to cheer him up, Dormand pointed out that he was bound to be back in the Cabinet before he turned 50. 'I believed him,' Hattersley wrote later. 'Even if we lost the election, Margaret Thatcher would not last for long.'[24]

The result could, of course, have been very different. If Harrison had insisted on bringing in Sir Alfred Broughton, or if he had taken up Jack Weatherill's offer, then the vote would have been tied, allowing the Speaker, George Thomas, to vote in favour of the government. But there were other possibilities, too. Perhaps Fitt or Maguire might have voted with the government in return for a promise to move Roy Mason after the election. Clement Freud might have abstained if the government had agreed to support his freedom of information bill. The Ulster Unionists could have abstained en bloc if Callaghan had been more accommodating over their cherished pipeline. There was even talk that the Tory MP Alan Glynn would have abstained if Callaghan had given him a peerage. And then, of course, there were the Scottish Nationalists: to the end of his days, Michael Foot believed that Callaghan could have found a compromise and avoided the entire confidence debate. And yet, as Kenneth Morgan points out, all of this is basically irrelevant, because the no-confidence vote of March 1979 was not really a turning point. Even if the government had won, Callaghan was seriously considering an early election in May or June. And even if he had staggered on to October, battered, bloodied and demoralized, the outcome would probably have been the same. As Callaghan knew, the damage had been done during the Winter of Discontent. A fighter to the last, he was ready to take his case to the people. But he must have guessed what their verdict would be.[25]

Heavy rain was falling as Margaret Thatcher left for work the morning after the no-confidence vote. 'I had no chance of a lie-in this morning,' she told the waiting journalists, her mood relieved rather than jubilant, 'but I did allow myself the luxury of a cooked breakfast – grilled, not fried.' A couple of miles away, Jim Callaghan was writing letters to Walter Harrison and Sir Alfred Broughton, reassuring them that by putting the latter's health ahead of the government's survival, they had done 'the right thing'. His political secretary Tom McNally, who caught a glimpse of the note to Broughton before Callaghan sealed the envelope, thought it showed 'the bigness of the man'.[26]

At ten, the Cabinet met to approve the election arrangements, the atmosphere 'subdued, but in no way depressed'. The date, the Prime Minister told his colleagues, would be 3 May, giving them a long campaign. After half an hour the meeting broke up and Callaghan prepared to leave for the Palace. One aide saw him standing alone in the hallway, looking 'incredibly old and tired'. But when he emerged into the noonday sunlight, he had resumed the public persona of Sunny Jim. 'I always look forward to a good fight,' he said cheerfully, grinning at the ranks of photographers. His meeting with the Queen did not last long; she had been 'very nice', he told his advisers. Then he recorded a brief television address, explaining the reasons for the election. The government's great achievement, Callaghan told the audience, had been to bring down inflation by more than half in just three years. 'The question you will have to consider', he said amiably, 'is whether we risk tearing everything up by the roots, scrapping the programmes that assist firms on which a million jobs depend, slashing spending that is needed for families and hospitals and schools, having an upheaval in industry and with the unions. The answer must surely be no.' It was good, sensible stuff, but it hardly sounded like crusading socialism. 'It was a straight appeal to conservatism – warning the public against taking the sudden lurches into radical policies that Thatcher would involve (some of which I personally sympathise with),' Donoughue wrote. 'We really are the party of caution and conservatism now!'[27]

For Callaghan, the next day's papers made gloomy reading. In the *Telegraph*, a Gallup poll gave the Conservatives a 7 per cent lead, while a MORI poll for the *Express* had Mrs Thatcher's party 9 per cent clear and an ORC poll for ITN even had them 18 per cent ahead. Despite his personal popularity, the bookmakers gave the Prime Minister little chance of clawing back the Tories' advantage: William Hill made them prohibitive 2–7 favourites to form the next government. Tellingly, too, the stock market was buoyant: on the day that Callaghan called the election, the FT30 Index closed at 540.8, a stark contrast with its low of 265.3 during the IMF crisis two and a half years earlier. And yet, despite the torrent of bad news, Callaghan seemed to be relishing the prospect of a showdown. A week after the debate that had brought down his government, he held a boisterous farewell party at Number 10. 'It's three years tomorrow since I became Leader,' he said, standing on a chair, 'and I want to thank you all and I hope you all enjoy the campaign.' He seemed 'full of vigour', Donoughue thought, 'and very keen to get cracking'. But Donoughue himself was less buoyant: Mrs Thatcher, he wrote in his diary, was 'much more effective than most of our people – or her advisers apparently – seem to realise'. After the party had broken up, he had a quiet drink with Harold Lever and got home after eleven. 'It is still very cold,' he added, 'and there have been more snowstorms in Kent. We need the spring soon.'[28]

33
The Winner Takes it All

*'Toast and marmalade.' She savoured the words happily . . .
'Lovely toast and marmalade. I can never eat that. Now and
then I eat chocolates, but I find it hard to stop at one.'*

*In our mind's eye, we both contemplated for a moment the
dark luxuries of a box of chocolates.*

*Then the image receded as she said: 'It's often best, you
know: to do without completely. You can't indulge. It will sit
on your hips.'*

Interview with Margaret Thatcher
('My Face, My Figure, My Diet'), *Sun*, 13 March 1979

MICHAEL COCKERELL: *Why did you say that you will not be
given another chance if you lose the election?*
MARGARET THATCHER: *There's only one chance in life for
women. It is the law of life.*

BBC interview, 27 April 1979

Two days after the no-confidence debate, Margaret Thatcher was in
Finchley, presenting new cars to disabled women. Thanks to the charity
Motability, she had a new Chrysler Avenger for Doris Cahill and a yellow Mini 1000 automatic for Beryl Ward. 'We want to say how much
we admire your courage and your tremendous cheerfulness,' Mrs
Thatcher told the two beaming women. 'This is our way of expressing
our tremendous admiration for you both.' She was delighted to see that
both ladies were wearing Conservative blue. 'I feel terribly guilty I am
not wearing blue, but I am going to the television studios and the background is bright turquoise – so I have to wear brown,' she said to

laughter from the photographers. 'We girls must think about these things.' A few moments later, as the meeting was winding to an end, one of her aides murmured something in her ear, and in that instant her expression completely changed. 'All we know is that there's one dead,' one of them muttered. 'Who?' she asked slowly, her eyes shining with disbelief, her face suddenly pale. 'In the *House*?'[1]

'Bloody Murder', read the next morning's headlines, announcing the shocking news that the Conservatives' Northern Ireland spokesman, Airey Neave, had been killed by an Irish National Liberation Army car bomb while driving his Vauxhall Cavalier up the ramp from the Palace of Westminster's underground car park. To politicians of all parties, this terrible atrocity was a reminder of the running sore of Northern Ireland, as well as a warning of the potential dangers that awaited them during the election campaign. It was a 'tragic, violent and despicable murder', Jim Callaghan told a hushed House of Commons, while Gerry Fitt told the press that this 'terrible and callous murder' had horrified 'everyone except the psychopaths of the IRA'. But to Margaret Thatcher above all, the loss of Airey Neave came as a devastating blow. 'Not only were they close personal friends,' one reporter wrote the next day, 'but he was the behind-the-scenes master strategist who put her in power.' It was no wonder that when the Tory leader faced the press after visiting Neave's grief-stricken widow, it was obvious that she had been crying. 'He was one of freedom's warriors,' she said quietly, biting her lip, her face ashen. 'No one knew what a great man he was, how great a man he was, except those nearest to him. He was staunch, brave, true, strong, but he was very gentle and kind and loyal ... I and so many other people owe so much to him. And now we must carry on for the things he fought for, and not let the people who got him triumph.'[2]

Mrs Thatcher had been due to address the nation that night, giving a brief reply to Jim Callaghan's broadcast announcing the election. Thanks to Neave's murder, the broadcast was postponed until the following Monday, when she opened with a brief tribute to her old friend. She thanked Callaghan for his generous tribute in the Commons, and she said how 'moved' she had been 'to see how the nation instinctively closes ranks. Anyone who thinks that terrorism is the way to divide us, or to weaken our resolve, doesn't know the British people.' But then it was back to business:

We've just had a devastating winter of industrial strife. Perhaps the worst in living memory. Certainly the worst in mine. We saw the sick refused admission to hospital, we saw people unable to bury their dead, we saw children locked out of their schools, we saw the country virtually at the mercy of secondary pickets and strike committees and we saw a Government apparently helpless to do anything about it. It's a thousand pities they didn't take up our offer of support to deal with some of these matters in January; together I believe we could have stopped them happening again. Now we'll just have to do the job ourselves.

If people put their faith in her, she would 'do more to stop this terrible rise in crime and vandalism, to raise standards in education, to give more families the chance to buy their own homes'. Under Labour, she claimed, Britain had not just been 'marking time'; it had been falling 'further and further behind'. Callaghan promised more of the same; she offered something new. 'We're at the springtime of the year, the traditional season of hope and new beginnings,' she ended. 'I think we all know in our hearts it's time for a change.'[3]

From the outset, Jim Callaghan was conscious that he faced a challenge no British party leader had ever confronted before. Old prejudices died hard: many people would undoubtedly have agreed with Betty Poynton, a Leicester machinist who told the press: 'I don't fancy a woman as Prime Minister. It's a fellow's job.' Yet Callaghan thought it was vital to avoid 'any wholesale attack on Mrs Thatcher', because female voters 'would be angered by anything which smacked of male chauvinist piggery'. Instead, he hoped that during the five-week campaign, he would be able to exploit her inexperience, giving her 'the opportunity to turn the voters off on her own initiative'. As the campaign wore on, some of Callaghan's aides chafed at his self-imposed restraint. It was time for some 'Thatcher bashing', Bernard Donoughue suggested on 21 April, urging him to be more aggressive in targeting women and young voters, and to use pro-Labour celebrities such as Marjorie Proops, Brian Clough and Elton John (although, he noted, John had a 'complicated image'). But Callaghan stood firm. He had no desire to be accused of sexism, and 'he would not himself attack her personally'.[4]

Callaghan's reluctance to bash Mrs Thatcher was not the only disappointment for his activists. At the beginning of April, he chaired a meeting to consider the National Executive's draft of the Labour manifesto. Ostensibly the meeting was dominated by the left, but it soon became clear that Callaghan was in fighting form. On issue after issue – compulsory planning, nationalization of the banks, criticism of the EEC, even the abolition of fox-hunting – he firmly shook his head. By the time they had reached the proposal to scrap the House of Lords, he had run out of patience. 'I won't have it, I won't have it,' he said firmly. 'I am the Leader of the Party . . . and I won't do it.' The left were furious, but Callaghan got his way. Even Tony Benn proved more supine than usual, largely because, as he put it, 'I have the most ghastly piles.' And when the manifesto was unveiled on 6 April, it was much more moderate than had been generally expected, taking a hard line on inflation and saying relatively little about full employment. *The Economist* hailed it as Labour's most moderate manifesto for eighty years; in the *Sunday Mirror*, the cartoonist Keith Waite had Callaghan saying: 'If you must have a Conservative Prime Minister, I'm your man.' But many Labour activists saw Callaghan's imposition of a 'right-wing' agenda as the ultimate symbol of the leadership's treachery. 'We have been betrayed by the Labour Government,' Tony Benn wrote even before the end of the campaign, 'and the manifesto doesn't say anything.' For many of Benn's followers, this was the last straw. From now on, they determined, the grass roots must control the party.[5]

While the left raged, Callaghan cut a remarkably laid-back figure. As though keen to banish his reputation as a bruiser, he ran an exceptionally restrained campaign, enjoying leisurely breakfasts with his family and the election team, spending his afternoons pottering around shopping centres, and occupying his evenings with worthy speeches to party rallies. To the press corps, he seemed 'elegiac', 'fastidious' and 'dignified'; some even thought he was 'half-hearted'. But although many observers thought he seemed ready to 'lose with dignity', and although he occasionally sank into pessimism, there was method in Callaghan's apparent lassitude. While Mrs Thatcher seemed brash and hyperactive, the Prime Minister appeared the soul of conservatism. Often he alluded directly to his experience: it had been a great boost to him, he said, that 'in a rather long political life' he had already been Chancellor, Home Secretary and Foreign Secretary, 'because experience in those offices is of the very greatest value'. All in all, said the *Sunday Telegraph*, Callaghan was 'the most accomplished purveyor of comfortable conservatism our politics has seen in many a long year'.[6]

There was, of course, a nice irony in the fact that Callaghan was running as the champion of the status quo against the forces of change. It was the Labour leader who talked of building gradually on the achievements of the past; it was the Conservative leader, meanwhile, who promised a 'fundamental change of course'. Callaghan's gamble was that, as in 1974, voters would recoil from the prospect of radical upheaval. But this inevitably meant that Labour's campaign often came over as nostalgic, even negative, with little idealism or even fresh ideas. To his critics, Callaghan seemed to be acquiescing in Britain's national decline; by contrast, Mrs Thatcher insisted again and again that 'we needn't go on as we are'. The easy option would be to stick with the status quo, 'but we could not do that for long. Year after year we have been falling further behind friends and neighbours ... If we go on declining, we shall sooner or later fall; and we shall become a quite different kind of country.' Change, Thatcher admitted, was 'often difficult and sometimes frightening', but the changes she had in mind 'should not be too difficult; and they should certainly not be frightening'. To her admirers, this was a much more invigorating formula than Callaghan's conservatism. 'If we want to carry on as we have been doing, getting poorer slowly and steadily, then Callaghan is the man we vote for,' wrote the arch-reactionary George Gale. By contrast, Mrs Thatcher was 'different' and 'disturbing', and 'not in the least comfortable or comforting'. That, Gale thought, was precisely what the country needed.[7]

Yet despite her promises of renewal and rebirth, Mrs Thatcher's manifesto was just as vague as Callaghan's. Her priorities, she claimed, were to control inflation and reform the unions; to restore economic incentives; 'to uphold Parliament and the rule of law'; to 'support family life'; and to 'strengthen Britain's defences'. For Tory diehards, however, the small print must have been disappointing. Her economic policy boiled down to vague promises to control the money supply, and though Mrs Thatcher talked a lot about tax cuts, her manifesto offered no specifics.* On spending, too, there were no hard figures: as usual, the manifesto pledged to cut 'waste, bureaucracy and over-government', but it also promised *not* to cut spending on the NHS. And even her proposed union reforms looked positively trivial compared with Heath's efforts in the early 1970s, with no mention of outlawing the closed shop or banning secondary picketing. Indeed, compared with Heath's manifesto in 1970, all this seemed pretty anodyne. There was no sense of a revolution in waiting, and no hint that her economic strategy would almost certainly involve severe hardship for those unfortunate enough to lose their jobs. It was no wonder that the *Telegraph*'s cartoonist Nicholas Garland drew Mrs Thatcher holding up two shopping bags,

---

* For example, she flatly denied that she planned to double VAT. 'We have no intention of doubling [it],' she told a press conference on 23 April. Two months later, Sir Geoffrey Howe raised the standard rate of VAT from 8 per cent to 15 per cent.

one containing Labour's record (strikes, crime and so on), the other, almost empty, labelled 'We'll let you know after we win'.[8]

One obvious reason for Mrs Thatcher's caution was that her aides were eager to reach out to former Labour voters, who would have been put off by more strident rhetoric. As her publicity guru Gordon Reece saw it, the keys to victory were young first-time voters and 'soft' Liberals and Labour voters. In particular, Reece thought it was crucial to appeal to working-class housewives, people who had just bought their first homes (or were keen to do so), and ambitious skilled workers (the 'C2s' of official statistics). These were people who read the *Sun* and the *Mirror*, watched ITV rather than the BBC and preferred *Coronation Street* to *Panorama*. They were not interested in ideology; what they wanted was a government that kept prices down and strikes to a minimum, banished the spectre of national decline and allowed them to pursue their dreams of the good life. They were often hard-working, law-abiding, patriotic and ambitious; they wanted to take more foreign holidays, to pay less tax, to move up the property ladder. And although many were trade union members, they were tired of being lectured by their ageing leaders and sick of seeing their living standards stagnate. As an internal Shadow Cabinet report put it, the Tories would never have a better opportunity to 'jump the class barrier'.[9]

It was an opportunity that the grocer's daughter seized with both hands. In her first rally of the campaign, cheekily arranged in the Prime Minister's Cardiff constituency, Mrs Thatcher appealed directly to 'Labour's traditional supporters'. Jim Callaghan's party, she said, was no longer 'the party of Clement Attlee, of Hugh Gaitskell, of Roy Jenkins', to whose legacy she now, almost incredibly, laid claim:

> There used to be, in this country, a Socialism which valued people. It had dignity and it had warmth. Its methods were those of the collective, of putting all decisions to the centre, which was why it was not our creed, but its aims to raise the living standards of the people were the same as ours. Well, what a world away that is from the officious, jargon-filled intolerant Socialism practised by Labour these last few years! What a world away it is! What a world away that sort of brotherhood is from flying pickets, from kangaroo courts, the merciless use of the closed shop power, and all the other ugly apparatus which has been strapped like a harness on our people and our country, turning worker against worker, and society against itself.

It would be hard, she acknowledged, for Labour supporters to 'cross the

Rubicon'. But their old party had been taken over by 'the extreme left wingers', who wanted to 'build a State in which the freedom of the individual is utterly destroyed'. For those voters still loyal to Attlee's legacy, she said earnestly, 'we offer you a political home where you can honourably realise the ideals which took you into the Labour party in the first place'.[10]

Overshadowing everything was the Winter of Discontent. One Conservative broadcast opened with images of rubbish in the streets, supermarket shelves bare, graveyards abandoned and airports closed, while a sepulchral voice intoned, again and again: 'Crisis? What crisis?' In her speeches, Mrs Thatcher rarely failed to mention the events of a few months previously. 'All of you have suffered under the rule of the pickets and the strikers this winter. We all saw at first hand that power and felt our own powerlessness,' she told a packed rally in Birmingham Town Hall. 'Well, you're not powerless now. This is a time when the ordinary people of this country in their tens of millions hold the future of our country in their hands. And when you come to decide that future on May the third, remember last winter.' Of course the trade union leaders, now back in line behind Labour, did not take this lying down, but as the winter had proved, their grasp of public relations was tenuous to say the least. 'I don't see how we can talk to Mrs Thatcher,' said the railwaymen's leader Sid Weighell. Should she get in, Weighell warned, 'I will say to the lads, come on, get your snouts in the trough.' In those last six words, he gave the Tories all the ammunition they needed. 'We have seen the gravediggers refusing to bury the dead,' thundered Lord Hailsham. 'We have seen the refuse accumulating in the streets . . . We have seen cancer patients having to postpone their operations . . . What is this but the law of the jungle? What is it due to but a selfish and materialistic view of the world? What is this but the weakest and most vulnerable, the old and the sick and the poor going to the wall?'[11]

The obvious weakness of the Conservative campaign was Mrs Thatcher herself. As her critics had long predicted, her Home Counties image did not play well with the voters, and in personal popularity she still lagged well behind Callaghan. Indeed, the more people saw the two leaders, the more they warmed to the Labour veteran. At the beginning of April the Prime Minister was 7 per cent ahead; by the beginning of May his lead had stretched to 19 per cent. Amazingly, even four out of ten *Conservatives* thought Callaghan would be the better Prime Minister. As a poll for *The Economist* showed, this was not just old-fashioned male chauvinism: voters saw Sunny Jim as a reassuring, avuncular figure, but perceived Mrs Thatcher as less experienced, less in touch with ordinary people, more strident and more condescending. Since Callaghan was so much more popular than his party, his aides urged him to talk in the first person, using '"I", not just "we" or "Labour"'. And since Thatcher was so much less popular than hers, the Tories always flanked her with moderate faces such as Willie Whitelaw and Jim Prior, keeping Sir Keith Joseph well out of sight. Even so, there were plenty of hints of the steel beneath the style. 'You must say something sometimes,' she upbraided Sir Geoffrey Howe at their first press confer- ence. 'Very good,' she murmured after he had roused himself. 'You should intervene more often.'[12]

The mere fact of Thatcher's gender meant that she dominated the campaign. As her biographer points out, her femininity proved a great asset, strengthening the impression that she offered something entirely new, a fresh start under a 'new broom' who knew better than anybody about the difficulty of managing a household budget and the import- ance of the family. Presented with a giant broom at a Bristol factory, she jabbed it at the cameras with the words 'We'll sweep them out of White- hall!' And although she had spent most of her career as the very antithesis of a submissive housewife, she was more than happy to play the part for the press. After all, the 'supreme common sense' of the housewife was an excellent frame for Conservative ideas, allowing her to appeal to precisely 'the sort of prudent, domestic, bill-paying, debt- avoiding, book-balancing maxims' that most people readily understood. 'They will turn to me,' she said of the voters, 'because they believe a woman knows about prices.' In Halifax, she even went shopping at the local supermarket, brandishing a bulging blue bag labelled 'February 1974' alongside a half-empty red bag labelled 'Today'. 'If Labour had five more years I would only need an envelope to carry the shopping, so don't let them lecture you on food prices,' she said firmly.[13]

More than any previous leader's itinerary, Mrs Thatcher's daily schedule was meticulously organized, with factory visits or walkabouts in key marginal constituencies, interviews with local radio stations and a big set-piece address to a Tory rally in the evening. The priority was to produce plenty of footage for the early evening news, which attracted large audiences among the Tories' target groups – women in Labour households, first-time voters and the C2 skilled workers. One typical morning, Thursday, 19 April, found her in Leicester. 'Dressed in a smart, gold-trimmed dark blue suit, her blonde hair perfectly in place,' wrote one reporter, 'she stepped out of her hotel precisely on schedule at

9 a.m.'* Her first port of call was Grahame Gardner Ltd, a small local clothing firm, where she asked one of the machinists to show her the art of lock-stitching. After a brief demonstration, she 'sat down to make a very good job of a pocket in a blue hospital overall', the cameras quietly whirring away. 'Straight through and blue,' Mrs Thatcher said delightedly as she fed the material to the needle. This went down very well with the factory staff. 'She's a lady, isn't she, but she'll have a go at anything,' said an admiring Beryl Jarvis, who had previously doubted the Tory leader's abilities. 'After all, she can't do much worse than the men.'[14]

From there Mrs Thatcher went on to give local Tory workers a pep talk, providing some snappy lines for the lunchtime radio bulletins. Then her battle bus took her to Coalville, a vital Leicestershire marginal, followed by 'dozens of journalists, ten television crews and a swarm of still photographers'. There she wandered around the shopping precinct, shaking hands and answering questions about 'everything from prices to punk'. When a teenager with a punk badge asked if she would scrap school uniforms, she replied: 'Some schools like them, some don't and you obviously don't. But punk is not my taste.' A local reporter asked if she was feeling tired. 'Any woman who has had to get up in the night to her children and still cope can stand this,' she insisted. 'By comparison, all this is a doddle.' After forty minutes or so, she was off to the Cadbury's factory in Birmingham, where she tried her hand at packing Creme Eggs on the assembly line. 'How many to the box?' she demanded over the roar of the machines. 'Forty-eight,' the supervisor said. That was far too many: after struggling to fill two boxes, Thatcher said apologetically: 'It takes concentration, doesn't it?'† Once again the workers were impressed by her efforts. 'She picked the job up very well,' said Betty Bowcott, who had worked as a Cadbury's instructor for twenty years. 'I'd certainly employ her if she loses.' Before she left, Mrs Thatcher presented a wedding card to 23-year-old Susan Bridgewater, who was getting married that weekend. 'I'll always treasure her card,' Susan said afterwards. 'She gave me a few tips on housework.'[15]

---

* It is worth noting that, with colour television sets having overtaken black-and-white three years earlier, Mrs Thatcher's outfits were chosen specifically for television, where they made for an obvious contrast with her opponent's dark suits.

† This incident offers a good example of the way in which Mrs Thatcher's legend was polished over the years. Looking back on the campaign in 2005, the *Guardian*'s Michael White recalled watching her 'stuffing chocolates into their boxes faster than the girls on the production line'. But his memory was playing tricks; in fact, and not very surprisingly, she made a mess of it.

In public at least, Callaghan found Mrs Thatcher's televised stunts highly amusing. He was especially entertained when she was photographed cuddling a calf for thirteen minutes on a Norfolk farm. ('If we're not careful,' Denis Thatcher had mordantly remarked, 'we'll have a dead calf on our hands.') As a keen farmer, Callaghan was properly scornful of the fact that she had held it the wrong way round. 'If you want to be photographed holding a calf the wrong way,' he joked, 'she'll oblige. But ask them to discuss the issues and all you get is a deathly silence. The truth is in this election the Tories are being sold as though they were Daz or Omo.' But this was an old tune; even the soap-powder parallel went back to the 1950s. And although Callaghan claimed that he had no time for media-friendly gimmicks, this was not strictly true. After all, his aides had arranged for him to be filmed talking to apprentices in a workshop and to pensioners in a retirement home, while he was also filmed attending an Easter service with his grandchildren. As the *Guardian* remarked, the very bulletin featuring Callaghan's mocking remarks about Thatcher and the calf also 'included a sequence in which the Prime Minister helped a pretty 21-year-old-voter to cut her birthday cake', while his much-feted 'meet-the-people tours ... sometimes seemed to involve not so much meeting the people as meeting the cameramen'. The truth is that both leaders were packaged: the only real difference was that Thatcher's packaging was rather glossier.[16]

For some of the Tory leader's admirers, the election represented the great showdown between freedom and collectivism. This was a chance, wrote Auberon Waugh, to declare war on 'the other side's front line', namely 'its ward "supervisors", its dwarves, ugly women, young men with squints and crooked minds, victims of broken homes or comprehensive education with impassive faces and staring eyes, its hunchbacks, sexual incompetents, militant "feminists", baby-bashers, trade unionists, teachers, lesbians, drunks, freaks, idlers, social workers, *New Statesman* journalists and Islington housewives'. In truth, though, very few people saw the election as a chance to lash out against hunchbacks, teachers and ugly women. Far from being a great ideological showdown, wrote the BBC's Michael Cockerell, the election was 'lower key and better mannered than most since the war'. Even the Tory newspapers were much more restrained than in 1974, and although the *Mail* and the *Express* launched ferocious attacks on trade union 'Reds', they were kinder to 'Uncle Jim' than they had been to Harold Wilson. Crime, schools and immigration were barely mentioned, and few ordinary people saw the election as a clash between two bitterly opposed philosophies. Only five out of ten thought there were 'important differences' between Labour and the Tories (compared with 71 per cent in 1945, 66 per cent in 1959 and 59 per cent in 1964), while four out of ten thought they were 'much of a muchness'. Labour's Dennis Skinner livened up the proceedings by writing his election address in verse, while the Liberals did their best for the gaiety of the nation by hiring an orange battle bus that kept breaking down. But despite the best efforts of Eric Sykes for the Tories and Brian Clough for Labour, most people found the campaign intolerably dull. 'Night after night the nation's living rooms are invaded by politicians endlessly contradicting each other – and frequently themselves as well,' sighed the *Express*. 'Switch off these TV bores!'[17]

From the outset, a Conservative victory seemed inevitable. No government had entered a general election lagging further behind in the polls, and when voters were asked what they thought of Labour's record on individual issues, the results were damning. On law and order, the government's approval rating was minus 21 per cent; on immigration minus 28 per cent; on the economy minus 48 per cent; on the cost of living minus 51 per cent; on strikes, not surprisingly, minus 62 per cent. And despite all the razzamatazz, the polls barely budged at all. Reading the morning papers on Sunday, 22 April, Bernard Donoughue noted that the *Sunday Telegraph* had the Conservatives 5½ per cent ahead, the *Sunday Times* gave them a lead of 9 per cent and the *Observer* had them fully 20 per cent clear. 'It looks as if we're making very little impact,' he wrote miserably. 'It is as though people have made up their minds: they are fed up with the unions and our craven attitude towards them; they want tax cuts even if it means price rises; they want a gamble on a new face; and no rational argument in the campaign will change this.' Not surprisingly, Callaghan was 'grumpy again' at their daily breakfast meeting the next morning. Mrs Thatcher, he complained, was 'the dominant character of the campaign'. But he still refused to take off the gloves, repeating that 'he would not attack her personally'.[18]

And yet in the next few days there came the first signs of a subtle shift in momentum. With nothing to lose, Labour began hammering at their opponents' economic plans, demanding to know where the money for tax cuts was coming from and asking how they intended to keep prices down. Bit by bit the polls began to move; from an average of 10 per cent, the Conservative lead was falling. For Margaret Thatcher this was the lowest point of the campaign, the dark moment when it seemed that victory was slipping away. Rattled by Callaghan's mockery of her tax plans, she 'seemed somewhat on the defensive', remarked the BBC's David Dimbleby on Wednesday, 25 April. That night, she was resting near Glasgow Airport when the party chairman, Peter Thorneycroft, rang to suggest inviting Edward Heath to her final press conference. At the critical moment, the old guard had lost confidence.[19]

'Margaret exploded in a mixture of fury and supreme contempt,' recalled her speechwriter, the veteran playwright Ronald Millar. 'Scared rabbits!' she raged. 'They're running scared, that's what's the matter with them! The very idea! How *dare* they?' Unwittingly, her colleagues had touched a nerve: in her memoirs, Thatcher wrote that this was 'the closest I came in the campaign to being really upset'. Her husband Denis told Millar the next morning that she had not slept a wink, but had lain awake in cold fury. He had 'never seen her in such a state', he said. Later that day, after touring Aberdeenshire, she told Central Office that there was no way she would share a platform with her predecessor. If they did not understand that 'what we were fighting for was a reversal not just of the Wilson–Callaghan approach but of the Heath Government's approach,' she thought, 'they had understood nothing.'[20]

On the evening of 30 April, with just three days to go, the BBC broke the scarcely believable news that the *Daily Mail* now gave Labour the tiniest of leads, amounting to just 0.7 per cent. That night the Prime Minister's aides were 'euphoric', and the next morning Callaghan seemed a man reborn, 'sparkling with humour and confidence'. Donoughue thought that even the reporters seemed swept up in the 'good mood'; indeed, in Wednesday's *Guardian*, Peter Jenkins wrote that 'it would no longer be amazing to see Mr Callaghan win by a whisker'. At lunch in Number 10, Donoughue raised with Ken Stowe the possibility of Labour suffering a 'close loss'. In that case, Stowe said reassuringly, he had already advised Callaghan that 'it was for *him* to try to create a new government, coalition, etc.' Just in case, the civil service had arranged to put a plane on standby to fly David Steel down from Scotland for coalition talks. Deep down, Donoughue knew this was all highly unlikely. Despite the erosion of the Conservative lead, the polls in London and the West Midlands, where the Tories had targeted working-class voters in the key marginals, were not quite so good. But after so much despair in recent months, at least Callaghan had given himself a sliver of hope.[21]

On Monday evening, Mrs Thatcher had made her last broadcast to the nation. Like many of her major speeches, it was largely the work of Ronald Millar, who brilliantly caught her blend of patriotic populism. 'We're coming to the moment of decision,' she began softly, her tone a long way from that of an Iron Lady:

> As the tumult and the shouting of the last few weeks die away and you sit at home wondering what to do on Thursday I can well imagine you saying to yourselves, 'If only the politicians would be quiet. If only we could sit peacefully for a few minutes and think about our country and its future and the decision you're asking us to make.'
>
> I know how you feel. The decision is crucial. The problems facing Britain are very grave. I can't remember when our people have approached an election quite as thoughtfully as this one.

Yet again she appealed to the thirst for a fresh start. 'If ever there was a need for change, it's now,' she said earnestly. 'I don't mean sudden change and I'm not talking about trying to bring back some nostalgic version of the past.' She talked of cutting taxes, 'limited but essential' union reforms, and the need for strong defence against the Soviet threat. She also addressed head-on the lingering suspicion of a woman Prime Minister. 'It's never happened before,' she said. 'And I know that despite all the changes in our society there are some who still feel a little bit uncertain about it. I also know that there are others who would welcome it.' But she ended on an unashamedly patriotic, even sentimental note:

> Somewhere ahead lies greatness for our country again; this I know in my heart. Look at Britain today and you may think that an impossible dream. But there's another Britain which may not make the daily news but which each one of us knows. It's a Britain of thoughtful people – oh, tantalisingly slow to act yet marvellously determined when they do. It's their voice which steadies each generation . . .
>
> Today, if you listen, you can hear that voice again . . . Its message is quiet but insistent. It says this: Let us make this a country safe to work in; let us make this a country safe to walk in; let us make it a country safe to grow up in; let us make it a country safe to grow old in.
>
> And it says, above all: May this land of ours, which we love so much, find dignity and greatness and peace again.

Inspired by Saatchi & Saatchi's research, many of these phrases had been written specifically to appeal to women, skilled workers and first-time voters. In Downing Street, Bernard Donoughue thought it was 'completely artificial, all sugary'. It was, he decided, a weak attempt 'to imitate the Queen's Christmas broadcast'. But as the Jubilee had shown, a lot of people liked the Queen.[22]

Wednesday, the last day, was bitterly cold. Across much of the country it rained. In many places hail and snow poured down. 'God really is a Tory,' Donoughue thought. In London, Mrs Thatcher again appealed for change, insisting that cutting taxes was 'a moral case as well as a material one'. Her opponent, too, devoted his last press conference to the theme of change. A Conservative vote was a vote for 'change with chaos', Callaghan explained. By contrast, a Labour vote was a vote for 'controlled' change, adapted for 'the ordinary worker and his family'.

> Change is coming to this country. It's happening all the time, and I think it will accelerate in the nineteen hundred and eighties, especially because of this trendy term we now have, the micro-processor revolution, and the silicon chip, which everybody talks about and hardly anybody has ever seen. But this is going to transform our working life in the 1980s, and I think what we have to do, and what we are preparing to do, is to meet that change in an orderly, sensible way.
>
> Change must come to this country. The question is whether you leave it to free-market forces which could throw a man and his family on the street overnight, or to try and control it, and make sure that through government partnership with industry, on both sides of industry, that you can make it come in a way that will help the people of this country – not create vast wealth for some and poverty for others.

Even as the Prime Minister was speaking, his backroom boys were studying the final auguries. That afternoon, working listlessly in a deserted Number 10, Donoughue heard rumours that the last opinion polls were bad. 'They may be wrong,' he thought, 'but it does not feel wrong. Basically people want a change and they hate the trade unions. All the other arguments are at the margin.'[23]

'This is D-Day. D for Decision. The first day of the rest of our lives,' declared the front page of Britain's biggest selling newspaper on Thursday morning. Appealing directly to 'traditional Labour supporters', a gigantic *Sun* headline said sternly: 'Vote Tory This Time. *It's the only way to stop the rot.*' As so often during the campaign, an editorial insisted that the *Sun* was 'not a Tory newspaper' but a 'RADICAL newspaper', and boasted of its pride in having 'the largest working-class readership of any daily paper'. Its message, however, could have come directly from Conservative Central Office, with Labour dismissed as 'the refuge of militants, Marxist bullies and class war warriors'. By contrast, the *Sun* said, Margaret Thatcher was offering 'FREEDOM to run your life as YOU want to run it ... to work, with or without a union card ... to spend your money or save it'. Many of its readers might be suspicious of a female leader. But 'to argue against a woman as Prime Minister is no argument at all – if the passion, the will and the ability are there'.[24]

The *Sun*'s enthusiasm for Mrs Thatcher did not go down well with the print unions. At first the editorial was set in the wrong measure and type size; then the compositors inserted what the editor, Larry Lamb, called 'substantial and arbitrary cuts'. Eventually he managed to get the paper out as planned, albeit a little late.* Of the other mass-market papers, the *Mail* hailed 'The Woman Who Can Save Britain', while the *Express* advised its readers: 'YOU can help Margaret Thatcher make Britain really GREAT again.' Only one paper, the *Mirror*, gave Labour an unambiguous endorsement. 'Back to the Tories, or FORWARD WITH THE PEOPLE?' asked its front page on polling day, above a small picture of a smiling Callaghan. The *Guardian*'s recommendation, however, was half-hearted at best. 'Since there is scant faith, only a gritty determination to make the best of what we have by learning and unlearning and struggling,' it said, 'Mr Callaghan, a compassionate struggler, is not merely the man we deserve but also, in all probability, the man we need.'[25]

It was a cool, cloudy morning. In Bristol, Tony Benn toured his constituency perched on the roof of his car, wrapped up in a blanket and wearing rubber overtrousers, a woolly hat and an anorak. 'It was freezing,' he recorded. 'We went round every single ward and it was terribly exhausting.' In general, however, the weather was better than many Labour strategists had feared, with only brief flurries of snow in Scotland and the west. In London, some of Mrs Thatcher's closest advisers were quietly gloomy, with Gordon Reece, Tim Bell and Alistair McAlpine all fearing a last-minute surge back to Labour. But they were wrong: across the South and the Midlands, skilled workers and middle-class voters were swinging to the right. Roy Jenkins, protesting against the government of which he had been a part, did not vote, while his wife

---

* As he wryly noted, everybody came out a winner: since the 'saboteurs' were on piecework, they got paid twice for their efforts.

Jennifer voted Liberal. In Hampstead, Harold Pinter, exasperated by 'union selfishness and violent behaviour at the National', cast his vote for the Conservatives. So did his wife, Lady Antonia Fraser, who wanted 'to see a woman walk into No. 10'. Peter Hall, after much agonizing the night before, voted Tory, too. 'It wasn't at all difficult,' he wrote in his diary, as though in wonder. 'In fact, it positively felt good: wanting change ... and we have to have change.'[26]

In Downing Street the mood was subdued, everybody waiting for the moment of decision. On his way into work, Bernard Donoughue visited his local polling station, and what he saw confirmed his worst fears:

> It seemed very quiet, just a trickle of old ladies. I could tell from the deter-
> mined look in their eyes that they had not come to vote FOR anybody.
> They had come to vote AGAINST Alan Fisher, Moss Evans and every trade
> union thug who stood in a picket line barring the way to the hospital or
> the graveyard that they feared might be their destination tomorrow. And
> against every Labour local authority which had left piles of rubbish in the
> way of their shopping. And against every union leader who had stared at
> them on the TV screen and said, 'To hell with the public, my members
> want as much as they can grab.' It was all very well for Labour – for us in
> the PM's speeches – to argue that Mrs Thatcher and the Tories preached
> the harsh doctrine of 'weakest to the wall'. As far as these weak old ladies
> were concerned, Labour and the unions practised it.

That afternoon a call came in from Cardiff. It was Callaghan. They had lost, he said bluntly. 'Mrs Thatcher [will] be in No. 10 as Prime Minister tomorrow. So we must be out by 3.30 pm.' In fact, the civil service had already made all the arrangements, keen to avoid the embarrassing scrambles that had marked the arrival and departure of the last Conservative Prime Minister. On Wednesday, Ken Stowe had held a secret meeting with Mrs Thatcher's aide Richard Ryder to finalize the arrangements for the transition. Already Stowe had made an appointment for Callaghan to see the Queen after lunch on Friday, with Mrs Thatcher scheduled to follow an hour later. Nothing would be left to chance: a 'buffet supper', Ryder reported, had been ordered for the new Prime Minister's first evening. 'Do you want to sleep at Downing Street on Friday night?' he asked. On his report she wrote her answer: 'NO'.[27]

At ten the polls closed. In Downing Street, Donoughue sat alone watching the results, the BBC opening with Rick Wakeman's splendid 'Arthur' instrumental. The first exit polls gave the Conservatives a majority of around 60, as predicted, but the polls had been badly wrong before. But by midnight results were flooding in from Middle England, and it was clear that they had been right after all. Across the country the Liberal vote had collapsed. In the affluent South-east, meanwhile, working-class voters had turned away from Labour in their droves. In Harlow the swing to the Tories was almost 13 per cent; in Thurrock and Basildon it was 11 per cent; in Dagenham, the home of the giant Ford plant, it was 13.4 per cent. From Hertfordshire came reports that Shirley Williams had lost her seat; in Cardiff, waiting for his count, Jim Callaghan told reporters that he was 'heartbroken' at the news. At Conservative Central Office 'the grins grew steadily broader'; in a corner, someone had put Bollinger on ice. On television, Denis Healey cut a typically bullish figure, as though confident that he would soon be wrestling with the nation's finances again. But at Transport House, Labour officials watched in a silence 'heavy with doom and despondency'. 'I felt completely numbed,' Bernard Donoughue recorded afterwards. 'Not bitterly disappointed – I never really thought we would win ... Just flat and numb. As if bereaved, as if somebody close to me had died, predictably but still a sad loss, leaving a void.'[28]

At half past two, smartly dressed in dark blue, her hair perfectly arranged, Mrs Thatcher took the stage for her Finchley count. By now she surely knew that she would be moving into Number 10, yet she looked unnaturally calm, even serene. 'I know what it's like to be on the losing side,' she told her opponents; 'but, you know, if you go to other seats, things might change.' An hour later the BBC cut to Cardiff, where Callaghan stood impassively on the platform, a weary-looking man in a dark business suit, his hands clasped behind his back. When his name was read out, the Independent Socialist candidate Pat Arrowsmith, who had dogged him during the last days, started shouting 'Troops out of Ireland!' Callaghan seemed barely to notice, but when he began to thank the returning officer, she started shouting about Ireland again. 'I'm sure that even the candidate who keeps interrupting would welcome a word of thanks to all those who have sat throughout the whole day to collect the votes,' the Prime Minister said mildly – at which point Arrowsmith started heckling again. 'You see what I've had to put up with for the last month going round the country,' Callaghan said with a weary grin, and the hall broke into applause. 'You're a silly woman!' somebody shouted. 'No, no, it's all right,' Callaghan said calmly. 'She has her own strong views.' To tumultuous applause, he invited her to take the microphone, and then led the other candidates off the stage.

'Strange scenes at the count,' the BBC's David Dimbleby said thought-fully as the coverage cut back to London.[29]

'It looks like a Tory victory!!' Kenneth Williams wrote on Friday morning, exulting that it was 'the first time since Macmillan that we've had a leader with style and dignity'. For the other Conservative diarists who had cursed the high taxes of the Wilson and Callaghan years, there seemed much to celebrate. Roy Strong gleefully recorded his 'euphoria', while James Lees-Milne wrote that he was 'wonderfully cheered by the victory'. 'Bloody good, eh?' a triumphant Kingsley Amis wrote to Philip Larkin. 'Not only that she got in but that those who were pushed out were pushed out: that murdering quean Thorpe, and that shouting bully Pardoe, and that tousle-haired totalitarian Shirley Williams – I bet she rued the day she turned up on the Grunwick picket line!' Amis's only regret was that 'they didn't get rid of Dr bloody Death (Owen)', although, like many people, he feared that Mrs Thatcher might go the way of Edward Heath. 'This lot should do quite well,' he added, 'until the miners go on strike for an increase of 250% now and 375% on 1st June and the power workers for 425% backdated to 1st January 1929.' In that case, he thought, the new Prime Minister should 'send for the guns and kill'.[30]

At the Stock Exchange, where the FT30 Index reached an all-time high of 558.6, there were reports of traders cheering as late Tory victories came through, some even singing 'Land of Hope and Glory'. But not everyone was similarly delighted. When the *Telegraph* asked one of Amis's old bêtes noires what he thought of Mrs Thatcher's victory, Enoch Powell simply replied: 'Grim.' Like millions of voters in Scotland, northern England and Labour's working-class heartlands, Powell was no admirer of Mrs Thatcher, who struck him as shallow, insincere about Europe and immigration, and slavishly pro-American. One of the first things he did after the election was to write a heartfelt letter to Callaghan ('My dear Jim'), commiserating on his defeat.[31]

Callaghan found it hard to disguise his shock at the scale of the Conservatives' victory. For the first time since 1966 the voters had produced a clear and unarguable mandate: indeed, the swing to the Tories of just over 5 per cent was a post-war record. When the dust settled the following day, they had 339 seats to Labour's 269, with the Liberals reduced to just 11 seats, the SNP and Plaid Cymru on two each and the Northern Irish parties on 12. Still, the Labour vote had certainly not collapsed: with 11.5 million votes, Callaghan had won only 100,000 votes fewer than Wilson in February 1974. The real story was Mrs Thatcher's success at taking almost 2 million votes from the Liberals, who paid a heavy price for the Thorpe–Scott fiasco – although it was a testament to David Steel's ability that they lost only two seats. After a decade in which the two-party system had seemed to be cracking apart, the Conservatives had reasserted their position as the party of Middle England, and of government.[32]

Behind these figures, however, were two trends hinting at the political and social cleavages of the decades to come. The first was Mrs Thatcher's spectacular success with young working-class voters. Among skilled workers (the C2s) there was a swing of 11 per cent to the Conservatives, with most of the defectors being young men and women in their twenties and early thirties. Even among unskilled manual workers, the bedrock of the Labour vote, there was a 9 per cent swing to the Conservatives, while among trade union members there was a pro-Tory swing of more than 8 per cent. It was not only the prosperous middle classes, in other words, who were drawn to Mrs Thatcher's rhetoric of change; she also attracted four out of ten skilled workers and one in three trade union members. Intriguingly, the swing was most marked in the New Towns of south-eastern England, the Lancashire and Yorkshire coalfields and the car-manufacturing heartlands of Birmingham, Oxford and Dagenham – precisely those places where skilled union members were sick of wage restraint, wanted a return to free collective bargaining and liked the sound of lower taxes.

Given her later reputation, Mrs Thatcher's appeal to trade unionists in 1979 was genuinely remarkable. In less than five years as party leader, she had slashed Labour's lead among union members from an apparently unassailable 42 per cent to just over 18 per cent. Later, *The Economist* suggested that the Tories' harder line on crime and immigration had much to do with it, especially in East London seats such as Barking, Dagenham and Stepney and Poplar. But this is surely only part of the explanation: after all, 51 per cent of union members thought the Tories had the best policies on tax, while 38 per cent preferred their policies on inflation and prices and 37 per cent of union members even thought they had the best strategy for handling unemployment. The truth is that affluence, ambition and sheer exasperation at wage restraint, as well as shock at the Winter of Discontent, had eaten away at Labour's core support. Revealingly, more than 60 per cent of people told a survey for the *Sunday Times* that they had voted, not out of class loyalty, but in accordance with their private interests.[33]

The other striking thing about the results, though, was the reappearance of what Disraeli had once called the 'two nations'. As the *Guardian* remarked after the election, there was no national pattern. While 'the moneyed South, the affluent Midlands and the shires' had rallied behind Mrs Thatcher, the industrial north remained staunchly Labour. In inner London, for example, the Tory swing was almost 7 per cent, yet in Scotland there was actually a swing to Labour of 0.7 per cent. In the West Midlands the pro-Tory swing was 7.1 per cent; in Tyneside, it was only 3.8 per cent. The obvious conclusion, the *Guardian* thought, was that 'the have-nots, the have-littles and the have-problems bent only slightly in the wind of change whilst the have-plentys and want-mores were eager to clip along with the Conservatives'. The paper's political editor Ian Aitken thought that this growing north–south divide might create 'real difficulties for a new Conservative Government pledged to make big cuts in public expenditure and to move toward a phasing out of job subsidies and support for failing industries'. This would surely blunt Mrs Thatcher's radicalism in office, he predicted, since she was bound to want to improve her position in the industrial north. Like most commentators, he had little sense of what was coming.[34]

Had the British people made a decisive turn to the right? In some ways it certainly felt like it. On immigration, law and order, educational standards and capital punishment, many voters had been well to the right of both major parties for years anyway – hence the popularity of Enoch Powell. Poll data suggest that public opinion moved further to the right between 1974 and 1979, particularly on 'social' issues such as immigration and crime. The British Election Survey found that support for public ownership had fallen dramatically, down from 32 per cent to 17 per cent in less than five years; meanwhile, support for privatization had risen from 22 per cent to 40 per cent, even though the Conservatives had not yet made it a major issue. What was most remarkable, though, was the fact that Labour supporters themselves were moving rightwards. In 1964, when Harold Wilson had first come to power, 57 per cent of Labour voters wanted more public ownership, yet by 1979 it was down to only 32 per cent. Similarly, in 1964 some 59 per cent of Labour voters did not believe the unions had 'too much power', yet by 1979, this was down to just 36 per cent. In later years, Labour leaders were often pilloried for leading a supposedly left-wing party to the right, an image some of them positively encouraged. The irony, though, is that millions of Labour voters had got there first.[35]

Even so, Britain was a long way from being a Thatcherite nation in

1979. On some issues, voters were clearly becoming more liberal: in the long run, support for the death penalty, for instance, was gradually falling. And on many economic issues, most people still held fairly social democratic views, not least because they were worried about unemployment. When Gallup asked voters whether they would prefer tax cuts (even if it meant reduced spending on health, education and welfare) or high social spending (even if it meant no tax cuts), seven out of ten said they would prefer spending. Deep down, most people still believed in high public spending on the social services they now took for granted. Only 8 per cent thought the government spent too much on education, while 52 per cent thought it should spend more. Only 4 per cent wanted cuts to the NHS, compared with 66 per cent who wanted more investment. And just 1 per cent supported cuts in pensions, while 44 per cent wanted more spending and 48 per cent thought the government had the balance about right. These voters may well have been angry at Britain's competitive decline, weary of the government's indulgence of the unions and eager for a fresh start under a new regime. But they were not, by any stretch of the imagination, card-carrying Thatcherites.[36]

Of course this contradicts Jim Callaghan's famous remark to Bernard Donoughue a few days before the election: 'You know there are times, perhaps once every thirty years, when there is a sea change in politics. It then does not matter what you say or what you do. There is a shift in what the public wants and what it approves of. I suspect there is now such a sea change – and it is for Mrs Thatcher.' But the relevant entry in Donoughue's diary – as opposed to his memoirs – shows that Callaghan has been misquoted. In fact, he was 'quite optimistic' that Labour would win, '*unless* there has been one of those sea changes in public opinion towards Thatcher' (my italics). The difference is crucial: these were not the words of somebody who thought that the country had swung irrevocably to the right. Indeed, even after the voters had kicked him into opposition, Callaghan refused to accept that there had been a great ideological shift. When, a week after the election, Tony Benn insisted that Labour hold an inquest into the reasons for their defeat, Callaghan snapped that the reasons were perfectly clear. 'I'll tell you what happened,' he said. 'We lost the Election because people didn't get their dustbins emptied, because commuters were angry about train disruption and because of too much union power. That's about it.'[37]

Things could, of course, have been very different. According to the most celebrated counterfactual in modern political history, if only Callaghan had gone to the country in October 1978, then Margaret

Thatcher would have been no more than a historical curiosity. But there is no evidence that Labour would have won a clear mandate: as Callaghan's own calculations had shown, an October election would probably have produced another hung parliament, with the Tories winning 304 seats and Labour 303. The most plausible alternative is that the Conservatives would have won a very narrow victory, perhaps as a minority government. In any case, it is a mistake to see the Winter of Discontent as a one-off: the reason it was such a disaster for Labour was precisely because it played on so many long-standing anxieties. At the height of the industrial turmoil, the *Guardian*'s Peter Jenkins identified the strikes as mere symptoms of a 'chronic British condition', rooted in 'falling production, eroding competitiveness and deteriorated productivity'. 'Wages in Britain *are* low, living standards *are* becoming inadequate,' he wrote grimly. 'We are living in an expensive and increasingly poor country. It is not much use lecturing people about paying themselves more than the country can afford. A better way of putting it is that increasingly the country cannot afford to pay people enough.' What Britain needed, he thought, was 'a bold government' and a 'psychological break' from the 'dreary cycle of failure'.[38]

Jenkins's frustration at Britain's 'loss of competitiveness' was widely shared, not just by proto-Thatcherites, but by millions of people from all backgrounds. People had been talking about degeneration and decay for a long time: ever since the Macmillan years, they had been telling each other that something was 'wrong' with the economy, that Britain's institutions were sclerotic and senescent, that the United Kingdom was breaking up, and that the future held only discontent and decline. At one level these fears seem overheated: after all, most people enjoyed more comfortable lives than ever before. But to voters reflecting on the turbulent events of the 1970s – the miners' strikes, the three-day week, the IRA bombing campaigns, the double-digit inflation, the corruption scandals, the IMF bailout and the Winter of Discontent – talk of the 'Sick Man of Europe' seemed disturbingly accurate. For anyone who was tired of reading about walkouts and stoppages, or was horrified by the bloodshed in Northern Ireland, or was disgusted by headlines about crime and corruption, or was disturbed by surging prices and stagnant salaries, or was anxious about the decline of the nation's industries, or was unhappy at the influx of so many immigrants, or was distressed by the spread of permissiveness and pornography, or was suspicious of comprehensive schools and progressive teaching methods, talk of

Wonder-Maggie prepares to take on the dreaded D-Kline: John Jensen in the
Sunday Telegraph, 6 May 1979

change naturally appealed. 'Unless we change our ways and our direction, our glories as a nation will soon be a footnote in the history books,'
Margaret Thatcher had said during the election campaign. And whether
they liked her or not, millions clearly agreed.[39]

Disquiet at the state of the nation went well beyond dyed-in-the-
wool Tories. The director Peter Hall had voted Labour since the 1950s
but now felt that it was 'the party of sectional interest; the party that
protects pressure groups and bully boys'. His colleague Michael Elliott
also voted Tory 'for the first time in his life', explaining that he 'could
not support a party that was allowing the corruption of trade unionism and the corruption of picketing'. Similarly, his friend Stephen Fay,
who worked for the *Sunday Times*, 'said that he was going to vote Tory,
too, for the first time, because he felt we needed a corrective'. Even Bernard Donoughue, the man in charge of dreaming up policies for Wilson
and Callaghan, saw the Winter of Discontent as proof that Britain
desperately needed change. The government had its achievements, he
wrote, but 'we left a country where society appeared divided, national
morale was low and group behaviour depressingly bad'. He was struck,
too, by how 'dismal certain aspects of life could be for many people in
the late 1970s', especially in the dilapidated cities and decaying industrial areas:

> Few public services, especially at local government level, worked adequately
> or as well as they had done twenty years earlier. Travelling on public trans-
> port ... could be a nightmare. Strikes were frequent in the public and
> private sectors. Manufacturing products were often shabby and unreliable,

with our domestic cars particularly prone to failure. Basically, customers were badly treated and so daily life for ordinary citizens could be very frustrating.

To all this, Donoughue felt, the Labour Party had no real answer. Tied to the 'old-fashioned unions and the shrinking old working classes', constantly 'looking over its shoulder to appease the left', it was unable to reach out to the 'growing new middle classes and the new young with their aspirations'. And although he was far from being a Tory himself, he hoped that Mrs Thatcher would 'restore some efficiency to our economy, some discipline to the public sector, some priority to the consumer as opposed to the producer, and some sense of responsibility in society as a whole'. He was not alone: polls showed that almost eight out of ten people agreed it was 'time for a change'.[40]

Exhausted after the drama of the small hours, Jim Callaghan returned to Downing Street from Cardiff at breakfast time on Friday morning, ushering his wife through the black door before a handful of bleary-eyed spectators. While Audrey went upstairs for a nap, Callaghan went out to the garden with the faithful Ken Stowe. Beneath the surface, Stowe said later, the Prime Minister seemed 'emotional and a bit wounded – feeling that he had been rejected'. After a while he went inside and wrote a message for his successor, as well as a minute authorizing her to see all his papers about the deal for Trident. By now the transition was well under way: when Donoughue arrived a few hours later, the secretaries were already shredding the Policy Unit papers. 'All those arguments about pay policy, the industrial strategy, the Health Service, the Price Commission, renegotiating the EEC terms of entry, down to saving the "pint" measurement, all into black plastic bags,' Donoughue recorded sadly. 'Thus go governments.'[41]

At twelve-thirty, the Prime Minister appeared in the doorway. 'Thank you, dear Bernard, for everything,' Callaghan said, grasping his hand. Then they all went upstairs for a farewell lunch of cottage pie – 'the last supper', as Callaghan jokingly called it. Perhaps Donoughue's mind went back to those first disastrous lunches under Harold Wilson; this time, though, the atmosphere was very different. Most of them had been expecting defeat: there was 'a buzz of conversation, some jokes and calm discussion about future plans'. They talked about the election, and Callaghan said he doubted 'there was much else we could do. "The people wanted a change."' He shook his head: 'The unions did it: people could not forget and would not forgive what they had to suffer from the unions last winter.' Donoughue said that Mrs Thatcher ought to give Alan Fisher and Moss Evans a life peerage each 'for services to the Conservative Party'. At that, he noted, Callaghan 'laughed easily and with pleasure'. At the end, Donoughue felt a rush of affection for his beaten leader. 'Everybody agrees he fought a brave, honourable and honest campaign,' he wrote. 'He has lived up to the office of Prime Minister, and history will write well of him.'

History certainly ought to write well of Jim Callaghan. It is grossly unfair that while Harold Wilson is remembered for winning four elections, Callaghan is written off as a loser. Given his atrocious inheritance and non-existent majority, he proved a surprisingly effective Prime Minister, and certainly a much straighter one than his predecessor. It is true that he might have done more to fight Trotskyite infiltration into the Labour Party, but his wafer-thin majority meant he was always dependent on left-wing support. It is also true that he was utterly at sea during the Winter of Discontent, but probably nobody could have coped with such an extraordinary surge of industrial unrest – and in any case, much of the blame surely lies with his supine colleagues and with the militants in the unions. Still, the fact remains that for most of his tenure, Callaghan had the courage to face up to the challenges of the day, acknowledging the primacy of bringing inflation down and frequently lecturing his own party about the need for change. It was a tragedy for Labour that, in the years that followed, it did not learn the appropriate lessons, preferring instead to dismiss him and Healey as 'traitors to socialism'. Yet although this serious, old-fashioned man remained without honour among his own activists, his opponents held him in high regard. Callaghan was not only 'much more confident' than Wilson, remarked Sir Geoffrey Howe years later, but he had made a bold start at 'addressing the real problems of the country'. Even Mrs Thatcher thought he had been 'dealt a bad hand by history and Harold Wilson'. Callaghan had a 'real feel for public opinion', she admitted, calling him 'a brilliant poker player' who 'employed skill, gamesmanship and simple bluff to spin out his defeat as long as possible'. Above all, she was impressed by his 'brave public break' with Keynesian economics – a reminder that the gulf between them was not as wide as people later imagined.[42]

Callaghan's defeat is often seen as the death rattle of a post-war consensus based on full employment and Keynesian management. As Labour's leading moderate throughout the 1960s and 1970s, he had always been 'a classic consensus man'. But even before he moved into Number 10, the cosy world of the post-war consensus had collapsed, a victim of surging world prices, rising unemployment, industrial decline, the death of deference and the emergence of a new generation who took affluence for granted and were no longer content to be told what to do. The man in Whitehall no longer knew best; increasingly, people were determined to take their lives into their own hands. And as Callaghan had warned in 1976, Britain's commitment to full employment was no longer sustainable without pushing inflation into double figures. The Labour left's answer was a siege economy, dressed up with a lot of ultra-proletarian rhetoric. But Callaghan's answer – spending cuts, cash limits, money-supply targets and lengthening dole queues – was much closer to Mrs Thatcher's than we often think. During the 1979 campaign, both made fighting inflation their chief priority, and both ruled out incomes policies. They were both keen admirers of the Atlantic alliance and reluctant supporters of Britain's EEC membership; they both championed law and order; they both spoke up for old-fashioned standards in education. If Callaghan had still been running the country in the early 1980s, he would not have restored the post-war consensus. Instead, he would have carried on reforming it – albeit much more slowly than the Tories did.[43]

Perhaps this helps to explain why, on the night of the election, there was surprisingly little sense that Mrs Thatcher's victory marked a sea change. Interviewed by the BBC while the results were coming in, senior Labour ministers like Denis Healey and Merlyn Rees remained remarkably upbeat. In the previous fifteen years, they had fought six elections, winning four of them. Modern governments came and went; nobody imagined that Labour would be out of power for the next eighteen years. The Conservative victory had been solid rather than spectacular: with just 44 per cent of the total vote, Mrs Thatcher had won a smaller share than Ted Heath in 1970 and barely more than Sir Alec Douglas-Home in 1964. Her manifesto had been vague, her approach was cautious and her colleagues were known to have their doubts. As Peregrine Worsthorne had already warned readers of the *Sunday Telegraph*, a Tory victory was 'not going to make all that much difference'. There would, he predicted, be 'neither revolution nor counter-revolution': should Mrs Thatcher make any changes, they would be measured 'in inches not miles'. In their review of the election, David Butler and Dennis Kavanagh agreed: in all probability, it would 'not prove to be a watershed'. Only a few observers detected signs of the extraordinary turbulence ahead. On the Sunday after the election, the *Express* group's cartoonist Michael Cummings drew Mrs Thatcher as an airline pilot, her Conservative colleagues strapped in nervously behind her. 'Fasten Your Seat Belts' reads a giant sign. In the distance, through the windscreen, storm clouds are gathering.[44]

Just before 2.30, Callaghan left Downing Street for the last time. By now, as if mocking him after the months of snow, the sun had come out. In the hallway of Number 10, the staff had gathered to bid him farewell, many of them crying. Callaghan himself was visibly moved – Donoughue thought 'there were clearly tears in the PM's eyes' – and reached out to clasp the hands of one of the messengers, a keen Labour supporter. Then he walked out of the door and into the sunlight, waving cheerfully at the crowd. He climbed into his black Rover and gave the staff one last wave; this time, mercifully, the window did not fall off. The car swept up towards the Palace. Then, after Callaghan had surrendered his office to the Queen, another car took him to Transport House for a final press conference. Now that he had shed the burden of power, he seemed remarkably relaxed. 'I want to congratulate Mrs Thatcher on becoming Prime Minister,' he said, smiling broadly. 'It's a great office, a wonderful privilege – and for a woman to occupy that office is, I think, a tremendous moment in the country's history.'[45]

Margaret Thatcher waited for the call in her room at Conservative Central Office. Around her bustled friends, family and hangers-on, yet she felt 'an odd sense of loneliness and anticipation', her mind full of minor anxieties about protocol. The phone rang: almost unbelievably, however, it was not Buckingham Palace, but Edward Heath, calling to offer his congratulations. Perhaps he was hoping that, if he kept her talking long enough, she might miss the appointment and he would be invited instead. In any case, she asked one of her aides to take the call. And then at last the phone rang again, and this time it was the Palace. It was just after three o'clock. A trim figure in royal blue, almost dwarfed by the crowd of photographers and supporters, Thatcher pushed her way through to the car outside. In her pocket she carried a little file-card with a few words scribbled in blue pen, suggested by her speechwriter, Ronald Millar. 'HM – accepted,' they began. 'Know great responsibilities – enter door . . . Discord – harmony . . .'[46]

It had just gone four when, to mingled cheers and boos from the large crowd, her own black Rover turned off Whitehall and into Down-ing Street. 'Good afternoon, Prime Minister,' shouted a BBC reporter, as the first woman to follow in the footsteps of Walpole, Gladstone and Churchill climbed out of the car and waved vigorously at the crowd. As Margaret Thatcher stepped towards the reporters, a group of burly policemen moved protectively around her. Not for the last time, how-ever, she seemed almost oblivious to her surroundings, her attention fixed on the cameras. 'How do you feel at this moment?' asked the man from the BBC. 'Very excited, very aware of the responsibilities,' she said quietly, almost humbly:

> Her Majesty the Queen has asked me to form a new administration and I have accepted.
>
> It is, of course, the greatest honour that can come to any citizen in a democracy. I know full well the responsibilities that await me as I enter the door of Number 10 and I'll strive unceasingly to try to fulfil the trust and confidence that the British people have placed in me, and the things in which I believe.
>
> And I would just like to remember some words of St Francis of Assisi, which I think are really just particularly apt at the moment:
>
> 'Where there is discord, may we bring harmony.
>
> Where there is error, may we bring truth.
>
> Where there is doubt, may we bring faith.
>
> And where there is despair, may we bring hope.'

By now she was looking right into the camera, her voice softer than ever, her gaze almost imploring:

> And to all the British people – howsoever they voted – may I say this. Now that the election is over, may we get together and strive to serve and strengthen the country of which we're so proud to be a part.
>
> And finally, finally, one last thing: in the words of Airey Neave, whom we had hoped to bring here with us, 'There is now work to be done.'

There was one more question, though, before she was free. 'Have you got any thoughts, Mrs Thatcher, at this moment about Mrs Pankhurst and your own mentor in political life, your own father?' one of the reporters asked. 'Well, of course, I just owe almost everything to my own father, I really do,' she said, frowning slightly.

> He brought me up to believe all the things that I do believe and they're just the values on which I've fought the election. And it's passionately

interesting to me that the things that I learned in a small town, in a very modest home, are just the things which I believe have won the election.

Gentlemen, you're very kind. May I just go, may I just go and have a word . . .

With that she went over to the crowd, and the cheers and the boos redoubled in the little street. And then, at last, she went in.[47]

Acknowledgements

There are worse places to be trapped, metaphorically speaking, than Britain in the late 1970s, but there are probably a lot better ones, too. Writing about Harold Wilson, a pudgy, shabby Little Englander locked away with his fears and his fantasies, I increasingly wondered whether we were, in fact, the same person. Fortunately for me, my aides and advisers were rather more harmonious than poor old Wilson's. While I schemed in the shadows, my government ministers – Stefan McGrath, Richard Duguid, Natalie Ramm, Caroline Elliker and Marina Kemp – did all the real work, while Simon Winder was a one-man Cabinet, combining the avuncular experience of Jim Callaghan, the irrepressible spirit of Denis Healey and the elegant insight of Roy Jenkins. And nobody could have dotted the i's and crossed the t's better than my brilliant chief speechwriter, Elizabeth Stratford.

At the Treasury, Andrew Wylie and James Pullen of the Wylie Agency struck terror into Britain's creditors and ensured that I had no need to apply to the IMF. In my political office, Mari Yamazaki made a splendid press secretary and Sue Ayton of Knight Ayton Management groomed me for the small screen. My first television campaign was a daunting but wonderfully enjoyable experience. My media supremo, Steve Condie, was a model of calm, dapper and decisive leadership, even keeping his cool as my expensive Gannex raincoat disintegrated. Our party political broadcasts were splendidly directed by Mary Crisp, Tom McCarthy, Fatima Salaria and Paul Tilzey, while Alex Mason, Sarah Ager and Zoe Jewell kept the party leader amused, entertained and (most importantly) well fed. Back at Transport House, Rebecca Maidens kept a tight hold of the purse strings, while the party chairman, Dominic Crossley-Holland, cast an avuncular eye over proceedings. As always, though, the real stars of the campaign were the activists who did all the real work: Briony hunched over the archives in her darkened back room, Catherine doing battle with the nation's taxi drivers, and Justin, Louis, Sam,

Ali and Adam pounding the streets in the key marginals. We'll always have Wigan – and Caerphilly, and Wolverhampton, and Torremolinos ...

On Fleet Street, Jason Cowley, Paul Dacre, Andrew Holgate, Leaf Kalfayan and Dave Musgrove allowed me to present my government's point of view. From the backbenches, Simon Hooper, Andrew Preston and Ted Vallance offered plenty of useful tips. At the TUC, Martin O'Neill occasionally denounced my pay policy as a betrayal of socialism, but he nevertheless joined me on election night to watch Mrs Thatcher's victory. Among other international statesmen, Kester Aspden, Rhys Evans, Martin Halliwell, Gary Kemp, David Kynaston, Liam McCarthy, Jack MacGowan and Richard Vinen all offered useful advice on beating inflation, while Lawrence Black and Hugh Pemberton invited me to address their G7 summit at the Centre for Contemporary British History. And all the time, across the Commons, my Tory opposite number, Tom Holland, waxed lyrical about the delights of yachts, organs and the city of Salisbury.

Like any good politician, I have probably overlooked dozens of people crucial to my enterprise. Fortunately, though, this doubtless rather tiresome metaphor begins to fall apart when it comes to my family. Unlike Herbert Wilson, my father, Rhys Sandbrook, has never been interested in politics. But he has never stinted in his encouragement, even during the most difficult circumstances. When my mother, Hilary Sandbrook, died unexpectedly in May 2011, he remained marvellously strong and steadfast. I would also like to thank Alex Sandbrook, Chelsea Naso, Rachel Morley, Ian and Kate Larkworthy and Steve and Sue Whiston. As for my wife, Catherine Morley, there may occasionally be a Marcia Williams-style glint in her eye after some particularly egregious behaviour on my part, but without her love and support, I would have remained the equivalent of an obscure backbencher – and there we are, back to the political metaphor again. To cut a long story short, I like to think of her as my Audrey Callaghan. But the reality, of course, is that I am merely her Denis Thatcher.

Notes

Documents marked PRO are from the National Archives (Public Record Office) in Kew. References to Hansard are from the website http://hansard.millbanksystems. com/sittings/1970s. Documents marked TFW are from the Margaret Thatcher Foundation website at www.margaretthatcher.org/. Place of publication is London, unless otherwise stated.

PREFACE

1. J. W. Rinzler, *The Making of Star Wars: The Definitive Story behind the Original Film* (2008), p. 182; Dale Pollock, *Skywalking: The Life and Films of George Lucas* (1990), pp. 153, 159; 'History of Studio', http://www.elstreefilmstudios. co.uk/studiohistory.aspx.

2. For the admissions figures, see http://www.bfi.org.uk/features/ultimatefilm/.

3. Pollock, *Skywalking*, pp. 161–2, 168; Rinzler, *The Making of Star Wars*, pp. 144, 164, 194; Peter Biskind, *Easy Riders, Raging Bulls: How the Sex 'n' Drugs 'n' Rock 'n' Roll Generation Saved Hollywood* (1998), pp. 329–30.

4. Rinzler, *The Making of Star Wars*, pp. 153, 186, 192, 196; *Sunday Times*, 2 May 1976.

5. Pollock, *Skywalking*, p. 169; Rinzler, *The Making of Star Wars*, p. 231; Zachary Leader (ed.), *The Letters of Kingsley Amis* (2000), p. 800.

6. *Time*, 19 May 1975; Robert Moss, 'Anglocommunism?', *Commentary*, February 1977, pp. 27–33; *The Times*, 8 May 1975; Bernard D. Nossiter, *Britain: A Future that Works* (1978), pp. 12–13; Pollock, *Skywalking*, p. 162; Rinzler, *The Making of Star Wars*, pp. 184, 193.

7. *Daily Express*, 3 June 1977, 22 October 1977; *The Times*, 28 December 1977; for the BBC clip (undated, but almost certainly from 26 December 1977), see the link 'London Feels Force' at http://news.bbc.co.uk/1/hi/england/7083045. stm.

8. *The Times*, 10 February 1978.

9. *Rolling Stone*, 25 August 1977, 5 November 1987; *The Times*, 6 April 1976.

10. Transcript of Conservative election broadcast, 7 June 1983, TFW; *Daily Mail*, 15 September 2009, 5 May 2010.

11. *Guardian*, 28 September 1978.

12. *The Times*, 6 April 1976, 29 September 1976; *Daily Express*, 6 April 1976; *The Times*, 29 September 1976; James Callaghan, *Time and Chance* (1987), pp. 425–7.

13. James Sullivan, 'Goodbye, Papa, It's Hard to Die', *Slate*, 16 March 2005, at http://www.slate.com/id/2114863/.

CHAPTER 1. BRAVE NEW WORLD

1. *Daily Express*, 4 March 1974, 5 March 1974; *The Times*, 4 March 1974, 5 March 1974; *Daily Mirror*, 4 March 1974, 5 March 1974.
2. Bernard Donoughue, *Downing Street Diary*, vol. 1: *With Harold Wilson in No. 10* (2005), pp. 43–9.
3. *Daily Mirror*, 5 March 1974; Donoughue, *Downing Street Diary*, pp. 52–3; and see Bernard Donoughue, *The Heat of the Kitchen: An Autobiography* (2003), p. 119; Roy Jenkins, *A Life at the Centre* (1991), pp. 369–70.
4. *The Times*, 5 March 1974; *Daily Mirror*, 5 March 1974; *Time*, 18 March 1974.
5. *Daily Mirror*, 5 March 1974; Richard Coopey and Nicholas Woodward, 'The British Economy in the 1970s', in Coopey and Woodward (eds.), *Britain in the 1970s: The Troubled Economy* (1996), p. 6; Max-Stephan Schulze and Nicholas Woodward, 'The Emergence of Rapid Inflation', ibid., p. 112; Alec Cairncross, 'The Heath Government and the British Economy', in Stuart Ball and Anthony Seldon (eds.), *The Heath Government 1970–1974: A Reappraisal* (Harlow, 1996); David Kynaston, *The City of London*, vol. 4: *A Club No More 1945–2000* (2001), pp. 470–71.
6. Niall Ferguson, *High Financier: The Lives and Time of Siegmund Warburg* (2010), p. 312; Hansard, 13 December 1973; *The Times*, 14 December 1973, 16 January 1974, 25 March 1974; Kynaston, *A Club No More*, pp. 488–90; Keith Middlemas, *Power, Competition and the State*, vol. 3: *The End of the Postwar Era: Britain since 1974* (Basingstoke, 1991), pp. 10, 14, 30, 33; PRO CAB 128/53, CM (73) 60, 12 December 1973; PRO CAB 128/53, CM (73) 61, 13 December 1973; David Butler and Dennis Kavanagh, *The British General Election of February 1974* (1974), pp. 140–41, 145; Anthony King and Robert J. Wybrow (eds.), *British Political Opinion 1937–2000: The Gallup Polls* (2001), p. 312; Barbara Castle, *The Castle Diaries 1974–1976* (1980), p. 23; Cecil King, *The Cecil King Diary 1970–1974* (1975), p. 332.
7. PRO CAB 128/53, CM (73) 60, 12 December 1973; PRO CAB 128/53, CM (73) 61, 13 December 1973; Hansard, 13 November 1973; *The Times*, 14 November 1973, 8 February 1974; John Campbell, *Edward Heath: A Biography* (1994), pp. 560–62, 563, 565, 572–3, 583–5, 595–6.
8. Kenneth O. Morgan, *Michael Foot: A Life* (2007), pp. 295–6; Chris Wrigley, 'Trade Unions, Strikes and the Government', in Coopey and Woodward (eds.), *Britain in the 1970s*, pp. 274–5; Geoffrey Owen, *From Empire to Europe: The Decline and Revival of British Industry since the Second World War* (1999), p. 437; Stephen Milligan, *The New Barons: Union Power in the 1970s* (1976), p. 7.
9. Vernon Bogdanor, '1974: The Crisis of Old Labour', in Anthony Seldon and Kevin Hickson (eds.), *New Labour, Old Labour: The Wilson and Callaghan Governments, 1974–1979* (2004), p. 12; Anthony Sampson, *The New Anatomy of Britain* (1971), pp. 628–9, 632; Milligan, *The New Barons*, pp. 87–8, 97–8, 130, 189; *Sun*, 4 January 1977; Andrew Thorpe, 'The Labour Party and the

Trade Unions', in John McIlroy, Nina Fishman and Alan Campbell (eds.), *The High Tide of British Trade Unionism: Trade Unions and Industrial Politics, 1964–1979* (Monmouth, 2007), p. 143; Andy Beckett, *When the Lights Went Out: Britain in the Seventies* (2009), pp. 294–5, 299–300. On Jones and the KGB, see Christopher Andrew, *The Defence of the Realm: The Authorized History of MI5* (2009), pp. 588, 657.

10. Robert Taylor, *The Fifth Estate: Britain's Unions in the Seventies* (1978), pp. 337–8, 353; Robert Taylor, 'The Rise and Fall of the Social Contract', in Seldon and Hickson (eds.), *New Labour, Old Labour*, pp. 92–3, 99, 101; John McIlroy and Alan Campbell, 'The High Tide of Trade Unionism: Mapping Industrial Politics, 1964–79', in McIlroy, Fishman and Campbell (eds.), *The High Tide of British Trade Unionism*, pp. 100, 106; Milligan, *The New Barons*, pp. 82, 220–22; Paul Ferris, *The New Militants: Crisis in the Trade Unions* (Harmondsworth, 1972), pp. 14, 48, 55; Nick Tiratsoo, 'You've Never Had It So Bad? Britain in the 1970s', in Nick Tiratsoo (ed.), *From Blitz to Blair: A New History of Britain since 1939* (1997), p. 178.

11. Eric Hobsbawm, 'The Forward March of Labour Halted?', *Marxism Today*, September 1978, pp. 279–86; Martin Jacques and Francis Mulhern (eds.), *The Forward March of Labour Halted?* (1981); Eric Hobsbawm, *Interesting Times: A Twentieth-century Life* (2002), pp. 264–6.

12. Geoffrey Moorhouse, *The Other England* (1964); Bernard D. Nossiter, *Britain: A Future that Works* (1978), pp. 68–9; Butler and Kavanagh, *The British General Election of February 1974*, p. 17; Arthur Marwick, *British Society since 1945* (Harmondsworth, 1982), pp. 121, 242–3; John Benson, *The Rise of Consumer Society in Britain, 1880–1980* (Harlow, 1994), p. 72.

13. Justin Smith, 'Glam, Spam and Uncle Sam: Funding Diversity in 1970s British Film Production', in Robert Shail (ed.), *Seventies British Cinema* (2008), p. 68; *Daily Mirror*, 3 March 1979.

14. *Sunday Times*, 1 May 1977; Ray Carney and Leonard Quart, *The Films of Mike Leigh: Embracing the World* (2000), pp. 96–115; Michael Billington, *State of the Nation: British Theatre since 1945* (2007), pp. 280–81.

15. Butler and Kavanagh, *The British General Election of February 1974*, p. 6; Michael Young and Peter Willmott, *The Symmetrical Family: A Study of Work and Leisure in the London Region* (1973), p. 48; Lawrence James, *The Middle Class: A History* (2006), p. 527; *Sunday Times*, 24 April 1977.

16. Marwick, *British Society since 1945*, p. 250; Jeremy Seabrook, *City Close-up* (Harmondsworth, 1971), p. 81; Margaret Drabble, *The Middle Ground* (Harmondsworth, pb. 1981), p. 199.

17. *The Times*, 29 May 1976, 2 June 1978.

18. Shamit Saggar, *Race and Politics in Britain* (Hemel Hempstead, 1992), pp. 41, 45; James, *The Middle Class*, p. 436; *The Good Food Guide 1977* (1977), p. ix; Kate Colquhoun, *Taste: The Story of Britain through its Cooking* (2007), p. 357; *The Times*, 8 April 1978.

19. *The Times*, 10 December 1977, 16 September 1978, 21 December 1979.

20. Miriam Akhtar and Steve Humphries, *Some Liked It Hot: The British on Holiday at Home and Abroad* (2000), pp. 101–2, 105–9, 115; Alwyn W. Turner, *Crisis? What Crisis? Britain in the 1970s* (2008), p. 165; John Burnett, *Liquid*

Pleasures: A Social History of Drinks in Modern Britain (1999), pp. 154–5; *The Times*, 29 November 1977, 21 December 1979.

21. Benson, *The Rise of Consumer Society*, p. 69; Roger Cox, 'Carrefour at Caerphilly: The Shoppers and the Competition', *International Journal of Retail and Distribution Management*, 3:3 (1975), pp. 39–41; *The Times*, 5 February 1972, 13 April 1973, 10 September 1973, 30 April 1974, 17 January 1983, 12 April 1983; Turner, *Crisis? What Crisis?*, p. 56; Ann Oakley, *Housewife* (1974), p. 131; Colquhoun, *Taste*, pp. 353, 365; Joe Moran, *Queuing for Beginners: The Story of Daily Life from Breakfast to Bedtime* (2007), pp. 153–4.

22. Elizabeth Wilson, *Only Halfway to Paradise: Women in Post-war Britain. 1945–1968* (1980), p. 40; Hera Cook, *The Long Sexual Revolution: English Women, Sex and Contraception 1800–1975* (Oxford, 2005), p. 336; interview for *Barnet Press*, 9 September 1978, TFW; *The Times*, 19 May 1975; interview for *Birmingham Evening Mail*, 4 August 1978, TFW; Moran, *Queuing for Beginners*, pp. 17, 154; *Independent*, 23 July 2009; *Daily Telegraph*, 10 October 2010.

23. Nossiter, *Britain: A Future that Works*, pp. 200–201; *Daily Mirror*, 10 March 1978; Moran, *Queuing for Beginners*, pp. 51, 77; Burnett, *Liquid Pleasures*, pp. 90–91; Simon Gunn and Rachel Bell, *Middle Classes: Their Rise and Sprawl* (2003), p. 201; Young and Willmott, *The Symmetrical Family*, pp. 166–7, 278–80.

24. *Observer*, 2 September 1975; Bart Moore-Gilbert, 'Cultural Closure or Post-Avantgardism?', in Bart Moore-Gilbert (ed.), *The Arts in the 1970s: Cultural Closure?* (1994), pp. 14–19; Stuart Laing, 'The Politics of Culture: Institutional Change in the 1970s', ibid., p. 43; Robert Hewison, *Too Much: Art and Culture in the Sixties 1960–75* (1986), pp. 269–71; Randall Stevenson, *The Oxford English Literary History*, vol. 12: *1960–2000: The Last of England?* (Oxford, 2004), pp. 127–8, 132, 137; John Sutherland, *Bestsellers: Popular Fiction of the 1970s* (1981), p. 28.

25. *Guardian*, 6 April 1976; Marwick, *British Society since 1945*, p. 250; Louis Barfe, *Turned Out Nice Again: The Story of British Light Entertainment* (2008), pp. 1, 237; Jonathan Coe, *The Rotters' Club* (2002), pp. 274–5. For viewing figures, see the British Film Institute's chart at 'Britain's Most Watched TV: The 1970s', http://www.bfi.org.uk/features/mostwatched/1970s.html; and see also Joe Moran, '"Stand Up and Be Counted": Hughie Green, the 1970s and Popular Memory', *History Workshop Journal*, 70 (2010), pp. 181, 189–90, 192.

26. Laing, 'The Politics of Culture', p. 32; Asa Briggs, *The History of Broadcasting in the United Kingdom*, vol. 5: *Competition* (Oxford, 1995), p. 959.

27. Hunter Davies, *The Creighton Report: A Year in the Life of a Comprehensive School* (Newton Abbot, 1977), pp. 278–80; *The Times*, 11 September 1971, 4 June 1980; 'Milestones in the Progress of Scouting', http://scouts.org.uk/documents/About/history/fs295306.pdf.

28. Dave Laing, *One Chord Wonders: Power and Meaning in Punk Rock* (Milton Keynes, 1985), pp. 32–4; Dave Harker, 'Blood on the Tracks: Popular Music in the 1970s', in Moore-Gilbert (ed.), *The Arts in the 1970s*, pp. 242–3; *The Times*, 13 December 1980; for chart data, see www.everyhit.com.

29. *Guardian*, 15 April 2010; Chris Hunt, 'The Story of Wigan Casino', http://www.chrishunt.biz/features05.html; Andy Wilson, *Northern Soul: Disco, Drugs and Subcultural Identity* (2007), pp. 14–81. The Granada film is on YouTube.

30. *The Times*, 7 November 1975, 13 September 1976, 1 September 1980; Jeremy Seabrook, *What Went Wrong? Working People and the Ideals of the Labour Movement* (1978), p. 29.

31. Ibid., pp. 9, 12–13, 27–8, 31, 115, 135.

32. Phil Wickham, *The Likely Lads* (Basingstoke, 2008), pp. 1–3; Gunn and Bell, *Middle Classes*, p. 219; Robert Colls, *Identity of England* (Oxford, 2002), p. 341; Phillip Whitehead, *The Writing on the Wall: Britain in the Seventies* (1985), pp. 411–13; Gordon Burn, *Somebody's Husband, Somebody's Son: The Story of Peter Sutcliffe* (1984), p. 74.

33. Seabrook, *What Went Wrong?*, pp. 38, 67, 135; Richard Hoggart, *The Uses of Literacy* (Harmondsworth, 1958), pp. 202–3, 248–9, 340.

34. Patrick Hutber, *The Decline and Fall of the Middle Class – and How It Can Fight Back* (Harmondsworth, pb. 1977), p. 20; Joe Rogaly, *Grunwick* (1977), pp. 111–12; Joseph Rowntree Foundation, *Income and Wealth: The Report of the JRF Inquiry Group* (1995), p. 13; Nicholas Timmins, *The Five Giants: A Biography of the Welfare State* (1996), p. 368; *The Times*, 27 April 1977; Jerry White, *London in the Twentieth Century* (2001), pp. 72–4.

35. Seabrook, *What Went Wrong?*, pp. 208–9; Clive Irving, *Pox Britannica: The Unmaking of the British* (New York, 1974), p. 168; Peter Townsend, *Poverty in the United Kingdom* (1979), pp. 305–10.

36. *The Times*, 28 April 1975, 2 March 1976, 16 December 1976; Dave Haslam, *Manchester, England: The Story of the Pop Cult City* (2000), p. xxii; Mike Leigh, *Ecstasy* (2011), pp. 94, 107; *Daily Telegraph*, 14 March 2011.

37. *The Times*, 20 January 1977, 25 July 1977; Nossiter, *Britain: A Future that Works*, pp. 17, 68–9; Whitehead, *The Writing on the Wall*, p. 392.

38. Sampson, *The New Anatomy of Britain*, pp. 559–60, 564; Anthony Sampson, *The Changing Anatomy of Britain* (1983), pp. 339–40; Whitehead, *The Writing on the Wall*, pp. 393–4; on Matthews, see *Daily Telegraph*, 26 November 2010; 'Our History' at http://www.bernardmatthews.com/.

39. *The Times*, 22 May 1975, 2 November 1977, 21 May 1980, 24 March 1984.

40. *The Times*, 4 July 1975, 29 June 1984; and see http://www.cambridgescience park.co.uk/about/history/.

41. *The Times*, 29 January 1973, 7 January 1976, 24 November 1976, 17 January 1977; 'Sinclair: A Corporate History', http://www.nvg.ntnu.no/sinclair/sinclair/corphist.htm; *Practical Computing*, July 1982, at http://www.worldofspectrum.org/CliveSinclairInterview1982/.

42. *The Times*, 30 January 1980, 11 February 1980, 22 September 1980; *Daily Express*, 3 November 1980.

43. *The Times*, 19 February 1981, 28 February 1981.

CHAPTER 2. THE SOCIAL CONTRACT

1. Barbara Castle, *The Castle Diaries 1974–1976* (1980), pp. 34–5; Marcia Falkender, *Downing Street in Perspective* (1983), pp. 104–5; John Campbell, *Edward Heath: A Biography* (1993), pp. 292–3.

2. See Ben Pimlott, *Harold Wilson* (1992), pp. 617–18.

3. Giles Radice, *Friends and Rivals: Crosland, Jenkins and Healey* (2002), p. 246; Bernard Donoughue, *The Heat of the Kitchen: An Autobiography* (2003), pp. 172–3; C. A. R. Crosland, *The Future of Socialism* (1956), pp. 520–24; David Marquand, *The Progressive Dilemma: From Lloyd George to Blair* (1999), pp. 172–4; Kevin Jefferys, *Anthony Crosland: A New Biography* (1999), pp. 172–6; Edmund Dell, *A Strange Eventful History: Democratic Socialism in Britain* (2000), pp. 404–5.

4. Ivor Crewe and Anthony King, *SDP: The Birth, Life and Death of the Social Democratic Party* (Oxford, 1995), pp. 14, 24; Marquand, *The Progressive Dilemma*, p. 177; Tony Benn, *Against the Tide: Diaries 1973–1976* (1989), pp. 4, 12, 15, 26, 46, 61; David Butler and Dennis Kavanagh, *The British General Election of February 1974* (1974), pp. 50–51. The text of the manifesto is reproduced in *The Times*, 9 February 1974, and at http://www.labour-party.org.uk/manifestos/1974/feb/; see also Michael Hatfield, *The House the Left Built: Inside Labour Policy Making 1970–1975* (1978), esp. pp. 171–229; Stuart Holland, 'The Industrial Strategy', in Anthony Seldon and Kevin Hickson (eds.), *New Labour, Old Labour: The Wilson and Callaghan Governments, 1974–1979* (2004), pp. 297–9.

5. Vernon Bogdanor, '1974: The Crisis of Old Labour', in Seldon and Hickson (eds.), *New Labour, Old Labour*, pp. 5–7; Pimlott, *Harold Wilson*, pp. 617–18; Edmund Dell, *A Hard Pounding: Politics and Economic Crisis, 1974–1976* (Oxford, 1991), p. 12; Dell, *A Strange Eventful History*, pp. 411, 434–5; Joel Barnett, *Inside the Treasury* (1982), p. 15; Bernard Donoughue, *Prime Minister: The Conduct of Policy under Harold Wilson and James Callaghan, 1974–1979* (1987), p. 51; Edmund Dell, *The Chancellors: A History of the Chancellors of the Exchequer, 1945–90* (1996, pb. 1997), p. 400.

6. Pimlott, *Harold Wilson*, pp. 11–13; Philip Ziegler, *Wilson: The Authorized Life* (1993), pp. xi, 5–6, 60–61; John Cole, *As It Seemed to Me: Political Memoirs* (1995), p. 47; Joe Haines, *Glimmers of Twilight: Harold Wilson in Decline* (2003), pp. xiii–xiv; *Daily Express*, 8 November 1962.

7. Castle, *The Castle Diaries*, pp. 32–3, 37; Pimlott, *Harold Wilson*, p. 616; Ziegler, *Wilson*, p. 412; Michael Cockerell, *Live from Number 10: The Inside Story of Prime Ministers and Television* (1989), p. 206.

8. *Sunday Times*, 17 February 1974; Pimlott, *Harold Wilson*, p. 648; Ziegler, *Wilson*, pp. 468–9; Haines, *Glimmers of Twilight*, pp. xiii, xvii, 116.

9. Ibid., p. xvii; Bernard Donoughue, *Downing Street Diary*, vol. 1: *With Harold Wilson in No. 10* (2005), pp. 72, 529, 547, 584.

10. Richard Clutterbuck, *Britain in Agony: The Growth of Political Violence* (1977), p. 112; Butler and Kavanagh, *The British General Election of February 1974*, pp. 67, 72; PRO CAB 128/54, CC (74) 1, 5 March 1974.

11. PRO CAB 128/54, CC (74) 2, 7 March 1974; Kenneth O. Morgan, *Michael Foot: A Life* (Oxford, 2007), pp. 298–9.

12. *The Times*, 7 March 1974; *Financial Times*, 8 March 1974; Donoughue, *The Heat of the Kitchen*, p. 126.

13. Morgan, *Michael Foot*, pp. 3–15, 282–3; Mervyn Jones, *Michael Foot* (1995), p. 350; Jack Jones, *Union Man: An Autobiography* (1986), p. 281.

14. Hansard, 18 March 1974; Donoughue, *The Heat of the Kitchen*, p. 124; Morgan, *Michael Foot*, pp. 284, 291–2; Dell, *A Strange Eventful History*, p. 435.

15. Tony Benn, *The New Politics: A Socialist Renaissance* (1970), p. 61; Clutterbuck, *Britain in Agony*, p. 171; Robert Taylor, *The Trade Union Question in British Politics: Government and Trade Unions since 1945* (Oxford, 1993), p. 230; Kenneth O. Morgan, *Callaghan: A Life* (Oxford, 1997), p. 390.

16. Bogdanor, '1974: The Crisis of Old Labour', pp. 7–8; Hatfield, *The House the Left Built*, pp. 77, 112–31, 136; Tony Benn, *Office without Power: Diaries 1968–1972* (1988), pp. 406–7; Benn, *Against the Tide*, p. 80; Castle, *The Castle Diaries*, pp. 9–10.

17. *The Times*, 24 January 1973; Gerald A. Dorfman, *Government versus Trade Unionism in British Politics since 1968* (1979), pp. 110–11; Taylor, *The Trade Union Question in British Politics*, p. 226; Dell, *A Hard Pounding*, p. 15; Pimlott, *Harold Wilson*, p. 604; Ziegler, *Wilson*, p. 392.

18. *The Times*, 27 June 1974, 26 September 1974; PRO CAB 129/77, C (74) 59, 'Voluntary Collective Bargaining in the Year Ahead', 18 June 1974; Clutterbuck, *Britain in Agony*, pp. 124, 171–4, 215–17; Stephen Milligan, *The New Barons: Union Power in the 1970s* (1976), pp. 74–6; Richard Coopey and Nicholas Woodward, 'The British Economy in the 1970s', in Coopey and Woodward (eds.), *Britain in the 1970s: The Troubled Economy* (1996), pp. 21–2; Jones, *Michael Foot*, p. 392; Morgan, *Michael Foot*, pp. 299–314, 347.

19. Ronald McIntosh, *Challenge to Democracy: Politics, Trade Union Power and Economic Failure in the 1970s* (2006), pp. 105–6; Robert Taylor, 'The Rise and Fall of the Social Contract', in Seldon and Hickson (eds.), *New Labour, Old Labour*, pp. 70–71, 74, 83, 98; Joe Gormley, *Battered Cherub: The Autobiography of Joe Gormley* (1982), p. 193; Dell, *The Chancellors*, p. 417.

20. Castle, *The Castle Diaries*, pp. 18, 157; Keith Middlemas, *Power, Competition and the State*, vol. 3: *The End of the Postwar Era: Britain since 1974* (Basingstoke, 1991), pp. 53–4, 92–3; Dell, *A Strange Eventful History*, pp. 444–5; PRO CAB 128/54, CC (74) 17, 23 May 1974; Jones, *Michael Foot*, pp. 354, 362; *The Times*, 4 October 1974, 5 October 1974; Phillip Whitehead, *The Writing on the Wall: Britain in the Seventies* (1985), p. 117.

21. Andy Beckett, *When the Lights Went Out: Britain in the Seventies* (2009), p. 290; Denis Healey, *The Time of My Life* (1989, pb. 1990), p. 394; Barnett, *Inside the Treasury*, p. 49; Dell, *The Chancellors*, p. 404; Roy Jenkins, *A Life at the Centre* (1991), pp. 427–8.

22. PRO CAB 128/54, CC (74) 3, 14 March 1974; Castle, *The Castle Diaries*, pp. 42–3; Healey, *The Time of My Life*, p. 392.

23. Edward Pearce, *The Lost Leaders: The Best Prime Ministers We Never Had* (1997), p. 136; Dell, *The Chancellors*, p. 402; and see Healey, *The Time of My Life*, and Edward Pearce, *Denis Healey: A Life in Our Times* (2002), passim.

24. Anthony Sampson, *The New Anatomy of Britain* (1971), p. 53; Cole, *As It Seemed to Me*, p. 181; Richard Holt, *Second amongst Equals: Chancellors of the Exchequer since the Second World War* (2002), pp. 53, 181, 279; Roy Hattersley, *Who Goes Home? Scenes from a Political Life* (1996), p. 185.

25. Healey, *The Time of My Life*, p. 392; Pearce, *Denis Healey*, pp. 390, 406, 410; Kenneth O. Morgan, *Labour People: Leaders and Lieutenants, Hardie to Kinnock* (Oxford, 1992), p. 313; Alan Watkins, *A Short Walk down Fleet Street*

(2000), pp. 157–8; Peter Hennessy, *The Prime Minister: The Office and its Holders since 1945* (2000), p. 361.

26. Dell, *The Chancellors*, pp. 405–6; Donald MacDougall, *Don and Mandarin: Memoirs of an Economist* (1987), p. 208.

27. Dell, *The Chancellors*, pp. 406–7; Healey, *The Time of My Life*, pp. 422–3; Barnett, *Inside the Treasury*, p. 23; David Smith, *The Rise and Fall of Monetarism: The Theory and Politics of an Economic Experiment* (1991), pp. 56, 61.

28. *The Times*, 27 March 1974; Alec Cairncross, *The British Economy since 1945: Economic Policy and Performance, 1945–1990* (Oxford, 1992), pp. 203–4; Dell, *The Chancellors*, p. 408; David Kynaston, *The City of London*, vol. 4: *A Club No More 1945–2000* (2001), p. 495; Middlemas, *Power, Competition and the State*, p. 28; James Lees-Milne, *Diaries, 1971–1983* (2008), p. 138.

29. Hansard, 26 March 1974; Dell, *The Chancellors*, p. 408; Healey, *The Time of My Life*, p. 393; Pearce, *Denis Healey*, p. 416; Whitehead, *The Writing on the Wall*, p. 127; Barnett, *Inside the Treasury*, p. 24.

30. Pearce, *Denis Healey*, pp. 414, 417; Nicholas Crafts, 'Economic Growth in the 1970s', in Coopey and Woodward (eds.), *Britain in the 1970s*, p. 102; Max-Stephan Schulze and Nicholas Woodward, 'The Emergence of Rapid Inflation', ibid., pp. 121, 132; Nicholas Woodward, 'The Retreat from Full Employment', ibid., pp. 136–62.

31. Castle, *The Castle Diaries*, pp. 81, 181; Dell, *The Chancellors*, p. 403; Pearce, *Denis Healey*, p. 414; *The Economist*, 27 April 1974.

32. *The Times*, 23 July 1974; Pearce, *Denis Healey*, pp. 417–18; Jenkins, *A Life at the Centre*, pp. 386–7; Dell, *A Hard Pounding*, p. 78; Barnett, *Inside the Treasury*, pp. 23, 32–3, 50.

33. Middlemas, *Power, Competition and the State*, pp. 7–8, 16, 187; Smith, *The Rise and Fall of Monetarism*, pp. 61–2; Nicholas Timmins, *The Five Giants: A Biography of the Welfare State* (1996), pp. 316–17; Healey, *The Time of My Life*, p. 393; Dilwyn Porter, 'Government and the Economy', in Coopey and Woodward (eds.), *Britain in the 1970s*, p. 44; Dell, *The Chancellors*, p. 407; Pearce, *Denis Healey*, p. 414; Holt, *Second amongst Equals*, pp. 248, 252.

34. Castle, *The Castle Diaries*, pp. 116–17; Donoughue, *The Heat of the Kitchen*, pp. 138–9; Niall Ferguson, *High Financier: The Lives and Time of Siegmund Warburg* (2010), p. 312; Donoughue, *Downing Street Diary*, pp. 134–5; Pearce, *Denis Healey*, pp. 415–16, 418.

35. David Butler and Dennis Kavanagh, *The British General Election of October 1974* (1975), p. 18; Kynaston, *A Club No More*, pp. 504–5; *The Economist*, 31 March 1973; *Banker*, March 1974; Jim Tomlinson, 'Economic Policy', in Seldon and Hickson (eds.), *New Labour, Old Labour*, p. 66.

36. Butler and Kavanagh, *The British General Election of October 1974*, p. 26; Pimlott, *Harold Wilson*, p. 635; Ziegler, *Wilson*, p. 418; Donoughue, *The Heat of the Kitchen*, p. 134.

37. *The Economist*, 20 July 1974; John Goodwin (ed.), *Peter Hall's Diaries: The Story of a Dramatic Battle* (1983), p. 103; Adam Sisman, *A. J. P. Taylor: A Biography* (1994), p. 369.

38. Ion Trewin (ed.), *The Hugo Young Papers: Thirty Years of British Politics – Off the Record* (2008), p. 37; *The Times*, 1 July 1974.

CHAPTER 3. KING RAT

1. Bernard Donoughue, *Downing Street Diary*, vol. 1: *With Harold Wilson in No. 10* (2005), pp. 61–2, 63–5.

2. Joe Haines, *The Politics of Power: The Inside Story of Life at No. 10* (1977), p. 158; Joe Haines, *Glimmers of Twilight: Harold Wilson in Decline* (2003), pp. 52–4, 134–5; Ben Pimlott, *Harold Wilson* (1992), pp. 199–200; Philip Ziegler, *Wilson: The Authorized Life* (1993), pp. 118–19.

3. Bernard Donoughue, *The Heat of the Kitchen: An Autobiography* (2003), pp. 201, 217, 226; Haines, *The Politics of Power*, pp. 157–9, 162, 164; Donoughue, *Downing Street Diary*, pp. 63–4; Haines, *Glimmers of Twilight*, pp. 94, 132.

4. Ibid., pp. 137–8; Donoughue, *The Heat of the Kitchen*, p. 213; Donoughue, *Downing Street Diary*, p. 143.

5. Ibid., p. 64.

6. *The Times*, 18 March 1974, 19 March 1974; Donoughue, *Downing Street Diary*, pp. 72–3; John Campbell, *Edward Heath: A Biography* (1993), pp. 625–6; Hailsham diary, 13 March 1974; Hailsham to Heath, 15 March 1974, both in Hailsham Papers, Churchill College, Cambridge.

7. *Daily Mail*, 18 March 1974; Haines, *The Politics of Power*, p. 200; Pimlott, *Harold Wilson*, pp. 625–7; *Financial Times*, 5 April 1974.

8. Donoughue, *Downing Street Diary*, pp. 83, 86–8.

9. Hansard, 4 April 1974; *The Times*, 5 April 1974; Barbara Castle, *The Castle Diaries 1974–1976* (1980), pp. 66, 70.

10. Haines, *The Politics of Power*, p. 202; Haines, *Glimmers of Twilight*, pp. 87–9; Donoughue, *The Heat of the Kitchen*, pp. 202–3; Donoughue, *Downing Street Diary*, pp. 93, 96–7.

11. Pimlott, *Harold Wilson*, pp. 628–9; *Observer*, 7 April 1974; *The Times*, 12 February 1974, 22 November 1973, 19 June 1974, 22 June 1974; Patrick Dunleavy, *The Politics of Mass Housing in Britain, 1945–1975* (Oxford, 1981), pp. 292–4; David Hare, *Plays I* (1996), pp. 234, 273–4, 291, 294; Michael Billington, *State of the Nation: British Theatre since 1945* (2007), pp. 218–19.

12. Pimlott, *Harold Wilson*, p. 629; *The Times*, 9 April 1974; Michael Cockerell, *Live from Number 10: The Inside Story of Prime Ministers and Television* (1989), p. 207; Donoughue, *The Heat of the Kitchen*, p. 208; Maureen Colquhoun, *A Woman in the House* (Shoreham-by-Sea, 1980), p. 28.

13. Haines, *The Politics of Power*, pp. 163, 195; *The Times*, 24 May 1974, 25 May 1974; Pimlott, *Harold Wilson*, pp. 630–31; Haines, *Glimmers of Twilight*, p. 90.

14. Donoughue, *Downing Street Diary*, pp. 127–8, 131, 145, 152; Nicholas Henderson, *Mandarin: The Diaries of an Ambassador, 1969–1982* (1994), pp. 69–72.

15. Tony Benn, *Against the Tide: Diaries 1973–1976* (1989), p. 137; Donoughue, *Downing Street Diary*, p. 96; Ziegler, *Wilson*, p. 477; and see Stephen Dorril and Robin Ramsay, *Smear! Wilson and the Secret State* (1992), pp. 291–5, 299–300.

16. Pimlott, *Harold Wilson*, pp. 407, 706; Dominic Sandbrook, *White Heat: A History of Britain in the Swinging Sixties* (2007), pp. 281, 645–58; Christopher Andrew, *The Defence of the Realm: The Authorized History of MI5* (2009), pp. 527–9; Tony Benn, *Office without Power: Diaries 1968–1972* (1988), p. 63.

17. Pimlott, *Harold Wilson*, pp. 698–9; Andrew, *The Defence of the Realm*, pp. 416–17; Ziegler, *Wilson*, p. 366; Donoughue, *Downing Street Diary*, p. 608.

18. Andrew, *The Defence of the Realm*, pp. 627–8, 630–31; Donoughue, *Downing Street Diary*, pp. 608–9, 710; Haines, *Glimmers of Twilight*, p. 161; Pimlott, *Harold Wilson*, pp. 708–9.

19. Andrew, *The Defence of the Realm*, pp. 503–21; Tom Mangold, *Cold Warrior: James Jesus Angleton. The CIA's Master Spy Hunter* (1991), pp. 74–6; Pimlott, *Harold Wilson*, pp. 703–4.

20. Andrew, *The Defence of the Realm*, pp. 596–7, 642; Peter Wright, *Spycatcher* (1987), p. 369; Bernard Porter, *Plots and Paranoia: A History of Political Espionage in Britain 1790–1988* (1989), pp. 191, 205–6, 213–14; Ziegler, *Wilson*, p. 476; *Guardian*, 11 September 2001; Hansard, 15 January 1988; and see Dorril and Ramsay, *Smear!*, pp. 244–55.

21. Andrew, *The Defence of the Realm*, pp. 642–3; Dorril and Ramsay, *Smear!*, pp. 256–9; Porter, *Plots and Paranoia*, p. 212; Pimlott, *Harold Wilson*, pp. 713–15.

22. Dorril and Ramsay, *Smear!*, pp. 203, 206–7, 276; Pimlott, *Harold Wilson*, p. 711; *News of the World*, 24 October 1971; *Spectator*, 19 June 1976; Francis Wheen, *Strange Days Indeed: The Golden Age of Paranoia* (2009), p. 264.

23. Patrick Marnham, *The Private Eye Story: The First 21 Years* (1982), pp. 155, 157, 192–3; Dorril and Ramsay, *Smear!*, pp. 239–41; Marcia Falkender, *Downing Street in Perspective* (1983), pp. 133, 141; *Mail on Sunday*, 3 May 1987; Pimlott, *Harold Wilson*, pp. 631–2, 718.

24. Andrew, *The Defence of the Realm*, pp. 632–3, 635; Pimlott, *Harold Wilson*, p. 720; Peter Hennessy, *Muddling Through: Power, Politics and the Quality of Government in Postwar Britain* (1997), pp. 264–5; Ziegler, *Wilson*, p. 478.

25. Donoughue, *Downing Street Diary*, pp. 670, 656; Haines, *Glimmers of Twilight*, pp. 146–7; Andy Beckett, *When the Lights Went Out: Britain in the Seventies* (2009), p. 166; Pimlott, *Harold Wilson*, p. 719; Andrew, *The Defence of the Realm*, p. 637; Tony Benn, *Conflicts of Interest: Diaries 1977–80* (1990), p. 378.

26. *The Times*, 24 August 1977; Hansard, 20 May 1976; Kenneth O. Morgan, *Callaghan: A Life* (Oxford, 1997), p. 606; Andrew, *The Defence of the Realm*, pp. xxi, 637; *Mail on Sunday*, 18 April 2010; *Guardian*, 18 April 2010.

CHAPTER 4. A THIRD WORLD COUNTRY

1. John le Carré, *Tinker Tailor Soldier Spy* (1974, pb. 1975), pp. 21–2; John le Carré, *Smiley's People* (1980), p. 40; John le Carré, *The Honourable Schoolboy* (1977), p. 533; and see Leroy Panek, *The Special Branch: The British Spy Novel, 1890–1980* (Bowling Green, Ohio, 1981), pp. 242–3, 246–7.

2. Le Carré, *Tinker Tailor Soldier Spy*, pp. 77, 124, 304; Panek, *The Special Branch*, pp. 238, 241, 248–9.

3. Jerry White, *London in the Twentieth Century* (2001), pp. 73, 75, 204–6; *The Times*, 16 October 1974, 14 March 1975, 19 April 1975, 5 June 1976; Clive Irving, *Pox Britannica: The Unmaking of the British* (New York, 1974), p. 159; Ronald McIntosh, *Challenge to Democracy: Politics, Trade Union Power and Economic Failure in the 1970s* (2006), p. 356.

4. *Weekend Telegraph*, 16 April 1965; *Time*, 15 April 1966; Martin Amis, *Success*

(1977), p. 118; Margaret Drabble, *The Ice Age* (1977), p. 67; Margaret Drabble, *The Middle Ground* (Harmondsworth, pb. 1981), p. 111; Jonathan Raban, *Soft City* (1974), pp. 169–70.

5. Dave Haslam, *Not Abba: The Real Story of the 1970s* (2005), p. 178; Phillip Whitehead, *The Writing on the Wall: Britain in the Seventies* (1985), p. 246; *The Times*, 13 June 1978, 8 June 1972; Geoffrey Moorhouse, *Britain in the Sixties: The Other England* (1964), pp. 95, 97; J. G. Ballard, *High Rise* (1975); Raban, *Soft City*, pp. 26–7; Christopher Booker, *The Seventies: Portrait of a Decade* (1980), pp. 300–301; on tower blocks, see also Gordon E. Cherry, *Town Planning in Britain since 1900: The Rise and Fall of the Planning Ideal* (Oxford, 1996), pp. 184–5; Peter Hall, *Cities of Tomorrow: An Intellectual History of Urban Planning in the Twentieth Century* (Oxford, 1996), pp. 226–7.

6. Kenneth O. Morgan, *The People's Peace: British History since 1945* (Oxford, 1999), p. 429; Whitehead, *The Writing on the Wall*, p. 403; John Goodwin (ed.), *Peter Hall's Diaries: The Story of a Dramatic Battle* (1983), p. 398.

7. Malcolm Bradbury, *The History Man* (1975), pp. 12–13, 66.

8. Colin Dexter, *Last Seen Wearing* (1977), pp. 8–9; Drabble, *The Ice Age*, p. 165; Piers Paul Read, *A Married Man* (1979), p. 11; Michael Palin, *Diaries 1969–1979: The Python Years* (2006), p. 441; Alan Clark, *Diaries: Into Politics 1972–1982*, ed. Ion Trewin (2001), p. 130.

9. Le Carré, *Tinker Tailor Soldier Spy*, p. 102; Denis Judd, *Empire: The British Imperial Experience from 1765 to the Present* (1996), pp. 388–391; *The Times*, 27 May 1978; Jan Morris, *Farewell the Trumpets: An Imperial Retreat* (1978), pp. 548–9, 554.

10. *The Times*, 28 January 1972, 31 January 1972, 30 March 1972, 6 April 1972; see also RCMS 32, Papers on the BBC *British Empire* series, Royal Commonwealth Society Library, Cambridge University Library, especially folders 2, 3 and 5.

11. D. J. Taylor, *After the War: The Novel and England since 1945* (1993), pp. 52–3; Steven Earnshaw, 'Novel Voices', in Clive Bloom and Gary Day (eds.), *Literature and Culture in Modern Britain*, vol. 3: *1956–1999* (Harlow, 2000), pp. 60–61; *The Times*, 20 October 1975; Patricia Waugh, *Harvest of the Sixties: English Literature and its Background, 1960 to 1990* (Oxford, 1995), pp. 201–2; Randall Stevenson, *The Oxford English Literary History*, vol. 12: *1960–2000: The Last of England?* (Oxford, 2004), pp. 485–6; *The Times*, 27 September 1973; J. G. Farrell, *The Siege of Krishnapur* (1973), p. 312.

12. Taylor, *After the War*, pp. 56–8; Simon Raven, *Sound the Retreat* (1971); George MacDonald Fraser, *Flashman* (1969), p. 11; John Sutherland, *Reading the Decades: Fifty Years of the Nation's Bestselling Books* (2002), pp. 123–5; *The Times*, 24 May 1969.

13. *The Times*, 10 April 1975, 20 June 1975, 10 July 1975; *Daily Express*, 12 June 1975, 20 June 1975, 24 June 1975; Kenneth O. Morgan, *Callaghan: A Life* (Oxford, 1997), p. 419; Drabble, *The Ice Age*, p. 92; le Carré, *Tinker Tailor Soldier Spy*, p. 297.

14. *Time*, 15 September 1975; Jeremy Seabrook, *What Went Wrong? Working People and the Ideals of the Labour Movement* (1978), pp. 187, 165.

15. Taylor, *After the War*, p. 189; John Sutherland, *Bestsellers: Popular Fiction of the 1970s* (1981), p. 101; James Chapman, *Licence to Thrill: A Cultural History of the James Bond Films* (1999), pp. 164, 173–4; *New York Times*, 18 December

1971; Robert Shail, '"More, Much More ... Roger Moore": A New Bond for a New Decade', in Robert Shail (ed.), *Seventies British Cinema* (2008), pp. 154–7; Simon Winder, *The Man Who Saved Britain: A Personal Journey into the Disturbing World of James Bond* (2006), p. 262; Palin, *Diaries*, p. 428.

16. Joel Krieger, *Reagan, Thatcher and the Politics of Decline* (Oxford, 1986), pp. 61–2; Krishan Kumar, *The Rise of Modern Society: Aspects of the Social and Political Development of the West* (Oxford, 1988), pp. 290–328; *Guardian*, 26 September 1978; Andrew Gamble, *Britain in Decline: Economic Policy, Political Strategy and the British State* (Basingstoke, 1994), pp. xv, 15, 17; Catherine R. Schenk, 'Britain and the Common Market', in Richard Coopey and Nicholas Woodward (eds.), *Britain in the 1970s: The Troubled Economy* (1996), p. 193; Tony Benn, *Against the Tide: Diaries 1973–1976* (1989), p. 142.

17. *Guardian*, 26 September 1978; Gamble, *Britain in Decline*, pp. xv, xx, 10, 12–13; W. A. P. Manser, *Britain in Balance* (1971), p. xiii; Andy Beckett, *When the Lights Went Out: Britain in the Seventies* (2009), p. 176. On 'declinism', see Jim Tomlinson, 'Inventing "Decline": The Falling Behind of the British Economy in the Post-war Years', *Economic History Review*, 49:4 (1996), pp. 731–57; Jim Tomlinson, *The Politics of Decline: Understanding Post-war Britain* (2000); Jim Tomlinson, 'Thrice Denied: "Declinism" as a Recurrent Theme in British History in the Long Twentieth Century,' *Twentieth Century British History*, 20:2 (2009), pp. 227–51.

18. Stevenson, *The Last of England?*, p. 476; Sutherland, *Reading the Decades*, p. 99; Alwyn W. Turner, *Crisis? What Crisis? Britain in the 1970s* (2008), pp. 24–5; Roy Carr and Charles Shaar Murray, *Bowie: An Illustrated Record* (New York, 1981), pp. 14, 64; Nicholas Pegg, *The Complete David Bowie* (2000), pp. 289–91; *NME*, 4 October 1975; Ian MacDonald, *The People's Music* (2003), pp. 142–3, 190–91; Mark Blake, *Comfortably Numb: The Inside Story of Pink Floyd* (Cambridge, Mass., 2008), p. 247.

19. Martin Amis, *Dead Babies* (1975), p. 137; Neil Powell, *Amis & Son: Two Literary Generations* (2008), pp. 303–8; Drabble, *The Ice Age*, pp. 62–3; John Fowles, *Daniel Martin* (1977), p. 265; Richard Critchfield, *An American Looks at Britain* (New York, 1990), p. 143; John Lahr (ed.), *The Diaries of Kenneth Tynan* (2002), p. 120.

20. Michael Billington, *State of the Nation: British Theatre since 1945* (2007), pp. 231–2, 249–50 (and see also pp. 210–13, 215, 221–2, 260–61); Trevor Griffiths, *Comedians* (pub. 1976), p. 7; Robert Hewison, *Too Much: Art and Culture in the Sixties, 1960–75* (1986), p. 206; Georg Gaston, 'Interview with David Hare', *Theatre Journal*, 45:2 (May 1993), p. 214; Waugh, *Harvest of the Sixties*, pp. 171–3; Stevenson, *The Last of England?*, p. 323.

21. *Sunday Times*, 6 November 1977; Stephen Citron, *Sondheim and Lloyd Webber: The New Musical* (Oxford, 2001), pp. 232–2; Goodwin (ed.), *Peter Hall's Diaries*, pp. 378–9; *The Times*, 20 September 1978.

22. Richard Weight, *Patriots: National Identity in Britain 1940–2000* (2002), pp. 543–4, 578; David Cannadine, 'The National Trust and the National Heritage', in David Cannadine, *In Churchill's Shadow: Confronting the Past in Modern Britain* (2002), pp. 238, 240; Turner, *Crisis? What Crisis?*, pp. 48, 67, 150–51; Lawrence James, *The Middle Class: A History* (2006), pp. 489, 534; Elizabeth Wilson, *Adorned in Dreams: Fashion and Modernity* (1985), pp. 114, 177; Sutherland,

Reading the Decades, pp. 88–9; Asa Briggs, *The History of Broadcasting in the United Kingdom*, vol. 5: *Competition* (Oxford, 1995), pp. 944–6; Ruth Barton, 'When the Chickens Came Home to Roost: British Thrillers of the 1970s', in Shail (ed.), *Seventies British Cinema*, p. 48; John Leggott, 'Nothing To Do around Here: British Realist Cinema in the 1970s', ibid., p. 100; Alexander Walker, *National Heroes: British Cinema in the Seventies and Eighties* (1985), pp. 129, 227–8. On audience figures for *Star Wars*, see http://www.bfi.org.uk/features/ultimatefilm/chart/index.php.

23. Hewison, *Too Much*, p. 301; Read, *A Married Man*, pp. 157–8; Walker, *National Heroes*, pp. 227–8; Goodwin (ed.), *Peter Hall's Diaries*, pp. 227–8; for more on *Akenfield*, see http://www.akenfield.com/.

24. Briggs, *Competition*, pp. 944–6; Patrick Cormack, *Heritage in Danger* (1978), p. 10.

25. Roy Strong, *The Roy Strong Diaries 1967–1987* (1997), pp. 139–40; Roy Strong, Marcus Binney and John Harris, *The Destruction of the Country House* (1974); *The Times*, 30 September 1974, 11 October 1974, 25 October 1974, 30 November 1974.

26. *The Times*, 20 January 1977, 7 February 1977, 11 March 1977, 7 April 1977, 28 May 1977, 22 November 1978.

27. *Daily Express*, 22 November 1978; *Guardian*, 27 September 1976; *Time*, 30 September 1974; Lewis Baston, *Reggie: The Life of Reginald Maudling* (Stroud, 2004), p. 309; David Kynaston, *The City of London*, vol. 4: *A Club No More 1945–2000* (2001), p. 527.

28. *Guardian*, 27 September 1976; White, *London in the Twentieth Century*, p. 140; the interview is from Adam Curtis's excellent BBC documentary *The Mayfair Set*, episode 1: *Who Pays Wins* (1999).

29. Amis, *Success*, p. 42; *New York Times*, 19 November 1978; Drabble, *The Middle Ground*, p. 188; Anthony Burgess, *1985* (1978), p. 121; Richard Ingrams and John Wells, *Mrs Wilson's Diary* (1975), entry for 10 January 1975.

30. John Cleese and Connie Booth, *The Complete Fawlty Towers* (1989), p. 150; Douglas Hurd, *Memoirs* (2003), p. 196; Francis Wheen, *Strange Days Indeed: The Golden Age of Paranoia* (2009), p. 18; James Lees-Milne, *Diaries, 1971–1983* (2008), p. 147; Tony Benn, *Conflicts of Interest: Diaries 1977–80* (1990), pp. 341–2.

31. Palin, *Diaries*, pp. 242–3; Graham McCann, *Fawlty Towers: The Story of Britain's Favourite Sitcom* (2007), pp. 9–22; Howard Sounes, *Seventies: The Sights, Sounds and Ideas of a Brilliant Decade* (2006), pp. 36–7.

32. Taylor, *After the War*, p. 37; Kingsley Amis, *The Amis Collection: Selected Non-fiction 1954–1990* (1990), pp. 229–40 (on hotels, see p. 234); Bernard Donoughue, *Downing Street Diary*, vol. 1: *With Harold Wilson in No. 10* (2005), p. 167.

33. Paul Bryers, *Hollow Target* (1976), pp. 105–6; Turner, *Crisis? What Crisis?*, p. 93; Stephen Haseler, *The Death of British Democracy: A Study of Britain's Political Present and Future* (1976), pp. 20, 200; Sir Keith Joseph, *Solving the Union Problem is the Key to Britain's Recovery* (1979), p. 5; speech to the Institute of Socio-Economic Studies, New York, 15 September 1975, TFW; speech to Conservative party conference, 14 October 1977, TFW.

34. Barbara Castle, *The Castle Diaries 1974–1976* (1980), pp. 159–60, 221; Donoughue, *Downing Street Diary*, pp. 143, 174, 303, 490; Hansard, 19 November 1975; E. H. H. Green, *Thatcher* (2006), p. 55; James Callaghan, *Time and Chance* (1987), p. 326.

35. *Newsweek*, 21 October 1974; Lawrence James, *The Rise and Fall of the British Empire* (1999), p. 619; *The Times*, 2 April 1974; *Daily Express*, 6 August 1976; Turner, *Crisis? What Crisis?*, pp. 261–2; Robert J. Wybrow, *Britain Speaks Out, 1937–87: A Social History as Seen through the Gallup Data* (1989), p. 115; Seabrook, *What Went Wrong?*, pp. 166, 119.

36. Speech at Alnwick Castle, 30 July 1975, TFW; Walker, *National Heroes*, pp. 132–3; *Screen International*, 9 September 1978; Chapman, *Licence to Thrill*, p. 180.

37. *Daily Express*, 9 August 1976, 10 August 1976; Philip Norman, *The Stones* (1993), p. 316; Bill Wyman, with Ray Coleman, *Stone Alone: The Story of a Rock 'n' Roll Band* (1990), pp. 9, 11.

38. *Daily Express*, 9 August 1976; *The Times*, 8 July 1974, 22 May 1975, 5 July 1975.

39. Irving, *Pox Britannica*, pp. 13–14, 18; Robert Moss, 'Anglocommunism?', *Commentary*, February 1977, pp. 27–33.

40. Bernard D. Nossiter, *Britain: A Future that Works* (1978), pp. 12–13; Wheen, *Strange Days Indeed*, p. 201; R. Emmett Tyrell, Jr. (ed.), *The Future that Doesn't Work: Social Democracy's Failure in Britain* (New York, 1977); *Time*, 19 May 1975; for domestic use of the 'sick man of Europe', see e.g. *The Times*, 24 October 1973, 15 March 1974, 13 February 1976, 8 July 1976.

41. Samuel H. Beer, *Britain Against Itself: The Political Contradictions of Collectivism* (New York, 1982), p. xi; *The Times*, 22 November 1974; Nossiter, *Britain: A Future that Works*, p. 30; Hudson Institute Europe, *The United Kingdom in 1980: The Hudson Report* (1974), p. 1.

42. *The Times*, 2 January 1976; Alan Greenspan to Gerald Ford, 23 April 1975, Box 56, CO160, Gerald R. Ford Library, Ann Arbor, Michigan; Dennis Kavanagh, *Thatcherism and British Politics: The End of Consensus?* (Oxford, 1987), p. 1.

43. Cleese and Booth, *The Complete Fawlty Towers*, pp. 224–6, 240–41; and see McCann, *Fawlty Towers*, pp. 203–7.

CHAPTER 5. ANARCHY IN THE UK

1. *The Times*, 11 March 1974, 15 March 1974, 16 March 1974, 18 March 1974; *Daily Express*, 18 March 1974; and see the invaluable but chilling Sutton Index of Deaths at http://cain.ulst.ac.uk/sutton/chron/1974.html.

2. Peter Taylor, *Provos: The IRA and Sinn Fein* (1998), pp. 153–5; Richard English, *Armed Struggle: The History of the IRA* (2003), p. 163; *The Times*, 9 March 1973.

3. *The Times*, 9 March 1973; Michael Cockerell, *Live from Number 10: The Inside Story of Prime Ministers and Television* (1989), pp. 181–3; Bernard Nossiter, *Britain: A Future that Works* (1978), p. 130.

4. PRONI, CJ 4/487, Statement by Northern Ireland Executive, 31 December 1973;

on Sunningdale, see *The Times*, 21 March 1973, 22 November 1973, 23 November 1973, 10 December 1973, 11 December 1973; David McKittrick and David McVea, *Making Sense of the Troubles* (2001), pp. 92-7; Paul Arthur, 'The Heath Government and Northern Ireland', in Stuart Ball and Anthony Seldon (eds.), *The Heath Government 1970-1974: A Reappraisal* (Harlow, 1996), pp. 236-7, 254-8; Henry Patterson, *Ireland since 1939: The Persistence of Conflict* (2007), pp. 240-41; 'Northern Ireland Constitutional Proposals', Cmnd. 5259, at http://cain.ulst.ac.uk/hmso/cmd5259.htm; text of the Sunningdale Agreement, 9 December 1973, at http://cain.ulst.ac.uk/events/sunningdale/agreement.htm.

5. Kevin Myers, *Watching the Door: Cheating Death in 1970s Belfast* (2009), pp. 65, 79, 166; *Sunday Telegraph*, 28 May 1972; interview on *Outlook*, BBC World Service, 9 July 1973, on the CD *Eyewitness: 1970-1979* (2005).

6. Arthur, 'The Heath Government and Northern Ireland', pp. 254-8; Patterson, *Ireland since 1939*, pp. 240-41; *The Times*, 5 January 1974. Paisley's words come from a clip in the second part of Peter Taylor's BBC series *Loyalists* (1999).

7. Brendan O'Leary, 'Northern Ireland', in Anthony Seldon and Kevin Hickson (eds.), *New Labour, Old Labour: The Wilson and Callaghan Governments, 1974-1979* (2004), p. 242; PRO PREM 16/145, Note of Meeting with the Northern Ireland Executive, 18 April 1974; Tony Benn, *Against the Tide: Diaries 1973-1976* (1989), pp. 137-8; Bernard Donoughue, *Downing Street Diary*, vol. 1: *With Harold Wilson in No. 10* (2005), p. 124.

8. Patterson, *Ireland since 1939*, pp. 248, 268-9; *Irish Independent*, 1 January 2006; Garret FitzGerald, 'The 1974-5 Threat of a British Withdrawal from Northern Ireland', *Irish Studies in International Affairs*, 17 (2006), pp. 141-50; Roy Foster, *Luck and the Irish: A Brief History of Change, c. 1970-2000* (2007), pp. 121, 123.

9. O'Leary, 'Northern Ireland', pp. 243-4; McKittrick and McVea, *Making Sense of the Troubles*, p. 106.

10. PRONI OE 1/24, Note of Meeting, 26 March 1974; PRO CAB 128/54, CC (74) 11, 10 April 1974; McKittrick and McVea, *Making Sense of the Troubles*, pp. 99, 102; Peter Taylor, *Loyalists* (1999, pb. 2000), pp. 125, 127.

11. *The Times*, 15 May 1974; Richard Clutterbuck, *Britain in Agony: The Growth of Political Violence* (1978), p. 137; Taylor, *Loyalists*, pp. 127-8; PRO PREM 16/146, Statement by Stanley Orme, 20 May 1974.

12. Ian S. Wood, *Crimes of Loyalty: A History of the UDA* (Edinburgh, 2006), pp. 32-6; Clutterbuck, *Britain in Agony*, pp. 136-7; Taylor, *Loyalists*, pp. 128-30.

13. *The Times*, 16 May 1974; Clutterbuck, *Britain in Agony*, pp. 137-8; Taylor, *Loyalists*, p. 130.

14. PRONI OE 1/16, Statement by Brian Faulkner, 15 May 1974; *The Times*, 17 May 1974; Nossiter, *Britain: A Future that Works*, p. 153; Clutterbuck, *Britain in Agony*, p. 139; Taylor, *Loyalists*, p. 130, 133; Wood, *Crimes of Loyalty*, pp. 37-8.

15. PRONI CJ 4/504, Note of Meeting, 17 May 1974; PRO PREM 16/146, 'Provision of Electric Power to Belfast', 17 May 1974; *The Times*, 18 May 1974; Taylor, *Loyalists*, pp. 131-2; Charles Brett, *Long Shadows Cast Before: Nine Lives in Ulster 1625-1977* (Edinburgh, 1978), p. 88.

16. *The Times*, 18 May 1974; Taylor, *Loyalists*, pp. 125-6; Taylor, *Provos*, p. 162.

17. *The Times*, 18 May 1974, 20 May 1974; Clutterbuck, *Britain in Agony*, p. 140; Taylor, *Loyalists*, pp. 132-4.

18. *The Times*, 20 May 1974, 21 May 1974, 22 May 1974; *Daily Express*, 21 May 1974, 22 May 1974; PRONI OE 2/25, Minutes of Executive Meeting, 21 May 1974; Taylor, *Loyalists*, pp. 135–6.

19. PRONI OE 1/16, Note of Meeting, 23 May 1974; PRO PREM 16/147, Note of Meeting at Chequers, 24 May 1974.

20. PRO CAB 129/177, CP (74) 56, 'Northern Ireland', 24 May 1974; PRO CAB 128/154, CC (74) 18, 24 May 1974.

21. PRO FCO 87/336, Harold Wilson to Liam Cosgrave, 25 May 1974; Ben Pimlott, *Harold Wilson* (1992), p. 634; Taylor, *Loyalists*, p. 136.

22. *The Times*, 27 May 1974, 28 May 1974; PRO PREM 16/148, Merlyn Rees to Harold Wilson, 27 May 1974; Wood, *Crimes of Loyalty*, p. 45.

23. PRO PREM 16/148, Idi Amin to Harold Wilson, 28 May 1974; PRONI OE 2/32, Minutes of Executive Meeting, 28 May 1974; *The Times*, 29 May 1974; Ken Bloomfield, *Stormont in Crisis: A Memoir* (Belfast, 1994), p. 220.

24. *The Times*, 29 May 1974; Clutterbuck, *Britain in Agony*, p. 143; PRO PREM 16/148, Memo from Harold Wilson, 30 May 1974.

25. *The Times*, 29 May 1974; McKittrick and McVea, *Making Sense of the Troubles*, p. 107; Clutterbuck, *Britain in Agony*, pp. 143–4; O'Leary, 'Northern Ireland', p. 256.

26. Taylor, *Loyalists*, p. 132; McKittrick and McVea, *Making Sense of the Troubles*, pp. 103–4, 106; Robert Fisk, *The Point of No Return: The Strike which Broke the British in Ulster* (1975); English, *Armed Struggle*, p. 165; Patterson, *Ireland since 1939*, p. 243.

27. McKittrick and McVea, *Making Sense of the Troubles*, p. 108; Taylor, *Provos*, pp. 177–97, 200–201; English, *Armed Struggle*, pp. 171–2, 179, 180–83.

28. PRO PREM 16/152, 'Northern Ireland', 22 November 1974; Taylor, *Provos*, pp. 202–3; Peter Taylor, *Brits: The War against the IRA* (2002), pp. 196–7; O'Leary, 'Northern Ireland', p. 244; McKittrick and McVea, *Making Sense of the Troubles*, pp. 118–19, 123; Bernard Donoughue, *Downing Street Diary*, vol. 2: *With James Callaghan in No. 10* (2008), pp. 298–9.

29. Roy Mason, *Paying the Price* (1999), p. 174; *Daily Telegraph*, 18 April 2004; McKittrick and McVea, *Making Sense of the Troubles*, pp. 122–3, 125, 130; Taylor, *Loyalists*, pp. 157, 159–60.

30. *The Times*, 29 December 1979.

CHAPTER 6. COULD IT HAPPEN HERE?

1. *The Times*, 28 May 1974; Robert Fisk, *The Point of No Return: The Strike which Broke the British in Ulster* (1975), p. 13; Richard Clutterbuck, *Britain in Agony: The Growth of Political Violence* (1978), p. 144.

2. Ibid., pp. 128, 152–67; *The Times*, 21 March 1974.

3. Clutterbuck, *Britain in Agony*, pp. 19, 146; Stephen Haseler, *The Death of British Democracy: A Study of Britain's Political Present and Future* (1976), pp. 19, 101.

4. *The Times*, 28 October 1975, 21 December 1975, 24 December 1974, 30 December 1975; and see Dave Haslam, *Not Abba: The Real Story of the 1970s* (2005), p. 192.

5. Mark Garnett, *From Anger to Apathy: The British Experience since 1975* (2007), p. 38; Stuart Ball, 'The Conservative Party and the Heath Government', in Stuart Ball and Anthony Seldon (eds.), *The Heath Government 1970–1974: A Reappraisal* (Harlow, 1996), pp. 326–7; Vernon Bogdanor, 'The Fall of Heath and the End of the Postwar Settlement', ibid., pp. 380–82; Haseler, *The Death of British Democracy*, p. 11.

6. Anthony King, 'The Problem of Overload', in Anthony King (ed.), *Why is Britain Becoming Harder to Govern?* (1976), pp. 7–8, 11, 15–16, 26; John Mackintosh, 'The Declining Respect for the Law', ibid., pp. 89, 92; and see Dilwyn Porter, 'Government and the Economy', in Richard Coopey and Nicholas Woodward (eds.), *Britain in the 1970s: The Troubled Economy* (1996), pp. 34–5, 49–50.

7. Samuel Brittan, 'The Economic Contradictions of Democracy', in King (ed.), *Why is Britain Becoming Harder to Govern?*, pp. 96–7, 106, 110, 113, 128; *The Times*, 1 July 1974, 4 September 1974. Brittan's article is also in *British Journal of Political Science*, 5:2 (April 1975), pp. 129–59.

8. Tony Benn, *Against the Tide: Diaries, 1973–1976* (1989), p. 464; Friedman on CBS *60 Minutes*, 28 November 1976, quoted in Bernard Nossiter, *Britain: A Future that Works* (1978), p. 13.

9. John Sutherland, *Bestsellers: Popular Fiction of the 1970s* (1981), pp. 179, 182–3; *Time*, 18 March 1974, 20 May 1974.

10. *The Times*, 3 April 1975; Len Deighton, *SS-GB* (1978); Sutherland, *Bestsellers*, pp. 240, 242–3; John Ramsden, *Don't Mention the War: The British and the Germans since 1890* (2006), pp. 380–81; Ruth Barton, 'When the Chickens Came Home to Roost: British Thrillers of the 1970s', in Robert Shail (ed.), *Seventies British Cinema* (2008), p. 52; *Radio Times*, 3 June 1978.

11. *Time*, 28 August 1972; Martin Walker, *The National Front* (1977), pp. 206–7, 211.

12. Alwyn W. Turner, *Crisis? What Crisis? Britain in the 1970s* (2008), pp. 27, 31–2, 65; Arthur Wise, *Who Killed Enoch Powell?* (1970), pp. 42, 121–2; George Shipway, *The Chilian Club* (1971), pp. 56, 86, 163–4.

13. Cecil King, *The Cecil King Diary 1970–1974* (1975), p. 332; James Lees-Milne, *Diaries, 1971–1983* (2008), p. 135; Lord Robens *et al.*, *Inflation: Causes, Consequences, Cures* (1974), p. 60; *Newsweek*, 21 October 1974; Ion Trewin (ed.), *The Hugo Young Papers: Thirty Years of British Politics – Off the Record* (2008), pp. 37–8. For other examples, see Ronald McIntosh, *Challenge to Democracy: Politics, Trade Union Power and Economic Failure in the 1970s* (2006), p. 176; *Guardian*, 8 January 1975.

14. Benn, *Against the Tide*, pp. 66, 68; *Spectator*, 22 December 1973; Francis Wheen, *Strange Days Indeed: The Golden Age of Paranoia* (2009), pp, 57–9; Walker, *The National Front*, pp. 207–8; Bernard Donoughue, *Downing Street Diary*, vol.1: *With Harold Wilson in No. 10* (2005), p. 100; Ben Pimlott, *Harold Wilson* (1992), p. 632.

15. Jack Woddis, *Armies and Politics* (1977), p. 275; Nossiter, *Britain: A Future that Works*, p. 139; Hew Strachan, *The Politics of the British Army* (Oxford, 1997), pp. 188–90; Stephen Dorril and Robin Ramsay, *Smear! Wilson and the Secret State* (1992), pp. 256–9; Bernard Porter, *Plots and Paranoia: A History of Political Espionage in Britain 1790–1988* (1989), pp. 199, 212; David Edgar, *Destiny* (1976, pub. 1978), pp. 23, 27, 70.

16. Dorril and Ramsay, *Smear!*, pp. 211–13; Peter Taylor, *Brits: The War against the IRA* (2001, pb. 2002), pp. 53–5; Frank Kitson, *Low Intensity Operations: Subversion, Insurgency and Peacekeeping* (1971), pp. 3, 24–5, 71, 93, 192; Strachan, *The Politics of the British Army*, pp. 186–8; *The Times*, 23 May 1972.

17. Andy Beckett, *Pinochet in Piccadilly* (2002), pp. 185–6; *Sunday Telegraph*, 19 November 1975; Benn, *Against the Tide*, p. 461; King, *The Cecil King Diary 1970–1974*, p. 387; *Daily Telegraph*, 21 April 1987; Ruth Dudley Edwards, *Newspapermen: Hugh Cudlipp, Cecil Harmsworth King and the Glory Days of Fleet Street* (2003), p. 409.

18. *The Times*, 26 March 1970, 3 December 1971, 29 June 1972; Sir Walter Walker, *Fighting On* (1997); *Daily Telegraph*, 13 August 2001; Beckett, *Pinochet in Piccadilly*, pp. 192–4.

19. Dorril and Ramsay, *Smear!*, pp. 264–6; *Daily Express*, 1 February 1974.

20. *Private Eye*, 8 February 1974; *The Times*, 29 July 1974; Barrie Penrose and Roger Courtiour, *The Pencourt File* (1978), pp. 243–6; Dorril and Ramsay, *Smear!*, pp. 268–9; Beckett, *Pinochet in Piccadilly*, pp. 196–7.

21. *The Times*, 10 August 1974, 24 August 1974, 28 August 1974, 4 November 1974; Walker, *The National Front*, p. 212; Beckett, *Pinochet in Piccadilly*, pp. 197–8.

22. *Guardian*, 25 June 1974, 22 August 1974; *The Times*, 23 August 1974, 24 August 1974; Dorril and Ramsay, *Smear!*, pp. 265, 267; Walker, *The National Front*, pp. 212–3; and see episode 1 of Adam Curtis's BBC documentary *The Mayfair Set*, 'Who Pays Wins' (1999).

23. *The Times*, 7 April 1975; Dorril and Ramsay, *Smear!*, pp. 268, 282–3; Beckett, *Pinochet in Piccadilly*, pp. 198–9; Wheen, *Strange Days Indeed*, p. 252.

24. The exchange comes in episode 3 of the second series of *The Fall and Rise of Reginald Perrin* (5 October 1977): see http://www.youtube.com/watch?v=Xb82v7wh1Fw, as well as the discussions in Turner, *Crisis? What Crisis?*, p. 128; Wheen, *Strange Days Indeed*, p. 253. On Civil Assistance and NAFF, see Neill Nugent, 'The National Association for Freedom', in Roger King and Neill Nugent (eds.), *Respectable Rebels: Middle-class Campaigns in Britain in the 1970s* (1979), p. 97.

25. *The Times*, 6 January 1975, 10 January 1975; Tony Benn, *Conflicts of Interest: Diaries 1977–80* (1990), p. 283; Donoughue, *Downing Street Diary*, p. 659. On the mercenaries in Angola, see *The Times*, 29 January 1976, 9 February 1976.

26. Howard Brenton, *The Churchill Play* (1974), pp. 19, 27, 29, 57, 61, 65, 88.

27. Bart Moore-Gilbert, 'Apocalypse Now? The Novel in the 1970s', in Bart Moore-Gilbert (ed.), *The Arts in the 1970s: Cultural Closure?* (1994), p. 152; Rosemary Dinnage, 'In the Disintegrating City', *New York Review of Books*, 17 July 1975; Patricia Waugh, *Harvest of the Sixties: English Literature and its Background, 1960–1990* (Oxford, 1995), pp. 138–9; Leon Hunt, *British Low Culture: From Safari Suits to Sexploitation* (1998), pp. 74–5, 85–6; Anthony Burgess, *1985* (1978), p. 117; Turner, *Crisis? What Crisis?*, pp. 157–8; *Guardian*, 11 April 2009.

28. Terry Nation, *Survivors* (1976), pp. 87–8, 95–6; Andy Sawyer, 'Everyday Life in the Post-catastrophe Future: Terry Nation's *Survivors*', in John R. Cook and Peter Wright (eds.), *British Science Fiction Television: A Hitchhiker's Guide* (2006), pp. 131–54; Alan Stevens and Fiona Moore, *Liberation: The Unofficial and Unauthorized Guide to Blake's 7* (2003), pp. 59–102; Una McCormack, 'Resist the Host:

Blake's 7 – a Very British Future', in Cook and Wright (eds.), *British Science Fiction Television*, pp. 174–92; Turner, *Crisis? What Crisis?*, pp. 202–3; *Daily Mail*, 10 January 1978; and see Alwyn W. Turner, *The Man Who Invented the Daleks: The Strange Worlds of Terry Nation* (2011), pp. 202–31, 236–44.

29. Maureen Gregson, *1990* (novelization, 1977), pp. 7–8, 11, 130, 113, 127, 17, 14, 36, 15, 50, 22, 80; Maureen Gregson, *1990: Book Two* (novelization, 1978), pp. 10–11.

30. *Radio Times*, 17 September 1977; see also the episode guide at http://www. startrader.co.uk/Action%20TV/guide70s/1990.htm.

31. Robert Moss, *The Collapse of Democracy* (1977), pp. 23–34.

32. Richard Cockett, *Thinking the Unthinkable: Think-tanks and the Economic Counter-revolution, 1931–1983* (1995), pp. 224–5; Dorril and Ramsay, *Smear!*, pp. 212–13; Beckett, *Pinochet in Piccadilly*, pp. 187, 191; Moss, *The Collapse of Democracy*, pp. 15–6, 27, 36; Robert Moss, 'Anglocommunism?', *Commentary*, February 1977, pp. 27–33.

33. Hansard, 26 February 1975; *The Times*, 20 January 1976; Benn, *Against the Tide*, p. 501.

34. Stuart Hall *et al.*, *Policing the Crisis: Mugging, the State and Law and Order* (Basingstoke, 1978), p. 310; *Birmingham Evening Mail*, 12 June 1975; Haseler, *The Death of British Democracy*, pp. 200–205.

35. *The Money Programme* (16 July 1976), quoted in Andy Beckett, *When the Lights Went Out: Britain in the Seventies* (2009), pp. 181–2; Haseler, *The Death of British Democracy*, p. 191.

36. Andrew Motion, *Philip Larkin: A Writer's Life* (1994), p. 459; Zachary Leader (ed.), *The Letters of Kingsley Amis* (2000), p. 767; Zachary Leader, *The Life of Kingsley Amis* (2006), pp. 661–6; John Lahr (ed.), *The Diaries of Kenneth Tynan* (2002), pp. 317–18.

37. Kingsley Amis, *Memoirs* (1991), p. 318.

CHAPTER 7. THE ELECTION THAT NEVER WAS

1. *Daily Express*, 7 October 1974; *The Times*, 7 October 1974, 19 September 1975.
2. Paul Bew and Gordon Gillespie, *Northern Ireland: A Chronology of the Troubles, 1968–1999* (Dublin, 1999), p. 90; Richard English, *Armed Struggle: The History of the IRA* (2003), pp. 167–9; *The Times*, 8 February 1977; *Irish Times*, 18 November 1974.
3. *The Times*, 19 September 1974.
4. Bernard Donoughue, *Downing Street Diary*, vol. 1: *With Harold Wilson in No. 10* (2005), pp. 188–90, 193, 195.
5. Ben Pimlott, *Harold Wilson* (1992), p. 643; David Butler and Dennis Kavanagh, *The British General Election of October 1974* (1975), pp. 83–4, 112–13, 255.
6. Tony Benn, *Against the Tide: Diaries 1973–1976* (1989), pp. 226–8, 244; Donoughue, *Downing Street Diary*, p. 210; Stephen Dorril and Robin Ramsay, *Smear! Wilson and the Secret State* (1992), pp. 270–71; Wheen, *Strange Days Indeed: The Golden Age of Paranoia* (2009), p. 222.
7. Mark Garnett and Ian Aitken, *Splendid! Splendid! The Authorized Biography of Willie Whitelaw* (2003), pp. 187–8; John Campbell, *Edward Heath: A Biog-*

raphy (1993), pp. 628–30, 635, 641–2, 658–9; Butler and Kavanagh, *The British General Election of October 1974*, pp. 41, 82, 266.

8. Ibid., pp. 43–4; Campbell, *Edward Heath*, pp. 633, 636.

9. John Cole, *As It Seemed to Me: Political Memoirs* (1995), p. 112; *Guardian*, 4 March 1974, 2 August 1974; *The Times*, 27 June 1974.

10. *The Times*, 2 May 1974, 4 May 1974, 27 June 1974, 29 June 1974, 1 July 1974, 10 September 1974, 11 September 1974; Butler and Kavanagh, *The British General Election of October 1974*, pp. 66–9; Campbell, *Edward Heath*, pp. 633, 637, 638–41; and see *Putting Britain First: A National Policy* (1974), reproduced online at http://www.conservativemanifesto.com/1974/Oct/october-1974-conservative-manifesto.shtml.

11. *The Times*, 1 October 1974, 3 October 1974; Campbell, *Edward Heath*, pp. 642–3, 646; Butler and Kavanagh, *The British General Election of October 1974*, pp. 72, 290.

12. *The Times*, 25 September 1974, 28 September 1974, 3 October 1974; *Spectator*, 11 October 1974; John Campbell, *Margaret Thatcher*, vol. 1: *The Grocer's Daughter* (2000), pp. 271–5; Butler and Kavanagh, *The British General Election of October 1974*, pp. 121, 156–7, 177, 259.

13. Michael Cockerell, *Live from Number 10: The Inside Story of Prime Ministers and Television* (1989), pp. 210, 212; Butler and Kavanagh, *The British General Election of October 1974*, pp. 88, 106, 115; *The Times*, 24 September 1974; *The Economist*, 28 September 1974; Campbell, *Edward Heath*, p. 645.

14. Butler and Kavanagh, *The British General Election of October 1974*, pp. 80, 102, 133, 135, 141, 192, 250, 291; *The Times*, 9 October 1974; Campbell, *Edward Heath*, pp. 643–4.

15. Butler and Kavanagh, *The British General Election of October 1974*, pp. 79, 272; *Time*, 30 September 1974.

16. *The Times*, 27 August 1974, 29 August 1974, 31 August 1974, 7 September 1974; Butler and Kavanagh, *The British General Election of October 1974*, p. 91.

17. *Sunday Times*, 6 October 1974; *The Times*, 7 October 1974; Butler and Kavanagh, *The British General Election of October 1974*, pp. 125–9; Campbell, *Edward Heath*, pp. 649–51; Garnett and Aitken, *Splendid! Splendid!*, pp. 192–3.

18. Donoughue, *Downing Street Diary*, pp. 209–14; see also Philip Ziegler, *Wilson: The Authorized Life* (1993), p. 421; Wheen, *Strange Days Indeed*, pp. 220–21.

19. *The Times*, 8 October 1974; *Guardian*, 9 October 1974; Butler and Kavanagh, *The British General Election of October 1974*, pp. 169–71; Larry Lamb, *Sunrise: The Remarkable Rise and Rise of the Bestselling Soaraway Sun* (1989), p. 159; *Observer*, 6 October 1974.

20. *The Times*, 10 October 1974, 11 October 1974; Benn, *Against the Tide*, p. 234; Campbell, *Edward Heath*, p. 652; Butler and Kavanagh, *The British General Election of October 1974*, p. 245; Donoughue, *Downing Street Diary*, pp. 215–17.

21. On the results, see Butler and Kavanagh, *The British General Election of October 1974*, pp. 251, 277–81.

22. Donoughue, *Downing Street Diary*, pp. 217–18; Bernard Donoughue, *The Heat of the Kitchen: An Autobiography* (2003), p. 145.

23. *The Times*, 12 October 1974; Donoughue, *Downing Street Diary*, pp. 218–19.

CHAPTER 8. FOR GOD'S SAKE, BRITAIN, WAKE UP!

1. *Daily Express*, 22 November 1974; *Daily Mirror*, 22 November 1974, 23 November 1974; *The Times*, 22 November 1974.

2. *The Times*, 22 November 1974, 23 November 1974; *Daily Mirror*, 22 November 1974; Richard Clutterbuck, *Britain in Agony: The Growth of Political Violence* (1978), p. 150.

3. Roy Jenkins, *A Life at the Centre* (1991), pp. 395, 397–8; *Daily Mirror*, 22 November 1974; *The Times*, 23 November 1974.

4. *The Times*, 23 November 1974; Clutterbuck, *Britain in Agony*, p. 150; *Daily Express*, 22 November 1974.

5. Jenkins, *A Life at the Centre*, p. 396; *Daily Express*, 22 November 1974; *The Times*, 23 November 1974; *Daily Mirror*, 23 November 1974.

6. Tony Benn, *Against the Tide: Diaries 1973–1976* (1989), pp. 270, 274; PRO CAB 128/55, CC (74) 49, 25 November 1974.

7. *Daily Mirror*, 23 November 1974; *The Times*, 22 November 1974, 23 November 1974; Jenkins, *A Life at the Centre*, pp. 394–5; Clutterbuck, *Britain in Agony*, p. 151; PRO CAB 129/180, C (74) 139, 'IRA Terrorism in Great Britain', 24 November 1974.

8. PRO CAB 129/180, C (74) 139, 'IRA Terrorism in Great Britain', 24 November 1974; Clutterbuck, *Britain in Agony*, p. 151; John Campbell, *Roy Jenkins: A Biography* (1983), p. 162.

9. Jenkins, *A Life at the Centre*, pp. 364, 388; Ronald McIntosh, *Challenge to Democracy: Politics, Trade Union Power and Economic Failure in the 1970s* (2006), pp. 87, 120, 130; Bernard Donoughue, *Downing Street Diary*, vol. 1: *With Harold Wilson in No. 10* (2005), pp. 158–9.

10. Jenkins, *A Life at the Centre*, pp. 389–91; Barbara Castle, *The Castle Diaries 1974–1976* (1980), pp. 192, 194; Benn, *Against the Tide*, pp. 239–41.

11. Ben Pimlott, *Harold Wilson* (1992), pp. 648, 674–5; Philip Ziegler, *Wilson: The Authorized Life* (1993), pp. 468–71; Joe Haines, *Glimmers of Twilight: Harold Wilson in Decline* (2003), pp. xiii, xvii, 116; Donoughue, *Downing Street Diary*, pp. 263, 225, 388.

12. Ibid., pp. 214, 237; *The Times*, 4 October 1974; Edward Pearce, *Denis Healey: A Life in Our Times* (2002), p. 422; PRO CAB 128/55, CC (74) 45, 11 November 1974; Castle, *The Castle Diaries*, p. 213; *The Times*, 13 November 1974.

13. Castle, *The Castle Diaries*, pp. 219–24; see also Benn, *Against the Tide*, pp. 264–7; James Callaghan, *Time and Chance* (1987), p. 326.

14. *Daily Mirror*, 27 November 1974, 24 December 1974; Hansard, 24 May 1974; Benn, *Against the Tide*, pp. 272–3; *Daily Express*, 24 December 1974, 27 December 1974; and see Matthew Parris, *Great Parliamentary Scandals: Four Centuries of Calumny, Smear and Innuendo* (1995), pp. 186–9; Mark Garnett, *From Anger to Apathy: The British Experience since 1975* (2007), pp. 26–7.

15. *Daily Mirror*, 16 November 1974; *The Times*, 17 November 1974; Christopher Andrew, *The Defence of the Realm: The Authorized History of MI5* (2009), pp. 707–8; Parris, *Great Parliamentary Scandals*, pp. 189–90; Garnett, *From Anger to Apathy*, pp. 28–30; Hansard, 4 November 1974, 20 October 1975, 20 November 1975.

16. David Kynaston, *The City of London*, vol. 4: *A Club No More 1945–2000* (2001), pp. 510, 512; Keith Middlemas, *Power, Competition and the State*, vol. 3: *The End of the Postwar Era: Britain since 1974* (Basingstoke, 1991), p. 65; Cathy Courtney and Paul Thompson, *City Lives: The Changing Voices of City Finance* (1996), p. 130.

17. Middlemas, *Power, Competition and the State*, pp. 60, 497; *Newsweek*, 21 October 1974; Pearce, *Denis Healey*, p. 421; Jim Tomlinson, 'Economic Policy', in Anthony Seldon and Kevin Hickson (eds.), *New Labour, Old Labour: The Wilson and Callaghan Governments, 1974–1979* (2004), p. 58; McIntosh, *Challenge to Democracy*, p. 181; *Daily Telegraph*, 30 December 2005.

18. Anthony King and Robert J. Wybrow (eds.), *British Political Opinion 1937–2000: The Gallup Polls* (2001), p. 312; *Daily Express*, 31 December 1974; Roy Strong, *The Roy Strong Diaries 1967–1987* (1997), pp. 142–3. The episode of *Crossroads* (no. 2247, 31 December 1974) is on YouTube.

19. Alwyn W. Turner, *Crisis? What Crisis? Britain in the 1970s* (2008), p. 104; Joe Moran, '"Stand Up and Be Counted": Hughie Green, the 1970s and Popular Memory', *History Workshop Journal*, 70 (2010), pp. 173–5.

20. *The Times*, 7 January 1975, 9 January 1975; Kynaston, *A Club No More*, p. 516; Michael Palin, *Diaries 1969–1979: The Python Years* (2006), p. 203.

21. McIntosh, *Challenge to Democracy*, pp. 191, 193, 197.

22. Dilwyn Porter, 'Government and the Economy', in Richard Coopey and Nicholas Woodward (eds.), *Britain in the 1970s: The Troubled Economy* (1996), pp. 43, 45; David Butler and Dennis Kavanagh, *The British General Election of October 1974* (1975), p. 15; Edmund Dell, *The Chancellors: A History of the Chancellors of the Exchequer, 1945–90* (1996, pb. 1997), pp. 413, 417; Gerald A. Dorfman, *Government versus Trade Unionism in British Politics since 1968* (1979), p. 115; Donoughue, *Downing Street Diary*, p. 267.

23. *The Times*, 14 February 1975, 3 June 1975; Dell, *The Chancellors*, p. 417; Donoughue, *Downing Street Diary*, p. 352; Joe Haines, *The Politics of Power: The Inside Story of Life at No. 10* (1977), p. 4.

24. Dorfman, *Government versus Trade Unionism*, p. 116; Max-Stephan Schulze and Nicholas Woodward, 'The Emergence of Rapid Inflation', in Coopey and Woodward (eds.), *Britain in the 1970s*, p. 114; Samuel Brittan, 'The Economic Contradictions of Democracy', *British Journal of Political Science*, 5:2 (April 1975), p. 132; Dell, *The Chancellors*, p. 417; Donoughue, *Downing Street Diary*, p. 358; Haines, *The Politics of Power*, p. 4.

25. Donoughue, *Downing Street Diary*, pp. 280, 312; Bernard Donoughue, *The Heat of the Kitchen: An Autobiography* (2003), p. 160; Phillip Whitehead, *The Writing on the Wall: Britain in the Seventies* (1985), p. 149; Castle, *The Castle Diaries*, pp. 318–19; *TUC Economic Review* (1975), p. 58; Tomlinson, 'Economic Policy', p. 60; Robert Taylor, 'The Rise and Fall of the Social Contract', in Seldon and Hickson (eds.), *New Labour, Old Labour*, p. 82.

26. Dell, *The Chancellors*, pp. 412–13; Pearce, *Denis Healey*, pp. 424–5; *The Times*, 11 January 1975, 14 January 1975, 16 January 1975; Castle, *The Castle Diaries*, p. 285.

27. Dell, *The Chancellors*, p. 414; Pearce, *Denis Healey*, p. 425; Joel Barnett, *Inside the Treasury* (1982), p. 62; Castle, *The Castle Diaries*, pp. 352–4, 359, 361; Benn, *Against the Tide*, pp. 356–7.

28. Hansard, 15 April 1975; *The Times*, 16 April 1975; Dell, *The Chancellors*, p. 416; Edmund Dell, *A Strange Eventful History: Democratic Socialism in Britain* (2000), p. 462; Tomlinson, 'Economic Policy', pp. 58–9; Pearce, *Denis Healey*, p. 427; Denis Healey, *The Time of My Life* (1989, pb. 1990), pp. 378–9.

29. Memorandum of Conversation, President Ford and Henry Kissinger, 8 January 1975, Box 8, National Security Adviser's Files, Gerald R. Ford Library, Ann Arbor, Michigan.

30. *Wall Street Journal*, 29 April 1975; *The Times*, 8 May 1975.

31. *The Times*, 8 May 1975; Harold Wilson, *Final Term: The Labour Government, 1974–1976* (1979), p. 113.

CHAPTER 9. A CLEVER BIT OF PROPAGANDA

1. Hunter Davies, *The Creighton Report: A Year in the Life of a Comprehensive School* (Newton Abbot, 1977), pp. 8–11.

2. Ibid., pp. 258, 3–5, 24–5, 39, 152.

3. Ibid., pp. 75, 91–3, 25, 50, 52–5, 102, 142, 204.

4. Ibid., pp. 16, 116, 147–8, 153, 158–60.

5. Ibid., pp. 146–7, 111–13, 22–3, 236.

6. Ibid., pp. 196, 282, 284, 227.

7. Simon Gunn and Rachel Bell, *Middle Classes: Their Rise and Sprawl* (2003), pp. 146–8; Graham McCann, *Dad's Army: The Story of a Classic Television Show* (2001), p. 116; Lawrence James, *The Middle Class: A History* (2006), p. 430.

8. Nicholas Timmins, *The Five Giants: A Biography of the Welfare State* (1996), pp. 99–100, 239–41; Ken Coates and Richard Silburn, *Poverty: The Forgotten Englishmen* (Harmondsworth, 1970), p. 124; R. A. Butler, *The Art of the Possible: The Memoirs of Lord Butler* (Harmondsworth, 1973), pp. 124–25; Anthony Sampson, *The New Anatomy of Britain* (1971), p. 129; Gunn and Bell, *Middle Classes*, p. 170; Peter Clarke, *Hope and Glory: Britain 1900–1990* (1996), p. 285.

9. C. A. R. Crosland, *The Future of Socialism* (1956), pp. 204–6; Timmins, *The Five Giants*, pp. 238, 242–3, 298–9; Peter Calvocoressi, *The British Experience 1945–75* (Harmondsworth, 1978), p. 158; Gunn and Bell, *Middle Classes*, pp. 170–71, 176; Susan Crosland, *Tony Crosland* (1982), pp. 146–8; Kevin Jefferys, *Anthony Crosland: A New Biography* (1999), pp. 203–7; John Campbell, *Edward Heath: A Biography* (1993), pp. 236–7; John Campbell, *Margaret Thatcher*, vol. 1: *The Grocer's Daughter* (2000), pp. 221–3, 225–6; Hugo Young, *One of Us: A Biography of Margaret Thatcher* (1990), pp. 68, 70.

10. *Britain Will Win with Labour* (1974), online at http://www.psr.keele.ac.uk/area/uk/man/lab74oct.htm; *The Times*, 12 March 1975, 13 March 1975; Sampson, *The New Anatomy of Britain*, pp. 140–45.

11. *The Times*, 24 January 1975, 13 March 1975.

12. *The Times*, 29 April 1975, 4 August 1975, 22 August 1975, 12 November 1975; *Observer*, 25 January 1976; Joe Moran, '"Stand Up and Be Counted": Hughie Green, the 1970s and Popular Memory', *History Workshop Journal*, 70 (2010), p. 175; Timmins, *The Five Giants*, p. 320.

13. Ibid., pp. 319–20; for a nicely balanced verdict, see Clarke, *Hope and Glory*, p. 286.

14. Gunn and Bell, *Middle Classes*, pp. 171, 174; *Daily Mail*, 28 April 1976.

15. *The Plowden Report: Children and their Primary Schools* (1967), paras 521, 523–5, 529, 505–6; Kathryn A. Riley, *Whose School is it Anyway?* (1998), pp. 12–14; Timmins, *The Five Giants*, p. 244; for a spectacularly vigorous attack on the report and its legacy, see Peter Hitchens, *The Abolition of Britain: The British Cultural Revolution from Lady Chatterley to Tony Blair* (2000), pp. 68–75.

16. Riley, *Whose School is it Anyway?*, pp. 14, 41; John Gretton and Mark Jackson, *William Tyndale: Collapse of a School – or a System?* (1976), pp. 50–51; *New Statesman*, 5 December 1975.

17. Gunn and Bell, *Middle Classes*, p. 174; *New Society*, 1 February 1973; Paul Ferris, *The New Militants: Crisis in the Trade Unions* (Harmondsworth, 1972), p. 73; *Guardian*, 11 November 1975.

18. *The Times*, 12 December 1970; Sampson, *The New Anatomy of Britain*, pp. 148–9; Gerald Bernbaum, 'Case Study: Countesthorpe College', in Alan Harris, Martin Lawn and William Prescott (eds.), *Curriculum Innovation* (1975), pp. 347–9, 365–71; and see also the essays in John Watt (ed.), *The Countesthorpe Experience* (1977).

19. C. B. Cox and A. E. Dyson (eds.), *The Black Papers in Education* (1971), pp. 9–11, 20, 33–4; Timmins, *The Five Giants*, pp. 269–71.

20. *New Statesman*, 18 April 1969; *Evening Standard*, 9 April 1969; *The Times*, 9 April 1969, 3 January 1972, 31 December 1974; Timmins, *The Five Giants*, p. 273.

21. Cox and Dyson (eds.), *The Black Papers*, pp. 17, 22, 26, 37–8, 65, 195, 215–23.

22. C. B. Cox and Rhodes Boyson (eds.), *Black Paper 1975: The Fight for Education* (1975), pp. 3, 25, 6.

23. *The Times*, 28 October 1975; Gretton and Jackson, *William Tyndale*, pp. 20, 40; Riley, *Whose School is it Anyway?*, pp. 28–9.

24. Ibid., pp. 21–2, 4, 58; *Daily Mail*, 29 October 1975; *Daily Telegraph*, 17 October 1975; *Daily Express*, 25 September 1975, 2 January 1976; *Evening News*, 28 October 1975.

25. Gretton and Jackson, *William Tyndale*, pp. 15–16, 27, 31–3.

26. Ibid., pp. 53, 18–19; Riley, *Whose School is it Anyway?*, p. 27.

27. *The Times*, 2 July 1975, 10 July 1975, 25 September 1975, 3 October 1975; *Daily Express*, 25 September 1975, 17 October 1975; Gretton and Jackson, *William Tyndale*, pp. 20–25, 27–9, 48–9; Riley, *Whose School is it Anyway?*, pp. 37, 40, 43.

28. Gretton and Jackson, *William Tyndale*, pp. 105–14, 56; *Daily Express*, 2 January 1976; Terry Ellis, Jackie McWhirter, Dorothy McColgan and Brian Haddow, *William Tyndale: The Teachers' Story* (1976), pp. 42–5.

29. Riley, *Whose School is it Anyway?*, pp. 24, 26, 28; *The Times*, 22 January 1976, 24 January 1976; *Daily Express*, 17 October 1975; Gretton and Jackson, *William Tyndale*, pp. 39–40.

30. Riley, *Whose School is it Anyway?*, pp. 23, 38, 45; Gretton and Jackson, *William Tyndale*, p. 37.

31. *Daily Express*, 17 July 1976; *The Times*, 17 July 1976, 19 July 1976, 16 October 1976, 18 January 1978, 7 November 1978; Gretton and Jackson, *William Tyndale*, pp. 117–21; for the text of the report, see Robert Auld, *William Tyndale, Junior and Infants School Public Inquiry* (1976).

32. Gretton and Jackson, *William Tyndale*, p. 121; Riley, *Whose School is it Anyway?*,

pp. 49, 21, 57–8; Timmins, *The Five Giants*, p. 322; *The Times*, 5 September 1977; *Daily Express*, 19 July 1976.

33. *News of the World*, 7 August 1977; *Daily Mail*, 4 March 1975, 18 January 1975, 27 April 1976; *Guardian*, 5 February 1976, 6 February 1976; Riley, *Whose School is it Anyway?*, p. 53; *Sunday Express*, 11 July 1976; and see Clyde Chitty, *Towards a New Education System: The Victory of the New Right?* (1989), pp. 65–6; Alwyn W. Turner, *Crisis? What Crisis? Britain in the 1970s* (2008), pp. 260–61.

34. *Guardian*, 27 October 1975.

35. Mike Phillips and Trevor Phillips, *Windrush: The Irresistible Rise of Multi-racial Britain* (1999), p. 204; Jonathon Green, *Them: Voices from the Immigrant Community in Contemporary Britain* (1990), pp. 238–9; Harry Golbourne, *Race Relations in Britain since 1945* (Basingstoke, 1998), p. 87; Gunn and Bell, *Middle Classes*, pp. 179–82.

36. *The Times*, 18 July 1974, 22 March 1977, 24 March 1977, 28 March 1977; Cox and Boyson (eds.), *Black Paper 1975*, pp. 62–3, 30.

37. Colin Dexter, *Last Seen Wearing* (1977), p. 49; Colin Dexter, *Service of All the Dead* (1980), p. 103; Piers Paul Read, *A Married Man* (1979), pp. 159–60, 162.

38. Maureen Gregson, *1990* (novelization, 1977), p. 101; Maureen Gregson, *1990: Book Two* (novelization, 1978), p. 56; Hitchens, *The Abolition of Britain*, pp. 255–6.

39. Gunn and Bell, *Middle Classes*, p. 173; Davies, *The Creighton Report*, pp. 261, 265, 101.

40. *Daily Express*, 10 January 1976; Davies, *The Creighton Report*, p. xii; Rachel Sharp and Anthony Green, *Education and Social Control: A Study in Progressive Primary Education* (1975); Alison Pressley, *The Seventies: Good Times, Bad Taste* (2002), p. 59.

41. Speech to Conservative party conference, 14 October 1977, TFW. The poster, which first appeared in 1978, is in the Bodleian Library's Conservative Party archive at http://www.bodley.ox.ac.uk/dept/scwmss/cpa/poster-home.html.

CHAPTER 10. NUTTY AS A FRUITCAKE

1. *Daily Mirror*, 14 October 1974; *Guardian*, 12 October 1974; *Daily Express*, 14 October 1974.

2. Jim Prior, *A Balance of Power* (1986), p. 98; John Campbell, *Edward Heath: A Biography* (1993), pp. 654–6; Mark Garnett and Ian Aitken, *Splendid! Splendid! The Authorized Biography of Willie Whitelaw* (2003), pp. 201–2; Hugo Young, *One of Us: A Biography of Margaret Thatcher* (1990), p. 91.

3. John Ranelagh, *Thatcher's People: An Insider's Account of the Politics, the Power and the Personalities* (1992), pp. 115–16; Campbell, *Edward Heath*, pp. 456, 471, 509–11; Simon Heffer, *Like the Roman: The Life of Enoch Powell* (1998), p. 657; John Ramsden, 'The Conservative Party and the Heath Government', in Stuart Ball and Anthony Seldon (eds.), *The Heath Government 1970–1974: A Reappraisal* (Harlow, 1996), pp. 323–4, 326–7, 334–5.

4. *Spectator*, 9 March 1974; Ronald McIntosh, *Challenge to Democracy: Politics, Trade Union Power and Economic Failure in the 1970s* (2006), p. 123; John Ramsden, *An Appetite for Power: A History of the Conservative Party since*

1830 (1999), pp. 415, 418; Phillip Whitehead, *The Writing on the Wall: Britain in the Seventies* (1985), p. 324; *The Times*, 20 January 1975.

5. *Spectator*, 2 December 1972; Campbell, *Edward Heath*, pp. 515–20; Heffer, *Like the Roman*, p. 615; Whitehead, *The Writing on the Wall*, p. 325; Prior, *A Balance of Power*, p. 98; Ion Trewin (ed.), *The Hugo Young Papers: Thirty Years of British Politics – Off the Record* (2008), p. 46; Alan Clark, *Diaries: Into Politics 1972–1982*, ed. Ion Trewin (2001), p. 56.

6. Young, *One of Us*, pp. 94–5; Campbell, *Edward Heath*, pp. 656–7, 659–60, 662; John Campbell, *Margaret Thatcher*, vol. 1: *The Grocer's Daughter* (2000), p. 286; Geoffrey Wheatcroft, *The Strange Death of Tory England* (2005), p. 87; *The Economist*, 2 November 1974; *The Times*, 16 October 1974, 8 November 1974, 11 November 1974, 15 November 1974.

7. *Daily Express*, 11 November 1974, 11 December 1974; *The Times*, 18 December 1974.

8. *Daily Express*, 6 January 1975; *The Times*, 15 October 1974, 25 November 1974, 1 February 1975.

9. Richard Cockett, *Thinking the Unthinkable: Think-tanks and the Economic Counter-revolution, 1931–1983* (1995), pp. 125, 132–5, 138 (and pp. 122–58 in general); and see also episode 1, 'Outsiders', of the excellent BBC Four series *Tory! Tory! Tory!* (2006).

10. Cockett, *Thinking the Unthinkable*, pp. 143, 146, 149, 178–9; Andrew Denham and Mark Garnett, *Keith Joseph* (Chesham, 2001, pb. 2002), pp. 137–8; Andy Beckett, *When the Lights Went Out: Britain in the Seventies* (2009), pp. 274–5.

11. Cockett, *Thinking the Unthinkable*, p. 164; Heffer, *Like the Roman*, pp. 645, 349, 366–8, 445, 476, 484–6; *The Times*, 2 September 1968, 12 October 1968; *Observer*, 13 October 1968; see also the thoughtful chapter on Powell in Richard Vinen, *Thatcher's Britain: The Politics and Social Upheaval of the 1980s* (2009), pp. 43–59.

12. Hansard, 5 April 1971, 28 June 1971, 11 October 1973, 23 July 1973; Heffer, *Like the Roman*, pp. 590–1, 597, 622–3, 645, 658–9, 672, 678; Tony Benn, *Against the Tide: Diaries 1973–1976* (1989), p. 55; *The Times*, 3 July 1974, 6 July 1974.

13. Milton Friedman, 'The Quantity Theory of Money: A Restatement', in Friedman (ed.), *Studies in the Quantity Theory of Money* (Chicago, 1956), pp. 3–21; Milton Friedman, 'The Role of Monetary Policy', *American Economic Review*, 58:1 (March 1968), pp. 1–17; Franco Modigliani, 'The Monetarist Controversy, or Should We Forsake Stabilization Policies?', *American Economic Review*, 67 (March 1977), pp. 1–19; Alan S. Blinder, 'The Rise and Fall of Keynesian Economics', *Economic Record*, December 1988, p. 278; David Smith, *The Rise and Fall of Monetarism: The Theory and Politics of an Economic Experiment* (1991), pp. 11–30. On Powell in the summer of 1974, see Heffer, *Like the Roman*, pp. 721–8.

14. Kevin Hickson, *The IMF Crisis of 1976 and British Politics* (2005), pp. 180–82; Smith, *The Rise and Fall of Monetarism*, p. 36; Cockett, *Thinking the Unthinkable*, pp. 150–54; *Daily Telegraph*, 5 January 2009; *The Times*, 7 August 1970, 17 September 1970.

15. Cockett, *Thinking the Unthinkable*, pp. 154–5, 157; Smith, *The Rise and Fall of Monetarism*, pp. 47–8, 50, 59, 76, 81; Noel Thompson, 'Economic Ideas and the

Development of Economic Opinion', in Richard Coopey and Nicholas Woodward (eds.), *Britain in the 1970s: The Troubled Economy* (1996), pp. 57–70.

16. Smith, *The Rise and Fall of Monetarism*, p. 35; Cockett, *Thinking the Unthinkable*, pp. 183–5.

17. Smith, *The Rise and Fall of Monetarism*, pp. 36, 51; Cockett, *Thinking the Unthinkable*, pp. 185–7; Beckett, *When the Lights Went Out*, pp. 337–8; *The Times*, 18 May 1968, 24 May 1973, 7 October 1974, 10 April 1975.

18. Dennis Kavanagh, *Thatcherism and British Politics: The End of Consensus?* (Oxford, 1987), pp. 92, 96, 102, 107; Cockett, *Thinking the Unthinkable*, pp. 196, 217; Robert Blake, 'A Changed Climate', in Robert Blake and John Patten (eds.), *The Conservative Opportunity* (1976), p. 3; *The Times*, 8 January 1976.

19. Denham and Garnett, *Keith Joseph*, pp. 14, 24, 48–50, 55, 134; Nicholas Timmins, *The Five Giants: A Biography of the Welfare State* (1996), pp. 285–6.

20. Denham and Garnett, *Keith Joseph*, pp. 78, 137–9, 159–61; Timmins, *The Five Giants*, pp. 286, 288, 290; *Sunday Mirror*, 25 March 1973; Ranelagh, *Thatcher's People*, pp. 106–7.

21. Sir Keith Joseph, *Reversing the Trend: A Critical Reappraisal of Conservative Economic and Social Policies* (1975), p. 6; Denham and Garnett, *Keith Joseph*, pp. 234–6, 250, 252; Sir Keith Joseph, 'This is Not the Time to be Mealymouthed' (Upminster speech), 22 June 1974, TFW; and see Cockett, *Thinking the Unthinkable*, pp. 240–42.

22. Young, *One of Us*, pp. 85–7; Denham and Garnett, *Keith Joseph*, pp. 238–44, 246–8; Campbell, *The Grocer's Daughter*, pp. 266–8; Sir Keith Joseph, Shadow Cabinet paper on inflation, 1 May 1974, TFW; minutes of the 10th Shadow Cabinet meeting, 3 May 1974, TFW. *The Times*, 31 August 2006. The famous account of the Shadow Cabinet meeting in Ranelagh, *Thatcher's People*, pp. 125–6, has been comprehensively debunked by Campbell, and by Denham and Garnett.

23. Denham and Garnett, *Keith Joseph*, pp. 255–7; Timmins, *The Five Giants*, pp. 357–8; Sir Keith Joseph, 'Inflation is Caused by Governments' (Preston speech), 5 September 1974, TFW.

24. Campbell, *The Grocer's Daughter*, p. 268; Denham and Garnett, *Keith Joseph*, pp. 257–9; *The Times*, 6 September 1974; *The Economist*, 7 September 1974; *New Statesman*, 13 September 1974; Reginald Maudling, *Memoirs* (1978), p. 209; Lewis Baston, *Reggie: The Life of Reginald Maudling* (Stroud, 2004), p. 466.

25. Ranelagh, *Thatcher's People*, pp. 132–3; Denham and Garnett, *Keith Joseph*, pp. 265–6, 219, 262–3; *Private Eye*, 18 October 1974.

26. Sir Keith Joseph, 'Our Human Stock is Threatened' (Edgbaston speech), 19 October 1974, TFW; *The Times*, 21 October 1974; Denham and Garnett, *Keith Joseph*, p. 267; Timmins, *The Five Giants*, p. 289.

27. Denham and Garnett, *Keith Joseph*, pp. 267–9; Max Caulfield, *Mary Whitehouse* (1975), p. 1; *The Times*, 21 October 1974, 26 October 1974; *Sunday Times*, 20 October 1974, 27 October 1974.

28. Heffer, *Like the Roman*, pp. 739, 741; Denham and Garnett, *Keith Joseph*, pp. 271–2, 274; *Private Eye*, 18 October 1974; Denis Healey, *The Time of My*

Life (1989, pb. 1990), p. 488; Lord Hailsham's diary, 9 March 1977, 29 March 1977, TFW.

29. Denham and Garnett, *Keith Joseph*, pp. 278, 281–2, 293, 294–5; Morrison Halcrow, *Keith Joseph: A Single Mind* (1989), p. 77; Simon Jenkins, *Thatcher and Sons: A Revolution in Three Acts* (2006), p. 42; Alwyn W. Turner, *Crisis? What Crisis? Britain in the 1970s* (2008), p. 120; *The Times*, 2 January 1975.

30. Denham and Garnett, *Keith Joseph*, pp. 274, 276; *Daily Express*, 15 November 1974; *Daily Mirror*, 15 November 1974; Margaret Thatcher, *The Path to Power* (1995), pp. 266–7; Campbell, *Edward Heath*, pp. 663–4.

CHAPTER 11. HOUSEWIFE OF THE YEAR

1. Hugo Young, *One of Us: A Biography of Margaret Thatcher* (1990), p. 3; John Campbell, *Margaret Thatcher*, vol. 1: *The Grocer's Daughter* (2000), pp. 3–4.

2. Young, *One of Us*, p. 16; Campbell, *The Grocer's Daughter*, pp. 31–2, 47, 50, 64; Richard Vinen, *Thatcher's Britain: The Politics and Social Upheaval of the 1980s* (2009), p. 17; Simon Jenkins, *Thatcher and Sons: A Revolution in Three Acts* (2006), p. 47.

3. Campbell, *The Grocer's Daughter*, pp. 15–17, 30–31; Peter Jenkins, *Mrs Thatcher's Revolution: The Ending of the Socialist Era* (1987), p. 83; Brenda Maddox, *Maggie: The First Lady* (2003), pp. 6–9; Young, *One of Us*, p. 6.

4. Jenkins, *Thatcher and Sons*, pp. 17, 19, 22; Campbell, *The Grocer's Daughter*, pp. 1–2, 29–30, 92; E. H. H. Green, *Thatcher* (2006), p. 17.

5. Campbell, *The Grocer's Daughter*, pp. 58, 80; Oxford University Conservative Association Policy Sub-committee report, 1 December 1945, TFW; report from Miss Cook to Conservative Central Office, 19 November 1951, TFW; Green, *Thatcher*, pp. 9–10, 13.

6. *Onward*, April 1954, TFW; Green, *Thatcher*, pp. 13–15; Jenkins, *Thatcher and Sons*, p. 46; Jim Prior, *A Balance of Power* (1986), p. 42; Campbell, *The Grocer's Daughter*, p. 176; *Sunday Mirror*, 28 December 1969.

7. Campbell, *The Grocer's Daughter*, p. 163; Young, *One of Us*, pp. 52, 220–21; John Ranelagh, *Thatcher's People: An Insider's Account of the Politics, the Power and the Personalities* (1992), pp. 24, 43; David Cannadine, *Class in Britain* (2000), pp. 176–7.

8. Campbell, *The Grocer's Daughter*, pp. 191–2; lecture to Conservative Political Centre, 11 October 1968, TFW; E. H. H. Green, *Ideologies of Conservatism: Conservative Political Ideas in the Twentieth Century* (Oxford, 2002), p. 249; Richard Cockett, *Thinking the Unthinkable: Think-tanks and the Economic Counter-revolution, 1931–1983* (1995), pp. 171–2.

9. Campbell, *The Grocer's Daughter*, pp. 212–13, 216, 243; *Guardian*, 14 February 1975; Maddox, *Maggie*, pp. 84–5; Roy Strong, *The Roy Strong Diaries 1967–1987* (1997), p. 169.

10. Cecil King, *The Cecil King Diary 1970–1974* (1975), p. 22; Lewis Baston, *Reggie: The Life of Reginald Maudling* (Stroud, 2004), p. 468; John Campbell, *Edward Heath: A Biography* (1993), pp. 214, 385–6; Ranelagh, *Thatcher's People*, p. 136; Campbell, *The Grocer's Daughter*, pp. 225–6, 229–30, 231–2,

256; Young, *One of Us*, p. 74; Nicholas Timmins, *The Five Giants: A Biography of the Welfare State* (1996), pp. 281, 298–9; *Guardian*, 14 January 1974.

11. Campbell, *The Grocer's Daughter*, pp. 244, 251, 255, 257; Young, *One of Us*, pp. 77–8; Jenkins, *Thatcher and Sons*, p. 33.

12. Campbell, *The Grocer's Daughter*, pp. 270–74, 276–7, 280–81; *The Times*, 29 September 1974; Alan Clark, *Diaries: Into Politics 1972–1982*, ed. Ion Trewin (2001), p. 47; Ronald McIntosh, *Challenge to Democracy: Politics, Trade Union Power and Economic Failure in the 1970s* (2006), p. 164; *Sunday Times*, 13 October 1974; *Finchley Press*, 26 June 1970.

13. Margaret Thatcher, *The Path to Power* (1995), pp. 266–7; Phillip Whitehead, *The Writing on the Wall: Britain in the Seventies* (1985), p. 327; *The Economist*, 30 November 1974; Campbell, *Edward Heath*, pp. 663–4; *Daily Mirror*, 24 January 1975; *Sunday Mirror*, 9 February 1975; Campbell, *The Grocer's Daughter*, p. 287; *The Times*, 31 January 1975, 11 September 1974.

14. Campbell, *Edward Heath*, pp. 661–2; Campbell, *The Grocer's Daughter*, pp. 298, 292–3; Hansard, 22 January 1975.

15. Nicholas Ridley, *My Style of Government: The Thatcher Years* (1991), p. 9; Francis Pym, *The Politics of Consent* (1984), p. 5; *The Times*, 23 January 1975.

16. Campbell, *The Grocer's Daughter*, pp. 291, 298, 301; Mark Wickham-Jones, 'Right Turn: A Revisionist Account of the 1975 Conservative Party Leadership Election', *Twentieth Century British History*, 8:1 (1997), p. 81; Ranelagh, *Thatcher's People*, p. 135; Norman Tebbit, *Upwardly Mobile* (1988), p. 179.

17. *Daily Mirror*, 3 February 1975; *Daily Mail*, 24 January 1975; Campbell, *The Grocer's Daughter*, pp. 296–7.

18. *Guardian*, 4 February 1975, 14 February 1975; Michael Cockerell, *Live from Number 10: The Inside Story of Prime Ministers and Television* (1989), pp. 217–18; Campbell, *The Grocer's Daughter*, pp. 80, 185–6, 293; *Daily Telegraph*, 30 January 1975; and see Green, *Thatcher*, pp. 29–30.

19. *The Times*, 31 January 1975; Campbell, *The Grocer's Daughter*, p. 287; Ion Trewin (ed.), *The Hugo Young Papers: Thirty Years of British Politics – Off the Record* (2008), p. 49; Campbell, *Edward Heath*, pp. 668–70, 673.

20. *Daily Express*, 3 February 1975; Campbell, *Edward Heath*, p. 672; *Daily Mail*, 1 February 1975; Campbell, *The Grocer's Daughter*, p. 299; Roy Greenslade, *Press Gang: How Newspapers Make Profits from Propaganda* (2004), p. 357; *The Times*, 4 February 1975.

21. Campbell, *Edward Heath*, p. 674; Prior, *A Balance of Power*, p. 100; *Daily Express*, 5 February 1975; Edward Heath, *The Course of My Life* (1998), p. 534.

22. Bernard Donoughue, *Downing Street Diary*, vol. 1: *With Harold Wilson in No. 10* (2005), p. 294; McIntosh, *Challenge to Democracy*, pp. 188–9; Tony Benn, *Against the Tide: Diaries 1973–1976* (1989), p. 311; Barbara Castle, *The Castle Diaries 1974–1976* (1980), p. 303.

23. Transcript of interview for ITN, 4 February 1975, TFW; *Yorkshire Post*, 6 February 1975.

24. *Daily Telegraph*, 6 February 1975; Campbell, *The Grocer's Daughter*, pp. 302–4; *The Times*, 10 February 1975, 11 February 1975; Cockerell, *Live from Number 10*, p. 218; Philip Cowley and Matthew Bailey, 'Peasants' Uprising or Religious War? Re-examining the 1975 Conservative Leadership Contest', *British Journal*

of Political Science, 30:4 (September 1999), p. 621; and see Mark Garnett and Ian Aitken, *Splendid! Splendid! The Authorized Biography of Willie Whitelaw* (2003), pp. 210–14.

25. Campbell, *The Grocer's Daughter*, p. 306; transcripts of Conservative Central Office press conference and interview for ITN, 11 February 1975, both from TFW; *The Times*, 11 February 1975; Cockerell, *Live from Number 10*, p. 219.

26. *Daily Mail*, 12 February 1975; Campbell, *The Grocer's Daughter*, p. 308; Marcia Falkender, *Downing Street in Perspective* (1983), p. 233; Benn, *Against the Tide*, p. 311; Castle, *The Castle Diaries*, p. 309; Donoughue, *Downing Street Diary*, p. 310.

27. Ranelagh, *Thatcher's People*, p. ix; Garnett and Aitken, *Splendid! Splendid!*, pp. 215–16; Jenkins, *Thatcher and Sons*, p. 46; Jenkins interview in the BBC documentary series *Tory! Tory! Tory!* (2006), episode 1; Campbell, *The Grocer's Daughter*, pp. 390–410; Alistair Horne, *Macmillan*, vol. 2: *1957–86* (1989), p. 616; Andrew Motion, *Philip Larkin: A Writer's Life* (1994), p. 479.

28. Jenkins, *Thatcher and Sons*, p. 46; Cowley and Bailey, 'Peasants' Uprising or Religious War?', p. 601; Young, *One of Us*, p. 92; Campbell, *Edward Heath*, p. 655; Julian Critchley, *Westminster Blues* (1985), p. 121; Whitehead, *The Writing on the Wall*, p. 330; Campbell, *The Grocer's Daughter*, pp. 34, 260–61.

29. Cowley and Bailey, 'Peasants' Uprising or Religious War?', pp. 610, 613, 624, 626, 629; Thatcher, *The Path to Power*, p. 277.

30. Vernon Bogdanor, 'The Fall of Heath and the End of the Postwar Settlement', in Stuart Ball and Anthony Seldon (eds.), *The Heath Government 1970–1974: A Reappraisal* (Harlow, 1996), pp. 377, 386; Green, *Ideologies of Conservatism*, pp. 237–8; David Edgar, *Destiny* (pub. 1978), p. 19; John Betjeman, 'Executive', in John Betjeman, *Collected Poems* (2001), pp. 312–13; Lawrence James, *The Middle Class: A History* (2006), p. 463; John Mortimer, *Paradise Postponed* (1985, pb. 1986), pp. 298–9; US Embassy in London to State Department, 'Margaret Thatcher: Some First Impressions', 16 February 1975, TFW.

31. Green, *Ideologies of Conservatism*, pp. 219–24, 229, 234–6; Green, *Thatcher*, pp. 38–40, 50–52; Vinen, *Thatcher's Britain*, pp. 6, 43–6, 48–9, 51–2; Campbell, *The Grocer's Daughter*, p. 264; Anthony Sampson, *The Changing Anatomy of Britain* (1983), pp. 43–4; Andrew Gamble, *Britain in Decline: Economic Policy, Political Strategy and the British State* (Basingstoke, 1994), pp. 142–3; Nigel Lawson, *The View from No. 11: Memoirs of a Tory Radical* (1992), p. 14; transcript of interview on Granada's *World in Action*, 3 February 1975, TFW.

32. Green, *Thatcher*, p. 18; Jenkins, *Thatcher and Sons*, pp. 22–3; Sampson, *The Changing Anatomy of Britain*, p. 41; *Daily Telegraph*, 12 February 1975; Andy Beckett, *When the Lights Went Out: Britain in the Seventies* (2009), p. 280.

33. *The Times*, 13 February 1975; Campbell, *Edward Heath*, pp. 676, 690; Garnett and Aitken, *Splendid! Splendid!*, p. 226; Ranelagh, *Thatcher's People*, pp. 158–9.

34. Campbell, *Edward Heath*, pp. 679–80; John Ramsden, *An Appetite for Power: A History of the Conservative Party since 1830* (1999), p. 423.

35. Donoughue, *Downing Street Diary*, pp. 310–11, 341, 357.

36. Campbell, *The Grocer's Daughter*, pp. 318, 343–4, 352; *Sunday Times*, 25 May 1975; Hansard, 22 May 1975, 28 October 1975; Ranelagh, *Thatcher's People*, p. 157.

CHAPTER 12. THE ECONOMICS OF PETER PAN

1. *The Times*, 5 August 1975, 13 August 1975, 14 August 1975, 2 September 1975, 3 September 1975, 30 October 1975; Hansard, 22 May 1975.

2. John Cleese and Connie Booth, *The Complete Fawlty Towers* (1989), pp. 129-30.

3. Ibid., pp. 251, 253; Michael Palin, *Diaries 1969-1979: The Python Years* (2006), p. 411; Bernard Donoughue, *Downing Street Diary*, vol. 2: *With James Callaghan in No. 10* (2008), pp. 353-4; Bernard Donoughue, *The Heat of the Kitchen: An Autobiography* (2003), p. 252.

4. Geoffrey Owen, *From Empire to Europe: The Decline and Revival of British Industry since the Second World War* (1999), pp. 214-15, 218-21, 230, 236-8, 246; J. F. Wright, *Britain in the Age of Economic Management: An Economic History since 1939* (Oxford, 1979), pp. 30, 33; Central Policy Review Staff, *The Future of the British Car Industry* (1975), pp. v, xi-xii, 80, 87; Geoffrey Tweedale, 'Industry and De-industrialization in the 1970s', in Richard Coopey and Nicholas Woodward (eds.), *Britain in the 1970s: The Troubled Economy* (1996), p. 259.

5. Owen, *From Empire to Europe*, pp. 227-9, 231; *Time*, 14 November 1977; Paul Ferris, *The New Militants: Crisis in the Trade Unions* (Harmondsworth, 1972), p. 53; Phillip Whitehead, *The Writing on the Wall: Britain in the Seventies* (1985), p. 264. On the Allegro and the TR7, as well as the history of British Leyland generally, see the terrific essays at http://www.aronline.co.uk/.

6. Owen, *From Empire to Europe*, pp. 137-9, 149; Tweedale, 'Industry and De-industrialization in the 1970s', pp. 257-8; *The Times*, 1 March 1976, 19 December 1977.

7. Tweedale, 'Industry and De-industrialization in the 1970s', pp. 266-7; Owen, *From Empire to Europe*, pp. 77, 87, 106-9, 198, 206; Brian Hogwood, *Government and Shipbuilding: The Politics of Industrial Change* (1979), p. 206.

8. Anthony Sampson, *The New Anatomy of Britain* (1971), p. 572; Jim Tomlinson, 'British Industrial Policy', in Coopey and Woodward (eds.), *Britain in the 1970s*, p. 171; Tweedale, 'Industry and De-industrialization in the 1970s', pp. 252-4; Lawrence James, *The Middle Class: A History* (2006), p. 438; *The Economist*, 25 December 1976; Simon Gunn and Rachel Bell, *Middle Classes: Their Rise and Sprawl* (2003), p. 200; Kenneth O. Morgan, *The People's Peace: British History since 1945* (Oxford, 1999), p. 428.

9. Owen, *From Empire to Europe*, pp. 431, 438-40; Chris Wrigley, 'Trade Unions, Strikes and the Government', in Coopey and Woodward (eds.), *Britain in the 1970s*, pp. 279-80; Chris Wrigley, 'Toil and Turmoil: Trade Unions in a Changing Economy, 1945-2000', in Felipe Fernández-Armesto (ed.), *England 1945-2000* (2001), pp. 219-20; Bernard Nossiter, *Britain: A Future that Works* (1978), p. 66.

10. Ibid., pp. 80, 86; Owen, *From Empire to Europe*, p. 441; *The Times*, 7 September 1970, 15 December 1976; Nick Tiratsoo, 'The Seventies', in Fernández-Armesto (ed.), *England 1945-2000*, p. 292.

11. Graham Turner, *Business in Britain* (1969), p. 431; David Childs, *Britain since 1945: A Political History* (1979), p. 258; Stephen Haseler, *The Death of British Democracy: A Study of Britain's Political Present and Future* (1976), p. 29; *Financial Times*, 3 May 1980; Anthony Sampson, *The Changing Anatomy of*

Britain (1983), pp. 305–6; Ronald McIntosh, *Challenge to Democracy: Politics, Trade Union Power and Economic Failure in the 1970s* (2006), p. 118.

12. Richard E. Caves and Lawrence B. Krause (eds.), *Britain's Economic Performance* (Washington, 1980), p. 19; *Fortune*, May 1974; Childs, *Britain since 1945*, pp. 258–9; Andrew Gamble, *Britain in Decline: Economic Policy, Political Strategy and the British State* (Basingstoke, 1994), pp. 38–9; Clive Irving, *Pox Britannica: The Unmaking of the British* (New York, 1974), p. 42; Nossiter, *Britain: A Future that Works*, p. 80; Martin J. Wiener, *English Culture and the Decline of the Industrial Spirit* (Cambridge, 1981); *The Times*, 22 February 1974, 1 May 1974, 30 September 1975; David Edgerton, 'The Prophet Militant and Industrial: The Peculiarities of Correlli Barnett', *Twentieth Century British History*, 2:3 (1991), pp. 360–79; Christopher Harvie, 'Liturgies of National Decadence: Wiener, Dahrendorf and the British Crisis', *Cencrastus*, 21 (1985), pp. 17–25; Owen, *From Empire to Europe*, pp. 9–29, 31, 422–3, 450; Gamble, *Britain in Decline*, pp. 83, 105, 109, 115.

13. Richard Coopey and Nicholas Woodward, 'The British Economy in the 1970s', in Coopey and Woodward (eds.), *Britain in the 1970s*, p. 9; Terry Gourvish, 'Beyond the Merger Mania: Merger and De-merger Activity', ibid., pp. 236–46; Sampson, *The Changing Anatomy of Britain*, pp. 350–2; Edmund Dell, *A Strange Eventful History: Democratic Socialism in Britain* (2000), pp. 364–5; Owen, *From Empire to Europe*, pp. 452–3.

14. Robert Taylor, 'The Heath Government, Industrial Policy and the "New Capitalism"', in Stuart Ball and Anthony Seldon (eds.), *The Heath Government 1970–1974: A Reappraisal* (Harlow, 1996), pp. 154–60; Owen, *From Empire to Europe*, pp. 453, 455; John Campbell, *Edward Heath: A Biography* (1993), pp. 452, 454, 460; Coopey and Woodward, 'The British Economy in the 1970s', pp. 9, 28; Tony Benn, *Against the Tide: Diaries 1973–1976* (1989), pp. 183–4.

15. *Daily Express*, 14 June 1970; *The Times*, 5 May 1975, 8 May 1975; Benn, *Against the Tide*, p. 331.

16. Michael Frayn, 'Festival', in Michael Sissons and Philip French (eds.), *Age of Austerity* (Oxford, 1963), p. 319; Edward Pearce, *The Lost Leaders: The Best Prime Ministers We Never Had* (1997), p. 225; Kenneth O. Morgan, *Labour People: Leaders and Lieutenants, Hardie to Kinnock* (Oxford, 1992), pp. 304–5.

17. Ibid., pp. 304–6; Austin Mitchell, *Four Years in the Death of the Labour Party* (1983), pp. 18, 30; Tony Benn, *Office without Power: Diaries 1968–1972* (1988), pp. 315, 322, 347–9; Alwyn W. Turner, *Crisis? What Crisis? Britain in the 1970s* (2008), p. 38.

18. Michael Hatfield, *The House the Left Built: Inside Labour Policy Making 1970–1975* (1978), pp. 67–8; *The Times*, 7 October 1972; *Sunday Express*, 8 October 1972; *Sunday Telegraph*, 13 May 1973; *Observer*, 18 February 1973; Benn, *Against the Tide*, pp. 50, 54; Susan Crosland, *Tony Crosland* (1982), p. 210; Benn, *Office without Power*, p. 443; Turner, *Crisis? What Crisis?*, p. 39.

19. *Guardian*, 19 March 1980; Benn, *Against the Tide*, pp. 4, 12, 15, 23–4, 61.

20. Ibid., pp. 3, 11, 26, 42, 56; Hatfield, *The House the Left Built*, pp. 39, 120–21, 146, 172–3, 188, 193, 197, 207, 228–9; Gamble, *Britain in Decline*, pp. 24, 179–80; Ben Pimlott, *Harold Wilson* (1992), pp. 602–3, 665; Noel Thompson, 'Economic Ideas and the Development of Economic Opinion', in Coopey and Woodward (eds.), *Britain in the 1970s*, pp. 69–70; Jim Tomlinson, 'British Industrial Policy',

ibid., p. 165; Robert Taylor, 'The Rise and Fall of the Social Contract', in Anthony Seldon and Kevin Hickson (eds.), *New Labour, Old Labour: The Wilson and Callaghan Governments, 1974–1979* (2004), pp. 73, 75–6. On the manifesto, see *The Times*, 9 February 1974, as well as http://www.labour-party.org.uk/manifestos/1974/feb/.

21. Benn, *Against the Tide*, pp. 114–15, 138, 152, 186–7, 211, 245.

22. Ivor Crewe and Anthony King, *SDP: The Birth, Life and Death of the Social Democratic Party* (Oxford, 1995), pp. 27–8; Barbara Castle, *The Castle Diaries 1974–1976* (1980), pp. 126, 128, 109; Benn, *Against the Tide*, pp. 172–3.

23. Whitehead, *The Writing on the Wall*, p. 130; Castle, *The Castle Diaries*, p. 24; Benn, *Against the Tide*, pp. 140–41, 144, 148.

24. *Daily Express*, 14 May 1974, 13 June 1974, 14 June 1974, 24 June 1974, 26 June 1974; Benn, *Against the Tide*, p. 184.

25. Whitehead, *The Writing on the Wall*, pp. 121–2; *The Times*, 15 May 1974; Bernard Donoughue, *Downing Street Diary*, vol. 1: *With Harold Wilson in No. 10* (2005), p. 144.

26. Pimlott, *Harold Wilson*, pp. 638–9; Donoughue, *Downing Street Diary*, vol. 1, p. 138; Benn, *Against the Tide*, pp. 173, 175, 177–9.

27. Harold Wilson, *Final Term: The Labour Government, 1974–1976* (1979), p. 33; Donoughue, *Downing Street Diary*, vol. 1, pp. 149–50, 158; Benn, *Against the Tide*, pp. 187–9, 194.

28. Donoughue, *Downing Street Diary*, vol. 1, pp. 171–2; Benn, *Against the Tide*, pp. 210, 212–14; Castle, *The Castle Diaries*, p. 167; PRO CAB 129/178, C (74) 88, 'Planning Agreements and the National Enterprise Board', 1 August 1974; PRO CAB 128/55, CC (74) 32, 2 August 1974.

29. Coopey and Woodward, 'The British Economy in the 1970s', p. 18; *New York Times*, 13 July 1984; Tomlinson, 'British Industrial Policy', pp. 177–8, 182–3; Nicholas Crafts, 'Economic Growth in the 1970s', in Coopey and Woodward (eds.), *Britain in the 1970s*, p. 98; Whitehead, *The Writing on the Wall*, pp. 140, 145; Keith Middlemas, *Power, Competition and the State*, vol. 3: *The End of the Postwar Era: Britain since 1974* (Basingstoke, 1991), p. 83. On INMOS, see the ex-employees' website at http://www.inmos.com/.

30. Benn, *Against the Tide*, p. 350; *The Times*, 13 July 1974, 23 July 1974, 27 July 1974; and on the occupations, see Malcolm Marks, 'The Battle at Fisher Bendix', *International Socialism*, 73 (December 1974), pp. 11–15; Joe Jacobs, 'Under New Management: The Fisher-Bendix Occupation, 1972', at http://libcom.org/library/under-new-management-fisher-bendix-occupation-1972.

31. Benn, *Against the Tide*, pp. 167, 172, 195–6, 203.

32. Ibid., pp. 221, 222–3, 242; PRO CAB 129/179, C (74) 118, Memorandum by the Secretary of State for Industry, 29 October 1974; PRO CAB 129/79, C (74) 115, Memorandum by the Chancellor of the Exchequer, 28 October 1974; PRO CAB 128/55, CC (74) 42, 31 October 1974; Donoughue, *Downing Street Diary*, vol. 1, p. 235.

33. Benn, *Against the Tide*, pp. 287, 292–4; Tony Benn, *Conflicts of Interest: Diaries 1977–80* (1990), p. 300; *The Times*, 6 January 1975, 18 August 1975, 27 April 1977, 19 September 1978, 17 November 1978; *New Internationalist*, December 1981; PRO 128/63, CM (78) 18, 11 May 1978.

34. Benn, *Against the Tide*, pp. 183, 226, 358, 459; Ron McKay and Brian Barr, *The Story of the Scottish Daily News* (1976), pp. 22–3, 70–71, 142–52; Roy Greenslade, *Press Gang: How Newspapers Make Profits from Propaganda* (2004), pp. 266–7; *The Times*, 5 May 1975, 6 May 1975, 30 May 1975, 8 October 1975, 7 November 1975, 10 November 1975, 12 November 1975, 17 December 1975, 17 November 1976; *New Internationalist*, December 1981.

35. Benn, *Against the Tide*, pp. 118, 121, 146, 172, 261–2; *The Times*, 14 June 1974, 2 August 1974, 9 November 1974, 11 November 1974, 12 November 1974, 13 November 1974. For the background to Meriden, see Chris Hemming, 'The Meriden Motorcycle Co-operative' (in two parts), at http://www.labourhistory.org.uk/.

36. Benn, *Against the Tide*, pp. 276, 308, 326; *The Times*, 31 January 1975, 1 February 1975, 27 February 1975.

37. Castle, *The Castle Diaries*, p. 424; Benn, *Against the Tide*, p. 423; Donoughue, *Downing Street Diary*, vol. 1, p. 478; *The Times*, 24 June 1975, 3 July 1975, 18 July 1975, 25 July 1975, 1 August 1975.

38. PRO CAB 128/57, CC (75) 38, 29 July 1975; and see Castle, *The Castle Diaries*, pp. 477–9; Benn, *Against the Tide*, p. 425; *The Times*, 1 August 1975.

39. *The Times*, 12 August 1975, 14 August 1975, 19 January 1976, 8 January 1977, 8 February 1977, 27 September 1980, 27 August 1983; on Meriden's struggle for survival, see John Rosamond, *Save the Triumph Bonneville: The Inside Story of the Meriden Workers' Co-op* (Dorchester, 2009), pp. 47–442.

40. Donoughue, *Downing Street Diary*, vol. 1, p. 243; *The Times*, 12 November 1975.

41. Robert Taylor, 'The Rise and Fall of the Social Contract', pp. 78–9; Michael Artis, David Cobham and Mark Wickham-Jones, 'Social Democracy in Hard Times: The Economic Record of the Labour Government 1974–1979', *Twentieth Century British History*, 3 (1992), p. 54; Paul Ormerod, 'Government Policy and Company Profitability', in Jonathan Michie (ed.), *The Economic Legacy 1979–1992* (1992), p. 293; Coopey and Woodward, 'The British Economy in the 1970s', p. 9; Donoughue, *The Heat of the Kitchen*, pp. 140–41.

42. Tweedale, 'Industry and De-industrialization in the 1970s', p. 259; Owen, *From Empire to Europe*, p. 232; Benn, *Against the Tide*, pp. 184, 278, 358, 367; PRO CAB 129/183, C (75) 53, 'British Leyland: The Ryder Report', 23 April 1975; PRO CAB 128/56, CC (75) 22, 22 April 1975; *The Times*, 25 April 1975; Castle, *The Castle Diaries*, p. 374.

43. Tweedale, 'Industry and De-industrialization in the 1970s', p. 260; Owen, *From Empire to Europe*, pp. 232–4; Castle, *The Castle Diaries*, p. 559; Donoughue, *Downing Street Diary*, vol. 2, p. 40; *Time*, 14 November 1977; *The Times*, 8 October 1976, 15 December 1976, 26 July 1977, 26 October 1977; Michael Edwardes, *Back from the Brink: An Apocalyptic Experience* (1983), pp. 40–41, 45.

44. *The Times*, 30 October 1975; Edward Pearce, *Denis Healey: A Life in Our Times* (2002), pp. 444–5; PRO CAB 129/186, C (75) 128, 'Chrysler UK', 21 November 1975; Castle, *The Castle Diaries*, p. 545; Benn, *Against the Tide*, p. 466.

45. Dell, *A Strange Eventful History*, p. 442; Castle, *The Castle Diaries*, pp. 454, 545, 563, 585; PRO CAB 128/57, CC (75) 47, 11 November 1975; PRO CAB 128/57, CC (75) 50, 25 November 1975; Benn, *Against the Tide*, pp. 466–7.

46. Castle, *The Castle Diaries*, p. 545; PRO CAB 129/186, C (75) 129, 'Chrysler', 21 November 1975; Donoughue, *Downing Street Diary*, vol. 1, pp. 577, 580, 610–11; Donoughue, *The Heat of the Kitchen*, pp. 170–71.

47. Donoughue, *Downing Street Diary*, vol. 1, pp. 588, 605–8, 610–11; PRO CAB 128/57, CC (75) 56, 12 December 1975; Pearce, *Denis Healey*, pp. 445–6.

48. Hansard, 16 December 1975; Pearce, *Denis Healey*, p. 446; *The Times*, 17 December 1975. For similarly caustic verdicts on the Chrysler deal, see Keith Middlemas, *Power, Competition and the State*, p. 85; Philip Ziegler, *Wilson: The Authorized Life* (1993), pp. 457–9; Dell, *A Strange Eventful History*, p. 443; Robert Taylor, 'The Rise and Fall of the Social Contract', p. 79.

CHAPTER 13. POWER TO THE PEOPLE!

1. Keith Jacka, Caroline Cox and John Marks, *Rape of Reason: The Corruption of the Polytechnic of North London* (1975), pp. 74–6; *Daily Express*, 22 September 1975.

2. *The Times*, 3 July 1975, 4 July 1975, 30 September 1975, 1 October 1975; *Daily Express*, 22 September 1975, 29 September 1975; speech at Conservative party conference, 10 October 1975, TFW.

3. *The Times*, 28 April 1975, 22 November 1979; Jacka, Cox and Marks, *Rape of Reason*, pp. v, 1, 2–6, 82–3.

4. Ibid., *passim*; *The Times*, 14 October 1972, 18 October 1973, 28 April 1975, 4 October 1975; and see the letters pages on 25 April 1975, 29 April 1975, 7 July 1975, 9 July 1975, 15 July 1975, 16 July 1975.

5. Jacka, Cox and Marks, *Rape of Reason*, pp. 6–8, 99–100.

6. Ibid., pp. 48–9, 68, 71–2, 80; *The Times*, 4 October 1975.

7. *The Times*, 22 November 1979; *Daily Express*, 22 September 1975.

8. Nicholas Timmins, *The Five Giants: A Biography of the Welfare State* (1996), pp. 302–3, 328–9; George L. Bernstein, *The Myth of Decline: The Rise of Britain since 1945* (2004), p. 334; and see *The Times*, 8 December 1975.

9. David Hare, *Writing Left-handed* (1991), p. 35; Arthur Marwick, *The Sixties: Cultural Revolution, in Britain, France, Italy and the United States, c. 1958– c. 1974* (Oxford, 1999), p. 752; *The Times*, 6 November 1973, 14 February 1974, 16 February 1974, 21 February 1974, 15 March 1974.

10. *New Society*, 20 February 1969; *The Times*, 19 March 1974, 21 March 1974, 23 March 1974, 24 April 1974, 19 March 1975, 25 April 1974; C. B. Cox and Rhodes Boyson (eds.), *Black Paper 1975: The Fight for Education* (1975), p. 64.

11. Robert J. Wybrow, *Britain Speaks Out, 1937–87: A Social History as Seen through the Gallup Data* (1989), p. 88; *Sunday Telegraph*, 10 March 1968; *Sun*, 28 October 1970; the *Rising Damp* quotations are from 'The New Tenant' (September 1974), 'Permissive Society' (November 1975) and 'Things that Go Bump in the Night' (December 1975).

12. Nick Thomas, 'Challenging Myths of the 1960s: The Case of Student Protest in Britain', *Twentieth Century British History*, 13:3 (2002), pp. 282–3, 286–7, 295–6; David Caute, *The Year of the Barricades: A Journey through 1968*

(1988), pp. 360–61; *Guardian*, 25 May 1968; Marwick, *The Sixties*, pp. 560, 286–7; *The Times*, 22 November 1974, 28 November 1974.

13. Anthony Sampson, *The New Anatomy of Britain* (1971), p. 179; Mark Garnett, *From Anger to Apathy: The British Experience since 1975* (2007), p. 64; *The Times*, 9 April 1975, 26 July 1975, 26 June 1976, 1 February 1978; Hare, *Writing Left-handed*, p. 35.

14. *The Times*, 14 November 1977, 15 November 1977.

15. Perry Anderson, 'A Culture in Contra-flow I', *New Left Review*, 180 (March–April 1990), p. 45; Stefan Collini, *Absent Minds: Intellectuals in Britain* (Oxford, 2006), pp. 189–90; Bart Moore-Gilbert, 'Cultural Closure or Post-Avantgardism?', in Moore-Gilbert (ed.), *The Arts in the 1970s: Cultural Closure?* (1994), pp. 18–19; Stuart Laing, 'The Politics of Culture: Institutional Change in the 1970s', ibid., p. 53; Anthony Easthope, 'The Impact of Radical Theory in Britain', ibid., pp. 57, 59, 65–6; *History Workshop Journal*, 1:1 (1976), pp. 1–3; Austin Mitchell, *Four Years in the Death of the Labour Party* (1983), p. 66.

16. Jacka, Cox and Marks, *Rape of Reason*, pp. 43, 124–5.

17. Malcolm Bradbury, *The History Man* (1975), pp. 128, 134, 138, 145; and see D. J. Taylor, *After the War: The Novel and England since 1945* (1993), pp. 204–5, 210–12.

18. Andy Beckett, *When the Lights Went Out: Britain in the Seventies* (2009), pp. 309–10; Jacka, Cox and Marks, *Rape of Reason*, pp. 41, 44–6, 78, 106.

19. Bradbury, *The History Man*, p. 3; Ivor Crewe and Anthony King, *SDP: The Birth, Life and Death of the Social Democratic Party* (Oxford, 1995), pp. 14–15; David Butler and Dennis Kavanagh, *The British General Election of 1979* (1980), pp. 57–8; Jeremy Seabrook, *What Went Wrong? Working People and the Ideals of the Labour Movement* (1978), p. 48.

20. Jerry White, *London in the Twentieth Century* (2001), pp. 393–4; David Kogan and Maurice Kogan, *The Battle for the Labour Party* (1982), pp. 122–5; and see Andrew Hosken, *Ken: The Ups and Downs of Ken Livingstone* (2008).

21. Bernard Donoughue, *Downing Street Diary*, vol. 2: *With James Callaghan in No. 10* (2008), pp. 43, 240; Anthony Sampson, *The Changing Anatomy of Britain* (1983), p. 87; Mitchell, *Four Years in the Death of the Labour Party*, pp. 21–2.

22. Kenneth O. Morgan, *Callaghan: A Life* (Oxford, 1997), pp. 514, 563, 569; Philip Ziegler, *Wilson: The Authorized Life* (1993), p. 442; Ben Pimlott, *Harold Wilson* (1992), p. 636; Crewe and King, *SDP*, p. 19; Robert Harris, *The Making of Neil Kinnock* (1984), pp. 71, 84; Hansard, 23 July 1975, 26 June 1975; Martin Westlake, *Kinnock: The Biography* (2001), pp. 100, 132.

23. John Tomlinson, *Left, Right: The March of Political Extremism in Britain* (1981), pp. 76, 78; *The Times*, 14 February 1974; Alwyn W. Turner, *Crisis? What Crisis? Britain in the 1970s* (2008), pp. 233–4; Francis Wheen, *Strange Days Indeed: The Golden Age of Paranoia* (2009), pp. 50–53; Vanessa Redgrave, *Vanessa Redgrave: An Autobiography* (1991), pp. 191–2; *Observer*, 19 March 2006.

24. Turner, *Crisis? What Crisis?*, pp. 233–4; Richard Clutterbuck, *Britain in Agony: The Growth of Political Violence* (1978), p. 237; *The Times*, 1 November 1974, 2 November 1974.

25. Edward Brown, 'Trevor Griffiths', in George W. Brandt (ed.), *British Television Drama* (Cambridge, 1981), p. 78; Paul Madden, 'Jim Allen', ibid., pp. 48–51;

Anthony Hayward, *Which Side Are You On? Ken Loach and his Films* (2005), pp. 134, 139–40; *Daily Telegraph*, 25 September 1975; *Daily Mail*, 23 September 1975.

26. Sampson, *The New Anatomy of Britain*, p. 58; Clutterbuck, *Britain in Agony*, pp. 213–14, 234–6; Tomlinson, *Left, Right*, pp. 85–6, 90, 123–4; and see Dave Renton, *When We Touched the Sky: The Anti-Nazi League 1977–1981* (2006).

27. Tomlinson, *Left, Right*, pp. 63, 67–75, 79; Michael Crick, *Militant* (1984), pp. 32, 46, 55–8, 60, 76, 122, 135; *The Times*, 12 December 1975.

28. Christopher Andrew, *The Defence of the Realm: The Authorized History of MI5* (2009), pp. 660–61; *The Times*, 1 October 1975; Harris, *Kinnock*, p. 81.

29. Crick, *Militant*, pp. 85–7; Tony Benn, *Against the Tide: Diaries 1973–1976* (1989), pp. 468–9; Kogan and Kogan, *The Battle for the Labour Party*, p. 20; Bernard Donoughue, *Downing Street Diary*, vol. 1: *With Harold Wilson in No. 10* (2005), pp. 578–9.

30. *The Times*, 12 December 1975; Crick, *Militant*, pp. 77–9, 87, 93–4; Tony Benn, *Conflicts of Interest: Diaries 1977–80* (1990), pp. 17, 151; Andrew, *The Defence of the Realm*, p. 663.

31. Kogan and Kogan, *The Battle for the Labour Party*, pp. 23–8, 32–4, 42–3, 47, 49; *The Times*, 4 October 1978.

32. *The Times*, 20 June 1972, 4 October 1972, 7 October 1972, 3 March 1973, 10 March 1973; John Ramsden and Richard Jay, 'Lincoln: The Background to Taverne's Triumph', in Chris Cook and John Ramsden (eds.), *By-elections in British Politics* (1973), pp. 264–315; Phillip Whitehead, *The Writing on the Wall: Britain in the Seventies* (1985), pp. 342–3; Roy Jenkins, *A Life at the Centre* (1991), pp. 351–2; and see Dick Taverne, *The Future of the Left: Lincoln and After* (1974).

33. *The Times*, 11 February 1974, 12 February 1974, 20 March 1975, 24 June 1975, 4 July 1975, 8 July 1975; Crick, *Militant*, pp. 88–9; Kogan and Kogan, *The Battle for the Labour Party*, p. 30; Jenkins, *A Life at the Centre*, p. 419; Paul McCormick, 'Prentice and the Newham North-East Constituency: The Making of Historical Myths', *Political Studies*, 29:1 (March 1981), pp. 73–90.

34. *The Times*, 18 July 1975, 19 July 1975, 22 July 1975, 23 July 1975, 12 September 1975; Jenkins, *A Life at the Centre*, pp. 428–9.

35. *Guardian*, 14 July 1977, 22 January 2001; *The Times*, 29 September 1975, 1 October 1975, 27 September 1976, 22 December 1976, 28 March 1977, 10 October 1977, 13 October 1977.

36. Kogan and Kogan, *The Battle for the Labour Party*, pp. 30–1; *The Times*, 22 December 1976, 10 October 1977, 11 October 1977; *Observer*, 9 October 1977; Reg Prentice, 'Right Turn', in Patrick Cormack (ed.), *Right Turn: Eight Men who Changed their Minds* (1978), pp. 3, 13.

37. John Ranelagh, *Thatcher's People: An Insider's Account of the Politics, the Power and the Personalities* (1992), pp. 67–8; *The Times*, 5 April 1974, 10 July 1974, 18 July 1974, 23 September 1974, 3 March 1976, 4 March 1976; Peter Paterson, *Tired and Emotional: The Life of Lord George-Brown* (1993), pp. 270–71.

38. Richard Cockett, *Thinking the Unthinkable: Think-tanks and the Economic Counter-revolution, 1931–1983* (1995), pp. 226–7, 258–9; Robert Hewison, *Too Much: Art and Culture in the Sixties, 1960–75* (1986), p. 293; Randall Stevenson, *The Oxford English Literary History*, vol. 12: *1960–2000: The Last*

of England? (Oxford, 2004), pp. 188–9; Kingsley Amis, 'Why Lucky Jim Turned Right' (1967), reprinted in Amis, *What Became of Jane Austen?* (1970), p. 217.

39. *The Times*, 22 March 1977; *New Statesman*, 16 May 1975, 9 September 1976; *Sunday Telegraph*, 11 September 1977; Christopher Booker, *The Seventies: Portrait of a Decade* (1980), pp. 238–44; Paul Johnson, 'Farewell to the Labour Party', in Cormack (ed.), *Right Turn*, pp. 78–9, 81, 83, 86; and see Cockett, *Thinking the Unthinkable*, pp. 227–8.

40. *New Statesman*, 28 February 1964; Patrick Cormack, 'A Society at Risk', in Cormack (ed.), *Right Turn*, p. v; Edward Pearce, 'A Shift to Malice', ibid., p. 68; Hugh Thomas, 'Letter to a Social Democrat', ibid., p. 99; Lord Chalfont, 'Our Security Menaced', ibid., pp. 45–6; Graham Hough, 'Freedom in Danger', ibid., p. 22.

41. *The Times*, 2 October 1978, 5 October 1978; Alfred Sherman to Margaret Thatcher, 25 October 1977, TFW; Richard Ryder to Alfred Sherman, 28 October 1977, TFW.

CHAPTER 14. THE GREAT REFERENDUM SIDESHOW

1. *The Times*, 1 December 1976, 2 December 1976; Barbara Castle, *The Castle Diaries 1974–1976* (1980), p. 241.

2. *Daily Express*, 2 December 1974; James Callaghan, *Time and Chance* (1987), p. 312; Tony Benn, *Against the Tide: Diaries 1973–1976* (1989), p. 277; Stephen Haseler, *The Death of British Democracy: A Study of Britain's Political Present and Future* (1976), p. 69.

3. Simon Winder, *The Man Who Saved Britain: A Personal Journey into the Disturbing World of James Bond* (2006), pp. 36, 38; John Ramsden, *Don't Mention the War: The British and the Germans since 1890* (2006), pp. 382, 387, 389; Asa Briggs, *The History of Broadcasting in the United Kingdom*, vol. 5: *Competition* (Oxford, 1995), p. 944; Alwyn W. Turner, *Crisis? What Crisis? Britain in the 1970s* (2008), p. 153.

4. *Daily Mail*, 3 September 1977; *Guardian*, 24 February 2005; Turner, *Crisis? What Crisis?*, p. 153; Andrew Gamble, *Britain in Decline: Economic Policy, Political Strategy and the British State* (Basingstoke, 1994), p. xx; Bernard Donoughue, *Downing Street Diary*, vol. 1: *With Harold Wilson in No. 10* (2005), p. 499; Adam Sisman, *A. J. P. Taylor: A Biography* (1994), pp. 371, 373.

5. Richard Coopey and Nicholas Woodward, 'The British Economy in the 1970s', in Coopey and Woodward (eds.), *Britain in the 1970s: The Troubled Economy* (1996), p. 3; *Daily Express*, 2 December 1974.

6. David Winner, *Those Feet: An Intimate History of English Football* (2005), p. 135; David Downing, *The Best of Enemies: England v Germany, a Century of Footballing Rivalry* (2000), p. 143; *Observer*, 30 April 1972; *Daily Mirror*, 12 May 1975; Donoughue, *Downing Street Diary*, p. 143; Richard Vinen, *Thatcher's Britain: The Politics and Social Upheaval of the 1980s* (2009), p. 92; Hansard, 19 November 1975.

7. *Guardian*, 30 September 1975; *Report of the Committee of Inquiry on Industrial Democracy*, Cmnd 6706 (1977), p. 57; Kenneth O. Morgan, *Callaghan: A Life* (Oxford, 1997), pp. 561–2; Edmund Dell, *A Strange Eventful History: Democratic Socialism in Britain* (2000), pp. 464–6; Robert Taylor, 'The Rise and

Fall of the Social Contract', in Anthony Seldon and Kevin Hickson (eds.), *New Labour, Old Labour: The Wilson and Callaghan Governments, 1974-1979* (2004), p. 81.

8. *Daily Mail*, 28 November 1973; Turner, *Crisis? What Crisis?*, p. 165; Steve Humphries and Miriam Akhtar, *Some Liked It Hot: The British on Holiday at Home and Abroad* (2000), pp. 109-10, 115; *Encounter*, January 1963; *The Times*, 1 January 1973; Neill Nugent, 'British Public Opinion and the European Community', in Stephen George (ed.), *Britain and the European Community: The Politics of Semi-detachment* (Oxford, 1992), p. 181; *Time*, 15 September 1975.

9. *The Times*, 9 February 1974, 16 May 1975; Bernard Donoughue, 'Harold Wilson and the Renegotiation of the EEC Terms of Membership, 1974-5: A Witness Account', in Brian Brivati and Harriet Jones (eds.), *From Reconstruction to Integration: Britain and Europe since 1945* (Leicester, 1993), p. 204; Donoughue, *Downing Street Diary*, p. 60.

10. *Le Point*, 17 March 1975; *Le Canard enchaîné*, 12 March 1975, both reprinted in David Butler and Uwe Kitzinger, *The 1975 Referendum* (1976), pp. 28, 44.

11. *The Times*, 2 April 1975; *Financial Times*, 2 April 1975; Butler and Kitzinger, *The 1975 Referendum*, pp. 29-30, 34, 46; Morgan, *Callaghan*, pp. 394-5, 416, 424-5, 428; Callaghan, *Time and Chance*, p. 304; John W. Young, 'Europe', in Seldon and Hickson (eds.), *New Labour, Old Labour*, pp. 142-5, 428; Hugo Young, *This Blessed Plot: Britain and Europe from Churchill to Blair* (1998), p. 281.

12. *Guardian*, 6 December 1974; Ben Pimlott, *Harold Wilson* (1992), p. 655; PRO CAB 128/56, CC (75) 13, 17 March 1975; PRO CAB 128/56, CC (75) 14, 18 March 1975; Benn, *Against the Tide*, pp. 342-3, 345-7; Donoughue, *Downing Street Diary*, p. 335.

13. Butler and Kitzinger, *The 1975 Referendum*, pp. 61, 95, 175-6; Philip Ziegler, *Wilson: The Authorized Life* (1993), p. 431; Donoughue, *Downing Street Diary*, p. 393.

14. Butler and Kitzinger, *The 1975 Referendum*, pp. 107, 111; Young, *This Blessed Plot*, p. 284; John Campbell, *Margaret Thatcher*, vol. 1: *The Grocer's Daughter* (2000), pp. 336-7; Hansard, 8 April 1975; speech to Conservative Group for Europe, 16 April 1975, TFW.

15. Ibid.; Campbell, *The Grocer's Daughter*, p. 337; Edward Heath, *The Course of My Life* (1998), p. 546.

16. Butler and Kitzinger, *The 1975 Referendum*, pp. 73-4, 78-9, 83, 85, 95-6, 173; *The Times*, 9 April 1975, 10 June 1975, 8 October 1975.

17. *The Times*, 8 May 1975, 14 May 1975; Butler and Kitzinger, *The 1975 Referendum*, pp. 32, 91, 93; Russell Davies (ed.), *The Kenneth Williams Diaries* (1993, pb. 1994), pp. 492-3.

18. Butler and Kitzinger, *The 1975 Referendum*, p. 256; Campbell, *Edward Heath*, pp. 685, 687; *The Times*, 2 June 1975.

19. Butler and Kitzinger, *The 1975 Referendum*, pp. 86-7; Roy Jenkins, *A Life at the Centre* (1991), pp. 410, 416, 424-6.

20. Young, *This Blessed Plot*, p. 290; *Sunday Times*, 27 April 1975; Butler and Kitzinger, *The 1975 Referendum*, pp. 118-22, 128, 131.

21. Ibid., pp. 97-9, 100, 102, 105, 110, 134-6; *Daily Mail*, 2 June 1975.

22. *Evening Standard*; 24 March 1975; Butler and Kitzinger, *The 1975 Referendum*,

pp. 108–9, 115, 256; Castle, *The Castle Diaries*, pp. 339, 361; Benn, *Against the Tide*, p. 362.

23. Butler and Kitzinger, *The 1975 Referendum*, pp. 236, 239, 241–3; *Daily Express*, 9 May 1975; *Sunday Telegraph*, 4 May 1975; *The Times*, 12 May 1975; *Daily Mirror*, 9 May 1975.

24. *The Times*, 19 May 1975, 21 May 1975, 28 May 1975; *Daily Mirror*, 20 May 1975, 26 May 1975, 29 May 1975; Hansard, 20 May 1975; Jenkins, *A Life at the Centre*, pp. 410–11; and see Butler and Kitzinger, *The 1975 Referendum*, pp. 180–81, 237, 144.

25. Benn, *Against the Tide*, pp. 378, 424–5; Castle, *The Castle Diaries*, p. 391; Butler and Kitzinger, *The 1975 Referendum*, pp. 243–4; *Daily Express*, 21 May 1975; *Daily Telegraph*, 5 June 1975; *Sun*, 26 May 1975, 4 June 1975.

26. Butler and Kitzinger, *The 1975 Referendum*, pp. 160, 182, 188, 191, 220–21; *The Times*, 28 May 1975; Mark Garnett, *From Anger to Apathy: The British Experience Since 1975* (2007), p. 32.

27. *Sunday Times*, 1 June 1975; Young, *This Blessed Plot*, pp. 287–9, 296; Michael Palin, *Diaries 1969–1979: The Python Years* (2006), pp. 238–9; *The Times*, 2 November 1974.

28. Butler and Kitzinger, *The 1975 Referendum*, pp. 247, 250; Anthony King and Robert J. Wybrow (eds.), *British Political Opinion 1937–2000: The Gallup Polls* (2001), p. 331; Roger Broad and Tim Geiger, 'The 1975 British Referendum on Europe: A Witness Seminar', *Contemporary British History*, 10:3 (1996), p. 98; Castle, *The Castle Diaries*, p. 403.

29. *Sun*, 4 June 1975; *Daily Mail*, 20 May 1975; *Daily Mirror*, 5 June 1975; Butler and Kitzinger, *The 1975 Referendum*, pp. 194, 226–7, 234–5; Roy Greenslade, *Press Gang: How Newspapers Make Profits from Propaganda* (2004), p. 295.

30. *The Times*, 2 June 1975, 3 June 1975; Butler and Kitzinger, *The 1975 Referendum*, p. 207; Jenkins, *A Life at the Centre*, pp. 412–3; Sir Robert Mark, *In the Office of Constable* (1978), p. 234; Turner, *Crisis? What Crisis?*, p. 173.

31. Castle, *The Castle Diaries*, pp. 405–6; *The Times*, 4 June 1975; Butler and Kitzinger, *The 1975 Referendum*, pp. 187, 205; Heath, *The Course of My Life*, p. 549.

32. *The Times*, 5 June 1975, 6 June 1975; *Evening Standard*, 5 June 1975; Butler and Kitzinger, *The 1975 Referendum*, pp. 188–9; Jenkins, *A Life at the Centre*, p. 414; Ziegler, *Wilson*, p. 433; Donoughue, *Downing Street Diary*, pp. 399–400.

33. *The Times*, 7 June 1975; Donoughue, *Downing Street Diary*, p. 401; Butler and Kitzinger, *The 1975 Referendum*, pp. 162, 252, 255, 265–6, 271, 280.

34. *Guardian*, 7 June 1975; *Daily Mail*, 7 June 1975; *Sunday Times*, 8 June 1975; *Daily Telegraph*, 7 June 1975; Donoughue, *Downing Street Diary*, pp. 402–3; and see Pimlott, *Harold Wilson*, pp. 654, 659–60.

35. *Observer*, 8 June 1975; Butler and Kitzinger, *The 1975 Referendum*, p. 273; Jenkins, *A Life at the Centre*, p. 415; *The Times*, 4 June 1975, 14 June 1975; *Sunday Express*, 8 June 1975; Hansard, 9 June 1975; Campbell, *Edward Heath*, p. 688.

36. Donoughue, *Downing Street Diary*, pp. 405–6, 411; Jenkins, *A Life at the Centre*, pp. 421–3; Bernard Donoughue, *The Heat of the Kitchen: An Autobiography* (2003), p. 159.

37. Donoughue, *Downing Street Diary*, pp. 355, 405–8; Benn, *Against the Tide*, pp. 389–95, 397.
38. Pimlott, *Harold Wilson*, pp. 667–8; *Time*, 23 June 1975; *Sun*, 7 June 1975.

CHAPTER 15. THE BELLS OF HELL

1. Jon Savage, *England's Dreaming: Sex Pistols and Punk Rock* (2005), pp. 115–20; John Lydon, with Keith and Kent Zimmerman, *Rotten: No Irish, No Blacks, No Dogs* (2008), p. 74; interview with Paul Cook, Steve Jones and Glen Matlock, c. 1977, reproduced at http://www.philjens.plus.com/pistols/pistols/pistols_origins.html.
2. *NME*, 25 June 1965, 4 December 1976; Alwyn W. Turner, *Crisis? What Crisis? Britain in the 1970s* (2008), p. 103; Ben Pimlott, *Harold Wilson* (1992), p. 674.
3. *NME*, 4 October 1975; *Daily Mirror*, 28 April 1976; *Playboy*, September 1976; Savage, *England's Dreaming*, p. 113; see also Ian MacDonald, *The People's Music* (2003), pp. 142–3.
4. Alan Clark, *Diaries: Into Politics 1972–1982*, ed. Ion Trewin (2001), p. 66; *Daily Mail*, 14 March 1975; Turner, *Crisis? What Crisis?*, p. 104; John Goodwin (ed.), *Peter Hall's Diaries: The Story of a Dramatic Battle* (1983), p. 188; Clive Irving, *Pox Britannica: The Unmaking of the British* (New York, 1974), pp. 13–14, 18.
5. Bernard Donoughue, *Downing Street Diary*, vol. 1: *With Harold Wilson in No. 10* (2005), pp. 458, 490, 503, 505.
6. Dilwyn Porter, 'Government and the Economy', in Richard Coopey and Nicholas Woodward (eds.), *Britain in the 1970s: The Troubled Economy* (1996), pp. 44–5; Max-Stephan Schulze and Nicholas Woodward, 'The Emergence of Rapid Inflation', ibid., p. 114; Edward Pearce, *Denis Healey: A Life in Our Times* (2002), pp. 429, 432; *Daily Mirror*, 10 May 1975; David Smith, *The Rise and Fall of Monetarism: The Theory and Politics of an Economic Experiment* (1991), pp. 62–3; Jim Tomlinson, 'Economic Policy', in Anthony Seldon and Kevin Hickson (eds.), *New Labour, Old Labour: The Wilson and Callaghan Governments, 1974–1979* (2004), p. 58.
7. *Daily Express*, 13 June 1975, 14 June 1975; *Daily Mirror*, 14 June 1975, 21 June 1975; Christian Wolmar, *Fire and Steam: A New History of the Railways in Britain* (2007), p. 291; *Daily Express*, 13 June 1975; Randall Stevenson, *The Oxford English Literary History*, vol. 12: *1960–2000: The Last of England?* (Oxford, 2004), p. 145.
8. *Daily Express*, 14 June 1975, 27 June 1975; Turner, *Crisis? What Crisis?*, p. 101.
9. *Daily Mirror*, 11 June 1975, 30 June 1975.
10. Denis Healey, *The Time of My Life* (1989, pb. 1990), p. 394; David Kynaston, *The City of London*, vol. 4: *A Club No More 1945–2000* (2001), pp. 520–21; Robert J. Wybrow, *Britain Speaks Out, 1937–87: A Social History as Seen through the Gallup Data* (1989), p. 110; *Daily Mirror*, 26 June 1975, 19 May 1975; *New Statesman*, 16 May 1975; Phillip Whitehead, *The Writing on the Wall: Britain in the Seventies* (1985), p. 149.
11. *Daily Mirror*, 13 May 1975; Larry Lamb, *Sunrise: The Remarkable Rise and Rise of the Bestselling Soaraway Sun* (1989), p. 172; *The Economist*, 17 May

1975; *Sunday Mirror*, 8 June 1975; Pearce, *Denis Healey*, p. 429; Donoughue, *Downing Street Diary*, pp. 483, 431.

12. Tony Benn, *Against the Tide: Diaries 1973–1976* (1989), p. 403; *Time*, 29 September 1975.

13. PRO CAB 128/56, CC (75) 29, 20 June 1975; Barbara Castle, *The Castle Diaries 1974–1976* (1980), pp. 426–8; Benn, *Against the Tide*, pp. 404–5.

14. *The Times*, 1 July 1975; Ronald McIntosh, *Challenge to Democracy: Politics, Trade Union Power and Economic Failure in the 1970s* (2006), p. 218; Michael Cockerell, *Live from Number 10: The Inside Story of Prime Ministers and Television* (1989), p. 224; Joe Haines, *The Politics of Power: The Inside Story of Life at No. 10* (1977), pp. 52–5; Donoughue, *Downing Street Diary*, pp. 437–9; Bernard Donoughue, *The Heat of the Kitchen: An Autobiography* (2003), p. 164.

15. *Time*, 23 June 1975; Donoughue, *Downing Street Diary*, pp. 442–4; Donoughue, *The Heat of the Kitchen*, pp. 164–6; Haines, *The Politics of Power*, pp. 55–60.

16. Castle, *The Castle Diaries*, pp. 439–43; Benn, *Against the Tide*, pp. 411–12; Donoughue, *Downing Street Diary*, pp. 412, 420–25; Stephen Milligan, *The New Barons: Union Power in the 1970s* (1976), pp. 99, 56; Whitehead, *The Writing on the Wall*, p. 150; Martin Holmes, *The Labour Government 1974–1979: Political Aims and Economic Reality* (Basingstoke, 1985), p. 27; *The Times*, 23 June 1975, 24 June 1975, 26 June 1975.

17. Edmund Dell, *The Chancellors: A History of the Chancellors of the Exchequer, 1945–90* (1996, pb. 1997), p. 418; Pearce, *Denis Healey*, pp. 438, 441; Castle, *The Castle Diaries*, pp. 453–6; PRO CAB CC (75) 77, Draft White Paper: 'The Attack on Inflation', 9 July 1975; PRO CAB 128/57, CC (75) 33, 10 July 1975; PRO CAB 128/57, CC (75) 34, 10 July 1975; Hansard, 11 July 1975; *Daily Mirror*, 12 July 1975; Benn, *Against the Tide*, pp. 414, 416, 417.

18. *Daily Mirror*, 12 July 1975; Edmund Dell, *A Strange Eventful History: Democratic Socialism in Britain* (2000), p. 447; Pearce, *Denis Healey*, p. 432; Dell, *The Chancellors*, p. 432; *Financial Times*, 12 July 1975; Alec Cairncross, *The British Economy since 1945: Economic Policy and Performance, 1945–1990* (1992), p. 203; Donoughue, *The Heat of the Kitchen*, p. 168.

19. *The Times*, 12 July 1975, 3 September 1975, 4 September 1975; Castle, *The Castle Diaries*, p. 438; Gerald A. Dorfman, *Government versus Trade Unionism in British Politics since 1968* (1979), pp. 121–2; Robert Taylor, 'The Rise and Fall of the Social Contract', in Seldon and Hickson (eds.), *New Labour, Old Labour*, p. 87.

20. Richard Clutterbuck, *Britain in Agony: The Growth of Political Violence* (1978), p. 173; *The Times*, 21 August 1975; Dell, *A Strange Eventful History*, p. 446; Whitehead, *The Writing on the Wall*, p. 153.

21. Dell, *The Chancellors*, p. 419; Smith, *The Rise and Fall of Monetarism*, pp. 61–2; Peter Clarke, *Hope and Glory: Britain, 1900–1990* (1996), p. 304; Kevin Hickson, *The IMF Crisis of 1976 and British Politics* (2005), p. 85; Pearce, *Denis Healey*, p. 442; Patrick Hutber, *The Decline and Fall of the Middle Class – and How It Can Fight Back* (Harmondsworth, pb. 1977), p. 151; Kathleen Burk and Alec Cairncross, *Goodbye, Great Britain: The 1976 IMF Crisis* (New Haven, 1992), p. 189; *Time*, 19 May 1975.

22. *The Times*, 10 May 1975, 24 January 1976; Tomlinson, 'Economic Policy', p. 60; Taylor, 'The Rise and Fall of the Social Contract', p. 82.

23. Hansard, 1 July 1975; Pearce, *Denis Healey*, pp. 437, 439–40, 442; Hickson, *The IMF Crisis*, pp. 57–8; Richard Holt, *Second amongst Equals: Chancellors of the Exchequer since the Second World War* (2002), p. 27; PRO CAB 128/57, CC (75) 31, 1 July 1975; PRO CAB 128/57, CC (75) 33, 10 July 1975; Benn, *Against the Tide*, pp. 414–15; Castle, *The Castle Diaries*, pp. 452, 463.

24. Clutterbuck, *Britain in Agony*, p. 174; Benn, *Against the Tide*, pp. 502, 406, 413, 486; Castle, *The Castle Diaries*, pp. 421–2, 428, 431, 441.

25. Robert Harris, *The Making of Neil Kinnock* (1984), pp. 71, 84; Hansard, 23 July 1975, 26 June 1975; *Guardian*, 21 November 1977; Martin Westlake, *Kinnock: The Biography* (2001), pp. 100, 132.

26. Donoughue, *Downing Street Diary*, p. 516; Pearce, *Denis Healey*, pp. 449–50; Mervyn Jones, *Michael Foot* (1995), pp. 390–1; Benn, *Against the Tide*, p. 442.

27. Ibid., p. 444; Castle, *The Castle Diaries*, pp. 511–12.

28. Dell, *A Strange Eventful History*, p. 447; *Wall Street Journal*, 20 August 1975; *The Times*, 21 August 1975; Cairncross, *The British Economy since 1945*, p. 213; Hickson, *The IMF Crisis*, pp. 58–9.

29. Savage, *England's Dreaming*, pp. 143–7.

30. Mark Garnett, *From Anger to Apathy: The British Experience since 1975* (2007), p. 169; *The Times*, 23 January 1975, 22 April 1975, 18 August 1975, 1 September 1975, 2 September 1975.

31. *Daily Mirror*, 29 August 1975, 30 August 1975, 24 October 1975, 30 October 1975, 20 November 1975; *Daily Express*, 6 September 1975, 10 October 1975, 4 November 1975, 13 November 1975, 19 November 1975; Michael Palin, *Diaries 1969–1979: The Python Years* (2006), p. 261; Benn, *Against the Tide*, p. 448; for *Time of Terror*, see the BFI's DVD set *Shadows of Progress* (2010).

32. Wybrow, *Britain Speaks Out*, p. 112; *Daily Express*, 2 January 1976; *Daily Mirror*, 2 January 1976; Donoughue, *Downing Street Diary*, p. 616.

CHAPTER 16. OUR WORLD IS IN DANGER

1. *Daily Mirror*, 5 November 1975; *The Times*, 5 November 1975, 28 November 1975; Hansard, 28 November 1975; and see also Mark Garnett, *From Anger to Apathy: The British Experience since 1975* (2007), pp. 72–6.

2. *The Times*, 8 December 1975, 13 December 1975; *Daily Mirror*, 8 December 1975, 9 December 1975, 10 December 1975, 13 December 1975; Michael Palin, *Diaries 1969–1979: The Python Years* (2006), p. 269; *Guardian*, 28 October 2009; for the 'death list', see PRO PREM 16/67, Bill Innes to Nigel Wicks, 19 December 1976.

3. *The Times*, 29 November 1975; Joe Rogaly, *Grunwick* (Harmondsworth, 1977), pp. 75–6; Neill Nugent, 'The National Association for Freedom', in Roger King and Neill Nugent (eds.), *Respectable Rebels: Middle-class Campaigns in Britain in the 1970s* (1979), pp. 81–2; Garnett, *From Anger to Apathy*, pp. 73–5; and see Lord Harris of High Cross's entry on McWhirter in the *Oxford Dictionary of National Biography*.

4. Patrick Hutber, *The Decline and Fall of the Middle Class – and How it Can Fight Back* (Harmondsworth, pb. 1977), pp. 9–10, 28, 30.

5. *Evening Standard*, 1 December 1974; Roger King, 'The Middle Class in Revolt?', in King and Nugent (eds.), *Respectable Rebels*, p. 1; *The Times*, 7 January 1975, 11 January 1975, 13 January 1975; Jeremy Seabrook, *City Close-up* (1971), pp. 83–4.

6. Hutber, *The Decline and Fall of the Middle Class*, p. 88; *The Times*, 12 November 1975; Piers Paul Read, *A Married Man* (1979), p. 15; John Lahr (ed.), *The Diaries of Kenneth Tynan* (2002), pp. 236–7; Dallas Cliff, 'Religion, Morality and the Middle Class', in King and Nugent (eds.), *Respectable Rebels*, p. 127; Roy Strong, *The Roy Strong Diaries 1967–1987* (1997), p. 209.

7. David Butler and Dennis Kavanagh, *The British General Election of 1979* (1980), pp. 13, 26; Keith Middlemas, *Power, Competition and the State*, vol. 3: *The End of the Postwar Era: Britain since 1974* (Basingstoke, 1991), pp. 4, 11; Andy Beckett, *When the Lights Went Out: Britain in the Seventies* (2009), p. 176; Margaret Drabble, *The Ice Age* (1977), pp. 13–14; Hutber, *The Decline and Fall of the Middle Class*, p. 37.

8. Ibid., pp. 23, 32–4, 47, 55; King, 'The Middle Class in Revolt?', p. 7.

9. Anthony Sampson, *The New Anatomy of Britain* (1971), pp. 510–11; Garnett, *From Anger to Apathy*, p. 234; Nicholas Crafts, 'Economic Growth in the 1970s', in Richard Coopey and Nicholas Woodward (eds.), *Britain in the 1970s: The Troubled Economy* (1996), pp. 94–5; Hutber, *The Decline and Fall of the Middle Class*, p. 43; Middlemas, *Power, Competition and the State*, p. 157; Nicholas Timmins, *The Five Giants: A Biography of the Welfare State* (1996), p. 316.

10. Anthony Crosland, *Socialism Now and Other Essays* (1974), p. 75; John Goodwin (ed.), *Peter Hall's Diaries: The Story of a Dramatic Battle* (1983), p. 109; Alwyn W. Turner, *Crisis? What Crisis? Britain in the 1970s* (2008), p. 102; Seabrook, *City Close-up*, p. 185; *Daily Mail*, 12 July 1977, 13 July 1977; *The Times*, 13 July 1977, 15 July 1977.

11. James Chapman, *Inside the TARDIS: The Worlds of Doctor Who* (2006), p. 128; and see also http://www.shannonsullivan.com/drwho/serials/4w.html.

12. Dennis Kavanagh, *Thatcherism and British Politics: The End of Consensus?* (Oxford, 1987), pp. 44, 46; Timmins, *The Five Giants*, p. 503; J. F. Wright, *Britain in the Age of Economic Management: An Economic History since 1939* (Oxford, 1979), pp. 166–7; Bernard Nossiter, *Britain: A Future that Works* (1978), pp. 51–2; *The Times*, 5 January 1984.

13. Timmins, *The Five Giants*, pp. 267, 352–3; David Donnison, *The Politics of Poverty* (Oxford, 1991), pp. 43, 66; Jeremy Seabrook, *What Went Wrong? Working People and the Ideals of the Labour Movement* (1978), pp. 73–4.

14. Seabrook, *City Close-up*, pp. 90, 25, 186–7, 241.

15. Bernard Donoughue, *The Heat of the Kitchen: An Autobiography* (2003), p. 271; Tony Benn, *Against the Tide: Diaries 1973–1976* (1989), p. 461.

16. King, 'The Middle Class in Revolt?', p. 18; Turner, *Crisis? What Crisis?*, pp. 126, 258; the *Rising Damp* episode (17 January 1975) is on YouTube.

17. Jane Devenson and Katherine Lindsay, *Voices from the Middle Class: A Study of Families in Two London Suburbs* (1975); Seabrook, *City Close-up*, pp. 83–4; Arthur Marwick, *Class: Image and Reality in Britain, France and the USA since 1930* (1980), pp. 323–4.

18. James Lees-Milne, *Diaries, 1971–1983* (2008), pp. 26, 129, 154.

19. Andrew Motion, *Philip Larkin: A Writer's Life* (1994), pp. 409, 415; Zachary

Leader, *The Life of Kingsley Amis* (2006), pp. 642–3; Kingsley Amis, *Girl, 20* (1971), pp. 126–7.

20. Kingsley Amis, *Jake's Thing* (1978), pp. 10–11, 14; Leader, *The Life of Kingsley Amis*, pp. 686–8.

21. D. J. Taylor, *After the War: The Novel and England since 1945* (1993), pp. 197–215; on Hines's fiction in the late 1970s, see the fine essay in the *Observer*, 4 December 2005.

22. Kenneth O. Morgan, *Michael Foot: A Life* (Oxford, 2007), pp. 300–301, 304–6; Richard Clutterbuck, *Britain in Agony: The Growth of Political Violence* (1978), pp. 124–7, 174–5; PRO CAB 129/185, C (75) 101, 'The Law on Picketing: Memorandum by the Secretary of State for Employment', 25 September 1975; PRO CAB 129/185, C (75) 102, 'The Law on Picketing: Memorandum by the Home Secretary', 1 October 1975; PRO CAB 128/57, CC (75) 42, 9 October 1975; John Campbell, *Roy Jenkins: A Biography* (1983), pp. 166–7; Rogaly, *Grunwick*, p. 130.

23. Stephen Milligan, *The New Barons: Union Power in the 1970s* (1976), pp. 74–6; Mervyn Jones, *Michael Foot* (1995), pp. 370–75, 391–3; Morgan, *Michael Foot*, pp. 307–13, 347; *The Times*, 1 December 1975, 2 December 1975, 3 December 1975; Hansard, 2 December 1975.

24. *New Statesman*, 16 May 1975; Paul Johnson, 'Farewell to the Labour Party', in Patrick Cormack (ed.), *Right Turn: Eight Men who Changed their Minds* (1978), pp. 78–9; Roy Greenslade, *Press Gang: How Newspapers Make Profits from Propaganda* (2004), p. 280; Benn, *Against the Tide*, p. 96.

25. Peregrine Worsthorne, 'New Lads on Top', in R. Emmett Tyrell Jr. (ed.), *The Future that Doesn't Work: Social Democracy's Failure in Britain* (New York, 1977), pp. 5, 7, 20.

26. Stuart Ball, 'The Conservative Party and the Heath Government', in Stuart Ball and Anthony Seldon (eds.), *The Heath Government 1970–1974: A Reappraisal* (Harlow, 1996), pp. 334–5; King, 'The Middle Class in Revolt?', pp. 4–5; Roger King, 'The Middle Class Revolt and the Established Parties', in King and Nugent (eds.), *Respectable Rebels*, p. 179.

27. King, 'The Middle Class in Revolt?', pp. 2, 4, 13–14; Nugent, 'The National Association for Freedom', pp. 77–83; Ross McKibbin, *Classes and Cultures: England, 1918–1951* (Oxford, 1998), pp. 53–67; Richard Cockett, *Thinking the Unthinkable: Think-tanks and the Economic Counter-revolution, 1931–1983* (1995), pp. 18–20, 68–74, 220–21.

28. *The Times*, 9 May 1974; Neill Nugent, 'The Ratepayers', in King and Nugent (eds.), *Respectable Rebels*, pp. 30–32, 34, 36–7; King, 'The Middle Class Revolt and the Established Parties', pp. 157–8; Kevin Theakston and Ed Gouge, 'Central and Local Government', in Anthony Seldon and Kevin Hickson (eds.), *New Labour, Old Labour: The Wilson and Callaghan Governments, 1974–1979* (2004), pp. 214–21; party political broadcast on housing and rates, 28 August 1974, TFW.

29. Hutber, *The Decline and Fall of the Middle Class*, pp. 79–80, 110–12; *Guardian*, 31 August 1974; John McHugh, 'The Self-employed and the Small Independent Entrepreneur', in King and Nugent (eds.), *Respectable Rebels*, pp. 50–51, 66; King, 'The Middle Class Revolt and the Established Parties', p. 162.

30. McHugh, 'The Self-employed and the Small Independent Entrepreneur', pp. 54–6, 70; speech to Conservative rally in Cardiff, 16 April 1979, TFW.

31. *The Times*, 12 November 1974, 8 September 1975, 9 September 1975, 5 November 1975; King, 'The Middle Class in Revolt?', p. 3; Hutber, *The Decline and Fall of the Middle Class*, pp. 108–10.

32. *The Times*, 29 November 1975, 3 December 1975; Nugent, 'The National Association for Freedom', pp. 76, 85; Jack McGowan, '"Dispute", "Battle", "Siege", "Farce"? Grunwick 30 Years On', *Contemporary British History*, 22:3 (2008), p. 394; Beckett, *When the Lights Went Out*, p. 379.

33. *The Times*, 17 December 1975; Nugent, 'The National Association for Freedom', pp. 76, 86, 91–2, 94; Rogaly, *Grunwick*, p. 74; Cockett, *Thinking the Unthinkable*, pp. 220–21, 223.

34. Nugent, 'The National Association for Freedom', p. 76; Andrew Gamble, *The Free Economy and the Strong State: The Politics of Thatcherism* (1994); Cockett, *Thinking the Unthinkable*, p. 222; *Daily Telegraph*, 13 September 2010; Phillip Whitehead, *The Writing on the Wall: Britain in the Seventies* (1985), p. 213; Beckett, *When the Lights Went Out*, pp. 381–2.

35. *The Times*, 24 July 1976, 13 August 1976, 6 June 1980; Nugent, 'The National Association for Freedom', pp. 88–89; Rogaly, *Grunwick*, pp. 76–7; Whitehead, *The Writing on the Wall*, p. 214; Cockett, *Thinking the Unthinkable*, p. 221; Beckett, *When the Lights Went Out*, pp. 375–6; George Ward, *Fort Grunwick* (1977), pp. 58–9.

CHAPTER 17. IT'S BLOODY WAR NOW

1. Michael Bilton, *Wicked beyond Belief: The Hunt for the Yorkshire Ripper* (2003), pp. 3, 9–10; Gordon Burn, *Somebody's Husband, Somebody's Son: The Story of Peter Sutcliffe* (1984), pp. 106–8.

2. Kester Aspden, *The Hounding of David Oluwale* (2008), pp. 28, 238; Martin Bell, *Complete Poems* (Newcastle upon Tyne, 1988), pp. 137–9; Burn, *Somebody's Husband, Somebody's Son*, pp. 105–6, 119–20; Bilton, *Wicked beyond Belief*, pp. 36, 40, 76; *Yorkshire Post*, 31 October 1975; *The Times*, 7 November 1975; *Daily Express*, 10 June 1976. I am also enormously grateful to Kester Aspden for letting me read his unpublished paper 'Women against Male Violence: The West Yorkshire Story'.

3. Bilton, *Wicked beyond Belief*, pp. 10–13, 16; *Daily Express*, 31 October 1975; *The Times*, 22 January 1976; *Sun*, 23 January 1976.

4. Bilton, *Wicked beyond Belief*, p. 32; Burn, *Somebody's Husband, Somebody's Son*, pp. 134–5.

5. Bilton, *Wicked Beyond Belief*, pp. 142–3; Burn, *Somebody's Husband, Somebody's Son*, pp. 131–4; *Daily Express*, 27 June 1976.

6. Burn, *Somebody's Husband, Somebody's Son*, pp. 137, 144, 149, 159–60; *Daily Express*, 22 September 1978; Bilton, *Wicked beyond Belief*, pp. 236, 272; *The Times*, 28 November 1979.

7. *Daily Express*, 27 June 1979, 30 June 1979, 5 September 1979; Burn, *Somebody's Husband, Somebody's Son*, pp. 178–9, 181, 190–92; Bilton, *Wicked beyond Belief*, pp. 384, 392–3.

8. Burn, *Somebody's Husband, Somebody's Son*, pp. 193, 209; Bilton, *Wicked beyond Belief*, p. 442; *Daily Express*, 21 November 1980; *The Times*, 21 November 1980, 25 November 1980, 28 November 1980, 1 December 1980, 3 December 1980, 4 December 1980, 5 December 1980; Aspden, 'Women against Male Violence'.

9. *New Statesman*, 5 March 2009; *Guardian*, 14 March 2009; *The Times*, 9 December 1980; and see Nicole Ward Jouve, *The Streetcleaner: The Yorkshire Ripper Case on Trial* (1986); Mark Garnett, *From Anger to Apathy: The British Experience since 1975* (2007), pp. 142–3.

10. Stuart Hall *et al.*, *Policing the Crisis: Mugging, the State and Law and Order* (Basingstoke, 1978), pp. 10, 14, quoting data from the annual reports of the Commissioner of the Metropolitan Police and the Chief Inspector of Constabulary; George L. Bernstein, *The Myth of Decline: The Rise of Britain since 1945* (2004), p. 437; Alan Sked and Chris Cook, *Post-war Britain: A Political History* (1988), p. 354; Nick Tiratsoo, 'The Seventies', in Felipe Fernández-Armesto (ed.), *England 1945–2000* (2001), p. 277; Central Statistical Office, *Social Trends 1982* (1981), pp. 205–6; Garnett, *From Anger to Apathy*, pp. 51–2; Robin Day, *Grand Inquisitor: Memoirs* (1989), pp. 191–2.

11. Geoffrey Pearson, *Hooligan: A History of Respectable Fears* (1983), pp. 4–5; *The Times*, 3 February 1975, 25 April 1978; Barbara Castle, *The Castle Diaries 1974–1976* (1980), p. 182.

12. Leif Jerram, *Streetlife: The Untold Story of Europe's Twentieth Century* (Oxford, 2011), p. 397; Margaret Drabble, *The Middle Ground* (Harmondsworth, pb. 1981), p. 223; *Daily Express*, 7 April 1977; *Daily Mirror*, 7 April 1977; Max Caulfield, *Mary Whitehouse* (1975), p. 125.

13. *The Times*, 16 February 1976; *Daily Express*, 14 April 1976; Ian Kennedy Martin, 'Sweeney: A Preamble', http://www.iankennedymartin.com/page3.htm; Alwyn W. Turner, *Crisis? What Crisis? Britain in the 1970s* (2008), pp. 62, 125; Anthony Clark, 'The Sweeney', http://www.screenonline.org.uk/tv/id/473709/.

14. *Daily Express*, 3 January 1975, 14 November 1975.

15. Garry Whannel, 'Television in the 1970s', in Bart Moore-Gilbert (ed.), *The Arts in the 1970s: Cultural Closure?* (1994), p. 185; James Chapman, *Saints and Avengers: British Adventure Series of the 1960s* (2002), pp. 224, 244–5; John Wagner *et al.*, *Judge Dredd: The Complete Case Files 01* (2005).

16. Charlotte Brunsdon, *Law and Order* (2010), pp. 7, 9–10, 12, 35–7, 56–7, 75, 102–8; *Radio Times*, 1–7 April 1978; *Daily Express*, 7 April 1978, 8 April 1978; *Daily Telegraph*, 19 June 1978; Hansard, 8 May 1978.

17. Jeremy Sandford, *Down and Out in Britain* (1971), p. 146; Daniel Lawrence, *Black Migrants: White Natives. A Study of Race Relations in Nottingham* (Cambridge, 1974), pp. 206–8; Mike Phillips and Trevor Phillips, *Windrush: The Irresistible Rise of Multi-racial Britain* (1999), pp. 301–2; Institute of Race Relations, *Deadly Silence: Black Deaths in Custody* (1991); Aspden, *The Hounding of David Oluwale*, p. 224.

18. *The Times*, 29 November 1969; Barry Cox, John Shirley and Martin Short, *The Fall of Scotland Yard* (Harmondsworth, 1977), pp. 10, 16, 21, 25, 31–2, 49, 129.

19. Ibid., pp. 13, 37, 44–6, 64, 68–9; *The Times*, 30 December 1998; *Independent*, 28 January 1999; and see Richard Hobbs's entry on Williamson in the *Oxford Dictionary of National Biography*.

20. Cox, Shirley and Short, *The Fall of Scotland Yard*, pp. 7, 86, 96, 126–7, 130, 157–9, 174, 178, 180–90, 208–9; *Daily Express*, 8 July 1977.

21. Cox, Shirley and Short, *The Fall of Scotland Yard*, pp. 132–7, 212–13; Lewis Baston, *Reggie: The Life of Reginald Maudling* (Stroud, 2004), p. 419; Sir Robert Mark, *In the Office of Constable* (1978), pp. 124, 127–31; Jerry White, *London in the Twentieth Century* (2001), pp. 304–6; *Independent*, 5 October 2010; *Daily Telegraph*, 1 October 2010.

22. Michael Palin, *Diaries 1969–1979: The Python Years* (2006), p. 195; *The Times*, 10 December 1979, 6 February 1980, 5 February 1982; *Daily Telegraph*, 3 December 2010; Robert Reiner, *The Politics of the Police* (Oxford, 2000), p. 63.

23. Clive Irving, *Pox Britannica: The Unmaking of the British* (New York, 1974), pp. 91–2; Hansard, 12 December 1977, 4 August 1980; *The Times*, 29 June 1978, 18 October 1978; William Belson, *The Public and the Police* (1975); Richard Clutterbuck, *Britain in Agony: The Growth of Political Violence* (1978), pp. 275–6.

24. *The Times*, 11 June 1977, 9 February 1978, 11 April 1978, 26 April 1978; *Daily Express*, 11 April 1978, 26 April 1978, 4 May 1978, 20 June 1978; and see Michael Prince, *God's Cop: The Biography of James Anderton* (1988).

25. Pearson, *Hooligan*, p. 4; Jeffrey Weeks, *Sex, Politics and Society: The Regulation of Sexuality since 1800* (Harlow, 1989), p. 249; Dallas Cliff, 'Religion, Morality and the Middle Class', in Roger King and Neill Nugent (eds.), *Respectable Rebels: Middle-class Campaigns in Britain in the 1970s* (1979), p. 148; *Daily Express*, 29 December 1977; *The Times*, 29 November 1975.

26. Robert J. Wybrow, *Britain Speaks Out, 1937–87: A Social History as Seen through the Gallup Data* (1989), p. 104; *The Times*, 24 September 1977; *Daily Express*, 28 June 1978, 29 December 1978; *Daily Mirror*, 28 June 1978; *Daily Mail*, 30 August 1977; Pearson, *Hooligan*, p. 10.

27. *The Times*, 25 March 1974, 5 April 1974; Cate Haste, *Rules of Desire: Sex in Britain, World War I to the Present* (1994), pp. 228, 238; Hera Cook, *The Long Sexual Revolution: English Women, Sex and Contraception 1800–1975* (Oxford, 2005), pp. 268–70, 320, 335; Kaye Wellings *et al.*, *Sexual Behaviour in Britain: The National Survey of Sexual Attitudes and Lifestyles* (1994), pp. 70, 235.

28. Weeks, *Sex, Politics and Society*, p. 274; Jane Lewis, 'Marriage', in Ina Zweiniger-Bargielowska (ed.), *Women in Twentieth-century Britain* (Harlow, 2001), p. 73; Haste, *Rules of Desire*, pp. 286, 288; Mary Abbott, *Family Affairs: A History of the Family in Twentieth-century England* (2003), p. 141; *The Times*, 24 October 1978, 28 April 1981; *Guardian*, 19 December 1979, 24 December 1979.

29. Jeremy Seabrook, *What Went Wrong? Working People and the Ideals of the Labour Movement* (1978), p. 34; *Sunday Times*, 2 March 1980; Haste, *Rules of Desire*, pp. 226, 234–5, 287; Michael Schofield, *Promiscuity* (1976); *The Times*, 21 May 1976.

30. Leon Hunt, *British Low Culture: From Safari Suits to Sexploitation* (1998), p. 48; John Cleese and Connie Booth, *The Complete Fawlty Towers* (1989), pp. 53–5, 59. The Rigsby lines are from the episodes 'Permissive Society' (7 November 1975), 'Fawcett's Python' (10 May 1977) and 'The Cocktail Hour' (17 May 1977).

31. Seabrook, *What Went Wrong?*, p. 31; Jeremy Seabrook, *City Close-up* (Harmondsworth, 1971), pp. 148–9.

32. Ian Jack, *Before the Oil Ran Out: Britain in the Brutal Years* (1997), p. 125; Seabrook, *What Went Wrong?*, p. 34; *The Times*, 7 December 1976.

33. *Daily Express*, 23 January 1975, 3 February 1976, 9 February 1976, 14 February 1976; *Daily Telegraph*, 3 September 2010; Turner, *Crisis? What Crisis?*, p. 250.

34. *Observer*, 15 August 1971; Haste, *Rules of Desire*, p. 256; *Report of the Committee on Obscenity and Film Censorship*, Cmnd 7772 (1979), pp. 44–5; *Sunday People*, 6 February 1972; Cox, Shirley and Short, *The Fall of Scotland Yard*, pp. 160–61, 165, 181–2, 184–5; Paul Ferris, *Sex and the British: A Twentieth-century History* (1993), pp. 232–5; *Sunday Times*, 30 December 1973; *The Times*, 31 January 1973, 22 May 1974, 3 February 1976.

35. *Daily Express*, 11 November 1976; Turner, *Crisis? What Crisis?*, p. 145; Hunt, *British Low Culture*, pp. 47–9; *New Statesman*, 30 May 1975; *Report of the Committee on Obscenity and Film Censorship*, pp. 44–5; Haste, *Rules of Desire*, p. 256; Ferris, *Sex and the British*, p. 245.

36. Richard Webber, *Fifty Years of Carry On* (2008), pp. 151, 169–75; *Observer*, 31 October 1976; *Daily Mail*, 22 February 1978; Russell Davies (ed.), *The Kenneth Williams Diaries* (1993, pb. 1994), pp. 553, 557–8; *Daily Express*, 19 April 1978.

37. *Sun*, 26 March 1975; Caulfield, *Mary Whitehouse*, pp. 120, 152, 170; Michael Tracey and David Morrison, *Whitehouse* (1979), pp. 85, 188–9; Cliff, 'Religion, Morality and the Middle Class', pp. 129–30; Turner, *Crisis? What Crisis?*, p. 134; *The Times*, 18 April 1973, 29 January 1975, 30 January 1975, 31 October 1977.

38. *News of the World*, 17 July 1977; Turner, *Crisis? What Crisis?*, p. 255; Sir Keith Joseph, 'Our Human Stock is Threatened' (Edgbaston speech), 19 October 1974, TFW.

39. Andrew Denham and Mark Garnett, *Keith Joseph* (Chesham, 2001, pb. 2002), pp. 282–3, 287–8; Sir Keith Joseph, 'Notes Towards the Definition of Policy', 4 April 1975, TFW.

40. Lord Hailsham's diary, 10 April 1975, 11 April 1975, TFW; minutes of Leader's Consultative Committee, 57th meeting, 11 April 1975, TFW; Ferris, *Sex and the British*, p. 250; *The Times*, 15 May 1978.

41. New Year message, 2 January 1970, TFW; John Campbell, *Margaret Thatcher*, vol. 1: *The Grocer's Daughter* (2000), pp. 191–2; Weeks, *Sex, Politics and Society*, p. 293.

42. *The Times*, 22 January 1976, 30 August 1977, 6 September 1977, 20 September 1977, 10 October 1977, 24 November 1977, 9 February 1978; Garnett, *From Anger to Apathy*, pp. 285, 299.

43. Tracey and Morrison, *Whitehouse*, pp. 3, 5–7; Rictor Norton, 'Mea Culpa', *Gay and Lesbian Humanist*, Summer 2002, at http://www.pinktriangle.org.uk/glh/214/norton.html.

44. Tracey and Morrison, *Whitehouse*, pp. 7, 11–13; *The Times*, 29 July 1977.

45. Norton, 'Mea Culpa'; *The Times*, 29 July 1977; Tracey and Morrison, *Whitehouse*, pp. 18–19; Weeks, *Sex, Politics and Society*, p. 280.

46. *The Times*, 12 July 1977, 13 July 1977, 18 August 1977; Tracey and Morrison, *Whitehouse*, pp. 15–17; Brett Humphreys, 'The Law that Dared to Lay the Blame', *Gay and Lesbian Humanist*, Summer 2002, at http://www.pinktriangle.org.uk/glh/214/humphreys.html.

47. Tracey and Morrison, *Whitehouse*, p. 17; *The Times*, 9 July 1977, 13 July 1977, 15 July 1977, 21 July 1977, 23 July 1977, 31 October 1977; Wybrow, *Britain*

Speaks Out, p. 116; Weeks, *Sex, Politics and Society*, p. 286; Haste, *Rules of Desire*, pp. 244–7; Turner, *Crisis? What Crisis?*, pp. 241–2.

48. *Daily Express*, 5 March 1976, 25 April 1978, 7 October 1978, 30 October 1978; Andy Medhurst, *A National Joke: Popular Comedy and English Cultural Identities* (2007), pp. 104–5; Louis Barfe, *Turned Out Nice Again: The Story of British Light Entertainment* (2008), pp. 284–8.

CHAPTER 18. EVENING ALL

1. Bernard Donoughue, *Downing Street Diary*, vol. 1: *With Harold Wilson in No. 10* (2005), pp. 593–4; Bernard Donoughue, *The Heat of the Kitchen: An Autobiography* (2003), p. 181.

2. Donoughue, *Downing Street Diary*, vol. 1, pp. 398, 473; Donoughue, *The Heat of the Kitchen*, pp. 178–9; Joe Haines, *The Politics of Power: The Inside Story of Life at No. 10* (1977), pp. 10, 220; Philip Ziegler, *Wilson: The Authorized Life* (1993), pp. 486–7.

3. Donoughue, *Downing Street Diary*, vol. 1, pp. 529, 547, 584, 637, 642, 683; Ben Pimlott, *Harold Wilson* (1992), pp. 675–6; Francis Wheen, *Strange Days Indeed: The Golden Age of Paranoia* (2009), pp. 270–71.

4. Ziegler, *Wilson*, pp. 482–3; Roy Jenkins, *A Life at the Centre* (1991), pp. 297–8; Denis Healey, *The Time of My Life* (1989, pb. 1990), p. 446; Pimlott, *Harold Wilson*, pp. 650–1; Donoughue, *The Heat of the Kitchen*, p. 128; Barbara Castle, *The Castle Diaries 1974–1976* (1980), pp. 671–2.

5. Haines, *The Politics of Power*, p. 220; Donoughue, *Downing Street Diary*, vol. 1 pp. 471, 483, 539–40; Joe Haines, *Glimmers of Twilight: Harold Wilson in Decline* (2003), pp. 116–17; Ziegler, *Wilson*, p. 483.

6. Haines to Wilson, 6 November 1975, reprinted in Haines, *Glimmers of Twilight*, pp. 120–23; Harold Wilson, *Final Term: The Labour Government, 1974–1976* (1979), p. 29; Ben Pimlott, *The Queen: A Biography of Elizabeth II* (1997), p. 430; Pimlott, *Harold Wilson*, p. 674; Ziegler, *Wilson*, p. 484.

7. Pimlott, *Harold Wilson*, p. 651 (see e.g. *News of the World*, 27 October 1974; *Daily Mail*, 31 October 1974, 13 January 1975); Jenkins, *A Life at the Centre*, p. 430; James Callaghan, *Time and Chance* (1987), pp. 386–7; *Observer*, 7 March 1976; Castle, *The Castle Diaries*, pp. 671–2, 674; Tony Benn, *Against the Tide: Diaries 1973–1976* (1989), p. 527.

8. Haines, *Glimmers of Twilight*, p. 118; Donoughue, *Downing Street Diary*, vol. 1, p. 687; *The Times*, 5 March 1976, 6 March 1976; Edmund Dell, *The Chancellors: A History of the Chancellors of the Exchequer, 1945–90* (1996, pb. 1997), pp. 422–3; David Kynaston, *The City of London*, vol. 4: *A Club No More 1945–2000* (2001), pp. 529–31; Kevin Hickson, *The IMF Crisis of 1976 and British Politics* (2005), pp. 74–8; Edward Pearce, *Denis Healey: A Life in Our Times* (2002), p. 455.

9. Edmund Dell, *A Hard Pounding: Politics and Economic Crisis, 1974–1976* (Oxford, 1991), p. 205; Dell, *The Chancellors*, p. 46; Hickson, *The IMF Crisis*, pp. 86–7; Max-Stephan Schulze and Nicholas Woodward, 'The Emergence of Rapid Inflation', in Richard Coopey and Nicholas Woodward (eds.), *Britain in the 1970s: The Troubled Economy* (1996), p. 123; Nicholas Woodward, 'The

Retreat from Full Employment', ibid., p. 145; Leo Pliatzky, *Getting and Spending: Public Expenditure, Employment and Inflation* (Oxford, 1982), p. 142; Martin Holmes, *The Labour Government 1974-1979: Political Aims and Economic Reality* (Basingstoke, 1985), p. 84; Keith Middlemas, *Power, Competition and the State*, vol. 3: *The End of the Postwar Era: Britain since 1974* (Basingstoke, 1991), pp. 105-6.

10. *The Times*, 11 March 1976; Kynaston, *A Club No More*, p. 530; Castle, *The Castle Diaries*, p. 681; Benn, *Against the Tide*, p. 529.

11. Callaghan, *Time and Chance*, pp. 390-91; Pimlott, *Harold Wilson*, pp. 678-9.

12. Castle, *The Castle Diaries*, pp. 682-3, 686; Benn, *Against the Tide*, p. 531; *The Times*, 12 March 1976, 15 March 1976; Hansard, 11 March 1976; Healey, *The Time of My Life*, p. 445; Pimlott, *Harold Wilson*, p. 678.

13. Donoughue, *Downing Street Diary*, vol. 1, pp. 696-9; PRO CAB 128/58, CC 76 (10), 16 March 1976; PRO PREM 16/1072, Action Plan and Timetable, 16 March 1976; PRO PREM 16/1072, Personal Minute M34/76, 16 March 1976; Healey, *The Time of My Life*, p. 446; Castle, *The Castle Diaries*, pp. 689-91; Benn, *Against the Tide*, p. 535; Donoughue, *The Heat of the Kitchen*, pp. 183-4.

14. *The Times*, 17 March 1976.

15. *Sunday Telegraph*, 21 March 1976; *The Times*, 18 March 1976; Pimlott, *Harold Wilson*, pp. 681-3, *Daily Express*, 17 March 1976.

16. Donoughue, *Downing Street Diary*, vol. 1, pp. 706-7; Castle, *The Castle Diaries*, pp. 699-700; Benn, *Against the Tide*, pp. 542-3.

17. Donoughue, *Downing Street Diary*, vol. 1, pp. 709, 715; Donoughue, *The Heat of the Kitchen*, p. 185.

18. Donoughue, *Downing Street Diary*, vol. 1, pp. 718-21.

19. *Spectator*, 20 March 1976; Ziegler, *Wilson*, pp. 502-3, 518; Pimlott, *Harold Wilson*, pp. 683-4; Hansard, 6 April 1976; Benn, *Against the Tide*, p. 557.

20. Christopher Booker, *The Seventies: Portrait of a Decade* (1980), p. 120; Bernard Donoughue, *Downing Street Diary*, vol. 2: *With James Callaghan in No. 10* (2008), p. 226; Donoughue, *The Heat of the Kitchen*, p. 128; David Marquand, *The Progressive Dilemma: From Lloyd George to Blair* (1999), pp. 156-7, 163; Andy Beckett, *When the Lights Went Out: Britain in the Seventies* (2009), p. 162.

21. Donoughue, *Downing Street Diary*, vol. 2, pp. 165, 403; Donoughue, *The Heat of the Kitchen*, p. 191; Pimlott, *Harold Wilson*, pp. 726, 729. Wilson's resignation interview with the BBC can be seen on YouTube.

22. John Goodwin (ed.), *Peter Hall's Diaries: The Story of a Dramatic Battle* (1983), p. 399; *Daily Mirror*, 27 December 1978; *Daily Express*, 27 December 1978.

23. *The Times*, 24 March 1976, 25 March 1976, 26 March 1976; Anthony Sampson, *The New Anatomy of Britain* (1971), pp. 50, 52; John Campbell, *Roy Jenkins: A Biography* (1983), pp. 176-7.

24. Donoughue, *Downing Street Diary*, vol. 1, p. 414; Ion Trewin (ed.), *The Hugo Young Papers: Thirty Years of British Politics – Off the Record* (2008), pp. 51-2; Kevin Jefferys, *Anthony Crosland: A New Biography* (1999), pp. 190-92; Susan Crosland, *Tony Crosland* (1982), pp. 314-16; Roy Hattersley, *Who Goes Home? Scenes from a Political Life* (1996), pp. 161-2.

25. Giles Radice, *Friends and Rivals: Crosland, Jenkins and Healey* (2002), pp. 236, 238-9; *The Times*, 18 March 1976, 19 March 1976; Healey, *The Time of My Life*, pp. 446-7.

26. Donoughue, *Downing Street Diary*, vol. 1, pp. 694, 701; Haines, *The Politics of Power*, p. 89; Kenneth O. Morgan, *Callaghan: A Life* (Oxford, 1997), pp. 462–3, 469, 470–71; *The Times*, 17 March 1976; *Daily Mirror*, 17 March 1976.

27. Jenkins, *A Life at the Centre*, p. 435; Morgan, *Callaghan*, pp. 473–5; *New Statesman*, 9 April 1976; Castle, *The Castle Diaries*, p. 711.

28. Morgan, *Callaghan*, p. 474; Peter Hennessy, *The Prime Minister: The Office and its Holders since 1945* (2000), pp. 378–9; *The Times*, 6 April 1976; Benn, *Against the Tide*, p. 553; Callaghan, *Time and Chance*, pp. 394–5.

29. Donoughue, *Downing Street Diary*, vol. 1, p. 723; *The Times*, 6 April 1976; *Daily Express*, 6 April 1976.

CHAPTER 19. A GREAT DETECTIVE EXERCISE

1. Bernard Donoughue, *Downing Street Diary*, vol. 1: *With Harold Wilson in No. 10* (2005), pp. 596, 601, 603, 714; Bernard Donoughue, *The Heat of the Kitchen: An Autobiography* (2003), p. 197.

2. Donoughue, *Downing Street Diary*, vol. 1, p. 715; Joe Haines, *The Politics of Power: The Inside Story of Life at No. 10* (1977), p. 150.

3. *Sunday Times*, 2 May 1976; *Sunday Express*, 23 May 1976; Ben Pimlott, *Harold Wilson* (1992), pp. 685–7; *The Times*, 27 May 1976; Tony Benn, *Against the Tide: Diaries 1973–1976* (1989), p. 571.

4. *The Times*, 27 May 1976; Hansard, 27 May 1976; Donoughue, *The Heat of the Kitchen*, p. 199; Pimlott, *Harold Wilson*, p. 688; *Daily Telegraph*, 26 May 1976; *Guardian*, 26 May 1976; Philip Ziegler, *Wilson: The Authorized Life* (1993), p. 498.

5. *The Times*, 29 May 1976, 31 May 1976; Haines, *The Politics of Power*, pp. 151–3.

6. Ibid., pp. 153–4; *The Times*, 7 February 1977, 8 February 1977, 9 February 1977, 12 February 1977, 14 February 1977; and see *Panorama*, 'Joe's Version', 14 February 1977; Pimlott, *Harold Wilson*, pp. 691–2.

7. Haines, *The Politics of Power*, pp. 155–6; Donoughue, *The Heat of the Kitchen*, pp. 194–5; *The Times*, 23 September 1977, 13 December 1980, 19 December 1980; Pimlott, *Harold Wilson*, pp. 688–9, 724, 726; on Kagan in prison, see the entry by John A. Hargreaves in the *Oxford Dictionary of National Biography*.

8. Bernard Donoughue, *Downing Street Diary*, vol. 2: *With James Callaghan in Number 10* (2008), pp. 238, 249; *Daily Mirror*, 6 September 1977, 7 September 1977, 8 September 1977; Andrew Mourant, *Don Revie: Portrait of a Footballing Enigma* (Edinburgh, 1990), pp. 64–5, 133–4, 204–5; Rob Bagchi and Paul Rogerson, *The Unforgiven: The Story of Don Revie's Leeds United* (2002), pp. 166–7.

9. Simon Freeman, with Barrie Penrose, *Rinkagate: The Rise and Fall of Jeremy Thorpe* (1996), pp. 19–20, 33, 36, 115, 110–1, 132; Christopher Andrew, *The Defence of the Realm: The Authorized History of MI5* (2009), p. 533.

10. Freeman, with Penrose, *Rinkagate*, pp. 96, 81–6, 36, 43–7, 59–60, 78; Andrew, *The Defence of the Realm*, pp. 533–4.

11. *Daily Express*, 21 November 1978, 30 November 1978; *Daily Mirror*, 21 November 1978; Freeman, with Penrose, *Rinkagate*, pp. 90, 94–6, 123–6, 130, 142, 145–6, 161–2, 169–82; Andrew, *The Defence of the Realm*, p. 636.

12. Freeman, with Penrose, *Rinkagate*, pp. 195–7; *Sunday Times*, 3 March 1974.

13. *Daily Express*, 28 November 1978; Freeman, with Penrose, *Rinkagate*, pp. 188–9, 206–8, 211–14.

14. Freeman, with Penrose, *Rinkagate*, pp. 215–17.

15. Ibid., pp. 220–21; *Private Eye*, 12 December 1975; Francis Wheen, *Strange Days Indeed: The Golden Age of Paranoia* (2009), pp. 208–9.

16. *Daily Mirror*, 30 January 1976; *The Times*, 31 January 1976, 2 February 1976; Freeman, with Penrose, *Rinkagate*, pp. 229–31.

17. *Daily Mirror*, 30 January 1976; Freeman, with Penrose, *Rinkagate*, pp. 122–3, 230–31; Wheen, *Strange Days Indeed*, pp. 270–1.

18. Donoughue, *Downing Street Diary*, vol. 1, pp. 652, 678; Andrew, *The Defence of the Realm*, pp. 636–7.

19. Barbara Castle, *The Castle Diaries 1974–1976* (1980), pp. 642, 648, 677–8; Hansard, 9 March 1976; Freeman, with Penrose, *Rinkagate*, pp. 231–2; for more on Jack Straw and the Thorpe case, see *Sunday Times*, 20 October 2002.

20. Freeman, with Penrose, *Rinkagate*, pp. 234–6, 239; *Daily Mirror*, 6 March 1976; *Sunday Times*, 14 March 1976.

21. *Sunday Times*, 9 May 1976; *The Times*, 10 May 1976; Freeman, with Penrose, *Rinkagate*, pp. 240–41.

22. Donoughue, *Downing Street Diary*, vol. 2, p. 32; *Daily Mirror*, 30 January 1978; Barrie Penrose and Roger Courtiour, *The Pencourt File* (1978), pp. 9, 13; Freeman, with Penrose, *Rinkagate*, pp. 242–5.

23. *The Times*, 2 February 1978; Pimlott, *Harold Wilson*, pp. 694–6; Freeman, with Penrose, *Rinkagate*, pp. 248–61, 268, 277–89; *Daily Mirror*, 30 January 1978, 31 January 1978, 1 February 1978, 2 February 1978; Andrew, *The Defence of the Realm*, pp. 639–40; Tony Benn, *Conflicts of Interest: Diaries 1977–80* (1990), p. 378.

24. *Evening News*, 19 October 1977, 20 October 1977; Freeman, with Penrose, *Rinkagate*, pp. 222–3, 237–8, 286–9.

25. *The Times*, 28 October 1977, 5 August 1978; Freeman, with Penrose, *Rinkagate*, pp. 295, 324–5.

26. *The Times*, 7 September 1978, 9 September 1978, 14 September 1978, 15 September 1978; Freeman, with Penrose, *Rinkagate*, pp. 333–4.

27. *Sunday Express*, 19 November 1978; *Daily Mirror*, 20 November 1978; *The Times*, 23 November 1978; Freeman, with Penrose, *Rinkagate*, pp. 337–8.

28. *The Times*, 21 November 1978, 23 November 1978, 24 November 1978, 28 November 1978, 30 November 1978; *Daily Express*, 14 November 1978; Freeman, with Penrose, *Rinkagate*, pp. 338–45.

29. *Sunday Express*, 15 April 1979, 29 April 1979; *Daily Mirror*, 27 April 1979; *The Times*, 30 April 1979.

30. *Daily Express*, 5 May 1979; and see Freeman, with Penrose, *Rinkagate*, p. 346.

31. Freeman, with Penrose, *Rinkagate*, pp. 347, 351, 356; *Daily Express*, 22 May 1979, 23 May 1979; *Daily Mirror*, 18 May 1979, 19 May 1979.

32. Freeman, with Penrose, *Rinkagate*, pp. 358–9, 365; *Daily Express*, 19 June 1979. Cook's sketch (now easily found on YouTube) was later released as a record, *Here Comes the Judge: Live* (1979).

33. *Daily Express*, 23 June 1979; Freeman, with Penrose, *Rinkagate*, pp. 362–4.

CHAPTER 20. JIM'S FACTS OF LIFE

1. Bernard Donoughue, *Downing Street Diary*, vol. 2: *With James Callaghan in No. 10* (2008), pp. 13, 15; Barbara Castle, *The Castle Diaries 1974–1976* (1980), p. 724.

2. Kenneth O. Morgan, *Callaghan: A Life* (Oxford, 1997), pp. 3, 6, 10, 22; John Cole, *As It Seemed to Me: Political Memoirs* (1995), p. 159; Peter Hennessy, *The Prime Minister: The Office and its Holders since 1945* (2000), p. 379.

3. Kenneth O. Morgan, *Labour People: Leaders and Lieutenants, Hardie to Kinnock* (Oxford, 1992), pp. 266–7; Hennessy, *The Prime Minister*, pp. 378–9; *Sunday Times*, 4 April 1976; Morgan, *Callaghan*, pp. 355–6; Richard Crossman, *The Diaries of a Cabinet Minister*, vol. 3: *Secretary of State for Social Services, 1968–70* (1977), p. 628.

4. Morgan, *Callaghan*, pp. 374–6, 381–2, 409; Joe Haines, *The Politics of Power: The Inside Story of Life at No. 10* (1977), p. 89.

5. Morgan, *Callaghan*, pp. 482, 496; Chris Ballinger and Anthony Seldon, 'Prime Ministers and Cabinet', in Anthony Seldon and Kevin Hickson (eds.), *New Labour, Old Labour: The Wilson and Callaghan Governments, 1974–1979* (2004), pp. 177–9; Bernard Donoughue, *The Heat of the Kitchen: An Autobiography* (2003), p. 234.

6. Donoughue, *Downing Street Diary*, pp. 244, 363, 435–6.

7. Morgan, *Callaghan*, pp. 15, 504; Hennessy, *The Prime Minister*, pp. 392, 395; Morgan, *Labour People*, pp. 272, 274; Cole, *As It Seemed to Me*, p. 96; Morgan, *Callaghan*, p. 517; *Guardian*, 31 March 1976; Anthony Sampson, *The New Anatomy of Britain* (1971), p. 54; Hennessy, *The Prime Minister*, p. 395.

8. Castle, *The Castle Diaries*, pp. 724–5; James Callaghan, *Time and Chance* (1987), pp. 400, 402; Morgan, *Callaghan*, pp. 477–8, 501; Giles Radice, *Friends and Rivals: Crosland, Jenkins and Healey* (2002), pp. 244–5.

9. Morgan, *Callaghan*, p. 478; Kenneth O. Morgan, *Michael Foot: A Life* (Oxford, 2007), pp. 316, 338; Simon Hoggart and David Leigh, *Michael Foot: A Portrait* (1981), p. 167; Callaghan, *Time and Chance*, p. 401; Donoughue, *Downing Street Diary*, p. 122.

10. Morgan, *Callaghan*, pp. 479–80, 498–500, 517; Donoughue, *Downing Street Diary*, pp. 2, 20, 24, 39, 178; Edmund Dell, *A Strange Eventful History: Democratic Socialism in Britain* (2000), p. 452; Donoughue, *The Heat of the Kitchen*, pp. 239, 262.

11. *Time*, 24 May 1976; Callaghan, *Time and Chance*, pp. 397–8.

12. *The Times*, 7 April 1976, 8 April 1976.

13. Hansard, 27 May 1976; Tony Benn, *Against the Tide: Diaries 1973–1976* (1989), p. 572; *The Times*, 28 May 1976, 29 May 1976.

14. Morgan, *Callaghan*, pp. 481, 523; *The Times*, 2 April 1975, 7 April 1976; Callaghan, *Time and Chance*, pp. 414–15.

15. Denis Healey, *The Time of My Life* (1989, pb. 1990), p. 427; David Kynaston, *The City of London*, vol. 4: *A Club No More 1945–2000* (2001), p. 543; Ronald McIntosh, *Challenge to Democracy: Politics, Trade Union Power and Economic Failure in the 1970s* (2006), p. 272.

16. *The Times*, 7 April 1976; Edmund Dell, *The Chancellors: A History of the Chancellors of the Exchequer, 1945–90* (1996, pb. 1997), p. 423; Edward Pearce,

Denis Healey: A Life in Our Times (2002), p. 459; Healey, *The Time of My Life*, p. 396; Donoughue, *Downing Street Diary*, pp. 28–9.

17. *The Times*, 6 May 1976, 17 June 1976; Pearce, *Denis Healey*, p. 462; Morgan, *Callaghan*, pp. 529–30.

18. Castle, *The Castle Diaries*, p. 687; Robert Taylor, 'The Rise and Fall of the Social Contract', in Seldon and Hickson (eds.), *New Labour, Old Labour*, p. 88; *The Times*, 21 June 1977.

19. Dell, *The Chancellors*, pp. 424–5; *The Economist*, 15 May 1976; Leo Pliatzky, *Getting and Spending: Public Expenditure, Employment and Inflation* (Oxford, 1982), p. 148; Edmund Dell, *A Hard Pounding: Politics and Economic Crisis, 1974–1976* (Oxford, 1991), p. 218; Kevin Hickson, *The IMF Crisis of 1976 and British Politics* (2005), p. 87.

20. Ibid., pp. 60, 64–5; Dell, *The Chancellors*, p. 424; Kathleen Burk and Alec Cairncross, *Goodbye, Great Britain: The 1976 IMF Crisis* (New Haven, 1992), p. 37; Mark D. Harmon, 'The 1976 UK–IMF Crisis: The Markets, the Americans and the IMF', *Contemporary British History*, 11:3 (Autumn 1997), pp. 1–17; William E. Simon, with John M. Caher, *A Time for Reflection: An Autobiography* (Washington, 2004), p. 152; Healey, *The Time of My Life*, pp. 419–20; Andy Beckett, *When the Lights Went Out: Britain in the Seventies* (2009), p. 320.

21. *The Times*, 7 June 1976; PRO CAB 128/59, CM (76) 8, 10 June 1976; Dell, *The Chancellors*, pp. 424–5; Hickson, *The IMF Crisis*, pp. 89–91; Dell, *A Hard Pounding*, pp. 219–20; Donoughue, *Downing Street Diary*, p. 37.

22. *Daily Express*, 26 June 1976; Donoughue, *Downing Street Diary*, pp. 45–6; Pliatzky, *Getting and Spending*, p. 149; PRO CAB 129/190, CP (76) 40, 'Public Expenditure to 1980–81', 1 July 1976; PRO CAB 129/190, CP (76) 42, 'Public Expenditure 1977–78 – The Economic Background', 2 July 1976; PRO CAB 128/59, CM (76) 13, 6 July 1976.

23. Donoughue, *Downing Street Diary*, pp. 52–3; David Marquand, *The Progressive Dilemma: From Lloyd George to Blair* (1999), pp. 175–6; Dell, *A Strange Eventful History*, pp. 357–8; Susan Crosland, *Tony Crosland* (1982), pp. 355–6, 372.

24. Cambridge Political Economy Group, *Britain's Economic Crisis* (1975); Stuart Holland, *The Socialist Challenge* (1975); Andrew Gamble, *Britain in Decline: Economic Policy, Political Strategy and the British State* (Basingstoke 1994), pp. 158, 171–85; Benn, *Against the Tide*, pp. 324–5 (and see Tony Benn, 'The Alternative Economic Strategy in Outline' (1975), repr. on pp. 725–7); Hickson, *The IMF Crisis*, pp. 171, 175; Dell, *A Strange Eventful History*, pp. 460–61; Stuart Holland, 'The Industrial Strategy', in Seldon and Hickson (eds.), *New Labour, Old Labour*, pp. 297–9; Joe Haines, *Glimmers of Twilight: Harold Wilson in Decline* (2003), p. 40.

25. Benn, *Against the Tide*, pp. 302, 591–2, 595; PRO CAB 128/59, CM (76) 15, 15 July 1976; Dell, *The Chancellors*, p. 426.

26. PRO CAB 128/59, CM (76) 19, 21 July 1976; PRO CAB 128/59, CM (76) 20, 21 July 1976; Hickson, *The IMF Crisis*, pp. 95–6; Morgan, *Callaghan*, pp. 531–2; Benn, *Against the Tide*, pp. 598–601; Donoughue, *Downing Street Diary*, vol. 2, p. 58.

27. Callaghan, *Time and Chance*, pp. 420–21.

28. Healey, *The Time of My Life*, p. 428; Hickson, *The IMF Crisis*, p. 99; *The Times*, 4 September 1976.

29. *The Times*, 7 September 1976, 8 September 1976, 9 September 1976, 11 September 1976; Donoughue, *Downing Street Diary*, pp. 66–7; Hickson, *The IMF Crisis*, pp. 99–100.

30. Kynaston, *A Club No More*, p. 547; Morgan, *Callaghan*, p. 533; Hickson, *The IMF Crisis*, p. 100; Donoughue, *Downing Street Diary*, p. 71.

31. *The Times*, 31 May 1976; Alan Clark, *Diaries: Into Politics 1972–1982*, ed. Ion Trewin (2001), p. 33.

32. Donoughue, *Downing Street Diary*, pp. 72–4; *The Times*, 28 September 1976; Benn, *Against the Tide*, pp. 615–16.

33. *The Times*, 29 September 1976; Donoughue, *Downing Street Diary*, p. 73; Callaghan, *Time and Chance*, pp. 425–7; Hickson, *The IMF Crisis*, pp. 102–3.

34. Richard Cockett, *Thinking the Unthinkable: Think-tanks and the Economic Counter-revolution, 1931–1983* (1995), pp. 185–7; Morgan, *Callaghan*, p. 535; *The Times*, 29 September 1976; Donoughue, *Downing Street Diary*, p. 73; Benn, *Against the Tide*, pp. 615–16; *Daily Express*, 29 September 1976; Callaghan, *Time and Chance*, p. 429; Beckett, *When the Lights Went Out*, p. 336.

35. David Smith, *The Rise and Fall of Monetarism: The Theory and Politics of an Economic Experiment* (1991), p. 65; Dell, *The Chancellors*, pp. 427–8; Hickson, *The IMF Crisis*, pp. 104, 106, 209; Morgan, *Callaghan*, pp. 507–8, 536–7.

36. *The Times*, 29 September 1976; *Daily Express*, 29 September 1976; Pearce, *Denis Healey*, p. 469; Beckett, *When the Lights Went Out*, pp. 333–4; Callaghan, *Time and Chance*, p. 428.

37. Healey, *The Time of My Life*, p. 429; Pearce, *Denis Healey*, p. 469; *Daily Express*, 29 September 1976, 30 September 1976, 1 October 1976; *The Times*, 30 September 1976.

38. *Daily Express*, 30 September 1976; Callaghan, *Time and Chance*, p. 428; Healey, *The Time of My Life*, p. 429; Pearce, *Denis Healey*, p. 470; Beckett, *When the Lights Went Out*, p. 340.

39. *The Times*, 1 October 1976; Pearce, *Denis Healey*, pp. 470–71; Healey, *The Time of My Life*, p. 429; Ivor Crewe and Anthony King, *SDP: The Birth, Life and Death of the Social Democratic Party* (Oxford, 1995), p. 26.

40. *The Times*, 1 October 1976; Healey, *The Time of My Life*, p. 429; Pearce, *Denis Healey*, pp. 471–2; Morgan, *Callaghan*, p. 534; Benn, *Against the Tide*, p. 616.

41. *Guardian*, 1 October 1976; Kynaston, *A Club No More*, p. 549; *The Times*, 1 October 1976; *Daily Express*, 1 October 1976; Robin Day, *Grand Inquisitor: Memoirs* (1989), p. 239.

CHAPTER 21. MONEY, MONEY, MONEY

1. Roy Strong, *The Roy Strong Diaries 1967–1987* (1997), p. 179.

2. *NME*, 11 September 1976; Jon Savage, *England's Dreaming: Sex Pistols and Punk Rock* (2005), pp. 221–3, 224, 231.

3. Bernard Donoughue, *Downing Street Diary*, vol. 2: *With James Callaghan in No. 10* (2008), pp. 75–6, 77, 79–80; Denis Healey, *The Time of My Life* (1989, pb. 1990), pp. 430–31; Edward Pearce, *Denis Healey: A Life in Our Times* (2002), p. 476; Kevin Hickson, *The IMF Crisis of 1976 and British Politics* (2005), p. 116; Bill Williamson, *The Temper of the Times: British Society since*

World War II (Oxford, 1990), pp. 202–4; Ben Pimlott, 'The North East: Back to the 1930s?', *Political Quarterly*, 52:1 (January–March 1981), pp. 51–63.

4. *Sunday Times*, 24 October 1976; Hickson, *The IMF Crisis*, pp. 116–17; John Goodwin (ed.), *Peter Hall's Diaries: The Story of a Dramatic Battle* (1983), pp. 265–6; John Lahr (ed.), *The Diaries of Kenneth Tynan* (2002), pp. 343–4; Strong, *The Roy Strong Diaries*, pp. 179–80.

5. *Daily Express*, 1 November 1976, 5 November 1976; Pearce, *Denis Healey*, p. 483; Hickson, *The IMF Crisis*, pp. 125–6; Andy Beckett, *When the Lights Went Out: Britain in the Seventies* (2009), pp. 343–4; *The Times*, 24 November 1976.

6. Kenneth O. Morgan, *Callaghan: A Life* (Oxford, 1997), pp. 537–8, 544–5; Edmund Dell, *A Hard Pounding: Politics and Economic Crisis, 1974–1976* (Oxford, 1991), p. 251; Pearce, *Denis Healey*, pp. 481, 486–8.

7. Edmund Dell, *The Chancellors: A History of the Chancellors of the Exchequer, 1945–90* (1996, pb. 1997), pp. 428, 430; Mark D. Harmon, 'The 1976 UK–IMF Crisis: The Markets, the Americans and the IMF', *Contemporary British History*, 11:13 (Autum 1997), pp. 10–12; Hickson, *The IMF Crisis*, pp. 118–24, 135–6; Kathleen Burk and Alec Cairncross, *Goodbye, Great Britain: The 1976 IMF Crisis* (New Haven, 1992), p. 82.

8. Pearce, *Denis Healey*, p. 483; Tony Benn, *Against the Tide: Diaries 1973–1976* (1989), pp. 636–8, 621, 641, 645, 609.

9. Hickson, *The IMF Crisis*, p. 133; PRO CAB 129/193, CP (76) 117, 'The Real Choices Facing the Cabinet', 29 November 1976; Edmund Dell, *A Strange Eventful History: Democratic Socialism in Britain* (2000), pp. 453–4; Kevin Jefferys, *Anthony Crosland: A New Biography* (1999), pp. 207–16.

10. PRO CAB 128/60, CM (76) 32, 18 November 1976; Pearce, *Denis Healey*, p. 489; Hickson, *The IMF Crisis*, p. 128; Susan Crosland, *Tony Crosland* (1982), pp. 377–8; Hansard, 11 October 1976; Dell, *The Chancellors*, p. 433.

11. Peter Hennessy, *The Prime Minister: The Office and its Holders since 1945* (2000), pp. 383–5; Giles Radice, *Friends and Rivals: Crosland, Jenkins and Healey* (2002), p. 259; Pearce, *Denis Healey*, p. 481.

12. Ibid., pp. 482, 487; Beckett, *When the Lights Went Out*, p. 353; Donoughue, *Downing Street Diary*, pp. 105–6; Dell, *The Chancellors*, pp. 430, 434.

13. Benn, *Against the Tide*, pp. 653–5; PRO CAB 129/193, CP (76) 111, 22 November 1976; PRO CAB 128/60, CM (76) 33, 23 November 1976; Donoughue, *Downing Street Diary*, p. 104; Crosland, *Tony Crosland*, pp. 377–8.

14. Hennessy, *The Prime Minister*, p. 387; Hickson, *The IMF Crisis*, pp. 131, 206; Dell, *The Chancellors*, pp. 430, 433; Dell, *A Strange Eventful History*, pp. 433, 458–9; Dell, *A Hard Pounding*, p. 261.

15. Hickson, *The IMF Crisis*, p. 132; Donoughue, *Downing Street Diary*, p. 104; Benn, *Against the Tide*, pp. 656–7.

16. *The Times*, 25 November 1976; Benn, *Against the Tide*, pp. 657–9; PRO CAB 128/60, CM (76) 34, 25 November 1976.

17. Pearce, *Denis Healey*, pp. 492–3; James Callaghan, *Time and Chance* (1987), pp. 437–8; Crosland, *Tony Crosland*, p. 379.

18. Donoughue, *Downing Street Diary*, pp. 108, 110; Morgan, *Callaghan*, p. 547; Pearce, *Denis Healey*, pp. 493–4.

19. Benn, *Against the Tide*, pp. 662–5; PRO CAB 128/60, CM (76) 35, 1 December 1976. The Benn paper is PRO CAB 129/193, CP (76) 117, 'The Real Choices Facing the Cabinet', 29 November 1976; the Policy Unit riposte is PRO CAB 129/193, CP (76) 116, 'The Case For and Against Import Controls', 30 November 1976.

20. Bill Rodgers, *Fourth among Equals: The Autobiography of Bill Rodgers* (2000), p. 166; Burk and Cairncross, *Goodbye, Great Britain*, p. 97; Hickson, *The IMF Crisis*, p. 138; Roy Hattersley, *Who Goes Home? Scenes from a Political Life* (1996), pp. 174–5.

21. PRO CAB 128/60, CM (76) 35, 1 December 1976; Benn, *Against the Tide*, pp. 665–8; Hickson, *The IMF Crisis*, p. 139; Pearce, *Denis Healey*, p. 496; and see PRO CAB 129/193, CP (76) 124, 'A Strategy for Planned Expansion', 30 November 1976 (Shore paper); PRO 129/193, CP (76) 118, 'Economic Strategy – The IMF', 29 November 1976 (Crosland paper).

22. Morgan, *Callaghan*, pp. 548–9; Hickson, *The IMF Crisis*, pp. 140–41; Crosland, *Tony Crosland*, pp. 380–81; Callaghan, *Time and Chance*, pp. 438–9; Hattersley, *Who Goes Home?*, p. 176.

23. *Daily Telegraph*, 2 December 1976; *Daily Mirror*, 2 December 1976; PRO CAB 128/60, CM (76) 36, 2 December 1976; Benn, *Against the Tide*, pp. 670–74, 677–8; Hickson, *The IMF Crisis*, pp. 141–3; Donoughue, *Downing Street Diary*, pp. 110–11.

24. Callaghan, *Time and Chance*, pp. 440–1; Pearce, *Denis Healey*, p. 495; Hickson, *The IMF Crisis*, pp. 144, 146; Burk and Cairncross, *Goodbye, Great Britain*, p. 103; PRO CAB 128/60, CM (76) 38, 7 December 1976; PRO CAB 128/60, CM (76) 39, 7 December 1976; Joel Barnett, *Inside the Treasury* (1982), pp. 105–6; Benn, *Against the Tide*, pp. 683–6; Donoughue, *Downing Street Diary*, pp. 114–15.

25. Callaghan, *Time and Chance*, p. 444; Healey, *The Time of My Life*, p. 431; Morgan, *Callaghan*, pp. 551–2; Benn, *Against the Tide*, p. 693.

26. Hansard, 15 December 1976; Barnett, *Inside the Treasury*, p. 110; Pearce, *Denis Healey*, pp. 498, 500; Hickson, *The IMF Crisis*, pp. 147–8; *Sun*, 16 December 1976; *The Times*, 16 December 1976; Healey, *The Time of My Life*, p. 432; *Daily Express*, 16 December 1976.

27. Kenneth O. Morgan, *The People's Peace: British History since 1945* (Oxford, 1999), pp. 385–6; Benn, *Against the Tide*, p. 690; Phillip Whitehead, *The Writing on the Wall: Britain in the Seventies* (1985), p. 200.

28. Healey, *The Time of My Life*, pp. 432–3; Beckett, *When the Lights Went Out*, pp. 355–6; Donoughue, *Downing Street Diary*, p. 117; on the Treasury's navigational difficulties, see Healey, *The Time of My Life*, pp. 380–81, 427; Jim Tomlinson, 'Economic Policy', in Anthony Seldon and Kevin Hickson (eds.), *New Labour, Old Labour: The Wilson and Callaghan Governments, 1974–1979* (2004), pp. 62–3.

29. Pearce, *Denis Healey*, p. 484; Keith Middlemas, *Power, Competition and the State*, vol. 3: *The End of the Postwar Era: Britain since 1974* (Basingstoke, 1991), pp. 156, 187; David Kynaston, *The City of London*, vol. 4: *A Club No More 1945–2000* (2001), p. 551; Dell, *The Chancellors*, pp. 430, 437; Radice, *Friends and Rivals*, p. 265.

30. Hansard, 15 December 1976; Ken Coates, 'The Choices before Labour', *New Left Review*, 131 (January–February 1982), p. 38.

31. Tony Benn, 'An Interview with Eric Hobsbawm', in Martin Jacques and Francis Mulhern (eds.), *The Forward March of Labour Halted?* (1981), p. 87; Benn, *Against the Tide*, p. xii; Tony Benn, *Conflicts of Interest: Diaries 1977–80* (1990), p. 270; Donoughue, *Downing Street Diary*, pp. 124–5.

32. Ion Trewin (ed.), *The Hugo Young Papers: Thirty Years of British Politics – Off the Record* (2008), p. 99; Dell, *A Strange Eventful History*, pp. 448–9, 452, 460–61; Benn, *Conflicts of Interest*, p. 477.

33. Burk and Cairncross, *Goodbye, Great Britain*, p. xi; Hickson, *The IMF Crisis*, pp. 195–6, 199; Steve Ludlam, 'The Gnomes of Washington: Four Myths of the 1976 IMF Crisis', *Political Studies*, 40 (1992), pp. 713–27; Tomlinson, 'Economic Policy', pp. 61, 66; Peter Hennessy, *Muddling Through: Power, Politics and the Quality of Government in Postwar Britain* (1997), p. 285.

34. David Smith, *The Rise and Fall of Monetarism: The Theory and Politics of an Economic Experiment* (1991), p. 59; Bernard Donoughue, *The Heat of the Kitchen: An Autobiography* (2003), pp. 249–50; Hickson, *The IMF Crisis*, p. 211; Hansard, 22 July 1976; *The Times*, 23 July 1976. On this point I am also indebted to a paper by Duncan Needham, 'Keynesian Consensus to "Sado-monetarism": UK Monetary Policy from Devaluation to Mrs Thatcher', delivered at the 'Reassessing the 1970s' conference at the Centre for Contemporary British History, 7 July 2010.

35. Healey, *The Time of My Life*, pp. 382–3, 434; Hickson, *The IMF Crisis*, pp. 200, 212–13; Kevin Hickson, 'Economic Thought', in Seldon and Hickson (eds.), *New Labour, Old Labour*, pp. 34–5, 46–7.

36. Healey, *The Time of My Life*, pp. 378–9; Richard Holt, *Second amongst Equals: Chancellors of the Exchequer since the Second World War* (2002), p. 183; Robert Skidelsky, 'The Fall of Keynesianism', in David Marquand and Anthony Seldon (eds.), *The Ideas that Shaped Post-war Britain* (1996), pp. 64–5; Benn, *Against the Tide*, p. 619; Donoughue, *Downing Street Diary*, pp. 182, 318.

37. Morgan, *Callaghan*, p. 553; Callaghan, *Time and Chance*, pp. 444–5.

38. *Daily Express*, 24 December 1976; *The Times*, 24 December 1976.

39. *Daily Express*, 3 December 1976; Anthony King and Robert J. Wybrow (eds.), *British Political Opinion 1937–2000: The Gallup Polls* (2001), pp. 171, 313; Alwyn W. Turner, *Crisis? What Crisis? Britain in the 1970s* (2008), p. 189. The Green single is online at http://www.youtube.com/watch?v=64z16Vd69Vs; on Green's departure, see *Daily Express*, 18 March 1978, 20 March 1978; Louis Barfe, *Turned Out Nice Again: The Story of British Light Entertainment* (2008), pp. 291–2; Jeremy Isaacs, *Look Me in the Eye: A Life in Television* (2006), p. 209; Joe Moran, '"Stand Up and Be Counted": Hughie Green, the 1970s and Popular Memory', *History Workshop Journal*, 70 (2010), pp. 173–98.

CHAPTER 22. THE BREAK-UP OF BRITAIN

1. *Daily Mirror*, 11 June 1974; *NME*, 27 April 1974, 9 November 1974.

2. *NME*, 2 November 1974, 19 April 1975; on nostalgia and the Bay City Rollers, see also Alwyn W. Turner, *Crisis? What Crisis? Britain in the 1970s* (2008), pp. 148–9.

3. *NME*, 2 November 1974, 9 November 1974, 19 April 1974.

4. *Daily Mirror*, 10 April 1975, 22 May 1975; *The Times*, 21 May 1975, 3 June 1975, 4 June 1975; *Time*, 22 September 1975.

5. Phillip Whitehead, *The Writing on the Wall: Britain in the Seventies* (1985), p. 296; Bernard Nossiter, *Britain: A Future that Works* (1978), p. 40; *Guardian*, 9 September 1975.

6. *The Times*, 6 February 1975; Kenneth O. Morgan, *Michael Foot: A Life* (2007), pp. 324–5.

7. D. Gareth Evans, *A History of Wales 1906–2000* (Cardiff, 2000), pp, 162–3; George L. Bernstein, *The Myth of Decline: The Rise of Britain since 1945* (2004), p. 484; *The Times*, 12 July 1975, 5 January 1976, 2 April 1976.

8. *The Times*, 6 May 1971; Andrew Marr, *The Battle for Scotland* (1992), pp. 133, 172; Whitehead, *The Writing on the Wall*, p. 287; Willy Maley, 'Cultural Devolution? Representing Scotland in the 1970s', in Bart Moore-Gilbert (ed.), *The Arts in the 1970s: Cultural Closure?* (1994), p. 83; Bernstein, *The Myth of Decline*, pp. 464, 470; David Childs, *Britain since 1945: A Political History* (1979), p. 269; Keith Middlemas, *Power, Competition and the State*, vol. 3: *The End of the Postwar Era: Britain since 1974* (Basingstoke, 1991), p. 189.

9. Martin Johnes, 'A Prince, a King and a Referendum: Rugby, Politics and Nationhood in Wales, 1969–1979', *Journal of British Studies*, 47 (2008), pp. 129–48; *The Times*, 19 March 1974, 21 March 1974; Trevor Fishlock, *Wales and the Welsh* (1972), p. 7; Phil Bennett, *The Autobiography* (2003), p. 33; Richard Holt, *Sport and the British: A Modern History* (Oxford, 1990), pp. 252–3; Martin Polley, *Moving the Goalposts: A History of Sport and Society since 1945* (1998), p. 60.

10. Trevor Fishlock, *Talking of Wales: A Companion to Wales and the Welsh* (1976), p. 47; Bernstein, *The Myth of Decline*, pp. 486–8; Kenneth O. Morgan, *Rebirth of a Nation: Wales, 1880–1980* (Cardiff, 1981), p. 389; Bernard Levin, *The Pendulum Years: Britain in the Sixties* (1970), p. 159; Rhys Evans, *Gwynfor Evans: A Portrait of a Patriot* (Talybont, 2008), pp. 259–66, 341.

11. Ibid., pp. 325–6, 335, 343–4; Kenneth O. Morgan, *Callaghan: A Life* (Oxford, 1997), p. 631; Hansard, 16 December 1976 (Abse), 3 February 1975 (Kinnock); Martin Westlake, *Kinnock: The Biography* (2001), pp. 122–3; Robert Harris, *The Making of Neil Kinnock* (1984), pp. 100–101; Morgan, *Rebirth of a Nation*, p. 134.

12. Marr, *The Battle for Scotland*, pp. 66–72, 74–5, 115, 117–20; James J. Kellas, 'Scottish Nationalism', in David Butler and Michael Pinto-Duschinsky (eds.), *The British General Election of 1970* (1971), pp. 446–62; Alan Sked and Chris Cook, *Post-war Britain: A Political History* (1988), pp. 240, 244; Whitehead, *The Writing on the Wall*, p. 290.

13. *Time*, 14 May 1973; Daniel Yergin, *The Prize: The Epic Quest for Oil, Money and Power* (New York, 1992), pp. 668–9; *The Times*, 15 May 1970, 28 May 1970, 3 June 1970, 20 October 1970; *Daily Express*, 21 October 1970.

14. *Time*, 14 May 1973, 19 September 1975; *New York Times Magazine*, 2 November 1975; Yergin, *The Prize*, p. 669; Tony Benn, *Against the Tide: Diaries 1973–1976* (1989), p. 419.

15. Andy Beckett, *When the Lights Went Out: Britain in the Seventies* (2009), pp. 188–9; *Time*, 29 September 1975; Edmund Dell, *A Strange Eventful History:*

Democratic Socialism in Britain (2000), p. 439; Yergin, *The Prize*, p. 670; *New York Times Magazine*, 2 November 1975.

16. *The Times*, 2 March 1973, 12 July 1974, 4 November 1975; Andrew Marr, *A History of Modern Britain* (2007), pp. 437–8; Christopher Harvie, *Fool's Gold: The Story of North Sea Oil* (1995), pp. 89–90 and *passim*; Beckett, *When the Lights Went Out*, p. 198; Marr, *The Battle for Scotland*, p. 132.

17. *The Times*, 18 June 1974, 12 December 1974, 24 June 1975; *Time*, 14 May 1973, 29 September 1975; Beckett, *When the Lights Went Out*, pp. 203–5.

18. Graham McColl, *'78: How a Nation Lost the World Cup* (2006), p. 83; *The Times*, 18 April 1974; *Time*, 8 April 1974, 30 September 1974; 'SNP Seizes on North Sea Oil Memo', 29 December 2005, http://news.bbc.co.uk/1/hi/scotland/4567138.stm; *Scotland on Sunday*, 1 January 2006; *Guardian*, 30 January 2006. The McCrone report ('The Economics of Nationalism Re-examined') is online at http://www.oilofscotland.org/MccronereportScottishOffice.pdf.

19. Marr, *The Battle for Scotland*, pp. 132, 135; *The Times*, 26 May 1973, 18 September 1973; Whitehead, *The Writing on the Wall*, pp. 292–3; Michael Billington, *State of the Nation: British Theatre since 1945* (2007), pp. 214–15.

20. *The Times*, 2 November 1973, 9 November 1973, 27 October 1974; *Time*, 28 October 1974; Marr, *The Battle for Scotland*, p. 137; David Butler and Dennis Kavanagh, *The British General Election of October 1974* (1975), pp. 345–9.

21. Marr, *The Battle for Scotland*, pp. 121–4, 136, 150; Dilys M. Hill, 'Devolution', in Anthony Seldon and Kevin Hickson (eds.), *New Labour, Old Labour: The Wilson and Callaghan Governments, 1974–1979* (2004), pp. 227–8; *The Times*, 4 October 1973, 27 September 1974; *Scotsman*, 10 August 2010.

22. Ivor Crewe, Bö Sarlvik and James Alt, 'Partisan Dealignment in Britain 1964–1974', *British Journal of Political Science*, 7:2 (1977), pp. 129–90; Dennis Kavanagh, *Thatcherism and British Politics: The End of Consensus?* (Oxford, 1987), pp. 144–5; Anthony Sampson, *The New Anatomy of Britain* (1971), p. 667; Tom Nairn, *The Break-up of Britain: Crisis and Neo-nationalism* (1977), pp. 13, 45, 51, 67, 69, 89; Peter Mandler, *The English National Character: The History of an Idea from Edmund Burke to Tony Blair* (New Haven, 2006), pp. 226–7; Sir Arthur Bryant, 'The Heart of a Nation', *Illustrated London News*, February 1981, p. 24.

23. Marr, *The Battle for Scotland*, p. 149; *The Times*, 17 November 1975; Peter Clarke, *Hope and Glory: Britain 1900–1990* (1996), p. 322; Sked and Cook, *Post-war Britain*, p. 326; *Time*, 28 October 1974.

24. Whitehead, *The Writing on the Wall*, p. 289; Maley, 'Cultural Devolution?', p. 84; H. M. Drucker and Gordon Brown, *The Politics of Nationalism and Devolution* (1980), p. 76; Marr, *The Battle for Scotland*, pp. 134–5, 148, 150–51; Evans, *Gwynfor Evans*, pp. 341–6, 351–2 and *passim*.

25. *Sunday Mail*, 27 February 1977; Maley, 'Cultural Devolution?', p. 84; David Butler and Dennis Kavanagh, *The British General Election of 1979* (1980), p. 100; Marr, *The Battle for Scotland*, p. 156; *The Times*, 3 February 1977, 5 May 1977, 7 May 1977; Whitehead, *The Writing on the Wall*, pp. 296–7.

26. Philip Ziegler, *Wilson: The Authorized Life* (1993), pp. 452–3; Barbara Castle, *The Castle Diaries 1974–1976* (1980), p. 153; Butler and Kavanagh, *The British*

General Election of 1979, p. 105; Bernard Donoughue, *Downing Street Diary*, vol. 1: *With Harold Wilson in No. 10* (2005), pp. 284–5.

27. *The Times*, 17 November 1975, 28 November 1975; Marr, *The Battle for Scotland*, p. 145.

28. Ibid., p. 155; Morgan, *Michael Foot*, pp. 355, 358; Hansard, 16 December 1976; *The Times*, 17 December 1976.

29. *The Times*, 14 November 1977; Whitehead, *The Writing on the Wall*, p. 295; Marr, *The Battle for Scotland*, pp. 141–8, 156–8; Hansard, 14 November 1977, 18 January 1977; Westlake, *Kinnock*, p. 122.

30. *The Times*, 22 February 1975, 2 December 1976, 9 December 1976; speech in Glasgow, 21 February 1975, TFW; Butler and Kavanagh, *The British General Election of 1979*, pp. 82, 109; John Campbell, *Margaret Thatcher*, vol. 1: *The Grocer's Daughter* (2000), pp. 396–8. For the Tory manifesto, see http://www.conservativemanifesto.com/1979/.

31. *The Times*, 23 February 1977, 26 January 1978, 27 January 1978; Hill, 'Devolution', pp. 230–31; Butler and Kavanagh, *The British General Election of 1979*, pp. 36, 107; Hansard, 25 January 1978; Morgan, *Michael Foot*, pp. 356–8.

32. Whitehead, *The Writing on the Wall*, p. 298; Morgan, *Michael Foot*, p. 358; Morgan, *Callaghan*, pp. 631–2; Evans, *Gwynfor Evans*, pp. 369–71.

33. *The Times*, 27 January 1978, 25 March 1978, 10 May 1978; McColl, '78, pp. 84–5.

34. *Daily Mail*, 16 January 1978; Turner, *Crisis? What Crisis?*, p. 228.

35. *The Times*, 11 May 1978, 26 May 1978, 27 May 1978, 29 May 1978.

36. *Scotsman*, 31 May 1978, 1 June 1978; *The Times*, 31 May 1978, 1 June 1978, 2 June 1978.

37. McColl, '78, pp. 2–4; *The Times*, 26 May 1978; *Scotsman*, 26 May 1978.

38. Holt, *Sport and the British*, pp. 259–61; Jeffrey Hill, *Sport, Leisure and Culture in Twentieth-century Britain* (Basingstoke, 2002), p. 15; McColl, '78, pp. 50–51, 81.

39. McColl, '78, pp. 7, 18, 23–6, 79, 198; *Daily Mirror*, 6 June 1977; *The Times*, 6 June 1977.

40. McColl, '78, pp. 54, 63, 69–71; *Daily Express*, 31 May 1978; *The Times*, 4 May 1978, 20 May 1978, 8 June 1978, 26 June 1978; *Daily Mirror*, 20 April 1978.

41. *Daily Express*, 12 May 1978; McColl, '78, pp. 56–7.

42. McColl, '78, pp. 90–92, 96–7, 152–6.

43. *Scotsman*, 30 December 2008; McColl, '78, pp. 114–24; *Observer*, 4 June 1978.

44. *Daily Express*, 5 June 1978, 6 June 1978; McColl, '78, pp. 129–48; *The Times*, 7 June 1978.

45. McColl, '78, pp. 149, 166; *The Times*, 8 June 1978; for the television footage, see http://www.youtube.com/watch?v=jWuOhv1XuSs.

46. McColl, '78, pp. 167–8, 184; *Daily Mirror*, 9 June 1978; *Daily Express*, 9 June 1978, 10 June 1978; *The Times*, 9 June 1978.

47. *The Times*, 13 June 1978; *Observer*, 11 June 1978.

48. *Scotsman*, 12 June 1978; *The Times*, 16 June 1978; McColl, '78, pp. 251–2.

49. *Daily Telegraph*, 29 December 2008; *Scotsman*, 31 December 2008; *Daily Express*, 7 June 1978.

50. *Daily Express*, 14 June 1978, 16 June 1978.

CHAPTER 23. NO FUN AT ALL

1. *Daily Express*, 9 January 1975; *The Times*, 2 June 1975; *Rolling Stone*, 17 July 1975.

2. *Rolling Stone*, 21 September 1973; *Time*, 9 July 1973, 31 December 1973; *The Times*, 29 July 1974; *Daily Express*, 9 January 1975.

3. Dave Laing, *One Chord Wonders: Power and Meaning in Punk Rock* (Milton Keynes, 1985), pp. 4–7; Jon Savage, *England's Dreaming: Sex Pistols and Punk Rock* (2005), p. 124; *Melody Maker*, 28 June 1975; for chart data, see www.everyhit.com.

4. Paul Hegarty and Martin Halliwell, *Beyond and Before: Progressive Rock since the 1960s* (2011), pp. 2, 75–7, 95, 99–100; and see Edward Macan, *Rocking the Classics: English Progressive Rock and the Counterculture* (Oxford, 1997); Paul Stump, *The Music's All that Matters: A History of Progressive Rock* (1997); Bill Martin, *Listening to the Future: The Time of Progressive Rock, 1968–1978* (Chicago, 1998).

5. Hegarty and Halliwell, *Beyond and Before*, p. 119; *Time*, 13 June 1977. Images of Gabriel as the Slipperman, which really have to be seen to be believed, are all over the Internet.

6. Dave Harker, 'Blood on the Tracks: Popular Music in the 1970s', in Bart Moore-Gilbert (ed.), *The Arts in the 1970s: Cultural Closure?* (1994), p. 245; Keith Emerson, *Pictures of an Exhibitionist* (2004), p. 292; *Daily Express*, 14 June 1977.

7. *NME*, 19 June 1976.

8. *The Times*, 30 July 1977.

9. Robert Walser, *Running with the Devil: Power, Gender and Madness in Heavy Metal Music* (1993), p. x; Deena Weinstein, *Heavy Metal: The Music and its Culture* (New York, 2000), pp. 75, 93–120; Dave Haslam, *Not Abba: The Real Story of the 1970s* (2005), pp. 47, 72; *Guardian*, 9 July 2011.

10. Laing, *One Chord Wonders*, pp. 6–9; Savage, *England's Dreaming*, pp. 81, 124; Haslam, *Not Abba*, p. 183.

11. Savage, *England's Dreaming*, pp. 8–11, 23–44, 47–69.

12. Laing, *One Chord Wonders*, pp. 11–13, 23, 40; Savage, *England's Dreaming*, pp. 58–65, 86–92, 131; *NME*, 27 November 1976. On the etymology of 'punk', see http://www.jonsavage.com/punk/punk-etymology/; on American punk, see Clinton Heylin, *From the Velvets to the Voidoids: The Birth of American Punk Rock* (2005).

13. Savage, *England's Dreaming*, pp. 71–2, 77–80, 124–9.

14. Ibid., pp. 143–7, 157, 191–2, 254–5.

15. *NME*, 27 December 1975, 21 February 1976, 11 September 1976.

16. Savage, *England's Dreaming*, pp. 150, 172, 222, 224, 255; *NME*, 2 October 1976.

17. *Guardian*, 3 December 1976; Savage, *England's Dreaming*, pp. 257–60.

18. Laing, *One Chord Wonders*, pp. 36–7; *Daily Mirror*, 2 December 1976; *Evening Standard*, 2 December 1976; Savage, *England's Dreaming*, pp. 263–4.

19. *Guardian*, 3 December 1976; *Daily Mail*, 3 December 1976; *Daily Express*, 3 December 1976; Savage, *England's Dreaming*, p. 266.

20. Ibid., pp. 267–8, 271–3, 357; *NME*, 11 December 1976.

21. Savage, *England's Dreaming*, pp. 270, 273, 286–8, 308, 315–20, 345; *Daily Express*, 11 March 1977; *Evening Standard*, 17 March 1977.

22. Savage, *England's Dreaming*, pp. 273, 278, 293–5, 301, 374; Laing, *One Chord Wonders*, p. 32; Peter York, *Style Wars* (1980), pp. 44–5.

23. Ibid., pp. 22, 32, 131; Savage, *England's Dreaming*, pp. 281–2, 330; *NME*, 13 November 1976, 19 March 1977.

24. *Observer*, 31 January 1977.

25. Laing, *One Chord Wonders*, pp. 27, 46–8, 66, 76; Savage, *England's Dreaming*, pp. 101, 189; Haslam, *Not Abba*, p. 229.

26. *NME*, 27 November 1976, 1 October 1977; York, *Style Wars*, p. 137; Laing, *One Chord Wonders*, p. 93; Savage, *England's Dreaming*, p. 241; John A. Walker, *Left Shift: Radical Art in 1970s Britain* (2002), p. 188.

27. *Melody Maker*, 4 June 1977; Laing, *One Chord Wonders*, pp. 82–3, 85; *NME*, 1 October 1977.

28. *The Times*, 21 November 1973; Laing, *One Chord Wonders*, pp. 22, 53, 60–61, 63; *NME*, 21 February 1976.

29. Haslam, *Not Abba*, pp. 239–40, 242, 252; Laing, *One Chord Wonders*, pp. 13–14, 16–17; Mark Perry, *Sniffin' Glue and Other Rock 'n' Roll Habits* (2009); James Nice, *Shadowplayers: The Rise and Fall of Factory Records* (2010), pp. 5–51.

30. Leon Hunt, *British Low Culture: From Safari Suits to Sexploitation* (1998), p. 58; Laing, *One Chord Wonders*, pp. 24–5; York, *Style Wars*, pp. 25, 48.

31. Savage, *England's Dreaming*, pp. 9, 39, 99; Iain Chambers, *Popular Culture: The Metropolitan Experience* (1986), pp. 171–2; *NME*, 21 February 1976; Laing, *One Chord Wonders*, pp. 22, 100; *Sounds*, 27 November 1976.

32. *Mix*, 1 January 1999; *NME*, 7 May 1977, 1 October 1977; *Daily Express*, 14 June 1977.

33. *NME*, 2 October 1976, 13 November 1976; *New Society*, 22 December 1977; Laing, *One Chord Wonders*, p. 119; *Time*, 11 July 1977; *Daily Mirror*, 22 June 1977.

34. Alexander Walker, *National Heroes: British Cinema in the Seventies and Eighties* (1985), p. 234; Bill Williamson, *The Temper of the Times: British Society since World War II* (Oxford, 1990), pp. 202–4; Ben Pimlott, 'The North East: Back to the 1930s?', *Political Quarterly*, 52:1 (January–March 1981), pp. 51–63; Alison Pressley, *The Seventies: Good Times, Bad Taste* (2002), p. 11.

35. Savage, *England's Dreaming*, pp. 30–6, 278; David Hatch and Stephen Milward, *From Blues to Rock: An Analytical History of Pop Music* (1989), p. 170.

36. Simon Frith, *Sound Effects* (New York, 1981), p. 161; Laing, *One Chord Wonders*, pp. 15, 57, 29, 71; Savage, *England's Dreaming*, p. xv; *NME*, 28 October 1978.

37. *Daily Express*, 14 June 1977; York, *Style Wars*, p. 206; Laing, *One Chord Wonders*, pp. 121–2.

38. Derek Jarman, *Dancing Ledge* (1993), p. 164; *The Times*, 5 July 1977.

39. *The Times*, 30 July 1977; Laing, *One Chord Wonders*, p. 126; *NME*, 4 December 1976.

40. Simon Reynolds, *Rip It up and Start Again: Post-punk, 1978–1984* (2005), pp. 6–11, 111; *NME*, 7 May 1977.

41. *NME*, 11 December 1976; Savage, *England's Dreaming*, pp. 232–3, 235, 330; Laing, *One Chord Wonders*, p. 29.

42. *NME*, 11 December 1976; Savage, *England's Dreaming*, pp. 237–8, 398, 488; Chambers, *Popular Culture*, pp. 166, 172, 178; and see Dick Hebdige, *Subculture: The Meaning of Style* (1979), if you dare.

43. Savage, *England's Dreaming*, pp. 314–15, 348–9, 364–5; for chart data, see www.everyhit.com.

44. Savage, *England's Dreaming*, pp. 230, 322, 365; *Daily Mirror*, 13 June 1977; *NME*, 15 July 1977; Hansard, 26 July 1977; Hebdige, *Subculture*, p. 158.

45. *Daily Mirror*, 21 June 1977; *The Times*, 22 June 1977; Savage, *England's Dreaming*, pp. 365–6, 425, 479; Walker, *National Heroes*, pp. 234–5; *Guardian*, 10 November 1977; *Sun*, 25 November 1977.

46. John Lydon, with Keith and Kent Zimmermann, *Rotten: No Irish, No Blacks, No Dogs* (2008), p. 244; *Daily Express*, 7 January 1978, 10 January 1978; *Daily Mirror*, 16 January 1978, 20 January 1978; Savage, *England's Dreaming*, pp. 443–69, 522–3, 528–9.

47. Laing, *One Chord Wonders*, pp. 106, 109, 120; York, *Style Wars*, p. 43; *The Times*, 18 November 1980.

48. Laing, *One Chord Wonders*, p. 117; Reynolds, *Rip It up and Start Again*, passim; *Guardian*, 20 October 2006; Ian MacDonald, *The People's Music* (2003), pp. 200–1.

49. Laing, *One Chord Wonders*, p. 33; Harker, 'Blood on the Tracks', pp. 242–3; for chart data, see www.everyhit.com.

50. Gary Kemp, *I Know This Much* (2009), p. 61; Hegarty and Halliwell, *Beyond and Before*, pp. 163–79; *NME*, 18 December 1976, 10 September 1977.

51. Laing, *One Chord Wonders*, p. 34; York, *Style Wars*, pp. 37–8.

52. *The Times*, 21 June 1975; Harker, 'Blood on the Tracks', pp. 243–4. For sales figures, see the BPI database at http://www.bpi.co.uk/visitors-area/article/certified-awards.aspx.

53. *The Times*, 7 June 1977; York, *Style Wars*, pp. 163–77.

CHAPTER 24. CARNIVAL TIME

1. *Daily Mirror*, 28 August 1976; *The Times*, 28 August 1976, 26 August 1975.

2. *Daily Mirror*, 30 August 1976; Emma Griffiths, 'Remembering the Notting Hill Riot', http://news.bbc.co.uk/1/hi/england/london/5275542.stm; *The Times*, 31 August 1976; *Daily Mirror*, 31 August 1976; Mike Phillips and Trevor Phillips, *Windrush: The Irresistible Rise of Multi-racial Britain* (1999), p. 282.

3. *Daily Mail*, 1 September 1976; *Daily Mirror*, 1 September 1976; *Daily Express*, 1 September 1976; *Daily Telegraph*, 1 September 1976, 2 September 1976; *Evening News*, 1 September 1976; and see the excellent analysis of the press coverage in Peter Jackson, 'Street Life: The Politics of Carnival', *Environment and Planning D: Society and Space*, 6 (1988), pp. 217–21.

4. *Daily Mirror*, 1 September 1976; *Evening Standard*, 1 September 1976; Jackson, 'Street Life', p. 219; John Muncie, Gordon Hughes and Eugene McLaughlin, *Youth Justice: Critical Readings* (2002), p. 62; Sir Robert Mark, *In the Office of Constable* (1978), p. 222; *Guardian*, 1 September 1976.

5. *Guardian*, 17 August 2002; *Daily Express*, 29 August 1977, 30 August 1977.

6. *The Times*, 1 September 1976.

7. Shamit Saggar, *Race and Politics in Britain* (Hemel Hempstead, 1992), pp. 41, 45, 53; *The Times*, 14 February 1978.

8. Hansard, 8 July 1976; *The Times*, 10 July 1976, 16 October 1980; Harry Golbourne, *Race Relations in Britain since 1945* (Basingstoke, 1998), pp. 102–3, 109; Alwyn W. Turner, *Crisis? What Crisis? Britain in the 1970s* (2008), pp. 207–8; Louis Barfe, *Turned Out Nice Again: The Story of British Light Entertainment* (2008), pp. 122–3, 289–90; Bernard Donoughue, *Downing Street Diary*, vol. 2: *With James Callaghan in No. 10* (2008), p. 152. On the Minstrels, see also the excellent BBC Four documentary *Black and White Minstrel Show: Revisited* (2004).

9. Bernard Nossiter, *Britain: A Future that Works* (1978), p. 168; Phillips and Phillips, *Windrush*, p. 256; Jerry White, *London in the Twentieth Century* (2001), p. 167; Robert Winder, *Bloody Foreigners: The Story of Immigration to Britain* (2004), p. 298; Martin Polley, *Moving the Goalposts: A History of Sport and Society since 1945* (1998), pp. 147–8; on the Three Degrees, see Dave Bowler and Jas Bains, *Samba in the Smethwick End: Regis, Cunningham, Batson and the Football Revolution* (2000). My thanks to Dr Joe Street for bringing to my attention this fine book about the Black Country's perennial whipping boys.

10. Hunter Davies, *The Glory Game* (1972), pp. 30, 172; Julian Shea, 'From Brisbane Road to the Bernabeu', http://news.bbc.co.uk/sport1/hi/football/8149282. stm; 'Inside Out: Black Flash', http://www.bbc.co.uk/insideout/westmidlands/series5/black_flash_footballers.shtml; *The Times*, 3 March 1981.

11. Stuart Hall *et al.*, *Policing the Crisis: Mugging, the State and Law and Order* (Basingstoke, 1978), pp. 342–3; Colin Brown, *Black and White Britain* (1984), p. 157; Golbourne, *Race Relations in Britain since 1945*; White, *London in the Twentieth Century*, pp. 163–4.

12. Paul Harrison, *Inside the Inner City: Life under the Cutting Edge* (1983), pp. 229–30, 382; *The Times*, 8 October 1985; White, *London in the Twentieth Century*, pp. 73, 163–4; 'History of Broadwater Farm', http://www.haringey.gov.uk/index/community_and_leisure/neighbourhoods/broadwaterfarm/historyofbroadwaterfarm.htm.

13. White, *London in the Twentieth Century*, pp. 163, 282; Hall *et al.*, *Policing the Crisis*, p. 244; Michael Pratt, *Mugging as a Social Problem* (1980).

14. *The Times*, 4 October 1975, 16 May 1975, 26 October 1976, 27 October 1976; Beatrix Campbell, *The Iron Ladies: Why Do Women Vote Tory?* (1987), p. 141.

15. Hansard, 10 July 1975; *The Times*, 14 April 1981, 28 December 1981, 26 October 1982; Turner, *Crisis? What Crisis?*, pp. 215–16; Zig Layton-Henry, *The Politics of Immigration: Immigration, Race and Race Relations in Post-war Britain* (Oxford, 1992), p. 126; Maureen Cain, *Society and the Policeman's Role* (1973), p. 117.

16. *The Times*, 1 September 1976, 4 December 1979; White, *London in the Twentieth Century*, pp. 297–8, 301; Phillips and Phillips, *Windrush*, pp. 302–3.

17. *The Times*, 8 January 1978, 9 January 1978; Turner, *Crisis? What Crisis?*, pp. 216–7; Phillips and Phillips, *Windrush*, pp. 295–9, 307–9; Hall *et al.*, *Policing the Crisis*, p. 357; Dave Haslam, *Not Abba: The Real Story of the 1970s* (2005), pp. 102, 159–60; Linton Kwesi Johnson, *Dread Beat an' Blood* (poems, pub. 1975); Linton Kwesi Johnson, *Inglan is a Bitch* (1980); interview with Linton Kwesi Johnson by

Debi Ghose, http://brixtonblog.wordpress.com/2011/04/28/interview-linton-kwesi-johnson/.

18. Nossiter, *Britain: A Future that Works*, p. 169; Ken Pryce, *Endless Pressure: A Study of West Indian Lifestyles in Bristol* (1979); Alexander Walker, *National Heroes: British Cinema in the Seventies and Eighties* (1985), p. 241; Julia Toppin, 'Pressure', www.screenonline.org.uk/film/id/480497/; Phillips and Phillips, *Windrush*, pp. 349–50, 352; *The Times*, 4 February 1978.

19. *New Society*, November 1969; Jeremy Seabrook, *What Went Wrong? Working People and the Ideals of the Labour Movement* (1978), pp. 160–4; Saggar, *Race and Politics in Britain*, pp. 177–8; Walker, *National Heroes*, p. 242.

20. Dennis Potter, *Brimstone and Treacle* (1978), pp. 32–3; Turner, *Crisis? What Crisis?*, p. 224. Note that there are slight differences between Potter's published text and what was actually said on screen.

21. David Butler and Dennis Kavanagh, *The British General Election of February 1974* (1974), p. 336; Martin Walker, *The National Front* (1977), pp. 9, 149–51, 153–4, 160, 166.

22. *The Times*, 17 June 1974, 28 February 1975; Richard Clutterbuck, *Britain in Agony: The Growth of Political Violence* (1978), pp. 152–3, 159–61, 162–3, 239; and see the files at PRO HO 233, Scarman Inquiry into Red Lion Square Disorders: minutes, evidence and papers.

23. John Tomlinson, *Left, Right: The March of Political Extremism in Britain* (1981), p. 37; Clutterbuck, *Britain in Agony*, pp. 238–9; Nossiter, *Britain: A Future that Works*, p. 177. This particular edition of *Panorama*, 'F Troop, Treatment and the Half-way Line' (14 November 1977) is on YouTube.

24. Martin Harrop, Judith England and Christopher T. Husbands, 'The Bases of National Front Support', *Political Studies*, 28:2 (June 1980), pp. 271–83; Annie Phizacklea and Robert Miles, *Labour and Racism* (1980); Saggar, *Race and Politics in Britain*, p. 181; Seabrook, *What Went Wrong?*, pp. 205, 222.

25. Walker, *The National Front*, p. 217; Tomlinson, *Left, Right*, p. 31; David Robins and Philip Cohen, *Knuckle Sandwich: Growing up in the Working-class City* (Harmondsworth, 1978), pp. 199, 202, 168; Seabrook, *What Went Wrong?* p. 93.

26. *The Times*, 5 May 1976, 18 May 1976, 19 May 1976, 22 May 1976; *Daily Express*, 5 May 1976, 7 May 1976; Hall *et al.*, *Policing the Crisis*, p. 335; Walker, *The National Front*, pp. 196–7; Hansard, 24 May 1976.

27. *The Times*, 27 May 1976, 1 June 1976; Walker, *The National Front*, pp. 198–9.

28. *The Times*, 7 June 1976, 8 June 1976; 17 June 1976; *Daily Mirror*, 7 June 1976; Hall *et al.*, *Policing the Crisis*, p. 337; Walker, *The National Front*, p. 199; Winder, *Bloody Foreigners*, pp. 301.

29. John Street, *Rebel Rock: The Politics of Popular Music* (Oxford, 1986), pp. 74–5; *Observer*, 20 April 2008; *NME*, 11 September 1976; Dave Laing, *One Chord Wonders: Power and Meaning in Punk Rock* (Milton Keynes, 1985), p. 110.

30. Clutterbuck, *Britain in Agony*, pp. 213–14, 234–6; Tomlinson, *Left, Right*, pp. 85–6, 90; *Observer*, 20 April 2008; Andy Beckett, *When the Lights Went Out: Britain in the Seventies* (2009), p. 450; Jon Savage, *England's Dreaming: Sex Pistols and Punk Rock* (2005), pp. 482, 484; Turner, *Crisis? What Crisis?*, p. 223; and see David Widgery, *Beating Time: Riot 'n' Race 'n' Rock 'n' Roll* (1986).

31. Tomlinson, *Left, Right*, p. 85; Clutterbuck, *Britain in Agony*, pp. 214–19; *The Times*, 15 August 1977, 20 August 1977.

32. *The Times*, 15 August 1977; *Guardian*, 15 August 1977; Clutterbuck, *Britain in Agony*, pp. 220–21; Saggar, *Race and Politics in Britain*, pp. 183–4; Dave Haslam, *Not Abba: The Real Story of the 1970s* (2005), p. 278; Tony Benn, *Conflicts of Interest: Diaries 1977–80* (1990), p. 345. On the ANL, Dave Renton, *When We Touched the Sky: The Anti-Nazi League 1977–1981* (2006) is vigorous but excessively partisan.

33. Ken Lunn, 'Complex Encounters: Trade Unions, Immigration and Racism', in John McIlroy, Nina Fishman and Alan Campbell (eds.), *The High Tide of British Trade Unionism: Trade Unions and Industrial Politics, 1964–1979* (Monmouth, 2007), p. 85; Phillip Whitehead, *The Writing on the Wall: Britain in the Seventies* (1985), p. 233; Tomlinson, *Left, Right*, pp. 123–4; Saggar, *Race and Politics in Britain*, pp. 182, 184; Mark Garnett, *From Anger to Apathy: The British Experience since 1975* (2007), pp. 81, 84.

34. Alan Clark, *Diaries: Into Politics 1972–1982*, ed. Ion Trewin (2001), p. 112; Hailsham diary, 2 November 1977, TFW.

35. Walker, *The National Front*, pp. 113, 115; Simon Heffer, *Like the Roman: The Life of Enoch Powell* (1998), p. 778; *The Times*, 5 October 1976, 6 October 1976; Jeremy Seabrook, *City Close-up* (Harmondsworth, 1971), p. 59.

36. Saggar, *Race and Politics in Britain*, pp. 120, 122; E. H. H. Green, *Thatcher* (2006), pp. 134–6; message to *CRC Journal*, 1 June 1976, TFW; *Finchley Times*, 9 November 1976, TFW; *The Times*, 14 February 1977.

37. Saggar, *Race and Politics in Britain*, pp. 121, 125, 135, 182; Green, *Thatcher*, pp. 131, 133, 135; Nigel Lawson, 'Thoughts on "Implementing Our Strategy"', 15 January 1978, TFW.

38. Interview for *World in Action*, 27 January 1978, TFW; *Observer*, 25 February 1979; John Campbell, *Margaret Thatcher*, vol. 1: *The Grocer's Daughter* (2000), pp. 399–400; Michael Cockerell, *Live from Number 10: The Inside Story of Prime Ministers and Television* (1989), p. 239; Andrew Denham and Mark Garnett, *Keith Joseph* (Chesham, 2001, pb. 2002), pp. 314–15.

39. Donoughue, *Downing Street Diary*, vol. 2, p. 284; Hansard, 7 February 1978, 25 July 1978; *Sunday Times*, 26 February 1978; Mark Garnett and Ian Aitken, *Splendid! Splendid! The Authorized Biography of Willie Whitelaw* (2003), pp. 231–2.

40. Campbell, *The Grocer's Daughter*, p. 400; Saggar, *Race and Politics in Britain*, p. 125; Green, *Thatcher*, p. 136; Donoughue, *Downing Street Diary*, p. 289.

41. *The Times*, 4 March 1978.

42. Radio interview for IRN, 3 March 1978, TFW; Campbell, *The Grocer's Daughter*, pp. 400–401.

CHAPTER 25. A HOT, HOT DAY

1. *Daily Mirror*, 24 June 1976, 25 June 1976; *Daily Express*, 25 June 1976.

2. *Time*, 6 September 1976; *Guardian*, 17 May 2006; Ian Currie, 'Understanding Weather: The 1976 Drought', http://www.bbc.co.uk/weather/features/understanding/1976_drought.shtml.

3. *The Times*, 5 August 1976, 6 August 1976, 14 August 1976, 1 September 1976; *Time*, 6 September 1976; *Independent*, 17 May 2006; *Guardian*, 17 May 2006.

4. Bernard Donoughue, *Downing Street Diary*, vol. 2: *With James Callaghan in No. 10* (2008), p. 50; Russell Davies (ed.), *The Kenneth Williams Diaries* (1993, pb. 1994), p. 521; Ian McEwan, *The Cement Garden* (1978), p. 71; and see Phil Tinline's insightful essay in the *Guardian*, 26 February 2005.

5. John Goodwin (ed.), *Peter Hall's Diaries: The Story of a Dramatic Battle* (1983), pp. 243, 247–51, 252–3.

6. Joe Rogaly, *Grunwick* (Harmondsworth, 1977), pp. 9–14; Lord Scarman, *Report of a Court of Inquiry under the Rt Hon Lord Justice Scarman*, Cmnd 6922 (1977), pp. 6–7; Andy Beckett, *When the Lights Went Out: Britain in the Seventies* (2009), pp. 360–2.

7. Scarman, *Report*, pp. 5, 15–16; Rogaly, *Grunwick*, pp. 29–33; *Sunday Times*, 26 June 1977; Richard Clutterbuck, *Britain in Agony: The Growth of Political Violence* (1978), pp. 193–4.

8. Scarman, *Report*, pp. 16–18; Rogaly, *Grunwick*, pp. 37–8; Clutterbuck, *Britain in Agony*, p. 194; George Ward, *Fort Grunwick* (1978), p. 5.

9. Scarman, *Report*, pp. 7–10; Rogaly, *Grunwick*, pp. 16–19, 171–2.

10. Scarman, *Report*, p. 8; Rogaly, *Grunwick*, pp. 17, 51–2, 54; Jack McGowan, '"Dispute", "Battle", "Siege", "Farce"? Grunwick 30 Years On', *Contemporary British History*, 22:3 (2008), p. 391.

11. Rogaly, *Grunwick*, pp. 60, 64, 69; Beckett, *When the Lights Went Out*, pp. 365–6, 372–3.

12. Rogaly, *Grunwick*, pp. 23–4, 28, 38.

13. Beckett, *When the Lights Went Out*, pp. 369–70; Clutterbuck, *Britain in Agony*, p. 197; Rogaly, *Grunwick*, p. 13.

14. Ibid., pp. 38–9; Scarman, *Report*, pp. 5, 18–19; McGowan, 'Grunwick 30 Years On', pp. 389–90; David McNee, *McNee's Law: The Memoirs of Sir David McNee* (1983), pp. 100–101.

15. Rogaly, *Grunwick*, pp. 21–2, 44, 46, 68; *The Times*, 30 June 1977; Beckett, *When the Lights Went Out*, pp. 375–6, 382.

16. Scarman, *Report*, pp. 12–14; *The Times*, 19 May 1977; Rogaly, *Grunwick*, p. 20; Clutterbuck, *Britain in Agony*, p. 198; Beckett, *When the Lights Went Out*, pp. 371, 373, 384, 391.

17. Rogaly, *Grunwick*, pp. 53, 81–2; Clutterbuck, *Britain in Agony*, pp. 198–9; John Tomlinson, *Left, Right: The Rise of Political Extremism in Britain* (1981), pp. 85–6.

18. *The Times*, 14 June 1977, 15 June 1977; Clutterbuck, *Britain in Agony*, p. 199; Beckett, *When the Lights Went Out*, p. 385.

19. Clutterbuck, *Britain in Agony*, p. 199; Beckett, *When the Lights Went Out*, pp. 387–8; Rogaly, *Grunwick*, pp. 84–5, 87.

20. *The Times*, 15 June 1977, 16 June 1977, 17 June 1977, 20 June 1977, 21 June 1977; Clutterbuck, *Britain in Agony*, pp. 190, 200–201; Beckett, *When the Lights Went Out*, p. 387; and see the BBC Four documentary *Time Shift: The Grunwick Strike* (2002).

21. Rogaly, *Grunwick*, pp. 80, 90–91, 99; PRO PREM 16/1491, Industrial Policy: Letter from Ken Stowe, 13 June 1977; 'The Grunwick Dispute', 21 June 1977;

Note of Meeting, 21 June 1977; Note of Meeting, 23 June 1977; Note for the Prime Minister, 6 July 1977; *The Times*, 24 June 1977.

22. Clutterbuck, *Britain in Agony*, pp. 193, 202; *Sunday Times*, 26 June 1977; Rogaly, *Grunwick*, p. 81; McGowan, 'Grunwick 30 Years On', p. 388.

23. *Daily Express*, 23 June 1977, 24 June 1977; *The Times*, 23 June 1977, 24 June 1977; PRO PREM 16/1491, Industrial Policy, Note of Meeting, 24 June 1977; *Time Shift: The Grunwick Strike*; *New Society*, 30 June 1977.

24. *The Times*, 24 June 1977; Paul Routledge, *Scargill: The Unauthorised Biography* (1993), p. 102; Beckett, *When the Lights Went Out*, p. 391.

25. *The Times*, 24 June 1977; Rogaly, *Grunwick*, p. 85; Clutterbuck, *Britain in Agony*, pp. 202–3; *The Listener*, 30 June 1977; and see the footage in *Time Shift: The Grunwick Strike*.

26. PRO PREM 16/1491, Industrial Policy, Note of Meeting at Chequers, 26 June 1977; Hansard, 23 June 1977; *Daily Express*, 24 June 1977.

27. PRO PREM 16/1491, Industrial Policy, Note for the Prime Minister, 5 July 1977; PRO PREM 16/1491, Industrial Policy, Note of Meeting, 11 July 1977; McGowan, 'Grunwick 30 Years On', p. 392; *The Times*, 12 July 1977; Rogaly, *Grunwick*, p. 82; Clutterbuck, *Britain in Agony*, p. 204; *Daily Express*, 12 July 1977.

28. Scarman, *Report*, p. 14; Rogaly, *Grunwick*, p. 109; *The Times*, 24 June 1977.

29. Ward, *Fort Grunwick*, p. 86; *The Times*, 12 July 1977; Hansard, 12 July 1977; Beckett, *When the Lights Went Out*, pp. 395–401.

30. Clutterbuck, *Britain in Agony*, p. 206; PRO PREM 16/1491, Industrial Policy, Note for the Prime Minister, 27 July 1977; Rogaly, *Grunwick*, p. 183; McGowan, 'Grunwick 30 Years On', p. 399; *The Times*, 30 July 1977, 8 November 1977, 24 November 1977.

31. *The Times*, 15 December 1977, 29 March 1978, 12 April 1978, 13 May 1978, 15 July 1978; Beckett, *When the Lights Went Out*, p. 402.

32. Sir Keith Joseph, speech at Doncaster Racecourse, 24 June 1977, TFW.

33. *The Times*, 12 September 1977; *Guardian*, 13 September 1977; Jim Prior, *A Balance of Power* (1986), p. 155; McGowan, 'Grunwick 30 Years On', pp. 396–7; 'Panorama: The Alternative Prime Minister', 11 July 1977, BBC Archive, http://www.bbc.co.uk/archive/thatcher/6330.shtml.

34. *The Times*, 1 September 1977; Clutterbuck, *Britain in Agony*, pp. 208, 241; Richard Cockett, *Thinking the Unthinkable: Think-tanks and the Economic Counter-revolution, 1931–1983* (1995), p. 222; Mark Garnett, *From Anger to Apathy: The British Experience since 1975* (2007), pp. 117–18; Phillip Whitehead, *The Writing on the Wall: Britain in the Seventies* (1985), pp. 219–20.

35. McGowan, 'Grunwick 30 Years On', pp. 384, 386; Rogaly, *Grunwick*, pp. 82, 111, 120–21; Kenneth O. Morgan, *Callaghan: A Life* (Oxford, 1997), pp. 582–3; *The Economist*, 10 January 1976; E. H. H. Green, *Thatcher* (2006), p. 123; Alwyn W. Turner, *Crisis? What Crisis? Britain in the 1970s* (2008), p. 257.

36. Louis Barfe, *Turned Out Nice Again: The Story of British Light Entertainment* (2008), p. 161; Graham McCann, *Fawlty Towers: The Story of Britain's Favourite Sitcom* (2007), pp. 216, 312; Glen Aylett, 'Strike Out', at http://www.transdiffusion.org/tmc/thames/strikeout.php.

37. Roy Greenslade, *Press Gang: How Newspapers Make Profits from Propaganda* (2004), pp. 247, 282–4, 310–11.

38. Ibid., pp. 329–30; *The Times*, 28 November 1978, 30 November 1978, 13 November 1979; and see Eric Jacobs, *Stop Press* (1980); John Grigg, *The History of The Times, 1966–1981* (1993).

39. Roy Strong, *The Roy Strong Diaries 1967–1987* (1997), p. 148; Goodwin (ed.), *Peter Hall's Diaries*, pp. 296, 298, 310; Dominic Shellard, *British Theatre since the War* (New Haven, 2000), pp. 168–9; Michael Billington, *State of the Nation: British Theatre since 1945* (2007), p. 254.

40. Goodwin (ed.), *Peter Hall's Diaries*, pp. 307, 312, 320–21, 386–7.

41. Ibid., pp. 389–90, 393.

42. Ibid., pp. 419, 421–2, 425–6, 431, 434.

CHAPTER 26. WHAT A TREAT TO LOOK AT YOU!

1. Tony Benn, *Conflicts of Interest: Diaries 1977–80* (1990), pp. 31, 76; and see Roy Hattersley, *Who Goes Home? Scenes from a Political Life* (1996), p. 171.

2. Kenneth O. Morgan, *Callaghan: A Life* (Oxford, 1997), p. 511; Ben Pimlott, *The Queen: A Biography of Elizabeth II* (1997), p. 434; Kenneth O. Morgan, *Michael Foot: A Life* (Oxford, 2007), pp. 333–4; *The Times*, 5 February 1972.

3. Pimlott, *The Queen*, pp. 400–406, 424–6; Barbara Castle, *The Castle Diaries 1974–1976* (1980), pp. 34–5; *The Times*, 22 January 1975, 30 January 1975, 27 February 1975; *Private Eye*, 21 February 1975; Willie Hamilton, *My Queen and I* (1975), pp. 187–95.

4. *Daily Mirror*, 16 December 1971; Piers Brendon and Phillip Whitehead, *The Windsors: A Dynasty Revealed* (2000), p. 182; Pimlott, *The Queen*, pp. 380–88, 415, 492; *Daily Express*, 23 April 1975.

5. *Daily Mirror*, 19 January 1977, 27 January 1977; for the 'bastard' incident, see *Daily Mirror*, 13 September 1976; *Daily Express*, 15 September 1976.

6. Pimlott, *The Queen*, pp. 435–7; *The Times*, 17 April 1976, 18 April 1976, 20 April 1976; *Daily Express*, 17 March 1976, 18 March 1976; for more on Margaret and Snowdon, who seem to have been utterly ghastly individuals, see Tim Heald, *Princess Margaret: A Life Unravelled* (2007) and Anne de Courcy, *Snowdon: The Biography* (2008).

7. *Daily Mirror*, 18 March 1976, 22 March 1976, 24 March 1976; *News of the World*, 21 March 1976; *Daily Express*, 29 March 1976, 10 October 1978; Pimlott, *The Queen*, pp. 438–9, 441.

8. *Sun*, 5 April 1978; Philip Ziegler, *Crown and People* (1978), p. 143; *The Times*, 5 April 1978, 11 May 1978; Pimlott, *The Queen*, pp. 439–40.

9. Ibid., pp. 444–5; Brendon and Whitehead, *The Windsors*, p. 189; *Director*, 18 January 1977; *The Times*, 18 January 1977, 19 January 1977; Mark Garnett, *From Anger to Apathy: The British Experience since 1975* (2007), pp. 167–8; Ronald McIntosh, *Challenge to Democracy: Politics, Trade Union Power and Economic Failure in the 1970s* (2006), p. 356.

10. PRO PREM 16/1439, Note of Meeting, 20 January 1977; PRO PREM 16/1439, W. J. Innes to David Holt, 18 June 1976.

11. Pimlott, *The Queen*, pp. 446–7; *The Economist*, 11 June 1977; *The Times*, 6 May 1977; Ziegler, *Crown and People*, p. 191; Brendon and Whitehead, *The Windsors*, pp. 189–90.

12. Richard Weight, *Patriots: National Identity in Britain 1940–2000* (2002), pp. 546, 548–9; Phillip Whitehead, *The Writing on the Wall: Britain in the Seventies* (1985), p. 305; *Time*, 20 June 1977; Jon Savage, *England's Dreaming: Sex Pistols and Punk Rock* (2005), pp. 351–5, 364–5; *Daily Telegraph*, 8 February 1977; *People* (US), 21 February 1977; Andrew Motion, *Philip Larkin: A Writer's Life* (1994), p. 410.

13. *Daily Mirror*, 7 June 1977; *Daily Express*, 7 June 1977; Benn, *Conflicts of Interest*, p. 160.

14. *The Times*, 8 June 1977; *Time*, 20 June 1977; Benn, *Conflicts of Interest*, p. 161; Weight, *Patriots*, p. 547.

15. Roy Strong, *The Roy Strong Diaries 1967–1987* (1997), p. 193; *The Times*, 8 June 1977.

16. *Time*, 20 June 1977; Ziegler, *Crown and People*, p. 187; *The Times*, 8 June 1977; on *Coronation Street* and the Jubilee, see http://coronationstreet.wikia.com/wiki/Silver_Jubilee.

17. *Sunday Times*, 10 July 1977; *Observer*, 2 June 2002; on Shilton, see Peter Heyworth's letter in the *London Review of Books*, 23 January 2003; on Shurdington, see the Jubilee Celebrations programme at http://www.shurdington.org/jubilee77.htm; on Chedworth, see *The Times*, 8 June 1977.

18. *The Times*, 11 June 1977, 15 August 1977; *New Statesman*, 3 June 1977; *Time*, 20 June 1977; Whitehead, *The Writing on the Wall*, p. 306; Brendon and Whitehead, *The Windsors*, pp. 190–91; Pimlott, *The Queen*, p. 446.

19. James Callaghan, *Time and Chance* (1987), p. 461.

20. Russell Davies (ed.), *The Kenneth Williams Diaries* (1993, pb. 1994), pp. 542–3; *The Times*, 13 August 1977; Pimlott, *The Queen*, pp. 447; *Time*, 20 June 1977.

21. Angus Maude *et al.*, Steering Committee paper on 'Themes', 16 February 1978, TFW; Pimlott, *The Queen*, pp. 450–51; *Observer*, 6 February 1977; *Sunday Times*, 29 May 1977; *Daily Telegraph*, 5 February 1977; *Daily Express*, 7 June 1977.

22. *Daily Mirror*, 2 June 1977; *The Times*, 7 June 1977.

23. Alwyn W. Turner, *Crisis? What Crisis? Britain in the 1970s* (2008), p. 193; *Time*, 20 June 1977.

CHAPTER 27. THE SHADES ARE CLOSING IN

1. Susan Crosland, *Tony Crosland* (1982), pp. 394–6, 399–400; David Owen, *Time to Declare* (1992), p. 252; Bernard Donoughue, *Downing Street Diary*, vol. 2: *With James Callaghan in No. 10* (2008), p. 146.

2. Hansard, 21 February 1977; Tony Benn, *Conflicts of Interest: Diaries 1977–80* (1990), pp. 34, 42; *Financial Times*, 21 February 1977; Donoughue, *Downing Street Diary*, p. 146; Kevin Jefferys, *Anthony Crosland: A New Biography* (1999), pp. 222, 224–5; Colin Welch, 'Crosland Reconsidered: The Man who Took Too Much for Granted', *Encounter*, 52:1 (1979), p. 95.

3. Owen, *Time to Declare*, pp. 256, 265; James Callaghan, *Time and Chance* (1987), p. 448; Benn, *Conflicts of Interest*, p. 43; Phillip Whitehead, *The Writing on the Wall: Britain in the Seventies* (1985), p. 257; Kenneth O. Morgan, *Callaghan: A Life* (Oxford, 1997), pp. 563–4; Philip Norton, 'Parliament', in Anthony

Seldon and Kevin Hickson (eds.), *New Labour, Old Labour: The Wilson and Callaghan Governments, 1974–1979* (2004), pp. 193–4; David Kogan and Maurice Kogan, *The Battle for the Labour Party* (1982), p. 141.

4. PRO PREM 16/1399, Philip Wood to Callaghan, 16 March 1977; Hansard, 17 March 1977, 18 March 1977; *The Times*, 18 March 1977, 19 March 1977, 21 March 1977; Whitehead, *The Writing on the Wall*, p. 258; Callaghan, *Time and Chance*, pp. 451–2; Donoughue, *Downing Street Diary*, p. 166.

5. *Daily Mirror*, 18 March 1977, 19 March 1977, 21 March 1977, 22 March 1977; Callaghan, *Time and Chance*, p. 453; *Daily Express*, 21 March 1977.

6. PRO PREM 16/1399, Note of Meeting (Foot–Molyneaux), 18 March 1977; PRO PREM 16/1399, Ken Stowe to Callaghan, 18 March 1977; PRO PREM 16/1399, Note for the Record (Rodgers), 21 March 1977; PRO PREM 16/1399, Note of Meeting (Callaghan–Foot–Molyneaux–Powell), 21 March 1977; Morgan, *Callaghan*, pp. 565–6; Donoughue, *Downing Street Diary*, pp. 166–7.

7. Whitehead, *The Writing on the Wall*, pp. 258–60; Donoughue, *Downing Street Diary*, p. 160; Morgan, *Callaghan*, p. 566.

8. PRO PREM 16/1399, Note of Meeting (Callaghan–Steel), 21 March 1977; Callaghan, *Time and Chance*, pp. 455–6; Donoughue, *Downing Street Diary*, p. 168; PRO PREM 16/1399, Note of Meeting (Callaghan–Steel), 22 March 1977; PRO PREM 16/1399, Note of Meeting (Callaghan–Foot–Steel–Pardoe), 22 March 1977; PRO PREM 16/1399, Note of Meeting, (Foot–Pardoe), 21 March 1977.

9. PRO CAB 128/61, CM (77) 12, 23 March 1977; Callaghan, *Time and Chance*, pp. 457–8; Benn, *Conflicts of Interest*, pp. 86–9; Donoughue, *Downing Street Diary*, p. 170.

10. Benn, *Conflicts of Interest*, pp. 88, 90–2, 94–5; Donoughue, *Downing Street Diary*, p. 170; PRO PREM 16/1399, Note of Telephone Conversation, 24 March 1977.

11. *Daily Express*, 24 March 1977; Hansard, 23 March 1977; Margaret Thatcher, *The Path to Power* (1995), pp. 327–8; Anne Perkins, *Red Queen: The Authorized Biography of Barbara Castle* (2003), p. 445; Donoughue, *Downing Street Diary*, pp. 171–2.

12. Whitehead, *The Writing on the Wall*, pp. 260–61; Denis Healey, *The Time of My Life* (1989, pb. 1990), p. 403; Joel Barnett, *Inside the Treasury* (1982), p. 142; Ion Trewin (ed.), *The Hugo Young Papers: Thirty Years of British Politics – Off the Record* (2008), p. 125; Morgan, *Callaghan*, pp. 568–9.

13. *The Times*, 2 February 1977, 23 February 1977.

14. Alec Cairncross, *The British Economy since 1945: Economic Policy and Performance, 1945–1990* (Oxford, 1992), pp. 217, 220; Edmund Dell, *The Chancellors: A History of the Chancellors of the Exchequer, 1945–90* (1996, pb. 1997), p. 436; Morgan, *Callaghan*, pp. 558–9, 563; *Time*, 2 January 1978.

15. *The Times*, 30 March 1977, 1 April 1977; Anthony King and Robert J. Wybrow (eds.), *British Political Opinion 1937–2000: The Gallup Polls* (2001), p. 234; Donoughue, *Downing Street Diary*, pp. 173–4; John Goodwin (ed.), *Peter Hall's Diaries: The Story of a Dramatic Battle* (1983), p. 291.

16. *Daily Mirror*, 24 March 1977, 25 March 1977; Michael Cockerell, *Live from Number 10: The Inside Story of Prime Ministers and Television* (1989), pp. 235–6.

17. *Daily Mirror*, 25 March 1977; Cockerell, *Live from Number 10*, p. 236; Donoughue, *Downing Street Diary*, p. 176; Trewin (ed.), *The Hugo Young Papers*, pp. 127–8.

18. *Daily Mirror*, 12 May 1977, 13 May 1977; *Daily Express*, 12 May 1977, 13 May 1977; Morgan, *Callaghan*, pp. 516–18, 559, 571; King and Wybrow (eds.), *British Political Opinion*, p. 191; *Financial Times*, 10 January 1977, 16 December 1977.

19. Hansard, 8 June 1976, 29 June 1976, 27 July 1976; John Campbell, *Margaret Thatcher*, vol 1: *The Grocer's Daughter* (2000), pp. 358–9; Cockerell, *Live from Number 10*, p. 230; Donoughue, *Downing Street Diary*, p. 59.

20. Ibid., pp. 232, 236, 279; Hansard, 26 October 1977; *The Times*, 27 October 1977; King and Wybrow (eds.), *British Political Opinion*, p. 13; Morgan, *Callaghan*, pp. 575–6.

21. *The Economist*, 13 August 1977; *Financial Times*, 15 September 1977; Morgan, *Callaghan*, p. 574; Hansard, 3 March 1978; David Butler and Dennis Kavanagh, *The British General Election of 1979* (1980), pp. 13, 26; *The Times*, 21 June 1977; Denis Barnes and Eileen Reed, *Government and the Trade Unions* (1980), p. 212.

22. Whitehead, *The Writing on the Wall*, p. 257; Keith Middlemas, *Power, Competition and the State*, vol. 3: *The End of the Postwar Era: Britain since 1974* (Basingstoke, 1991), p. 157.

23. Robert Taylor, 'The Rise and Fall of the Social Contract', in Seldon and Hickson (eds.), *New Labour, Old Labour*, pp. 83, 90; Dilwyn Porter, 'Government and the Economy', in Richard Coopey and Nicholas Woodward (eds.), *Britain in the 1970s: The Troubled Economy* (1996), p. 46; Jack Jones, *Union Man: An Autobiography* (1986), p. 307; Chris Wrigley, 'Trade Unions, Strikes and the Government', in Coopey and Woodward (eds.), *Britain in the 1970s*, p. 287; Richard Clutterbuck, *Britain in Agony: The Growth of Political Violence* (1978) pp. 182, 187.

24. *The Times*, 21 March 1977; Robert Taylor, *The Fifth Estate: Britain's Unions in the Seventies* (1978), p. 125; Taylor, 'The Rise and Fall of the Social Contract', pp. 83–6, 88, 97; Middlemas, *Power, Competition and the State*, pp. 98, 159; Andrew Thorpe, 'The Labour Party and the Trade Unions', in John McIlroy, Nina Fishman and Alan Campbell (eds.), *The High Tide of British Trade Unionism: Trade Unions and Industrial Politics, 1964–1979* (Monmouth, 2007), pp. 144–5.

25. Clutterbuck, *Britain in Agony*, p. 188; Joel Krieger, *Reagan, Thatcher and the Politics of Decline* (Oxford, 1986), p. 48; *The Times*, 19 January 1977, 3 February 1977, 11 February 1977, 1 March 1977, 17 March 1977.

26. Donoughue, *Downing Street Diary*, pp. 216, 218; Benn, *Conflicts of Interest*, p. 192; *The Times*, 12 July 1977.

27. *Daily Express*, 14 July 1977; PRO CAB 128/62, CM 77 (25), 14 July 1977; Benn, *Conflicts of Interest*, pp. 194–5; Hansard, 20 July 1977; *The Times*, 21 July 1977; Donoughue, *Downing Street Diary*, p. 224; Krieger, *Reagan, Thatcher and the Politics of Decline*, pp. 8–9.

28. Whitehead, *The Writing on the Wall*, pp. 257, 267; *The Times*, 5 September 1977; *Time*, 18 July 1977; Alastair J. Reid, *United We Stand: A History of Britain's Trade Unions* (2004), p. 330; Robert Taylor, 'The Rise and Fall of the Social Contract', pp. 91–2; John McIlroy and Alan Campbell, 'The High Tide of Trade

Unionism: Mapping Industrial Politics, 1964–79', in McIlroy, Fishman and Campbell (eds.), *The High Tide of British Trade Unionism*, pp. 103–4.

29. *The Times*, 5 September 1977, 6 September 1977, 8 September 1977.

30. *The Times*, 7 September 1977, 27 August 1977; PRO PREM 16/1406, Note of Telephone Conversation, 23 October 1977; PRO PREM 16/1406, Draft of Home Secretary's Speech, 25 October 1977.

31. *Daily Mirror*, 17 November 1977.

32. *The Times*, 10 November 1977.

33. Benn, *Conflicts of Interest*, p. 248; *Daily Mirror*, 17 November 1977.

34. PRO CAB 128/62, CM (77) 35, 10 November 1977; PRO CAB 128/62, CM (77) 36, 17 November 1977; Morgan, *Callaghan*, pp. 581–2.

35. *Time*, 28 November 1977; *The Times*, 13 January 1978; *Daily Express*, 10 November 1977.

CHAPTER 28. MAGGIE ISN'T WORKING

1. The original posters can be viewed online at the Bodleian Library's Conservative Party Archive Poster Collection site, http://www.bodley.ox.ac.uk/dept/scwmss/cpa/poster-home.html.

2. *The Times*, 11 January 1978, 16 June 1978; Hugo Young, *One of Us: A Biography of Margaret Thatcher* (1990), p. 126; David Butler and Dennis Kavanagh, *The British General Election of 1979* (1980), pp. 138–9; John Campbell, *Margaret Thatcher*, vol. 1: *The Grocer's Daughter* (2000), p. 413; on Saatchi & Saatchi more generally, see Ivan Fallon, *The Brothers: The Rise of Saatchi & Saatchi* (1988).

3. Ibid., p. 188; Nick Clarke, *The Shadow of a Nation: The Changing Face of Britain* (2003), pp. 104–5; Campbell, *The Grocer's Daughter*, p. 413; Margaret Thatcher, *The Path to Power* (1995), p. 411.

4. *The Times*, 31 July 1978, 1 August 1978, 3 August 1978; *Daily Express*, 2 August 1978; Campbell, *The Grocer's Daughter*, p. 413; Joe Moran, *Queuing for Beginners: The Story of Daily Life from Breakfast to Bedtime* (2007), p. 65.

5. Campbell, *The Grocer's Daughter*, pp. 395, 413; party political broadcast (Scotland), 4 May 1977, TFW.

6. Campbell, *The Grocer's Daughter*, pp. 312–24; Mark Garnett and Ian Aitken, *Splendid! Splendid! The Authorized Biography of Willie Whitelaw* (2003), pp. 216, 218–19; John Ranelagh, *Thatcher's People: An Insider's Account of the Politics, the Power and the Personalities* (1992), p. 159; *Daily Mirror*, 7 March 1975; *Sunday Times*, 10 October 1976; Brenda Maddox, *Maggie: The First Lady* (2003), pp. 101, 107.

7. *Sunday Times*, 18 November 1984; Michael Cockerell, *Live from Number 10: The Inside Story of Prime Ministers and Television* (1989), p. 234; Campbell, *The Grocer's Daughter*, pp. 347, 402–3.

8. Alwyn W. Turner, *Crisis? What Crisis? Britain in the 1970s* (2008), p. 123; *Sun*, 16 March 1979; Campbell, *The Grocer's Daughter*, p. 406.

9. Ibid., pp. 408–9; speech to Shipley Conservatives, 28 June 1975, TFW; *Conservative Monthly News*, September 1975, TFW; interview for Granada TV, 1 September 1977, TFW.

10. Campbell, *The Grocer's Daughter*, p. 409; remarks receiving Valentine card,

13 February 1975, TFW; *Daily Mirror*, 14 February 1974; speech to Finchley Conservatives, 31 January 1976, TFW.

11. Campbell, *The Grocer's Daughter*, pp. 339–41, 353–4; Margaret Thatcher, *The Downing Street Years* (1993), p. 157; Young, *One of Us*, p. 250; *The Economist*, 15 February 1975; *Sunday Telegraph*, 14 May 1978; Butler and Kavanagh, *The British General Election of 1979*, pp. 66–7. On Thatcher's anti-détente rhetoric, see speech to Chelsea Conservative Association, 26 July 1975, TFW; speech at Kensington Town Hall, 19 January 1976, TFW.

12. Lewis Baston, *Reggie: The Life of Reginald Maudling* (Stroud, 2004), pp. 470–71, 477, 483; Jim Prior, *A Balance of Power* (1986), p. 108; Thatcher, *The Path to Power*, p. 319.

13. Nigel Lawson, *The View from No. 11: Memoirs of a Tory Radical* (1992), p. 64; interview for *Panorama*, 8 June 1987, Thatcher CD-ROM; E. H. H. Green, *Thatcher* (2006), pp. 26–7; Andrew Gamble, *Britain in Decline: Economic Policy, Political Strategy and the British State* (Basingstoke, 1994), pp. 138–9, 144–6; Dennis Kavanagh, *Thatcherism and British Politics: The End of Consensus?* (Oxford, 1987), pp. 11–13; Richard Vinen, *Thatcher's Britain: The Politics and Social Upheaval of the 1980s* (2009), p. 7; Ranelagh, *Thatcher's People*, p. 71.

14. Ibid., p. ix; Richard Cockett, *Thinking the Unthinkable: Think-tanks and the Economic Counter-revolution, 1931–1983* (1995), pp. 173–4; Andy Beckett, *When the Lights Went Out: Britain in the Seventies* (2009), p. 280; Vinen, *Thatcher's Britain*, p. 7; *Spectator*, 24 May 1986; Nicholas Timmins, *The Five Giants: A Biography of the Welfare State* (1996), pp. 249–55, 265; E. H. H. Green, *Ideologies of Conservatism: Conservative Political Ideas in the Twentieth Century* (Oxford, 2002), pp. 219, 223–5, 236; Green, *Thatcher*, pp. 30–31, 34–40.

15. Ian Gilmour, *Dancing with Dogma: Britain under Thatcherism* (1993), p. 11; Alan Sked and Chris Cook, *Post-war Britain: A Political History* (1988), p. 328; Green, *Thatcher*, p. 33; Campbell, *The Grocer's Daughter*, p. 11; Ranelagh, *Thatcher's People*, p. ix; Cockett, *Thinking the Unthinkable*, p. 250; Vernon Bogdanor, 'The Fall of Heath and the End of the Postwar Settlement', in Stuart Ball and Anthony Seldon (eds.), *The Heath Government 1970–1974: A Reappraisal* (Harlow, 1996), p. 377; Green, *Thatcher*, pp. 48, 50–51; and see generally David Cannadine, *Class in Britain* (2000), pp. 173–4; Green, *Ideologies of Conservatism*, pp. 214–39; Green, *Thatcher*, pp. 21–54.

16. Campbell, *The Grocer's Daughter*, pp. 365, 374–5, 377–8; speech to Junior Carlton Club Political Council, 4 May 1976, TFW; speech to Conservative party conference, 8 October 1976, TFW; Zachary Leader (ed.), *The Letters of Kingsley Amis* (2000), pp. 839–40.

17. *Daily Telegraph*, 30 January 1975; *Evening Standard*, 18 October 1974; *Daily Express*, 3 January 1975; Green, *Thatcher*, pp. 18–19; speech to Conservative Central Council, 15 March 1975, TFW; Campbell, *The Grocer's Daughter*, p. 334.

18. Speech to Conservative party conference, 10 October 1975, TFW.

19. Interview for *World in Action*, 31 January 1975, TFW; and see Green, *Thatcher*, pp. 18–21.

20. Speech at Preston, 15 September 1974, TFW; general election press conference, 2 May 1979, TFW; Sir Keith Joseph, Shadow Cabinet paper on inflation, 1 May 1974, TFW; Green, *Thatcher*, pp. 66–7.

21. Speech to Conservative Central Council, 15 March 1975, TFW; speech to Conservative National Union, 11 June 1975, TFW; Nigel Lawson to Margaret Thatcher, 19 July 1978, TFW; Green, *Thatcher*, pp. 68–9; interview for ITN, 11 February 1975, TFW.

22. Lecture to Conservative Political Centre, 11 October 1968, TFW; David Smith, *The Rise and Fall of Monetarism: The Theory and Politics of an Economic Experiment* (1991), pp. 73–4; Cockett, *Thinking the Unthinkable*, pp. 172–4, 183–5; *The Times*, 10 April 1975.

23. Sir Geoffrey Howe, Shadow Cabinet paper on 'Economic Prospects and the Party's Political Position', 16 December 1975, TFW; Joseph to Thatcher, 22 July 1976, TFW; Green, *Thatcher*, p. 60; Hansard, 22 May 1975; 'The Right Approach to the Economy', 8 October 1977, TFW.

24. Howe, Shadow Cabinet paper on 'Economic Prospects and the Party's Political Position'; Campbell, *The Grocer's Daughter*, pp. 366, 386–7; Green, *Ideologies of Conservatism*, p. 215; Simon Jenkins, *Thatcher and Sons: A Revolution in Three Acts* (2006), pp. 50–51.

25. Sir Keith Joseph, 'Monetarism is Not Enough' (Stockton lecture), 5 April 1976, TFW; speech at St Lawrence Jewry ('I Believe: A Speech on Christianity and Politics'), 30 March 1978; Timmins, *The Five Giants*, pp. 358, 360–62, 364; and see the various Shadow Cabinet minutes online at TFW.

26. Cockett, *Thinking the Unthinkable*, p. 266; *Daily Telegraph*, 3 August 1988; Campbell, *The Grocer's Daughter*, pp. 364–5, 382–93; Kavanagh, *Thatcherism and British Politics*, pp. 201–2; Vinen, *Thatcher's Britain*, pp. 7–8, 93, 292–4; speech to Conservative party conference, 8 October 1976, TFW; speech to Conservative party conference, 14 October 1977, TFW.

27. Angus Maude *et al.*, Steering Committee paper on 'Themes', 16 February 1978, TFW; Campbell, *The Grocer's Daughter*, p. 385.

28. Green, *Thatcher*, pp. 102–5; speech in Finchley, 14 March 1966, TFW; John Hoskyns, 'Policy-making for the Next Conservative Government', 14 October 1975, TFW; Hoskyns to Sherman, 3 October 1975, TFW; Hoskyns to Sherman, 24 February 1976, TFW; Joseph to Thatcher, 6 August 1976, TFW; and see Young, *One of Us*, pp. 114–15; Ranelagh, *Thatcher's People*, pp. 218–19; Cockett, *Thinking the Unthinkable*, pp. 259–62, 265–6.

29. 'Stepping Stones', 14 November 1977, TFW (pp. S-1, 5, 6–7, 13, 17, 30, A12–A13); for more analysis, see Young, *One of Us*, pp. 114–15; Ranelagh, *Thatcher's People*, pp. 219–20; Cockett, *Thinking the Unthinkable*, pp. 272–4; Green, *Thatcher*, pp. 115–16.

30. Cockett, *Thinking the Unthinkable*, p. 285; minutes of Leader's Steering Committee, 51st meeting, 30 January 1978, TFW; Campbell, *The Grocer's Daughter*, p. 394; Green, *Thatcher*, p. 116.

31. Authority of Government Policy Group: Final Report, 22 June 1978, TFW; *The Times*, 18 April 1978, 19 April 1978; Ranelagh, *Thatcher's People*, pp. 220–21; interview for *Panorama*, 23 February 1976, Thatcher CD-ROM; Campbell, *The Grocer's Daughter*, pp. 393–4; speech to Conservative party conference, 14 October 1977, TFW.

32. Anthony King and Robert J. Wybrow (eds.), *British Political Opinion 1937–2000: The Gallup Polls* (2001), pp. 198–9, 208; *The Times*, 10 October 1978.

33. John Goodwin (ed.), *Peter Hall's Diaries: The Story of a Dramatic Battle* (1983), p. 365; radio interview for LBC, 28 April 1979, TFW; Kingsley Amis, *Memoirs* (1991), pp. 315–16.

CHAPTER 29. WE'LL BEAT THE BASTARDS YET

1. James Callaghan, *Time and Chance* (1987), pp. 34–5; Kenneth O. Morgan, *Callaghan: A Life* (Oxford, 1997), pp. 12, 16; *Guardian*, 5 April 2005.

2. Bernard Donoughue, *Downing Street Diary*, vol. 2: *With James Callaghan in No. 10* (2008), pp. 22–3; Bernard Donoughue, *The Heat of the Kitchen: An Autobiography* (2003), pp. 235–6, 240–41; *Guardian*, 16 October 2001; Kathryn A. Riley, *Whose School is it Anyway?* (1998), pp. 56, 58–9.

3. *TES*, 23 January 1976, 8 October 1976; Clyde Chitty, *Towards a New Education System: The Victory of the New Right?* (1989), pp. 62–3; Roy Lowe, 'Education Policy', in Anthony Seldon and Kevin Hickson (eds.), *New Labour, Old Labour: The Wilson and Callaghan Governments, 1974–1979* (2004), pp. 130–31; Conservative Central Office, *The Right Approach* (1976), p. 61.

4. Morgan, *Callaghan*, p. 502; Lowe, 'Education Policy', pp. 132, 134; Nicholas Timmins, *The Five Giants: A Biography of the Welfare State* (1996), pp. 324–5.

5. *TES*, 15 October 1976; Callaghan, *Time and Chance*, p. 410; *Guardian*, 13 October 1976.

6. Donoughue, *Downing Street Diary*, p. 84; *The Times*, 19 October 1976. For the complete text of the speech, see *Guardian*, 15 October 2001.

7. Tony Benn, *Against the Tide: Diaries 1973–1976* (1989), pp. 626–7; *TES*, 15 October 1976; and see Timmins, *The Five Giants*, pp. 325–7; Riley, *Whose School is it Anyway?*, pp. 65–6; Morgan, *Callaghan*, p. 541.

8. Riley, *Whose School is it Anyway?*, p. 66; *The Times*, 19 October 1976; Benn, *Against the Tide*, p. 629; *TES*, 14 January 1977; Lowe, 'Education Policy', pp. 135–6; Timmins, *The Five Giants*, pp. 326–8.

9. Ibid., p. 328; *Guardian*, 16 October 2001; see also Riley, *Whose School is it Anyway?*, pp. 69–70.

10. Tony Benn, *Conflicts of Interest: Diaries 1977–80* (1990), pp. 268, 196; Ion Trewin (ed.), *The Hugo Young Papers: Thirty Years of British Politics – Off the Record* (2008), pp. 102, 121–2.

11. Benn, *Conflicts of Interest*, pp. 270, 226, 250; Mervyn Jones, *Michael Foot* (1995), pp. 418–19; Kenneth O. Morgan, *Michael Foot: A Life* (Oxford, 2007), p. 350.

12. Donoughue, *Downing Street Diary*, pp. 289, 307; David Butler and Dennis Kavanagh, *The British General Election of 1979* (1980), p. 5; Phillip Whitehead, *The Writing on the Wall: Britain in the Seventies* (1985), pp. 269–70; Morgan, *Callaghan*, p. 503; *Daily Express*, 21 August 1978, 4 October 1978; *The Times*, 25 May 1978.

13. Donoughue, *Downing Street Diary*, pp. 15, 25; Bernard Donoughue, *Downing Street Diary*, vol. 1: *With Harold Wilson in No. 10* (2005), p. 568; Morgan, *Callaghan*, pp. 492–3; Peter Hennessy, *The Prime Minister: The Office and its Holders since 1945* (2000), p. 381.

14. Noel Thompson, 'Economic Ideas and the Development of Economic Opinion', in Richard Coopey and Nicholas Woodward (eds.), *Britain in the 1970s: The Troubled Economy* (1996), p. 77; Edward Pearce, *Denis Healey: A Life in Our Times* (2002), p. 510; Andy Beckett, *When the Lights Went Out: Britain in the Seventies* (2009), p. 406; Jim Tomlinson, 'Economic Policy', in Seldon and Hickson (eds.), *New Labour, Old Labour*, pp. 59, 64–5; Dilwyn Porter, 'Government and the Economy', in Coopey and Woodward (eds.), *Britain in the 1970s*, pp. 47, 51; Timmins, *The Five Giants*, p. 378.

15. Kevin Hickson, *The IMF Crisis of 1976 and British Politics* (2005), pp. 212–13; David Smith, *The Rise and Fall of Monetarism: The Theory and Politics of an Economic Experiment* (1991), pp. 59, 70; Thompson, 'Economic Ideas and the Development of Economic Opinion', p. 77; Keith Middlemas, *Power, Competition and the State*, vol. 3: *The End of the Postwar Era: Britain since 1974* (Basingstoke, 1991), p. 142; David Kynaston, *The City of London*, vol. 4: *A Club No More 1945–2000* (2001), pp. 553–4; Austin Mitchell, *Four Years in the Death of the Labour Party* (1983), p. 18; Simon Heffer, *Like the Roman: The Life of Enoch Powell* (1998), p. 793; Hansard, 20 July 1977.

16. Nicholas Woodward, 'The Retreat from Full Employment', in Coopey and Woodward (eds.), *Britain in the 1970s*, pp. 136, 142; Alec Cairncross, *The British Economy since 1945: Economic Policy and Performance, 1945–1990* (Oxford, 1992), pp. 35, 230; Richard Coopey and Nicholas Woodward, 'The British Economy in the 1970s', in Coopey and Woodward (eds.), *Britain in the 1970s*, p. 25; *The Times*, 24 April 1978; Ben Pimlott, 'The North East: Back to the 1930s?', *Political Quarterly*, 52:1 (January–March 1981), pp. 51–63.

17. Joseph Rowntree Foundation, *Income and Wealth: The Report of the JRF Inquiry Group* (1995), p. 13; Timmins, *The Five Giants*, p. 368; *Guardian*, 28 September 1978.

18. Paul Madden, 'Jim Allen', in George W. Brandt (ed.), *British Television Drama* (Cambridge, 1981), pp. 52–3; Dave Rolinson, 'The Spongers', at http://www.screenonline.org.uk/tv/id/557920/index.html.

19. *The Times*, 26 January 1978; *Daily Express*, 25 January 1978; on the *Scum* affair, see *The Times*, 12 January 1978, 24 January 1978; Justin Hobday, 'Scum', http://www.screenonline.org.uk/tv/id/439310/; and Mark Kermode's Radio Four documentary of the same name, 5 October 2009.

20. *Daily Express*, 9 February 1978.

21. Anthony King and Robert J. Wybrow (eds.), *British Political Opinion 1937–2000: The Gallup Polls* (2001), pp. 264–6; Robert J. Wybrow, *Britain Speaks Out, 1937–87: A Social History as Seen through the Gallup Data* (1989), p. 118; Dennis Kavanagh, *Thatcherism and British Politics: The End of Consensus?* (Oxford, 1987), p. 169; *Guardian*, 28 September 1978.

22. Edmund Dell, *The Chancellors: A History of the Chancellors of the Exchequer, 1945–90* (1996, pb. 1997), p. 454; Richard Holt, *Second amongst Equals: Chancellors of the Exchequer since the Second World War* (2002), p. 183; Beckett, *When the Lights Went Out*, p. 421; Joel Krieger, *Reagan, Thatcher and the Politics of Decline* (Oxford, 1986), p. 94; John Campbell, *Margaret Thatcher*, vol. 1: *The Grocer's Daughter* (2000), p. 363; interview for *Jimmy Young Show*, 31 January 1978, *Thatcher* CD-ROM. On the similarities between Callaghan

and Thatcher, see Butler and Kavanagh, *The British General Election of 1979*, p. 5; Phillip Whitehead, 'The Labour Governments, 1974–1979', in Peter Hennessy and Anthony Seldon (eds.), *Ruling Performance: British Governments from Attlee to Thatcher* (1989), p. 264; Andrew Gamble, *Britain in Decline: Economic Policy, Political Strategy and the British State* (Basingstoke, 1994), p. 194; Richard Cockett, *Thinking the Unthinkable: Think-tanks and the Economic Counter-revolution, 1931–1983* (1995), pp. 216–17; Steven Fielding, 'The 1974–9 Governments and "New" Labour', in Seldon and Hickson (eds.), *New Labour, Old Labour*, p. 290.

23. Timmins, *The Five Giants*, pp. 365–7; *Guardian*, 16 June 1971; Donoughue, *The Heat of the Kitchen*, p. 173.

24. Ibid., pp. 172–3; Beckett, *When the Lights Went Out*, pp. 421–2; Joe Haines, *The Politics of Power: The Inside Story of Life at No. 10* (1977), pp. 96–100.

25. Donoughue, *Downing Street Diary*, vol. 1, p. 535; Donoughue, *The Heat of the Kitchen*, pp. 174–5; Haines, *The Politics of Power*, pp. 96, 108–11; *The Times*, 30 September 1976; Morgan, *Callaghan*, p. 502; Timmins, *The Five Giants*, pp. 366–7; Beckett, *When the Lights Went Out*, p. 423.

26. Michael Palin, *Diaries 1969–1979: The Python Years* (2006), p. 469; Smith, *The Rise and Fall of Monetarism*, p. 69; *Time*, 2 January 1978; King and Wybrow (eds.), *British Political Opinion*, p. 313; *The Times*, 12 April 1978; Cairncross, *The British Economy since 1945*, p. 223; Dell, *The Chancellors*, pp. 446–7; Morgan, *Callaghan*, p. 578; MORI Post-Budget Poll, 12–13 April 1978, http://www.ipsos-mori.com/researchpublications/researcharchive/poll.aspx?oItemId=2498; *Daily Express*, 14 August 1978.

27. Palin, *Diaries*, p. 469; *Guardian*, 26 September 1978, 27 September 1978; on the underlying problems beneath the apparent prosperity of 1977–8, see also Kenneth O. Morgan, *The People's Peace: British History since 1945* (Oxford, 1999), pp. 405–6.

28. Richard Clutterbuck, *Britain in Agony: The Growth of Political Violence* (1978), pp. 182, 187–8; Robert Taylor, 'The Rise and Fall of the Social Contract', in Seldon and Hickson (eds.), *New Labour, Old Labour*, pp. 83, 90; *The Economist*, 8 January 1978; Porter, 'Government and the Economy', p. 48; Morgan, *Callaghan*, p. 632.

29. *Daily Mirror*, 21 February 1978.

30. Morgan, *Callaghan*, pp. 557, 578–9; Donoughue, *Downing Street Diary*, vol. 2, pp. 282, 297, 307; Denis Healey, *The Time of My Life* (1989, pb. 1990), p. 442.

31. Donoughue, *Downing Street Diary*, vol. 2, p. 293; *Daily Express*, 5 April 1978; Butler and Kavanagh, *The British General Election of 1979*, pp. 31, 39; Michael Cockerell, *Live from Number 10: The Inside Story of Prime Ministers and Television* (1989), p. 239; Morgan, *Callaghan*, pp. 583–4; Campbell, *The Grocer's Daughter*, p. 411; *The Times*, 25 May 1978.

32. Donoughue, *Downing Street Diary*, vol. 2, pp. 349–50; Hansard, 25 July 1978; *Daily Express*, 26 July 1978; *Financial Times*, 26 July 1978; *The Times*, 26 July 1978; *Daily Mirror*, 26 July 1978; Campbell, *The Grocer's Daughter*, pp. 412–13; Norman Tebbit, *Upwardly Mobile* (1988), p. 157.

33. Donoughue, *Downing Street Diary*, vol. 2, pp. 279, 287; Morgan, *Callaghan*, p. 636; *The Times*, 20 July 1978; Benn, *Conflicts of Interest*, pp. 305–6.

34. *The Times*, 21 July 1978, 3 September 1978; Morgan, *Callaghan*, pp. 628, 636–8, 640; Donoughue, *Downing Street Diary*, vol. 2, p. 354.

35. Callaghan, *Time and Chance*, p. 517; *The Times*, 2 September 1978, 6 September 1978; Morgan, *Callaghan*, pp. 641–3.

36. *Daily Express*, 6 September 1978; *The Times*, 6 September 1978, 7 September 1978; Donoughue, *Downing Street Diary*, vol. 2, pp. 356–7; Morgan, *Callaghan*, p. 643.

CHAPTER 30. SIEGE CONDITIONS

1. Bernard Donoughue, *Downing Street Diary*, vol. 2: *With James Callaghan in No. 10* (2008), pp. 358–9; Joel Barnett, *Inside the Treasury* (1982), p. 154; Tony Benn, *Conflicts of Interest: Diaries 1977–80* (1990), p. 334; Roy Hattersley, *Who Goes Home? Scenes from a Political Life* (1996), pp. 207–8.

2. James Callaghan, *Time and Chance* (1987), pp. 517–18; Michael Cockerell, *Live from Number 10: The Inside Story of Prime Ministers and Television* (1989), p. 241.

3. Donoughue, *Downing Street Diary*, p. 359; *Daily Mirror*, 8 September 1978; *Financial Times*, 8 September 1978; *The Times*, 8 September 1978, 9 September 1978; Kenneth O. Morgan, *Callaghan: A Life* (Oxford, 1997), p. 644; *Time*, 18 September 1978.

4. Callaghan, *Time and Chance*, pp. 511, 515; Morgan, *Callaghan*, pp. 638–40; Kenneth O. Morgan, *Michael Foot: A Life* (Oxford, 2007), pp. 360–61; David Owen, *Time to Declare* (1992), p. 382.

5. Callaghan, *Time and Chance*, pp. 516–17; Morgan, *Callaghan*, pp. 638–9, 648; Denis Healey, *The Time of My Life* (1989, pb. 1990), p. 462; David Butler and Dennis Kavanagh, *The British General Election of 1979* (1980), pp. 44–5.

6. Donoughue, *Downing Street Diary*, pp. 361–2, 366; Morgan, *Callaghan*, pp. 649–50.

7. *Guardian*, 23 January 1979; on Chelmsley Wood, see Lynsey Hanley, *Estates: An Intimate History* (2007).

8. Robert Taylor, 'The Rise and Fall of the Social Contract', in Anthony Seldon and Kevin Hickson (eds.), *New Labour, Old Labour: The Wilson and Callaghan Governments, 1974–1979* (2004), p. 100; *Observer*, 10 December 1978, 28 January 1979; *New Society*, 18 January 1979; Samuel H. Beer, *Britain Against Itself: The Political Contradictions of Collectivism* (New York, 1982), pp. 57–60.

9. Donoughue, *Downing Street Diary*, p. 260; Healey, *The Time of My Life*, p. 398; PRO CAB 129/198, CP (77) 116, 'The Pay Scene', 20 December 1977.

10. PRO CAB 128/63, CM (77) 41, 22 December 1977; Callaghan, *Time and Chance*, pp. 474, 519, 522; Benn, *Conflicts of Interest*, pp. 266, 308, 326; Morgan, *Callaghan*, pp. 633–4; Donoughue, *Downing Street Diary*, pp. 307, 346; PRO CAB 128/64, CM 78 (21), 8 June 1978; *The Times*, 8 June 1978, 12 June 1978, 19 June 1978, 22 June 1978; PRO CAB 129/203, CP (78) 83, 'Pay Policy after July', 19 July 1978; PRO 128/64, CM 78 (27), 20 June 1978.

11. *Guardian*, 26 January 1979; Eric Hobsbawm, 'The Forward March of Labour Halted?', *Marxism Today*, September 1978, pp. 279–86; Martin Jacques and Francis Mulhern (eds.), *The Forward March of Labour Halted?* (1981); Eric

Hobsbawm, *Interesting Times: A Twentieth-century Life* (2002), pp. 264–6; Beer, *Britain Against Itself*, pp. 154–5; Keith Middlemas, *Power, Competition and the State*, vol. 3: *The End of the Postwar Era: Britain since 1974* (Basingstoke, 1991), pp. 158–9, 166–7; Morgan, *Callaghan*, pp. 658, 672; Andrew Thorpe, 'The Labour Party and the Trade Unions', in John McIlroy, Nina Fishman and Alan Campbell (eds.), *The High Tide of British Trade Unionism: Trade Unions and Industrial Politics, 1964–1979* (Monmouth, 2007), p. 146.

12. Richard Coopey and Nicholas Woodward, 'The British Economy in the 1970s', in Richard Coopey and Nicholas Woodward (eds.), *Britain in the 1970s: The Troubled Economy* (1996), pp. 9, 15; Morgan, *Callaghan*, p. 632; *The Times*, 24 June 1978, 3 July 1978, 4 September 1978.

13. Callaghan, *Time and Chance*, pp. 520–21; Morgan, *Callaghan*, p. 635; Taylor, 'The Rise and Fall of the Social Contract', p. 94; John McIlroy and Alan Campbell, 'The High Tide of Trade Unionism: Mapping Industrial Politics, 1964–79', in McIlroy, Fishman and Campbell (eds.), *The High Tide of British Trade Unionism*, p. 117; Healey, *The Time of My Life*, p. 468; Edward Pearce, *Denis Healey: A Life in Our Times* (2002), pp. 513, 518.

14. McIlroy and Campbell, 'The High Tide of Trade Unionism', p. 117; Healey, *The Time of My Life*, pp. 398, 462; Phillip Whitehead, *The Writing on the Wall: Britain in the Seventies* (1985), pp. 277, 279; Lawrence Black and Hugh Pemberton, 'The Winter of Discontent in British Politics', *Political Quarterly*, 80:4 (October–December 2009), p. 561. For a well-argued alternative view, see Pearce, *Denis Healey*, pp. 513–16.

15. Black and Pemberton, 'The Winter of Discontent in British Politics', p. 561; Donoughue, *Downing Street Diary*, p. 346; Bernard Donoughue, *The Heat of the Kitchen: An Autobiography* (2003), pp. 263–4; Morgan, *Callaghan*, p. 647; Taylor, 'The Rise and Fall of the Social Contract', p. 100.

16. *The Times*, 22 September 1978, 23 September 1978, 26 September 1978.

17. Donoughue, *Downing Street Diary*, p. 366; *The Times*, 27 September 1978, 30 September 1978; Morgan, *Callaghan*, p. 655; Benn, *Conflicts of Interest*, pp. 347–8.

18. *The Times*, 3 October 1978; Morgan, *Callaghan*, p. 645; Whitehead, *The Writing on the Wall*, pp. 279–80; Donoughue, *Downing Street Diary*, pp. 369–70; Callaghan, *Time and Chance*, pp. 524–5; Robert Harris, *The Making of Neil Kinnock* (1984), p. 116; Benn, *Conflicts of Interest*, p. 355.

19. *The Times*, 4 October 1978; Donoughue, *Downing Street Diary*, pp. 370, 380, 383; Morgan, *Callaghan*, pp. 645–6; Taylor, 'The Rise and Fall of the Social Contract', p. 100; Callaghan, *Time and Chance*, pp. 526–8; PRO CAB 128/64, CM (78) 38, 9 November 1978; Benn, *Conflicts of Interest*, pp. 388–9.

20. Donoughue, *Downing Street Diary*, p. 389; *The Times*, 15 November 1978; Morgan, *Callaghan*, p. 656; Morgan, *Michael Foot*, pp. 362–3; Callaghan, *Time and Chance*, p. 533; Benn, *Conflicts of Interest*, p. 391.

21. *Financial Times*, 4 November 1978; *Daily Express*, 3 November 1978, 4 November 1978, 8 November 1978, 16 November 1978, 21 November 1978; Morgan, *Callaghan*, pp. 655–6.

22. Callaghan, *Time and Chance*, p. 534; Donoughue, *Downing Street Diary*, pp. 398, 401; PRO CAB 129/204, CP (78) 125, Memorandum by the Chancellor of the Exchequer, 4 December 1978; PRO CAB 128/64, CM (78) 42, 7 December

1978; Butler and Kavanagh, *The British General Election of 1979*, p. 120; Morgan, *Callaghan*, p. 659; Owen, *Time to Declare*, p. 384.

23. Callaghan, *Time and Chance*, p. 533; *Daily Express*, 13 November 1978; Morgan, *Callaghan*, pp. 657–8; PRO PREM 16/1707, Industrial Policy, Albert Booth to Roy Hattersley, 15 November 1978; PRO PREM 16/1707, Industrial Policy, Tim Lankester to I. A. Fair, 17 November 1978.

24. Callaghan, *Time and Chance*, pp. 536–7; Morgan, *Callaghan*, p. 656; PRO PREM 16/1707, Industrial Policy, Roy Hattersley: 'Oil Tanker Drivers', 1 December 1978, 5 December 1978, 14 December 1978; PRO PREM 16/1707, Industrial Policy, Note to the Prime Minister, 11 December 1978; PRO PREM 16/1707, 'Effects of Industrial Action by Oil Tanker Drivers', 11 December 1978.

25. PRO PREM 16/1707, Industrial Policy, 'Oil Tanker Drivers Dispute: Contingency Plans', 21 November 1978; PRO PREM 16/1707, Industrial Policy, 'Oil Tanker Drivers: Contingency Planning against Industrial Action', 22 November 1978; PRO PREM 16/1707, Industrial Policy, Ken Stowe to Callaghan, 12 December 1978; PRO PREM, 16/707, Industrial Policy, Sir John Hunt to Callaghan, 13 December 1978; Donoughue, *Downing Street Diary*, p. 406.

26. PRO CAB 128/64, CM (78) 44, 1 December 1978; Benn, *Conflicts of Interest*, pp. 419–25; *Guardian*, 21 December 1978, 22 December 1978.

27. Donoughue, *Downing Street Diary*, p. 407; *Daily Telegraph*, 21 December 1978, 22 December 1978, 23 December 1978; Butler and Kavanagh, *The British General Election of 1979*, p. 120.

28. Michael Palin, *Diaries 1969–1979: The Python Years* (2006), pp. 517, 519–20; *Guardian*, 2 January 1979; *Daily Telegraph*, 2 January 1979; *Daily Express*, 2 January 1979, 3 January 1979; Dave Haslam, *Not Abba: The Real Story of the 1970s* (2005), p. 289; Alwyn W. Turner, *Crisis? What Crisis? Britain in the 1970s* (2008), pp. 263–4.

29. Benn, *Conflicts of Interest*, p. 428; Donoughue, *Downing Street Diary*, p. 411; *Guardian*, 3 January 1979; Haslam, *Not Abba*, p. 290.

30. Donoughue, *Downing Street Diary*, pp. 411–14; *Daily Express*, 3 January 1979; *Guardian*, 3 January 1979.

31. Donoughue, *Downing Street Diary*, pp. 415–16; *Daily Express*, 4 January 1979, 5 January 1979; *Guardian*, 5 January 1979; Morgan, *Callaghan*, p. 660; Benn, *Conflicts of Interest*, pp. 428–9.

32. Ibid., p. 411; Callaghan, *Time and Chance*, p. 554; Morgan, *Callaghan*, pp. 616, 660–61; Cockerell, *Live from Number 10*, p. 242; Andy Beckett, *When the Lights Went Out: Britain in the Seventies* (2009), pp. 480, 482; *Daily Express*, 5 January 1979.

33. *Daily Express*, 6 January 1979, 8 January 1979; *Guardian*, 6 January 1979; *Sunday Express*, 7 January 1979; Benn, *Conflicts of Interest*, pp. 430–31; Palin, *Diaries*, p. 521.

34. Donoughue, *Downing Street Diary*, pp. 416–18.

35. *Daily Express*, 10 January 1979; *Guardian*, 10 January 1979, 11 January 1979; Cockerell, *Live from Number 10*, pp. 242–3; Morgan, *Callaghan*, pp. 661–2.

36. Russel Davies (ed.), *The Kenneth Williams Diaries* (1993, pb. 1994), p. 575; Donoughue, *Downing Street Diary*, p. 423; Cockerell, *Live from Number 10*,

p. 243; *Guardian*, 11 January 1979; *Daily Express*, 11 January 1979; *Daily Mirror*, 12 January 1979.

37. *Sun*, 10 January 1979; Roy Greenslade, *Press Gang: How Newspapers Make Profits from Propaganda* (2004), pp. 309, 337, 359; Turner, *Crisis? What Crisis?*, pp. 264–6.

CHAPTER 31. RATS ON THE TOWN

1. *Evening Standard*, 24 January 1980; *Observer Music Monthly*, 4 October 2009; Gary Kemp, *I Know This Much* (2009), pp. 93–4; Steve Strange, *Blitzed* (2002), pp. 39–40; and see David Johnson's invaluable website www.shapersofthe80s. com.

2. Kemp, *I Know This Much*, pp. 53, 83, 86, 92; *Observer Music Monthly*, 4 October 2009.

3. Ibid.; Michael Hann, 'Spandau Ballet: The Sound of Thatcherism', http://www. guardian.co.uk/music/musicblog/2009/mar/25/spandau-ballet-thatcherism; Kemp, *I Know This Much*, pp. 15–16, 176–7.

4. Kenneth O. Morgan, *Callaghan: A Life* (Oxford, 1997), pp. 662–3; *Guardian*, 11 January 1979, 12 January 1979; Bernard Donoughue, *Downing Street Diary*, vol. 2: *With James Callaghan in No. 10* (2008), p. 419.

5. Tony Benn, *Conflicts of Interest: Diaries 1977–80* (1990), pp. 433–6; PRO CAB 128/65, CM (79) 1, 11 January 1979; Donoughue, *Downing Street Diary*, pp. 419–20.

6. *Guardian*, 12 January 1979, 13 January 1979, 15 January 1979; Benn, *Conflicts of Interest*, p. 436.

7. PRO PREM 16/2128, Industrial Policy, Daily Situation Report by MAFF, 15 January 1979; PRO PREM 16/2128, Industrial Policy, Report by the Scottish Office and SCCC, 15 January 1979; PRO PREM 16/2128, Industrial Policy, Daily Situation Report by the Department of Industry, 15 January 1979; *Guardian*, 15 January 1979, 16 January 1979; PRO PREM 16/2128, Industrial Policy, H. B. Greenborough to Callaghan, 16 January 1979; PRO PREM 16/2128, Industrial Policy, 'Railways and Road Haulage', 16 January 1979; PRO PREM 16/2128, Industrial Policy, 'Major Employers', 16 January 1979.

8. Hansard, 16 January 1979; Morgan, *Callaghan*, p. 665; *Guardian*, 17 January 1979, 24 January 1979; Donoughue, *Downing Street Diary*, p. 424.

9. *Guardian*, 6 January 1979, 8 January 1979, 16 January 1979, 18 January 1979, 23 January 1979; Michael Palin, *Diaries 1969–1979: The Python Years* (2006), p. 524.

10. Ibid., p. 524; John Goodwin (ed.), *Peter Hall's Diaries: The Story of a Dramatic Battle* (1983), pp. 407–8.

11. Robert Harris, *The Making of Neil Kinnock* (1984), p. 117; Kevin Jefferys, *Finest and Darkest Hours: The Decisive Events in British Politics from Churchill to Blair* (2002), p. 193; Andy Beckett, *When the Lights Went Out: Britain in the Seventies* (2009), pp. 484–7, 490, 493; *Sunday Telegraph*, 21 January 1979; *Daily Express*, 10 January 1979.

12. *Independent*, 18 October 1992; Zachary Leader (ed.), *The Letters of Kingsley*

Amis (2000), p. 865; Morgan, *Callaghan*, p. 663; *Guardian*, 7 January 1984, 15 January 1979.

13. *Guardian*, 18 January 1979.

14. PRO PREM 16/2128, Industrial Policy, Department of Transport: Emergency Situation Report, 17 January 1979; PRO PREM 16/2128, Industrial Policy, Emergency Daily Situation Report by the Department of Energy, 17 January 1979; PRO PREM 16/2128, Industrial Policy, Bill Rodgers to Alec Kitson, 17 January 1979; PRO PREM 16/2128, Industrial Policy, Daily Situation Report by the Department of Industry, 17 January 1979; *Guardian*, 18 January 1979; Donoughue, *Downing Street Diary*, pp. 424–5.

15. PRO PREM 16/2128, Industrial Policy, Road Haulage Situation, 17 January 1979; PRO PREM 16/2128, Industrial Policy, Note of Meeting (6 pm), 17 January 1979; Anthony King and Robert J. Wybrow (eds), *British Political Opinion 1937–2000: The Gallup Polls* (2001), p. 333; Morgan, *Callaghan*, pp. 666–9; PRO PREM 16/2128, Industrial Policy, Note of Meeting (7.15 pm), 17 January 1979.

16. *Guardian*, 18 January 1979, 19 January 1979; PRO PREM 16/2128, Industrial Policy, Daily Situation Report by the Scottish Office: Annexe B, 18 January 1979; PRO CAB 129/65, CM (79) 3, 18 January 1979; Benn, *Conflicts of Interest*, pp. 440–42; PRO PREM 16/2128, Industrial Policy, Bill Rodgers to Callaghan, 18 January 1979.

17. *Guardian*, 19 January 1979; Donoughue, *Downing Street Diary*, pp. 425–6, 429; Morgan, *Callaghan*, pp. 664–5; Peter Hennessy, *The Prime Minister: The Office and its Holders since 1945* (2000), p. 394; Joel Barnett, *Inside the Treasury* (1982), p. 175.

18. David Butler and Dennis Kavanagh, *The British General Election of 1979* (1980), pp. 122–3; Morgan, *Callaghan*, pp. 664–5; Donoughue, *Downing Street Diary*, p. 427; Bernard Donoughue, *The Heat of the Kitchen: An Autobiography* (2003), pp. 267–9.

19. *Guardian*, 23 January 1979.

20. *New Statesman*, 26 January 1979; *Guardian*, 23 January 1979; Jefferys, *Finest and Darkest Hours*, p. 196.

21. Peter Clarke, *Hope and Glory: Britain, 1900–1990* (1996), pp. 304, 355; John McIlroy and Alan Campbell, 'The High Tide of Trade Unionism: Mapping Industrial Politics, 1964–79', in John McIlroy, Nina Fishman and Alan Campbell (eds.), *The High Tide of British Trade Unionism: Trade Unions and Industrial Politics, 1964–1979* (Monmouth, 2007), pp. 105, 120–21; Alex Callinicos, 'Alan Fisher, NUPE and the New Reformism', *International Socialism*, 96 (March 1977), pp. 9–13; and see also Tara Martin, 'The Beginning of Labor's End? Britain's Winter of Discontent and Working-class Women's Activism', *International Labor and Working-class History*, 75:1 (2009), pp. 49–67.

22. Edward Pearce, *Denis Healey: A Life in Our Times* (2002), p. 516; Benn, *Conflicts of Interest*, p. 412; *Guardian*, 19 January 1979; Keith Middlemas, *Power, Competition and the State*, vol. 3: *The End of the Postwar Era: Britain since 1974* (Basingstoke, 1991), p. 531, n. 520.

23. *Guardian*, 22 January 1979, 23 January 1979; Benn, *Conflicts of Interest*, p. 444.

24. Donoughue, *Downing Street Diary*, p. 428; *Guardian*, 23 January 1979.

25. *Guardian*, 23 January 1979, 24 January 1979; Benn, *Conflicts of Interest*, p. 445; Donoughue, *Downing Street Diary*, p. 430.

26. Morgan, *Callaghan*, pp. 663, 670; *Guardian*, 24 January 1979; *Time*, 12 February 1979; *Daily Express*, 2 February 1979, 8 February 1979, 9 February 1979; Phillip Whitehead, *The Writing on the Wall: Britain in the Seventies* (1985), pp. 282–3; *Daily Mail*, 2 February 1979.

27. Morgan, *Callaghan*, p. 665; Donoughue, *The Heat of the Kitchen*, pp. 266–7; 'Symposium: The Winter of Discontent', *Contemporary Record*, 1:3 (Autumn 1987), p. 43; Donoughue, *Downing Street Diary*, pp. 434, 436, 441.

28. *Daily Express*, 9 February 1979; Palin, *Diaries*, pp. 531, 533; Jefferys, *Finest and Darkest Hours*, p. 197; Alison Pressley, *The Seventies: Good Times, Bad Taste* (2002), p. 95; the ITN news reports, from 6 February 1979 and 30 January 1979, can be seen at www.itnsource.com and on YouTube.

29. *Guardian*, 24 January 1979, 30 December 2009; *Daily Express*, 1 February 1979; Jefferys, *Finest and Darkest Hours*, p. 197.

30. *Daily Mail*, 1 February 1979; *Daily Express*, 1 February 1979; Jefferys, *Finest and Darkest Hours*, p. 197; Hansard, 31 January 1979; James Callaghan, *Time and Chance* (1987), p. 537; Roy Hattersley, *Who Goes Home? Scenes from a Political Life* (1996), p. 202.

31. Donoughue, *Downing Street Diary*, pp. 437, 447; Benn, *Conflicts of Interest*, pp. 446–8, 449–51; PRO CAB 129/65, CM (79) 5, 30 January 1979; PRO CAB 129/65, CM (79) 6, 1 February 1979; Barnett, *Inside the Treasury*, p. 175.

32. Donoughue, *Downing Street Diary*, pp. 432, 437.

33. Ibid., p. 444; *Guardian*, 15 February 1979; Morgan, *Callaghan*, pp. 671–2; Ian Gilmour, *Dancing with Dogma: Britain under Thatcherism* (1993), p. 96; Jefferys, *Finest and Darkest Hours*, p. 198; *The Economist*, 10 March 1979; *Daily Mail*, 15 February 1979.

34. Callaghan, *Time and Chance*, pp. 162–3; Lewis Baston, *Reggie: The Life of Reginald Maudling* (Stroud, 2004), pp. 484–5, 504.

35. Morgan, *Callaghan*, p. 671; *Guardian*, 24 February 1979; Benn, *Conflicts of Interest*, p. 464; Donoughue, *The Heat of the Kitchen*, pp. 269–70; Donoughue, *Downing Street Diary*, pp. 463–4.

36. *Guardian*, 7 March 1979, 8 March 1979; *Daily Express*, 7 March 1979, 8 March 1979, 9 March 1979; Jefferys, *Finest and Darkest Hours*, p. 199; Beckett, *When the Lights Went Out*, pp. 473–5, 477; *Sunday Express*, 11 March 1979.

37. Jefferys, *Finest and Darkest Hours*, pp. 199–200; Alwyn W. Turner, *Crisis? What Crisis? Britain in the 1970s* (2008), p. 257; *Daily Mirror*, 30 January 1979; Beckett, *When the Lights Went Out*, p. 496; *Guardian*, 24 January 1979; and see the Channel Four programme *Secret History: The Winter of Discontent* (1998).

38. Denis Healey, *The Time of My Life* (1989, pb. 1990), p. 463.

39. *Guardian*, 26 January 1979; *Time*, 12 February 1979; *Daily Mail*, 12 February 1979; Turner, *Crisis? What Crisis?*, p. 267; Andrew Taylor, 'The Conservative Party and the Trade Unions', in McIlroy, Fishman and Campbell (eds.), *The High Tide of British Trade Unionism*, pp. 174–5; Donoughue, *Downing Street Diary*, p. 452.

40. Healey, *The Time of My Life*, p. 462; Morgan, *Callaghan*, p. 673; Paul Foot, *The Vote: How it was Won and How it was Undermined* (2005), p. 396; Eric Hobsbawm, *Interesting Times: A Twentieth-century Life* (2002), p. 264.

41. Whitehead, *The Writing on the Wall*, p. 284; Donoughue, *Downing Street Diary*, p. 439.

42. Robert J. Wybrow, *Britain Speaks Out, 1937–87: A Social History as Seen through the Gallup Data* (1989), p. 119; King and Wybrow (eds), *British Political Opinion*, pp. 13, 172, 266; Donoughue, *Downing Street Diary*, p. 441; Robin Day, *Grand Inquisitor: Memoirs* (1989), p. 245.

43. Alfred Sherman, 'Our Exposed Flank: Free Collective Bargaining – October–November 1978', 11 December 1978, TFW; *Daily Express*, 9 January 1979; Lord Hailsham, *The Dilemma of Democracy: Diagnosis and Prescription* (1978), p. 64; Richard Cockett, *Thinking the Unthinkable: Think-tanks and the Economic Counter-revolution, 1931–1983* (1995), pp. 268–70.

44. Interview for *Weekend World*, 7 January 1979, TFW; *Daily Express*, 8 January 1979; speech to Glasgow Conservatives, 19 January 1979, TFW; Conservative party political broadcast, 17 January 1979, TFW.

45. *Guardian*, 18 January 1979, 19 January 1979; Michael Cockerell, *Live from Number 10: The Inside Story of Prime Ministers and Television* (1989), p. 244; John Campbell, *Margaret Thatcher*, vol. 1: *The Grocer's Daughter* (2000), pp. 422–3; *Daily Express*, 1 February 1979.

CHAPTER 32. NO CONFIDENCE

1. *Daily Express*, 1 March 1979; *Daily Mirror*, 1 March 1979; Andrew Marr, *The Battle for Scotland* (1992), p. 159.

2. *Time*, 12 March 1979; Marr, *The Battle for Scotland*, pp. 159–61; David Butler and Dennis Kavanagh, *The British General Election of 1979* (1980), pp. 110–11, 113; Kenneth O. Morgan, *Callaghan: A Life* (Oxford, 1997), p. 678.

3. *Sunday Post*, 25 February 1979; message to Russell Sanderson (president of the Scottish Conservatives), 27 February 1979, TFW; Butler and Kavanagh, *The British General Election of 1979*, p. 110; *Sunday Express*, 25 February 1979; *Daily Express*, 28 February 1979.

4. Rhys Evans, *Gwynfor Evans: A Portrait of a Patriot* (Talybont, 2008), pp. 378–9, 381; *Daily Mirror*, 1 March 1979.

5. *Daily Express*, 3 April 1979; *Daily Telegraph*, 3 March 1979; Morgan, *Callaghan*, p. 679; Evans, *Gwynfor Evans*, pp. 383–3.

6. Morgan, *Callaghan*, pp. 677–8; Kenneth O. Morgan, *Michael Foot: A Life* (Oxford, 2007), p. 358; Butler and Kavanagh, *The British General Election of 1979*, pp. 115–16; Marr, *The Battle for Scotland*, pp. 161–2.

7. *Daily Express*, 3 March 1979; Russell Davies (ed.), *The Kenneth Williams Diaries* (1993, pb. 1994), p. 577; speech to Conservative local government conference, 3 March 1979, TFW; Bernard Donoughue, *Downing Street Diary*, vol. 2: *With James Callaghan in No. 10* (2008), p. 453.

8. *Daily Telegraph*, 19 March 1979; *Western Mail*, 14 February 2009; Morgan, *Callaghan*, p. 680.

9. Ibid., p. 681; PRO CAB 128/65, CM (79) 11, 8 March 1979; Dilys M. Hill, 'Devolution', in Anthony Seldon and Kevin Hickson (eds.), *New Labour, Old Labour: The Wilson and Callaghan Governments, 1974–1979* (2004), p. 234.

10. Donoughue, *Downing Street Diary*, pp. 458, 461–2; Tony Benn, *Conflicts of Interest: Diaries 1977–80* (1990), pp. 471–2; Bernard Donoughue, *The Heat of the Kitchen: An Autobiography* (2003), p. 271; Morgan, *Callaghan*, p. 674.

11. Ibid., p. 682; Morgan, *Michael Foot*, pp. 366–7; PRO CAB 128/65, CM (79) 13, 22 March 1979; Benn, *Conflicts of Interest*, pp. 475–6; Donoughue, *Downing Street Diary*, pp. 464–5.

12. Ibid., pp. 465–7.

13. Morgan, *Callaghan*, p. 679; James Callaghan, *Time and Chance* (1987), p. 561; Donoughue, *Downing Street Diary*, p. 467; Mervyn Jones, *Michael Foot* (1995), p. 428.

14. *Daily Telegraph*, 28 March 1979; Evans, *Gwynfor Evans*, pp. 384–7; Morgan, *Callaghan*, p. 683; Callaghan, *Time and Chance*, p. 683; *Observer*, 22 March 2009.

15. Morgan, *Callaghan*, pp. 683–4; *Observer*, 22 March 2009.

16. Donoughue, *Downing Street Diary*, p. 472; on Maguire, see http://www.agendani.com/the-mp-notes.

17. Hansard, 28 March 1979; Morgan, *Callaghan*, p. 684; Donoughue, *Downing Street Diary*, p. 470.

18. *Observer*, 22 March 2009.

19. Donoughue, *Downing Street Diary*, pp. 468–70.

20. Ibid., pp. 470–71; *Time*, 9 April 1979; Hansard, 28 March 1979.

21. Donoughue, *Downing Street Diary*, p. 471; John Campbell, *Margaret Thatcher*, vol. 1: *The Grocer's Daughter* (2000), p. 426; Hansard, 28 March 1979.

22. Andy Beckett, *When the Lights Went Out: Britain in the Seventies* (2009), pp. 498–9; *Daily Telegraph*, 8 May 2007; *Observer*, 22 March 2009; the final quotations are from the BBC Radio Four documentary *The Night the Government Fell* (2004).

23. Hansard, 28 March 1979; *Daily Mirror*, 29 March 1979; *Daily Telegraph*, 29 March 1979; Donoughue, *Downing Street Diary*, p. 472; Callaghan, *Time and Chance*, p. 563; *Observer*, 22 May 2009.

24. Callaghan, *Time and Chance*, p. 563; Phillip Whitehead, *The Writing on the Wall: Britain in the Seventies* (1985), p. 286; Donoughue, *Downing Street Diary*, pp. 472–3; *Observer*, 22 May 2009.

25. Butler and Kavanagh, *The British General Election of 1979*, pp. 126–7; Morgan, *Callaghan*, pp. 685–6.

26. *Daily Express*, 30 March 1979; *Guardian*, 28 March 2005; *Observer*, 22 March 2009.

27. Donoughue, *Downing Street Diary*, pp. 473–4; PRO CAB 128/65, CM (79) 14, 29 March 1979; John Cole, *As It Seemed to Me: Political Memoirs* (1995), p. 186; *Time*, 9 April 1979; *Guardian*, 30 March 1979.

28. *Daily Express*, 30 March 1979; *Daily Telegraph*, 30 March 1979; *Daily Mirror*, 29 March 1979; David Kynaston, *The City of London*, vol. 4: *A Club No More 1945–2000* (2001), p. 579; Benn, *Conflicts of Interest*, pp. 484–5; Donoughue, *Downing Street Diary*, p. 477.

CHAPTER 33. THE WINNER TAKES IT ALL

1. Remarks presenting charity cars to the disabled, 30 March 1979, TFW; *Daily Telegraph*, 2 April 1979; *Daily Express*, 31 March 1979; *Daily Mirror*, 31 March 1979; and see the ITN news clip at http://www.youtube.com/watch?v=IAgMR_gC9IY.

2. *Daily Express*, 31 March 1979; *Daily Mirror*, 31 March 1979; Hansard, 2 April 1979; written statement following Neave's assassination, 30 March 1979, TFW; remarks after visiting Neave's widow, 30 March 1979, TFW.

3. Broadcast in reply to the Prime Minister, 2 April 1979, TFW.

4. *Time*, 7 May 1979; *Guardian*, 30 March 1979; Kenneth O. Morgan, *Callaghan: A Life* (Oxford, 1997), pp. 686, 691; Bernard Donoughue, *Downing Street Diary*, vol. 2: *With James Callaghan in No. 10* (2008), pp. 488, 490.

5. Morgan, *Callaghan*, pp. 686–8, 690; Tony Benn, *Conflicts of Interest: Diaries 1977–80* (1990), pp. 481–4, 489; Eric Shaw, 'The Labour Party', in Anthony Seldon and Kevin Hickson (eds.), *New Labour, Old Labour: The Wilson and Callaghan Governments, 1974–1979* (2004), pp. 269–70; David Butler and Dennis Kavanagh, *The British General Election of 1979* (1980), pp. 149–50, 152–3; *Sunday Mirror*, 8 April 1979. For the manifesto itself, see 'The Labour Way is the Better Way' (1979), http://www.labourmanifesto.com/1979/.

6. Butler and Kavanagh, *The British General Election of 1979*, pp. 174, 184, 194, 253; Morgan, *Callaghan*, pp. 690, 697; Bernard Donoughue, *The Heat of the Kitchen: An Autobiography* (2003), p. 274; Michael Cockerell, *Live from Number 10: The Inside Story of Prime Ministers and Television* (1989), pp. 247, 249; *Sunday Telegraph*, 29 April 1979.

7. Butler and Kavanagh, *The British General Election of 1979*, p. 330; *Guardian*, 2 May 1979; David Cannadine, 'Statecraft: The Haunting Fear of National Decline', in David Cannadine, *In Churchill's Shadow: Confronting the Past in Modern Britain* (2002), pp. 38–9; message to the people of Britain, 16 April 1979, TFW; *Daily Express*, 29 March 1979.

8. Conservative general election manifesto, 11 April 1979, TFW; Butler and Kavanagh, *The British General Election of 1979*, pp. 156–8; Dennis Kavanagh, *Thatcherism and British Politics: The End of Consensus?* (Oxford, 1987), p. 205; John Campbell, *Margaret Thatcher*, vol 1: *The Grocer's Daughter* (2000), pp. 430–31; *Daily Telegraph*, 26 April 1979.

9. Butler and Kavanagh, *The British General Election of 1979*, p. 138; Campbell, *The Grocer's Daughter*, p. 432; E. H. H. Green, *Thatcher* (2006), pp. 128–9; minutes of Shadow Cabinet meeting, 17 April 1978, TFW.

10. Speech to Conservative rally in Cardiff, 16 April 1979, TFW; speech to Conservative rally in Edinburgh, 25 April 1979, TFW; Campbell, *The Grocer's Daughter*, p. 433.

11. Butler and Kavanagh, *The British General Election of 1979*, pp. 183, 189–90, 223–4; speech to Conservative rally in Birmingham, 19 April 1979, TFW; *Daily Express*, 11 April 1979.

12. Butler and Kavanagh, *The British General Election of 1979*, p. 323; *Time*, 23 April 1979; Morgan, *Callaghan*, p. 692; Campbell, *The Grocer's Daughter*, p. 434; *Guardian*, 1 May 1979.

13. Campbell, *The Grocer's Daughter*, pp. 429–30; remarks visiting Bristol, 17 April 1979, TFW; Peter Clarke, *Hope and Glory: Britain 1900–1990* (1996), p. 360; John Cole, *As It Seemed to Me: Political Memoirs* (1995), p. 187; remarks on food prices, 24 April 1979, TFW.

14. Campbell, *The Grocer's Daughter*, pp. 435–7; Cockerell, *Live from Number 10*, p. 247; Butler and Kavanagh, *The British General Election of 1979*, pp. 171–2, 205; *Time*, 7 May 1979; *Leicester Mercury*, 19 April 1979; speech to Leicester Conservatives, 19 April 1979, TFW.

15. Speech to Leicester Conservatives, 19 April 1979, TFW; interview for *Leicester Mercury*, 19 April 1979, TFW; remarks visiting Coalville, 19 April 1979, TFW; remarks visiting Cadbury's, 19 April 1979, TFW; *Birmingham Post*, 20 April 1979; *Time*, 7 May 1979.

16. *Time*, 23 April 1979, 7 May 1979; *Guardian*, 3 May 1979; Butler and Kavanagh, *The British General Election of 1979*, p. 172; Cockerell, *Live from Number 10*, p. 249.

17. *Spectator*, 14 May 1979; Cockerell, *Live from Number 10*, p. 249; Butler and Kavanagh, *The British General Election of 1979*, pp. 38, 178, 185, 236, 252–3, 305, 319; Kavanagh, *Thatcherism and British Politics*, p. 36; Alwyn W. Turner, *Crisis? What Crisis? Britain in the 1970s* (2008), p. 234; *Guardian*, 1 May 1979, 2 May 1979; *Daily Express*, 26 April 1979.

18. Butler and Kavanagh, *The British General Election of 1979*, pp. 130, 264; Donoughue, *The Heat of the Kitchen*, p. 274; Donoughue, *Downing Street Diary*, pp. 489–90.

19. Butler and Kavanagh, *The British General Election of 1979*, pp. 187–8, 192; *Guardian*, 26 April 1979; Donoughue, *Downing Street Diary*, pp. 491–2; general election press conference (BBC TV campaign report), 25 April 1979, TFW.

20. Campbell, *The Grocer's Daughter*, pp. 439–40; Ronnie Millar, *A View from the Wings* (1993), p. 262; Margaret Thatcher, *The Path to Power* (1995), p. 456.

21. Donoughue, *Downing Street Diary*, pp. 495–7; *Guardian*, 2 May 1979; Morgan, *Callaghan*, p. 696.

22. Party election broadcast, 30 April 1979, TFW; *Daily Telegraph*, 1 May 1979; Butler and Kavanagh, *The British General Election of 1979*, p. 195; Cockerell, *Live from Number 10*, pp. 250–51; Campbell, *The Grocer's Daughter*, pp. 348, 441–2; Donoughue, *Downing Street Diary*, p. 495.

23. General election press conference, 2 May 1979, TFW; 'Election: Who Will Win?', 2 May 1979, BBC Archive, http://www.bbc.co.uk/archive/thatcher/6332.shtml; *Guardian*, 3 May 1979; Donoughue, *Downing Street Diary*, p. 497.

24. *Sun*, 3 May 1979.

25. Larry Lamb, *Sunrise: The Remarkable Rise and Rise of the Bestselling Soaraway Sun* (1989), pp. 154–8; *Daily Mail*, 3 May 1979; *Daily Express*, 3 May 1979; *Daily Mirror*, 3 May 1979; *Guardian*, 2 May 1979; and see Butler and Kavanagh, *The British General Election of 1979*, pp. 231–60; Roy Greenslade, *Press Gang: How Newspapers Make Profits from Propaganda* (2004), pp. 360–61.

26. Benn, *Conflicts of Interest*, p. 493; Butler and Kavanagh, *The British General Election of 1979*, p. 197; Campbell, *The Grocer's Daughter*, p. 444; *London Review of Books*, 25 February 2010; Roy Jenkins, *A Life at the Centre* (1991),

p. 493; John Goodwin (ed.), *Peter Hall's Diaries: The Story of a Dramatic Battle* (1983), p. 434.

27. Donoughue, *Downing Street Diary*, pp. 498–9; Richard Ryder note for Mrs Thatcher, 2 May 1979, TFW.

28. Donoughue, *Downing Street Diary*, pp. 499–500; Butler and Kavanagh, *The British General Election of 1979*, pp. 197–9, 363, 368; *Guardian*, 4 May 1979; Morgan, *Callaghan*, p. 698.

29. See the footage from the BBC's election night programme, *Decision 79*, on YouTube.

30. Russell Davies (ed.), *The Kenneth Williams Diaries* (1993, pb. 1994), p. 581; Roy Strong, *The Roy Strong Diaries 1967–1987* (1997), p. 235; James Lees-Milne, *Diaries, 1971–1983* (2008), p. 294; Zachary Leader (ed.), *The Letters of Kingsley Amis* (2000), p. 870.

31. *Daily Telegraph*, 5 May 1979; *Sunday Telegraph*, 6 May 1979; David Kynaston, *The City of London*, vol. 4: *A Club No More 1945–2000* (2001), p. 580; Simon Heffer, *Like the Roman: The Life of Enoch Powell* (1998), pp. 820–21.

32. For detailed election figures and analysis, see Butler and Kavanagh, *The British General Election of 1979*, pp. 353–431.

33. Ibid., pp. 163, 343, 345, 350; *Sunday Times*, 6 May 1979; Robert Taylor, 'The Rise and Fall of the Social Contract', in Seldon and Hickson (eds.), *New Labour, Old Labour*, p. 97; Andrew Taylor, 'The Conservative Party and the Trade Unions', in John McIlroy, Nina Fishman and Alan Campbell (eds.), *The High Tide of British Trade Unionism: Trade Unions and Industrial Politics, 1964–1979* (Monmouth, 2007), p. 175; *The Economist*, 2 June 1979.

34. Butler and Kavanagh, *The British General Election of 1979*, p. 394; *Guardian*, 4 May 1979, 5 May 1979.

35. Anthony Heath, Roger Jowell and John Curtice, *How Britain Votes* (Oxford, 1985), p. 132; Kavanagh, *Thatcherism and British Politics*, pp. 73, 118, 169, 293.

36. Ibid., pp. 294–5; Butler and Kavanagh, *The British General Election of 1979*, p. 342; Anthony King and Robert J. Wybrow (eds.), *British Political Opinion 1937–2000: The Gallup Polls* (2001).

37. Bernard Donoughue, *Prime Minister: The Conduct of Policy under Harold Wilson and James Callaghan, 1974–1979* (1987), p. 191; Donoughue, *Downing Street Diary*, pp. 483–4; Benn, *Conflicts of Interest*, p. 499.

38. James Callaghan, *Time and Chance* (1987), p. 516; Morgan, *Callaghan*, p. 638; Campbell, *The Grocer's Daughter*, p. 414; *Guardian*, 26 September 1978, 27 September 1978; and see the profile at the beginning of Peter Jenkins, *Anatomy of Decline* (1995), a posthumous collection of some of his best pieces.

39. Speech to Conservative rally in Bolton, 1 May 1979, TFW.

40. Richard Vinen, *Thatcher's Britain: The Politics and Social Upheaval of the 1980s* (2009), p. 98; Goodwin (ed.), *Peter Hall's Diaries*, p. 429; Donoughue, *The Heat of the Kitchen*, pp. 280–81.

41. Ibid., p. 279; David Owen, *Time to Declare* (1992), p. 403; Donoughue, *Downing Street Diary*, p. 501.

42. Denis Healey, *The Time of My Life* (1989, pb. 1990), p. 447; Edmund Dell, *A Strange Eventful History: Democratic Socialism in Britain* (2000), pp. 473–4; Andy Beckett, *When the Lights Went Out: Britain in the Seventies* (2009), p. 405; Thatcher, *The Path to Power*, pp. 313, 419.

43. Morgan, *Callaghan*, p. 699; Butler and Kavanagh, *The British General Election of 1979*, pp. 5–6; and see Austin Mitchell, *Four Years in the Death of the Labour Party* (1983), pp. 16–17, 20; Ivor Crewe and Anthony King, *SDP: The Birth, Life and Death of the Social Democratic Party* (Oxford, 1995), pp. 23–4; Robert Skidelsky, 'The Worst of Governments', in Seldon and Hickson (eds.), *New Labour, Old Labour*, pp. 316, 319–20.

44. *Sunday Telegraph*, 29 April 1979; Butler and Kavanagh, *The British General Election of 1979*, pp. 332, 338–9; Kavanagh, *Thatcherism and British Politics*, pp. 206–7; *Sunday Express*, 6 May 1979.

45. Donoughue, *Downing Street Diary*, pp. 502–3; *Time*, 14 May 1979; 'Official Announcement of Win', 4 May 1979, BBC Archive, http://www.bbc.co.uk/arch ive/thatcher/6327.shtml, and see the election footage on YouTube.

46. Millar, *A View from the Wings*, pp. 266–8; Margaret Thatcher, *The Downing Street Years* (1993), p. 17; Campbell, *The Grocer's Daughter*, pp. 445–6; aide-memoire for St Francis prayer, 4 May 1979, TFW.

47. 'Thatcher Arrives at Downing Street', 4 May 1979, BBC Archive, http://www. bbc.co.uk/archive/thatcher/6328.shtml; remarks on becoming Prime Minister, 4 May 1979, TFW; and see also Campbell, *The Grocer's Daughter*, pp. 446–7.

Further Reading

Although historians love to boast about the originality of their research – and I am no exception – it would be sheer folly to pretend that nobody has written about this period before. Like the three previous volumes in this series, *Seasons in the Sun* naturally draws on the work of scores of historians, journalists and biographers, many of whose books I also used when writing *State of Emergency*. It seems a bit pointless merely to type out the same list again, but it would be churlish not to acknowledge particular debts, and some readers may appreciate hints for further reading.

The obvious starting point, I suppose, is now the Internet. For newspapers from the 1970s, subscribers can consult the online digital archives of *The Times*, the *Guardian* and the *Observer*, while the archives of the *Express* and *Mirror* group papers are online at www.ukpressonline.co.uk. Parliamentary debates from the 1970s are at http://hansard.millbanksystems.com/sittings/1970s, while the University of Ulster's CAIN archive (http://cain.ulst.ac.uk/) has an enormous amount of material on the conflict in Northern Ireland. All Cabinet minutes and papers are online at www.nationalarchives.gov.uk/cabinetpapers, while there are plenty of other records at www.nationalarchives.gov.uk/documentsonline. The BBC have a Margaret Thatcher archive, including plenty of clips, at www.bbc.co.uk/archive/thatcher, and there is a tremendous television news archive at http://www.itnsource.com/. In many ways, though, the single most useful resource – especially for people interested in politics – is the vast archive of speeches, documents and broadcasts organized by the Margaret Thatcher Foundation at www.margaretthatcher.org/archive. Even people who loathe Mrs Thatcher should give it a whirl.

As for books and articles, it makes sense to start with the broad general histories of the period. The best is still Phillip Whitehead, *The Writing on the Wall: Britain in the Seventies* (1985), a wonderfully evocative survey by a former Labour MP, with plenty of good stories about his party's time in office. Of the more recent surveys, Francis Wheen's *Strange Days Indeed: The Golden Age of Paranoia* (2009) is tremendously funny about Harold Wilson and Marcia Williams, Alwyn W. Turner's *Crisis? What Crisis? Britain in the 1970s* (2008) is a hugely entertaining synthesis of high politics and pop culture, and Andy Beckett's *When the Lights Went Out: Britain in the Seventies* (2009) has some useful material on Grunwick. Despite its world-class gloominess, Richard Clutterbuck, *Britain in Agony: The Growth of Political Violence* (1978), is indispensable. And if there is one article worth singling out, it is surely Joe Moran's splendid ' "Stand Up and Be Counted": Hughie Green, the 1970s and Popular Memory', *History Workshop Journal*, 70 (2010), pp. 173–98, which pulls off the amazing feat of viewing the entire decade through the prism of its least lovable television presenter.

For the Wilson and Callaghan governments, readers should start with the excellent biographies of the major figures. Ben Pimlott's *Harold Wilson* (1992) and Philip Ziegler's *Wilson: The Authorized Life* (1993) are both very good, but Kenneth O. Morgan's *Callaghan: A Life* (Oxford, 1997) is even better. The same author's *Michael Foot: A Life* (2007) is well worth reading, and you can while away many happy hours laughing at the relevant volumes of Tony Benn's diaries, *Against the Tide* (1989) and *Conflicts of Interest* (1990). By far the most useful diaries for the period, though, are the two volumes of Bernard Donoughue's gripping *Downing Street Diary* (2005 and 2008), which should be supplemented by Joe Haines's characteristically acerbic *Glimmers of Twilight: Harold Wilson in Decline* (2003). Among autobiographies, Denis Healey's boisterous *The Time of My Life* (1989, pb. 1990) and Roy Jenkins's stylish *A Life at the Centre* (1991) are outstanding. There are some excellent essays in Anthony Seldon and Kevin Hickson (eds.), *New Labour, Old Labour: The Wilson and Callaghan Governments, 1974–1979* (2004), while Michael Hatfield, *The House the Left Built: Inside Labour Policy Making 1970–1975* (1978) is very good on the rise and fall of Tony Benn's industrial policy. Ronald McIntosh, *Challenge to Democracy: Politics, Trade Union Power and Economic Failure in the 1970s* (2006) gives the view from across Whitehall. The Jeremy Thorpe affair is covered in ghastly but hilarious detail in Simon Freeman, with Barrie Penrose, *Rinkagate: The Rise and Fall of Jeremy Thorpe* (1996).

On the Tories, John Campbell's *Edward Heath: A Biography* (1993) does a fine job of humanizing this very grumpy man, while Andrew Denham and Mark Garnett, *Keith Joseph* (Chesham, 2001, pb. 2002) and Mark Garnett and Ian Aitken, *Splendid! Splendid! The Authorized Biography of Willie Whitelaw* (2003) are model political biographies. Among a host of books on Margaret Thatcher, the outstanding titles are E. H. H. Green's slim but brilliant *Thatcher* (2006), Richard Vinen's insightful *Thatcher's Britain: The Politics and Social Upheaval of the 1980s* (2009), and John Campbell's definitive *Margaret Thatcher*, vol. 1: *The Grocer's Daughter* (2000). (In fact, Campbell really deserves a bibliographical essay all to himself.) On the 'middle-class revolt', see Patrick Hutber, *The Decline and Fall of the Middle Class – and How It Can Fight Back* (Harmondsworth, 1976, pb. 1977), and Roger King and Neill Nugent (eds.), *Respectable Rebels: Middle-class Campaigns in Britain in the 1970s* (1979). On the evolution of free-market ideas, see Richard Cockett, *Thinking the Unthinkable: Think-tanks and the Economic Counter-revolution, 1931–1983* (1995), while David Smith, *The Rise and Fall of Monetarism: The Theory and Politics of an Economic Experiment* (1991), is a clear and persuasive diagnosis by one of Britain's best economics writers.

For the economic picture more generally, there are rich pickings among the essays in Richard Coopey and Nicholas Woodward (eds.), *Britain in the 1970s: The Troubled Economy* (1996). On the plight of industry, Geoffrey Owen, *From Empire to Europe: The Decline and Revival of British Industry since the Second World War* (1999) is a splendid read. On the City of London, see David Kynaston's definitive *The City of London*, vol. 4: *A Club No More 1945–2000* (2001), while for a very caustic view of life at the Treasury, see Edmund Dell, *The Chancellors: A History of the Chancellors of the Exchequer, 1945–90* (1996, pb. 1997). The various essays in John McIlroy, Nina Fishman and Alan Campbell (eds.), *The High Tide of British Trade Unionism: Trade Unions and Industrial Politics, 1964–1979* (Monmouth, 2007) do their best to stick up for the trade unions. Surprisingly little has been written on the Winter of Discontent, but the IMF crisis is now a very crowded field. Edmund Dell, *A Hard Pounding: Politics and Economic Crisis, 1974–1976* (Oxford, 1991) and Kathleen Burk and Alec Cairncross, *Goodbye, Great Britain: The 1976 IMF Crisis* (New Haven, 1992) are superb, but should be supplemented by Steve Ludlam, 'The Gnomes of Washington: Four Myths of the 1976 IMF Crisis', *Political Studies*, 40 (1992), pp. 713–27, and Mark D. Harmon, 'The 1976 UK–IMF Crisis: The Markets, the Americans and the IMF', *Contemporary British History*, 11:3 (Autumn 1997), pp. 1–17. The best recent overview is Kevin Hickson, *The IMF Crisis of 1976 and British Politics* (2005).

For the UWC strike, I used Robert Fisk, *The Point of No Return: The Strike which Broke the British in Ulster* (1975) and Peter Taylor, *Loyalists* (1999, pb. 2000). For the European referendum, I relied on David Butler and Uwe Kitzinger, *The 1975 Referendum* (1976). On schools, the best places to start are Hunter Davies, *The Creighton Report: A Year in the Life of a Comprehensive School* (Newton Abbot, 1977), John Gretton and Mark Jackson, *William Tyndale: Collapse of a School – or a System?* (1976) and Kathryn A. Riley, *Whose School is it Anyway?* (1998). Keith Jacka, Caroline Cox and John Marks, *Rape of Reason: The Corruption of the Polytechnic of North London* (1975) makes pretty blood-curdling reading. On the rise of the Scottish National Party, Andrew Marr, *The Battle for Scotland* (1992) is a fine read. Jerry White's definitive *London in the Twentieth Century* (2001) is a magnificent account of life in the capital, while Barry Cox, John Shirley and Martin Short, *The Fall of Scotland Yard* (Harmondsworth, 1977) and Sir Robert Mark, *In the Office of Constable* (1978) are excellent on the Metropolitan Police.

On fears of crime, Stuart Hall *et al.*, *Policing the Crisis: Mugging, the State and Law and Order* (Basingstoke, 1978) is entertainingly dated but full of good material. Geoffrey Pearson, *Hooligan: A History of Respectable Fears* (1983) is essential, while Michael Tracey and David Morrison, *Whitehouse* (1979) gets under the skin of this controversial woman. For the Yorkshire Ripper, I relied on Gordon Burn, *Somebody's Husband, Somebody's Son: The Story of Peter Sutcliffe* (1984) and Michael Bilton, *Wicked beyond Belief: The Hunt for the Yorkshire Ripper* (2003). On race and immigration, Mike Phillips and Trevor Phillips, *Windrush: The Irresistible Rise of Multi-racial Britain* (1999) is full of fascinating recollections, while Martin Walker, *The National Front* (1977) and John Tomlinson, *Left, Right: The March of Political Extremism in Britain* (1981) are very good on the far right and far left. On the Grunwick affair, Joe Rogaly's excellent *Grunwick* (Harmondsworth, 1977) is the obvious place to start, but I am also indebted to Jack McGowan's article '"Dispute", "Battle", "Siege", "Farce"? Grunwick 30 Years On', *Contemporary British History*, 22:3 (2008), pp. 383–406.

Nobody interested in the 1970s could possibly doubt that in terms of popular culture, this was a very rich period indeed. Bart Moore-Gilbert (ed.), *The Arts in the 1970s: Cultural Closure?* (1994) is a nice collection of essays, while Alexander Walker, *National Heroes: British Cinema in the Seventies and Eighties* (1985) and Robert Shail (ed.), *Seventies British Cinema* (2008) are full of insights into the dying film industry.

Louis Barfe, *Turned Out Nice Again: The Story of British Light Entertainment* (2008) brings alive the world of Morecambe and Wise and *The Generation Game*. Michael Billington, *State of the Nation: British Theatre since 1945* (2007) is an excellent survey of life on stage, and D. J. Taylor, *After the War: The Novel and England since 1945* (1993) is the best of a number of books on the post-war novel. Scottish readers should probably avoid Graham McColl's hilarious *'78: How a Nation Lost the World Cup* (2006). And there are, of course, hundreds of books on pop music and punk rock. Dave Laing, *One Chord Wonders: Power and Meaning in Punk Rock* (Milton Keynes, 1985) and Jon Savage, *England's Dreaming: Sex Pistols and Punk Rock* (2005) are the pick of the bunch. Peter York, *Style Wars* (1980) is annoying but indispensable, while Simon Reynolds, *Rip It up and Start Again: Post-punk, 1978–1984* (2005) is brilliant on what came next. On progressive rock, Paul Hegarty and Martin Halliwell, *Beyond and Before: Progressive Rock since the 1960s* (2011) makes a valiant but surely doomed effort to defend this much maligned genre, while Gary Kemp's elegant memoir *I Know This Much* (2009) is very good on the New Romantics.

Perhaps the greatest pleasures, though, lie in the diaries and novels of the period. Among the more well-known diaries, Alan Clark, *Diaries: Into Politics 1972–1982*, ed. Ion Trewin (2001), Michael Palin, *Diaries 1969–1979: The Python Years* (2006), Roy Strong, *The Roy Strong Diaries 1967–1987* (1997) and John Lahr (ed.), *The Diaries of Kenneth Tynan* (2002) are full of insights, but by far the most compelling are John Goodwin (ed.), *Peter Hall's Diaries: The Story of a Dramatic Battle* (1983) and Russell Davies (ed.), *The Kenneth Williams Diaries* (1993, pb. 1994). In fiction, I found Malcolm Bradbury's *The History Man* (1975), Margaret Drabble's *The Ice Age* (1977) and *The Middle Ground* (Harmondsworth, 1980, pb. 1981) and Kingsley Amis's *Jake's Thing* (1978) to be especially useful, but the most evocative and powerful book of the period is surely John le Carré's classic *Tinker Tailor Soldier Spy* (1974, pb. 1975). Finally, my editor, Simon Winder, would never forgive me if I neglected to mention his marvellously funny *The Man Who Saved Britain: A Personal Journey into the Disturbing World of James Bond* (2006), which kicks off with an unforgettable scene of the 10-year-old Winder eating an Old Jamaica bar while watching *Live and Let Die* in 1973. In its way, that moment tells you all you need to know about 1970s Britain.

Index

Page references in *italic* indicate illustrations.